ICELANDIC

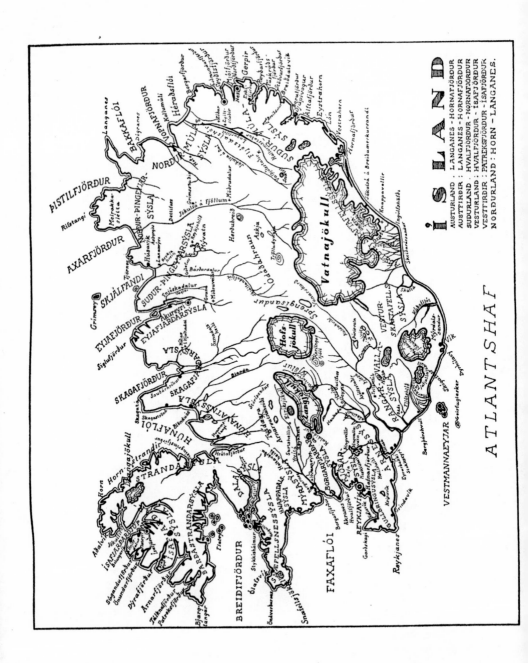

ICELANDIC

GRAMMAR
TEXTS
GLOSSARY

BY

STEFÁN EINARSSON

THE JOHNS HOPKINS UNIVERSITY PRESS
BALTIMORE AND LONDON

The Icelandic Course published by the Linguaphone Institute has this book as one of its elements.
The Linguaphone Icelandic Course includes recordings illustrating the chapter on Pronunciation in this book, and also recordings of the tales numbered 65, 66, 67, and 71 in this book (p. 288 ff.).

The Johns Hopkins University Press
2715 North Charles Street
Baltimore, Maryland 21218-4319
The Johns Hopkins Press Ltd., London

ORIGINALLY PUBLISHED, 1945
ELEVENTH IMPRESSION, 1994

A catalog record for this book is available from the British Library.

To

KEMP MALONE

PREFACE.

This book owes its inception to the decision of the American Council of Learned Societies to sponsor emergency foreign language courses in the Johns Hopkins University in the academic year 1941-42. Icelandic was to be one of these languages, and it was expected that the course would be taken by some American officers going to Iceland.

Owing to this purpose the book was designed to give a fair proportion of the common everyday language which foreigners would need in their contacts with the Icelandic people in town and in country, as well as some selections from newspapers. This is given in the topical selections *Daglegt líf og daglegt tal.* There is nothing literary in these selections (some purists might, indeed, find them too colloquial), except the last chapters, which contain some specimens of simple Icelandic folk tales.

Next came the question of the grammar. Was it to be abbreviated or full? Since Snæbjörn Jónsson had already written a short grammar for his *Primer of Modern Icelandic* and since no full grammar of Icelandic was in existence in English—or for that matter in any language—it was decided to make the grammar comparatively full. As a matter of fact it is now the only Icelandic grammar giving fairly full information on Pronunciation, Inflexions, and Syntax.* This grammar, too, gives fair prominence to colloquial speech. It was ready by June 1942.

The next task was to write exercises for use in grammatical drill. An attempt was made to write connected colloquial prose rather than incoherent sentences. The matter must of course be graded in difficulty. The task is not an easy one in a language as complicated in structure as the Icelandic.

The texts were all written and excerpted for the glossary in the summer of 1942. It remained to design the glossary. There came the question, whether pronunciation should be shown or not. At first it had not been considered necessary. But the feeble response to the planned Icelandic course at the Johns Hopkins University seemed to indicate that the book would be used chiefly by two classes of people: (1) by soldiers or others actually in Iceland, and (2) by

* This is still (1949) true in spite of Blöndal and Stemann's Danish textbook of 1943, unknown to me in 1945.

linguistic students in this country and elsewhere, especially teachers who are also interested in Old Norse-Icelandic. An earnest plea from one of the latter class, Professor Einar Haugen, at the University of Wisconsin, made me decide to include phonetic transcription. Considerable thought was given to adopting a notation similar to that used for English in *Webster's Collegiate Dictionary*, but this was not found practicable, and so a modified International Phonetic Alphabet was chosen. Apart from the notation of the stops (*p, t, k, b, d, g*), it is quite similar to the system used by Jón Ófeigsson in Blöndal's *Íslensk-dönsk orðabók* 1920-24.

Not only a phonetical notation, but also a phonetical standard had to be decided upon. The one chosen is essentially my own Eastern pronunciation. It agrees with the Northern in some points against the Southern of Reykjavík (which is put first in Blöndal's dictionary). The relation will be seen from the following table, where the first column represents the pronunciation put first in the glossary:

1. Intervocalic *p, t, k* North & East become *b, d, g* South & West (Rvík).
2. Voiced *l, m, n* + *p, t, k* North & East become voiceless *l, m, n* + *p, t, k* South & West (Rvík).
3. *hv* [hw] South & East become *kv* North & West (Rvík).
4. *fð* [v.ð], *gð* [q.ð] South & East (Rvík) become [b̥.ð, g̊.ð] North.
5. *agi, egi* [ai:jɪ, ei:jɪ] North & West (Rvík) become [a:jɪ, ɛ:jɪ] South & East.

Points (1) and (3) recommend themselves to beginning foreigners as they are in agreement with the orthography and therefore less confusing. Point (2) because the voiced sounds come easier in pronunciation to most foreigners, and certainly to all English-speaking peoples. Should a conservative Standard of Pronunciation ever be adopted in Iceland, it would be similar to this.

Yet, whoever wants from the beginning to acquire the pronunciation of Reykjavík (Southern) can do so easily, as it is in all cases indicated, either in full or by abbreviation, after the first pronunciation given. For though it is not officially recognized as a standard pronunciation, it has the advantage of numbers as well as the influence of the capital.

The adoption of phonetic spelling necessitated a rewriting of the chapter of pronunciation, but no attempt was made to introduce the pronunciation into the exercises or the grammar otherwise. The Glossary will, however, always give the desired information.

The orthography is the official Icelandic one. But since it is not always well defined, and authorities (Freysteinn Gunnarsson,

Björn Guðfinnsson) differ, there may be difference of opinion about details. By oversight the verb *skifta* and its derivatives have been so spelled throughout the book instead of the official spelling *skipta*.

The works of my predecessors have benefited me greatly. For the Inflexions I am most indebted to Valtýr Guðmundsson's Grammar, whose classification in nouns I have adopted. Otherwise I have followed the common classification in Germanic grammars. In the Syntax I owe most to Jakob Jóh. Smári's full book. Heusler's excellent grammar of Old Icelandic has often been helpful; so has Björn Guðfinnsson's grammar of Modern Icelandic. For the English Otto Jespersen's *Essentials of English Grammar* has been specially helpful.

The typing, checking, and proofreading of the book has been a very time-consuming task. But in spite of much work the writer has no illusions of having been able to eliminate all errors and inconsistencies. He can only hope that these are not so grave as to hamper seriously the usefulness of the book.

I am indebted to many people for help and advice. My wife has done some of the checking for me. Several Icelandic friends: Professor Halldór Hermannsson, Þorvaldur Þórarinsson, M. A., Þórhallur Ásgeirsson, M. A., Ólafur Jóhann Sigurðsson, and Benedikt Þórarinsson have read my texts in manuscript or proofs and given me good advice. Dr. Björn Guðfinnsson has generously read proof not only of the grammar and the texts but also of the very difficult glossary with the phonetic transcription. I am also much indebted to Dr. Phillip P. Mitchell for a critical reading of the grammar and the exercises, which has eliminated many an un-English idiom. But I owe the greatest thanks to my friend Professor Kemp Malone. Not only is he largely responsible for the fact that this task was undertaken, but he gave me freely of his valuable time to discuss matters, and read the whole manuscript before it went to the printer. For all this it is most fitting that the work be dedicated to him.

I am, moreover, deeply grateful to President Isaiah Bowman and to the authorities of the Johns Hopkins Press for their very generous decision to defray the costs of publication. Without this support the work might not have been published at all.

Thanks are also due to the Icelandic Alþingi for a subvention to keep the price of the book down.

Finally, I should like to express my thanks to the young Icelandic artist, Halldór Pétursson, for his fine illustrations and maps, and to the printers for their excellent workmanship in printing a most difficult text under trying wartime conditions.

PREFACE TO THE SECOND EDITION.

Apart from a page added to the Glossary and a few corrections in the Grammar, a very slight revision of the *Æfingar,* has been undertaken.

I should like to thank my reviewers for encouragement and advice—taken whenever feasible. That the book has filled a need is obvious, not only from the reviews, but also by its comparatively quick sale.

I note with gratification that in 1947 Dr. Björn Guðfinnsson, foremost authority on Current Icelandic Grammar and Pronunciation, has proposed a Standard of Pronunciation, practically agreeing with the one used by me in this book (cf. p. viii).

STEFÁN EINARSSON.

April 1949.

HOW TO USE THE BOOK.

It goes without saying that the beginner had better start with
the *Æfingar* (Exercises), if he intends to get a working knowledge
of the language. Should he find them too hard, he might begin
by memorizing simple sentences from the Syntax. The longer
Exercises may also profitably be broken up into two or more assign-
ments. Any one who intends to stay in Iceland had also better work
carefully through most of the topical chapters of *Daglegt líf og
daglegt tal* (Everyday Life and Colloquial Speech).

The student who is specially interested in the language, the
literature, and the specific culture of Iceland may skip many of the
topical lists, especially those that are mostly enumeration of things
(*Íslenzkur matur; Bankar, búðir, verzlanir*) or otherwise too specialized for him (e. g. *Reikningur; Hjá klæðskera; Viðgerðir, þvottar,
hreinsun*). The topical headings will in most cases indicate to him
what he wants, but he should not forget that some of the most
interesting topics are already dealt with in the Exercises (e. g.
Gömlu bæirnir). To facilitate the finding of different topics, an
index of them in English is here added.

The bibliography is added for the use of teachers and students.
After this book a beginner might read the texts in Snæbjörn Jónsson's *Primer* with the aid of his glossary. He might even read the
Old Icelandic texts in Gordon's *Introduction to Old Norse*, since
Gordon, too, has a glossary. The Old Icelandic forms (*at, ok, ek,
mik, þik, -t, -r* for Modern *að, og, ég, mig, þig, -ð, -ur*) will hardly
bother him, and he can use the modern pronunciation. With the
help of Zoëga's Icelandic-English Dictionary, the beginner can
tackle any Icelandic text, preferably one that has been translated
into English, for the dictionary is after all small. Aside from the
Bible, which always is available, I have listed some anthologies, plays
and novels to select from. Some of Nordal's selections are translated
in Beck's *Icelandic Poems and Stories*. Of the rest Jóhann Sigurjónsson's plays are probably the easiest readings.

But first of all the beginner should get himself one of the two
picture books on Iceland to get an idea what the country and its
people are like.

To use the grammar one must refer to the Contents of the Grammar. Many references have also been given to it in the Glossary,
though this is by no means an index of it.

Warning: Due to the inflation caused by the war, the prices
nentioned in the book may be considered quite imaginary.

In somewhat greater detail the chief formal differences between Old and Modern Icelandic are as follows:

1. In endings after consonants *-r* > *-ur* : *hest(u)r, ak(u)r, Hild(u)r, lif(u)r, hreið(u)r, fæt(u)r, vík(u)r* (but O. Icel. *sögur* wf.1.pl.) ; *gul(u)r; okk(u)r, ykk(u)r, yð(u)r; þú, hann bít(u)r*.

Note: *-rr* > *-r* : *her(r), Gunnar(r), annar(r)* ; *þú, hann berr* > *þú berð, hann ber*; *-ss* > *-s* : *ís(s), haus(s)*; *þú, hann kýs(s)*; *-nn* > *-n* sometimes in verbs: *þú, hann skín(n)*.

2. *K* > *g* in *ek, mik, þik, sik*; *mjök*; now *ég, mig*, etc.

3. *T* > *ð* in *at; þat, hvat, þat, vit, þit*; now *að*, etc.; also in the types *annat, mikit; farit, talit, lifat, kallat*; now *annað*, etc.

4. *Vá* > *vo* : *ván, vár; hvárr, tvá; svá; þvá, várum*; now *von, vor, hvor*, etc.

5. Contractions like *blán, blám, trúm, snjóm* (for *bláan, bláum, trúum, snjóum*) were the rule in O. Icel.; now they are exceptional (*skóm, trjám*).

6. In nouns the types *heiðr* and *köttr:köttu* (u-stem) are now *heiði* f.1 and *köttur:ketti* (i-stem plurals).

7. In pronouns *hon, hánum, þessar, nökkur* (*nekkverr, nakkvarr*), *hvárgi* are now *hún, honum, þessarar, nokkur, hvorugur*. *Sjá* is now *þessi*.

8. In numerals *tvau, sjau* is now *tvö, sjö*.

9. In verbs these changes take place:

(a) The first person ending of the present subjunctives ended in *-a*; now it ends in *-i*: *ek bera, telja, kalla*, now *beri*, etc.

(b) The first person ending of the preterite indicative in weak verbs, and the preterite subjunctive in all verbs, ended in *-a*; now *-i*: *ek talda; bæra, telda, kallaða*, now *taldi; bæri*, etc.

(c) The first, second, and third plural of the preterite subjunctive in all verbs ended in *-im, -ið, -i*; now *-um, -uð, -u* (*-i*) : *bærim, -ið, -i, kallaðim, -ið, -i*; now *bærum, kölluðum*, etc.

(d) The first person singular present or preterite middle voice ended in *-umk* (later *-umz*) ; now *-st(-zt)*. The first person plural ending was *-um(s)k* (later *-umz*) ; now *-umst*. The other forms of the middle voice ended in *-sk* or *zk* (later *-z*) ; now *-st* or *-zt*.

10. In spelling O. Icelandic had *æ* and *œ* for Modern *æ*, *ǫ* and *ø* for Modern *ö*. Sometimes *ø* has become Modern *e*. E. g. *bœr, fœtr*, now *bær, fætur; lǫnd, snøri*, now *lönd, snöri; kømr*, now *kemur*.

TOPICAL INDEX.

xiii

BIBLIOGRAPHY

BIBLIOGRAPHY:
Cornell University Library: *Catalogue of the Icelandic Collection bequeathed by Willard Fiske*. Compiled by Halldór Hermannsson. 3 vols. Ithaca, N. Y., Cornell University Press, 1914, 1927, 1943.
Lingua Islandica-Íslenzk tunga. Tímarit um íslenzka og almenna málfræði. Ritstjóri: Hreinn Benediktsson. 1. árg. — (1959–   ).   Reykjavík, Bókaútgáfa Menningarsjóðs og Félag íslenzkra fræða, 1959–
[Bibliography annually or biannually.]
Bibliography of Old Norse-Icelandic studies 1963–   Edited by Hans Bekker-Nielsen and Thorkil Damsgaard Olsen. Copenhagen, Munksgaard, 1964–

DICTIONARIES:
*Íslenzk-ensk orðabók eftir G. T. Zoëga. 2. útgáfa. Reykjavík, Sigurður Kristjánsson, 1922.
[Only existing Modern Icelandic-English dictionary.]
*Ensk-íslenzk orðabók eftir G. T. Zoëga. 3. útgáfa. Reykjavík, Sigurður Kristjánsson, 1932.
Íslensk-dönsk orðabók [eftir] Sigfús Blöndal . . . Reykjavík, Kaupmannahöfn og Kristíaníu, Þór. B. Þorláksson og H. Aschehoug & Co. (W. Nygaard), 1920-24. Offset printing 1954.
[The biggest and best of all modern Icelandic dictionaries; gives pronunciation.]
Isländisches etymologisches Wörterbuch von Dr. Alexander Jóhannesson. Bern, A. Francke A. G. Verlag. 1951- [under publication].
Ensk-íslenzk orðabók [eftir] Sigurð Örn Bogason. Reykjavík, Útgefandi Ísafoldarprentsmiðja h.f., 1966. [2nd ed.]
Íslenzk-dönsk orðabók [eftir] Sigfús Blöndal . . . Reykjavík, Kaupmannahöfn og Kristíaníu, Þór. B. Þorláksson og H. Aschehoug & Co. (W. Nygaard), 1920-24. — *Viðbætir*. Ritstjórar Halldór Halldórsson og Jakob Benediktsson. Samverkamenn Árni Böðvarsson og Erik Sønderholm. Reykjavík, Útgefandi Íslenzkdanskur orðabókarsjóður, 1963.
Íslenzk orðabók handa skólum og almenningi. Ritstjóri: Árni Böðvarsson. Reykjavík, Bókaútgáfa Menningarsjóðs, 1963.

GRAMMARS AND READERS:
*A Primer of Modern Icelandic by Snæbjörn Jónsson. Oxford University Press, London, Humphrey Milford, 1927 (reprint 1941).
[Grammar, exercises, selected readings, glossaries; up to now the only textbook in English.]
Islandsk Grammatik, islandsk Nutidssprog af Valtýr Guðmundsson. København, Hagerups Forlag, 1922.
[Phonology with pronunciation, inflexions, the fullest treatment, but no syntax.]

---

* Books, marked with an asterisk (*), are for serious beginners.

xix

Íslenzk málfræði [eftir] Jakob Jóh. Smára. Reykjavík, Ársæll Árnason, 1923.
[Phonology, inflexions, word formation, metrics.]
Íslenzk málfræði handa æðri skólum eftir Halldór Halldórsson. Reykjavík,
Ísafoldarprentsmiðja H. F., 1950. [Contains a chapter on semasiology.]
Praktisk Lærebog i islandsk Nutidssprog af Sigfús Blöndal og Ingeborg
Stemann. København, Ejnar Munksgaards Forlag, 1943.
[The best textbook in a Scandinavian language.]
Linguaphone Icelandic Course—Námsskeið í íslenzku—Samið hefur dr. Stefán
Einarsson. (I: Textar á talplötum, II: Vocabularies and Text of Sounds
Record, III: Explanatory Notes.) London, [W.1] Linguaphone Institute
Ltd., 207-209 Regent Street, [1955].
Laut- und Formenlehre des Isländisches, von Bruno Kress. Halle (Saale), 1963.

ORTHOGRAPHY:
Stafsetningar orðabók. Samið hefur Freysteinn Gunnarsson. 3. útgáfa
Akureyri, Þorsteinn M. Jónsson, 1945.
Stafsetningar orðabók með skýringum [eftir] Halldór Halldórsson. Akureyri,
Þorsteinn M. Jónsson, 1947.

PHONETICS:
The Phonology of Modern Icelandic by Kemp Malone. Menasha, Wisconsin,
The Collegiate Press, George Banta Publishing Co., 1923. New York
University, Ottendorfer Memorial Series of Germanic Monographs No. 15.
[Fine analysis, but analphabetic system hard to use.]
Træk af moderne islandsk Lydlære, af Jón Ófeigsson, in Sigfús Blöndal's
Íslensk-dönsk orðabók 1920-24.
[First useful system of phonetical writing; excellent.]
Beiträge zur Phonetik der isländischen Sprache [von] Stefán Einarsson. Oslo,
A. W. Bröggers Boktrykkeri A/S, 1927.
[Experimental studies on nasality, voice (tonality), length (quantity);
also a description of the sounds, based partly on palatograms; useful for
the consonants.]
Icelandic Phonetics by Sveinbjörn Sveinbjörnsson in collaboration with the
editor Ole Olesen. Universitetsforlaget i Aarhus, C. A. Reitzels Forlag,
København. 1933. Acta Jutlandica V. Supplementum.
[Otto Jespersen's analphabetical system used to some extent; useful
for the vowels.]
Die Laute des modernen Isländischen. Inaug.-Diss. von Bruno Kresz. Berlin,
Druck von C. Schulze & Co., 1937.
[Good; especially useful for the extensive bibliography.]
Grundfragen der isländischen Satzphonetik von Sveinn Bergsveinsson.
Kopenhagen, Einar Munksgaard, Berlin, Verlagsanstalt Metten & Co.,
1941.
Mállýzkur I [eftir] Björn Guðfinnsson. *Reykjavik,* Útgefandi: Ísafoldar-
prentsmiðja H.F., 1946.
[Best work on Icelandic dialects. With a phonetic introduction.]
Breytingar á framburði og stafsetningu [eftir]Björn Guðfinnsson. Reykjavík,
Útgefandi: Ísafoldarprentsmiðja H.F., 1947.
[Suggests a standard of pronunciation based on a good survey of the
dialects.]

---

* Books, marked with an asterisk (*), are for serious beginners.

Um kerfisbundnar hljóðbreytingar í íslenzku eftir Stefán Einarsson. With a Summary in English. Reykjavík, H.F. Leiftur, 1949. = *Studia Islandica* 10.
Mállýzkur I [eftir] Björn Guðfinnsson. Reykjavík, Útgefandi: Ísafoldarprentsmiðja h.f., 1946.
Mállýzkur II. Um íslenzkan framburð. Ólafur M. Ólafsson og Óskar Ó. Halldórsson unnu úr gögnum höfundar og bjuggu til prentunar. (Studia Islandica 23.) Reykjavík, Heimspekideild Háskóla Íslands og Bókaútgáfa Menningarsjóðs, 1964.

SYNTAX
Íslenzk setningafræði [eftir] Jakob Jóh. Smára. Reykjavík, Ársæll Árnason, 1920.
  [Biggest and best modern syntax with examples from the literature.]
Íslenzk setningafræði handa skólum og útvarpi [eftir] Björn Guðfinnsson. Reykjavík, Útgefandi Ríkisútvarpið, 1938.

WORD FORMATION
  Die Komposita im Isländischen von Alexander Jóhannesson. Reykjavík, 1929. Rit Vísindafélags Íslendinga IV.
  Die Suffixe im Isländischen von Alexander Jóhannesson. Fylgir *Árbók Háskóla Íslands* 1926-27. Reykjavík, 1928.

SEMASIOLOGY:
  Íslenzk orðtök. Drög að rannsóknum á myndhverfum orðtökum í íslenzku. Reykjavík, Ísafoldarprentsmiðja H.F., 1954. [Metaphorical idioms.]

HISTORY OF THE LANGUAGE:
  An Introduction to Old Norse by E. V. Gordon. Oxford, Clarendon Press, 1927 (reprint 1938).
  [Introduction, texts, grammar, glossary.]
  Altisländisches Elementarbuch von Andreas Heusler. 3. Auflage. Heidelberg, Carl Winter, 1932.
  [Phonology, inflexions, syntax; excellent.]
  Altisländische und altnorwegische Grammatik (Laut- und Flexionslehre) .. von Adolf Noreen. 4. Auflage. Halle (Saale), Max Niemeyer, 1923.
  [The fullest handbook in existence.]
  Íslenzk tunga í fornöld eftir Alexander Jóhannesson. Reykjavík, Ársæll Árnason, 1924.
  Nokkrar sögulegar athuganir um helztu hljóðbreytingar o. fl. í íslenzku, einkum í miðaldarmálinu (1300-1600) eftir Jóhannes L.L. Jóhannsson, Reykjavík, Félagsprentsmiðjan, 1924.
  Um íslenskar orðmyndir á 14. og 15. öld og breytingar þeirra úr fornmálinu. Með viðauka um nýjungar í orðmyndum á 16. öld og síðar. [eftir] Björn K. Þórólfsson. Reykjavík, Fjelagsprentsmiðjan, 1925.
  Modern Icelandic, an Essay by Halldór Hermannson. Ithaca, N. Y., Cornell University Library, 1919. = *Islandica* vol. XII.
  [The only cultural history of the language. Excellent.]
  Málið á Nýja testamenti Odds Gottskálkssonar, [eftir] Jón Helgason. (Safn Fræðafjelagsins, VII. bindi.) Kaupmannahöfn, gefið út af Hinu íslenzka fræðafjelagi í Kaupmannahöfn, 1929.

* Books, marked with an asterisk (*), are for serious beginners.

Die Sprache der Guðbrandsbiblía. Orthographie und Laute. Formen. (Bibliotheca Arnamagnæana, Vol. XVII.) Kopenhagen, Ejnar Munksgaard, 1956.

Early Icelandic Script as illustrated in vernacular texts from the twelfth and thirteenth centuries, by Hreinn Benediktsson. (Íslenzk handrit—Icelandic Manuscripts, Series in folio, Vol. II.) Reykjavík, The Manuscript Institute of Iceland, 1965.

Íslenzk málfræði handa æðri skólum [eftir] Halldór Halldórsson. Reykjavík, Útgefandi: Ísafoldarprentsmiðja h.f., 1950.

Þættir um íslenzkt mál eftir nokkra íslenzka málfræðinga. Ritstjórn annaðist Halldór Halldórsson. Reykjavík, Almenna bókafélagið, 1964.

---

* Books, marked with an asterisk (*), are for serious beginners.

ABBREVIATIONS.

acc.	accusative.	n	in references to the Grammar: note.
adj.	adjective.		
adv.	adverb.	nom.	nominative.
advs	adverbs.	oppos.	opposite.
approx.	approximately.	part.	participle.
art.	article.	pass.	passive.
cf.	confer.	patr.	patronymic.
coll.	collective.	pers.	person, personal.
compar.	comparative.	pl.	plural.
conj.	conjunction.	poss.	possessive.
cp.	compare.	Pr.	Pronunciation.
dat.	dative.	pref.	prefix.
def.	definite.	prep.	preposition.
dem.	demonstrative.	preps	prepositions.
e-ð	*eitthvað.*	pres.	present.
e. g.	for instance.	pret.	preterite.
e-m	*einhverjum.*	pret. pres. v.	preterite present verb(s).
e-n	*einhvern.*	pron.	pronoun.
Engl.	English.	pp.	pages.
e-r	*einhver.*	pp.	past participle.
e-u	*einhverju.*	ppn.	past participle neuter.
e-s	*einhvers.*	pr. p.	present participle.
etc.	et cetera.	q. v.	quod vide.
f., fem.	feminine, in Glossary: strong feminine.	recipr.	reciprocal.
		refl.	reflexive.
gen.	genitive.	S.	Syntax.
Germ.	German.	Sc.	Scottish.
Icel.	Icelandic.	sbdy	somebody.
i. e.	id est.	sg.	singular.
impers.	impersonal.	st.	strong.
In.	Inflexions.	stf.	strong feminine, = f. in Glossary.
ind.	indicative.		
indef.	indefinite.	sth	something.
indic.	indicative.	stm.	strong masculine, = m. in Glossary.
inf.	infinitive.		
interj.	interjection.	stn.	strong neuter, = n. in Glossary.
interr.	interrogative.		
interrog.	interrogative.	subj.	subjunctive.
intr.	intransitive.	superl.	superlative.
lit.	literally.	v.	verb.
m., masc.	masculine, in Glossary: strong masculine.	w.	weak.
		wf.	weak feminine.
math.	mathematics.	wm.	weak masculine.
midv.	middle voice.	wn.	weak neuter.
mus.	music.	wv.	weak verb.
n.	neuter, in Glossary: strong neuter.		

xxiii

CONTENTS.

LIST OF ILLUSTRATIONS.

GRAMMAR AND TEXT

CONTENTS OF GRAMMAR.

PART I. PRONUNCIATION.

1. Introduction.

1. The Icelandic Alphabet.

With the exception of the accented vowels and *ð, þ, æ, ö,* the Icelandic alphabet has no symbols not employed in English. But a number of the letters have a pronunciation foreign to English. Below the letters, with their Icelandic names, are listed. Since some of the letters have many sound values, and these will be given in detail later, no attempt is here made to indicate their pronunciation. But the pronunciation of the names of the letters is given here respelled in the alphabet of the International Phonetic Association slightly modified.

Letter	Name	Letter	Name	Letter	Name	Letter	Name
a	a [a:]	g	ge [g,ɛ:]	o	o [ɔ:]	v	vaff [vaf:]
á	á [au:]	h	há [hau:]	ó	ó [ou:]	w	tvöfalt vaff
b	bé [bjɛ:]	i	i [ɪ:]	p	pé [pʰjɛ:]		[tʰvö:falt vaf:]
c	sé [sjɛ:]	í	í [i:]	q	kú [kʰu:]	x	ex [ɛx·s]
d	dé [djɛ:]	j	joð [jɔ:ð]	r	err [ɛr:]	y	upsílon [ʏf·si·lɔ·n]
ð	eð [ɛ:ð]	k	ká [kʰau:]	s	ess [ɛs:]	ý	[y:]
e	e [ɛ:]	l	ell [ɛd·l̥]	t	té [tʰjɛ:]	z	seta [sɛ:tʰa; sɛ:d̥a]
é	é (je) [jɛ:]	m	emm [ɛm:]	u	u [ʏ:]	þ	þorn [þɔd·n̥]
f	eff [ɛf:]	n	enn [ɛn:]	ú	ú [u:]	æ	æ [ai:]
						ö	ö [ö:]

Of these letters *c, q,* and *w* are never used in Icelandic words. *a, á, e, é, i, í, o, ó, u, ú, y, ý, æ, ö* are vowels, *b, d, ð, f, g, h, j, l, m, n, p, r, s, t, v, x, z,* and *þ* consonants. The accent mark (´) over a vowel does not mean that it is stressed, but marks it as different in quality from the unaccented vowel.

2. Key to the modified International Phonetic Alphabet.

Length of sounds (vowels or consonants) is marked by a following : (colon), half-length by a following . (period). Stress is not marked, because it falls regularly on the first syllable of a word. Voicelessness of a consonant is indicated by a subscribed (or a superscribed) °. Half-voiced consonants are italicized. Aspiration, a breath (ʰ) following or preceding (preaspiration) the stops *p, t, k,* is indicated by an ʰ.

1

Vowels. Monophthongs.

[a] English *a* in f*a*ther or (Boston) *a*sk.

[ɛ] Engl. *e* in *e*nd, s*e*t.

[ɪ] Engl. *i* in p*i*n, s*i*t.

[i] Engl. *ee* in f*ee*l.

[ɔ] Eng. *o* in h*o*rse, *aw* in l*aw*.

[u] Engl. *oo* in sch*oo*l.

[ʏ] similar, but more open than German *ü* in M*ü*tter.

[y] German *ü* in k*ü*hn, French *u* in *u*ne.

[ö] German *ö* in h*ö*ren, French *eu* in p*eu*r.

Vowels. Diphthongs, ending in [i], [y], and [u].

[ai] Engl. *i* in *i*ce.

[ei] Engl. *a* in *a*le, f*a*te.

[(ɪ)i] a combination of *i* in s*i*t and *ee* in f*ee*l.

[ɔi] Engl. *oy* in b*oy*.

[(ʏ)y] *u* in French t*u*er.

[öy] a combination of [ö] and [y] as in French f*eui*lle.

[au] Engl. *ou, ow* in *ou*t, c*ow*.

[ou] Engl. *o* in *o*ld, n*o*te.

Consonants.

[b] Engl. *b*oy.

[b̥] between Engl. *b* and *p*, French *p*.

[d] Engl. *d*ay.

[d̥] between Engl. *d* and *t*, French *t*.

[ð] Engl. *th*is, brea*th*e.

[f] Engl. *f*eel, pu*ff*.

[g] Engl. *g*o.

[g̊] between Engl. *g* and *k*, French *k*.

[gⱼ] Engl. *g*eese (*g* or *gy*).

[g̊ⱼ] between Engl. *g* (*gy*) and *k* (*ky*).

[q] voiced spirant, N. German sa*g*en.

[x] voiceless spirant, slightly more to the front than German a*ch*, Scottish lo*ch*.

[h] Engl. *h*and. Before consonants a breath, making them voiceless: [hl̥, hn̥, hr̥]. Also [hj̊] = [ç] approx. Engl. *h*ue; [hw̥] = [xw̥] = Engl. *wh*at.

[ʰ] Aspiration and preaspiration—the latter not found in English—are puffs of breath, following or preceding stops (*p, t, k*). When a preaspiration follows [i] or [u] (alone, or in diphthongs) it may sound like [j̊] and [(x)w̥] respectively.

[j] Engl. *y*es.

[j̊] only after [h] which see.

[kʰ] Engl. *c*o*ck*.

[kⱼʰ] approx. Engl. *k*een (*k* or *ky*).

[k] Engl. s*k*ull, ras*c*al.

[kⱼ] approx. Engl. s*k*ein, as*k*ing (*ky*).

[ʰk] *hk*, lacking in Engl.

[ʰkⱼ] *hky*, lacking in Engl.

[l] approx. Engl. *l*ip.

[l̥] lacking in Engl., Welsh *ll*.

[m] Engl. *m*an.

[m̥] lacking in Engl.

[n] Engl. *n*anny.

[n̥] lacking in Engl.

[ŋ] Engl. si*ng*, si*ng*er, ba*n*k.
[ŋ̊] lacking in Engl.
[n̥] an [n] with the oral articulation of the following
  [s], a nasalized [s]; similarly [nᵛ, n̪, nⱼ, n̠] before
  [v/f, þ, j/hj̊, hw̥]. Lacking in English. These
  pronunciations are dis-
  regarded in the Glossary.
[pʰ] Engl. *p*a*p*a, *p*e*p*.
[p] Engl. s*p*in, ves*p*er.
[ʰp] *hp*, lacking in English.

[r] Scottish *r* *r*un, ve*r*y.
[r̥] lacking in English.
[s] Engl. *s*o, ha*s*te (never as in
  ro*s*e).
[tʰ] Engl. *t*ime, bai*t*.
[t] Engl. s*t*and, hos*t*ess.
[ʰt] *ht*, lacking in English.
[v] Engl. *v*an, re*v*ive, but
  weaker.
[w̥] only in [hw̥]==*wh* in Engl.
  *wh*at.
[þ] Engl. *th*in.

Note: Description in greater detail follows under the Icelandic sounds in **2** and **3** below.

3. *Words and Syllables.*

Icelandic words, like English, may be of one syllable (mono-syllabic), two syllables (disyllabic), or more syllables (polysyllabic): *bók* [bou:kʰ] book, *bækur* [bai:kʰʏr̥] books, *bókstafir* [bou:kʰ-sta.vɪr̥] letters. Most words are made up of a stem syllable and an ending: *sigl-a* [sɪg̊.la] sail, *vind-ur* [vɪn.d̥ʏr̥] wind. Such words are simple or uncompounded, while *Ís-land* [i:sland̥], Ice-land, is a disyllabic compound word. Most polysyllabic words are compounds: *Reykja-vík* [rei:kⱼʰavi:kʰ] 'Smoke Bay,' *Hafnar-fjörður* [hab̥·nar̥fjör·ðʏr̥] 'Haven Fjord,' *Sel-tjarnar-nes* [sɛl·-tʰjad̥narnɛ:s] 'Seal Pond Ness.'

None of these words is ordinarily hyphenated, but the hyphen is here used to indicate the conventional division of syllables in simple and compound words. In dividing simple words (*sigl-a*) the con-sonants between vowels always go with the preceding vowel. In compound words one divides between the compounding parts (*Ís-land*).

4. *Stress.*

Stress or accent (marked here only with ' before the syllable) in Icelandic falls regularly on the first syllable of a word: 'vindur [vɪn.d̥ʏr̥] wind, 'Ísland [i:sland̥]. In compound words some (secondary) stress also may fall on the second or third part: 'Hafnar'fjörður [hab̥·nar̥fjör·ðʏr̥], 'Seltjarnar'nes [sɛl·tʰjad̥-narnɛ:s]. Endings (-*a*, -*i*, -*u*, -*ar*, -*ir*, -*ur*, -*um*, etc.) are never stressed, yet they are never as short and clipped as endings may be

3

in English.   In general there is much less difference between stressed and unstressed syllables in Icelandic than in English. A few prefixes (*hálf-* [haul·*v*] half, *jafn-* [jab·n̥] even, equal, and *ó-* [ou:] un-), usually stressed, may be unstressed under certain conditions. The prefix *all-* [aḍ.l̥], rather, quite, is always unstressed.

5. Length.

1. In Icelandic both vowels and (most) consonants may be differentiated by length.   The spelling does not express length in vowels, but consonants are doubled to indicate that they are long, cp. *ana* [a:na], rush forward, with *Anna* [an:a] Ann.   The first word has a long stem vowel *a* + short *n* + a half long end vowel *a*. The second has a short *a* + a long (double) *n* + a half long *a*.

Note: The customary English terms 'long *a*,' 'short *a*' (in *ale*, b*a*ck) mean something quite different from the Icelandic long *a* [a:], short *a* [a]. In English the vowels are actually different in pronunciation, while in Icelandic both have nearly the same pronunciation (quality), but differ in duration or length, the long vowel being about twice as long as the short (in musical notation: long ♩, short ♪).

2. All Icelandic vowels may be either long or short.   They are *long*

(a) if no consonant follows;
(b) if followed by a single consonant;
(c) if followed by two consonants, the first of which is *p, t, k̇, s* [pʰ, tʰ, kʲʰ, kʰ, s] and the second of which is *j, r* or *v* [j, r, v].

They are *short*, if followed by more than one consonant, except as stated in (c). Before *pp, tt, kk* [ʰp:, ʰt:, ʰkʲ:, ʰk:] or *p, t, k* [ʰp·, ʰt·, ʰk·] followed by *l* or *n* [l, n] the vowels are especially clipped, because of the preaspiration [ʰ] that has developed before these sounds.   Instances:

(a) *þú* [þu:] thou, *nú* [nu:] now, *svo* [svɔ:] so; the names of the vowels: *a* [a:], *á* [au:], etc. (cf. *1*); *búa* [bu:a] farm, *lóa* [lou:a] plover.

(b) Long vowels:	Short vowels:
hatur [ha:tʰʏr̥] hate	*hattur* [haʰt:ʏr̥] hat
Ása [au:sa] fem. proper name	*Ásta* [aus·ta] fem. proper name
Keli [kʲʰɛ:lɪ] masc. pet name	*Ella* [ɛl:a] fem. pet name
hann lét [han: lje:tʰ] he let	*þú lézt* [þu: ljɛs·t] you let
ef [ɛ:v] if	*eff* [ɛf:] the letter *f*
hiti [hɪ:tʰɪ] heat	*hitti* [hɪʰt:ɪ] (he) hit

4

líta [liːtʰa] (to) look

okur [ɔːkʰʏɹ̩] usury

hól [houːl] praise

bruni [brʏːnɪ] fire

súpa [suːpʰa] (to) sip

sæl [saiːl] happy f.

völur [vöːlʏɹ̩] rod

haus [höyːs] head

heitur [heiːtʰʏɹ̩] hot m.

eyða [eiːða] spend

líttu [liʰtːʏ] look!

okkur [ɔʰkːʏɹ̩] us

hóll [houd̥l̩] hill, knoll

brunni [brʏnːɪ] dat. of *brunnur*
          m. well

súptu [sufˑtʏ] sip!

sæll [said̥l̩] happy m.

völlur [vöd̥lʏɹ̩] plain, field

gen. *hauss* [höysː] of a head

heitt [heiʰtː] hot n.

eyddi [eid̥ːɪ] spent

(c) Before *p, t, k, s + j, r, v*: *lepja* [leːpʰja] lap up, *vitja* [vɪːtʰja] visit, *vekja* [vɛːkjʰa] awaken, *Esja* [ɛːsja] a mountain, *skopra* [skɔːpʰra] roll, *titra* [tʰɪːtʰra] shiver, vibrate, *akrar* [aːkʰraɹ̩] fields, *tvisvar* [tʰvɪːsvaˑr] twice, *uppgötva* [ʏʰpːgöːtʰva] discover, *vökva* [vöːkʰva] water (flowers).

These rules apply to vowels in stem syllables and in endings (in final position, not within the sentence). There are few exceptions in stem syllables: *en* [ɛnː] but, *fram* [framː] forth, forward, *um* [ʏmː] about; all these have short vowels and long consonants in spite of the spelling. The ending *-um* [-ʏmː] likewise has a short vowel and long (or at any rate a half-long) consonant.

When stressed, endings have fully as long vowels as root syllables, hence *-ar* may rime with *þar*. Usually, however, the length of the vowels in endings is somewhat reduced (to half-length). Within the sentence the end vowel may become short, and it is frequently elided before another vowel. Hence the length of vowels (and consonants) in endings has been left unmarked. The consonants in the endings *-inn* [-ɪn] and *-um* [-ʏm] retain some length and are voiced, at least in careful speech.

3. When a monosyllabic word of the type *til* [tʰɪːl] to, *við* [vɪːð] with, at, *haf* [haːv] sea, ocean (having a long vowel plus a short consonant) comes to stand before a consonant in the second part of a compound word, then the vowel is shortened and the consonant lengthened. Examples: *til* [tʰɪːl] : *tilbúinn* [tʰɪlˑbuˑɪn] ready, ready made, *við* [vɪːð] : *viðkoma* [vɪðˑkʰɔˑma] touch, *haf* [haːv] : *hafgola* [havˑgɔˑla] breeze from the sea (as if written *till-, viðð-, havv-*). The same shift in length may happen within the sentence: *til komi þitt ríki* [tʰɪlˑ kʰɔˑmɪ þɪʰtˑ riːkjʰɪ] thy kingdom come (as if written *till komi . . .*). But before vowels, and *h* + vowel, there is no such change: *við*: *viðundur* [vɪːðʏnd̥ʏɹ̩]

fool, *viðhöfn* [vɪːðhöb̦n̦] show, ceremony, *til: til hans* [tʰɪːl (h)ans] to him.

Long vowels in monosyllabic words, ending in *p, t, k, s* [pʰ, tʰ, kʰ, s] are usually not susceptible to change in length: *laus* [löyːs] loose: *lauslega* [löyːslɛ·qa] loosely, approximately, *matur* [maːtʰɣɾ] food: *matmálstími* [maːtʰmaulstʰiːmɪ] time for meals.   Yet the change occurs in some very common words as *kaupmaður* [kʰöyʰpːma·ðɣɾ] merchant (as if written *kaupp-*), *kaupfélag* either [kʰöyː-fjɛ·laq] or [kʰöyf:jɛ·laq] co-operative society.

2. Survey of the Vowels.

1. *Pronunciation of the Vowels.*

The pronunciation of the Icelandic vowels is approximately as follows:

1. *a* [a]: as in English f*a*ther (long) or the Boston or Southern English pronunciation of *a*sk. Long: *faðir* [faːðɪɾ] father, *hatur* [haːtʰɣɾ] hate; short: *mann* [mannː] acc. of *maður* [maːðɣɾ] man, *hattur* [haʰtːɣɾ] hat. The American (not British!) *o* in st*o*pping may, perhaps, approach the Icelandic short *a* [a].

   Note 1: The combinations *ang, ank* are pronounced as if spelled *áng, ánk* [auŋ· g̊, auŋ·kʰ, auŋ·k], cf. the Special Remarks below.

   Note 2: The combination *agi* is pronounced as if spelled *ægi* or *æi* [aiːjɪ], more rarely [aːjɪ]; cf. the Special Remarks below.

2. *á* [au]: a diphthong, composed of Icelandic *a* and *ú*, as in c*o*w (long); the short variety is not found in English. Long: *skál* [skauːl] bowl, skoal, *bátur* [bauːtʰɣɾ] boat; short: *skáld* [skaul·d̦] poet, *átt* [auʰtː] direction.

3. *e* [ɛ]: as in *a*ir (long), g*e*tting (short). Long: *vera* [vɛːra] to be, *meta* [mɛːtʰa] to value; short: *verri* [vɛrːɪ] worse, *mettur* [mɛʰtːɣɾ] satisfied (by food).

   Note 1: The combinations *eng, enk, egi, egj-* are pronounced as if spelled *eing, eink, eigi, eigj-* [eiŋ· g̊, eiŋ·kʰ, eiŋ·k, eiːjɪ, eiːj-]; cf. Special Remarks below.

   Note 2: The interrogative pronoun *hver* [hwɛ̥ːr, hwɣ̥ːr], who, and its derivatives are usually pronounced as if spelled with *u*: *hvur* [hwɣ̥ːr] who, *hvergi* [hwɣ̥r· g̥̊jɪ] nowhere, *hvernig* [hwɣ̥d̦·nɪq or hwɣ̥d̦·nɪn] how, *hversslags* [hwɣ̥ɾ·slaxs] what kind of, *hvert* [hwɣ̥ɾ·t] whither, *einhver* [eiŋ·hwɣ̥r] somebody, *hvenær* [hwɣ̥ːna(i)ɾ] when. These are all colloquial forms.

But *hve* [hwɛ:] and *hversu* [hwɛ̣r·sɤ], how, being more literary, retain *e* [ɛ̣] as all the others may do, too, in a higher type of speech.

4. *é* [jɛ] : a diphthong, or rather a combination of Icelandic *j* and *e,* often spelled *je* (cf. *j*), as in *ye*s (long), *ye*sterday (shorter). Long: *hér* [hjɛ:r] here, *él* [jɛ:l] squall; short: *hérna* [hjɛd̦·na] here, *fékk* [fjɛʰk:] got.

5. *i* [ɪ] : as in b*i*d (longer), p*i*ty (shorter). Long: *vinur* [vɪ:nɤ̣r] friend, *vita* [vɪ:tʰa] know; short: *vinna* [vɪn:a] work, *hitta* [hɪʰt:a] hit.

Note 1: The combinations *ing, ink, igi, igj-* are pronounced as if spelled *íng, ínk,* (*i*)*ígi,* (*i*)*ígj-* [iŋ·g̊, iŋ·kʰ, iŋ·k, (ɪ)i:jɪ, (ɪ)i:j-]; cf. Special Remarks below.

Note 2: *illur* [ɪd̦·lɤ̣r], bad, evil, and words derived from it are often pronounced as if spelled *íllur* [id̦·lɤ̣r].

Note 3: Long *i* in *vinur* [vɪ:nɤ̣r] etc., tends to be pronounced like long *e* (above) : *venur* [vɛ:nɤ̣r], but such pronunciation is considered vulgar. Cf. Special Remarks 3 (c)·

6. *í* [i] : as in gr*ee*n (long) ; a short *ee* is not found in English. Long: *ís* [i:s] ice, *hvítur* [hwi:tʰɤ̣r] white; short: *á ísnum* [is·nɤm] on the ice, *hvítt* [hwi̦ʰt:] white n.

7. *o* [ɔ] : as in l*aw* (long) ; the short vowel is somewhat like *o* in English (not American!) kn*o*tty. Long: *gola* [gɔ:la] breeze, *votur* [vɔ:tʰɤ̣r] wet; short: *volgur* [vɔl·g̊ɤ̣r] tepid, lukewarm, *gott* [gɔʰt:] good n.

Note 1: The combination *ong* is pronounced as if spelled *óng* [ouŋ·g̊]; cf. Special Remarks below.

Note 2: The combination *ogi* is pronounced as if spelled *oíji* or *oji* [ɔi:jɪ, ɔ:jɪ]. Cf. Special Remarks below.

Note 3: The interrogative pronoun *hvor*, which of two, is sometimes pronounced *hvur* [hwɤ:r], but this pronunciation should not be adopted because of confusion with *hver* [hwɤ̣:r] (see 3. *e* above). Similarly with *u*: *hvorugur* [hwɤ:rɤqɤ̣r], neither of two, and *hvorki . . . né* [hwɤ̣r·kjɪ . . . njɛ:] neither . . . nor.

8. *ó* [ou] : a diphthong, composed of Icelandic *o* (better: English *o* in n*o*te) and *ú,* as in sl*ow,* n*o*te (long) ; the short diphthong does not occur in English. Long: *skóli* [skou:lɪ] school, *mót* [mou:tʰ] meeting; short: *hóll* [houd̦·l] hill, *flótti* [flouʰt:ɪ] flight.

9. *u* [ʏ]: is somewhat similar to German *ü* in m*ü*ssen, M*ü*tter (slightly more open), but nothing similar is found in English. It is really a rounded Icelandic *i*. To pronounce it pronounce t*i*n with unchanged tongue position but with pursed lips. The result should be *tun* as in *tunna* [tʰʏnːa] barrel. Long: *munur* [mʏːnʏ̦r] difference, *lukum* [lʏːkʰʏm] we finished; short: *munnur* [mʏnːʏ̦r] mouth, *lukka* [lʏʰkːa] luck, happiness.

Note 1: The combinations *ung, unk* are pronounced as if spelled *úng, únk* [uŋ·g̊, uŋ·kʰ, uŋ̊·k]. Cf. Special Remarks below.

Note 2: The combination *ugi* may be pronounced as if spelled *uiji* or *uji* [ʏyːjɪ or ʏːjɪ]. A third very common pronunciation [yːjɪ] cannot be spelled with Icelandic letters, but here the *ug* has the sound of French *u* in *tuer*. Cf. Special Remarks below.

Note 3: The dative plural ending of nouns with a suffixed article *-unum* is often pronounced as if spelled *-onum*: *mönnunum* [mönːʏnʏm or mönːɔnʏm] to the men.

Note 4: Long *u*, as in *munur*, tends to be pronounced as long *ö*, but such pronunciation is considered vulgar. Cf. Special Remarks 3 (c).

10. *ú* [u]: as in sch*oo*l (long); short *oo* is not found in English except with a different quality in f*u*lly. Long: *hún* [huːn] she, *hús* [huːs] house; short: *brúnni* [brunːɪ] dative singular of *brú-in* [bruːɪn] the bridge, *stúlka* [stul·kʰa, stul̦·ka] girl.

11. *y* and *ý* are pronounced like Icelandic *i* and *í* (above).

Note: In a few words *y* is pronounced like Icelandic *u*, but only colloquially: *spyrja* [spɪr·ja, spʏr·ja] ask, *smyrja* [smɪr·ja, smʏr·ja] spread butter on, grease, *kyrr* [kjʰɪr:, kjʰʏr:] quiet, *ykkur* [ɪʰk·ʏ̦r, ʏʰk·ʏ̦r] acc., dat., *ykkar* [ɪʰk·ar̦, ʏʰk·ar̦] gen. of *þið* [þɪːð] you.

12. *æ* [ai]: a diphthong, composed of Icelandic *a* and *i*, as in h*i*gh (long); a short *i* does not occur in English. Long: *mæla* [maiːla] measure, *mæta* [maiːtʰa] meet; short: *mældi* [mail·d̦ɪ] measured, *hætta* [haiʰtːa] cease.

Note: *ætla*, intend, be going to, is often pronounced as if spelled *attla* [aʰtːla].

13. *ö* [ö]: as in German h*ö*ren, French p*eu*r (perhaps slightly less open). Somewhat similar to English f*ur*, b*ur*n. To pronounce Icelandic *ö* try pronouncing English *men* with pursed lips (rounded). The result should be *mön* as in *mönnum* [mönːʏm] dat. pl. of *maður* [maːðʏ̦r] man. Long: *vör* [vöːr] lip, *vök*

[vö:kʰ] a hole in the ice; short: *börn* [böḍ·ṇ] children, *sökk* [söʰk:] sank.

Note: The combinations *öng, önk, ögi* are pronounced as if spelled *aung, aunk, augi* [öyŋ·g̊, öyŋ·kʰ, öyṇ·k, öy:jɪ]. Cf. Special Remarks below.

14. *au* [öy]: a diphthong as in French *feuille*, not found in English, composed of Icelandic *ö* and *i* (or rather [y]). To imitate the Icelandic sound try to pronounce *bay* with pursed instead of spread lips. The result should be Icelandic *bau* as in *bauja* [böy:ja] buoy. Long: *aurar* [öy:raṛ] sandy plains, small coins, *havs* [höy:s] head; short: *haust* [höys·t] fall, autumn.

15. *ei* [ei]: a diphthong, composed of Icelandic *e* (better: English *a* in hate) and *i*, as in English *ale* (long); the short variety is lacking in English. Long: *ein* [ei:n] one f., *reipi* [rei:pʰɪ] rope; short: *einn* [eiḍ·ṇ] one m., *heitt* [heiʰt:] hot n.

16. *ey* is pronounced like *ei*.

2. Special Remarks on the Vowels.

1. Vowels before *ng, nk.*—Before *ng, nk* [ŋ·g̊, ŋ·kʰ, ṇ·k] the vowels *a, e, i, o, u, y, ö* [a, ɛ, ɪ, ɔ, ʏ, ɪ, ö] are pronounced as (short) *á, ei, í, ó, ú, ý, au* [au, ei, i, ou, u, i, öy] and by some writers are so spelled. Examples: *langur* (*lángur*) [lauŋ·g̊ʏṛ] long, *banki* (*bánki*) [bauŋ·kⱼʰɪ, bauṇ·kⱼɪ] bank, *enginn* (*einginn*) [eiŋ·g̊ⱼɪn] nobody, *þing* (*þíng*) [þiŋ·g̊] parliament, assembly, convention, *kongur* (*kóngur*) [kʰouŋ·g̊ʏṛ] king, *ungur* (*úngur*) [uŋ·g̊ʏṛ] young, *munkur* (*múnkur*) [muŋ·kʰʏṛ, muṇ·kʏṛ] monk, *yngri* (*ýngri*) [iŋ·g̊rɪ] younger, *þröngur* (*þraungur*) [þröyŋ·g̊ʏṛ] narrow. If *n* and *g* (or *k*) belong to different syllables, the vowels remain unchanged: *van-gá* [vaŋ·gau·] inadvertence, *vin-gjarnlega* [vɪŋ·-g̊ⱼaḍnlɛ:qa] in a friendly way. Occasional exceptions, like *vingast* [vɪŋ·g̊ast] get friendly, are due to association with words where the change does not take place, in this case *vinur* [vɪ:nʏṛ] friend.

2. Vowels before *gi, gj.*—Before *gi, gj* (pronounced *ji, j* [jɪ, j]) *a, e, i, o, u, y, ö* [a, ɛ, ɪ, ɔ, ʏ, ɪ, ö] are often pronounced as (long) *æ, ei, í, oí, uí, ý, au* [ai:, ei:, (ɪ)i:, ɔi:, (ʏ)y:, (ɪ)i:, öy:]. Thus *daginn* [dai:jɪn] acc., the day, rhymes with *bæinn* [bai:jɪn] acc., the farm; *segja* [sei:ja], say, with *eyja* [ei:ja] island; *segir* [sei:jɪṛ], he says, with *eigir* [ei:jɪṛ] (that) you own; *stigi* [st(ɪ)i:jɪ], ladder, with *mýi* [mi:jɪ] dat. of *mý* [mi:] mosquito swarm. *Bogi* [bɔi:jɪ], bow, and *hugi* [h(ʏ)y:ɪ], mind, rhyme only with words in *-ogi, -ugi*, but *lögin* [löy:jɪn], the law, rhymes with *hauginn* [höy:jɪn] the

mound, heap. (If the vowels and the *gi, gj* belong to different syllables, nothing happens: *hé-gilja* [hje̞:gjɪlja] trifle, superstition). From such forms as starting points *œ, ei, i* are sometimes extended to other forms: *laginn* [lai:jɪn] adept, skilful, pl. *lagnir* [la(i)g̊·nɪr̥]; *spegill* [spei:jɪd̥l̩] mirror, pl. *speglar* [speig̊·lar̥]; *megir* [mei:jɪr̥] (that) you may, infinitive *mega* [mei:qa] be able to; *siginn* [s(ɪ)i:jɪn] sunk, drained, pl. *signir* [sig̊·nɪr̥].

Dialectally *a, e, i, o, u, y, ö* are kept and pronounced long before *gi, gj*: *daginn* [da:jɪn], *tregi* [tʰrɛ:jɪ] grief, *stigi* [stɪ:jɪ], *bogi* [bɔ:jɪ], *hugi* [hɤ:jɪ], *lögin* [lö:jɪn].

3. The Icelandic Vowel System.—(a) Phonetically the Icelandic vowels can be arranged as follows in the conventional vowel triangle:

Monophthongs	Front Central		Back	Diphthongs
High (close)	*i* [i]		*ú* [u]	Ending in *i*: *œ* [ai], *ei* [ei],
High mid	*i* [ɪ] *u* [ɤ]			*ig*(*i*) [(ɪ)i:], *og*(*i*) [ɔi:]
Low mid	*e* [ɛ] *ö* [ö]		*o* [ɔ]	Ending in [y]: *au* [öy],
				ug(*i*) [(ɤ)y:]
Low (open)	*a* [a]			Ending in *ú*: *á* [au], *ó* [ou]

u [ɤ] and *ö* [ö] are rounded front vowels; *o* [ɔ] and *ú* [u] rounded back vowels. *é* = *je* [jɛ] is not here included; like *ja* [ja], *jö* [jö], *jó* [jou], etc., it is a combination of *j* + vowel.

(b) The first elements in the diphthongs *ei* [ei], *ó* [ou] are slightly higher (closer) than the simple Icelandic vowels *e* [ɛ], *o* [ɔ]. These diphthongs correspond closely to the American-English vowels in *a*le, h*o*le. British *o* in h*o*le is different.

The second elements [i, y, u] of the diphthongs are, perhaps, never fully [i, y, u], except before *j* ([i, y]) and *g* [q] ([u]), and at the end of words. Before consonants, and especially when short, the second element is considerably lowered, but not so as to be readily identifiable with Icelandic *i* [ɪ], *u* [ɤ] (an [ʊ], as in English f*u*ll, is completely lacking in Icelandic). When the diphthongs are short, the second element is often obscured or reduced, sometimes lost or merged with the first element in a new sound. Thus *œtla* [aiʰt·la], intend, is usually pronounced as if spelled *attla* [aʰt·la] and *austur* [öys·tɤr̥], east, is sometimes pronounced *ustur* [ɤs·tɤr̥].

The mastering of the short diphthongs is undoubtedly one of the most difficult tasks in learning Icelandic. A few examples to bring out the differences between long and short, and between *i* [ɪ],

10

i [i], *u* [ɤ]-[y] respectively would therefore not seem to be out of place:

Long:			Short:		
sit [sɪːtʰ] *sýti* [siːtʰɪ]		*sœti* [saiːtʰɪ]	*sitt* [sɪʰtː]	*sitt* [siʰtː]	*sœtt* [saiʰtː]
nutum [nɤːtʰɤm]		*naut* [nöyːtʰ]	*rutt* [rɤʰtː]		*autt* [öyʰtː]
slúta [sluːtʰa] *áta* [auːtʰa]		*sóti* [souːtʰɪ]	*slútti* [sluʰtːɪ] *átti* [auʰtːɪ]		*sótti* [souʰtːɪ]

Note, that before *tt* [ʰtː] the second elements of the diphthongs are unvoiced and may give the impression of voiceless spirants: [i] > [j̊] or [ç], [y] likewise, but [u] > [w̥] or [xw̥]. This spirantisation of the vowel is also plainly observable in case of simple *í* [i], *ú* [u], but not after *i* [ɪ], *u* [ɤ].

(c) The high mid and low mid vowels (the "lax" vowels, see below) all tend to be diphthongized when long. The resulting diphthongs begin with a closer position and end with a more open (or at least equally open) position than the corresponding short vowels. Thus *i* [ɪː] becomes [iɛː], *e* [ɛː] becomes [iɛː, ɛæː], *u* [ɤː] becomes [ɤöː], *ö* becomes [ɤöː, ööː], and *o* [ɔː] becomes [uɔː, ɔaː].

Besides, *i* [ɪː] and *u* [ɤː] show a widespread tendency to become *e* [ɛː] and *ö* [öː], which in turn are hit by the just mentioned diphthongization (very common among Icelandic-Americans), but that tendency is considered vulgar.

The Icelandic vowels may be divided into two groups, called "tense" (*breiðir* broad) or "lax" (*grannir* thin). The first group consists of *í, ú* and the diphthongs, ending in [i, y, u]; these were all originally long vowels, diphthongs, or short vowels + *g*. The second group comprises the rest; these were originally short vowels. Each group can be arranged in triplets as follows:

Breið sérhljóð Tense vowels				*Grönn sérhljóð* Lax vowels		
High	*í* [i]	*ú* [u]	*ug*(*i*) [(ɤ)yː]	High mid *i* [ɪ]	*u* [ɤ]
High mid *ei* [ei]	*ó* [ou]	*au*	[öy]	Low mid *e* [ɛ]	*ö* [ö]
Low	*æ* [ai]	*á* [au]	*og*(*i*) [ɔiː]	Low *a* [a]	*o* [ɔ]

In this table *ig*(*i*) [(ɪ)iː] is neglected, but it may roughly be classified with *í* [i]. Likewise, there is a discrepancy in the third row of the tense vowels, the two first diphthongs ending in [y] but the last in *í* [i]. But [y] may be considered to be a variant of the Icelandic *í* phoneme, and in Icelandic orthography the diphthongs in question would be written phonetically *ui, öi, oi*.

It follows from the definition above, that the terms "lax" and "tense" are here used in a special sense, different from that in other grammatical works. But in the older language the difference was actually that between a lax and a tense vowel.

11

3. Survey of Consonants.

1. *Preliminary Note.*

Most consonants may be short, half-long, and long (doubled in the orthography) ; in the following, examples to illustrate all these stages of length will be given, if they exist.

The Icelandic orthography usually indicates full length of a consonant by doubling it; but sometimes the doubling of a consonant is retained, when it is actually pronounced only half-long; this happens when an original double consonant comes to stand before another consonant e. g. *kyssa* [kjʰɪsːa] kiss, preterite *kyssti* [kjʰɪs·tɪ]. This is now the official orthography; at other times it has called for the simplification of double consonants before other consonants, i. e. *kysti*, and many writers follow that practice.

A *stop* is a consonant made by full closure of the mouth (*p, t, k* [pʰ, tʰ, kjʰ, kʰ]—*b, d, g* [b̥, d̥, g̊j, g̊]) ; a *spirant* is made by narrowing of the oral passage at some point (*f, þ, s, hj, hv, k/g + t* [f, þ, s, hj̊ or ç, hw̥ or xw̥, x]--*v, ð, j, g* [v, ð, j, q]). In the *liquids* (*l, r* [l, r]), too, there is a narrowing of the oral passage, but in *l* the opening is on the side, and in *r* the tip of the tongue is trilled (Scottish *r*). The nasals (*m, n, n(g)* [m, n, ŋ]) are, like the stops, made by closure in the mouth, but the nasal passage is left open.

Note: The accompanying palatograms picture the roof of the mouth (the palate—front—and part of the velum—back) under àrticulation of several stops and spirants, etc. The shaded parts show where the tongue has touched in articulation.

A consonant is *voiceless* if the vocal cords are left wide open, giving free passage to the air from the lungs. The result is a breath or an aspiration, as in *h* [h], unchecked except for the stoppage or narrowing in the mouth which marks the particular consonant. A consonant is *voiced* if the vocal cords vibrate, producing a singing or humming tone. Compare *pit*: *bid, fat*: *vat, thin*: *this, seal*: *zeal*; the first word of each pair contains a voiceless, the second a voiced consonant.

The place of a consonant in a given word (phrase) is often of prime importance for pronunciation. For the sake of shortness we shall use *initial(ly)*, *medial(ly)*, *final(ly)* to designate position at the beginning of a word, within a word, and at the end of a word.

2. *Pronunciation of the Consonants.*

1. *b*: *b* is always voiceless. Initially it sounds like English *b* [b]:

1. dama
   tap

2. nef
   Anna
   hnefi

3. ana

4. eða
   ennþá

5. sama
   vansa

6. Ara
   rama

7. mala
   lama
   álpa

8. gef
   kef

9. gaf
   kaf

10. ja
    hja

**PALATO-
GRAMS**

11. aga
    hva

1 and 2: dental d, t, n, nn, hn;
3: supra-dental n;   4: interdental ð, þ, nþ;
5: supra-dental s, ns;   6: supra-dental r;
7: supra-dental l;   8: palatal (front) g, k;
9: velar (back) g, k;   10: palatal j, hj;
            11: velar g, hv.

bera [bɛːra] carry. Medially and finally it sounds more like *p* (French *p*) and is marked [b̥]; short: *lamb* [lam·b̥] lamb; long: *kobbi* [kʰɔb·ɪ] young seal.

Note: *b* is lost between *m* and *d, t, s, g*: *kemba* [kjʰɛm·ba] comb, preterite *kembdi* [kjʰɛm·d̥ɪ], past participle *kembt* [kjʰɛm·tʰ, kjʰɛm̥·t].

2. *d*: *d* is always voiceless. Initially it sounds like English *d* [d]: *dagur* [da:qʏr̥] day. Medially and finally it sounds more like *t* (French *t*) and is marked [d̥]. Short: *landi* [lan·d̥ɪ] compatriot, *öld* [öl·d̥] century; long: *saddur* [sad̥:ʏr̥] satisfied.

Note 1: *d* is lost between *l, n* and *g, n, l, k, s*: *holdgun* [hɔl·g̊ʏn] incarnation, *úldna* [ul·(d̥)na] get putrid, *sundla* [sʏn·(d̥)la] get dizzy, *lands* [lan·s] gen. of *land* [lan·d̥] land, etc.

Note 2: Beware of using the weak or slurred American *d* in ol*d* and ru*dd*er!

3. *ð*: *ð* is a voiced spirant [ð] as in brea*the*, slightly weaker than the English sound. Occurs medially or finally only; short: *eða* [ɛ:ða] or; half-long: *fjaðrir* [fjað·rɪr̥] feathers. Before *k* it may remain or become voiceless, i. e. [þ]: *blaðka* [blað·kʰa, blaþ·ka] leaf, leaflet. It is only half-voiced in final position *bað* [ba:ð] bath.

Note: *ð* is lost between *r* and *n, g* and *s*: *harðna* [hard̥na] harden (see *rn* 13 (d)), *bragðs* [brax·s] gen. of *bragð* [braq·ð] trick.

4. *f*: (a) *f* is a voiceless spirant [f] as in *f*ather; short initially: *faðir* [fa:ðɪr̥] father; half-long medially before voiceless consonants (*t, k, s*): *oft* [ɔf·t] often, *ofsi* [ɔf·sɪ] violence; long medially and finally: *kaffi* [kʰaf:ɪ] coffee, *offra* [ɔf:ra] sacrifice, *eff* [ɛf:] the letter *f*.

(b) *f* is a voiced spirant [v] (= *v*) as in ha*v*en; short between vowels or between a voiced consonant and a vowel (voiced consonant): *hafa* [ha:va] have, *horfa* [hɔr·va] look, *ýlfra* [il·(v)ra] howl; half-long before voiced consonants and *g*: *hafði* [hav·ðɪ] had, *lífga* [liv·g̊a] call to life.

(c) *f* is a half-voiced spirant [v] (short) finally after vowels and voiced consonants: *haf* [ha:v] ocean, *horf* [hɔr·v] direction.

(d) The combinations *fl, fn* (sometimes *fð*) are pronounced [b̥·l, b̥·n, (b̥·ð)] between vowels or [b̥·l, b̥·n, (b̥·þ)] at the end of a word: *efla* [ɛb̥·la] strengthen, *hefna* [hɛb̥·na] avenge, *afl* [ab̥·l̥] strength, *höfn* [höb̥·n̥] harbor (*hafði* [hab̥·ðɪ] had, *hefð* [hɛb·þ] title). Before consonants *fl, fn* are pronounced [vl or lv]/[fl̥ or l̥f], [m· or f·] : *efldi* [ɛvld̥ɪ, ɛlvd̥ɪ] strengthened, *eflt* [ɛfl̥t, ɛl̥ft] strengthened pp., *hefndi* [hɛm·d̥ɪ] avenged, *hefnt* [hɛm·tʰ, hɛm·t] avenged pp., *jafnt* [jam·tʰ, jam·t or jaf·t] even n., *hrafns* [hr̥af·s] gen. of *hrafn* [hr̥ab·n̥] raven.

Note: *f* is lost (a) between *l* and *n, r, s, t*: *hálfna* [haul·na] finish half of, *hálfri* [haul·(v)rɪ] dat. fem. of *hálfur* [haul·vɣr̥] half, *hálfs* [haul·(f)s] gen. of *hálfur, hálft* [haul̥·(f)t] neuter of *hálfur*; (b) sometimes after *á, ó, ú*: *lófi* [lou:(v)ɪ] palm of the hand, *húfa* [hu:a] cap.

5. *g*: (a) *g* is a voiceless short back stop [g], sounding like English *g* in *good*, initially before back vowels and consonants: *gata* [ga:tʰa] road, street, *grár* [grau:r] grey; in other positions it sounds more like *k* (French *k*) and is marked [g̊]: medially (half-long) before *n, l* and sometimes *ð*: *rigna* [rɪg̊·na] rain, *sigla* [sɪg̊·la] sail, *sagði* [saq·ðɪ or sag̊·ðɪ] said; medially (short) after consonants and before *a, u*, or finally (short) after consonants: *blóðga* [blouð·g̊a] draw blood, *lífga* [liv·g̊a] revive, *Helga* [hɛl·g̊a] fem. proper name, *hanga* [hauŋ·g̊a] hang, *bjarga* [bjar·g̊a] save. It is a long voiceless back stop, written double, between vowels, if the following vowel is *a, u*, before *r, v*, or at the end of a word: *Sigga* [sɪg̊:a] fem. pet name, gen. *Siggu* [sɪg̊:ɣ]; *naggra* [nag̊·ra] reach (scrape) bottom (of boats); *höggva* [hög̊·va] hew, *högg* [hög̊:] blow. *Guð* [gvɣ:ð], god, and words compounded with it, insert a *v* [v] after the *g*.

(b) *g* is a voiceless short front stop [gⱼ], sounding like English *y* in *geese* (or *gy* in Virginian *gy*arden): initially before the front vowels *e, i, í, y, ý, æ, ei, ey*, and *j*: *geta* [gⱼɛ:tʰa] be able to, *Gísli* [gⱼis·lɪ] m. proper name, *gylla* [gⱼɪd·la] gild, *Geysir* [gⱼei·sɪr̥] a famous hot spring (the Gusher), *gæta* [gⱼai:tʰa] watch, *geit* [gⱼei:tʰ] goat, *gjamma* [gⱼam:a] yelp. Elsewhere *g* sounds more like an English *ky* (in *cyan*) (French *qui*) and is marked [g̊ⱼ]: medially (short) after consonants before *i* or *j*: *Helgi* [hɛl·g̊ⱼɪ] masc. proper name, *bjargi* [bjar·g̊ⱼɪ] dat. of *bjarg* [bjar·g̊] rock, cliff, *syngja* [sɪŋ·g̊ⱼa] sing; medially long, written double, before *i* and *j*: *Siggi* [sɪg̊ⱼ:ɪ] masc. pet name, *beggja* [bɛg̊ⱼ:a] of both.

(c) *g* is a voiced short back spirant [q], as in German sa*g*en (not quite that far back), after vowels before *a, u* in endings: *eiga* [ei:qa] own, *eigum* [ei:qɣm] we own; half-long before the consonants *ð, r* (shortened before *ld*): *sagði* [saq·ðɪ] said, *sigra* [sɪq·ra] win the victory (*sigldi* [sɪqld̥ɪ] sailed). In final position the spirant is short and half-voiced: *lag* [la:q] layer, *sög* [sö:q] saw.

(d) *g* is a voiceless half-long back spirant [x], as in German *ach* (not quite that far back) or Scottish lo*ch*, before the consonants *s, t* (shortened before *lt*): *hugsa* [hɤx·sa] think, *sagt* [sax·t] said pp. (*siglt* [sɪxl̥t] sailed pp.).

(e) *g* is a voiced short front spirant [j], as in English *y*es (= Icelandic *j*) after vowels before *i* and *j*: *leigi* [lei:jɪ] I rent, *segi* [sei:jɪ] I say, *leigja* [lei:ja] rent, *segja* [sei:ja] say.

Note: *g* is lost (a) between *l* and *d, t, n, s*: *fylgdi* [fɪl·(q)d̥ɪ] followed, *fylgt* [fɪl̥·(x)t] followed pp., *bólgna* [boul·(q)na] be inflamed, etc.; (b) between *r* and *ð, t, n*: *birgðir* [bir·(q)ðɪr̥] provisions, *margt* [mar̥·t], many n., *morgni* [mɔd̥·nɪ] dat. of *morgunn* [mɔr·g̊ɤn] morning; (c) in the combinations *ng* and *gn* before consonants: *hringdi* [hr̥ɪŋ·d̥ɪ] rang, *rigndi* [rɪŋ·d̥ɪ] rained; (d) in final position after *á, ó, ú*, medially between these vowels and *a, u* of the ending: *lág* [lau:] hollow, *dróg* [drou:] bad horse, *súg* [su:] draft (acc. sg.), *drógar* [drou:ar̥] hacks (horses), *drógu* [drou:ɤ] they drew.

6. *h*: *h* is a (short) breath, as in English *h*ome, [h]: *heima* [hei:ma] at home. It occurs only initially, and not only before vowels but also before consonants in the combinations *hl, hn, hr, hj, hv*. *Hl* sounds like Welsh *Ll* in *Lloyd*; *hj* is similar to English *h* in *h*ue; *hv* is like *wh* in *wh*at in North English and General American. Examples: *hjarta* [hjar̥·ta] heart, *hér* [hjɛːr] here, *hlutur* [hl̥ɤ:tʰɤr̥] thing, *hnífur* [hn̥i:vɤr̥] knive, *hrútur* [hr̥u:tʰɤr̥] ram, *hvað* [hw̥a:ð] what, *hvíld* [hwil·d̥] rest. Note that *hv* is frequently pronounced as *kv* [kʰva:ð], [kʰvil·d̥].

Note: *h* is usually lost in pronouns within the sentence: *er (h)ann* is he; it is also lost in the second part of compound words, especially after voiceless consonants: *hest(h)ús* [hɛs·tu·s] stable for horses.

7. *j*: *j* is a short front spirant, as English *y* in *y*es [j]: *já* [jau:] yes, *Björn* [bjöd̥·n̥] masc. proper name, literally Bear, *brjóta* [brjou:tʰa] break, *fljúga* [fl̥ju:(q)a] fly, *snjór* [snjou:r] snow, *hrjóta* [hr̥jou:tʰa] snore, *jakka* [ja^hk:a] acc. of *jakki* [ja^hkj:ɪ] jacket, *hjakka* [hja^hk:a] hack again and again, *telja* [tʰɛl·ja] count, *temja* [tʰɛm·ja] break in, *erja* [ɛr·ja] plow, *efja* [ɛv·ja] mud. When *j* follows the stops *g* and *k* it fronts them, almost disappearing itself: *bergja* [bɛr·g̊ja] taste, *leggja* [lɛg̊j:a] lay, *velkja* [vɛl·kj^ha] soil, *ekkja* [ɛ^hkj:a] widow. In the combinations

15

-gj- and *-gi, g* becomes *j*. After *h, j* becomes voiceless: *hér* [hjɛːr] here, *hjakka* [hjḁʰkːa] hack.

8. *k*: (a) *k* is a voiceless aspirated short back stop [kʰ], as in English *cow*, initially before back vowels and consonants: *kaka* [kʰaːkʰa] cake, acc. *köku* [kʰöːkʰʏ], *koma* [kʰɔːma] come; *króna* [kʰrouːna] crown, *klippa* [kʰlɪʰpːa] clip, *Knútur* [kʰnuːtʰʏr̥] Canute; medially between vowels, or between a vowel and *r, v*: *taka* [tʰaːkʰa] take, *akrar* [aːkʰrar̥] fields, *vökva* [vöːkʰva] water; also medially after voiced consonants: *bliðka* [blið·kʰa] soften, *bankar* [bauŋ·kʰar̥] banks; finally after a vowel or a voiced consonant: *tak* [tʰaːkʰ] hold, *hönk* [höyŋ·kʰ] hank, coil.

(b) Double *k* (*kk*) is a long preaspirated voiceless back stop [ʰkː], not found in English. It occurs between vowels, if the following vowel is *a* or *u*, or between a vowel and a following *r, v*, or in final position: *brekka* [brɛʰkːa] slope, acc. *brekku* [brɛʰkːʏ]; *þykkra* [þɪʰkːra] gen. pl. of *þykkur* [þɪʰkːʏr̥] thick, *sökkva* [söʰkːva] sink; *þökk* [þöʰkː] thanks. Before *l, n* a *kk* or *k* is here marked only half-long [ʰk·] (though it has very nearly full length): *ökkli* [öʰk·lɪ] ankle, *ekla* [ɛʰk·la] lack, dearth, *þykkna* [þɪʰk·na] become thick, *lækna* [laiʰk·na] cure, heal.

(c) *k* is a voiceless aspirated short front stop [kjʰ], similar to *k* in English *keen* (or *ky* in dialectic *cyan*), before the front vowels *e, i, í, y, ý, æ, ei, ey*, and *j*. Examples: *kenna* [kjʰɛnːa] teach, *kista* [kjʰɪsta] chest, *kíkir* [kjʰiːkjʰɪr̥] field glass, *kýr* [kjʰiːr] cow, *kæra* [kjʰaiːra] accuse, *keyra* [kjʰeiːra] drive, *Kjartan* [kjʰar̥·tan] masc. proper name, *Kjós* [kjʰouːs] place name, *Reykjavík* [rei·kjʰaviːkʰ] 'Smoke Bay,' *Reykir* [rei·kjʰɪr̥] 'Smokes.'

(d) Double *k* (*kk*) is a long preaspirated voiceless front stop [ʰkjː], not found in English. It occurs only between a vowel and a following *i* or *j*: *þekkir* [þɛʰkjːɪr̥] knows, *þekkja* [þɛʰkjːa] know.

(e) *k* is a voiceless unaspirated stop—back or front according to the following vowel as explained above—as in English *scan, skein*, if preceded by a voiceless spirant, liquid, or nasal: *skamma* [skamːa] scold, *skemma* [skjɛmːa] spoil; *rífka* [rif·ka] enlarge, *rífki* [rif·kjɪ] (that I) enlarge, *askur* [as·kʏr̥] ash (the tree), *eski* [ɛs·kjɪ] ash (the wood); *verka* [vɛr̥·ka] gen. pl., *verki* [vɛr̥·kjɪ] dat. sg. of *verk* [vɛr̥·k] work. Since *l, m, n* may be either voiced or voiceless before *k*, the *k* is either aspirated or not after these sounds: *hálka* [haul·kʰa or hauḷ·ka] slipperiness, *aumkva* [öym·kʰva or öyṃ·kva] pity, *Rænka* [raiŋ·kʰa or raíŋ·ka] familiar name for *Ragnheiður* [rag̊·ṇ(h)ɛi·ðyŗ] fem. proper name.

(f) *k* is a half-long back spirant [x], as in German a*ch* (not quite that far back), Scottish lo*ch*, before *t* and *s* : *slíkt* [slix·t] such, *taktu* [tʰax·tɤ] take!, *flaksa* [flax·sa] flap.

(g) *k* is often pronounced like an Icelandic *g* (i. e. like a French *k*), that is, as a voiceless unaspirated stop—back or front according to the following vowel—after long vowels: *taka* [tʰa:g̊a] take, *akrar* [a:g̊raŗ] fields, *vökva* [vö:g̊va] water, *tekinn* [tʰɛ:g̊ʲɪn] taken, *tekjur* [tʰɛ:g̊ʲyŗ] income; *ók* [ou:g̊] drove.

Note: *k* is lost usually between *l, n, r, s* and *t, st*: *velkt* [vɛḷ·t] soiled, *skenkt* [skʲeiŋ·tʰ, skʲeiŋ̊·t] poured pp., *enskt* [ɛn·st] English n., etc.

9. *l*: (a) *l* is a voiced liquid [l], like French and German *l*, but never as hollow (retracted) as the English *l* in fi*ll*; *l* in lea*ve* is, perhaps, slightly more like the Icelandic sound. It is short in *lifa* [lɪ:va] live, *ljúfur* [lju:vyŗ] dear, *tala* [tʰa:la] speak, and, half-voiceless, in final position: *öl* [ö:l̥] ale, bear. It is half-long before voiced consonants and *b, d, g*: *eldur* [ɛl·d̥yŗ] fire, *volgur* [vɔl·g̊yŗ] lukewarm, *ólmur* [oul·myŗ] eager, mad.

(b) *l* is a voiceless liquid [l̥], not found in English, short initially after *h* : *hlaupa* [hl̥öy:pʰa] run; medially (half-long) always before *t*, often before *p* and *k* : *elta* [ɛl̥·ta] pursue, *stelpa* [stɛl̥·pʰa or stɛḷ·pa] girl (disrespectfully), *stúlka* [stul·kʰa or stuḷ·ka] girl. Also (short) in final position, if preceded by a stop or an *s* : *dufl* [dɤb̥·l̥] buoy, *fugl* [fɤg̊·l̥] bird, *rupl* [rɤʰp·l̥] plundering, *gutl* [gɤʰt·l̥] dabbling, *hekl* [hɛʰk·l̥] crocheting, *rusl* [rɤs·l̥] rubbish.

(c) Double *l* (*ll*) is pronounced as Icelandic *dl* (i. e. nearly *tl*) with voiced short [l] between vowels or between vowels and *r, n*, with voiceless short [l̥] in final position : *allur* [ad·lyŗ] all, gen. pl. *allra* [ad·lra] of all, *hella* [hɛd·la] flat stone, flat rock, gen. pl. *hellna* [hɛd·lna] ; *fjall* [fjad·l̥] mountain. Before other consonants than *r, n* double *l* (*ll*) is pronounced as a half-long *l*, voiced or voiceless depending upon the consonants (cf. (a) and (b) above): *alls* [al·s] gen. of *allur*, *allt* [al̥·t] neuter of *allur*.

Note: In a few loanwords *ll* is pronounced as long [l:]: *mylla* [mɪl:a] mill, *ball* [bal:] ball, dance; likewise in familiar or pet names: *Kalli* [kʰal:ɪ] pet name for *Karl* [kʰa(r)d̥l̥] Charles, *Ella* [ɛl:a] familiar name for *Elín*.

17

(d) For the combination *rl*, see *r* below.

10. *m* : (a) *m* is a voiced nasal, as in English *m*an, short: *maður* [ma:ðɤr̥] man, *koma* [kʰɔ:ma] come, *hólmur* [houl·mɤr̥] small island, half-voiced: *höm* [hö:m̥] haunch, buttock. It is half-long before voiced consonants and *b, d, g*: *kemba* [kʲʰɛm·ba] comb. It is long, when written double: *komma* [kʰɔm:a] comma, *fimm* [fɪm:] five, unless followed by a consonant, then only half-long: *fimmti* [fɪm·tʰɪ] fifth.

(b) *m* is a voiceless nasal [m̥], not found in English, sometimes before *p, t, k* : *hempa* [hɛm·pʰa or hɛm̥·pa] cassock, *aumkva* [öym·kʰva or öym̥·kva] pity, *fimmti* [fɪm·tʰɪ or fɪm̥·tɪ] fifth.

11. *n* : (a) *n* is a voiced nasal [n], as in English *n*ame; short initially: *nál* [nau:l] needle, medially: *vani* [va:nɪ] habit, (after consonants) *hólnum* [houl·nɤm] dat. of *hóll* [houd·l̥] hill; half-voiced in final position after voiced sounds: *lán* [lau:n] loan, *iðn* [ɪð·n] trade. It is half-long before voiced consonants and *d*: *sandur* [san·dɤr̥] sand. It is long, written double, between vowels and in final position, if it follows the vowels *a, e, i, o, u, y*: *manni* [man:ɪ] dat., *mann* [man:] acc. of *maður* [ma:ðɤr̥] man; *menn* [mɛn:] pl. of *maður*, *minna* [mɪn:a] less, *unna* [ɤn:a] love, *ynni* [ɪn:ɪ] (though I) loved.

(b) *n* is a voiceless nasal [n̥], not found in English, short initially after *h* : *hnífur* [hn̥i:vɤr̥] knive; finally, if preceded by a stop or *s* : *höfn* [höb·n̥] harbor, *vagn* [vaɡ·n̥] wagon, *vopn* [vɔʰp·n̥] weapon, *vatn* [vaʰt·n̥] water, *bákn* [bauʰk·n̥] a huge thing, *rausn* [röys·n̥] munificence. It is a half-long voiceless nasal sometimes medially before *t*: *vanta* [van·tʰa or van·ta] lack.

(c) Double *n* (*nn*) is pronounced as Icelandic *dn* (i. e. nearly *tn*), if preceded by the vowels *á, é, í, ó, ú, ý, œ, au, ei, ey* and followed by a vowel or *r*, or if in final position. The *n* is voiced before vowels and *r*, voiceless in final position : *Spánn* [spaud·n̥] Spain, *brúnn* [brud·n̥] brown, *einni* [eið·nɪ] dat. fem., (shortened in) *einnri* [eið·nrɪ] dat. fem. colloquially of *einn* [eið·n̥] one, *tónn* [tʰoud·n̥] tone. Excepted from this rule are the *nn*-forms of the definite article (because originally preceded by *i*, cf. (a) above): *brúnni* [brun:ɪ] from *brú-inni* dat. of *brú-in* [bru:ɪn] the bridge.

(d) For the combination *rn*, see *r*.

(e) *n* before *g* is a voiced nasal—back before [g], front

before [gⱼ]—like English *ng* in si*ng*, but the *g* is never lost in pronunciation, unless a consonant follows, then it is dropped: *þing* [þiŋ·g̊] assembly, convention, dat. *þingi* [þiŋ·g̊ⱼɪ], gen. *þings* [þiŋ·s], *hringur* [hr̥iŋ·g̊ʏr̥] ring, *hringja* [hr̥iŋ·g̊ⱼa] ring, pret. *hringdi* [hr̥iŋ·d̥ɪ].

(f) *n* before *k* is sometimes a voiceless nasal—back before [k], front before [kⱼ]—not found in English; the *k* may be lost in pronunciation before *t*; the combination *ng* [ŋ] also turns voiceless before *t* : *banki* [bauŋ·kⱼʰɪ or bauŋ̊·kⱼɪ] bank, *krankur* [kʰrauŋ·kʰʏr̥, kʰrauŋ̊·kʏr̥] sick, neuter: *krankt* [kʰrauŋ.tʰ or kʰrauŋ̊·t], *hringja* [hr̥iŋg̊ⱼa] ring, *hringt* [hr̥iŋ·tʰ or hr̥iŋ̊·t] rung pp.

(g) *gn* before consonants is pronounced like *ng*, sometimes voiceless before *t*, otherwise voiced: *rigna* [rɪg̊·na] rain, *rigndi* [rɪŋ·d̥ɪ] rained, *rignt* [rɪŋ·tʰ or rɪŋ̊·t] rained pp.

(h) *n* tends to lose its stoppage before *s* and to become a voiced half-long nasalized spirant (with the same oral articulation as *s* itself) : *dansa* [danᵤ·sa] dance, *vinza* [vɪnᵤ·sa] winnow, *hundsa* [hʏnᵤ·sa] to ignore (as a dog). A similar transformation of final *n* before other consonants (spirants) occurs within the sentence: *Jón Jónsson* [jounⱼ· jounᵤ·sɔn], *Jón Finnsson* [jounᵥ· fɪnᵤ·sɔn], *Jón Vigfússon* [jounᵥ· vɪx·fus·ɔn], *Jón Sveinsson* [jounᵤ· sveinᵤ·sɔn]. Before *b* and *g*, *n* turns into *m* and [ŋ] under similar circumstances: *Jón Björnsson* [joum· bjös:ɔn], *Jón Guðmundsson* [jouŋ· gvʏð·mʏn(d̥)sɔn].

These sounds are ignored in the Glossary.

Note: *n* is lost (a) between *r*, *t* and *s* : *barns* [bas:] of a child, *vatns* [vas:] of water; (b) sometimes between *r* and *sk* : *bernska* [ber̥ska] childhood; (c) between *f*, *g* and *s*: *hrafns* [hr̥af·s] of a raven, *gagns* [gax·s] of use.

12. *p* : (a) *p* is a voiceless aspirated short stop [pʰ], as in English *p*en, initially: *penni* [pʰen:ɪ] pen, *Pétur* [pʰjɛ:tʰʏr̥] Peter, *plata* [pʰla:tʰa] plate; medially between vowels, or between a vowel and *j, r* : *api* [a:pʰɪ] ape, *lepja* [lɛ:pʰja] lap up, *liprir* [lɪ:pʰrɪr̥] nimble pl.; also medially after voiced consonants: *hampur* [ham·pʰʏr̥] hemp; finally after a vowel or a voiced consonant: *tap* [tʰa:pʰ] loss, *hamp* [ham·pʰ] hemp acc.

(b) Double *p* (*pp*) is a long preaspirated voiceless stop [ʰp:], not found in English. It occurs between vowels, or between a vowel and *r*; or in final position: *heppinn* [hɛʰp:ɪn] lucky, *krappra* [kʰraʰp:ra] gen. pl. of *krappur* [kʰraʰp:ʏr̥] narrow,

19

strait, *happ* [haʰp:] luck, lucky strike. Before *l, n* a *pp* or *p* is here marked only half-long [ʰp·] (though it has very nearly full length) : *heppni* [heʰp·nɪ] luck, *epli* [eʰp·lɪ] apple, *skepna* [skjeʰp·na] creature.

(c) *p* is a voiceless unaspirated short stop [p], as in English *spin,* gras*p*ing, if preceded by a voiceless spirant, liquid or nasal: *spinna* [spɪn:a] spin, *hespa* [hɛs·pa] hasp, *verpa* [vɛr̥·pa] throw. Since *l, m, (n)* may be either voiced or voiceless before *p,* it follows that *p* is either aspirated or not after these sounds: *stelpa* [stɛl·pʰa or stɛl̥·pa] girl (disrespectfully), *hempa* [hɛm·pʰa or hɛm̥·pa] cassock.

(d) *p* is pronounced *f* [f·] (half-long) before *s, t,* and *k* : *skips* [skjɪf·s] gen. of *skip* [skjɪ:pʰ] ship; *keypti* [kjʰeif·tɪ] pret. of *kaupa* [kʰöy:pʰa] buy; *dýpka* [dif·ka] deepen.

(e) *p* is often pronounced like an Icelandic *b* [b̥] (i. e. like a French *p*), that is, as a voiceless unaspirated (short) stop after long vowels: *api* [a:b̥ɪ] ape, *lepja* [lɛ:b̥ja] lap up, *liprir* [lɪ:b̥rɪr̥] nimble pl.; *tap* [tʰa:b̥] loss.

13.*r* : (a) *r* is a short trilled voiced liquid [r], like Scottish *r,* initially : *renna* [rɛn:a] run, *rjúka* [rju:kʰa] smoke, emit smoke; medially between vowels and after voiced consonants: *brenna* [brɛn:a] burn, *vera* [vɛ·ra] to be, *efri* [ɛv·rɪ] upper, *neðri* [nɛð·rɪ] lower. It is half-voiced in final position after vowels (in root syllables) : *vor* [vɔ:r] spring. It is half-long before voiced consonants and *g*: *erfa* [ɛr·va] inherit, *jörð* [jör·ð] earth, *arga* [ar·g̊a] to sick (dogs) ; it is long, written double, between vowels and at the end of a word: *verri* [vɛr:ɪ] worse, *kyrr* [kjʰɪr:] quiet.

(b) *r* is a trilled voiceless short liquid [r̥], not found in English, initially after *h* : *hrifa* [hr̥i:va] rake. It is half-long medially before the consonants *p, t, k,* and *s* : *verpa* [vɛr̥·pa] throw, *erta* [ɛr̥·ta] tease, *verk* [vɛr̥·k] work, *vers* [vɛr̥·s] verse; but it is often assimilated to (lost before) *s* : *versna* [vɛ(r̥)sna] grow worse, *þyrstur* [þɪs·tyr̥] thirsty. In endings (*-ar, -ir, -ur* [-ar̥, -ir̥, -yr̥]) *r* is voiceless and short.

(c) *rl,* between vowels and in final position, may be pronounced in three ways: as *rl* [-r·l-, -r·l], *rdl* [-rd̥l-, -rd̥l̥], and *dl* [-d̥·l-, -d̥·l̥] : *Karl* [kʰar·l, kʰard̥l̥, kʰad̥·l̥] Charles, *árla* [aur·la, aurd̥la] early, *varla* [vard̥la, vad̥·la] hardly. The pronunciation [r·l] is literary or dialectal, the other two are general, but common words tend to have the last pronunciation. Before consonants the combination is pronounced either [rl] or [l·], the second being more common: *Karls* [kʰarls, kʰal·s] gen. of *Karl*.

(d) *rn*, between vowels and in final position, may be pronounced in three ways: as *rn* [-r·n-, -r·n], *rdn* [-rd̥n-, -rd̥n̥], and *dn* [-d̥·n-, -d̥·n̥]: *horn* [hɔr·n, hɔrd̥n̥, hɔd̥·n̥] horn, *barn* [bad̥·n̥] child, *stjórna* [stjourd̥na] govern. The pronunciation [r·n] is literary or dialectal, the other two are general, but common words tend to have the last pronunciation [d̥·n]. Before consonants the combination *rn* usually loses one or both of its consonants: *vernda* [vɛ(r)nd̥a] protect, *fernt* [fɛ(r̥)nt, fɛʰt:] four together, *bernska* [bɛr(n)ska] childhood, *barns* [bas:] of a child.

Note: r is lost before *s, sk, sn, st*; *nd, nt*; cf. (b) and (d) above.

14. *s* : *s* is a voiceless spirant, as in English *s*un (never voiced as in ro*s*e!); it is short in *sól* [sou:l], *snjór* [snjou:r] snow, *spinna* [spɪn:a] spin, *vasi* [va:sɪ] pocket, *Esja* [ɛ:sja] name of a mountain, *tvisvar* [tʰvɪ:svar] twice, *lausra* [löy:sra] gen. pl. of *laus* [löy:s] loose; *dansa* [danᵪsa] dance, *flaksa* [flax·sa] flap; *hús* [hu:s] house, *dans* [danᵪs] dance. It is half-long before consonants in *hestur* [hɛs·tʏr̥] horse, *visna* [vɪs·na] wither, *kyssti* [kjʰɪs·tɪ] kissed, pret. of *kyssa* [kjʰɪs:a] kiss. It is long, written double, between vowels, between a vowel and a following *j, r, v*, and at the end of a word: *hissa* [hɪs:a] astonished, *hvassra* [hʷas:ra] gen. pl. of *hvass* [hʷas:] keen, acute, strong (of wind).

15. *t* : (a) *t* is a voiceless aspirated short stop [tʰ], as in English *t*ime (never slurred as in American moun*t*ain, twen*t*y, bu*tt*er, wa*t*er!), initially: *tími* [tʰi:mɪ] time, *tjón* [tʰjou:n] damage, *trjóna* [tʰrjou:na] snout, ram; medially between vowels, or between a vowel and *j, r, v*: *ata* [a:tʰa] soil, *etja* [ɛ:tʰja] egg on, *vitrir* [vɪ:tʰrir̥] wise pl., *uppgötva* [ʏʰp:gö·tʰva] discover; also medially after voiced consonants: *vanta* [van·tʰa] lack; finally after a vowel or a voiced consonant: *met* [mɛ:tʰ] record, *mynt* [mɪn·tʰ] coin.

(b) Double *t* (*tt*) is a long preaspirated voiceless stop [ʰt:], not found in English. It occurs between vowels, or between a vowel and *r*, or in final position: *hittinn* [hɪʰt:ɪn] clever at hitting, *brattra* [braʰt:ra] gen. pl. of *brattur* [braʰt:ʏr̥] steep, neuter: *bratt* [braʰt:]. Before *l, n* a *tt* or *t* is here marked only half-long [ʰt·] (though it has very nearly full length):

hittni [hɪʰt·nɪ] the ability to hit, *vitni* [vɪʰt·nɪ] witness, *vettlingur* [vɛʰt·lingy̥r̥] mitten, *vatn* [vaʰt·n̥] water.

(c) *t* is a voiceless unaspirated short stop [t], as in English s*t*and, las*t*ing, if preceded by a voiceless spirant, liquid or nasal: *standa* [stan·d̥a] stand, *hefta* [hɛf·ta] put hobble on, hobble, *hestur* [hɛs·tyr̥] horse, *vigt* [vɪx·t] weight, *lykta* [lɪx·ta] smell; *hertur* [hɛr̥·tyr̥] hardened, dried, *eltur* [ɛl̥·tyr̥] pursued pp. Since *m, n, ng* may be either voiced or voiceless before *t*, the *t* is either aspirated or not after these sounds: *skemmta* [skjɛm·tʰa or skjɛm·ta] amuse, *vanta* [van·tʰa or van̥·ta] lack, *langtum* [lauŋ·tʰʏm or lauŋ̊·tʏm] far more.

(d) *t* is often pronounced like an Icelandic *d* [d̥] (i. e. like French *t*), that is, as a voiceless unaspirated (short) stop after long vowels: *ata* [a:d̥a] soil, *etja* [ɛ:d̥ja] egg on, *vitrir* [vɪ:d̥rɪr̥] wise pl., *uppgötva* [ʏʰp:gö·d̥va] discover; *met* [mɛ:d̥] record.

Note: *t* is lost usually before *s, st, z, zt*: *báts* [baus:] of a boat, *stytztur* [stɪs·tyr̥] shortest; also between *s* and a following consonant, except *r*: *prests* [pʰrɛs:] parson's, *systkin* [sɪs·kjɪn] brother and sister, but *vestra* [vɛstra] in the west.

16. *v*: *v* is a voiced short spirant [v], like English *v* in va*t*, have (but less energetic): *vera* [vɛ:ra] to be, *svara* [sva:ra] answer, *því* [þvi:] therefore, *höggva* [hög:va] hew, *sökkva* [söʰk:va] sink. In *hvað* (after *h*) *v* sounds like [w̥], but the combination *hv* may also be pronounced *kv* [kʰv]: [kʰva:ð].

Note: *v* is lost (a) after *á, ó*: *sjávar* [sjau:(v)ar̥] of the sea, *sljóvan* [sljou:an] acc. of *sljór* [sljou:r] dull; (b) in unstressed particles: *svo* [sɔ:] so, *því* [þi:] therefore.

17. *x*: *x* is a voiceless back spirant [x], as in German a*ch* (not quite that far back), followed by an *s*: *sex* [sɛx·s] six, *lax* [lax·s] salmon. Though not quite the same, English *x* may be substituted for it.

18. *z*: *z* = *s*. It is never like English *z*. In the present Icelandic official orthography *z* represents the assimilation of *ð, d, t* to *s*: *sézt* for *séðst* [sjɛs·t] been seen, *elzt* for *eldst* [ɛlst] aged pp., *veizt* for *veitst* [veis·t] you know, *stytzt* for *styttst* [stɪs·t] shortest. Many writers never use *z*, writing simply *s* in its place.

19. *þ*: *þ* is a voiceless short spirant [þ] like English *th* in *th*in; it occurs only initially: *þunnur* [þʏn:yr̥] thin, *þykkur* [þɪʰk:yr̥] thick. In unstressed pronouns and adverbs (after voiced sounds) *þ* has the sound of [ð] (as in English *th*is): *ég 'sagði þér það*

[jε(x) saq·ðɪ ðjɛr ða(ð)] I told you that (so); 'er það·satt
[ɛr·ða saʰt:] is it true? (Stress, marked with ' on sagði and er).

Note: For ð pronounced like þ, see 3 above.

3. Voiced and Voiceless Consonants.

1. In Icelandic the tendency to voicelessness in consonants is
much stronger than in English. In the following classification the
classes of sounds (or single sounds) marked with * are not found
in English.

p, t, k [pʰ, tʰ, kⱼʰ, kʰ] hard voiceless aspirated stops.
*[ʰp, ʰt, ʰkⱼ, ʰk] hard voiceless preaspirated stops.
voicel. cons. + [p, t, kⱼ, k] hard voiceless unaspirated stops.
b, d, g [b-, d-, gⱼ-, g-] soft voiceless unaspirated stops, similar to
          English b-, d-, g-.
*[b̥, d̥, g̊ⱼ, g̊] soft voiceless unaspirated stops; to the English-
          speaking they may sound like p, t, k.
f, þ, s, hj, hv, *k/g + t [f, þ, s, hj̥ or ç, hw̥ or xw, x] voiceless spirants.
v, ð, j, *g [v, ð, j, q] voiced spirants.
*hr, hl, hn, r, l, m, n, ng [hr̥, hl̥, hn̥, r̥, l̥, m̥, n̥, ŋ̥] voiceless liquids
          and nasals.
r, l, m, n, ng [r, l, m, n, ŋ] voiced liquids and nasals.

2. The strong voiceless quality of p, t, k is manifested in many
ways:

(a) They are aspirated (i. e. followed by an aspiration or a puff
of breath) initially (as in English), and, medially and finally,
after long vowels·or voiced consonants: *koma* [kʰɔ:ma] come, *aka*
[a:kʰa] drive, *ók* [ou:kʰ] drove, *banki* [bauŋ·kⱼʰɪ] bank, *hönk*
[höyŋ·kʰ] hank, coil.

(b) They are preaspirated (i. e. preceded by a puff of breath)
when written double or, even if not doubled, before l, n : pp, tt,
kk and p, t, k + l, n : *heppinn* [hɛʰp:ɪn] lucky, *happ* [haʰp:] luck,
krappra [kʰraʰp:ra] gen. pl. of *krappur* [kʰraʰp:ʏr̥] narrow, *heppni*
[hɛʰp·nɪ] luck, *vopna* [vɔʰp·na] to weapon, *ætla* [a(i)ʰt·la] intend,
vatn [vaʰt·n̥] water.

(c) They turn preceding voiced spirants, liquids, and nasals into
voiceless sounds: ð (often), f (= v), g (always); r (always), l, m, n
(often): *blíðka* [blið·kʰa or blið·ka] soften, mitigate, *haft* [haf·t]
pp. of *hafa* [ha:va] to have, *sagt* [sax·t] pp. of *segja* [sei:ja] to say,
vertu [vɛr̥·tʏ] be! *elta* [ɛl̥·ta] pursue, *skemmta* [skⱼɛm·tʰa or
skⱼɛm̥·ta] to entertain, *vanta* [van·tʰa or van̥·ta] to lack, *hjálpa*

23

[hjaul·pʰa or hjauḷ·pa] to help (Note: *l* in *lt* is almost always, in *lp, lk,* often voiceless).

Note: This rule is really only a variation of rule (b), since in both cases the *p, t, k* are preceded by puffs of breath: after vowels we call this a preaspiration, it devoices the end of the vowel, after consonants we call it the voicelessness of the consonants.

(d) Only *p, t, k*—never *b, d, g*—can stand after *s* : *spyrja* [spɪr·ja] ask, *hestur* [hɛs·tʏr̥] horse, *askur* [as·kʏr̥] ash.

Note 1: The difference between *p, t, k* and *b, d, g* is precisely this: that the former are either aspirated or preaspirated, while the latter are neither. To this there is one exception: at the end of a word before a pause (in absolute final position) all stops, *b, d, g* as well as *p, t, k,* show aspiration. But this end aspiration disappears within the sentence and is therefore not indicated in the phonetic spelling.

Note 2: After long vowels (see **1,** *5* (Length) above) the aspirated *p, t, k* [pʰ, tʰ, kⱼʰ, kʰ] lose the aspiration and become *b, d, g* [b̥, d̥, g̥ⱼ, g̥]. This is common in the South and West of Iceland, but not in the North and the East. Since it is easier to follow the orthography, the foreigner may just as well learn the Northern form.

3. The strong voiceless character of *s* is manifested—not only by (d) above—but also by the fact, that it turns preceding voiced *f* (=*v*) [v], *g* [q], and *r* [r] into voiceless sounds: *hafs* [haf·s] gen. of *haf* [ha:v] ocean, *dags* [dax·s] gen. of *dagur* [da:qʏr̥] day, *hers* [hɛr̥·s] gen. of *her* [hɛːr] army.

4. Voiced spirants, liquids, and nasals may become half-voiceless or voiceless.

Short:

(a) They are half-voiceless at the end of words (in absolute final position) when preceded by vowels or voiced consonants. Compare *gala* [ga:la] crow, pret. *gól* [gou:l̥]; *hafa* [ha:va] have, *haf* [ha:v] ocean; *jörðu* [jör·ðʏ] dat. of *jörð* [jör·ð] earth; *saga* [sa:qa] to saw, *sag* [sa:q] sawdust; *harmur* [har·mʏr̥] sorrow, acc. *harm* [har·m̥]; *eina* [ei:na] acc. of *ein* [ei:n̥] fem. one.

(b) They are voiceless after stops (*p, t, k* and *b, d, g*) and *s* at the end of a word (absolute final position): *vatn* [vaʰt·n̥] water, *vopn* [vɔʰp·n̥] weapon, *gutl* [gʏʰt·l̥] dabbling, *bákn* [bauʰk·n̥] a huge thing; *höfn* [höb·n̥] harbor, *barn* [bad·n̥] child, *einn* [eid·n̥] one, *lygn* [lɪg̥·n̥] calm (sea), *afl* [ab·l̥] strength, *höll* [höd̥·l̥] palace, *fugl* [fʏg̥·l̥] bird.

Note: The half-voiceless and the voiceless sounds, described in

(a) and (b), become voiced within the sentence before voiced sounds. Long (double) liquids and nasals always retain their voice in a root syllable and often in endings: *ball* [bal:] dance, *menn* [mɛn:] men; *gefinn* [gjɛːvɪn] given, *mönnum* [mönːʏm] dat. pl. to men. Cf. 1, 5 (Length) above.

Half-long:

(c) They become voiceless before *p, t, k,* and, to some extent, *s*; cf. 2(c) and 3 above.

Note: The extent to which this change takes place is dialectal. In the South and West of Iceland *all* voiced spirants, liquids, and nasals turn voiceless before *p, t, k* : thus we have there *ft, fk; ðk* [þk], *gt* [xt]; *rp, rt, rk* [r̥p, r̥t, r̥k]; *lp, lt, lk* [l̥p, l̥t, l̥k]; *mp, mt, mk* [m̥p, m̥t, m̥k]; *nt, nk* [n̥t, ŋ̊k] while in the North only *ft, fk, gt; rp, rt, rk* and *lt* are voiceless, all the rest voiced. The difference is seen in words like *bliðka* [N bliðˑkʰa, S bliþˑka] soften, *hjálpa* [N hjaulˑpʰa, S hjaul̥ˑpa] help, *hálka* [N haulˑkʰa, S haul̥ˑka] slipperiness, *hempa* [N hɛmˑpʰa, S hɛm̥ˑpa] cassock, *skemmta* [N skjɛmˑtʰa, S skjɛm̥ˑta] to entertain, *aumka* [N öymˑkʰa, S öym̥ˑka] to pity, *vanta* [N vanˑtʰa, S van̥ˑta] lack, *banka* [N bauŋˑkʰa, S bauŋ̊ˑka] to knock. There is no variation before *s*, cf. 3 above.

Since the Northern voiced pronunciation is easier for foreigners to acquire, I have given it first in this book.

4. Loss of Consonants.

1. In simple words (*barn* [baḍ·n̥] child, *systir* [sɪsˑtɪr̥] sister) the great majority of consonant clusters contains only two consonants. If this number is exceeded, there is a tendency to drop one of the consonants, often the middle one, sometimes the first, but never the last one. This loss has been mentioned in notes to the respective consonants (above: Pronunciation of the Consonants), but a comprehensive view of the chief cases is here added:

b: *kemba* [kjʰɛmˑba] comb, preterite *kem(b)di* [kjʰɛmˑḍɪ], pp. *kem(b)t* [kjʰɛmˑtʰ, kjʰɛm̥ˑt]; *lamb* [lamˑb̥] lamb, gen. *lam(b)s* [lamˑs].

d: *sun(d)la* [sʏnˑla] get dizzy, *syn(d)ga* [sɪŋˑg̊a] to sin, *sandur* [sanˑḍʏr̥] sand, gen. *san(d)s* [sanˑs].

ð: *har(ð)na* [harḍna] harden, *bragð* [braqˑð] trick, gen. *brag(ð)s* [braxˑs], *Nor(ð)lendingur* [nɔrḍlɛnḍiŋg̊ʏr̥] inhabitant of the North of Iceland.

Note: The [ḍ] in [harḍna] is not a continuation of the *ð*, but is developed out of the cluster *rn*; cf. *r* above, 2, 13.

f: *þar(f)nast* [þarḍnast] to need, *þarfur* [þar·vɤr̥] useful, n.
þar(f)t [þar̥·t]; *hál(f)na* [haul·na] finish one half, *hálfur*
[haul·vɤr̥] half, gen. *hál(f)s* [haul·s], gen. pl. *hál(f)ra* [haul·-
ra], n. *hál(f)t* [hauḷ·t]; *hvolfa* [hwɔl·va] capsize, pret. *hvol(f)di*
[hwɔl·dɪ]; *horfa* [hɔr·va] look, pret. *hor(f)ði* [hɔr·ðɪ]; *hvarfla*
[hwarḍla] waver.

g: *fylgja* [fɪl·g̊ja] follow, pret. *fyl(g)di* [fɪl·dɪ], pp. *fyl(g)t*
[fɪl̥·(x)t]; *vol(g)na* [vɔl·na] get lukewarm, warm up, *fylgsni*
[fɪlsnɪ] hiding place, hideout, *syrgja* [sɪr·g̊ja] to mourn, pret.
syr(g)ði [sɪr·ðɪ], pp. *syr(g)t* [sɪr̥·(x)t]; *margur* [mar·g̊ɤr̥]
many (a), n. *margt* [mar̥·t]; *morgunn* [mɔr·g̊ɤn] morning,
dat. *mor(g)ni* [mɔrḍnɪ or mɔḍ·nɪ].

k: *velkja* [vɛl·kjʰa, veḷ·kja] soil, pret. *vel(k)ti* [veḷ·(x)tɪ]; *skenkja*
[skjeiŋ·kjʰa, skjeiŋ·kja] to pour (wine, tea), give, pret. *skenkti*
[skjeiŋ·tʰɪ, skjeiŋ·tɪ]; *merkja* [mer̥·kja] mark, pp. *mer(k)t*
[mer̥·(x)t]; *falskur* [falskɤr̥] false, n. *fals(k)t* [falst]; *enskur*
[enₛskɤr̥] English, n. *ens(k)t* [enₛst]; *vel(k)zt* [veḷ·(x)st] pp.
middle voice of *velkja*; *styr(k)zt* [stɪr̥st] pp. middle voice of
styrkja [stɪr̥·kja] strengthen; *reykví(k)skur* [rei:kʰviskɤr̥] of
Reykjavík.

m: *kaldaver(m)sl* [kʰal·daver̥sḷ] wellspring, cold in summer, not
freezing in winter.

n: *barn* [baḍ·n̥] child, gen. *barns* [bas:]; *vatn* [vaʰt·n̥] water, gen.
vatns [vas:]; *hrafn* [hrab·n̥] raven, gen. *hrafns* [hr̥af·s]; *til
gagns* [tʰɪl· gax·s] of avail; *jafn* [jab·n̥] even, gen. *jafns* [jaf·s
or jabns], n. *jafnt* [jam·tʰ, jam·t or jaf·t]; *olnbogi* [ɔl·bɔi·jɪ]
elbow.

r: *barn* [baḍ·n̥] child, *karl* [kʰaḍ·ḷ] old man, *hverndags-* [hwɤn·-
daxs-] everyday-, *stirndur* [stɪn·dɤr̥] full of stars, *gjarn* [gjaḍ·n̥]
eager, willing, n. *gjarnt* [gjan·tʰ, gjan·t]; *vers* [ver̥·s or ves:]
verse, *þorskur* [þɔs·kɤr̥] cod, *fyrst* [fɪs·t] first, *versna* [ves·na]
get worse.

t: *vatn* [vaʰt·n̥] water, gen. *vatns* [vas:], *prestur* [pʰres·tɤr̥] parson, clergyman, pastor, priest, gen. *prests* [pʰres:]; *fljót* [fljou:tʰ]
big river, gen. *fljóts* [fljou:tʰs] or [fljous:]; *stuttur* [stɤʰt:ɤr̥]
short, superlative *stytztur* [stɪs·tɤr̥] shortest; *systkin* [sɪs·kjɪn]
brother and sister; *hestbak* [hes·ba·kʰ] horse-back.

2. Consonants are sometimes lost through assimilation to similar
vowels:

f (= *v*) [v] is rarely lost after *á, ó, ú* [au, ou, u]: *áfir* or *áir* [au:ɪr̥]
buttermilk, *lófi* [lou:(v)ɪ] palm of the hand, *húfa* [hu:a] cap.

g [q], the back spirant, is always lost after *á, ó, ú* [au, ou, u] : *lágur* [lau:ɣʀ or lau:r] low, fem. *lág* [lau:], neuter *lágt* [lauʰt: or laux·t] ; *lágum* [lau:ɣm] we lay; *skógur* [skou:ɣʀ] woods, acc. *skóg* [skou:], gen. *skógar* [skou:ar] ; *súgur* [su:ɣʀ] draft, acc. *súg* [su: or su:q] ; *fljúga* [flju:a] fly.

Note: *g* (= *j*), the front spirant before *i* and *j*, is not lost, except mostly after *jú* : *fljúgi* [flju:ɪ] first person singular subjunctive of *fljúga*, but *súgi* [su:jɪ] dat. of *súgur*.

4. Changes in Connected Speech.

1. Elision.

Unstressed vowels of endings are often elided before initial vowels of the next word :

'*Ertu* '*búinn?* [ɛʀ·tɣ bu:ɪn] are you ready? '*Ertu ekki* '*búinn?* [ɛʀ·tɛʰkⱼ·ɪ bu:ɪn] aren't you ready? '*Ertu ekki* '*enn búinn?* [ɛʀ·tɛʰkⱼ ɛn: bu·ɪn] aren't you ready yet? '*Ekki er að* '*tala um*'*það* [ɛʰkⱼ:ɛra tʰa:lɣm þa:(ð)] no need to discuss that, I know it!

2. Loss of Consonants.

In unstressed forms of conjunctions, prepositions, pronouns, and endings consonants (*ð, g, r* [ð, q, r]) are lost before initial consonants (not *h* + vowel) of the next words: *og* [ɔ:q, ɔ(·)], and, *að* [a:ð, a(·)] to, that, at, *með* [mɛ:ð, mɛ(·)] with, *við* [vɪ:ð, vɪ(·)] we, at, with, *ég* (or *eg*) [jɛ:q, jɛ(·)] I, *það* [þa:ð, þa(·)] that, it, *hvað* [hwa:ð, hwa(·)] what, *eitthvað* [eiʰt·hwa·ð, eixw:a·(ð)] something, *þið* [þɪ:ð, þɪ(·)] you, *hingað* [hiŋ·ga(ð)] hither, here, *þangað* [þauŋ·ga(ð)] thither, there, *fyrir* [fɪ:rɪ(ʀ)] for, before, *gerir* [gⱼɛ:rɪ(ʀ)] does, *gerið* [gⱼɛ:rɪ(ð)] you do. Examples:

Þú og '*hann* [þu: ɔq han:] you and he : *hingað og* '*þangað* [hiŋ·gað ɔ þauŋ·gað] hither and thither; *að* '*eiga* [að ei:qa] to own, *að* '*hafa* [að ha:va] to have : *að* '*vera* [a vɛ:ra] to be; *með* '*engu móti* [mɛð eiŋ·ɣɣ mou:tʰɪ] by no means : *með* '*smjöri* [mɛ smjö:rɪ] with butter; *við* '*Eyjafjörð* [vɪð ei:jafjör·ð] at Eyjafjörður, *við* '*Horn* [vɪð hɔd·n̥] at Horn : *við* '*Snæfellsnes* [vɪ· snai:fɛlsnɛ·s] at Snæfellsnes; *hingað og* '*þangað* [hiŋ·gað ɔ þauŋ·gað] hither and thither : '*hingað til* [hiŋ·ga(ð) tʰɪ·l] up to now; *ég á að* '*fara* [jɛ·q au·a(ð) fa:ra] I am to go : *ég* '*veit ekki* [jɛ vei:tʰ ɛʰkⱼ·ɪ] I don't know; '*það er bezt að* ... [þa:ð ɛr bɛs·t a(ð) ...] it is best to ... : *það veit* '*enginn* [þa· vei·tʰ eiŋ·gⱼɪn] nobody knows (it); '*hvað er* '*að?* [hwa:ð ɛr a:ð] what is the matter? : '*hvað gerir* '*það til?* [hwa·

27

gȷɛrɪ(r̥) þa: tʰɪl] what does that matter? *er eitthvað 'að?* [ɛr eiʰt·hwað a:ð] is anything wrong? : *'finna sér 'eitthvað 'til* [fɪn:a sjɛr eiʰt·hwa(ð) tʰɪ:l] find some excuse (or pretext); *við erum 'tíu* [vɪð ɛ·rɣm tʰi:jɣ] we are ten : *við vorum 'tíu* [vɪ(ð) vɔ·rɣm tʰi:jɣ] we were ten; *þið 'eruð* [þɪ·ð ɛ:rɣð] you are : *þið 'farið* [þɪ· fa:rɪð] you go.

3. Weakened Words.

Unstressed forms of conjunctions, prepositions, pronouns, and auxiliary verbs often show loss of consonants, assimilations, contractions or other signs of weakening. Examples: *svo, so* [s(v)ɔ:] thus, so; *svona* [s(v)ɔ:na] so, thus, enough! *því* [þ(v)i:] (dat. of *það* [þa:ð] that, it) because; *svo sem* or *svosem* or *sosum* [sɔ:sɛ·m or sɔ:sɣm] certainly, indeed; *aftur* [aʰt:ɣr̥] after, again, back; *aftan* [aʰt:an] from behind; *eftir* [ɛʰt:ɪr̥] after; *ofan í* or *oní* [ɔ:vani· or ɔ:ni·] down into; *ofan á* or *oná* [ɔ:vanau· or ɔ:nau·] on the top of; *ofan um* or *onum* [ɔ:vanɣm or ɔ:nɣm] down through; *ofan yfir* or *onyfir* [ɔ:vanɪvɪr̥ or ɔ:nɪvɪr̥] down over; but *ofan fyrir* [ɔ:van fɪ:rɪr̥] down below (motion) : there is no contraction when the following word begins with a consonant. Similarly: *yfir í* or *yfrí* (*ufrí*) [ɪ:vɪri· or ɪv·ri·, ɣv·ri·] over into (motion); *yfir á* or *yfrá* [ɪ:vɪrau· or ɪv·rau·] over onto; *yfir um* or *yfrum* [ɪ:vɪrɣm or ɪv·rɣm] over through; but before consonant: *yfir frá* [ɪ:vɪr̥ frau:] over yonder (no contraction). The third person pronouns *hann, hún* [han:, hu:n] he, she, usually drop their *h*'es: *er* (*h*)*ann 'heima?* [ɛ·r an· hei:ma] is he at home? *er hún 'farin?* [ɛ·r un· fa:rɪn] has she gone? *'sástu hana?* [saus·t ana] did you see her? *'taktu hann* [tʰax·t an·] take him! *'á hann gott 'bókasafn?* [au· an gɔʰt· bou:kʰasab̥·n̥] has he a good library?

4. Enclitic þú.

Assimilations are frequent between monsyllabic verb forms and a following unstressed *þú*, thou, you, thus especially in the second person singular imperative, but also in the second person singular indicative when the pronoun follows (in questions and the like).

Examples:

	Imperative	Present
tala [tʰa:la] speak	: *talaðu* [tʰa:laðɣ]	: *talarðu*
gefa [gȷɛ:va] give	: *gefðu* [gȷɛv·ðɣ]	: *gefurðu*
segja [sei:ja] say	: *segðu* [seiq·ðɣ]	: *segirðu*
skera [skȷɛ:ra] cut	: *skerðu* [skȷɛr·ðɣ]	: *skerðu*
biðja [bɪð·ja] ask	: *biddu* [bɪd:ɣ]	
telja [tʰɛl·ja] count	: *teldu* [tʰɛl·d̥ɣ]	

dæma [dai:ma] judge   : *dæmdu* [daim·d̥ɤ]
koma [kʰɔ:ma] come   : *komdu* [kʰɔn·d̥ɤ]
venja [vɛn·ja] make used to   : *vendu* [vɛn·d̥ɤ]
mæla [mai:la] measure   : *mældu* [mail·d̥ɤ]
mæla [mai:la] speak   : *mæltu* [maiļ·tɤ]
standa [stan·d̥a] stand   : *stattu* [staʰt:ɤ]
sleppa [slɛʰp:a] let go   : *slepptu* [slɛf·tɤ]
bíta [bi:tʰa] bite   : *bíttu* [biʰt:ɤ]
taka [tʰa:kʰa] take   : *taktu* [tʰax·tɤ]
lesa [lɛ:sa] read   : *lestu* [lɛs·tɤ]   : *lestu*
vera [vɛ:ra] be   : *vertu* [vɛŗ·tɤ]   : *ertu*

The assimilations in the above forms are usually expressed in writing, and more commonly so in the imperative than in the present: *talar þú?* do you speak? *gefur þú?* do you give? It will be seen that the form of *þ* as *ð, d, t* is dependant upon the preceding consonants; this is also the case with the *ð, d, t* in the preterite (and past participle) suffix of weak verbs. But the following assimilations are not expressed in writing: *komið þið* [kʰɔ:mɪðɪð] come! (pl.), *hafið þið 'séð þá?* [ha:vɪðɪ sjɛð:au·] have you seen them?

5. Weakening of -m, -n.

Nasals at the end of a word have a tendency to become partially assimilated to following consonants; *n* is especially susceptible. It becomes *m* before *p, b* and *ng* [ŋ] before *k, g* : *Jón'Björnsson* [joum· bjös:ɔn], *Jón 'Guðmundsson* [jouŋ· gvɤð·mɤn(d̥)sɔn]. Before open consonants (spirants and liquids) the oral stoppage of *n* is loosened up so as to produce the effect of a nasalized spirant or liquid (cf. the pronunciation of *n* above: 3, 2, 11(h)) : *Jón 'Þórðar-son* [jounꝸ· þour·ðaŗsɔn], *Jón 'Sveinsson* [jounᵤ· sveinᵤ·sɔn], *Jón 'Jónsson* [jounⱼ· jounᵤ·sɔn], *Jón 'Friðriksson* [jounᵥ· frɪð·rɪxsɔn], *Jón 'Vigfússon* [jounᵥ· vɪx·fus·ɔn]. The same thing happens in compound words: *beinprjónn* [beim·prjoud̥n̩] bone needle, *andskotinn* [anᵤ·skɔ·tʰɪn] the devil.

Instances with *m* : *komum við* [kʰɔ:mɤnᵥ vɪ:ð] we come; *umfram* [ɤnᵥ·fram·] in addition, to boot.

These sounds are disregarded in the Glossary.

5. Vowel Shifts.

In Icelandic vowels often interchange in different forms of the same word. This interchange is due to sound changes in more or less remote times.

29

1. The Old Shift.

The Old Shift (*hljóðskifti* ablaut, gradation) occurs regularly in the principal parts (inf., pret. sg., pret. pl., pp.) of the strong verbs as in English ride, rode, ridden:

1. *bíta* bite,   *beit, bitum, bitinn*
2. *bjóða* offer,   *bauð, buðum, boðinn*
3. *bresta* burst,   *brast, brustum, brostinn*
4. *bera* bear,   *bar, bárum, borinn*
5. *gefa* give,   *gaf, gáfum, gefinn*
6. *fara* go,   *fór, fórum, farinn*
7. *heita* be called, *hét, hétum, heitinn*

Cognate or related words are often differentiated by this Old Shift: 1. *heitur* hot : *hiti* heat, 2. *sjóða* to cook : *sauður* sheep : *suða* boiling : *soð* broth, 5. *sitja* to sit : *sess* seat : *sáta* haystack (small) : *set* seat, etc.

2. The I-Shift.

The I-Shift (*i-hljóðvarp*, i-umlaut, i-mutation) is so called because it was caused by an *i* or a *j*—now often lost—in the ending of a word. The *i* (*j*) affected and changed the vowel of the root syllable. The i-shift occurs in the pres. sg. indic. of the strong verbs and elsewhere. The following vowels were affected:

a becomes *e* : *taka* to take : *ég tek* I take, *maður* man : pl. *menn*.
á   "   *æ* : *hár* high : *hærri* higher, *á* acc. of *ær* ewe.
e   "   *i* : pp. *selinn* : inf. *sitja* to sit.
o   "   *e* : *koma* to come : *ég kem* I come.
o(u) "   *y* : *sonur* son : pl. *synir*.
ó   "   *œ* : *stór* big : *stœrri* bigger.
u   "   *y* : *fullur* full : *fyllri* fuller.
ú   "   *ý* : *mús* mouse : pl. *mýs* mice, *kú* acc. of *kýr* cow.
ju   "   *y* : *við bjuggum* we lived : *við byggjum* subjunctive.
jú   "   *ý* : *ljúga* to lie : *ég lýg* I lie.
jó   "   *ý* : *bjóða* to offer : *ég býð* I offer.
au   "   *ey* : *ausa* to dip, scoop : *ég eys* I dip.

In all of the above examples, except *synir*, the *i* (*j*) that caused the shift is lost. Instances of preserved *i, j* : *vanur* accustomed : *venja* custom, *dagur* day : dat. *degi*, *taka* take : pp. *tekinn*, *dómur* judgement : *dæmir* (he) judges, *ból* bed : *bæli* lair, *taldi* counted : *telja* to count, *lugum* (we) lied : *lygi* a lie, *auður* desert : *eyði* state of wilderness, *ljós* light : *lýsi* cod liver oil, etc. It will be seen from these examples that related words are often differentiated (in the root syllable) by the i-shift.

Many *i*'s, though in endings, do not cause the i-shift because they are more recent than it: *hani* a rooster, *garði*, dat. of *garður* yard, garden.

3. *The U-Shift.*

The U-Shift (*u-hljóðvarp*, u-umlaut, u-mutation) affects only the root vowel *a* which becomes *ö*. It was caused by a *u* or *v* in the ending, sometimes lost : *land* land : pl. *lönd*, sometimes preserved: dat. pl. *löndum*. If *a* occurs in a suffix or an inflexional ending, it is changed to *u* (which in turn changes a preceding *a* of the root syllable to *ö*) : *kallaði* I called : *kölluðum* we called, *kjallari* cellar, basement : *kjöllurum* dat. pl. The sg. nom. ending *-ur* never causes a u-shift, because it is a later development of *-r*.

4. *Breaking.*

Breaking (*klofning*, fracture) affects only the rootvowel *e* which becomes *ja* and—by u-shift—*jö*. It is found in root syllables before *a* and *u* (that may be lost) in endings. Examples: *gefa* to give : *gjöf* gift, gen. *gjafar*, dat. pl. *gjöfum*. Sometimes it looks as if *i* is broken to *ja* and *jö* : *skildir* shields : nom. sg. *skjöldur*, gen. sg. *skjaldar*, *girnast* to desire : *gjarn* eager, f. *gjörn*, but actually the *i* here represents an original *e*.

31

PART II. INFLEXIONS.

I. NOUN DECLENSIONS.

1. Preliminary Remarks.

1. Icelandic nouns, like English, show three *genders*: masculine, feminine, and neuter, and two *numbers*: singular and plural. But Icelandic has four *cases*: nominative, accusative, dative, and genitive, where English has only three: nominative, accusative, and genitive (in the pronouns: he, him, his).

2. The agreement of the three genders is also deceptive. English has the so-called natural gender, i. e. living beings are either masculine or feminine according to sex, while inanimate things are neuter. Icelandic has mostly grammatical gender, i. e. gender depends upon the inflexional endings of the nouns. It is impossible to give exhaustive rules, but here are a few distinctive endings:

Masculines end in: *-ur* (exceptions: strong feminines, class 1, types *Hildur, lifur,* and strong neuters, type *hreiður*); *-aður, -uður; -aldur* (also neuter); *-angur* (also neuter), *-ingur, -ungur; -undur; -dómur; -leikur; háttur; -skapur; -all, -ill, -ull; -ann, -inn, -unn* (also feminine); *-ar* (except *sumar* n.), *-ir* (except *móðir, dóttir, systir,* all feminine); *-andi* (except *kveðandi* f. and a few others); *-ingi, -ungi; -ari* (except *altari* n.); *-ji.*

Feminines end in: *-ing, -ung; -úð; -un (-an); -yn; -und; -urð; -semd; -a* (excepting weak neuters, type *auga*), *-ja, -ynja, -sla, -átta, -usta, -ka, -ska, -eskja; -fræði.*

Neuters end in: *-al, -að, -ald, -an, -ang, -arn, -in; -erni, -elsi, -indi; -gin, -orð.*

3. There are two main kinds of noun declensions in Icelandic, called the *strong* and the *weak*. In the *Strong Declension*, the genitive singular always ends in a consonant (*-s, -ar*); in the *Weak Declension* all the cases of the singular end in a vowel (*-i, -a, -u*). Both are divided into subclasses based on the gender and the case endings, notably the endings of the nominative (accusative) plural, and the genitive singular.

2. Strong Declension, Masculine Nouns.

1. Class 1: genitive singular *-s (-ar)*, plural *-ar.*

32

(a) Paradigms:

Sg. nom.	*hest-ur* horse	*hatt-ur* hat	*mó-r* peat,	*hver* geyser	*akur* field
acc.	*hest*	*hatt*	*mó* heath	*hver*	*akur*
dat.	*hest-i*	*hatt-i*	*mó*	*hver*	*akr-i*
gen.	*hest-s*	*hatt-s*	*mó-s*	*hver-s*	*akur-s*
Pl. nom.	*hest-ar*	*hatt-ar*	*mó-ar*	*hver-ar*	*akr-ar*
acc.	*hest-a*	*hatt-a*	*mó-a*	*hver-a*	*akr-a*
dat.	*hest-um*	*hött-um*	*mó-um*	*hver-um*	*ökr-um*
gen.	*hest-a*	*hatt-a*	*mó-a*	*hver-a*	*akr-a*

Sg. nom.	*stól-l* chair	*himin-n* heaven	*lækn-i-r* doctor	*söng-ur* song
acc.	*stól*	*himin*	*lækn-i*	*söng*
dat.	*stól-i*	*himn-i*	*lækn-i*	*söng-(v-i)*
gen.	*stól-s*	*himin-s*	*lækn-i-s*	*söng-s*
Pl. nom.	*stól-ar*	*himn-ar*	*lækn-ar*	*söng-v-ar*
acc.	*stól-a*	*himn-a*	*lækn-a*	*söng-v-a*
dat.	*stól-um*	*himn-um*	*lækn-um*	*söng-v-um*
gen.	*stól-a*	*himn-a*	*lækn-a*	*söng-v-a*

(b) Remarks on the Paradigms.

The Frequency of the Types.

1. *Hestur* is most frequent of all these types. Thus go words in *-ingur, -ungur, -dómur, -leikur* (dative singular *-i* missing), and *-undur*. *Hattur* (words with *a* in the root syllable) is a fairly common type. Like *mór* go only few words (stem vowel *á, ó, æ, ý*), mostly literary, except *skór* shoe (cf. 7 below), and *Valtýr* personal name. Like *hver* go monosyllabic words like *bjór* skin, *ás* ace, *karl* old man, *vagn* wagon, *Jón* John, and disyllabic nouns that do not drop the vowel of the suffix: e. g. *biskup* bishop, *krystall* crystal, *stúdent* student (B. A.), graduate of a Gymnasium; some personal names in *-an(n), -ar*: *Kjartan, Ragnar, Einar, Gunnar,* and the (foreign) names *Jóhann, Stefán* (all, except *bjór*, have *-i* in dative singular). *Hver* itself often has the second class plural *hverir*. Like *akur* go several words in *-ur, -aldur, -angur*; similarly words in *-ar* (but cf. above): *hamar: hamri* hammer. Like *stóll* go monosyllables in *-l-l, -n-n*, e. g. *bíll* auto, *stýll* style, and disyllabic words that do not drop the vowel of their suffix (or second part), e. g. *magáll* flank (of mutton, beef), *Þorkell, Þorsteinn*. Like *himinn* go words in *-all, -ill, -ull; -ann, -inn, -unn*, dropping their suffix vowel, cf. 6 below. *Læknir* (cf. 8 below) is rather common, *söngur* (9 below) a very rare type.

Sound Shifts, Assimilations, and Stem Forms.

2. The *-ur* of the nominative singular was originally *-r*. But *-r*

(here and elsewhere) changed to *-ur* after consonants and between consonants, while it remained *-r* after a vowel and before a vowel. Hence *hest-ur*, but *mó-r*, hence also *akur, akur-s*, but *akr-i*, where the *-r* was not a nominative case ending but belonged to the stem. (By stem is meant that part of the word which is left when the inflexional endings—here case endings—are subtracted.) The old nominative *-r* was assimilated and lost after *r, s*, hence *hver* geyser, *ís* ice, *háls* neck; it was assimilated to *l, n*, giving *ll, nn* after vowels: *stóll, steinn* stone, *himinn*; but *l, n* only, after consonants: *fugl* bird, *hrafn* raven.

Note: In the following *-ur* from *-r* will often be referred to as the expanded *-r*.

3. The genitive *-s* is added to a stem ending in vowel + *s*, but is lost after a stem ending in consonant + *s*: *ís* ice, genitive *íss*, but *háls* neck, genitive *háls*.

4. The dative singular of *dagur* is *degi* (i-shift Pr. **5**, *2*).

5. The dative plural of words with *a* as a root vowel shows u-shift (Pr. **5**, *3*): *hattur* : *höttum, akur* : *ökrum*.

6. Words like *himinn* are made up of a root syllable, a suffix, and the case ending, thus: *him-in-n*. Whenever the case ending begins with a vowel, the vowel of the suffix is dropped, hence nominative plural *him-n-ar*. Thus *gaffall* : *gafflar* fork; *lykill* : *lyklar* key; *jökull* : *jöklar* glacier; *aftan*(*n*) : *aftnar* evening; *drottinn* : *drottnar* lord; *morgun*(*n*) : *morgnar* morning. With i-shift before the (preserved) *i* of the suffix: *ketill* kettle, accusative *ketil*, dative *katli*, plural *katlar, katla, kötlum, katla*.

7. *Skór* goes like *mór* in the singular, but shows contracted forms in the plural: *skór, skó, skóm, skóa*.

8. The stem of *læknir* is really *lækn-i-* in the singular, *lækn-* in the plural. But colloquially it is *læknir-*, so that the word goes like *hver*: genitive singular *læknir-s*, plural *læknir-ar*. But though very common, this is not considered good form even in conversation. When the *-ir* in these words is preceded by a *g* or *k*, a *j* is added to the stem throughout the plural, but instances are not common: *beyk-i-r* cooper, plural *beyk-j-ar, -j-um, -j-a*.

Note: *Eyrir* a coin (0.01 *króna*) goes like *læknir* in the singular, but the plural is *aurar, aura, aurum, aura*.

9. In several words the stem ends in *v* in the plural and, sometimes, in the dative singular: *söngur* : *söng-v-ar*. To these *v*-stems

belong the very irregular words *sjór* sea, and *snjór* snow, whose forms are as follows:

Sg. nom.	*sjór, sær, sjár*	*snjór, snær, snjár*
acc.	*sjó, sæ, sjá*	*snjó, snæ, snjá*
dat.	*sjó, sæ(vi), sjá(vi)*	*snjó, snæ(vi), snjá(vi)*
gen.	*sjóar, sævar, sjávar, sjós*	*snjóar, snævar, snjávar, snjóvar*
Pl. nom.	*sjóar, sjóir* waves,	*snjóar* snowfalls, the snow left
acc.	*sjóa, sjói* breakers	*snjóa* on the ground after a
dat.	*sjóum*	*snjóum* snowfall
gen.	*sjóa*	*snjóa*

The stems *sjó-, snjó-* are most common in colloquial use; the others are mostly poetical or literary.

Peculiarities of Inflexion.

10. The *-i* of the dative singular is often missing. After the *-i* of the stem in *lækn-i-r* it is lost.

11. The genitive singular is often *-ar*, either exclusively, or by the side of *-s*. Thus: *grautur* porridge, cereal, genitive *grautar*; *skógur* woods, birch copse, genitive *skógar* (*skógs*), and words in *-undur*: *höfundur, -ar*, author. Many personal names have the ending *-ar*, but take the *-s* when compounded with *-son* to make the masculine patronymic: *Sigurður*, genitive *Sigurðar*, but *Sigurðsson*. Thus: *Höskuldur, Guðmundur, Jörundur, Eyvindur, Guðbrandur, Haraldur, Þorvarður*, and others similarly compounded. When compounded with *-dóttir*, some of these names have *-s* others *-ar*: *Guðmundsdóttir* but *Sigurðardóttir*.

Note: Many of the above remarks are equally pertinent in the following classes of nouns, but will not be repeated.

2. *Class 2*: genitive singular *-s* (*-jar*), plural *-ir*.

(a) Paradigms:

Sg. nom.	*smið-ur* smith	*dal-ur* valley	*leik-ur* play	*vegg-ur* wall
acc.	*smið*	*dal*	*leik*	*vegg*
dat.	*smið*	*dal*	*leik*	*vegg*
gen.	*smið-s*	*dal-s*	*leik-s*	*vegg-j-ar*
Pl. nom.	*smið-ir*	*dal-ir*	*leik-ir*	*vegg-ir*
acc.	*smið-i*	*dal-i*	*leik-i*	*vegg-i*
dat.	*smið-um*	*döl-um*	*leik-j-um*	*vegg-j-um*
gen.	*smið-a*	*dal-a*	*leik-j-a*	*vegg-j-a*

35

(b) Remarks on the Paradigms.

1. None of these types is especially common; *smiður* and *veggur* are perhaps most common.

2. Words without *-(u)r* in nominative singular (cf. class 1(b)2): *guð, -s, -ir* God; *grís* pig, *her* army; words with *-r* only: *ljár* scythe (dative plural *ljá(u)m*); *blœr, -s, -ir* soft wind, breeze; *bœr, -jar, -ir* farm(stead), town. As to *dölum,* cf. class 1(b)5.

3. Words the stems of which end in *k* or *g* (or *œ, ey, ý*), like *leikur, veggur, (bœr),* have a *j* appearing before the endings *-ar, -um, -a* only, but a *j* is heard in pronunciation even before the ending *-ir, -i.*

4. Lack of dative singular *-i* is characteristic of this class, though some words, like *gestur* guest, have it.

5. Words of the types *leikur, veggur* fluctuate between genitive singular in *-s* or *-jar. Bœr* has only *bœjar.*

3. Class 3: genitive singular *-ar,* plural *-ir.*

(a) Paradigms:

Sg. nom.	*hlut-ur* thing	*stað-ur* place	*fatnað-ur* clothing	*söfnuð-ur* congregation
acc.	*hlut*	*stað*	*fatnað*	*söfnuð*
dat.	*hlut*	*stað*	*fatnað-i*	*söfnuð-i*
gen.	*hlut-ar*	*stað-ar*	*fatnað-ar*	*safnað-ar*
Pl. nom.	*hlut-ir*	*stað-ir*	*fatnað-ir*	*söfnuð-ir*
acc.	*hlut-i*	*stað-i*	*fatnað-i*	*söfnuð-i*
dat.	*hlut-um*	*stöð-um*	*fötnuð-um*	*söfnuð-um*
gen.	*hlut-a*	*stað-a*	*fatnað-a*	*safnað-a*

Sg. nom.	*kött-ur* cat	*fjörð-ur* firth	*hátt-ur* mode	*spón-n* spoon	*son-ur* son
acc.	*kött*	*fjörð*	*hátt*	*spón*	*son*
dat.	*kett-i*	*firð-i*	*hœtt-i*	*spœn-i*	*syn-i*
gen.	*katt-ar*	*fjarð-ar*	*hátt-ar*	*spón-s*	*son-ar*
Pl. nom.	*kett-ir*	*firð-ir*	*hœtt-ir*	*spœn-ir*	*syn-ir*
acc.	*kett-i*	*firð-i*	*hœtt-i*	*spœn-i*	*syn-i*
dat.	*kött-um*	*fjörð-um*	*hátt-um*	*spón-um*	*son-um*
gen.	*katt-a*	*fjarð-a*	*hátt-a*	*spón-a*	*son-a*

(b) Remarks on the Paradigms.

1. Lack of dative singular *-i* marks the most common of these types: *hlutur, staður,* though several words have it sometimes (*kviður* belly, *liður* joint) or always (*fundur* meeting, *kostur* choice, advantage). As to *stöðum,* cf. class 1(b)5.

2. *Fatnaður* is a more common type than *söfnuður* (the first has the u-shift (Pr. **5**, *3*) only in dative plural; the second everywhere, except in genitive singular and plural). Like *söfnuður* go *fögnuður* joy, *mánuður* month, and *söknuður* sorrow.

3. The last five types, *köttur*, etc., originally had a stem ending in *-u*, which appeared in accusative plural: *köttu, fjörðu, háttu, spónu, sonu*. These forms are still found in the literary language. Dialectally the form *fjörðu* has been changed to *fjörður* (f. pl.): *norður á fjörður* (= *firði*) north into the firths.

4. The original root vowel *a* is seen in the genitive singular and plural of *köttur*. Before *-i*, *-ir* the vowels are i-shifted (*a* to *e*, [*e*] to *i*, *á* to *æ*, *ó* to *æ*, [*o*] to *y*). In the other cases it is u-shifted (*a* to *ö*). In *fjörður, fjarðar* there is a breaking of an original *e*. Cf. the i-shift, the u-shift, and the breaking (Pr. **5**, *2-4*).

5. Like *fjörður* goes the common personal name *Björn* Bear (genitive usually *Björns*), and the less common *Hjörtur* Hart. No other words go like *spónn, sonur*. The latter is always *-son* in compounds (sometimes also the simplex: *son minn* my son).

4. Class 4: plural in *-ur*.

(a) Paradigms: only these six common words: father, brother, foot, finger, winter, man.

Sg.	nom.	*faðir*	*bróðir*	*fót-ur*	*fingur*	*vetur*	*mað-ur*
	acc.	*föður*	*bróður*	*fót*	*fingur*	*vetur*	*mann*
	dat.	*föður*	*bróður*	*fæt-i*	*fingr-i*	*vetr-i*	*mann-i*
	gen.	*föður(-s)*	*bróður(-s)*	*fót-ar*	*fingur-s*	*vetr-ar*	*mann-s*
Pl.	nom.	*feður*	*bræður*	*fæt-ur*	*fingur*	*vetur*	*menn(-ir)*
	acc.	*feður*	*bræður*	*fæt-ur*	*fingur*	*vetur*	*menn*
	dat.	*feðr-um*	*bræðr-um*	*fót-um*	*fingr-um*	*vetr-um*	*mönn-um*
	gen.	*feðr-a*	*bræðr-a*	*fót-a*	*fingr-a*	*vetr-a*	*mann-a*

(b) Remarks on the Words.

1. The genitives *föðurs, bróðurs*, and the nominative plural *mennir* are only (and always) used with the suffixed article: *föðursins, bróðursins, mennirnir* (pronounced [-ı̣d·nı̣r̥, -ıṛd̠nı̣r̥, -ı·nı̣r̥]).

2. Colloquially the plurals *vetur, fingur, fætur* are often feminine, especially with the suffixed article: *veturnar*, etc., instead of *veturnir*. And colloquially the nominative singular *bróðir* may be used in the accusative and dative singular also. But none of these colloquial forms is to be recommended.

37

3. In *faðir, bróðir, fingur, vetur,* r belongs to the stem (expanded to -*ur* after consonants). *Mað-ur* comes from *mað-r* from *mann-r,* and *menn* from *menn-r.* Cf. class 1(b)2.

3. Strong Declension, Feminine Nouns.

1. Class 1: genitive singular -*ar* (-*r*), plural -*ar*.

(a) Paradigms:

Sg. nom.	*kinn* cheek	*kerling* old	*lifur* liver	*Hild-ur*	*heið-i* heath,
acc.	*kinn*	*kerling-u* woman	*lifur*	*Hild-i*	*heið-i* mountain
dat.	*kinn*	*kerling-u*	*lifur*	*Hild-i*	*heið-i*
gen.	*kinn-ar*	*kerling-ar*	*lifr-ar*	*Hild-ar*	*heið-ar*
Pl. nom.	*kinn-ar*	*kerling-ar*	*lifr-ar*	*Hild-ar*	*heið-ar*
acc.	*kinn-ar*	*kerling-ar*	*lifr-ar*	*Hild-ar*	*heið-ar*
dat.	*kinn-um*	*kerling-um*	*lifr-um*	*Hild-um*	*heið-um*
gen.	*kinn-a*	*kerling-a*	*lifr-a*	*Hild-a*	*heið-a*

Sg. nom.	*á* river	*stöð* station	*skel* shell
acc.	*á*	*stöð*	*skel*
dat.	*á*	*stöð*	*skel*
gen.	*á-r*	*stöð-v-ar*	*skel-j-ar*
Pl. nom.	*á-r*	*stöð-v-ar*	*skel-j-ar*
acc.	*á-r*	*stöð-v-ar*	*skel-j-ar*
dat.	*á-m*	*stöð-v-um*	*skel-j-um*
gen.	*á-a*	*stöð-v-a*	*skel-j-a*

(b) Remarks on the Paradigms.

1. *Kinn* is the most common type; in *lifur* the -*ur* is an expanded -*r* belonging to the stem (cf. **2**, class 1(b)2). Like *kerling* go words in -*ing*, while those in -*ung* may or may not have -*u* in dative singular only: *djörfung* (dative -*u*) courage.

2. -*u* in the accusative and dative singular have, besides *kerling*, many feminine personal names, e. g. *Áslaug, Bergljót, Katrín, Guðrún, Rannveig, Ingileif*, and other similar.

3. *Heið-i* was originally *heið-r* exactly like *Hild*(-*u*)*r*, but most words of this class have replaced the nominative -(*u*)*r* by -*i*, which is the stem ending (cf. *lækn-i-r*) of the accusative and dative singular. A few, mostly literary words, still have -*ur*, the only colloquial are *reyður* salmon trout, *æður* eider duck, and *brúður* bride (but plural *brúðir*). The -*ur* persists mostly in personal names, e. g. *Guðríður, Hólmfríður, Ingveldur, Jarþrúður, Ragnheiður, Ragnhildur, Þorgerður*, and other similar. Without the -*ur* but otherwise like *Hildur* go names in -*dís*, -*un*(*n*): *Þórdís, Þórunn*.

Note: These feminine nouns (names) with nominative *-ur* constitute a major exception to the rule that all nouns in *-ur* (nominative singular) are masculine. In all other nouns, feminine or neuter, that now end in *-ur*, the *-ur* is an expanded *-r*, belonging to the stem, e. g. *lifur* f., *hreiður* n. nest. Cf. also the Definite Article, II, 3, 1 (c).

4. Like *á* go words with the stem vowels *á, ó, ú*: *brá* eyelash, *stó* iron stove. In most of them the vowel of the ending is dropped, except in the genitive plural. But sometimes the loss does not take place as expected, thus *frú*, genitive singular *frúar* (plural regular *frúr, frúm, frúa*) lady. When used as a title before the personal name, *frú* is indeclinable: *frú Kristín* : *til frú Kristínar* to Mrs. Kr. (genitive singular). Likewise *ungfrú* Miss. Cf. the indeclinable titles *herra* Mr. and *séra* the Rev.

5. *Stöð* and *skel* show a stem ending in *v* and *j* respectively before a vowel in the case ending. Neither type is very common. Like *skel*, but with accusative and dative singular in *-ju*, go names like *Þórey, Guðný*, etc.

2. *Class 2*: genitive singular *-ar*, plural *-ir*.

(a) Paradigms:

Sg. nom.	*tíð* time	*gjöf* gift	*verzlun* trade	*pöntun* order	*alin* ell
acc.	*tíð*	*gjöf*	*verzlun*	*pöntun*	*alin*
dat.	*tíð*	*gjöf*	*verzlun*	*pöntun*	*alin*
gen.	*tíð-ar*	*gjaf-ar*	*verzlun-ar*	*pöntun-ar*	*áln-ar*
Pl. nom.	*tíð-ir*	*gjaf-ir*	*verzlan-ir*	*pantan-ir*	*áln-ir*
acc.	*tíð-ir*	*gjaf-ir*	*verzlan-ir*	*pantan-ir*	*áln-ir*
dat.	*tíð-um*	*gjöf-um*	*verzlun-um*	*pöntun-um*	*áln-um*
gen.	*tíð-a*	*gjaf-a*	*verzlan-a*	*pantan-a*	*áln-a*

(b) Remarks on the Paradigms.

1. The majority of Icelandic feminines goes like *tíð*, thus words ending in *-semd, -úð, -und, -un(n)*, and *-urð*, e. g. *meinsemd* disease, tumor, *varúð* caution, *tegund* species, *vorkun(n)* excuse, pity, *fegurð* beauty. Also personal names like *Vilborg*.

2. *Gjöf* illustrates the type of words having *a* in the root syllable; these are u-shifted in nominative, accusative, and dative singular and dative plural. Cf. the u-shift (Pr. 5, 3). Thus go *sök* guilt, case, sake, *höfn* harbor, the personal names like *Ingibjörg*. The type is not uncommon.

3. Words like *verzlun* are common; the suffix *-un-* is u-shifted

from original *-an-*; in the literary language many of these words have actually *-an-* throughout the paradigm, except in the dative plural, which always has *-un-*. *Pöntun* illustrates the type having *a* in the root syllable u-shifted to *ö*. *Alin* is quite irregular, a unique formation.

4. Some words of the types *tíð*, *gjöf* take *-u* in accusative and dative singular. Thus *sól*: *sólu* sun (poetic), and especially the personal names: *Björg*: *Björg(u)*, *Vilborg*: *-borgu*.

3. Class 3: genitive singular *-ar* (*-ur*, *-r*), plural *-ur* (*-r*).

(a) Paradigms:

Sg.	nom.	*steik* roast	*mörk* pint	*bók* book	*brú* bridge	*ký-r* cow	*móðir* mother
	acc.	*steik*	*mörk*	*bók*	*brú*	*kú*	*móður*
	dat.	*steik*	*mörk*	*bók*	*brú*	*kú*	*móður*
	gen.	*steik-ar*(*-ur*)	*mark-ar*, *merk-ur*	*bók-ar*	*brú-ar*	*ký-r*	*móður*
Pl.	nom.	*steik-ur*	*merk-ur*	*bœk-ur*	*brý-r*	*ký-r*	*mœður*
	acc.	*steik-ur*	*merk-ur*	*bœk-ur*	*brý-r*	*ký-r*	*mœður*
	dat.	*steik-um*	*mörk-um*	*bók-um*	*brú-m*	*kú-m*	*mœðr-um*
	gen.	*steik-a*	*mark-a*	*bók-a*	*brú-a*	*kú-a*	*mœðr-a*

(b) Remarks on the Paradigms.

1. Comparatively few words belong to this class. Like *ký́r* goes *ær* ewe (*ær, á, á, ær*, plural *ær, ær, ám, áa*) and the obsolete *sýr* sow. Like *móðir* go only *dóttir* daughter and *systir* sister (plural *dœtur*, *systur*). Colloquially these three family nouns may be indeclinable throughout the singular: *móðir* (or *móður*), *dóttir, systir* (cf. *faðir*, *bróðir*, Strong masculines (2, class 4)).

2. All these words have in common the nominative and accusative plural in *-ur* (originally *-r*, thus preserved after vowels: *brú-r*, *ký-r*; sometimes assimilated to *-(u)r* or *-s* of the stem: *mœður*, *mýs*, plural of *mús* mouse). But the genitive singular fluctuates between *-ar* and *-(u)r* (from original *-r*).

3. All these words have i-shifted root vowels before the *-(u)r* of the nominative and accusative plural, and all, except the family nouns, have it also before an *-(u)r* of the genitive singular. The family nouns are i-shifted throughout the plural. Words with *a* in the root syllable have a u-shift in the nominative, accusative, and dative singular, as well as in the dative plural.

4. Though few in numbers, some nouns belonging to this class are exceedingly common, and some of these common words have minor irregularities of inflexion. Like *steik*: *mjólk, -ur* (no plural)

milk; *sæng, -ur, -ur* bed, blanket, mattress; like *mörk*: *nögl, naglar, neglur* nail; *tönn, tannar, tennur* tooth; *hönd*, dative *hendi*, genitive *handar*, plural *hendur* hand (nominative, accusative, and dative singular may all be *hendi*); *nótt*, genitive *nætur*, plural *nætur* night (with the same vowel shift as *bók*, and a change of *tt* to *t* before -(*u*)*r* in the ending, cf. Strong masculines (2, class 1(b)2)). Dative singular of *nótt* may be *nóttu*; and, in the literary language chiefly, another stem form may be used: *nátt, náttar*, plural *nætur, náttum, nátta*. Like *brú*: *tá*, genitive *táar* or *tár*, plural *tær, tám, táa* toe; *kló, klóar*, plural *klær, klóm, klóa* claw.

4. Strong Declension, Neuter Nouns.

One class only: genitive singular -*s*, plural without ending.

(a) Paradigms:

Sg. nom.	*borð* table	*barn* child	*kyn* kin	*tré* tree	*hreiður* nest
acc.	*borð*	*barn*	*kyn*	*tré*	*hreiður*
dat.	*borð-i*	*barn-i*	*kyn-i*	*tré*	*hreiðr-i*
gen.	*borð-s*	*barn-s*	*kyn-s*	*tré-s*	*hreiður-s*
Pl. nom.	*borð*	*börn*	*kyn*	*tré*	*hreiður*
acc.	*borð*	*börn*	*kyn*	*tré*	*hreiður*
dat.	*borð-um*	*börn-um*	*kyn-j-um*	*trjá-m*	*hreiðr-um*
gen.	*borð-a*	*barn-a*	*kyn-j-a*	*trjá-a*	*hreiðr-a*
Sg. nom.	*meðal* medicine	*sumar* summer	*kvæð-i* poem	*rík-i* state	
acc.	*meðal*	*sumar*	*kvæð-i*	*rík-i*	
dat.	*meðal-i*	*sumr-i*	*kvæð-i*	*rík-i*	
gen.	*meðal-s*	*sumar-s*	*kvæð-i-s*	*rík-i-s*	
Pl. nom.	*meðöl, -ul*	*sumur*	*kvæð-i*	*rík-i*	
acc.	*meðöl, -ul*	*sumur*	*kvæð-i*	*rík-i*	
dat.	*meðöl-um, -ulum*	*sumr-um*	*kvæð-um*	*rík-j-um*	
gen.	*meðal-a*	*sumr-a*	*kvæð-a*	*rík-j-a*	

(b) Remarks on the Paradigms.

1. *Borð* is a very common type. Like *barn* go words with *a* in the root syllable (u-shift in nominative, accusative, and dative plural).

2. In words like *kyn* (not numerous) *j* appears in the stem before -*u* and -*a* in the ending. Similarly a few words, mostly literary, show a *v* belonging to the stem, especially before -*i* and -*a* in the ending: *böl*, dative *böl*(*v*)*i*, genitive plural *bölva* calamity, harm; *fjör*, dative *fjör*(*v*)*i* zest, spirit.

3. Like *tré* go only *hné* knee, *hlé* lee, shelter (but dat. *hlé*(*i*)),

and the irregular *fé,* genitive *fjár* cattle, especially sheep; property, money; plural *fé, fjám, fjáa* property, moneys (antiquated).

4. The disyllabic types are less common. In *hreiður,* -*r* belongs to the stem but is expanded to -*ur* except before a vowel in the case ending; cf. Strong masculines (2, class 1(b)2). In the other two the suffixes -*al-,* -*ar-* show u-shift (-*öl-,* -*ul-*; -*ur-*) in the same cases as *barn;* the suffix -*ar-* also drops its vowel before vowels in the case endings. Like *meðal* go words in -*að,* -*al,* -*ald,* -*an,* -*ang:* *hérað* district, *folald* foal, *fargan* racket, *hunang* honey.

5. Since the type *hreiður* makes another major exception from the rule that words ending in -*ur* are masculine, it may be well to list here several of the most common words: *austur* (*vestur, norður, suður*) the east (west, etc.), *daður* flirting, *eitur* poison, *fóður* fodder, *hreistur* scales (of fish), *jórtur* (chewing the) cud, *klaustur* monastery, *leður* leather, *myrkur* darkness, *okur* usury, *púður* powder, *rökkur* twilight, *silfur* silver, *slíður* scabbard, *sykur* (also m.) sugar, *tötur* tatter, rag, poor fellow, *tjóður* tether, *veður* weather, *þvaður* gossip, *öskur* cry, roar. Cf. also the Definite Article, II, 3, 1(c).

6. *Kvæð-i* and *rík-i* are fairly common types. In them -*i* really belongs to the stem, cf. *lækn-i-r* and *heið-i.* *Kvæð-i* loses the -*i* of the stem before the endings -*um,* -*a,* while *ríki* shows a *j* in the stem before these same endings. Like *rík-i* go words ending in -*ki,* -*gi*: *virki* fortress, *vígi* fortress, fastness.

Note: *Altari,* plural *ölturu* altar; *lát* giving way, death, plural *lát;* but plural *læti,* dative *látum,* genitive *láta* noise, racket.

5. Weak Declension, Masculine Nouns.

1. *Class 1:* genitive singular-*a,* plural -*ar.*

(a) Paradigms:

Sg. nom.	*tím-i* time	*af-i* grand-	*vilj-i* will	*dómar-i* judge	*bakar-i* baker
acc.	*tím-a*	*af-a* father	*vilj-a*	*dómar-a*	*bakar-a*
dat.	*tím-a*	*af-a*	*vilj-a*	*dómar-a*	*bakar-a*
gen.	*tím-a*	*af-a*	*vilj-a*	*dómar-a*	*bakar-a*
Pl. nom.	*tím-ar*	*af-ar*	*vilj-ar*	*dómar-ar*	*bakar-ar*
acc.	*tím-a*	*af-a*	*vilj-a*	*dómar-a*	*bakar-a*
dat.	*tím-um*	*öf-um*	*vilj-um*	*dómur-um*	*bökur-um*
gen.	*tím-a*	*af-a*	*vilj-a*	*dómar-a*	*bakar-a*

(b) Remarks on the Paradigms.

1. These types, except *vilji,* are very common.

42

2. Afi displays the usual u-shift of *a* before *-um*. In a corresponding case, there is u-shift of the suffix *-ar-* in *dómurum*, and of root syllable and suffix in *bökurum* (Cf. u-shift, Pr. **5**, *3*).

3. Words with stems ending in *j* go like *vilji*, unless the *j* is preceded by *g* or *k*, in which case *j* is lost in writing (but not in pronunciation) before *-i*: *kunningi*, accusative *kunningja* acquaintance; *einyrki*, accusative *-yrkja* a farmer without help.

4. *Herra* Mr., and *séra* (or *síra*) (the) Reverend, are indeclinable in the singular; in plural *herra* is *herrar*. Both words are used as titles; cf. the title *frú*, Strong feminines (**3**, class 1(b)4), *herra* being the general title for Mr., *séra* being the title of ordained clergymen only: *séra Eiríkur á Vogsósum* the Rev. E. at V.

2. Class 2: genitive singular *-a*, plural *-ur* (with i-shift of the preceding syllable).

(a) Paradigms:

Sg. nom.	*nemand-i* pupil	*bónd-i* farmer, husband
acc.	*nemand-a*	*bónd-a*
dat.	*nemand-a*	*bónd-a*
gen.	*nemand-a*	*bónd-a*
Pl. nom.	*nemend-ur*	*bænd-ur*
acc.	*nemend-ur*	*bænd-ur*
dat.	*nemend-um* (ö)	*bænd-um*
gen.	*nemend-a* (*a*)	*bænd-a*

(b) Remarks on the Paradigms.

These types are originally present participles that have become nouns. Occasionally the older dative and genitive plural endings *-öndum* and *-anda* are found in the literature. *Bóndi* is an older contracted type for *búandi* dweller, farmer (from *búa* to dwell). Like it are *frændi* relative, cousin (originally friend, lover); and *fjandi*, plural *fjendur, fjandur, fjandar; fjendum, fjöndum; fjenda, fjanda* enemy, fiend (=hater), devil. The plural *fjendur* means enemies, *fjandar* devils.

6. Weak Declension, Feminine Nouns.

1. Class 1: genitive singular *-u*, plural *-ur*.

Sg. nom.	*tung-a* tongue	*sag-a* story	*lilj-a* lily	*amm-a* grandmother
acc.	*tung-u*	*sög-u*	*lilj-u*	*ömm-u*
dat.	*tung-u*	*sög-u*	*lilj-u*	*ömm-u*
gen.	*tung-u*	*sög-u*	*lilj-u*	*ömm-u*

Pl. nom.	*tung-ur*	*sög-ur*	*lilj-ur*	*ömm-ur*
acc.	*tung-ur*	*sög-ur*	*lilj-ur*	*ömm-ur*
dat.	*tung-um*	*sög-um*	*lilj-um*	*ömm-um*
gen.	*tungn-a*	*sagn-a*	*lilj-a*	*amm-a*

(b) Remarks on the Paradigms.

The types *lilja, amma* are extremely common. The only difference between them and *tunga, saga* is, that the latter have preserved the old stem suffix -*n*- in genitive plural. Of common words having -*na* in genitive plural note: *fluga* fly, *gáfa* gift, talent, *kista* chest, *klukka* clock, bell, *kúla* ball, projectile, *leiga* rent, *messa* mass, *míla* mile, *mínúta* minute, *pípa* pipe, *ríma* ballad, *rjúpa* ptarmigan, *rófa* tail, rutabaga, *sála* soul, *skeifa* horseshoe, *skrúfa* screw, *skýrsla* report, *stelpa* hussy, gal, *stúlka* girl, *telpa* (little) girl, *sýsla* district, county, *vika* week; also a few in -*gja*, -*kja*: *ekkja* (genitive plural *ekkna*) widow, *rekkja* bed, *kirkja* church, kirk.

Note: Quite irregular is *kona*, genitive plural *kvenna* woman, wife.

2. Class 2: genitive singular -*i* (or -*is*), plural lacking (or -*ar*, -*ir*).

(a) Paradigms:

Sg. nom.	*lyg-i* lie	*æf-i* (*æv-i*) life	*fræð-i* learning, -logy
acc.	*lyg-i*	*æf-i*	*fræð-i*
dat.	*lyg-i*	*æf-i*	*fræð-i*
gen.	*lyg-i*	*æf-i*	*fræð-i*
Pl. nom.	*lyg-ar*	*æf-ir*	lacking
acc.	*lyg-ar*	*æf-ir*	
dat.	*lyg-um*	*æf-um*	*fræði* may also be
gen.	*lyg-a*	*æf-a*	neuter like *kvæði*.

(b) Remarks on the Paradigms.

1. Like *lygi* go only *festi* chain, plural *festar* chains, betrothal, and *gersemi* (genitive -*is* in compounds) a precious thing, a gem.

2. Like *æfi* go *fylli* fullness, satisfaction, surfeit, and *gleði* comedy. *Gleði* gladness has no plural.

3. Like *fræði* go many abstract nouns formed from adjectives, e. g. *gleði* gladness from *glaður* glad. In compounds -*fræði* corresponds to -logy: *jarðfræði* geology, *gerlafræði* bacteriology. Like *fræði* go, moreover, words in -*andi*, -*gi*, -*li*, -*ni*, -*semi*, -*vísi*: *kveðandi* metrum, *græðgi* greed, *athygli* attention, *beiðni* request, *hófsemi* moderation, *smekkvísi* taste, good taste.

7. Weak Declension, Neuter Nouns.

Only one class of few words:

Sg. nom.	*aug-a* eye	*hjart-a* heart	Pl.	*aug-u*	*hjört-u*
acc.	*aug-a*	*hjart-a*		*aug-u*	*hjört-u*
dat.	*aug-a*	*hjart-a*		*aug-um*	*hjört-um*
gen.	*aug-a*	*hjart-a*		*augn-a*	*hjartn-a*

Thus go *bjúga* sausage, *eista* testicle, *eyra* ear, *hnoða* ball of yarn, *lunga* lung, *milta* milt, *nýra* kidney.

8. A Review of the Case Endings.

A review of the case endings may be of some help in memorizing the preceding classes of nouns. Since the classes are distinguished by certain case endings only, it follows that these endings must be distinctive. Case endings occurring in all or most classes of nouns are either less distinctive or quite non-distinctive.

1. Common to all nouns (and adjectives), strong and weak, hence non-distinctive, are the endings *-um* of the dative, *-a* of the genitive plural (*hestum, hesta,* etc.).

2. Common to most strong nouns of all genders is the lack of any ending in the accusative singular. A few feminines have *-u* (*Björgu*). Otherwise: *hest* m., *lækni* m., *heiði* f., *nótt* f., *land* n.

3. In all neuter nouns (and pronouns and adjectives) the nominative and accusative singular are alike (without ending: *land*: *land*), and the nominative and accusative plural are alike (without ending: *lönd* : *lönd*).

4. In most feminine nouns of the strong declension the nominative and accusative singular are alike (without ending: *tíð* : *tíð*, but *Hildur* : *Hildi, kýr* : *kú*!), and the nominative and accusative endings of the plural are alike (*kinnar* : *kinnar, tíðir* : *tíðir, nætur* : *nætur*). The identity of the nominative and accusative plural also holds for the weak feminine declension (*tungur* : *tungur, lygar* : *lygar*).

5. In most masculine nouns of the strong declension the nominative singular ends in *-ur* (*-r,* or *-r* is assimilated to the stem). Contrasting with this, strong neuters have no ending in nominative singular (in *hreiður* the ending is apparent only), and most strong feminines have none (*Hildur* is a real, *lifur* an apparent exception).

6. In strong masculine and neuter nouns the dative ending *-i* is often found (*hesti* m., *landi* n.). If not, the dative, like the accusative, is without ending (*smið* m.).

45

7. In strong feminine nouns the dative ending *-u* is sometimes found (*Björgu*). If not, the dative, like the nominative and accusative, shows no ending (*gjöf*).

8. The genitive singular ending *-s* is found: in all strong neuter nouns (*lands, kvæðis*), in most of the strong masculine nouns of the first class (*hests, læknis*), in many of the second class (*smiðs*), and in four of the fourth class (*fingurs*).

9. The genitive singular ending *-ar* is found: in all feminine strong nouns, except a few of the third class (*kinnar, tíðar,* but *merkur*), in all of the strong masculines of the third class (*hlutar, kattar*), and in some of those of the second class (*bekkjar*).

10. The genitive singular ending *-ur* is found in the fourth class strong masculines *föður, bróður,* and in some strong feminine nouns of the third class (*merkur, nætur*).

11. The plural ending *-ar* is found in strong masculines (*hestar*) and feminines (*kinnar*) of the first class, respectively, in weak masculines of the first class (*tímar*), and in weak feminines of the second class (*gersemar*).

12. The plural ending *-ir* is found: in strong masculine nouns of the second and third classes (*staðir, hlutir*), in strong feminine nouns of the second class (*gjafir*), and in some weak feminines of the second class (*æfir*).

13. The plural ending *-ur* is found: in strong masculine nouns of the fourth class (*vetur*), in strong feminines of the third class (*nætur*), in weak masculine nouns of the second class (*nemendur*), and in weak feminine nouns of the first class (*tungur*).

14. The plural ending *-u* is confined to a few weak neuter nouns (*hjörtu*).

15. The plural without an ending is confined to the strong neuter nouns (*lönd, kvæði*).

16. In all feminine and neuter nouns the accusative plural is identical with the nominative plural (cf. 3 and 4 above). The same thing is true of masculines having the nominative plural ending *-ur* (strong, fourth class: *vetur,* weak, second class: *nemendur*). But masculines, having *-ar, -ir* in nominative plural, have *-a, -i* in accusative plural (a few *-ir* nouns may have *-u*: *hestar : hesta, staðir : staði, kettir : ketti (köttu)*).

17. All the singular cases of the weak nouns end in vowels: the masculine nouns: nominative *-i* other cases *-a,* the feminine nouns: nominative *-a* other cases *-u,* or *-i* in all cases, the neuter nouns: *-a* in all cases (*tími : tíma; tunga : tungu, lygi; auga*).

18. Types of words ending in *-i* are: *heiði* strong feminine, first class, *kvæði* strong neuter, *tími*, *nemandi* weak masculines, and *lygi* weak feminine, second class.

19. Synopsis of Noun Declensions.

Strong . . . .

Masculine. . . . .

Class.	1.		2.	3.
Sg. nom.	*-ur* (*-r*, *-l*, *-n*, -),	*-i-r*	*-ur* (*-r*, -)	*-ur* (*-r*, *-n*, -)
acc.	-	*-i-*	-	-
dat.	*-i*, -	*-i-* *-v-i*	- (*-i*)	*-i*
gen.	*-s* (*-ar*)	*-i-s*	*-s*, *-j-ar*	*-ar*
Pl. nom.	*-ar*	(*-j*)*-ar* *-v-ar*	*-ir*	*-ir*
acc.	*-a*	(*-j*)*-a* *-v-a*	*-i*	*-i* (*-u*)
dat.	*-um*	(*-j*)*-um* *-v-um*	*-um* (*-j-um*)	*-um*
gen.	*-a*	(*-j*)*-a* *-v-a*	*-a* (*-j-a*)	*-a*

Masculine. . . . . .Neuter. . . . .

Class	4.				
Sg. nom.	*-ir-*	*-ur* and	-		*-i-*
acc.	*-ur-*	-	-		*-i-*
dat.	*-ur-*	*-i* other	*-i*		*-i-*
gen.	*-ur-* (*s*)	*-s*	*-s*		*-i-s*
Pl. nom.	*-ur-*	*-n* types	-		*-i-*
acc.	*-ur-*	*-n*	-		*-i-*
dat.	*-r-um*	*-n-um*	*-um*, *-j-um*		*-um*, *-j-um*
gen.	*-r-a*	*-n-a*	*-a*, *-j-a*		*-a*, *-j-a*

Feminine. . . . .

Class	1.					2.	3.	
Sg. nom.	-,	*-ur*, *-n*, *-i*				-	-	- *-ir-*
acc.	- (*-u*)	*-i-*				-	-	- *-ur-*
dat.	- (*-u*)	*-i-*				-	-	- *-ur-*
gen.	*-ar*	*-ar*	*-j-ar*	*-v-ar*	*-ar*	*-ar*, *-ur*	*-ur-*
Pl. nom.		*-ar*	*-j-ar*	*-v-ar*	*-ir*	*-ur*	*-ur-*
acc.		*-ar*	*-j-ar*	*-v-ar*	*-ir*	*-ur*	*-ur-*
dat.		*-um*	*-j-um*	*-v-um*	*-um*	*-um*	*-r-um*
gen.		*-a*	*-j-a*	*-v-a*	*-a*	*-a*	*-r-a*

Weak . . . .

Masculine. . . . . .Feminine. . . . . .Neuter

Class	1.	2.	1.	2	
Sg. nom.	*-i*	*-i*	*-a*	*-i*	*-a*
acc.	*-a*	*-a*	*-u*	*-i*	*-a*
dat.	*-a*	*-a*	*-u*	*-i*	*-a*
gen.	*-a*	*-a*	*-u*	*-i*	*-a*

47

Pl. nom.	-ar	-ur		-ur	(-ir, -ar)	-u
acc.	-a	-ur		-ur	(-ir, -ar)	-um
dat.	-um	-um		-um	(-um)	-u
gen.	-a (-n-a)	-a		-a (-n-a)	(-a)	-n-a

Note: When a hyphen (-) follows the apparent ending, it is to indicate that that ending really is part of the stem. E. g. *-i-, -ir-, -ur-*. This has not, however, been done in case of the weak declension, although all the end vowels there may be so regarded.

II. THE DEFINITE ARTICLE.

1. The Free Definite Article.

Icelandic has only one article, the definite article *hinn* m., *hin* f., *hið* n. It may be placed before its noun, as in English, but only if an adjective intervenes: *hinn góði maður* the good man. In this position we shall call it the free definite article. But it may also be suffixed to its noun: *góði maður-inn* the good man, and if there is no adjective it must be suffixed: *maður-inn* the man. The first of the three possibilities is very rare in the spoken language, but common enough in literary or elevated style. When suffixed, the article always lacks the *h*, and even when free, it is by some authors written *inn, in, ið*. In its normal form it does not differ from the demonstrative pronoun *hinn, hin, hitt* that one, except in nominative and accusative singular neuter. The declension is as follows:

Sg. nom.	hin-n m.	hin f.	hið n.	Pl.	hin-ir	hin-ar	hin
acc.	hin-n	hin-a	hið		hin-a	hin-ar	hin
dat.	hin-um	hin-ni	hin-u			hin-um	
gen.	hin-s	hin-nar	hin-s			hin-na	

2. The Suffixed Definite Article.

In the combination noun + suffixed article, both the noun and the article are inflected as may be seen from the following examples:

(a) Masculine Nouns:

Sg. nom.	hestur-inn	staður-inn	skór-inn	tími-nn
acc.	hest-inn	stað-inn	skó-inn	tíma-nn
dat.	hesti-num	stað-num	skó-num	tíma-num
gen.	hests-ins	staðar-ins	skós-ins	tíma-ns

Pl. nom.	hestar-nir	staðir-nir	skór-nir	tímar-nir
acc.	hesta-na	staði-na	skó-na	tíma-na
dat.	hestu-num	stöðu-num	skó-num	tímu-num
gen.	hesta-nna	staða-nna	skó-nna	tíma-nna

(b) Feminine Nouns:

Sg. nom.	kinn-in	á-in	œr-in	lifr-in	lilja-n
acc.	kinn-ina	á-na	á-na	lifr-ina	lilju-na
dat.	kinn-inni	á-nni	á-nni	lifr-inni	lilju-nni
gen.	kinnar-innar	ár-innar	œr-innar	lifrar-innar	lilju-nnar

Pl. nom.	kinnar-nar	ár-nar	œr-nar	lifrar-nar	liljur-nar
acc.	kinnar-nar	ár-nar	œr-nar	lifrar-nar	liljur-nar
dat.	kinnu-num	á-num	á-num	lifru-num	lilju-num
gen.	kinna-nna	á-nna	á-nna	lifra-nna	lilja-nna

(c) Neuter Nouns:

Sg. nom.	barn-ið	tré-ð	te-ið the tea	hreiðr-ið	auga-ð
acc.	barn-ið	tré-ð	te-ið	hreiðr-ið	auga-ð
dat.	barni-nu	tré-nu	te-inu	hreiðri-nu	auga-nu
gen.	barns-ins	trés-ins	tes-ins	hreiðurs-ins	auga-ns

Pl. nom.	börn-in	tré-n		hreiðr-in	augu-n
acc.	börn-in	tré-n		hreiðr-in	augu-n
dat.	börnu-num	trjá-num		hreiðru-num	augu-num
gen.	barna-nna	trjá-nna		hreiðra-nna	augna-nna

3. Remarks on the Inflexion.

1. In the nouns with suffixed article three changes take place:

(a) The -m of the dative plural is lost in all nouns.

(b) The -a of the genitive plural is lost after -á, -ó, -ú in all feminine nouns: á-nna of the rivers, of the ewes; kló-nna of the claws; brú-nna of the bridges; in the masculines skó-nna of the shoes and ljá-nna of the scythes; in the neuter nouns trjá-nna of the trees; fé fee, property, livestock: fjá-nna; hné knee : hnjá-nna; and strá straw : strá-nna (or stráa-nna).

(c) Feminine and neuter nouns with a stem ending in consonant + r (which is expanded to -ur, unless followed by a vowel in the case ending) retain the original -r unexpanded before the vowel of the definite article: lifur f. liver : lifr-in the liver; hreiður n. nest : hreiðr-ið.

2. The -i of the suffixed article is retained:

(a) In monosyllabic forms of the article, -inn, -in, -ið, -ins, after consonants and all stem vowels, except sometimes -é : hestur-

inn, hest-inn, hests-ins; *á-in*; *bú-ið* the estate, plural *bú-in*; *te-ið* the tea, but *tré-ð, fé-ð, kné-ð* the tree, the livestock, the knee.

(b) In disyllabic forms of the article: accusative, dative, genitive singular feminine *-ina, -inni, -innar,* but only after consonants.

3. The *-i* of the suffixed article is lost:

(a) In monosyllabic forms of the article: after the endings *-a, -i, -u,* and after the stem vowel *-é* (cf. above): *tími-nn, tíma-nn, augu-n, tré-ð, tré-n.*

(b) In disyllabic forms of the article: in all the cases of the plural in all genders, in dative singular masculine and neuter (whether or not preceded by a consonant or a vowel: *stað-num* the place, *búi-nu* the estate), and in the accusative dative, genitive singular feminine after vowels: *á-na, á-nni, lilju-nnar.*

Note: The *-nn* of the definite article is always pronounced as long (or short) *n,* never as [d̦·n]; cf. Pr. **3, 2,** 11(c).

III. ADJECTIVE DECLENSIONS.

1. Preliminary Remarks.

A normal adjective in Icelandic has a great variety of forms. This variety is created by several factors combined.

First there is the matter of agreement. An adjective must agree in gender, case, and number with its noun. Since nouns fall into three genders, and each noun has four cases in singular and four in plural, it follows that an adjective has to have three genders with four cases in singular and four in plural for each gender.

Then there is the matter of two types of inflexions, the so-called *strong* and *weak declensions.* Any adjective, as a rule, assumes the form of one or the other of these two declensions according to context. The strong declension is used when the adjective modifies indefinite nouns, or when the adjective is predicative. The weak declension is used when the adjective modifies a noun that is defined or determined in some way (by the definite article, etc.; see Syntax III, **2**). E. g. *góður maður* a good man, *maðurinn er góður* the man is good; *hinn góði maður* the good man = *góði maðurinn*; *þessi góði maður* this good man. But here, too, the meaning of adjectives plays a role. Only the so-called descriptive adjectives (e. g. *rauður* red) follow these rules, the so-called limiting adjectives (e. g. *allur* all, *tveir* two) show the strong declension only.

In the third place there is *comparison* (of descriptive adjectives chiefly) with special suffixes to show the *comparative* and *superlative* degree. The comparative is always weak. But the superlative, like the positive, may be inflected either weak or strong.

Comparison (by suffixes) alone, is found in English.

2. The Strong Declension of Adjectives.

(a) Paradigms:

1. *gulur* yellow.

Sg. nom.	gul-ur m.	gul f.	gul-t n.	Pl.	gul-ir	gul-ar	gul
acc.	gul-an	gul-a	gul-t		gul-a	gul-ar	gul
dat.	gul-um	gul-ri	gul-u			gul-um	
gen.	gul-s	gul-rar	gul-s			gul-ra	

Thus goes the great majority of adjectives ending in *-ur* in nominative singular masculine, among them those in *-aður*, *-agur*, *-eyg(ð)ur*, *-faldur*, *-látur*, *-legur*, *-leitur*, *-lyndur*, *-neskur*, *-óttur*, *-ráður*, *-ræður*, *-samur*, *-skur*, *-tugur*, *-ugur*, *-verður*, *-verskur*, *-ýgur*. Adjectives with *a* in the root syllable u-shift this to *ö* according to the pattern of the next paradigm; *a* in suffixes is similarly u-shifted to *u*.

2. *fagur* beautiful, fair.

Sg. nom.	fagur m.	fögur f.	fagur-t n.	Pl.	fagr-ir	fagr-ar	fögur
acc.	fagr-an	fagr-a	fagur-t		fagr-a	fagr-ar	fögur
dat.	fögr-um	fagur-ri	fögr-u			fögr-um	
gen.	fagur-s	fagur-rar	fagur-s			fagur-ra	

Thus go adjectives in which *-(u)r* belongs to the stem (expanded *-r*), e. g. *magur* lean, *digur* thick, *lipur* nimble, *snotur* nice-looking, *vitur* wise, sage. All root vowels other than *a* are unchanged throughout the inflexion.

3. *hár* high, tall, loud.

Sg. nom.	há-r m.	há f.	há-tt n.	Pl.	há-ir	há-ar	há
acc.	há-an	há-a	há-tt		há-a	há-ar	há
dat.	há-um	há-rri	há-u			há-um	
gen.	há-s	há-rrar	há-s			há-rra	

Thus go adjectives with the stem vowels *-á, -ó, -ú* : *blár* blue, *grár* grey, *hrár* raw, *smár* small, *mjór* thin, slender, *trúr* faithful.

4. *nýr* new.

Sg. nom.	*ný-r* m.	*ný* f.	*ný-tt* n.	Pl.	*ný-ir*	*ný-j-ar*	*ný*
acc.	*ný-j-an*	*ný-j-a*	*ný-tt*		*ný-j-a*	*ný-j-ar*	*ný*
dat.	*ný-j-um*	*ný-rri*	*ný-j-u*			*ný-j-um*	
gen.	*ný-s*	*ný-rrar*	*ný-s*			*ný-rra*	

Thus go adjectives with the stem vowels *-ý* and *-œ* : *hlýr* warm, *-sœr* visible, *auðsœr* evident; and similarly goes *mið-ur, mið, mit-t* mid-, in the middle, accusative *mið-j-an, mið-j-a, mit-t,* but nominative plural masculine *mið-j-ir.*

5. *dýr* dear, expensive.

Sg. nom.	*dýr* m.	*dýr* f.	*dýr-t* n.	Pl.	*dýr-ir*	*dýr-ar*	*dýr*
acc.	*dýr-an*	*dýr-a*	*dýr-t*		*dýr-a*	*dýr-ar*	*dýr*
dat.	*dýr-um*	*dýr-ri*	*dýr-u*			*dýr-um*	
gen.	*dýr-s*	*dýr-rar*	*dýr-s*			*dýr-ra*	

Thus go adjectives the stems of which end in *-r, -s,* and (consonant +) *-n* : *stór* big, great, *kyr(r)* quiet, *þurr* dry, *fús* willing, eager, *laus* loose, *hvass* keen-edged, strong (of wind) ; *gjarn* eager, *jafn* even.

6. *seinn* slow, late.

Sg. nom.	*sein-n* m.	*sein* f.	*sein-t* n.	Pl.	*sein-ir*	*sein-ar*	*sein*
acc.	*sein-an*	*sein-a*	*sein-t*		*sein-a*	*sein-ar*	*sein*
dat.	*sein-um*	*sein-ni*	*sein-u*			*sein-um*	
gen.	*sein-s*	*sein-nar*	*sein-s*			*sein-na*	

Thus go monosyllabic adjectives in *-nn, -ll* : *hreinn* clean, *sœll* happy; disyllabic adjectives in *-ull* : *þögull* taciturn, and one disyllabic adjective in *-ill* : *heimill* at free disposal (sometimes *heimull*).

7. *gamall* old.

Sg. nom.	*gamal-l* m.	*gömul* f.	*gamal-t* n.	Pl.	*gaml-ir*	*gaml-ar*	*gömul*
acc.	*gaml-an*	*gaml-a*	*gamal-t*		*gaml-a*	*gaml-ar*	*gömul*
dat.	*göml-um*	*gamal-li*	*göml-u*			*göml-um*	
gen.	*gamal-s*	*gamal-lar*	*gamal-s*			*gamal-la*	

Thus go *einsamall* alone, *vesall* sick(ly), ailing (but *vesœll* goes like *seinn*), and adjectives in *-ugur, -ull,* if they drop the suffix vowel at all.

8. *mikill* great, large, big; n. also: much.

Sg.					Pl.			
nom.	*mikil-l* m.	*mikil* f.	*miki-ð* n.		*mikl-ir*	*mikl-ar*	*mikil*	
acc.	*mikin-n*	*mikl-a*	*miki-ð*		*mikl-a*	*mikl-ar*	*mikil*	
dat.	*mikl-um*	*mikil-li*	*mikl-u*			*mikl-um*		
gen.	*mikil-s*	*mikil-lar*	*mikil-s*			*mikil-la*		

Thus goes, aside from *mikill*, only *lítill* little, small, but the *í* of the root syllable becomes *i* when the following suffix vowel drops.

9. *heiðinn* heathen.

Sg.					Pl.			
nom.	*heiðin-n* m.	*heiðin* f.	*heiði-ð* n.		*heiðn-ir*	*heiðn-ar*	*heiðin*	
acc.	*heiðin-n*	*heiðn-a*	*heiði-ð*		*heiðn-a*	*heiðn-ar*	*heiðin*	
dat.	*heiðn-um*	*heiðin-ni*	*heiðn-u*			*heiðn-um*		
gen.	*heiðin-s*	*heiðin-nar*	*heiðin-s*			*heiðin-na*		

Thus go disyllabic adjectives in *-inn*, most past participles of strong verbs, and a few past participles of weak (or partly weak) verbs: *heppinn* lucky, *fundinn* found, *farinn* gone, *flúinn* fled, *snúinn* turned.

10. *talinn*, pp. of *telja*, told.

Sg.					Pl.			
nom.	*talin-n* m.	*talin* f.	*tali-ð* n.		*tald-ir*	*tald-ar*	*talin*	
acc.	*talin-n*	*tald-a*	*tali-ð*		*tald-a*	*tald-ar*	*talin*	
dat.	*töld-um*	*talin-ni*	*töld-u*			*töld-um*		
gen.	*talin-s*	*talin-nar*	*talin-s*			*talin-na*		

Thus are declined the past participles of weak verbs of the first class ending in *-ja*: *telja* count, tell. Also the past participles of two strong verbs: *alinn* fed (from *ala*), and *galinn* crazy, insane (from *gala* enchant).

(b) Remarks on the Declension.

1. Some of the adjective case endings are obviously the same as the noun case endings; thus the nominative masculine singular in *-ur*, the nominative feminine singular without ending, the genitive masculine and neuter singular in *-s*, the nominative and accusative feminine plural in *-ar*, the nominative and accusative neuter plural with no ending, the masculine accusative plural in *-a,* and the dative plural of all genders in *-um*. The other endings differ from those of the nouns, but agree with the corresponding endings of the pronouns; obviously, the adjective endings are a mixture of noun and pronoun case endings.

2. Note (a) that the dative and genitive plural *-um*, *-ra* are

alike in all genders; (b) that the genitive singular masculine and neuter are alike, -*s*; (c) that the nominative and accusative neuter are alike in the singular and also in the plural; and (d) that there is a formal agreement between the nominative singular feminine and the nominative and accusative plural neuter, as well as (e) between the accusative singular feminine and the accusative plural masculine.

3. The nominative singular masculine ends in -*ur* after most consonants: *gulur*; in -*r* after vowels (*á, ó, ú, ý, æ*): *há-r*. After a tense root vowel and any suffix vowel + *l* or *n*, the -(*u*)*r* has been assimilated to the consonants, giving -*ll*, -*nn*: *sæll, seinn, mikill, heiðinn*. After a consonant + *l* or *n*, after simple or expanded *r* (-*ur*) belonging to the stem, and after *s*, the nominative -*ur* has been lost altogether: *jafn* even; *dýr* expensive; *fagur* fair; *frjáls* free,

4. The nominative singular feminine has no ending, but if there is an *a* in the root syllable this undergoes u-shift to *ö*: *fagur* becomes *fögur* fair.

5. The nominative and accusative singular neuter has the ending -*t*: *allur*: *all-t* all; *hress*: *hress-t* in good spirits. But often either the final sounds of the stem or the ending are modified; this depends on the nature of the final sounds of the stem.

(a) A vowel + *ð* or *dd* + *t* gives *tt*: *góður* m.: *got-t* n. good (note also the changed vowel!); *glað-ur* m.: *glat-t* n. glad; *gladd-ur* m.: *glat-t* n. gladdened.

(b) A consonant + *ð*, *d*, or *t* + *t* gives *t*: *harð-ur* m.: *hart* n. hard; *vond-ur* m.: *vont* n. bad, evil; *fast-ur* m.: *fast* n. fast, firm.

(c) Doubled *t* (i. e. *tt*)+*t* gives *tt*: *bratt-ur* m.: *bratt* n. steep.

(d) After tense (cf. Pr. **2**, *2*, 3) stem vowels (*á, ó, ú, ý, æ*) the -*t* is doubled: *há-r* m.: *há-tt* n. high; *mjó-r* m.: *mjó-tt* n. thin; *nýr* m.: *ný-tt* n. new. Since *g* is usually lost in the adjectives *bá(g)ur* pitiful, and *lá(g)ur* low, the neuter forms, though spelled *bágt* and *lágt*, are often pronounced *bátt* and *látt*.

(e) In the adjective *sannur* true, the numeral *einn* one, and the pronouns *minn* my, *þinn* thy, your, *sinn* his, *hinn* the other, the combination *n(n)*+*t* becomes *tt*: *satt, eitt, mitt, þitt, hitt*. This is an exceptional treatment, cf. *seinn*: *seint* above.

(f) When added to the suffixes -*il*-, -*in*-, -*ar*-, and -*að*-, a *t* assimilates the preceding consonant and is, in turn, weakened to *ð*: *mikil-l* m.: *miki-ð* n. great; *heiðin-n* m.: *heiði-ð* n. heathen; *gefin-n* m. : *gefi-ð* n. given; *annar* m. : *ann-að* n. other; *kallað-ur* m.: *kallað* n. called. The same treatment is given the always unstressed definite article: (*h*)*in-n* m.: (*h*)*ið* n. the. Exception: *heimil-l* m. *heimil-t* n. free.

6. In the endings -ri, -rar, -ra (dative and genitive singular feminine, genitive plural all genders), the -r is doubled when the stem ends in a tense (Pr. 2, 2, 3) vowel (á, ó, ú, ý, æ): há-rri, há-rrar, há-rra high; the r is assimilated to the preceding (vowel +) l or n: sæl-li, sæl-lar, sæl-la happy; sein-ni, etc. slow. (Colloquially the regular -ri, -rar, -ra endings are here often superimposed upon the doubled consonants: sæll-ri, seinn-ri.) But if l or n are preceded by consonants, or if they are doubled, no assimilation takes place: megn m.: megn-ri pungent; full-ur m.: full-ri full; sann-ur m.: sann-ri true.

When added to the suffixes -ar-, -ur-, the expected doubled r-r is sometimes simplified to r: annar m.: annar-i, annar-ar, annar-a other; nokkur m.: nokkur-(r)i, nokkur-(r)ar, nokkur-(r)a any.

7. Adjectives ending in ss or a consonant + s do not add the -s of the genitive singular masculine and neuter: hvass m., gen. hvass keen, acute, stormy; frjáls m., gen. frjáls free; but fús m., gen. fúss eager.

8. Disyllabic adjectives ending in -inn have the same ending in the accusative singular masculine: heiðin-n, accusative heiðin-n (instead of the usual ending -an: gaml-an) heathen. Only two words in -ill: mikill great, and litill small, have this peculiar accusative singular ending: mikin-n, litin-n, but it is also found in pronouns such as hin-n, min-n, vor-n the other, my, our, etc.

9. Disyllabic adjectives with the suffixes -al-, -in-, -ar-, -ur- (i. e. the expanded r; cf. Noun Declensions, I, 2, 1 (b) 2) drop the vowel of the suffix when the case ending begins with a vowel: gamal-l: gaml-ir old; heiðin-n: heiðn-ir heathen; annar: aðr-ir (for annr-ir, cf. maður for mannr, Noun Declensions, I, 2, 4) other, another; fagur: fagr-ir fair, beautiful. Only two words in -il- show this loss of the suffix vowel: mikil-l: mikl-ir great, and lítil-l: litl-ir small, the latter with a concomitant change of í to i in its root syllable.

Adjectives with the suffixes -ug-, -ul- may or may not drop the suffix vowel: auðug-ur: auðug-ir or auðg-ir wealthy; þögul-l: þögul-ir or þögl-ir silent, taciturn. The full forms are used in conversation and in ordinary prose, while the contracted forms are literary and poetical. Occasionally the two forms have split into two words, one colloquial, the other of higher style: heilagur: helgur holy; máttugur: máttkur mighty.

10. In ný-r, new, -sær, visible, j appears as a stem ending before -a and -u of the case endings, but, though audible, it is not

55

written before *i* in the ending: *nýr*: *ný-j-an, ný-j-um,* but `ný-ir`. In *mið-ur*, in the middle, *j* appears not only before *-a* and *-u*, but also before *-i*: *mið-j-an, mið-j-um, mið-j-ir.*

In a similar way, *v*, originally belonging to the stem, appears before all vowels of the endings: *dökk-ur* dark: *dökk(v)-an, dökk(v)-um, dökk(v)-ir.* But colloquially this *v* is seldom heard.

Note: If the nominative masculine *-ur* seems to be an exception to these rules, it is because it is really an expanded *r*.

11. The declension of the past participles of the first class of weak verbs in *-ja*, like *talinn* from *telja* count, shows a mixture of two stems, the first disyllabic like *heiðinn*, the second monosyllabic like *gulur*. The monosyllabic stem *tald-* appears where the case ending begins with a vowel; the *a* of the root is u-shifted to *ö* before *u* in the ending. The stem *tald-* may also be used throughout the whole declension; in that case the past participle really has two forms: *talinn* and *taldur*.

12. Synopsis of the Strong Adjective Declension.

Masculine		Feminine	Neuter
Sg. nom.	*-ur, -r, -l, -n, -*	-	*-t, -tt, -ð*
acc.	*-an, -n*	*-a*	*-t, -tt, -ð*
dat.	*-um (-m)*	*-ri, -li, -ni*	*-u*
gen.	*-s, -*	*-rar, -lar, -nar*	*-s, -*
Pl. nom.	*-ir*	*-ar*	-
acc.	*-a*	*-ar*	-
dat.	*-um (-m)*	*-um (-m)*	*-um (-m)*
gen.	*-ra, -la, -na*	*-ra, -la, -na*	*-ra, -la, -na*

3. The Weak Declension of Adjectives.

1. Class 1:

1. This declension is very similar to the weak declension of nouns, the masculine being inflected on the pattern of *tími*, the feminine like *tunga*, and the neuter like *hjarta*—in the singular. In the plural all genders alike end in *-u* in all cases. Examples: *latur* lazy, and *fagur* beautiful (*-ur* expanded *r* belonging to the stem):

Sg. nom.	*lat-i* m.	*lat-a* f.	*lat-a* n.	Pl. *löt-u*
other cases	*lat-a*	*löt-u*	*lat-a*	*löt-u*
Sg. nom.	*fagr-i* m.	*fagr-a* f.	*fagr-a* n.	Pl. *fögr-u*
other cases	*fagr-a*	*fögr-u*	*fagr-a*	*fögr-u*

2. The above examples, having *a* in the root syllable, show u-shift. All other root syllable vowels are unchanged.

3. Disyllabic words that drop the suffixal vowel before a vowel in the case ending do so here throughout the inflexion: *fagur*: *hinn fagri, heiðinn* heathen: *hinn heiðni, lítill* little: *hinn litli* (note the change of *í* to *i*), *gamall* old: *hinn gamli*.

4. Most limiting adjectives are never weak; thus *allur* all, *miður* mid-, *nógur* enough, *sjálfur* self, *sumur* some. *Fár* and *margur* (the singulars of *fáir* few, *margir* many) may be weak in the plural, but never in the singular. Cf. In. III, 1.

5. Superlatives, when weak, take this inflexion: *hinn latasti maður* the most lazy man. Likewise past participles: *kærður* accused, *hinn kærði* the accused, from *kæra* accuse.

2. Class 2:

In the comparative, adjectives are always declined weak, but the declension is different from the one above:

Sg. nom.	*latar-i* m.	*latar-i* f.	*latar-a* n.	Pl. *latar-i*
other cases	*latar-i*(-*a*)	*latar-i*	*latar-a*	*latar-i*

Note: Dative plural of *fleiri* more, is either *fleiri* or *fleirum*.

3. Class 3:

Many adjectives are wholly indeclinable. Such are *eigin* own (except in nom. acc. sg. neuter: *eigið*), *hugsi* lost in thought; but most of these indeclinable adjectives end in -*a* : *aflaga* out of order, *andvaka* sleepless, *einstaka* single, solitary, *forviða, hissa, hlessa* astonished, surprised, *hvumsa* startled, taken aback, and many more.

Present participles, when used as adjectives, are indeclinable: *rennandi vatn* running water, pl. *rennandi vötn.* Formerly these were declined like the comparatives (class 2), such forms are still found in the written language.

4. Comparison of Adjectives.

1. Suffixes of Comparison.

Most adjectives form their comparative and superlative degree by adding the suffixes -*ari* and -*astur* to the stem of the positive. This corresponds to the regular comparison of adjectives in English. A smaller group adds the suffixes -*ri* and -*stur* with i-shift of the root vowel, doubling of the *r* after the tense (Pr. **2, 2,** 3) stem vowels (*á, ó, ú, ý, œ*), and assimilation of *r* to a preceding *l* or *n* (in this last case *r* is often colloquially restored and added to the *ll, nn* : *sælli* happier, colloquially *sællri*). This smaller Icelandic group is represented in English by the solitary old, elder, eldest.

In disyllabic adjectives the suffix drops its vowel (or an expanded -(*u*)*r* reverts to -*r*) before the vowels in -*ari*, -*astur*.

Note: As to these sound changes, cf. above **2** (b) 6 and 9.

2. *Adjectives with* comparative -*ari*, superlative -*astur*.

lat-ur lazy	*lat-ari*	*lat-astur*
snotur nice, handsome	*snotr-ari*	*snotr-astur*
dýr expensive	*dýr-ari*	*dýr-astur*
fús eager	*fús-ari*	*fús-astur*
lasin-n sick (ly)	*lasn-ari*	*lasn-astur*
ör liberal, sensitive	*ör(v)-ari*	*ör(v)-astur* (*v* literary)

3. *Adjectives with* comparative -*ri* superlative -*stur*.

(a) With i-shift comparative and superlative:

grann-ur slender	*grenn-ri*	*grenn-stur*
lang-ur long	*leng-ri*	*leng-stur*
fá-r sg. of few	*fœ-rri*	*fœ-stur*
há-r high	*hœ-rri*	*hœ-stur*
smá-r small	*smœ-rri*	*smœ-stur*
lág-ur low	*lœg-ri*	*lœg-stur*
stór big	*stœr-ri*	*stœr-stuŕ*
stutt-ur short	*stytt-ri*	*styt-ztur* (pronounced *stystur*)
ung-ur young	*yng-ri*	*yng-stur*
þunn-ur thin	*þynn-ri*	*þynn-stur*
mjúk-ur soft	*mýk-ri*	*mýk-stur*
þröng-ur narrow	*þreng-ri*	*þreng-stur*

(b) With i-shift in all forms:

sýn-n obvious	*sýn-ni*	*sýn-stur*
væn-n good, good-looking	*væn-ni*	*væn-stur*

(c) Without i-shift:

frá-r swift of foot	*frá-rri*	*frá-stur*
kná-r strong	*kná-rri*	*kná-stur*
mjó-r slender, thin	*mjó-rri*	*mjó-stur*

Note: These words originally had -*ari*, -*astur*, but the suffix vowel was dropped after the tense stem vowels. Hence the lack of i-shift.

4. Mixed Comparison.

Some adjectives have a mixed comparison, drawn from the two chief types.

(a) Comparison with *-ri, -astur* is found in the following types:

falleg-ur handsome	*falleg-ri*	*falleg-astur* (words in *-legur*)
kunnug-ur familiar with	*kunnug-ri*	*kunnug-astur* (words in *-ugur*)
sæl-l happy	*sæl-li*	*sæl-astur* (words in vowel + *ll*)
sein-n slow	*sein-ni*	*sein-astur* (words in vowel + *nn*, except
		sýnn, vænn, cf. 3(b))
þögul-l silent	*þögul-li*	*þögul-astur* (words in *-ull*)

Adjectives with the stem vowels *á, ó, ú, ý, æ* (except *frár, knár, mjór,* cf. *3*(c)):

þrá-r stubborn	*þrá-rri*	*þrá-astur*
sljó-r dull, insensitive	*sljó-rri*	*sljó-astur*
trú-r faithful	*trú-rri*	*trú-astur*
hlý-r cosy, warm	*hlý-rri*	*hlý-j-astur*
ný-r new	*ný-rri*	*ný-j-astur*
auðsæ-r evident	*auðsæ-rri*	*auðsæ-j-astur*

(b) Comparison with *-ari/-ri, -astur/-stur*:

auðug-ur wealthy	*auð(u)g-ari*	*auð(u)g-astur*
	auðug-ri	(thus some adjectives in *-ugur*)
vesæl-l sick	*vesæl-li*	*vesæl-astur* (some adjectives in
vesal-l wretched	*vesl-ari*	*vesl-astur* vowel + *ll*)

Adjectives in (expanded) *-(u)r*:

dýr expensive	*dýr-ari*	*dýr-astur*
	dýr-ri	*dýr-stur*
kær dear	*kær-ari*	*kær-astur*
	kær-ri	*kær-stur*
fagur beautiful	*feg(ur)-ri*	*fegur-stur*
	fagr-ari	*fagr-astur*
magur lean	*magr-ari*	*magr-astur*
	meg(ur)-ri	*megur-stur*

In some others:

fræg-ur famous	*fræg-ari*	*fræg-astur*
	fræg-ri	*fræg-stur*
glögg-ur observant	*glegg-ri*	*glegg-stur*
	glögg(v)-ari	*glögg(v)-astur*
þykk-ur thick	*þykk-ri*	*þykk-stur*
	þykk(v)-ari	*þykk(v)-astur*
(fram-ur) outstanding	*frem-ri*	*frem-stur*
fram-ur arrogant	*fram-ari*	*fram-astur*
djúp-ur deep	*dýp-ri*	*dýp-stur*
	djúp-ari	*djúp-astur*

In this list the commoner forms have been put first.

5. Irregular Comparison.

gamall old	*eldri* elder	*elztur* eldest
góður good	*betri* better	*beztur* best
lítill little	*minni* less	*minnstur* least
margur many (sg.)	*fleiri* more	*flestur* most
mikill great	*meiri* more, greater	*mestur* most, greatest
vondur bad, evil, } *illur* ill }	*verri* worse	*verstur* worst.

IV. ADVERBS AND THEIR COMPARISON.

1. Preliminary Remarks.

1. There are a number of characteristic adverb suffixes in Icelandic. Among these -*ar*, -*u*, -*um*, -*s*, -*is* are noun or adjective case endings: *reyndar* in fact (genitive of *reynd* experience); *hálfu* by half, twice as much (dative), *hálfu fleiri* twice as many; *stórum* (dative) greatly, *stundum* (dative plural) sometimes; *annars* (genitive) otherwise; *umhverfis* (genitive) around. In adverbs of place, the endings -*i* and -(*u*)*r* mean: dwelling in the place : *inni* inside, *þar* there, *norður* (*á landi*) in the North of Iceland. The ending -*an* means: motion from a place: *innan* from the inside, *þaðan* thence, *norðan* from the north. Apart from 'dwelling in' the ending -(*u*)*r* may also mean motion to a place: *norður* north, to the north, etc.

2. Many adverbs have patently pronominal case forms:

Interrogative:		Demonstrative:	
Cause:	*hví, því* why?	*því, þess vegna* therefore
Mode:	*hve, hversu* how?	*þannig* thus
Time:	*hvenær* when?	*þá* then
Place:	*hvar, hvert, hvaðan* where, wither, whence?	*þar, þangað, þaðan* there, thither, thence

3. Adverbs of place fall into well defined patterns in Icelandic:

Rest:	*hér* here	*þar* there	*hvar* where?
Motion to:	*hingað* hither	*þangað* thither	*hvert* whither, where?
Motion from:	*héðan* hence	*þaðan* thence	*hvaðan* whence?

Rest:	*uppi* up above	*niðri* down below	*úti* outside	*inni* inside
Motion to:	*upp* up	*niður* down	*út* out	*inn* in(to)
Motion from:	*ofan* down, from above	*neðan* up, from below	*utan* from the outside	*innan* from the inside

Rest:	*norður* in the north	*suður* in the s.	*austur*	*vestur*
Motion to:	*norður* (to the) n.	*suður* to the s.	*austur*	*vestur*
Motion from:	*norðan* from the n.	*sunnan* from the s.	*austan*	*vestan*

Note 1. *Norður* 'in the north' is so used almost only with prepositions: *norður á landi* in the North of Iceland. When it should be used alone, *nyrðra* must be substituted: *hann er nyrðra* he is in the North (of Iceland, in the northern regions). *Í norðri* to the north (of the direction only, *í hánorðri* due north). *Suður, austur, vestur* are treated in the same way. Parallel to *nyrðra* (weak comparative, accusative neuter) are the expressions *í efra* in the upper regions, *í neðra, í ytra, í innra* (for older *hið efra,* etc.). *Hann er niðri í Fjörðum* he is down in the Firths = *hann er í neðra,* common expression in the East of Iceland. Like *inni—inn—innan* are the adverbial patterns *frammi—fram—framan* near the interior—to the interior—from the interior (so in the North of Iceland), or near the sea—toward the sea—from the sea (South of Iceland), *heima—heim—heiman* at home—home—from home, and *handan* from beyond.

Note 2: In Old Icelandic times it was idiomatic to speak of *fara frá Noregi út til Íslands* go (i. e. sail) from Norway out to Iceland, and the opposite: *fara utan frá Íslandi til Noregs* sail 'from the outside' from Iceland to Norway. Cp. the American usage 'out west.' From this usage *fara utan* came to get the meaning 'go abroad' which was extended even to *vera utan* be abroad. Since *út* in Norway was equivalent to west, this sense has been retained, not only in the West of Iceland, where it fits, but also in the South of Iceland, where *fram,* towards the sea, takes the place of *út,* out, in other parts of the country.

Note 3: In speaking of travelling to different parts of the country only the cardinal directions *norður, suður, austur, vestur* are used, hence often in a very distorted sense. But in determining directions and speaking about the weather the intermediate directions, both the old ones: *landnorður, landsuður, útnorður, útsuður* (Norwegian terms) and the more modern: *norðaustur, suðaustur, norðvestur, suðvestur* are used.

Note 4: The preposition *fyrir* combines with adverbs of motion in two different ways: (a) *fyrir* preceding adverbs in *-an* expresses rest: *fyrir ofan* (with acc.) above, *fyrir neðan* below, *fyrir utan* outside (of), *fyrir innan* inside (of), *fyrir norðan* north of, in the North, etc.; (b) *fyrir* following, especially, adverbs of motion to (but also others) always indicates the crossing of a definite limit (also with acc.): *upp fyrir* up above (a certain limit), *niður fyrir* down below, *út fyrir* out beyond (a certain limit), *inn fyrir* in beyond; *norður fyrir* north beyond (over) etc. Examples: *fyrir norðan á* north of the river (rest); *norður fyrir á* north over the

61

river (motion to the northern bank); also *norðan fyrir á* from the north over the river (i. e. crossing the river from the north to the south bank).

4. Of the types mentioned above, only certain adverbs of place have comparison. Comparison is more frequent, though not universal, in adverbs derived from adjectives by the suffixes *-a*, *-la*, and *-lega*, the last type from the adjectives in *-legur* : *víða* widely, in many places (from *víður* wide), *varla* (pron. *valla*, sometimes so spelled) hardly (from *var* cautious), *fallega* well, beautifully (from *fallegur* beautiful). Moreover, the neuter of adjectives in all degrees may be used adverbially : *fljótt* quickly, *fljótar(a)* more quickly, *fljótast* most quickly; but, as here indicated, the *-a* of the neuter comparative is often lost. It is not lost, however, if the neuter adjective has the endings *-ra*, *-st* : *langt* long (way), *lengra* longer (way), *lengst* longest; *hátt* high, loudly, *hærra* higher, louder, *hæst* highest, loudest. Here belong also the neuter comparative forms *nyrðra*, *syðra*, *eystra*, *vestra* in the North, etc., mentioned above.

2. Comparison of Adverbs.

The comparison of adverbs corresponds closely to that of adjectives. There are two groups: the more common one ending in *-ar*, *-ast* : *fallega* beautifully, *falleg-ar*, *falleg-ast*; the less common one ending in *-(u)r*, *-st* with i-shift of the root vowel: *lengi* long, *leng-ur*, *leng-st*. Examples:

(a) Comparison in *-ar*, *-ast* :

aust-ur to (in) the east	*aust-ar* more to the east	*aust-ast* most to the east
vest-ur to (in) the west	*vest-ar*	*vest-ast*
fram forward, forth *frammi* in a forward position }	*fram-ar* more forward	*fram-ast* most forward
aft-ur back	*aft-ar* further back	*aft-ast* furthest back
oft often	*oft-ar* more often	*oft-ast* most often
síð, *síð-la* late	*síð-ar* later	*síð-ast* latest, last
s(k)jaldan seldom	*s(k)jaldn-ar* more seldom	*s(k)jaldn-ast* most seldom
víð-a widely	*víð-ar* more widely	*víð-ast* most widely

(b) Comparison in *-(u)r*, *-st* :

leng-i long (time)	*leng-ur* longer	*leng-st* longest
skamm-t short	*skem-ur* shorter	*skemm-st* shortest
fjar-ri far (away)	*fir-r* farther	*fir-st* farthest
nær, *nær-ri* near	*næ-r* nearer	*næ-st* nearest
fjær, *fjær-ri* far (away)	*fjær* farther	*fjær-st* farthest

gjör-la, ger-la clearly, thoroughly	*gjör, ger* more clearly, more thoroughly	*gjör-st, ger-st* most clearly, thoroughly
	ská-r better under the circumstances	*ská-st* best under the circumstances

(c) Mixed Comparison in *-ar, -st* :

suð-ur to the south	*sunn-ar* more to the south	*syð-st* most to the south
norð-ur to the north	*norð-ar*	*nyr-zt*
inn into *inni* inside	*inn-ar* inner	*inn-st* innermost
út out *úti* outside	*ut-ar* outer	*yzt* outermost
of-an from above *upp* up *uppi* up above	*of-ar* higher up	*ef-st* highest up, topmost
neð-an from below *nið-ur* down to *nið-ri* down below	*neð-ar* lower	*neð-st* lowest

(d) Irregular Comparison:

vel well	*betur* better	*bezt* best
illa badly	*verr* worse	*verst* worst
lítið little	*minna* less	*minnst* least (literal)
lítt little	*miður* less	*minnst* least (derived sense)
mjög (mikið) very	*meir* more	*mest* most
gjarna(n) willingly	*heldur* rather	*helzt* most willingly, preferably
varla (valla) hardly	*síður* less (willingly)	*sízt* least (willingly)
har(ð)la very much	*fremur* even more	*fremst* first of all
snemma early	*fyrr* earlier	*fyrst* earliest, first
árla early	———————	———————
———————	*fyrrmeir* of old	*hinzt* last

V. NUMERALS.

1. Cardinals and Ordinals.

In Icelandic the cardinals, if written in ciphers, have no mark, but the ordinals are marked by a period, following the number, corresponding to the English 1st, 2nd, 3rd, 4th, etc.

0 *núll* n.

1 *einn* m., *ein* f., *eitt* n.	1. *fyrsti* m., *fyrsta* f., *fyrsta* n.
2 *tveir* m., *tvær* f., *tvö* n.	2. *annar* m., *önnur* f., *annað* n.
3 *þrír* m., *þrjár* f., *þrjú* n.	3. *þriðji* m., *þriðja* f., *þriðja* n.
4 *fjórir* m., *fjórar* f., *fjögur* n.	4. *fjórði* m., *fjórða* f., *fjórða* n.

5 *fimm*	5. *fimmti, -a, -a,* etc.
·6 *sex*	6. *sjötti, sétti*
7 *sjö*	7. *sjöundi*
8 *átta*	8. *áttundi*
9 *níu*	9. *níundi*
10 *tíu*	1.. *tíundi*
11 *ellefu*	11. *ellefti*
12 *tólf*	12. *tólfti*
13 *þrettán*	13. *þrettándi*
14 *fjórtán*	14. *fjórtándi*
15 *fimmtán*	15. *fimmtándi*
16 *sextán*	16. *sextándi*
17 *sautján, seytján*	17. *sautjándi, seytjándi*
18 *átján*	18. *átjándi*
19 *nítján*	19. *nítjándi*
20 *tuttugu (tveir tugir, tigir)*	20. *tuttugasti (tvítugasti)*
21 *tuttugu og einn (ein, eitt)*	21. *tuttugasti og fyrsti*
22 *tuttugu og tveir*	22. *tuttugasti og annar*
29 *tuttugu og níu*	29. *tuttugasti og níundi*
30 *þrjátíu (þrír tugir, tigir)*	30. *þrítugasti*
31 *þrjátíu og einn*	31. *þrítugasti og fyrsti*
40 *fjörutíu (fjórir tugir)*	40. *fertugasti*
50 *fimmtíu (fimm tugir)*	50. *fimmtugasti*
60 *sextíu (sex tugir)*	60. *sextugasti*
70 *sjötíu (sjö tugir)*	70. *sjötugasti*
80 *áttatíu (átta tugir)*	80. *áttugasti*
90 *níutíu (níu tugir)*	90. *nítugasti*
100 *hundrað, eitt hundrað*	100. *hundraðasti*
101 *hundrað og einn*	101. *hundraðasti og fyrsti*
110 *hundrað og tíu*	110. *hundraðasti og tíundi*
111 *hundrað og ellefu*	111. *hundraðasti og ellefti*
120 *hundrað og tuttugu*	120. *hundrað og tuttugasti*
121 *hundrað tuttugu og einn*	121. *hundrað tuttugasti og fyrsti*
130 *hundrað og þrjátíu*	130. *hundrað og þrítugasti*
131 *hundrað þrjátíu og einn*	131. *hundrað þrítugasti og fyrsti*
190 *hundrað og níutíu*	190. *hundrað og nítugasti*
200 *tvö hundruð*	200. *tvö hundraðasti*
201 *tvö hundruð og einn*	201. *tvö hundraðasti og fyrsti*
220 *tvö hundruð og tuttugu*	220. *tvö hundruð og tuttugasti*
300 *þrjú hundruð*	300. *þrjú hundraðasti*
900 *níu hundruð*	900. *níu hundraðasti*
1000 *þúsund, eitt þúsund, ein þúsund, tíu hundruð*	1000. *þúsundasti*
1200 *eitt þúsund og tvö hundruð, tólf hundruð*	1200. *eitt þúsund og tvö hundraðasti*
1225 *eitt þúsund tvö hundruð tuttugu og fimm, tólf hundruð tuttugu og fimm*	1225. *eitt þúsund tvö hundruð tuttugasti og fimmti*
10.000 *tíu þúsund*	10.000. *tíu þúsundasti*
100.000 *hundrað þúsund*	100.000. *hundrað þúsundasti* .
1.000.000 *(ein) milljón*	1.000.000. *milljónasti*
1.000.000.000 *(ein) billjón*	1.000.000.000. *billjónasti*

Note: *Skipið sökk 29. apríl 1941* (*tuttugasta og níunda apríl nítján hundruð fjörutíu og eitt*) the ship sank April 29th, 1941. *Skipið sökk þann 29.* the ship sank on the 29th (of a known month, often: *þ. m. = þessa mánaðar* of this month, *inst.*). Dates of letters: (*hinn*) *29. apríl 1941* April 29, 1941.

2. Declension of Numerals.

1. Both cardinals, denoting definite number, and ordinals, indicating position in a series, are limiting adjectives with the exception of *hundrað*, which is a neuter noun, and *þúsund*, which is either a feminine or a neuter noun: *mörg hundruð* many hundreds, *mörg þúsund* or *margar þúsundir* many thousands. In *hundrað menn, þúsund menn* hundred, thousand men, the words are used as adjectives (indeclinable), but they can also be used as substantives: *hundrað manns* or *manna, þúsund*(*ir*) *manna* a hundred, thousand(s) of people. Like *þúsund, milljón* and *billjón* are feminine nouns, they all belong to the second class of strong feminines (*-ar, -ir*).

2. The first four cardinals are inflected, the rest are indeclinable. These indeclinable cardinals may be used as nouns taking genitive (partitive) of the thing counted: *fimm* (adj.) *menn* or *fimm manns* five (of) men, five persons. The first four take an adjective declension as follows:

(a) *Einn* one.

Sg. nom.	*ein-n* m.	*ein* f.	*eit-t* n.	Pl.	*ein-ir*	*ein-ar*	*ein*
acc.	*ein-n, ein-an*	*ein-a*	*eit-t*		*ein-a*	*ein-ar*	*ein*
dat.	*ein-um*	*ein-ni*	*ein-u*			*ein-um*	
gen.	*ein-s*	*ein-nar*	*ein-s*			*ein-na*	

Accusative masculine *einan* is used as a predicative with the object: *þeir skildu hann eftir einan* they left him alone. The plural is used in the following cases: *þeir skildu þá eftir eina* they left them alone; *þeir einir, sem tekið hafa próf, fá inngöngu í skólann* only those who have taken the examination gain admission to the school; *einir vettlingar* one pair of mittens. *Einn* may also have a weak form: *hann er sá eini, sem veit nokkuð um þetta* he is the only one who knows something about this; in the same sense it can even have a superlative: *sá einasti* the only one.

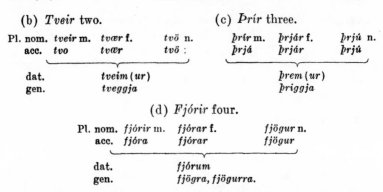

(b) *Tveir* two.   (c) *Þrír* three.

Pl. nom.	*tveir* m.	*tvær* f.	*tvö* n.	*þrír* m.	*þrjár* f.	*þrjú* n.
acc.	*tvo*	*tvær*	*tvö* :	*þrjá*	*þrjár*	*þrjú*

dat.   *tveim* (*ur*)   *þrem* (*ur*)
gen.   *tveggja*   *þriggja*

(d) *Fjórir* four.

Pl. nom.	*fjórir* m.	*fjórar* f.	*fjögur* n.
acc.	*fjóra*	*fjórar*	*fjögur*

dat.   *fjórum*
gen.   *fjögra, fjögurra.*

3. All the ordinals, except *annar* the second, are declined like weak adjectives (first class: *fyrsti* m., *fyrsta* f., *fyrsta* n.). But *annar* is always strong:

Sg. nom.	*annar* m.	*önnur* f.	*anna-ð* n.	Pl.	*aðr-ir*	*aðr-ar*	*önnur*
acc.	*anna-n*	*aðr-a*	*anna-ð*		*aðr-a*	*aðr-ar*	*önnur*
dat.	*öðr-um*	*annar-i*	*öðr-u*			*öðr-um*	
gen.	*annar-s*	*annar-ar*	*annar-s*			*annar-a*	

It will be seen that the consonant group *nnr* always changes to *ðr*, but since the suffix, in the customary way, only drops its vowel before a case ending beginning with a vowel, the *nnr* to *ðr* will only appear in such places. The u-shift appears as usually in adjectives with *a* in the root and suffix syllables (Adjective Declension, III, 2 (a) 1 and 2 and 7).

3. Other Numerals.

1. Adjectives expressing age, length, height, and depth in decades from 20-70 end in *-tugur*: *tvítugur maður* a man of twenty; *tvítugur hvalur* a whale twenty ells long; *klífa þritugan hamarinn* (proverbial) climb the cliff thirty fathoms high, i. e. attempt and accomplish the impossible; *á fertugu dýpi* at a depth of forty fathoms. Furthermore: *fimmtugur* fifty (years old), *sextugur* sixty, *sjötugur* seventy. From the decades 80-120 such adjectives are formed in *-ræður*: *áttræður, níræður, tíræður, tólfræður*; e. g. *níræður öldungur* an old man of ninety; *tírætt kvæði* a poem of 100 stanzas; *tólfrætt færi* a fishing line of 120 fathoms.

The neuter *tvítugt* and the noun *tvítugs-aldur* denote the age of twenty: *vera um tvítugt = vera á tvítugsaldri* be in the late teens, about twenty. *Vera milli tvítugs og þrítugs* (n.) be between twenty and thirty, be in the twenties = *vera á þrítugs-aldri. Hálf-þrítugur* is 25, similarly *hálf-fertugur* 35, *hálf-fimmtugur* 45, *hálf-áttrœður* 75. This agrees with the customary counting by halves in Icelandic: 1½ is rarely *einn og hálfur*, but usually *hálfur annar* (i. e. half (of) the second one), 2½ = *hálfur þriðji*, 3½ = *hálfur fjórði*. Likewise about time : 1:30 p. m.: *klukkan hálftvö e. h.* (= *eftir hádegi*).

Otherwise fractions are read in much the same way as in English : 1⅓, 2⅔ *einn og einn hálfur, tveir og tveir þriðju,* etc.; and decimals 12,05 *tólf komma núll fimm,* 3,61 *þrír komma sex einn.*

Note : In the eighties, nineties : *á níunda, tíunda tug aldarinnar.*

2. Multiplicative adjectives are formed by the suffix *-faldur* (*-föld* f., *-falt* n.) : *einfaldur* simple, *tvöfaldur* twofold, double, false, *þrefaldur* threefold, triple, *ferfaldur* fourfold, *fimmfaldur, sexfaldur, sjöfaldur, áttfaldur, nífaldur, tífaldur,* and so on, but higher numbers are rare. Cf., however, *þrítugfaldur* thirtyfold, *hundraðfaldur* hundredfold, *þúsundfaldur* thousandfold.

3. Distributive numerals (adjectives) are formed from the numbers 2-4 to count groups or quantities; the plural of *einn* is also used in that sense: *einir sokkar* one pair of stockings; *tvenn gleraugu* two pair of glasses; *tvenn spil* two packs of cards; *fernir skór* four pair of shoes; *tvennir tímar* two (different) times.

These distributive numerals are rarely used in the singular, unless neuter: *tvennt, þrennt, fernt* a group of two, three, four; *tvennt ólíkt* two entirely different things; *skifta í tvennt* divide in two parts; *í tvennu lagi* in two parts (places) ; *með tvennu móti* in two ways; *tvenns konar* two kinds of.

Tvennur fatnaður (m.) two suits of clothing.

4. The only multiplicative numeral adverbs are *tvisvar* twice, and *þrisvar* thrice. For all others the cardinal number plus the dative of *sinn* n. time, occasion, is used: *einu sinni* once, *fjórum sinnum* four times, *fimm sinnum* five times. *Fjórum sinnum fimm eru tuttugu* 4 x 5 = 20.

5. In addition to *tugur* (*tigur*), *-ar, -ir* m. decade, *hundrað, -aðs, -uð* n., *þúsund, -ar, -ir* f., *milljón, -ar, -ir* f., *billjón, -ar, -ir* f., there are several other numerical nouns in Icelandic. Masculines in *-ingur, -ungur* denote parts or fractions of something: *helmingur* ½, *þriðjungur* ⅓, *fjórðungur* (cf. Engl. farthing) ¼, *fimmtungur* ⅕, *sjöttungur* ⅙, *áttungur* ⅛, *tólftungur* 1⁄12 ; these are formed from the stems of the ordinals *þriðj-i, fjórð-i,* etc., and only if that stem is monosyllabic, hence 1⁄7 is either *einn sjöund-i* or *sjöundi partur,* likewise 1⁄10, 1⁄11, etc., *einn tíundi, ellefti.* Feminine are *eining* unit, unity, *þrenning* trinity, and *tíund* tithe.

67

6. The names of cards are as follows: *tvistur* m. deuce, *þristur* m. trey, *fjarki* m. four, *fimma* f. five, *sexa* f. six, *sjöa* f. seven, *átta* f. eight, *nía* f. nine, *tía* f. ten. Variant names are: *fimm* n., *sex* n., *sjö* n.

7. In counting the hours the numerals *eitt, tvö, þrjú, fjögur fimm*, . . . *tólf* are indeclinable neuter nouns: *klukkan er eitt* it is one (o'clock), *frá eitt til tvö* from one to two, *milli eitt og tvö* between one and two.

VI. PRONOUNS.

1. Personal Pronouns.

1. Person.

Sg. nom.	*ég, eg* I	Pl.	*við* we	Honorific Pl.	*vér* we
acc.	*mig* me		*okkur* us		*oss* us
dat.	*mér* me		*okkur* us		*oss* us
gen.	*mín*		*okkar* (our)		*vor* (our)

2. Person.

Sg. nom.	*þú* you (thou)	Pl.	*þið* you	Honorific Pl.	*þér* you
acc.	*þig* you (thee)		*ykkur* you		*yður* you
dat.	*þér* you (thee)		*ykkur* you		*yður* you
gen.	*þín*		*ykkar* (your)		*yðar* (your)

3. Person.   Reflexive.

Sg. nom.	*hann* he	*hún* she	*það* it		——
acc.	*hann* him	*hana* her	*það* it		*sig* him(her,it) self
dat.	*honum* him	*henni* her	*því* (*þí*) it		*sér* him(her,it) self
gen.	*hans* his	*hennar* her	*þess* its		*sín*
Pl. nom.	*þeir* they	*þær* they	*þau*(*g*) they		——
acc.	*þá* them	*þær* them	*þau*(*g*) them		*sig* themselves
dat.		*þeim* them			*sér* themselves
gen.		*þeirra* their			*sín* themselves

Note: The forms *þí, þaug* (for *því, þau*) are colloquial, but only *þí* is common.

(a) The plurals *við, þið* were originally duals (we two, you two), while *vér, þér* were plurals. Now the latter are only honorific plurals, concerning the use of which, see the Syntax.

(b) The genitives *mín, þín, sín,* and *vor* are used only after prepositions and as objects of verbs: *hér er bréf til þín* here is a letter to you; *bíddu* (*biðið þér*) *mín* wait for me. For the possessive function the corresponding possessive pronouns are used. But the other genitives are used in all these functions: *til hans* to him, *bíða hans* wait for him, *húsið hans* his house.

(c) The reflexive pronoun *sig, sér, sín* refers to the third person singular and plural. As reflexives referring to *ég, þú; við, þið; vér, þér* the oblique cases of these pronouns are used: *ég meiddi mig* I hurt myself, *fáið yður sæti* (you) take a seat.

Note: Here may be mentioned the pronoun *sjálfur, sjálf, sjálft* self, which is declined like an ordinary adjective (*gulur*).

2. Possessive Pronouns.

(a) The possessive pronouns are formed from the stems of the genitives of the personal pronouns. They are *minn* my, mine, *þinn* your, yours (thy, thine), *sinn* his, her, its own, and *vor* our, ours (in elevated style). Their declension is similar to that of the strong adjective *heiðinn*, but note the vowel shift in the root syllable! (*minn, þinn, sinn* are inflected alike).

Sg.						
nom.	*min-n* m.	*mín* f.	*mit-t* n.	*vor* m.	*vor* f.	*vor-t* n.
acc.	*min-n*	*mín-a*	*mit-t*	*vor-n*	*vor-a*	*vor-t*
dat.	*mín-um*	*mín-ni*	*mín-u*	*vor-um*	*vor-ri*	*vor-u*
gen.	*mín-s*	*mín-nar*	*mín-s*	*vor-s*	*vor-rar*	*vor-s*
Pl. nom.	*mín-ir*	*mín-ar*	*mín*	*vor-ir*	*vor-ar*	*vor*
acc.	*mín-a*	*mín-ar*	*mín*	*vor-a*	*vor-ar*	*vor*
dat.		*mín-um*			*vor-um*	
gen.		*mín-na*			*vor-ra*	

(b) These possessive pronouns (adjectives) refer to *ég; þú; hann, hún, það;* and *vér. Sinn* refers to the third person pronoun only if this is the subject of the sentence: *hann tók hattinn sinn* he took his hat, while *hann tók hattinn hans* means: he took his (i. e. somebody else's) hat. Here *hans* is the genitive of the third person pronoun *hann*, not a possessive adjective. Likewise *okkar, ykkar,* and the honorific *yðar* are the genitives of the personal pronouns to which they refer: *við, þið,* and the honorific *þér.* Likewise, too, when not referring to the subject of the sentence, the genitives *hans, hennar, þess, þeirra* are used for English his, her, its, their.

3. Demonstrative Pronouns.

There are three demonstrative pronouns in Icelandic: *sá* the, he (who), this, that, *þessi* this, this here, and *hinn* that (one), the other (one). *Hinn* is declined exactly like the definite article *hinn,* with the exception that the nom.-acc. sg. neuter is *hitt*. *Sá* and *þessi* are declined as follows:

Sg. nom.	*sá* m.	*sú* f.	*það* n.	*þess-i* m.	*þess-i* f.	*þett-a(ð)* n.
acc.	*þann*	*þá*	*það*	*þenn-a(n)*	*þess-a*	*þett-a(ð)*
dat.	*þeim*	*þei-rri*	*því (þí)*	*þess-um*	*þess-ari*	*þess-u*
gen.	*þess*	*þei-rrar*	*þess*	*þess-a*	*þess-arar*	*þess-a*
Pl. nom.	*þeir*	*þær*	*þau(g)*	*þess-ir*	*þess-ar*	*þess-i*
acc.	*þá*	*þær*	*þau(g)*	*þess-a*	*þess-ar*	*þess-i*
dat.	*þeim*			*þess-um*		
gen.	*þei-rra*			*þess-ara*		

It will be noticed that the neuter singular and the whole plural of *sá* is identical with the same forms of the third personal pronoun: actually the demonstrative pronoun is used for the third person pronoun.

Note 1: The forms *þí, þaug, þennan, þettað* are colloquial, the other forms are more literary. *Þaug*, however, is not common.

Note 2: With the demonstrative pronouns are sometimes listed: the pronoun of identity *samur, söm, samt* the same, and the pronouns of similarity *slíkur, slík, slíkt* such, and *þvílíkur, -lí -líkt* such.

4. Relative Pronouns.

Like the English *that*, the Icelandic relative pronouns are indeclinable. The most common is *sem*; *er* is common in the written language, but not colloquial; *að, eð* are only used in certain rare combinations (*þar eð* since). Since these pronouns have no genitive, the translation of the English *whose* (*of which*) is often a ticklish job. Neither can the Icelandic pronouns be preceded by a preposition as can the English *whom, which*. But in all this they resemble the English *that*, and by making shift with *that* the speaker of English will usually be able to form a sentence directly translatable into Icelandic. Examples: *maðurinn, sem sá mig* the man who saw me; *maðurinn, sem ég sá* the man (that) I saw; *húsið, sem hann bjó í* the house that he lived in.

Note: There is no way of referring especially to persons or inanimate things, as can be done in English; note also that a relative pronoun is always preceded by a comma in Icelandic.

5. Interrogative Pronouns.

These are *hver* (noun) who (of an undetermined number), *hvor* (noun) which (of two), *hvaða* (indeclinable adjective) what kind of, and *hvílíkur* (adjective) what kind of, what a; the last one is not much used colloquially (replaced by *hvaða*). *Hvílíkur* goes like an ordinary adjective (*gulur*); *hver* is declined as follows:

Sg.	nom.	*hver* m.	*hver* f.	*hver-t* n. (adj.)	*hvað* n. (noun)
	acc.	*hver-n*	*hver-j-a*	*hver-t*	*hvað*
	dat.	*hver-j-um*	*hver-ri*	*hver-j-u*	
	gen.	*hver-s*	*hver-rar*	*hver-s*	
Pl.	nom.	*hver-j-ir*	*hver-j-ar*	*hver*	
	acc.	*hver-j-a*	*hver-j-ar*	*hver*	
	dat.		*hver-j-um*		
	gen.		*hver-ra*		

As mentioned in the Pronunciation 2, *1*, 3n2, *hve-* in this pronoun is always pronounced *hvu-*: [hw̥ʏ:r̥, hw̥ʏd̥·n̥], etc. *Hvor* is also often so pronounced. It is declined exactly like the possessive pronoun *vor*, 2 above. The only difference is one of pronunciation. Because *vor* is literary, *vorn* is pronounced [vɔrd̥n̥]. But because *hvor* is common, the corresponding form is [hw̥ɔd̥·n̥] or [hw̥ʏd̥·n̥].

6. Indefinite Pronouns.

1. There are several indefinite pronouns in Icelandic: *einn* one; (*ekki*) *neinn* (not) any (one); *nokkur* any(one), some, certain; *sumur*, mostly in pl. *sumir* some; *hver* whoever (of many); *hvor* whichever (of two); *einhver* somebody, some (one); *annar* another, other, someone else; *annarhver* every other (of many); *annarhvor* every other (of two), one of two; *annartveggja* (*-i*) one of two; *báðir* both; *hvortveggja* (*-i*) each of two, both; *hvorugur* neither of two; *enginn* nobody, no (one), none. For the meaning and use of these pronouns, see the Syntax, IV, **6**.

Note: Several other words are also sometimes indefinite pronouns by their use, thus *allur* all, *maður* one, *þeir* they, *hann*, *það* with impersonal verbs: it.

2. These indefinite pronouns have different types of inflexions

(a) *Einn, neinn* go like the numeral *einn*, acc. masc. *einn, neinn* (not *nein-an*!).

(b) *Sumur, hvorugur* go like the adjective *gulur*; *nokkur* is declined as follows:

Sg.	nom.	*nokkur* m.	*nokkur* f.	*nokkur-t* n. (adj.)	*nokku-ð* n. (noun)
	acc.	*nokkur-n*	*nokkr-a*	*nokkur-t*	*nokku-ð*
	dat.	*nokkr-um*	*nokku(r)-ri*	*nokkr-u*	
	gen.	*nokkur-s*	*nokku(r)-rar*	*nokkur-s*	

71

Pl. nom.	*nokkr-ir*	*nokkr-ar*	*nokkur*
acc.	*nokkr-a*	*nokkr-ar*	*nokkur*

dat.	*nokkr-um*
gen.	*nokkur-ra*

Note: The dat. sg. masc. and dat. pl. may be colloquially *nokkur-j-um*, likewise dat. sg. neuter *nokkur-j-u*. These forms are not to be imitated.

(c) *Annar* is declined like the numeral *annar*; *hver*, *sérhver*, and *einhver* are declined like the interrogative pronoun *hver*, with double forms *hvert*, *hvað* in the nom.-acc. sg. neuter. *Einhver* has, besides, the irregular forms *eitt-hvert* and *eitt-hvað* in the nom.-acc. sg. neuter. The reason for this is that originally *einhver* was two words: *einn* and *hver* with both words inflected. In the following there will be other instances of these doubly inflected compounds.

(d) *Annarhver* and *annarhvor* have such a double inflection, the first part going like *annar* the second like *hver*, *hvor*. For the sake of clearness the full inflexion of *annar-hvor* is here given:

Sg. nom.	*annar-hvor* m.	*önnur-hvor* f.	*annað-hvort* n.
acc.	*annan-hvorn*	*aðra-hvora*	*annað-hvort*
dat.	*öðrum-hvorum*	*annari-hvorri*	*öðru-hvoru*
gen.	*annars-hvors*	*annarar-hvorrar*	*annars-hvors*

Pl. nom.	*aðrir-hvorir*	*aðrar-hvorar*	*önnur-hvor*
acc.	*aðra-hvora*	*aðrar-hvorar*	*önnur-hvor*

dat.	*öðrum-hvorum*
gen.	*annara-hvorra*

(e) In *annar-tveggja*, *hvor-tveggja* the first part only is inflected, *tveggja* being the gen. pl. of *tveir* two. Sometimes, however, *tveggja* is felt to be a weak adjective, having *-tveggi* in nom. sg. masc. But the feminine hardly ever shows *-tveggju* in the oblique cases. Instead of *hvor-tveggja*, *hvoru-tveggja* may be used, *hvoru-* being indeclinable. The pronunciation *hvur-tveggja*, *hvuru-tveggja* is common, but need not be imitated.

(f) *Báðir* goes as follows:

Pl. nom.	*báð-ir* m.	*báð-ar* f.	*bæð-i* n.
acc.	*báð-a*	*báð-ar*	*bæð-i*

dat.	*báð-um*
gen.	*beggj-a*

Cf. the inflexion of the numeral *tveir* two.

(g) *Enginn,* like *annar-tveggja,* originally was a compound (*einn* + *gi*) where the first part was inflected, but the second part indeclinable. Now fusion of the two parts has taken place, and the inflexion is added to the end in agreement with the general custom of the language. This accounts for the irregularities of inflexion.

Sg. nom.	*enginn (engi)* m.	*engin (engi)* f.	*ekkert (ekki)* n.
acc.	*engan, öngvan*	*enga, öngva*	*ekkert (ekki)*
dat.	*engum, öngvum*	*engri, öngri*	*engu, öngvu*
gen.	*einskis, einkis, eingis*	*engrar, öngrar*	*einskis, einkis, eingis*
Pl. nom.	*engir, öngvir*	*engar, öngvar*	*engin*
acc.	*enga, öngva*	*engar, öngvar*	*engin*
dat.		*engum, öngvum*	
gen.		*engra, öngra*	

The forms enclosed in parentheses are literary or old. *Ekki* is the most common negation ('not') in Icelandic, but in the sense 'nothing' it survives only in a few idiomatic expressions: *seint er betra en ekki* 'late is better than nothing' i. e. better late than never, *allt kom fyrir ekki* everything was in vain, *lítið sem ekki* hardly anything. The forms with *eng-* are both literary and colloquial, those with *öngv-* only colloquial. Only colloquial, too, and dialectal is a pronunciation of *öng-* (pronounced *aung-*) for *eng-* (*eing-*) throughout the paradigm. It is advisable to use *eng-* in speaking as well as writing.

VII. THE CONJUGATION OF VERBS.

1. Preliminary Remarks.

1. *Verb Categories.*

Icelandic verbs, like the English verbs, have *tenses, moods, verbals, voices, numbers,* and *persons.*

(a) Of *tenses* Icelandic, like English, has two that are differentiated by inflexion: the *present* and the *preterite.* The other tenses are formed with the auxiliary verbs: *hafa* to have, *vera* to be, *munu* shall, will, and others.

(b) Of *moods* Icelandic, like English, has three: *indicative, subjunctive,* and *imperative.* In Icelandic these moods are distinct by form, whereas they are only partly so in English. The subjunctive, too, is very rare in English, while it is common in Icelandic.

(c) Of *verbals* Icelandic has three: the *infinitive* (a noun) and the present and past *participles* (adjectives). English has all these and a verbal noun (the *gerund*) in addition; in Icelandic its function is often taken by the infinitive: smoking is forbidden: *það er bannað að reykja.*

(d) Of voices English has two: *active* and *passive,* but Icelandic three: *active, middle,* and *passive.* The two first named are differentiated by inflexional endings; the passive, as in English, is formed by an auxiliary verb: to be (shot): *að vera (skotinn).*

(e) Icelandic verbs, like English verbs, have two numbers: *singular* and *plural* in all the moods and tenses. Contrary to English usage these numbers are found also in the participles when they take the adjective inflexion.

(f) Icelandic, like English, has three *persons,* first, second, and third, in all tenses of the indicative, subjunctive, and, partly, of the imperative. But whereas English (in most verbs) has only one inflexional ending, namely that of the third person present (I, you, we, they come; he comes), Icelandic has two or three different personal endings in the singular, and three in the plural: *ég kem, þú, hann kemur; við komum, þið komið, þeir koma.* There are, furthermore, different sets of personal endings for the different tenses (present, preterite), for the different moods (indicative, subjunctive, imperative) and for two of the voices (active and middle).

2. Strong and Weak Verbs.

As in English, it is possible in Icelandic to divide all verbs into two large groups, called *strong* and *weak* verbs. In English the great majority of verbs is weak, hence they are often called the regular verbs. In Icelandic the same is true to a lesser extent. Actually both the strong and the weak verbs fall into many smaller classes, at least seven for the strong verbs, and four for the weak. There are subdivisions within the classes.

The strong verbs are characterized by the old shift of vowels (Pr. 5, *1*). There are four different stem forms, called the principal parts of the strong verbs: infinitive *bresta,* first (and third) person preterite indicative singular *brast,* first person preterite indicative plural *brustum,* and past participle *brostinn.* The strong verbs are also marked by no ending in the first (and third) person preterite indicative singular, and by the ending *-inn* in the past participle.

The weak verbs have root vowels unchanged by the old shift; in the first (and third) person preterite singular indicative they have the endings *-ði, -di, -ti, -aði,* and their past participles end in *-ður, -dur, -tur, -aður,* and *-inn.*

74

Both strong and weak verbs may have their root vowels in certain forms affected by i-shift and u-shift (Pr. **5**, *2* and *3*). Since the present singular of strong verbs often is affected by the i-shift, it is advisable to quote the first (or the third) person present singular indicative in addition to the four principal parts.

2. Strong Verbs.

1. Principal Parts.

There are as many classes of strong verbs as there are types of the old shift of vowels (see Pr. **5**, *1*) or seven in all.

From the four principal parts (stem forms) of the strong verbs all other forms are derived in the following manner, illustrated by the verb *bjóða* to offer.

(a) From the infinitive (or present stem) *bjóð-a*:

1. The present indicative active, i-shifted (Pr. **5**, *2*) in the singular, without i-shift in the plural: *ég býð, við bjóð-um*. Likewise the middle: *ég býð-st, við bjóð-um-st*.

2. The present subjunctive active and middle (without i-shift): *ég bjóð-i; ég bjóð-i-st*.

3. The imperative active and middle (without i-shift): *bjóð þú* or *bjód-du; bjóð-st þú*.

4. The present participle (as a rule only in the active): *bjóð-andi*.

(b) From the preterite singular stem *bauð* are formed only the first, second and third persons of the preterite singular indicative active and middle: *ég, hann bauð, þú bauð-st; ég, þú, hann bauð-st*.

(c) From the preterite plural stem *buð-um* are formed:

1. The first, second, and third person plural active and middle: *við buð-um, þið buð-uð, þeir buð-u; við buð-um-st*, etc.

2. The preterite subjunctive active and middle, with i-shift of the root vowel: *ég byð-i; ég byð-i-st*.

(d) The past participle, *boð-inn*, is not used to form any other parts of the verb by endings (though it is itself inflected as an adjective). But its neuter form *boð-ið* (middle *boð-i-zt*) is used to form compound tenses in combination with the auxiliary verb *hafa: ég hef boðið* I have offered, *ég hafði boðið* I had offered, *ég mun hafa boðið* I have probably offered, *ég mundi hafa boðið* I would have offered; see the Syntax VI, 1, *2*.

Note 1. I-shift (Pr. **5**, *2*) takes place only if the root vowels are susceptible to it: *i, í, e, ei* are not. Hence there is no i-shift in

the present of verbs of the first, third, fourth, and fifth classes:
bíta bite, *ég bít*; *dett-a* fall, *ég dett*; *bera* bear, *ég ber* I bear;
stela steal, *ég stel*.

Note 2. Verbs, having breaking (Pr. **5**, *4*) in the infinitive,
give it up in the present singular indicative, replacing it with the
original *e*: *gjalda* pay, *ég geld* I pay. In the present plural breaking returns: *við gjöldum* we pay (u-shift, Pr. **5**, *3*), *þið gjaldið*
you pay, *þeir gjalda* they pay.

2. Class 1: *bíta.* Vowel Shift: *i—ei/é—i—i*; root vowel followed
by one consonant.

Type a: *bíta* bite, *bít, beit, bitum, bitinn.*

Thus go: *bíða* wait (past participle irregularly *beðinn*, usually
only in neuter *beðið*), *drífa* drive, drift, snow, *grípa* seize, catch,
grip, *hrífa* have effect, fascinate, *hrína* cry, *hvína* whiz, *kvíða* fear
for, *líða* pass (of time), glide, *líta* look, see, *ríða* ride, *rísa* rise,
skína shine, *skríða* creep, *slíta* tear, *sníða* cut, *svífa* soar, hover,
þrífa catch, *þrífast* thrive.

Type b: *stíga* step, ascend, *stíg, steig/sté, stigum, stiginn.*

Thus go: *hníga* fall gently, *míga* piss, *síga* fall, sink (run slowly
like molasses), *svíkja* betray, *víkja* deviate, turn, yield. But the
forms *hné, sté*, etc., are mostly literary or rare.

Note: *Rísta* cut (literary) is the only verb of this class having
more than one consonant following the root vowel. Usually it is
weak: *rista, risti, rist.*

3. Class 2: *bjóða.* Vowel Shift: *jó/jú/ú—au/ó—u—o*; root vowel
followed by one consonant.

Type a: *bjóða* offer, *býð, bauð, buðum, boðinn.*

Thus go: *brjóta* break, *fljóta* float, *frjósa* freeze, *gjósa* gush,
spout, *hljóta* must, have to, *hnjóta* stumble, *kjósa* choose, *njóta*
enjoy, *sjóða* cook, boil, seethe, *þjóta* rush, speed, *þrjóta* give out,
cease.

Type b: *drjúpa* drip, *draup, drupum, dropinn.*

Thus go: *fjúka* be blown away, *kljúfa* split, cleave, *ljúga* lie (tell
a lie), *ljúka* finish, *rjúfa* break, tear up, *sjúga* suck.

Type c: *súpa* sip, drink, *sýp, saup, supum, sopinn.*

Thus go: *lúka* pay up, *lúta* bend over forward, bow, incline.

Type d: *fljúga* fly, *flýg, flaug/fló, flugum, floginn*
        smjúga creep, *smýg, smaug/smó, smugum, smoginn.*

Fló, smó are literary forms.

Note: *Ljósta* strike (literary) is the only verb of this class having two consonants following the root vowel.

4. *Class 3*: *bresta*. Vowel Shift: *e/i/ja/ö/y—a/ö—u—o/u*; root vowel followed by two consonants.

Type a¹: *bresta* burst, *brest, brast, brustum, brostinn*.

Thus go: *detta* fall, *skella* clash, fall, *skreppa* slip, dash for, *sleppa* let go of, *smella* clash, crack, *snerta* touch, *spretta* sprout, grow, sprint. *Bregða*, move quickly, is irregular: *bregð, brá, brugðum, brugðinn*.

Type a²: *verða* become, *verð, varð, urðum, orðinn*.

Thus go verbs in which *v* precedes the root vowel, dropping the *v* before the *u* of the preterite plural and the *o* of the past participle: *hverfa* disappear, *svelgja* swallow, *svelta* starve, *sverfa* file (iron, etc.), *vella* cook, boil, well up, *velta* turn over, *verpa* throw, *þverra* dwindle, diminish.

Type b¹: *spinna* spin, *spinn, spann, spunnum, spunninn*

     b²: *finna* find, *finn, fann, fundum, fundinn*

     b³: *vinna* work, win, *vinn, vann, unnum, unninn*

     b⁴: *binda* bind, *bind, batt, bundum, bundinn*.

Thus go: *vinda* wind, twist, *hrinda* push, *springa* (preterite *sprakk*) burst, *stinga* (preterite *stakk*) prick, pierce.

Note 1: The *i* of the infinitive and the *u* of the past participle (instead of the regular *e, o* of type a) show a shift caused by the following *n*+consonant. A *v* is lost before *u* in pret. pl. and pp.

Note 2: The preterite singular *batt* comes from *bant* which in turn is from *band*. Similarly *stakk* from *stank* from *stang*.

Type c: *drekka* drink, *drekk, drakk, drukkum, drukkinn*
            brenna burn (intr.), *brenn, brann, brunnum, brunninn*
            renna run (intr.), *renn, rann, runnum, runninn*.

Note: Since *kk* in *drekka* was originally *nk*, this type is really a subdivision of b with the original *e* restored in the infinitive. *Brenna, renna* (transitive) burn, run are weak: *brenndi, renndi*.

Type d: *bjarga* save, *berg, barg, burgum, borginn*
            gjalda pay, *geld, galt, guldum, goldinn*
            gjalla resound, *gell, gall, gullum, gollinn*
            skjálfa shiver, *skelf, skalf, skulfum, skolfinn*.

Note 1: *Bjarga* is usually weak, preterite *bjargaði*, likewise *gjalla*, *gjallaði* in the sense: speak loudly. In their strong form, these verbs are all literary, except *skjálfa*. The common verb for *gjalda*, pay, is *borga*.

Note 2: Preterite singular *galt* shows the same hardening (unvoicing) of the original *-d* as *batt* above.

Note 3: The *ja* of the infinitive is broken (see breaking Pr. **5**, *4*) from an original *e*, which always appears in the present indicative singular—the present plural has the breaking again.

Type e: *hrökkva* flinch, break, *hrekk, hrökk, hrukkum, hrokkinn*
           slökkva put out, quench, *slekk, (slökk, slukkum, slokkinn)*
           stökkva jump, gallop, *stekk, stökk, stukkum, stokkinn*
           sökkva sink (intr.), *sekk, sökk, sukkum, sokkinn*.

Note 1: The *ö* of the infinitive is a u-shifted *e*, the *ö* of the preterite singular a u-shifted *a*.

Note 2: *Slökkva* usually has a weak preterite and past participle: *slökkti, slökktur.*   *Stökkva, sökkva*, when transitive, are weak: *stökkti, sökkti*.

Type f: *syngja* sing, *syng, söng, sungum, sunginn*
           tyggja chew, *tygg* —— —— *tugginn*.

Note 1: The *y* in *syngja* (*tyggja*) is a u-shifted *i* (from *e*, cf. type b, note 1).

Note 2. *Tyggja* usually has a weak preterite: *tuggði*.

5.   *Class 4*: *bera*. Vowel Shifts: *e/o—a/o—á/o—o/u*; root vowel followed by one liquid or nasal (*l, r, m, n*).

Type a: *bera* bear, carry, *ber, bar, bárum, borinn*.

Thus go: *skera* cut, *stela* steal, *fela* conceal (past participle *fólginn*; the verb is also weak: *fela, faldi, falinn*), and *nema* take, learn (past participle *numinn*).

Type b: *koma* come, *kem, kom, komum, kominn*
           sofa sleep, *sef, svaf, sváfum, sofinn*
           troða step, tread, *treð, trað, tráðum, troðinn*.

Note: These verbs are marked by an old *o* in the infinitive; *kom, komum* is from older *kvam, kvámum*; *troða* usually has *tróð, tróðum* in preterite singular and plural according to class 6.

6.   *Class 5*: *gefa*. Vowel Shift: *e/i/é—a/á—á/o—e/é*; root vowel followed by any one consonant, except *l, r, m, n*.

Type a: *gefa* give, *gef, gaf, gáfum, gefinn*.

Thus go: *drepa* kill, knock, *geta* beget, guess, also *geta* be able to, with the exception of the past participle, whose neuter form is *getað*; *kveða* chant, compose poetry, say, *leka* leak, *lesa* read, *meta* estimate, esteem (also weak: *matti*), *reka* drive.

Note: Vera to be, has not only a very irregular present, but also an irregular preterite plural, because an original *vá-* has turned to *vo-*: *vera*; *er, em*; *var, vorum, verið.* See Irregular Verbs, 5 below.

Type b¹: *biðja* ask, beg, pray, *bið, bað, báðum, beðinn*
      sitja sit, *sit, sat, sátum, setinn*
   b²: *liggja* lie, *ligg, lá, lágum, leginn*
      þiggja accept, *þigg, þá, þágum, þeginn.*

Note 1: Biðja, sitja, liggja, þiggja are called *j*-presents because their present stem terminates in *j*; in all these verbs the root vowel was originally *e* as in *gefa,* but has been shifted to *i* by the following *j*. In *liggja, þiggja* an original single *g* has been doubled by the following *j*.

Note 2: The preterites *lá, þá* stand for original *lag, þag*; *þiggja* has also a weak preterite and past participle :*þáði, þáður*; the weak preterite is more common than the strong one.

Type c: *sjá (séa)* see, *sé, sá, sáum, séður (sénn)*
      éta, eta eat,. *ét, et*; *át*; *átum*; *étinn, etinn.*

Note: Sjá and éta are quite irregular. *Séa, sénn* are old forms now never used, *séður* is a weak past participle. *Éta* is colloquial, slightly vulgar; *borða* (literally: eat at a table) is polite, *eta* is literary.

7. *Class 6: fara.* Vowel Shift: *a/e/á/o/ey/œ—ó—ó—a/e*; root vowel followed by one consonant.

Type a¹: *fara* go, fare, *fer, fór, fórum, farinn.*

Thus go: *ala* give birth to, feed, *gala* crow (more commonly weak: *galaði, galað*), *grafa* dig, bury, *hlaða* build (a wall), *kala* freeze (to death, or so as to be hurt), *mala* grind (more commonly weak: *malaði, malað*), *skafa* scrape, *skapa* create, shape (literary, more commonly weak: *skapaði, skapaður*).

Type a²: *taka* take, *tek, tók, tókum, tekinn.*

Thus go: *aka* drive, *draga* draw, drag (preterite singular *dró* from *dróg*; cf. class 5, type b, note 2), *skaka* shake, churn. The *e* of the past participle is an i-shifted *a* that occurs only before *-ki* and *-gi* (see *hleginn,* below).

Type b¹: *hefja* lift, heave, *hef, hóf, hófum, hafinn*
      kefja suffocate, suppress, *kef, (kóf, kófum), kafinn*

skekja shake (rare), *skek, skók, skókum, skekinn* (cf. type a²)

sverja swear, *sver, sór, sórum, svarinn* (*v* lost before *ó*).

Type b²: *deyja* die, *dey, dó, dóum, dáinn*
geyja bark (literary), *gey, gó, góum,* ——
hlæja laugh, *hlæ, hló, hlógum, hlegið* (cf. type a²)
klæja itch, *klæ, kló, klógum, klegið* (cf. type a²).

Note 1: All the verbs of type b are *j*-presents (cf. class 5, type b) with *e* from i-shifted *a* in the infinitive (originally *hafja, dauja, hlahja*).

Note 2: In *hlæja, klæja* an *h* corresponding to the *g* in the preterite plural and past participle has been lost in the present and preterite singular.

Note 3: *Kefja* and *klæja* are usually weak: *kafði, kafinn, klæjaði, klæjað*.

Type c: *flá* flay, *flæ, fló, flógum, fleginn*
slá beat, *slæ, sló, slógum, sleginn*
þvo wash, *þvæ, þó, þógum, þveginn.*

Note 1: These verbs had an *h* in the present and preterite singular, corresponding to the *g* in the preterite plural and past participle. The *h* has been lost as in *hlæja, klæja* above.

Note 2: *Þvo* was originally *þvá; v* is, as usually, lost before the *ó* in the preterite singular and plural. But sometimes it is restored by analogy, giving *þvó, þvógum.* Most commonly, however, the verb is weak in the preterite: *þvoði.*

Type d: Irregular verbs, originally belonging to classes 4 and 5.
fela hide, conceal, *fel, fól, fólum, falinn*
troða tread, stuff, *treð, tróð, tróðum, troðinn* (also class 4, type b)
vefa weave, *vef, óf, ófum, ofinn* (*v* lost before *ó, o*)
vega weigh, kill, *veg; óg, vó(g); ógum, vógum; veginn.*

Note: Since *g* is lost in pronunciation after *ó*, there is colloquially no difference between the singular and plural stem in *-ó, -óg-.* Hence there is a tendency to confusion in writing, and wrong spellings like *dróg, slóg* are occasionally seen in print. In *vó(g), vógum v* is restored by analogy with the *v*-forms.

8. *Class* 7: *heita.* Verbs with *é—é* or *jó/ó—ju/u* in preterite singular and plural. Stems of infinitive and past participle are as a rule alike.

Type a¹: *heita* be called, *heiti, hét, hétum, heitinn*
    leika play, *leik, lék, lékum, leikinn.*

Type a²: *falla* fall, *fell, féll, féllum, fallinn*
    halda hold, *held, hélt, héldum, haldinn*
    hanga hang, *hangi, hékk, héngum, hanginn*
    fá get, *fæ, fékk, fengum, fenginn*
    ganga (*gá*) go, walk, *geng, gekk, gengum, genginn.*

Type a³: *blása* blow, *blæs, blés, blésum, blásinn*
    gráta weep, *græt, grét, grétum, grátinn*
    láta let, *læt, lét, létum, látinn*
    ráða advise, *ræð, réð, réðum, ráðinn.*

Note 1: *Heiti, hangi* are weak presents, like *dæmi* of *dæma. Ráða* may have a weak preterite *réði.*

Note 2: *Hélt* comes from *held, hékk* from *henk* from *heng,* cf. *batt* of class 3, above. Similarly *fékk, gekk* from *feng, geng.*

Note 3: *Fá* and *ganga* are irregular, *fá* in the present and preterite plural, *ganga* in the preterite singular and plural. In the past participle both these verbs have *e* from an i-shifted *a.*

Note 4: *Valda* cause, *veld, olli, ollum, valdið* has an irregular weak preterite.

Type b¹: *auka* increase, *eyk, jók, jukum* (*ukum*), *jyki* (*yki*), *aukinn*
    ausa dip, ladle, *eys, jós, jusum* (*usum*), *jysi* (*ysi*), *ausinn*
    hlaupa run, *hleyp, hljóp, hlupum, hlypi, hlaupinn.*

Type b²: *búa* prepare, live, *bý, bjó, bjuggum, b* (*j*) *yggi, búinn*
    spýja spew, vomit, *spý, spjó* —— *spúið.*

Type b³: *höggva* hew, *hegg, hjó, hjuggum, h* (*j*) *yggi, högg* (*v*) *inn*
    vaxa grow, *vex,* (*v*) *óx,* (*v*) *uxum, yxi, vaxinn.*

Note 1: *Spýja* has a *j*-present with i-shift of the root vowel from *ú* (cf. class 5, type b, note 1); it is also often weak: *spúði,* so always in preterite plural *spúðum.*

Note 2: The forms following the preterite plurals are preterite subjunctives. *Ukum, yki, usum, ysi, byggi, hyggi, vóx, vuxum* are unusual forms, mostly literary.

3. Weak Verbs.

1. Preliminary Remarks.

1. Weak verbs have only three principal parts (or stem forms): the infinitive (the present stem) *tel-j-a* count, *dæm-a* judge; the

preterite singular indicative (preterite stem) *tal-di, dæm-di*; and
the past participle *tal-inn, tal-dur, dæm-dur.*

2. But, as mentioned above, the preterite (and the past participle)
of the weak verbs is formed by addition of the suffix *-ði, -di, -ti,* or
-aði (past participle *-ður, -dur, -tur, -aður,* or *-inn*) to the (sometimes slightly changed) present stem of the verb. Whether the verb
adds *-ði, -di,* or *-ti* to the present stem, depends on the nature of
the sounds before the ending.

(a) *-ði* is used:

(1) After vowels, thus also in the ending *-aði*: *kall-a*: *kall-a-ði*
call, *strá*: *strá-ði* strew.

(2) After voiced spirants (except *ð*) and soft (not dental) stops:
haf-a: *haf-ði* (also pronounced *habb-ði*) have; *seg-j-a*: *sag-ði* (also
pronounced *sagg-ði*) say; *ybb-a* : *ybb-ði* show hostility; *hygg-j-a* :
hug-ði (also pronounced *hugg-ði*) think.

(3) After (vowel+) *r, rf,* and *rg* : *lær-a*: *lær-ði* learn; *horf-a* :
horf-ði look; *byrg-j-a* : *byrg-ði* (also pronounced *byr-ði*) lock up.

(4) Sometimes after *rr*: *þerr-a* : *þerr-ði* dry, wipe; but *sperr-a* :
sperr-ti stretch out (a foot), perk up.

(b) *-di* is used:

(1) After (vowel +) *ð*, which turns to *d*: *beið-a* : *beid-di* ask, beg.

(2) After *dd* (with assimilation and loss of *d*) : *brydd-a* : *brydd-i*
furnish with a border (*brydding* f.) or a point (*broddur* m.).

(3) After (vowel +) *n, fn, gn,* and *ng*: *reyn-a* : *reyn-di* try;
nefn-a : *nefn-di* (pronounced *nem-di*) name; *rign-a* : *rign-di* (pronounced *ring-di*) rain; *hring-j-a* : *hring-di* ring.

(4) After (vowel +) *m, mm, lm, rm,* and *mb*: *dæm-a* : *dæm-di*
judge; *dimm-a* : *dimm-di* darken; *hylm-a* : *hylm-di* conceal (a
thievery); *verm-a* : *verm-di* warm; *kemb-a* : *kemb-di* (pronounced
kem-di) comb.

(5) After *lf, fl, lg, gl*: *skelf-a* : *skelf-di* frighten; *skefl-a* : *skefl-di*
form snowdrifts; *velg-j-a* : *velg-di* warm up; *sigl-a* : *sigl-di* sail.
(Note: in all these combinations the *f* and *g* tends to be lost in
the preterite before the consonant (see Pronunciation **3**, *4*)).

(6) Usually after (vowel +) *l*: *mæl-a* : *mæl-di* measure; sometimes
after *rn*: *stirn-a* : *sti(r)n-di* glitter; rarely after *ld, nd* (with
assimilation and loss of *d*), *ll,* and *nn*: *ýld-a* : *ýld-i* putrify; *send-a* :
send-i send; *fell-a* : *fell-di* fell; *brenn-a* : *brenn-di* burn (transitive).

(c) *-ti* is used:

(1) After the hard stops *p, t, k,* and after *s*: *kaup-a*: *keyp-ti* buy; *mæt-a* : *mæt-ti* meet; *vak-a* : *vak-ti* be awake; *reis-a* : *reis-ti* raise.

Note: If the stem ends in consonant + *t*, the suffix is lost by assimilation: *svelt-a* : *svelt-i* starve (transitive), *hitt-a* : *hitt-i* hit, meet.

(2) After *rð* (with assimilation and loss of *ð*): *girð-a* : *gir-ti* gird, span, enclose.

(3) Usually after *ll, nn; ld, nd* (with assimilation and loss of *d*): *vill-a* : *vill-ti* lead astray; *spenn-a* : *spenn-ti* span; *gild-a* : *gil-ti* be worth; *synd-a* : *syn-ti* swim; rarely after (vowel +) *l*: *mæl-a* : *mæl-ti* speak; sometimes after *rr* and *rn*: *sperr-a* : *sperr-ti* stretch out, perk up; *girn-ast* : *girn-tist* desire.

Note 1. Loss of consonants is frequent in the groups that arise through the addition of the *ð, d* or *t* of the preterite suffix. See the Pronunciation **3**, *4*.

Note 2. For the student it may be easiest to memorize the cases listed under (a) and (c) as having respectively *-ði,* and *-ti,* while all the rest (b) have *-di.*

3. Before *-ði, -di, -ti* the following changes in the verb stem take place:

(a) A *j* or *v* of the present stem is dropped: *tel-j-a* : *tal-di* count; *sökk-v-a* : *sökk-ti* sink (transitive).

(b) The dentals *ð, d, t,* if preceded by a consonant, are assimilated and lost: *herð-a*: *her-ti* harden; *synd-a*: *syn-ti* swim; *svelt-a*: *svelt-i* starve (transitive).

(c) If preceded by a vowel, *ð* becomes *d* by assimilation: *hræð-a*: *hræd-di* frighten.

(d) In a few verbs the consonant of the preterite suffix is fully assimilated to an *ll* or *nn* of the verb stem: *skroll-a* : *skroll-i* hang loosely; *vald-a* : *oll-i* cause; *kunn-a* : *kunn-i* know (how to) ; *unn-a*: *unn-i* love. Similarly *t-t* turns into *s-s* in *vit-a* : *viss-i* know.

4. The weak verbs are divided into four classes on the basis of their present stem:

1. *tel-j-a* count, *tel, tal-di, tal-inn (tal-dur)*
2. *dæm-a* judge, *dæm-i, dæm-di, dæm-dur*
3. *lif-a* live, *lif-i, lif-ði, lif-að*
4. *kall-a* call, *kall-a, kall-aði, kall-aður.*

2. Class 1: *tel-j-a* count, *tel, tal-di, tal-inn (tal-dur)*.

1. The root syllable of these verbs contains a lax vowel (cf. Pronunciation **2**, *2*, 3(c)) followed by one consonant (not counting the *j*), or a tense vowel with no consonant following. Like some of the strong verbs, these verbs are *j*-presents, the *j* appearing in the infinitive (*tel-j-a*), in the present plural indicative (*tel-j-um*, etc.), in the present subjunctive (*tel-j-i*, etc.), and in the present participle (*tel-j-andi*). If the stem ends in a tense vowel or *k* or *g*, the *j* is not written (though pronounced) before *-i* in the ending (*flý-j-a* flee, *þið flý-ið* you flee; *vek-j-a* awaken, *þið vek-ið*).

The first person singular indicative is monosyllabic (*tel*); the second and third person singular end in *-ur* (*tel-ur*). This *-ur* is really an expanded *-r*, which will appear as such after a vowel of the stem (*flý-r*), and which will be lost after *-r* of the stem (*berj-a* beat, *hann ber* he beats). To the forms *flý-r, ber* an *ð* is usually added in the second person, giving *flý-r-ð, ber-ð,* this *ð* has been drawn over to the verb from a following pronoun: *þú.*

The whole present (indicative, subjunctive, imperative, infinitive, and participle) has an i-shifted (Pr. **5**, *2*) root vowel, which appears unshifted in the preterite indicative and the past participle.

Note: Verbs with *g* in the stem double it before the *j*, or rather throughout the present. Thus: *leggja* lay, *ég legg* I lay; *þiggja* accept, *hyggja* think; preterites: *lag-ði, þá-ði* (irregular), *hug-ði. Tyggja, tuggði* chew, has *gg* in the stem.

2. Normally these verbs have a past participle ending in *-inn* with a mixed inflexion, as shown in the Adjectives, III, **2** (a), paradigm 10. But there are other possibilities:

(a) Some verbs show two past participles, one in *-inn*, the other in *-ður, -dur, -tur*, e. g. *berja* beat, *barinn (barður)*; *leggja* lay, *lagður (laginn)*; *knýja* compel, propel, *knúinn (knúður)*; *núa* rub, *núinn (núður)*; *telja* count, *talinn (taldur)*; *velja* choose, *valinn (valdur)*; *dylja* conceal, *dulinn (duldur)*; *hrekja* treat roughly, *hrakinn (hraktur)*; *vekja* awaken, *vakinn (vaktur)*; *þekja* cover up, thatch, *þakinn (þaktur)*.

(b) Other verbs show only the weak past participle, e. g. *flá* skin, flay, **fláður; ná* reach, *náð* n.; *þiggja* accept, **þáður; hyggja* think, *hugað* n.; *spyrja* ask, *spurður; ljá* lend, *léður; tjá* tell, *téður; gleðja* gladden, *gladdur; kveðja* say goodbye, *kvaddur; seðja* satisfy (hunger), *saddur; bryðja* crunch, *bruddur; ryðja* clear (out of the way), *ruddur; styðja* support, *studdur; fletja* flatten, cut open (fish), *flattur*; *hvetja* exhort, encourage, whet, *hvattur*; *flytja* move, *fluttur*; *lykja* lock up, (en)close, *luktur*.

Note: The verbs marked with (*) are also strong: *flá* : *fleginn*, *þiggja* : *þeginn*. Likewise *þvo* wash, *þvoð*, or strong *þveginn*.

3. The following types of stems are found in the first class of weak verbs:

Type a: *vefja* wrap, *vef, vafði, vafinn*
       telja count, *tel, taldi, talinn (taldur)*
       vekja awaken, *vek, vakti, vakinn (vaktur)*.

Note: This is the most common type.

Type b: *smyrja* butter, smear, grease, *smyr, smurði, smurinn*
         (smurður)
       mylja crush, *myl, muldi, mulinn*
       styðja support, *styð, studdi, studdur*
       flytja move, *flyt, flutti, fluttur*.

Note: This, too, is a common type.

Type c: *flýja (flúa)* flee, fly, *flúði (flýði), flúinn*
       gnýja storm, rage, *gný, gnúði, gnúinn*
       knýja compel, *kný, knúði, knúinn*
       núa rub, *ný, núði, núinn*
       rýja shear (the wool), *rý, rúði, rúinn* (also Weak class 3).

Note: A less common type. Similar is:
       tæja tease, pick the wool, *tæ, táði, táinn* (also Weak·class 3).

Type d: *selja* sell, *sel, seldi, seldur*
       skilja understand, *skil, skildi, skilinn*
       setja set, *set, setti, settur*
       deyja die, *dey, deyði, (deyður)* (usually Strong class 6).

Note: These verbs have i-shifted root vowels, even in the preterite. The vowel of *skilja*, however, is not subject to i-shift at all.

Type e: Verbs with irregular infinitives.
       flá flay, skin, *flæ, fláði, fláður* (also Strong class 6)
       ná reach, get, *næ, náði, náð* n.
       þvo wash, *þvæ, þvoði, þvoð* n. (also Strong class 6)
       ljá lend, *ljæ, léði, léður*
       hafa have, *hef, hafði, hafður* (also Weak class 3)
       fela conceal, *fel, faldi, falinn* (also Strong class 4 and 6).

Note: The older forms of the infinitives *ljá, tjá* were *léa, téa*.

3. Class 2: *dæm-a* judge, *dæm-i, dæm-di, dæm-dur.*

1. Verbs of this class either have (a) a tense root vowel (cf. Pronunciation **2**, *2*, 3(c)) followed by one or more consonants, or (b) a lax root vowel followed by two or more consonants. Whenever possible, the root vowel is i-shifted throughout the conjugation.

The present indicative is disyllabic (*dæm-i*, etc.).

2. Verbs, whose stems terminate in *g* or *k*, insert a *j* between the *g* and *k* and a following *-a, -u* in the ending: *víg-j-a* : *víg-j-um* consecrate; *steik-j-a* : *steik-j-um* roast. Before an *-i* in the ending this *j* is dropped in writing, but not in pronunciation: *víg-i, steik-i.* But before consonants it is dropped both in writing and in pronunciation: *víg-ði, steik-ti.*

Note: These *ja*-verbs can be distinguished from the verbs of the first class by observing the type of the stem. Class 1 has a type consisting of a lax vowel (Pr. **2**, *2*, 3) + one consonant, with the one exception of *ggj*. It may also have a tense stem vowel followed by no consonant.

3. Three verbs have an infinitive in *-va*:

slökkva put out (the light), *slökkvi, slökkti, slekkti, slökktur*
stökkva spray, *stökkvi, stökkti, stekkti, stökkt* n.
sökkva sink (trans.), *sökkvi, sökkti, sekkti, sökkt* n.

All these verbs may also go according to Strong class 3, but *stökkva* and *sökkva* are then intransitive: to jump, to sink. The forms *slekkti, stekkti, sekkti* are (i-shifted) preterite subjunctives.

4. Apart from these *-ja* and *-va* verbs, there are really no variant types of inflexion in this class, to which a great number of the weak verbs belongs. They all go like *dæma* with preterites in *-ði, -di, -ti* according to the rules in the Preliminary Remarks 2.

Instances:

heyra hear, *heyri, heyrði, heyrður*
þreyja wait patiently for, *þreyi, þreyði, þreyður* (rare type)
dæma judge, *dæmi, dæmdi, dæmdur*
byggja build, *byggi, byggði, byggður*
breiða spread out, *breiði, breiddi, breiddur*
þekkja know, recognize, *þekki, þekkti, þekktur*
kyssa kiss, *kyssi, kyssti, kysstur.*

5. A few irregular, but very common verbs, that may be classed here because of affinities with this class, are:

kaupa buy, *kaupi, keypti, keyptur*
meina mean, *meina, meinti, meintur*

sækja seek, fetch, *sæki, sótti,* (*sækti*), *sóttur*
yrkja compose a poem, *yrki, orti,* (*yrkti*), *ortur*
þykja think, feel, seem, *þyki, þótti,* (*þætti*), *þótt* n.

Note: Sækti, yrkti, þætti are preterite subjunctives.

4. Class 3: lif-a live, *lif-i, lif-ði, lif-að.*

1. Like the verbs of the second class (preceding), these verbs
have a disyllabic present with the same endings. But unlike the
verbs of the second class, these verbs, with the exception of a few
j-presents, have no i-shift of the root vowel (Pr. **5, 2**).

Verbs having *a* in the root syllable u-shift (Pr. **5, 3**) this *a* to *ö*
before *u* in the endings: *vak-a* to be awake, *við vök-um* we are
awake, *við vök-t-um* we were awake.

In the majority of verbs the preterite subjunctive is not i-shifted,
but several common verbs have an i-shifted preterite subjunctive,
among them: *segja* : *segði* say; *þegja* : *þegði* to be silent; *þora* :
þyrði dare; *duga* : *dygði* avail; *trúa* : *tryði* believe; *þola* : *þyldi*
endure, suffer; *una* : *yndi* like, enjoy; *vaka* : *vekti* be awake.

The past participle in *-að* n. is similar to that of class 4: *kalla* :
kall-aður to call.

2. Because of the intransitive meaning of most of these verbs,
the past participle has usually only its neuter form: *lif-að* lived,
sá-ð sown, *hvolf-t* capsized. But when transitive, these verbs have
past participles in *-aður, -ður, -dur, -tur,* e. g. *segja* : *sagður* say.
More instances: *há* : *háður* hold (a meeting); *má* : *máður* erase,
make fade; *skrá* : *skráður* write, register; *snjá* : *snjáður* wear
threadbare; *strá* : *stráður* strew; *tjá* : *tjáður* tell, say; *þjá* : *þjáður*
afflict, torment; *þrá* : *þráður* long for, yearn; *rýja* (*rúa*) : *rúður*
shear (the wool).

3. Past participles in *-að*(*ur*) belong to verbs whose stems are
made up of a lax root vowel (Pr. **2, 2, 3**) and a consonant: *lif-a* :
lif-að. (Cf. class 1 above). Past participles in *-ð*(*ur*) (originally
-að(*ur*)) belong to the many verbs with the stem vowel *á* : *sá* :
sá-ð sow (cf. 2. above), and the few with the stem vowels *ó, ú* :
gló-a : *gló-ð* glow; *spú-a* : *spú-ð* spew, but *trú-a* : *trú-að.* Past
participles in *-t* (*-ður, -dur, -tur*) belong to verbs whose stems contain (a) a lax vowel + two consonants (*horf-a* : *horf-t* look) or
(b) a tense vowel + one or more consonants (*slór-a* : *slór-t* loaf,
tarry). (Cf. class 2 above). But many of these verbs have also a
past participle in *-að* : *slór-að.* Those having *-t* only are: *horfa*

look, *hanga* hang, *góna* stare, *glápa* stare, *glotta* grin, *skorta* lack, *drúpa* droop, *húka* squat, *skúta* overhang, *slúta* project, hang down.

4. Belonging to this class are several verbs with *j*-presents:

segja say, *segi, sagði, (e), sagður*

þegja be silent, *þegi, þagði, (e), þagað (þagður)*

æja rest and graze (horses), *æi, áði, (á), áð*; also *á, ái*

heyja hold (a meeting), *heyi, háði, (æ), háður*; also *há, hái*

tæja tease, pick (wool), *tæi, táði, (æ), táður, táinn*

dýja shake (of quicksand), *dýi, dúði, (ú), dúð, dúað*; also *dúa, dúi*

hlýja warm, cover up, *hlýi, hlúði, (ú), hlúð*; also *hlú(a), hlúi*

lýja tire, *lýi, lúði, (ú), lúinn, lúður*

rýja shear (the wool), *rýi, rúði, (ú), rúinn, rúður*; also *rúa, rúi*

spýja spew, vomit, *spýi, spúði, (ú), spúinn, spúður*; also *spúa, spúi.*

Note: Most of these verbs, from *æja* on, also may have first class presents: *æ*, etc. Enclosed in parentheses: preterite subjunctive vowels.

5. Otherwise the verbs of this class can be arranged in the following types on the basis of their stems:

Type a[1]: Stems in -*á* (with loss of the infinitive ending -*a*):

á rest and graze (horses), *ái, áði, (á), áð*; also *æja, æi*

gá look, look out, *gái, gáði, (á), gáð(ur).*

Note: Thus go some thirty-five verbs, of which these are the most common: *gljá* shine, glitter; *há* handicap; *hvá* say *hvað* (= what), beg your pardon; *lá* blame somebody for something (*e-m e-ð*); *má* erase; *sá* sow; *skrá* write, register; *snjá(st)* become threadbare; *spá* prophesy; *strá* strew; *tjá* avail, tell; *þjá* torment; *þrá* long for.

Type a[2]: Stems in -*ú* and -*ó*:

dúa angle, *dúi, dúði, (ú), dúð, dúað*

glóa glow, shine, *glói, glóði, (ó), glóð, glóað*

Note: *Dúa* shake also has a *j*-present *dýja*; thus all other verbs of this type; cf. 4 above.

Type b: Stems made up of a lax vowel (Pr. **2, 2,** 3)+a consonant:

lifa live, *lifi, lifði, lifað*

hjara vegetate, *hjari, hjarði, hjarað*

þora dare, *þori, þorði, (y), þorað*

loða stick to, *loði, loddi, (y), loðað*

þola endure, *þoli, þoldi, (y), þolað*

vaka be awake, *vaki, vakti, (e), vakað.*

Note: Thus go several common verbs: *lafa* hang limply; *stara* stare; *vara* suspect; *vofa* (*yfir*) threaten, hang over; *blasa* (*við*) lie open before the eye; *flaka* flap; *brosa* smile.

Note 2: Here, too, belongs the (auxiliary) verb *hafa* have:

hafa have, *hefi* or *hef, hafði, (hefði), hafður.*

The form *hefi* is literary only, *hef* (like *tel* from *telja*) is both literary and colloquial.

Type c: Stems made up of a lax vowel (Pr. **2, 2, 3**)+two consonants, or a tense vowel + one or more consonants (like *dœma*) :

horfa look, *horfi, horfði, horft.*

Note: Thus go the verbs of this type enumerated in 3 above; exception :

tolla stick to, cleave, *tolli, tolldi, (tylldi), tollað.*

Type d: Irregular preterites:

olla cause, *olli, olli, (ylli), ollað*; also *valda, veld, olli, valdið*
skolla hang loosely, *skolli, skolli, (o), skollað*
skrolla hang loosely, *skrolli, skrolli, (o), skrollað.*

5. *Class 4*: *kall-a* call, *kall-a, kall-aði, kall-aður.*

1. The greatest number of weak verbs belongs to this class. The disyllabic present ends in *-a*, the preterite in *-aði*, the past participle in *-aður*. Unless the verb is compounded of a root syllable and a suffix (e. g. *hýr-g-a* gladden), an i-shift (Pr. **5, 2**) is never found in the root syllables of this class. Neither is the preterite subjunctive formed by i-shift, as in almost all other classes of verbs, weak and strong.

Before *u* in the ending, an *a* of the root syllable is u-shifted (Pr. **5, 3**) to *ö*, while the *a* of the preterite (and past participle) suffix is turned to *u*: *við köll-um* we call; *við köll-uð-um* we called.

2. The past participle, too, when inflected as an adjective, has u-shift of *a* in root syllable and suffix in the cases which ordinarily show u-shift (cp. *fagur*, Adjectives, III, **2** (a), paradigm 2). The suffix vowel is never dropped:

Sg. nom.	*kall-að-ur* m.	*köll-uð* f.	*kall-að* n.
acc.	*kall-að-an*	*kall-að-a*	*kall-að*
dat.	*köll-uð-um*	*kall-að-ri*	*köll-uð-u*
gen.	*kall-að-s*	*kall-að-rar*	*kall-að-s*
Pl. nom.	*kall-að-ir*	*kall-að-ar*	*köll-uð*
acc.	*kall-að-a*	*kall-að-ar*	*köll-uð*
dat.		*köll-uð-um*	
gen.		*kall-að-ra*	

89

Note: All other vowels of the root syllable remain unchanged, e. g. *hýrg-að-ur, hýrg-uð, hýrg-að.*

3. All the verbs of this class go like *kalla* or *hýrga*; like *kalla* if they have *a* in the root syllable.

A great many of these verbs are uncompounded (derivations of nouns *kall-a,* from *kall* n. call), but a number of them are formed with the following suffixes: *-ga, -ka, -la, -na, -ra,* and *-sa,* as well as with *-ja* and *-va.*

4. The verbs in *-ja* belonging to this class are naturally hard to distinguish (most of them have i-shift) in the infinitive from the *j*-verbs of other classes. But most of the forms are quite distinct, and in this class the *j* goes through the whole conjugation:

> *byrja* begin, *byrja, byrjaði, byrjaður.*

Likewise the *-va* verbs:

> *bölva* curse, damn, *bölva, bölvaði, bölvaður.*

Thus: *döggva* bedew, *fölva* cover with a film of snow, *glöggva* make clear, *mölva* break, smash, *rökkva* grow dark, fall (of dusk), *skrökva* not tell the truth, *slöngva* sling, hurl, *stöðva* stop, *uppgötva* discover, *vökva* water, wet, *þröngva* compel, *ölvast* become intoxicated, *örva* encourage.

4. Inflexional Endings of the Verbs.

1. Synopsis of the Endings of the Active Voice.

Present...

Indicative				Subjunctive....
Strong & Weak 1	Weak 2 & 3	Weak 4		Strong & Weak
Sg. 1 —	-i	-a		-i
2 -ur (-rð, -ð, -t, -)	-i-r	-a-r		-ir
3 -ur (-r, -)	-i-r	-a-r		-i
Pl. 1	-um			-um
2	-ið			-ið
3	-a			-i

Imperative.. Infinitive..... Participle

	Strong & Weak 1 & 2	Weak 3	Weak 4	All Verbs	All Verbs
Sg. 2	—	-i	-a	-a (-u, -)	-andi (-ndi)
Pl. 1	-um	-um	-um		
2	-ið	-ið	-ið		

Preterite...

Indicative................Subjunctive.......Past Participle.........

Strong		Weak	Strong & Weak	Strong		Weak
Sg. 1	—	-i	-i	-inn	1	-inn
2	-st (-zt, -t, -)	-ir	-ir		2	-ður, -dur, -tur
3	—	-i	-i		3	-ður, -dur, -tur
					4	-aður
Pl. 1		-um				
2		-uð				
3		-u	(-i)			

Note: In this table Sg. (Pl.) 1, 2, 3, means singular (plural) first, second, and third person, while Weak 1, 2, 3, 4 means weak verbs of first, second, third, and fourth class.

2. The Present Indicative.

(a) The present indicative singular shows the greatest variety of endings. Seemingly it has a different set of endings for (a) all the strong verbs and the weak verbs of the first class, (b) for the weak verbs of the second and third classes, and (c) for the weak verbs of the fourth class. If, however, we look upon the vowels of the endings in the second, third, and fourth classes (-i and -a) as belonging to the stem of these verbs (as they originally did), the picture is considerably simplified. We see then that:

1. The first person has no ending: *ég gef* I give, *tel* count, *dæm-i* judge, *vak-i* am awake, *kall-a* call.

2. The second person ends in -r after vowels: *þú dæm-i-r* you judge, *kall-a-r* you call; and in an expanded -r (= ur) after consonants: *þú gef-ur* you give, *tel-ur* count.

But there are exceptions in the monosyllabic stem forms of the strong verbs and the weak verbs of the first class: (a) After a vowel -rð is added: *þú fæ-rð* you get. This is the normal personal ending -r plus an ð which is drawn over from the pronoun *þú* in phrases like *fær þú* (becoming *færðu* and, by faulty analysis, *færð þú*). (b) -r is assimilated and lost after the consonants -r, -s, -x, and -n, while -ð, -t (from *þú*) is added to -r, -s (but not to -x, -n): *þú ber-ð* you bear, carry; *þú kýs-t* you choose, elect; *þú vex* you grow; *þú hrín* you cry.

Note: In the literary and poetic language the forms without -ð, -t are not uncommon.

3. The third person ends in -r after vowels (also after root vowels!) *hann fæ-r* he gets, *sný-r* turns; *dæm-i-r* judges, *kall-a-r* calls. It ends in expanded -r (= ur) after consonants, except -r, -s, -x, -n after which it is lost: *hann gef-ur* he gives, but *hann ber* he carries, *kýs* chooses, *vex* grows, *hrín* cries.

4. Verbs with infinitives in *-ja, -va* always drop the *j* and *v* in the present singular, if they are strong or belong to the first class of the weak verbs: *ligg-j-a* lie, *ég ligg; sökk-v-a* sink, *ég sekk; tel-j-a* count, *ég tel.* If they belong to the second and third weak classes, they keep the *v* but drop the *j*: *sökk-v-a* sink (transitive), *ég sökk-v-i*; *víg-j-a* consecrate, *ég víg-i*; *seg-j-a* say, *ég seg-i.* (Though *j* is dropped in writing it is kept in pronunciation.) If they belong to the fourth class of the weak verbs, they keep both *j* and *v*: *fer-j-a* ferry, *ég fer-j-a*; *vök-v-a* water, *ég vök-v-a.*

(b) The present indicative plural endings are alike for all verbs, strong and weak: *-um, -ið, -a,* the third person being identical with the infinitive: *gef-a* to give, they give, *kall-a* to (they) call, also *fá* to (they) get (with loss of the end vowel from *fá-a*). As to the plural stem forms, these rules are to be noted:

1. Unlike the singular stem (in strong verbs) which has the root vowel i-shifted or without breaking (Pr. **5**), (e. g. *ég kýs* I choose, *tek* take, *geld* pay), the plural stem shows no i-shift, but breaking: *við kjós-um* we choose, *við tök-um* we take, *við gjöld-um* we pay. These examples also show u-shift of the root vowel before *-um*; the second and third person *tak-ið, -a; bjarg-ið, -a* are not u-shifted (there being no *u* in the ending).

Note 1: Exceptions are *j*-presents, having i-shift both in singular and plural: *sverja* swear, *ég sver, við sverjum.*

Note 2: Verbs with *í, i, e, ei* as root vowels keep them unchanged in singular and plural: *bíta* bite, *ég bít, við bítum; finna* find, *ég finn, við finnum; bera* bear, carry, *ég ber, við berum; heita* be called, *ég heiti.*

Note 3: Though always spelled *-ið* the second person present plural ending often drops the *-ð* before its pronoun: *komi(ð) þið,* or rather *komiðið?* do you come (are you coming)?

Note 4: Verbs dropping the *-a* of the infinitive, also drop it in the third person present plural: *flá* to flay, they flay; *þvo* to wash, they wash; *flú(a)* to flee, they flee.

2. Verbs with *j*-presents, whether strong (*sver-j-a* swear) or weak (regardless of class) show their *j* before the plural endings, except before *-ið*, if the *j* is preceded by a (tense, Pr. **2**, *2*, 3) vowel, *k* or *g*: *sver-j-um, sver-j-ið, sver-j-a*; but *svík-j-a* deceive, betray, *svík-j-um : svík-ið; víg-j-a* consecrate, *víg-j-um : víg-ið; kný-j-a* compel, *kný-j-um : kný-ið.* In pronunciation, however, *j* is retained even before *-ið*.

3. Verbs of all classes, whether strong or weak, having *v* in their present stem show this *v* before the present plural personal endings: *sökk-v-a* sink, *sökk-v-um, sökk-v-ið, sökk-v-a*; *böl-v-a* curse, *böl-v-um, böl-v-ið, böl-v-a*.

3. The Present Subjunctive.

1. Only one set of endings is used in this inflexion. The singular endings *-i, -ir, -i* are added to the infinitive (present) stem without i-shift (Pr. **5**, *2*): *kjós-a* choose, *ég kjós-i*, etc. The first and second person plural are like the corresponding indicative forms: *við kjós-um, þið kjós-ið*, with u-shift (Pr. **5**, *3*) before *-um*: *við tök-um* we take. The third person plural is like the first and third person singular: *þeir kjós-i, tak-i*.

2. Verbs with infinitives in *-ja* and *-va* retain their *j* and *v* both in singular and plural, except that *j* is dropped (but pronounced!) before *-i* in the ending, if preceded by a (tense, Pr. **2**, *2*, 3) vowel, *k*, or *g*: *sver-j-a* swear, *sver-j-i*; *tel-j-a* count: *tel-j-i*; *sökk-v-a* sink, *sökk-v-i*; but *frý-j-a* taunt, *frý-i*; *seg-j-a* say, *seg-i*; *vek-j-a* awaken, *vek-i*.

4. The Preterite Indicative.

(a) The preterite indicative singular has two sets of endings, one for the strong, the other for the weak verbs.

1. The strong verbs have no endings in the first and the third person, while the normal ending of the second person is *-st*: *ég, hann gaf* I, he gave; *þú gaf-st* you gave (thou gavest). But if the preterite stem terminates in *-s*, the ending is only *-t*: *kjós-a* choose, *ég kaus* I chose, *þú kaus-t* you chose; if it terminates in *-t*, an assimilation takes place and the ending is *-z-t*: *skjót-a* shoot, *ég skaut, þú skau-z-t*; *hald-a* hold, *ég hélt, þú hél-z-t*; if it ends in *-tt*, the ending is *-t-zt*: *bind-a* bind, *ég batt, þú bat-zt*; and if it, finally, ends in *-st*, there is no ending: *brest-a* burst, *ég brast, þú brast*.

Note: Not only *-zt*, but also *-tzt* is always pronounced *-st*, and by many authors so spelled.

2. The weak verbs have invariably *-i, -ir, -i* in preterite singular (a set of endings that is also used in the present singular subjunctive, and in the preterite singular subjunctive of all verbs): *tel-j-a* count, *ég tal-d-i, þú tal-d-ir, hann tal-d-i* I, you, he counted.

(b) The preterite plural indicative has the same set of endings: *-um, -uð, -u* for all verbs strong and weak (these endings are also used for the preterite plural subjunctive): *far-a* go, *við fór-um*, *þið fór-uð, þeir fór-u; tel-j-a* count, *við töl-d-um, þið töl-d-uð, þeir töl-d-u; kall-a* call, *við köll-uð-um, þið köll-uð-uð, þeir köll-uð-u.* The two last examples show that an *a*, whether in the root or the suffix syllable, is always u-shifted (Pr. **5,** *3*) before these endings.

5. *The Preterite Subjunctive.*

The preterite subjunctive, whose stem in strong and weak verbs alike is identical with that of the preterite plural indicative, but i-shifted (Pr. **5,** *2*) (except in the fourth class of weak verbs and in some of the verbs of the third weak class), has the endings -*i*, -*ir*, -*i* in the singular, and -*um*, -*uð*, -*u* (or -*i*) in the plural: *kjós-a* choose, preterite plural: *við kus-um,* preterite subjunctive: *ég kys-i, þú kys-ir, hann kys-i, við kys-um, þið kys-uð, þeir kys-u (kys-i)*; *tel-j-a* count, preterite indicative: *ég tal-d-i, við töl-d-um,* preterite subjunctive: *ég tel-d-i, við tel-d-um,* etc.; but *kall-a* call, preterite indicative: *ég kall-að-i, við köll-uð-um,* preterite subjunctive the same. It will be observed that the plural endings cause no u-shift (Pr. **5,** *3*), except in the third and fourth classes of weak verbs, when the i-shift is lacking. But strong verbs, whose stems end in a tense (Pr. **2,** *2, 3*) vowel, *g* or *k*, add a *j* before the *u* of the plural endings: *sjá* see, preterite plural: *við sá-um,* preterite subjunctive: *ég sæ-i, við sæ-j-um; tak-a* take, *við tók-um, ég tæk-i, við tæk-j-um; ljúg-a* lie, *við lug-um, ég lyg-i, við lyg-j-um; gang-a* go, *við geng-um, ég geng-i, við geng-j-um.*

6. *The Imperative.*

1. The second person singular is without ending in all strong verbs (*tak-a* take, *tak* (you) take!), and in the first and second classes of weak verbs (*tel-j-a* count, *tel* count! *dæm-a* judge, *dæm* judge!). But in some verbs of the third weak class it has the ending -*i*: *þeg-j-a* be silent, *þeg-i þú* you be silent (but *seg-j-a* say, *seg þú!* without ending!); and in the verbs of the fourth weak class it has the ending -*a*: *kall-a* call, *kall-a þú* (you) call! Since, however, the -*i* and the -*a* of these imperatives originally belonged to the stem, it may be said that they, too, are without ending.

Note 1: The above forms are mostly literary. Usually *þú* is added to these imperatives as an ending. The resulting forms are given in Pronunciation **4,** *4.* Whether *þú* becomes -*ðu*, -*du*, or -*tu* depends upon much the same rules as govern the formation of the preterite suffix (see Weak Verbs, Preliminary Remarks, **3,** *1* above).

Note 2: Verbs in *-ja* or *-va* never show the *j* or *v* in the imperative singular, unless they belong to the fourth class of weak verbs: *her-j-a* plunder, *bö-l-va* curse, imperatives *her-j-a þú, böl-v-a þú*. But *tel-j-a* count, *tel þú*, and *sökk-v-a* sink, *sökk þú*, regularly.

Note 3: The verbs *binda* bind, *standa* stand, *vinda* wind, turn, and *hrinda* push, have *bitt*(*u*), *statt*(*u*), *vitt*(*u*), *hritt*(*u*), or *hrint*(*u*) as imperatives; the verbs *ganga* go, and *stinga* stab, pierce, have *gakk* or *gáttu*, and *stíktu*. All other verbs in *-nd* and *-ng* retain these sounds unchanged.

2. The first and second person plural are identical with the corresponding indicative forms: *tak-a* take, *tök-um við*! *tak-ið þið*! let us take! you take!

7. *The Infinitive.*

The infinitive of all verbs ends in *-a*, before which a *j* or *v* of the present stem appears, if it exists: *far-a* go, *tel-j-a* count, *sökk-v-a* sink. In *kall-a* the *-a* really belongs to the stem, so that the *-a* of the ending is dropped. It is also dropped after *á* (in many verbs: *fá* get, *sá* sow, *slá* beat), *o* (originally *á*: *þvo* wash, from *þvá*), *e* (in *ske* happen), and partly after *ú* (*flú*(*a*) flee, *snú*(*a*) turn).

Note: Two verbs have an infinitive in *-u*: *munu* shall, will, and *skulu* shall; see the Preterite present verbs, 5 below. These two verbs as well as *vilja* (rarely) also have a preterite infinitive: *mundu, skyldu, vildu* with the same *-u* ending. Sometimes, however, these preterite infinitives end in *-i*, but that is chiefly colloquial.

8. *The Participles.*

1. Present participles ending in *-andi* (*-ndi*) are indeclinable when used as adjectives (weak declension, third class); when used as nouns they go like *nemandi* (weak masculine, second class). Verbs in *-ja, -va* retain *j* and *v* throughout the inflexion: *vel-j-a* choose, vote, *vel-j-andi* voter, pl. *vel-j-endur* (not *vel-éndur*! though otherwise *je* is always spelled *é*).

2. Past participles, whether strong: *-inn*, or weak: *-inn, -ður, -dur, -tur, -aður*, go like adjectives (see Adjectives, III, 2 (a), paradigms 9 and 10: *heiðinn, talinn*; and *kallaður* under the third class of weak verbs), strong and weak. They also take comparison: *lúinn* tired (from *lýja* tire out), *lún-ari* more tired, *lún-astur* most tired; *ryðgaður* rusty, *ryðgaðri, ryðgaðastur*, from *ryðga* rust.

9. Paradigms of the Strong Verbs.

Present.

Indicative.

Class	1	2	3¹	3²	4	5	6	7¹	7²
Sg. 1	skín	kýs	brest	geld	ber	gef	tek	fœ	hǫgg
2	skín	kýs-t	brest-ur	geld-ur	ber-ð	gef-ur	tek-ur	fœ-rð	hǫgg-ur
3	skín	kýs	brest-ur	geld-ur	ber	gef-ur	tek-ur	fœ-r	hǫgg-ur
Pl. 1	skín-um	kjós-um	brest-um	gjöld-um	ber-um	gef-um	tök-um	fá-um	hǫgg-o-um
2	skín-ið	kjós-ið	brest-ið	gjald-ið	ber-ið	gef-ið	tak-ið	fá-ið	hǫgg-o-ið
3	skín-a	kjós-a	brest-a	gjald-a	ber-a	gef-a	tak-a	fá	hǫgg-o-a

Subjunctive.

Class	1	2	3¹	3²	4	5	6	7¹	7²
Sg. 1	skín-i	kjós-i	brest-i	gjald-i	ber-i	gef-i	tak-i	fá-i	hǫgg-o-i
2	skín-ir	kjós-ir	brest-ir	gjald-ir	ber-ir	gef-ir	tak-ir	fá-ir	hǫgg-o-ir
3	skín-i	kjós-i	brest-i	gjald-i	ber-i	gef-i	tak-i	fá-i	hǫgg-o-i
Pl. 1	skín-um	kjós-um	brest-um	gjöld-um	ber-um	gef-um	tök-um	fá-um	hǫgg-o-um
2	skín-ið	kjós-ið	brest-ið	gjald-ið	ber-ið	gef-ið	tak-ið	fá-ið	hǫgg-o-ið
3	skín-i	kjós-i	brest-i	gjald-i	ber-i	gef-i	tak-i	fá-i	hǫgg-o-i

Imperative.

Class	1	2	3¹	3²	4	5	6	7¹	7²
Sg. 2	skín, skíndu	kjós(tu)	brest(u)	gjald, gjaltu	ber(ðu)	gef(ðu)	tak(tu)	fá(ðu)	hǫgg(ðu)
Pl. 1	skín-um	kjós-um	brest-um	gjöld-um	ber-um	gef-um	tök-um	fá-um	hǫgg-o-um
2	skín-ið	kjós-ið	brest-ið	gjald-ið	ber-ið	gef-ið	tak-ið	fá-ið	hǫgg-o-ið

Infinitive.

Class	1	2	3¹	3²	4	5	6	7¹	7²
	skín-a	kjós-a	brest-a	gjald-a	ber-a	gef-a	tak-a	fá	hǫgg-o-a

Present Participle.

Class	1	2	3¹	3²	4	5	6	7¹	7²
	skín-andi	kjós-andi	brest-andi	gjald-andi	ber-andi	gef-andi	tak-andi	fá-andi	hǫgg-o-andi

96

9. *Paradigms of the Strong Verbs (continued).*

Preterite.

Indicative.

	1	2	3¹	3²	4	5	6	7¹	7²
Sg. 1	skein	kaus	brast	galt	bar	gaf	tók	fékk	hjó
2 skein-st	skein-st	kaus-t	brast	gal-zt	bar-st	gaf-st	tók-st	fékk-st	hjó-st
3 skein	skein	kaus	brast	galt	bar	gaf	tók	fékk	hjó
Pl. 1 skin-um	skin-um	kus-um	brust-um	guld-um	bár-um	gáf-um	tók-um	feng-um	hjugg-um
2 skin-uð	skin-uð	kus-uð	brust-uð	guld-uð	bár-uð	gáf-uð	tók-uð	feng-uð	hjugg-uð
3 skin-u	skin-u	kus-u	brust-u	guld-u	bár-u	gáf-u	tók-u	feng-u	hjugg-u
Subjunctive.									
Sg. 1 skin-i	skin-i	kys-i	bryst-i	gyld-i	bœr-i	gœf-i	tœk-i	feng-i	hjygg-i
2 skin-ir	skin-ir	kys-ir	bryst-ir	gyld-ir	bœr-ir	gœf-ir	tœk-ir	feng-ir	hjygg-ir
3 skin-i	skin-i	kys-i	bryst-i	gyld-i	bœr-i	gœf-i	tœk-i	feng-i	hjygg-i
Pl. 1 skin-um	skin-um	kys-um	bryst-um	gyld-um	bœr-um	gœf-um	tœk-j-um	feng-j-um	hjygg-j-um
2 skin-uð	skin-uð	kys-uð	bryst-uð	gyld-uð	bœr-uð	gœf-uð	tœk-j-uð	feng-j-uð	hjygg-j-uð
3 skin-u(-i)	skin-u(-i)	kys-u(-i)	bryst-u(-i)	gyld-u(-i)	bœr-u(-i)	gœf-u(-i)	tœk-j-u(-i)	feng-j-u(-i)	hjygg-j-u(-i)
Past Participle.	skin-inn	kos-inn	brost-inn	gold-inn	bor-inn	gef-inn	tek-inn	feng-inn	högg-v-inn

0. Paradigms of the Weak Verbs.

Present.

Indicative.

Class	1¹	1²	1³	2¹	2²	3¹	3²	3³	4¹	4²
Sg. 1	tel	spyr	flý	dæm-i	sökk-v-i	lif-i	seg-i	vak-i	kall-a	hýrg-a
2	tel-ur	spyr-ð	flý-rð	dæm-i-r	sökk-v-o-i-r	lif-i-r	seg-i-r	vak-i-r	kall-a-r	hýrg-a-r
3	tel-ur	spyr	flý-r	dæm-i-r	sökk-v-o-i-r	lif-i-r	seg-i-r	vak-i-r	kall-a-r	hýrg-a-r
Pl. 1	tel-j-um	spyr-j-um	flýj-j-um	dæm-um	sökk-v-o-um	lif-um	seg-j-um	vök-um	köll-um	hýrg-um
2	tel-j-ið	spyr-j-ið	flýj-j-ið	dæm-ið	sökk-v-o-ið	lif-ið	seg-ið	vak-ið	kall-ið	hýrg-ið
3	tel-j-a	spyr-j-a	flýj-j-a	dæm-a	sökk-v-o-a	lif-a	seg-j-a	vak-a	kall-a	hýrg-a

Subjunctive.

Class	1¹	1²	1³	2¹	2²	3¹	3²	3³	4¹	4²
Sg. 1	tel-j-i	spyr-j-i	flýj-i	dæm-i	sökk-v-o-i	lif-i	seg-i	vak-i	kall-i	hýrg-i
2	tel-j-ir	spyr-j-ir	flýj-ir	dæm-ir	sökk-v-o-ir	lif-ir	seg-ir	vak-ir	kall-ir	hýrg-ir
3	tel-j-i	spyr-j-i	flýj-i	dæm-i	sökk-v-o-i	lif-i	seg-i	vak-i	kall-i	hýrg-i
Pl. 1	tel-j-um	spyr-j-um	flýj-j-um	dæm-um	sökk-v-o-um	lif-um	seg-j-um	vök-um	köll-um	hýrg-um
2	tel-j-ið	spyr-j-ið	flýj-j-ið	dæm-ið	sökk-v-o-ið	lif-ið	seg-ið	vak-ið	kall-ið	hýrg-ið
3	tel-j-i	spyr-j-i	flýj-j-i	dæm-i	sökk-v-o-i	lif-i	seg-i	vak-i	kall-i	hýrg-i

Imperative.

Class	1¹	1²	1³	2¹	2²	3¹	3²	3³	4¹	4²
Sg. 2	tel (du)	spyr (ðu)	flý (ðu)	dæm (du)	sökk (tu)	lif (ðu)	seg (ðu)	vak (tu)	kall-a (ðu)	hýrg-a (ðu)
Pl. 1	tel-j-um	spyr-j-um	flýj-j-um	dæm-um	sökk-v-o-um	lif-um	seg-j-um	vök-um	köll-um	hýrg-um
2	tel-j-ið	spyr-j-ið	flýj-j-ið	dæm-ið	sökk-v-o-ið	lif-ið	seg-ið	vak-ið	kall-ið	hýrg-ið

Infinitive.

Class	1¹	1²	1³	2¹	2²	3¹	3²	3³	4¹	4²
	tel-j-a	spyr-j-a	flýj-j-a	dæm-a	sökk-v-o-a	lif-a	seg-j-a	vak-a	kall-a	hýrg-a

Present Participle.

Class	1¹	1²	1³	2¹	2²	3¹	3²	3³	4¹	4²
	tel-j-andi	spyr-j-andi	flýj-j-andi	dæm-andi	sökk-v-andi	lif-andi	seg-j-andi	vak-andi	kall-andi	nýrg-andi

10. Paradigms of the Weak Verbs (continued).

Preterite.

	Class 1¹	1²	1³	2¹	2²	3¹	3²	3³	4¹	4²
Indicative										
Sg. 1	tal-d-i	spur-ð-i	flú-ð-i	dæm-d-i	sökk-t-i	líf-ð-i	sag-ð-i	vak-t-i	kall-að-i	hýrg-að-i
2	tal-d-ir	spur-ð-ir	flú-ð-ir	dæm-d-ir	sökk-t-ir	líf-ð-ir	sag-ð-ir	vak-t-ir	kall-að-ir	hýrg-að-ir
3	tal-d-i	spur-ð-i	flú-ð-i	dæm-d-i	sökk-t-i	líf-ð-i	sag-ð-i	vak-t-i	kall-að-i	hýrg-að-i
Pl. 1	tól-d-um	spur-ð-um	flú-ð-um	dæm-d-um	sökk-t-um	líf-ð-um	sög-ð-um	vök-t-um	köll-uð-um	hýrg-uð-um
2	tól-d-uð	spur-ð-uð	flú-ð-uð	dæm-d-uð	sökk-t-uð	líf-ð-uð	sög-ð-uð	vök-t-uð	köll-uð-uð	hýrg-uð-uð
3	tól-d-u	spur-ð-u	flú-ð-u	dæm-d-u	sökk-t-u	líf-ð-u	sög-ð-u	vök-t-u	köll-uð-u	hýrg-uð-u
Subjunctive										
Sg. 1	tel-d-i	spyr-ð-i	flý-ð-i	dæm-d-i	sekk-t-i	líf-ð-i	seg-ð-i	vek-t-i	kall-að-i	hýrg-að-i
2	tel-d-ir	spyr-ð-ir	flý-ð-ir	dæm-d-ir	sekk-t-ir	líf-ð-ir	seg-ð-ir	vek-t-ir	kall-að-ir	hýrg-að-ir
3	tel-d-i	spyr-ð-i	flý-ð-i	dæm-d-i	sekk-t-i	líf-ð-i	seg-ð-i	vek-t-i	kall-að-i	hýrg-að-i
Pl. 1	tel-d-um	spyr-ð-um	flý-ð-um	dæm-d-um	sekk-t-um	líf-ð-um	seg-ð-um	vek-t-um	köll-uð-um	hýrg-uð-um
2	tel-d-uð	spyr-ð-uð	flý-ð-uð	dæm-d-uð	sekk-t-uð	líf-ð-uð	seg-ð-uð	vek-t-uð	köll-uð-uð	hýrg-uð-uð
3	tel-d-u(-i)	spyr-ð-u(-i)	flý-ð-u(-i)	dæm-d-u(-i)	sekk-t-u(-i)	líf-ð-u(-i)	seg-ð-u(-i)	vek-t-u(-i)	köll-uð-u(-i) (kall-að-i)	hýrg-uð-u (hýrg-að-i)
Past Participle	tal-inn, tal-d-ur	spur-ð-ur	flú-inn	dæm-d-ur	sökk-t-ur	líf-ð-ur	sag-ð-ur	vak-inn, vak-t-ur	kall-að-ur	hýrg-að-ur

99

11. The Middle Voice.

1. The middle voice is originally a reflexive, formed by addition of *sik* (the old form of the reflexive pronoun *sig*) to all forms of the verb in the active voice. *Sik* in these endings was contracted to *-sk* which in turn has given the modern *-st* or *-zt*. The middle forms are made as follows:

2. After vowels, whether in stems or endings, *-st* is added. Thus in infinitives: *-(a)-st*; first person present indicative: *-i-st, -a-st*; third person plural indicative: *-(a)-st*; first and third person singular of (a) present subjunctive, (b) weak preterite indicative, and (c) preterite subjunctive: *-i-st*; third person plural preterite indicative and subjunctive: *-u-st*; third person plural present (and preterite) subjunctive: *-i-st*; singular imperative: *kalla-st*.

3. The second and third persons singular present indicative drop the endings *-ur (-r, -ð, -rð, -t)*, leaving a stem form identical with the first person, to which the *-st* (or *-zt*) is added. Likewise the *-ir* of the second person present subjunctive, preterite subjunctive, and weak preterite indicative, drops its *-r*, adding *-st* to the vowel: *-i-st*.

4. The first person plural *-um*, regardless of tense or mood, always becomes *-um-st*, or colloquially *-ust-um*, a form that is hardly to be recommended.

The second person plural present ending *-ið* becomes *-izt* in all three moods, and the preterite *-uð* becomes *-uzt* both in indicative and subjunctive.

5. In the present indicative singular of strong verbs and weak verbs of the first class, as well as in the preterite singular of strong verbs (all three persons), the middle ending is added directly to the (monosyllabic) stem. It is then always *-st* unless the stem terminates in the consonants *-d, -t, -tt,* and (consonant +) *-ð*. In these special cases the *-st* combines with the specified consonants to make *-zt*, or, in the case of *-tt, -t-zt*. Examples:

hald-a hold,   present: *ég hel-zt (helst)*, from *held-st*
                 preterite: *ég hél-zt (hélst)*, from *hélt-st*
lát-a let,   present: *ég læ-zt (læst)*, from *læt-st*
                 preterite: *ég lé-zt (lést)*, from *lét-st*
vind-a wind,   present: *ég vin-zt (vinst)*, from *vind-st*
                 preterite: *ég vat-zt (vast)*, from *vatt-st*
bregð-a jerk, present: *ég breg-zt (bregst)*, from *bregð-st*
                 preterite: *ég brá-st (brást)*.

100

6. The second person preterite indicative (active), which now has the ending *-st*, formerly ended in *-t*: *gaf-st* you gave, formerly *gaf-t*. Hence the middle ending could be spelled *-zt* to distinguish it from the active; but both are spelled and pronounced alike. Example: *gef-a* give, active and middle *gaf-st*.

7. The present participles are now hardly used in the middle voice, except facetiously in imitation of the old learned style: *berjandisk ok bölvandisk* beating and cursing.

The past participles are found only in a neuter form, used to make up the compound tenses of the verbs. Since the neuter form of the (active) past participle ends either in *-ið, -ð, -t,* (*-tt*), or *-að*, it is obvious that the assimilations described in 5 above always take place. Examples:

taka take	pp. *tekinn, tekið*	middle	*tekizt* (*tekist*)	from	*tekið-st*
kalla call	" *kallaður, kallað*	"	*kallazt* (*kallast*)	"	*kallað-st*
skrá book	" *skráður, skrá*	"	*skráðst* (!)	"	*skráð-st*
sjá see	" *séður, séð*	"	*sézt* (!) (*sést*)	"	*séð-st*
dæma judge	" *dæmdur, dæmt*	"	*dæmzt* (*dæmst*)	"	*dæmt-st*
þekkja know	" *þekktur, þekkt*	"	*þekkzt* (*þekkst*)	"	*þekkt-st*
breiða spread	" *breiddur, breitt*	"	*breiðzt* (!) (*breiðst*)	"	*breitt-st*
hitta hit	" *hittur, hitt*	"	*hitzt* (*hist*)	"	*hitt-st*
kyssa kiss	" *kysstur, kysst*	"	*kysstst* (*kysst*)	"	*kysst-st*

Note 1: One would expect *séðst, breitzt,* and *kysszt,* but these forms are never so spelled. Verbs like *breiða, breiddi, breiddur,* with *ð* in the present stem and *dd* in the preterite and past participle, always have *ð* in the past participle middle. It will be seen that the past participles in the middle voice always have *-z,* except in *skráðst* (in weak verbs after *á* in stem) and *kysstst.*

Note 2. Two verbs, *leggja* and *setja* lay and set, have expanded their past participles in the middle voice with case endings of adjectives, i. e. the indeclinable neuter form *lagzt* and *setzt* take the ordinary strong adjective endings: *lagzt-ur, lögzt, lagzt; setztur, setzt, setzt. Ég er lagztur* I have taken to bed.

Note 3. It should not be forgotten that the above rules about where to place *-zt* and *-tzt* are simply orthographical, and that these combinations are always pronounced, and by many writers spelled *-st.* I have added these forms in parentheses.

8. Not all verbs may have the middle voice; this depends upon their meaning (of which more in the Syntax). Thus *vera* be, and *verða* become, lack it. On the other hand, there are verbs, appearing only in the form of the middle voice; thus *óttast* fear.

9. Paradigm of a Verb in the Middle Voice:

Present...

Indicative	Subjunctive	Indicative	Subjunctive
Sg. 1,2,3 *fer-st*	*far-i-st*	*kall-a-st*	*kall-i-st*
Pl. 1	*för-um-st*	*för-um-st*	*köll-um-st*	*köll-um-st*
2	*far-i-zt*	*far-i-zt*	*kall-i-zt*	*kall-i-zt*
3	*far-a-st*	*far-i-st*	*kall-a-st*	*kall-i-st*

Preterite..

Sg. 1	*fór-st*	*fær-i-st*	*kall-aði-st*	The same
2	*fór-st*	*fær-i-st*	*kall-aði-st*	as
3	*fór-st*	*fær-i-st*	*kall-aði-st*	indicative
Pl. 1	*fór-um-st*	*fær-um-st*	*köll-uðum-st*	except
2	*fór-u-zt*	*fær-u-zt*	*köll-uðu-zt*	sometimes
3	*fór-u-st*	*fær-u-st*	*köll-uðu-st*	*kall-aði-st*

Imperative...

Sg. 2	*far-st* (does not occur)	*kall-a-st*	
Pl. 1	*för-um-st*	*köll-um-st*	
2	*far-i-zt*	*kall-i-zt*	

Infinitive..

	far-a-st perish	*kall-a-st*	be called

Past Participle...

	far-i-zt	*kall-a-zt*

5. Irregular Verbs.

1. *Preterite Present Verbs.*

These are verbs, few in number but very common, whose present has the same form as the preterite of a strong verb, and whose preterite is weak. As a rule, in these verbs the infinitive, the (weak) preterite, and the past participle (if found) are formed from the present plural stem.

These verbs are *vita* know; *kunna* know, know how to, *unna* love, *þurfa* need; *muna* remember, *munu* shall, will, *skulu* shall; *mega* may, *eiga* own, have (to), and *vilja* will, want to. They are inflected as follows:

	vita	kunna	unna	muna	þurfa	munu	skulu	mega	eiga	vilja
Present Indicative										
Sg. 1	veit	kann	ann	man	þarf	mun	skal	má	á	vil
2	veizt	kannt	annt	manst	þarft	munt	skalt	mátt	átt	vilt
3	veit	kann	ann	man	þarf	mun	skal	má	á	vill
Pl. 1	vitum	kunnum	unnum	munum	þurfum	munum	skulum	megum	eigum	viljum
2	vitið	kunnið	unnið	munuð	þurfið	munuð	skuluð	megið	eigið	viljið
3	vita	kunna	unna	muna	þurfa	munu	skulu	mega	eiga	vilja
Present Subjunctive										
Sg. 1	vit-i	kunn-i	unn-i	mun-i	þurf-i	mun-i	skul-i	meg-i	eig-i	vilj-i

etc.: -ir, -i; -um, -ið, -i.

	vita	kunna	unna	muna	þurfa	munu	skulu	mega	eiga	vilja
Preterite Indicative										
Sg. 1	viss-i	kunn-i	unn-i	mund-i	þurft-i		—	mátt-i	átt-i	vild-i

etc.: -ir, -i; -um, -uð, -u.

	vita	kunna	unna	muna	þurfa	munu	skulu	mega	eiga	vilja
Preterite Subjunctive										
Sg. 1	viss-i	kynn-i	ynn-i	mynd-i	þyrft-i	mynd-i	skyld-i	mætt-i	ætt-i	vild-i

etc.: -ir, -i; -um, -uð, -u (-i).

	vita	kunna	unna	muna	þurfa	munu	skulu	mega	eiga	vilja
Imperative										
Sg. 2	vit(tu)	—	unn(tu)	mun(du)		—	—			
Pl. 1	vitum	—	unnum	munum		—	—			
2	vitið	—	unnið	munið		—	—			
Infinitive	vita	kunna	unna	muna	þurfa	munu	skulu	mega	eiga	vilja
Present Participle	vitandi	kunnandi	unnandi	munandi	þurfandi	—	—	megandi	eigandi	viljandi
Past Participle	vitaður	kunnað	unnað, unnt	munað	þurft	—	—	mátt	átt	viljað

103

Note: For the infinitive forms *munu, skulu* the subjunctive forms *muni, skuli* are sometimes substituted: *hún segist skuli reyna það* she says she'll try it.

The verbs *munu, skulu,* and *vilja* also have the preterite infinitives *mundu, skyldu,* and *vildu* (*mundi, skyldi, vildi*).

The form *mundi* (of *munu*) was originally and indicative form, but has now only subjunctive meaning.

2. Preterites in -ri.

A few verbs have preterites in *-ri.* As is most clearly seen in *róa* row, *re-ri,* these are traces of reduplicating preterites. The verbs are as follows:

Infinitive	Present	Preterite	Past Participle
kjósa choose, vote	*kýs*	*kjöri (keri)*	*kjörinn (kerinn)* also strong, class 2
róa row	*rœ*	*reri (réri, röri)*	*róinn*
gróa grow	*grœ*	*greri (gréri, gröri)*	*gróinn*
núa rub	*nú*	*neri (néri, nöri)*	*núinn*
snúa turn	*snú*	*sneri (snéri, snöri)*	*snúinn*

Note: These preterites in *-ri* take the endings of the weak preterites: *-i, -ir, -i; -um, -uð, -u.* The preterite subjunctive is identical with the indicative, except for an occasional third person plural in *-i.* The form *reri* is literal, but *réri* is a common and *röri* a dialectal colloquial form. The same is true of the variants of the other verbs.

3. The Verb *vera* to be.

Present.......................   Preterite...... ....

Indicative	Subjunctive		Indicative	Subjunctive
Sg. 1 *er, em*	*sé*	*veri*	*var*	*væri*
2 *ert*	*sért*	*verir*	*varst*	*værir*
3 *er*	*sé*	*veri*	*var*	*væri*
Pl. 1 *erum*	*séum*	*verum*	*vorum, vórum*	*værum*
2 *eruð*	*séuð*	*verið*	*voruð, vóruð*	*væruð*
3 *eru*	*sé(u)*	*veri*	*voru, vóru*	*væru, væri*

Imperative	Infinitive	Present Participle	Past Participle
Sg. 2 *ver(tu)*			
Pl. 1 *verum*	*vera*	*verandi*	*verið*
2 *verið*			

PART III. SYNTAX.

I. CASES AND THEIR USES.

1. Nominative.

Icelandic agrees with English in using the nominative as a subject of a sentence. As a rule, the object is put in the accusative, but some verbs take a dative or even a genitive object. The normal use of the dative is for the indirect object, and the normal function of the genitive is as a possessive.

In English the functions of the parts of the sentence are determined by the word order: subject, verb, indirect object, object, e. g. he gave me the book. This, too, is the normal order in Icelandic: *hann gaf mér bókina*, but it need not be as strictly observed as in English. See Word Order, VII below.

2. Accusative.

1. *Accusative with Verbs.*

1. The accusative normally marks the object of transitive verbs: *taka bókina* take the book; transitive verbs in the middle voice also take accusative: *hræðast dauðann* dread death.

2. Some verbs take double accusative, e. g. *þeir kusu hann borgarstjóra* (or: *fyrir borgarstjóra*) they elected him (as) mayor; *ég taldi hann góðan* I considered him good.

Note: In the passive the object (accusative) becomes subject (nominative), and the subject is turned into a prepositional phrase (much as in English): *hann var kosinn borgarstjóri* (*af þeim*) he was elected mayor (by them); the verbs of the middle voice cannot be so converted.

3. Some verbs take the logical subject in the accusative, and the (logical) object in the accusative. These are really impersonal verbs (q. v. VI, **14** below) with two accusatives; they tend to have the (logically normal) word order: logical subject, verb, object. Examples:

mig vantar skó I lack (need) shoes (literally: 'it lacks me shoes');
mig skortir ekkert I lack nothing;
mig dreymdi draum I dreamt (had) a dream.

105

Thus also the verbs *mig minnir* I think I remember, *mig grunar* I suspect, *mig langar* I want, I'd like to, *mig syfjar* I get sleepy, drowsy, *mig þyrstir* I get thirsty.

Note: None of these verbs is ever used in the passive.

4. A seemingly reflexive accusative is sometimes used after intransitive verbs of motion (colloquially): *ég labbaði mig upp í skóla* I strolled up to the school.

2. *Adverbial Accusative.*

The accusative is used adverbially to answer the questions (1) when? (2) how long? and (3) in what direction?

1. *Það rigndi vikuna, sem leið* it rained last week; *hann kemur annað kvöld* he will come tomorrow evening; but with prepositional phrases: *í gær* yesterday, *í dag* today, *á morgun* tomorrow.

2. *Ég var þar tvo daga, tvær nætur, tvö ár* I was there two days, two nights, two years.

3. *Þeir fóru þessa leið, veginn til Þingvalla, Hellisheiði* they went this way (took this road), the way to Þ., over H.

Note: Though originally adverbial, this accusative has now often become objective, as may be seen by the passive construction: *þessi leið var farin* this road was taken.

3. *Accusative with Prepositions.*

The accusative is used after the following prepositions:

1. *Um* round, over; during; concerning, about; *gegnum, í gegnum* through; *kringum* around; *umfram* above, beyond, in excess of; *umhverfis* round.

2. It is used after *á* on, onto; to; *í* in, into; *undir* under; *yfir* over, above; when these prepositions are in phrases linked with verbs of motion. It is also used after the prepositions *eftir* after, in succession to; by; *fyrir* before, in front of; along; for, on behalf of; *með* with (somebody or something in one's power); *við* near by, at; with; to, towards. All these prepositions may be used with the dative, in a different sense.

Note: *Fyrir norðan á* north of the river; *norður fyrir á* (motion) crossing the river to the north; likewise: *fyrir sunnan* south of, etc., *fyrir innan* inside (something), on the inner, landward side of something; *suður fyrir* crossing to the south, *inn fyrir* crossing toward the inside, or: towards the interior.

3. The accusative is used after the adverbs *fram* forth, up; *heim* home; *inn* in, towards the interior; *út* out, towards the outside (towards the sea); *upp* up; *niður* down; also after their opposites: *framan* from the outside, from the interior; *heiman* from home; *innan* from the inside, from the interior, *utan* from the outside, from the sea, from Iceland to Europe, etc. Since these adverbs are mostly linked with verbs of motion, the accusative may be considered to be governed by the verbs (accusative of direction *2*, *3* above). But when the verbs are lacking, the adverbs may be looked upon as prepositions: *út dalinn* (on the way) down the valley.

3. Dative.

1. Dative with Verbs.

1. The dative is normally the indirect object, the person for whom something is done or to whom something happens: *hann gaf mér bókina* he gave me the book. In the passive, unlike English, the dative remains: *mér var gefin bókin (af honum)* I was given the book (by him). *Hann sagði mér að fara* he told me to go, in the passive: *mér var sagt að fara (af honum)* I was told to go (by him). The two passive constructions are common, when the logical subject *(af honum)* is not expressed.

Thus the dative is used with the verbs *gefa e-m e-ð* give somebody something, *lána* lend, *bjóða* offer, *fá* give, *rétta* hand, *afhenda* deliver, *færa* bring; *segja* tell, *sýna* show; *selja* sell, *launa* reward; *skipa* command, *heita* promise, *lofa* permit.

2. The dative alone may be used as object to verbs:

(a) Verbs like *hjálpa e-m* help somebody, *hlífa* spare, *gagna* help, avail, *gegna* obey; *játa e-u* say yes to something, *neita* deny; *eyða e-u* spend something, *týna* lose, *gleyma* forget.

Note: Some of these verbs may take a double dative, the first being indirect object (a person), the second a direct object (a thing): *lofa e-m e-u* promise something to somebody.

(b) Verbs denoting mental states, both impersonal and personal.

Impersonal: *mér líkar, mislíkar e-ð* something pleases, displeases me, or: I like, dislike something; *hvað þóknast yður?* what would you like?

Note: Here the dative is really the logical subject. Cf. also Dative as Possessive, *4* below.

Personal: *kvíða e-u* fear for; *ég kvíði því* I hate to think of it; *fagna* rejoice, *unna* love, *trúa* believe, *treysta* trust.

107

(c) Verbs like *stjórna* govern, *stýra* steer, *ráða* have one's way about, be responsible for, *halda* keep; *taka e-m* receive somebody, *fylgja* follow.

(d) Verbs denoting (quick) movement: *koma e-u* (*e-m*) *e-ð* get something (somebody) to some place, *bregða sverði* unsheath, brandish a sword, *kasta steini* throw a stone, *fleygja* throw; *skjóta kúlu* shoot a projectile, *dreifa heyi* spread hay, *velta tunnu* roll a barrell, *hrinda* push, *sökkva skipi* sink a ship, *snúa sér* turn (oneself), *ríða hesti* ride a horse, *róa* (*á*) *báti* row a boat, *leggja báti að bryggju* lay a boat up at the pier.

Some of these datives are close to the instrumental sense (throw 'with' a stone, etc.) in (e).

(e) The instrumental ('with') sense is clear in certain set phrases: *beita e-n brögðum* use dishonest means in dealing with somebody, trick somebody; *taka e-n höndum* seize, arrest somebody; *taka e-m tveim höndum* receive somebody with both hands, welcome; *ganga þurrum fótum* walk with dry feet; *bæta fullum bótum* make full amends. Also with past participles: *grasi vaxinn* grown (covered) with grass, *búinn gulli* adorned with gold (= *gullbúinn*). But prepositions may also be used: *ég tók steininn upp með annari hendi* I lifted the stone with one hand; *standa á öðrum fæti* stand on one foot.

(f) The dative has an ablative sense after verbs denoting depriving, robbing somebody (accusative) of something (dative): *svipta e-n e-u* deprive somebody of something, *ræna e-n e-u* rob, *firra e-n e-u* deprive somebody of something, avert something from somebody. But *stela e-u frá e-m* steal something from somebody, with a preposition; likewise sometimes *ræna* rob.

2. Dative with Adjectives and Adverbs.

1. The dative is commonly used with adjectives (and adverbs) where English has to, with, or from. But even in Icelandic prepositional phrases often take the place of the dative. Examples: *þarfur—óþarfur mér* useful—detrimental to me; *ljúfur* (*við mig*)—*leiður* (*við mig*) dear—hateful to me; *nytsamur* (*fyrir mig*) useful to me; *skæður* dangerous to; *kær* dear; *þægur* (*við mig*) obedient to me.—*Góður* (*við mig*) good to me; *vondur, illur* (*við mig*) unkind, bad to me; *gramur* (*við mig*) peeved at, angry with me; *reiður* (*við mig*) angry with me; *vinveittur* friendly to.— *Nálægur mér* near to me, *nálægt* (adv.) *mér* near (to) me, *nærri* near, *nær* nearer, *næst* nearest; *fjarlægur mér* far away from me, *fjarri* (adv.) far, *fjær* further away, *fjærst* furthest away.—*Skyldur*

mér related to me; *tengdur, venzlaður mér* a relative by marriage to me.—*Líkur mér* like, similar to me; *ólíkur mér* unlike, dissimilar to me; *svipaður mér* similar to me; *jafn mér* equal to me.—*Hlýðinn mér* obedient to me; *óhlýðinn mér* (*við mig*) disobedient to me; *tryggur* (*við mig*), *trúr mér* faithful to me.—*Andstæður mér* opposed to me; *jafngamall mér* of the same age as I; *jafnfætis* (adv.) *mér* on equal standing (footing) with me; *samtímis* (adv.) *mér* coeval with me.—*Vanur e-u* (*við e-ð*) used to something.

2. The dative indicates cause in *ég varð því feginn* I was glad at that.

3. The dative indicates 'with respect to' in *mikill vexti* great in (with respect to) stature. But prepositional phrases often take its place: *svartur á hár* black-haired.

4. The thing or (more rarely) the person compared to another thing or person is put in the dative of comparison (before comparatives of adjectives and adverbs):

Fáir munu vera honum meiri few will be greater than he, or: *fáir munu vera meiri en hann*; this alternative construction is more common colloquially.

5. The dative of difference is also used with (before) comparatives to indicate the difference between the things compared:

Hann er mér miklu reyndari he is much more experienced than I, or: *hann er miklu reyndari en ég* (more colloquial); here *mér* is the dative of comparison, *miklu* the dative of difference. Likewise: *tveim árum yngri* younger by two years; *þrem dögum síðar* (*áður*) three days later (earlier); *engu síður* no less. In chains of comparisons: *því meir(a)* . . . *því meir(a)* the more . . . the more; *því meira sem rigndi, því meiri varð forin* the more it rained, the more (worse) the mud became. Also: *þeim mun meira sem hann las, því heimskari þóttist hann verða* the more he read, the more stupid he thought he became. A very high degree without a real comparison is expressed in *ónáðaðu mig ekki, nema því meira liggi við* do not disturb me unless something very serious is at stake; this use of *því meira* is only found after *nema* (conj.).

2(a). Adverbial Dative.

An adverbial dative of time occurs in *einu sinni* once, *stundum* at times.

3. Dative with Prepositions.

The dative is used after the following prepositions:

1. *Að* to; *af* of, off, from; *frá* from; *hjá* at, with, of; *úr* out of, of; *andspænis* opposite; *ásamt* together with; *gagnvart* opposite; *gegn*

109

against; *gegnt* opposite; *handa* for; *meðfram* along; *mót, móti* against, towards; *undan* in front of.

2. It is used after *á* on, in; *í* in; *undir* below; *yfir* above; when these prepositions are linked with verbs of rest; also after *eftir* after, according to; *fyrir* in front of, on account of; *með* with (accompanying somebody); *við* against, at, from. All these prepositions can be used with the accusative in a different sense.

Note: In addressing letters, the place names are usually put in dative without any preposition: *Herra Jón Jónsson, Höskulds-stöðum, Breiðdal, Suður-Múlasýslu,* but: *Jón býr á Höskulds-stöðum í Breiðdal í Suður-Múlasýslu.*

4. Dative as a Possessive.

Sometimes dative is used in Icelandic where English requires the genitive. See the Genitive *1*, 5 below.

4. Genitive.

1. Differences in Icelandic and English Usage.

1. No difference is made in Icelandic—as is done in English—between persons and things in the genitive construction in its possessive sense: Persons: *hús Jóns* John's house, *bréf mömmu* mother's letter; things: *morgunn lífsins* the morning of life. The Icelandic genitive corresponds thus both to the English -*s* genitive and the *of* genitive; but the word order is reversed in Icelandic as compared to the English -*s* genitive. This holds good also of possessive pronouns: *faðir minn* my father, *móðir hans* his mother, *húsið þeirra* their house; *þau fluttu í nýja húsið sitt* they moved into their new house.

2. The English genitive ' at St. Paul's, at Smith's' is not found in Icelandic, where *í St. Pálskirkju, hjá Smith* is used instead. Neither is the so-called group genitive found in Icelandic: ' the King of Iceland and Denmark's birthday' is: *afmælisdagur konungs Íslands og Danmerkur.*

3. Often English uses the genitive of a personal pronoun or a possessive pronoun where Icelandic uses the suffixed definite article only: *hann tók ofan hattinn* he took off his hat; *hún fór úr kápunni* she took off her coat; *ég fór á (í) nýju skóna* I put on my new shoes; *mig svíður í augun* my eyes hurt me; *mig tekur í bakið (fótinn)* I have a piercing (sudden) pain in my back (foot); *mig verkjar í fótinn* I have a constant pain in my foot.

110

4. Instead of *my* nose, eyes, ears, hair, arm, foot, toe (etc., of parts of the human body), the Icelanders say: *nefið á mér* (the nose on me), *augun í mér; eyrun, hárið, handleggurinn, fóturinn, táin á mér.* Likewise: *tungan, hjartað, maginn í mér* my tongue, heart, stomach (inside the body, hence *í* as also of the eyes). Also of animals: *skottið á hundinum* the tail of (on) the dog. Similarly: *hjá* in one's possession: *hestarnir hjá honum, karlinum, eru alltaf vel hirtir* the horses of his—of the old fellow—are always well groomed, or: his horses are always well groomed.

Parts of other wholes (than the human or animal bodies) may be treated likewise: *gluggarnir á húsinu* the windows of (on) the house; *herbergin í húsinu* the rooms of (in) the house; *trén í skóginum* the trees of (in) the woods.

5. When the parts of the human body are governed by a preposition, the English genitive is sometimes replaced, not by a prepositional phrase as above, but by a dative; this usage is, however, not colloquial, except in some fixed phrases or idiomatic expressions. Examples: *hann barði sér á brjóst* he beat his breast; *mér vöknaði um augu* my eyes grew moist; *þeir ráku óvinina af höndum sér* they drove their enemies off (their hands); *hafa allt illt á hornum sér* (literally: have everything evil on one's horns) be sour as a pickle; *telja á fingrum sér* count on one's fingers, but *kunna upp á sína tíu fingur* have something at one's fingers' ends.

2. *Different Meanings of the Genitive.*

Apart from indicating possession, which has been sufficiently illustrated above, the genitive is also used to express:

1. Measure in space and time: *þriggja pela flaska* a bottle of one and a half pints, a one and a half pint bottle; *fjögra faðma dýpi* a depth of four fathoms; *tveggja tíma reið* a ride of two hours.

2. Value: *Eignin er 3000 króna virði* the property is worth 3000 crowns; *einskis, mikils virði* worth nothing, much; of little, great value.

3. Description: *mikils háttar maður* a man of note; *tveggja ára barn* a two years old child; *tveggja vetra tryppi* a two years old colt. Note that *ár* is used of humans, *vetur* of animals.

4. Material: *fjórtán álnir vaðmála* fourteen ells of homespun; often a prepositional phrase is used instead: *fimm metrar af lérefti* five meters of linen; *glas af vatni* a glass of water (*vatnsglas* may mean the same, but also: a glass for water).

111

5. The whole (of which a part is taken: Partitive Genitive):

mörg hundruð manna (or *manns*) many hundreds of persons;
tvö hundruð manna (*manns*) two hundred persons (men);
enginn þeirra none of them (also: *enginn af þeim*);
fyrstur allra first of all (also: *fyrstur af öllum*);
hvað er tíðinda? what news? (literally: what is of tidings?);
ógrynni fjár immeasurable wealth.

Also with adverbs: *snemma dags* early in the day, but *snemma um daginn* early that day; *lengi sumars* for a good part of the summer.

6. Objective genitive: *ótti drottins er upphaf vizkunnar* the fear of God is the beginning of wisdom. In compounds: *ættjarðar-ást* love of country.

7. Genitive of Naming: (mostly in compounds) *Reykjavíkur-bær* the city of Reykjavík.

Note: The genitives of 1-3 are, like adjectives with which they have much in common, placed before their nouns, those of 4-5 after their nouns, as is also the possessive genitive: *hús Jóns*.

3. Genitive with Verbs.

1. Verbs like *vænta e-s* expect something; *örvænta* (also *um e-ð*) despair of something; *bíða* (also *eftir e-u*) wait for something; *óska, æskja* (also *eftir e-u*) wish for something; *biðja* (also *um e-ð*), *beiðast* ask for something; *leita* (also *eftir e-u*) seek, look for something.

2. Verbs like *afla e-s* procure something; *fá konunnar* marry the woman; *njóta* enjoy; *þurfa* (also *e-ð*), *þarfnast* need something; *sakna* miss; *gá* (also *að e-u*) heed, look after; *gæta* (also *að e-u*) take care of, look after; *geyma* (also *e-ð*) take care of, preserve; *vitja* (also *um e-ð*) visit; *geta* (also *um e-ð*) mention; *minnast* remember.

3. In fixed phrases: *nema staðar* (literally: take a place) stop; *fara ferða sinna* go about one's business.

4. Verbs with accusative of the person, genitive of the thing:

biðja e-n e-s ask somebody for something (also *um e-ð*);
spyrja e-n e-s ask (question) somebody about something (also *um e-ð*);
dylja e-n e-s conceal something from somebody.

112

5. Verbs with dative of the person, genitive of the thing:

unna e-m e-s not grudge (= grant) somebody something;
varna e-m e-s deny something to somebody;
synja e-m e-s deny something to somebody (also *synja um e-ð*).

6. Verbs like *meta, virða mikils, einskis* value highly, not at all; *gjalda e-s* pay for something, have to take the consequences of something; *njóta e-s* reap the fruit of something; *iðrast e-s* repent of something; *hefna e-s* avenge something or somebody; also *iðrast eftir, hefna fyrir e-ð.*

4. Genitive with Adjectives.

1. Measure in space and time: *tveggja metra langur* two meters long; *sex feta hár, djúpur, síður, þykkur, víður, breiður* six feet high, deep, low, thick, wide, broad; *mánaðar gamall* a month old.

2. Value: *mikils verður* worth much, important; *mikils, lítils metinn* highly, little esteemed.

3. Other adjectives: *fullur illsku* full of evil (also *af e-u, með e-ð*); *saddur lífdaga* satisfied with one's life's days (i. e. of ripe old age, ready to die), but *saddur af mat* appetite satisfied; *einskis þurfi* needing nothing; *matar-þurfi* in need of food (compound); *laus allra mála* free from all concern with (obligation), *alls-laus* destitute, but *laus við e-ð* free from something.

Verða e-s var become aware of something; *verða e-s vís, vísari* learn of something.

5. Adverbial Genitive.

The genitive is sometimes used adverbially of space and time, but mostly in fixed phrases: *annars staðar* elsewhere; *þessa heims og annars* in this and the other world; *beggja vegna* on both sides; *annars vegar* on the one hand, *hins vegar* on the other hand; *loks(ins)* finally, at last. Some of these terms are also written as compounds: *annarsstaðar*, etc.

6. Genitive with Prepositions.

The genitive is used after the following prepositions: *til* to, *án* without, *auk* in addition to, *meðal* among, *megin* on . . . side, *milli, millum* between, *sakir, sökum* on account of, *vegna* because of, on account of; *handan* on the other side of, *innan* inside of, within, *utan* outside of, *ofan* above, *neðan* below, *sunnan* to the south of, *norðan* to the north of, *vestan* to the west of, *austan* to the east of.

113

II. THE USE OF THE DEFINITE ARTICLE.

1. English has two articles, the indefinite *a*(*n*) and the definite *the*. Icelandic has nothing corresponding to the indefinite article (*maður* a man), but it has a definite article in full form (the free definite article) before adjectives: *hinn, hin, hið* (colloquially *sá, sú, það*) and in weakened form suffixed to nouns: *-inn, -in, -ið.*

Note 1: *Einn maður,* a man, is old-fashioned and not good form; *maður einn,* a certain man, is literary. But *í einu orði sagt* in a word; *einn eða tvo daga* one or two days, a day or two.

Note 2: *Tvisvar á dag* twice a day, *einu sinni á ári* once a year (here the English *a* is only apparently the indefinite article, in reality it is the preposition on = *á*).

2. As in English the definite article (free or suffixed) is used, when the noun represents something known, already mentioned or defined. *Einu sinni var karl og kerling; karlinn hét Jón, en kerlingin Guðrún* once upon a time there was an old man and an old woman; the old man was called J., and the old woman G.; *leika sér í garðinum, á götunni* play in the garden, in the street.

Other examples: *grái hesturinn* the grey horse; *grái hesturinn, sem týndist í gær* the grey horse that got lost yesterday; *hesturinn hans Jóns* John's horse (also *hestur Jóns*); *hesturinn minn* my horse; *þetta er minn hestur, en ekki yðar* this is my horse, not yours (no article, cf. 4 below); *maðurinn minn* my husband, but *maður minn* my dear fellow! (address); *sonur minn* my son, my son!

3. Like English, Icelandic has no article with proper names, including God (but not the devil), titles, members of the family; feastdays, days and months, days or seasons in prepositional phrases; collective words.

Examples: *herra Jón Jónsson* Mr. J. J.; *frú* (Mrs.) *Anna Bjarnadóttir; séra* (the Rev.) *Þorsteinn Þórarinsson, prófessor Magnús Jónsson; guð* God, *djöfullinn* the devil; *pabbi* daddy, father, *mamma* mummy, mother, *afi* grandpa, grandfather, *amma* grandma, grandmother, but *faðir minn* my father, *móðir mín* my mother; *viku fyrir jól* a week before Christmas, *fyrir, eftir páska* before, after Easter, but *á jólunum, páskunum, hvítasunnunni* at Christmas, Easter, Whitsunday; *í dag* today, *í kvöld* tonight, *í nótt* tonight, *í morgun* this morning, *á morgun* tomorrow, *í sumar* (*vor, haust, vetur*) this summer (spring, fall, autumn, winter); *glas af vatni*

114

a glass of water, *hringur úr gulli* a ring of gold; *á ensku, dönsku, þýsku* in English, Danish, German.

Note: The titles *herra, frú, séra,* always precede the given name. But *bóndi, prestur, biskup, prófessor* often are placed between the given name and the patronymic: *Guðmundur bóndi Friðjónsson.*

4. When modified by a genitive, a possessive or demonstrative pronoun (except *hinn*), or by *annar, annarhver, (sér)hver,* a noun usually has no article (as in English mostly).

Examples: *hús Jóns* (or *húsið hans Jóns*) John's house; *mitt hús* my house, but *húsið mitt;* *þetta hús* this house, but *hitt húsið* the other house; *annað hús* another house, but *annað húsið* one of the two houses; *annaðhvert hús* every other house (of many); *(sér)-hvert hús* every house.

Note: There is no difference in meaning between *mitt hús* and *húsið mitt* my house. The appearance of the article depends entirely on the word order. This rule affects the possessive pronouns only.

5. Unlike English, Icelandic often has no article with generic nouns, with place names that border on proper nouns, with names of parts of the human body, parts of a house, parts of a ship, and with certain collective words.

Examples: *bóndi var ekki heima* the farmer was not at home; *bændur* the farmers, *piltar* the boys, the farmhands, *stúlkur* the girls, the farm girls, *biskup* the bishop, *prestur* the parson, *kaupmaður* the merchant.—*Fara heiðar* travel over the heaths (the mountains) ; *austur yfir fjall* east over the Mountain (from Reykjavík to the Southern Lowlands).—*Vera á fótum* to be on one's feet; *skera sig í fingur* cut one's finger; *hafa hatt á höfði* have a hat on one's head (note the absence of the genitive in these Icelandic constructions).—*Frammi í stofu* (out) in the parlor; *í búri og eldhúsi* in the pantry and the kitchen.—*Vinda upp segl og setja stýri fyrir* hoist the sail and set the rudder.—*Lög* neuter plural, the law; *alþýða* the people, the public; *veður* the weather; *veður var gott, kalt, heitt* the weather was good, cold, warm.

6. In Icelandic the definite article sometimes takes the place of the genitive in English (cf. the Genitive, I, **4**, *1*, 3). This is especially the case with nouns denoting parts of the human body, clothing, or any part of some greater whole.

Examples: *þér skáruð yður í fingurinn* you cut your finger; *fór sandur (sandkorn) í augað á yður?* did (a grain of) sand enter your eye? *viljið þér ekki fara úr kápunni?* won't you take off your coat? *það glampar á gluggana á húsinu* the windows of the house gleam; *skipið týndi stýrinu* the ship lost its rudder.

115

7. After words denoting number or amount (limiting adjectives) as a part of a whole, the generic noun denoting the whole may be added as an apposition, and then with the suffixed article:

einn sjómaðurinn (common)
einn af sjómönnunum (common) ⎫ one of the sailors,
einn sjómannanna (literary) ⎭
but *einn sjómaður* one sailor.

Likewise: *einhvern daginn* one of these days; *fyrstu nóttina, sem þeir voru þar* the first night (first of the nights) they stayed there; *nokkur skipin fórust* some of the boats were lost; *þetta má margur maðurinn hafa* many a man has to take (suffer) this; *þér eigið hálft skipið* you own half the boat; *ég skal selja yður það húsið, sem þér viljið heldur* I will sell you the house you prefer; *annað bréfið* one of the letters; *hvort augað er blint?* which of the eyes is blind? *hvorugt augað* neither of the two eyes; *annaðhvort augað* one of the two eyes; *það er ekki þetta auga, heldur hitt augað* it is not this eye, but the other one.

8. On the use of the definite article in connection with adjectives, see the Weak Adjectives below (III, 2).

III. ADJECTIVES.

1. Strong Adjectives.

1. Adjectives are strong (i.e. take the strong declension), generally speaking, when they modify indeterminate nouns (nouns without the definite article): *rauður hestur* a red horse.

Note: In vivid literary style a strong adjective may modify a noun with the definite article: *blátt hafið* the blue sea, the sea that is (just now) blue. This is an inverted apposition, cf. 3 below.

2. Adjectives are always strong in predicative position: *hann er ríkur* he is rich; *hún er falleg* she is handsome; *íslenzka flaggið er blátt, hvítt og rautt* the Icelandic flag is blue, white, and red.

Note: Indeclinable adjectives in *-i, -a* are used mostly as predicatives: *hann var hugsi* he was pensive; *ég er hissa* I am surprised.

3. Adjectives are strong in appositive position: *Jón var fluttur veikur á spítalann* John was taken, sick, to the hospital; *þeir fluttu á hestinum, meiddum* they used the horse, [though] injured, for transport.

4. Most limiting adjectives have a strong form, thus *allur* all,

annar (an)other, and the pronouns: *hver* each, every, *einhver* some, *sérhver* each, every, *nokkur* any, *hvorugur* neither, *annarhver* every other, *enginn* no, *neinn* (not) any, *báðir* both. Most of these adjectives can, nevertheless, modify nouns with the definite article (cf. the Definite article, II, 7): *er það allur galdurinn?* is that the whole hocus-pocus? i. e. is that all there is to it? *annar maðurinn var dökkklæddur* one of the two men wore a dark suit of clothes; *hvert fíflið getur þetta* any fool can do this.

Note: The singulars *fár* (few), *margur* (many) are always strong, but the plurals can be weak *þeir mörgu, sem* the many, who.

2. Weak Adjectives.

1. Adjectives are weak (i. e. take the weak declension) after the (literary) definite article *hinn, hin, hið*: *hin rósfingraða morgungyðja* the rose-fingered morning goddess.

2. Adjectives are weak with nouns that have the suffixed article (but cf. 1, 1, note, and 4 above): *hvíti dauðinn* the white death, i. e. tuberculosis; *rauði hesturinn hans Páls* Paul's red horse (*Páls rauði hestur* is bad style).

3. Adjectives are weak after the demonstrative pronouns *sá* the, that one, *þessi* this: *Hann er fallegur, þessi rauði hestur. Viljið þér ekki selja mér þann rauða?* He is fine-looking, this red horse. Wouldn't you like to sell me the red one?

Note: After *hinn,* the other, the definite suffixed article is retained: *ég vil heldur kaupa hinn rauða hestinn* I prefer to buy the other red horse. Cf. S. II, 7 above.

4. Adjectives are weak after the possessive pronouns: *minn* my, *þinn* (thy) your, *sinn* his, her, its, *vor* our; also after the genitives of the personal pronouns: *hans* his, *hennar* her, *þess* its, *okkar* our, *ykkar* your, *yðar* your, and even after genitives of nouns. But these constructions are rare and not good form, for, as a rule, the possessive pronouns (and the genitives) are placed after the noun they modify (cf. 2 above). Examples: *Jóns (hennar, minn) rauði hestur,* bad form for: *rauði hesturinn hans Jóns (hennar, minn)* John's (her, my) red horse; *Jóns (hennar, minn) bezti hestur,* rare for: *bezti hesturinn hans Jóns (hennar, minn)* John's (her, my) best horse.

Note 1: In the definite statement: *bréfið er frá mínum gamla, góða vini, Sveinbirni,* the front position of *mínum* is good enough form, while in the indefinite statement: *bréfið er frá góðum, gömlum vini mínum, Sveinbirni,* the letter is from a good old friend of mine, S., the adjectives remain strong in spite of the following *mínum*.

Note 2: At the end of a letter one can write: *þinn gamli vinur*
your old friend, but the usual informal but not intimate formula is:
þinn, yðar einlægur yours sincerely, with a strong adjective.

5. Adjectives are usually weak in direct address: *góða frú, ég ætla
að biðja yður að hafa nú ekki mikið fyrir mér* dear Mrs. X, please,
don't put yourself out on my account; *heyrðu góði minn* listen
my dear; beginnings of letters: *kæri vinur, góði vinur* dear friend;
kæri herra dear Sir.

Note: Even here strong forms are sometimes used: *drottinn minn
góður!* good Lord! *góðir hálsar!* Gentlemen!

6. Ordinals, from *þriðji* onwards, and comparatives are always
weak, whether the noun they modify has the definite article or not.
Weak are also usually (even without the article) the ordinal *fyrsti*
(strong: *fyrstur*) and superlatives of adjectives in attributive
position. But as predicatives they are strong. Examples: *Íslendingar
fengu sjálfstæði sitt fyrsta desember 1918* the Icelanders got their
independence on December first, 1918; *næsta sunnudag ætlum við
til kirkju* next Sunday we are going to church; *í síðustu viku
sumars* in the last week of summer; *elzta systir mín hét Rósa*
my oldest sister was called R.; *elzta systirin* the oldest sister (of
many); *elzta systir* Oldest Sister (used almost as a proper name).
Ég þarf að skreppa til næsta bæjar I have to make a short visit
(trip) to the next farmstead (town).

In predicative position: *systir mín er elzt* my sister is oldest (of
the lot); *hann er efstur í bekk* he leads the class; but *hún er eldri
en ég* she is older than I; *hann er þriðji í röðinni* he is the third
in the order (row).

Note: Superlatives (and *fyrstur*) are sometimes strong even in
attributive position: *Jón Sigurðsson hefur verið mestur stjórnmálamaður á Íslandi* J. S. was (has been) the greatest statesman in
Iceland (i. e. that Iceland has produced); *hún er fegurst kona á
Íslandi* she is the most beautiful woman in Iceland. But these
constructions are literary.

7. With proper names (place names, personal names) or words
that border on proper names, the adjectives are weak without any
definite article: *Efsti-Bær* The Uppermost Farm, *Fremsti-Bær*
The Innermost Farm, *Neðsti-Bær* The Lowest Farm; *Eiríkur rauði*
Eric the Red, *Jón lærði* John the Learned, *Stóri-Eiríkur* Big-Eric;
afi gamli Old Grandpa, *stóra systir* Big Sister; *Litli-Rauður* Little-
Red (a horse name), *Stóra-Brúnka* Big-Blackie (a mare's name),
rauða kussa the Red Cow, *svarta kussa* the Black Cow.

118

3. Adjectives used as Nouns.

1. Adjectives denoting number are used as nouns in their masculine singular and plural strong forms. Examples: *Allir vita, að Eiríkur rauði byggði Grænland. Flestir hafa heyrt, að Leifur heppni fann Ameríku; trúa því margir, þó að sumir efi það, en fáir geta neitað því með rökum*: All know that Eric the Red settled Greenland. Most (people) have heard that Leif the Lucky found America; many believe it, though some doubt it, but few (litotes = none) can deny it with good reason. In all those cases English has a parallel usage of all, most, many, some, few. English can also match the singular in *margur er knár, þó hann sé smár* many a man is strong, though he is small, but not in *fár veit, hverju fagna skal* few know what to welcome (proverbial: one never knows what turns out to be good for him).

2. The neuter singular of adjectives (and pronouns) is often used as a noun to denote number or amount, ideas and qualities, also in fixed prepositional phrases: *þar var margt (fátt) manna* there was a great (small) number of people; *þaðan er skammt til Hafnarfjarðar* from there it is a short way to H.; *skömmu síðar* a little while later; *fyrir skömmu* a short while ago; *löngu áður* long before; *skömmu áður* a short while before; *segja satt* tell the truth; *segja rétt frá* tell (the story) correctly; *eiga gott, illt* be well, badly off; *launa illt með góðu* requite evil with good; *gera manni bilt við* scare one; *verði þér (yður) að góðu* 'may this turn to good for you' (a phrase, used by the host, when his guest thanks him for the food; also a greeting used by someone entering a place where people are eating) ; *þetta er að vísu rétt* true enough, this is right; *með réttu eða röngu* right or wrong, rightly or wrongly; *með góðu eða illu* by fair means or foul; *frelsa oss frá illu* deliver us from evil.

3. Adjectives can be given noun function by a preceding *sá, sú, það* (or by the literary *hinn, hin, hið*). This is common in referring to something previously mentioned (in order to avoid repetition of the noun), and in referring to well known persons, animals, or things. In English the same is done with the prop word *one*. Examples: *Tvær kerlingar voru að tala saman. Þá segir sú eldri . . .* two old women were conversing; then the older one says . . . ; *sá dauði* the dead one, *þeir dauðu* (plural) the dead; *hið fagra* the beautiful, Beauty, *hið illa* the evil, Evil. Especially common of animals: *sá grái* the grey one, i. e. the grey horse = *Gráni*; *sá rauði* the red one = *Rauður*; *sá skjótti* the piebald one = *Skjóni*; *sá jarpi* the bay one = *Jarpur*.

Note 1: The strong forms of the adjectives may also be used as nouns: *blindir fá sýn, haltir ganga* the blind get sight, the lame walk; but this usage is more literary, unless the adjective denotes number, cf. 1 above.

Note 2: Unlike English, Icelandic usually does not use adjectives to denote nationalities. *Þeir ensku, dönsku, þýzku,* or *enskir danskir, þýzkir* is old-fashioned and bad form for *Englendingar. Danir, Þjóðverjar* the English, the Danes, the Germans.

4. Comparatives.

1. Comparatives of adjectives always have the weak declension.

2. In comparisons of two, the comparative is always used, never the superlative as sometimes in English: *það voru tveir bræður; Jón var eldri* there were two brothers; John was the older one; *hann var eldri* he was oldest (of two).

3. Comparison can be made in two ways:

> *Jón var eldri og reyndari en ég* (more common), or:
> *Jón var mér eldri og reyndari* (more literary; cf. Dative
> with adjectives, I, **3**, *2*)
> John was older and more experienced than I (was).

Note: English speakers who tend to use me (him, her) in such a comparison instead of I (he, she) should beware, for even colloquial Icelandic follows here the same rule as formal English.

4. Chains of comparisons: *því hærra sem við gengum á fjallinu, því verri varð færðin, en því víðara varð útsýnið* the higher we climbed up the mountain, the worse the going became and the wider the view; *draugagangurinn jókst því meira, sem lengra leið* the haunting increased, as time passed; *eftir því sem hann las lengur, eftir því varð hann vissari í sinni sök* 'according as he read longer, accordingly he became more certain of this matter,' i. e. the longer he read, the more certain he became of the matter.

5. The dative of difference is used with comparatives: *fjörðurinn er miklu (tveim mílum) lengri* the firth is much (two miles) longer. Instead of the dative, an accusative or adverbs may be used: *hann er dálítið hærri en ég* he is a little taller than I; *hann er heldur hærri* he is a little taller; *þessi aðferð er langtum (ennþá) betri* this method is by far (still) the better. *Ég fer, nema veðrið verði því verra* I am going, unless the weather gets very bad indeed (a high degree, so only after *nema* unless, and *ef ekki* if not).

6. The comparison is vague in *heldri menn* better people; *þeir*

120

munu (vera) færri, sem mundu láta hafa sig til þess they would
be few (indeed) who would let themselves be used to do that.

Note: Heldur margir (a) rather many, quite a few = *all-margir*,
(b) too many.

5. Superlatives.

1. Superlatives of adjectives take both the strong and the weak
declension: *þeim var ég verst, er ég unni mest* I was worst to him
I loved the most (cf. **1**, 2; **2**, 6); *yngsta dóttir prests hét Sigrún*
the parson's youngest daughter was called S. (cf. **2**, 6); *allir beztu
menn sjá, að þetta er heimska* all the best men see that this is
foolishness (cf. **2**, 6).

2. A high degree without comparison: *hann er (allra) bezti karl*
he is a very good (fine) fellow; *hann var manna sterkastur* he was
a very strong man (literally: the strongest of men; this expression
is literary).

3. The very highest degree may be indicated by a preceding *allra*
of all, or by the prefixes *al-, lang-* completely, by far: *hann er allra
skemmtilegastur (al-, lang-sk.) þeirra manna, sem ég hef kynnst*
he is by far the most interesting fellow I have ever known (literally:
become acquainted with).

Note 1: To weaken the effect of the superlative, *einna* or *hvað*
perhaps, may be put before it: *veðrið er einna (hvað) skást í dag*
the weather is, perhaps, most tolerable today.

Note 2: *Þegar veðrið var sem verst, var barið að dyrum* when
the weather was at its worst (as bad as possible), there was a knock
at the door; *komdu sem fyrst* come as soon as possible.

IV. PRONOUNS.

1. Personal Pronouns.

1. When used predicatively, the personal pronouns always agree
in case with the (provisory) subject. This is in agreement with
formal English, but against colloquial English usage. Examples:
Hver er þar? Who is there? *Það er ég (hann, hún)* It is I (he,
she), colloquial: It is me (him, her).

Likewise in comparisons after *en* than: *Björn er hærri en ég
(þú, hann, hún)* B. is taller than I (you, he, she), colloquial:
B. is taller than me (you, him, her).

2. The Honorific Plurals. *Vér*, we, is used in royal letters and proclamations; it is also used by editors of newspapers, and by some writers.

Þér, you, is used in elevated prose as a plural of the second person (= *þið*), but it is also common in everyday speech in addressing one person with whom one is not on familiar terms. It thus corresponds to the use of the last name in address in English, while the use of the singular *þú* (thou), you, corresponds to the English use of the given name. Such a distinction between the last name and the given name does not exist in Icelandic. If the last name is a patronymic, *Jón Björnsson* John the son of Björn, it is never used alone in address or reference; usually the first name is so used alone, or both together. If the last name is a family name, *Sigurður Nordal*, either or both names may be used, but the use of the last name is probably more frequent. Using the given name alone carries no implication of familiarity, nor does the use of the family name imply respect or unfamiliarity.

Using *þú* in familiar address is called *að þúast*, to say *þú* to each other; transitive: *að þúa einhvern* to 'thou' somebody. Using *þér* is *að þérast*; *að þéra einhvern*.

The practice *að þérast* is very common in Icelandic towns; in the country it is less common, and among Icelandic Americans the practice *að þúast* is general—in imitation of the general English *you*.

The honorific *þér* (of one person) takes the verb in the plural, but the predicative sometimes in the plural, sometimes in the singular: *komið þér sælir* (plural) how do you do (literally: come you blessed!); *ég hélt, að þér væruð farinn* I thought you had gone (*farinn* singular, but *farnir* plural may also be used).

3. Idiomatic are the abbreviated pronominal expressions:

við Gunnar we, Gunnar and I;
þið Gunnar you, you (one or more) and Gunnar;
þeir Gunnar (a) they, somebody just mentioned and Gunnar, or (b) they, Gunnar and his companions.

Likewise: *við bræður(nir)* we, the brothers; *þau hjónin* they, the married couple; *þau systkinin* they, the brother and the sister; *þau Gunnar* they, Gunnar and a woman.

4. (a) *Hann*, he, and *hún*, she, are sometimes used in a way that reminds one of the definite article—but chiefly with proper names: *þar kemur hann Jón ríðandi á honum Grána* there comes (our) John riding on (our) Gráni; *hún Katla er farin að gjósa* Katla (the well known volcano) has begun erupting; *kröftugur er*

hann Satan mighty is the Devil. Also with generic names that are so common or familiar as to border on proper names: *hún kussa* the cow, *hann boli* the bull. In all cases the usage expresses familiarity.

(b) *Hann*, he, is used as an indefinite subject in statements about the weather (alternating with *það* it): *hann (það) snjóar* it is snowing; *ljótur er hann núna* what ugly weather! (literally: ugly is it now); *hann (það) er að ganga í byl* it is turning into a blizzard; *hann er að hvessa* the storm is rising.

5. (a) *Það*, it, is much more widely used as an indefinite subject than *hann* (it can also be used for *hann* in most of the above mentioned cases): *það dimmir* it is getting dark; *það hlýnar seint* it warms up slowly.

(b) *Það* is also used as a preparatory or provisory subject (object) referring to a following infinitive or an *að*-clause: *það er bezt að hætta* it is best to cease; *það er réttast, að þér farið heim* it is best (literally: most right) that you go home; *ég geri mér það* (object) *að reglu að lesa Njálu einu sinni á ári* I make it a rule to read *Njála* once a year.

(c) *Það* is, finally, used as a preparatory subject, where English uses *there* standing for a following noun: *það var enginn maður þar* there was nobody (no man) there (also: *þar var enginn maður*); *það var einu sinni karl og kerling* there was once upon a time an old man and an old woman (also: *einu sinni var karl og kerling*); *það er víða pottur brotinn* (proverbial) in most places there is something amiss (literally: a broken pot or pan) (also: *víða er pottur brotinn*).

This last use of *það* for 'there,' though colloquially common, is avoided in the written language. Note, that there must be some adverbial modification of the verb in such sentences: *það var maður*, there was a man, alone would seem incomplete in Icelandic.

6. The pronominal adjective *sjálfur, sjálf, sjálft*, self, is used for emphasis with personal pronouns, agreeing with them in gender, case, and number: *ég sjálf(ur)* I myself, *þú sjálf(ur)* you yourself, *þér sjálfir (-ar)* you yourself (polite), *hann sjálfur* he himself, *hún sjálf* she herself, *það sjálft* it itself; accusative: *mig sjálfan* me myself, dative: *mér sjálfum* (to) me myself, etc. In reflexive constructions *sjálfur* usually agrees with the object (the reflexive pronoun) rather than with the subject: *hann hengdi (sjálfan) sig* he hanged himself; *hver er sjálfum sér næstur* each is nearest to himself, i. e. everybody for himself.

123

2. Reflexive and Possessive Pronouns.

1. The reflexive pronoun *sig, sér, sín* refers to the third person, while the oblique cases of *ég* and *þú, við* and *þið, vér* and *þér* are used as reflexive pronouns referring to these persons. Examples: *ég meiddi mig* I hurt myself, *þú meiddir þig* you hurt yourself; *hann* (*hún, það*) *meiddi sig* he (she, it) hurt himself (herself, itself); *við meiddum okkur* we hurt ourselves, *þið meidduð ykkur* you hurt yourselves, *þeir* (*þær, þau*) *meiddu sig* they hurt themselves; (*vér meiddum oss* we hurt ourselves), *þér meidduð yður* you hurt yourself. With dative: *ég greiddi mér* I combed myself, etc. With genitive: *ég naut mín ekki* I did not enjoy my faculties, i. e. I was not myself, etc.

2. The reflexive pronouns rarely have a reciprocal sense: *þeir réðu það með sér* they decided (that) between them (among themselves); *þeir töluðu sín á milli* they spoke to each other (among themselves).

3. The possessive-reflexive pronoun *sinn, sín, sitt* always refers to the subject of the sentence: *þegar gestur kemur á bæ, taka drengirnir hestinn hans; sjaldan er hann sjálfur látinn hirða um hestinn sinn* when a guest arrives at a farmstead, the boys take his horse; seldom is he allowed to take care of his horse himself.

4. *Sinn, sín, sitt* (his) combines with *hver, hvor, hvað* (each) to give a distributive sense: *rétt er að gjalda hverjum sitt* it is right to pay each his due; *Björn og Jón tóku sinn hestinn hvor* Björn and John took each a horse (*tóku hvor sinn hest* would mean: took each his own horse); *það er sitt hvað gæfa eða gjörvuleikur* good luck and talent are different things (proverbial, i. e. a gifted man is not always the luckiest one).

5. In dependent clauses a reflexive (-possessive) pronoun referring to the subject of the principal clause is used, if the clause is in the subjunctive mood. If it is in the indicative, the genitive of the third person pronoun is used (as in English):

hana dreymdi, að bróðir sinn kæmi til sín (subjunctive),
hana dreymdi, að bróðir hennar kom til hennar (indicative) she dreamt that her brother came to her.

But there is vacillation in this point.

6. In scolding, the possessive pronoun answers to the personal pronoun in English: *þrjóturinn þinn* you rascal; *kjáninn þinn* you (little) fool.

124

7. In Icelandic the formal difference, found in English my/mine, our/ours, your/yours, her/hers, their/theirs, is lacking. *Er þetta kápan þín? Nei, það er mín (kápa)* Is this your coat? No, it is mine. *Þetta eru víst mín gleraugu, en ekki yðar* these are probably my glasses, not yours. In this respect the Icelandic pronouns resemble the English *his*, which does not change: his horse; the horse is his. But the noun function (*hesturinn er minn*) is rare in Icelandic.

Note: As a rule a possessive pronoun, like a genitive, is placed after the noun it modifies. When stressed, it may be put before it.

3. Demonstrative Pronouns.

1. The weakest of the demonstrative pronouns is really the definite article (q. v. II above). As in English it has two functions, that of determining in itself, and that of determining in connection with a following word: *þetta er maðurinn* this is the man, and: *maðurinn, sem ég sá í gær* the man I saw yesterday. In the latter case its place is sometimes taken by the demonstrative *sá, sú, það*: *sá maður, sem fann púðrið, var ekki óparfur mannkyninu* the man who invented gunpowder was not quite useless (litotes) to mankind. Before adjectives the free definite article is also quite often replaced by *sá, sú, það*: *sá gamli* the old one; *þeir gömlu* the old ones, the ancients. This use of *sá* for *hinn* is more colloquial than literary. The possessive and demonstrative pronouns are limiting adjectives.

2. *Sá, sú, það* are used both as substantives and as adjectives: *sá er góður!* he is a good one! (sarcastically); *sá góði maður* that good man. It may refer to something preceding it (though the third person pronoun is principally so used), or to something following: *maður gekk niður Laugaveg; sá (hann) var ekki lítill vexti* a man walked down Laugavegur; he was not small of stature (litotes); *á þeim degi* (previously mentioned) *urðu Heródes og Pílatus vinir* on that day Herod and Pilate became friends; *þeir verða að missa, sem eiga* those who own (something) must take losses (proverbial); *sá, sem finnur úrið, er beðinn að skila því* he who finds the watch is asked to return it.

Sá, sú, það sometimes means: such a (one): *ég var sá klaufi, að láta þetta heyrast á mér* I was such a fool as to give a hint about this; *því einu mun hann lofa, sem hann mun efna* he will promise such things only as he will carry out.

En sá (sú, það) is used in exclamations: *en sá hiti!* what heat! *en það veður!* what weather! It is also used in exclamations of

125

wonder and admiration with adjectives: *sá gamli!* (look at) the old one! (i. e. he could do this in spite of his age).

Það (and the plural *þeir þær, þau*) is also used as a third person pronoun (q. v. **1,** 5 above). The border-line between the two usages is not always clear, but by and large the personal pronoun corresponds to the English *it,* the demonstrative to the English *that.* Moreover, the personal pronoun is always a noun, while the demonstrative may be an adjective. Examples of the demonstrative: *það er það sama* it is (all) the same (cf. *sá sami* the same one) ; *afdrif hans urðu þau, að hann drukknaði* what in the end became of him was that he drowned.—*Það* to such an extent (= *svo* so) : *áin var það mikil, að hún var ekki reið* the river was that much (to such an extent) swollen that it could not be forded.—*Það* by that much (= *þeim mun, því*) : *Árni var það vitrari en Björn, að hann gat þagað* Á. was that much wiser than B. that he could keep silent.— *Og það* and that, moreover, even: *hann las á bók níræður, og það gleraugnalaust* he could read a book (literally : he read on a book) at ninety, and that without glasses. *Því fremur* all the more (so) ; *því (þess) meir* the more.—*Rétt er það* that is right, oh yes ; *einmitt það* just so, is that so? *það er nú það* that is that.

Því (dat. of *það*) is colloquially often used for the interrogative adverb *hví* why. Literal: *hví slær þú mig?* why do you strike me? Colloquial: *því læturðu svona?* why do you carry on like that?

3. *Þessi, þessi, þetta* this, that. It can be used as a noun or as an adjective: *þetta er vitleysa* this is foolishness; *þetta skip er íslenzkt* this boat is Icelandic. It may also refer to something that came before, or something following: *nú fréttist lát biskups, og þóttu þetta ill tíðindi* now the news of the bishop's death is heard, and people consider that very bad tidings; *þessir menn, sem áttu að stjórna landinu, voru bráðókunnugir og einskis nýtir* these men who were to govern the land were grossly unfamiliar with conditions and of no use.—*Þessi hérna* this . . . here, *þessi þarna* this . . . there.—*Þetta gengur* this is the common thing, that is the way it goes; *hann baxar þetta í áttina* he tries his best to move ('it') in the right direction.—*Heyrðuð þér ólætin á götunum í gær? Þessi líka litlu læti (eða hitt þó heldur)* Did you hear the racket on the streets yesterday? Quite a little disturbance (or rather the opposite) (litotes).

4. *Hinn, hin, hitt* that one, that, the other one. Contrasting with *þessi: þér fáið ekki þessa bók, heldur hina* you do not get this book, but the other one; *það er víst satt, að bílslys hafi orðið, en hitt er lygi, að nokkrir hafi meiðzt* it is probably true that there was an automobile accident, but it is a lie to say that anybody was hurt.—*Hinir og þessir* some, *hitt og þetta* this and that; *mér líkaði þar vel, heldur en hitt* I liked it there, rather than not; *það hefði verið vitlegt, eða hitt þó heldur* that would have been wise, or rather the opposite; *ekki á morgun, heldur hinn daginn* not tomorrow but the day after tomorrow; *í hitt eð fyrra* two years ago.

5. The pronoun of identity: *samur, söm, samt* is more commonly used in its weak form: *sami maður* the same man, but: *hann varð aldrei samur eftir slysið* he never was the same after the accident. *Gleðileg jól!* *Ég óska þér þess (hins) sama* Merry Christmas! I wish you the same. *Sama er mér* it is all the same to me. *Samt* adverbially: nevertheless, however; *þakk fyrir samt* thank you anyway. *Samur . . . og* same . . . as.

The pronouns of similarity: *slíkur* and *þvílíkur* such. *Slíkur maður hafði aldrei sést þar fyrri* such a man had never appeared there before; *sem slíkur* as such; *þvílíkur fjöldi* such a multitude, what a multitude; *slíkt og þvílíkt* what things! the idea of it!

4. Relative Pronouns.

Malkus, sem missti eyrað M. who lost his ear; *þjófurinn, sem var dæmdur* the thief who was condemned; *húsið, sem við bjuggum í* the house we lived in; *eruð þér maðurinn, sem átti húsið, er selt var á uppboðinu?* are you the man who owned the house that was sold at the auction? (better: . . . whose house was sold . . .) ; *sá, sem ekki vill vinna . . .* he who does not want to work . . . ; *þeir vildu ekki láta undan, sem ég get ekki láð þeim* they would not give in, which I cannot blame them for; *maðurinn, sem ég sá* the man I saw; note that in Icelandic the relative is not dropped in such cases, though there are a few exceptions: *á sunnudaginn(sem)kemur* next Sunday; *á laugardaginn (sem) var* last Saturday, but: *vikuna, sem leið* last week.

Þar sem where, *hvar sem* wherever, *hvert sem* wherever, *hvaðan sem* wherever . . . from.

In the literary language *er* is used everywhere by the side of *sem*. *Að* is old-fashioned and very rare, *eð* is used only in the conjunction *þar eð* since, but it is fairly common.

Not to be confused with *sem* the relative is the conjunction *sem* as, like: *rauður sem blóð* red as blood; *ríða sem skjótast* ride as quickly as possible.

5. Interrogative Pronouns.

1. *Hver, hver, hvert, hvað* who, which, what. *Hver er hann?*

who is he? *Hver er þar?* who is there? *Hann spurði, hver þar
væri* he asked who was there. *Hver okkar á að gefa?* which of us is
to deal (the cards)? *Hvert í logandi!* what in hell!

Hvað segið þér? what do you say? *Hvað er að frétta?* what is
the news? *Nú er bezt að vita, hvað hann segir* it is best to find
out what he says. *Hvað?* what, excuse me, what did you say? (also
Ha? or *A?*). *Við skulum sjá, hvað kaffinu líður* let us see what
progress the coffee has made (how nearly the coffee is done). *Hvað
um það* even so, in spite of everything; *hvað er að tarna!* what is
this, is that so! *Hvað* is also used adverbially instead of *hve* how:
en hvað hún er falleg! how beautiful she is!

2. *Hvaða* what kind of (=*hversslags*). *Hvaða maður er þetta?*
what kind of a man is this? who is this? *Hvaða vitleysa!* what
foolishness! *Enginn veit, hvaða lög verða samþykkt á næsta þingi*
nobody knows what laws will be enacted by the next Congress.

3. *Hvor, hvor, hvort* which of two. *Hvorn eiðinn á ég að rjúfa?*
which of the two oaths shall 1 break? *Hvor þeirra var það?* which
of them (the two) was it? *Hvort á ég að gera?* which (of the two
things) shall I do? *Ég vissi ekki, hvort ég átti að gera, vera heima,
eða fara út* I did not know which (of the two things) I should do,
stay at home or go out.

4. *Hvílíkur, hvílík, hvílíkt* what kind of, what. It is mostly used
in subordinate interrogative clauses: *fáir vissu, hvílíkt góðmenni
Jón var* few knew how kindhearted a man John was. Also in
exclamations (literary): *hvílík fegurð!* what beauty! *hvílík bölvuð
læti!* what infernal racket!

Note: The usual colloquial expression for the last example is:
þvílík bölvuð læti! Similarly the place of the interrogative adverb
hví, why, is usually taken by the demonstrative *því: því lætur þú
svona?* why do you act like that?

6. Indefinite Pronouns.

1. Indefinite pronouns may be classified in different ways.
There are pronouns of indefinite unity (*einn*), of difference (*annar*),
of discretion (*einn, nokkur*), of unspecified quantity (*einhver,
sumir*), and of totality (inclusive: *allir, báðir,* individualizing:
hver, hvor, negative: *enginn, hvorugur*). This classification will
not be used here, but the only noun among the lot will be discussed
first: *maður,* while the (limiting) adjectives (sometimes with noun
function) will follow in alphabetical order.

Maður m. 4 one; *maður má ekki reykja* one must not smoke;

manni verður kalt one gets cold; *maður sér nú til* we will see; *maður heyrir* one hears; *menn segja* people say.

2. *Allur, öll, allt* singular: all, whole, (neuter) everything; plural: all. *Allur bærinn* the whole town; *vinna allan daginn* work all the day (the whole day); *allt eða ekkert* all or nothing; *allt er, þegar þrennt er* three times makes the thing complete (proverbial). Complete(ly): *allur annar maður* a completely different man; *allur á bak og burt* completely vanished; *hann er ekki allur, þar sem hann er séður* (proverbial) he is not all where you see him, i. e. you never know where you have him. Plural: *allir vilja hann heldur* all prefer him (everybody prefers him); *þarna eru þeir allir* there they are, all of them; *hestarnir eru allir* the number of horses is complete, i. e. none is lacking.

Allur saman, öll saman, allt saman all together, complete(ly); in the nominative feminine singular and in the nominative-accusative neuter plural these words often become *öllsömun* or even *öllsömul*. *Komið þið öllsömul blessuð og sæl!* how are you, all of you (greeting to a familiar company of men and women); *hún var öllsömul klædd í hvítt* she was all completely dressed in white.

In prepositional phrases: *með öllu* completely; *með öllu móti* in every way; *umfram allt* above all; *þrátt fyrir allt* in spite of everything.

Neuter *allt*: *allt* all the way, *ég lenti allt suður í Fjörð* I got all the way south to Fjörður; so with adverbs or prepositions of direction: *allt frá sjó upp að fjöllum*, or: *frá sjó allt upp að fjöllum* from the sea all the way up to the mountains; also of time: *allt til jóla* all the time up to Christmas; *allt að því* almost; *allt til þess að (er)* until. Genitive: *alls* altogether, *þeir voru alls fimmtíu* they were fifty in all; *alls ekki* not at all; *alls ekkert* nothing at all. Dative: *öllu* (with comparatives) somewhat; *öllu styttri* a bit shorter; *öllu heldur* rather.

Plural: *alla vega* in various ways; *alla vega litur* varicolored; genitive *allra* of all; with superlatives: *allra-bezt* best of all; *allra-versta veður* nasty weather; *allra-bezti maður* a fine man. Often in one word: *allavega, allrabeztur*.

3. *Annar, önnur, annað* other, another, someone else, a different one. *Þar kemur annar og enn annar* there another one comes, and yet another; *enginn er annars bróðir í leik* (proverbial) nobody is another's brother in play, i. e. each for himself and the devil take the hindmost; *það var eitthvað annað* that was something else; *hann var allur annar maður eftir uppskurðinn* he was quite a different man after the operation; *það var enginn (ekki neinn)*

annar en hann it was no one else than he; *hesturinn var haltur á
öðrum afturfæti* the horse was lame in one hind foot; *lúðan er
svört á annað borðið, hvít á hitt* the flounder is black on one side,
white on the other; *hann og sumir (einhverjir) aðrir* he and some
others; *hitt og annað (eitt og annað)* this and that; *hver sagði
öðrum* each told the other; *öðru hvoru* every now and then; *í annað
sinn (öðru sinni)* for the second time, another time, some other
time; *einn af öðrum* one after another; *aðrir (sumir) segja . . .
aðrir segja* some say . . . others say; *annars* otherwise, by the way.

4. *Annarhver, -hver, -hvert* (also separately: *annar hver*) every
other (of many): *annarhver maður féll* every other man fell.

5. *Annarhvor, -hvor, -hvort* (also: *annar hvor*) one of two.
Annaðhvort . . . eða either . . . or: *ég man ekki hvað hann heitir,
en það var annaðhvort Jóhann eða Jóhannes* I do not remember
his name, but it was either J. or J. *Það væri nú annaðhvort!* (*þó
ég gerði þetta*) why, of course (I will do this).

6. *Annartveggja* (also *annar tveggja*) one of two, either (literary).

7. *Báðir, báðar, bæði* both. *Báðir drengirnir* both the boys;
hjónin eru bæði gestrisin the husband and wife are both hospitable.
Bæði . . . og both . . . and: *hesturinn var bæði fljótur og fótviss*
the horse was both swift and surefooted. *Báðu megin (báðumegin)
við ána* on both sides of the river (= *beggja vegna við ána*). Also
báðum megin.

8. *Enginn, engin, ekkert* no one, nobody, none, no, nothing.
Hér er enginn (maður) here is nobody (no one, no man); *þetta
máttu fyrir engan mun gera* you must not do this on any account;
þeir áttu sér einskis ills von they were completely unsuspecting of
evil; *enginn veit, hvað átt hefur, fyrr en misst hefur* no one knows
what he has had before he has lost it (proverbial); *svara engu*
answer nothing; *segja ekkert* say nothing; *þetta er engu að síður
satt* this is, none the less, true; *hann er engu síður fjármálamaður
en prestur* he is no less a financier than a clergyman; *það er ekkert
síður yður að kenna en honum* it is just as much your fault as his.

9. *Einhver, -hver, -hvert, -hvað* somebody, some one, some. It
is used mostly in affirmative sentences: *einhver kemur* somebody is
coming; rarely in questions: *kemur einhver?* (usually *kemur
nokkur?*) is anybody coming? but never in negative sentences
(where *ekki neinn, ekki nokkur* or *enginn* is used). *Einhvern
daginn langar mig til að heimsækja þig (yður)* one of these days
I would like to visit you; *hittuð þér nokkra ókunnuga hjá presti?*

130

Já, þar var eitthvað af fólki did you meet any guests (literally: non-acquaintances) at the parson's? Yes, there were some people; *þar var eitthvað hundrað manns* there were some (about) one hundred people; *það var eitthvað annað* that was something else (quite a different story).

10. *Einn, ein, eitt* one. *Einn* may be used after a negation: *ekki einn* not one (more emphatic than the common *ekki neinn* not any); in partitive phrases: *einn þeirra* one of them; *einn vinur (vina) hans* one of his friends; *þetta er ein sú versta hríð, sem komið hefur í vetur* this is one of the very worst blizzards that has come this winter; *einn góðan veðurdag* one fine day. *Einna* (with superlatives) perhaps: *veðrið er einna bezt undir kvöldið* the weather is perhaps best towards evening. *Eitt og annað* (= *hitt og annað*) this and that. *Maður einn* (= *maður nokkur*) a certain man (note the word order!), but *maðurinn einn* (*af öllum dýrum jarðarinnar*) *getur gengið uppréttur* man alone (of all the animals of the earth) can walk erect.

11. *Hver, hver, hvert, hvað* whoever, whatever, each, every, any. *Hver* is used as an antecedent for relative pronouns: *hver, sem flýr, er ragur* whoever flees is cowardly; *hvað, sem á gengur* whatever is going on. *Hver* each, every: *gefa hverjum sitt* give every one his due; *hver maður á rétt á því* every man has a right to it (thereto); *skattur á hvert nef* a tax on each nose, i. e. per head. *Hann fer nú að koma hvað af hverju* he will be coming any time now; *það var farið með hann eins og hvern annan glæpamann* he was treated like any other criminal; *annar hver maður féll* every other man fell; reciprocal: *þeir réðust hver á annan* they attacked each other.

12. *Hvor, hvor, hvort* whichever, each of two, either. *Það mátti einu gilda, hvor var* it was all the same whichever of the two it was; *mér er sama, hvort heldur er* it is all the same to me which of the two things happens; *ég ætlaði ofan hvort sem var, sagði kerlingin; hún datt ofan og hálsbrotnaði* I was going downstairs anyway, said the old woman; she fell down and broke her neck; *hestarnir fengu sína tugguna hvor* the horses got each (of the two) a wisp of hay; *þeir gengu hvor á eftir öðrum* they walked one behind the other; *þeir börðu hvor annan* (reciprocal) they beat each other; *þeim sýndist sinn veg hvorum* they (two) differed in their opinions (each looked at it in his own way).

13. *Hvorugur, hvorug, hvorugt* neither (of two): *hvorugt skipið kom með póst* neither boat brought mail; *hvorugt okkar* neither

of us (man and woman); *við erum með hvorugum* we are for neither of the parties.

14. *Hvortveggja, hvor-, hvort-* either of two, both. *Hvortveggja maðurinn* either man, both men; *hvernig líkaði þér við þá? Og svona hvorttveggja og bæði* how did you like them? Oh, only so so. *Það er hvorttveggja, að stúlkan er lagleg, enda veit hún af því* the girl is not only good-looking, but she knows it, too.

15. *Neinn, nein, neitt* (not) anybody, (not) any one, (not) anything. *Neinn* is used only after negations: *hann er ekki neinn* (= *enginn*) *lærdómsmaður* he is not any (= no) scholar; *það var ekki neitt* it was not anything, it was nothing; *það er ekki til neins* it is (of) no use. *Af hverju lætur þú svona? Og ekki af neinu* why do you carry on like that? Oh, for no (special) reason.

16. *Nokkur, nokkur, nokkurt, nokkuð* any one, anybody, anything. *Nokkur* in the singular is used in questions and negative sentences: *er nokkur hér?* is there anybody here? *ekki nokkur sál* not a soul; the plural *nokkrir* has also the meaning some, several: *nokkrir menn* some men; *nokkrir segja* some say; the neuter singular *nokkuð* is a noun, meaning a certain amount of: *er nokkuð að frétta* (= *í fréttum*)? is there any news? *hún keypti nokkuð af kaffi og sykri* she bought some coffee and sugar; *nokkru fyrir jól* a short time before Christmas; *þó nokkuð* quite a bit; the neuter *nokkurt* is an adjective: *er nokkurt lag á þessu?* is this in any shape, i. e. is there any rime and reason in this? Finally: *maður nokkur* (note the word order!) *ferðaðist milli Jerúsalem og Jeríkó* a certain man travelled between J. and J. (more common than *maður einn*, but both are literary).

17. *Sérhver, -hver, -hvert, -hvað* whoever, whatever, every, each, any; a literary counterpart to the common *hver* (q. v.).

18. *Sumur, sum, sumt* some. With the exception of the neuter, this pronoun is hardly used in the singular, except in archaisms or fixed phrases (*sums staðar, sumsstaðar* some place). *Sumt* means something, some things: *sumt var gott, sumt var afleitt* some things were fine, some were bad indeed; *að sumu leyti* in some respects; *það er allt og sumt* that is all; the plural: *sumir segja að Japanar séu skræfur, aðrir að þeir séu ósigrandi* some say that the Japanese are cowards, others that they are invincible. *Sumir* certain people (in veiled references to well known persons).

132

V. CONCORD.

1. Concord in Case.

Nouns used as modifiers, predicatives or appositives of other nouns, must agree in case, and often agree in number (sometimes in gender) with the nouns they modify or describe. *Kristján póstur* K. the mailman; *Kristján var póstur* K. was a mailman; *hafið þér heyrt af Kristjáni pósti?* have you heard of K. the mailman? *séra Jón Helgason, prestur að Mosfelli* the Rev. J. H., parson of Mosfell; *hann kenndi mér, stráknum, að lesa* he taught me, the boy (when I was a boy), to read; *hún er kennari* (or *kennslukona*) *við barnaskólann* she is a teacher at the primary school.

Note: The same is true of any other words (pronouns, adjectives) used as nouns.

2. Concord in Case, Gender, and Number.

1. Adjectives (and pronouns used as adjectives) must agree in case, gender, and number with the nouns (pronouns) they modify (as attributives, predicatives, or appositives). Attributives: *góður maður* a good man; plural: *góðir menn* good men; *góð kona* a good woman; genitive plural: *góðra kvenna* of good women; *gott barn* a good child; dative plural: *góðum börnum* to good children. Predicative: *skipið er gott* the ship is good; appositive: *hann kenndi mér, ungum, að skrifa* he taught me, when I was young, to write.

2. When an adjective (or a pronoun) modifies or refers to two or more nouns of different genders, it is put in the neuter. This is possible only if the adjective is predicative or appositive, not if it is attributive: *ég sá svarta á* (f.) *og svart lamb* (n.) I saw a black ewe, and a black lamb, or: *ég sá á og lamb, bæði svört* I saw a ewe and a lamb, both black (or: *þau voru bæði svört* they were both black). However, it is sometimes possible to let the adjective modify one of the two things, though modification of both is really meant: *kona mín og börn* my wife and children. And two (or more) nouns of the same gender can, of course, be modified by one adjective: *á Þingvöllum eru margar gjár og sprungur* at Þingvellir there are many chasms and clefts.

3. Concord in Number, Nouns.

1. Nouns. There are some discrepancies between Icelandic and English in the use of the plural and the singular. Thus in Icelandic it is *átjánda og nítjánda öldin* (singular), in English: the eighteenth

and nineteenth centuries; *þér björguðuð lífi* (singular) *okkar* you saved our lives *tveir menn með hatta á höfði* (singular) *gengu fram hjá* two men with hats on their heads passed by.

2. In Icelandic plural, not singular as often in English, is used regularly after numerals: *tvær tylftir* two dozen; *tvö hundruð sinnum* two hundred times; *fimm feta og sex þumlunga hár* five foot six.

4. Concord in Number, Verbs.

1. As in English, the chief rule in Icelandic is that the verb agrees with the subject in number and person: *hann fór heim* he went home; *þeir fóru heim* they went home; *Björn og Árni fóru heim* B. and Á. went home; *ég og þú (við) fórum* I and you (we) went; *þú og hann (þið) fóruð* you and he (you) went.

2. In English several nouns, though singular in form, take (or may take) the plural of the verb (because they are collectives). Thus: the family, government, nation, people were.... In Icelandic they take a singular verb: *fjölskyldan, stjórnin, þjóðin, fólkið var*. ... The clergy *klerkarnir* is a plural and takes a plural verb: *klerkarnir voru*....

3. After *það, þetta, hitt, slíkt, hvað, annað* the copula (*vera, verða*) often is in the plural, if the predicative is in the plural: *það eru engin undur* it is no wonder; *þetta eru ljótu ólætin* this is a terrible racket (what a racket!); *þetta er satt, en hitt eru ýkjur* this is true, but the other is an exaggeration; *hvað eru Röntgengeislar?* what are X-ray? *það verða engin vandræði* there will be no difficulties.

4. The verb *þykja* is usually used in the third person singular, although the subject is in the plural, when it means: seem, think, and takes the logical subject in the dative: *mér þótti þið fljótir* I thought (that) you were quick, it seemed to me that you were quick; *okkur þótti þeir latir* we thought they were lazy, we thought them lazy. But: *þeir þykja latir* they are considered lazy.

5. After the honorific plural *þér,* you, the number in an adjective vacillates. Always: *komið þér sælir* (m.) *sælar* (f.), *verið þér sælir (sælar)* (plural) how are you, good-bye; but: *eruð þér búinn* (singular, or: *búnir* plural)? are you ready? *eruð þér reiður* (masculine singular) *við mig?* are you angry with me?

6. With many subjects, the verb may be attracted to the nearest one and appear in the singular. This is more likely to happen, when

the verb precedes the subjects than if it follows them: *sat* (singular) *konungur og drottning í hásœti og drukku* (plural) *saman um kvöldið* the king and queen sat in the high seat and drank together during the evening.

VI. VERBS.

1. The Compound Tenses of the Verbs in all Moods and Voices.

1. Simple and Compound Tenses.

1. Of the tenses, only present and preterite are distinguished by specific simple forms (see the Inflexions VII, 1, *1*). All other tenses of the verb, as well as the complete passive voice, are formed by auxiliary verbs combined with certain forms (past participles, infinitive) of the verb that is being conjugated.

2. The chief auxiliary verbs are *hafa* have, *munu* shall/will, *vera* be, and *verða* be (in the future), become. The first two are used to form the compound tenses of the past and the future. *Vera* is used to form a past conjugation of intransitive verbs of motion and the passive of all transitive verbs.

The conjugation of *hafa* and *vera* is given below. *Munu* is a preterite present verb, whose inflexion is given in the Irregular Verbs. *Verða, varð, urðum, orðinn* is a strong verb of class three, it is conjugated like *bresta* (see paradigms in Inflexions VII, 4, *9*) with the exception that it loses its *v* before the vowels *u, y,* and *o* in the preterite plural indicative, preterite subjunctive, and the past participle.

2. Conjugation of the Auxiliaries hafa and vera.

Indicative	Subjunctive	Indicative	Subjunctive
Present........			
Sg. 1 *hef, hefi* I have	*hafi* I have	*er, em* I am	*sé* I be
2 *hefur, hefir*	*hafir* have	*ert* (art) are	*sért* you be
3 *hefur, hefir*	*hafi* have	*er* he is	*sé* he be
Pl. 1 *höfum* have	*höfum* have	*erum* we are	*séum* we be
2 *hafið* have	*hafið* have	*eruð* you are	*séuð* you be
3 *hafa* have	*hafi* have	*eru* they are	*sé(u)* they be
Preterite........			
Sg. 1 *hafði* I had	*hefði* I had	*var* I was	*væri* I were
2 *hafðir*	*hefðir*	*varst* were	*værir*
3 *hafði*	*hefði*	*var* was	*væri*
Pl. 1 *höfðum*	*hefðum*	*vorum* were	*værum*
2 *höfðuð*	*hefðuð*	*voruð* were	*væruð*
3 *höfðu*	*hefðu*	*voru* were	*væru*

135

Perfect . . . .

Sg. 1 *hef haft*	*hafi haft*	*hef verið*	*hafi verið*
I have had	I have had	I have been	I have been, etc.

Past Perfect . . . .

Sg. 1 *hafði haft*	*hefði haft*	*hafði verið*	*hefði verið*
I had had	I had had	I had been	I had been, etc.

Future . . . .

Sg. 1 *mun hafa*	*muni hafa*	*mun vera*	*muni vera*
I shall/may have	I shall/may have	I shall/may be	I shall/may be, etc.

Perfect Future (Futurum exactum) . . . .

Sg. 1 *mun hafa haft*	*muni hafa haft*	*mun hafa verið*	*muni hafa verið*
I may/shall have had	I may/shall have had	I may/shall have been	I may/shall have been

Past Future (First Conditional) . . . .

Sg. 1	*mundi (y) hafa*	*mundi (y) vera*
	I would have	I would be, etc.

Past Perfect Future (Second Conditional) . . . .

Sg. 1	*mundi (y) hafa haft*	*mundi (y) hafa verið*
	I would have had	I would have been, etc.

Note: Of *hafa* only the present and the preterite (indicative and subjunctive) as well as the infinitive *hafa* are used as auxiliaries. The compound tenses above, the imperative (*hafðu* have, *hafið þið* have), the middle voice (*hafast* have oneself), and the passive (*vera hafður* be had) are not so used.

But the complete conjugation of *vera*, simple and compound tenses alike, is used as an auxiliary in one way or another. The only exception is the subjunctive *veri*, listed above under the conjugation of the verb *vera* to be (Inflexions VII, 5, 3).

3. *Synopsis of Voices, Tenses, and Moods (Transitive Verbs).*

	Active	Middle	Passive
Present			
Indicative	*ég ber* I beat	*ég berst* I fight	*ég er barinn* I am beaten
Subjunctive	*ég berji*	*ég berjist*	*ég sé barinn*
Infinitive	*berja*	*berjast*	*vera barinn*
Preterite			
Indicative	*ég barði* I beat	*ég barðist* I fought	*ég var barinn* I was beaten
Subjunctive	*ég berði*	*ég berðist*	*ég væri barinn* I were beaten
Perfect			
Indicative	*ég hef barið* I have beaten	*ég hef barizt* I have fought	*ég hef verið barinn* I have been beaten

136

| Subjunctive | *ég hafi barið* | *ég hafi barizt* | *ég hafi verið barinn* |
| Infinitive | *hafa barið* | *hafa barizt* | *hafa verið barinn* |

Past Perfect...

Indicative	*ég hafði barið*	*ég hafði barizt*	*ég hafði verið barinn*
	I had beaten	I had fought	I had been beaten
Subjunctive	*ég hefði barið*	*ég hefði barizt*	*ég hefði verið barinn*

Future ....

Indicative	*ég mun berja*	*ég mun berjast*	*ég mun vera (verða) barinn*
	I shall (may) beat	I shall (may) fight	I shall (may) be beaten
Subjunctive	*ég muni berja*	*ég muni berjast*	*ég muni vera (verða) barinn*
Infinitive	*munu berja*	*munu berjast*	*munu vera (verða) barinn*

Perfect Future (Futurum exactum).................................

Indicative	*ég mun hafa barið* I (shall) may have beaten	*ég mun hafa barizt* I (shall) may have fought	*ég mun hafa verið barinn* I (shall) may have been beaten
Subjunctive	*ég muni hafa barið*	*ég muni hafa barizt*	*ég muni hafa verið barinn*
Infinitive	*munu hafa barið*	*munu hafa barizt* ‹	*munu hafa verið barinn*

Past Future (First Conditional)..................................

| Subjunctive | *ég mundi (y) berja* I would beat | *ég mundi (y) berjast* I would fight | *ég mundi (y) vera (yrði) barinn* I would be beaten |
| Infinitive | *mundu berja* | *mundu berjast* | *mundu vera (verða) barinn* |

Past Perfect Future (Second Conditional)..........................

| Subjunctive | *ég mundi (y) hafa barið* I would have beaten | *ég mundi (y) hafa barizt* I would have fought | *ég mundi (y) hafa verið barinn* I would have been beaten |
| Infinitive | *mundu hafa barið barið* | *mundu hafa barizt* | *mundu hafa verið barinn* |

2. The Indicative and the Meaning of its Tenses.

1. *The Present.*

The present tense has at least three meanings:

(a) present time: *hann sefur* he sleeps, he is sleeping;

(b) future time: *ég sé þig (yður) á morgun* I (shall) see you tomorrow.

(c) past time (historical or dramatic present): *báturinn kom inn fyrir oddann á hraðri siglingu, en allt í einu hvolfir honum* the boat rounded the cape in swift sailing, but all of a sudden it capsizes.

137

These three meanings of the present are also found in English, but (b) and especially (c) are more used in Icelandic, spoken and written, than in English. (c) is common in animated narrative. The present is also used to denote the customary and the timeless states or actions: *maður er manns gaman* (proverbial) man is pleased (consoled) by man; *stutt er líf, en listin löng* ars longa, vita brevis.

Note 1: *Ég sé í blöðunum* I see in the papers (= I have seen); *ég heyri* (= *ég hef heyrt*), *að þeir séu farnir að sökkva skipum* I hear (have heard) that they are beginning to sink boats. This agrees with English usage. But the English ' I forget ' is always: *ég man ekki* I do not remember.

Note 2: *Ég kem, þegar ég er tilbúinn* I shall come, when I am ready. Here English uses future in the principal clause, present in the subordinate clause, while Icelandic has present in both. Likewise: *ég fer hvergi, ef* (*að*) *rignir* I shall go nowhere, if it rains.

Note 3: For the present as imperative, see **10** below.

2. The Preterite.

The preterite tense usually denotes simple past time without reference to present time: *ég kom í gær* I came yesterday; *ég kom til Ameríku fyrir fimmtán árum* I came to America fifteen years ago; *lastu blaðið í morgun?* did you read the paper this morning? (said in the afternoon). *Einu sinni var . . .* once there was. . . .

Note 1: *Ég þekkti móður hans vel* I knew his mother well, or: I used to know his mother well. Otherwise ' I used to ' is: *ég var vanur að.*

Note 2: The preterite may sometimes stand for a perfect, even for a past perfect tense: *Eiríkur konungur réð einn vetur fyrir Noregi, áður en Hákon kom til Noregs* King E. reigned (= had reigned) one winter over Norway, before H. came to Norway.

Note 3: *Var það nokkuð fyrir yður?* literally: ' Was there anything for you?' Can I help you? a polite question of sales-girls in stores. *Gaztu fundið mig?* Could you see me? (dialectal).

3. The Perfect.

The perfect tense denotes a past time with reference to, or stretching into the present: *ég hef ekki lokið við bókina* I have not finished the book; *hvað mörg ár hefur þú* (*hafið þér*) *átt heima í Reykjavík* how many years have you lived in R.; *hefurðu* (*hafið þér*) *lesið blaðið í morgun* have you read the paper this morning? (said in the morning).

Note: In stating a past event with some doubt, the perfect future

138

is often used for the perfect with an adverb of doubt: *ég mun hafa séð hann fyrir tveim árum* (*ég hef víst séð hann*) I probably have (may have) seen him (or: saw him) two years ago. If there is no doubt, a simple preterite is used: *ég sá hann fyrir tveimur árum* I saw him two years ago. Thus, apart from the present doubt about the past event, there is neither a reference to the present, nor a stretching into the present in these cases of the perfect future or the perfect with an adverb of doubt. Perfect of doubt would be a fit name for it.

4. The Past Perfect.

The past perfect tense refers to a time before the past time (expressed through the preterite); its relation to the preterite is thus the same as that of the perfect tense to the present. *Tveir bátar fórust í laugardagsbylnum; þeir höfðu róið um morguninn, en komu ekki aftur* two boats were lost in the Saturday blizzard; they had rowed out in the morning, but they did not come back. This tense is not very common in the indicative (direct narrative), instead of it a simple preterite is often used: *þeir réru um morguninn* they rowed out in the morning.

Note: Intransitive verbs of motion also form tenses roughly corresponding to the perfect and past perfect with the auxiliary *vera* to be: *ég er* (*var*) *kominn* I have (had) come; cf. the Conjugation of the Intransitive Verbs of Motion, 3 below.

5. The Future.

The future tense, formed with *munu* and the infinitive of the verb conjugated, rarely is used for the simple future time: *samt mun ég vaka* yet I shall stay awake (poetic). Colloquially the present tense is most commonly used for the future: *ég fer* I (shall) go; *munu* usually implies doubt: *ég mun fara* I shall probably go; *eitthvað annað mun undir búa* something else must be (= probably is) lurking under this, i. e. there must be a hidden reason for this; *þetta mun satt vera* this is probably true.

Note: A future more or less modified in meaning is often formed by the auxiliaries *skulu* shall, *eiga* have to, *vilja* will, want to, *verða* must, have to, *þurfa* have to, *mega* may, *ætla* intend; see the Auxiliary Verbs, 13 below. The present subjunctive and the imperative often have a definitely future meaning.

6. The Perfect Future (Futurum exactum).

The perfect future is formed with *munu hafa* and the past

139

participle of the verb conjugated. Usually it is only in form a perfect future, in reality a perfect of doubt (cf. *3*, note above): *ég mun hafa lagt af stað klukkan tólf í gær* I started probably at twelve o'clock yesterday.

A true perfect future is, however, sometimes possible: *Jesús sagði við Pétur: áður en haninn galar tvisvar, munt þú hafa afneitað mér þrisvar* J. said to P.: before the cock has crowed twice you shall have denied me three times.

A true perfect future is, finally, common in the intransitive verbs of motion, formed with the auxiliaries *vera* or *verða*: *ég mun verða kominn austur yfir fjörð fyrir hádegi á morgun* I shall have crossed east over the firth before noon tomorrow morning. Cf. Conjugation of Intransitive Verbs of Motion.

7. *The Past Future and Past Perfect Future.*

The past future and the past perfect future, though often formed with the originally indicative form *mundi* instead of the subjunctive form *myndi*, have really a subjunctive sense in any case, and should therefore be treated under the subjunctive. They are sometimes called the first and second conditional.

3. Compound Conjugation with *vera* of Intransitive Verbs of Motion.

1. *The Form.*

Intransitive verbs of motion and change form a special compound conjugation, in addition to the ordinary one, by combining their past participle (which agrees with the subject) with all tenses (and moods) of the verb *vera* be:

Present	*ég er farinn*	I am (have) gone
Preterite	" *var farinn*	" was (had) gone
Perfect	" *hef verið farinn*	" have been gone
Past Perfect	" *hafði verið farinn*	" had been gone
Future	" *mun [vera/verða] farinn*	" shall be gone
Perfect Future	" *mun hafa verið farinn*	" shall (may) have been gone
Past Future	" *mundi [vera/verða] farinn*	" should be gone
Past Perfect Future	" *mundi hafa verið farinn*	" should have been gone

Note 1: The verbs *vera*, *verða* may be omitted in the future and the past future. These tenses may also be formed by present and preterite (subjunctive) of *verða*, future: *ég verð farinn* I shall be gone, past future: *ég yrði farinn* I should (have) be(en) gone.

Note 2 : The subjunctive is formed by substituting the subjunctive of *vera* (*verða*) in all the tenses: *ég sé farinn* I be gone, etc. Imperative: *vertu farinn, áður en ég kem* be gone before I come.

2. The Meaning.

This compound conjugation agrees perfectly in form with the passive voice of transitive verbs (q. v. **8** below) :

> *ég er kominn* I have come,
> *ég er meiddur* I am hurt (passive),

but the meaning of the present and the preterite of this compound conjugation is somewhat similar to the perfect and the past perfect of transitive verbs and must often be so translated into English. Yet, there is a difference in meaning:

Present: *hann er kominn* he has come (and he is here) ;

*Perfect: *hann hefur komið* he has come (at some time in the past, but he is not here now) ;

Preterite: *hann var kominn* he had come (when we came home) ;

*Past Perfect: *hann hafði komið* he had come (at some time in the past).

Likewise, there is a difference in meaning between the two types of future tenses (future and perfect future) :

Future: *hann mun* [*vera*] *kominn* he has probably come (he is probably here) ;

         hann mun [*verða*] *kominn* he will probably have come (before you leave) (a true perfect future, cf. **2**, *6* above) ;

         **hann mun koma* he will probably come (at some time in the future) ;

Perfect Future: *hann mun hafa verið kominn* he has probably come (before I left yesterday, but I did not see him) ;

         * *hann mun hafa komið* he has probably come (at some time in the past).

And, finally, the past future and past perfect future:

Past Future: *hann mundi vera kominn* he would have come (now, if . . .) ;

         hann mundi verða kominn he would have come (tomorrow, if . . .) ;

141

> * *hann mundi koma* he would come (tomorrow, if . . .).

Past Perfect   *hann mundi hafa verið kominn* he would have
Future :   come (= been here) (now, if . . .) ;
                  * *hann mundi hafa komið* he would have come (then, if . . .).

Note 1 : To avoid confusion, the tenses of the ordinary simple conjugation are marked with an asterisk (*), while those of the compound conjugation are left unmarked.

Note 2 : Apart from a few verbs like *go*, English has now usually nothing to correspond to this compound conjugation with *vera*, since English forms its perfect and past perfect with *have* in verbs of motion as well as in transitive verbs.

3. Examples.

1. Thus go intransitive verbs of motion and change: *detta, falla* fall, *fljúga* fly, *ganga* go, *hlaupa* run, *fara* go; *byrja* begin, *verða* become.

2. Ordinarily verbs of the middle voice cannot take this conjugation, even if they are intransitive verbs of motion: *ferðast* travel, *ég hef ferðazt* I have travelled. The reason seems to be that the past participle of the middle voice is an indeclinable neuter, incapable of agreement with the subject, unless it is a neuter. And in that case, one finds that the middle voice can take this compound conjugation: with *það* as an indefinite subject of intransitive verbs: *það er (var, hefur verið, hafði verið*, etc.) *skreiðzt upp á þak* one (somebody) creeps up on the roof; *það er (var, hefur verið, hafði verið*, etc.) *barizt* they (men, people) fight; *það er glaðzt meira á himnum yfir einum syndara, sem bœtir ráð sitt, heldur en yfir níutíu og níu réttlátum* in heaven they rejoice more over one sinner, who makes amends, than over ninety-nine righteous. The two verbs, finally, which have declinable past participles in the middle voice, being besides verbs of motion, take the compound conjugation. These are: *leggjast* lie down, and *setjast* sit down; *ég er (var, hef verið, hafði verið*, etc.) *setztur* I am (was, have been, had been) seated. Cf. the Middle Voice, *7, 4* and *6* below.

3. When ordinary transitive verbs become intransitive, their passive voice may acquire the meaning of this conjugation: *leggja af stað* start, *hann er lagður af stað* he has started. Likewise impersonally: *það er (var,* etc.) *barið* literally: it is (was, etc.)

knocked, i. e. somebody is (was) knocking (at the door). Cf. the
Passive Voice, 8 below.

4. Durative Action, indicated by *vera að*.

1. *The Form.*

Icelandic, like English, has developed an expanded conjugation
along with the ordinary one in order to express duration of an
action (or simultaneity of action), something going on, something
on the point of happening, or, finally, in order to give the action
affective (emotional) emphasis. This expanded conjugation is
formed in Icelandic by the verb *vera* (in all its forms) and an
infinitive with *að* of the verb conjugated. In English the present
participle takes the place of this infinitive.

Present	*ég er að lesa*	I am reading
Preterite	*ég var að lesa*	I was reading
Perfect	*ég hef verið að lesa*	I have been reading
Past Perfect	*ég hafði verið að lesa*	I had been reading
Future	*ég mun vera/verða að lesa*	I shall probably be reading
	or: *ég verð að lesa* (common)	I shall be reading
Perfect Future	*ég mun hafa verið að lesa*	I may/shall have been reading
Past Future	*ég mundi (y) vera/verða að lesa*	I would be reading
	ég yrði að lesa, ef . . .	I would be reading, if . . .
Past Perfect Future	*ég mundi (y) hafa verið að lesa ef . . .*	I would have been reading, if . . .

Note 1: Of the three possible forms of the future, the two formed
with *verða* are most common colloquially, especially the last one.
But *ég mun verða að lesa* has not only the meaning: I may/shall
be reading, but also: I may/shall have to read. Likewise: *ég verð
að lesa* means either: I shall be reading, or: I shall have to read.
In a similar way the past future is formed with *vera, verða,* or *yrði.*

Note 2: The perfect future is commonly a perfect of doubt: *ég
mun hafa verið að lesa, þegar hann kom* I was probably reading
when he came.

Note 3: The subjunctive is formed by replacing the indicative
forms of *vera* with its subjunctive forms: *ég sé að lesa* I be reading,
etc. The imperative: *vertu að lesa* be reading, keep reading, *verið
þið (þér) að lesa* ' be you reading,' keep (on) reading.

2. *Verbs taking vera að.*

Verbs denoting action or change (sudden or gradual) can express
durative action by tenses expanded with *vera að.* Examples: *ég*

borða morgunmat klukkan níu I eat breakfast at nine: *ég var að borða, þegar þér komuð* I was eating, when you came. *Við fórum af (á) stað um sjöleytið* we started about seven o'clock: *við vorum að fara af stað, þegar hann reið í hlaðið* we were on the point of starting when he rode up to the place (in front of the house). *Hvernig líður yður? Mér er að batna* how are you? I am getting better (improving). *Ég var að sofna* I was (just) falling asleep; *hann er að deyja* he is (on the point of) dying; *við erum að fara* we are about to go; *hann er að hvessa* it is about to storm. The first two of these examples show the ordinary tenses and the expanded ones side by side.

Note: The immediate past is sometimes expressed by the preterite of *vera að* + the verb: *Ég var (einmitt) að fá bréf að heiman* I have just received a letter from home.

3. Verbs not taking vera að.

As in English, there are several verbs that are not capable of expanding their tenses with *vera að* in order to indicate durative action. Thus the preterite present verbs (*vita; kunna, unna, þurfa; skulu, munu, muna; mega, eiga; vilja*), likewise the auxiliaries *hafa* and *vera*. Generally speaking, verbs expressing extended states of being (duratives) or states of mind do not take the expanded tenses (though some of them do in English). Thus: *vera* to be, to stay; *búa* *live, *dwell, *farm; *dvelja(st)* *dwell, *sitja* *sit, *liggja* *lie, *verða* *remain (but not *verða* become), *vaka* be awake, *sofa* *sleep, *lifa* *live;—*óttast* fear, *líka, mislíka* be pleased, displeased, *elska* love, *hata* hate, *leiðast* be bored;—*þekkja* recognize, *álíta, skoða* look upon, consider, *ætla* intend, consider, etc. (the verbs marked by the asterisk (*) do take the expanded tenses in English: I am sitting, etc.).

Likewise verbs of the weather (impersonal): *hann rignir, það rignir* it rains; *hann (það) snjóar* it snows, it is snowing; *það hríðar* it is snowing (sleeting); *það suddar, það ýrir úr honum* it drizzles, is drizzling. But some of these may take *vera að*.

4. Use for Emphasis.

The tenses expanded with *vera að* are sometimes used to give affective (i. e. emotional) emphasis to statements. This is common in half-angry or surprised questions, exclamations, or commands. Verbs, that otherwise would not take *vera að* (cf. *3* above) may do so under these circumstances. Examples:

1. *Ég bý á Ási* I live (farm) at Ás; *ég bjó á Ási* I lived at Á.;

2. *ég bý ekki á Ási lengur en þetta árið* I shall not live at Ás longer than this year;
3. *ég verð ekki að búa á Ási lengur* I shall not be living at Ás longer;
4. *ég er ekkert að búa á Ási lengur* I am not living at Ás any longer;
5. *til hvers ertu að búa á Ási?* why are you living at Ás?
6. *þú ættir ekki að vera að búa á Ási* you should not be living at Ás;
7. *ég veit ekki, hvað hann vill vera að búa á Ási* I (certainly) do not know why he should be wanting to live at Ás.

The two statements in (1) express simple facts, present and past. The statement of future in (2) may or may not be affective. And because the verb *búa* has a durative sense, it does not take the expanded tenses with *vera að* in those unaffected statements. But all the following cases are more or less affective: (3-4) express disgust, (5) wonder or disgust, and (6-7) dissatisfaction or moral indignation.

Commands: *Vertu ekki að skæla, krakki!* don't be crying, you brat! *Komið þið (þér) inn! Verið þið (þér) ekki að standa úti* please come in, don't keep standing outside.

Segir þú satt? Are you telling the truth? *Nei, nú ertu ekki að segja satt* no, now you are not telling the truth.

5. Beginning Action, indicated by *fara að*.

1. Form.

Some verbs may be used to indicate that the action of the verb conjugated (in the infinitive) is to begin or is beginning. Such are *byrja* begin, *taka*, *hefja* begin, but especially *fara*, which alone may be considered to be an auxiliary in the colloquial language (*taka* and *hefja* are literary).

Present	*ég fer að sofa* I (am) go(ing) to sleep	
Preterite	*ég fór að sofa* I went to sleep	
Perfect 1	*ég er farinn að sofa* I have gone to sleep (now)	
Perfect 2	*ég hef farið að sofa* I have gone to sleep (at some time)	
Past Perfect 1	*ég var farinn að sofa* I had gone to sleep (then)	
Past Perfect 2	*ég hafði farið að sofa* I had gone to sleep	
Future	*ég mun fara að sofa* I shall go to sleep	
Perfect Future	*ég mun hafa farið að sofa* I may/shall have gone to sleep	
Past Future	*ég mundi fara að sofa* I would go to sleep	
Past Perfect Future	*ég mundi hafa farið að sofa* I would have gone to sleep.	

Note 1: The verb *fara* so used can take the expanded conjugation

145

of durative action: *eg er að fara að sofa* I am on the point of going to sleep.

Note 2: *Fara* with the infinitive has two or three distinct senses:

(a) to begin: *ég fór að lesa* I began to read;

(b) simple future: *hann fer að koma* he will soon come (be here);

(c) affective (emotional) emphasis (especially the preterite): *hann fór að gifta sig*! he had to marry! (shouldn't have done so).

2. Usage.

Fara að can be used with many verbs of action, including those which themselves have a sense of beginning: *vakna* awaken, *sofna* fall asleep. One can even say: *ég held mér sé betra að fara að byrja að klæða mig* I think I had better begin (to begin) dressing, though such redundancy naturally would not be considered elegant.

But *fara að* cannot be used with the preterite present verbs or the auxiliaries *hafa* and *vera*. There seems also to be a tendency not to use it with several other verbs that cannot take *vera að* either (durative verbs: *sitja* sit, *liggja* lie, *standa* stand, *vaka* be awake). But: *hann fer að rigna* it is going to rain.

6. Completed Action, indicated by *vera búinn að*.

1. Form.

Ég er búinn að lesa bókina, I have finished reading the book, illustrates the way *vera búinn* with infinitive can be used to indicate completed action.

Present	*ég er búinn að borða* I am through eating	
Preterite	*ég var búinn að borða* I was through eating	
Perfect	*ég hef verið búinn að borða* I have been through eating	
Past Perfect	*ég hafði verið búinn að borða* I had been through eating	
Future	*ég mun vera/verða (verð) búinn að borða* I shall be through eating	
Perfect Future	*ég mun hafa verið búinn að borða* I may/shall have been through eating	
Past Future	*ég mundi vera/verða (yrði) búinn að borða* I would be through eating	
Past Perfect Future	*ég mundi hafa verið búinn að borða* I would have been through eating	

Note 1. For the variants in the future, the past future, and the meaning of the perfect future, see these tenses in the Indicative, **2** above. Subjunctive is formed by substituting the subjunctive forms of *vera* for those of the indicative: *ég sé búinn,* etc. Imperative: *vertu búinn að borða, áður en kennarinn kemur* have eaten before the teacher comes; *verið þið (þér) búnir að borða* (plural).

Note 2: Originally *búinn* (past participle of *búa* prepare) meant: prepared, ready (= *tilbúinn*): *voru menn þá búnir til bardaga* men were then ready for the fight.

2. Usage.

Many verbs take *vera búinn* to indicate completed action: *gera* do, *slá túnið* mow the home-field, *sjá* see, *segja* say, tell, *ganga* go, *fara* go.

But it is not possible to use *vera búinn* with some verbs, for example the durative verbs *vera* be, stay, *sofa* sleep, *standa* stand, *sitja* sit, *liggja* lie, unless the duration is specified: *ég er búinn að sofa tvo tíma* I have slept two hours, *ég er búinn að standa hér síðan í morgun* I have stood here since this morning, *hann er búinn að vera* he is through, but *ég hef staðið hér* I have been standing here. Verbs indicating state of mind of indefinite duration cannot take *vera búinn*: *mér hefur leiðzt* I have been bored. Likewise, verbs indicating either the beginning or the end of an action rarely take *vera búinn*: thus either *ég er sofnaður, vaknaður* or: *ég hef sofnað, vaknað* I have fallen asleep, I have awakened, rarely *ég er búinn að sofna*. Likewise: *hann er dáinn, hann hefur dáið* he is dead, he has (probably) died, never: *hann er búinn að deyja*.

7. The Meaning of the Middle Voice.

1. Reflexive.

The original meaning of the middle voice is reflexive, as is indicated by its origin *klæða sik > klæðask > klæðast* dress oneself; also in active with the reflexive pronoun: *klæða sig*. Likewise, even if the reflexive pronoun is in the dative (as an object) *snúast = snúa sér* turn oneself. More rarely if the dative is an indirect object: *taka sér ferð á hendur = takast ferð á hendur* undertake a journey (literally: take a journey on one's hands).

2. Reciprocal.

The middle voice also has a reciprocal meaning: *þeir berjast = þeir berja hvor annan* they fight each other; *þeir heilsast = þeir heilsa hvor öðrum* they greet each other. *Þau talast við = þau tala hvort við annað* they (a man and a woman) speak to each other.

3. Passive.

The middle voice also has a passive meaning: *ekkert heyrist fyrir*

147

fossinum nothing is heard on account of the waterfall. Thus *fréttast* be heard (of news), *spyrjast* be heard (by asking), *sjást* be seen, *virðast* seem, *fást* be to be had, *fœðast* be born, *reynast* be proven, *finnast* be found, *skiljast* be understood.

4. Intransitive Sense.

Several transitive verbs (indicating change from one state to another) have intransitive counterparts in the middle voice:

kvelja e-n torture somebody	*kveljast* suffer (pain, torture)
gleðja e-n gladden somebody	*gleðjast* be glad, rejoice
minna e-n á e-ð remind somebody of something	*minnast e-s* remember something
hrœða e-n terrify somebody	*hrœðast* be afraid
mata e-n feed somebody	*matast* eat
hefja e-ð begin something	*hefjast* begin
týna e-u lose something	*týnast* be lost, get lost
" *e-m* destroy somebody	" perish
koma e-u e-ð get, move something somewhere	*komast* get somewhere
þrífa til tidy up	*þrífast* thrive

In some verbs the difference in meaning between the active and the middle voice is negligible, e. g. *skilja/skiljast* part, *dvelja/dveljast* stay, dwell.

5. Middle Voice Verbs.

Some verbs are found only in the middle voice, e. g. *mér missýnist* my eyes deceive me, *ég nálgast e-ð* I approach something, *mér skjátlast (e-ð)* I am mistaken (in something), *ég eldist* I grow old, *ég ferðast* I travel, *ég óttast* I fear, *mér leiðist þetta* I am bored with this, etc.

6. Impersonal Intransitives.

Some impersonal intransitive verbs in the middle voice (cf. 4 above) form tenses with the auxiliaries *vera (verða)* and their own past middle participles: *nú heyrir Jón, að setzt er í körfustólinn* now J. hears that somebody seats himself in the wicker chair; *nú er farið upp á þak og setzt klofvega á mæninn* now somebody climbs the roof and sets himself astride the ridge of the roof; *ekki verður um villzt* there can be no mistake about it.

Note: Only two verbs *leggjast* and *setjast* lie down and sit down, have past middle participles which can be used in all genders like adjectives agreeing with the subjects: *hann er lagztur* he has lain down (also: he has taken to bed because of sickness), *hún var setzt* she had sat down. Cf. the Compound Conjugation of Intransitive Verbs of Motion, **3** above.

148

8. The Passive Voice.

1. *Form.*

The passive voice in Icelandic, as in English, is formed by conjugating the verb *vera*, be, and adding the past participle of the verb that is being conjugated. Thus the passive infinitive of *berja* beat is: *vera barinn* be beaten (cf. the Synopsis of Voices, Tenses, and Moods, **1**, *3* above).

2. *Transitive Verbs.*

Normally a passive voice can only be formed of transitive verbs or, rather, verbs which have an accusative object:

Active: *Jón tók bókina* John took the book,
Passive: *bókin var tekin af Jóni* the book was taken by John (this is ambiguous, since *taka af* also means: take from).

Note: The past participle agrees (in gender, case, and number) with the (converted) subject in the passive sentence.

Note 2: Very often no logical subject is given in the passive voice: *bókin var tekin* the book was taken. This agrees with English usage; it is, indeed, almost the only way that one can suppress the logical subject in English, while there are many more ways in Icelandic; cf. the Impersonal Verb Constructions, **14** below.

3. *Indirect Objects.*

An indirect object remains unchanged in the passive:

Active: *Jón gaf mér (Pétri) bókina* John gave me (Peter) the book,
or: John gave the book to me (to Peter).
Passive: *bókin var gefin mér (Pétri) af Jóni*
(a) the book was given me (to Peter) by John,
(b) I (Peter) was given the book by John.

Note: The last mode of expression is unthinkable in Icelandic, but it may be approached, and actually often is, by putting the indirect object first: *mér var gefin bókin (af Jóni)*.

4. *Direct Objects in Dative and Genitive.*

If the verb has an object in the dative or genitive, this remains unchanged in the passive, but the past participle of the passive verb is put in the neuter gender, whereby the verb becomes impersonal:

Active: *Jón kastaði steini* John threw a stone,
Passive: *steini var kastað (af Jóni)* a stone was thrown by John.
Active: *Jón beið mín* John awaited me, John waited for me,

149

Passive: *mín var beðið (af Jóni)* I was awaited (by J.).

Note: The logical subject of a verb in the passive can be added with the preposition *af* by. But passives without the logical subject are much more common.

5. Passive with verða.

Instead of *vera* with the past participle, *verða* with the past participle is sometimes used, but there is a difference in meaning:

Þú ert dæmdur you are condemned	*Þú verður dæmdur* you will be condemned
Þú varst dæmdur you were condemned	*Þú varðst ekki dæmdur* you could not be condemned (usually with negation)
Þú hefur verið dæmdur you have been condemned	*Þú hefur ekki orðið dæmdur* it has not been possible to condemn you
Þú munt vera dæmdur you probably are condemned	*Þú munt verða dæmdur* you will be condemned
Þeim var ekki bjargað they were not saved	*Þeim varð ekki bjargað* it was not possible to save them.

6. Intransitive Verbs of Motion.

Intransitive verbs of motion have no passive voice. But they form a system of compound conjugation in exactly the same way, with a wholly different meaning (as shown in **3** above).

9. Use of the Subjunctive.

1. The Subjunctive Tenses.

The subjunctive has all the tenses that the indicative has: present, preterite, perfect, past perfect, future, and perfect future. In addition it has two more: the past future (first conditional) and the past perfect future (second conditional). As will be seen in the following, these tenses do not always represent the time values that their names imply.

2. Use of the Tenses in Principal Clauses.

1. Present Subjunctive.—The present subjunctive is used to express wish, exhortation, admonition, or command: *gangi þér (yður) vel!* may it go well with you, good luck! *drottinn blessi heimilið* (may) God bless the home; *fari hann bölvaður* let him be (literally: go) damned, damn him.

Note 1: In this sense the present subjunctive complements the imperative which is found only in the second person singular:

farðu heim go home, and in the first and second person plural:
grátum ekki let us not weep, *verið þið (þér) kyrrir* be quiet;
but third person plural subjunctive: *fari þeir sem fara vilja, komi
þeir sem koma vilja* let those go who will, let those come who will
(a formula, addressed to the elfs on New Year's Eve).

Note 2: To express pleasure or displeasure at a thing done by
somebody, one can use a perfect subjunctive or imperative: *hafi
hún sæl gert!* good for her, to have done this! *hafðu sæll gert!*
good for you, to have done this! But this is rare.

Note 3: Command in the second and third person, promise in the
first person singular, exhortation in the first person plural is often
expressed by the auxiliary *skulu* (q. v.).

Note 4: The time value of the present subjunctive in principal
clauses, if not general as in *drottinn blessi heimilið*, is nearest to
being a future, since the fulfilment of the wish, exhortation, or
command must lie in the future. The same is true of the imperative
and of *skulu*.

Note 5: In subordinate clauses the present subjunctive is chiefly
used after present in the principal clause: *það er sagt, að hann
komi á morgun* it is said that he will come tomorrow.

2. Preterite Subjunctive.—The preterite subjunctive is used to
express potentiality (possibility): that something could or might
take place; it is used to express suggestions, polite opinion, and in
questions. The verbs so used are chiefly: *vera* be, *vilja* will, want,
wish, *mega* may, *þykja* think, seem, *þurfa* need, *eiga* owe, ought,
have to, *geta* to able to, *skulu* shall.

Examples: *það væri ágætt* that would be fine; *þér (yður) væri
nær (betra) að fara að hætta* you had better stop; *nú væri gaman
að fara út* now it would be fun to go out; *vildir þú ekki heldur
fara heim?* wouldn't you rather like to go home? *mætti eg spyrja?*
might I ask? (a shade more polite than *má eg spyrja?* may I ask?);
þá þætti mér verr farið en heima setið then I would consider that
journey worse than sitting at home, i. e. this would have been
better not done; *þú þyrftir (þér þyrftuð) að vera hér um tíma*
you should (you would need to) stay here for a while; *þú ættir
(þér ættuð) að heimsækja mig oftar* you should visit me more
often; *gæti ég fengið að líta á blaðið?* could I (might I) have a
look at the paper? *það gæti verið* that might be; *skyldu þeir (þær,
þau) fara að koma?* would they be coming soon? I wonder whether
they would be coming soon; *hún gifti sig, sem aldrei skyldi verið
hafa* she married, as she should never have done; *það skyldi þó*

aldrei hafa verið Jón? it couldn't have been John, could it? *það kæmi mér ekki á óvart* I would not be surprised.

Note 1: A past perfect subjunctive is used much like the preterite subjunctive: *hver hefði trúað því?* who would have believed it? The past perfect subjunctive may sometimes be replaced by a past perfect future (second conditional): *hver mundi hafa trúað því?* exactly as in English.

Note 2: Instead of the preterite subjunctive a past future (first conditional) (*mundi* + infinitive) may be used: *vildir þú fara* = *mundir þú vilja fara?* would you like to go? *mér var sagt, að þér ættuð að fara* = *mér var sagt, að þér mynduð eiga að fara* I was told that you were (would have) to go. The difference, if any, is a slight expression of doubt (diffidence) in the *mundi* construction.

Note 3: The time value of the preterite subjunctive is mostly present or future; it may alternate with the present (as in English): *viltu heldur fara?* (present) do you prefer to go? *vildir þú heldur fara?* (preterite) would you prefer to go? The past future, as described in note 2, also has a future meaning.

Note 4: In subordinate clauses the preterite subjunctive is used ('a) if it would have been used in direct speech: *hann segir, að það kynni að vera hægt* he says that it might be possible (direct speech: *það kynni að vera hægt* it might be possible); (b) following a preterite (subjunctive) in the principal clause: *það væri betur, að satt væri* (abbreviated: *betur satt væri*) it would be better, if it were true.

3. Use of the Subjunctive in Conditions.

1. Real Conditions.—When condition and effect are thought of as something real, the effect naturally following if the condition holds, the indicative (usually present, but also perfect, perfect future or even preterite) is used in both the principal clause (effect) and in the if-clause (condition). If, however, the *ef*, if, is dropped, then a subjunctive (present, etc.) is used and placed first in the subordinate clause.

Examples:

Ég skal koma (ég kem), ef ég get I shall come, if I am able to; *geti ég gert það, skal ég koma* if I can do it, I shall come.
Ef hann snjóar, verður heiðin ófær if it snows, the heath will be impassable;
snjói hann í nótt, verður heiðin ófær if it snows tonight, the heath ...

Ef allt hefur farið sem ætlað var, þá sjáum við hann á morgun
   if all has gone, as planned, we shall see him tomorrow;
hafi allt gengið sem ætlað var, þá sjáum við hann . . .
Hann fór alltaf, ef honum var boðið he always went, if he was
   invited; *væri honum boðið, fór hann alltaf* if he was invited,
   he always went.

2. Imaginary Conditions.—When condition and effect are both
imaginary, something supposed, then preterite subjunctive (or
past perfect, or past future, or past perfect future) is used both
in the principal clause (effect) and in the if-clause (condition).
Here too, *ef*, if, may be omitted, but the verb must then be placed
first in the subordinate clause.

Examples:

Ég skyldi koma (ég kæmi), ef ég gæti, en ég get það ekki I should
   come, if I could, but I cannot;
gæti ég gert það, skyldi ég koma (kæmi ég) . . . could I do it,
   I would come.
Heiðin yrði ófær, ef hann snjóaði the heath would become impassable, if it should snow;
snjóaði hann nú, yrði heiðin ófær if it snowed now, the heath
   would become impassable.
Ef báturinn hefði ekki brotnað, þá hefðu mennirnir komizt í land
   if the boat had not been damaged, the men would have reached
   shore;
hefði báturinn ekki brotnað, þá . . . had the boat not been damaged,
   the men . . . , or: *hefði báturinn ekki brotnað, þá mundu mennirnir hafa komizt á land* had the boat not been damaged, the
   men would have reached shore.

Note 1: The last phrasing with the past perfect future (second
conditional, *mundu hafa komizt*) in the principal clause, agrees
with English usage, as the translation shows, but is not as common
as the phrasing with the perfect (*hefðu komizt*).

Note 2: As the translations show, English sometimes (in case of
have, shall, etc.) can match the Icelandic change of word order
(if I had . . . = had I . . .), but in most cases it cannot do so (*ef ég
get* . . . = *geti ég* . . . if I am able to).

Note 3: In the English: if I was mad, I did not show it, the
if-clause is not a condition, neither is the principal clause an effect.
Here 'if' signifies admittance, concession, rendered by *þó (að)*
in Icelandic: *þó ég væri reiður, lét ég ekki á því bera.*

3. *Nema*-clauses.—*Nema*, unless, is used to imply an exceptional condition; it is not used except after a negation (or a negative sense) in the principal clause. When combined with *ef*: *nema ef,* except that, unless, the mood in the conditional clause is indicative or subjunctive, according to the rules above:

Ég kem ekki, nema ef ég get I shall not come, unless I can;
hann fór aldrei neitt, nema ef honum var boðið he never went
anywhere, except that (unless) he was invited.

When *nema* alone is used (not followed by *ef*), subjunctive is always used:

Ég kem ekki, nema ég geti I shall not come, unless I can;
hann fór aldrei neitt, nema honum væri boðið he never went
anywhere, unless he was invited.

4. Use of the Subjunctive in Subordinate Clauses.

1. *Að*-Clauses.—The subjunctive is frequently used in *að*-clauses after verbs of wishing, commanding, needing—thinking, fearing, expecting—feeling, seeming—saying:

Við óskum þess, að þér skiftið við okkur (formal) we wish that you
deal with us (or: that you were dealing . . . , or: that you
would deal . . .);
það vildi ég, að veðrið færi að skána (common) I wish the weather
would (begin to) improve;
hún þarf þess með, að henni fari að batna (common) 'she (certainly) needs, that she should be getting better,' i. e. she needs
to get better;
hann hélt (sagði, bjóst við), að skipið kæmi á morgun he thought
(said, expected) that the boat would come tomorrow;
mér virðist, sýnist (formal), *ég held* (informal), *að þetta sé rétt*
it seems to me, I think, I feel, that this is right.

Note 1: Present is used after present, preterite after preterite in the principal clause.

Note 2: When, however, the *að*-clause states a fact, not a supposition, the indicative is used:

Björn heyrði, að menn sungu í næsta herbergi (or: *heyrði menn
syngja*) Björn heard that men sang (heard men sing) in the
next room, but:
Birni heyrðist, að menn syngi í næsta herbergi (or: *heyrðist menn
syngja*) Björn thought he heard that men sang (heard men
sing). . . .

154

The first is a fact, the second an impression one is not certain of. Often there is a choice of either expression. Thus often after the verbs *sjá* see, *heyra* hear, *skilja* understand, *vita* know. But after *sýnast* think one sees, *heyrast* think one hears, *skiljast* think one understands, subjunctive is used.

2. Interrogative Clauses.—The subjunctive is used in interrogative clauses, headed by an interrogative pronoun, adjective, or adverb, especially after verbs of asking:

Finnur spyr, hvað sé í pokanum (present) F. asks, what is in the bag;
Finnur spurði, hvað væri í pokanum (preterite) F. asked, what
    was. . . .
Maðurinn spurði, hver ég væri, hvaðan ég kæmi, hvert ég ætlaði
    og hvort ég ætlaði lengra í kvöld the man asked, who I was,
    whence I came, where I was going, and whether I was going to
    travel further tonight.

Note: After the verbs *sjá* see, *heyra* hear, *skilja* understand, *vita* know, the indicative is often used, because the content of the interrogative clause is then (usually) a fact:

Ég sá og heyrði, hvað fram fór (*hvað um var að vera*) I saw and
    heard, what was going on;
þér skiljið, hvers vegna ég get ekki komið you understand, why I
    cannot come.

3. Causal Clauses.—The subjunctive is used in causal clauses (beginning with *af því að*), if the cause is imaginary and denied in the principal clause; a real cause is put in the indicative: *Hann fór ekki til Vesturheims, af því að honum liði svo illa heima, heldur af því að hann langaði til að litast um í veröldinni* he did not go to America, because he was doing so badly at home, but because he wanted to look about in the world.

Note: On causal clauses beginning with *ef*, if, see the Use of the Subjunctive in Conditions, *3* above.

4. Result Clauses.—The subjunctive is used in a result clause (beginning with *svo að*), if the preceding principal clause contains a denial, a question, or a command:

Þeir voru ekki svo grunnhyggnir, að þeir tryðu þessu they were
    not so gullible that they believed this, but:
þeir voru svo grunnhyggnir, að þeir trúðu they were so gullible
    that they believed (indicative).
Eru þeir svo grunnhyggnir, að þeir trúi þessu? are they so gullible
    as to believe this?

Þið skuluð skifta verkum, svo að tveir séu alltaf á verði divide your work so that two are always on guard.

Note: Otherwise a result clause (in direct speech) is usually in the indicative: *hún var svo glöð, að hún réð sér ekki fyrir fögnuði* she was so happy that she was beside herself with joy.

5. Clauses of Purpose.—The subjunctive is always used in clauses of purpose, beginning with *til (þess) að, svo að, að* (the last mostly literary):

Hann tekur lán, til þess að sonur hans geti haldið áfram námi he borrows a sum in order that his son may continue studying; in the preterite: *hann tók lán, til (þess) að sonur hans gæti . . .* he borrowed a sum so that (in order that) his son might. . . .
Farðu frá birtunni, svo (að) ég sjái til að lesa get out of my light so that I may see to read.

Note: Thus with different subjects in the principal and the subordinate clause. When the subject is the same in both, an infinitive often replaces the clause of purpose: *Hann tók lán til (þess) að senda son sinn í skóla* he borrowed in order to send his son to a school.

6. Concessive Clauses.—The subjunctive is always used in concessive clauses headed by *þó (að)*, *þótt* although, *enda þótt (þó að)* even if, *jafnvel þótt (þó að)* even if, *þó aldrei nema* even if. Of these forms *þó* is colloquial, *þó að* and *þótt* literary. Examples:

Ekki batnar veðrið, þó (að) loftvogin sé að stíga (hún er að stíga) the weather does not improve, although the barometer is rising (it is actually rising; hence the present).
Þó höfnin sé stór (hún er stór), þá tekur hún ekki fleiri skip although the harbor is large (it is actually large), it will not hold any more ships.
Þó höfnin væri stór (hún er ekki stór), þá tæki hún ekki fleiri skip even if the harbor were big (it is not; hence the preterite), it would not hold more ships.

Þó svo væri even so, even if it were so; *ekki er sopið kálið, þó í ausuna sé komið* (proverb) there is many a slip betwixt cup and lip.

7. Clauses of Comparison.—The subjunctive is used in clauses of comparison, headed by *sem, og, eins og*, if the comparison is with something imaginary—otherwise the indicative is used:

Hann fór hratt, sem fugl flygi, á skíðunum he traveled fast as (if) a bird (were flying) on the skis; but with indicative:
eg fór eins hratt og ég gat I traveled as fast as I could do;

hann er jafngamall og ég er he is as old as I am (usually *jafn-gamall og ég,* or: *jafngamall mér*).

Note 1: After *virðast* (literary), *sýnast* seem, *heyrast* think one hears, *finnast, þykja* think, feel, a clause of comparison, beginning with *sem, eins og* always has the subjunctive:

Mér virtist sem öll sund væri lokuð it seemed to me (I felt) that all paths were barred; *mér heyrist eins og skotið sé í suðurátt,* it sounds to me as if they were shooting in the south; *honum fannst eins og gripið væri (maður gripi) utan um hann* it seemed to him (he felt) as if someone embraced him (were embracing him).

Note 2: After comparatives and *annar* the conjunction (*heldur*) *en,* (rather) than, is used; the clause has the subjunctive if the compared thing is imaginary and especially after a negation, in which case *heldur en* means: any more than:

Það er ekki annað (heldur) en (að) hann fari heim there is no other choice for him than to go home;
það var ekki meira heldur en svo, að ég gat vel gert það, or:
það var ekki meira heldur en svo, að eg gæti vel gert það it was not more than (so) that I could well do it (the first stated as a fact, the latter as a supposition);
hann leit ekki á hana, heldur en hún væri ekki til he did not look at her any more than if she did not exist.

5. Indirect Speech.

1. Reporter not Subject of Indirect Speech.—The subjunctive is always used in indirect speech when the reporter is not the same person as the subject of the indirect speech clause (always an *að*-clause). English, too, has a that-clause, but the *that* is often dropped.

Direct Speech	Indirect Speech
Hún fer heim á morgun	*Hann segir, að hún fari heim á morgun* (present)
she goes home tomorrow	*Hann sagði, að hún færi heim á morgun* (preterite)
	he says (that) she is going home . . .
	he said (that) she was going home . . .
Hún kom heim í gær	*Hann segir, að hún hafi komið heim í gær*
she came home yesterday	*Hann sagði, að hún hefði komið heim í gær*
	he says (that) she came home . . .
	he said (that) she came home . . .
Hún hefur lesið bókina	*Hann segir, að hún hafi lesið bókina*
she has read the book	*Hann sagði, að hún hefði lesið bókina*
	he says (that) she has read the book
	he said (that) she had read the book

157

Hún hafði séð þetta	*Hann segir, að hún hafi séð þetta*
she had seen this	*Hann sagði, að hún hefði séð þetta*
	he says (that) she has seen this
	he said (that) she had seen this
Hún verður orðin góð	*Hann segir, að hún verði orðin góð*
she will have got well	*Hann sagði, að hún yrði orðin góð*
	he says (that) she will have got well
	he said (that) she would have got well

2. Reporter Subject of Indirect Speech.—When the subject of the indirect speech clause is the same as the reporter, the indirect speech is not put in the subjunctive, but in the infinitive, whose grammatical subject is the middle ending of the verb of saying (*hann segist vera = hann segir sig vera* an accusative with infinitive: he declares himself to be). Unlike Icelandic, English here has the that-clause, precisely as in the cases above.

Direct Speech	Indirect Speech
Ég er ekki heima	*Ég segist (sagðist) ekki vera heima*
I am not at home	I say that I am not at home
	I said that I was not at home
	Þú segist (sagðist) ekki vera heima
	you say that you are not at home
	you said that you were not at home
	Hann segist (sagðist) ekki vera heima
	he says that he is not at home
	he said that he was not at home
Ég var ekki heima	*Hann segist (sagðist) ekki hafa verið heima*
I was not at home	he says (said) that he was not at home
Ég hef ekki lesið bókina	*Hann segist (sagðist) ekki hafa lesið bókina*
I have not read the book	he says (said) that he has (had) not read . . .
Ég hafði séð þetta	*Hann segist (sagðist) hafa séð þetta*
I had seen this	he says (said) that he had seen this
Ég verð orðinn góður	*Hann segist (sagðist) verða orðinn góður*
I will have got well	he says (said) that he will (would) have . . .
Þá mundi ég hlæja	*Hann segist (sagðist) þá mundu (-i) hlæja*
then I would laugh	he says (said) that he would laugh then
Ég mundi hafa hlegið	*Hann segist (sagðist) mundu (-i) hafa hlegið*
I would have laughed	he says (said) that he would have laughed

Likewise *kveðast* say (literary), *þykjast* pretend, let on, *látast* pretend, let on:

Hann kvaðst vera (sagðist vera) veikur he said that he was sick; *hann læzt vera veikur*; *hann þykist vera veikur* he pretends to be sick.

Note 1: These examples show the predicative adjective agreeing in case with the reporter in such sentences, rather than with the latent accusative of the middle ending. In true accusative with infinitive constructions, this is not the case:

Indirect Speech: *hann segist vera veikur* (same subject, latent accusative).

Accusative with Infinitive: *hann segir sig vera veikan* (same subject)
hann segir hana vera veika (two subjects).

Note 2: The student should note the interplay of tenses between principal and subordinate clause in the indirect speech of type 1:

Hann segir (hefur sagt, mun segja, mun hafa sagt), að hún fari á morgun he says (has said, will say, will have said) that she goes tomorrow.

Hann sagði (hafði sagt, mundi segja, mundi hafa sagt), að hún færi á morgun he said (had said, would say, would have said) that she would go tomorrow.

This arrangement of the tenses agrees with English usage.

In indirect speech of the second type, the infinitive, which takes the place of the subordinate clause, remains the same regardless of the preceding tenses.

10. Use of the Imperative.

1. The imperative is used in commands; it is normally put before its subject, which is not as often omitted as in English: *Komdu (kondu)* come; *komið þið* (plural) come; *kom inn* come in. The missing persons are to a certain extent supplied by the present subjunctive (q. v. *9, 2*): *komi þeir, sem koma vilja* let those come who will.

2. With a certain emphasis of command, it is possible to use the indicative for the imperative: *þú kemur strax!* you come at once! *þið komið undir eins!* you come immediately!

3. After negation it is possible to use the infinitive instead of the imperative: *ekki að gráta* don't weep; *ekki að hrekkja!* no teasing! no pranks!

4. The expanded conjugation with *vera að* (see Durative Action, **4** above) is commonly used for emphasis in the imperative: *vertu ekki að hrekkja mig (stríða mér)* don't be playing your pranks on me! don't be teasing me! This is especially common after a negation.

5. The perfect imperative *hafðu sæll (bölvaður) gert!* expressing approval or disapproval of something done: good boy, to have done this! (damned fellow), is rarely used. A present imperative in a similar sense is, perhaps, a little more common, but literary: *njóttu heill handa!* bravo for you, to do this!

11. Use of the Infinitive.

1. Tenses.

The infinitive has the following tenses: present, perfect, future, perfect future, past future, past perfect future, for which see the Synopsis of Voices, Tenses, and Moods, *1, 3* above. A preterite tense is lacking, except of the verbs *munu* and *skulu* : *mundu* and *skyldu*; e. g. *hann sagðist mundu* (colloquial: *mundi*) *koma á morgun* he said he would come tomorrow; *mundi* is probably a subjunctive form, mistakenly substituted for the infinitive, from such sentences as *hann sagði, að hann mundi koma* (see Indirect Speech, *9, 5* above) he said that he would come. *Ég sagðist skyldu* (*skyldi*) *kenna honum* I said I would teach him. The subjunctive form *muni, skuli* is similarly substituted for *munu, skulu*.

2. The Infinitive a Noun.

The infinitive is a nominal form of the verb and is often used as a noun (subject, object, predicative, after prepositions, etc.) mostly as in English:

Að heyra til þín núna er ekki fallegt to listen to you now is not nice (at all) ; (often: *að heyra til þín!* listen to you!).

Að hika er sama og tapa to hesitate is (the same as) to lose.

Reynið þið að taka hestinn try (plural) to take the horse.

Þér getið ekki aftrað mér frá (*því*) *að lesa ritið* you cannot keep (hinder) me from reading the work.

Má ég tala við yður? may I speak to you? *hann nennir ekki að læra* he does not care to exert himself in learning, he does not want to learn; *ég bað hann að hjálpa mér* I asked him to help me; *hann bauð mér að hjálpa mér* he offered to help me; *hún lét hann hjálpa sér* she let (or: had) him help her.

3. The Infinitive of Purpose.

Very often the infinitive expresses goal or purpose, as in English. In that case it is frequently preceded by *til þess að, til að*, or simply *að* in order to, to: *ég varð að fara tvær dagleiðir til þess að* (*til að*) *ná þeim* I had to travel a two days' journey in order to catch up with them; *tveir menn voru sendir að leita* two men were sent (in order) to search; *bóndi er farinn út á tún að slá* the farmer has gone out in the homefield to mow (it).

4. Accusative with Infinitive.

A so-called accusative with infinitive is often used in Icelandic

instead of an *að*-clause (English that-clause). In these constructions the subject of the clause is put in the accusative, the verb in
the infinitive—as is common in English, too, with certain verbs:

Accusative with Infinitive: *ég sá hann koma* I saw him come;
Að-clause: *ég sá, að hann kom* I saw that he came.

Thus after *sjá* see, *heyra* hear, *álíta* consider, *segja* say, *kalla*
declare, *telja* declare, consider, *láta* let, have, say, *vilja* will, and
others less common: *við heyrðum prest messa* we heard the parson
sing mass; *ég álít þetta rangt (vera)* I consider this wrong (= *ég
álít, að þetta sé rangt)* ; *hann lét það gott heita* he said that this
was all right; *karl sagði (taldi) sig (vera) sjötugan* the old man
claimed to be seventy; but also: *karl sagðist (vera) sjötugur* the
old man said he was seventy.

5. The Infinitive in Indirect Speech.

The example: *karl sagðist vera sjötugur* the old man said he
was seventy, shows that a predicative, following the infinitive, is
put in the nominative to agree with the subject of the verb of
saying, if that subject is the same as that of the infinitive. This is
really indirect speech (of the second type, *9, 5, 2,* which see).

Other instances of a nominative as a subject of an infinitive:
*hann var kallaður (talinn, haldinn, álitinn) (vera) sonur séra
Péturs* he was considered (to be) the son of the Rev. P. Also:
mér finnst þetta (vera) rangt I feel this is wrong; *þessi læknir
þykir góður* this doctor is considered good—not to be confused
with: *þessi læknir þykist góður* this doctor thinks that he is good,
or: this doctor thinks himself good.

6. Að with the Infinitive.

The mark of the infinitive is *að* to : *að lesa* to read. As in English,
it is often dropped; thus after the verbs *munu* shall/will, *skulu*
shall, *mega* may, *vilja* will, *láta* let. *Þetta mun vera rétt* this will
be right, this is probably right.

It is also dropped in the accusative with infinitive construction,
and in the nominative with infinitive construction (indirect speech):
hann segir sig vera veikan he claims (gives himself out) to be sick,
hann segist vera veikur he says he is sick.

Note 1: Infinitives are sometimes dropped. This is especially
common in case of *vera* as will be seen in the paragraphs above.
Vera is also commonly dropped in the future, and past future of
the passive and of the intransitive verbs of motion: *hann mun*

161

(*vera*) *barinn* (*farinn*) he will be beaten, he has probably been beaten; he may be gone, he has probably gone.

Note 2: In English a verbal noun (a gerund in -*ing*) is often used where Icelandic has the infinitive: *viljið þér gera svo vel að segja mér* would you mind telling me; *ég gat ekki að mér gert að hlæja* I could not help laughing; *að lesa og skrifa list er góð* reading and writing is a useful art; *við hættum að kaupa blaðið* we stopped buying the newspaper; *hann þreyttist aldrei á að dást að landinu* he never got tired of admiring the country. Thus often when the infinitive follows (is governed by) a preposition: *ég hlakka til að fara* I look forward to going.

Note 3: Some English infinitives are expressed in a different way in Icelandic: this has nothing to do with it = *það kemur þessu* (*máli*) *ekkert við*; nothing to speak of = *ekkert, sem heitir*, or: *ekkert að kalla*.

Note 4: As in English (rarely), an infinitive is sometimes used in what seems to be a passive sense; but this usage is much more widespread in Icelandic (cf. Impersonal Verb Construction, **14** below): *hér er ekkert að gera* here is nothing to be done; *hér er nóg að gera* here is enough to do (= to be done).

12. The Participles.

1. The Present Participle.

1. The present participle is common with verbs of motion, as in English: *koma gangandi* come walking, *koma labbandi, ríðandi*; *akandi, keyrandi*; *siglandi* come sauntering, riding, driving (a car), sailing; *liggja sofandi* lie sleeping, *sitja þegjandi* sit silent, *standa másandi og glápandi* stand wheezing and staring.

2. *Ekki nokkur lifandi maður* not a living soul. From this expression *lifandi* has spread as an expletive: *lifandi skelfing, lifandi ósköp* how awfully, how frightfully, *ekki lifandi vitund* not a bit. *Mikil lifandi skelfingar ósköp er gaman að vera svolítið hífaður* gee, whiz! how positively (perfectly) divine it is to be a tiny bit tight.

3. The present participle sometimes is used in a passive sense: *þreifandi myrkur* groping darkness (i. e. darkness such that one must feel one's way), but *þreifandi fullur* groping tipsy; *þetta er ómissandi bók* this is an indispensable (invaluable) book; *óskandi væri, að tíðin færi að batna* it is to be hoped that the weather will get better.

162

Note 1: An English present participle corresponds to an Icelandic infinitive in the expanded conjugation of Durative Action with *vera að*: *þér eruð að missa úrið yðar* you are losing your watch.

Note 2: The frequent use in English of present participles to form absolute nominatives, and participial clauses (including the infamous dangling participles) is unknown in Icelandic, which always resolves the participles into clauses with finite verb forms:

Time: *þegar ég kom fyrir húshornið, sá ég hann* rounding the corner of the house, I saw him;

Cause: *af því að Jón var ekki við, talaði ég við son hans* because John was not at home (present) (dangling: John not being present), I spoke to his son;

Condition: *ef þetta er satt, getum við eins vel hætt að vinna* this being true, we can just as well quit working;

Concession: *þó að ég verði að játa þetta, þá neita ég að hætta að vinna* admitting this, I refuse to quit working.

2. The Past Participle.

1. The past participle has an active sense in intransitive verbs (e. g. *kominn* come, *farinn* gone), but in transitive verbs it has a passive sense (e. g. *barinn* beaten, *mikið lesin bók* a much read book). Some verbs waver: *hann er vel lesinn* (active) he is well read (has read widely); *ærin er borin* (active) the ewe has lambed, but *lambið var ný-borið* (passive) the lamb was newly born. Likewise of other animals: *hryssan er köstuð* the mare has foaled, *kýrin er borin* the cow has calved, *tíkin er gotin* the bitch (tyke) has had her whelps.

2. The past participle is used with the auxiliaries *vera*, (*verða*), *hafa* to form compound tenses of verbs; after *vera*, (*verða*) it agrees with the subject: *hann er farinn, hún er farin* he (she) has gone; after *hafa* its neuter form alone (accusative) is now used *hann hefur aukið eldana* he has stoked the fires, but in the older language the past participle could in such position agree with the object (as in French): *hann hefir aukna eldana*.

3. The past participle is also used after the verbs *eiga, fá, geta*: *þér eigið gott skilið af mér* you deserve good things (thanks) from me; *enginn fær gert við því* (literary) *enginn getur gert við því* (colloquial) nobody can help that; *enginn getur gizkað á* nobody can guess.

163

13. Auxiliary Verbs.

1. Besides the auxiliaries *hafa, munu, vera, verða, fara,* which are used to form all the compound and expanded conjugations of the verbs as shown before, there are still several very common verbs that come very near to being auxiliary verbs for forming a future variously modified, and expressing some of the modal effects otherwise indicated by the subjunctive and the imperative. These verbs are the preterite present verbs *eiga, kunna, mega, skulu, vilja, þurfa,* and the common verbs *geta, verða, ætla.* It is convenient to list them below in alphabetical order.

2. *Eiga,* be to, expresses mild necessity, except in the first person present in a question, where it also means: shall I not? or: don't you want me to? Question: *á ég (ekki) að fara?* (a) shall I (not) go? (b) am I (not) to go? Answer to (a): *ég skal fara* I will go; to (b): *ég á (ekki) að fara. Átt þú (ekki) að fara?* are you (not) to go? *á hann (ekki) að fara?* is he (not) to go? *Eigum við að fara?* (a) shall we go? (b) are we to go? Answer (a) *við skulum (viskum, vuskum) fara* we shall go, let us go; (b) *við eigum að fara* we are to go. *Eigið þið (þér) að fara?* are you to go? *Eiga þeir að fara?* are they to go? *Þið (þér) eigið að fara* you are to go; *þeir eiga að fara* they are to go. Preterite: *ég (hann) átti að fara* I (he) was to go; *átti ég að fara?* was I to go? Present subjunctive is not found in this sense, except in subordinate clauses: *mér er sagt, að þér eigið að fara* I am told that you are to go. Preterite subjunctive expresses advice in the second and third person, (moral) duty in the first: *þú ættir að fara, hann ætti að fara* you (he) ought to go, you (he) should go; *ég ætti að fara* I should (ought to) go.

Note: Eiga also means: (a) be supposed to, (b) own, possess: (a) *þeir eiga að hafa séð sjö flugvélar* they are supposed to have seen seven airplanes (also: *þeir áttu að hafa séð . . .* they were supposed to have . . .), so only with perfect of verbs; (b) *hann á hús í Reykjavík* he has a house in R. (common).

3. *Geta* be able to, can, may. It is followed by a past participle. (a) *Hann getur (ekki) komið* he is (not) able to come, he can(not) come; *getur hann lesið?* can he (is he able to) read? *það er ómissandi að geta brugðið sér á sjóinn* it is indispensable to be able to make quick jaunts out to sea (for fishing).

(b) *Það getur verið* it may be; *það getur verið, að ég verði að skreppa til næsta bæjar* it may be that I have to take a trip to the next farm (town). *Það getur ekki verið!* that is impossible!

4. *Kunna* know, know how to, may. (a) *Hann kann fyrsta boðorðið* he knows the first commandment; *hann kunni ensku* he knew English. (b) *Kunnið þér að skrifa íslenzku?* do you know how to write Icelandic? *Nei, ég kann það ekki* no, I do not know how to. (c) *Hann kann að koma* he may come (= *það getur verið, að hann komi* it may be that he comes). This sense is used only in affirmative sentences, not in questions nor after a negation; *hann kann ekki að koma* would mean: he does not know how to come. *Hann kynni að koma, ef hann vissi, að sér væri óhætt* he might come, if he knew that he was safe.

5. *Mega*, may, be allowed to; be able, possible; have to.

(a) *Ég má (ekki) fara* I may (am allowed to) go/I must not go; *þið (þér) megið (ekki) fara* you may go/you must not go; *má ég biðja um smjör?* may I have (ask for) the butter?

(b) *Þetta má ekki* this is not allowed (impersonal); *hér má ekki reykja* smoking is forbidden here; *má vera*, or: *vera má* may be; *það má vel vera* that is quite possible.

(c) *Þeir mega vara sig* they should (had better) beware; *hann mátti lesa upp og læra betur* he had to read everything once more and learn it better; *þér megið trúa mér* you may (must) believe me.

6. *Skulu* shall/will. *Skulu* expresses a promise in the first person (also an exhortation in the first person plural), a command in the second and third:

Ég skal (ekki) fara I will (not) go;
þú skalt (ekki) fara you shall (not) go, don't you go;
hann skal (ekki) fara he shall (not) go;
við skulum (colloquially: *viskum, vuskum*) *(ekki) fara*
    (a) we will (not) go, (b) let us (not) go!
þið (þér) skuluð (ekki) fara you shall (not) go (= *farið þið/þér ekki* don't you go);
þeir skulu (ekki) fara they shall (not) go.

By stressing *skulu* the statements are made peremptory or threatening.

The third person present is sometimes used in questions: *skal hann ætla að fara að rigna* = *ætli hann fari að rigna?* will it begin to rain? I wonder; *skulu þeir ná landi* = *ætli þeir nái landi?* will they reach the shore? one wonders. The first and second persons can not be so used.

Present subjunctive can be used only in subordinate clauses: *ég er hissa, að þú skulir geta látið svona* I am astonished, that

165

you should be able to carry on like that; also with the principal clause unexpressed, as an exclamation: *að þú skulir geta látið svona!* how can you carry on like that!

The preterite is found only in the subjunctive; in principal clauses it is used in questions or after negations: *skyldi pósturinn fara að koma?* I wonder whether the mailman will be coming; *skyldi það? = ætli það?* I wonder if it is so; *það skyldi aldrei verið hafa* that should never have been; *það skyldi maður ætla* one would think so; narrative in indirect speech: *maður hét Jón, hann skyldi vera prestur þeirra* a man was called John, he was to be (*átti að vera*) their parson.

7. *Verða* must, have to, have got to. *Hann verður að fara* he must go; *verður hann að fara?* must he go? *Nei, hann parf ekki að fara* no, he need not go; *já, hann verður að fara* yes, he must go.

Note 1: In this sense *verða* does not take the negation; instead *þurfa* is used.

Note 2: *Það varð að vera = það hlaut að vera* that must have been so, that must have been the reason.

8. *Vilja* will, want. This verb keeps its original meaning of will (volition) better than its English counterpart, which usually denotes a mere future time: *ég vil ekki fara* I do not want to go; *viljið þið (þér) fara?* do you want to go? Preterite subjunctive: *Vilduð þér finna mig?* would you kindly speak to me (literally: meet me)? *Hvað viljið þér mér?* what do you want me about? (of me).

Note: Impersonal, with *verða*: *þetta fór, eins og oft vill verða, menn skiftust í flokka um málið* it came about, as often will happen, that people were divided on the matter. *Mikið má, ef vel vill* (proverbial) much can be done, with good will, or: if things turn out well. *Ef til vill* if it so happens, perhaps.

9. *Þurfa* need, have to. It expresses a strong necessity (stronger than *eiga* be (supposed) to): *allir þurfa að borða* all need to eat;

    ég parf (ekki) að fara I must go/I need not go;
    purfið þið (þér) að fara? must you go?/need you go?
    ég þurfti að fara I had to go.

Preterite subjunctive: *ég þyrfti að fara í búð* I ought (should need) to go to a store. Impersonal: *það þarf að gera við úrið* it is necessary to mend the watch.

10. *Ætla* intend to, be going to.

    Ég ætla (ekki) að fara I am (not) going to go;
    ætlarðu, ætlið þið, ætlið þér að fara? are you going to go?

A verb of motion is often omitted after *ætla*: *Ólafur muður, ætlarðu suður?* Ó. muður (mouth), are you going south? *Hvert ætlarðu?* where are you going?

Note: *Ætli,* third person present subjunctive, is used adverbially to introduce questions; it is followed by a subjunctive (= *skyldi* + infinitive) : *ætli hann fari?* = *skyldi hann fara?* I wonder whether he will go. *Hvað ætli klukkan sé?* I wonder what o'clock it is (what time it is).

11. Verbs in Affirmative Sentences, Negative Sentences, and Questions.

In English, verbs fall into two groups, one small, consisting of the very frequent auxiliaries: have, be, can, may, shall, will (dare, need), the other big, consisting of all other verbs:

Group 1 employs no auxiliary:

Affirmative: I am sick *ég er veikur*;
Negative: I am not sick *ég er ekki veikur*;
Question: Are you sick? *ertu veikur? eruð þér veikur?*

Group 2 employs the auxiliary *do* in negative sentences and questions:

Affirmative: I go home *ég fer heim*;
Negative: I do not go home *ég fer ekki heim*;
Question: Do you go home? *fer þú heim? farið þér heim?*

It will be seen that in the second group English uses the auxiliary *do* in negative sentences and in questions. Not so the Icelandic, where all verbs are treated like the first group in English. The verb *gera, gjöra* corresponding to *do* is sometimes used as an auxiliary in old poetry, but it is not the only one. Others are *nema, ná, ráða*—all used like *do* in English, but in all types of sentences.

14. Impersonal Verb Constructions.

1. Preliminary Remarks.

As in English, it is often desired to use verbs without mentioning any subject—if a subject exists at all. Two methods are open: either to use some kind of an indefinite noun or pronoun as a formal subject, or nothing at all except the verb of the third person singular. In Icelandic both methods are used, English is confined to the first. A logical subject of such a verb may in Icelandic be expressed in dative or accusative, in English in a prepositional phrase: *mér virðist það rangt* to me it seems wrong.

167

A logical subject may be expressed in a prepositional phrase or, more frequently, omitted in Icelandic and English alike in the passive voice: *hann var barinn (af ræningjanum)* he was beaten (by the robber). The omission of the logical subject in the English passive is certainly the easiest (if not the only) way to render, not only a similar Icelandic passive construction, but also many of the Icelandic impersonal verb constructions, whether they are of' the active or of the middle voice. This will be seen in what follows.

2. Indefinite Subjects.

Indefinite nominal and pronominal subjects are as common in Icelandic as in English: *sumir segja, að* . . . some say that . . . ; *menn segja, fólk segir, að* . . . men say, people say that . . . ; *þeir segja, að Katla sé farin að gjósa* they say that Katla (the volcano) has begun erupting; *það er sagt, að* . . . it is said that . . . (passive).

Note: In the last example the saying (the *að* . . . clause) is the real subject instead of which a provisory subject (*það*) is used, just as in English. In Icelandic *það* can be omitted by putting the past participle first: *sagt er, að.* . . . The first method is colloquial, the latter literary. *Það* falls automatically, if an adverb comes to stand before the verb: *nú er sagt, að.* . . .

3. Nature, etc.

Verbs expressing processes of nature (no demonstrable subject), variations of day and night, the seasons, the weather take either the indefinite subjects *það, hann* (b), or none at all:

(a) *Það dagar* it dawns, *það dimmir* it darkens, night falls; *það vorar, haustar, vetrar* spring, fall (autumn), winter comes. *Nú er farið að dimma af nótt* now the night has begun to encroach upon the day (in late August).

(b) *Það rignir, suddar, snjóar, fennir, hríðar, fýkur, hlánar, hlýnar* it rains, drizzles, snows, drifts, snows in a blizzard, drifts, thaws, gets warm. Even more commonly these verbs have *hann* (sometimes personified as the air: *hann Loftur*, formed from *loft* n. air, sometimes even alluding to the ruler of the world: God) as a subject: *hann rignir, snjóar, hlýnar. Hvass er hann og kaldur* the wind (storm) is cold and keen; *hann er að rífa sig upp í norðangarra* the weather is deteriorating into persistent northerly storms. *Það* is often replaced by an adverb (cf. the note of *2* above): *nú snjóar*, but *hann* cannot be omitted: *nú snjóar hann; enn er hann á norðan* it is still blowing from the north.

(c) The verbs of (a) and (b) are intransitive. But here are transitive impersonal verbs: *daginn* (accusative) *lengir* the day(s) grow(s) longer, literally: it lengthens the days, or, in passive: the day is lengthened; *það er farið að bregða birtu* (dative) the day-light is beginning to fail; *þokunni* (dative) *léttir* the fog clears; *þó að hann snjóaði í allan gærdag, þá festi ekki snjó* (accusative) even if it snowed all yesterday, the snow did not remain (on the ground); *á vorin, þegar snjóa* (accusative plural) *leysir* in spring, when the snow melts. *Reykinn* (accusative) *leggur út á sjóinn* the smoke is carried out to sea; *skipið* (accusative) *rak á land* the ship drifted ashore. In most of these cases the Icelandic object is converted into an English subject, and the transitive verb into an intransitive. And even in Icelandic there is a feeling that the objects of these verbs are really the logical subjects; this is indicated by the tendency to put the object before the verb as any other subject.

4. Happenings, etc.

Verbs expressing not too well defined happenings, turning, beginning and end, events, passing of time, difference and lack, are impersonal, with or without *það*:

(a) *Ekkert ber við* nothing happens, *svo bar við, að* . . . it happened that . . . ; *því víkur svo við, að* . . . it so happens that . . . , the point is that . . . ; *hér hefur Íslendingabók* here begins Í.; *nú víkur sögunni til Englendinga* now the tale turns to the English; *hér lýkur sögunni* here the story ends.

(b) *Norðmenn veittu hraustlegt viðnám, en svo fór, að Þjóð-verjar unnu* the Norwegians offered a spirited resistance, but it so turned out that the Germans won; *nú er svo komið, að þeir eru heimilislausir* now things have come to such a pass that they are without homes.

(c) *Nú var komið að kvöldi* now it was near evening; *það líður á veturinn, sumarið, daginn* the winter, summer, day passes; *þaðan var skammt til bæja* from there it was a short way to the farm-steads; *nú er ekki langt til páska* now it is not long to Easter.

(d) *Hér vantar það, sem við á að éta* (proverbial) here is lacking what should be eaten with (the bread, i. e. butter, fat); i. e. the main thing is lacking; *þá* (accusative) *skildi á (greindi á) um pólitík* they differed (fell out) about politics.

5. Mind, etc.

Verbs expressing processes of the mind, sensations, thoughts,

feelings, etc. are often impersonal. With these verbs the logical
subject (the man who senses, thinks, feels) is put in the accusative
or the dative, while the sensation, thought, feeling often is treated
as a subject (a pronoun: *það*, an *að*-clause, etc.). That the accusative or dative is the logical subject is indicated by its fairly
consistent position before the verb. Cp. English: methinks = it
seems to me = I think.

(a) *Mig þyrstir* I get thirsty, I am thirsty; *mig langar í mjólk
að drekka* I (crave) would like to have milk to drink; *mig syfjar*
I get drowsy; *mig grunar* I suspect; *mig minnir* I think I remember; *mig dreymdi, að* . . . I dreamt that. . . .

Mér lízt svo á manninn, að . . . it is my impression of the man
that . . . ; *mér sýnist, heyrist* it seems to me, I think I hear;
mér þykir vænt um hann I like (love) him; *mér þykir illt (leitt),
að* . . . I am sorry that. . . .

(b) *Mér er (verður) heitt, kalt, illt* I am (get) warm, cold, sick;
honum varð illt (bilt) við he was startled; *henni brá (við, í brún)*
she was startled; *þeim batnar, versnar* they get better, worse; *okkur
kom vel saman* we hit it off well (with each other) ; *mér svelgdist
á (vatninu)* I swallowed it (the water) the wrong way; *mér varð
það á að sofna undir messunni* I happened to go to sleep involun-
tarily during the mass.

6. *Compound Tenses with vera.*

The third person singular of ·*vera* (in any tense, indicative and
subjunctive) can be used impersonally in all the compound forms
made up by *vera* (and *verða*).

(a) Passive of transitive verbs: *Það var byggt af kappi, meðan
efni var til* building went on eagerly, while there was material at
hand; *það var sungið* there was singing, people sang; *þeim var
fylgt til næsta bæjar* they were guided to the next farmstead (object
of active verb in dative: *fylgja e-m*) ; *þessa verður minnzt* this will
be remembered (object of active verb genitive: *minnast e-s*).

(b) Compound tenses with *vera* of intransitive verbs of motion:
Nú var riðið í hlað, stigið af baki, gengið að bæjardyrum og barið
now somebody rode up to the front of the house, alighted from the
horse, walked up to the door, and knocked (literally: now was
ridden . . .).

(c) Compound tenses with *vera* of intransitive middle voice verbs:
Þar var barizt tvo daga there they fought two days; *síðan hefur
ekki verið að hafzt* since then nothing has been done.

7. Sensations, Sayings.

Verbs of seeing, hearing, feeling, considering, and saying often are impersonal, with or without the indefinite subject *það*:

(a) *Það sér (sést) ekki á þér, að þú sért veikur* 'it cannot be seen on you that you are sick,' you do not look like a sick man; *það var að heyra á honum, að hann kynni vel við sig* one gathered (by hearing him) that he liked it well there; *það var að finna á (fannst) á henni, að hún vildi komast burt* one felt from what she said that she wanted to get away; *það þykir ókurteisi að taka ekki ofan* it is considered impolite not to doff one's hat; *það lítur ekki út fyrir annað en rigningu* it does not look like anything else but rain; *það sér ekki út úr augunum fyrir þoku* (also: *það sést ekki . . .*) one cannot see out of one's eyes on account of (the) fog; *þar sér (sjást) enn spor hans í sandinum* his tracks (footprints) are still seen there in the sand.

(b) *Nú segir ekki af þeim, fyrr en þeir koma til bæja* now nothing is said (heard) of them, until they get to the farmsteads (= *nú er ekkert sagt af þeim*); *þess getur ekki, hvar þeir kæmu að landi* it is not mentioned where they landed (= *þess er ekki getið*).

Note: In Icelandic these impersonal third person active verbs are replaced, sometimes, by the middle voice (*sér: sést*), sometimes by the passive (*segir: er sagt*). In English the passive usually is employed.

8. Preterite Present Verbs, etc.

The preterite present verbs *eiga, mega, skulu, verða, þurfa*, and the verb *vera* are often impersonal with or without *það*: *Hvað á að borða?* what is there to be eaten? *það á að borða fisk og kartöflur* fish and potatoes are to be eaten; *ekki mátti borða kjöt um föstuna* meat could not (must not) be eaten during lent; *hvað skal segja?* what is to be said? what is to be decided? *hér skal staðar numið* here one must stop; *hér verður að taka í taumana* here the reins must be seized, i. e. something has to be done; *það þarf ekki* that is not necessary; *nú þarf að spara* now people must save; *þá er að hætta* the thing to do is to stop now, you can stop now.

9. Infinitives with Passive Meaning.

Hvað á að borða, what is to be eaten, and other examples in the last paragraph show that, in order to retain the effect of the impersonal verb in English, one must either add an indefinite subject (what is one to eat) or convert the active infinitive into a passive one. This situation is common, too, with active infinitives

171

after verbs of commanding: *látið þér færa mér mjólk* have milk brought to me; *þeir skipa að slökkva öll ljós* they command all lights to be put out.

VII. WORD ORDER.

1. Preliminary Remarks.

The simple and most common word order in Icelandic is quite similar to that of English, but it is much less rigid. This is mostly owing to the fact that distinguishing case forms are still clear in Icelandic, whether they stand in the common order or not, while in English nothing but the word order indicates the function of individual words. When the rules of common word order are broken in Icelandic, it is almost always to emphasize certain words by moving them to the beginning (or the end) of the sentence, or to give a vivid or dramatic tone to the narrative. The account of the deviations from the common word order belongs therefore primarily in the realm of stylistics.

Examples:

Common normal
     word order: *Ari las Njálu*   Ari read Njála
Common inverted
     word order: *las Ari Njálu*   "   "   "   (lively narrative)
Uncommon inverted.
     word order: *Njálu las Ari*   "   "   "   (stressing *Njála*)

2. Normal Word Order (Subject-Verb).

1. Normal word order is used in affirmative sentences (plain narrative):

(a) Subject-verb: *Gísli svaf* G. was sleeping.
(b) Subject-verb-predicative: *Gísli var veikur* G. was sick.
(c) Subject-verb-object-predicative: *Gísli las kverið allt* G. read the booklet complete(ly).
(d) Subject-verb-object-object: *þeir sviftu Gísla launum* they deprived G. of (his) salary.
(e) Subject-verb-indirect object-object: *Gísli gaf honum (Pétri) kverið* G. gave him the booklet/G. gave the booklet to Peter.

Note: Here one type of word order in Icelandic corresponds to two in English.

172

(f) Subject-verb-indirect object-predicative with subject: *Gísli var öllum góður* G. was good to everybody (all).

(g) Impersonal verb-(indirect) object-object with the omitted subject: *vantar Gísla vinnu* G. lacks work.

Note: Though normal, this is not the common word order. That is: *Gísla vantar vinnu* (inverted, see below).

2. Normal word order is used in questions that begin with interrogative pronouns: *hver kom?* who came? *hvaða maður var þetta?* what man (who) was that?

3. Normal word order is usual in subordinate clauses beginning with a conjunction, an interrogative pronoun or adverb, or a relative pronoun. In all these the subject-verb follows right after the conjunction or the pronoun, unless the pronoun itself (interrogative or relative) is subject.

Þeir sögðu, að Gísli væri veikur they said that G. was sick. Thus after *fyrr en* before, *þar eð* since, *því að* because, *þó (að)* although, even if, etc.

Þeir spurðu, hvort Gísli væri kominn they asked, whether G. had come.

Þeir spurðu, hver væri kominn (also inverted: *hver kominn væri*) they asked who had come?

Það var Gísli, sem var kominn (also inverted: *sem kominn var*) it was G. who had come.

Bókin, sem Gísli var að lesa, hét Njála the book G. was reading was called Njála.

Note: Inversion of auxiliary verb and past participle is possible only when the pronoun (interrogative, relative) is subject.

3. Inverted Word Order (Verb-Subject).

1. Inverted word order is common in affirmative sentences with impersonal verbs, where the sentence takes the form: indirect or direct object-verb-object or predicative (with the subject, latent in the verb): *Björn* (acc.) *vantar vinnu* B. needs work; *Birni* (dat.) *varð illt* B. was taken ill.

Note: Though inverted from a grammatical point of view, this order is really normal from the logical point of view: logical subject-verb-logical object. Hence it usually is preferred to the normal order in 2, 1 (g) above.

2. Inverted word order is common in dramatic or vivid narrative, also, as in English, in the short intercalated 'says he': *leið nú til sumarmála, fór húsfreyja þá að ógleðjast; spurði bóndi hana,*

hverju það sætti. "*Það má ég ekki segja þér,*" *segir hún* time was approaching the first day of summer, then the lady of the house began to flag in spirit; her husband asked her what was the matter with her. "I cannot tell you that," she says (i. e. she said).

3. Inverted word order is the rule in the uncommon affirmative sentences, where parts of the sentence other than the subject are placed first, mostly for emphasis or, perhaps, for rhythmical reasons. *Sterkur var Gísli!* G. certainly was strong! *Bókina las hann spjaldanna á milli* the book he read from cover to cover; *honum gaf hann dóttur sína* to him he gave his daughter; *stundum var mér* (logical subject) *allt of heitt* at times I was much too warm; *þrettán nóttum fyrir jól koma jólasveinar af fjöllunum* thirteen nights before Christmas the Yule Goblins come from the mountains.

Note: The normal order of auxiliary and main verb (past participle, infinitive) may be seen from the different compound conjugations. E. g. normal: *ég hef séð hann* I have seen him; inverted: *hef ég séð hann* (1) lively, (2) question; *séð hef ég hann, hann hef ég séð* uncommon, dramatic expressions.

4. Inverted word order is used in questions, not introduced by pronominal subjects (cf. 2, 2 above): *Er Gísli heima?* is G. at home? *Kemur hann í kvöld?* does he come tonight? *Hvar verður hann í nótt?* where is he going to stay overnight?

Note: Sometimes questions are expressed with tone alone, without changing word order.

5. Inverted word order is used in commands with the imperative, sometimes with the subjunctive: *Farðu heim* (= *far þú heim*)! go home! *fari hann bölvaður*! let him be damned! but: *drottinn blessi heimilið* God bless the home.

6. Inverted word order is used in main clauses that follow their subordinate clauses; these postponed main or principal clauses often begin with (a redundant) *þá*: *þegar við vorum búin að borða, þá fórum við að hátta* when we (a mixed company) had eaten, we went to bed, but: *við fórum að hátta, þegar*. . . .

Also in co-ordinated sentences beginning with *enda, heldur*: *hann var ljótur í gær, enda fór hann að snjóa í dag* the weather was threatening yesterday, and, sure enough, it began to snow today: *þau vildu ekki búa þar lengur, heldur fóru þau til Reykjavíkur* they did not want to live there any longer, instead they went to Reykjavík.

7. Inverted word order is used in conditional clauses, when *ef*, if, is omitted: *nú skyldi ég hlæja, væri ég ekki dauður* (= *ef ég væri ekki dauður*), *sagði karlinn* now I would laugh, were I not dead (= if I were not dead), said the old man.

4. Adverbs.

1. Adverbs, when modifying verbs, usually follow the verb (or the object or the indirect object of the verb): *Gísli las vel G.* read well; *Gísli las bókina vel G.* read the book well.

2. When modifying adjectives or other adverbs, the adverbs precede the word modified: *Gísli las mjög vel G.* read very well; *Gísli var hættulega veikur G.* was dangerously ill. But *mjög, nokkuð* somewhat, and *vel* may also follow the word: *syfjaður mjög* very sleepy; *gamall nokkuð* somewhat old; *ríkur vel* quite rich.

3. When subject and verb are inverted (a) in questions, (b) in commands, (c) in vivid or dramatic narrative, the adverb follows the subject, not the verb: *Las Gísli vel?* did G. read well? *Lestu (les þú) vel!* read (you) well! *nú lætur prestur Gísla stafa, og las hann mjög vel* now the parson had G. spell, and he read well indeed.

4. But it is also possible to put the adverb in front of verb and subject, which then invariably are inverted: *vel las Gísli* well did G. read. This emphasizes the adverb; it is especially common in case of adverbs of time, place and mood.

Normal:
það var einu sinni maður
there was once a man
hann var þar um nóttina
he was there during the night.

Inverted:
einu sinni var maður
once there was a man
þar var hann um nóttina
there he was during the night.

VIII. CONJUNCTIONS.

1. Conjunctions may be divided into two groups according to whether they connect coordinated sentences or subordinated clauses.

2. Coordinating Conjunctions.—Of these there are two kinds, the simple and the correlative.

Simple conjunctions are in order of frequency: *og* and, *en* but, *eða* or, *heldur* but, *ellegar* or (else), *enda* and also, and indeed, and that is why.

Correlative conjunctions are in order of frequency: *bæði . . . og* both . . . and, *hvorki . . . né* neither . . . nor, *annaðhvort . . . eða* either . . . or, *hvort heldur . . . eða* whether . . . or, *ýmist . . . eða* either . . . or, sometimes . . . sometimes, *ekki (eigi) aðeins . . . heldur einnig* not only . . . but also.

Note: Occasionally *en* is used where English would have *and*: *Jón var sonur hans, en Ása dóttir* J. was his son and Á. his daughter.

175

3. Subordinating Conjunctions.—Some of these conjunctions are followed by the indicative, some by the indicative and the subjunctive, and some by the subjunctive only (see Use of the Subjunctive in Conditions and in Subordinate Clauses, VI, 9, 4 above). In the following it will be indicated which mood follows each conjunction.

(a) The conjunction *að*, that, is a subordinating conjunction *par excellence*. It is not only used alone in that-clauses, which usually take the subjunctive, rarely the indicative, but it is also frequently used as the last element in composite conjunctions, many of which will be seen in the following. But in these composite conjunctions it often is dropped in the colloquial language, though it is usually kept in writing. This dropping is indicated by square brackets. Even alone *að* may be dropped, though more rarely: *ég held [að] ég sé* I think I am.

(b) Causal conjunctions: *af því [að]*, *því [að]*, *fyrir því að*, *sökum þess að*, *sakir þess að*, *vegna þess að* (ind. and subj.) because; *því [að]* (ind. and subj.) for, because; *með því [að]*, *sökum þess að*, *úr því [að]*, *þar eð*, *þar sem*, *fyrst* (ind.) since.

(c) Conditional conjunctions: *ef* (ind. and subj.) if, *nema* (subj.) unless, *svo framarlega sem* (ind. and subj.) provided.

(d) Result conjunctions: *svo [að]*, *að* (ind. and subj.) so that.

(e) Concessive conjunctions: *þó [að]*, *þótt*, *enda þótt* (subj.) although, though, even if; *þrátt fyrir það að* (ind.) in spite of the fact that.

(f) Purpose conjunctions: *til að, til þess að* (subj. or inf.) in order that, or: in order to; *svo [að]* (subj. and ind.) so that.

(g) Comparison conjunctions: *eins og* as if, as, *eins . . . og* as . . . as, *as . . . as* if, *og* as; *sem* as, like, *svo sem* as, *svo . . . sem* as (so) . . . as; *en* than, *heldur en* than; *því . . . því* tne . . . the, *því . . . þeim mun* the . . . the, *þess . . . þess* the . . . the.

(h) Temporal conjunctions: *þegar, þá er, er* when; *áður en, fyrr en* before; *á meðan* while; *eftir að* after; *sem* as, when; *frá því [að]* from the time that, *jafnskjótt og, jafnskjótt sem* as soon as, *óðara en, undir eins og, strax og*, as soon as; *um leið og* as soon as, at the same time as; *síðan* since; *þangað til að, þar til að, þar til er, til þess er, unz* until.

(i) Interrogative conjunctions: *hvort* whether, *hvort . . . eða* whether . . . or, *hvort heldur . . . eða* whether . . . or; *hvort sem . . . eða* whether . . . or.

(j) Relative conjunctions: *þar sem* (or *er*) 'there where,' where; *þangað sem* (*er*) 'thither where,' whither, where; *þaðan sem* (*er*) 'thence where,' whence; *hvert sem* (*er*) wherever (motion); *hvar sem* wherever; *hvaðan sem* 'whence-so-ever,' wherever . . . from; *hvernig sem* however; *hvenær sem* whenever.

4. Conjunctions and Adverbs.—Conjunctions and adverbs are often alike, i. e. the same words sometimes function as conjunctions, sometimes as adverbs. Usually the word order will reveal whether one has to do with one or the other (cf. Word Order, VII, 4, adverbs). It is inverted when adverbs stand at the head of a sentence, but normal after conjunctions in a subordinate clause.

Adverbs:	Conjunctions:
þó however, still	*þó* [*að*] although
þó kom hann still he came (= *hann kom þó*);	*þó* [*að*] *hann kæmi* . . . even if he came;
þegar at once	*þegar* when
þegar batnaði honum he got well at once (= *honum batnaði þegar*);	*þegar honum batnaði* . . . when he got well;
áður before, formerly	*áður en* before
áður var hér óbyggt before, this place was not settled (= *hér var óbyggt áður*);	*áður en hér var byggt* . . . before this place was settled;
á meðan meanwhile	*á meðan* while
á meðan var kaffið hitað meanwhile, the coffee was made (= *kaffið var hitað á meðan*);	*á meðan kaffið var hitað* . . . while the coffee was being made;
jafnskjótt, strax, undir eins at once	*jafnskjótt og, strax og, undir eins og* as soon as
strax tók hann til máls at once, he began to speak.	*strax og hann tók til máls* . . . as soon as he began to speak.

IX. APPENDIX. WORD FORMATION.

1. Words in Icelandic are mainly formed in two different ways: by derivation (in a narrow sense of the word) or by composition. By derivation a great many words can be formed from the same stem or root; thus from the verbal stem of the strong verb *sitja* (root *set-*), to sit, we have the following derived words: *setja* to set, *seta* f. seat, *set* n. sitting place, *setur* n. a dwelling place, *sessa* f. pillow, *sess* m. seat, *sessi* m. sitting companion, *sáta* f. small haystack, *sæti* n. (collective) a group of *sáta*'s, *sót* n. soot, *Sóti* m. rustbrown horse, *sjatna* to settle down. The vowel shifts involved in these formations are: the old shift (*set-*:*sat-*:*sát-*: *sót-*), the i-shift (*sitja, sæti*), and the breaking (*sjatna*).

No attempt will here be made to describe the laws of derivation, but it may be remarked that the borderline between it and composition as defined below, is not always clear.

2. Composition of words is done mainly by compounding with three elements: prefixes, suffixes, and word stems, or words unchanged. By this definition a prefix is a (short) compounding element that occurs only prefixed to words, e. g. *tor-sóttur* difficult to get. Likewise, a suffix is a (short) compounding element that occurs only at the end of words, e. g. *bú-andi* farmer, *gam-all* old. The borderline between prepositions or adverbs and prefixes is often vague, hence I have in the glossary given any prefixed element the name of prefix.

Since inflexional endings are added directly to the suffixes, and since gender and class in nouns and adjectives, as well as class in verbs, is determined by the inflexional ending, most suffixes are mentioned in connection with the different classes of inflexions so that there is no need to enumerate them here.

3. As there is no such opportunity to mention the prefixes, a short list may be given here:

aðal- chief; *aðaldalur* chief valley.
afar- very, awfully; *afarstór* very (awfully) big, huge.
al- all, complete; *alvitur* omniscient, knowing all.
all- quite; *allvitur* quite wise.
and- anti-, opposite; *andstæðingur* adversary, opponent.
auð- easily; *auðsær* evident, *auðveldur* easy (easily wielded).
einka- private, special; *einkasonur* only son, *einkasala* monopoly.
fjöl- multi-, poly-; *fjölfræðingur* polymath.
for- fore, pro-; *forboði* foreboding, precursor, *forboðinn* prohibited.
frum- proto-, primeval; *frumskógur* primeval forest; *frumkvæði* initiative.
gagn- through; *gagnsær* transparent, also *gegn-sær*.
mis- mis-; *misskilja* misunderstand.
ó- un-, in-; *ófær* impassable, *óvinur* enemy, *ófriður* war.
of- too, too much; *ofdrykkja* too much drinking, intemperance.
sí- always, continually; *síungur* always young.
sví- derogatory prefix; *svívirða* dishonor, disgrace.
tor- difficult; *torsóttur* hard to come by, hard to get.
van- negative prefix; *vanheilsa* bad health.
var- negative prefix; *vargefin* (of a woman) ill matched (in marriage).

ör- negative and intensive prefix; *örmagna* exhausted, *örmjór* very slender.

Prepositions and adverbs often are used as prefixes: *úti-hús* outhouse, *til-búinn* prepared.

4. Words, of all classes, may be joined to other words to make compound words. Usually the word at the end is unchanged: it retains its gender and class features, if it is a noun, its class features, if it is an adjective or a verb: *skóli* m. school : *barna-skóli* m. school for children; *gamall* adj. old: *fjör-gamall* very old; *brenna* wv. burn : *skað-brenna* wv. burn to damage, burn dangerously. A few words change their gender or class by derivation: *þing* n. meeting, assembly : *Al-þingi* n. the national assembly, the Icelandic Parliament; *nótt* f. night : *mið-nætti* n. mid-night.

5. Words, which do not stand at the end, but either first or in the middle (if the compound word has more than two parts), are joined in three different ways to the last element:

(a) The stem (or root) may be joined directly to the following element: *sól* f. sun : *sól-skin* n. sunshine; *kýr* f. cow : *kú-gildi* n. the value of a cow; *til* prep., adv. to : *til-finning* f. feeling.

(b) The word (stem or root) may be connected by a so-called connective vowel, that otherwise does not appear: *ráð* n. advice : *ráðu-nautur* m. adviser.

(c) Some case forms of the word may be used (never the nominative, if it is different from the stem), especially the genitive: *barn* n. child : *barns-skór* m. pl. the shoes of a child, *barna-skóli* m. school for children; *höfn* f. harbor : *hafnar-garður* 'harbor wall,' a mole.

6. As a rule the first element in a compound word remains unchanged throughout the flexion. But there are certain exceptions. In some of the pronouns both parts are inflected, e. g. *annar-hvor*. In place names, composed of a weak adjective and a noun, the weak adjective usually retains its inflexion, at least in colloquial speech, e. g. *Breiði-fjörður*, gen. *Breiða-fjarðar* 'Broad Firth,' *Langa-brekka*, gen. *Löngu-brekku* 'Long Slope.' But in the old language there was a tendency to substitute the stem form of the adjective, hence: *Breiða-fjörður, Langa-brekka,* and this is by some considered the more correct form. There must, finally, often be an agreement in number between the two parts of a compound word, thus *manns-nafn* a personal name (lit. ' man's name ') has the plural *manna-nöfn* ' men's names.'

7. As will be seen from the above paragraphs, compound words in Icelandic are, by and large, made by the same rules as compound words in English. But compound words are more common in Icelandic and that for several reasons:

(a) In English there is a tendency to keep the elements of compound words separated in writing (the first word may then be looked upon as an adjective): stone wall = *grjót-garður*. In Icelandic the tendency is directly opposite.

(b) In English an adjective + a noun often correspond to a compound word in Icelandic: golden anniversary = *gull-brúðkaup*.

(c) In English the of-genitive often corresponds to an Icelandic genitive (or stem) that enters as a first element into a compound word: mistress of the house = *hús-freyja*, love of country = *ættjarðar-ást*.

(d) It follows from the above-mentioned points that frequently an Icelandic compound will interchange with the uncompounded last element: *kirkju-staður* = *staður* parsonage, literally 'church place.'

8. It would lead too far to enumerate even the common types of Icelandic compounds. In the main the same types can be found in English, though English possesses some types that are not found in Icelandic, e. g. cut-throat, hold-up, left-overs, father-in-law. Of the Icelandic types that are not found in English only one shall here be mentioned, because it is very frequent in colloquial speech. Formally, it looks like *grjót-garður* stone wall, or *kirkju-staður* parsonage, that is, it is composed of two nouns. But it is really the second element (noun) which modifies the first in the type *mann-skratti* deuce of a fellow. It is a type very expressive of emotions: it is used in terms of scolding, disparaging, invective, but also in terms of condescending, pitying, and even endearment and petting. Examples: *mann-skratti* deuce of a fellow, devil of a man, *strák-grey* poor boy, *hunds-garmur* poor dog, wretch of a dog, *krakka-skinn* poor children, *móður-mynd* what is supposed to be a mother, *karl-tötrið* the poor (rag of an) old man.

9. Compounds of verb-adverb combinations are found in Icelandic as well as in English: *utan-á-skrift* address from *skrifa utan á*, cp. English *down-pour* from pour down.

180

TEXTS I.

ÆFINGAR MEÐ MÁLFRÆÐI.

1.

Hvað eigum við að lesa í málfræðinni? What are we to read in the grammar?

Þið eigið að lesa nútíð framsöguháttar af sögninni að vera (í setningafræðinni), persónufornöfnin og veika beygingu karlkyns og kvennkyns nafnorða í beygingafræðinni. Lesið líka atviksorðin og athugið, að nafnhættir sagna enda á -a.

You are to read the present indicative of the verb to be (in the Syntax: S. VI, 1, *2*), the personal pronouns, and the weak declensions of masculine and feminine nouns in the Inflexions (In. VI, 1; In. I, 5, *1*; 6, *1*). Read also the adverbs (In. IV, 1, 1-3), and note that the infinitives of verbs end in *-a.*

Æfing. Exercise.

Björssi, Siggi, Gunna og Valdi eru að leika sér. Björssi er kennari; þau Siggi, Gunna og Valdi eru að læra hjá honum. Björssi er einn í skólastofunni, en þau eru þar ekki; þau eru úti. Björssi: Hvar eruð þið? Siggi (úti): Ég er hér. Björssi: Ertu þarna einn? Siggi: Já, ég er hérna einn. Björssi: Hvar eru þau Gunna og Valdi? Siggi: Valdi er úti á götu, en Gunna er uppi hjá mömmu. Björssi: Hvar er pabbi? Siggi: Pabbi er ekki heima. Björssi: Hvar eru þau afi og amma? Siggi: Þau eru líka uppi hjá mömmu. Björssi: Tíminn er að byrja; þið Gunna verðið að koma inn í skólann. Gunna og Siggi (við gluggann): Við erum að koma.

Preliminary note to the Exercise Glossaries:

The grammatical tags following the catchwords should be used as references to the Grammar. The designation of gender (m., f., n.) is preceded by an indication whether the noun is *strong* or *weak* (st or w) and followed by the class number. Thus wm.1 means ' weak masculine first class,' and stf.2 ' strong feminine second class.' Likewise verbs (v.) are marked *strong* or *weak* (st,w) with the class number added, thus: stv.1 is ' strong verb first class,' and wv.4 ' weak verb fourth class.'

In the General Glossary at the end, weak nouns and verbs are marked exactly as above, but the *strong* nouns and verbs are not marked with st. Hence simple m., f., n., v. in the General Glossary corresponds to stm., stf., stn., and stv. in the Exercises. This is in agreement with general dictionary practice.

á prep. with dat. on; in.
að with infinitives: to.
afi wm.1 grandpa.
amma wf.1 grandma.
Bjössi wm.1 pet name for *Björn*.
að byrja to begin, beginning.
einn alone.
ekki adv. not.
en conj. but.
ertu = ert þú. Pr. **4**, *4*.
gata wf.1 street.
að gera to do, doing.
gluggi wm.1 window.
Gunna wf.1 pet name for *Guðrún.*
heima adv. at home.
hér adv. here.
hérna adv. here (pointing).
hjá prep. with dat. with.
hvað interr. pron. what.
hvar adv. where.
í prep. with dat. in, at; with acc. into.
inn adv. into.
já adv. yes.

kennari wm.1 teacher.
að koma to come, coming.
að leika sér to play, playing.
líka adv. also, too.
að læra to learn, study; learning.
mamma wf.1 mother, mummy.
og conj. and.
pabbi wm.1 father, daddy.
Siggi wm.1 pet name for *Sigurður.*
skólastofa wf.1 schoolroom.
skóli wm.1 school.
tími wm.1 time, hour, class period.
uppi adv. up above, upstairs.
úti adv. outside.
Valdi wm.1 pet name for *Þorvaldur,* *Valdimar.*
að vera to be; with infinitive: *að vera að læra* to be learning (present participle, cf. S. VI, **4**).
að verða to have to; *þið verðið* you must.
við prep. with acc. at.
þar adv. there.
þarna adv. there (pointing).

Note 1: *Í skólastofu-nni* in the schoolroom; *í skóla-nn* into the school; *við glugga-nn* at the window; *tími-nn* the hour, the period. These are forms of the suffixed definite article; see In. II, **2**.

Translate into Icelandic:

What (*hvað*) is Bjössi doing (*að gera*)? He is a teacher. Where is he? He is up at the school (*uppi í skóla*). Where are Siggi, Gunna and Valdi? Siggi and Valdi are outside, Valdi is out in the street, but Gunna is upstairs. She is with mother. Where are grandma and grandpa? They are upstairs with mother, too. Where is father? He is not at home, he is out. Who (*hver*) is studying? Siggi, Gunna, and Valdi.

Note 2: Siggi and Valdi are here (1) *Siggi og Valdi eru hér,* (2) *þeir Siggi og Valdi eru hér* (literally: they, S. and V.). Cf. S. IV, **1**, 3. Siggi and Gunna, they . . . *Siggi og Gunna, þau* . . . Cf. S. V, **2**, 2: persons of different sex (or nouns of different gender) are referred to with the neuter plural personal pronoun.

2.

Hvað eigum við að lesa í málfræði? What are we to read in the grammar?

Lesið þið annan flokk af veikum kvennkynsorðum (fræði) og

182

sterk hvorugkynsorð (borð, barn, kyn). Lesið um dvöl verknaðar í setningafræðinni (vera að koma).

Read the second class of feminines, weak declension (In. I, **6**, **2**) and the strong neuters (In. I, **4**). Read about durative action in the syntax (S. VI, **4**).

Æfing.

Bjössi: Eruð þið nú til? Gunna og Siggi: Já, við erum til. Bjössi: Þá er að byrja. Siggi, ertu góður í málfræði? Siggi: Nei, ég er ekki góður í henni. Bjössi: En í dýrafræði? Siggi: Nei, ekki heldur. Bjössi: Ertu ekki góð í landafræði, Gunna? Gunna: Jú, ég er góð í henni. Bjössi: Hvar er Ísland? Gunna: Ísland er þarna á þilinu. Bjössi: Nei, ekki kortið af Íslandi, heldur landið sjálft. Gunna: Ísland er norðarlega í Atlantshafi. Bjössi: Hvar er Grænland? Gunna: Grænland er fyrir vestan Ísland. Bjössi: Hvar er England? Gunna: England er fyrir suðaustan Ísland. Bjössi: En hvar eru þau á kortinu? Gunna: Ísland er hér, Grænland þarna og England þarna hinu megin niðri á kortinu.

á prep. with dat. on; *á kortinu* on the map.
Atlantshaf stn. the Atlantic ocean.
að byrja to begin.
dýrafræði wf.2 zoology.
England stn. England.
fyrir prep. with acc. for; *fyrir vestan* west of, *fyrir suðaustan* southeast of.
góður m. *góð* f. good; *góð(ur)* í good at.
Grænland stn. Greenland.
heldur adv. either, *ekki heldur* not either.
heldur conj. but.
hinu megin adv. on the other side.
í prep. with dat. at, in.
Ísland stn. Iceland.
já adv. yes (answering a positive question).
jú adv. yes (answering a negative question).

kort stn. map.
land stn. land, country.
landafræði wf.2 geography.
málfræði wf.2 grammar.
nei adv. no.
niðri adv. down, below.
norðarlega adv. northerly; *n. í Atlantshafi* in the northern Atlantic.
nú adv. now.
sjálft adj. n. itself.
suðaustan adv. from the southeast; *fyrir s.* southeast of.
til adv. ready.
um prep. with acc. about.
að vera til be ready; *þá er að byrja* then let us begin. S. VI, **14**, 8.
vestan adv. from the west; *fyrir vestan* west of.
þá adv. then.
þessi dem. pron. this, these.
þil stn. (like *kyn*) wall, partition.

Note: *Á þili-nu* on the wall; *kort-ið* the map; *land-ið* the country; *á korti-nu* on the map. These are forms of the suffixed definite article (In. II, **2**).

Translate into Icelandic:

Gunna and Valdi are studying with Bjössi. He is a good (*góður*) teacher. They are studying (*eru að læra*) grammar and geography, but they are not good (*góð*) at grammar. Valdi is studying about (*að læra um*) Iceland, Gunna about England. Where are these (*þessi*) countries? They are in the Atlantic. Are they on the map? Yes, they are (omit 'they are' in Icelandic). Where is the map? The map is on the wall.

3.

Hvað á ég að lesa í málfræði? What am I to read in the grammar?

Lesið þér þátíðina af sögninni að vera, annan flokk af veikum karlkynsorðum (nemandi, bóndi), veik hvorugkynsorð (auga), sterk hvorugkynsorð (borð, barn, kyn) og tilsvarandi myndir af viðskeytta ákveðna greininum.

Read the preterite of the verb to be (S. VI, **1**, *2*), the second class of masculines, weak declension (In. I, **5**, *2*), the weak neuters (In. I, **7**), the strong neuters (In. I, **4**), and corresponding forms of the suffixed definite article (In. II, **2**).

Æfing.

Hvað voru börnin að gera? Þau voru að leika sér. Bjössi var kennari, Siggi og Gunna nemendur, Valdi var bóndi. Hann var úti, en þau voru uppi í skóla. Í skólastofunni var borð; á borðinu voru blöð, blek og pennar. Á þilinu í stofunni voru kort og myndir af dýrum. Þar var mynd af krumma, sem var að kroppa augu úr lambi. Bjössi var að prófa Gunnu í dýrafræði. Hvaða dýr er þetta? En Gunna var utan við sig; hún var að horfa út í gluggann. Í glugganum voru blóm, og á honum var fluga. Út um gluggann sá Gunna fyrst hafið, með skipum á, þar næst fjallið á móti. Yfir í fjallinu var fé, líklega lömb með mömmum sínum. Féð var að kroppa gras í fjallinu. En Gunna sá ekki krumma; hann var að kroppa augu úr lambi í fjallinu.

Note: *Út um gluggann sá Gunna hafið* inverted word order; cf. S. VII, **3**, 3; normal word order: *Gunna sá hafið út um gluggann* G. saw the sea (out) through the window.

af prep. with dat. of.
auga wn. eye; *augu úr lambi* the eyes (out) of a lamb.
barn stn. child.
blað stn. paper, newspaper.
blek stn. ink.
blóm stn. flower.
bóndi wm.2 farmer.
borð stn. table.

dýr stn. animal.
en conj. but.
fé stn. collective: sheep.
fjall stn. mountain.
fluga wf.1 fly.
fyrst adv. first.
að gera to do, doing.
gras stn. grass.
haf stn. sea, ocean.

að horfa to look, looking.
hvað interr.pron.n. what.
hvaða interr.pron.indecl. what, what
kind of.
í prep. with dat. in, on.
að kroppa to graze, crop; pick, peck.
krummi wm.1 pet name for *hrafn*
raven; *krummi* the raven; cf. S.
II, 5.
lamb stn. lamb.
líklega adv. probably, likely.
með prep. with dat. with; *m. mömmum sínum* with their mothers.
mót stn. meeting; *á móti* adv.
phrase: opposite.
mynd stf.2 picture; pl. *myndir* pictures.
nemandi wm.2 pupil.
næst adv. next; *þar næst* thereupon.

penni wm.1 pen.
að prófa to examine, examining.
sá pret. of *sjá* to see.
sem rel.pron.indecl. who, that.
skip stn. ship, boat; *með skipum á*
with ships on it.
um prep. with acc. through.
uppi í skóla up at the school.
úr prep. with dat. out of.
út adv. out (motion to a place);
út í out into, out in; *út um* out
through, out.
utan adv. from the outside; *utan
við* outside of; *u. við sig* absentminded, distracted.
yfir adv. over; *y. í* over yonder in.
þar næst adv. (= *þarnæst*) thereupon.
þetta dem.pron.n. this.

Translate into Icelandic:

What were the children doing? They were playing. What was
Bjössi? He was a teacher. What was Valdi? He was a farmer.
Where was he? He was out. Where were the others (*hin*)? They
were in the school. What was in the schoolroom? A table. What
was on the table? Pens and ink. What was on the wall of the
schoolroom? A picture of the raven (*krumma*). What was he
doing? He was picking an eye out of a lamb. Did Gunna see (*sá
Gunna*) the raven? No, she was looking out of (*út um*) the window.
She saw the sea and the mountains opposite.

4.

Hvað á að lesa í málfræði? What is there to be read in the
grammar?

*Lesið nútíð af sögninni að hafa, eignarfornöfnin og ákveðna
greininn (einkum tími-nn, lilja-n og hvorugkynsorðin). Lærið líka
beygingardæmin tré, hreiður og kvæði.* Read the present of the
verb to have (S. VI, 1, 2), the possessive pronouns (In. VI, 2),
and the definite article (In. II, 1 and 2, especially *tími-nn, lilja-n*
and the neuter nouns). Learn also the strong neuter paradigms
tré, hreiður, kvæði (In. I, **4**).

Æfing.

Pabbi Gunnu er skipstjóri; hann hefur skip til umráða. Eitt
kvöld hefur hann boð á skipinu, og Gunna er í boðinu. Hún hefur
gaman af að vera úti á skipi pabba síns; hún hefur leiksystkin

185

sín með sér. Þau eru krakkar eins og hún; þau hafa líka gaman
af að vera úti á skipi. Á meðal krakkanna er Bjössi. Gunna
(við Bjössa): Er ekki gaman að vera hér? B.: Jú. G.: Hefur þú
verið á skipi áður?. B.: Já, og ég á líka sjálfur skip. G.: Hvaða
skip eru það? B.: Það eru smáskip; ég hef fjölda af þeim á vatninu
fyrir ofan skólann. G.: Hefur þú mastur og akkeri og stýri á þínum
skipum eins og pabbi hefur á sínu skipi? B.: Já. G.: En hefur
þú ljós á þeim á kvöldin í myrkrinu? B.: Nei, það hef ég ekki.
G.: Úr hverju eru þín skip? B.: Þau eru úr tré. G.: Já, en skip
pabba míns er úr járni og stáli. Hefur þú háseta á þínum skipum
eins og pabbi hefur á sínu? B.: Nei.

á verb; *ég á* I have, own.

á prep. *á meðal* compound prep. with gen. among; *á skipinu* on the ship, on board the boat.

aðeins adv. only.

áður adv. before.

akkeri stn. (like *klæði*) anchor.

boð stn. invitation, party; *í boðinu* at the party.

eins og conj. like.

einu sinni adv. once.

eitt one (neuter).

fjöldi wm.1 multitude, a great many.

fyrir prep. with acc. for; *f. ofan* above.

gaman stn. (like *sumar*) fun; *hafa g. af* be fond of, be happy over.

hafa v. to have; *h. verið* have been.

háseti wm.1 sailor.

hvaða interrog. pron. what.

í prep. with dat. in, at.

járn stn. iron.

jú adv. yes, answering negative questions.

krakki wm.1 a familiar (pet) word for the more polite *barn* child.

kvöld stn. evening; *á kvöldin* in the evening.

leiksystkin stn. pl. playmates.

líka adv. also.

ljós stn. light.

mastur stn. (*hreiður*) mast.

með sér with her.

meðal prep. with gen. among.

mjög adv. very.

myrkur stn. (*hreiður*) darkness.

sjálfur my-, your-, him-, her-, it-self.

skipstjóri wm.1 captain.

smáskip stn. a small ship, little boat.

stál stn. steel.

stýri stn. (*kvæði*) rudder.

til prep. with gen. to, for, at.

tré stn. tree, wood; pl. trees.

umráð stn. disposal; *til u-a* at one's disposal.

úr prep. with dat. out of, of; *úr hverju* of what material; *vera úr* be made of.

úti á skipi out on the boat.

vatn stn. water; lake.

við prep. with acc. to.

það it, that; *það eru skip* they are ships; *það hef ég ekki* that I have not.

Translate into Icelandic:

What (*hvað*) is Gunna's father? He is a captain. Does he have a
ship? Yes, he has a great many ships (*fjölda af skipum* or *fjölda skipa*). Once (*einu sinni*) he had (*hafði*) a party on the ship for
(*fyrir*) Gunna and her playmates; they were (*höfðu*) very (*mjög*)
happy over it (*því*). Bjössi was among them. His father has no
(*ekkert*) ship; but he himself has many (*mörg*) small ships on a

186

PEYSUFÖT OG UPPHLUTUR.

lake above the school. Of what material were Bjössi's ships? Not of iron and steel, but only (*aðeins*) of wood. Is Bjössi fond of his ships (*skipunum sínum*)? Yes, he is (he is: omited in Icelandic).

5.

Hvað eigum við að hafa í málfræði? What (assignment) are we to have in the grammar?

Lesið þið núliðna tíð af sögninni að vera, sterka beygingu lýsingarorða (gulur, hár, dýr, seinn, mikill), og lesið um ' það ' notað sem óákveðið fornafn.

Read the perfect of the verb to be (S. VI, **1**, *2*), the strong declension of adjectives (In. III, **2**), and of *það* used as indefinite pronoun (S. IV, **1**, 5). For *blátt hafið*, see S. III, **1**, 1.

Note: The neuter of adjectives is often used adverbially.

Æfing.

Gunna er lítil stúlka. Mamma hennar er ennþá ung kona. Þær eru mjög laglegar; Gunna er lík mömmu sinni. Mamma hennar er alltaf á svörtum peysufötum; hún hefur litla, svarta skotthúfu, stórt, hvítt slifsi og fallega, rósótta silkisvuntu.

Þær mæðgur hafa verið inni í húsinu, en nú eru þær úti að ganga. Veðrið er svo gott; það hefur verið ágætt upp á síðkastið. Það hefur verið dálítið kalt, en nú er bara heitt.

Þær Gunna eru að ganga á grænum bölum skammt fyrir innan húsið. Þaðan er mjög fallegt útsýni: næst er svart hraun, svo er blátt hafið og í fjarska eru fjöllin, blá með grænum brekkum. Þar er sjálfsagt mjög skemmtilegt að vera.

á prep. with dat. *vera á peysufötum* wear *p.* habitually.
ágætur adj. (*gulur*) excellent.
alltaf adv. always.
bali wm.1 field, lawn.
bara adv. just; quite.
blár adj. (*hár*) blue.
brekka wf.1 slope.
dálítið adv. neuter (of *dálítill*) a little.
ennþá adv. still, yet.
fallegur adj. handsome, beautiful.
fjarski wm.1 the distance; *í f-a* in the distance.
fyrir innan compound prep. with acc. inside, on the inner side (towards the interior, up above).
föt stn.pl. clothes.

að ganga to walk; *að g. úti* to take a walk.
góður, góð, gott adj. good.
grænn adj. (*seinn*) green.
heitur adj. (*gulur*) hot, warm.
hraun stn. lava (field).
húfa wf.1 cap.
hús stn. house.
hvítur adj. (*gulur*) white.
inni adv. inside, indoors.
kaldur, köld, kalt adj. cold.
kona wf.1, gen. pl. *kvenna*, woman.
laglegur adj. (*gulur*) handsome, good-looking.
líkur adj. (*gulur*) like.
lítill adj. (*mikill*) little, small.
mjög adv. very.
mæðgur wf.1.pl. mother and daughter.

187

næst adv. nearest, next.
peysuföt stn.pl. a national costume.
rósóttur, -ótt, -ótt adj. with floral
design.
stökast stn. only in the phrase: *upp
á s-ið* lately, of late.
silkisvunta wf.1 silk apron.
sjálfsagt adv. of course, undoubtedly.
skammur,skömm,skammt adj. short;
skammt a short distance.
skemmtilegur adj. (*gulur*) pleasant,
nice, interesting.
skotthúfa wf.1 a tasseled cap, used
with *peysuföt*.

slifsi stn. (*kvæði*) a broad tie or
scarf, used with *peysuföt*.
stór adj. (*dýr*) big, great.
stúlka wf.1 girl.
svartur, svört, svart adj. black.
svo adv.(1) so; (2) thereupon, then.
svunta wf.1 apron.
ungur adj. (*gulur*) young.
útsýni stn. (*kvæði*) view.
veður stn. (*hreiður*) weather.
vinkona wf.1 (female) friend.
þaðan adv. from there, thence.
þegar conj. when.

Translate into Icelandic:

Gunna is a beautiful little girl. Her mother is handsome, too.
They have always been good friends (*vinkonur*). Gunna wears
handsome clothes (*er í . . . fötum*). Her cap is blue, and she has
a blue apron. Gunna is fond of taking a walk (*að ganga úti*) with
her mother, when (*þegar*) the weather is fine (*gott*). When the
weather is not fine, they stay inside (*eru þær inni*: inverted word
order). Their house is handsome; it is a good house, too, and not
cold. There is (*það er*) an excellent view from its windows (*úr
gluggunum*).

6.

The present indicative of *verða* (like *bresta*) : In. VII, **4**, *9*.

The preterite and perfect indicative of *hafa*: S. VI, **1**, *2*.

Strong masculines, first class (*hestur, hattur, stóll*) : In. I, **2**, *1*.

Æfing.

Íslenzkir hestar eru litlir, en fallegir. Þeir verða seint þreyttir;
það er ótrúleg seigla í þeim. Þeir hafa fallegan haus, stuttan
makka (eða háls) og þykkt tagl og fax. Og þeir hafa harða hófa.
Hópur af hálf-villtum hestum er kallað stóð. Þegar ég var strákur,
hafði ég mjög gaman af hestum.

Hafið þér nokkurn tíma verið heilan dag á hestbaki? Nei, ég
hef aldrei haft hest. Það er gaman, og ef hesturinn er þýður, þá
verður maður ekki þreyttur. En þér verðið líka að hafa góðan
hnakk (söðul). Slæmur hnakkur er eins og vondur stóll. Að vera
á þýðum hesti er næstum eins og að vera í bíl. En hastir og latir
hestar eru afleitir. Maður verður dauðþreyttur á þeim.

afleitur adj. (*gulur*) terrible.
aldrei adv. never.
Ameríka wf.1 America.
ár stn. year.
bíll stm.1 (*stóll*) dat. *bíl* car, automobile.
dagur stm.1 (*hattur*), dat. *degi*, day.
dauðþreyttur adj. dead tired, exhausted; *d. á þeim* dead tired of them.
ef conj. if.
fax stn. mane of a horse.
fimm num. five.
fótviss, -viss, -visst adj. sure of foot.
fremur adv. rather.
haft pp. of *hafa* have.
hálf-villtur adj. half wild.
háls stm.1 (*hver*) dat. *-i* neck.
harður, hörð, hart adj. hard.
hastur, höst, hast adj. rough, hard-trotting.
haus stm.1 (*hver*) dat. *-i* head, less polite than *höfuð* stn.
heill adj. (*seinn*) whole, all.
hestbak stn. horseback.
hestur stm.1 horse, pony.
hnakkur stm.1 (*hattur*) saddle.
hófur stm.1 (*hestur*) hoof.
hópur stm.1 (*hestur*) flock.
hvað adv. how; *hvað lengi* how long.
íslenzkur adj. (*gulur*) Icelandic.
kallaður, kölluð, kallað pp. of *kalla* call (cf. In. VII, 3, 5, 2).
laglegur, -leg, -legt adj. good-looking.
latur, löt, latt adj. lazy.
lengi adv. long.

maður stm.4 man; as indef.pron.: one.
makki wm.1 neck of a horse.
nokkur indef. pron. any; *nokkurn tíma* ever.
nokkurntíma adv. ever.
næstum adv. almost.
ótrúlega adv. incredibly.
ótrúlegur adj. incredible.
seigla wf.1 toughness.
seigur adj. (*gulur*) tough.
seinn, sein, seint adj. slow, late; *þeir verða seint þreyttir* they don't easily get tired.
slæmur adj. (*gulur*) bad.
stóð stn. flock of (breeding) horses.
stóll stm.1 chair.
strákur stm.1 boy; less polite than *drengur* stm.2.
stuttur, stutt, stutt adj. short.
söðull stm.1 (*himinn*) lady's saddle.
tagl stn. tail of a horse.
tími wm.1 time; *nokkurn tíma* anytime, ever.
verða v. become, get; must, have to.
villtur, villt, villt adj. wild.
vondur, vond, vont adj. bad, evil.
þá adv. then; at the beginning of a main clause, which follows its subordinate clause, it is often to be omitted in the English translation.
þegar conj. when.
þreyttur, þreytt, þreytt adj. tired.
þýður, þýð, þýtt adj. smooth-paced (of horses).
þykkur adj. (*gulur*) thick.

Have you (*þú, þér*) ever had an Icelandic horse? They are fine (*góðir*), but they are not big. They are incredibly tough and sure of foot (*fótvissir*). The Icelanders (*Íslendingar*) have always had fine horses. What is the neck of a horse (*hálsinn á hestinum*) called in (*á*) Iceland? It is called *makki*. Do other (*önnur*) Icelandic animals have a *makki*? No, only the horses have it. They also have a mane and a thick tail.

Have you ever had a car? Yes, I had an excellent car. Was it a big car? No, it was rather (*fremur*) small, but it was good-looking (*laglegur*). Where (*hvaðan*) was it from? It was from America (*frá Ameríku*). How long (*hvað lengi*) did you have it? I had it five years (*fimm ár*).

189

Note: The question: how long (*hvað lengi*)? is answered by an accusative of time: *fimm ár* (for) five years.

7.

The present indicative of *skulu, eiga, mega*: In. VII, **5**, *1*; S. VI, **13**, 2, 5, and 6.

Strong masculines of the first and second classes (*mór, læknir, dalur, leikur*) : In. I, **2**, *1* and *2*).

Enclitic *þú*: Pr. **4**, *4*.

All verbs in Icelandic are treated like the English verb *to be* in questions and after negations. Cf. S. VI, **13**, 11.

Æfing.

Nonni á heima í stórum dal norður í landi. Pabbi hans er læknir í stóru læknishéraði. Hann á bíl, eins og margir íslenzkir læknar, og eins og allir drengir, er Nonni vitlaus í að keyra í bílnum. Læknirinn hefur hann þess vegna stundum með sér, þegar hann er að vitja um sjúklinga. Nonni er of ungur til þess að keyra, en hann á að þurka ryk af bílnum og þvo hjólin, þegar þau verða óhrein. Nonni er ekki vel ánægður með þetta. "Á ég ekki að keyra fyrir þig, pabbi," segir hann, "bara einu sinni? Ef ég má það, þá skal ég aldrei vera vondur strákur." "Nei, þú mátt það ekki," segir læknirinn, "og nú ertu gestur hér, en gestir verða að vera kurteisir. Ef þú verður góður drengur, þá máttu fara í berjamó með börnunum hérna, meðan ég er hjá sjúklingnum. Hér er svo mikið af berjum. En þið megið ekki vera of sein." "Nei, við skulum ekki vera of sein," segir Nonni. En í berjamónum var fullt af kræk iberjum og bláberjum—og Nonni varð of seinn.

Note 1: Inverted word order (S. VII, **3**) when any part of the sentence (even a subordinate clause) but the subject is put first: *eins og allir drengir, er Nonni vitlaus í að keyra*, normal: *Nonni er vitlaus í að keyra, eins og allir drengir* (a phrase of comparison); *ef þú verður góður drengur, þá* (redundant) *máttu fara*, normal: *þú mátt fara, ef þú verður góður* (an *ef*-clause).

Note 2: Infinitive of purpose: *til þess að keyra* (S. VI, **11**, *3*); infinitives without *að*: *þá máttu fara* (S. VI, **11**, *6*).

áður adv. before.
af prep. with dat. of, off, from.
alltof adv. too, far too (= *allt of*).
allur, öll, allt adj. (indef. pron.) all; *allt of* all too, far too.
ánægður, ánægð, ánægt adj. pleased, content with (*á. með*).

bara adv. just, only.
ber stn. (*kyn*) berry.
berjamór stm.1 (*mór*) a heath where berries grow.
bláber stn. (*kyn*) blueberry (whortleberry).
dalur stm.2 valley.

190

drengur stm.2 (*leikur*) boy.
ef conj. if; *ef þú verður* if you will be.
eiga pret.pres.v. (1) own; *eiga heima* live, (have a home); (2) be (supposed) to; (3) shall, *á ég?* shall I?
fara stv.6 go; *f. í berjamó* go picking berries.
fullur, full, fullt adj. full.
fyrir prep. with acc. for.
fyrri adv. before, of old.
gestur stm.2 guest.
hafa með sér take with one, take along.
hérað stn. district.
hérna adv. here.
hjá prep. with dat. with.
hjól stn. wheel.
keyra wv.2 to drive.
krækiber stn. crowberry.
kurteis, -eis, -eist adj. polite.
líka adv. too, also.
læknir stm.1 doctor, physician.
læknishérað stn. district of a (country) doctor.
margur, mörg, margt adj. many.
meðan conj. while.
mikill, -il, -ið adj. great, much; *mikið af* great amount of.

Nonni wm.1 pet name for *Jón* John.
norður adv. north; *n. í landi* in the North (of Iceland).
of adv. too.
óhreinn adj. (*seinn*) dirty.
ryk stn. dust.
segja wv.3 say; *segir* says.
sjúklingur stm.1 patient.
stór, stór, stórt adj. big, large.
stundum adv. sometimes.
svo adv. so; *svo mikið* so much.
til þess að with inf. in order to.
varð pret. of *verða* became, was.
vel adv. quite; well.
vitja wv.4 visit; *v. um* visit.
vitlaus, -laus, -laust adj. witless, mad; *v. í e-ð* (or: *að gera e-ð*) madly eager to do something.
vondur, vond, vont adj. bad, evil.
þá adv. then; often placed at the beginning of a main clause when it follows the dependent clause; then it need not be translated.
þegar conj. when.
þess vegna adv. therefore.
þetta this.
þurrka wv.4 dry, wipe.
þvo stv.6 and wv.1 wash.

Translate into Icelandic:

Where does Nonni live? In the North. What is (the profession of) his father? He is a doctor. Are there (*Eru*) many doctors in Iceland? Yes. Do they have cars? Yes, they now have cars, but formerly (*áður fyrri*) they did not have (*höfðu*) them. What did they have then? They had horses. Is Nonni allowed (*má Nonni*) to drive the car? No, he is far too (*allt of*) young. He is supposed to wash the wheels of the car (*á bílnum*), but he is not too well pleased with it (*það*). He is also allowed to go picking berries. Shall we, too, go picking berries? Yes, let us go, it is so nice here in the valley.

8.

Demonstrative and relative pronouns: In. VI, 3 and 4; S. IV, 3 and 4.

Weak adjectives: In. III, 3.

Strong masculines, third class: In. I, 2, *3*.

Æfing.

Hafið þér nokkurn tíma verið farþegi á íslenzku skipunum? Nei. Þau eru ekki stór, en þessi litlu skip fara milli New York og Íslands

(Reykjavíkur) á tíu til tólf dögum. Farið er ekki dýrt, en maturinn er ekki innifalinn í farinu, eins og venja er til á amerískum skipum. Sá, sem er vanur íslenzka matnum, hann vill ekki annan mat. En útlendingar verða að læra átið á þessum ágæta mat, eins og til dæmis hangikjöti, harðfiski, slátri og skyri. Hangikjöt og kartöflujafningur, harðfiskur og smjör, skyr og rjómi: þetta eru uppáhaldsréttir Íslendinga. Annars er nóg á skipunum af þessum vanalega, alþjóðlega mat fyrir þá, sem ekki eru vanir hinum. Á ég að fara með Lagarfossi? Nei, þér skuluð heldur fara með hinu skipinu, sem nú er í New York, Gullfossi. Þegar þér komið til Íslands, þá verðið þér að fara hringinn í kringum landið með skipi til þess að sjá firðina. Sá, sem ekki hefur séð hina hrikalegu firði á Norður- og Austurlandi, hann á mikið eftir. Sums staðar rísa fjöllin þverhnípt úr sjó, stundum eru í þeim margir litir, en oftast er dökki liturinn yfirgnæfandi.

á prep. with dat. in (of time); of.

að prep. with dat., see *vera*.

allur adj. all; *allt í lagi* all right, O. K.

alþjóðlegur adj. international.

annar, önnur, annað adj. another; other.

annars adv. otherwise, besides.

át stn. eating; *læra átið á* learn to eat.

dýr, dýr, dýrt adj. expensive.

dæmi stn. (*kvæði*) example; *til d-is*, abbreviated *t. d.*, for example.

dökkur adj. dark.

eiga eftir have left (in store), have missed.

éta stv.5 eat; *étið* eaten.

far stn. fare, passage.

fara stv.6 fare, travel, go.

farþegi wm.1 passenger.

fjörður stm.3 firth, fjord.

Gullfoss stm.1 'Gold Falls,' an Icelandic boat; these are often named after waterfalls (*fossar*).

hangikjöt stn. smoked meat (mutton).

harðfiskur stm.1 hard (dried) fish.

heldur adv. rather; *h. ekki* not . . . either.

hrikalegur adj. awe-inspiring.

hringur stm.2 ring, round.

hvernig adv. how.

í kringum compound prep. with acc. around, round about; *hringinn í k.* all around.

innifalinn í included in.

jafnvel adv. even.

kartöflujafningur stm.1 creamed potatoes.

ket (*kjöt*) stn. meat.

Lagarfoss stm.1 'Loch Falls,' an Icel. boat; *með L.-i* on the L.

litur stm.3 (*hlutur*) color.

læra, lærði, lært wv.2 learn.

matur stm.3 (*hlutur*) food.

með skipi by boat.

milli . . . og prep. with gen. between . . . and.

nógur adj. enough.

nóg stn. enough; *nóg er af e-u* there is enough of something.

oft, oftar, oftast adv. often, more, most often.

réttur stm.3 (*hlutur*) dish.

rjómi wm.1 cream.

rísa stv.1 rise.

sá, sú, það that one; *sá sem* he who.

sjá stv.5 see; *séð* seen.

sjór stm.1 sea.

skyr stn. Icelandic curds, cottage cheese (smooth); *skyr og rjómi* curds and cream, curds with cream.

slátur stn. (*hreiður*) blood and liver sausages.

smjör stn. butter.

sums staðar adv. in places.

til conj. to.

til (*þess*) *að* in order to.

tíu num. ten.

tólf num. twelve.

uppáhaldsréttur stm. 3 favorite dish.

útlendingur stm.1 foreigner.

vanalegur adj. usual; *þessi vanalegi* the usual.

vanur, vön, vant adj. with dat. used to.

venja wf.1 custom; *v. er til* it is customary.

vera að : *e-ð er að e-u* something is wrong with something.

vill present of *vilja* want.

víst adv. certainly.

yfirgnæfandi adj. dominating.

þessi, þessi, þetta this, that.

þverhníptur adj. perpendicular.

Translate into Icelandic:

Did you ever go to Iceland (*hafið þér nokkurn tíma farið*)? Yes, once (*einu sinni*). Were you on one of (*einu af*) the Icelandic boats? Yes. How (*hvernig*) was it? It was fine (*ágætt*), only, it was too small for the big waves (*sjóa*) of the Atlantic (*Atlantshafsins*). How long (*hvað . . . lengi*) was it (' were you ') from New York to Iceland? Ten days. How (*hvernig*) was the food? It was good, but I could not (*gat ekki étið*) eat all the Icelandic food. What was wrong with it (*hvað var að honum*)? Oh, I suppose it was all right (*Og það var víst allt í lagi með hann*), but I am not used to it. You will get (*verðið*) used to it; it is really fine (*bara ágætur*).

Note: *Hvað lengi* how long? *Tíu daga* (accusative of time) ten days.

9.

The preterite indicative of strong verbs, personal endings: Sg. 1 —, 2 -*st*, 3 —; Pl. 1 -*um*, 2 -*uð*, 3 -*u* (see synopsis, In. VII, **4**, *1*).

The most common strong verbs in Icelandic in order of frequency: *vera, fara, koma, sjá, verða, fá, geta, taka, ganga, halda, heita* (In. VII, **1**, *2*). Learn the list of strong verbs: Pr. **5**, *1*.

Interrogative pronouns: In. VI, **5**; S. IV, **5**.

Æfing.

Sáuð þið skipið, sem var að koma? Við sáum til þess inn fyrir Gróttu, en það er of stórt til að komast inn í höfnina. Hvert fór það? Það fór bara á ytri höfnina. Tókuð þið eftir, hvaða flagg það hafði? Nei, en það var víst amerískt. Amerísk ferðamannaskip hafa komið hingað á hverju sumri í mörg ár. Í fyrra fengum við að fara um borð í skipið, sem þá kom. Það hét Scandia. Það tók okkur langan tíma að skoða það allt; við gengum um það allt. Það varð líka að liggja úti, því það gat ekki komizt inn á innri höfnina. Ferðamennirnir voru ekki nema rúman dag í landi; þeir

193

fóru samt til Þingvalla, Geysis og Gullfoss, eins og vant er. En
þeir fengu vont veður og urðu víst fegnir, þegar þeir komust um
borð í skipið aftur. En þarna er bátur að koma frá borði,, við
skulum spyrja þá, sem í honum eru: Hvaða skip er þetta? Hvað
heitir það? Hver er skipstjóri? Hverjir eiga það? Hvað marga
farþega hefur það? Hvað lengi verða þeir hér? Hvenær á skipið
að fara? Hvort eigum við að fara út í það í kvöld eða á morgun?

á prep. with acc. *á morgun* tomorrow.

aftur adv. again.

amerískur adj. American.

ár stn. year.

bátur stm.1 boat.

borð stn. board; *um b. í* on board;
frá borði from the boat.

enskur, ensk, enskt adj. English.

fá, fékk, fengum, fenginn stv.7 (1)
be allowed; (2) get.

fara, fór, fórum, farinn stv.6 go.

feginn, -in, -ið adj. glad, fain.

ferðamaður stm.4 traveller, tourist.

ferðamannaskip stn. tourist boat.

flagg stn. flag.

fyrra only in *í fyrra* last year.

ganga, gekk, gengum, genginn stv.7
go, walk.

geta, gat, gátum, getað stv.5 be able
to. Takes a past participle,
whereas the English *can* takes infinitive: *ég get komið* I can come.

Geysir stm.1 a famous geyser, from
which the English name for hot
springs is derived.

Grótta wf.1 low headland, near
Reykjavík.

Gullfoss stm.1 'Gold Falls,' a famous waterfall in the South.

héðan adv. hence, from here.

heita, hét, hétum, heitinn stv.7 be
called.

hingað adv. hither, here.

hvað (1) interr.pron. what; (2) adv.
(with adj. or adv.) how; *h. lengi*
how long.

hvaða interr. pron. adj. what, what
kind of.

hvaðan adv. whence, where . . . from.

hvenær adv. when.

hver interr.pron. who, which.

hver indef. pron. every.

hvert n. of *hver* (1) which; (2) adv.
whither, where; *af hverju* why,
hvers vegna why.

hvor interr.pron. which of two; n.
hvort (1) which of two; (2)
conj. *hvort . . eða* whether . . or.

höfn stf.2 harbor; *á h-ina* into the
harbor.

í prep. with acc. *í mörg ár* for many
years; *í kvöld* tonight.

inn fyrir prep. with acc. (moving)
inwards (passing) by (a point).

innri adj. inner.

koma, kom, komum, kominn stv.4
come; *komast* (middle voice) get,
reach.

land stn. land; *í l.* ashore.

langur, löng, langt adj. long.

lengi adv. long.

liggja, lá, lágum, leginn stv.5 lie.

morgunn stm.1 (*himinn*) morning.

náttúrufegurð stf.2 natural beauty.

nema conj. but, except; *ekki n.* not
more than.

rúmur adj. roomy, a little over.

samt adv. however, yet, still.

sjá, sá, sáum, séð stv.5 see; *sjá til
e-s* see, discover, watch.

skoða wv.4 look at, inspect.

spyrja, spurði, spurður wv.1 ask.

sögustaður stm.3 an historic place.

sumar stn. summer.

taka, tók, tókum, tekinn stv.6 with
double acc.: *það tók mig langan
tíma* it took me a long time;
t. eftir e-u notice something.

um prep. with acc. over.

vera, var, vorum, verið stv.5 be.

verða, varð, urðum, orðinn stv.3 become, will be; stay; *v. feginn* be
glad.

194

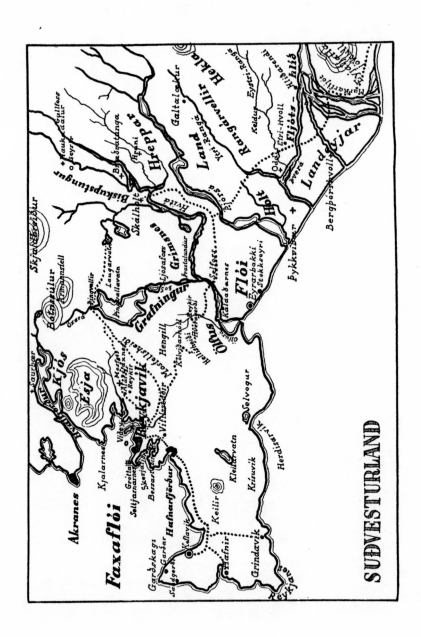

SUÐVESTURLAND

víst adv. surely, probably.
ytri adj.compar. outer.
þá adv. then.
Þingvellir stm.3 the famous plains

(*vellir*) where the old *Alþingi* (parliament) met.
því for, because.
ætla wv.4 intend.

Translate into Icelandic:

What ship was coming? Where did you see it? Where did it come from? Where is it to go from here (*héðan*)? How many passengers does it have? Who came ashore with the boat? The captain came ashore. Who is the captain? How long, I wonder, will he (*skal hann*) stay here? Only a short (*stuttan*) time. Who (pl.) came with the captain from the boat? Some (*nokkrir*) passengers, who are (*ætla*) going (*að fara*) to Þingvellir tomorrow morning (*á morgun*). All tourists go to (*fara til*) Þingvellir. Why (*af hverju, hvers vegna*)? Because (*af því að*) the Þingvellir is (are) a historic place. Why do they go (*fara þeir*) to Geysir and Gullfoss? Because these places have great natural beauty (*náttúrufegurð* f.). Is Geysir not an English (*enskt*) word (*orð*)? No, it is Icelandic.

10.

The preterite indicative of weak verbs, personal endings: Sg. 1 *-i*, 2 *-ir*, 3 *-i*; Pl. 1 *-um*, 2 *-uð*, 3 *-u* (In. VII, **4**, *1*).

The preterite suffixes of weak verbs: *-ð-i*, *-d-i*, *-t-i*, *-að-i* (In. VII, **1**, *2* and VII, **3**, *1*). Inverted Word Order S. VII, **3**, *2*.

The most common weak verbs in Icelandic: *hafa, segja, gera, leggja, kalla*. Learn the list of weak verbs, In. VII, **3**, *1*, *4*.

Strong feminines, first and second class: In. I, **3**, *1* and *2*.

Æfing.

Skipið, sem lagðist hérna á ytri höfninni í fyrra dag, er á förum. Ferðamennirnir, sem með því voru, fóru í gær austur yfir heiðar í bílum til að skoða sögustaði. Lögðu menn af stað snemma um morguninn. Annar flokkurinn fór Mosfellsheiði til Þingvalla, hinn fór Hellisheiði austur í sveitir. Veðrið var ekki gott framan af: rigning á fjallinu, en þoka í byggð. En eftir litla stund gerði gott veður, sólskin og hita, og jörðin glitraði í sólskininu. Ferðin varð því mjög skemmtileg. Bílarnir, sem fóru austur í sveitir, stönzuðu fyrst við Grýlu í Ölfusi, og tók fólkið myndir af hvernum. Þar fóru sumir af ferðamönnunum á símastöðina, hringdu upp höfðu fengið nóg af veðrinu. En flestir héldu áfram alla leið austur í Fljótshlíð, skoðuðu bæ Gunnars á Hlíðarenda, og nutu hins dýrðlega útsýnis til Eyjafjallajökuls. Höfðu þeir ágæta skemmtun af.

195

á stöðina to the station.

annar . . . hinn one . . . the other.

austur adv. (to the) east; *a. í* east into; *a. yfir* east over.

bílastöð stf.1 (*stöð*) automobile station, taxicab stand.

byggð stf.2 inhabited, settled part (of land).

byrja, -aði, -aður wv.4 begin; *til að b. með* to begin with.

bær stm.2 farmstead; town.

dýrðlegur adj. magnificent, glorious.

eftir prep. with acc. after; with dat. for.

Eyjafjallajökull stm.1 (*himinn*) 'Eyjafjalla Glacier.'

fá stv.7 get; *fá nóg af e-u* get enough of sth.

ferð stf.2 journey.

flestir adj.pl. most.

Fljótshlíð stf.1 'Fleet Slope,' a district of the South.

flokkur stm.1 flock; party.

fólk stn. people, folks.

framan af in the beginning, to begin with.

för stf.2 (*gjöf*) journey; going; *vera á förum* be on the point of going.

gera (*gjöra*), *gerði, gerður* wv.2 do, make; *gerði* (impersonal) *gott veður* (acc.) literally: it made good weather, i. e. the weather became fine.

glitra, -aði, -að wv.4 glitter.

Grýla wf.1 bugbear; name of a geyser.

Gunnar stm.1 a hero from *Njála*; he lived at Hlíðarendi.

gær adv. yesterday = *í gær*.

halda, hélt, héldum, haldinn stv.7 keep; *halda áfram* keep going.

heiði stf.1 heath, mountain.

Hellisheiði stf.1 'Cave Heath.'

hiti wm.1 heat, warmth.

Hlíðarendi wm.1 'Slope's End.'

hringja, hringdi, hringt wv.2 ring; *h. upp* call up (on the telephone).

hver stm.1 and 2 geyser, hot spring.

í prep. with acc. at a certain time: *í fyrra dag* the day before yesterday; *í gær* yesterday.

jökull stm.1 (*himinn*) glacier.

jörð stf.2 (*gjöf*) earth, ground.

leggja, lagði, lagður wv.1 lay; *l. af stað* start a journey; *leggjast* (of ships) cast anchor.

leið stf.2 way, road; *alla leið* all the way.

Mosfellsheiði stf.1 'Moss Fell Heath.'

njóta, naut, nutum, notinn stv.2 enjoy (*e-s*).

næst adv. next.

rigning stf.1 (*kerling*) rain.

senda, sendi, sendur (*sent*) wv.2 send; *s. eftir* send for.

símastöð stf.1 (*stöð*) telephone station (*sími* wm.1 telephone).

skemmtun stf.2 (*verzlun*) enjoyment, fun; *hafa skemmtun af e-u* enjoy something.

snemma adv. early.

sól stf.2 sun.

sólskin stn. sunshine.

stanza, -aði, -aður wv.4 stop.

stund stf.2 hour, while.

sumir indef.pron.adj. some.

sveit stf.2 rural district.

sögustaður stm.3 historic place.

taka stv.6 take; *t. mynd* take a picture.

tala, -aði, -aður wv.4 speak.

útsýni til view of.

við prep. with acc. at.

þoka wf.1 fog.

Ölfus stn. a district of the South.

Translate into Icelandic:

Were you one of the party (*einn af hópnum*) that went to Hlíðarendi the other day (*um daginn*)? Yes (, I was). Where could you get taxicabs (*bíla*)? At (*á*) a taxicab station in Reykjavík. How was the weather? It was not so good to begin with, but it became fine after a while. How many hours were you on the mountain? Two or three (*tvær eða þrjár*). How far (*langt*) did

you go? All the way east to Fljótshlíð, and we got a glorious
view of the glacier (*jökulsins*). How were the roads (*vegirnir*)?
Fine. We had great fun on the journey (= *við höfðum mikla
skemmtun af förinni*).

11.

Strong masculines, fourth class: In. I, **2**, *4.*

Strong feminines, third class: In. I, **3**, *3.*

Reflexive and possessive pronouns: S. IV, **2**, 4.

Compound words: S. IX. Numerals: In. V, **2**, *2.*

Æfing: Fjölskyldan og frændfólkið.

Faðir minn heitir Jón Guðmundsson, og móðir mín Guðrún
Sigurðardóttir. Við erum þrjú systkinin, systir mín Sigríður
(Jónsdóttir), bróðir minn Sigurður (Jónsson) og ég, Guðmundur
(Jónsson). Systir mín er gift manni, sem heitir Magnús Ólafsson;
hann er þess vegna mágur minn og tengdasonur foreldra minna.
Sigurður bróðir minn á Margréti Ólafsdóttur, systur Magnúsar;
hún er því mágkona mín og tengdadóttir foreldra minna: faðir
minn er tengdafaðir hennar, og móðir mín er tengdamóðir hennar.
Konan mín heitir Kristín Ólafsdóttir; hún er systir Margrétar;
við bræðurnir eigum þá sína systurina hvor og erum svilar.

Ég og faðir minn erum feðgar, ég og móðir mín mæðgin.
Systir mín og móðir mín eru mæðgur, systir mín og faðir minn
eru feðgin. Systir föður míns er föðursystir mín, bróðir föður
míns föðurbróðir minn. Á sama hátt á ég móðursystur og
móðurbróður. Sjálfur er ég bróðursonur föðurbróður míns og
föðursystur, systursonur móðurbróður míns og móðursystur. En
systir mín er bróðurdóttir eða systurdóttir þeirra. Svo á ég afa og
ömmur: föðurafa og föðurömmu, móðurafa og móðurömmu. Enn
fremur langafa og langömmu, langa-langafa o.s.frv. Börn mín og
bróður míns eru bræðrabörn, börn mín og systur minnar systkinabörn. Ef það eru drengir, þá eru þeir bræðra- og systkinasynir,
ef það eru stúlkur, þá bræðra- og systkinadætur. Börn systra eru
á sama hátt systrabörn, -synir eða -dætur.

Af öllu því fólki, sem nú var talið, er fjölskyldan sjálf:
faðir og móðir, afi og amma, sonur og dóttir, bróðir og systir. Allt
hitt fólkið er kallað skyldfólk eða frændfólk, karlmennirnir frændur,
kvennfólkið frændkonur eða frænkur. Tengdafólk er fólk, sem
maður tengist með mægðum: mágar, mágkonur, tengdafaðir og
tengdamóðir. Enn fremur má nefna stjúpmóður, -föður, -dóttur
og -son.

197

amma wf.1 grandmother.
afi wm.1 grandfather.
bróðir stm.4 brother.
bróðurdóttir stf.3 niece.
bróðursonur stm.3 nephew.
bræðrabörn, -synir, -dætur first cousins.
dóttir stf.3 daughter.
eiga pret.pres.v. own; be married to.
enn fremur adv. furthermore.
faðir stm.4 father.
feðgar wm.1.pl. father and son.
feðgin stn.pl. father and daughter.
fjölskylda wf.1 family.
foreldrar wm.1.pl. parents.
frændfólk stn. relatives.
frændi wm.2 cousin, relative.
frændkona wf.1 cousin, relative.
frænka wf.1 cousin, relative.
föður- paternal, *-afi, -amma, -bróðir* uncle, *-systir* aunt.
giftur, gift married to.
Guðmundur, -ar stm.1, but in patronymic: *Guðmundsson, -dóttir.*
Guðrún stf.1&2 Gudrun.
háttur stm.3 mode, manner, way; *á sama h.* in the same way.
heita stv.7 be called; *ég heiti* my name is; *sem heitir* whose name is.
Jón stm.1 John; patr. *Jónsson, -dóttir.*
karlmaður stm.4 man, oppos. woman.
kona wf.1 wife.
Kristín stf.1 Christine.
kvennfólk stn. women (folks).
langafi great-grandfather.
langamma great-grandmother.
langa-langafi great-great-grandfather.
líf stn. life; *á lífi* alive.
maður stm.4 man; one.
Magnús stm.1 Magnus; patr. *Magnús(s)son, -dóttir.*
mágkona wf.1 sister-in-law.
mágur stm.1 brother-in-law.
Margrét stf.1 Margaret.
móðir stf.3 mother.
móður- maternal; *-afi, -amma, -bróðir* uncle, *-systir* aunt.

mæðgin stn.pl. mother and son.
mæðgur wf.1.pl. mother and daughter.
mægð stf.2 usually in pl. *-ir* relationship by marriage.
mægjast, mægðist, mægzt wv.2 middle voice: become related by marriage.
nefna, nefndi, nefndur wv.2 name, mention; *má nefna* may be mentioned: after impersonal *mega* an active infinitive must be translated by the passive. See Impersonal Verbs in the Syntax.
o. s. frv. = og svo framvegis and so on.
Ólafur stm.1 Olaf, patr. *Ólafsson, -dóttir.*
sannarlega adv. certainly.
Sigríður stf.1 (*Hildur*) Sigrid.
Sigurður stm.1 Sigurd, patr. *Sigurðsson, Sigurðardóttir.*
sjálfur, sjálf, sjálft dem.pron. self, my-(your-, him-, her-, it-)self.
skyldfólk stn. relatives.
sonur stm.3 son; as a part of patr. always *-son.*
stjúp- step-, *-faðir, -móðir, -dóttir, -sonur.*
stjúpa wf.1 stepmother.
stjúpi wm.1 stepfather.
svili wm.1 a man married to another man's wife's sister.
svo (enumerating) then.
systir stf.3 sister.
systkin stn.pl. brother and sister.
systkinabörn, -synir, -dætur first cousins.
systrabörn,-synir,-dætur first cousins.
telja, taldi, talinn wv.1 enumerate.
tengdafaðir, -móðir, -dóttir, -sonur father, mother, daughter, son-in-law.
tengdafólk stn. people related by marriage, in-laws.
tengjast, tengdist, tengzt wv.2 middle voice: become related by marriage.
þess vegna adv. therefore.
þrír, þrjár, þrjú num. three.
því adv. therefore.

Translate into Icelandic:

Is your family big? Yes, I have a big family: my parents, five (*fimm*) brothers, and six (*sex*) sisters. My grand-parents (*afi minn og amma*) are also still living (*á lífi*). What is your name, please (*hvað heitið þér, með leyfi*)? My name is (*ég heiti*) Guðmundur, and I am the son of John (*og er Jónsson*). Have (*eigið*) you any (*nokkra*) uncles living? Yes. I have two (*tvo*) paternal [uncles] and two maternal uncles. Have you also aunts? Yes, I have (*á*) one (*eina*) maternal aunt. But have you any (*nokkrar*) nieces? I have one niece who is the daughter of my brother, and another who is the daughter of my sister (*Ég á eina bróðurdóttur og eina systurdóttur*). You certainly (*sannarlega*) have many relatives.

12.

The present indicative of weak verbs, second, third, and fourth class: In. VII, **4**, *1* and *2*. Personal endings:

Class 2 and 3: Sg. 1 -*i*,2 -*i-r*,3 -*i-r*

Pl. 1 -*um*,2 -*ið*,3 -*a*.

4   : Sg. 1 -*a*,2 -*a-r*,3 -*a-r*

The meaning of the present tense: S. VI, **2**, *1*.

Indefinite pronouns: *allur, annar, nokkur, neinn*; In. VI, **6**; S. IV, **6**.

Æfing.

Heyrið þér, fréttið þér nokkuð nýtt? Nei, það er lítið um það. Hvernig líkar yður lífið? Ágætlega. Hvað segir Morgunblaðið um stríðið? Og svo sem ekki neitt; þeir tapa eins og fyrri daginn. Hvað segja veðurfregnirnar? Þær þegja um veðrið. Hvernig er það annars? Hann rignir eða suddar núna, en líklega styttir hann upp með hádeginu. Kannske skánar veðrið nú á morgun; það veitir ekki af því, ef Ferðafélagið hugsar til að fara í fjallgöngu. O jæja, ég kalla þetta nú ekki slæmt veður. Það má vel ganga á fjöll í því, ef maður klæðir sig vel og passar að hafa allt í lagi. Já, nú skal ég segja yður, hvað við gerum. Við sendum þá Björn og Ólaf í búðir í dag. Björn kaupir olíuföt og bakpoka, Ólafur útvegar nesti. Ekki dugir (*dugar*) annað en að vera vel nestaður. Við hitum okkur kaffi og borðum á fjallinu. Við mælum okkur allir mót á bílastöðinni. Ég síma þangað og panta bíl. Björn mætir okkur þar, en Ólafur og hinir, sem ætla með okkur, hitta okkur rétt fyrir utan bæinn. Þér skrifið þeim í dag um þetta. Já. Allt í lagi; þá hittumst við á morgun; ég er strax farinn að hlakka til. Allir hlakka til að fara á fjöll. Hverjir ætla að fara? Ég ætla, þú ætlar, þér ætlið, Björn ætlar, við ætlum allir.

á prep. with acc. onto, into.

ágætlega adv. fine (from *ágæt-ur*).

annars anyway.

bakpoki wm.1 knapsack.

borða, -aði, -aður wv.4 eᵃt.

búð stf.2 shop.

duga, -ði, -að wv.3 avail, help, do.

en conj. than; *ekki annað en* nothing else than (but).

fara stv.6 (1) go, climb, travel; (2) with inf. begin (S. VI, **5**).

Ferðafélagið stn. with art. 'The Tourist Society.'

fjallganga wf.1 mountain climbing, *fara í f-göngu* go climb the mountains.

frétt stf.2 news.

frétta, frétti, frétt wv.2 hear (news).

fyrir utan prep. with acc. outside of.

fyrri adj. former; *eins og f. daginn* as usual.

hádegi stn. (*kvæði*) noon, midday.

heyra, -ði, -ður wv.2 hear, listen.

hita, -aði, -aður wv.4 heat, make (by boiling).

hitta, hitti, hittur wv.2 hit, meet; *hittast* middle voice, meet each other.

hlakka, -aði, -að wv.4 *h. til e-s* look forward to something.

hugsa, -aði, -aður wv.4 think; *h. til* think of.

í dag today.

kaffi stn. (*kvæði*) coffee.

kalla, -aði, -aður wv.4 with double acc. call, consider.

kannske adv. perhaps.

kaupa, keypti, keyptur wv.2 (irreg.) buy. Cf. In. VII, **3**, *3*, **5**.

klæða, klæddi, klæddur wv.2 cloth, dress; *k. sig* dress oneself.

lag stn. order; *allt í lagi* everything in order, O. K.

líka, -aði, -að wv.4 please; logical subj. in dat.; cf. S. I, **3**, *1*, 2b.

lítið um e-ð little of something; *það er l. u. það* not much, not at all.

með prep. with dat. with; *m. hádeginu* toward noon, at noon.

mega S. VI, **13**, 5; *það má ganga* it is possible to go.

Morgunblaðið stn. with art. 'The Morning Paper.'

mót stn. meeting; *mæla sér m.* appoint a meeting place.

mæla, mælti, mæltur wv.2 speak, appoint.

mæta, mætti, mættur wv.2 meet (*e-m*).

nesta, -aði, -aður wv.4 provide with food.

nesti stn. (*kvæði*) provisions.

nú adv. really; now.

núna adv. now.

nýr, nú, nýtt adj. new.

og (1) and, (2) oh.

o jæja interj. well; sure; why yes, but.

olíuföt stn.pl. coats of oil skin.

panta, -aði, -aður wv.4 order.

passa, -aði, -aður wv.4 take care.

rétt adv. just.

rigna, -di, -t wv.2 rain; *hann rignir* it rains. Cf. S. VI, **14**, *3*.

segja, sagði, sagður wv.3 say, tell.

senda, sendi, sendur wv.2 send.

síma, -aði, -að wv.4 telephone.

sjálfsagt adv. surely.

skána, -aði, -aður wv.4 get better (weaker than *batna*).

skrifa, -aði, -aður wv.4 write; *s. e-m* w. to somebody.

strax adv. at once.

stríð stn. war.

stytta, stytti, styttur wv.2 shorten; *s. upp* cease to rain.

stöð stf.1 station, = *bílastöð* taxicab station (stand, company).

sudda, -aði, -að wv.4 drizzle; *hann s.* it drizzles.

svo sem (sosum) adv. just about.

tapa, -aði, -aður wv.4 lose (*e-u*).

til prep. with gen. to.

um prep. with acc. about.

útvega, -aði, -að wv.4 procure.

veðurfregn stf.2 weather forecast, weather news.

veita, veitti, veittur wv.2 grant, afford; *ekki v. af því* one has use for it, one could use it, there is nothing to spare.

viðskiftavinur stm.3 customer.

þangað adv. thither, there.

þegja, þagði, þagað wv.3 be silent.

ætla, -aði, -aður wv.4 intend; *æ. að*

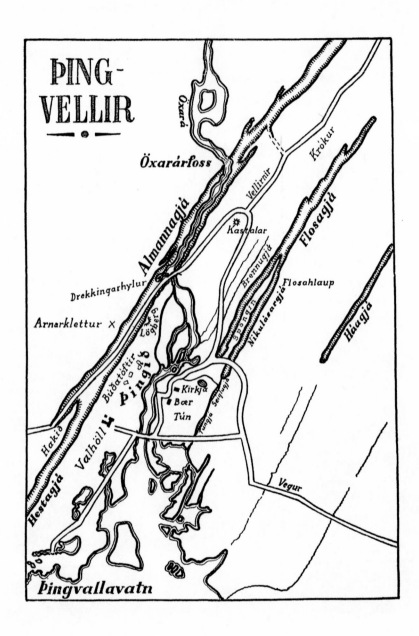

fara intend to go. Verbs of motion, like this, are often dropped after *ætla*, which then means: intend to go: *ég ætla út* I am going out.

Translate into Icelandic:

What is the news (*hvað er að frétta*, or *hvað er (segið þér) í fréttum*)? Everything (*allt*) fine (*gott*). What does the 'Morning Paper' say? Oh, it says nothing. How is the weather? Bad as always? No, it is fine, sunshine and heat (*hiti*). Are you not going to (*til*) Hafnarfjörður today? Yes (*jú*), I was going there (intended to go). Is anybody (*nokkur*) going with you? Yes, Björn is going with me. Do you intend to go in a car? Yes, I was just ordering one from the (automobile) 'station' (*stöð*). The 'station' will surely send it (*sendir . . . sjálfsagt*) at once. This 'station' is careful (takes good (*vel*) care) not to lose customers (*viðskiftavinum*). Well (*jæja*), I have to go, you write me to-morrow. Goodbye (*verið þér sælir*).

13.

The present, preterite, and perfect indicative of weak verbs, first class *telja*: In. VII, **3**, **2**.

Present endings: Sg. 1 —, 2 *-ur*, 3 *-ur*; Pl. 1 *-j-um*, 2 *-j-ið*, 3 *-j-a*.

Comparison of adjectives, *-ari, -astur*; *-ri, -stur*: In. III, **4**.

The comparative is always weak (second class), the superlative strong or weak.

Æfing. Þingvellir.

Á Íslandi eru margir merkir staðir, en Þingvellir eru merkastir. Þingvellir eru hinn forni Alþingisstaður Íslendinga, en Alþingi er elzta þing í Norðurálfu. Þeir, sem völdu staðinn, hafa haft gott vit á náttúrufegurð, því Þingvellir eru fegurri og tilkomumeiri en flestir aðrir staðir á landinu. Af vestri bakka Almannagjár er hið fegursta útsýni austur yfir vellina og suður um Þingvallavatn. Eystri gjárbakkinn er að vísu miklu lægri, en þaðan er hljóðbært um alla vellina. Hér telja menn hið forna Lögberg hafa verið; þar sagði lögsögumaður upp lögin, og þaðan fluttu menn ræður og erindi, meðan þingheimur þakti brekkuna og vellina fyrir neðan. Þeir, sem þingið settu, hafa því eigi aðeins kunnað að meta fegurð staðarins, heldur einnig hina hentugu staðhætti. Þeir ruddu líka, að sögn, Öxará farveg niður í Almannagjá; þar fellur hún enn í fögrum fossi. Hins vegar hafa nútímamenn rutt og lagt veg þann, sem nú liggur ofan í gjána, yfir ána og ofan á vellina. Sjálfir vellirnir eru ekki mjög víðir. Þeir eru rétt austan við Almannagjá;

sunnan þeirra er Þingvallavatn, en að austan er hraun. Á heitum sumardegi hylur blámóða landið svo langt sem augað eygir. Úti við sjóndeildarhringinn eru blá fjöll, í norðri Ármannsfell og Skjaldbreiður.

Á Þingvöllum er nú prestssetur og gistihús; gistihúsið (Valhöll) selur gestum fæði og annan greiða við sanngjörnu verði.

á stf.1 river.

að prep. with dat. at.

að prep. with dat. according to; *a. vísu* to be sure, *a. sögn* according to what is said.

að austan adv. to the east.

af prep. with dat. of; from.

Almannagjá stf.2 'Gorge of the Commons.'

Alþingi stn. (*kvæði*) the old national convention of the Icelanders.

Alþingisstaður stm.3 the place of the national convention.

Ármannsfell stn. 'Fell of Ármann,' a mountain.

auga wn. eye; *svo langt sem augað eygir* as far as eye can see.

austan við prep. with acc. east of, to the east of.

austur yfir prep. with acc. east across, east over.

bakki wm.1 bank, brink.

(*blá*)*móða* wf.1 (blue) mist.

brekka wf.1 slope.

brú, brúar, brýr stf.3 bridge.

eigi adv. = *ekki* not; *e. aðeins . . . heldur einnig* not only . . . but also.

einnig adv. also.

en conj. than.

enn adv. still, yet.

erindi stn. (*kvæði*) address, speech.

eygja, eygði, eygt wv.2 (be able to) see.

eystri, austastur adj. (*austur*) eastern, more easterly, most easterly.

fagur, fegurri, fegurstur adj. beautiful, fair.

falla, féll, féllum, fallinn stv.7 fall.

farvegur stm.3 (river) bed.

fegurð stf.2 beauty.

flytja, flutti, fluttur wv.1 move; deliver (a speech).

forn, forn, fornt adj. ancient, old.

foss stm.1 waterfall.

fyrir neðan adv. down below.

fæði stn. (*kvæði*) food.

gamall, eldri, elztur adj. old.

gistihús stn. hotel, inn.

gjá, gjár, gjár stf.3 chasm, gorge.

gjárbakki wm.1 bank, brink of a gorge.

greiði wm.1 favor, good turn, service.

heldur conj. but.

hentugur, -ugri, -ugastur adj. practical, handy.

hins vegar adv. on the other hand.

hljóðbær, -ari, -astur adj. carrying sound; *h-t er* sound is easily carried.

hylja, huldi, hulinn wv.1 cover.

Íslendingur stm.1 Icelander.

kunna, kann, kunni, kunnað pret. pres.v. know how to, with inf.

lágur, lægri, lægstur adj. low.

leggja, lagði, lagður wv.1 lay, lay out.

liggja, lá, lágum, leginn stv.5 lie; lead.

lög stn.pl. law(s).

Lögberg stn. 'Law Rock.'

lögsögumaður stm.4 law-speaker; see *segja*.

margur, fleiri, flestur adj. many, more, most.

meðan conj. while.

merkur, merkari, merkastur adj. important, significant.

meta, mat, mátum, metinn stv.5 value, esteem.

miklu lægri much lower. S. III, **4**, 5.

náttúrufegurð stf.2 beauty of nature.

niður í prep. with acc. down into.

norður stn. north; *í norðri* in the north, to the north.

Norðurálfa wf.1 Europe.

nútímamenn stm.4 modern men.

ofan á, -i preps. with acc. down onto, into.

prestssetur stn. (*hreiður*) parsonage.

ryðja, ruddi, ruddur wv.1 clear (a road), excavate (a river bed).

ræða wf.1 speech.

saga wf.1 history.

sanngjarn, -gjarnari, -gjarnastur adj. fair (price).

segja, sagði, sagður wv.3 say; *s. upp lög* recite, proclaim the laws; this was the duty of the old lawspeaker (*lögsögumaður*).

selja, seldi, seldur wv.1 sell.

setja, setti, settur wv.1 set, establish.

sjóndeildarhringur stm.2 horizon.

Skjaldbreiður stm. 'Broad Shield,' a mountain.

staðháttur stm.3 usually in pl. qualities of a place.

staður stm.3 place.

suður um prep. with acc. south across, over.

sumardagur stm.1 summer day.

sunnan prep. with gen. (to the) south of.

sögn stf.2 (*gjöf*) story, (hear)say.

telja, taldi, talinn wv.1 count; consider. S. VI, 11, *4.*

tilkomumikill, -meiri, -mestur adj. grand, impressive.

um prep. with acc. over across.

Valhöll stf.2 'Valhall,' the hall of Odin; name of a hotel.

vatn stn. water; lake.

vegur stm.3 way, road.

velja, valdi, valinn wv.1 select.

verð stn. price.

vestri, vestastur adj. (*vestur*) western; more westerly, most westerly.

við prep. (1) with acc. at: *austan við* east of; *úti við* out near; (2) with dat. against, for: *við góðu verði* for a good price.

viður, viðari, viðastur adj. wide.

vís, vísari, vísastur adj. wise, certain; *að vísu* according to what is certain, to be sure.

vit stn. intelligence; *hafa v. á e-u* be a judge of something.

völlur stm.3 plain, field.

yfir prep. with acc. over, across.

þekja, þakti, þaktur, þakinn wv.1 cover, thatch.

þing stn. meeting, convention of the people, thing; congress, parliament.

þingheimur stm.1 assembly, the people participating in a *þing.*

Þingvallavatn stn. 'Lake of Thingvellir.'

Þingvellir stm.3 pl. 'Plains of the Thing.'

Öxará stf.1 'Axe River.'

Translate into Icelandic:

Have you ever been at (*á* with dat.) Þingvellir? It is a most beautiful (*hinn fegursti*) place. It is also a most important place in the history (*í sögu*) of the country (*landsins*). There the Icelanders established the Alþingi more than 1000 years ago (*fyrir meira en þúsund árum*). The lawspeaker proclaimed the law from the Law Rock, while the people covered the slope and the plains below. Alþingi is considered the oldest national assembly (*þing*) in Europe; it is much older than the British (*brezka*) Parliament (*þingið*). It has therefore been called (*kallað*) the grandmother of parliaments (*amma þinganna*).

14.

Normal present endings of strong verbs and weak verbs of the first class: Sg. 1 —, 2 -*ur,* 3 -*ur*; Pl. 1 -*um,* 2 -*ið,* 3 -*a.*

Preterite present verb *vita*: In. VII, **5**, *1*.

Indefinite pronouns *annar, enginn, hver, nokkur*: In. VI, **6**, 2(b), (c), and (g), and S. IV, **6**, 3, 8, 11, 16.

Numerals: In. V, **1**, **2** and **3**, 7.

Æfing. Hvað er framorðið?

Hvað er framorðið? Hvað er klukkan? Klukkan er eitt (tvö, þrjú, fjögur, fimm, o. s. frv.). Klukkan er farin að ganga tvö; hún er langt gengin tvö; hún er kortér gengin (til) tvö. Klukkan er eitt; hún er tíu mínútur yfir eitt (= tíu mínútur gengin tvö); hún er fimmtán mínútur yfir eitt (= kortér yfir eitt = kortér gengin tvö); hún er tuttugu og fimm mínútur yfir eitt (= hana vantar fimm mínútur í hálftvö). Klukkan er rétt hálftvö. Hún er fimm mínútur yfir hálftvö; hana vantar kortér í tvö. Á klukkum og úrum er hvít skífa með svörtum tölustöfum; þau hafa líka vís(ir)a; litli vísirinn bendir á stundirnar, langi vísirinn á mínúturnar. Á flestum klukkum og úrum, jafnvel armbandsúrum, er líka sekúnduvísir.

Í gamla daga, þegar hvorki voru til úr né klukkur, urðu menn að fara eftir sólinni; þegar hún var í hádegisstað eða hásuðri, vissu menn, að klukkan var tólf; þá var, með öðrum orðum, hádegi. Í þá daga var deginum skift í átta eyktir; svaraði hver eykt til þriggja stunda nú. Næsta eykt eftir hádegi var nón, klukkan þrjú, þá miðaftan, eða miður aftan, klukkan sex, þá náttmál, klukkan níu, miðnætti, klukkan tólf að nóttu, þá ótta, klukkan þrjú, þá rismál, klukkan sex, og loks dagmál, klukkan níu að morgni. Öll þessi heiti, nema ótta, og kannske rismál og náttmál, eru enn algeng í sveitum á Íslandi.

Þegar menn vissu ekki nákvæmlega, hvað tímanum leið, urðu menn að gizka á: það er nokkru (skömmu, rétt) fyrir (eftir) hádegi. Það er komið fram undir hádegi, það er komið yfir hádegi. Það stendur á hádegi, sögðu þeir, sem voru vissir í sinni sök. Aðrir sögðu: það var um hádegisbilið, um hádegisleytið.

Menn skifta oft deginum í fyrir og eftir hádegi (f. h., e. h.); morgunn heitir fyrir hádegi, eftirmiðdagur eftir hádegi, en kvöld eftir klukkan sex. Ég svaf vel í nótt, fór á fætur snemma í morgun, át morgunverð klukkan níu, miðdagsmat um hádegi. Ég fór í heimsókn síðdegis og drakk miðaftanskaffi hjá kunningja mínum. Ég ætla að borða kvöldmat klukkan sex til sjö, en í kvöld ætla ég í leikhúsið. Svo vonast ég til að sofa vel í nótt.

að conj. that.
að morgni in the morning.
aftan(n) stm.1 (*himinn*) evening.

algengur, -geng, -gengt adj. common.
armband stn. bracelet.
armbandsúr stn. wrist watch.

benda, benti, bent wv.2 *b. á* point to, show.

borða, -aði, -aður wv.4 eat, have a meal.

dagmál stn.pl. nine in the morning.

dálítið adv. a little.

drekka, drekkur, drakk, drukkum, drukkinn stv.3 drink.

eftir prep. with acc. after.

eftirmiðdagur stm.1 afternoon (pronounced *ettirmiddagur*); the word is common in towns, but not as good as *eftir hádegi, seinni hluti dags.*

éta, étur, át, átum, étinn stv.5 eat.

eykt stf.2 a period of three hours, the old Latin *hora.*

fara á fætur get up; *f. í rúmið* go to bed.

fara eftir e-u go according to something, follow something.

fram adv. forth; *f. undir* prep. with acc. up to; *f. yfir* prep. with acc. over, past (a certain time).

framorðið adj.n. advanced (of time); *hvað er f.* what time is it.

fyrir prep. with acc. before (of time).

ganga, gengur, gekk, gengum, genginn stv.7 (of clocks) go, run; *klukkan er farin að ganga tvö* it is past one o'clock; *langt gengin tvö* near two. Cf. S. VI, 5.

gizka, -aði, -að wv.4 guess (*á e-ð*) something.

hádegi stn. (*kvæði*) noon.

hádegisbil stn. =

hádegisleyti stn. about noon.

hádegisstaður stm.3 the place where the sun is at noon; south.

hálf- half; *hálftvö* 1:30 or 1½. Likewise: *hálfþrjú* 2:30, *-fjögur* 3:30. Note the indeclinable neuter!

hásuður stn. (*hreiður*) due south.

heimsókn stf.2 visit; *fara í h.* to visit.

heiti stn. name, term.

hvorki . . . né neither . . . nor.

í prep. with. acc (of time) *í gamla daga* in the old days, of old; *í morgun* this morning; *í dag* today; *í kvöld* tonight; *í nótt* tonight, last night.

klukka wf.1 clock; *k-an þrjú* three o'clock.

koma, kemur, kom, komum, kominn stv.4 come; (of time) pass, advance *það er komið fram undir hádegi* it is almost noon.

kortér stn. quarter of an hour.

kunningi wm.1 acquaintance.

kvöld stn. evening.

kvöldmatur (*-verður*) stm.3 supper.

leikhús stn. theater; *í l-ið* to the th.

líða, líður, leið, liðum, liðinn stv.1 pass (of time); *hvað líður tímanum?* what time is it?

loks adv. finally.

miðaftan(*n*) stm.1 or stn. four to six o'clock.

miðaftanskaffi stn. afternoon coffee; commonly in the towns called *eftirmiðdagskaffi* (not so good).

miðdagsmatur stm.3 lunch (at twelve to one), dinner.

miðdagur stm.1 dinner (at six) (pronounced *middagur*).

miðnætti stn. (*kvæði*) twelve at night, midnight.

miður, mið, mitt adj. (acc. *miðjan*) mid-.

miður adv.comparative: less; *því m.* unfortunately.

mínúta wf.1 minute.

morgunmatur (*-verður*) stm.3 breakfast.

nákvæmlega adv. exactly.

náttmál stn.pl. nine in the evening.

nema conj. except.

nón stn. three in the afternoon. This was the original time for noon, even in England, where noon was later advanced three hours to accommodate hungry monks.

nótt stf.3 night, *að n-u* at n.

næstur, næst, næst adj. next, nearest.

orð stn. word; *með öðrum orðum* in other words.

ótta wf.1 three o'clock in the morning.

rétt adv. just, exactly.

rismál stn.pl. six in the morning; time to rise.

sekúnda wf.1 second.

sekúnduvísir stm.1 secondhand.

síðdegis adv. in the afternoon.

skammur, skömm, skammt adj. short, neuter used as noun: a short while. Concerning the dative, see S. I, 3, 2, 5.

skífa wf.1 dial, face.

skifta, skifti, skiftur wv.2 divide (*e-u í e-ð* sth into sth).

sofa, sefur, svaf, sváfum, sofið stv.4 sleep; *fara að s.* go to sleep.

sól stf.2 sun.

standa, stendur, stóð, stóðum, staðinn stv.6 stand; impers. be exactly.

svara, -aði, -að wv.4 answer; *s. til* correspond to.

sök stf.2 matter, thing; cf. *viss* below.

tala, -aði, -aður wv.4 speak (*um* about).

tölustafur stm.2 cipher, numeral.

um prep. with acc. about, circa.

úr stn. watch.

vanta, -aði, -að wv.4 impers.v. with double acc.: lack; *hana vantar kortér í tvö* it is quarter of (to) two.

vasaúr stn. pocket watch.

vera til exist.

verða stv.3 must, have to.

vísir stm.1 (*læknir*) hand (on a clock).

viss, viss, visst adj. certain; *vera v. í sinni sök* be certain (positive) about something.

vita, veit, vitum, vissi, vitað pret. pres.v. know.

vona, -aði, -að wv.1 hope; *vonast* (middle voice) *til* hope, expect.

yfir prep. with acc. over, past.

þá adv. then . . . then (in enumerating things).

ætla, -aði, -aður wv.4 be going to, intend to.

Translate into Icelandic:

What time is it? what o'clock is it? It is one, two, etc. o'clock. It is five minutes past twelve; it is quarter past two; it is twenty minutes past three; it is half past four; it is quarter of five; it is five o'clock. Do you have a wrist watch? No, I have only a pocket watch (*vasaúr*). When did you rise this morning? I rose at seven o'clock. And when did you have (*borðuðuð þér*) breakfast? I had breakfast at nine, lunch at twelve, afternoon coffee at four, and I am going to have supper at six or seven. Tonight I shall go (am going) early to bed (*fara . . . í rúmið*), read a little (*lesa dálítið*) and go to sleep. But I am going to the theater with my mother and sister; they live (*búa*) in the country (*uppi í sveit*), but they came for a visit (*í heimsókn*) today.

15.

Strong verbs with unchanged vowels in the present: *i, í, e, ei.*

Verbs of the first (*i*), third (*e, i*), fourth and fifth (*e, i*), and the seventh (*ei*) classes: In. VII, **2**; VII, **4**, *2*.

Normal endings: Sg. 1 —,2 *-ur*,3 *-ur*; Pl. 1 *-um*,2 *-ið, -a.*

The meaning of the present tense: S. VI, **2**, *1*.

Indefinite pronouns (*annar, neinn, nokkur*): S, IV, **6**.

Æfing. Samtal.

Björn er í Menntaskólanum, Anna systir hans í Kvennaskólanum. Í dag verður Björn átján ára, svo þetta er afmælið hans. Þau

systkinin eru að tala saman. B.: Hvað gefur þú mér í afmælisgjöf?
A.: Ég gef þér ekki neitt! B.: Þú getur nú ekki verið þekkt fyrir
það, fyrst pabbi og mamma gefa mér úr, og Siggi bróðir gefur mér
skáldsögu. A.: Til hvers er það, þú lítur aldrei í bók. B.: Lít
ég aldrei í bók! Ég, sem les frá morgni til kvölds. A.: Já, en
þú lest aldrei annað en kennslubækurnar. B.: Víst les ég aðrar
bækur, ég les þær á kvöldin í rúminu, meðan þú sefur. A.: Og
svo geturðu aldrei komizt á fætur á morgnana!

B.: Jæja, tíminn líður; eigum við ekki að hætta þessu rifrildi?
Ég verð að fara upp á (bóka)safn. A.: Ef þú biður mig vel.
B.: Auðvitað bið ég þig vel, og heyrðu mig, geturðu gefið mér
að drekka? A.: Hvað drekkur þú, mjólk eða vatn? B.: Ef þú
finnur mjólk í búrinu, þá drekk ég hana heldur. A.: Gerðu svo
vel. En nú mátt þú til með að koma með mér í leikhúsið í kvöld,
og ef þú situr of lengi uppi á safni, þá sit ég heima. B.: Af hverju
ætlar þú í leikhúsið í kvöld? A.: Til að sjá hann Harald leika,
hann leikur bara í kvöld. B.: Jæja, þú bíður þá eftir mér. A.:
Já, og ég skal meira að segja hafa afmælisgjöfina til handa þér í
kvöld, ef þú kemur með mér. B.: Vertu bless(uð)! A.: Sæll og
bless(aður)!

á prep. with acc. (1) onto, into;
  upp á safn up to the library; (2)
  at a certain time, in: *á kvöldin,
  morgnana* in the evening, morning; (3) with dat. *á safni* in the
  library.
afmæli stn. (*kvæði*) birthday, anniversary (pronounced *ammæli*).
afmælisgjöf stf.2 birthday present.
átján num. eighteen.
auðvitað adv. of course (literally:
  easily known).
biða, *bíður, beið, biðum, beðið* stv.1
  wait; *b. eftir* wait for.
biðja, *biður, bað, báðum, beðinn* stv.
  5 ask, pray, request. Cf. In. VII,
  4, 2, (b) 2.
blessaður, *blessuð, blessað* pp. of
  blessa wv.4 bless. Used in greetings between friends, also abbreviated: *bless; komdu bless(aður)*
  hello, how do you do; *vertu b.*
  goodbye.
bók stf.3 book.
(*bóka*)*safn* stn. library.
búr stn. pantry.

drekka, *drekkur, drakk, drukkum,
  drukkinn* stv.3 drink.
eða conj. or.
eftir prep. with dat. after; for.
finna, *finnur, fann, fundum, fundinn*
  stv.3 find.
fótur stm.4 foot; *komast á fætur*
  get up.
frá prep. with dat. from.
fyrir prep. with acc. for.
fyrst conj. since.
gefa, *gefur, gaf, gáfum, gefinn* stv.5
  give (*e-m e-ð* sbdy sth).
gera, *gerði, gerður* wv.2 do; *gerðu
  svo vel* literally: do so well (as
  to); please.
geta, *getur, gat, gátum, getað* stv.5
  be able to. Takes a past. part.
hafa til (*tilbúinn*) have ready.
handa prep. with dat. for.
hann Haraldur cf. S. IV, 1, 4.
heldur adv. rather, preferably.
heyrðu mig listen!
hætta, *hætti, hættur* wv.2 cease.
í prep. with acc. (1) *í bók* into a
  book; (2) *í gjöf* as a gift.

207

jæja interj. well.

kennslubók stf.3 textbook.

komast middle voice of *koma*; get.

kvennaskóli wm.1 school for girls; high school for girls.

leika, leikur, lék, lékum, leikinn stv.7 play, act.

lesa, les, las, lásum, lesinn stv.5 read; second person *lest*; cf. In. VII, **4**, *2*(a), 2b.

líða, líður, leið, liðum, liðinn stv.1 pass (of time).

líta, lítur, leit, litum, litinn stv.1 look.

menntaskóli wm.1 gymnasium, college.

mega til (*með*) must, have to.

mikill, -il, -ið; meiri, mestur adj. great; more, most; *meira að segja* even, believe it or not.

mjólk stf.3 milk.

nemandi wm.2 student, pupil.

nú adv. referring to the whole sentence, marking a transition: now, really, you cannot do that.

rifrildi stn. (*kvæði*) quarrel, banter.

rúm stn. bed.

safn stn. collection, library.

saman adv. together.

samtal stn. talk, conversation.

sitja, situr, sat, sátum, setinn stv.5 sit, stay. Cf. In. VII, **4**, *2*(b), 2.

skáldsaga wf.1 novel.

svo (1) conj. so that, (2) adv. then.

sæll, sæl, sælt adj. happy; in greetings: *komdu, vertu sæll* how do you do; goodbye.

til prep. with gen. to, for; *til hvers* what for = *af hverju* why; *til* (*þess*) *að* in order to; *til* adv. ready.

um prep. with acc. about; adv. for.

þekktur, þekkt, þekkt adj. known; *þ. fyrir e-ð* known for (on account of) something; *þú getur ekki verið þ. f. það* you cannot be known to do that; you should be ashamed of doing it.

þyrstur, þyrst, þyrst adj. thirsty.

Translate into Icelandic:

Who is Björn? He is a student (*nemandi*) in the Gymnasium. And who is Anna? His sister and a student in the High School for Girls. What are they doing? Speaking [together] about (*um*) the birthday present, which Anna is to (*á að*) give Björn. Is she giving him anything (translate: does she give ... *nokkuð*)? Not yet. Are his parents giving him anything (= do his parents give ...)? Yes, they are giving (= they give) him a watch. Are you (*þú, þér*) giving (= do you give) him anything? No, nothing at all (*alls ekkert*). Björn is thirsty, he asks his sister for (*um*) a drink (*að drekka*). What does he drink? Milk. What do you drink? Water. We, too, ask for a glass of (*glas af*) water. If you (*þú, þér*) ask Anna for a glass of water, she will give (*þá gefur hún*) it to you. No, I shall wait (= I wait) no longer (*ekki lengur*).

16.

Numerals. Cardinals. In. V, 1 and **2**.

Dative of difference: S. I, **3**, *2*, 5.

Genitive of measure or description: S. I, **4**, *2*.

Passive of verbs: present and preterite: S. VI, **1**, *3*; VI, **8**.

Æfing. Tímatal.

Eitt dægur er tólf klukkutímar, tvö dægur eru einn sólarhringur eða tuttugu og fjórir tímar. Stundum er dagur notaður í sömu merkingu og sólarhringur. Ein vika er sjö dagar; vikudagarnir heita sunnudagur, mánudagur, þriðjudagur, miðvikudagur, fimmtudagur, föstudagur, laugardagur. Ef þriðjudagur er í dag, þá var mánudagur í gær, sunnudagur í fyrradag, laugardagur daginn fyrir í fyrradag, en á morgun er miðvikudagur og fimmtudagur hinn daginn. Eg svaf yfir mig í morgun, í dag ætla ég að kaupa mér vekjaraklukku til þess að vekja mig á réttum tíma á morgun (með morgninum).

Tólf mánuðir eru í einu ári, þeir heita janúar, febrúar, marz, apríl, maí, júní, júlí, ágúst, september, október, nóvember, desember. Hvað ert þú gamall? Ég er fjörutíu og fimm ára. Hvenær ertu fæddur? Níunda júní 1897. Hvenær varstu fermdur? Þegar ég var fjórtán ára. Og hvenær giftist þú? Tuttugasta og sjötta ágúst 1935. Hvað eru börnin gömul? Björssi er fjögra og Sigga tveggja ára.

Árstíðirnar eru vetur, sumar, vor og haust. En Íslendingar skifta líka árinu í tvö misseri: vetur og sumar, og er sumardagurinn fyrsti allmikill hátíðisdagur á Íslandi, hann ber jafnan upp á fimmtudag. Sumarið er tuttugu og sex vikur og endar á miðvikudegi. Vetur byrjar næsta laugardag. Verða þá milli sumars og vetrar nokkrir dagar, sem nefndir eru veturnætur. Sumarmál eru kallaðir dagarnir milli vetrar og sumars á vorin. Frá miðjum vetri hér um bil eru taldir þrír mánuðir þrítugnættir til sumars, þeir heita þorri, góa og einmánuður. Harpa heitir fyrsti mánuður í sumri. Um allt þetta má lesa í íslenzka almanakinu.

Íslenzka tímatalið er einkum notað í sveitum. Bændur rýja kannske ærnar í tíundu viku sumars og fara að slá, þegar tólf vikur eru af (sumri). Það fer eftir tíðarfari. Það er og gamall siður í sveitum að telja aldur dýra og jafnvel manna í nóttum og vetrum fremur en í dögum og árum.

af adv. or prep. with dat. off, passed of.
af því að conj. because.
ágúst m.indecl. August.
aldur stm.1 (*akur*) age.
allmikill, -il, -ið adj. rather important.
almanak stn. calender.
apríl m. indecl. April.
árstíð stf.2 season.
auðvitað adv. of course.
bað stn. bath.
bera, ber, bar bárum, borinn stv.4

bear; *b. upp á* coincide with (impers. with two acc.).
byrja, -aði, -aður wv.4 begin.
daginn fyrir the day before.
desember m.indecl. December.
dægur stn. (*hreiður*) twelve hours, night or day.
einkum adv. especially.
einmánuður stm.3 March-April, last month of winter.
eins adv. alike.
enda, -aði, -aður wv.4 end.
fara eftir go according to.

fasta wf.1 fast.

febrúar m.indecl. February.

ferma, fermdi, fermdur wv.2 confirm (a child).

fimmtudagur stm.1 Thursday.

fremur en rather than.

fyrradagur stm.1 day before yesterday; *í f-g* the day . . .

fœða, fœddi, fœddur wv.2 bear (a child), feed, bring up.

föstudagur stm.1 Friday.

gifta, gifti, giftur wv.2 marry (transitive: a father marries his daughter, a parson marries the couple), *giftast* marry (take a husband or wife).

góa wf.1 February-March, last but one month before summer.

harpa wf.1 April-May, first month in summer.

hátíð stf.2 festival, feastday.

hátíðisdagur stm.1 the same.

haust stn. autumn, fall.

hérumbil, hér um bil adv. about, ca.

hinn daginn the day after tomorrow.

í prep. with acc. *í dag* today, etc.

jafnan adv. always.

janúar m.indecl. January.

júlí m.indecl. July.

júní m.indecl. June.

kaupa, keypti, keyptur wv.2 (irreg.) buy; *k. sér* buy (for oneself).

klukkutími wm.1 hour = *stund.*

laug stf.1 bath.

laugardagur stm.1 Saturday.

maí m.indecl. May.

mál stn. language.

mánudagur stm.1 Monday.

mánuður stm.3 month.

marz m.indecl. March.

með prep. with dat. *með morgninum* first thing in the morning.

merking stf.1 significance, meaning.

miður, mið, mitt adj. mid-, in the middle of.

miðvikudagur stm.1 Wednesday.

misseri stn. (*kvœði*) half-year, semester.

nafn stn. name.

nota, -aði, -aður wv.4 use.

nóvember m.indecl. November.

og adv. also.

og conj. *samur . . . og* same as.

október m.indecl. October.

réttur, rétt, rétt adj. right, correct.

rúja, rú, rúði, rúinn wv.1 shear (the sheep).

samur, söm, samt adj. pronoun of identity: same. S. IV, **3**, 5.

september m.indecl. September.

siður stm.3 custom.

skrifa, -aði, -að wv.4 write.

slá, slœr, sló, slógum, sleginn stv.6 strike; mow (grass).

sofa yfir sig oversleep.

sólarhringur stm.2 day and night, twenty-four hours.

stafur stm.2 letter.

stundum adv. sometimes.

sumar stn. summer; *í s-ri* of the s.

sumardagur stm.1 summer day; *s-inn fyrsti* the first day of summer. Cf. S. II, 7.

sumarmál stn.pl. a few days before the first day of summer.

sunnudagur stm.1 Sunday.

telja, taldi, talinn wv.1 count (*í* in).

tíðarfar stn. weather conditions.

tímatal stn. chronology.

tími wm.1 hour; time, *á réttum t-a* at the right t.

vekja, vakti, vakinn wv.1 awaken.

vekjaraklukka wf.1 alarm clock.

verða þá then there will be.

vetur stm.4 winter.

veturnœtur a few days before the first day of winter.

vika wf.1 week.

vikudagur stm.1 weekday.

vikulok stn. end of the week.

vor stn. spring; *á vorin* in spring.

þorri wm.1 January-February, the first month after midwinter.

þriðjudagur stm.1 Tuesday.

þrítugnœttur, -nœtt, -nœtt adj. having thirty nights.

œr stf.3 ewe.

Translate into Icelandic:

In Icelandic (*á íslenzku*) the names of days and months are not written (*skrifuð*) with capitals (= big letters *stórum stöfum*) as in English. The names of the months are otherwise (*annars*) the same, but the names of the days are to some extent (*að nokkru leyti*) different (*ólik*). Sunday and Monday are alike (*eins*) in both languages (*mál-unum* with the definite article). Tuesday is called the third day, of the week of course (*auðvitað*). Wednesday is so called (*kallaður það*), because (*af því að*) it is in the middle (*í miðri*) of the week. Friday is fast (*föstu*) day, because then people were not allowed (*fólki var ekki leyft*) to eat meat. Saturday was called the day of bathing, because people took their baths (*fólk tók bað eða laug*) at the end of the week (*í vikulokin*).

17.

Strong verbs with i-shifted vowels in the present singular: *a-e-ö, á-æ, o-e, jó-ý, jú-ý, au-ey, ja-e-jö* (Pr. 5, 2).

Verbs of the second (*jó, jú-ý*), third (*ja-e-jö*), sixth (*a-e-ö*), and seventh (*a-e-ö, á-æ, au-ey*) classes. In. VII, 2; VII, 4, 2.

Normal endings: Sg. 1 —,2 -*ur*,3 -*ur*; Pl. 1 -*um*,2 -*ið*,3 -*a*.

Æfing. Sjóferð.

Þeir Siggi og Nonni ætla að róa á sjó. Nonni á lítinn bát, sem stendur niðri í fjöru. Þar standa líka margir aðrir bátar. Nonni býður Sigga að fara með sér á sjóinn; "ég ræð ekki við bátinn einn," segir hann. Siggi tekur boðinu með þökkum; þeir ganga niður að bátunum; Nonni fer að líta eftir árunum, en Siggi gáir til veðurs. "Hvað heldur þú um veðrið?" segir Nonni. "Það verður gott, held ég," segir Siggi, "hann dregur nú samt upp bliku í suðrinu." "Við höldum þá af stað," segir Nonni. Svo taka þeir skorðurnar undan bátnum og skjóta honum á flot. Siggi hleypur fyrst upp í bátinn, Nonni stekkur á eftir honum. Nú flýtur báturinn, drengirnir setja sig niður á þóftunum, taka til ára og róa út á sjó. Þeir róa fram hjá æðarkollum; þær eru spakar og fljúga ekki upp; þær fljóta eins og korkar á öldunum. Drengirnir láta þær eiga sig. Einn máfur flýgur eftir bátnum; þeir láta hann líka vera. Nú koma þeir út á miðið, hætta að róa og renna færum í sjó. Þeim gengur vel, þeir draga þorsk og ýsu. Nonni dregur líka eina spröku, þá er báturinn hlaðinn. "Nú drögum við ekki meira," segir hann, "heldur höldum í land." Svo róa þeir í land og skifta milli sín fiskinum. Hvor um sig heldur á stórri fiskkippu í hendinni, þegar þeir ganga heim neðan úr fjörunni.

211

á eftir adv. and prep. with dat. after.

af prep. with dat. from; *af stað* away, from the place.

alda wf.1 wave.

ár stf.1 oar.

bjóða, býður, bauð, buðum, boðinn stv.2 offer (*e-m e-ð* sbdy sth.).

blika wf.1 a cover of clouds.

boð stn. offer.

draga, dregur, dró, drógum, dreginn stv.6 draw; *hann dregur upp bliku* the sky is becoming overcast; *d. fisk* pull up fish.

eftir prep. with dat. after.

ég . . . einn I . . . alone.

eiga sig only after *láta*, which see.

fara, fer, fór, fórum, farinn stv.6 (1) go; (2) with infinitive: begin.

fiska, -aði, -að wv.4 to fish.

fiskkippa wf.1 a bunch (mess) of fish.

fiskur stm.1 fish.

fjara wf.1 shore, beach, ebb.

fljóta, flýtur, flaut, flutum, flotinn stv.2 float.

fljúga, flýgur, flaug, flugum, floginn stv.2 fly.

flot stn. floating; *á flot* afloat.

fram hjá prep. with dat. (forth) by.

færi stn. (*kvæði*) fishing line.

gá, gáir, gáði, gáður wv.3 look; *gá til veðurs* look at the weather.

ganga, gengur, gekk, gengum, genginn stv.7 (1) go, walk; (2) go so and so, *e-m gengur vel* (impersonal) 'it goes well for somebody,' somebody has good luck.

halda, heldur, hélt, héldum, haldinn stv.7 hold; (1) *h. á e-u* hold something (in the hand); (2) hold, consider, suppose; *h. um e-ð* think about something; (3) go, proceed, *h. í land, h. af stað* go (row) ashore, start.

heldur conj. but.

hlaða, hleður, hlóð, hlóðum, hlaðinn stv.6 load.

hlaupa, hleypur, hljóp, hlupum, hlaupinn stv.7 run; jump.

hvor um sig each.

hætta, hætti, hættur wv.1 cease, stop.

hönd stf.3 hand; *í hendinni* in the hand.

í prep. with dat. on; *í fjöru(nni)*.

korkur stm.1 cork.

láta, lætur, lét, létum, látinn stv.7 let; *l. vera* let be; *l. eiga sig* (literally: let one own oneself) let be.

líta eftir e-u look after something, take care of.

máfur stm.1 sea gull.

mið stn. (fishing) bank, landmark.

milli prep. with gen. between.

niður adv. down to (*að*).

ráða, ræður, réð, réðum, ráðinn stv.7 wield; *r. við* manage.

renna, renndi, renndur wv.2 let run; run out a fishing line.

róa, rær, reri, róinn irreg.v.2 row; *r. á sjó* row out on the sea (fishing).

róður, róðrar, róðrar stm.1 rowing; trip in a rowboat.

setja, setti, settur wv.2 set; *s. sig niður* sit down.

sjóferð stf.2 boat trip; fishing trip.

skifta, skifti, skiftur wv.2 divide (*e-u*).

skjóta, skýtur, skaut, skutum, skotinn stv.2 (1) shoot; (2) shove (with dat.).

skorða wf.1 prop, shore.

spakur, spök, spakt adj. tame, quiet.

spraka wf.1 flounder, halibut.

standa, stendur, stóð, stóðum, staðinn stv.6 stand, be standing.

stökkva, stekkur, stökk, stukkum, stokkinn stv.3 jump.

suður stn. (*hreiður*) south.

taka, tekur, tók, tókum, tekinn stv.6 take; (1) *t. e-u* accept something; (2) *t. til ára* take to the oars.

undan prep. with dat. from under.

úr prep. with dat. out of , *neðan úr* out from below, up.

ýsa wf.1 haddock.

þófta wf.1 thwart (pronounced *þótta*).

þorskur stm.1 cod.

þökk stf.2 thanks.

æðarkolla wf.1 eider duck.

212

KINDUR VIÐ FJÁRHÚS.

Translate into Icelandic:

Where are (*ætla*) the boys going? They are going out to (*út á* or *á*)
sea fishing (*að fiska*). Who owns the boat that is standing (*stendur*)
on the beach? It is Nonni's boat. Is Nonni going alone (*einn*) out
to sea? No, he is inviting (= invites) Siggi to go with him. Are
the boys inviting (= do the boys invite) you (*þú, þér*) to go with
them? No. But have you offered [them] to go with them? No.
Does Nonni's boat stand alone (*einn*) on the beach? No, many
other boats are standing there. Are there (*eru*) any birds on the
beach? Yes, there are eider ducks on the beach. Do the boys shoot
them? No, nobody is allowed (*má*) to shoot them, but Nonni sometimes shoots a gull. The eider ducks are tame, and they do not fly
much, but a gull flies the whole day. On the fishing bank, the first
fish that Siggi pulls up is a haddock, and the first fish that Nonni
gets (*fær*) is a cod. They load the boat with fish, and then they go
(*fara, halda*) home.

18.

Strong verbs and weak verbs, first class, ending in vowels, *-r, -s,*
-x, or *-n,* and taking *-rð, -ð, -t* or no ending in the second person
singular. In. VII, **4**, **2**.

Beginning action, indicated by *fara að*: S. VI, **5**.

Intransitive verbs of motion: S. VI, **3**.

Personal pronouns: S. IV, **1**.

Æfing. Á bóndabæ.

Þau Björn og Sigríður búa á stórri jörð, hafa margar kýr, marga
hesta og margt fé. Því miður deyr féð stundum úr fjárpestinni hjá
Birni. Nú eru ærnar farnar að bera, og Björn gengur við þær daglega til að missa ekki lömbin. "Sérðu forustuána, hana Bíldu?"
segir Björn við Siggu dóttur sína, "hún er víst að setja sig til
burðar." Sigga: "Já, hún ber víst í dag; fæ ég lambið undan
henni, ef ég næ henni?" "Já, þú færð það, en þú nærð henni
aldrei ein, held ég; við náum henni kannske bæði." Svo leggja þau
af stað bæði, ná henni, áður en hún ber, og setja hana inn í fjárhús.
Það er gott, því veðrið er að versna. Sólin skín að vísu, en hann
er farinn að vinda af norðri. Hann frýs á hverri nóttu í norðanátt.

Þegar þau feðginin koma heim, þá er kominn gestur, bóndi af
næsta bæ. Húsfreyja gefur honum kaffi, og þeir bændurnir skrafa
um landsins gagn og nauðsynjar. "Þú býrð nú vel hérna, Björn
minn," segir gesturinn. "O jæja, ég læt það vera, meðan pestin

drepur ekki féð fyrir manni." "Hún kemur nú við fleiri; ef þú
lest blöðin, sérðu hvernig hún geisar fyrir vestan." "Já, ég held
nú það," segir Björn. "En fréttir þú nokkuð af kosningunum?"
"Já," segir gestur; "það á að kjósa í næstu viku." "Einmitt
það; hvern ætlar þú að kjósa? Þú kýst víst framsóknarmanninn
eins og flestir hér um slóðir." "Nei, ég kýs sjálfstæðismanninn
(íhaldsmanninn)." "Það er annars gagn, að þessar kosningar verða
búnar, áður en við förum að slá." "Já, þú segir það satt; hvenær
gerir þú ráð fyrir að byrja?" "O svona eftir hálfan mánuð eða
þrjár vikur." "Hvað ertu lengi með túnið?" "Ég slæ mitt tún á
hálfum mánuði, en þú slærð víst ekki þitt á minna en þrem vikum?"
"Nei, mér veitir ekki af þrem vikum. En hvað er ég að hugsa,
mér er betra að fara að komast heim. Þakk fyrir mig, og verið þið
blessuð og sæl."

á prep. with dat. in (a week).
áður en conj. before.
af e-u from, about sth.
annars adv. really.
bera, ber, bar, bárum, borinn stv.4
    bear; lamb.
Bílda wf.1 a ewe with black spots
    around the eyes.
blað stn. newspaper.
bóndabær stm.2 farmstead.
búa, býr, bjó, bjuggum, búinn stv.7
    farm, live on a farm; pp. *búinn*
    done.
burður stm.3 birth (of the lambs),
    lambing (season).
bæði n. of *báðir* indef.pron. both.
daglega adv. daily.
deyja, deyr, dó, dóum, dáinn stv.6
    die; *d. úr pest* die of plague.
drepa, drepur, drap, drápum, drepinn
    stv.5 kill.
eftir prep. with acc. after (a week).
einmitt adv. just; *e. það* is that so?
    quite so.
einn, ein, eitt num. one; alone.
fá, fær, fékk, fengum, fenginn stv.7
    get.
fara, fer, fór, fórum, farinn stv.6 (1)
    go; *f. á undan* lead; (2) begin.
fjárhús stn. sheep barn (shed).
fjárpest stf.2 sheep plague.
forustuær stf.3 a ewe that leads the
    others; cf. bell-wether.
framsóknarmaður stm.4 progressive,

a man belonging to the party
    Framsókn stf.2.
frjósa, frýs, fraus, frusum, frosinn
    stv.2 freeze; *hann f.* it freezes;
    cf. S. IV, 1, 4(b).
fyrir vestan adv. in the west.
gagn stn. use, advantage; *það er g.*
    it is fortunate, fortunately;
    landsins g. og nauðsynjar the
    public weal.
ganga við walk among (to inspect).
geisa, -aði, -að wv.4 ravage.
gera, gerði, gerður wv.2 do, make.
gripur stm.2 (domestic) animal; pl.
    livestock.
hálfur, hálf, hálft adj. half.
heim adv. home.
hey stn. hay.
hjá prep. with dat. with, at; *féð ...*
    hjá Birni B.'s sheep.
hjálp stf.2 help, aid.
húsdýr stn. domestic animal.
húsfreyja wf.1 mistress of a house.
í næstu viku next week.
íhaldsmaður stm.4 a conservative.
jörð stf.2 farm, estate.
kaffi stn. coffee.
kjósa, kýs, kaus, kusum, kosinn stv.2
    choose, elect.
koma, kemur, kom, komum, kominn
    stv.4 come; *k. við e-n* touch,
    affect; *komast* get (home).
kosningar stf.1.pl. election(s).
kýr stf.3 cow.

láta, lætur, lét, létum, látinn stv.7 let; *ég læt það vera* (lit.I let it be) that is all right, I cannot complain.

lítill, -il, -ið; minni, minnstur adj. little, less, least.

mér er betra I had better.

miður adv. compar. less, worse; *því miður* unfortunately.

missa, missti, misstur wv.2 lose.

ná, nær, náði, náð wv.1 and 3 get, reach, catch (with dat.).

nauðsynjar stf.1.pl. necessities.

nóg stn. enough.

norðanátt stf.2 wind from the north.

norður stn. north.

o interj. oh.

o jæja interj. oh, why, well.

pest stf.2 plague; = *fjárpest.*

ráð stn. plan; *gera r. fyrir e-u* plan something, also with inf. (*að byrja*).

sannur, sönn, satt adj. true; *segja e-ð satt* tell the truth about something.

setja, setur, setti, settur wv.1 set, place; *s. inn* put into; *s. sig til*

burðar (about ewes) run away to lamb.

sjálfstæðismaður stm.4 an independent, a man of the Independence party (*Sjálfstæðisflokkur*).

skína, skín, skein, skinum, skininn stv.1 shine.

skrafa, -aði, -að wv.4 talk (*um* about).

slá, slær, sló, slógum, sleginn stv.6 strike, beat, slay; mow.

slóð stf.2 track; tract, *hér um s-ir* in these parts.

svona adv. about, perhaps; I suppose.

tún stn. homefield.

undan prep. with dat. from under; *u. e-m* (only of animals) born of.

veita, veitti, veittur wv.2 grant; *e-m veitir ekki af* one cannot do with less than.

vera með e-ð be occupied with.

versna, -aði, -aður wv.4 get worse, deteriorate.

vinda, vindar, -aði, -að wv.4 begin to blow (impersonal).

þakk fyrir mig thanks.

ær stf.3 ewe.

Translate into Icelandic:

Where do Björn and Sigríður live? They live on a big farm. Do they have any livestock (*nokkra gripi*)? Yes, they have cows, horses, and sheep. Most Icelandic farmers have these domestic animals (*húsdýr*). When do the ewes lamb? In spring (*á vorin*). What does a *forustuær* do? It leads (*fer á undan* = goes in front of) the sheep. What is Sigga going to do with Bílda? She is going to catch her. Does she get her? Yes, with the help (*hjálp*) of her father. What is Sigga supposed (*á S.*) to get, if she catches Bílda? She gets her lamb. Why do they put Bílda into the sheep barn? Because the weather is getting worse, the sun no longer shines. On Björn's farm there is (*er*) a big homefield (*tún*) which he mows every summer. Thus he gets hay enough (*nóg hey*) for the livestock.

19.

Perfect and past perfect indicative of all verbs is formed with the present and preterite of the verb *hafa* and the past participle neuter (ppn.) of the verbs conjugated. S. VI, 1, *3*; VI, 2, *3* and *4.*

Ppn. of strong verbs and weak verbs, first class, ends in *-ið.*

Ppn. of weak verbs, fourth class (and a few of third class) ends in -að.

Ppn. of verbs, whose stem ends in a vowel, strong or weak, ends in -ð.

Ppn. of weak verbs, second and (many) third classes, ends in -t.

Æfing. Alþingishátíð 1930.

Hvað hafið þér heyrt eða lesið um Ísland? Ég hef lesið mikið um það og talað við marga, sem hafa komið þangað. Hafið þér komið þar sjálfir? Já, ég hef heimsótt það einu sinni; það var árið 1930, þegar Íslendingar héldu mikla hátíð á Þingvöllum til minningar um stofnun Alþingis fyrir þúsund árum. Við konan mín tókum okkur far með skipi, sem Vestur-Íslendingar höfðu leigt til fararinnar. Þeir ætluðu að fjölmenna heim; þeir höfðu haft mikinn undirbúning, haldið fundi og deilt hart um málið. Þeir höfðu klofnað í tvo flokka um málið. Loks höfðu þeir samið við tvö skip um að flytja sig; við hjónin vorum svo heppin að ná í fyrra skipið. Okkur hefur sjaldan liðið betur á sjó, og við höfum aldrei skemmt okkur betur. Ég hafði aldrei séð eins marga Vestur-Íslendinga saman komna. Gamla menn og konur, sem ekki höfðu séð ættjörðina svo áratugum skifti. Ungt fólk, sem aldrei hafði séð hana, nema í anda. En allir höfðu tekið ástfóstri við landið, og allir biðu fullir eftirvæntingar eftir landsýn. Loks kom landsýn: grár veðurbarinn hólmi í regnskúrum. Svona hafði fólkið ekki hugsað sér landið. En það átti eftir að sjá landið stráð geislum sumarsólar, klætt grænu grasi og sveipað blárri móðu. Það átti eftir að sjá tinda og jökla eins skínandi hvíta og þeir höfðu verið í sögum gamla fólksins. Þetta var draumalandið.

Note: Stráð geislum strewn with rays, *klætt grasi* clothed with grass, *sveipað móðu* wrapped in mist; cf. S. I, 3, 1, 2(e) (instrumental dative).

Alþingishátíð stf.2 (millenary) celebration of the *Alþingi.*
andi wm.1 spirit; *í a-a* in (the) s.
ár stn. year.
áratugur stm.3 decade.
ástfóstur stn. loving care, affection; *taka á-i við e-n* center one's affections on somebody.
bíða, beið, biðum, beðinn, ppn. *beðið* stv.1 wait; *b. eftir* wait for.
byggja, byggði, byggður, ppn. *byggt* wv.2 build.
deila, deildi, deildur, ppn. *deilt* wv.2 fight, quarrel; *d. um* fight about.

draumaland stn. land of dreams.
eiga eftir be to, have in store, have left.
eins as; *eins og* as . . . as.
einu sinni adv. once.
eftirvænting stf.1 expectation.
för stf.2 journey.
fjölmenna, -mennti, -menntur, ppn. *-mennt* wv.2 crowd, flock.
flokkur stm.1 faction, party.
flytja, flutti, fluttur, ppn. *flutt* wv.1 transport.
fullur, full, fullt adj. full of (*e-s*).
fundur stm.3 meeting.

ÞINGVELLIR OG ALMANNAGJÁ.

fyrir prep. with dat. *f.* . . . *árum* . . . years ago.

fyrri adj. compar. first of two.

geisli wm.1 ray.

grár, grá, grátt adj. grey.

halda, hélt, héldum, haldinn, ppn. *haldið* stv.7 hold; *h. hátíð* celebrate a festival; *h. fund* hold a meeting.

harður, hörð, hart adj. hard; *hart* adv. hard, violently.

hátíð stf.2 festival, celebration.

heimsœkja, -sótti, -sóttur, ppn. *-sótt* wv.2 visit.

heppinn, -in, -ið adj. lucky; *h. með e-ð* lucky with respect to sth.

hjón stn.pl. married couple.

hólmi wm.1 islet, small island.

hugsa, -aði, -aður, ppn. *-að* wv.4 think; *h. sér* imagine.

hver stm.1 and 2 geyser.

jafnvel adv. even.

klœða, klœddi, klœddur, ppn. *klœtt* wv.2 cloth, cover (with dat.).

klofna, -aði, -aður, ppn. *-að* wv.4 split, be divided.

koma til come to, be to.

landsýn stf.2 landfall; sight of land.

leggja veg build a road.

leigja, leigði, leigður, ppn. *leigt* wv.2 rent, hire, charter.

líða, leið, liðum, liðinn, ppn. *liðið* stv.1 feel, *mér líður vel* I feel well.

loks adv. finally.

mál stn. case, matter, issue.

minning stf.1 memory.

móða wf.1 mist.

ná, nái, náður, ppn. *náð* wv.1 get; *ná í* get, reach.

regnskúr stf.2 rain, shower.

saman adv. together; *koma s.* gather.

semja, samdi, saminn, ppn. *samið* wv.1 agree, settle, come to terms; *s. um* about, *s. við e-n* with sbdy.

sjaldan adv. seldom.

skemmta, skemmti, skemmt (ppn.) wv.2 with dat. divert (*sér* oneself), have a good time.

skifta, skifti, skiftur, ppn. *skift* wv.2 divide, exchange, share; *svo árum skiftir* for years.

stofnun stf.2 establishment.

strá, stráði, stráður, ppn. *stráð* wv.3 strew, scatter.

sumarsól stf.2 summer sun.

sveipa, -aði, -aður, ppn. *-að* wv.4 cover, wrap in (with dat.).

svona adv. thus.

taka, tók, tókum, tekinn, ppn. *tekið* stv.6 take; *t. sér far* take a passage; *t. ástfóstri við* center one's affections in.

tala við speak to.

til prep. with gen. *t. minningar um* in memory of; *t. fararinnar* for the journey.

tindur stm.1 peak, summit.

tjaldborg stf.2 city of tents.

undirbúningur stm.1 preparation.

út af e-u on account of sth.

veðurbarinn, -in, -ið adj. weather-beaten, weathered.

Vestur-Íslendingar stm.1.pl. Icelandic-Americans.

þúsundárahátíð stf.2 millenary.

ættjörð stf.2 native land.

Translate into Icelandic:

Have you ever been (*komið til*) to Iceland? Yes, I have been there once. It was in 1930 when the Icelanders were celebrating (*héldu*) the millenary of the Alþingi (without the article). I had never seen the country before, and never heard of the Alþingi, but I had read some books about the hot springs (*hverana*) in Iceland. I had intended to go to Geysir, but I could not get passage (*far*) there from Reykjavík. All the cars had more than enough [to do] (*höfðu meira en nóg með að*) transporting (*að flytja*) the people from Reykjavík to Þingvellir. The Icelanders had made great

217

preparations. They had built a city of tents (*tjaldborg*) on Þingvellir. They had built (*lagt*) new roads. They had rented hundreds
(*hundruð*) of cars (*bíla*) to transport the people. And they were
very lucky with respect to (*með*) the weather.

20.

Future and perfect future of verbs: S. VI, **2**, *5* and *6*.

Future: *ég mun vera, hafa, fara* (1) I shall probably be, (2) I
shall be.

Perfect future: *ég mun hafa verið, haft, farið* (1) I may have
been, I probably was; (2) I shall have been (rare).

Compound conjugation of intransitive verbs of motion and change:

Present: *hann er farinn, kominn, byrjaður* he is gone, he has
come, begun.

Preterite: *hann var farinn, kominn, byrjaður* he was gone, he
had come, begun.

See S. VI, **3**.

Preterite present verbs: *vita, þurfa, munu, muna, vilja* (In. VII,
5, *1*).

Æfing. Kaupstaðarferð.

Ég man það ekki fyrir víst, en ég mun hafa verið á níunda eða
tíunda ári, þegar ég fékk að fara í kaupstaðinn í fyrsta sinn. Það
var um vor, pabbi var að flytja ullina í kaupstaðinn og lofaði mér
að fara með sér. Ég hafði að vísu oft farið þá ferð áður, en aðeins í
huganum. Eg hafði horft á eftir lestinni, þar sem hún fór í hægðum
sínum suður yfir ána og upp skarðsbrekkurnar. Hún varð minni
og minni, þar til hún hvarf sjónum, þar sem skarðið bar við loft.
Eftir það varð fullorðna fólkið að segja okkur börnunum, hvernig
lestinni gekk; það vissi allt. Nú er hann pabbi þinn kominn suður
fyrir Skarðið. Nú er hann víst að fara ofan með Svartagili. Nú
mun hann vera kominn ofan að Berufirði. Þar ætlar hann að hvíla
hestana, áður en hann leggur á leirurnar. Hann varð nokkuð seinn
fyrir, en hann mun samt hafa komizt yfir leirurnar, áður en flæddi
til muna. Svo þarf hann að komast yfir Fossá á fjöru, en þá er
hann líka sloppinn. Allt veit fullorðna fólkið, hugsuðum við
krakkarnir með öfund. Við vildum öll komast í kaupstaðinn sjálf
til þess að sjá alla dýrðina í búðinni, kaupa okkur rúsínur, eða
hnífa, eða jafnvel bók. Allt þetta hafði ég í huganum, þegar ég
lagði í fyrstu kaupstaðarferð mína. Ég hafði hlakkað mikið til
hennar, og ég varð ekki fyrir vonbrigðum.

KAUPSTAÐARFERÐ.

á prep. with dat. *á níunda ári* in my ninth year; *á eftir e-u* after; *á fjöru* on the beach, at ebbtide.

bera, bar, bárum, borinn stv.4 *e-ð* (acc.) *ber við loft* something looms, is seen against the sky (impers.).

Berufjörður stm.3 ' Bear Firth,' East Iceland.

búð stf.2 shop, general store.

dýrð stf.2 glory; wonderful things.

fá, fékk, fengum, fenginn stv.7 with inf. be allowed to.

fara ferð make a trip.

fara yfir cross, go through.

fjara wf.1 beach, ebb tide.

fjarðarendi wm.1 end of a firth.

flóð stn. flood, flood tide.

flytja, flutti, fluttur wv.1 transport.

flæða, flæddi, flæddur, ppn. *flætt* wv. 2 impers. *það flæðir* the flood comes in.

Fossá stf.1 ' Falls River.'

fullorðinn, -in, -ið adj. grown-up.

fyrir prep. with acc. *f. víst* for certain, surely.

fyrir adv. *seinn f.* late.

ganga, gekk, gengum, genginn stv.7 impers. *e-m gengur vel, illa* one fares well, badly.

gleyma, gleymdi, gleymdur wv.2 forget.

hann pabbi þinn your father.

heldur en conj. than.

hlakka, -aði, -að wv.4 *h. til* look forward to.

hnífur stm.1 knife.

horfa, horfði, horft wv.3 look; *h. á eftir e-m* watch somebody going.

hugi wm.1 =

hugur stm.3 mind, imagination.

hverfa, hvarf, hurfum, horfinn stv.3 disappear (*sjónum* from sight).

hvíla, hvíldi, hvíldur, ppn. *hvílt* wv.2 rest (transitive).

hægð stf.2 ease; *í hægðum sínum* at a leisurely pace, slowly.

í prep. with dat. in, at (cf. *hægð*); acc. *leggja í ferð* start a journey; *'í kaupstaðinn* to the town.

kaupa, keypti, keyptur, ppn. *keypt* wv.2 buy, = *k. sér.*

kaupstaðarferð stf.2 journey, trip to the trading place, the town.

kaupstaður stm.3 trading place, town.

komast, middle voice of *koma,* get.

leggja, lagði, lagður, ppn. *lagt* wv.1 lay; *l. á skarðið, leiruna, fjörðinn* start going over the pass, the mud flat, the firth; *l. í ferð* start a journey.

leira wf.1 mud flat at the end of a firth.

lest stf.2 caravan of pack-horses.

líka adv. really.

lofa, -aði, -aður wv.4 with dat. allow somebody (*e-m*) to do something.

loft stn. air, sky.

muna, man, munum, mundi, munað pret.pres.v. remember.

munu, mun, munum, mundi pret.pres. v. shall, will, may.

munur stm.3 difference; *til m-a* to a great extent.

níundi num. ninth.

ofan að with dat. down to.

ofan með with dat. down along.

poki wm.1 bag.

ríða, reið, riðum, riðinn stv.1 ride.

rúsínur wf.1.pl. raisins.

samt adv. nevertheless, all the same.

segja e-m tell some one.

sinn stn. time; *í fyrsta sinn* for the first time.

sjón stf.2 sight, vision; *hverfa s-um* disappear from sight.

skarð stn. mountain pass, ' Pass.'

skarðsbrekkur wf.1.pl. the slopes of the mountain, leading to a pass.

skemmtilegur adj. interesting, full of fun.

sleppa, slapp, sluppum, sloppinn stv. 3 escape.

suður fyrir with acc. south beyond.

suður yfir with acc. south beyond.

Svartagil stn. ' Black Ravine.'

til prep. with gen. *t. muna* to a considerable or great extent.

tíundi num. tenth.

ull stf.1 wool.

um prep. with acc. *u. vor* one spring, during one spring.

venjulega adv. usually.
verða fyrir e-u be hit by, affected by,
   v. f. vonbrigðum be disappointed,
   disillusioned.
vilja, vil, viljum, vildi pret.pres.v.
   want to, wish to.
vita, veit, vitum, vissi, vitað pret.
   pres.v. know.

vonbrigði stn.pl. disappointment.
þar sem (there) where.
þar til conj. until.
þegar conj. when.
þurfa, þarf, þurfum, þurfti, þurft
   pret.pres.v. need.
æfintýri stn. (*kvæði*) adventure.
öfund stf.2 envy.

Translate into Icelandic:

Few things (*fátt er*) are greater fun (*skemmtilegra*) for an Icelandic boy than (*heldur en*) to be allowed to go to town. There he can buy whatever (*hvað sem*) he wants, it need not be much, perhaps a knife or a bag of (*poki með*) raisins. He is allowed to ride his horse (*ríða hestinum sínum*); for the way to the trading place is usually (*venjulega*) long, and the journey will be (*verður*) full of adventures (*æfintýrum*) for the boy. He may (*kann*) have to (*þurfa*) cross a river (*fara yfir á*) on horseback (*ríðandi*). He may have to cross mountain passes and long mud flats at the end of a firth (*við fjarðarenda*), if he is lucky enough to get there before the flood tide sets in (*flæðir*). He will hardly (*varla*) forget (*gleyma*) his first journey to town.

21.

The Definite article: S. II.
Genitive: S. I, **4**.
Passive voice: S. VI, **8**.
Compound words: S. IX (Appendix).

Æfing. Húsið okkar.

Húsið okkar er nýtt. Það er byggt úr steinsteypu; slík hús eru kölluð steinhús. Í Reykjavík er það á móti lögum að byggja timburhús. Veggirnir á húsinu eru gráir, en þakið er lagt grænum þakhellum. Gluggar og dyr eru máluð græn. Húsið er tvær hæðir (= tveggja hæða hús, tvílyft hús), með kjallara undir og efsta lofti undir þaki. Í húsinu er miðstöðvarhitun; miðstöðin er í kjallaranum, en við erum að hugsa um að fá okkur laugahitun, áður en langt um líður. Í kjallaranum er líka þvottahús og kolageymsla, en þvotturinn er þurrkaður á efsta lofti. Í húsinu eru tvær íbúðir. Við búum niðri, en íbúðin á loftinu er leigð út. Báðar íbúðirnar eru svipaðar að tilhögun. Dyrnar, eða aðaldyrnar, eru á miðri hlið hússins, en stórir gluggar með fjórum rúðum til beggja handa. Gluggarnir

220

opnast út, en á vetrum eru þeir hafðir tvöfaldir, þá eru bara efri rúðurnar opnaðar. Á stöfnum eða göflum hússins eru líka gluggar (stafngluggar). Upp að dyrunum liggja tröppur með handriði. Hurðin í útidyrunum er úr þungum viði, hún opnast inn. Dyrabjalla er fest á dyrastafinn. Þegar hurðin er opnuð, tekur við forstofa. Þar hengja menn yfirhafnir sínar á snaga og fara af skóhlífum. Úr forstofunni liggja dyr inn í borðstofuna á hægri hönd, en inn í setustofuna (dagstofuna, stássstofuna) á vinstri hönd. Fólkið uppi á loftinu notar þessa stofu fyrir skrifstofu (eða bókaherbergi). Upp úr forstofunni liggur stigi upp á loftið, en meðfram stiganum er gangur þvert í gegn um húsið út að bakdyrunum. Á hægri hönd við þann gang er búr og eldhús, en á vinstri hönd baðherbergi og svefnherbergi. Milli setustofunnar og svefnherbergisins eru dyr, sömuleiðis milli eldhúss og borðstofu. Nú ratið þér víst um húsið, eða hvað?

á prep. with dat. (1) *á húsinu* on the house; (2) *á húsinu* of the house; (3) *á vetrum* in the winter; *á móti* with dat. against.
að prep. with dat. as to; to.
aðaldyr stf.3.pl. chief door, entrance.
baðherbergi stn. bathroom.
bakdyr stf.3.pl. back door.
bókaherbergi stn. library, study.
borðstofa wf.1 dining room.
búa, býr, bjó, bjuggum, búinn stv.7 (in the country) farm; (in town) live; inhabit.
búr stn. pantry.
byggja, byggði, byggður wv.2 build.
dagstofa wf.1 living room.
dyr stf.3.pl. door (= doorway).
dyrabjalla wf.1 doorbell.
dyrastafur stm.2 doorpost.
efri, efstur adj. upper, top-.
efsta loft attic.
eldhús stn. kitchen.
fá, fær, fékk, fengum, fenginn stv.7 *fá sér* get (for oneself).
fara af take off.
festa, festi, festur wv.2 fasten.
forstofa wf.1 hall.
fyrir prep. with acc. for; as.
gafl stm.1 gable, end of a house.
gangur stm.1 corridor.
hafa, hafði, hafður wv.3 have; keep.
handrið stn. railing.

hengja, hengdi, hengdur wv.2 hang (trans.).
herbergi stn. room.
hlið stf.1 side.
hugsa um think of, plan.
hurð stf.2 door.
hæð stf.2 floor, story.
hægri adj. comparative right.
hönd stf.3 hand; side; *til beggja handa* on both sides.
í gegnum prep. with acc. through.
íbúð stf.2 apartment.
kjallari wm.1 cellar.
kol stn. coal.
kolageymsla wf.1 coal storage.
laglegur adj. handsome, pretty, nice.
laugahitun stf.2 heating by water from hot springs.
leggja, lagði, lagður wv.1 lay; *l. e-ð e-u* cover something with something.
leigja, leigði, leigður wv.2 rent, = *l. út,* ▭ let, lease.
líða, líður, leið, liðum, liðinn stv.1 pass (of time); *áður en langt um líður* before long.
liggja, liggur, lá, lágum, leginn stv.5 lie; (of doorways, passages, roads) lead.
loft stn. loft, second floor, upper story; air.
lög stn.pl. the law.

221

mála, -aði, -aður wv.4 paint.
meðfram prep. with dat. along.
miðstöð stf.1 central heating (plant).
miðstöðvarhitun stf.2 central heating.
mót stn. meeting; *á móti* prep. with dat. against.
neðri, neðstur adj. lower, lowest.
nota, -aði, -aður wv.4 use (*fyrir* as).
notalegur adj. comfortable, cozy.
opna, -aði, -aður wv.4 open; *opnast* middle voice: be opened.
rata, -aði, -að wv.4 find one's way.
rúða wf.1 (window) pane.
setustofa wf.1 sitting room.
skóhlíf stf.1 galosh, rubber.
skrifstofa wf.1 study.
slíkur, slík, slíkt adj.pron. of similarity: such.
snagi wm.1 clothes-peg.
stafn stm.1 = *gafl*.
stafngluggi wm.1 window in a gable (end of a house).
stássstofa wf.1 drawing room.
steinhús stn. stone house; house made of concrete.
steinsteypa wf.1 concrete.
stigi wm.1 flight of stairs, ladder.
stofa wf.1 room; drawing room.
svefnherbergi stn. bedroom.
svipaður, -uð, -að adj. similar.
sömuleiðis adv. likewise.

taka við (*af e-u*) be next (in order).
tilhögun stf.2 arrangement.
timburhús stn. wooden house, frame house.
trappa wf.1 step; pl. *tröppur* steps, short flight of steps.
tvílyftur, -lyft, -lyft adj. two-story.
tvöfaldur, -föld, -falt adj. num. double.
undir prep. with dat. or adv. below, underneath.
útidyr stf.3.pl. front door.
veggur stm.2 wall.
vegna prep. with gen. because of.
við prep. with acc. at; *á hægri hönd við hann* on the right side of him (on his right side).
viður stm.3 wood.
vilja heldur prefer.
vinstri adj. compar. left; *á v. hönd* to the left.
yfirhöfn stf.2 overcoat.
þak stn. roof.
þakhella wf.1 slate, tile.
þungur; þyngri, þyngstur adj. heavy.
þurrka, -aði, -aður wv.4 dry.
þver, þver, þvert adj. crosswise; *þvert* (adv.) *í gegn um* straight through.
þvottahús stm. washroom.
þvottur stm.3 wash.

Translate into Icelandic:

Have you seen our new house (*nýja húsið okkar*) ? It is built of concrete. Most houses in Reykjavík are now built of concrete. It is a two-story house with a cellar and an attic. The walls are painted grey. The roof is covered with tiles. We live on the ground floor (*neðri hæðinni*), but we rent the apartment on the second floor to relatives of ours. It is a very nice (*lagleg*) apartment. It has (is = *eru*) three rooms, a kitchen and a bathroom. The rooms are large, especially (*einkum*) the dining room and the bedroom. They have big windows, too, so that there is (*það er*) plenty (*nóg*) of sun and air in the apartment. There is a central heating plant in the house, so that it is always very warm and comfortable (*notalegt*). I prefer (*vil heldur*) to live on the second floor, but my mother prefers the ground floor because of (*vegna*) the stairs.

22.

Use of the definite article: S. II, especially 7.

Concord: S. V, **4.**

Word order: (inverted) S. VII, **3,** especially 3.

Compound words: S. IX (Appendix).

Æfing. Íbúðin og húsgögnin okkar.

Við leigjum þriggja herbergja íbúð með baðherbergi og eldhúsi. Henni fylgir ljós og hiti, en hún er án húsgagna; þau eigum við sjálf. Við notum eitt herbergið fyrir dagstofu. Í henni höfum við einn legubekk (sófa, dívan) og tvo hægindastóla, stórt borð með þykkum dúki á miðju gólfi, en lítið reykingaborð með vindlum, sígarettum (vindlingum) og öskubakka í einu horninu. Í öðru horni stendur útvarpstæki. Á einum veggnum hangir málverk eftir Kjarval. Á gólfinu er fallegt gólfteppi (gólfábreiða), og snotur gluggatjöld eru hengd fyrir gluggana (gardínur). Niður úr loftinu hangir rafljósakróna. Úr dagstofunni lítum við inn í annað herbergið, það sem við höfum fyrir svefnherbergi. Þar eru tvö rúm, náttborð, stólar, dragkista (kommóða) og snyrtiborð með spegli. Veggfóðrið í svefnherberginu er ljósleitt. Svo göngum við yfir í þriðja herbergið: borðstofuna. Þar eru borð og stólar, hlaðborð (buffett) og skápur fyrir glös, postulín og leirtau. Á hlaðborðinu stendur silfurbakki með kaffikönnu, rjómakönnu og sykurkeri, en í skúffunni er geymdur borðbúnaður, líka úr silfri: hnífapör (hnífar og gafflar), (mat)skeiðar og teskeiðar. Þar er líka geymdur borðdúkur og servíettur. Í skápnum með glerhurðunum eru geymdir diskar, djúpir og grunnir, stórir og smáir, föt stór og smá, skálar, þar af ein stór súpuskál, vatnskönnur og vatnsglös, bollapör (bollar og undirskálar) úr postulíni, tekanna, kökudiskar o.m.fl. Í eldhúsinu er fyrst og fremst góð eldstó (rafeldstó, rafmagnseldavél), eldhússbekkur með mörgum lokuðum skápum og skúffum, eldhússskápur fyrir leirtau, potta og pönnur. Þar er líka þvottaþró (vaskur) með skólprennu og tvöfaldri vatnsleiðslu með heitu og köldu vatni. Í baðherberginu er baðker og vatnssalerni (kamar).

án prep. with gen. without.
auk prep. with gen. besides.
baðker stn. bathtub.
bollapar stn. cup and saucer.
bolli wm.1 cup.
bólstraður adj. upholstered.
borð stn. table.
borðbúnaður stm.3 table service.
borðdúkur stm.1 tablecloth.

borðstofuborð stn. dining room table.
buffett stn. buffet, sideboard.
dagstofu húsgögn stn.pl. living room furniture.
diskur stm.1 plate.
dívan stm.1 divan, couch.
djúpur, dýpri, dýpstur adj. deep; d.*diskur* or *djúpdiskur* soup plate.
dragkista wf.1 chest of drawers.

dúkur stm.1 (table) cloth.
eftir prep. with acc. by.
eigin adj. indecl. own.
eldavél stf.1 kitchen stove.
eldhússbekkur stm.2 kitchen bench, kitchen table.
eldhússskápur stm.1 kitchen cupboard, kitchen cabinet.
eldstó stf.2 = *eldavél.*
fat stn. platter.
fylgja, fylgdi, fylgt wv.2 follow; be in the bargain, be included.
fyrst og fremst in the first place.
gaffall stm.1 (*himinn*) fork.
gardína wf.1 curtain.
geyma, geymdi, geymdur wv.2 put away, store.
glas stn. glass; tumbler.
glerhurð stf.2 glass door.
gluggatjald stn. = *gardína.*
gólf stn. floor.
gólfábreiða wf.1 rug.
gólfteppi stn. rug.
grunnur, grynnri, grynnstur adj. shallow, flat; *g. diskur* (flat) plate; also *grunndiskur.*
hafa fyrir use as.
hanga, hangir, hékk, héngum, hanginn stv.7 hang (intr.).
heitur adj. hot.
hengja fyrir glugga put up curtains.
hiti wm.1 heat, heating.
hlaðborð stn. = *buffett.*
hnífapar stn. knife and fork.
hnífur stm.1 knife.
horn stn. corner.
húsgögn stn.pl. furniture; *án h-gagna* unfurnished.
hægindastóll stm.1 easy chair.
kaffikanna wf.1 coffeepot.
kaffistell stn. coffee set.
kaldur, köld, kalt adj. cold.
kamar stm.1 (*himinn*) toilet, W. C.
Kjarval stm.1 a famous Icelandic painter: *Jóhannes Kjarval.*
kommóða wf.1 = *dragkista.*
kökudiskur stm.1 cake plate.
legubekkur stm.2 sofa, couch.
leirtau stn. crockery, porcelain.
lita, lítur, leit, litum, litið stv.1 look.
ljós stn. light.
ljósleitur adj. light-colored.

loft stn. ceiling.
loka, -aði, -aður wv.4 close.
málverk stn. painting.
matskeið stf.1 tablespoon.
náttborð stn. night table.
o. m. fl. = og margt fleira.
panna wf.1 pan, skillet, frying pan.
postulín stn. porcelain, china.
pottur stm.1 pot.
rafeldstó stf.1 =
rafmagnseldavél stf.1 =
rafstó stf.1 electric stove.
rafljós stn. electric light.
rafljósakróna wf.1 electric chandelier.
reykingaborð stn. smoking stand.
rjómakanna wf.1 cream pitcher.
rjómi wm.1 cream.
rúm stn. bed.
salerni stn. toilet, W. C. (polite).
samstæða wf.1 set.
servíetta wf.1 table napkin.
sígaretta wf.1 cigaret.
silfur stn. (*hreiður*) silver.
silfurbakki wm.1 silver tray.
skál stf.1 and 2 bowl.
skápur stm.1 cupboard.
skeið stf.1 spoon.
skólprenna wf.1 waste pipe, gutter.
skúffa wf.1 drawer.
smár, smá, smátt adj. small, little.
snotur, snotur, snoturt; snotrari -astur adj. handsome, nice-looking.
snyrtiborð stn. dressing table, dresser.
sófi (sóffi) wm.1 sofa.
spegill stm.1 (*himinn*) mirror.
stóll stm.1 chair.
súpuskál stf.1 and 2 tureen.
sykurker stn. sugar bowl.
te stn. tea.
tekanna wf.1 teapot.
teppi stn. rug = *gólfteppi.*
teskeið stf.1 teaspoon.
undirskál stf.1 saucer.
úr prep. with dat. out of, from, of.
útvarp stn. broadcasting.
útvarpstæki stn. radio, receiving set.
vaskur stm.1 sink.
vatnsglas stn. tumbler.
vatnskanna wf.1 pitcher, jug.
vatnsleiðsla wf.1 water pipes, running water (in the houses).
vatnssalerni stn. W. C. (polite).

veggfóður stn. (*hreiður*) wallpaper.   *þvottaþró* stf.1 sink = *vaskur.*
vindill stm.1 (*himinn*) cigar.   *þægilegur* adj. comfortable.
vindlingur stm.1 cigaret.   *öskubakki* wm.1 ashtray.

Translate into Icelandic:

We are going to show (*sýna*) you our apartment. It has (there is in it) three rooms, a kitchen and a bath. Light and heat are included, but it is unfurnished. We bought our own (*eigin*) furniture. Our living room furniture (*dagstofu húsgögn*) consists of (*eru*) a sofa, two easy chairs, a big table, and some upholstered (*nokkrir bólstraðir*) chairs. In the dining room we have a dining room table (*borðstofuborð*) with six chairs, a buffet, and a cupboard. In the kitchen we have a small kitchen cabinet, besides the kitchen table and its closed cupboards. There is a sink with hot and cold running water (*með heitu og köldu vatni*). It is quite a comfortable (*mjög þægilegt*) kitchen. Have you seen our china? It is in the dining room cupboard. We have a set (*samstæðu*) for eight; there are nice cups and saucers, a beautiful teapot with a sugar bowl and a cream pitcher.

23.

Reflexive verbs: S. VI, 7.

Completed action, indicated by *vera búinn að* have done: S. VI, 6.

Indefinite pronoun *maður, allur saman, hver*: S. IV, 6. S. VI, 14, 2.

Genitive: S. I, 4, especially 1.

Æfing. Dagsverk barnanna.

Við förum á fætur klukkan sjö á morgnana. Stundum færir mamma okkur þá morgunkaffið í rúmið. Þegar við erum búin að drekka það, flýtum við okkur í fötin. Fyrst klæðum við okkur í nærfötin, svo þvoum við okkur upp úr köldu vatni og sápu og þurrkum okkur í framan og um hendurnar á handklæði. Svo fara drengirnir í buxur, vesti og jakka, en telpurnar í kjóla; síðan greiða þær sér vel og vandlega og stelast til að mála á sér varirnar með varalit og púðra sig í framan. Þegar þetta er búið, tökum við bækurnar okkar og nestið og förum í skólann. Elzti bróðir okkar fer í Menntaskólann og elzta systir okkar í Kvennaskólann, en við yngri systkinin göngum ennþá í barnaskólann. Þegar hringt er inn í kennslustund förum við inn í bekkinn okkar—ég er í sjötta bekk— og setjum okkur, hver við sitt borð. Við eigum öll að vera komin inn í bekkinn, áður en kennarinn kemur og sezt í kennarasætið. Hann hlýðir okkur yfir lexíurnar og segir okkur ýmislegt, auk

225

þess setur hann okkur fyrir til næsta dags. Hann tekur mig ekki
upp í dag, því hann gerði það í gær, og ég stóð mig heldur vel. Í
frímínútunum hlaupa allir krakkarnir út á gang. Stundum gera þau
at á ganginum, þá má maður vara sig að meiða sig ekki. Um hádegisbilið er matmálsfrí, og við borðum nestið okkar. Svo er aftur kennt
þar til klukkan tvö eða þrjú; þá er skólinn búinn, og við förum heim.
Skömmu seinna fáum við miðaftanskaffi (eftirmiðdagskaffi) með
kökum. Það sem eftir er dagsins eigum við að lesa undir morgundaginn og leika okkur. Bezt er að keppast við að lesa, þá getur
maður verið búinn fyrir kvöldmat, og þá fær maður máske að fara
út, annaðhvort á bíó eða á skauta á tjörninni. Svo labbar maður sig
heim, steinuppgefinn, og fer að hátta. Það er að segja, fyrst verður
maður að þvo sér í framan, um hendur og fætur og bursta tennurnar
á sér. Þegar maður er búinn að því öllu saman, þá má maður
afklæða sig og fara í rúmið. Og þá er maður ekki lengi að sofna.

á handklæði with a towel.

á morgnana in the morning.

afklæða, -klæddi, -klæddur wv.2 refl.
a. *sig* undress (oneself).

annaðhvort . . . eða either . . . or.

at stn. stampede, fight, riot.

augnablik stn. twinkling of an eye;
moment.

auk prep. with gen. in addition
(*þess* to that).

barnaskóli wm.1 primary school; elementary school.

bekkur stm.2 class, grade; form.

bíó stn. movie (= *kvikmyndahús*).

búinn, -in, -ið adj. (pp. of *búa* prepare) ready, finished, done, *vera
búinn* be over, be done, have done,
have finished, be finished.

bursta, -aði, -aður wv.4 brush.

bursti wm.1 brush; *tann-b.* toothbrush.

buxur wf.1.pl. trousers.

dagsverk stn. day's work.

eftirmiðdagskaffi (*-te*) stn. afternoon
coffee (tea).

fara á fætur rise; *í rúmið* go to bed;
á skauta go skating; *í skóla* go
to school; *í föt* put on clothes.

flýta, flýtti, flýtt wv.2 speed up,
hasten; *f. sér* refl. hasten, hurry.

framan adv. from the front; *í framan*
in front, the face.

frí stn. free time, holiday, vacation,
recess.

frímínútur wf.1.pl. recess of ten
minutes at the end of each hour
in schools.

færa, færði, færður wv.2 *f. e-m e-ð*
bring somebody something.

föt stn.pl. clothes.

ganga í skóla go to school.

gangur stm.1 corridor, passage.

gera at stir up a stampede.

greiða, greiddi, greiddur wv.2 with
dat. comb; *g. sér* refl. comb one's
hair, = *g. hárið á sér.*

handklæði stn. towel (= *þurrka*).

hátta, -aði, -aður wv.4 intr. go to
bed; trans.: put to bed.

heim adv. home.

hlýða, hlýddi, hlýtt wv.2 listen; *h.
e-m yfir e-ð* hear somebody repeat
his lesson, examine somebody in
something; *h. e-m* obey somebody.

hringja, hringdi, hringt wv.2 ring,
sound the bell; *h. inn* to enter
class, *h. út* to go out.

ís stm.1 ice.

jakki wm.1 jacket.

kaka wf.1 cake.

kenna, kenndi, kennt wv.2 with dat.
teach (*e-m e-ð*).

kennarasæti stn. teacher's chair, pulpit, rostrum.

kennslustund stf.2 hour (of teaching),
= *tími.*

keppast, kepptist, keppzt wv.2 *k. við
að* exert oneself in.

kjóll stm.1 dress.

klæða, klæddi, klæddur wv.2 clothe,
refl.: *k. sig* clothe oneself, dress;
k. sig í put on.

kunna e-ð know sth.

kvöldmatur stm.3 supper.

labba, -aði, -að wv.4 walk (leisurely),
saunter, = *l. sig* refl.

lesa undir (*e-ð*) prepare one's lessons
for.

lexía wf.1 lesson.

máske adv. = *kannske* perhaps.

matmálsfrí stn. recess for eating
(lunch).

mega, má, megum, mátti, mátt pret.
pres.v. may; must.

meiða, meiddi, meiddur wv.2 hurt;
refl. *m. sig* hurt oneself.

miðaftanskaffi stn. afternoon coffee.

morgundagur stm.1 (the day) tomorrow.

morgunkaffi stn. morning coffee;
breakfast.

morgunmatur stm.3 breakfast; *borða
m.* breakfast (v.).

nesti stn. provisions (lunch).

nærföt stn.pl. underwear.

næstum því adv. almost.

púðra, -aði, -aður wv.4 powder.

púður stn. (*hreiður*) powder.

rúm stn. bed.

sápa wf.1 soap.

segja, sagði, sagt wv.3 say; tell; *það
er að segja* that is.

setja, setti, settur wv.2 set; *s. sig*
refl., more commonly *setjast*,
middle voice: set oneself, sit
down, take a seat (= *sæti*).

setja (*e-m e-ð*) *fyrir* assign (a lesson to somebody).

síðan adv. thereupon, then.

*skammur, skömm, skammt; skemmri,
skemmstur* adj. short; *skammt* a
short way, a short while, *skömmu
seinna* a little later.

skauti pl. *skautar* wm.1 skate(s);
fara á s-a go skating (*s-um* skate).

sofna, -aði, -aður wv.4 fall asleep.

*standa, stendur, stóð, stóðum, stað-
inn* stv.6 stand; *s. sig* (*vel, illa*)
refl. acquit oneself (with honor,
badly).

stein-uppgefinn, -in, -ið adj. dog-tired,
exhausted (*stein-* intensive prefix).

stela, stelur, stal, stálum, stolinn
stv.4 steal; *stelast til að* middle
voice: do something by stealth.

taka e-n upp call on somebody (in
the class).

telpa wf.1 little girl.

tilbúinn, -in, -ið adj. ready.

tjörn stf.2 tarn, small lake, pond.

tönn stf.3 tooth.

undir prep. with acc. in preparation
for; *undir eins* at once.

upp úr prep. with dat. out of; *u. úr
vatni* with water.

vandlega adv. carefully.

vara, -aði, -að wv.4 warn (*e-n við
e-u* somebody of something); *v.
sig* refl. beware.

varalitur stm.3 lipstick.

vera eftir be left, remain; *það* (acc.,
cf. S. I, 2, 2) *sem eftir er dagsins*
(gen., cf. S. I, 4, 2, 5) in what is
left of the day.

vesti stn. vest, waistcoat.

vör stf.2 lip.

ýmislegur, -leg, -legt adj. different,
various; n. *ýmislegt* as a noun
(cf. S. III, 3, 2); various things.

þurrka, -aði, -aður wv.4 dry, wipe
dry; *þ. sér* wipe, dry oneself;
þ. sér í framan wipe one's face;
um hendur wipe one's hands; *um
munninn, augun, nefið* wipe one's
mouth, eyes, nose. Cf. S. I, 4, 1,
3-5.

þvo, þvær, þvoði (*þó*), *þvoðum*
(*þógum*), *þveginn* wv.1 and stv.6
wash; *þ. sér* refl. wash (oneself);
þ. sér í framan, um hendur, fætur,
etc. as *þurrka* above.

Translate into Icelandic:

When do you rise in the morning? We rise at seven. Do you have breakfast (*borðið þið morgunmat*) then? No, not at once (*undir eins*), first we have to dress (ourselves), wash our faces and hands, and brush our teeth. We must also comb our hair (*greiða hárið á okkur*) before we can have breakfast. Have you finished dressing? Yes. And have you finished eating? Almost (*næstum því*), I will be ready in a minute (*tilbúinn, búinn eftir augnablik*). Then let us go out (*þá skulum við . . .*). I cannot go out with you because (*af því að*) I must go to school. How long does it take you (*ert þú, eruð þér*) to walk to the school? Ten minutes. And when will school be over (*verður skólinn búinn*)? At two. I will see (*sé*) you when you come back (*aftur*). One must not (*má ekki*) be too late, and one must know (*verður að kunna*) one's (*sínar*) lessons. When school is over one must study (*lesa*) first, and then one may play. But one should (*ætti*) not skate, if the ice (*ísinn*) is too weak (*veikur*). I would have (*hefði*) gone skating yesterday, if the ice had (*hefði*) not been so unsafe (*ótraustur, ótryggur*).

24.

Present subjunctive of *vera* and *hafa*. S. VI, 1, 2.

Present subjunctive endings of all verbs (In. VII, **4**, *3*): Sg. 1 -*i*, 2 -*ir*, 3 -*i*; Pl. 1 -*um*, 2 -*ið*, 3 -*i*.

Subjunctive in *að*-clauses. S. VI, **9**, *4*, 1.

Subjunctive in *þó* (*að*)-clauses. S. VI, **9**, *4*, 6.

Subjunctive in interrogative clauses. S. VI, **9**, *4*, 2.

Æfing. Hvað halda útlendingar um Ísland?

Margir útlendingar, sem aldrei hafa komið til Íslands, halda, að landið sé heimskautaland, þakið ís og jöklum. Þeir álíta, að þar sé svo kalt, að siðaðir menn geti ekki lifað þar. Þeir hafa þá hugmynd, að hafnir frjósi þar á hverju ári, eða séu jafnvel ísi lagðar árið um kring. Sú skoðun hefur einhvern veginn bitið sig í þá, að ísbirnir og rostungar spóki sig um göturnar í Reykjavík og það um hásumarið. Þeir hafa líka heyrt, að Íslendingar byggi hús sín úr snjó og klaka og skríði inn í þau á fjórum fótum. Þeir segja, að Íslendingar séu Eskimóar eða Skrælingjar, sem klæði sig í selskinnsföt, smyrji sig úr sellýsi og lifi af keti af selum, rostungum og hvítabjörnum. Sumir halda þó, að Íslendingar séu smávaxin þjóð, sem lifi í tjöldum, og aki í litlum sleðum með hreindýrum fyrir um fjöll og firnindi í tunglsljósi og norðurljósum. Ef maður spyr þessa menn, hvaðan þeir hafi þessa þekkingu, þá svara flestir, að þeir hafi heyrt það sagt, sumir, að þeir hafi lesið um það í bókum, og nokkrir segjast hafa séð íslenzka Eskimóa með eigin augum á hringleikasýningum eða í kvikmyndum. Þó að þessum hugmyndum sé mótmælt, eru þær ótrúlega lífseigar. Orsakirnar til þess liggja í augum uppi. Fyrst er nafn landsins: Ísland. Í öðru lagi liggur landið nálægt Grænlandi og er oftast nefnt í sömu andrá í landafræðisbókum. Í þriðja lagi er landið venjulega talið til norðurheimskautslandanna, þó að það liggi allt sunnan við nyrðri heimskautsbauginn. En þessi lönd eru einmitt heimkynni þjóðanna, sem menn ætla, að búi á Íslandi. Eskimóar byggja Grænland og norðurströnd Ameríku, en Lappar búa í nyrztu héruðum Noregs, Svíþjóðar og Finnlands.

aka, ekur, ók, ókum, ekinn stv.6 drive (in a car, sleigh).

álíta, -lítur, -leit, -litum, -litinn stv.1 consider.

ályktun stf.2 conclusion; *draga á. af e-u* draw a conclusion from sth.

andrá stf.1 (*á*) moment.

árið um kring the year round.

ástæða wf.1 reason.

auga wn. eye; *liggja í a-um uppi* lie open for inspection, be obvious.

bíta, bítur, beit, bitum, bitinn stv.1 bite; *b. sig í e-ð* bite into, take hold of.

byggja, byggði, byggður wv.2(1) build; (2) inhabit = *búa á, í*.

eigin adj.indecl. own.

einhvern veginn, einhvernveginn adv. somehow.

Eskimói wm.1 Eskimo.

Finnland stn. Finland.

firnindi stn.pl. wilderness; usually in the phrase: *fjöll og f.* mountains and w.

flestir adj.m.pl. most; most people.

fótur stm.4 foot; *á fjórum f-um* on all fours.

fyrir adv. in front (as a team).

Grænland stn. Greenland.

halda, heldur, hélt, héldum, haldinn stv.7 hold, consider, think.

hásumar stn. high summer.

heimkynni stn. home.

heimskautaland stn. arctic country; polar region; *heimskaut* stn. pole.

heimskautsbaugur stm.1 polar circle; *nyrðri h.* the arctic circle.

hérað stn. region.

hreindýr stn. reindeer.

hringleikasýning stf.1 circus show.

hugmynd stf.2 idea.

hvítabjörn stm.3 polar bear.

ís stm.1 ice.

ísbjörn stm.3 polar bear.

jökull stm.1 glacier.

ket (*kjöt*) stn. meat, flesh.

klaki wm.1 ice.

kvikmynd stf.2 cinema, movie, motion picture.

lag stn. *í fyrsta* (*öðru*) *lagi* in the first (second) place.

land(*a*)*fræðisbók* stf.3 book of geography.

Lappi wm.1 a Lap.

leggja, lagði, lagður wv.1 lay; *ísi lagður* overlaid (covered) with ice.

lifa, lifði, lifað wv.3 live; *l. á* live by.

lífseigur adj. tough, tenacious.

liggja, liggur, lá, lágum, leginn stv.5 lie; be situated.

mótmæla, -mælti, -mæltur wv.2 deny (*e-u*).

nafn stn. name.

nálægur adj. near; *nálægt* adv. near (*e-u*).

náttúrlega adv. naturally, of course.

nefna, nefndi, nefndur wv.2 name; mention, speak of.

norðurheimskaut stn. north pole.

norðurheimskautsland stn. north polar (arctic) region.

norðurljós stn. aurora borealis.

norðurströnd stf.3 northern shore.

Noregur stm.2 Norway.

nyrðri, nyrztur adj. more, most northerly.

og það and that.

orsök stf.2 cause (*til* for).

ótrúlega adv. incredibly.

rangur, röng, rangt adj. wrong, mistaken; adv. *ranglega.*
rostungur stm.1 walrus.
samt adv. however.
segjast hafa say that they have.
sellýsi stn. seal oil.
selskinn stn. sealskin.
selskinnsföt stn.pl. sealskin, sealskin clothes.
selur stm.2 seal.
siðaður, -uð, -að; -aðri, -aðastur adj. civilized.
skoðun stf.2 view, opinion.
skríða, skríður, skreið, skriðum, skriðinn stv. 1 creep, crawl.
skrælingi wm.1 (1) barbarian, (2) Eskimo.
sleði wm.1 sleigh.
smávaxinn, -in, -ið; -vaxnari, -astur adj. small, little (of stature).
smyrja, smurði, smurður wv.1 smear, anoint; *s. úr* anoint with.
snjór stm.1 snow.

spóka, -aði, -að wv.4 stalk (refl.) sport one self.
sunnan við prep. with acc. south of.
svara, -aði, -að wv.4 answer.
Svíþjóð stf.2 Sweden.
telja, taldi, talinn wv.1 count; *t. til* count as, include in.
tjald stn. tent.
tungl stn. moon; heavenly body.
tunglsljós stn.moonlight (pronounced *tungsljós*).
trúa, trúði, trúað wv.3 believe (*e-u*).
um göturnar in the streets; *um sumarið* during the summer.
útlendingur stm.1 foreigner.
þekking stf.1 knowledge.
þjóð stf.2 nation, people.
þó adv. nevertheless, however; *þó nokkrir* quite a few.
þó (að) conj. with subj. though, although, even if.
ætla, -aði, -aður wv.4 think, believe.

Translate into Icelandic:

What ideas do foreigners have about Iceland? Most people (*flestir*) know naturally (*náttúrlega*) very little about it, but from its name they draw (*af nafninu draga þeir*) the (*þá*) wrong conclusion (*ályktun*) that it is an arctic country. They think that it is covered with snow and ice, and quite a few (*þó nokkrir*) have the mistaken (*þá röngu*) idea that it is inhabited by Eskimos. Do you believe these stories? I have never believed them, though I have often heard them. It is, however, obvious what is (*hver sé*) the reason for them (*ástæðan fyrir þeim* or *orsök þeirra*). Greenland is inhabited by Eskimos, and Greenland is very near to Iceland. But although it is not far between the countries, there has (*hafa*) for centuries (*svo öldum skiftir*) been no (*ekki . . . neinar*) intercourse (*samgöngur*) between them. The Eskimos have never come to Iceland, though Greenland was settled (*væri numið*) by Icelanders in the tenth century.

25.

Imperative with the second person pronoun attached (cf. Pr. **4**, *4*) is common in written and spoken language, but not used in elevated style (Bible etc.): In VII, **4**, *6*; S. VI, **10**.

Endings: Sg. 2 none in all verbs except: third class weak -(*i*) and fourth class weak always -*a*. Pl. 1 -*um*, 2 -*ið*.

Æfing. Heilræði Benjamíns Franklins.

Sparneytni: Borðaðu aldrei svo mikið, að starf þitt verði þér erfiðara á eftir, og drekktu aldrei svo mikið áfengi, að þú verðir kenndur. Þagmælska: Segðu aðeins það, sem þú eða aðrir hafa gagn af, en hafðu ekki orð á því, sem er einskis vert, eða öðrum til skaða. Reglusemi: Láttu hvert verk hafa sinn tíma og hvern hlut sinn stað. Ákvörðun: Einsettu þér að gera það, sem skyldan krefur, og framkvæmdu nákvæmlega það, sem þú hefur einsett þér. Sparsemi: Neitaðu þér um útgjöld, sem hvorki verða þér né öðrum að sönnu gagni. Eyddu engu til ónýtis. Iðjusemi: Eyddu aldrei tímanum til ónýtis, vertu sívinnandi að því, sem þér og öðrum er til gagns. Hreinskilni: Vertu ráðvandur og hreinn í huga og talaðu samkvæmt því. Réttlæti: Gerðu það ekki öðrum, sem þú vilt ekki, að þér sé gert. Dæmdu ekki aðra hart. Jafnlyndi: Vertu ekki reiðigjarn né hefnigjarn. Stilltu þig, þegar þér virðist aðrir gera á hluta þinn. Temdu þér glaðlyndi og jafnaðargeð. Vertu stilltur í mótgangi. Hreinlæti: Forðastu óhreinindi á líkama þínum, á fötum þínum, á heimili þínu. Auðmýkt: Reyndu að líkjast Jesú.

In the above (1) eliminate the attached second person pronoun (*borða, seg*, etc.), (2) substitute the second person plural pronoun or the honorific plural (*borðið þið, þér . . . starf ykkar, yðar*, etc.), (3) substitute the first person plural pronoun (hortative: *borðum . . . starf okkar*, etc.).

á eftir adv. afterwards.

af prep. with dat. from, by.

áfengi stn. intoxicating drinks.

ákvörðun stf.2 resolution.

auðmýkt stf.2 humility.

dæma, dæmdi, dæmdur wv.2 judge.

einsetja, -setti, -sett wv.1 *e. sér* determine (for oneself).

erfiður, -ið, -itt adj. difficult.

eyða, eyddi, eyddur wv.2 spend (*e-u*).

fara með read, say (a prayer).

forða, -aði, -að wv.4 save; *forðast* middle voice: avoid.

framkvæma, -kvæmdi, -kvæmdur wv. 2 carry out.

gagn stn. gain, advantage; *hafa g. af* gain by; *vera til g-s* be advantageous.

gera, gerði, gerður wv.2 do; *g. e-m e-ð* do something to somebody.

glaðlyndi stn. cheerfulness, sunny disposition.

hart adj.n. used as adv. harshly.

hefnigjarn, -gjörn, -gjarnt adj. revengeful.

heilræði stn. wholesome advice, wise counsel.

heimili stn. home.

hluti wm.1 part, lot; *gera á h-a e-s* wrong one.

hlutur stm.3 thing.

hreinlæti stn. cleanliness.

hreinn, hreinni, hreinastur adj. clean.

hreinskilni wf.2 sincerity, candor.

iðjusemi wf.2 industry.

jafnaðargeð stn. even temper.

jafnlyndi stn. equanimity, even temper.

Jesús, Jesú stm. pers. name.

kenndur adj. (slightly) tipsy.

krefja, krafði, krafður wv.1 demand.

kunna e-ð know something.

líkami wm.1 body.

líkjast, líktist, líkzt wv.2 be similar to (*e-m*).

mótgangur stm.1 adversity.

nákvæmlega adv. exactly.

neita, -aði, -að wv.4 *n. e-m um e-ð* deny somebody something.

óhreinindi stn.pl. dirt.

ónýti stn. a useless thing; *til ó-is* in vain, for no purpose.

orð stn. word; *hafa o. á e-u* mention something.

ráðvandur, -vönd, -vant adj. honest.

reglusemi wf.2 orderliness, regularity.

reiðigjarn, -gjörn, -gjarnt adj. hot-tempered, irascible.

réttlæti stn. justice.

reyna, reyndi, reyndur wv.2 try.

samkvæmt adj.n. with dat. according to.

sannur, sönn, satt adj. true.

sí-vinnandi pres.part. continually working.

skaði wm.1 detriment, harm.

skylda wf.1 duty.

sparneytni wf.2 frugality.

sparsemi wf.2 thrift, economy.

starf stn. work.

stilla, stillti, stilltur wv.2 calm; *s. sig* calm, control oneself.

stilltur, stillt, stillt adj. calm, quiet.

temja, tamdi, taminn wv.1 tame; *t.*

sér e-ð exercise oneself in something.

útgjöld stn.pl. expenditure, expenses.

verður, verð, vert adj. worth; *einskis v.* worth nothing, of no value.

verk stn. work.

virða, virti, virtur wv.2 estimate; *virðast* middle voice: *e-m virðist e-ð* it seems to somebody, somebody thinks.

þagmælska wf.1 reticence, discreetness.

Glossary of the Lord's Prayer:

brauð stn. bread.

daglegur, -leg, -legt adj. daily.

dýrð stf.2 glory.

eilífur adj. eternal; *að eilífu* for ever.

faðirvor stn. the Lord's Prayer.

freistni wf.2 temptation.

frelsa, -aði, -aður wv.4 save.

fyrirgefa, -gaf, -gáfum, -gefinn stv.5 forgive.

helga, -aði, - aður wv.4 hallow, sanctify.

koma til come.

leiða, leiddi, leiddur wv.2 lead.

máttur stm.3 might.

og adv. also.

ríki stn. realm, kingdom.

skuld stf.2 debt.

skuldunautur stm.1 debtor.

svo . . . sem so . . . as, as.

svona adv. thus, like this.

verða stv.3 be, become.

Translate into Icelandic:

Even Icelanders know (*kunna*) the wise counsels of Benjamin Franklin. Do you (*þú, þér* etc.) know them? If not, read them and learn them. Here are some of them: Do not eat too much; do not drink intoxicating liquors; do not say anything that may (*kann*) harm (*að skaða e-n* or *að verða e-m til skaða*) anybody; let every task have its appointed hour (*sína ákveðnu stund*), and if you have determined to do something, carry it out. Do not spend too much; be honest; don't judge others; be calm and clean in body and spirit (*á sál og líkama*).

Do you (*þú, þér*), perhaps, know the Lord's Prayer (*faðirvorið*) in Icelandic? If not, learn it and say it (*fara með e-ð*) every evening. It is like this (*svona*):

Faðir vor, þú sem ert á himnum; helgist þitt nafn; til komi

þitt ríki; verði þinn vilji, svo á jörðu, sem á himnum; gef oss í dag vort daglegt brauð; og fyrirgef oss vorar skuldir, svo sem vér og fyrirgefum vorum skuldunautum; og eigi leið þú oss í freistni, heldur frelsa oss frá illu; því að þitt er ríkið, mátturinn og dýrðin að eilífu. Amen.

Note the interchange of imperative and present subjunctive in the Lord's Prayer.

26.

Preterite subjunctive endings: In. VII, **4**, *5*. Sg. 1 -*i*, 2 -*ir*, 3 -*i*; Pl. 1 -*um*, 2 -*uð*, 3 -*u* (-*i*).

Preterite subjunctive of *vera, hafa* (S. VI, **1**, *2*), the preterite present verbs (In. VII, **5**, *1* and S. VI, **13**), and other verbs.

Use of subjunctive in main sentences of suggestion, polite opinion, and question (S. VI, **9**, *2*, 2); in imaginary conditions (S. VI, **9**, *3*, 2), and in subordinate clauses (*að*-clauses etc. S. VI, **9**, *4*, 1).

Æfing. Ráðagerðir á sunnudag.

Anna: Hvað eigum við að gera í dag? Björn: Já, hvað ættum við að gera? Ef veðrið væri skárra, þá mundi ég leggja til, að við gengjum inn fyrir bæ og færum í laugarnar. A.: Já, það væri fyrirtak, en ég er hrædd um, að veðrið fari ekki batnandi. B.: Hvað gætum við þá gert? Ættum við að fara í Sundhöllina? A.: Það væri ekki svo afleitt, ef hún væri ekki alltof full af fólki. B.: Ætli börnin úr barnaskólanum séu þar í dag? A.: Það tel ég víst. B.: Hvað annað getum við gert? A.: Hvernig væri að fara í kirkju? B.: Hver messar? A.: Séra Bjarni. B.: Það væri nú svo sem ekkert á móti því að hlusta á séra Bjarna, en, eins og þú veizt, þá leiðist mér að fara í kirkju. A.: Við kynnum að geta farið á bíó. B.: Hvað ætli sé á bíó? A.: Það er mynd með Grétu Garbo. B.: Veiztu, hvaða mynd það er? A.: Nei, en ég hitti hana Stínu frænku í gær, og hún sagði mér, að myndin væri mjög skemmtileg, og að við skyldum fyrir alla muni ekki missa af henni. B.: Ég vildi (að) við gætum heldur farið út að labba; það er drepandi að sitja inni á skrifstofu alla daga; og hvaða gagn er þá að því, þó maður fari á bíó og sitji þar? A.: Nei, nú man ég, að ég hitti Hrafnagils-hjónin á götu í gær—hver hefði trúað því, að þau væru í bænum?— og þau vildu endilega, að við kæmum til þeirra sem fyrst. B.: Hjónin frá Hrafnagili! Hvað skyldu þau annars ætla sér að verða lengi í bænum? A.: Það veit ég ekki, en ætli okkur sé ekki bezt að nota daginn til að fara til þeirra? B.: Jú, það skulum við einmitt gera.

233

á móti e-u against sth.

að prep. with dat. in.

afleitur, -leit, -leitt adj. out of the question, impossible; *ekki svo a.* not so bad, quite good (litotes).

alltof adv. (all) too.

annar, önnur, annað indef.pron. *annað* else; *annars* adv. really.

barnaskóli wm.1 primary school, elementary school.

batna, -aði, -aður wv.4 get better, improve; *fara b-andi* be improving.

drepa, drepur, drap, drápum, drepinn stv.5 kill; *d-andi* intolerable.

einmitt adv. just.

endilega adv. by all means.

fara í laugar go into the swimming pool; *í kirkju* to church; *á bíó* to the movies.

fullur, fyllri, fyllstur adj. full; *f. af e-u* full of something.

fyrirtak stn. an excellent thing.

gagn stn. advantage, help; *það er g. að e-u* there is help in something; something helps, avails.

ganga go; walk.

gata wf.1 street.

Gréta, -u wf.1 pet name for *Margrét*.

hitta, hitti, hitt wv.2 meet.

hlusta, -aði, -að wv.4 listen (*á* to).

Hrafnagils-hjónin stn.pl. with art. the couple from *Hrafnagil* (a farm).

hræddur, hrædd, hrætt adj. afraid; *vera h. um* be afraid, fear that.

hvað annað what else.

inn fyrir prep. with acc. across the (city) limits towards the interior.

kirkja wf.1 church.

kunna (1) know; (2) may; see S. VI, **13**, 4.

laug stf.1 bath; hot spring; *laugarnar* the hot springs near Reykjavík (a swimming pool).

leggja til propose.

leiðast, leiddist, leiðzt wv.2 middle voice, impersonal: *mér leiðist* I am bored.

messa, -aði, -að wv.4 hold service.

missa, missti, misstur wv.2 lose; *m. af e-u* miss something.

munur stm.3 thing; *fyrir alla m-i* by all means.

mynd stf.2 picture, movie (short for *kvikmynd*).

ráðagerð stf.2 plan, planning.

sem fyrst as soon as possible.

séra m.indecl. Reverend.

skárri, skástur adj. better, best under the (bad) circumstances.

skrifstofa wf.1 office.

Stína, -u wf.1 pet name for *Kristín*.

sundhöll stf.2 swimming hall, indoor swimming pool (in Rvík).

svo sem or *svosem* (*sosum*) adv. really.

verða stv.3 stay.

telja víst consider certain.

til (*þess*) *að* with inf. for.

þó conj. with subj. if.

ætla sér intend.

ætli interrog. adv. with subj. I wonder if.

Translate into Icelandic:

What do you (*þú, þér*) want to do today? Do you think (that) we ought to go out or stay at home? I would go out, if I knew when I could be back (*verið kominn aftur*). You ought to be able to be back before noon. Perhaps you had better (*kannske væri bezt fyrir þig (yður), að*) stay at home and read the new book (that) you got yesterday. I wonder whether that is a good book. It should be; it is by (*eftir* with acc.) a well-known author (*höfund*). No, I think I would rather (*vildi heldur*) go out for a walk (*fara út að labba*). Where should I go? You could go out of the town until you come to the hot springs swimming pool. That would be fine; I wonder whether anybody might be swimming there (*að synda þar*). Yes, somebody told me that the children were swimming there. Well, maybe I better go (*kannske ég fari heldur*) to the Swimming Hall. Yes, I think you could do that.

27.

The middle voice: In. VII, **4**, *11*; S. VI, **7**.

Indirect speech: S. VI, **9**, *5*.

Æfing. Fagnaðarfundur.

Þau systkinin, Anna og Björn, höfðu ekki sézt um langan tíma. Anna var nýgift kona í Reykjavík, en Björn hafði verið utanlands við nám. Það varð því heldur en ekki fagnaðarfundur með þeim, þegar þau fundust niðri við skip. Það lá við, að þau færust á mis í þrönginni, sem myndazt hafði á hafnarbakkanum, en þegar þau loksins hittust, þá heilsuðust þau með kossi. Anna sagði, að sér hefði leiðzt svo mikið, að ekkert hefði frétzt af honum í langan tíma; hún sagðist alltaf hafa verið að búast við bréfi frá honum. Hún sagðist jafnvel hafa verið farin að óttast, að hann hefði kannske veikzt snögglega, eða slysazt; bílslys eru ekki lengi að vilja til nú á dögum. Björn kvaðst hafa verið að ferðast síðustu mánuðina, og hann þóttist ekki hafa komizt til að skrifa—annars höfðu þau systkinin alltaf skrifazt á. Hann sagðist hafa verið að vonast eftir því, að hann kæmist heim, áður en Anna giftist, en því miður hefði hann orðið of seinn. Nú skyldu þau flýta sér að komast heim til hennar, því hann væri að sálast úr forvitni að sjá nýja húsið hennar og vita, hvernig sér litist á það. Þetta reyndist vera nýtízkuhús með stórum, spegilskyggðum gluggum og einföldum stálhúsgögnum. Björn gat ekki nógsamlega dáðst að því öllu saman. Hann sagðist varla tíma að setjast í stólana eða leggjast í legubekkinn, allt væri svo fínt og fágað. En Anna hélt, að það væri ekki of gott handa honum, enda fyndist sér hér allt fullt af ryki, hvernig sem hún hamaðist við að þurrka það af. Hann skyldi nú bara láta fara vel um sig, því nú ætlaði hún að skjótast fram í eldhús að hita þeim kaffi.

af prep. with dat. from; adv. off.

bílslys stn. automobile accident.

bráðlega adv. shortly, soon.

bréf stn. letter.

búa, býr, bjó, bjuggum, búinn stv.7 prepare; *búast við* expect (literally: prepare oneself for).

dá, dáði, dáður wv.3 admire; *dást að e-u* admire sth (midv.intr.).

dagur stm.1 *nú á dögum* nowadays.

einfaldur, -föld, -falt adj. simple.

enda conj. and . . . indeed.

fága, -aði, -aður wv.4 polish, cleanse.

fagnaðarfundur stm.3 happy meeting, happy reunion.

fara stv.6 go; *farast á mis* midv. recipr.: pass each other without meeting; *farast* intr. perish.

ferðast, -aðist, -azt wv.4 midv. only: travel.

fínn, fín, fínt; fínni, fínastur adj. fine.

finna, finnur, fann, fundum, fundinn stv.3 find; *finnast* midv. recipr.: find each other, meet; *e-m finnst e-ð* it seems to somebody, somebody thinks, feels.

flýta, flýtti, flýtt wv.2 hasten, speed up, *f. sér* hasten, make haste.

forvitni wf.2 curiosity.

fram í out into. .

frétta, frétti, frétt wv.2 hear (by asking); *fréttast* midv. pass. or intr.: be heard, be rumored.

gifta, gifti, giftur wv.2 marry; *giftast* midv. pass. or intr.: be married, marry.

hafnarbakki wm.1 quay.

hamast, -aðist, -azt wv.4 midv. only: *hamast við e-ð* work like a fury at something.

handa prep. with dat. for.

heilsa, -aði, -að wv.4 greet; *heilsast* midv.recipr. greet each other.

heldur en ekki rather than not (litotes = very great(ly)).

hita, -aði, -að wv.4 heat; *h. kaffi* make coffee.

hitta, hitti, hittur wv.2 hit, meet; *hittast* midv.recipr. meet each other (= *finnast*).

hvernig sem however much.

í prep. with acc. *í langan tíma* for a long time (= *um l. t.*).

koma stv.4 come; *komast* midv.intr. get (to a place); *k-ast til* find time to, get around to do sth.

koss stm.1 kiss.

kveða, kveður, kvað, kváðum, kveðinn stv.5 say; *kveðast* midv.refl. followed by indirect speech with infinitive and nominative: *hann kvaðst vera latur* he said he was lazy.

láta fara vel um sig make oneself comfortable.

leggja, lagði, lagður wv.1 lay; midv.

refl.: *leggjast* 'lay oneself,' lie down.

leiðast, leiddist, leiðzt wv2. midv. only: be bored, be sorry.

liggja, liggur, lá, lágum, leginn stv.5 lie; *það liggur við, að . . .* it almost happens that . . . , someone barely escapes doing something.

líta, lítur, leit, litum, litið stv.1 look; *líta á* look at; *e-m lízt á e-ð* midv. intr. sbdy thinks well of sth.

loksins adv. finally.

með prep. with dat. with; between.

mynda, -aði, -aður wv.4 form (trans.); *myndast* midv.intr.: form, take shape.

nám stn. study.

nógsamlega adv. enough.

ný- prefix newly, recently.

nýgiftur, -gift, -gift adj. newly wed, recently married.

nýtízkuhús stn. house after the newest fashion, modernistic house.

óttast, -aðist, -azt wv.4 midv. fear.

reyna, reyndi, reyndur wv.2 try; *reynast* midv.intr. prove (to be).

ryk stn. dust.

sálast, -aðist, -azt wv.4 die; pp. *sálaður* dead.

segja, sagði, sagður wv.3 say; *segjast* midv.refl. followed by indirect speech (cf. *kveðast*) say that. . . .

setja, setti, settur wv.1 set; *setjast* midv.refl. set, seat oneself, sit down, take a seat.

siðastur, -ust, -ast adj. last.

sjá, sér, sá, sáum, séður stv.5 see; *sjást* midv.recipr. see each other; pass. be seen.

skjóta, skýtur, skaut, skutum, skotinn stv.2 shoot; *skjótast* midv.intr. dart, run.

skrifa, -aði, -aður wv.4 write; *skrifast á* midv.recipr. write to each other.

slysa, -aði, -að wv.4 make one have an accident (*slys* stn.); *slysast* midv. pass. or intr. have an accident.

snögglega adv. suddenly.

spegilskyggður, -skyggð, -skyggt adj. polished like a mirror.

stálhúsgögn stn.pl. steel furniture.

tíma, tímdi, tímt wv.2 *tíma að gera
e-ð* make oneself do something
(with negation only).
um prep. with acc. *um tíma* for a
time (while).
úr prep. with dat. *sálast úr forvitni*
die from curiosity.
utanlands adv. abroad.
varla adv. hardly.
veikja, veikti, veiktur wv.2 weaken;
veikjast midv.intr.: get sick, be
taken ill.

við prep. with acc. at, occupied with;
við nám studying.
vilja til happen.
vita hvernig find out how.
vona, -aði, -að wv.4 hope; *vonast
eftir e-u* midv.intr.: hope for sth.
þröng stf.2 crowd.
þykja, þótti, þótt wv.2 impers. *mér
þykir* it seems to me, I think;
þykjast midv.intr.: say, give as
one's opinion, pretend.

Translate into Icelandic:

Do you ever write to your sister? Yes, we (brother and sister)
have always written to each other. What did she write the last time,
any news? Yes, she wrote that she had married a well-to-do
(*efnuðum*) merchant in Reykjavík, and that they had bought (themselves) a new house. She was, of course, very happy over (*mjög
ánægð yfir því að*) being married, and having the house, but she
was so sorry never to be able to see us. She said she could never
forget (*gleymt*) when we all met for the last time (*í síðasta sinn*)
in Reykjavík. But she said that she was expecting our sister from
the country to visit her shortly (*bráðlega*). She said that she had
heard that she (the sister) had been taken ill, but fortunately (*til
allrar hamingju*) it proved to be wrong. Well, if you write back
to your sister, please (*blessaður* = blessed), give her my regards
(*heilsaðu henni frá mér*). Tell her also that I would have (*hefði*)
written her long ago, if I had had anything to write about.

28.

Compound words: S. IX (Appendix).

Interrelationship of indefinite and reflexive (possessive) pronouns.
S. IV, 2 and 6.

Æfing. Gömlu bæirnir.

Gömlu íslenzku bæirnir voru mjög ólíkir nýju bæjunum, sem
byggðir eru eftir fyrirmyndum úr kaupstöðunum. Gömlu bæirnir
voru byggðir úr torfi og grjóti með þykkum veggjum eins og virki.
Orsökin til þess, að menn byggðu svo, var fyrst og fremst timburskortur. Vegna skorts á timbri var heldur ekki byggt eitt stórt hús
og hólfað í sundur með skilrúmum úr timbri, heldur var hvert
herbergi byggt út af fyrir sig sem sérstakt hús, enda var það kallað
hús, og allur bærinn varð samsafn af mörgum húsum. Þetta gaf
bæjunum svip. Húsin, sem ætluð voru til íbúðar og geymslu, voru

byggð saman og kölluð heimahús, eða bæjarhús. Fjósið handa kúnum var og oft byggt með bæjarhúsunum, enda var oftast innangengt í það. Kom það sér vel fyrir mjaltakonur á vetrum. Hin gripahúsin voru byggð á víð og dreif um túnið og kölluð útihús; það voru fjárhús (ærhús, sauðhús, lambhús og hrútakofi) og hesthús. Oftast voru líka skemma og smiðja taldar með útihúsum, því þó að þær væru byggðar með bæjarhúsunum, eða í bæjarþorpinu, eins og það var kallað, þá var venjulega ekki innangengt í þær, heldur voru dyr á hvorri um sig.

Bæjarhúsin voru annaðhvort byggð í röð meðfram hlaðinu, og sneru þá stöfnum fram á hlaðið, eða þau voru byggð sitt hvoru megin við löng göng, sem lágu inn úr bæjardyrum. Þrjú voru þau hús, sem enginn bær mátti án vera: baðstofa, eldhús og búr. Í búrinu var geymdur matur. Í eldhúsinu var eldað í opnu eldstæði, sem kallað var hlóðir, en reykinn lagði upp um stromp í þakinu. Baðstofan var bæði svefn- og setustofa; þar sátu menn á rúmum sínum, sem stóðu í röðum meðfram veggjunum, og unnu tóvinnu. Karlmenn kembdu ull í kömbum, konur spunnu á rokk. Baðstofan var venjulega þiljuð í hólf og gólf og með skarsúð að þaki. En utan á skarsúðinni var þykkt torfþak, eins og á öllum öðrum húsum á bænum. Þegar vel var byggt, var ekki kalt í bæjum þessum á veturna, því þeir héldu vel á hita. En í rigningatíð eða rigningasveitum, var erfitt að verja þá leka.

á prep. with dat. in (certain respect), of, *skortur á timbri* lack of timber; *á vetrum* in winter.

að prep. with dat. for, as a.

aðal- prefix chief, main.

án adv. without.

baðstofa wf.1 lit. ' bathroom,' a combined bed- and sitting room in old Icelandic farmsteads.

byggja, byggði, byggður wv.2 build.

bæjardyr stf.3.pl. doorway, entrance hall of a farmstead.

bæjarhús stn. a ' house ' or room in the farmstead group of houses; pl. the main group of houses on a farmstead.

bæjarþorp stn. the main group of houses on a farmstead (=*bæjarhús* pl.).

dreif stf.1 scattering; see *við.*

eftir prep. with dat. according to.

elda, -aði, -aður wv.4 cook.

eldstæði stn. fireplace.

eldur stm.1 fire.

enda conj. . . . also . . . , . . . indeed . . . ; *e. var það* it was also (indeed); and that is why it was.

erfiður, -ið, -itt adj. difficult.

fjárhús stn. sheep shed, barn.

fjós stn. cattle stable, cow stable.

fyrirmynd stf.2 pattern, model.

fyrst og fremst first and foremost, above all.

geymsla wf.1 storeroom, storage.

gólf stn. floor; *í hólf og gólf* walls and floor alike.

gripahús stn.pl. houses, sheds, barns, stables for the animals (*gripir*).

grjót stn.coll. stones, rocks.

göng stn.pl. corridor, passage.

halda á e-u keep something; *h. e-u úti* keep something out.

heimahús stn.pl. = *bæjarhús*, lit. ' home houses.'

heldur ekki not either.

hesthús stn. stable, horse shed.

GÖMUL BAÐSTOFA.

[Karlinn er að kemba í kömbum, konan að spinna á rokk.]

hlað stn. a place, partly paved, in front of a farmhouse.

hlóðir stf.2.pl. fireplace.

hlýindi stn.pl. warmth, coziness.

hólf stn. compartment.

hólfa, -aði, -aður wv.4 divide into compartments.

hrútakofi wm.1 ram shed.

hrútur stm.1 wether, ram.

hvor um sig each.

íbúð stf.2 habitation.

innangengt adj.n. having a passage from within; connected by a passage with the *bæjarhús.*

kambar stm.1.pl. cards.

kemba, kembdi, kembdur wv.2 comb; card, *kemba ull í kömbum* card wool in cards.

kofi wm.1 hut, shed.

koma sér vel come in handy.

lambhús stn. lamb shed.

leggja lay, *e-ð* (acc.) *leggur upp* something is carried up (impersonal transitive).

leki wm.1 leak.

liggja lead.

meðfram prep. with dat. along.

mjaltakona wf.1 milkmaid.

mjaltir stf.2 milking time.

ólíkur adj. unlike.

opinn, -in, -ið adj. open.

orsök stf.2 cause, reason; *o. til e-s* reason why.

reykur stm.2 smoke.

rigningasveit stf.2 rainy district.

rigningatíð stf.2 rainy spell.

rokkur stm.1 spinning wheel.

röð stf.2 row.

samsafn stn. collection, group.

sauðhús stn. sheep barn, shed.

sauður stm.3 sheep; especially a castrated ram.

sem conj. as.

sérstakur, -stök, -stakt adj. separate.

sitt hvoru megin við each on one side of, on both sides of.

skarsúð stf.2 clincher roof.

skemma wf.1 a storeroom.

skilrúm stn. partition.

skortur stm.1 lack (*á* of).

smiðja wf.1 smithy, forge.

snúa, snýr, sneri, snúinn ri-verb (In VII, 5, 2) turn (*e-u*) in a certain direction.

spinna, spinnur, spann, spunnum, spunninn stv.3 spin; *spinna á rokk* spin on a spinning wheel.

strompur stm.1 chimney pot, skylight.

sundur adv. asunder = *í sundur.*

svefn stm.1 sleep.

svipur stm.2 characteristic appearance.

til prep. with gen. for.

timbur stn. (*hreiður*) timber, wood.

timburskortur stm.1 lack of timber.

torf stn. green turf, sod.

torfþak stn. roof thatched with sod.

tóvinna wf.1 wool home industry.

tún stn. cultivated field near the houses, homefield.

úr prep. with dat. from, of.

út af fyrir sig by oneself, apart, separated from others.

utan á on the outside of.

útihús stn. outhouse, a house far from the central group on the farm.

verja, varði, varinn wv.1 defend; *v. e-n e-u* guard something against something.

við only in the phrase: *á víð og dreif* scattered.

vinna, vinnur, vann, unnum, unninn stv.3 work (at).

virki stn. fortress.

virkisveggur stm.2 fortress wall.

ým(i)s, ým(i)s, ýmist adj. different, several.

þak stn. roof; *að þaki* as a roof, for a roof.

þilja, -aði, -aður wv.4 line (with wooden boards).

þorp stn. town, village.

ærhús stn. shed for the ewes.

ætla til intend for.

Translate into Icelandic:

Did you ever see an old Icelandic farmstead? Yes, they are

very different from the modern (*nýju*) ones (*bæjunum*). The
modern farmhouses are built of (*úr*) timber or concrete like the
houses in the towns (*kaupstöðunum*). But the old farmhouses
were built of sod and stones with thick walls. Do you know why
they were so built? There were several (*ýmsar*) reasons (*ástæður*) ;
lack of timber was one, the coziness of the houses (*hlýindin í
húsunum*) another. Thick walls and thick sod roofs keep out
(*halda úti*) the cold, and, if they are well built, even the rain,
especially in winter. Do you know what were the main (*aðal-*)
rooms or houses on an old Icelandic farmstead? The so-called
'bathroom' was the chief (*aðal-*) house, next to that (*þar næst*)
was the kitchen and the pantry. A storeroom and a forge were
also often (found) on a farmstead.

29.

Impersonal verbs: S. VI, **14**.   Middle voice: S. VI, **7**.
Accusative with Infinitive: S. VI, **11**, *4*.
Passive voice: S. VI, **8**.

Æfing. Draugagangurinn á Nesi.

Hefurðu heyrt söguna um drauganganginn á Nesi? Ekki það?
Ja, ég vil ekki ábyrgjast, að hún sé sönn, en hún er höfð eftir greindu
fólki og ólygnu. Gamli Jón í Nesi var efnakarl, menn töldu hann
efnaðri en hann léti í veðri vaka, og héldu, að hann geymdi peninga
í kistuhandraða frammi á skemmulofti. Og eftir að karl dó, þóttust
menn fara að verða varir við draugagang á loftinu og í stofunni.
Það var gengið upp stigann, og inn eftir loftinu, sumir sögðu, að
það væri sezt á kistuna, en aðrir, að hún væri opnuð. Síðan var
hringlað í einhverju, sem menn álitu vera peningana. Stundum
heyrðist mönnum skellt hleranum á uppgöngunni, en þegar að var
komið, sást ekkert, og hlerinn var kræktur aftur. Þó sagði karl
einn, sem menn héldu vera skyggnan, að sér hefði einu sinni sýnzt
vofa standa við stofuhurðina; kvaðst hann hafa hastað á hana, og
hefði hún þá liðið upp stigann og horfið. Karl hafði átt að sofa í
stofunni, en honum varð svo bilt við þetta, að hann bað heimafólkið
blessað að lofa sér að sofa inni í baðstofu hjá því. Meðan björt
var nótt, bar lítið á drauganganginum, en hann jók um allan helming,
þegar fór að dimma af nótt. Eitt haust voru tveir menn nætursakir
í Nesi. Þeir þóttu miklir á lofti, enda þóttust þeir ekki uppnæmir
fyrir smámunum, og létust ekki trúa því, að þeir gætu ekki sofið í
náðum í stofunni. Þeim var fylgt til rúms í stofuna, og segir ekki
af þeim, fyrr en næsta morgun. Þá sögðu þeir sínar farir ekki

sléttar. Þeim hafði ekki komið dúr á auga fyrir ólátunum á loftinu. Tvisvar höfðu þeir farið upp á loftið, og í bæði skiftin sló öllu í dúnalogn. En þeir voru ekki fyrr komnir í rúmið en ólætin hófust á ný, og héldust þau, þar til komið var fram undir morgun. Sóru þeir og sárt við lögðu, að þeir skyldu aldrei sofa í þeirri stofu framar. Loks var það ráð tekið að brenna kistuna. Eftir það tókst með öllu af draugagangurinn í Nesi.

á prep. with dat. on, in, at; of.

ábyrgjast, -byrgðist, -byrgzt wv.2 midv. only: guarantee.

aldrei framar nevermore.

álíta, -lítur, -leit, -litum, -litinn stv.1 consider, think (*á. e-n vera e-ð* acc. with inf.).

allur helmingur full half; *um a-n h-g* by a full half; more than twice as much; *með öllu* altogether, for good.

auka, eykur, jók, jukum, aukinn stv.7 increase; impers.: *hann* (acc.) *eykur* it increases; but more commonly midv.: *hann eykst* it increases.

bera, ber, bar, bárum, borinn stv.4 bear; impers.: *það ber á e-u* something is noticeable, puts in appearance.

biðja, biður, bað, báðum, beðinn stv.5 ask, pray; *b. e-n blessaðan, að* ask somebody, please, to. . . .

bilt adj.n. only in the phrase: *verða b. við (e-ð)* be startled (amazed) at (something).

bjartur, björt, bjart adj. bright, light.

blessaður, -uð, -að; -aðri, -aðastur adj. blessed. *Blessaður, gerðu þetta!* lit. 'blessed (fellow), do this,' be a good boy and do this, = please, do this. Acc. with inf.: *ég bað hann blessaðan að gera þetta* I asked him, please, to do this.

brenna, brenndi, brenndur wv.2 burn (transitive).

deyja, deyr, dó, dóum, dáinn stv.6 die.

dimma, dimmdi, -aði, dimmt, -að wv. 2 or 4 impers.: *það dimmir* it gets dark; *það dimmir af nótt* the nights get longer.

draugagangur stm.1 lit. walking of ghosts, visitation of ghosts.

draugasaga wf.1 ghost story.

draugur stm.1 ghost, spook.

dúnalogn stn. dead calm (quiet).

dúr stm.1 nap; *e-m kemur ekki d. á auga* one does not sleep a wink.

efnaður, -uð, -að; -aðri, -aðastur adj. well-to-do.

efnakarl stm.1 an old man of means.

efni stn.pl. means.

ekki það(?) not so(?), no(?).

fram hjá adv. by; *f. undir* up to.

frammi adv. away from the center of *bæjarhús*; out.

fylgja e-m til rúms show sbdy to his bed.

fyrr adv. sooner; *ekki fyrr . . . en* no sooner . . . than.

greindur, greind, greint adj. intelligent.

hafa e-ð eftir e-m repeat (quote) something after somebody; *hafði átt* was supposed to have.

halda, heldur, hélt, héldum, haldinn stv.7 hold; think (with *að*-clause: that . . .), consider, think (with acc. and inf.: *h. e-n vera e-ð*); *haldast* keep on.

hasta, -aði, -að wv.4 *h. á e-n* rebuke one (to silence).

hefja, hefur, hóf, hófum, hafinn stv. 6 heave; begin; *hefjast* midv.intr. begin.

heimafólk stn. people of the household.

helmingur stm.1 half; *um allan helming* by a full half; by leaps and bounds.

heyra, heyrði, heyrður wv.2 hear; *heyrast* midv. *mér heyrist e-ð* (*að* . . .) I think I hear something (that . . .).

hleri wm.1 trap door.

hringla, -aði, -aður wv.4 jingle, rattle.

hverfa, hverfur, hvarf, hurfum, horf-
inn stv.3 disappear.
ja interj. well.
kista wf.1 chest.
kistuhandraði wm.1 locker.
koma að get, come to (a place).
krœkja, krœkti, krœktur wv.2 hook,
clasp (*aftur*) (a door).
láta, lœtur, lét, létum, látinn stv.7
let; *látast* midv. pretend, say.
leggja, lagði, lagður wv.1 lay;
sverja og sárt við leggja swear,
invoking heavy (sore) penalties
for oneself if the oath be not true.
líða, líður, leið, liðum, liðinn stv.1
glide.
lofa, -aði, -aður wv.4 allow (*e-m e-ð*).
loft stn. loft; *skemmu-* storage room
loft; air, *vera mikill á l-i* be conceited, give oneself airs.
myrkfœlinn, -in, -ið adj. afraid of
the darkness.
náð stf.2 grace (*drottins n.* grace of
God); pl. *náðir* peace.
Nes stn. Ness.
nœtursakir stf.2.pl. over night; *vera*
n. stay over night.
ólyginn, -in, -ið; -lygnari, -astur adj.
truthful.
ólœti (gen. *-láta*) stn. noise, racket.
óvanalegur adj. unusual, uncommon.
peningur stm.1 money, coin; pl.
money.
ráð stn. plan, decision; *taka r.* decide.
saga wf.1 story, tale, saga (*um*
about).
sár, sár, sárt adj. sore, wounded.
segja wv.3 impers.: *segir ekki af*
honum nothing is said about him,
told about him, heard about him;
ég vil ekki segja I would not say.
sjá stv.5 see; *sjást* midv.pass. be seen.
skella, skellti, skellt wv.2 slam (*e-u*)
(a door).
skemmuloft stn. storeroom loft.

skifti stn. time; *í bæði s-in* both times.
skyggn, skyggn, skyggnt adj. clairvoyant.
slá, slær, sló, slógum, sleginn stv.6
strike, smite; *öllu slær í dúnalogn*
everything becomes dead quiet.
sléttur, slétt, slétt adj. smooth; *segja*
sínar farir eigi sléttar complain
of the rough going one has had.
smámunur stm.3 a little thing, trifle.
stofuhurð stf.2 guest room door.
sverja, sver, sór, sórum, svarinn stv.
6 swear; *s. og sárt við leggja*
swear, invoking heavy (sore)
penalties for oneself in case the
oath be not true.
sýna, sýndi, sýndur wv.2 show;
sýnast midv. *mér s-ist e-ð* something seems to me, I think that
I see something.
taka stv.6 take; *takast af* cease.
telja wv.1 *t. e-n* (*vera*) *e-ð* (acc.
with inf.) consider somebody (to
be) something.
tvisvar adv. twice.
uppganga wf.1 stairway.
uppnœmur, -nœm, -nœmt adj. taken
aback (*fyrir e-u* at something).
vaka, vakti, vakað wv.3 be awake;
láta í veðri vaka intimate, make
believe, hint.
var, vör, vart adj. aware; *verða var*
við become aware of, notice.
vera is often omitted in acc. with
infinitive phrases: *þeir töldu hann*
(*vera*) *efnaðan*; *þeir sögðu hann*
(*vera*) *dauðan*, etc.
vofa wf.1 wraith, spirit.
yfirleitt adv. generally.
þykja, þótti, þótt wv.2 seem; be considered: *þeir þóttu góðir* they
were considered good; *þykjast*
midv. think of oneself (that),
think (that . . .).

Translate into Icelandic:

Did you know that there were ghosts in Iceland? No, I did not
know that. Well, there are ghost stories, at any rate (*að minnsta*
kosti), and they are quite common, but I would not say (*ég vil ekki*
segja) that people believed them generally (*yfirleitt*). But it is
not uncommon (*óvanalegt*) for people to think (that) (*að menn*

haldi að) they hear or see something in the old farmhouses. They think they hear (*heyrist*) somebody walking, or they think they see (*sýnist*) a spirit gliding by (*fram hjá*). They are afraid of the darkness (*hræddir við myrkrið* or *myrkfælnir*), especially when the nights begin to get longer. But they are very fond of the ghost stories, nevertheless (*samt sem áður*).

30.

Impersonal verbs and other verbs with the logical subject in dative or accusative, the logical object in nominative or other cases. See S. I, 2, *1, 3*; I, 3, *1,* 2b; VI, 14, *5*.

Genitive not used where the English would expect it: S. I, 4, *1*.

Use of definite article instead of a genitive: S. II, 6.

Æfing. Veikindi, kvillar og sóttir.

Mér hefur sjaldan orðið misdægurt um dagana. Ég hef aldrei fengið landfarssóttir, eins og t. d. barnaveiki, kíghósta, mislinga, hettusótt, eða skarlatssótt. Ég hef aldrei veikzt af lungnabólgu og hvorki látið skera úr mér hálskirtla né botnlanga. Ég hef aldrei verið skorinn upp. En ég hef stundum orðið lasinn af kvefi, innflúenzu, eða hálsbólgu, og ég hef átt vanda fyrir höfuðverk með uppköstum.

Höfuðverkurinn byrjar oft með því, að mig fer að verkja í ennið, eða gagnaugun, eða hnakkann. Svo fæ ég velgju og loks kasta ég upp. Eftir það batnar mér venjulega fljótt. Meðan á þessu stendur, missi ég alla matarlyst. Mér býður (velgir) við öllu, nema súrri (skyr)blöndu. Hana drekk ég, þegar mig þyrstir.

Þegar ég var strákur, fékk ég stundum hlustarverk í eyrun, aftur á móti varð mér aldrei illt í augunum, nema hvað mig sveið í þau, ef reykur komst að þeim. Þess vegna hef ég aldrei getað þolað (liðið) tóbaksreyk. Tannpínu (-verk) fékk ég aldrei, enda hefur aldrei verið dregin úr mér tönn. Blóðnasir fékk ég oft (mér blæddu oft nasir) í gamla daga.

Manni varð sjaldan illt í maganum, nema maður ofæti sig á einhverju góðgæti eins og berjaskyri eða nýjum sviðum. Þá gat maður fengið magaverk og kveisu. Stundum fékk maður brjóstsviða af kaffi og steiktu brauði.

Hita fæ ég ekki, nema með innflúenzu eða vondu kvefi. Tak í brjóst og bak hef ég aldrei fengið, enda fylgir það bara lungnabólgu. En mig hefur oft tekið í axlirnar, lærin, eða kálfana af mikilli áreynslu, það er kölluð harðsperra. Stundum hef ég fengið verk í hrygginn; það hefur kannske verið gigt.

Oft hefur maður nú meitt sig lítils háttar. Ég geng enn með ör
á öllum fingrum eftir skurði og ígerðir. Einu sinni marði ég mig
á hægra þumalfingri. Ég átti lengi í því, og nöglina rak fram af
fingrinum. Ég hef viðbeinsbrotnað, en hvorki fót- né handleggs-
brotnað.

Manni var oft kalt á fótum, þegar maður stóð í blautu heila daga.
Á vetrum frusu sokkar og skór að fótunum, svo að maður fann
ekki til tánna á sér, en aldrei kól mig samt. Fæturnir voru fyrst svo
dofnir, að maður fann ekkert til, en þegar fór að færast ylur í þá,
þá fór mann að klæja og svíða í tærnar. Einu sinni vatzt fóturinn
á mér um ökklaliðinn, hann bólgnaði strax og sárnaði, svo að ég
gat ekki stigið í hann. Mig verkjaði í ökklann vikutíma, en svo
var það búið.

aftur á móti on the other hand.
áreynsla wf.1 exertion.
axlir pl. of *öxl.*
bak stn. back (= *hryggur*).
barnaveiki wf.2 diphtheria.
batna, -*aði,* -*að* wv.4 impers.: *mér
batnar* I get better, I get well;
pers.: *mér batnar e-ð* (nom.) I
get over something, I get well.
berjaskyr stn. Icelandic curds with
berries.
bjóða, býður, bauð, buðum, boðinn
stv.2 offer; impers.: *mér býður
við e-u* I am nauseated at, I abhor something.
blanda wf.1 whey; a drink mixed
from sour whey or *skyr* and water.
blautur, blaut, blautt adj. wet; *í
blautu* in wet socks (clothes).
blóðnasir stf.3.pl. bleeding nose, nosebleed.
blæða, blæddi, blætt wv.2 bleed; impers.: *mér blæðir* I am bleeding.
bólga wf.1 inflammation.
bólgna, -*aði,* -*aður* wv.4 be (get)
inflamed.
botnlangabólga wf.1 appendicitis.
botnlangi wm.1 appendix.
brjóst stn. breast.
brjóstsviði wm.1 heartburn.
dagur stm.1 day; *um dagana* in my
life.
dofi wm.1 numbness.
dofinn, -*in,* -*ið* adj. numb.
dofna, -*aði,* -*aður* wv.4 become numb
(dead, of limbs).

draga, dregur, dró, drógum, dreginn
stv.6 drag, pull; *draga tönn (úr
e-m)* pull (somebody's) tooth.
eiga pret.pres.v. own, have; *eiga
vanda fyrir e-u* be liable to get
something (a sickness), be prone
to something; *eiga lengi í e-u* be
sick with something (suffering
from something) for a long time.
enni stn. forehead.
eyra wn. ear.
finna stv.3 find; *finna til* feel something, be hurt; *finna til fótanna
(á sér)* feel one's feet; *finna til
kulda* feel the cold.
fljótur, fljót, fljótt adj. quick; *fljótt*
adv. quickly.
fótbrotna, -*aði,* -*að* wv.4 break a leg.
friskur, frisk, friskt adj. well; *ekki
friskur* unwell.
færa, færði, færður wv.2 move
(trans.) *færast í* midv.intr.
move into, enter.
gagnauga wn. temple.
ganga stv.7 go; *ganga að* be the
matter with, *hvað gengur að þér?*
what is the matter with you?
ganga með ör have a scar.
gigt stf.2 rheumatism, arthritis.
góðgæti stn. (coll.) things good to
eat, goodies.
háls stm.1 neck; throat (= *kok*).
hálsbólga wf.1 tonsilitis, inflammation of the throat.
hálskirtill stm.1 tonsil.

244

handleggsbrotna, -aði, -að wv.4 break
an arm.

handleggur stm.2 arm (= *armur*).

harðsperra wf.1 or pl. *-ur* aching or
stiffness in limbs and muscles.

hettusótt stf.2 mumps.

hiti wm.1 fever; *fá hita* get a fever,
hafa hita have a fever.

hlust stf.2 passage of the ear.

hlustarverkur stm.2 earache.

hnakki wm.1 back of the head.

hryggur stm.2 back, spine.

höfuðverkur stm.2 headache.

ígerð stf.2 boil, abscess.

illur, ill, illt; verri, verstur adj. bad,
ill; *mér er illt* I am sick; *mér
verður illt* I will get sick, I am
getting sick.

innflúenza wf.1 influenza (*flenza* = flu).

kala, kelur or *kell, kól, kólum, kalinn* stv.6 *mig kelur* (*kell*) impers.: I freeze, I am freezing, I
become frostbitten.

kaldur, köld, kalt adj. cold; *mér er
kalt* I am cold; *mér er kalt á
höndum, fótum*, etc. my hands,
feet, etc. are cold, I have cold
hands, feet.

kálfi wm.1 calf of the leg.

kasta, -aði, -að wv.4 throw; *kasta
upp* throw up, vomit.

kíghósti (*kík-*) wm.1 whooping cough.

kirtill stm.1 (*himinn*) gland.

kok stn. throat, pharynx.

klæja, -aði, -að wv.4 itch; *mig klæjar*
I itch; *mig klæjar lófann* (acc.)
the palm of my hand itches; *mig
klæjar á tánum* (*í tærnar*) my
toes itch.

kvef stn. cold; *fá kvef* catch cold.

kveisa wf.1 bellyache.

kvilli wm.1 ailment, malady.

landfarssótt stf.2 epidemic.

lasinn, -in, -ið, lasnari, lasnastur
adj. sick, ill, not well, indisposed.

láta skera have operated.

líða, líður, leið, liðum, liðinn stv.1
suffer, stand; *líða frá* pass away.

lítils háttar a little, a bit.

lunga wn. lung.

lungnabólga wf.1 (pronounced *lúna-*)
pneumonia.

lyst stf.2 appetite = *matarlyst*.

lær (*læri*) stn. thigh.

magaverkur stm.2 stomach ache.

magi wm.1 stomach.

matarlyst stf.2 appetite.

meiða, meiddi, meiddur wv.2 hurt;
meiða sig hurt oneself.

merja, marði, marinn wv.1 crush;
merja sig crush a part of one's
anatomy; *m. sig á fingri, fæti*,
etc. crush a finger, a foot, etc.

misdægurt adj.n. only in: *verða aldrei
misdægurt* 'never have a day
different from another,' never get
sick.

mislingar stm.1.pl. measles.

nasir pl. of *nös; mér blæða nasir*
my nose bleeds.

nef stn. nose.

nema hvað except that.

nögl stf.3 nail.

nös stf.2 nostril.

oféta, -étur, -át, -átum, -étinn stv.5
eat too much; *oféta sig* overeat
(oneself); *o. s. á* over-indulge in.

reka, rekur, rak, rákum, rekinn stv.5
drive; impers.trans.: *e-ð rekur*
something is driven, *nöglina rekur
fram* the nail 'is driven forth,'
the nail falls away.

sár stn. wound.

sárna, -aði, -að wv.4 get sore, get
tender.

skarlatssótt stf.2 scarlet fever.

skera, sker, skar, skárum, skorinn
stv.4 cut; *skera upp* operate upon; *skera úr* cut away.

skór stm.1 shoe.

skurður stm.3 cut; operation.

skyr stn. Icelandic curds.

skyrblanda wf.1 sour curds mixed
with water.

sokkur stm.1 sock, stocking.

sótt stf.2 sickness, malady.

standa stv.6 stand; *standa í blautu*
keep the wet clothes (socks) on;
meðan stendur á e-u while something lasts.

steikja, steikti, steiktur wv.2 roast,
cook in (deep) fat; *steikt brauð*
bread cooked in fat.

stíga, stígur, steig, stigum, stiginn

245

stv.1 step; *stíga í fótinn* step on the (= one's own) foot; *stíga á fótinn* step on somebody else's foot.

strax adv. at once.

súr, súr, súrt adj. sour; pickled.

svið stn.pl. head and feet of sheep (cattle) singed over a fire before cooking.

svíða, svíður, sveið, sviðum, sviðinn stv.1 singe, burn; impers.: *mig svíður* I have a burning sensation in (*í fótinn, augað,* acc. the foot, the eye).

sviði wm.1 burning sensation.

tá stf.3 toe.

tak stn. piercing, stabbing pain.

taka stv.6 take; *mig tekur í bakið,* etc. I feel a stabbing pain in my back, etc.

tannpína (*-verkur*) wf.1 (stm.2) toothache.

tóbaksreykur stm.2 tobacco smoke.

uppköst stn.pl. vomiting.

vandi wm.1 custom, habit; *eiga vanda fyrir e-u* get something (a sickness) habitually, be prone to (get) something.

veiki wf.2 sickness, malady.

veikindi stn.pl. sickness.

veikja, veikti, veiktur wv.2 weaken (trans.); *veikjast* (*af*) midv.intr. get sick, ill (with).

veikur, veik, veikt adj. sick, ill.

velgja wf.1 nausea; *fá velgju* get nauseated; *hafa velgju* be, feel nauseated.

velgja, velgdi, velgt wv.2 impers.: *mig velgir við e-u* I am nauseated at something.

verkja, -aði, -að wv.4 impers.: *mig verkjar* (*í fótinn,* etc.) I have a pain (in the foot, etc.).

verkur stm.2 pain.

viðbein stn. collarbone.

viðbeinsbrotna, -aði, -að wv.4 break the collarbone.

vikutími wm.1 week's time.

vinda, vindur, vatt, undum, undinn stv.3 twist, turn; *vindast* get twisted; *vindast um ökklann* turn one's ankle.

ylur stm.2 warmth.

þola, þoldi, þolað wv.3 suffer, stand (= *líða*).

þumalfingur stm.4 thumb.

þumall stm.1 thumb; thumb of a mitten or glove.

þyrsta, þyrsti, þyrst wv.2 impers.: *mig þyrstir* I am (I am getting) thirsty.

þyrstur, þyrst, þyrst adj. thirsty; *ég er þyrstur* I am thirsty.

ökklaliður stm.3 (the joint of) the ankle.

ökkli wm.1 ankle.

ör stn. scar.

öxl stf.2 shoulder.

Translate into Icelandic:

Are you sick? Are you ill? No, I am only a little indisposed. What is the matter with you (*hvað gengur að þér, yður*)? I have a slight headache, and I feel (*hef*) a bit (*svolítla*) nauseated (*velgju*). I hope it will pass (over) (*að það líði frá*). Do you think (*heldur þú, haldið þér*) that you have a fever? I feel as if I have a fever (*mér finnst ég hafa ...*). I feel that I have (*ég finn, að ég hef*) a fever. You ought to (*ættir að*) go to bed at once. You should not have (*þú hefðir ekki átt, þér hefðuð ekki átt*) stayed up (*að vera á fótum*) so late. You should have taken better care (*fara betur með*) of yourself. Where do you think (*hvar finnst þér, yður*) the headache is (*vera*)? In the forehead above the right eye. Well, I am sure that you will get better (*þér, yður batnar*), if you go to bed and sleep well. Yes, tomorrow I shall be well (*frískur*). Well, let us (*við skulum*) hope so (*það*). Good night.

246

TEXTS II.

DAGLEGT LÍF OG DAGLEGT TAL.

31. Kveðjur. Að heilsast og kveðjast.

Fyrir hádegi og jafnvel fram undir kvöld má alltaf bjóða góðan dag: "Góðan daginn"; (svar) "Góðan dag(inn)." Þegar líður á daginn, er boðið "gott kvöld" á sama hátt, og þegar menn skiljast að kvöldi, "góða nótt." Menn heilsast með "góðan daginn," "gott kvöld," en kveðjast með "góða nótt."

Komumaður getur kastað á mann kveðju, en venjulegra er að heilsa með handabandi. Ef menn þúast, segir hann þá: "Komdu sæll (sæl)," "Sæll (sæl) vertu," "Sæll (sæl)." Við fleiri en einn mann: "Komið þið sælir," "Sælir verið þið," "Sælir." Við fleiri en eina konu: "Komið þið sælar," "Sælar verið þið," "Sælar," og við menn og konur: "Komið þið sæl," "Sæl verið þið," "Sæl," eða: "Sælt veri fólkið." Ef menn þérast er sagt: "Komið þér sælir," "Sælir verið þér," "Sælir."

Maður, sem er að fara, getur líka kastað á mann kveðju, eða kvatt með handabandi; hann segir, ef menn þúast: "Vertu sæll (sæl) "; við fleiri menn: "Verið þið sælir," við konur: "Verið þið sælar," og við menn og konur: "Verið þið sæl." Ef menn þérast, þá er sagt: "Verið þér sælir (sælar)."

Kunningjar segja oft "Sæli(r) nú," þegar þeir finnast, en "Vertu bless(aður)," eða "Blessi þig," þegar þeir skilja.

Ef menn hafa verið saman fyrir skömmu, þá þakka menn fyrir síðast: "Þakka þér (yður) fyrir síðast," (svar) "Já, það er nú sjálfþakkað," eða bara "Sjálfþakkað." Annars t. d.: "Langt er nú síðan við höfum sézt." "Hvernig líður þér (yður)?" eða "Hvernig sæki ég að þér (yður)?" (Svar) "Vel, en hvernig líður þér (yður)?" "Hvað er í fréttum (að frétta)?" (Svar) "Allt gott," "Allt bærilegt," eða "Og svosem ekki neitt." Að heimsókn lokinni kveður maður, þakkar fyrir góðgerðirnar eða skemmtunina, og biður að heilsa konunni, ef hún er ekki viðstödd.

32. Kynning. Að kynna fólk.

Áður fyrr var alsiða að spyrja menn að heiti: "Hvað heitið þér (með leyfi)?" eða: "Hvað heitir maðurinn?" "Ég heiti Jón Stefánsson." Þessi siður mun enn tíðkast í sveitum. En í bæjum munu kynningar vera venjulegri. "Viltu gera svo vel að kynna

mig prófessor Valtý Guðmundssyni? (... frú Önnu Jónsdóttur?)."
"Þekkizt þið ekki?" "Hafið þið sézt?" "(Þetta er) Gunnar
Stefánsson, stúdent—prófessor Valtýr Guðmundsson (frú Anna
Jónsdóttir)." G. S.: "Komið þér sælir (sælar)." V. G.: "Sælir."
Kynni menn sig sjálfir, heilsa menn fyrst og segja svo nafn sitt:
"Komið þér sælir—(ég heiti) Gunnar Stefánsson," eða öfugt.

Vestur-Íslendingar segja eins og Ameríkumenn: "Það gleður
mig að kynnast þér," og þegar þeir kveðja: "Mér þykir vænt um
að hafa hitt þig," eða: "Það gleður mig að hafa mætt þér." Á
Íslandi er þetta aldrei sagt við ókunnuga, nema þegar hugur fylgir
máli. Að segja það við hvern sem er, mundi verða talin hræsni.

33. Íslenzk mannanöfn.

Íslendingar hafa skírnarnöfn, föðurnöfn, ættarnöfn, gælunöfn og
viðurnefni. Öll þessi nöfn eru líka notuð á ensku, nema föðurnöfnin.
En af því að föðurnafnið fer á eftir skírnarnafninu, þá álykta
flestir útlendingar, að það sé eftirnafn mannsins (eða konunnar),
og sé eins notað og hin venjulegu erlendu eftirnöfn. En svo er
ekki. Föðurnafnið er ekki eiginlega heiti, heldur segir það til, hvers
sonur (eða dóttir) maðurinn (eða konan) er. Ef spurt er "Hvað
heitið þér?" þá er svarið: "Ég heiti Jón." En ef spurt er: "Hvers
son eruð þér?" er svarið: "Ég er Guðmundsson." En svarið við
fyrri spurningunni getur líka verið í einu lagi: "Ég heiti Jón (og
er) Guðmundsson." Í ávarpi og umtali má nota bæði skírnar- og
föðurnafnið, en venjulega er skírnarnafnið eitt notað. Hins vegar
er ómögulegt að nota föðurnafnið eitt—nema það sé orðið að
ættarnafni.

Ættarnöfn eru notuð af allmörgum á svipaðan hátt eins og í
ensku, en á síðustu áratugum hefur það verið á móti lögum að taka
upp ný ættarnöfn. Til dæmis um ættarnöfnin má nefna: Jón
Thoroddsen, Einar H. Kvaran, Vilhjálmur Þ. Gíslason (föðurnafn
gert að ættarnafni).

Gælunöfn á börnum og unglingum eru mjög algeng eins og í
ensku. Dæmi: Siggi, Bjössi, Óli, Mundi, Nonni af Sigurður, Björn,
Ólafur, Jón. Stúlkur: Sigga, Gunna, Rúna, Rænka af Sigríður,
Guðrún, Sigrún, Ragnheiður eða Ragnhildur. Önnur yngri
gælunöfn, ekki ótíð í Reykjavík, eru tæpitungunöfn eins og Dídí,
Lóló, o. s. frv. Ekki verður af þeim ráðið, hvað barnið heitir, því
þau eru sjaldnast dregin af skírnarnafninu.

Viðurnefni eða auknefni gefa skólapiltar hver öðrum og gár-
ungar náunganum. Oft eru þau alveg meinlaus, eins og þegar tveir
Sigurðar til aðgreiningar eru kallaðir Siggi grái og Siggi svarti

eftir háralit. En stundum eru þau gefin af illfýsi og eru þá síður
en svo meinlaus. Viðurnefni eru auðvitað aldrei notuð, nema í
kunningjahóp, eða meðal óvina mannsins, sem ber það.

Algengustu mannanöfn 1910.

Karlmannsnöfn: Jón, Guðmundur, Sigurður, Ólafur, Magnús,
Kristján, Einar, Bjarni, Jóhann, Björn, Gísli, Árni, Stefán, Þor-
steinn, Helgi, Guðjón, Halldór, Kristinn, Páll, Jóhannes, Pétur,
Þórður, Sveinn, Gunnar, Jónas, Ágúst, Sigurjón.

Kvennmannsnöfn: Guðrún, Sigríður, Kristín, Margrét, Ingibjörg,
Anna, Helga, Jóhanna, Guðbjörg, Jónína, María, Guðný, Halldóra,
Guðríður, Steinunn, Elín, Þórunn, Guðlaug, Ólöf, Sigurbjörg,
Valgerður, Þuríður, Hólmfríður, Ragnheiður, Þorbjörg, Kristjana,
Elísabet, Þóra, Björg, Solveig, Katrín.

34. Heimsókn. Að heimsækja fólk.

Heimsóknartími. Ef maður á erindi við einhvern, sem maður
þekkir ekki, mun réttast að skrifa honum bréf eða hringja hann
upp í síma og spyrja, hvenær maður megi heimsækja hann. Til
kunningja sinna getur maður farið um miðaftansleytið. Að
ákveðnum tíma hringir maður dyrabjöllunni eða ber (bankar) að
dyrum. Stúlka kemur út.

Góðan daginn. Er húsbóndinn (frúin, húsfreyja) heima? Væri
hægt að fá að tala við Steindór Sigurðsson? Ég skal vita, hvort
hann er viðlátinn, en ég er hrædd um, að hann hafi skroppið út
í bæ. Já, hann var nýfarinn út í bæ, en frúin er heima. Ég á nú
eiginlega ekkert erindi við hana, en hvenær haldið þér, að væri
bezt að hitta Steindór? Ég held hann komi rétt strax, kannske
þér vilduð koma inn og bíða eftir honum. Þakk fyrir, ég held
það væri réttast. Gerið þér svo vel. Komið þér sælar frú, (ég
heiti) Steingrímur Jónsson. Sælir; gerið þér svo vel og fáið yður
sæti. Má bjóða yður vindil? Nei þakk, ég reyki ekki. En kaffisopa?
Takk, en það er nú annars hreinasti óþarfi, og ég er svo hræddur
um, að þér hafið of mikið fyrir mér. Alls ekki, við erum með kaffi
á könnunni. Gerið þér svo vel. Takk. Þér borðið ekki neitt; hvað
má ég rétta yður? kleinur, pönnukökur? Takk, ekki meira. Ég er
hrædd um, að kaffið sé ekki nógu sterkt. Jú, þetta er fyrirtakskaffi,
og pönnukökurnar eru ágætar. Nú er Steindór að koma. Það var
ágætt... þakk fyrir kaffið (þakkar með handabandi). Fyrirgefið þér
(verði yður að góðu). Komið þér sælir. Sælir; hvað get ég gert fyrir
yður. Mig langaði til að spyrja yður (leita ráða yðar) um dálítið,
sem ég hef verið að hugsa um. Það er velkomið. ... Jæja, þakka

249

yður nú fyrir upplýsingarnar, og verið þér sælir. Ég bið að heilsa konunni yðar með þakklæti fyrir góðgerðirnar.

35. Talið þér íslenzku?

Talið þér íslenzku? Það er nú lítið; ég get dálítið (rétt aðeins) fleytt (bjargað) mér. Nú, mér heyrist þér tala nógu vel. Fyrirgefið þér, en ég skil ekki vel, hvað þér segið; nei, þér þurfið ekki að tala hærra, en þér talið of hratt fyrir mig. Viljið þér gera svo vel að tala hægara? . . . já, þetta er betra; nú skil ég yður miklu betur. Hvað lengi hafið þér verið að læra íslenzku? Ekki nema tvo mánuði. Og hvað er langt síðan þér komuð til Íslands? Aðeins ein vika. Þér verðið þá víst ekki lengi að komast upp á að læra að tala og skilja málið. Þér ættuð að koma yður fyrir uppi í sveit, því þar kunna færri ensku, og þar verðið þér að tala málið allan tímann. Já, hér í Reykjavík eru því miður svo margir, sem skilja og tala ensku, að maður fær sjaldan tækifæri til að nota íslenzku.

Hvernig á að bera þetta orð fram? Þakka yður fyrir. Segir maður hann, hún, eða það um orðið 'höfn'? Maður segir hún höfnin. Og hvernig beygist sögnin 'að liggja'? Liggja, ligg, lá, lágum, leginn. Það er alveg furða, hvað þér berið rétt fram og hvað þér talið málfræðislega rétt.

Hvað heitir þetta (bendir á hlutinn)? Þetta heitir (nú) úr. Hvað er þetta kallað? Þetta er kallað úr. Hvernig lesið þér þetta? Hvað þýðir þetta? Ég finn það ekki í orðabókinni. Það er ekki von, það er ekki í orðabókinni.

36. Bréf.

Kunningjabréf.   Smáragötu 12, Reykjavík
                                                     12. júní 1937

Kæri vinur!

Ég má ekki láta skipið fara svo, að ég skrifi þér ekki línu. Við komum til Reykjavíkur í gær eftir þriggja daga skemmtilega sjóferð frá Edinborg. Við vorum stálheppin með veður, og jöklarnir stóðu hvítir í sólskininu, þegar við komum í landsýn. Og þú hefðir bara átt að sjá Vestmannaeyjar: gulmórauðir klettarnir risu þverhníptir úr grængolandi sjónum, krýndir dökkgrænum grastóm, þar sem hvítar, lagðsíðar kindur virtust hanga eins og flugur á vegg. Og svo fuglarnir í bjarginu! Þvílíkt líf og þvílík læti!

Morguninn eftir komum við til Reykjavíkur. Jón og kona hans voru niðri á bryggju að taka á móti mér, þau tóku mér eins og ég væri sonur þeirra. Ég fæ að vera hjá þeim, meðan ég er í Reykjavík.

VESTMANNAEYJAR.

Ég bý í litlu gaflherbergi með útsýni yfir garðinn og Tjörnina. Á morgun fer ég að hitta prófessorana og spyrja þá, hvaða tíma ég ætti að taka hjá þeim næsta vetur. Jón segir mér, að mér sé bezt að koma mér í sumarfrí austur í sveitir, annaðhvort hjá einhverjum presti eða hjá sýslumanninum á Efra-Hvoli; hann kvað vera með afbrigðum gestrisinn. Það verður haldið hálfsmánaðar námskeið í íslenzku seinna í sumar austur á Laugarvatni; prófessor Alexander kvað ætla að halda fyrirlestra um íslenzka málfræði, prófessor Nordal um Snorra Sturluson og doktor Einar Ólafur Sveinsson um Sturlungu. Þú getur því nærri, að ég muni reyna að komast þangað.

Skipið er að fara, og ég verð að slá botn í þetta rugl. Ég bið að heilsa foreldrum þínum og Siggu systur þinni.

Með beztu kveðjum,

þinn einlægur

S. S.

Bréf til ókunnugs manns.

Smáragötu 12, Reykjavík
12. júní 1937.

Herra prófessor Sigurður Nordal,
Háskóla Íslands,
Reykjavík.

Heiðraði herra:

Mér hefur verið ráðlagt að hitta yður og tala við yður um nám mitt hér á Íslandi bæði í sumar og næsta vetur. Ég er með meðmælabréf frá manni, sem þér þekkið, vestan hafs. Vilduð þér gera svo vel að láta mig vita, hvenær ég megi koma og tala við yður.

Virðingarfyllst,

S. S.

Upphöf á bréfum: Kæri vinur, góði vinur, kæri herra, heiðraði herra, nafnið eitt (í verzlunarbréfum).

Endir á bréfum: Með beztu kveðjum, þinn einlægur; kærar kveðjur, þinn einlægur; innilegar hamingjuóskir og beztu kveðjur, yðar einlægur; með vinsemd, yðar einlægur; með vinsemd og virðingu; virðingarfyllst.

Í verzlunarbréfum er ekki notað annað ávarp en nafn mannsins (firmans) og utanáskrift: Herra Jón Gíslason, Bankastræti 9, Reykjavík.

Utanáskrift (heimilisfang) á bréfum: Herra Jón Jónsson, Þorvaldsstöðum, Breiðdal, Suður-Múlasýslu.

37. Göturnar í Reykjavík og helztu byggingar.

Flestar götur í Reykjavík eru malbikaðar, nokkrar eru steyptar og enn aðrar eru gerðar úr eintómri möl; þær verða forugar í rigningatíð, og þeim hættir við sandfoki í þurrkum. Meðfram götunum eru gangstéttir og göturennur (göturæsi).

Nöfn á götum (götunöfn) enda á -gata, -stígur, -stræti og -vegur. Örfá enda á -sund, og ein gata, sem liggur hringinn í kring um bæinn, er kölluð Hringbraut. Nokkur ný götunöfn enda á -tún, -melur og -holt.

Miðbærinn er elzti hluti Reykjavíkur. Hann nær norðan frá höfn suður að Tjörn, austan frá Lækjargötu og vestur að Aðalstræti. Elzta gatan í Miðbænum er Austurstræti milli Aðalstrætis og Lækjargötu.

Ein af aðalgötum Vesturbæjarins, og elzt þeirra, er Vesturgata. Vestan Tjarnar liggur Suðurgata suður á Mela. Laugavegur og Hverfisgata eru helztar götur í Austurbænum; af götum, sem liggja í suður og suðaustur, má nefna Laufásveg og Skólavörðustíg.

Elztu opinberar byggingar í Reykjavík munu vera Menntaskólinn, Dómkirkjan og Alþingishúsið, allar í Miðbænum. Við Hverfisgötu er Safnahúsið, með Landsbókasafninu og Þjóðminjasafninu, og Þjóðleikhúsið. Í Vesturbænum gnæfir kaþólska Kristskirkjan við loft, en á Skólavörðuholtinu stendur hið einkennilega hús Einars Jónssonar myndhöggvara, Hnitbjörg. Háskólinn nýi stendur suður á Melum, en Landsspítalinn sunnan við Austurbæinn. Sundhöllin er í Austurbænum við Barónsstíg.

Myndastytta Ingólfs Arnarsonar, fyrsta landnámsmanns á Íslandi og fyrsta búanda í Reykjavík, stendur á Arnarhóli; stytta Jóns Sigurðssonar, mesta stjórnmálamanns sem landið hefur átt, stendur á Austurvelli fram undan Alþingishúsinu. Styttur af Kristjáni konungi IX og Hannesi Hafstein ráðherra standa á blettinum fyrir framan Stjórnarráðshúsið. Litlu sunnar við Lækjargötu er líkan af Jónasi skáldi Hallgrímssyni. Allar þessar styttur eru eftir Einar Jónsson myndhöggvara. Stytta af Albert Thorvaldsen, hinum fræga dansk-íslenzka myndhöggvara, eftir sjálfan hann, stendur í Hljómskálagarðinum, en líkan af Leifi heppna, gefið landinu á 1000 ára afmæli Alþingis 1930 af stjórn Bandaríkjanna, stendur uppi á Skólavörðuholtinu.

38. Umferð í Reykjavík.

Í Reykjavík geta menn hjólað (farið á hjóli, hjólhesti, reiðhjóli), farið í strætisvagni, eða leigt sér bíl. Öll umferð er vinstra megin á götunni.

INGÓLFUR ARNARSON.

Strætisvagnar Reykjavíkur ganga víða um bæinn og út úr honum. Farmiðar eru ódýrir. Viðkomustaðir (áfangastaðir, stoppstaðir) eru merktir með skiltum, er bera áletrunina S. V. R., hvíta á svörtum grunni. Bílstjóri kallar upp nafn áfangastaðarins: " Sundhöllin "; farþegi, sem ætlar út, svarar: " Já."

Leigubílar bera nafn bifreiðastöðvarinnar (skammstafað eða fullu nafni) á miða, sem límdur er á framglugga bílsins (t. d. B. S. R. = Bifreiðastöð Reykjavíkur, Litla Bílastöðin, Steindór, o. s. frv.). Ekki er hægt að taka leigubíla á götunni; menn verða að síma á stöðina og panta þá.

Bifreiðastöðvarnar (bílastöðvarnar) leigja bíla með bílstjóra, sjaldan án þeirra, og þá dýrara. Bílaviðgerðastofur (bílaverkstæði) gera við bíla og reiðhjól, skifta um olíu og smyrja þá. Benzínstöðvar selja benzín og olíu, en skifta hvorki um olíu né smyrja bíla.

39. Að spyrjast til vegar.

Fyrirgefið þér, ég er hræddur um, að ég sé villtur, gætuð þér vísað mér á rétta leið (sagt mér til vegar)? Hvert ætlið þér? Ég ætlaði ofan á Pósthús, en ég veit ekki einu sinni, hvað gatan heitir, sem við erum (staddir) á. Þetta er Lækjargata, og þér getið gengið beint áfram (beint af augum) þar til þér komið að næsta götuhorni. Þar beygið (snúið) þér til vinstri inn í Austurstræti, gangið svo þar til þér komið að næstu þvergötu; það er Pósthússtræti, og þar beygið þér til hægri fyrir hornið, þaðan er örskammt að dyrum Pósthússins. Þakka yður fyrir. Ekkert að þakka.

Heyrðu drengur minn, hvað er skemmsta leið inn í Laugar? Það er skemmst að fara Laugaveginn. Og hvað ætli það sé lengi gengið? Það er röskur hálftímagangur. En er það ekki vandratað? Nei, það er ómögulegt að villast, ekki er annað en að halda sér alltaf við Laugaveginn. Heldur þú, að þú mættir vera að fylgja mér þangað? Nei, ég hef því miður ekki tíma til þess.

Hvar er Háskólinn? Hann er suður á Melum, yður er bezt að fara Suðurgötu til að komast þangað. En hvar er Símastöðin? Hún er niðri í Miðbæ, rétt vestan við Austurvöll; ef þér vitið, hvar Alþingishúsið er, þá hljótið þér að finna hana.

40. Tóbak.

Hvað má bjóða yður, sígarettur (vindlinga) eða vindil? Þakka yður fyrir, ég reyki venjulega pípu; mér verður ekki gott af sígarettum, og vindla reyki ég mjög sjaldan, helzt þegar mér eru boðnir þeir. Mér finnst vindlar venjulega of sterkir. Yður væri nú óhætt að reykja þessa vindla, því þeir eru mildir.

Ég er alveg að verða tóbakslaus (búinn, uppiskroppa með tóbak) ; hvar getur maður fengið tóbak keypt? Í hvaða tóbaksbúð sem er ; þær selja reyktóbak í pökkum og dósum, vindla af öllum tegundum, og svo auðvitað sígarettur, bæði amerískar, enskar, egypzkar og tyrkneskar.

Hafið þér eldspýtu? Það dó í pípunni minni. Já, gerið þér svo vel. Hérna er líka öskubakki, ef þér viljið slá úr pípunni öskuna.

Tóbaksverzlanirnar hafa líka munntóbak og neftóbak, því hér eru allmargir karlar, sem annaðhvort taka upp í sig (tyggja tóbak) eða taka (það) í nefið. Þér ættuð að sjá tóbaksbaukana (ponturnar) hjá þeim sumum, körlunum, þeir (þær) eru oft hreinustu listaverk. Fást þeir (þær) í tóbaksbúðunum? Nei en þar getið þér fengið pípur, vindlahylki, munnstykki, eldspýtur o. m. fl.

Reykingar eru bannaðar í strætisvögnunum og víðar vegna ólofts og eldhættu.

41. Á rakarastofunni. Hjá rakara eða hárskera.

Ég þarf að láta klippa mig ; er nokkur rakarastofa hér í grennd-inni? Já, það er rakari á næsta götuhorni. Góðan daginn. Gæti ég fengið mig klipptan? Já, ég er rétt að segja búinn að raka þennan mann (viðskiftavin), og þér eruð næstur. Gerið þér svo vel og fáið yður sæti á meðan ; þarna eru blöð, Vikan og Fálk-inn. . . . Hvernig viljið þér hafa það? Þér getið snöggklippt mig á hliðunum og hnakkanum og stýft dálítið ofan af höfðinu. Hvar á eg að skifta hárinu, hægra megin? Nei, ég skifti því ekki, heldur greiði það beint aftur. Viljið þér fá höfuðbað (hárþvott)? Ekki núna, þakk fyrir. En viljið þér ekki fá hárvatn (hárspíritus, feiti) í hárið, það er nokkuð óþægt? Þér getið bara vætt það í vatni. Kannske ég láti raka mig um leið. Það er velkomið. Þér verðið að passa að raka ekki af mér efrivararskeggið. Þessi hnífur er sár, hafið þér ekki annan betri? Viljið þér fá andlitsnudd? Nei þakk, þetta er nóg. Hvað skulda ég? Klippingin (stýfingin) kostar tvær krónur sjötíu og fimm (aura) og raksturinn sjötíu (aura) ; það verða þrjár fjörutíu og fimm alls.* Þakk. Sælir.

Á hárgreiðslustofu.

Konur síma á hárgreiðslustofuna og panta hárþvott og greiðslu eða liðun (lagningu) á hárinu. Hárgreiðslustúlkurnar þvo hárið, greiða það, liða það eða leggja það. Þær lita hár og augabrúnir og þær snyrta hendurnar (handsnyrting).

* Due to the inflation caused by the war, these and other prices mentioned in the book may be considered quite imaginary.

42. Í gistihúsinu (Á hótelinu).

Getið þér vísað mér á gott gistihús? Já, Hótel Borg er bezta gistihúsið í bænum. Úr því að þér hafið farangur með yður, er bezt fyrir yður að taka bíl þangað, þó það sé ekki langt. Þarna er dyravörðurinn; hann tekur við dótinu yðar og vísar yður á afgreiðsluna. Dyravörðurinn tekur handtöskurnar og fær (hótel)þjónana til að hjálpa sér með koffortin (fatakoffortið). Við afgreiðsluborðið. Góðan daginn. Gæti ég fengið herbergi hér með heitu og köldu vatni, helzt á móti suðri? Já, það eru herbergi laus bæði á þriðju og fjórðu hæð; þjónn, farðu upp með manninum og sýndu honum herbergin númer 110 og 220; hérna eru lyklarnir. Hvað kosta þau? Annað kostar tuttugu en hitt þrjátíu krónur á dag. Mér þykir það nokkuð dýrt; en það er bezt, að ég líti á herbergin. Mér lízt ekki vel á þetta herbergi, það er of stórt handa mér, og ég er hræddur um, að það sé ónæðissamt; hér er talsverður hávaði af götunni; viljið þér gera svo vel að sýna mér hitt herbergið? Já, það er betra; hér er enginn hávaði (kyrrt og gott); auk þess er það ódýrara; hitt var of dýrt. Viljið þér gera svo vel og láta vekja mig klukkan átta á morgun, og haldið þér (að þér) vilduð láta bursta skóna mína? Já, þér skuluð bara láta þá út fyrir herbergisdyrnar, áður en þér farið að sofa. Getið þér látið mig hafa ábreiðu í viðbót? Ég er hræddur um, að mér verði kalt í nótt. Hafið þér nú allt, sem þér þurfið? Hér er vatnskanna, og í baðherberginu er sápa og handklæði. Viljið þér láta færa yður kaffi (morgunkaffi) upp í herbergið, eða ætlið þér að koma ofan að borða? Það er bezt ég komi ofan.

Gestir gefa þjónum og stúlkum á gistihúsum og matsöluhúsum 10% af reikningnum í drykkjupeninga.

43. Reikningur. Að reikna.

Að leggja saman heitir samlagning. Ef ég legg saman tvo og tvo, fæ ég út fjóra (verður útkoman eða summan fjórir) : $2 + 2 = 4$, tveir og tveir eru fjórir.

Að draga frá heitir frádráttur. Ef ég dreg tvo frá fjórum, fæ ég út tvo (verður útkoman eða afgangurinn tveir) : $4 - 2 = 2$, tveir frá fjórum eru tveir.

Að margfalda heitir margföldun. Ef þú margfaldar fimm með tveimur, færð þú út (kemur út) tíu: $5 . 2 = 10$, tvisvar fimm eru tíu, eða fimm sinnum tveir eru tíu. Allir verða að kunna litlu margföldunartöfluna, hún byrjar svona: einu sinni tveir eru tveir; tvisvar tveir eru fjórir; þrisvar tveir eru sex; fjórum sinnum tveir eru átta; og hún endar á: níu sinnum níu eru áttatíu og einn; níu sinnum tíu eru níutíu.

255

Að deila heitir deiling. Ef maður deilir tveim í tólf, fær maður út (verður útkoman) sex: 12 : 2 = 6, tólf deilt með tveimur er sex, eða tvo í tólf hefur maður sex sinnum.

Ef deiling gengur ekki upp, þá er afgangurinn brot. Ef tveim er deilt í þrjá, þá er útkoman 1½, einn og einn hálfur. Brotin heita: ½ (einn) hálfur, ⅓ einn þriðji, ⅔ tveir þriðju, ¼ einn fjórði, ⅕ einn fimmti, o. s. frv.

Talan, sem er fyrir ofan brotstrikið, heitir teljari, en sú fyrir neðan er kölluð nefnari.

Þegar nefnarinn er tíu, hundrað, þúsund, o. s. frv., verður brotið tugabrot. Almennum brotum má breyta í tugabrot. Þannig er ½ = 0,5, núll komma fimm; ⅓ = 0,33, núll komma þrjátíu og þrír (þrír þrír); ¼ = 0,25, núll komma tuttugu og fimm (tveir fimm) o.s.frv. Íslenzk mynt, mál og vog eru öll í tugabrotum, og léttir það mjög reikning og viðskifti.

Í daglegu tali er 1½ *ekki* einn og einn hálfur, heldur hálfur annar. Á sama hátt: 2½, hálfur þriðji, 3½, hálfur fjórði, o.s.frv. En 1⅓ er *ávallt* einn og einn þriðji.

44. Íslenzkir peningar, mál og vog.

Ein króna er hundrað aurar. Algengustu myntir eru: einseyringur, tveggjaeyringur, fimmeyringur, tíeyringur, tuttugu-og-fimm-eyring-ur, króna og tveggja króna peningur. Af seðlum (bankaseðlum) eru þessir venjulegastir: fimm króna seðill, tíu króna seðill, fimmtíu króna seðill og hundrað króna seðill. Krónur og aurar úr kopar eða nikkel er oft kölluð skiftimynt, smápeningar, eða bara smátt. " Getið þér skift krónu í smátt? " " Ég hef, því miður, ekki svo mikið í smáu." Gengið er skráð í bönkunum og birt í blöðunum.

Bæði mál og vog eru eftir metrakerfinu, sem innleitt var á Íslandi 1912. Áður var mælt í þumlungum, fetum, álnum, föðmum og (dönskum) mílum. Lögur var mældur í pelum, mörkum og pottum, en þyngd í pundum, fjórðungum og vættum. Ein alin var tuttugu og fjórir þumlungar eða tvö fet; þrjár álnir voru í faðmi. Ein míla var 24000 fet. Í potti voru fjórir pelar, en tvær merkur í potti. Einn fjórðungur var tíu pund, en átta eða tíu fjórðungar voru í vætt.

Nú er eining lengdarmálsins metri. Hann skiftist í desímetra (0,1), sentímetra (0,01) og millímetra (0,001), en desímetri mun sjaldan hafður í daglegu tali. Tíu metrar eru í dekametra, 100 í hektómetra, en hvorugt þessara nafna er notað í daglegu tali. Hins-vegar er kílómetri (1000 m.) mjög algengur. Dönsk míla er rúmir 7,5 km. eða um 4,12 enskar mílur.

Lögur er nú mældur í lítrum. Önnur mál eru lítt eða ekki notuð
í daglegu tali. Einn lítri er nálægt því að vera sama sem pottur
(=1,06 quart).

Þyngd er mæld í grömmum, en þau eru helzt notuð á pósthúsinu,
í lyfjafræði og í matreiðslubókum. Þungavara er mæld í kílóum
(kílógrömmum = 1000 gr.). Eitt kíló er hér um bil sama og tvö
pund (= 2,20 amerísk pund).

45. Póstur.

Ég þarf að láta bréf í póstinn. Hvar er pósthúsið? Niðri í bæ.
Eru nokkrir póstkassar hér nálægt, sem ég gæti stungið bréfinu í?
Já, en er þetta almennt bréf? Já, en ég er hræddur um, að það
sé tvöfalt, og ég hef ekki nóg í frímerkjum til að borga undir það.
Hvað er burðargjald fyrir almenn bréf? Tuttugu og fimm aurar
innanlands undir einfalt bréf, fimmtíu aurar undir tvöfalt. Hvað
er burðargjald til útlanda? Fjörutíu og fimm aurar undir einfalt,
níutíu aurar undir tvöfalt bréf. En hvað kostar undir bréfspjald?
Tuttugu aura innanlands, tuttugu og fimm aura til útlanda. Jæja,
ég verð víst að kaupa mér frímerki.

Sendið þér peninga í bréfinu? Nei, en ég lagði innan í það ávísun.
Þá er réttara að setja bréfið í ábyrgð (skrásetja það). Hvað kostar
ábyrgð á bréf? Fjörutíu aura auk burðargjalds, hvort sem er til
útlanda eða innanlands. Ég vil ekki senda peninga í ábyrgðar-
bréfi; er ekki hægt að senda póstávísun hvert sem er? Jú, innanlands er það hægt, en ég veit ekki, hvort hægt er að senda þær til
Englands eða til Ameríku. Þér verðið að spyrja mennina á pósthúsinu (póstþjónana) um það.

Er pósturinn kominn? Ég átti von á bréfi (sendingu, böggli)
með honum. Þér verðið að bíða, þangað til pósturinn er borinn út.
Nei, það er ekki til neins, bréfið bíður mín á pósthúsinu; ég lét
skrifa mér *poste restante*, Reykjavík. Nú—ef svo er, þá verðið
þér að sækja það sjálfur. Ég átti líka von á böggli, ætli böggla-
afgreiðslan sé á sama stað og bréfaafgreiðslan? Spyrjið þér um
það á pósthúsinu.

Nú fór verr en skyldi (Nú er illt í efni), ég er að verða of seinn
að koma bréfunum í póstinn. Skipið fer í fyrramálið, og ég held,
að það sé búið að loka pósthúsinu. Farið þér bara með bréfin og
setjið þau í póstkassann á pósthúsinu.

Er hægt að leigja sér pósthólf hér á pósthúsinu? Já, en spyrjið
þér póstþjónana um það.

Hvernig er með póstinn upp til sveita? Þar eru bæði póstaf-
greiðslur og bréfhirðingar. Það er ekki hægt að afgreiða póst-
ávísanir og póstkröfur á bréfhirðingunum.

46. Sími.

Get ég fengið lánaðan síma hér? Já, gerið þér svo vel. Vitið þér númerið? Nei. Hérna er símaskráin. Ætlið þér að hringja (síma) til einhvers hérna í bænum? Já. Funduð þér númerið? Já. Jæja, hérna er síminn; þér veljið númerið á honum.

Halló, er þetta Jón Helgason? Já, hver er þetta? Komið þér sælir—þetta er John Smith. Já, komið þér nú sælir. Hvað get ég gert fyrir yður? Hvað var það? Vilduð þér tala við mig? Hvern ætluðuð þér að ná í? Ha, ég heyri ekki. Hvað segið þér? Talið þér svolítið hærra, sambandið er svo slæmt.

Þurfið þér að síma út á land? Þá veljið þér töluna 02 (núll tvo) á símanum (símatækinu), en miðstöðvarstúlka svarar. Halló, halló. Má ég fá Landssímann (Landssímastöðina, langlínuna)? Landssíminn! Get ég fengið að tala við Akureyri? Getið þér náð í Akureyri fyrir mig? Ég skal reyna. Akureyri er á tali; á ég að hringja yður upp seinna, þegar Akureyri er laus? Hvaða númer hafið þér? Ég var að spyrja eftir símanúmerinu yðar. Það er 1224, tólf tuttugu og fjórir. Þakka yður fyrir.

Sjálfvirkur sími er aðeins í Reykjavík og Hafnarfirði. Annars staðar hringja menn á miðstöð og biðja um númerið. Halló, má ég fá 124, hundrað tuttugu og fjóra?

Ef þér viljið senda símskeyti (skeyti), farið þér á Landssímastöðina og skrifið skeytið á símskeytaform (eyðublað), sem þeir hafa þar. Ef þér viljið það síður, getið þér hringt á stöðina og beðið þá að taka skeytið og senda yður reikning fyrir því.

Skeyti til útlanda eru send af Ritsímastöðinni. Verð fer eftir því, hvað mörg orð skeytið er.

47. Matsöluhús. Kaffihús.

Í Reykjavík er allmikið af litlum matsöluhúsum, er taka fasta gesti í fæði fyrir visst gjald um mánuðinn, en selja ekki einstakar máltíðir. Á stærri matsöluhúsum og hótelum geta menn keypt fæði yfir mánuðinn, eða til skemmri tíma, og auk þess einstakar máltíðir. Sum af þessum matsöluhúsum kalla sig kaffihús, af því að þau hafa einkum á boðstólum miðaftanskaffi (eftirmiðdagskaffi eða -te) fyrir gesti sína. Miðaftanskaffi (-te) er oftast drukkið frá 3—4, en oft sitja menn lengi yfir því, reykja og rabba saman eða hlusta á útvarpið eða hljómleika (músík) hljómsveitarinnar, ef hún er nokkur. Á kvöldin fæst líka kaffi, te súkkulaði og kökur á kaffihúsunum; fara menn þangað inn, þegar menn koma af kvikmyndahúsunum (bíóunum) eða leikhúsinu. Kaffihúsin koma þannig að nokkru í stað amerískra 'drugstores,' þar sem hægt er að skreppa inn, á hvaða tíma dags sem er, að fá sér hressingu, að nokkru leyti svara þau til 'næturklúbba.' Á sumum þeirra er dans eftir kl. 9, en þeim er öllum lokað kl. 11½ á kvöldin.

Venjulegur matmálstími á matsöluhúsum er:

morgunverður (morgunkaffi)	kl. 8-9
miðdagsmatur	kl. 12-1
miðaftanskaffi (eftirmiðdagskaffi)	kl. 3-4
kvöldmatur	kl. 7-8

Við hátíðleg tækifæri (í veizlum, boðum) er miðdegisverður etinn kl. 6-7, og er sú máltíð oft nefnd miðdagur (middagur).

48. Á matsöluhúsi.

Morgunverður (-matur). Þjónn, ungfrú, fröken! Heyrið þér; get ég fengið að borða? Já, gerið þér svo vel; hérna er autt borð—nei, ekki þarna; þetta borð er upptekið (pantað). Hvað má bjóða yður? Má ég sjá matseðilinn? Gerið þér svo vel—nei, fyrirgefið þér; við höfum víst engan matseðil. Hvað hafið þið þá að borða? Við höfum hafragraut og mjólk (út á), te og smurt brauð með marmelaði, eða sultutaui; þér getið líka fengið kaffi eða mjólk í staðinn fyrir te; svo höfum við egg, linsoðin, harðsoðin, eða steikt. Hafið þér steikt egg og svínsflesk? Nei, því miður; við höfum ekkert flesk núna. Látið þér mig hafa tvö steikt egg, te og brauð með marmelaði—en hvaða brauð hafið þið? Við höfum venjulegt brauð (rúgbrauð), normalbrauð, súrbrauð og franskbrauð. Hafið þér ekki hveitibrauð? Jú, súrbrauð og franskbrauð eru hveitibrauð. Látið þér mig fá þrjár sneiðar af hvoru, og mér þætti vænt um, ef þér vilduð rista (glóðarsteikja) brauðið fyrir mig. Ég skal sjá til þess. Bíðið þér við; ég sé, að þið hafið sykur og rjóma þarna á borðinu, en gæti ég fengið sneið af sítrónu með teinu? Já, það getið þér fengið. Annar gestur: Heyrið þér ungfrú; gætuð þér útvegað mér glas af mjólk, smurt rúgbrauð með rúllupylsu, tvær sneiðar, og smurt flatbrauð með mysuosti? Við höfum ekkert flatbrauð. Jæja, þá tvær sneiðar til af rúgbrauði með mysuosti.

Þegar gesturinn er búinn að borða, kallar hann á þjóninn eða ungfrúna: Þjónn, viljið þér láta mig fá reikninginn? Gerið þér svo vel. Takk, getið þér skift tíu króna seðli í smátt? Ég skal sjá til. Þakka yður fyrir, þér getið tekið afganginn (í drykkjupeninga, þjórfé, það er minnst 10% af upphæð reikningsins). Verið þér sælir. Sælir.

Miðdegisverður. Ungfrú! Gæti ég fengið miðdagsmat hér? Já, gerið þér svo vel. Hvað hafið þið í dag? Við höfum sætsúpu á undan, fisk og kartöflur með bræddu smjöri, og kaffi á eftir. Við höfum hrísgrjónavelling með kanel og sykri og mjólk út á, lambasteik (rifjasteik) með brúnuðum kartöflum, og ávexti eða kaffi á eftir.

Súpan er fyrsti réttur, fiskurinn eða kjötið með grænmeti aðalrétturinn (aðalmaturinn), en kaffið, ávextirnir (eða skyr) eftirréttur (eftirmatur).

49. Íslenzkur matur.

Á Íslandi eru kjöt og fiskur algengustu fæðutegundirnar. Af kjöti er sauðakjöt algengast. Það er líka kallað kindakjöt, og, ef það er af lömbum, lambakjöt eða dilkakjöt. Næst því gengur nautakjöt, þar næst hrossakjöt og svínakjöt (flesk, svínslæri), sem til skamms tíma a. m. k. hefur verið heldur sjaldgæft. Hænsnakjöt er ekki almennt, í stað þess má stundum fá rjúpur, sem þykja hátíðamatur. Kjöt er étið nýtt, fryst, saltað og reykt eða hangið. Hangikjöt (sauðarlæri) er uppáhaldsmatur Íslendinga.

Fiskur. Algengustu fisktegundirnar eru þorskur, ýsa og heilagfiski (flyðra, spraka, lúða, lúra, koli), en auk þess má fá síld og ufsa, lax og silung (urriða, bleikju, murtu). Fiskur er étinn nýr, frystur, saltaður (saltfiskur), hertur (harðfiskur), reyktur og niðursoðinn. Niðursoðin síld (kryddsíld, gaffalbitar) er herramannsmatur. Harðfiskur og smjör er þjóðréttur Íslendinga.

Grænmeti. Algengast grænmeti eru kartöflur og rófur. Auk þess má fá: næpur, gulrætur, rauðrófur, hreðkur (radísur), hvítkál, blómkál, rauðkál, grænkál, spínat og salat. Rabarbari er algengur, en tómatar, gúrkur, melónur og jafnvel vínber vaxa í gróðurhúsum við laugahita.

Súpur, grautar og vellingar. Súpur eða grautar eru oft étin á undan (eða eftir) aðalmatnum. Hafragrautur með mjólk er venjulegur morgunmatur (áður bankabyggsgrautur). Til miðdagsmatar eru ýmsir mjólkurgrautar algengir: hrísgrjónagrautur, hrísmjölsgrautur, rjómagrautur, þ. e. þykkur hrísgrjónavellingur með rúsínum, kanel og sykri út á, sem er algengur jólamatur um öll Norðurlönd. Ennfremur áfasúpa og smjörgrautur. Sætsúpa úr kirsiberja- eða hindberjasaft, bláberjasúpa og rabarbarasúpa. Rauðgrautur, rabarbaragrautur, eplagrautur og sveskjugrautur. Kjötsúpa er oft borðuð með nýju eða söltu kjöti, súrsæt fiskisúpa með nýjum fiski (einkum hrognkelsum), baunir með feitu saltkjöti (saltkjöt og baunir).

Mjólkurmatur. Mest af nýmjólkinni er gerilsneytt og selt í mjólkurbúðum. Annars er mjólkin skilin í rjóma og undanrennu. Úr rjómanum er búið til smjör, úr undanrennunni (stundum líka úr nýmjólkinni) mjólkurostur af ýmsum gerðum eða skyr. Þegar ostur er tekinn úr mjólkinni, verður eftir mysa; úr henni er búinn til mysuostur. Áfir verða eftir, þegar smjör er tekið úr rjómanum. Skyr er hvergi notað nema á Íslandi og í Frakklandi, það er uppáhaldsréttur Íslendinga, þeir éta það nýtt með sykri eða berjum og rjóma út á.

Ávextir. Algengust íslenzk ber eru: kræk iber, bláber, aðalbláber; hrútaber eru sjaldgæfari, en jarðarber sjaldgæfust. Algengustu innfluttir ávextir eru: epli, appelsínur (glóaldin), perur, bananar og sítrónur. Þurrkaðir ávextir: rúsínur, sveskjur, gráfíkjur (fíkjur), döðlur, kúrenur, epli. Niðursoðnir ávextir: ananas (granaldin), perur, ferskjur, apríkósur, jarðarber. Á krepputímum hafa Íslendingar orðið að banna innflutning á ávöxtum.

Brauð: rúgbrauð, seytt (hverabrauð) og óseytt (venjulegt brauð), sigtibrauð, normalbrauð, súrbrauð, franskbrauð. Í sveitum var siður að baka brauð undir potti (pottbrauð) eða á glóð; glóðarbakaða brauðið var ósýrt og bakað í þunnum kringlóttum kökum, sem kallaðar voru flatkökur, eða flatbrauð. Það er bezt heitt eða volgt með smjöri. Hart brauð: kex, kringlur, tvíbökur; sænskt hrökkbrauð.

Kökur. Jólakaka, sódakaka, pönnukökur, lummur og kleinur eru mjög vinsælar kökur (kaffibrauð) um allt land. Algeng í bæjunum eru vínarbrauð, snúðar, bollur og sykurkringlur. Smákökur eða kaffibrauð: gyðingakökur, piparkökur, hálfmánar. Ennþá fínni eru rjómakökur og tertur (rjómaterta).

50. Bankar, búðir, verzlanir.

Árið 1939 voru í Reykjavík þrír bankar (Landsbankinn, Útvegsbankinn, og Búnaðarbankinn), 70 heildsölur og 543 smásölur. Heildsöluverzlanirnar selja í heildsölu, smásöluverzlanirnar í smásölu.

Af þessum búðum eru engar 5 og 10 senta búðir, en til er þó ein verzlun, sem líkist þeim: hið svo nefnda Nora-magasín. Engin stór vörudeildahús (department stores) á amerískan mælikvarða eru þar heldur, en margar stærri verzlanir, ekki sízt vefnaðarvöruverzlanir (Haraldur Árnason, Vöruhúsið, o. fl.), eru að vaxa í þá átt og hafa undirdeildir með óskyldum vörutegundum. Amerískar lyfjabúðir (drugstores) eru alveg óþekktar, því íslenzkar lyfjabúðir (apótek) selja aðeins lyf (meðul) og hreinlætis- eða snyrtivörur. Miklu minna kveður að verzlunum með útibúum (chain stores) heldur en í Ameríku (A & P Stores, American Stores), en þó eru þær til í Reykjavík (t. d. Silli og Valdi, Kiddabúðir). Svipuð útibús-

261

verzlununum eru líka kaupfélögin, sem eru mjög mikill og sterkur
þáttur í íslenzkri verzlun, bæði í Reykjavík og einkum úti um land.
Þau eru flest í Sambandi hinna íslenzku samvinnufélaga (SÍS),
sem hefur miðstöð sína í Reykjavík. Annars eru helztu samvinnu-
félög í Reykjavík: Kaupfélag Reykjavíkur og nágrennis (KRON)
og Sláturfélag Suðurlands (SS), sem selur kjöt og landbúnaðar-
afurðir fyrir bændur á Suðurlandsundirlendinu.

Einkasölur, reknar til hagsmuna fyrir ríkið, eru áfengisverzlunin,
bifreiðaeinkasalan, viðtækjaverzlun ríkisins og tóbakseinkasalan.

Í litlum kaupstöðum úti um land hafa verzlanir eða kaupfélög
allt, sem á annað borð er selt á staðnum í einni búð (general store).
Slíkar búðir eru enn til, einkum í útjöðrum Reykjavíkur.

Af því, sem nú hefur verið sagt, er auðséð, að verzlanir í Reykjavík eru nú meira eða minna sérhæfðar, án þess þó, að þær bindi
sig að öllu við eina vörutegund.

Matvöruverzlanir má einkum flokka eftir því, hvort þær verzla
mestmegnis með innlendan eða útlendan mat.

Þær, sem verzla með innlendan mat, eru helzt fiskverzlanir,
kjötbúðir (oft í nýlenduvöruverzlunum) og mjólkurbúðir. Mjólkur-
búðirnar selja oft brauð, og á hinn bóginn er oft seld mjólk í
brauðbúðum eða bakaríum. Grænmeti er ekki selt í sérstökum
búðum, heldur annaðhvort í kjötbúðunum, eða í nýlenduvöru-
verzlununum.

Verzlanir, sem selja útlenda matvöru, eru kallaðar nýlenduvöruverzlanir. Þær hafa t. d. kaffi, te, sykur; kornvörur: hveiti, rúgmjöl,
hrísgrjón, haframjöl, bygggrjón, maís, baunir, ertur, sagógrjón; alls
konar niðursoðinn mat (dósamat): ávexti, fisk (sardínur) og kjöt.
Auk þess selja þær oft innlendan mat: kjöt og grænmeti, sjaldnar
fisk. Stundum selja nýlenduvöruverzlanir líka hreinlætisvörur eins
og sápu o. fl., en til eru líka búðir, sem verzla eingöngu með þær.

Sápuhúsið og Sápubúðin eru slíkar hreinlætisvörubúðir. Þar
geta menn keypt sápur: handsápu og þvottasápur. Ennfremur
snyrtivörur svo sem raksápu, rakvélar, rakbursta, hárgreiður; tann-
bursta, tannduft, tannpasta; ilmvötn, hárvötn, ilmsmyrsl, andlits-
farða, varalit o. s. frv.

Vefnaðarvöruverzlanir eru með stærstu fyrirtækjum í Reykjavík.
Þær kalla sig stundum vöruhús, vefnaðarvörudeildir, eða fatabúðir.
Í þeim eru seld (tilbúin) föt eða fataefni, innlend og útlend. Af
innlendum fataefnum eru dúkar og efni frá Álafossi og Gefjun,
tveim stærstu klæðaverksmiðjum landsins, merkust. Efni í föt getur
verið vaðmál, klæði, ullardúkar, tvisttau, baðmullartau, léreft, sirz,
silki o. s. frv.

SKAUTBÚNINGUR.

Tilbúin karlmannsföt: jakkaföt (eða bara föt), smóking, kjólföt, eru sjaldgæf; menn láta sauma þau á sig. En peysur, frakkar, yfirfrakkar, regnkápur, regnfrakkar og reiðföt eru venjulega keypt tilbúin. Nærföt eru: nærskyrtur, nærbuxur (brækur), skyrtur (mannséttskyrtur) með linum eða hörðum flibba. Þar með fylgja slaufur (við kjólföt), slifsi eða hálsbindi, skyrtuhnappar. Enn er að nefna sokka, sokkabönd, axlabönd og belti. Hattar eru ýmist harðir eða linir, auk pípuhattanna, sem fylgja kjólfötunum. Loks eru hanzkar, fingravettlingar og belgvettlingar eða bara vettlingar. Íslenzkir ullarsokkar og ullarvettlingar eru miklu hlýrri en útlendir sokkar og vettlingar.

Kvennmannsföt eru: kjólar, útiföt (dragtir), jakkar, treyjur, blússur, peysur, pils og svuntur; kápur, regnkápur, loðkápur; kjólkragar, loðkragar, refir. Nærföt: nærskyrtur, nærbuxur, sokkabandsbelti, undirkjólar eða millipils. Sokkar: silkisokkar, baðmullarsokkar, ullarsokkar. Hattar, húfur og hanzkar eða vettlingar.

Íslenzku búningarnir fást víst sjaldan eða aldrei í búðum, heldur eru saumaðir fyrir þá eða þær, sem vilja. Þeir eru þrenns konar og allir einkennilegir og fallegir. Fyrsti og algengasti búningurinn er upphlutur með millum, treyju, pilsi og svuntu. Ungar stúlkur ganga oft á upphlut. Annar algengur búningur eru peysufötin með skotthúfu, treyju, slifsi, brjóstnál, pilsi og svuntu. Rosknar konur bera oft peysuföt, og fer þeim vel. Loks er skautbúningurinn. Það er sjaldséður hátíðabúningur, sem konur bera helzt við fermingu eða giftingu. Hann er með hvítu skauti og hvítri slæðu. Honum fylgir skauttreyja og pils með stokkabelti úr silfri eða gulli. Stundum fylgir honum möttull.

Skóverzlanir selja skó, stígvél, gúmmískó, gúmmístígvél, reiðstígvél; brúna, gula hvíta og svarta skó; brúnan, gulan, hvítan og svartan skóáburð (skósvertu); skóhlífar og inniskó. Skóverzlanir hafa líka oft sokka. Íslenzkir skór (sauðskinnsskór) munu nú ekki sjást nema sums staðar í sveitum, þeir voru léttir og liprir, en héldu illa vatni.

Af öðrum verzlunum er helzt ástæða til að nefna sportvöruverzlanir, er selja ferðaföt, tjöld, byssur, fiskistengur, veiðarfæri, sjónauka, ljósmyndavélar o. fl., sem ferðamenn og íþróttamenn mega ekki án vera. Annars má rétt nefna járnvöruverzlanir, glervöruverzlanir, timburverzlanir, húsgagnaverzlanir og bókaverzlanir, sem bæði eru margar og tiltölulega góðar í Reykjavík.

51. Að fara í búðir.

Ég þarf að fara í búðir og gera innkaup í dag; vilduð þér nú

ekki gera svo vel að koma með mér? Það er velkomið, en hvert
ætlið þér? Fyrst þarf ég að fara í banka og fá dollurum (enskum
pundum) skift í íslenzka peninga; ég er með 100 dollara ávísun
frá banka í New York. (Í bankanum) Góðan daginn. Vilduð þér
gera svo vel að kaupa þessa ávísun af mér? Já, það er víst hægt.
Hvað er gengið núna? Það er 6.51 kr. (fyrir dollarann), en þér
verðið að borga lítils háttar afföll af ávísuninni í innheimtukostnað.
Það er allt í lagi. Viljið þér fá peningana í stórum seðlum eða
smáum? Látið þér mig fá fimm hundrað króna seðla, en hitt í
smáu, helzt í tíu króna seðlum. Gerið þér svo vel.

Hvar fær maður sápu og rakáhöld? Við gætum reynt í Sápu-
húsinu. Góðan daginn. Hvað var það fyrir yður? Má ég sjá
rakvélarnar ykkar? Já, gerið þér svo vel. Hvernig eru blöðin í
þessari? Þau bíta mjög vel, segja þeir, sem brúka þau. Þá held ég,
að ég taki hana, en svo þarf ég líka að fá rakbursta, raksápu og
handsápu. Gerið þér svo vel. Hvað kostar þetta allt? Augnablik;
þetta verður alls fimmtán krónur og fjörutíu aurar (15.40 kr.).
Takk. Sælar. Sælir.

Svo þarf ég endilega að kaupa mér nærföt og sokka. Þá er bezt
að fara í Vöruhúsið eða til Haraldar (Árnasonar). Góðan daginn.
Má ég fá að líta á nærfötin hjá ykkur? Það er velkomið, áttu það
að vera nærföt úr ull eða bómull (baðmull)? Ég vil þau heldur
úr ull. Svo þarf ég líka að fá mér skyrtur með linum flibba. Áttu
þær að vera hvítar eða mislitar? Ég vil helst ljósar röndóttar
skyrtur. Hvaða númer brúkið þér? Númer 16. Gerið þér svo vel.
Var það nokkuð fleira? Já, hafið þið lagleg slifsi? Við höfum
heilmikið úrval af slifsum, þetta hérna fer yður vel. Já. Þér
ætluðuð að taka sokka líka? Já. Áttu það að vera silkisokkar eða
ullarsokkar? Ullarsokkar, helzt gráir. Gerið þér svo vel.

Þá á ég nú eftir að fá mér skó; hvert ætti maður að fara til
þess? Ætli það sé ekki bezt að fara til Lárusar Lúðvígssonar?
Góðan daginn. Má ég fá að líta á skó hjá yður? Augnablik. Nú
skal ég strax afgreiða yður. Hvers konar skó voruð þér að hugsa
um, góða skó, eða sterka gönguskó? Hafið þér brúna skó, létta og
ekki of stirða? Já, hvernig passa þessir? Þeir meiða mig á tánum;
þeir eru víst of þröngir. Við skulum nú sjá; yfirleðrið á þessum
skóm er mýkra og þeir eru ívið breiðari. Já, ég held, að þeir séu
ágætir. Hvað á ég að borga? 65.50 kr. Takk. Verið þér sælir.
Sælir.

52. Hjá klæðskera.

Ég þarf nauðsynlega að fá mér föt; ætti ég að kaupa þau tilbúin í búð eða láta klæðskera sauma þau á mig? Tilbúin föt eru auðvitað nokkuð ódýrari, en flestir láta sauma sér föt, því þau fara betur.

(Hjá klæðskeranum.) Góðan daginn. Sælir. Ég vildi gjarnan kaupa af yður föt, má ég sjá fataefnin yðar? Hvernig ætti þau að vera, blá föt úr kambgarni eða séfíoti? Nei, ég vil helzt grátt efni úr alull, ekki of þykkt. Hérna hef ég ljómandi fallegt grátt ullartau, hvernig lízt yður á það? Vel, held ég; hvað kostar það? Það er fjörutíu krónur metrinn. Ég held ég megi taka það. Jæja; þá er að taka mál af yður. Viljið þér hafa uppbrot á buxunum? Já, og passið þér að hafa skálmirnar hvorki of víðar né of síðar. Vestið má heldur ekki vera of sítt, þetta er mátulegt. Ég vil hafa jakkann einhnepptan, ég kann ekki við mig í tvíhnepptum fötum. Og hann má ekki vera of þröngur um herðarnar. Viljið þér hafa ermarnar langar eða stuttar? Ekki of langar. Viljið þér hafa loku á vösunum, eða ekki? Ég kann betur við að hafa loku. Jæja, þá er allt í lagi. Hvenær geta fötin orðið tilbúin? Ekki fyrr en eftir þrjár vikur. Það er nokkuð seint. Já, en við höfum svo mikið að gera. Og hvað eiga fötin að kosta? 360 kr. Já, það er sanngjarnt verð. Verið þér nú sælir. Sælir.

53. Viðgerðir, þvottar, hreinsun.

Ef úrið yðar stanzar (hættir að ganga), þá farið þér með það til úrsmiðs. Hann hreinsar það, setur í það fjöður eða hjól, og gerir við hvað annað í því, sem kann að vera bilað.

Ef þér þurfið að láta gera við skóna yðar, þá farið þér til skósmiðs. Þér getið líka farið í skóverzlunina, sem seldi yður skóna, ef hún hefur skóverkstæði. Þeir sóla skóna, hálfsóla þá eða setja á þá hæla.

Ef þér þurfið að láta þvo þvott (nærföt, skyrtur, sokka), þá farið þér með hann í þvottahús, eða útvegið yður þvottakonu. Og ef þér þurfið að láta hreinsa föt, þá farið þér með þau í gufuhreinsun, sem hreinsar þau og pressar, eða í efnalaug, sem hreinsar þau án þess að þvo þau upp úr vatni.

54. Skemmtanir.

Í Reykjavík er helzta skemmtun manna að fara í kvikmyndahúsin (bíóin) og í leikhúsið. Í kvikmyndahúsunum eru sýndar amerískar, enskar, franskar, þýzkar og norrænar myndir. Leikhúsið sýnir íslenzk og útlend leikrit; flest þeirra eru leikin af Leikfélagi Reykjavíkur, sem hefur nokkrum góðum leikurum á að skipa. Mjög vinsælir eru skopleikirnir, sem kallaðir eru ' revýur,' þeir eru venjulega teknir beint út úr bæjarlífinu. Stundum leika mennta-skólapiltar eða aðrir. Verð á aðgöngumiðum fer eftir því, hve mikil aðsókn er að sýningunni; það fer líka eftir því, hver sætin eru: ódýrustu sæti voru aftast niðri; önnur sæti niðri voru oft ódýrari en sæti á svölunum; en sæti í stúkum eru dýrust. Að reykja, tala eða blístra í leikhúsi eða kvikmyndahúsi þykir ósvinna.

Hljómleikar eru alltíðir. Reykjavík á vísi til hljómsveitar, hljómlistarskóla og allmarga hljómlistarmenn: organleikara, píanóleikara, fiðluleikara og söngvara. Kirkjuhljómleikar eru oft ágætir, sömuleiðis einsöngvar með píanóundirspili eða einleikur á fiðlu með undirspili. En það sem helzt einkennir sönglíf á Íslandi eru hinir ágætu karlakórar í Reykjavík og úti um land. Þeir hafa mjög þjálfaðar raddir og syngja svo hreint, að unun er á að hlýða. Hljómleikar eru nú haldnir í sal Háskólans, auk þess eru hljómleikar fastur liður á skemmtiskrá útvarpsins, sem notar bæði innlenda söngkrafta og útlendar grammófónplötur (symfóníur o. s. frv.).

Reykjavík er full af listamönnum, einkum málurum. Frægastur listamannanna mun vera myndhöggvarinn Einar Jónsson, og enginn, sem til Reykjavíkur kemur, má láta undir höfuð leggjast að heimsækja listasafn hans í Hnitbjörgum. Af málurum, sem búa í Reykjavík, má nefna Ásgrím Jónsson, sem mun vera þeirra elztur, og Jóhannes Kjarval, sem tvímælalaust er þeirra fjölhæfastur. Málararnir hafa stundum málverkasýningar, og má telja það með beztu skemmtunum í Reykjavík. Annars eru verk þeirra vinsæl, og hús flestra betri borgara í Reykjavík eru full af málverkum. Málverkasafn ríkisins er í Alþingishúsinu.

Dansleikir eru algeng skemmtun alls staðar. Karlmenn (herrar) bjóða stúlkum (dömum) á dansleikinn (dansinn), en í danssalnum bjóða þeir þeim upp og dansa við þær. Dansar eru alþjóðlegir; menn dansa vals, tangó, foxtrott, rumbu, eða hvað þeir nú heita þessir nýju dansar.

Á vetrum fara menn á skautum og skíðum. Skíðabrekkurnar eru alllangt frá Reykjavík, menn fara þangað í bílum.

Á sumrin fara menn í ferðalög upp í sveitir, eða jafnvel upp um fjöll og firnindi. Ferðafélagið stendur oft fyrir þessum ferðum, það hefur skrifstofu í Reykjavík og auglýsir ferðir sínar í blöðunum. Menn fara með áætlunarbílum eins langt og þeir fara eða leigja sér bíla til fararinnar. Í sveitunum leigja menn sér hesta til að ríða inn í óbyggðir, eða á fjöllin, eða hvert sem bílar komast ekki. Stundum hafa menn með sér tjöld og liggja úti svo dögum skiftir. Sumir fara í sumarfrí og dvelja um tíma í alþýðuskólunum, sem reistir hafa verið víða um land og eru notaðir fyrir gistihús á sumrin. Til eru og önnur gistihús við þjóðveginn, en þau eru fremur misjöfn að gæðum. Menn geta líka stundum komið sér

266

fyrir á bóndabæjum eða prestsetrum til sumardvalar um lengri eða skemmri tíma.

Lax- og silungsveiðar eru ágæt skemmtun, enda hafa efnaðir Englendingar, auk landsmanna sjálfra, svo árum skiftir lagt stund á þær í beztu veiðiám landsins. Góðar laxár eru uppi í Borgarfirði og víðar um landið. Menn verða að kaupa réttinn til að veiða eða veiðileyfið af eiganda árinnar. Lax og silungur er veiddur með stöng og flugu eða annari beitu. Nóg er af ánamöðkum. Við Mývatn og við Sogið er og mikil silungsveiði, en þar er líka mikið mýbit (mikill mývargur), og er bezt að búa sig út með verjur gegn því (honum).

Þeim, sem gaman hafa af fuglum, mun seint leiðast á Íslandi, því þar er geysimargt af fuglum, og fjölbreytt fuglalíf bæði til lands og sjávar. Sumt af þessum fuglum eru staðfuglar, en margt eru farfuglar. Sumir lifa við sjó eða vötn, aðrir á landi uppi. Af landfuglum ber mest á lóum, spóum, og hrossagaukum að sumrinu til; hrafninn er algengur árið um kring. Smáfuglar algengir við bæi eru máríuerlur, snjótittlingar (sólskríkjur) og steindeplar. Svanir og alls konar tegundir af öndum eru algengir á vötnum og ám; óðinshanar sjást oft á litlum lækjum eða síkjum. Við sjóinn eru ýmsar tegundir af máfum og svartfugli, skarfar og kjóar. En mest ber þó á kríunni á vorin og æðarfuglinum árið um kring. Æðarfuglinn er friðaður árið um kring, því hann er mesti nytjafugl, gefur af sér egg og dún. Mikill fjöldi íslenzkra fugla er friðaður, og Íslendingar gera lítið að því að skjóta þá, sem ófriðaðir eru, nema helzt rjúpur, sem skotnar eru á vetrum, og ýmsa sjófugla, sem annaðhvort eru skaðlegir eða eru góðir til átu. Af ránfuglum má nefna örninn, sem er sjaldgæfur, og fálkann eða valinn, sem er frægur mjög sem veiðifugl og kóngsgersemi að fornu og nýju.

55. Kirkja og hátíðir.

Íslendingar eru langflestir lúterstrúar og hafa verið það síðan um miðja sextándu öld. Kirkjan er þjóðkirkja, en fáeinir söfnuðir hafa myndað fríkirkju. Lúterskir helgisiðir koma sumum amerískum mótmælendum einkennilega fyrir sjónir. Þar á meðal er skrúði prestsins. Hann er í skósíðri hempu, svartri, með hvítan pípukraga um hálsinn. Í þessum búningi stígur hann í stólinn og fremur öll prestsverk utan kirkju: skírir, gefur saman hjón (giftir) og jarðar. En undir sjálfri messunni, fyrir altarinu, ber prestur hvítt rykkilín, sem hylur alla hempuna, og yfir rykkilíníð steypir hann hökli, lítilli útsaumaðri kápu, er liggur laus á öxlunum, en hylur bak og brjóst að nokkru.

267

Þegar hringt hefur verið til messu, gengur fólk í kirkju, en með-hjálparinn les bæn í kórdyrum. Þá er sunginn sálmur, og síðan hefst messan. Prestur stendur alskrýddur fyrir altari og ávarpar söfnuðinn: "Drottinn sé með yður." Forsöngvarinn og fólkið anzar: "Og með þínum anda." Þá tónar prestur bæn ("Látum oss biðja"), en söfnuðurinn syngur amen. Því næst tónar klerkur pistilinn ("Pistilinn skrifar postulinn Páll"). Þá er sunginn sálmur, og eftir það ávarpar prestur söfnuðinn aftur, sem í byrjun messu, og tónar síðan guðspjallið ("Guðspjallið skrifar guðspjalla-maðurinn Matteus," söfnuðurinn tekur þá undir: "Guði sé lof og dýrð fyrir hans gleðilegan boðskap"). Eftir guðspjall er enn sunginn sálmur, síðan stígur prestur í stólinn og prédikar (flytur prédikun). Á eftir prédikun les prestur bæn, en söfnuðurinn syngur sálm. Þá fer prestur fyrir altarið og tónar bæn. Að henni lokinni ávarpar hann söfnuðinn í þriðja sinn og blessar hann (seinni blessunin). Þá er útgöngusálmurinn sunginn, meðhjálpari les bæn í kórdyrum og hringir til útgöngu: guðsþjónustunni er lokið. Hljóð-fallið í íslenzkum kirkjusöng er hægara og hátíðlegra en í ensk-amerískum kirkjusöng.

Stórhátíðir ársins eru jól, nýjár, páskar og hvítasunna. Jólin eru þríheilög, þau byrja á jólanóttina, sem hefur á sér hina mestu helgi af öllum hátíðisdögum ársins. Jólanóttin er kvöld aðfangadags jóla. Þá kemur jóladagurinn (25. desember). Þá kemur annar í jólum, og í gamla daga var haldið heilagt allt fram á þrettánda í jólum, eða þrettándann, sem nú er svo kallaður. Enn halda menn stundum upp á þrettándann með brennum og (álfa)dönsum. Gamlárskvöld er kvöldið fyrir nýjársdaginn. Næsti sunnudagur fyrir páska er pálmasunnudagur, en fimmtudagurinn í páskavikunni heitir skírdagur; næsti dagur er föstudagurinn langi. Tvíheilagt er bæði á páskum og hvítasunnu, en milli þeirra er uppstigningar-dagurinn. Börn eru oft fermd á hvítasunnunni.

Á hátíðum er siður að óska mönnum gleðilegrar hátíðar: "Gleði-leg jól!" "Þakk, ég óska þér þess sama. Þakk í sama máta." "Gleðilegt nýjár, og þakka þér fyrir gamla árið!" "Þakk, sömuleiðis; þakka þér sjálfum." Um jól og nýjár senda menn kunningjum og vinum jóla- og nýjárskort: Gleðileg jól og gott nýjár! Gleðileg jól og farsælt nýjár! Innilegar óskir um gleðileg jól og gott nýjár, frá (þínum elskandi syni) Bjössa. Á páskum og hvítasunnu: "Góðan dag og gleðilega hátíð!" "Þakk, sömuleiðis."

56. Skólar, bækur, rithöfundar.

Íslenzk börn eru skólaskyld; þau fara í barnaskóla, þegar þau eru sjö ára, og eru í honum, þar til þau eru fjórtán ára. Þá geta þau farið í miðskólana: gagnfræðaskóla og lýðskóla fyrir pilta og stúlkur og kvennaskóla fyrir stúlkur. Síðar geta þau farið í kennaraskóla, verzlunarskóla, samvinnuskóla, stýrimannaskóla, vélstjóraskóla og iðnskóla eða hússtjórnarskóla. Þau, sem vilja halda áfram námi, fara úr gagnfræðaskólunum í lærdómsdeildir menntaskólanna tveggja í Reykjavík og á Akureyri. Upp úr þeim taka þau stúdentspróf (og eru þá kölluð stúdentar), og eiga þau þá rétt á inntöku í Háskólann.

Í lægri skólum er lesið: íslenzka, danska (eða sænska), enska, kristin fræði, saga, náttúrufræði, landafræði og stærðfræði. En í lærdómsdeildum menntaskólanna bætast hér við: latína, þýzka og franska, auk áframhaldandi náms í hinum námsgreinunum. Lærdómsdeild menntaskólanna er skift í tvær deildir, máladeild og stærðfræðideild.

Í Háskólanum lesa allir forspjallsvísindi (rökfræði, sálarfræði) fyrsta veturinn, en annars er skólanum skift í deildir: heimspekideild, er auk forspjallsvísinda kennir norrænu og íslenzku (sögu, málfræði og bókmenntir), guðfræðideild, laga- og hagfræði-deild, læknadeild og verkfræðideild, sem enn er í bernsku. Þeir, sem lokið hafa námi í þessum deildum, eru kallaðir kandídatar (cand. mag., theol., juris., med., polyt.) eða norrænufræðingar, guðfræðingar, lögfræðingar, læknar og verkfræðingar. Þeir eiga rétt til embætta í landinu. Aðeins norrænudeildin útskrifar líka meistara (mag. art.), en allar eldri deildirnar hafa gefið mönnum doktorspróf (dr. phil., theol., jur., med.).

Í Reykjavík er beztur bókakostur á landinu. Stærst bókasafn er Landsbókasafnið; í því eru bæði bækur og handrit; það er í Safnahúsinu; þar eru líka Þjóðskjalasafnið, Þjóðminjasafnið og Náttúrugripasafnið. Önnur bókasöfn í Reykjavík eru Alþýðubókasafnið og Háskólabókasafnið.

Bókaútgáfa er meiri á Íslandi að tiltölu við fólksfjölda en í flestum, ef ekki öllum, öðrum löndum,[1] enda er margt af bókabúðum (-verzlunum) í Reykjavík. Þær, sem hafa gamlar bækur til sölu, eru kallaðar fornsölur eða fornbókaverzlanir. Hljóðfæraverzlanir verzla með hljóðfæri, hljómplötur og nótur.

Bókaútgefendur eru líka allmargir, en hér skal aðeins minnzt á nokkur bókaútgáfufélög. Elzt þeirra er Hið íslenzka bókmenntafélag (1816—). Það gefur meðal annars út tímaritið Skírni, sem nú er elzta tímarit á Norðurlöndum. Næstelzt er Hið íslenzka þjóðvinafélag (1869—). Það gefur út vinsælt almanak (Almanak hins

[1] In 1930 one book per 12,497 persons was published in the U. S. A. In Iceland it was one book per 466 persons.

269

íslenzka þjóðvinafélags) og tímaritið Andvara. Hið íslenzka fornleifafélag (1879—) og Ferðafélag Íslands (1928—) gefa út árbækur.
Fornritafélag Íslands (1928—) gefur út íslenzk fornrit í prýðilegum
útgáfum. Mál og menning (1938—) gefur út Tímarit Máls og
menningar og aðrar bækur. Bókaútgáfa Menningarsjóðs (1940—)
tók að sér útgáfu Þjóðvinafélagsins og gefur auk þess út þýðingar
og aðrar bækur.

Ísland hefur alltaf átt mjög mörg skáld og rithöfunda að tiltölu
við fólksfjölda. Á tólftu og þrettándu öld var Ísland miðstöð
andlegrar menningar á Norðurlöndum, og enn byrjar bókmenntasaga allra þjóða á Norðurlöndum, og einkum Norðmanna, á bók-
menntum Íslendinga. Eddurnar og sögurnar eru kunnar um allan
hinn menntaða heim, og þeirra vegna er forníslenzka kennd í nær
þrjátíu háskólum í Bandaríkjunum. Skáldskapur og bókvísi dóu
aldrei út á Íslandi, en hér er ekki rúm til annars en að benda á
helztu núlifandi íslenzka höfunda. Davíð Stefánsson mun vera
vinsælastur af skáldunum. Af öðrum má nefna Jakob Thórarenssen,
Jón Magnússon,[1] Jóhannes úr Kötlum og Tómas Guðmundsson, sem
er þeirra mestur formsnillingur. Af skáldsagnahöfundum er Guðmundur bóndi Friðjónsson á Sandi elztur.[1] Hann hefur skrifað
smásögur og ljóð. Frægastur er Gunnar Gunnarsson, einn af
þekktustu höfundum á Norðurlöndum. Af yngri mönnum má nefna
Guðmund G. Hagalín, sem skrifar sjómannasögur, Kristmann Guðmundsson, sem er snjall ástarsöguhöfundur, og Halldór Kiljan
Laxness, sem vera mun þeirra gáfaðastur og slyngastur rithöfundur.
Ekki má heldur gleyma Þórbergi Þórðarsyni, sem hefur skrifað
merkilega sjálfsæfisögu.

57. Uppi í sveit.

Íslenzkir bændur búa ekki í þorpum, heldur á bæjum, hver út af
fyrir sig. Það hafa þeir gert síðan á landnámstíð, enda eru bæirnir
margir svo gamlir og bera sömu nöfnin og þeir hafa í Landnámu,
því íslenzkir bæir heita alltaf einhverju nafni, þvert á móti því
sem tíðkast í Ameríku, þar sem bæir eru venjulega nafnlausir.

Íslenzk bæjanöfn enda oft á -staðir, -kot, -gerði, -hús, -bær, -land,
-búð. Þessi nöfn gefa það í skyn, að búið hafi verið á staðnum
(sömuleiðis -ból, -bú). Önnur nöfn eru dregin af húsum, mann-
virkjum, eða búskaparháttum, svo sem -naust, -tóft, -fjós, -hlaða,
-skemma; -sel, -stekkur, -stöðull, -tún. Sum eru dregin af vegum:
-gata, -tröð, og loks eru mörg dregin af landslagi, eins og Bakki,
Hóll, Holt, Tunga, Eyri, Fell, Nes, Foss, Borg, o. fl.

Langflest eru heitin, sem enda á -staðir, og er fyrri liður þeirra

[1] Died 1944.

GAMALL BÆR.

oftast mannsnafn, t. d. Þorvaldsstaðir; það þýðir auðvitað 'staður eða bær Þorvalds.' Eintala er sjaldan notuð í þessum nöfnum, nema um kirkjustað sé að ræða. Dæmi um önnur nöfn: Múlakot, Bakka-gerði, Miðhús, Kirkjubær, Eyrarland, Kirkjuból, Nautabú, Tóarsel, Gilsárstekkur, Ártún.

En víkjum nú aftur að bændunum. Þeir hafa um langan aldur lifað, og lifa enn flestir, á kvikfjárrækt. Þeir hafa sauðfé, nautgripi og hesta og framleiða ull, kjöt og mjólk. Þessi húsdýr eru fóðruð á heyi, enda eru störf sveitabóndans mest í því falin að afla heyja (að heyja) handa skepnunum að sumrinu og hirða þær að vetrinum. Á síðustu árum hafa menn tekið upp svínarækt og loðdýrabúskap (á refabúum).

Hver bóndi á venjulega víðáttumikið land (til jafnaðar um 1500 ekrur). Næst bænum er þetta land ræktað með áburði og afgirt til að verja það fyrir skepnunum. Þetta land er kallað tún; það er sama orð og *town* og þýðir eiginlega afgirtur blettur. Hey af túninu er kallað taða; það er bezta fóðrið, notað handa kúm, ám og reiðhestum. Túnið sprettur fyrst og er slegið fyrst. Næst koma engjar, grasgefnir en óræktaðir hlutar af landinu. Þær eru slegnar síðar en túnið (túnasláttur og útengjasláttur). Allt annað land (úthagi) er notað fyrir beitiland, bæði sumar og vetur, ef það er nógu grösugt til þess.

Um húsaskipun á gömlu bæjunum er þegar talað.[1] Á nýju bæjunum eru húsin annaðhvort úr timbri eða steinsteypu.

Þegar menn koma á bæi, er venjan að kasta kveðju á fólkið, ef það er úti við: "Komið þið sæl!" Þá er spurt eftir þeim, sem maður vill finna, oftast húsbónda eða húsfreyju. "Gæti ég fengið að tala við húsbóndann eða konuna (húsfreyjuna) á bænum?" Ef enginn er úti, verða menn að berja að dyrum; í gömlu bæjunum var siður að berja þrjú föst högg, því oft var langt úr bæjardyrum inn í eldhús eða baðstofu. Ef hundarnir hafa ekki verið úti og gelt að gestunum, þá koma þeir nú fram með miklum gangi, en venjulega bíta þeir ekki, þó þeir láti grimmilega, enda reynir bóndi allt hvað hann getur að þagga niður í þeim: "Skammastu þín! þegiðu hvuti! farðu í bæinn! snáfaðu burt! svei þér!" Hundar eru allmargir á bæjum, enda ómissandi til að smala fénu vor og haust.

Nú heilsast menn: gestirnir biðja um að lofa sér að vera, ef þeir koma seint að kvöldi dags. "Við erum að hugsa um að biðja yður um að lofa okkur að vera." "Það er velkomið, ef þið getið gert ykkur það að góðu. Við höfum því miður ekki nema eitt rúm handa gestum, en þið eruð fjórir; kannske geta félagar yðar sofið

---

[1] *Gömlu bæirnir.* 28. *Æfing.*

úti í hlöðu. Þeir mega bara ekki reykja þar, því þeir gætu kveikt í heyinu. Gerið þið svo vel að koma inn." Bóndi fylgir nú gestunum til stofu, og ef þeir eru votir eftir ferðalagið, býður hann þeim að fara úr blautu fötunum og láta þurrka þau frammi í eldhúsi. Á meðan eru þeim lánaðir þurrir sokkar og skór. Svo færir húsfreyja gestunum kaffi og kleinur eða pönnukökur eða smákökur, eða kvöld-mat, ef þeir hafa komið mjög seint. Kvöldmatur í sveitum er oft grautur (hafragrautur) og mjólk með slátri eða smurðu brauði, en gestum er oft gefið kjöt, salt eða nýtt, ef til er, kannske með kjötsúpu, rófum og kartöflum; brauð og smjör og kaffi á eftir. Nýtt kjöt og annað nýmeti er helzt til á haustin í sláturtíðinni; þá er líka nóg af nýju slátri (blóðmör og lifrarpylsu) og nýjum sviðum, en hvorttveggja er sett ofan í súrt og geymt til næstu sláturtíðar, ef vel á að vera. Fæstir útlendingar geta étið mat upp úr súru, aftur á móti þykir þeim gott að fá brauð og smjör, mjólk og nýtt skyr. Þegar gestirnir eru búnir að borða, vísar bóndi þeim til rúms. Rúm í sveitum eru oft með strádýnu í botni og fiðurundir-sæng, í þeim eru línlök og (yfir)sængur úr fiðri eða dún. Koddar eru stoppaðir úr fiðri. Þeir, sem vanir eru að sofa við teppi, kjósa það heldur, nema mjög kalt sé. Að sumrinu er ágætt að sofa í hlöðum, nema heitt sé í heyinu og vott ofan á, en venjulega má skara því frá og láta vindaugað standa opið til að hafa nægt loft.

Meðan vegir voru vondir og landferðir erfiðar, voru bæirnir einu gistihúsin í sveitum. Gestrisni var mikil, fólkið vildi allt fyrir gestina gera, enda voru þeir helzta skemmtun í einveru sveitalífsins. En síðan vegir hafa verið lagðir um landið og ár brúaðar, svo að bílar geta farið landshornanna milli, hafa bæirnir hætt að geta hýst gesti, nema þeir hafi gert sér það að atvinnu. Í stað þeirra hafa komið gistihús, sem því miður eru nokkuð misjöfn að gæðum. Aðeins í afskekktum sveitum, sem enn eru ófærar bílum, fyrir vegleysu sakir eða vatna, er hægt að búast við að hitta bæina eins og þeir voru áður, ef þar er þá ekki svo mikil fátækt, að þeir geti ekki sinnt gestum.

Í þessum sveitum er íslenzki hesturinn enn í sínu forna gildi. Hann er notaður til áburðar, reiðar og kannske til dráttar. Hann er enn aðalfararskjótinn, ef menn þurfa að fara yfir jökulárnar, sem enn belja óbrúaðar yfir sandana sunnanlands. Yfir þær ríða menn helzt á góðum vatnahestum, og ókunnugir fara þær ekki fylgdarlaust.

58. Íslenzk náttúra.

Landslag á Íslandi er allólíkt í ýmsum hlutum landsins. Á Suðurlandi eru víðáttumiklar sléttur og lágir hálsar eða holt fram

andan fjalllendinu. Á Norðurlandi eru djúpir, langir og breiðir
dalir inn af fjörðunum. Á Vestfjörðum er blágrýtis-hásléttan
sundurgrafin af sæbröttum fjörðum, og sama er að segja um
Austfirði, nema hvað þar eru fjöllin ennþá sundurtættari og tind-
óttari. Í Skaftafellssýslunum liggur breið láglendisræma milli fjalls
og fjöru; ströndin er bein, sendin og hafnlaus, en jöklarnir gnæfa
að baki og senda breiðar skriðjökuls-tungur og fjölda kolmórauðra
jökulvatna beljandi fram á sandana.

Ár og lækir. Landið er ótrúlega auðugt að fljótum eða stórám,
ám, þverám og lækjum—þetta eru allt rennandi vötn. Af stöðuvötn-
um eða vötnum eru Þingvallavatn og Mývatn stærst. Mývatn dregur
nafn af mýinu (mýbitinu, mývarginum), sem þar er mjög mikið.
Við Sogið, sem rennur úr Þingvallavatni, er líka mjög mikið af
mýi. Bæði þessi vötn eru mikil veiðivötn. Vötn, tjarnir, pollar,
pyttir eru nöfn á kyrru vatni, sem stundum getur verið staðnað.
Vötnin eru stærst, pyttirnir minnstir, en oft djúpir. Lón eða hóp
heita vötn, sem stíflazt hafa við sjó, oft gengur sjórinn upp í þau
um ósa. Lónin eru venjulega aflöng. Síki, ræsi, keldur, kílar og
lænur eru vatnsrásir í mýrum og flóum af náttúrunnar hendi, en
skurðir eða grafningar eru gerðir af mannahöndum vegna áveitu
eða afrennslis, t. d. meðfram vegum og brautum.

Mýrar og flóar. Rótlausir flóar, forir eða forarflóar, eins og t. d.
í Ölfusinu, geta verið mjög illir yfirferðar, ef ekki ófærir mönnum
og skepnum. Í þeim eru oft breiðar rótlausar keldur, leirkeldur,
milli grasigróinna þúfna. Stundum er rótarsvörðurinn ófúinn og
seigur, er þá oft hægt að ganga eða ríða yfir mýrina, þó allur jarð-
vegurinn dúi undir fæti: það er kallað kviksyndi; en því er sjaldan
trúandi. Vatnið er venjulega heldur minna í mýrum, sem ekki eru
sundurgrafnar af keldum og leirpyttum. Þær eru samt ávallt blautar,
oft mosavaxnar og þýfðar, og láta undan fæti, þó hvergi sökkvi í.
Dý, með ljósgulum dýjamosa, eru þar, sem kaldavermsl er í jörðu;
venjulega er kviksyndi, stundum rótlaust, í dýjum. Oft má vara
sig á dýjum að vetrinum, þegar mýrar og flóar eru lagðir og stál-
heldir. Á sumrum er oftast illfært um mýrar og flóa. Stundum eru
mýrar líka góðar engjar.

Þurrlendi. Stundum er þurrlendið slétt, en mjög oft er það
þýft. Túnin eru þurrlend og venjulega sléttuð, því mörg tún voru
upphaflega þýfð. Þúfurnar eru mjög einkennandi fyrir íslenzkt
landslag. Þegar þær eru háar, og djúpar skorur milli þeirra, eru
þær kallaðar kargaþýfi, eða þúfnakargi. Stundum eru þúfurnar
blásnar upp, og skín í svart moldarflag í hverri þúfu gegnt vindátt-
inni. Slétt harðvelli er oft á árbökkum; oft eru líka harðvellisbalar

273

og grundir undir fjallsrótum, stundum uppgróin gömul hlaup eða hraun, oft með mýrum neðan undir.

Sandar. Á Suðurlandi, í Skaftafellssýslum og á Fjöllum er allmikið af söndum. Sums staðar eru þetta foksandar, eða flugsandur, svo til dæmis á Rangárvöllum. Annars staðar eru sandarnir flatar eða lítt hallandi malarsléttur, eins og hinir frægu sandar í Skaftafellssýslunum, Skeiðarársandur og Breiðamerkursandur.

Skógar. Það, sem Íslendingar kalla skóg, er venjulega birkikjarr, sjaldan hærra en í mitt lær eða mitti. Það vex á þurrlendi í holtum, ásum, sundum og hlíðarslökkum. Fjalldrapi og víðikjarr þekur víða mýrar eða móa, einkum á Norður- og Austurlandi. Mestu skógar (birki) eru annars í Borgarfirði vestra, á Vöglum í Fnjóskadal, á Hallormsstað og víðar á Fljótsdalshéraði og Bæjarstaðaskógur í Öræfum. Þetta eru skógar líka á útlendan mælikvarða. Íslendingar reyna eftir föngum að vernda skógarleifar sínar.

Hverar og laugar eru víða um land. Bezt þekktar eru laugarnar í kring um Reykjavík. Þær voru lengi notaðar til þvotta (þvottalaugarnar). Síðan var vatni veitt úr þeim í sundlaug skammt frá (sundlaugarnar). Loks var vatni úr þeim og öðrum heitum uppsprettum veitt til Reykjavíkur og notað í Sundhöllina og til þess að hita part af bænum. Nú er allur bærinn hitaður með laugavatni. Á seinni árum hafa margir héraðsskólar verið byggðir víðsvegar um landið. Þar sem völ hefur verið á, hafa þeir verið hitaðir með laugavatni. Laugavatn hefur líka víða verið notað til að hita gróðurreiti og gróðurhús. Má rækta í þeim jafnvel suðrænar plöntur og ávexti. Frægastur allra hvera á Íslandi er Geysir, og af hans nafni draga hverar víða um lönd nafn sitt. Margt er minni hvera og lauga í kring um Geysi í Haukadal. Önnur hverasvæði eru t. d. Hveragerði í Ölfusi, með Grýlu, og Hveravellir milli jökla uppi á hálendinu. Brennisteinshverir og gufuhverir eru ekki ótíðir sums staðar á landinu.

Hraun. Í nágrenni Reykjavíkur og Hafnarfjarðar er mikið af hraunum. Þau eru víða úfin og ill yfirferðar með holum og skútum eða geysistórum hraundröngum. Stundum eru þau flöt helluhraun, stundum eins og úfinn sjór, sem hefur storknað á augabragði. Oft er þurrt í hraununum, en talsverður gróður getur verið í hraungjótunum.

Fjöll. Íslenzk fjöll hafa ýmsan svip, en öll eru þau, eins og landið allt, mynduð af áhrifum elds, vatns og jökla, eða veðurs. Í blágrýtisfjöllunum á Austfjörðum, Vestfjörðum og Norðurlandi eru blágrýtislögin gömul lög af hrauni, er hlaðizt hafa hvert ofan á annað og hafa síðan verið skorin sundur—eins og lagkaka—af

LÓMAGNÚPUR. BLÁGRÝTISFJALL.

jöklum og vatni. Þessi fjöll eru tindótt (full af tindum), með hvössum eggjum og djúpum giljum og gljúfrum, sem hafa spýtt fram úr sér stórum hlaupum ofan í dalina. Í þeim eru raðir af klettum efst, og niður úr klettunum ganga langar skriður ofan í hlíðarnar. Þessar skriður eru stórgrýttar efst, en á milli þeirra ganga lyngi vaxnir geirar, af móum eða grasi, hátt upp í fjöllin. Slík fjöll eru einna verst yfirferðar, en víða liggja þó vegir yfir þau um heiðar og skörð. Annars staðar eru fjöllin eldfjöll af ýmsu tæi eða móbergsfjöll. Sum eldfjöllin eru keilumynduð, eins og Keilir á Reykjanesi og Helgafell í Vestmannaeyjum. Önnur eru langir hryggir, eins og Hekla. Loks eru enn önnur breiðar bungur, eins og Skjaldbreiður. Móbergsfjöllin eru ekki eins stökk í sér eins og blágrýtisfjöllin, því móbergið líkist mjög steinsteypu. Fjöllin eru því oft kollótt, stundum grasi vaxin upp á koll. Ef vatn eða vindur sverfur þau, þá eru klettarnir ekki lagskiftir eins og í blágrýtisfjöllunum. Mjög fallegir klettar úr móbergi eru í Heimakletti í Vestmannaeyjum.

59. Saga Íslands.

Þegar Norðmenn fundu Ísland á síðara hluta níundu aldar, komu þeir að óbyggðu landi. Með stofnun Alþingis settu þeir á fót lýðveldi, sem stóð þar til um miðja þrettándu öld. Þá hafði um nokkur ár verið ófriður innanlands meðal höfðingja, og endaði hann með því, að landið gekk Noregskonungi á hönd 1264. Með norsku krúnunni komst landið undir dönsk yfirráð 1380. Þó varðveittu Íslendingar eigi aðeins tungu sína og bókmenntir, heldur einnig talsverða sjálfstjórn. Þannig hélt Alþingi áfram störfum sínum, í breyttum myndum að vísu, allt þar til um 1800, að það var lagt niður. En á nítjándu öldinni bárust frelsishreyfingar frá Evrópu til Íslands, og landsmenn hófu sjálfstæðisbaráttu sína undir forustu Jóns Sigurðssonar (1811-1879). Alþingi var endurreist 1845, konungur gaf landinu nýja stjórnarskrá á þúsund ára afmæli þess 1874, heimastjórn, með ráðherra búsettum í landinu, vannst 1904, og loks viðurkenndi Danmörk (og önnur ríki) sjálfstæði Íslands með sambandslögunum 1918. Samkvæmt þeim áttu bæði ríkin að hafa sama konung og nokkur gagnkvæm réttindi, en Danmörk fór a. n. l. með utanríkismálin fyrir hönd Íslands. Samningurinn gilti til tuttugu og fimm ára, að þeim tíma liðnum var það ætlun Íslendinga að slíta sambandinu við Danmörku og endurreisa lýðveldi í landinu. En þá skall á heimsstríðið síðara. Þjóðverjar hertóku Danmörku, en Englendingar Ísland 1940. Næsta sumar báðu Íslendingar Bandaríkjamenn um vernd sína; þeir komu til landsins í júlí 1941. Bæði Englendingar og Bandaríkjamenn lýstu því yfir, að þeir mundu hverfa úr landinu að stríðinu loknu, og lofuðu því, að landið fengi að halda sjálfstæði sínu.

Vorið 1944 slitu Íslendingar, eins og þeir höfðu ætlað, sambandinu við Dani. Var lýðveldið síðan stofnað og forseti kosinn með miklum hátíðahöldum í Reykjavík og á Þingvöllum 17. júní 1944.

60. Pólitík.

Fram til 1918 skiftust menn í pólitíska flokka á Íslandi um afstöðuna til Danmerkur. Hinir róttækari kröfðust sjálfstæðis og skilnaðar, hinir hægfara vildu litlar breytingar eða engar. En eftir 1918 tóku menn að skiftast í flokka um innanlandsmálin. Aukinn sjávarútvegur skapaði þorp og bæi, sem lifðu á fiskiveiðum í stórum stíl (mótorbáta- og togaraútgerð), þar sem landbúnaður og smáútræði höfðu verið aðalatvinnuvegir þjóðarinnar frá landnámstíð. Reykjavík hefur einkum vaxið ört síðan um aldamót; nú býr þar fullur þriðjungur þjóðarinnar (yfir 40 þúsund). Með þessum breytingum á atvinnuháttum sköpuðust nýjar stéttir, sem brátt fengu fulltrúa í pólitískum flokkum. Bændur sameinuðust fyrst um hagsmuni sína í kaupfélögunum og síðar í Framsóknar-flokknum. Gegn þeim fylktu sér kaupmenn og útgerðarmenn ásamt efnaðri borgurum bæjanna í flokki, sem um skeið kallaði sig Íhaldsflokk, og var það að nokkru leyti réttnefni. Flokkurinn hefur annars lengst gengið undir nafninu Sjálfstæðisflokkur. En verka-menn og öreigar í bæjunum mynduðu Alþýðuflokk og börðust fyrir hugsjónum jafnaðarmanna og umbótum á sínum hag. Um 1930 mynduðu róttækari jafnaðarmenn Kommúnistaflokkinn og kölluðu þá hina hægfara félaga sína sósíaldemókrata. Og 1933 stökk upp í hægra fylkingararmi sjálfstæðismanna flokkur Þjóðernis-sinna undir áhrifum frá Þýskalandi. En þeir fengu lítið fylgi og eru nú alveg úr sögunni.

Þótt Ísland hafi haft þingbundna konungsstjórn í orði kveðnu, þá hefur fullt lýðræði verið í landinu síðan 1918, eða jafnvel fyrr. Aldurstakmark kosningaréttar og kjörgengis hefur verið lágt (21 ár), og þátttaka í kosningum mjög almenn. Þingið hefur skipað stjórnina (þrjá til fimm menn) eftir reglum þingræðisins. Á síð-ustu árum fyrir stríðið var skipuð þjóðstjórn með samkomulagi stærstu flokkanna. Í reyndinni hefur flokksræðið gerzt sterkasta valdið. Í kapphlaupi flokkanna um hylli þjóðarinnar hefur geysi-mikið verið gert til þjóðþrifa. Vegir hafa verið lagðir, og brýr byggðar. Íslenzk skip sigla nú eigi aðeins með ströndum fram, heldur einnig milli landa. Skólar hafa verið byggðir í bæjum og í sveitum. Flestir þeirra eru að meira eða minna leyti styrktir af ríkinu, og veita því ódýra eða ókeypis kennslu. Spítalar hafa verið byggðir, og ríkið hefur styrkt almenn sjúkrasamlög og veitt ellistyrki og örorkubætur gömlu fólki og farlama. Landbúnaðurinn hefur notið styrkja um langa hríð, og ríkið hefur hlaupið undir bagga með útgerðarmönnum togaranna og tekið þátt í byggingu nýrra síldarverksmiðja. Það hefur rekið einkasölur og styrkt bókagerð í landinu. Og það hefur styrkt listamenn og rithöfunda. En á hinn bóginn hefur flokksræðið haft sína galla. Landið átti í vök að verjast fjárhagslega milli styrjaldanna. Að miklu leyti var það útlendum kreppum að kenna, að nokkru leyti óvarkárni landsmanna sjálfra. Hin mikla þátttaka lýðsins í flokkapólitíkinni hefur heldur ekki verið ómenguð blessun. Síðasti flokkurinn, sem stofnaður var í landinu, hefur það því meðal annars á stefnuskrá sinni að reyna að takmarka flokksvaldið en auka þjóðveldið. Hann kallar sig Landsmálasamtök Þjóðveldismanna (1942).

Aðalvopn flokkanna eru blöðin. Helztu blöðin í Reykjavík eru: Morgunblaðið og Vísir, bæði málgögn Sjálfstæðisflokksins. Tíminn er blað Framsóknarflokksins, en Alþýðublaðið málgagn Alþýðuflokksins (sósíaldemókratanna), Þjóðviljinn er blað sósíalista (= kommúnista), en Þjóðólfur er blað Þjóðveldismanna. Mörg fleiri blöð, flest pólitísk, koma út bæði í Reykjavík og í bæjum úti um land, og er ekki ástæða til að minnast á neitt þeirra, nema Spegilinn, sem segist vera samvizka þjóðarinnar, góð og vond eftir ástæðum.

61. Dagbók. Úr Morgunblaðinu 1941.

Næturlæknir er í nótt Úlfar Þórðarson, Sólvallagötu 18. Sími 4411. Aðra nótt Halldór Stefánsson, Ránargötu 12. Sími 2234.

Helgidagslæknir er María Hallgrímsdóttir, Grundarstíg 17. Sími 4384.

Næturvörður er í Reykjavíkur Apóteki og Lyfjabúðinni Iðunn.

" Gyllir." Menn voru í gær farnir að óttast um togarann " Gylli," vegna þess að ekkert hafði heyrzt til hans eftir vonda veðrið nú í vikunni. En Mbl. hafði í gærkvöldi sannar fregnir af því, að ekkert hafði orðið að hjá " Gylli "; loftskeytatækin voru hins vegar biluð, og var það ástæðan til þess, að ekki heyrðist frá skipinu.

Fimmtugur er í dag Sigurgísli Guðnason kaupm., Tjarnargötu 38. Sigurgísli er vinsæll maður og vel látinn af þeim, sem hann þekkja, og þeir eru margir hér í bæ.

Trúlofun. Nýlega hafa opinberað trúlofun sína ungfrú Alda Ágústsdóttir, Klapparstíg 13, og Rolf Holth í norska flughernum.

Hjónaefni. Nýlega hafa opinberað trúlofun sína Berta Valdimarsdóttir og Jón Pétursson bílstjóri.—Enn fremur Solveig Sigurðardóttir og Óskar Þórarinsson, Hlíð, Vestmannaeyjum.

Tilkynning frá brezka setuliðinu: Skotæfingar fara fram á Sandskeiði og fyrir norðan það dagana 8. til 13. þ. m.

Blindravinafélagi Íslands voru nýlega færðar kr. 25,00 að gjöf frá Ó. S., til blindraheimilis þess, sem félagið hefir í hyggju að stofnsetja. Stjórn félagsins biður blaðið að færa gefandanum alúðarþakkir og einnig öllum þeim mörgu, sem með góðvild og hjálpsemi hlynna að starfsemi Blindravinafélags Íslands.

5. hefti 14. árgangs Tímarits Iðnaðarmanna er fyrir nokkru komið út. Er efni þess þetta m. a.: Sjötta Iðnþing Íslendinga, Iðnmál á Alþingi, Mál rædd á Iðnþinginu, Minningarorð um Guðmund Eiríksson húsasmíðameistara o. fl. Tímaritið er hið vandaðasta að öllum frágangi. Er það gefið út af Landssambandi Iðnaðarmanna, en Sveinbjörn Jónsson byggingameistari er ritstjóri þess.

Dr. Cyril Jackson flytur háskólafyrirlestur í 1. kennslustofu Háskólans klukkan 8.15 í kvöld. Fyrirlesturinn verður um héraðið Sommerset í Englandi, sem er eitt fegursta hérað landsins. Þar eru og margar sögulegar minjar og sögustaðir. Dr. Jackson sýnir margar fallegar skuggamyndir til skýringar.

"Andy Hardy á biðilsbuxum" heitir myndin sem Gamla Bíó sýnir þessi kvöldin. Er þetta ein af hinum vinsælu framhaldsmyndum Hardy-fjölskyldunnar, þar sem Mickey Rooney leikur aðalhlutverkið. Þessi mynd er full af fjöri og græskulausu gamni.

Útvarpið í dag:

10.00 Morguntónleikar (plötur): Sónata í As-dúr og kvintett í g-moll eftir Mozart.

11.00 Messa í Dómkirkjunni (séra Friðrik Hallgrímsson).

12.15—13.00 Hádegisútvarp.

14.00 Mozart-tónleikar Tónlistarfélagsins í Gamla Bíó; 150 ára dánarminning (Hljómsveit Reykjavíkur; stjórn.: dr. Urbantschitsch. Einl.: Björn Ólafsson).

15.30—16.30 Miðdegistónleikar (plötur): Álfa-, dverga- og nornalög.

18.30 Barnatími (Nemendur kennaraskólans).

19.25 Hljómplötur: Etudes, Op. 25 eftir Chopin.

20.00 Fréttir.

20.20 Einsöngur (Bjarni Bjarnason læknir) : Lög eftir Skúla Hall-dórsson við ljóð eftir Jón Thoroddsen: a) Smalastúlkan. b) Kossa-leit. c) Fjöllin blá. d) Barmahlíð. e) Sortna þú, ský. f) Stúlkan mín. g) Drykkjuvísa.

20.45 Erindi: Nýjar listastefnur (Jóhann Briem listmálari).

21.10 Hljómplötur: Íslenzk lög, leikin á hljóðfæri.

21.20 Upplestur: "Rauða kýrin" smásaga eftir Theódóru Thor-oddsen (Kristján Gunnarsson kennari).

21.30 Hljómplötur: Lúðra-konsert eftir Mozart.

21.50 Fréttir.

62. Auglýsingar. Úr Morgunblaðinu 1941.

Ungur reglusamur maður, sem hefir góða verzlunarmenntun og talsverða æfingu í skrifstofustörfum, óskar eftir atvinnu. Tilboð auðkennt " Skrifstofumaður " sendist Morgunblaðinu.

Ung stúlka óskar eftir vinnu við afgreiðslustörf, helzt í vefnað-arvöruverzlun. Tilboð leggist inn á afgreiðslu blaðsins fyrir 10. þ. m. merkt: " 333."

Atvinna. Tvo vana sjómenn vantar skiprúm í utanlandssiglingar. Uppl. í síma 3332 kl. 2—4.

Af sérstökum ástæðum er 5 manna *fólksbíll* í góðu lagi til sölu og sýnis í Shellportinu við Lækjargötu frá kl. 1—6 í dag.

Lán óskast. Tveir vanir bílstjórar með meira prófi óska eftir 15 til 20 þúsund kr. láni til bílkaupa. Trygging: 1. veðréttur í tveimur til þremur bílum og veð í fasteign. Háir vextir. Tilboð merkt " Traust " leggist inn á afgreiðslu Morgunblaðsins fyrir föstudag.

Ung barnlaus hjón óska eftir einu *herbergi* helzt með einhverjum húsgögnum og aðgangi að eldhúsi til áramóta. Fyrirfram greiðsla. Uppl. í síma 4091 kl. 1—4 e. hád.

" Herbergi." 300 kr. fær sá, sem getur útvegað 2 reglusömum og ábyggilegum, ungum mönnum herbergi. Fyrirfram greiðsla. Tilboð merkt " 300 " leggist inn á afgreiðslu blaðsins fyrir mánudagskvöld.

" Lagarfoss " fer væntanlega vestur og norður eftir miðja næstu viku. Þeir, sem ætla að senda vörur með skipinu, tilkynni oss það í síðasta lagi fyrir þriðjudagskvöld 3. desember. Viðkomustaðir: Ísafjörður, Siglufjörður og Akureyri.

Tapað—fundið. Böggull með tveimur skóm, svörtum og brúnum, hefir tapazt. Skilist vinsamlegast á Framnesveg 17.

Kennsla. Kenni íslenzku, dönsku, ensku, þýzku og frönsku. Bjarnþór Þórðarson cand. phil., Laufásvegi 49.—Sími 4530.

Málverkasýningu opnar Finnur Jónsson í vinnustofu sinni í Íþöku við Menntaskólann í dag, sunnudaginn þ. 7. des. Sýningin verður opin daglega frá 11—12 árdegis og 1—10 síðdegis. Inngangur um Menntaskólahliðið við Bókhlöðustíg.

63. Fréttir. Úr Morgunblaðinu 1935-41.

Veðrið í gær: Við suðvesturströnd Íslands er lægðarmiðja, sem hefir mjög lítið færzt úr stað í dag, en virðist vera á hægri hreyfingu austur eftir. Vindur er fremur hægur SA með regni á S- og A-landi, en norðvestanlands er hæg NA-átt og úrkomulaust. N-átt mun vera til hafsins skammt fyrir vestan landið, og er útlit fyrir, að hún muni ná hingað innan skamms.

Veðurútlit í Rvík í dag: Léttir til með NV- eða N-kalda.

Háflóð er í dag kl. 5 og á morgun kl. 5.40.

Esja kom úr strandferð í gær.

Laxveiðin. Sigbjörn Ármann kaupmaður, sem skipaður hefir verið til þess að hafa lögreglueftirlit með því, að ákvæðum laxveiðilaganna frá 1932 sé fylgt í Hvítá í Borgarfirði og hinum laxveiðaánum þar, hefir beðið Morgunblaðið fyrir nokkrar athugasemdir viðvíkjandi fregn, sem stóð í blaðinu, um laxveiðina í ánum. Segir hann, að nú sé nógur lax bæði í Grímsá og Þverá, og fyrir þremur dögum hafi Englendingar t. d. fengið 25 pd. lax í Langadrætti, sem er norður undir Tvídægru. Eins og stóð í blaðinu, verpti fyrir ós Grímsár; en þá fékk Sigbjörn menn til þess að grafa ósinn út og sá um verkið. Síðan hefir laxinn runnið upp í ána. Síðan rigningarnar byrjuðu, hefir hlaupið vöxtur í árnar í Borgarfirði, og hefir laxinn því runnið upp þær, og nóg var af honum í Hvítá, meðan þurrkatíðin var sem mest.—Sigbjörn Ármann getur þess líka, að hugmynd sín sé sú, að fá Hvítá algerlega friðaða fyrir netjalagningu, og ádráttur í öllum þverám hennar sé bannaður með lögum. Þá verði þarna bezta laxveiðasvæði í heimi, og þá þurfi ekkert að vera að hugsa um laxaklak þar, þegar rányrkjan er útilokuð.

Um Fjallabaksveg nyrðri (Landmannaleið) ráðgerir Ferðafélag Íslands 6 daga skemmtiför í næstu viku. Verður ekið að Vík í Mýrdal fyrsta daginn og gist þar um nóttina. Þriðjudagsmorgun verður haldið áfram austur yfir Mýrdalssand og að Kirkjubæjarklaustri, en viðstöður verða í Hafursey á Mýrdalssandi og við Hólmsárbrú hjá Hrísnesi. Þriðja daginn verður haldið (á bifreið) frá Kirkjubæjarklaustri um Foss og Dverghamra að Fossnúp og

snúið þar vestur, að Hlíð í Skaftártungu. Gist þar um nóttina. Fjórða daginn verður haldið inn í óbyggðirnar, Landmannaleið, í Kýlinga, og gist þar. Staðið við í Eldgjánni og farið inn að Ófærufossi. Fimmta daginn verður haldið áfram vestur, og riðið inn í Jökulgil, svo langt sem tími endist til, og staðið við í Laugum í bakaleið og skoðað Laugahraun. Að Landmannahelli um kvöldið.— Sjötta daginn verður gengið á Loðmund snemma morguns, ef útsýni leyfir, og ekið síðan frá Landmannahelli að Galtalæk á Landi og þaðan til Reykjavíkur um kvöldið. Farmiðar og nánari upplýsingar um ferðina fást í Bókaverzlun Sigfúsar Eymundssonar frá deginum í dag til laugardags kl. 4.

Íslandsglíman 1935. Hún verður háð á Íþróttavellinum annað kvöld. Kl. 8 leikur Lúðrasveit Reykjavíkur á Austurvelli, og þar safnast fólk saman. Verður síðan gengið út á völl. Þar sýnir fyrst Drengjaflokkur Ármanns undir stjórn Vignis Andréssonar, og að þeirri sýningu lokinni hefst Íslandsglíman.

Keppendur eru aðeins sex, Sigurður Thorarensen glímukóngur, Ágúst Kristjánsson glímusnillingur, Lárus Salómonsson fyrrv. glímukóngur, Skúli Þorleifsson, Gunnar Salómonsson, allir úr Glímufélaginu Ármanni, og Steindór Gíslason úr U. M. F. Samhygð í Árnessýslu.

Íslandsglíman á að vera merkasti íþróttaviðburðurinn hér á landi á hverju ári, en það er leiðinlegt, að ekki skuli koma fleiri glímukappar utan af landi til þess að keppa í henni. Því að Íslandsglíman á að vera fyrir allt Ísland. En það er nú svo, að glímumenn utan af landi munu eigi þykjast sækja gull í greipar reykvísku glímumannanna, enda er það viðurkennt, að hér sé beztir glímumenn. Meiri þátttaka mundi í Íslandsglímunni, ef hún væri flokkaglíma, og mönnum skift niður eftir þunga.

Þrátt fyrir þetta vita allir, að glíman er merkur viðburður, því að þar verður skorið úr því, hver eigi að heita mestur glímugarpur á Íslandi, og hver glími af mestri list.

Það er því enginn efi á því, að fjölmennt verður á Íþróttavellinum annað kvöld.

Íþróttaskólinn á Álafossi. Í gær var lokið fyrsta námskeiði drengja í sumar. Voru á því nám skeiði 37, en nokkrir fóru, áður en því var lokið. Drengir þessir voru á aldrinum 8—14 ára.

Í gær gengu 26 drengir undir nokkurs konar burtfararpróf, og voru foreldrar þeirra og vandamenn komnir til að sjá, hverjum framförum þeir hefði tekið, og taka við þeim.

Fyrst sýndu drengirnir fimleika í stóra tjaldinu, undir stjórn kennara síns, Ólafs Péturssonar.—Tókst það vel, einkum þegar þess

281

er gætt, að fæstir drengjanna höfðu neina hugmynd um fimleika, eða að hlýða skipunum, fyrr en þeir komu að Álafossi fyrir mánuði.

Síðan var sundsýning í útilauginni, undir stjórn sundkennarans, ungfrú Klöru Klængsdóttur. Allir voru drengirnir syndir og sumir ágætlega. Höfðu þó margir ekki komið í vatn fyrr en þar upp frá. Voru þeir mjög óragir og stukku allir af háa stökkpallinum við laugina. Þeir sýndu bringusund, baksund, skriðsund og bjargsund.

Sigurjón skýrði frá því, hvernig skólanum er háttað, kvaðst vera ánægður með árangurinn—og það voru foreldrarnir líka. Mátti heyra mæðurnar vera að tala um það sín á milli, og allar voru þær hrifnar af því, hvað drengjunum sínum hefði farið fram.

Á þessum mánuði þyngdust drengirnir um ½—2 kg., brjóstvídd þeirra jókst um 1—2½ cm., og þeir hækkuðu um ½—2 cm., en það var aðallega vegna þess, að þeim var kennt að rétta úr sér.

Á morgun hefst nýtt námskeið á Álafossi. Er það fyrir telpur og verða þær 40 saman.

Íþróttaskólinn á Álafossi er eini skólinn á Norðurlöndum, sem tekur til kennslu börn á aldrinum 8—14 ára, kennir þeim leikfimi, sund, heilsufræði og prúðmennsku, en á það er lagt mikið kapp að hafa góð áhrif á börnin.

Ný skip. Vér Íslendingar höfum á þessu ári fært þungar fórnir. Vér eigum á bak að sjá tugum hraustra drengja, sem fallið hafa fyrir harðýðgi miskunnarlausrar styrjaldar. Og vér höfum misst tilfinnanlegan hluta af veiðiskipaflota vorum. Nemur tjónið samt. 2661 rúmlesta. Þar að auki hefir eitt skip, 749 rúmlestir, verið selt útlendingum. Nemur því rýrnun flotans samtals 3410 rúmlestum eða 8% af allri skipaeign Íslendinga, sem við síðustu áramót var 42933 rúmlestir.

Hér er um að ræða mjög alvarlegt mál. Velferð þjóðarinnar er á marga vegu undir því komin, að vér eigum nægan og góðan skipastól. Skipin eru ein þýðingarmestu framleiðslutæki vor. Að-flutningar til landsins byggjast allir á því, að til séu skip til að annast þá. Hér verður því vissulega að snúast við í samræmi við þá nauðsyn, sem fyrir hendi er. Hefir áður verið á það bent hér í blaðinu, að hverju beri að stefna. Vér verðum að leggja á það allt kapp að koma á fót skipasmíðastöðvum í landinu sjálfu, sem færar séu um það að endurnýja og byggja veiðiskipaflota vorn. Að undirbúningi þessara framkvæmda verður að vinda bráðan bug. Á s. l. reglulegu Alþingi var samþykkt þingsályktunartillaga um undirbúning á öflun efnis til skipasmíðastöðva, sem byggt gætu skip úr tré og járni. Hér er um stórkostlegt framfaramál að ræða og þess vert, að því sé fyllsti gaumur gefinn.

Niðursuðuverksmiðja á Akranesi. Haraldur Böðvarsson & Co. á
Akranesi hafa látið byggja niðursuðuverksmiðju með vélum og
öllum útbúnaði af nýjustu gerð, ásamt reykhúsi til að reykja í
síld og fisk.

Vélarnar eru að mestu leyti sjálfvirkar og ganga fyrir raforku,
en niðursuðuvörurnar eru soðnar við gufu og afkældar með nýrri
aðferð. Verksmiðjustjóri er Pétur Jóhannsson. Firmað hefir látið
skrásetja vörumerkið " Hekla " fyrir niðursuðuvörur sínar, og eru
fiskabollur frá verksmiðjunni þegar komnar í flestar verzlanir landsins, en á næstunni er von á fleiri tegundum, t. d. reyktum síldar-
flökum (Kippers), fiskbúðingum o. fl.

Firmað Eggert Kristjánsson & Co. hefir söluumboð til kaup-
manna og kaupfélaga um land allt.

Á Akranesi eru hin beztu skilyrði fyrir þenna rekstur, glænýr
fiskurinn og síldin úr sjónum og nýmjólkin á staðnum og úr nær-
sveitum í bollurnar.

Við flökun, reykingu og niðursuðu á síld, þarf um 70 manns til
vinnu, og afkasta vélarnar þá 20—30 þúsund dósum á dag. En af
fiskabollum getur verksmiðjan búið til 7500 heildósir á dag, og í
þær fara m. a. 3000 lítrar af nýmjólk.

Þessi starfsemi getur hjálpað bændunum í nágrenni Akraness
all-verulega með sölu mjólkurinnar; það vill svo heppilega til, að
þegar mest er af mjólkinni, þá eru bezt skilyrðin fyrir þessa fram-
leiðslu, þá er ýsan feitust og bezt og mest af henni.

Þessi starfsemi er aðallega byggð upp með útlenda markaðinn fyrir
augum, en að sjálfsögðu verður líka selt á innlenda markaðnum
eftir þörfum.

Douglas Fairbanks yngri í Reykjavík. Ameríski kvikmyndaleikarinn Douglas Fairbanks yngri var staddur hér í bænum í gærdag.
Hann snæddi hádegisverð að Hótel Borg með nokkrum félögum
sínum. Kvikmyndaleikarinn hafði hér stutta viðdvöl, og fáir munu
hafa vitað um dvöl hans í bænum.

Douglas Fairbanks er liðsforingi í ameríska sjóliðinu og hefir
hann tvisvar komið hingað til bæjarins, á meðan skip hans hefir
dvalið hér við land. En vegna þess, að landleyfi er ekki gefið, nema
nokkrar klukkustundir um hádaginn í hvert sinn, hefir hann ekki
haft tækifæri til að skoða sig mikið um.

Blaðamaður frá Morgunblaðinu átti stutt viðtal við Douglas Fairbanks að Hótel Borg í gærdag. Lét hann vel yfir ferð sinni hingað og
kvaðst hafa orðið snortinn af sérkennilegri fegurð landsins og hinu
hrikalega landslagi. Hann kvaðst hafa lesið um Ísland, en eigin
sjón og reynd hefði sannað sér, að ekki hafi verið ofsögum sagt
af Sögueyjunni.

283

—Mig hefði langað til að ferðast hér um landið og sjá sögustaði, sagði Douglas Fairbanks, en úr því getur ekki orðið að þessu sinni, til þess er árstíminn óhentugur og landleyfi mitt í hvert sinn of stutt. En ég hefi fengið tækifæri til að koma inn í hið sögufræga Alþingi ykkar og var ég svo heppinn, að fundur stóð yfir.

Douglas Fairbanks kvaðst hafa verið 1½ ár í ameríska flotanum. Hann hefir aðallega unnið í flotamálaráðuneytinu í Washington, en er nú um stundarsakir um borð í herskipi.

Ég spurði hann, hvort ekki væri von á kvikmynd, sem hann léki í, bráðlega.

—Jú, það er verið að ljúka við kvikmynd, sem ég leik í. Fékk ég nokkurra mánaða leyfi til að leika í þessari kvikmynd í sumar, og ætti hún að koma á markaðinn um áramótin.

Douglas Fairbanks er maður mjög viðfeldinn í allri framkomu og hinn alúðlegasti. Hann er alveg eins og hann er í kvikmyndum, sem hann hefir sézt í hér. Hann er hár og grannvaxinn, með skolleitt hár og lítið yfirvararskegg.

64. Þjóðtrú og þjóðsögur.

Þjóðtrú Íslendinga er að mörgu leyti einkennileg, þó að hún raunar minni allmikið á þjóðtrú á Norðurlöndum og á Bretlandseyjum.

Einn þáttur þjóðtrúarinnar er trúin á álfa eða huldufólk. Huldufólkið á að búa í hólum og klettum. Þeir, sem þykjast hafa séð það, lýsa því svo, að það sé í útliti og háttum líkt mennskum mönnum, nema hvað það sé heldur betur búið, heldur vænna álitum, og lifi yfirleitt við betri kjör en fólk í mannheimum. Menn mega vara sig að láta ekki heillast af græn- eða bláklæddum álfkonum á fjöllum uppi, og stundum hafa huldumenn numið bóndadætur úr byggðum. Venjulega sjá aðeins skyggnir menn huldufólkið, en út af þeirri reglu getur þó brugðið. Algengt er, að huldukonur í barnsnauð láti vitja mennskra kvenna til þess að leysa barnið frá móðurinni. Stundum taka álfkonur börn úr vöggu, en skilja sín eigin börn, eða jafnvel karla sína, eftir í staðinn. Slík börn verða ekki að manni og heita umskiftingar. Til að forða því, er gott að krossa barnið í bak og brjóst. Einu sinni gekk móðir frá barni sínu í vöggu, en skildi eftir hjá því son sinn sjö vetra gamlan. Þá komu þar tvær huldukonur, og sagði önnur: "Tökum á, tökum á." Hin svaraði: "Ekki má, ekki má, því kross er undir og ofan á, og sjövetlingur situr hjá og segir frá."

Um jól og nýjár er talið, að álfarnir flytji sig búferlum. Fara þeir þá í hópum um sveitirnar, koma við á bæjunum og slá þar upp dansi. Er sagt, að þeir hafi það þá til að æra fólk, sem verður á vegi þeirra. Það var því ekki vinsælt verk að vaka heima á jóla eða nýjársnótt, þegar allt fólkið fór annars til kirkjunnar. Til að koma í veg fyrir óhöpp, höfðu konur þann sið að ganga hringinn í kringum bæinn og segja: "Veri þeir, sem vera vilja," eða: "Komi þeir, sem koma vilja, fari þeir, sem fara vilja, mér og mínum að meinlausu." Álfatrúin er forn, en virðist hafa staðið í blóma á 15. og 16. öld.

Annar aðalþáttur íslenzkrar þjóðtrúar er tröllatrúin. Talið er, að trúin á tröllin sé enn eldri en álfatrúin, enda er hún orðin daufari nú á dögum. Tröllum var svo lýst, að þau væri stórskorin og stórvaxin mjög; trúðu menn því, að þau ættu heima í fjöllum, hömrum og giljum, stundum undir fossum. Sagt var, að nátttröll væri á ferðinni að nóttu til aðeins, og ef dagur tæki þau á ferða-lögum sínum, þá yrðu þau að steinum eða dröngum. Var það kallað, að þau dagaði uppi. Meðfram ströndum Íslands er fjöldi dranga og skerja, sem menn kalla karla og kerlingar og telja vera steingerð nátttröll. Sama er að segja um dranga og kletta á fjöll-um uppi. Menn trúðu, að tröllin lifðu á hrossaketi og manna-, og þau voru ávallt hundheiðin, þar sem álfarnir stundum ræktu kirkjur og kristni. Tröllskessur áttu það til að taka smalamenn á jólanótt-inni, og það gerði skessan fræga, sem Grettir glímdi við. Jafnvel prestarnir á stólnum voru ekki óhultir fyrir þeim; en þá var þó hægt um vik að hringja kirkjuklukkunum, því það álitu menn, að tröllin stæðust ekki. En þó að tröllin gæti þannig verið grimm og hættuleg, þá voru þau stundum meinlaus, og jafnvel greiðvikin, við mennska menn. Og væri þeim gerður greiði, þá voru þau svo trygg, að til þess hefur ávallt verið jafnað, og hafa menn því kallað tröllatryggð hina traustustu vináttu.

Þriðji þáttur íslenzkrar þjóðtrúar er trúin á drauga. Drauga-trúin er gömul, eins og sjá má af sögunni um Gretti og glímu hans við Glám. En hún magnaðist mjög á 17. öld, galdraöldinni svo nefndu. Stundum gengu misendismenn aftur, eins og Glámur, og ásóttu fólk og fé. Stundum vöktu kunnáttumenn upp drauga til að senda óvinum sínum. Hinir fyrrnefndu draugar voru kallaðir afturgöngur, hinir síðarnefndu sendingar. Draugar lögðust á kvik-fénað og drápu hann, þeir riðu húsum, svo að fólk hélzt ekki við, en bæirnir eyddust. Kæmi það fyrir, að menn yrðu úti eða færust í óveðrum á fjöllum uppi, þá varð þar oft reimt síðan; var talið, að draugarnir villtu fyrir vegfarendum. Menn, sem fórust af bátum, urðu sjódraugar, ekki sízt, ef líkin rak upp. Sumir draugar fylgdu mönnum og afkomendum þeirra allt í níunda lið. Helzt voru það uppvakningar og sendingar, sem það gerðu; fylgdu þessir draugar þá annaðhvort manni þeim, sem þeir voru sendir, eða galdramanninum, sem vakti þá upp. Þetta voru kallaðar fylgjur manna, sáust þær oft á undan mönnum þeim, er þær fylgdu, í líki mórauðra stráka, sem kallaðir voru Mórar, eða í gervi stuttpilsaðra stelpna, er Skottur nefndust. Sóttu þær að fólki og gerðu því eða gripum á bænum glettur (aðsókn). Ef fólk syfjaði, eða var eitthvað ómótt, áður en gestur kom á bæinn, kenndu menn það fylgju gestsins og töldu hann hafa sótt illa að sér. Þess vegna voru gestir vanir—og eru enn—að spyrja, hvernig þeir sæktu að þeim, sem þeir voru að heimsækja.

Skyldir draugum, afturgöngum og uppvakningum eru svipir manna eða vofur. Þeir sjást oft, eftir að menn hafa farizt voveiflega á sjó eða landi, en venjulega eru þeir alveg meinlausir. Á síðasta mannsaldri hefur drauga- og svipa-trú glæðzt í nokkuð breyttri mynd undir áhrifum hinnar amerísk-ensku andatrúar.

Nátengd draugatrúnni er trúin á galdra og galdramenn; þessi trú varð líka sterkust á 17. öldinni, en hún er eldri, eins og sjá má af fornsögunum og sögnunum um Sæmund fróða. Sæmundur var lærður af kölska sjálfum í Svartaskóla í Frakklandi; eftir það áttust þeir kölski jafnan glettingar við, þó svo, að Sæmundur hafði ávallt betur. Fara síðan margar sögur af því, hvernig leikið hefur verið á kölska af kunnáttumönnum eða öðrum, sem vissu lengra en nef þeirra náði. Eftir siðaskifti er þó svo að sjá sem kölski hafi farið að færast í aukana; þá er nokkrum kirkjum sökkt fyrir þá sök, að prestarnir dansa þar út jólanóttina með söfnuðinum í stað þess að rækja helgar tíðir (Dansinn í Hruna). Og þá selja nokkrir drottnunargjarnir áhugamenn kölska sál sína—og tapa henni fyrir fullt og allt, eins og Galdra-Loftur. En seinni alda galdramenn hafa minna með kölska að gera en með uppvakninga og sendingar, sem þeir senda hver öðrum. Stefnuvargur í tófugervi eða hrafna- er sendur á fé manna, og menn veikjast sjálfir af ókennilegum sjúkdómum, sem menn kenna göldrum. Á 17. öldinni eru menn brenndir fyrir galdra; á þeirri öld eru líka uppi kraftaskáld, eins og Hallgrímur Pétursson, sem sagt er, að ort hafi svo heitt um tófu, sem hann sá vera að bíta lamb af prédikunarstólnum, að hún drapst þar sem hún stóð. En fyrir þetta var skáldgáfan tekin af Hallgrími, sem bæði þá og síðar hefur verið talinn mesta sálmaskáld Íslands (Passíusálmarnir).

Fjórði höfuðþáttur íslenzkrar þjóðtrúar er trúin á útilegumenn. Hennar gætir þegar í fornöld, eins og sést af Grettis sögu, Gísla sögu og fleiri sögum. Bæði Grettir og Gísli voru útlagar, skógar-menn, óalandi, óferjandi og óráðandi nokkrum bjargráðum. Þeir lögðust út og lifðu á fjöllum uppi á veiðum og af því að stela fé byggðarmanna. Á öllum öldum hafa menn strokið á fjöll til að flýja refsingu; frægastur útilegumaður á seinni öldum var Fjalla-Eyvindur. Trúin á útilegumenn glæddist af því, að mönnum voru öræfin lítt kunn, en fjárheimtur voru hins vegar oft illar á haustin. Var það þá kennt útilegumönnum. Saman við þetta blandaðist svo trú á fjallavætti og tröll eða huldufólk, ásamt trúnni á sæludali, sem huldir væri í fjöllunum. Útilegumennirnir bjuggu oft í þessum kostamiklu huldudölum; þeir voru stærri og sterkari en aðrir menn, og stundum rammgöldróttir. Höfðu þeir það til að bregða yfir sig myrkva eða þokum, er þeir voru á flótta undan byggðamönnum. Auk þess að stela fé og ræna ferðamenn voru þeir vanir að ræna bóndadætrum úr byggð; eru margar sögur um það, hvernig röskir piltar úr sveitum hættu lífi sínu til að bjarga þeim úr klóm ræningjanna. Aftur á móti reyndust útilegumennirnir stundum hinir mestu heiðursmenn, sem vöruðust eins og heitan eld að gera á hluta nokkurs manns; með ungum útilegumönnum af þessu tagi og bóndadætrum, er þeir námu burt, tókust oft góðar ástir, unnust þau vel og lengi í sæludalnum, eða komust að lokum farsællega til byggða. Útilegumannatrú lifði fram á 19. öld. Jón frá Hlíðarendakoti, fylgdarmaður enska skáldsins William Morris, sótti um styrk til Alþingis til að fara á hendur þeim og útrýma þeim.

Mikið af íslenzkum þjóðsögum sækir efni sitt í þjóðtrú þá, sem lýst hefur verið hér að framan. Allmargar sögur eru þó alveg ósnortnar af þjóðtrúnni, t. d. sögur um einkennilega menn. Slíkar sögur eru mjög raunsæjar og minna stundum nokkuð á Íslendinga-sögurnar gömlu. Aðrar eru allt annað en raunsæjar, þær eru jafnvel enn rómantískari en hinar rómantískustu útilegumanna- eða huldu-fólks-sögur. Þetta eru æfintýrin. Þau geta verið blönduð þjóðtrú, en eru annars ekki við eina fjölina felld. Ótal æfintýri eru til um kóng og drottning í ríki sínu og karl og kerlingu í koti. Þau enda með því, að karlssonurinn fær kóngsdótturina. Þá eru ekki fáar sögur um karlsdæturnar þrjár, Ásu, Signýju og Helgu; Helga er vngst og fallegust, en hún er höfð útundan; samt fær hún kóngs-soninn á endanum. Svo eru stjúpmæðrasögurnar. Kóngur missir drottningu sína og leggst í rúmið af harmi. Ráðgjafar hans sjá, að svo búið má ekki standa. Þeir fara að leita honum annarar drottningar. En þó að þeir séu varaðir við að taka hana af eyjum eða annesjum, þá fer svo, að þeir finna hana einmitt á eyðiey, eftir langar hafvillur. Kóngur gerir samt brúðkaup til hennar og tekur

287

aftur gleði sína. En áður en langt um líður, sýnir drottning sinn innri mann, og leggur á kóngsbörnin, að þau verði að dýrum eða ófreskjum, ef hún sendir þau þá ekki til flagðsins systur sinnar. Í þessum álögum verða kóngsbörnin að vera, þar til einhver karlsson, eða kóngsson verður til að leysa þau úr þeim. Fær drottningar-flagðið þá makleg málagjöld og er brennd á báli.

65. Kirkjusmiðurinn á Reyni.

Einu sinni bjó maður nokkur á Reyni í Mýrdal; átti hann að byggja þar kirkju, en varð naumt fyrir með timburaðdrætti til hennar; var komið að slætti, en engir smiðir fengnir, svo hann tók að ugga að sér, að kirkjunni yrði komið upp fyrir veturinn. Einn dag var hann að reika út um tún í þungu skapi. Þá kom maður til hans og bauð honum að byggja kirkjuna fyrir hann. Skyldi bóndi segja honum nafn hans, áður en smíðinni væri lokið, en að öðrum kosti skyldi bóndi láta af hendi við hann einkason sinn á sjötta ári. Þessu keyptu þeir; tók aðkomumaðurinn til verka; skifti hann sér af engu nema smíðum sínum, og var fáorður mjög, enda vannst smíðin undarlega fljótt, og sá bóndi, að henni mundi lokið nálægt sláttulokum. Tók bóndi þá að ógleðjast mjög, en gat eigi að gert. Um haustið, þegar kirkjan var nærri fullsmíðuð, ráfaði bóndi út fyrir tún; lagðist hann þar fyrir, utan í hól nokkurn. Heyrði hann þá kveðið í hólnum, sem móðir kvæði við barn sitt, og var það þetta:

> Senn kemur hann Finnur,
> faðir þinn frá Reyn,
> með þinn litla leiksvein.

Var þetta kveðið upp aftur og aftur. Bóndi hresstist nú mjög og gekk heim til kirkju. Var smiðurinn þá búinn að telgja hina seinustu fjöl yfir altarinu, og ætlaði að festa hana. Bóndi mælti: "Senn ertu búinn, Finnur minn." Við þessi orð varð smiðnum svo bilt, að hann felldi fjölina niður og hvarf; hefir hann ekki sézt síðan.

66. Ýsa var það heillin!

Einu sinn mættust tvær kerlingar á ferð. Þær áttu heima langt hvor frá annari, svo þær þurftu nú svo sem að setjast niður og segja hvor annari tíðindin úr sinni sveit. Þær sáu, að þær gátu slegið tvær flugur í einu höggi, svo þær tóku upp hjá sér sjálf-skeiðinga og mat, og fóru að fá sér bita. Þeim bar nú margt á góma, og meðal annars segir önnur kerlingin, að það hafi nýlega

288

rekið fjarskalega fágætan fisk í sinni sveit. Hin spyr, hvaða fiskur
það hafi verið, en það man hún ómögulega. Þá fer hin að telja
upp ýmsa fiska, sem hún mundi eftir, en aldrei átti hún kollgátuna.
" Ekki vænti ég, að það hafi nú verið stökkull? " " Og sussu nei."
" Það skyldi þó aldrei hafa verið marhnútur? " " Vertu í eilífri
náðinni, ekki hét hann það." " Það hefur þó víst ekki verið skata? "
" Issi, sissi, nei." " Nú, það mun þó ekki hafa verið ýsa? " " Jú,
ýsa var það, heillin!" sagði þá hin, og hnippti í lagskonu sína;
en til allrar óhamingju mundi hún ekki eftir því, að hún var með
opinn hníf í hendinni, svo hnífurinn fór á hol í síðuna á hinni
kerlingunni, og sálaðist hún þar að vörmu spori.

67. Nátttröllið.

Það var á einum stað, að sá sem gæta átti bæjarins á jólanóttina,
meðan hitt fólkið var við aftansöng, fannst annaðhvort dauður
að morgni eða æðisgenginn. Þótti heimamönnum þetta illt, og vildu
fáir verða til að vera heima jólanóttina. Einu sinni býðst stúlka
ein til að gæta bæjarins. Urðu hinir því fegnir og fóru burtu.
Stúlkan sat á palli í baðstofu og kvað við barn, sem hún sat undir.
Um nóttina er komið á gluggann og sagt:

> Fögur þykir mér hönd þín,
> snör mín en snarpa, og dillidó.

Þá segir hún:

> Hún hefir aldrei saur sópað,
> ári minn Kári, og korriró.

Þá er sagt á glugganum:

> Fagurt þykir mér auga þitt,
> snör mín en snarpa, og dillidó.

Þá segir hún:

> Aldrei hefir það illt séð,
> ári minn Kári, og korriró.

Þá er sagt á glugganum:

> Fagur þykir mér fótur þinn,
> snör mín en snarpa, og dillidó.

Þá segir hún:

> Aldrei hefir hann saur troðið,
> ári minn Kári, og korriró.

Þá er sagt á glugganum:

> Dagur er í austri,
> snör mín en snarpa, og dillidó.

289

Þá segir hún:

> Stattu og vertu að steini,
> en engum þó að meini,
> ári minn Kári, og korriró.

Hvarf þá vætturin af glugganum. En um morguninn, þegar fólkið kom heim, var kominn steinn mikill í bæjarsundið, og stóð hann þar æ síðan. Sagði þá stúlkan frá því, sem hún hafði heyrt (en ekkert sá hún, því hún leit aldrei við), og hafði það verið nátttröll, sem á gluggann kom.

68. Smalastúlkan.

Það bar til vestur í Dalasýslu, að smalastúlka ein fór til kirkju og var til altaris. Þegar hún kom frá kirkjunni, fór hún undir eins að smala, og gaf sér ekki tíma til að borða áður. Hún gekk með klettum nokkrum. Þá heyrir hún, að sagt er í klettunum: "Ragnhildur í Rauðhömrum." Þá er svarað í öðrum klettum: "Hvað viltu, þussinn í Þríhömrum?" Þá segir hann: "Hér hleypur steik um stiga, tökum hana, tökum hana." Þá er svarað í hinum klettunum: "Svei henni, láttu hana fara, hún er kolug um kjaftinn." Stúlkan fór sinn veg og heyrði ekki meira af samtali hjúa þessara.

69. Sending.

Einu sinni var kona. Hún sat á baðstofupallinum við vinnu sína, og var enginn maður í bænum nema hún ein. Bóndi var ekki heima; hann hafði farið eitthvað af bæ, en vinnufólkið var allt úti við, sitt hvað að sýsla. Þá kom inn í baðstofuna drengur, ekki hár, en heldur gildvaxinn. Hann spyr konuna, hvar bóndi sé, en hún var ekki svo fljót á sér að segja til þess; því henni leizt ekki vel á strákinn. Hann spurði þá enn að bónda, því hann sagðist eiga að finna hann, og finna hann duglega, og megi hann ekki tefja. Konan spurði hann þá um erindið, og hvort hún gæti ekki afgreitt hann. Þegar strákur neitaði því, þá segir konan: "Ég held, að slíkur hnokki, sem þú ert, hafi ekki mikið að gera í hendurnar á manninum mínum. Eða getur þú orðið stærri en þú ert nú?" Strákur sagði það vera. Hún bað hann að sýna sér það; annars tryði hún því ekki.

Smá-óx þá strákur, þangað til hann varð sem tröll og náði upp í mæni. Konan sagði, að hann væri ekki allur, þar sem hann væri séður, og bað hann nú fara í samt lag aftur. Hann gerir svo. Þá spyr konan, hvort hann geti gert sig eins lítinn að sínu leyti og hann gæti gert sig stóran, og bað hann sýna sér það. Hann játar

HÉR HLEYPUR STEIK UM STIGA.

KERLINGIN MEÐ SENDINGUNA.

því, og smá-minnkar hann nú, þangað til hann var orðinn á stærð
við tittling. Þá tók konan upp dálítið glas, og spurði, hvort hann
gæti orðið svo lítill, að hann kæmist ofan í glasið. Þá gerði strákur
sig að flugu og fór ofan í glasið; en konan var ekki sein á sér, heldur
brá þegar líknarbelg yfir glasið, og mátti svo kauði kúra þar niðri
í. Þegar bóndi kom heim, fékk konan honum glasið, og sagði
honum upp alla sögu. Bónda þótti vænt um bragð konu sinnar,
tók við glasinu og fór með það, og vissi enginn framar, hvað um
það varð.

70. Sæmundur fróði fær Oddann.

Þegar þeir Sæmundur, Kálfur og Hálfdán komu úr Svartaskóla,
var Oddinn laus, og báðu þeir þá allir kónginn að veita sér hann.
Kóngurinn vissi dável, við hverja hann átti, og segir, að sá þeirra
skuli hafa Oddann, sem fljótastur verði að komast þangað. Fer þá
Sæmundur undir eins og kallar á kölska og segir: "Syntu nú með
mig til Íslands, og ef þú kemur mér þar á land án þess að væta
kjóllafið mitt í sjónum, þá máttu eiga mig." Kölski gekk að þessu,
brá sér í selslíki og fór með Sæmund á bakinu. En á leiðinni var
Sæmundur alltaf að lesa í Saltaranum. Voru þeir eftir lítinn
tíma komnir undir land á Íslandi. Þá slær Sæmundur Saltaranum
í hausinn á selnum, svo hann sökk, en Sæmundur fór í kaf og synti
til lands. Með þessu varð kölski af kaupinu, en Sæmundur fékk
Oddann.

71. Heyhirðingin.

Einu sinni átti Sæmundur fróði mikið af þurri töðu undir, en
rigningarlega leit út. Hann biður því allt heimafólk sitt að reyna
að ná heyinu saman undan rigningunni.

Kerling ein var hjá honum í Odda mjög gömul, er Þórhildur hét.
Prestur gengur til hennar og biður hana að reyna að haltra út á
túnið og raka þar dreifar. Hún segist skuli reyna það, tekur hrífu
og bindur á hrífuskaftsendann hettu þá, sem hún var vön að hafa
á höfðinu, og skjöktir svo út á túnið. Áður en hún fór, segir hún
við Sæmund prest, að hann skuli vera í garðinum og taka á móti
heyinu; því vinnumennirnir verði ekki svo lengi að binda og bera
heim. Prestur segist skuli fylgja ráðum hennar í því, enda muni
þá bezt fara.

Þegar kerlingin kemur út á túnið, rekur hún hrífuendann undir
hverja sátu, sem sætt var, og segir: "Upp í garð til Sæmundar!"
Það varð að áhrinsorðum, því hver baggi, sem kerling renndi hrífu-

skaftinu undir með þessum ummælum, hvarf jafnóðum heim í garð. Sæmundur segir þá við kölska og ára hans, að nú sé þörf að duga að hlaða úr. Að skömmum tíma liðnum var allt heyið komið í garð undan rigningunni.

Á eftir sagði Sæmundur við kerlingu: " Eitthvað kannt þú, Þórhildur mín." Hún segir: " Það er nú lítið og mestallt gleymt, sem ég kunni í ungdæmi mínu."

72. Búkolla.

Einu sinni var karl og kerling í koti sínu. Þau áttu einn son, en þótti ekkert vænt um hann. Ekki voru fleiri menn en þau þrjú í kotinu. Eina kú áttu þau karl og kerling; það voru allar skepnurnar. Kýrin hét Búkolla.

Einu sinni bar kýrin, og sat kerlingin sjálf yfir henni. En þegar kýrin var borin og heil orðin, hljóp kerling inn í bæinn. Skömmu seinna kom hún út aftur til að vitja um kúna. En þá var hún horfin. Fara þau nú bæði, karlinn og kerlingin, að leita kýrinnar, og leituðu víða og lengi, en komu jafnnær aftur. Voru þau stygg í skapi og skipuðu stráknum að fara, og koma ekki fyrir sín augu aftur, fyrr en hann kæmi með kúna. Bjuggu þau strák út með nesti og nýja skó, og nú lagði hann af stað eitthvað út í bláinn.

Hann gekk lengi, lengi, þangað til hann settist niður og fór að éta. Þá segir hann: "Baulaðu nú, Búkolla mín, ef þú ert nokkurs staðar á lífi." Þá heyrir hann, að kýrin baular langt, langt í burtu.

Gengur karlsson enn lengi, lengi. Sezt hann þá enn niður til að éta og segir: " Baulaðu nú, Búkolla mín, ef þú ert nokkurs staðar á lífi." Heyrir hann þá, að Búkolla baular dálítið nær en í fyrra sinn.

Enn gengur karlsson lengi, lengi, þangað til hann kemur fram á fjarskalega háa hamra, þar sezt hann niður til að éta og segir um leið: " Baulaðu nú, Búkolla mín, ef þú ert nokkurs staðar á lífi." Þá heyrir hann, að kýrin baular undir fótum sér. Hann klifrast þá ofan hamrana og sér í þeim helli mjög stóran. Þar gengur hann inn og sér Búkollu bundna undir bálki í hellinum. Hann leysir hana undir eins og leiðir hana út á eftir sér og heldur heimleiðis.

Þegar hann er kominn nokkuð á veg, sér hann, hvar kemur ógnastór tröllskessa á eftir sér og önnur minni með henni. Hann sér, að stóra skessan er svo stórstíg, að hún muni undir eins ná sér. Þá segir hann: " Hvað eigum við nú að gera, Búkolla mín?" Hún segir: " Taktu hár úr hala mínum og leggðu það á jörðina." Hann gerir það. Þá segir kýrin við hárið: " Legg ég á og mæli ég um,

292

SÆMUNDUR FRÓÐI Á SELNUM

BÚKOLLA OG STRÁKUR.

að þú verðir að svo stórri móðu, að ekki komist yfir, nema fuglinn fljúgandi." Í sama bili varð hárið að ógnastórri móðu.

Þegar skessan kom að móðunni, segir hún: "Ekki skal þér þetta duga, strákur. Skrepptu heim, stelpa," segir hún við minni skessuna, "og sæktu stóra nautið hans föður míns." Stelpan fer, og kemur með ógnastórt naut. Nautið drakk undir eins upp alla móðuna.

Þá sér karlsson, að skessan muni þegar ná sér, því hún var svo stórstíg. Þá segir hann: "Hvað eigum við nú að gera, Búkolla mín?" "Taktu hár úr hala mínum og leggðu það á jörðina," segir hún. Hann gerir það. Þá segir Búkolla við hárið: "Legg ég á og mæli ég um, að þú verðir að svo stóru báli, að enginn komist yfir, nema fuglinn fljúgandi." Og undir eins varð hárið að báli.

Þegar skessan kom að bálinu segir hún: "Ekki skal þér þetta duga, strákur. Farðu og sæktu stóra nautið hans föður míns, stelpa," segir hún við minni skessuna. Hún fer og kemur með nautið. En nautið meig þá öllu vatninu, sem það drakk úr móðunni, og slökkti bálið. Nú sér karlsson, að skessan muni strax ná sér, því hún var svo stórstíg. Þá segir hann: "Hvað eigum við nú að gera, Búkolla mín?" "Taktu hár úr hala mínum og leggðu það á jörðina," segir hún. Síðan segir hún við hárið: "Legg ég á og mæli ég um, að þú verðir að svo stóru fjalli, sem enginn kemst yfir, nema fuglinn fljúgandi." Varð þá hárið að svo háu fjalli, að karlsson sá ekki nema upp í heiðan himininn.

Þegar skessan kemur að fjallinu, segir hún: "Ekki skal þér þetta duga, strákur. Sæktu stóra borjárnið hans föður míns, stelpa," segir hún við minni skessuna. Stelpan fer og kemur með borjárnið. Borar þá skessan gat á fjallið, en varð of bráð á sér, þegar hún sá í gegn, og tróð sér inn í gatið, en það var of þröngt, svo hún stóð þar föst og varð loks að steini í gatinu, og þar er hún enn. En karlsson komst heim með Búkollu sína, og urðu karl og kerling því ósköp fegin.

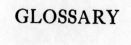

GLOSSARY

GLOSSARY

Besides containing the words of the preceding texts, a few terms, mostly connected with the war, culled from newspapers, and the most common place names of Iceland, this glossary also contains the vocabulary of the grammar. It is not an index to the grammar, although several references, mostly to the Syntax, ought to help those who want such information to get it.

In general the glossary is designed to help the beginner as much as possible to find and learn the correct grammatical form and syntactical construction. In nouns are given not only the endings according to which the noun is classified (as in Zoëga's *Íslenzk-ensk orðabók*), e. g. *dagur, -s, -ar*, but also gender and class number: m.1 (masculine first class), which may be used as a reference to the grammar. The adjectives are, for the benefit of the beginner, given in all three genders. The same rule is followed in the adjectival pronouns, while full inflexions are given of the personal pronouns and some others, mostly in order to show the pronunciation. The comparison of adjectives (and adverbs) is also given whenever it is not the regular one of *-ar(i), -ast(ur)*.

For the verbs three principal parts are given of the weak and four of the strong, e. g. *telja, taldi, talinn(ið)* wv.1, and *bjóða, býð, bauð, buðum, boðinn(-ið)* v.2. In addition the 1.pers. present of the strong verb is given (*býð* [1]), because of its frequent i-shift; of the past participle both the masculine and the neuter forms are given, again a feature to ease the task of the beginner. The abbreviations should not be hard to understand, e. g. *talinn(-ið)* = *talinn* m., *talið* n.; *kallað(ur)* = *kallaður* m., *kallað* n.; *breiddur (breitt)* = *breiddur* m., *breitt* n. Some verbs, as will be seen, have only the neuter form: these verbs never take an accusative object, and are mostly intransitive. Besides giving the forms in full to the above extent, the class marks, e. g. wv.1, v.2 = *weak* verb first class, *strong* verb second class, are always added and may be used as a direct reference to the grammar.

Both in nouns and verbs the mark w is used to designate the *weak* inflexion (declension, conjugation), while the *strong* is left unmarked: wm.1 = weak masculine first class, wv.1 = weak verb first class, and v.1 = strong verb first class.

[1] In the *Æfingar* (Exercises) the 3.pers. present is usually given because of the variety of its form.

Furthermore: forms of nouns, adjectives, adverbs, pronouns, and verbs that either have a totally different stem (*góður*: *betri*), or a considerably changed one by vowel or consonant shifts (*bjóða*: *býð*; *góður*: *gott*) are listed in alphabetical order with reference to the catch-word. E. g. *öll*, see *allur*; *axar, -ir*, see *öx*; *lönd*, see *land*; *mín*, see *ég* and *minn*. Here the beginner should be warned that he will find listed thus specially (with few exceptions) only such forms, as are actually entered in the glossary under the catch-word, e. g. *lönd*, because the catchword is *land, -s, lönd*, but not *öpum*, because the catchword is *api, -a, -ar*.

In many compound words, especially adverbs and conjunctions, usage varies as to writing them in one or more words. The present official orthography favors the latter expedient, and I have followed that rule in my texts. But in the glossary I have entered these words as compounds with the uncompounded form as a variant. E. g. *allsstaðar*, also *alls staðar*.

It is hoped that most of the personal and place names found in the grammar and the texts have found their way into the glossary. In addition the most common place names of Iceland have been added, chiefly for the sake of pronunciation, but also because a translation (in single quotation marks) has been given of the place names, if their meaning was perspicuous, as it usually is. This translation is not offered for adoption by translators, still less map makers of Iceland, but only because the foreign student should as a matter of course know their meaning.

In the phonetical notation the ' recommended ' pronunciation (cf. the Preface) is put first, the other pronunciations after a semicolon. E. g. [stul·kʰa, -ɤ(r̥) ; stul̬ka]. Sometimes the other pronunciation is abbreviated in some way, e. g. [ba:kʰarɪ, -a(r̥) ; ba:g̊-] which, written in full, would be: [ba:kʰarɪ, ba:kʰara, ba:kʰarar̥; ba:g̊arɪ, etc.]. At times the abbreviations entail a change in the order of the forms, e. g. *dilkur, -s, -ar* [dɪl·kʰɤr̥, -ar̥, dɪlkʰs]. In long words the chief break is indicated by a hyphen, e. g. [stjourd̥nmau·la-ma:ðɤr̥]. Full consequence in the notation of assimilations at the junction of two words has not been attained.

The alphabetical order is the English one with as slight modifications as possible, accented vowels being treated as the unaccented ones (*á = a*, etc.) and *ð* being entered as *d*. Only at the end are added the specific Icelandic letters *þ, æ, ö* in that order. ·

For abbreviations see the list of Abbreviations.

GLOSSARY.

3. **á, áði, áð** [au:, au:ðɪ, au:ð] wv.3
á hestum rest and graze horses.

a [a:] interr. ınterj. (= *ha*) what?
beg your pardon?

1. **á, ár, ár** [au:(r)] f.1 river; also
in place names: -*á, Ar-*.

2. **á, ám, áa,** see 1. *á* and *ær*.

4. **á,** see *eiga*.

5. **á** [au:] **A.** prep. with acc. (S. I,
2, 3, 2) (1) of place: on(to), in(to):
ganga á fjöll go up into the mountains, climb mountains; *upp á safn*
up to the library; *sauma á e-n* sew
for sbdy (sew clothes to be put on
sbdy); (2) of time: at, in, per:
á morgun tomorrow; *á kvöldin,
morgnana* in the evening, morning;
tvisvar á dag twice a day (S. II,
1n2); *króna á dag* one crown per
day. **B.** prep. with dat. (S. I, **3,
3, 2**) (1) of place: on, in, at: *á
húsinu* on the house; *á bœnum* at
the farm; *á Íslandi* in Iceland; *á
Norðurlöndum* in Scandinavia; *á
Laugavatni* at L-vatn; *á (bóka)-
safninu* at (in) the library, *á fjöru*
on the beach, at ebbtide; (2) on,
in, of: *eyrun á mér* my ears (S. I,
4, 1, 3); *þeir meiða mig á tánum*
they hurt my toes (literally: me on
the toes); *gluggarnir á húsinu* the
windows of the house; *nafn á e-u*
name of sth, the term for sth;
niðursuða á síld canning of herring;
(3) in: *vera á peysufötum* wear
peysuföt habitually; *vera á hreyfingu*
be in motion, be moving; (4) as
respects, of : *skortur á timbri* lack
of timber; (5) of time: on, in, at:
á níunda ári in (my, the) ninth
year; *á vetrum* in winter; *á jólunum,
páskunum* at Christmas, Easter; *á
viku* in a week's time; (6) with
verbs: *byrja á e-u* begin with sth;

þurrka á handklæði wipe (dry)
with a napkin. **C.** With preps and
advs: *á eftir* afterwards; *á eftir e-u*
after sth; *á meðal þeirra* among
them; *á meðan* adv. in the meantime, for the time being; *á meðan*
conj. while (S. VIII, 3(h)); *á
móti suðri* facing south; *á undan
e-u* before (in front of) sth; *á
undan* adv. before.

6. **á** [au:] interj. well! is that so! *á,
varstu feginn að flú?* well, you did
scram after all, did you!

ábreiða, -u, -ur [au:brei·ða, -ɤ(r̥)]
wf.1 cover, bedcover, blanket,
= *teppi*.

áburður, -ar [au:bʏrðʏr̥, -ar̥] m.3
manure; carrying of burdens, *til
á-ar* for carrying burdens, as a beast
of burden.

ábyggilegur [au:bɪg̊ˌɪ-lɛ:qʏr̥] adj.
(see -*legur*) reliable, dependable.

ábyrgð, -ar, -ir [au:bɪr(q)ð, -ðar̥, -ðɪr̥]
f.2 insurance; *setja bréf í ábyrgð*
insure a letter, register a letter;
á. á bréf registration of a letter;
ábyrgðarbréf registered letter.

ábyrgjast, -byrgðist, -byrgzt [au:bɪr̥-
g̊ˌast, -bɪr(q)ðɪst, -bɪr̥(x)st] wv.2
(middle voice only) *á. e-ð* guarantee
something.

1. **að, eð** [a:ð, ɛ:ð] rel. pron. that,
who, which (In. VI, 4; S. IV, 4).

2. **að** [a(:ð)] (Pr.4, 2) **A.** prep. with
dat. (1) of place: to, towards: *að
Kirkjubæjarklaustri* to K-klaustur;
at, in: *að Klaustri* at K-ur; (2) of
time: at, in: *að kvöldi (dags)* in
the evening; *að vetrinum (til)* in
winter, during the winter; *að þessu
sinni* this time, for the time being;
að þeim tíma liðnum that time having passed, after that (time); (3)
in, concerning: *að öllum frágangi*
in all make-up; *svipaður að gerð*

Consonants: [ð] brea*th*e; [g] *g*ood; [gɪ] *gy*arden (garden); [hw̥] *wh*at; [j] *y*es; [kɪ] *cy*an
(can); [ŋ] thi*ng*; [q] N. Germ. sa*g*en; [r] Scottish *r*; [x] approx. Germ. a*ch*; [þ] *th*in.
Voiceless: ○; [b̥, d̥, g̊] approx. *p, t, k.* Half-voiced: *italics*. Aspiration and preaspiration:
[ʰ]; [pʰ, tʰ, kʰ] *p-, t-, k-*. Others as in English.

similar in (as to) make; *vera gagn að e-u* be help in something; *ekki er gagn að því* it is of no avail; (4) according to: *að vísu* to be sure; *að sögn* according to what is said; (5) for, as: *með skarsúð að þaki* with a clincher roof as a roof. **B.** With inf.: to; in order to: *að hafa* to have, *vera að gera e-ð* be doing something (S. VI, **11**, *6*). **C.** Adverbially: *koma að* come up from somewhere, esp. from the sea; *vera að* keep on, but: *e-ð er að e-u* something is wrong with something, something is the matter with something; *að austan* from the east; *koma að austan* come from the east; *að austan* (= *austan við*) *er hraun* lava is to the east.

3. **að** [a(:ð)] conj. that, so that; *þó að* although; *því að* for; *af því að* [af·þi·jað] because; *til þess að* in order that, in order to; *til þess að . . . ekki* lest; *svo að* [sɔ:að] so that; *með því að* [mɛþ:i·jað], *úr því að* [ur·þi·jað] since (S. VI, **9**, *4*, 1 and *5*, 1; VII, 2, 3; VIII, 3 (a)).

áð, áði, see *æja* and 3. *á.*

aðal- [a:ðal-] pref. chief.

aðalatvinnuvegur, -ar, -ir [a:ðal-a:tʰvɪn·ʏvɛ:qʏr̥, -ar̥, -vei:jɪr̥; -a:d̥·] m.3 chief business, chief livelihood.

aðalbláber, -s, -, (-ja) [a:ðal-blau:bɛr, -bɛr̥s, -bɛrja] n. whortleberry.

aðaldalur, -s, -ir [a:ðal-da:lʏr̥, -dal·s, -da:lɪr̥] m.2 chief, main valley..

aðaldyr [a:ðal-dɪ:r] f.3.pl. chief door, entrance.

aðalfararskjóti, -a, -ar [a:ðal-fa:rar̥-skjou:tʰɪ, -a, -ar̥; -skjou:dɪ] wm.1 chief means of communication.

aðalgata, -götu, -ur [a:ðal-ga:tʰa, -gö:tʰʏ(r̥); -ga:d̥a, -gö:d̥ʏ] wf.1 chief street, main street, main thoroughfare.

aðalhlutverk, -s [a:ðal-hl̥ʏ:tʰvɛr̥k, -s; -hl̥ʏ:d̥·] n. chief role.

aðallega [a:ðal-ɛ:qa] adv. chiefly.

aðalmatur, -ar [a:ðal-ma:tʰʏr̥, -ar̥, -ma:d̥·] m.3 the chief course (meal).

aðalréttur, -ar, -ir [a:ðal-rjɛʰt:ʏr̥, -ar̥, -ɪr̥] m.3 the chief course.

Aðalstræti, -s [a:ðal-strai:tʰɪ, -ɪs; -strai:d̥·] n. 'Main Street.'

aðalvopn, -s [a:ðal-vɔʰp·n̥, -vɔʰp̩n̥s] n. chief weapon.

aðalþáttur, -ar, -þættir [a:ðal-þauʰt:-ʏr̥, -ar̥, -þaiʰt:ɪr̥] m.3 chief, main strand; chief part, element.

aðdráttur, -ar, -drættir [að-drauʰt·ʏr̥, -ar̥, -draiʰt·ɪr̥] m.3 transport(ing) to a place.

aðeins [a:ðeins] adv. only.

aðfangadagur, -s, -ar [að-fauŋga-da:qʏr̥, -dax·s; af:auŋga-] m.1 the day before a holiday, especially before Christmas.

aðferð, -ar, -ir [að-fɛrð, -ðar̥, -ðɪr̥] f.2 method.

aðflutningur, -s, -ar [að-flʏʰtnɪŋgʏr̥, -ɪŋs, -ɪŋgar̥] m.1 import, transport to the country.

aðgangur, -s [að-gauŋgʏr̥, -gauŋs] m.1 entrance, entrance fee; *a. að eldhúsi* access to (the use of) a kitchen.

aðgreining, -ar [að-grei:nɪŋg, -ɪŋgar̥] f.1 distinction; *til a-ar* for distinction.

aðgöngumiði, -a, -ar [að-göyŋgʏ-mɪ:ðɪ, -a(r̥)] wm.1 ticket.

aðra, -ar, -ir, see 1. *annar.*

ádráttur, -ar, -drættir [au:drauʰt·ʏr̥, -ar̥, -draiʰt·ɪr̥] m.3 draught of a (drag)net, dragging (a river) with dragnet.

aðsókn, -ar, -ir [að-souʰkn̥, -nar̥, -nɪr̥] f.2 attendance; *a. draugs* visitation, attack of a ghost (see *sækja að*).

áður [au:ðʏr] (1) adv. before, formerly, *á. fyrr* earlier, of old; (2) conj. before (S. VIII, 3 (h) and 4), *á. en* conj. before; *á. en langt um liður* before long.

af [a:v, av., af.] **A.** prep. with dat. of, off, from, by, with; (1) of: *einn af þeim* one of them; *glas af vatni* glass of water; (2) from: *af (á) stað* away, from the place; *hafa gagn af e-u* gain (profit) from sth; *dregið af e-u* derived from sth;

Vowels: *a* [a] approx. father; *á* [au] cow; *e* [ɛ] set; *é* [jɛ] yes; *i, y* [ɪ] sit; *í, ý* [i] feel; *o* [ɔ] law; *ó* [ou] note; *u* [ʏ] approx. Germ. Mütter; *ú* [u] school; *y* = *i; ý* = *í; æ* [ai] ice; *ö* [ö] Germ. hören; *au* [öy] French *feuille;* *ei, ey* [ei] ale. Length [:]; half-length [·].

kaupa af e-m buy from sbdy; *fréttast af e-m* be heard from sbdy; *sjá af e-u* see from sth; *þurrka af* wipe off; (3) to form the passive: *af* by: *af góðum var hann gefinn mér* it was given me by a good person (S. VI, 8); (4) by, with: *glíma af snilld, list* wrestle artistically, *af kröftum* with strength, (brute) force. B. *Af því að* conj. because (S. VI, 9, 4, 3; VIII, 3(b)); *af því, sem* . . . from what. . . .

áfangastaður, -ar, -ir [au: fauŋ̊a‧sta: ðүɽ, -aɽ, -ıɽ] m.3 (bus) stop.

afar- [a:vaɽ‧] pref. very.

afarstór, -stór, -stórt [a: vaɽ‧stou: r, -stoυɽ.t] adj. awfully big, huge.

áfasúpa, -u [au: (v)a‧su: pʰa, -ʏ; -su: b‧] wf.1 buttermilk soup.

afbrigði, -s, - [av‧brıqðı, -ıs; ab:rıqðı] n. exception; *með afbrigðum* exceedingly, exceptionally.

afdrif [av.drı‧v] n. pl. the end, the fate (of sbdy).

áfengi, -s [au: feiŋ̊ĝˌı, -ıs] n. intoxicating drinks.

áfengisverzlun, -unar, -anir [au:feiŋ̊ĝˌıs‧verslʏn, -ʏnaɽ, -anıɽ] f.2 liquor store; *Á. ríkisins* 'State Monopoly of Wines and Spirits.'

afföll, -falla [af:öðl, af:aðla] n. pl. discount.

afgangur, -s, -ar [av.gauŋ̊ĝʏɽ, -gauŋs, -gauŋ̊ĝaɽ] m.1 remainder.

afgirða, -girti, -girt(ur) [av.gˌırða, -gˌıɽtı, -gˌıɽtʏɽ] wv. 2 inclose, fence in or fence off.

afgr. = *afgreiðsla.*

afgreiða, -greiddi, -greiddur (-greitt) [av‧grei‧ða, -greid‧ı, -ʏɽ, -greiʰt‧] wv. 2 help, dispatch, expedite; wait on (in stores, offices).

afgreiðsla, -u, -ur [av.greiðsla, -ʏ(ɽ)] wf. 1 office; *a. blaðs* office of a newspaper, *a. hótelsins* office of the hotel; delivery.

afgreiðsluborð, -s, [av‧greiðslʏ‧bɔr‧ð, -bɔrðs] n. office desk.

afgreiðslustörf, -starfa [av.greiðslʏ‧stör.v, -star.va] n. pl. delivery; waiting on, selling.

afhenda, -henti, -hent(ur) [a: vhenda, -hentʰ(ı), -ʏɽ; -hentı, -ʏɽ] wv.2 *a. e-m e-ð* deliver sth to sbdy.

afi, -a, -ar [a: vı, -a(ɽ)] wm. 1 grandpa, grandfather.

áfir [au: (v)ıɽ] f. 2. pl. buttermilk (Pr. 3, 4, 2).

afkasta, -aði, -að [af‧kʰasta, -aðı, -að] wv. 4 accomplish, perform, be able to produce.

afklæða, -klæddi, -klæddur (-klætt) [af.kʰlai.ða,-kʰlaid.ɪ,-ʏɽ,-kʰlaiʰt.] wv. 2 refl. *a.sig* undress (oneself).

afkomandi, -a, -endur [af.kʰɔ.mandı, -a, -endʏɽ] wm. 2 descendant.

afkæla, -kældi, -kældur (-kælt) [af.‧kˌʰai.la, -kˌʰaildı, -ʏɽ, -kˌʰailt] wv. 2 cool (= *kæla*).

afl, -s, öfl [ab̥.l, ab̥ls, öb̥.l] n. strength, force.

afla, -aði, -að [ab̥.la, -aðı, -að] wv.4 earn, acquire, get; *a. e-s* procure sth, get sth.

aflaga [av.la.qa] adj. indecl. out of order (In. III, 3, 3).

aflangur, -löng, -langt [av.lauŋ̊ĝʏɽ, -löyŋ̊ĝ, -lauŋtʰ; -lauŋ̊t] adj. oblong.

afleitur, -leit, -leitt [av.lei.tʰʏɽ, -lei.tʰ, -leiʰt.; -lei.d̥-] adj. outrageous, terrible, out of the question, impossible; *ekki svo a.* not so bad, quite good (litotes).

afmæli, -s, - [av.mai.lı, am: ai.lı] n. birthday, anniversary.

afmælisgjöf, -gjafar, -gjafir [av.mai‧‧lıs-gˌö:v, -gˌa:vaɽ, -ıɽ; am:ai‧lıs-] f. 2 birthday present.

afneita, -aði, -að [av.nei.tʰa, -aðı, -að; -nei.d̥-] wv. 4 deny, *a. e-m* deny, abjure sbdy.

áfram [au: fram(.)] adv. ahead, forth.

áframhaldandi [au:fram‧haldandı] adj. indecl. continuing.

afrennsli, -s, - [av.rensl̥ı, -ıs] n. draining, drainage.

afskekktur, -skekkt, -skekkt [af.‧skˌextʏɽ, -skˌext] adj. out-of-the-way.

afstaða, -stöðu, -ur [af.sta.ða, -stö.‧ðʏ(ɽ)] wf. 1 reaction, attitude.

1. aftan(n), -ans, -nar [af.tan (-an), -ans, aftnaɽ] m. 1 evening.

Consonants: [ð] brea*the*; [g] *g*ood; [gˌ] *gy*arden (garden); [hʍ] *wh*at; [j] *y*es; [kˌ] *cy*an (can); [ŋ] thi*ng*; [q] N. Germ. sa*g*en; [r] Scottish *r*; [x] approx. Germ. a*ch*; [þ] *th*in. Voiceless: ○; [b̥, d̥, ĝ] approx. *p, t, k.* Half-voiced: *italics.* Aspiration and preaspiration: [ʰ]; [pʰ, tʰ, kʰ] *p-, t-, k-.* Others as in English.

301

2. aftan [aʰt: an, af.tan] adv. from behind (Pr. **4**, *3*).

aftansöngur, -s, -var [af.tan-söyŋ.ģyɼ, -söyŋ.s, -söyŋ.ģvaɼ] m. 1 evening service, evensong.

aftra, -aði, -að [af.tra, -aðɪ, -að] wv. 4 hinder, hold back from, *a. e-m frá e-u* hinder one from (doing) sth.

aftur [aʰt:yɼ, af.tyɼ] adv. (Pr. **4**, *3*) again, back; *komdu aftur* come back; *upp aftur og aftur* over and over again; *a. á móti* on the other hand.

afturfótur, -ar, -fætur [aʰt:yɼ-fou:tʰyɼ, -aɼ, -fai:tʰyɼ; af.tyɼ-; fou:d̥-, -fai:d̥-] m.4 hind foot, hind leg; *haltur á öðrum afturfæti* lame in one hind leg.

afturganga, -göngu, -ur [aʰt:yr-gauŋ.ģa, -göyŋ.ģy(ɼ); af.tyr-] wf.1 ghost, apparition; 'one who walks again,' revenant.

ág.=

ágúst [au:gust] m.indecl. August (the month; a pers. name).

ágætlega [au:g₁aitʰle:qa; -g₁aid̥-] adv. excellently, fine.

ágætur, -gæt, -gætt [au:g₁ai.tʰyɼ, -g₁ai.tʰ, -g₁aiʰt.; -g₁ai.d̥-] adj. excellent.

áhald, -s, -höld [au:hald̥, -hal(d̥)s, -höld̥] n. instrument.

áheyrn, -ar, -ir [au:heirdn̥, -naɼ, -nɪɼ] f.2 audience.

áhlaup, -s [au:hl̥öy.pʰ, -s; -hl̥öy.b̥] n. attack.

áhrif [au:hɼɪ.v] n.pl. influence; *hafa góð á. á e-n* influence somebody for the good, exert wholesome influence on somebody; *af áhrifum e-s* under the influence of somebody; *undir áhrifum* under the influence.

áhrinsorð [au:hɼɪns-or.ð] n.pl. words that come true; *verða að áhrinsorðum* come true, take effect.

áhugamaður, -manns, -menn [au:hy-qa-ma:ðyɼ, -man.s, -men:] m.4 aspirant, zealot; amateur.

áhöfn, -hafnar, -ir [au:höbn̥, -habnaɼ, -ɪɼ] f.2 crew.

áir = áfir.

---

aka, ek, ók, ókum, ekinn (-ið) [a:kʰa, ɛ:kʰ, ou:kʰ(ym), ɛ:k₁ʰɪn, -ɪð; a:ģa, ɛ:ģ, ou:ģ(ym), ɛ:ģ₁ɪn] v.6 drive (in a car, sleigh); *aka sleða* drive a sleigh; (*það*) *verður ekið* (impers.) people will drive.

akkeri, -s, - [aʰk₁:ɛ·rɪ, -ɪs] n. anchor.

Akranes, -s [a:kʰra-nɛ:s, -nɛs:; a:ģra-] n. 'Field Ness.'

akur, -urs, -rar [a:kʰyɼ, -yɼs, a:kʰraɼ; a:ģ-] m.1 field.

Akureyri, -ar [a:kʰyr-ei:rɪ, -ar; a:ģ-] f.1 'Field Spit.'

ákveðnari, -in, -ið; ákveðnari, -astur [au:kʰvɛ.ðɪn, -ɪn, -ɪð, -kʰvɛðnarɪ, -astyɼ] adj. determined; *að ákveðnum tíma* at the appointed time.

ákvæði, -s, - [au:kʰvai.ðɪ, -ɪs] n. regulation, provision of the law.

ákvörðun, -unar, -kvarðanir [au:-kʰvörðyn, -ynaɼ, -kʰvarðanɪɼ] f.2 resolution.

al- [a:l-] pref. completely, by far (S. III, **5**, 3).

ala, el, ól, ólum, alinn (-ið) [a:la, ɛ:l, ou:l, ou:lym, a:lɪn, -ɪð] v.6 give birth to; feed.

Álafoss [au:la-fɔs:] m.1 'Eel Falls.' álaga, see *álög.*

A-land = *Austurland.*

Albert, -s [al.bert(s)] m.1 Albert.

alda, öldu, -ur [al.d̥a, öl.d̥y, -yɼ] wf.1 wave; also pers. name: *Alda.*

aldamót [al.d̥a-mou:tʰ; -mou:d̥] n.pl. turn of the century.

aldur, -ir, see *öld.*

aldrei [al.drei·] adv. never; *aldrei framar* nevermore; never again.

aldur, -urs, -rar [al.d̥yɼ(s), aldraɼ] m.1 age, time; *á aldrinum* at the age, aged; *um langan aldur* for a long time.

aldurstakmark, -s, -mörk [al.d̥yɼs-tʰa:kʰmaɼk, -s, -möɼk; -tʰa:ģ-] n. age limit.

áleit, see *álíta.*

áletrun, -unar, -anir [au:le.tʰryn, -ynaɼ, -anɪɼ; au:le.d̥r-] f.2 legend, inscription.

Alexander, -s [a:lexsan.d̥eɼ, -eɼs] m.1

Vowels: *a* [a] approx. *father*; *á* [au] *cow*; *e* [ɛ] *set*; *é* [jɛ] *yes*; *i, y* [ɪ] *sit*; *í, ý* [i] *feel*; *o* [ɔ] *law*; *ó* [ou] *note*; *u* [y] approx. Germ. *Mütter*; *ú* [u] *school*; *y* = *i*; *ý* = *í*; *æ* [ai] *ice*; *ö* [ö] Germ. *hören*; *au* [öy] French *feuille*; *ei, ey* [ei] *ale*. Length [:]; half-length [·].

Alexander; *prófessor A. Jóhannesson,*
an authority on Icelandic grammar.

álfadans, -, -ar [aul·va·dan·s, -aɾ] m.l
elf-dance; a masquerade usually held
in the open on Twelfth-night; the
'elves' dancing around a bonfire.

álfalög, -laga [aul·va·lö:q, -la:qa]
n. pl. elf, fairy melodies.

álfatrú, -ar [aul·va·tʰru:, -aɾ] f.l belief in fairies, elves.

álfkona, -u, -ur [aul·(f)kʰɔ·na, -ɤ, -ɤɾ]
wf.l fairy (woman).

álft, -ar, -ir [aul·t, -aɾ, -ɪɾ] f.2 swan.

Álftafjörður, -fjarðar [aul·ta·fjör·ðɤɾ,
-fjar·ðaɾ] m.3 'Swan Fjord.'

álfur, -s, -ar [aul·vɤɾ, aul·(v)s, aul·vaɾ]
m.l elf, fairy.

algengur, -geng, -gengt [al·ɡ₁eiŋ̊g̊(ɤɾ),
-ɡ₁eiŋtʰ; -ɡ₁eiŋt] adj. common, ordinary.

algerlega, -gjör- [al·ɡ₁erlc:qa, -ɡ₁ör-]
adv. completely.

alin, álnar, -ir [a:lɪn, aul·naɾ, -ɪɾ] f.2
ell (a measure) (In. I, 3, 2).

álit, -s, - [au:lɪ·tʰ; -lɪ·d̥] n. appearance, looks: *vænn álitum* handsome
in appearance.

álíta, -lít, -leit, -litum, -litinn (-ið)
[au:li·tʰa, -li·tʰ, -lei·tʰ, -lɪ·tʰɤm, -ɪn,
-ɪð; -li·d̥-, -lei·d̥, -lɪ·d̥-] v.l consider,
think; *á. e-n vera e-ð* consider somebody to be something (S. VI, 4, 3);
ég álít þetta (vera) rangt I consider this (to be) wrong (S. VI, 11,
4).

all- [ad̥·l-] pref. quite, rather.

allavega [ad̥·la·vc:qa] adv. (= *alla
vega*) in various ways.

allangur, -löng, -langt [ad̥·lauŋ·g̊ɤɾ,
-löyŋ·g̊, -lauŋ·tʰ; -lauŋ̊·t] adj. quite
long; *alllangt frá* a considerable
way from.

allmargur, -mörg, -margt [ad̥·l·mar·g̊ɤɾ,
-mör·g̊, -maɾ·t] adj. quite many.

allmikill, -il, -ið [ad̥·l·mɪ:k₁ʰɪd̥l, -ɪl,
-ɪð; -mɪ:g̊₁-] adj. quite great, quite
big, quite some; *-ið* adv. considerably,
quite a bit.

allólíkur, -lík, -líkt [ad̥·l·ou:li·kʰɤɾ,

-li·kʰ, -lixt; -li·g̊·] adj. quite different.

alls [al·s] adv. altogether; *alls ólíkur*
quite different from.

allskonar [al·skʰɔ·naɾ] adv. (also *alls
konar*) all kinds of.

allslaus, -laus, -laust [al·slöy·s, -löyst]
adj. destitute.

allsstaðar [al·sta·ðaɾ] adv. (also *alls
staðar*) everywhere.

alltaf [al·ta·v] adv. always, continually; *a. að lesa* continually reading.

alltíður, -tíð, -títt [ad̥·l·tʰi:ðɤɾ, -tʰi:ð,
-tʰiʰt:] adj. quite frequent.

alltof [al·tɔ·v] adv. (all) too (also
allt of).

allur, öll, allt [ad̥·lɤɾ, öd̥·l, al·t], acc.
allan, alla, allt [ad̥·lan, ad̥·la], dat.
öllum, allri, öllu [öd̥·lɤm, adlrɪ,
öd̥·lɤ], gen. *alls, allrar, alls* [al·s,
adlraɾ]; pl. *allir, allar, öll* [ad̥·lɪɾ,
ad̥·laɾ, öd̥·l], acc. *alla, allar, öll*
[ad̥·la], dat. *öllum* [öd̥·lɤm], gen.
allra [adlra] adj. and indef. pron.
(always strong) (In. III, 3, 1, 4)
all, whole, complete, full; *allt Ísland*
the whole of Iceland; *allt fólkið*
the whole household, people; *allan
tímann* all the time; *allan daginn*
the whole day; *hann er ekki allur,
þar sem hann er séður* (proverbial)
he is not all he seems to be (he is
quite shrewd); *allur helmingur* full
half, *um allan helming* by a full half,
more than twice as much, by leaps
and bounds; pl. *allir: allir þeir
mörgu, sem* . . . all the many who
. . . ; *fyrstur allra* first of all (S.
I, 4, 2, 5); *hann er allra bezti karl*
he is a very good fellow (S. III, 5,
2-3); n. *allt: allt í lagi* all right,
O. K.; *allt gott* everything fine
(answer to *hvað er í fréttum?* what
news?); *þakka þér fyrir allt gott*
(a polite phrase) thanks for all the
kind things you have done for me;
allt annað en everything but; *allt,
sem* all that; *allt að því* almost;
allt þar til up to, until; *allt til jóla*

Consonants: [ð] breathe; [g] good; [g₁] garden (garden); [hw] what; [j] yes; [k₁] cyan
(can); [ŋ] thing; [q] N. Germ. sagen; [r] Scottish r; [x] approx. Germ. ach; [þ] thin.
Voiceless: ○; [b̥, d̥, g̊] approx. p, t, k. Half-voiced: italics. Aspiration and preaspiration:
[ʰ]; [pʰ, tʰ, kʰ] p-, t-, k-. Others as in English.

303

up to Christmas; *allt suður í Fjörð* all the way south to F.; *öllu hærri* a bit taller, a little taller; *umfram allt* above all; *þrátt fyrir allt* in spite of all (everything); *að* (*með*) *öllu* completely, withal; *alls* adv. altogether; *alls ekki* (*ekkert*) not (nothing) at all; *allur saman* all together, complete(ly). See also S. III, 1, 4; **3**, 1; IV, **6**, 2.

allursaman, öllsömul, -un, alltsaman, see *allur saman* above.

allverulega [að·l·vɛ:rʏlɛ:qa] adv. considerably, to a considerable extent.

allvitur, -vitur, -viturt [að·l·vɪ:tʰʏɾ, -vɪ:tʰʏɾt; -vɪ:d̦·] adj. quite wise.

almanak, -s, -nök [al·ma·na:kʰ, -nax·s, -nö:kʰ; -na:g̦, -nö:g̦] n. calendar.

Almannagjá, -r [al·man·a·g̦ˌau:, -g̦ˌau:r] f.1 'Gorge of the Commons,' famous chasm at Þingvellir.

almennur, -menn, -mennt [al·mɛn·(ʏɾ), -mɛntʰ; -mɛnt] adj. common, general; *a·t bréf* common, unregistered letter, opposed to *ábyrgðarbréf* registered letter; *almenn brot* common fractions.

álnar, -ir, see *alin.*

alsiða [al·sɪ·ða] adj. indecl. customary everywhere.

alskrýddur, -skrýdd, -skrýtt [al·skrid·(ʏɾ), -skriʰt·] adj. in full vestments.

alstaðar = *allsstaðar.*

altari, -s, ölturu [al·tarɪ, -ɪs, öl·tʏrʏ] n. altar; *fyrir altari* in front of the altar; *ganga til a-is* go to Communion; *vera til a-is* receive Communion (In. I, 4, (b)6n).

alúðar- [a:lu·ðaɾ·] pref. sincere, cordial; *a-þakkir* cordial thanks.

alúðlegur [a:luðlɛ:qʏɾ] adj. (see *-legur*) cordial, friendly.

alull, -ar [a:lʏdl, -ʏdlaɾ] f.1 all wool, 100% wool.

alvara, -vöru [al·va·ra, -vö·rʏ] wf.1 earnest, seriousness; *er þér alvara?* are you serious?

alvarlegur [al·varlɛ:qʏɾ] adj. (see *-legur*) serious, earnest.

alveg [al·vɛ·q] adv. completely, quite.

alvitur, -vitur, -viturt [al·vɪ·tʰʏɾ(t); -vɪ·d̦·] adj. omniscient.

álykta, -aði, -að [au:lɪxta, -aðɪ, -að] wv.4 conclude.

ályktun, -unar, -anir [au:lɪxtʏn, -ʏnaɾ, -anɪɾ] f.2 conclusion.

Alþingi, -s [al·þiŋg̦ˌɪ, -ɪs] n. the (old) national convention or parliament of the Icelanders.

Alþingishátíð, -ar [al·þiŋg̦ˌɪs·hau:tʰi·ð, -ðaɾ] f.2 (millenary) celebration of the Alþingi.

Alþingishús, -s [al·þiŋg̦ˌɪs·hu:s, -hus:] n. the House of Alþingi.

alþingisstaður, -ar [al·þiŋg̦ˌɪ·sta:ðʏɾ, -aɾ] m.3 the place of the old Alþingi.

alþjóðlegur [al·þjouðlɛ:qʏɾ] adj. (see *-legur*) international; common all over the nation.

alþýða, -u, -ur [al·þi·ða] wf.1 the people, the public.

Alþýðublaðið [al·þi·ðʏ·bla:ðɪð] n. with def. art. 'The People's Paper.'

Alþýðubókasafnið [al·þi·ðʏ·bou:kʰa·sabnɪð; -bou:g̦·] n. with def. art. 'The Public Library.'

alþýðuflokkur, -s, -ar [al·þi·ðʏ·flɔʰk:ʏɾ, -flɔʰk·s, -flɔʰk:aɾ] m.1 labor party; *A·inn* 'The Labor party.'

alþýðuskóli, -a, -ar [al·þi·ðʏ·skou:lɪ, -a(ɾ)] wm.1 a rural district school, 'Folk High School.'

álög, -laga [au:lö·q, -la·qa] n.pl. spell, enchantment; *vera í álögum* be spellbound, enchanted.

amen [a:mɛ.n] n. amen.

Ameríka, -u [a:mɛri·kʰa, -ʏ; -ri·g̦·] wf.1 America; *Ameríku-maður* American.

Ameríkani, -a, -ar [a:mɛrikʰa:nɪ, -a(ɾ)] wm.1 American.

amerískur, -ísk, -ískt [a:mɛrisk·(ʏɾ), -ist] adj. American.

a.m.k. = *að minnsta kosti* at least.

amma, ömmu, -ur [am:a, öm:ʏ(ɾ)] wf.1 grandma, grandmother.

án [au:n, aun] prep. with gen. without; *án þess þó að* (clause) without,

---

Vowels: *a* [a] approx. *father*; *á* [au] *cow*; *e* [ɛ] *set*; *é* [jɛ] *yes*; *i, y* [ɪ] *sit*; *í, ý* [i] *feel*; *o* [ɔ] *law*; *ó* [ou] *note*; *u* [ʏ] approx. Germ. *Mütter*; *ú* [u] *school*; *y* = *i*; *ý* = *í*; *æ* [ai] *ice*; *ö* [ö] Germ. *hören*; *au* [öy] French *feuille*; *ei, ey* [ei] *ale*. Length [:]; half-length [·].

however, (pres. part.); *án þess að*
gera e-ð without doing something.
ana, -aði, -að [a:na, -aðɪ, -að] wv.4
rush (foolishly) forward.
ánamaðkur, -s, -ar [au:na-mað·kʰʏɽ,
-s, -aɽ; -maþ·k-] m.1 angleworm.
ananas [a:nana·s] m.(?) pineapple.
and- [an·d̥·] pref. anti-, opposite.
andar, see *önd* 1. and 2.
andatrú, -ar [an·d̥a-tʰru:, -aɽ] f.1
spiritualism.
andi, -a, -ar [an·d̥ɪ, -a(ɽ)] wm.1 spirit;
í anda in the spirit.
andlegur, -leg, -legt [an·d̥le·qʏɽ, -le·q,
-lext] adj. spiritual, clerical.
andlit, -s, - [an·d̥lɪ·tʰ(s), -lɪ·d̥] n. face.
andlitsfarði, -a, -ar [an·d̥lɪ(tʰ)s-far·ðɪ,
-a(ɽ)] wm.1 face cream, rouge.
andlitsnudd,   -s   [an·d̥lɪ(tʰ)s-nʏd̥:,
-nʏd̥·s] n. facial massage.
andrá [an·d̥rau·] f.1 moment; only in
the phrase: *í sömu andrá(nni)* in
the same moment.
Andrés, -ar(-s) [an·d̥rjɛ·s, -d̥rjɛ·saɽ,
-d̥rjɛs·] m.1 Andrew, Andrews;
patronymic: *Andrésson.*
andskoti, -a, -ar [an·sko·tʰɪ, -a(ɽ);
-skɔ·d̥ɪ] wm.1 devil.
andspænis [an·d̥spai·nɪs] prep. with
dat. opposite.
andstæðingur, -s, -ar [an·d̥stai·ðiŋ̊g̊ʏɽ,
-iŋs, -iŋg̊aɽ] m.1 opponent.
andstæður, -stæð, -stætt [an·d̥stai·ðʏɽ,
-stai·ð, -staiʰt·] adj. opposed; *a.*
e-m opposed to someone.
andvaka [an·d̥va·kʰa, -va·g̊a] adj. indecl. sleepless.
andvari, -a, -ar [an·d̥va·rɪ, -a(ɽ)] wm.1
soft breeze; *Andvari* dwarf in the
old Icelandic mythology; a modern
periodical.
a. n. l. = *að nokkru leyti.*
ann, see *unna.*
Anna, Önnu, -ur [an:a, ön:ʏ(ɽ)] wf.1
pers. name: Ann.
annaðhvort . . . eða conj. either . . .
or; see *annarhvor.*
1. annar, önnur, annað [an:aɽ, ön:ʏɽ,
an:að], acc. *annan, aðra, annað*

[an:an, að·ra, an:að], dat. *öðrum,*
annari, öðru [öð·rʏm, an:arɪ, öð·rʏ],
gen. *annars, annarar, annars* [an:aɽs,
an:araɽ]; pl. *aðrir, aðrar, önnur*
[að·rɪɽ, að·raɽ, ön:ʏɽ], acc. *aðra,*
aðrar, önnur [að·ra], dat. *öðrum*
[öð·rʏm], gen. *annara* [an:ara]
num. ord. (In. V, 2, 3) second; *a.*
í jólum, páskum, hvítasunnu the
second day of Christmas, Easter,
Whitsun; *hálfur annar* = 1½ ; *annað*
kvöld tomorrow night (S. I, 2, 2, 1);
aðra nótt the night after tomorrow.
2. annar, önnur, annað [pronunciation,
see above] indef. pron. (only strong)
(In. VI, 6, 2(c)) another, one of
two;   *hvað   annað?*   what   else?
annað hús another house, but: *annað*
húsið one of the two houses (S. II,
4); *annað bréfið* one of the two
letters (S. II, 7); *með annari hendi*
with one hand; *annað en* other than,
else but, *það er ekki annað en að*
hann fari heim there is no other
choice for him but to go home (S.
VI, 9, 4, 7); *allt annað en* anything (everything) but; *enginn*
annar en none other than; *það var*
eitthvað annað that was something
else, i. e. something quite different;
allur annar maður a completely
different man; *hver sagði öðrum*
each told the other; *aðrir (sumir)*
. . . aðrir some . . . others; *annar . . .*
hinn one . . . the other; *hitt (eitt)*
og annað this and that; *sumir*
aðrir some others; *öðru hverju* every
now and then; *annars staðar* elsewhere (S. I, 4, 5). See also S. III,
1, 4; IV, 6, 3.
annarhver, önnurhver,   annaðhvert
[an:ar-hwʏ·r, ön:ʏɽ-hwʏ·r, an:að-
hwʏrt; -hwɛ·r, etc.; -kʰʏ·r, -kʰvɛ·r,
etc.] indef. pron. (only strong)
every other of many. See In. VI, 6,
2(d); S. III, 1, 4; IV, 6, 4. Also
annar hver, etc.
annarhvor, önnurhvor,   annaðhvort
[an:ar-hwɔ·r, ön:ʏɽ-hwɔ·r, an:að-

Consonants: [ð] brea*th*e; [g] *g*ood; [gj] *gy*arden (garden); [hw] *wh*at; [j] *y*es; [kj] *cy*an
(can); [ŋ] thi*ng*; [q] N. Germ. sa*g*en; [r] Scottish *r*; [x] approx. Germ. a*ch*; [þ] *th*in.
Voiceless: ○: [b̥, d̥, g̊] approx. *p, t, k*. Half-voiced: *italics*. Aspiration and preaspiration:
[ʰ]; [pʰ, tʰ, kʰ] *p-, t-, k-*. Others as in English.

hwɔrt; -hwɣ·r, etc.; -kʰvɔ·r, -kʰvɣ·r,
etc.] indef. pron. (only strong) one
of two, either (or); *annaðhvort
augað* one of the two eyes; *annaðhvort . . . eða* conj. either . . . or
(S. VIII, 2). See also In. VI, **6**,
2(d); S. IV, **6**, 5. Also *annar hvor,*
etc.

annars [an:aɽs] adv. (gen. of *annað*)
otherwise, or else; besides, really;
anyway; *það er nú annars hreinasti
óþarfi* but that is most unnecessary.

annarsstaðar [an:aɽ-sta:ðaɽ] adv. (=
annars staðar) elsewhere.

annartveggja, önnurtveggja, annað-
tveggja [an:aɽ-tʰvcg̊₁:a, ön:ɣɽ-
tʰvcg̊₁:a, an:að-tʰvcg̊₁:a] indef. pron.
one of two, either of two. See In.
VI, **6**, 2(e); S. IV, **6**, 6. Also
annar tveggja, etc.

annast, -aðist, -azt [an:ast, -aðɪst,
-ast] wv.4 (middle voice only) take
care of.

annes, -s, - [an:ɛ.s, -n:ɛs.] n. headland, promontory, peninsula.

anza, -aði, -að [an·sa, -aðɪ, -að] wv.4
respond.

ánægður, -nægð, -nægt [au:naiqðɣɽ,
-naiqð, -naixt; -naig̊ð-] adj. pleased,
content with; *ánægður með e-ð (yfir
e-u)* satisfied with something, happy
over something.

api, -a, -ar [a:pʰɪ, -a(ɽ); a:b̥ɪ] wm.1
ape.

appelsína, -u, -ur [aʰp:ɛlsi:na, -ɣ(ɽ)]
wf.1 orange.

apótek, -s, - [a:pʰou·tʰɛ:kʰ, -s; a:bou·-
tʰɛ:g̊] n. (=*lyfjabúð*) drugstore.

apr. = *apríl.*

apríkósa, -u, -ur [a:pʰri·kʰou:sa,
-ɣ(ɽ)] wf.1 apricot.

apríl [a:pʰri·l] m.indecl. April.

ár, -s, - [au:r, auɽ·s] n. year; *á sjötta
árinu* going on six; *árið um kring*
the year round; *einu sinni á ári*
once a year (S. II, 1n2); *tveggja
ára barn* a child two years old (S.
I, 4, 2, 3).

áramót [au:ra·mou:tʰ; -mou:d̥] n.pl.

end (and beginning) of the year,
new year.

árangur, (-ri), -urs [au:rauŋg̊ɣɽ(s),
-auŋg̊rɪ] m.1 result.

árás, -ar, -ir [au:rau.s, -aɽ, -ɪɽ] f.2
attack, raid.

áratugur, -ar, -ir [au:ra-tʰɣ:qɣɽ, -aɽ,
-tʰɣɣ:jɪɽ] m.3 decade.

árbakki, -a, -ar [aur·baʰk₁·ɪ,-baʰk·a(ɽ)]
wm.1 bank of a river.

árbók, -ar, -bækur [aur·bou·kʰ, -aɽ,
-bai·kʰɣɽ; -bou·g̊-, -bai·g̊-] f.3 year-
book.

árdegis [aur·dei·jɪs] adv. early in the
day, a. m.

áreynsla, -u, -ur [au:reinsla, -ɣ(ɽ)]
wf.1 exertion.

arga, -aði, -að [ar·g̊a, -aðɪ, -að] wv.4
sick (on); *a. hundum (á)* sick
dogs (on); *argast í e-u* raise a
rumpus about something (to get it
done).

árgangur, -s, -ar [aur·gauŋg̊ɣɽ, -gauŋs,
-gauŋg̊aɽ] m.1 year (of a periodical),
volume.

ári, -a, -ar [au:rɪ, -a(ɽ)] wm.1 evil
spirit, demon; *kölski og árar hans*
the devil and his demons.

árla; fyrr, fyrst [aur·dla, fɪr:, fɪ(ɽ)st]
adv. early (In. IV, **2**(d)).

Ármann, -s [aur·man·(s)] m.4 name
of a giant; pers. name; name of a
wrestling society.

Ármannsfell, -s [aur·mans-fed·l, -fel·s]
n. 'Fell of Ármann,' a mountain
near Þingvellir.

armband, -s, -bönd [ar·mband, -s,
-bönd] n. bracelet.

armbandsúr, -s, - [ar·mban(d̥)s-u:r,
-ur·s] n. wrist watch.

armur, -s, -ar [ar·mɣɽ, arms, -aɽ] m.1
arm.

arnar, see *örn.*

Arnarfjörður, -fjarðar [a(r)dnaɽ-
fjör·ðɣɽ, -fjar·ðaɽ] m.3 'Eagle's
Fjord.'

Arnarhóll, -hóls [a(r)dnar-houd·l,
-houl·s] m.1 'Eagle Hill' in
Reykjavík.

Vowels: *a* [a] approx. father; *á* [au] *cow*; *e* [ɛ] set; *é* [jɛ] *yes*; *i, y* [ɪ] sit; *í, ý* [i] feel;
o [ɔ] *law*; *ó* [ou] note; *u* [ɣ] approx. Germ. Mütter; *ú* [u] school; *y* = *i*; *ý* = *í*; *æ* [ai] ice;
ö [ö] Germ. hören; *au* [öy] French feuille; *ei, ey* [ei] ale. Length [:]; half-length [·].

Arndís, -ar [ad̥ndi·s(aṛ)] f.1 pers.
name.
Árnessýsla, -u [aur(d̥)nɛ(s)-sis·la, -ʏ]
wf.1 ' District of Árnes.'
Árni, -a [aud·nɪ, -a] wm.1 pers. name.
árstíð, -ar, -ir [auṛ·stʰi·ð, -ðaṛ, -ðɪṛ]
f.2 season.
árstími, -a, -ar [auṛ·stʰi·mɪ, -a(ṛ)]
wm.1 season.
ás, áss, ásar [au:s, aus:, au:saṛ] m.1
ridge; foothill; ace (in cards).
Ása, -u, -ur [au:sa, -ʏ (ṛ)] wf.1 pers.
name.
ásamt [au:samtʰ; au:saṇt] prep.with
dat. together with.
Ásgrímur, -s [au:sgri·mʏṛ, -grims] m.1
pers. name.
aska, ösku [as·ka, ös·kʏ] wf.1 ash.
askur, -s, -ar [as·kʏṛ, asks, as·kaṛ]
m.1 ash (the tree); a carved wooden
box, originally used for a food uten-
sil, now for decoration.
Áslaug, -ar [au:slöy·q, -qaṛ] f.1 pers.
name.
ásótti, see ásækja.
ást, -ar, -ir [aus·t, -aṛ, -ɪṛ] f.2 love;
tókust ástir góðar með þeim they
began to love each other well; *hafa
ást á e-m* love somebody.
Ásta, -u, -ur [aus·ta, -ʏ(ṛ)] wf.1 pers.
name.
ástarsaga, -sögu, -ur [aus·taṛ·sa:qa,
sö:qʏ(ṛ)] wf.1 love story.
ástarsöguhöfundur, -ar, -ar [aus·taṛ·
sö·qʏ-hö:vʏndʏṛ, -aṛ] m.1 writer of
love stories (In. I, 2, *1*(b)11).
ástfóstur, (-ri), -urs [aus·tfoustʏṛ(s),
-foustrɪ] n. loving care, affection;
taka ástfóstri við e-n center one's
affections in somebody.
ástæða, -u, -ur [au:stai·ða, -ʏ(ṛ)]
wf.1 ground, reason, pl. reasons, circumstances; *ástæða til að* reason
to (do something); *af ástæðum* for
reasons; *ástæða til e-s* the reason
why; *eftir ástæðum* depending upon
circumstances, considering circumstances.
ásækja, -sótti, -sótt(ur) [au:sai·k,ʰa,

-souʰt·ɪ, -souʰt·(ʏṛ)] wv.2 attack,
molest.
at, ats, öt [a:tʰ, ɐ·tʰs, ö:tʰ; a:d̥, ö:d̥]
n. fight, riot; stampede.
1. át, -s [au:tʰ(s); au:d̥] n. eating;
át á e-u the eating of sth.
2. át, -um, see *éta*.
ata, -aði, -að(ur) [a:tʰa, -aðɪ, -að,
-aðʏṛ; a:d̥a] wv.4 soil.
áta, -u, -ur [au:tʰa, -ʏ(ṛ); au:d̥a]
wf.1 food, eating; *til átu* for eating, to eat; *á. í sjó* food (plancton)
in the sea.
athugasemð,-ar,-ir [a:tʰ(h)ʏ·qa-sem·d̥,
-aṛ, -ɪṛ] f.2 note, notice, remark.
athygli [a:tʰ(h)ɪg̊lɪ] wf.2 attention.
athöfn, -hafnar, -ir [a:tʰ(h)öbn̥,
-(h)abn̥aṛ, -ɪṛ] f.2 ceremony.
átján [au:tʰjau·n; au:d̥-] num. card.
eighteen.
átjándi [au:tʰjaundɪ; au:d̥-] num.ord.
eighteenth.
Atlantshaf,-s[aʰt·lan(t)s-ha:v,-haf·s]
n. the Atlantic ocean.
átt, -ar, -ir [auʰt:, -aṛ, -ɪṛ] f.2 direction, direction of the wind, the wind;
norðanátt northwind (prevailing).
att, atti, see *etja*.
átt, -i, see *eiga*.
1. átta [auʰt:a] num. card. eight.
2. átta, -u, -ur [auʰt:a, -ʏ(ṛ)] wf.1
eight in cards.
áttatíu [auʰt:a-tʰi:jʏ] num. card.
eighty.
áttfaldur, -föld, -falt [auʰt:faldʏṛ,
-föld, -falt] adj. eightfold.
áttræður, -ræð, -rætt [auʰt:rai·ðʏṛ,
-rai·ð, -raiʰt·] adj. eighty years old;
eighty fathoms deep, high.
áttugasti [auʰt:ʏqastɪ] num. ord.
eightieth.
áttundi [auʰt:ʏndɪ] num. ord. eighth.
áttungur, -s, -ar [auʰt:uŋg̊ʏṛ, -uŋs,
-uŋg̊aṛ] m.1 one eighth.
atvinna, -u [a:tʰvɪn·a, -ʏ; a:d̥-]
wf.1 work, occupation, living; *gera
sér e-ð að atvinnu* make a living
by (out of) something.
atvinnuhættir [a:tʰvɪn·ʏ-haiʰt:ɪṛ;

Consonants: [ð] brea*th*e; [g] *g*ood; [gⱼ] *g*arden (garden); [hw̥] *wh*at; [j] *y*es; [kⱼ] *c*yan
(can); [ŋ] thi*ng*; [q] N. Germ. sa*g*en; [r] Scottish *r*; [x] approx. Germ. ach; [þ] *th*in.
Voiceless: ○; [b̥, d̥, g̊] approx. *p, t, k*. Half-voiced: *italics*. Aspiration and preaspiration:
[ʰ]; [pʰ, tʰ, kʰ] *p*-, *t*-, *k*-. Others as in English.

a:d̦-] m.3.pl. modes of occupation;
breytingar á atvinnuháttum occu-
pational changes.

auð- [öy:ð̦-] pref. easily.

auðkenna, -kenndi, -kenndur (-kennt)
[öyð̦·k̦ʰɛn·a, -k̦ʰend̦ɪ, -ʏ̣̦, -k̦ʰɛntʰ;
-k̦ʰɛnt] wv.2 mark.

auðmýkt, -ar [öyð̦·mıxt, -a̦] f.2
humility.

auðséður, -séð, -séð [öyð̦·sjɛ·ð̦ʏ̣,
-sjɛ·ð̦] adj. evident, obvious, clear.

auðsýna, -sýndi, -sýndur (-sýnt) [öyð̦·-
si·na, -sind̦ɪ, -ʏ̣̦, -sintʰ; -sinț] wv.2
show, express.

auðsær, -sæ, -sætt; -særri, -sæjastur
[öyð̦·sai·r, -sai·, -saiʰt·, -sair·ɪ,
-sai·jastʏ̣̦] adj. evident (In. III,
2(a)4 and (b)5; 4, *4*).

auðugur [öy:ð̦ʏqʏ̣̦] adj. (see -*ugur*)
wealthy, rich; *a. að e-u* rich in
something.

Auðunn, -unar (-uns) [öy:ð̦ʏn(-ʏn),
-ʏna̦ (-ʏns)] m.1 pers. name;
Auden, Edwin.

auður, auð, autt [öy·ð̦ʏ̣, öy:ð̦, öyʰt:]
adj. empty, unoccupied; snowfree.

auðveldur, -veld, -velt [öyð̦·veld̦ʏ̣,
-veld̦, -velt] adj. easy.

auðvitað [öyð̦·vɪ·tʰað, -vɪ·d̦·] adv. of
course (literally: easily known).

auga, -, -u, (-na) [öy:qa, -ʏ, öyg̊·na]
wn. eye; *koma ekki fyrir sín augu*
not to come back in their sight;
fyrir augum in view; *liggja í augum
uppi* 'lie open for inspection,' be
obvious; *augun í mér* my eyes (S.
I, 4, *1*, 4); *svo langt, sem augað
eygir* as far as eye can see.

augabragð, -s [öy:qa·braq·ð̦, -ð̦s;
-brag̊·þ] n. twinkling of an eye.

augabrún, -ar, -ir [öy:qa·bru:n, -na̦,
-nɪ̦] f.2 eyebrow.

auglýsa, -lýsti, -lýst(ur) [öyq·li·sa,
-listɪ, -list(ʏ̣)] wv.2 announce,
advertise.

auglýsing, -ar, -ar [öyq·li·sing̊, -a̦] f.1
advertisement.

auglýsingablað, -s, -blöð [öyq·li·sing̊a-
bla:ð̦, -blað·s, -blö:ð̦] n. (news)-

paper devoted chiefly to advertise-
ments (or announcements).

augnablik, -s, - [öyg̊·na·blɪ:kʰ, -s;
-blɪ:g̊] n. twinkling of an eye; just
a moment!

auk [öy:kʰ; öy:g̊] prep. with gen. in
addition to, besides; *auk þess* in
addition to that, besides; *þar að
auki* in addition thereto, besides
that (*auki* here is a dat. of an
otherwise non-existent *auk* n.).

auka, eyk, jók, jukum, aukinn (-ið)
[öy:kʰa, ei:kʰ, jou:kʰ, jʏ:kʰʏm,
öy:k̦ʰɪn, -ɪð̦; öy:g̊-, ei:g̊, jou:g̊]
v.7 increase (trans.); *aukast* be increased, increase (intr.); impers.:
hann (acc.) *jók um allan helming*
it was doubled, it became twice as
much, it increased by leaps and
bounds.

auki, -a, -ar [öy:k̦ʰɪ, öy:kʰa(̦);
öy:g̦̊ɪ, öy:g̊a(̦)] wm.1 increase;
færast í aukana grow, grow in
power.

aukið, -inn, see *auka*.

auknefni, -s, - [öy:kʰnɛb̦nɪ, -s; öy:g̊-]
n. nickname.

aumk(v)a, -aði, -að(ur) [öym·kʰ(v)a,
-að̦ɪ, -að̦, -að̦ʏ̣; öym̦·k-] wv.4 to
pity, *a. e-n* pity somebody.

aur, -s, -ar [öy:r, öyʏ̣·s, öy:ra̦] m.1
gravel, sandy plain.

aurar, see *eyrir*.

1. ausa, -u, -ur [öy:sa, -ʏ(̦)] wf.1
ladle, spoon.

2. ausa, eys, jós, jusum, ausinn (-ið)
[öy:sa, ei:s, jou:s, jʏ:sʏm, öy:sɪn,
-ɪð̦] v.7 dip, scoop, ladle.

austan [öys·ta̦n; ʏs·ta̦n] (1) adv.
from the east; *a. við mána* east of
the moon; (2) prep. with acc.
austan sléttuna from the east across
the plain; (3) prep. with gen. *a. ár*
east of the river (In. IV, 1, 3).

austastur, see *eystri*.

Austfirðir, -fjarða [öys·tfɪrð̦ɪ̦, -fjarð̦a]
m.3.pl. 'The East Fjords.'

1. austur, (-ri), -urs [öys·tʏ̣(s),
öystrɪ] n. east, the east.

Vowels: *a* [a] approx. father; *á* [au] cow; *e* [ɛ] set; *é* [jɛ] yes; *i, y* [ɪ] sit; *í, ý* [i] feel;
o [ɔ] law; *ó* [ou] note; *u* [ʏ] approx. Germ. Mütter; *ú* [u] school; *y* = *i*; *ý* = *í*; *æ* [ai] ice;
ö [ö] Germ. hören; *au* [öy] French feuille; *ei, ey* [ei] ale. Length [:]; half-length [·].

2. **austur** [öys.tʏɾ; ʏs.tʏɾ] adv. east, to the east, in the east; *a. í east into; a. yfir* east across, east over; *a. eftir* towards the east; *a. í sveitir* east into the rural districts (east of Reykjavík); *a. í sveitum* east in the rural districts (In. IV, 1, 3).

Austurbærinn, -bæjarins [öys.tʏr bai:rɪn, -bai:jarɪns] m.2 'The East Town' in Reykjavík.

Austurland,-s [öys.tʏr-lan.d̥,-lan.(d̥)s] n. 'The East' (of Iceland).

Austurstræti, -s [öys.tʏɾ-strai:tʰɪ(s); -strai:dɪ] n. 'East Street.'

Austurvöllur, -vallar [öys.tʏr-vöd.lʏɾ, -vad.laɾ] m.3 'East Field,' or 'East Common,' a square in Reykjavík.

autt, see *auður*.

ávallt [au:valt] adv. always.

ávarp, -s, -vörp [au:vaɾp(s), -vöɾp] n. address.

ávarpa, -aði, -að(ur) [au:vaɾpa, -aðɪ, -að, -aðʏɾ] wv.4 address.

áveita, -u, -ur [au:vei.tʰa, -ʏ(ɾ); -vei.d̥a] wf.1 irrigation.

ávísun, -unar, -anir [au:vi.sʏn, -ʏnaɾ, -anɪɾ] f.2 check, money order.

ávöxtur, -vaxtar, -vextir [au:vöxstʏɾ, -vaxstaɾ, -vɛxstɪɾ] m.3 fruit.

axar, -ir, see *öxi*.

Axarfjörður, -fjarðar [ax.saɾ-fjör.ðʏɾ, -fjar.ðaɾ] m.3 'Ax Fjord.'

axlabönd,-banda [axsla-bön.d̥, -ban.d̥a] n.pl. suspenders.

axlar, -ir, see *öxl*.

áætlun, -unar, -anir [au:aiʰtlʏn, -ʏnaɾ, -anɪɾ] f.2 plan, time table (of boats, busses, etc.), schedule.

áætlunarbíll,-bíls,-bílar [au:aiʰtlʏnar bid.l, -bil.s, -bi:laɾ] m.1 bus (long distance), a bus plying country routes according to schedule.

B.

1. **bað, -s, böð** [ba:ð, bað.s, bö:ð] n. bath.

2. **bað, báðum**, see *biðja*.

baðherbergi, -s, - [ba:ðhɛrbɛr.g̊,ɪ(s)] n. bathroom.

báðir, báðar, bæði, acc. **báða, báðar, bæði**, dat. **báðum**, gen. **beggja** [bau:ðɪɾ, -a(ɾ), -ʏm, bai:ðɪ, bɛg̊,:a] indef. pron. (only strong) both; *bæði . . . og* conj. both . . . and; *báðum (báðu) megin* on both sides (of). See In. VI, 6, 2(f); S. III, 1, 4; IV, 6, 7.

baðker, -s, - [bað.k,ʰɛ.r, -k,ʰɛrs] n. bathtub.

baðmull, -ar [bað.mʏdl, -ʏd̥laɾ] f.1 (= *bómull*) cotton.

baðmullarsokkur, -s, -ar [bað.mʏdlaɾ sɔʰk:ʏɾ, -sɔʰk.s, -sɔʰk:aɾ] m.1 cotton sock, stocking, hose; = *bómullar-*.

baðmullartau, -s, - [bað.mʏdlaɾ-tʰöy:, -s] n. cotton goods; *bómullar-*.

baðstofa, -u, -ur [bað.stɔ.va, -ʏ(ɾ); bas.t-] wf.1 literally: 'bathroom,' a combined bed- and sitting room in old Icelandic farmsteads.

baðstofupallur, -s [bað.stɔ-vʏ-pʰad.lʏɾ, -pʰal.s; bas.t-] m.1 the loft (upstairs room) of *baðstofa*.

báðumegin [bau:ðʏ-mei:jɪn] (1) adv. on both sides; (2) prep. with gen. on both sides of. Also *báðum megin* and *báðu megin*.

baggi, -a, -ar [bag̊,:ɪ, bag̊,:a(ɾ)] wm.1 pack, bundle (of hay, etc.).

bágur, bág, bágt; bág(a)ri (bárri), bágastur [bau:(q)ʏɾ, bau:(q), bauʰt:, bau:(q)arɪ, bau(q).rɪ, baur:ɪ, bau:(q)astʏɾ] adj. pitiful (In. III, 2(b)5d).

bak, -s, bök [ba:kʰ(s), bö:kʰ; ba:g̊, bö:g̊] n. back (= *hryggur*); *í bak og brjóst* behind and in front; *vera allur á bak og burt* have completely vanished; *að baki* behind, in the background; *eiga e-m á bak að sjá* lose somebody, meet with loss of somebody.

baka, -aði, -að(ur) [ba:kʰa, -aðɪ, -að, -aðʏɾ; ba:g̊a] wv.4 bake.

bakaleið, -ar [ba:kʰa-lei:ð, -aɾ; ba:g̊a-] f.2 way back; *í b.* on the way back.

Consonants: [ð] brea*the*; [g] *g*ood; [g̊ɟ] *gy*arden (garden); [hʍ] *wh*at; [j] *y*es; [kɟ] *cy*an (can); [ŋ] thi*ng*; [q] N. Germ. sa*g*en; [r] Scottish *r*; [x] approx. Germ. a*ch*; [þ] *th*in. Voiceless: ○; [b̥, d̥, g̊] approx. *p, t, k*. Half-voiced: *italics*. Aspiration and preaspiration: [ʰ]; [pʰ, tʰ, kʰ] *p-, t-, k-*. Others as in English.

309

bakari, -a, -ar [ba:kʰarɪ, -a(r̥); ba:g̊-] wm.1 baker.

bakarí, -íis, - [ba:kʰari:, -i:jɪs: ba:g̊-] n. bakery.

bakdyr [ba:kʰdɪ·r; ba:g̊-] f.3.pl. backdoor, back entrance.

bakki, -a, -ar [baʰkⱼ:ɪ, baʰk:a(r̥)] wm.1 brink, bank (of a river); also in place names -bakki, Bakka-.

bákn, -s, - [bauʰk·n̥(s)] n. a huge thing.

bakpoki, -a, -ar [ba:kʰpʰɔ·kⱼʰɪ, -pʰɔ·kʰa(r̥); ba:g̊pʰɔ·g̊ⱼɪ, -pʰɔ·g̊a(r̥)] wm.1 knapsack.

baksund, -s [ba:kʰsʏnd̥(s); ba:g̊-] n. back stroke.

bál, -s, - [bau:l, baul·s] n. fire, pyre.

bali, -a, -ar [ba:lɪ, -a(r̥)] wm.1 lawn, field.

bálkur, -s, -ar [baul·kʰʏr̥, -ar̥, baulkʰs; baul·k-] m.1 partition; undir bálki beside a partition (or: below a crossbar).

ball, -s, böll [bal:(s), böl:] n. =dansleikur, dance (Pr. 3, 2, 9n).

banani, -a, -ar [ba:na·nɪ, -a(r̥)] wm.1 banana.

Bandaríkin [ban·da·ri:kⱼʰɪn; -ri:g̊ⱼɪn] n.pl. with the def. art. the U. S. A.; Bandaríkja-menn Americans.

banka, -aði, -að [bauŋ·kʰa, -aðɪ, -að; bauŋ̊·ka] wv.4 knock; b. að dyrum knock (rap) at the door.

bankabygg, -s [bauŋ·kʰa-bɪg̊:(s); bauŋ̊·ka-] n. (peeled) barley.

bankabyggsgrautur, -ar, -ar [bauŋ·kʰa-bɪg̊·s-gröy:tʰʏr̥, -ar̥; bauŋ̊·ka -gröy:d-] m.1 barley porridge.

bankaseðill, -ils, -lar [bauŋ·kʰa-sɛ:ðɪdl, -ɪls, -sɛð·lar̥; bauŋ̊·ka-] m.1 bill, banknote.

Bankastræti, -s [bauŋ·kʰa-strai:tʰɪ(s); bauŋ̊·ka-strai:dɪ] n. 'Bank Street.'

banki, -a, -ar [bauŋ·kⱼʰɪ, bauŋ·kʰa(r̥); bauŋ̊·kⱼɪ, bauŋ̊·ka] wm.1 bank.

banna, -aði, -að(ur) [ban:a, -aðɪ, -að, -aðʏr̥] wv.4 forbid, prohibit (by law =með lögum).

bar, bárum, see bera.

bara [ba:ra] adv. just, only; quite; eða bara or just.

bardagi, -a, -ar [bar·dai·jɪ, -da·qa(r̥); -da·jɪ] wm.1 fight, battle; menn búnir til bardaga men ready to fight.

barði, barið, -inn see berja.

barg, see 2. bjarga.

Barmahlíð, -ar [bar·ma·hl̥i:ð, -ðar̥] f.1 'Bosom Slope,' a place name; name of a poem.

barmur, -s, -ar [bar·mʏr̥, barms, bar·mar̥] m.1 bosom.

barn, -s, börn [bað·n̥, bas:, böð·n̥; barð̥n, bar̥·s, börð̥n] n. child.

barnaskóli, -a, -ar [bað·na-skou:lɪ, -a(r̥)] wm.1 elementary school, primary school.

barnatími, -a, -ar [bad·na-tʰi:mɪ, -a(r̥)] wm.1 children's hour (instruction for children over the radio).

barnaveiki [bad·na-vei:kⱼʰɪ; -vei:g̊ⱼɪ] wf.2 diphtheria.

barnlaus, -laus, -laust [bað·nlöy·s, -löyst] adj. without children.

barnsnauð, -ar [bas:nöy·ð, -ðar̥; bar̥·s-] f.2 travail, labor.

barnsskór [bas:kou·r; bar̥·s-] m.1.pl. the shoes of a child.

Barónsstígur, -s [ba:roun-sti:qʏr̥, -stix·s] m.1 'Baron's Path.'

batna, -aði, -að [baʰt·na, -aðɪ, -að] wv.4 get better, improve; impers.: fara batnandi be improving; mér batnar I get better, well; mér batnar e-ð (nom.) I am recovering from something.

batt, see binda.

bátur, -s, -ar [bau:tʰʏr̥, -s, baus:, bau:tʰar̥; bau:dʏr̥] m.1 boat.

bauð,· see bjóða.

bauja, -u, -ur [böy:ja,-ʏ(r̥)] wf.1 buoy.

baula, -aði, -að [böy:la, -aðɪ, -að] wv.4 low; kýr baular a cow lows.

baun, -ar, -ir [böy:n, -nar̥, -nɪr̥] f.2 bean, pea; baunir beans, peas, peasoup.

baxa, -aði, -að [bax·sa, -aðɪ, -að] wv.4 move with difficulty, strive against (the wind, difficulties, etc.).

Vowels: a [a] approx. father; á [au] cow; e [ɛ] set; é [jɛ] yes; i, y [ɪ] sit; í, ý [i] feel; o [ɔ] law; ó [ou] note; u [ʏ] approx. Germ. Mütter; ú [u] school; y = i; ý = í; æ [ai] ice; ö [ö] Germ. hören; au [öy] French feuille; ei, ey [ei] ale. Length [:]; half-length [·].

1. beðið, see *bíða*.
2. beðið, -inn see *biðja*.
beggja, see *báðir*.
beið, see *bíða*.
beiða, beiddi, beiddur (beitt) [bei:ða, beid:ɪ, -ɪɾ, beiʰt:] wv.2 ask; *beiðast e-s* ask for something.
beiðni [beið·nɪ] wf.2 request.
beinn, bein, beint; beinni, beinastur [beid·n,bei:n,bein·tʰ; bein·t; beid·nɪ, bei:nastɪɾ] adj. straight, direct; *beint* adv. directly; *beint af augum* directly, straight forward, straight ahead; *beint áfram* straight ahead.
beinprjónn, -s, -ar [bein·pʰrjoudn̥, -pʰrjouns, -pʰrjou·naɾ; beim·-] m.1 bone needle.
beit, see *bíta*.
1. beita,-u,-ur [bei:tʰa, -ʏ(ɾ); bei:da] wf.1 bait.
2. beita, beitti, beitt(ur) [bei:tʰa, beiʰt:ɪ, -ʏɾ; bei:da] wv.2 *b. e-n brögðum* trick somebody (S. I, 3, *1*, 2(e)).
beitiland, -s, -lönd [bei:tʰɪ-lan·d, -lan·s, -lön·d; bei:dɪ-] n. pasture, grazing land.
beitiskip, -s, - [bei:tʰɪ-skᵢɪ:pʰ, -skᵢɪf·s; bei:dɪ-] n. cruiser.
beitt, see *beiða* and *beita*.
beizli, -s, - [beis·lɪ(s)] n. bridle.
bekkur, bekkjar(-s), bekkir [beʰk:ʏɾ, beʰkᵢ:aɾ, beʰk·s, beʰkᵢ:ɪɾ] m.2 bench; class, grade, form.
belgvettlingur, -s, -ar [bɛl·g̊veʰt·liŋg̊ʏɾ, -iŋs, -iŋg̊aɾ] m.1 = *vettlingur*, mitten.
belja, -aði, -að [bɛl·ja, -aðɪ, -að] wv.4 low, roar; go roaring.
belti, -s, - [bɛl·tɪ(s)] n. belt.
benda, benti, bent [ben·da, ben·tʰɪ, ben·tʰ; ben·t(ɪ)] wv.2 point (to), show; *b. á* point to, point out, mention.
Benjamín, -s [ben·jami·n, -mins] m.1 Benjamin.
benzín, -s [ben·si·n, -sins] n. gasoline, gas.
benzínstöð, -stöðvar, -var [ben·sin-stö:ð, -stöð·vaɾ] f.1 filling station.
ber, -s, -, (-ja) [bɛ:r, beɾ·s, ber·ja] n. berry.
bera, ber, bar, bárum, borinn (-ið) [bɛ:ra, bɛ:r, ba:r, bau:rʏm, bɔ:rɪn, -ɪð] v.4 bear, carry, transport; wear, have; bear (lamb, calve, foal); behove; happen, etc. (1) carry: *b. heim (hey)* carry home hay; *b. út póst* deliver mail; *berast* be carried, transported; spread; *b. nafn* have a name; be named; *b. áletrun* carry the legend (inscription); (2) wear: *b. föt* wear clothes; (3) bear, give birth to: *vera borin* have calved, lambed; (4) *b. fram* pronounce; (5) impersonal uses: behove: *það (mér) ber að gera það* it should be done (I should do it); *það ber á e·u* something is noticeable, puts in appearance, is prominent; *ég lét ekki á því bera* I did not let it be noticed, I did not show it; *það bar til* (or *við*) it happened; *sumardaginn fyrsta* (acc.) *ber jafnan upp á fimmtudag* the first day of summer always coincides with (= is) a Thursday; *þeim bar margt á góma* see *gómur*; *e·ð* (acc.) *ber við loft* something looms, is seen against the sky; *b. við* happen, *e·ð ber við* something happens (S. VI, 14, *4*). See also In. VII, 2, *5* and 4, *9*.
1. berg, -s, - [ber·g̊(s)] n. (= *bjarg*) rock, cliff.
2. berg, see 2. *bjarga*.
bergja, bergði, bergður (bergt) [ber·g̊ᵢa, ber·(q)ðɪ, -ʏɾ, beɾ·(x)t] wv.2 taste.
Bergljót, -ar [ber·g̊ljou·tʰ, -aɾ; -ljou·d] f.1 personal name.
berja, barði, barinn (-ið) [ber·ja, bar·ðɪ, ba:rɪn, -ɪð] wv.1 strike, beat, knock, rap; *b. að dyrum* knock at the door; *hann barði sér á brjóst* he beat his chest (breast) (S. I, 4, *1*, 5); *þeir berjast* (1) they fight, (2) they fight each other; *berjast fyrir hugsjónum* fight for ideals. See also S. VI, 1, *3*.

Consonants: [ð] brea*th*e; [g] *g*ood; [gᵢ] *gy*arden (garden); [hw] *wh*at; [j] *y*es; [kᵢ] *cy*an (can); [ŋ] thi*ng*; [q] N. Germ. sa*g*en; [r] Scottish *r*; [x] approx. Germ. a*ch*; [þ] *th*in. Voiceless: ○; [b̥, d̥, g̊] approx. *p, t, k*. Half-voiced: *italics*. Aspiration and preaspiration: [ʰ]; [pʰ, tʰ, kʰ] *p-, t-, k-*. Others as in English.

berjamór, -mós, -móar [berˑjaˑmouːr, -mouːs, -mouːaɾ] m.1 a heath where berries grow; *fara í b-mó* go picking berries.

berjaskyr, -s [berˑjaˑskjɪːr, -skjɪrˑs] n. Icelandic curds with berries.

bernska, -u [bernska, beɾska, -ɤ] wf.1 youth, childhood.

Berta, -u [berˑta, -ɤ] wf.1 Bertha.

Berufjörður, -fjarðar [beːrɤ-fjörˑðɤɾ, -fjarˑðaɾ] m.3 'Bear Fjord' (*bera* = female bear).

betri, beztur, see *góður*.

betur [beːtʰɤɾ; beːdɤɾ] adv. (comparative of *vel*) better; *b. satt væri!* would it were true!

beygja, beygði, beygður (beygt) [beiːja, beiqˑðɪ, -ɤɾ, beixˑt; beiǥ̊ˑðɪ] wv.2 turn (= *snúa*); *beygjast* be declined, conjugated; go.

beykir, -s, -jar [beiːkjʰɪɾ, -ɪs, -aɾ; beiːg̊ˏ-] m.1 cooper (In. I, **2**, *1*(b)8).

beykisstöð, -stöðvar, -var [beiːkjʰɪstöːð, -stöðˑvaɾ; beiːg̊ˏɪ-] f.1 headquarters.

bezt, -ur, see *vel*, *góður*.

bíða, bíð, beið, biðum, beðið [biːða, biːð, beiːð, bɪːðɤm, beːðɪð] v.1 wait; *bíðið þér við!* wait a minute! *b. e-s* wait for something (somebody); *mín var beðið* I was waited for, I was awaited (S. VI, **8**, *4*), *b. eftir e-m* wait for somebody.

biðill, -ils, -lar [bɪːðɪdl̥, -ɪls, bɪðˑlaɾ] m.1 suitor.

biðilsbuxur [bɪːðɪls-bɤxˑsɤɾ] wf.1.pl. literally: ' wooer's trousers,' only in: *vera á b-buxunum* 'wear wooer's trousers,' carry on courtship, make love.

biðja, bið, bað, báðum, beðinn (-ið) [bɪðˑja, bɪːð, baːð, bauːðɤm, beːðɪn, -ið] v.5 ask, pray, request; *b. e-n e-s = b. e-n um e-ð (að gera e-ð)* ask somebody for something (to do something); *b. e-n fyrir e-ð* ask somebody to take care of something, e. g. ask a newspaper to publish something; *b. e-n blessaðan að gera*

e-ð ask somebody to, please, do something; *ég bið að heilsa e-m* give my regards to somebody.

bifreið, -ar, -ir (-ar) [bɪvˑreiˑð, -ðaɾ, -ðɪɾ] f.2(1) automobile.

bifreiðaeinkasala, -sölu [bɪvˑreiˑðaeinˑkʰasaːla, -söːlɤ; -einˑkaˑ] wf.1 monopoly of automobiles; *b-salan = Bifreiða-einkasala ríkisins* 'The State Monopoly of Automobiles.'

bifreiðastöð, -stöðvar, -var [bɪvˑreiˑðastöːð, -stöðˑvaɾ] f.1 automobile station, taxi stand, taxicab company.

bil, -s, - [bɪːl, bɪlˑs] n. moment; *í sama bili* at that moment, at once.

bila, -aði, -að(ur) [bɪːla, -aðɪ, -að, -aðɤɾ] wv.4 break, crack, give way, fail, be damaged.

bílastöð, -stöðvar, -var [biːla-stöːð, -stöðˑvaɾ] f.1 automobile station, taxicab station, = *bifreiðastöð*.

bílaverkstæði, - [biːla-veɾˑkstaiˑðɪ, -ɪs] n. automobile service station.

bílaviðgerðastofa, -u, -ur [biːla-vɪðˑgˏerða-stɔːva, -ɤ(ɾ)] wf.1 automobile service station.

Bílda, -u, -ur [bilˑda, -ɤ(ɾ)] wf.1 a ewe (cow) with black spots around the eyes (*bíldótt ær, kýr*).

bíldóttur, -ótt, -ótt [bilˑdouʰtˑ(ɤɾ)] adj. with black (or colored) spots around the eyes.

bílkaup, -s, - [bilˑkʰöyˑpʰ(s), -kʰöyfˑs; -köyˑb] n. buying a car; mostly in pl.: *til bílkaupa* for buying a car.

bíll, -s, -ar [bidˑl, bilˑs, biːlaɾ] m.1 automobile, auto, car (In. I, **2**, *1*(b)).

billjón, -ar, -ir [bɪlˑjouˑn, -naɾ, -nɪɾ] f.2 billion.

bílslys, -s, - [bilˑslɪˑs, -slɪsˑ] n. automobile accident.

bílstjóri, -a, -ar [bilˑstjouˑrɪ, -a(ɾ)] wm.1 driver, chauffeur.

bilt [bɪlˑt] adj.n. only in the phrases: *verða bilt við* be startled at something; *gera e-m bilt við* scare one (S. III, **3**, 2).

binda, bind, batt, bundum, bundinn (-ið) [bɪnˑda, bɪnˑd̥, baʰtˑ, bɤnˑdɤm,

Vowels: *a* [a] approx. *father*; *á* [au] *cow*; *e* [ɛ] *set*; *é* [jɛ] *yes*; *i, y* [ɪ] *sit*; *í, ý* [i] *feel*; *o* [ɔ] *law*; *ó* [ou] *note*; *u* [ɤ] approx. Germ. *Mutter*; *ú* [u] *school*; *y* = *i*; *ý* = *í*; *æ* [ai] *ice*; *ö* [ð] Germ. *hören*; *au* [öy] French *feuille*; *ei, ey* [ei] *ale*. Length [ː]; half-length [ˑ].

-ın, -ıð] v.3 bind, tie, fetter; *binda á e-ð* tie to something; *b. sig við* 'tie oneself to,' limit, restrict oneself to; *binda* bind hay in bundles (*baggar*) of 100 pounds; *bitt þú, bittu* (imperative) bind, tie! (In. VII, 4, *6*, 1n3).

bindi, -s, - [bɪn·dɪ(s)] n. tie, bow.

bíó, -s, - [bi:jou·(s)] n. = *kvikmyndahús,* movie.

birgðaskip, -s, - [bɪr·(q)ða-skˌɪ:pʰ, -skˌɪf·s; -skˌɪ:b̥] n. supply ship, transport.

birgðir [bɪr·(q)ðɪr] f.2.pl. provisions, stores, stocks.

birki, -s [bɪr·kˌɪ(s)] n. birch(wood).

birkikjarr, -s, -kjörr [bɪr·kˌɪ-kˌʰar:, -kˌʰar:s, -kˌʰör:] n. birch copse.

birni(r), see *björn.*

1. birta, -u [bɪr·ta, -ʏ] wf.1 light, *fara frá birtunni* get out of one's light.

2. birta, birti, birt(ur) [bɪr·ta, -ɪ, -ʏr, bɪr·t] wv.2 get bright, brighten; publish, announce.

biskup, -s, -ar [bɪs·kʏpʰ, -ʏfs, -ʏpʰar; -ʏb̥(ar)] m.1 bishop.

bíta, bít, beit, bitum, bitinn (-ið) [bi:tʰa, bi:tʰ, bei:tʰ, bɪ:tʰʏm, -ın, -ıð; bi:d̥-, bei:d̥, bɪ:d̥-] v.1 bite; be sharp (of knives).

biti, -a, -ar [bɪ:tʰɪ, -a(r); bɪ:dɪ] wm.1 bite; *fá sér bita* take a bite.

bjarg, -s, björg [bjar·g̊(s), björ·g̊] n. rock, cliff.

1. bjarga, -aði, -að [bjar·g̊a, -aðɪ, -að] wv.4 or (rarely) :

2. bjarga, berg, barg, burgum, borginn (-ið) [bjar·g̊a, bɛr·g̊, bar·g̊, bʏr·gʏm, bɔr·g̊ˌın, -ıð] v.3 *b. e-m* save sbdy; *b. sér* 'save oneself,' get by.

bjargar, -ir, see 1. *björg.*

bjargráð [bjar·g̊rau·ð] n.pl. means of helping, helpful advice.

bjargsund, -s [bjar·g̊sʏnd̥] n. life saving (by swimming).

bjarnar, see *björn.*

Bjarni, -a [bjad̥·nɪ, -a] wm.1 personal name.

Bjarnþór, -s [bjad̥·n̥þou·r, -þour·s] m.1 personal name.

bjartur, björt, bjart [bjar·tʏr, björ·t, bjar·t] adj. bright, light; *meðan björt var nótt* while the (summer) nights were still bright.

bjó, see *búa.*

bjóða, býð, bauð, buðum, boðinn (-ið) [bjou:ða, bi:ð, böy:ð, bʏ:ðʏm, bɔ:ðın, -ıð] v.2 offer, invite; *b. e-m e-ð* offer sbdy sth; *má ég bjóða yður* or (impersonal) : *má bjóða yður* may I offer you; *b. e-m að gera e-ð* offer sbdy to do sth; *bjóðast til e-s* (*til að gera e-ð*) offer to do sth; *bjóða góðan dag, góða nótt, gott kvöld* greet with good morning, good night, good evening; *bjóða á dans(leik), ball* invite to a dance; *bjóða upp* ask (a girl) for a dance; impersonal: *mér býður við e-u* I am nauseated at, I abhor sth.

bjór, -s, -ar [bjou:r, bjour·s, bjou:rar] m.1 beer; skin.

bjúga, -, -u, (-na) [bju:(q)a, -ʏ, bjug̊·na] wn. sausage.

bjuggum, see *búa.*

1. björg, bjargar, -ir [björ·g̊, bjar·g̊ar, bjar·g̊ˌɪr] f.2 help; provisions, stocks; also personal name *Björg.*

2. björg, see *bjarg.*

björn, bjarnar, birnir [bjöd̥·n̥, bjad̥·nar, bɪd̥·nɪr; björdn, bjardnar, bɪrdnɪr] m.3 bear; also personal name: *Björn, -s* [bjös:] (In 1, 2, *3*(b)5).

björt, see *bjartur.*

Bjössi, -a, -ar [bjös:ɪ, -a(r)] wm.1 pet name for *Björn.*

blá, see *blár.*

bláber, -s, -, (-ja) [blau:bɛ·r, -bɛrs, -bɛrja] n. blueberry (whortleberry, bilberry).

bláberjasúpa, -u [blau:bɛrja-su:pʰa, -ʏ; -su:ba] wf.1 blueberry soup.

blað, -s, blöð [bla:ð, blað·s, blö:ð] n. leaf; paper, newspaper; blade (of grass etc.); *blaðið* the present newspaper, this newspaper; blade (of knives, razors, etc.).

Consonants: [ð] brea*th*e; [g] *g*ood; [gˌ] *gy*arden (garden); [hw] *wh*at; [j] *y*es; [kˌ] *cy*an (can); [ŋ] thi*ng*; [q] N. Germ. sa*g*en; [r] Scottish *r*; [x] approx. Germ. a*ch*; [þ] *th*in. Voiceless: o; [b̥, d̥, g̊] approx. *p, t, k*. Half-voiced: *italics*. Aspiration and preaspiration: [ʰ]; [pʰ, tʰ, kʰ] *p-, t-, k-*. Others as in English.

313

blaðamaður, -manns, -menn [bla:ða-
ma:ðyṛ, -man·s, -mɛn:] m.4 jour-
nalist, reporter.
blaðka, blöðku, -ur [blað·kʰa, blöð.-
kʰʏ(ṛ); blaþ·ka, blöþ·kʏ] wf.1 leaf,
leaflet, snip.
blágrýti, -s [blau:gri·tʰɪ(s); -gri:dɪ]
n. basalt.
blágrýtisfjall, -s, -fjöll [blau:gri·tʰɪs-
fjad·l, -fjal·s, -fjöd·l; -gri·d-] n.
basalt mountain; blágrýtis-háslétta
basalt plateau.
blágrýtislag, -s, -lög [blau:gri·tʰɪs-
la:q, -lax·s, -lö:q; -gri·d·] n. basalt
layer.
bláklæddur, -klædd, -klætt [blau:-
kʰlaid·ʏṛ, -kʰlaid·, -kʰlaiʰt·] adj. clad
in blue.
blámóða, -u, -ur [blau:mou·ða, -ʏ(ṛ)]
wf.1 blue mist (= móða).
1. blanda, blöndu, -ur [blan·da,
blön·dʏ(ṛ)] wf.1 a mixture; a drink
mixed with sour whey or sour skyr
and water; sour whey.
2. blanda, -aði, -að(ur) [blan·da, -aðɪ,
-að, -aðʏṛ] wv.4 mix, mingle;
blanda saman við mingle together
with, mix up with (= blanda e-u).
1. blár [blau:r] m.1 the blue air, the
blue distance; only in: út í bláinn
'out into the blue distance,' far
away; also: at random.
2. blár, blá, blátt; blárri, bláastur
[blau:r, blau:, blauʰt:, blaur:ɪ,
blau:astʏṛ] adj. blue (In. III,
2(a)3 & (b)5).
blasa, blasti, blasað [bla:sa, blas·tɪ,
bla:sað] wv.3 b. við lie before one's
eyes, be open to view.
blása, blæs, blés, blésum, blásinn (-ið)
[blau:sa, blai:s, blje:s, -ʏm, blau:-
sɪn, -ɪð] v.7 blow; b. upp erode.
blautur, blaut, blautt [blöy:tʰʏṛ,
blöy:tʰ, blöyʰt:; blöy:d(ʏṛ)] adj.
wet soggy; í blautu in wet clothes.
bleikja, -u, -ur [blei:k₁ʰa, -ʏ, -ʏṛ;
blei:g₁a] wf.1 charr, a species of
trout.
blek, -s [blɛ:kʰ, -s; blɛ:g̊] n. ink.
blés, -um, see blása.

blessa, -aði, -að(ur) [blɛs:a, -aðɪ, -að
-aðʏṛ] wv.4 bless; pp. blessaður
(abbreviated bless) is used in greetings between friends: komdu blessaður how do you do, hello; vertu
bless(aður) goodbye; blessaður,
gerðu þetta literally: 'blessed
(fellow), do this,' i. e. ·be a good
boy and do this, please, do this;
acc. with inf.: ég bað hann blessaðan að gera þetta I asked him,
please, to do this.
blessun, -unar, -anir [blɛs:ʏn, -ʏnaṛ,
-anɪṛ] f.2 blessing, benediction;
blessunin hún Anna mín my dear
(blessed) A.; benefit, ómenguð blessun an unmixed boon.
blettur, -s, -ir [blɛʰt:ʏṛ, blɛʰt·s,
blɛʰt:ɪṛ] m.2 patch; patch of lawn,
ground.
blíðka, -aði, -að(ur) [blið·kʰa, -aðɪ,
-að, -aðʏṛ; bliþ·ka] wv.4 soften,
mollify.
blika, -u, -ur [blɪ:kʰa, -ʏ(ṛ); blɪ:g̊a]
wf.1 a cover of clouds, often fore
boding storm or rain.
blindraheimili, -s, - [blɪn·dra-hei:-
mɪlɪ(s)] n. home for the blind.
Blindravinafélag Íslands [blɪn·dra-
vɪ:na-fjɛ:laq i:slan(d)s] n. 'The
Icelandic Friends of the Blind
Society.'
blindur, blind, blint [blɪn·dʏṛ, blɪn·d,
blɪn·tʰ; blɪn·t] adj. blind.
blístra, -aði, -að [blis·tra, -aðɪ, -að]
wv.4 whistle, hoot.
blóð, -s [blou:ð, blouð·s] n. blood.
blóðga, -aði, -að(ur) [blouð·g̊a, -aðɪ,
-að, -aðʏṛ] wv.4 draw blood.
blóðmör, -s [blouð·mö·r, -möṛs; blou:-
mʏṛ(s)] m.1 blood sausage, made
of blood, water, rye flour and suet,
eaten fresh or pickled.
blóðnasir [blouð·na·sɪṛ] f.2.pl. bleeding nose, nosebleed.
blóðugur [blou:ðʏqʏṛ] adj. (see
-ugur) bloody.
blóm, -s, - [blou:m, bloum·s] n. flower.
blómi, -a [blou:mɪ, -a] wm.1 flower
flowering; standa í blóma flourish

Vowels: a [a] approx. father; á [au] cow; e [ɛ] set; é [jɛ] yes; i, y [ɪ] sit; í, ý [i] feel;
o [ɔ] law; ó [ou] note; u [ʏ] approx. Germ. Mütter; ú [u] school; y = i; ý = i; æ [ai] ice;
ö [ö] Germ. hören; au [öy] French feuille; ei, ey [ei] ale. Length [:]; half-length [·].

blómkál, -s, - [bloum·kʰau·l, -kʰauls]
n. cauliflower.

blússa, -u, -ur [blus:a, -ʏ(r̥)] wf.1
blouse.

blæða, blæddi, blæddur(blætt) [blai:ða,
blaid̥:ɪ, -ʏr̥, blaiʰt:] wv.2 bleed;
impersonal: mér blœðir I bleed, I
am bleeding.

blær, -s, -ir [blai:r, blai:s, blai:jɪr̥]
m.2 soft wind, breeze (In. I, 2,
2(b)2).

blæs, see blása.

blöð, see blað.

blöðku, see blaðka.

blöndu, -ur, see blanda.

boð, -s, - [bɔ:ð, bɔð·s] n. offer, invitation, party.

boðið, -inn, see bjóða.

boðskapur, -ar [bɔð·ska·pʰʏr̥, -ar̥;
-ska·b·] m.3 message, tidings; gleðilegur boðskapur joyous tidings,
evangelium.

boðstólar [bɔð·stou·lar̥] m.1.pl. ' stands
of offering,' only in the phrase:
hafa e-ð á boðstólum have sth for
sale, offer sth for sale.

bogi, -a, -ar [bɔi:jɪ, bɔ:qa(r̥); bɔ:jɪ]
wm.1 bow; also personal name
Bogi.

bógur, -s (-ar), -ar (bægir) [bou:(q)ʏr̥,
boux·s, bou:(q)ar̥, bai:jɪr̥] m.1 (& 3)
shoulder (of an animal), bow, side
(of a ship); á hinn bóginn on the
other hand (side).

bók, -ar, bækur [bou:kʰ, -ar̥, bai:kʰʏr̥;
bou:g̊-, bai:g̊-] f.3 book (In. I, 3, 3).

bókabúð, -ar, -ir [bou:kʰa-bu:ð₁
-bu:ðar̥; bou:g̊a-] f.2 bookstore.

bókagerð, -ar [bou:kʰa-g̊ɪer·ð, -ðar̥;
bou:g̊a-] f.2 making, publishing of
books.

bókaherbergi, -s, - [bou:kʰa-her·-
berg̊₁ɪ(s); bou:g̊a-] n. library, study.

bókakostur, -ar [bou:kʰa-kʰɔs·tʏr̥,
-ar̥; bou:g̊a-] m.3 book facilities.

bókasafn, -s, -söfn [bou:kʰa-sab·n̥,
-sabns, -söb·n̥; bou:g̊a-] n. library.

bókaútgáfa, -u, -ur [bou:kʰa-u:tʰgau-
va, -ʏ(r̥); bou:g̊a-u:d̥-] wf.1 publishing of books; Bókaútgáfa Menn-

ingarsjóðs 'The Culture Fund
Publications.'

bókaútgáfufélag, -s, -lög [bou:kʰa·
u:tʰgau:vʏ-fje:laq, -laxs, -löq:
bou:g̊a-u:d̥-] n. publishing society
(company).

bókaútgefandi, -a, -endur [bou:kʰa·
u:tʰg̊₁e·vand̥ɪ, -a, -end̥ʏr̥; bou:g̊a-
u:d̥-] wm.2 publisher.

bókaverzlun, -unar, -anir [bou:kʰa-
verslʏn, -ʏnar̥, -anɪr̥; bou:g̊a-] f.2
bookstore (= bókabúð).

Bókhlöðustígur, -s [bou:kʰhlö·ðʏ-
sti:qʏr̥, -stix·s] m.1 'Library Path,
in Reykjavík.

bókmenntafélag, -s, -lög [bou:kʰmentʰa-
fje:laq, -laxs, -löq; bou:g̊menta-] n.
literary society; Hið íslenzka bókmenntafélag (= Bókmenntafélagið)
'The Icelandic Literary Society.'

bókmenntasaga, -sögu, -ur [bou:kʰ-
mentʰa-sa:qa, -sö:qʏ(r̥); bou:g̊-
menta-] wf.1 literary history.

bókmenntir [bou:kʰmentʰɪr̥; bou:g̊-
mentɪr̥] f.2.pl. literature.

bókstafur, -s, -ir [bou:kʰsta·vʏr̥, -stafs,
-sta·vɪr̥; bou:g̊-] m.2 letter.

bókvísi [bou:kʰvi·sɪ; bou:g̊-] wf.2
book culture, literature.

ból, -s, - [bou:l, boul·s] n. bed; dwelling place; in place names -ból.

bólga, -u, -ur [boul·g̊a, -ʏ(r̥)] wf.1
inflammation.

bólgna, -aði, -að(ur) [boul·na, -aðɪ,
-að, -aðʏr̥] wv.4 inflame, get inflamed.

boli, -a, -ar [bɔ:lɪ, -a(r̥)] wm.1 bull.

bolla, -u, -ur [bɔl:a, -ʏ(r̥)] wf.1 ball
(meat-, fish-); cross bun (Pr. 3, 2,
9n).

bollapar, -s, -pör [bɔd̥·la-pʰa:r, -pʰar̥·s,
-pʰö:r] n. cup and saucer.

bolli, -a, -ar [bɔd̥·lɪ, -a(r̥)] wm.1 cup.

bólstraður, -uð, -að [boul·straðʏr̥,
-ʏð, -að] adj. upholstered.

bómull, -ar [bou:mʏd̥l, -ʏd̥lar̥] f.1
= baðmull, also in compounds
bómullar-.

bóndabær, -bæjar, -bæir [boun·d̥a-

Consonants: [ð] breathe; [g] good; [g̊ɪ] gyarden (garden); [hw̥] what; [j] yes; [kɪ] cyan
(can); [ŋ] thing; [q] N. Germ. sagen; [r] Scottish r; [x] approx. Germ. ach; [þ] thin.
Voiceless: ○; [b̥, d̥, g̊] approx. p, t, k. Half-voiced: italics. Aspiration and preaspiration:
[ʰ]; [pʰ, tʰ, kʰ] p-, t-, k-. Others as in English.

315

bai:*r*, -bai:ja*ŗ*, -bai:jı*ŗ*] m.2 farmstead, farm.

bóndadóttir, -ur, -dætur [boun·da-
dou*ʰ*t:ı*ŗ*, -y*ŗ*, -dai:t*ʰ*y*ŗ*; -dai:d*ỵ̊ŗ*]
f.3 farmer's daughter.

bóndi, -a, bændur [boun·dı, -a, bain·-
d*ẙŗ*] wm.2 farmer, master, husband
(In. I, 5, 2).

bora, -aði, -að(ur) [bɔ:ra, -aðı, -að,
-aðy*ŗ*] wv.4 bore, drill.

borð, -s, - [bɔr·ð, bɔrðs] n. table,
board, plank, side; *um borð (í)* on
board; *frá borði* from the boat;
á annað borðið on one side; *á
annað borð* at all.

borða, -aði, -að(ur) [bɔr·ða, -aðı, -að,
-aðy*ŗ*] wv.4 eat; breakfast, lunch,
dine, sup; *get ég fengið að borða?*
can I get [something] to eat?

borðbúnaður, -aðar [bɔr·ðbu·naðy*ŗ*,
-aða*ŗ*] m.3 table service.

borðdúkur, -s, -ar [bɔr·ðdu·k*ʰ*y*ŗ*,
-du·k*ʰ*s, -a*ŗ*; -du·g̣-] m.1 tablecloth.

borðstofa, -u, -ur [bɔr·ðstɔ·va, -y(*ŗ*),
bɔ*ŗ*·s-] wf.1 dining room.

borðstofuborð [bɔr·ðstɔvɣ·bɔr·ð, -ðs]
n. dining room table.

borg, -ar, -ir [bɔr·g̣, -a*ŗ*, bɔr·g̣ı*ŗ*]
f.2 town, city; rocky hill, knoll;
thus in place names.

borga, -aði, -að(ur) [bɔr·g̣a, -aðı, -að,
-aðy*ŗ*] wv.4 pay; *b. undir bréf* pay
postage on a letter.

borgaréttur, -ar [bɔr·g̣ara-rje*ʰ*t:y*ŗ*,
-a*ŗ*] m.3 citizenship, civil rights;
license to trade.

Borgarfjörður, -fjarðar [bɔr·g̣ar-
fjör·ðy*ŗ*, -fjar·ða*ŗ*] m.3 'Borg Fjord.'

borgari, -a, -ar [bɔr·g̣arı, -a(*ŗ*)] wm.1
citizen, burgess, merchant.

borgið, -inn, see 2. *bjarga*.

borgun, -ar [bɔr·g̣ʏn, -ʏna*ŗ*] wf.2 payment.

borið, -inn, see *bera*.

borjárn, -s, - [bɔr·jau(r)dn(s)] n. iron
gimlet, bore, drill.

botn, -s, -ar [bɔ*ʰ*t·n, bɔs:, bɔ*ʰ*t·na*ŗ*]
m.1 bottom; end (of a valley or
fjord).

botnlangabólga, -u [bɔ*ʰ*t·(n)lauŋg̣a-
boul·g̣a, -ʏ] wf.1 appendicitis.

botnlangi, -a, -ar [bɔ*ʰ*t·(n)lauŋg̣ˌı,
-lauŋg̣a(*ŗ*)] wm.1 appendix.

1. brá, brár, brár [brau:(r)] f.1 eyelash.

2. brá, see *bregða*.

bráð- [brau:ð-] pref. exceedingly,
grossly.

bráðlega [brauð·le·qa] adv. soon.

bráðókunnugur[brau:ð-ou:k*ʰ*ʏn·ʏqʏ*ŗ*]
adj. (see *-ugur*) grossly unfamiliar
with; totally unknown.

bráður, bráð, brátt [brau:ðy*ŗ*, brau:ð,
brau*ʰ*t:] adj. quick, rash; *of bráð*
(f.) *á sér* too rash; *brátt* adv. soon.

bragð, -s, brögð [braq·ð, braqðs or
brax·s, bröq·ð; brag̣·þ, brög·þ] n.
trick, hold (in wrestling); *hvað á
nú til bragðs að taka?* what is now
to be done?

brann, see 2. *brenna*.

brast, see *bresta*.

brátt[brau*ʰ*t:] adv. soon; see *bráður*.

brattur, brött, bratt [bra*ʰ*t:y*ŗ*, brö*ʰ*t:,
bra*ʰ*t:] adj. steep.

brauð, -s, - [bröy:ð, bröyð·s] n. bread
(black bread, rye bread); benefice.

brauðbúð, -ar, -ir [bröyð·bu·ð, -ða*ŗ*,
-ðı*ŗ*] f.2 bread store, bakery store.

1. braut, -ar, -ir [bröy:t*ʰ*, -a*ŗ*, -ı*ŗ*;
bröy:d] f.2 road (a built or broken
way in contrast to the natural horse-
paths); in street-names *-braut*.

2. braut, see *brjóta*.

bréf, -s, - [brjɛ:v, brjɛf·s] n. letter.

bréfaafgreiðsla, -u, -ur [brjɛ:va-
av·greiðsla, -ʏ(*ŗ*)] wf.1 letter delivery.

bréfhirðing, -ar, -ar[brjɛ:vhırðiŋg̣, -a*ŗ*]
f.1 second class post office.

bréfspjald, -s, -spjöld [brjɛf·spjald(s),
-spjöld] n. post card.

bregða, bregð, brá, brugðum, brugðinn (-ið) [breq·ða, breq·ð, brau:,
brʏq·ðʏm, brʏq·ðın, -ıð; breg̣·ða,
breg̣·þ, brʏg̣·ðʏm, -ın, -ıð] v.3 move
quickly; *bregða sverði* unsheath,
brandish a sword; *bregða e-u yfir
sig* throw sth over oneself, as a

Vowels: *a* [a] approx. father; *á* [au] cow; *e* [ɛ] set; *é* [jɛ] yes; *i, y* [ɪ] sit; *í, ý* [i] feel;
o [ɔ] law; *ó* [ou] note; *u* [ʏ] approx. Germ. Mütter; *ú* [u] school; *y* = *i*; *ý* = *í*; *æ* [ai] ice;
ö [ö] Germ. hören; *au* [öy] French feuille; *ei, ey* [ei] ale. Length [:]; half-length [·].

316

cloak, a smokescreen; *bregða líkn-arbelg yfir glasið* lock up the bottle with an amnion (a membrane with magic properties); *henni brá (við, í brún)* she was startled (S. VI, **14**, *5*); *bregða sér í selslíki* turn oneself into the shape of a seal; *það er farið að bregða birtu* the daylight is beginning to fail (S. VI, **14**, *3*); *bregða út af e-u* deviate from something.

breiða, breiddi, breiddur (breitt) [brei:ða, breid̥:ɪ, breid̥:ʏɾ, breiʰt:] wv.2 spread out.

Breiðafjörður, -fjarðar [brei:ða-fjör-ðʏɾ, -fjar-ðar] m.3 'Broad Fjord'; also: *Breiðifjörður, Breiðafjarðar.*

Breiðamerkursandur, -s [brei:ðamer̥-kʏɾ-san-dʏɾ, -san-(d̥)s] m.1 'The Sand of Breiðamörk' (= 'Broad Woods').

Breiðdalur, -s [breið̥-da-lʏɾ, -dals; breid̥:a-lʏɾ] m.2 'Broad Dale;' dat. *Breiðdal = í Breiðdal* in B. (S. I, *3, 3*, 2n).

breiður, breið, breitt [brei:ðʏɾ, brei:ð̥, breiʰt:] adj. broad, wide, 'tense' (of vowels, cf. Pr. **2**, 3).

brekka, -u, -ur, (-na) [breʰk:a, -ʏ(ɾ), bre̥ʰk-na] wf.1 slope.

1. brenna, -u, -ur [bren:a, -ʏ(ɾ)] wf.1 fire, bonfire.

2. brenna, brenn, brann, brunnum, brunninn (-ið) [bren:a, bren:, bran:, brʏn:ʏm, brʏn:ɪn, -ɪð̥] v.3 burn (intr.).

3. brenna, brenndi, brenndur (brennt) [bren:a, bren-d̥ɪ, -ʏɾ, bren-tʰ; bren-t] wv.2 burn (trans.); *brenna e-u* burn sth; *brenna e-n* burn sbdy.

brennisteinn,-s [bren:ɪ-steid̥-n̥,-stein-s] m.1 sulphur.

brennisteinshver, -s, -ir (-ar) [bren:ɪ-steins-hwɛ:r, -hwɛr-s, -hwɛ:rar, -ɪr̥; -kʰvɛ:r, etc.] m.2(1) sulphur spring, solfatara.

bresta, brest, brast, brustum, brostinn (-ið) [brɛs-ta, brɛs-t, bras-t, brʏs-tʏm, brɔs-tɪn, -ɪð̥] v.3 burst (intr.).

Bretland, -s [brɛ:tʰland̥, -lan(d̥)s; brɛ:d̥-] n. Britain.

Bretlandseyjar [brɛ:tʰlan(d̥)s-ei:jar; brɛ:d̥-] f.1.pl. the British Islands.

brezkur, brezk, brezkt [brɛs-kʏɾ, brɛs-k, brɛs-t] adj. British.

breyta, breytti, breytt(ur) [brei:tʰa, breiʰt:ɪ, -ʏɾ, breiʰt:; brei:d̥a] wv.2 alter, change; *breyttur* altered, changed.

breyting, -ar, -ar [brei:tʰiŋ̊, -aɾ; brei:diŋ̊] f.1 change.

Briem, -s [bri:m, brim-s] m.1 family name.

bringa, -u, -ur [briŋ-g̊a, -ʏ(ɾ)] wf.1 breast.

bringusund, -s [briŋ-g̊ʏ-sʏn-d̥, -sʏn-(d̥)s] n. breast stroke.

brjóst, -s, - [brjous-t(s)] n. breast.

brjóstnál, -ar, -ar [brjous-tnau-l, -laɾ] f.1 brooch.

brjóstsvið, -a [brjous-tsvɪ-ð̥ɪ, brjous:vɪ-ð̥ɪ] wm.1 heartburn.

brjóstvídd, -ar, -ir [brjous-tvid̥-, -aɾ, -ɪr̥] f.2 breast measurement, girth.

brjóta, brýt, braut, brutum, brotinn (-ið) [brjou:tʰa, bri:tʰ, bröy:tʰ, brʏ:tʰʏm, brɔ:tʰɪn, -ɪð̥; brjou:d̥a, bri:d̥, bröy:d̥, brʏ:d̥ʏm, brɔ:d̥ɪn] v.2 break, damage.

bróðir, -ur, bræður [brou:ðɪɾ, -ʏɾ, brai:ðʏɾ] m.4 brother; *enginn er annars bróðir í leik* (proverbial) 'nobody is another's brother in play,' i. e. each for himself. . . .

bróðurdóttir, -ur, -dætur [brou:ðʏr-douʰt:ɪɾ, -ʏɾ, -dai:tʰʏɾ; -dai:d̥ʏɾ] f.3 niece, 'brother's daughter.'

bróðursonur, -ar, -synir [brou:ðʏɾ-sɔ:nʏɾ, -aɾ, -sɪ:nɪɾ] m.3 nephew, 'brother's son.'

brók, -ar, -brækur [brou:kʰ, -aɾ, brai:kʰʏɾ; brou:g̊, brai:g̊ʏɾ] f.3 drawers, pants.

brosa, brosti, brosað [brɔ:sa, brɔs-tɪ, brɔ:sað̥] wv.3 smile.

brostið, -inn, see *bresta.*

brot, -s, - [brɔ:tʰ(s); brɔ:d̥] n. frac-

Consonants: [ð] brea*th*e; [g] *g*ood; [gʲ] *gy*arden (garden); [hw] *wh*at; [j] *y*es; [kʲ] *cy*an (can); [ŋ] thi*ng*; [q] N. Germ. sa*g*en; [r] Scottish *r*; [x] approx. Germ. a*ch*; [þ] *th*in. Voiceless: ○; [b̥, d̥, g̊] approx. *p, t, k*. Half-voiced: *italics*. Aspiration and preaspiration: [ʰ]; [pʰ, tʰ, kʰ] *p-, t-, k-*. Others as in English.

317

tion, fragment; fold, crease; ford on a river.

brotasprengikúla, -u, -ur [brɔ:tʰa-spreiŋ̊ˌɪkʰu:la, -ʏ(r̥); brɔ:d̥a-] wf.1 shrapnel shell.

brotið, -inn, see *brjóta.*

brotna, -aði, -að [brɔʰt·na, -aðɪ, -að] wv.4 break (intr.), be damaged.

brotstrik, -s, - [brɔ:tʰstrɪ·kʰ(s); brɔ:dstrɪ·g̊] n. line (in fractions, e. g. ½).

brú, -ar, brýr [bru:(ar̥), bri:r] f.3 bridge.

brúa, -aði, -að(ur) [bru:a, -aðɪ, -að, -aðʏr̥] wv.4 to bridge.

bruddi, -ur, see *bryðja.*

brúðkaup, -s, - [bruð·kʰöy·pʰ, -kʰöyfs; -köy·b̥] n. wedding, bridal; *gera b. til konu* marry a woman.

brúður, -ar, -ir [bru:ðʏr̥, -ar̥, -ir̥] f.1 & 2 bride.

brugðið, -inn, -um, see *bregða.*

brúka, -aði, -að(ur) [bru:kʰa, -aðɪ, -að, -aðʏr̥; bru:g̊a] wv.4 use.

brúna, -aði, -aður [bru:na, -aðɪ, -að, -aðʏr̥] wv.4 to brown.

bruni, -a, -ar [brʏ:nɪ, -a(r̥)] wm.1 fire; burning.

brúnn, brún, brúnt; brúnni, brúnastur [brud̥·n̥, bru:n, brun·tʰ; brun̥·t; brud̥·nɪ, bru:nastʏr̥] adj. brown; black (of horses): *sá brúni = Brúnn* the black horse.

brunnið, -inn, -um, see 2. *brenna.*

brunnur, -s, -ar [brʏn:ʏr̥, brʏn·s, brʏn:ar̥] m.1 well, spring.

brustum, see *bresta.*

brutum, see *brjóta.*

bryðja, bruddi, bruddur (brutt) [brɪð·ja, bryd̥:ɪ, -ʏr̥, brʏʰt:] wv.1 crunch (between the teeth).

bryggja, -u, -ur [brɪg̊ˌ:a, brɪg̊ˌ:ʏ(r̥)] wf.1 pier, mole.

brynja, -u, -ur [brɪn·ja, -ʏ(r̥)] wf.1 byrnie, coat of mail; armor.

brynsprengja, -u, -ur [brɪn·spreiŋ̊ˌa, -g̊ˌʏʏ(r̥)] wf.1 armor-piercing shell.

brynvagn, -s, -ar [brɪn·vag̊n̥(s), -vag̊nar̥] m.1 tank.

brynvarinn, -in, -ið [brɪn·va·rɪn, -ɪn,

-ɪð] adj. armored; *b-inn vagn* armored car.

brýr, see *brú.*

brýt, see *brjóta.*

bræða, bræddi, bræddur (brætt) [brai:ða, braid̥·ɪ, -ʏr̥, braiʰt:] wv.2 melt; *brætt smjör* melted butter.

bræðrabörn, -barna [braið·ra-böd̥·n̥, -bad·na] n.pl. first cousins, ' children of brothers.'

bræðradætur, -dætra [braið·ra-dai:-tʰʏr̥, -dai:tʰra; -dai:d̥-] f.3.pl. first cousins, ' daughters of brothers.'

bræðrasynir, -sona [braið·ra-sɪ:nɪr̥, -sɔ:na] m.3.pl. first cousins, ' sons of brothers.'

bræður, see *bróðir.*

brögð, see *bragð.*

brött, -u, -um, see *brattur.*

bú, -s, - [bu:(s)] n. household, farming, housekeeping; estate; in place names *-bú* dwelling place (In. II, 3, 2).

búa, bý, bjó, bjuggum, búinn (-ið) [bu:a, bi:, bjou:, bjʏg̊:ʏm, bu:ɪn, -ɪð] v.7 farm, live on a farm; live, dwell; lurk; keep house; prepare, make; (1) farm, live: *búa á (að) Reyni* farm, live at R.; *búa í Reykjavík* live in R.; *búa í hvíta húsinu* live in the white house; *e-ð býr undir þessu* something is lurking under this; (2) prepare: *búa til* make; *búa sig* dress (oneself); *búa sig út með e-ð* provide oneself with something; be provided with something; *búa e-n út með e-ð* fit somebody out with, provide somebody with something; (3) middle voice: *búast við e-u* expect something (literally: ' prepare oneself for something '); (4) pp. *búinn*: prepared, ready, having finished; clad, dressed; *vera búinn að gera e-ð* have done something (S. VI, 6); *vera búinn (með e-ð)* have finished (with something), be through (with something), be out of something; *e-ð er búið* something is finished, something is over; *svo búið* such,

Vowels: *a* [a] approx. father; *á* [au] cow; *e* [ɛ] set; *é* [iɛ] yes; *i, y* [ɪ] sit; *í, ý* [i] feel; *o* [ɔ] law; *ó* [ou] note; *u* [ʏ] approx. Germ. Mütter; *ú* [u] school; *y = i; ý = í;* æ [ai] ice; *ö* [ö] Germ. hören; *au* [öy] French *feuille; ei, ey* [ei] ale. Length [:]; half-length [·].

as matters stand; *búinn gulli* adorned with gold = *gullbúinn*.

búandi, -a, -endur [bu:andɪ, -a, -endγr̥] wm.2 inhabitant, farmer (= *bóndi*).

búð, -ar, -ir [bu:ð, bu:ðar̥, -ɪr̥] f.2 shop, store; general store; temporary dwelling place of fishermen (*verbúðir*) or traders (*búðir*); also in place names -*búð*, -*búðir*; *fara í búðir* go shopping.

buðum, see *bjóða*.

búferli [bu:ferdlɪ] n. pl. only in: *flytja sig búferlum* moves.

buffett, -s, - [bʏf:ɛʰt·(s)] n. buffet, = *hlaðborð*.

bugur, -s, -ir [bʏ:qʏr̥, bʏx·s, bʏʏ:jɪr̥; bʏ:jɪr̥] m.2 loop, turn; *vinda bráðan bug að e-u* act quickly about something.

búinn, see *búa*.

Búkolla, -u [bu:kʰɔd·la, -ʏ] wf.1 name of a cow (*bú* + *kolla* = *kollótt kýr* cow without horns).

Búnaðarbanki Íslands [bu:naðar- bauŋ·kjʰɪ; -bauŋ·kjɪ; i:slan(d)s] wm.1 'The Rural Bank of Iceland.'

búnaður, -ar [bu:naðʏr̥, -ar̥] m.3 farming, agriculture, animal husbandry.

bundið, -inn, -um, see *binda*.

bunga, -u, -ur [buŋ·ga -ʏ(r̥)] wf.1 bulge, dome.

búningur, -s, -ar [bu:niŋ̊ʏr̥, -iŋs, -iŋar̥] m.1 attire, dress, apparel; (national) costume (= *þjóðbúningur*).

búr, -s, - [bu:r, bur̥·s] n. pantry; cage (for birds etc.); bower.

burðargjald, -s, -gjöld [bʏr·ðar-gjal·d, -gjal(d)s, -gjöl·d] n. postage, rate.

burður, -ar, -ir [bʏr·ðʏr̥, -ar̥, -ɪr̥] m.3 carrying; load; birth (of lambs, etc.); lambing season (= *sauðburður*).

burgum, see 2. *bjarga*.

bursta, -aði, -að(ur) [bʏ(r̥)sta, -aðɪ, -að, -aðʏr̥] wv.4 brush.

bursti, -a, -ar [bʏ(r̥)stɪ, -a(r̥)] wm.1 brush; *tannbursti* tooth brush.

burt [bʏr̥·t] adv. away.

burtfararpróf, -s, - [bʏr̥·tfa·rar̥-pʰrou:v, -pʰrouf·s] n. final examination.

burtu [bʏr̥·tʏ] adv. = *burt*; *langt í burtu* far away.

búsettur, -sett, -sett [bu:sɛʰt·ʏr̥, -sɛʰt·] adj. resident, domiciled.

búskaparháttur, -ar, -hættir [bu:ska- pʰar̥-hauʰt:ʏr̥, -ar̥, -haiʰt:ɪr̥; -ska·b-] m.3 manner, type of farming.

búskapur, -ar [bu:ska·pʰʏr̥, -ar̥; -ska- bʏr̥] m.3 farming, keeping house.

buxur, buxna [bʏx·sʏr̥, bʏxsna] wf.1. pl. trousers.

bý, see *búa*.

býð, see *bjóða*.

bygg, -s [bɪg̊:, bɪg̊:s] n. barley.

byggð, -ar, -ir [bɪq·ð, -ðar̥, -ðɪr̥; bɪg̊·þ] f.2 habitation, settlement; pl. *byggðir* the inhabited parts of the country (opposite *ó-byggðir*).

byggða(r)menn, -manna [bɪq·ða(r)- men:, -man:a; bɪg̊·ð-] m.4.pl. people of the inhabited districts (opposite *útilegumenn* outlaws).

bygggrjón [bɪg̊:rjou·n] n.pl. barley (grain).

byggingameistari, -a, -ar [bɪg̊ː:iŋa- meis·tarɪ, -a(r̥)] wm.1 builder, architect, designer of buildings.

byggja, byggði, byggður (byggt) [bɪg̊ː:a, bɪq·ðɪ, -ʏr̥, bɪx·t; bɪg̊·ð-] wv.2 build; settle (*b. Grænland* settle Greenland), inhabit; *b. upp* build up; *byggjast á e-u* be based on sth, depend on.

bylur, -s, byljir [bɪ:lʏr̥, bɪl·s, bɪl·jɪr̥] m.2 blizzard, snowstorm.

byrja, -aði, -að(ur) [bɪr·ja, -aðɪ, -að, -aðʏr̥] wv.4 begin; *b. e-ð* begin sth; *b. á e-u* (*með e-u*) begin with sth; *til að b. með* to begin with (S. VI, 3, 3).

byrjun, -ar, -ir [bɪr·jʏn, -ʏnar̥, -anɪr̥] f.2 beginning.

byssa, -u, -ur [bɪs:a, -ʏ(r̥)] wf.1 gun.

byssustingur, -s, -ir [bɪs:ʏ-stiŋ·g̊ʏr̥, -stiŋ·s, -stiŋ·g̊jɪr̥] m.2 bayonet.

bæði, see *báðir*; *bæði ... og* both ... and (S. VIII, 2)·

bægir, see *bógur*.

Consonants: [ð] brea*th*e; [g] *g*ood; [gj] *gy*arden (garden); [hw] *wh*at; [j] *y*es; [kj] *cy*an (can); [ŋ] thi*ng*; [q] N. Germ. sa*g*en; [r] Scottish *r*; [x] approx. Germ. a*ch*; [þ] *th*in. Voiceless: ○; [b̥, d̥, g̊] approx. *p, t, k*. Half-voiced: *italics*. Aspiration and preaspiration. [ʰ]; [pʰ, tʰ, kʰ] *p-, t-, k-*. Others as in English.

319

bæir, see *bær.*

bæjanöfn [bai:ja-nöb·n̥] n.pl. (of *bæjarnafn*) farm names.

bæjar, see *bær.*

bæjardyr [bai:jar-dɪ:r] f.3.pl. doorway, entrance hall of a farm house.

bæjarhús, -s, - [bai:jar̥-hu:s] n. a 'house' or room in a farmstead group of houses; pl. the main group of houses on a farmstead.

bæjarlíf, -s [bai:jar-li:v] n. town life.

Bæjarstaðaskógur, -ar [bai:jar̥sta:ða-skou:(q)ʏr̥, -ar̥] m.1 'Farm Stead Woods,' in Öræfi, one of the few woods in Iceland.

bæjarsund, -s, - [bai:jar̥-sʏn-d̥(s)] n. láne between two houses on a farmstead.

bæjarþorp, -s, - [bai:jar̥-þɔr̥·p(s)] n. the main group of houses on a farmstead (= *bæjarhús* pl.).

bækistöð [bai:kʰɪ-stö:ð; bai:g̊ʲɪ·] = *beykistöð.*

bækur, see *bók.*

bæli, -s, - [bai:lɪ(s)] n. lair, bed; also in place names *-bæli,* dwelling place.

bæn, -ar, -ir [bai:n, bai:nar̥, -ɪr̥] f.2 prayer.

bændur, see *bóndi.*

bær, bæjar, bæir [bai:r, bai:jar̥, bai:-jɪr̥] m.2 (In. I, 2, 2(b)) farmstead, farm; in place names: *-bær* farm; *fara af bæ* leave the farmstead; town: *austur í bæ* to (or in) the eastern part of the town.

bærilegur [bai:rɪ-lɛ:qʏr̥] adj. (see *-legur*) tolerable, pretty good (litotes = fine); adv. *bærilega.*

bæta, bætti, bætt(ur) [bai:tʰa, baiʰt:ɪ, -ʏr̥, baiʰt:; bai:d̥a] wv.2 mend, repair, improve; make amends; *b. ráð sitt* mend one's ways; *b. fullum bótum* make full amends (S. I, 3, 1, 2(e)); *bæta við* add to, *hér við bætist* to this is added.

böð, see 1. *bað.*

Böðvar, -s [böð·var̥, -var̥s] m.1 personal name.

bögglaafgreiðsla, -u, -ur [bög̊:la-av-

greiðsla, -ʏ(r̥)] wf.1 parcel post delivery.

böggull, -uls, -lar [bög̊:ʏd̥l, -ʏls, bög̊·lar̥] m.1 parcel, package, packet.

bök, see *bak.*

böl, (bölvi), -s [bö:l, böl·vɪ, böl·s] n. calamity (In. I, 4(b)2).

böll, see *ball.*

bölva, -aði, -að(ur) [böl·va, -aðɪ, -að, -aðʏr̥] wv.4 curse; *b. e-m (e-u)* curse sbdy (sth); *fari hann bölvaður* [fa:r an. böl·vaðʏr̥] damn him.

börn, see *barn.*

D.

dá, dáði, dáð(ur) [dau:, dau:ðɪ, dau:ð, dau:ðʏr̥] wv.3 admire; *dást að e-u* (= *dá e-ð*) admire sth.

daðla, döðlu, -ur [dað·la, döð·lʏ(r̥)] wf.1 date (the fruit).

daður, (-ri), -urs [da:ðʏr̥(s), dað·rɪ] n. flirting.

daga, -aði, -að [da:qa, -aðɪ, -að] wv.4 dawn; *það dagar* it dawns, it is dawning; *daga uppi* be overtaken by dawn (of trolls that turn into stone at the break of day) (S. VI, 14, 3).

dagblað, -s, -blöð [daq·bla·ð, -blaðs, -blö·ð] n. daily (newspaper).

dagbók, -ar, -bækur [daq·bou·kʰ, -ar̥, -bai·kʰʏr̥; -bou·g̊, -bai·g̊ʏr̥] f.3 diary.

daglega [daq·lɛ·qa] adv. daily.

daglegur [daq·lɛ·qʏr̥] adj. (see *-legur*) daily; *daglegt tal* everyday language, colloquial speech.

dagleið, -ar, -ir [daq·lei·ð, -ðar̥, -ðɪr̥] f.2 day's journey.

dagmál [daq·mau·l] n.pl. nine in the morning.

dagskrá, -r, -r [dax·skrau·(r)] f.1 order of the day, program.

dagstofa, -u, -ur [dax·stɔ·va, -ʏ(r̥)] wf.1 living room.

dagstofuhúsgögn [dax·stɔ·vʏ-hu:s-gög̊n̥] n.pl. living room furniture.

dagsverk, -s, - [dax·sverk(s)] n. day's work.

dagur, (degi), -s, -ar [da:qʏr̥, dei:jɪ, dax·s, da:qar̥] m.1 day; *ég var þar*

Vowels: *a* [a] approx. father; *á* [au] cow; *e* [ɛ] set; *é* [jɛ] yes; *i, y* [ɪ] sit; *í, ý* [i] feel; *o* [ɔ] law; *ó* [ou] note; *u* [ʏ] approx. Germ. Mütter; *ú* [u] school; *y* = *i*; *ý* = *í*; *æ* [ai] ice; *ö* [ö] Germ. hören; *au* [öy] French feuille; *ei, ey* [ei] ale. Length [:]; half-length [·].

320

tvo daga (adv. acc.) I was there two days (S. I, 2, 2, 2); *góðan dag* (*góðan daginn*)! good morning, good day (used only at meeting, not at departure, as 'good day' is used in English); dawn: *dagur ljómar* the day (= dawn) illuminates the sky; *dagurinn í dag* '(the day) today,' this very day; *einhvern daginn* some day, one of these days; *nú á dögum* nowadays; *um dagana* in my (his) life; *í gamla daga* in the (good) old days; *á dag* per day·

dáið, -inn, see *deyja*.

Dalasýsla, -u [da:la·sis·la, -ʏ] wf.1 'District of Dalir.'

dálítill, -il, -ið [dau:li·tʰɪdl, -ɪl, -ɪð; -li·d-] adj. very small, a little; *dálítið* a little thing; *dálítið hærri* a little taller, a little bit taller.

dalur, -s, -ir [da:lʏr, dal·s, da:lɪr] m.2 valley, dale.

dama, dömu, -ur [da:ma, dö:mʏ(r̥)] wf.1 lady.

dánarminning, -ar, -ar [dau:nar·mɪn:iŋg, -ar̥] f.1 commemoration of death, obituary.

Dani, -a, -ir [da:nɪ, -a, -ɪr̥] wm.1 & m.2.pl. a Dane, usually in pl. *Danir* (the) Danes (S. III, 3, 3n2).

Danmörk, -merkur [dan·mör̥k, -mer̥·kʏr̥] f.3 Denmark·

dans, -, -ar [dan·s(ar̥)] m.1 dance.

dansa, -aði, -að(ur) [dan·sa, -aðɪ, -að, -aðʏr̥] wv.4 dance.

danska, dönsku [danska, dönskʏ] wf.1 Danish.

dansk-íslenzkur, -lenzk, -lenzkt [dansk·i:slenskʏr̥, -lensk, -lenst] adj. Danish-Icelandic.

danskur, dönsk, danskt [danskʏr̥, dönsk, danst] adj. Danish.

dansleikur, -s, -ar (-ir) [dan·slei·kʰʏr̥, -lei·kʰs, -lei·kʰar̥, -lei·k₁ʰɪr̥; -lei·g̊·, -lei·g̊₁-] m.1 & 2 dance.

danssalur, -s, -ir [dan·(s)sa·lʏr̥, -sals, -sa·lɪr̥] m.2 dance hall.

dáti, -a, -ar [dau:tʰɪ, -a(r̥); dau:dɪ] wm.1 sailor (in the navy).

datt, see *detta*.

dauði, -a [döy:ðɪ, -a] wm.1 death; *hvíti dauðinn* white death, i. e. tuberculosis; *svarti dauðinn* Black Death.

dauður, dauð, dautt [döy:ðʏr̥, döy:ð, döyʰt:] adj. dead; *þeir dauðu* the dead.

dauðþreyttur, -þreytt, -þreytt [döyð-·þreiʰt:ʏr̥, -þreiʰt:; döyþ·-] adj. dead tired, dog tired, exhausted.

daufur, dauf, dauft [döy:vʏr̥, döy:v, döyf·t] adj. weak; flat; not vigorous, *daufari* less vigorous.

dável [dau:vɛ·l] adv. pretty well.

Davíð, -s [da:vi·ð, -vɪðs] m.1 David.

degi, see *dagur*.

deila, deildi, deildur (deilt) [dei:la, deil·dɪ, deil·dʏr̥, deil·t] wv.2 dispute, fight, quarrel; divide; *d. um e-ð* fight about sth; dispute about sth; *deila (með)* divide (by); *d. tveim-(ur) í tólf = d. tólf með tveim(ur)* divide twelve by two.

deild, -ar, -ir [deil·d, -ar̥, -ɪr̥] f.2 part, department, division; faculty (in the University); division or battalion (in the army).

deiling, -ar, -ar [dei:liŋg, -ar̥] f.1 division (math.).

dekametri, -a, -ar [dɛ:kʰa-mɛ:tʰrɪ, -a(r̥); dɛ:g̊a-mɛ:d̥rɪ] wm.1 dekameter.

des. =

desember [dɛ:sɛmbɛ·r] m.indecl. December.

desímetri, -a, -ar [dɛ:si-mɛ:tʰrɪ, -a(r̥); -mɛ:d̥rɪ] wm.1 decimeter.

detta, dett, datt, duttum, dottinn (-ið) [dɛʰt:a, dɛʰt:, daʰt:, dʏʰt:ʏm, doʰt:ɪn, -ɪð] v.3 fall; *d. ofan* fall down (stairs) (S. VI, 3, 3).

deyja, dey, dó, dóum, dáinn (-ið) [dei:ja, dei:, dou:, dou:ʏm, dau:-ɪn, -ɪð] v.6 (rarely *deyja, deyði, deyð(ur)* [dei:ðɪ, -ʏr̥, dei:ð] wv.1) die (S. VI, 6, 2); (of fire) go out, be extinguished; *eldurinn* (the fire), *ljósið* (the light) *dó* went out; *d. út* become extinct.

Consonants: [ð] brea*th*e; [g] *g*ood; [g₁] *gy*arden (garden); [hʍ] *wh*at; [j] *y*es; [k₁] *cy*an (can); [ŋ] thi*ng*; [q] N. Germ. sa*g*en; [r] Scottish *r*; [x] approx. Germ. a*ch*; [þ] *th*in. Voiceless: ○; [b̥, d̥, g̊] approx. *p, t, k*. Half-voiced: *italics*. Aspiration and preaspiration: [ʰ]; [pʰ, tʰ, kʰ] *p-, t-, k-*. Others as in English.

Dídí [di:di:] f.indecl. pet name.

digur, digur, digurt; digrari (digurri), digrastur (digurstur) [dɪ:qɣ̯ɪ, dɪ:-qɣ̯ɪt; dɪq·rarɪ, -astɣ̯ɪ; dɪ:qɣ̯ɪ·ɪ, dɪ:qɣ̯ɪstɣ̯ɪ] adj. thick.

díki, -s, - [di:kⱼʰɪ(s); di:g̊ⱼɪ] n. ditch.

dilkaket (-kjöt), -s [dɪl·kʰa-kⱼʰɛ:tʰ(s); -kⱼʰö:tʰ(s); dɪl·ka-kⱼʰɛ:d̥, -kⱼʰö:d̥] n. lamb (meat).

dilkur, -s, -ar [dɪl·kʰɣ̯ɪ, -ar̥, dɪlkʰs; dɪl·kɣ̯ɪ, -s] m.1 sucking lamb.

dillidó [dɪd̥·lɪ-dou:] interj. hushaby, lullaby.

dimma, dimmdi, dimmt, or -aði, -að [dɪm:a, dɪm·d̥ɪ, dɪm·tʰ; dɪm̥·t; dɪm:aðɪ, -að] wv.2 or 4 get dark; impersonal: það dimmir it is getting dark (S. IV, 1, 5(a)); það er farið að dimma af nótt the night has begun to gain on the day, the nights are getting longer (S. VI, 14, 3).

diskur, -s, -ar [dɪs·kɣ̯ɪ, dɪsks, dɪs·kar̥] m.1 plate.

dívan, -s, -ar [di:van, di:vans, di:-vanar̥] m.1 divan, couch.

djúpsprengja, -u, -ur [dju:pʰspreiŋg̊ⱼa, -ɣ(r̥)] wf.1 depth bomb.

djúpur, djúp, djúpt; dýpri (djúpari), dýpstur (djúpastur) [dju:pʰɣ̯ɪ, dju:pʰ, djuf·t; di:pʰrɪ, dif·stɣ̯ɪ; dju:pʰarɪ, -astɣ̯ɪ; dju:b-, di:b-] adj. deep; djúpur diskur (= djúpdiskur) soup plate.

djöfull, -uls, -lar [djö:vɣ̯d̥l, -ɣls, djöb·lar̥] m.1 devil.

djörfung, -ar [djör·vuŋg̊, -ar̥] f.1 courage.

dó, -um, see deyja.

dofi, -a [dɔ:vɪ, -a] wm.1 numbness.

dofinn, -in, -ið [dɔ:vɪn, -ɪn, -ɪð] adj. numb.

dofna, -aði, -að(ur) [dɔb·na, -aðɪ, -að, -aðɣ̯ɪ] wv.4 become numb (dead, of limbs).

doktor, -s, -ar [dɔx·tɔr̥, -ɔrs, -ɔrar̥] m.1 doctor, physician.

doktorspróf, -s, - [dɔx·tɔrs-pʰrou:v, -pʰrouf·s] n. doctor's examination.

dollari, -a, -ar [dɔl:arɪ, -a(r̥)] wm.1 dollar (Pr. 3, 2, 9n).

dómari, -a, -ar [dou:marɪ, -a(r̥)] wm.1 judge.

dómkirkja, -u, -ur [doum·kⱼʰɪrkⱼa, -kⱼɣ(r)] wf.1 cathedral; Dómkirkjan 'The Cathedral' in Reykjavík.

dómur, -s, -ar [dou:mɣ̯ɪ, doum·s, dou:mar̥] m.1 judgment, verdict.

dós, -ar, -ir [dou:s, -ar̥, -ɪr̥] f.2 can, tin; box.

dósamatur, -ar [dou:sa-ma:tʰɣ̯ɪ, -ar̥; -ma:d̥-] m.3 canned goods (food).

dót, -s [dou:tʰ(s); dou:d̥(s)] n. things, baggage, belongings.

dottið, -inn, see detta.

dóttir, -ur, dætur [douʰt:ɪr̥, -ɣ̯ɪ, dai:-tʰɣ̯ɪ; dai:d̥ɣ̯ɪ] f.3 daughter.

dr. = doktor.

draga, dreg, dró, drógum, dreginn (-ið) [dra:qa, drɛ:q, drou:, drou:(q)ɣm, drei:jɪn, -ɪð] v.6 draw, drag, pull; d. tönn (úr manni) pull a tooth ('from a person'); impersonal: hann (það) dregur upp bliku the sky is becoming overcast; draga fisk pull up fish; draga nafn (sitt) af e-u derive one's name from sth; draga frá subtract.

dragkista, -u, -ur [drax·kⱼʰɪsta, -ɣ(r̥)] wf.1 chest of drawers.

dragt, -ar, -ir [drax·t, -ar̥, -ɪr̥] f.2 (tailored) suit.

drakk, see drekka.

drangur, -s, -ar [drauŋ·g̊ɣ̯ɪ, drauŋ·s, drauŋ·g̊ar̥] m.1 rock, pinnacle.

drap, drápum, see drepa.

dráttarvél, -ar, -ar [drauʰt:ar-vjɛ:l, -vjɛ:lar̥] f.1 tractor, caterpillar tractor.

dráttur, -ar, drættir [drauʰt:ɣ̯ɪ, -ar̥, draiʰt:ɪr̥] m.3 pulling; til dráttar for hauling (wagons, carts).

draugagangur, -s [dröy:qa-gauŋ·g̊ɣ̯ɪ, -gauŋ·s] m.1 literally: walking of ghosts; visitation of ghosts, haunting.

draugasaga, -sögu, -ur [dröy:qa-sa:qa, -sö:qɣ(r̥)] wf.1 ghost story.

draugatrú, -ar [dröy:qa-tʰru:, -ar̥] f.1 belief in ghosts.

Vowels: a [a] approx. father; á [au] cow; e [ɛ] set; é [jɛ] yes; i, y [ɪ] sit; í, ý [i] feel; o [ɔ] law; ó [ou] note; u [ɣ] approx. Germ. Mütter; ú [u] school; y = i; ý = í; æ [ai] ice; ö [ö] Germ. hören; au [öy] French feuille; ei, ey [ei] ale. Length [:]; half-length [·].

draugur, -s, -ar [dröy:qᵣ̥, dröyx·s, dröy:qar̥] m.1 ghost, spook.
draumaland, -s, -lönd [dröy:ma-lan·d̥, -lan·(d̥)s, -lön·d̥] n. land of dreams.
draup, see *drjúpa*.
dreg, dregið, -inn, see *draga*.
1. dreif, -ar, -ar [drei:v, drei:var̥] f.1 scattered remnants, remnants of hay; see *við*.
2. dreif, see *drífa*.
dreifa, dreifði, dreifður (dreift) [drei:-va, dreiv·ðɪ, -ᵣ̥, dreif·t; dreib̥·ð̥-] wv.2 scatter, spread.
drekka, drekk, drakk, drukkum, drukk-inn (-ið) [drɛʰk:a, drɛʰk:, draʰk:, drᵧʰk:ʏm, drᵧʰk̞:ɪn, -ɪð] v.3 drink; *drekka upp* drink up.
drengjaflokkur, -s, -ar [dreiŋ·g̊ˌa-flɔʰk:ʏr̥, -flɔʰk·s, -flɔʰk:ar̥] m.1 flock of boys, boys.
drengur, -s, -ir, (-ja) [dreiŋ·g̊ʏr̥, dreiŋ·s, dreiŋ·g̊ˌɪr̥, -g̊ˌa] m.2 boy, young man; man; *hraustur drengur* a valiant man; *góður drengur* a gentleman.
drepa, drep, drap, drápum, drepinn (-ið) [drɛ:pʰa, drɛ:pʰ, dra:pʰ, drau:pʰʏm, drɛ:pʰɪn, -ɪð; drɛ:b̥-, dra:b̥, drau:b̥ʏm] v.5 kill; *drepast* be killed, die (of animals).
dreyma, dreymdi, dreymt [drei:ma, dreim·d̥ɪ, dreim·tʰ; dreim̥·t] wv.2 dream; *mig dreymir* I dream; I am dreaming (S. VI, 14, 5); *hann* (acc.) *dreymdi draum* he had a dream (S. I, 2, 1, 3).
drífa, dríf, dreif, drifum, drifinn (-ið) [dri:va, dri:v, drei:v, drɪ:vʏm, drɪ:vɪn, -ɪð] v.1 drive, drift, snow.
drjúpa, drýp, draup, drupum, dropinn (-ið) [drju:pʰa, dri:pʰ, dröy:pʰ, drʏ:pʰʏm, drɔ:pʰɪn, -ɪð; drju:ba, dri:b, dröy:b̥, drʏ:b̥ʏm, drɔ:bɪn] v.2 drip.
dró, drógum, see *draga*.
dróg, -ar, -ar (-ir) [drou:(q), drou:-(q)ar̥, drou:jɪr̥] f.1 & 2 hack, work horse.
dropið, -inn, see *drjúpa*.
drottinn, -ins, -nar [drɔʰt:ɪn, -ɪns,

drɔʰt·nar̥] m.1 Lord, God, pl. lords.
drottinn minn góður! my God! good Lord! (S. III, 2, 5n).
drottning, -ar, -ar [drɔʰt·niŋ̊, -ar̥] f.1 queen (also in cards); *drottning-ar-flagð* monster queen.
drottnunargjarn, -gjörn, -gjarnt [drɔʰt·nʏnar-g̊ˌad·n̥, -g̊ˌöd·n̥, -g̊ˌan·tʰ; -g̊ˌan·t] adj. ambitious, aspiring, imperious, domineering.
drukkið, -inn, -um, see *drekka*.
drukkna, -aði, -að(ur) [drᵧʰk·na, -aðɪ, -að, -aðʏr̥] wv.4 drown.
drúpa, drúpti, drúpt [dru:pʰa, druf·tɪ, druf·t; dru:ptʰ(ɪ); dru:ba] wv.3 droop.
drupum, see *drjúpa*.
drykkjupeningar [drɪʰkˌ:ʏ-pʰɛ:niŋ̊ar̥] m.1.pl. tip; *í d-a* as a tip.
drykkjuvísa, -u, -ur [drɪʰkˌ:ʏ-vi:sa, -ʏ(r̥)] wf.1 drinking song.
drýp, see *drjúpa*.
drættir, see *dráttur*.
1. dúa, -aði, -að [du:a, -aðɪ, -að] wv.4 shake, quiver under foot.
2. dúa, dúði, dúð [du:a, du:ðɪ, -du:ð] wv.3 angle, fish; see also *dúja*.
duga, dugði, dugað (or dugaði, -að) [dʏ:qa, dʏq·ðɪ, dʏ:qað; -aðɪ, dʏg̊·ðɪ] wv.3 & 4 avail, help; *duga e-m* help sbdy; *duga* show what one is good for, *nú er að duga eða drepast* (proverbial) now, show your mettle or be killed; *duga ekki* not avail; *þetta dugir (-ar) ekki* this must not go on, this won't do.
duglega [dʏq·lɛ·qa] adv. energetically, with a vengeance.
dúkur, -s, -ar [du:kʰʏr̥; du:kʰs, dux·s; du:kʰar̥; du:g̊·] m.1 cloth, stuff, fabric; tablecloth.
duldi, dulið, -inn, see *dylja*.
dúnalogn, -s [du:na-lɔg̊·n̥(s)] n. dead calm (quiet).
dúnn, -s [dud·n̥, dun·s] m.1 down, (eider) down.
dúnsæng, -ur, -ur [dun·saiŋ̊, -ʏr̥] f. 3 bedcover or mattress with down in it.
dúnyfirsæng, -ur, -ur [du:nɪ·vɪr̥saiŋ·g̊,

Consonants: [ð] brea*th*e; [g] *g*ood; [gˌ] *gy*arden (garden); [hw] *wh*at; [j] *y*es; [kˌ] *cy*an (can); [ŋ] thi*ng*; [q] N. Germ. sa*g*en; [r] Scottish *r*; [x] approx. Germ. a*ch*; [þ] *th*in. Voiceless: ○; [b̥, d̥, g̊] approx. *p, t, k*. Half-voiced: *italics*. Aspiration and preaspiration: [ʰ]; [pʰ, tʰ, kʰ] *p-, t-, k-*. Others as in English.

323

-ʏr̥] f.3 bedcover (comfort) with down in it.

1. dúr, -s, -ar [du:r, dur̥·s, du:rar̥] m. 1 nap; *e·m kemur ekki dúr á auga* sbdy does not sleep a wink.

2. dúr, -s [du:r, dur̥·s] m. 1 major (mus·).

duttum, see *detta*.

dvalar, -ir, see *dvöl*.

dvelja, dvaldi, dvalið [dvɛl·ja, dval·dɪ, dva:lɪð] wv. 1 = *dveljast* stay, sojourn, dwell (S. VI, 4, *3*; 7, *4*).

dvergalög [dver·g̊a-lö:q] n.pl. 'dwarf melodies.'

Dverghamrar [dver·g̊ham·rar̥] m.l.pl. 'Dwarf Rocks.'

dvergur, -s, -ar [dver·g̊ʏr̥, dver·g̊s, dver·g̊ar̥] m. 1 dwarf.

dvöl, dvalar, -ir [dvö:l, dva:lar̥, ·ɪr̥] f.2 stay, sojourn, duration.

dý, -s, -, (dýja) [di:(s), di:ja] n. quagmire, bog, mudhole, covered with bright green mosses.

dýja, dúði, dúð [di:ja, du:ðɪ, -du:ð] wv.1 shake, tremble (of quicksand or quagmire); see also 2. *dúa*.

dýjamosi, -a, -ar [di:ja-mɔ:sɪ, -a(r̥)] wm.1 moss, usually bright green, growing in quagmires (*dý*).

dylja, duldi, dulinn (-ið) [dɪl·ja, dʏl·dɪ, dʏ:lɪn, -ɪð] wv.1 conceal, hide; *dylja e·n e·s* conceal sth from sbdy.

dýpi, -s, - [di:pʰɪ(s); di:bɪ] n. depth.

dýpka, -aði, -að(ur) [dif·ka, -aðɪ, -að, -aðʏr̥] wv.4 deepen.

dýpri, dýpstur, see *djúpur*.

dyr [dɪ:r] f.3.pl. door (= doorway).

1. dýr, -s, - [di:r, dir̥·s] n. animal.

2. dýr, dýr, dýrt; dýrari, -astur; dýrri, dýrstur [di:r, dir̥·t, di:rarɪ, -astʏr̥, dir:ɪ, dirstʏr̥] adj. expensive, dear (In. III, *2*, (a)5; 4, *4*).

dyrabjalla, -bjöllu, -ur [dɪ:ra-bjað·la, ·bjöd·lʏ(r̥)] wf.1 doorbell.

Dýrafjörður, -fjarðar [di:ra-fjör·ðʏr̥, -fjar·ðar̥] m.3 'Dýri's Fjord.'

dýrafræði, - (-s) [di:ra-frai:ðɪ] wf.2 zoology.

dyrastafur, -s, -ir [dɪ:ra-sta:vʏr̥, -staf·s, -sta:vɪr̥] m.2 doorpost.

dyravörður, -varðar, -verðir [dɪ:ra-vör·ðʏr̥, -var·ðar̥, -ver·ðɪr̥] m.3 doorkeeper.

dýrð, -ar, -ir [dir·ð, -ðar̥, -ðɪr̥] f.2 glory.

dýrðlegur [dir·ðlɛ·qʏr̥] adj. (see *-legur*) glorious, magnificent.

dægur, (-ri), -urs, -ur [dai:qʏr̥(s), daiq·rɪ] n. twelve hours, night or day.

dæma, dæmdi, dæmdur (dæmt) [dai:ma, daim·dɪ, daim·tʰ; daim̥·t] wv.2 judge.

dæmi, -s, - [dai:mɪ(s)] n. example; *t. d. = til dæmis* for example.

dætur, see *dóttir*.

döðlur, see *daðla*.

döggva, -aði, -að(ur) [dög:va, -aðɪ, -að, -aðʏr̥] wv.4 bedew.

dökkgrænn, -græn, -grænt [döʰk:-graidn, -grai·n, -graintʰ; -graint̥] adj. dark green.

dökkklæddur, -klædd, -klætt [döʰkʰ:-laid·ʏr̥, -kʰ:laid·, -kʰ:laiʰt·] adj. in dark (clothes).

dökkur, dökk, dökkt; dekkri, dekkstur [döʰk:ʏr̥, döʰk:, döx·t; deʰk:rɪ, dex·stʏr̥] adj. dark.

dömu(r), see *dama*.

dönsk, see *danskur*.

E.

eð [ɛ:ð] rel.pron. only in *þar eð* since (S. IV, 4).

eða [ɛ:ða] conj. or (S. VIII, 2); *eða jafnvel* or even.

Edda, -u, -ur [ɛd:a, -ʏ(r̥)] wf.1 *Edda*. There are two books of this name: the *Edda* of Snorri Sturluson is a textbook of poetics, famous for its Old Icelandic mythology. The '*Poetic Edda*,' often called in Icelandic *Sæmundar Edda*, is a collection of songs dealing with Old Icelandic (Scandinavian) gods, and Germanic heroes.

Edinborg, -ar [ɛ:din-bɔr·g̊, -ar̥] f.2 Edinburgh.

eðlisfræði [ɛð·lɪs-frai:ðɪ] wf.2 physics.

Vowels: *a* [a] approx. father; *á* [au] cow; *e* [ɛ] set; *é* [jɛ] yes; *i, y* [ɪ] sit; *í, ý* [i] feel; *o* [ɔ] law; *ó* [ou] note; *u* [ʏ] approx. Germ. Mütter; *ú* [u] school; *y = i*; *ý = í*; *æ* [ai] ice; *ö* [ö] Germ. hören; *au* [öy] French *feuille*; *ei, ey* [ei] ale. Length [:]; half-length [·].

ef [ɛːv] conj. if, in case, provided; *ef ekki* if not (S. VI, **9**, *3*; VIII, 3(c); *ef svo er* if it is that way, if so.

efa, -aði, -að [ɛːva, -aðɪ, -að] wv.4 doubt, *efa e-ð* doubt sth.

efi, -a [ɛːvɪ, -a] wm.1 doubt; *það er enginn efi á því, að* . . . there is no doubt (about it) that. . . .

efja, -u, -ur [ɛv·ja, -ɣ(r̥)] wf.1 mud.

efla, efldi, efldur (eflt) [ɛb̥·la, ɛvldɪ, ɛl·(v)dɪ, -ɣr̥, ɛvltʰ, ɛflt, ɛl·(v)tʰ, ɛl·(f)t] wv.2 strengthen, reinforce.

efna, efndi, efndur (efnt) [ɛb̥·na, ɛm·dɪ, -ɣr̥, ɛm·tʰ; ɛm̥·t] wv.2 carry out, fulfil (a promise).

efnaður, -uð, -að [ɛb̥·naðʏr̥, -ɣð, -að] adj. well-to-do, well off.

efnafræði [ɛb̥·na-frai:ðɪ] wf.2 chemistry.

efnakarl, -s, -ar [ɛb̥·na-kʰad̥·l̥, -kʰal·s, -kʰad̥·lar̥] m.1 a(n old) man of means.

efnalaug, -ar, -ar [ɛb̥·na-löy:q, -qar̥] f.1 dry cleaning.

efni, -s, - [ɛb̥·nɪ(s)] n. matter, material (e. g. for building); stuff, fabric; subject, contents (of a book); pl. means, wealth; *nú er illt í efni* worse luck!

efri, efstur [ɛv·rɪ, ɛfstʏr̥] adj. compar. and superl. upper, top-, uppermost, topmost.

Efri-Hvoll, Efra-Hvols [ɛv·rɪ-hwɔd̥·l̥, ɛv·ra-hwɔl·s] m.1 'Upper Hill.'

efrivararskegg, -s, - [ɛv·rɪva-rar̥sk̩ɛg̊:(s)] n. moustache.

efstaloft, -s [ɛfsta-lɔf·t, -s]n. top floor, attic.

efstur [ɛfstʏr̥] superl. of *efri*; topmost, at the top; *vera efstur í bekk* lead the class.

eftir [ɛʰt:ɪr̥, ɛf·tɪr̥] (Pr. **4**, *3*) (1) prep. with acc. (S. I, **2**, *3*, 2); after, by: *eftir það* (= *þar eftir*) after that, thereafter; *eftir Chopin* by Chopin; (2) prep. with dat. (S. I, **3**, *3*, 2); after, for, according to, along: *hlaupa á eftir honum* run after him; *bíða eftir e-m* wait for sbdy; *eftir háralit* according to the color of the hair; *eftir metrakerfinu* according to the metric system; *eftir því, hvort* . . . according as . . . , depending upon whether . . . ; *eftir því, sem* . . . *eftir því* according as . . . accordingly, the . . . the (S. III, **4**, 4); (3) adv. (or prep. with dat.) *austur eftir* eastwards, *austur eftir dalnum* east along the valley, and similarly *vestur, norður, suður eftir (dalnum)*; also *út eftir* outwards, *út eftir dalnum* down (out) the valley; likewise: *inn, upp, niður, ofan eftir*; *á eftir* afterwards; (4) *eftir að* conj. after (S. VIII, 3(h)).

eftirlit, -s [ɛʰt:ɪr-lɪ:tʰ(s), ɛf·tɪr-; -lɪ:d] n. control.

eftirmatur, -ar [ɛʰt:ɪr-ma:tʰʏr̥, ɛf·tɪr-; -ma:dʏr̥, -ar̥] m.3 dessert.

eftirmiðdagur, -s, -ar [ɛʰt:ɪr-mɪd̥:a·qʏr̥, -daxs, -da·qar̥; ɛf·tɪr-mɪð·d̥·] m.1 afternoon. The word is common in towns, but not as good as *eftir hádegi, seinni hluti dags*. Compounds: *eftirmiðdags-kaffi, -te* afternoon coffee, tea.

eftirnafn, -s, -nöfn [ɛʰt:ɪr-nab̥·n̩(s), -nöb̥·n̩; ɛf·tɪr-] n. last name.

eftirréttur, -ar, -ir [ɛʰt:ɪ(r)-rjɛʰt:ʏr̥, -ar̥, -ɪr̥; ɛf·tɪr-] m.3 dessert.

eftirvænting, -ar [ɛʰt:ɪr-vain·tʰiŋg̊, -ar̥; ɛf·tɪr-, -vain·t-] f.1 expectation, hope.

ég, mig, mér, mín [je:q, je(·); mɪ:q, mɪq, mɪx, mɪ(·); mje:r, mjɛr, mjɛr̥; mi:n] first pers. pron. sg.: I, me, me, of me; plural (originally dual): **við, okkur, okkur, okkar** [vɪ:ð, vɪð, vɪþ, vɪ(·); ɔʰk:ʏr̥, ɔʰk:ar̥] we, us, us; of us, our, ours; honorific plural: **vér, oss, oss, vor** [vjɛ:r, vjɛr, vjɛr̥; ɔs:; vɔ:r] we, us, us; of us, our, ours (Pr. **4**, *2*; In. VI, 1, 1); *það er ég* it is I (me) (S. IV, 1, 1); *ég meiddi mig* I hurt myself; *bíddu mín* wait for me; pl. *við*: *við Gunnar* we, Gunnar and I (S. IV, 1, 3); honorific pl.: *vér, Kristján X, af guðs náð konungur* We, Christian

Consonants: [ð] brea*th*e; [g] *g*ood; [gj] *gy*arden (garden); [hw] *wh*at; [j] *y*es; [kj] *cy*an (can); [ŋ] thi*ng*; [q] N. Germ. sa*g*en; [r] Scottish *r*; [x] approx. Germ. a*ch*; [þ] *th*in. Voiceless: ○; [b̥, d̥, g̊] approx. *p, t, k*. Half-voiced: *italics*. Aspiration and preaspiration: [ʰ]; [pʰ, tʰ, kʰ] *p-, t-, k-*. Others as in English.

325

the Tenth, by the grace of God, king (S. IV, **1**, 2).

1. egg, -s, - [eǥ:(s)] n. egg.
2. egg, eggjar, -jar [eǥ:, eǥ̢:aɽ] f.1 edge, ridge.

egypzkur, egypzk, egypzkt [e:g̢ˌɪfskyɽ, e:g̢ˌɪfsk, e:g̢ˌɪfst] adj. Egyptian.

e. h., e. hád. = *eftir hádegi* = p. m.

eiður, -s, -ar [ei:ðyɽ, eið·s, ei:ðaɽ] m.1 oath.

eiga, á, eigum, átti, átt(ur) [ei:qa, au:, ei:qɣm, auʰt:ɪ, auʰt:(ɣɽ)] pret. pres. v. (In. VII, **5**, *1*) (1) own, possess, have: *enginn veit, hvað átt hefur, fyrr en misst hefur* (proverbial) no one knows what he has had before he has lost it; be married to, have for spouse: *hann átti Guðrúnu* he was married to G., he and G. were man and wife; *eiga hey undir* own hay outside (not fully dried or harvested); *eiga rétt á e-u* (*til e-s*) have a right to sth; *eiga gott skilið af e-m* deserve good things (thanks) from sbdy; *hann á það skilið* he deserves it S. VI, **12**, *2*, 3); *eiga það til að gera e-ð* be liable (prone) to do sth; *eiga vanda fyrir e-u* be prone to (get) sth (a sickness); *eiga von á e-u* expect sth; *eiga e-ð eftir* have sth left, have sth in store; *þá áttu mikið eftir* then you have much in store for you; *þú mátt eiga mig* you may have me; *eiga sig* only after *láta* (which see): *láta e-n eiga sig* leave sbdy alone, leave sbdy to his own resources; (2) with preps and advs: *eiga heima* live (have a home); *eiga lengi í e-u* be for a long time sick with sth (suffering from sth); *eiga við e-n* deal with sbdy; *eigast glettingar við* play pranks upon each other; (3) auxiliary: be to, be intended to, have to, be going to, be supposed to: *eiga að vera* be intended to be; *hann á að vera* he is to be, he should be; *ég á að gera e-ð* I am to do sth; *á ég að fara?* am I to

go? shall I go?; *eigum við að fara?* shall we go? are we to go?; *hann ætti að fara* he should go; *seinna á að hita bæinn* later the city is (supposed) to be heated, is going to be heated; *eiga í vök að verjast* ' have to defend oneself in an icehole,' i. e. face difficulties, be in straits, be hard pressed; *eiga að finna e-n* be supposed to visit sbdy; *huldufólkið á að búa í hólum* the ' hidden folk ' (elves) is supposed to live in hills; *þeir áttu að hafa séð hann* they were supposed to have seen him. See Syntax VI, **2**, 5n; **4**, *3*; **9**, *2*, 2; **13**, 2; **14**, 8.

eigandi, -a, -endur [ei:qand̦ɪ, -a, -end̦yɽ] wm.2 owner.

eigi [ei:jɪ] adv. = *ekki*, not; *eigi aðeins . . . heldur einnig* not only . . . but also.

eigin(n), eigin, eigið [ei:jɪn, ei:jɪð] adj. indecl. except in nom., acc. sg. n. own (In. III, **3**, *3*).

eiginlega [ei:jɪn-le:qa] adv. properly (speaking), really, in reality.

eign, -ar, -ir [eiǥ·n̦, eiǥ·naɽ, -ɪɽ] f.2 property, possession.

eilífur, -líf, -líft [ei:li·vyɽ, -li·v, -lift] adj. eternal; *vertu í eilífri náðinni* ' be in eternal grace,' (a mild oath) i. e. by all means! (= *og blessaður!*).

Einar, -ars [ei:naɽ(s)] m.1 personal name.

einfaldur, -föld, -falt [ein·faldyɽ, -föld̦, -falt] adj. simple, simplex, not double; *einfalt bréf* a letter weighing 20 grams or less.

eingöngu [eiŋ·göyŋǥɣ] adv. exclusively, only.

einhnepptur, -hneppt, -hneppt [ein·· hneftyɽ, -hneft] adj. single-breasted.

einhver, -hver, eitthvert; eitthvað [eiŋ·hwyɽ, eiŋ·hwe·r, eiŋ·kʰvyɽ, -kʰve·r, eiŋ·kv-; eiʰt·hwyɽt, eiʰt·· hwert, eix:(w)ɣrt; eiʰt·kʰvyɽt, -kʰvert, eiʰk:vyɽt,-k:vert; eiʰt·hwa·ð, eix:(w)að, eiʰk:va(·)ð] (Pr. **2**, *1*, 3n2; **4**, *2*) indef. pron. (only strong) (In. VI, **6**, 2(c)) some, someone,

Vowels: *a* [a] approx. father; *á* [au] cow; *e* [e] set; *é* [je] yes; *i, y* [ɪ] sit; *í, ý* [i] feel; *o* [ɔ] law; *ó* [ou] note; *u* [ɣ] approx. Germ. Mütter; *ú* [u] school; *y = i*; *ý = í*; *æ* [ai] ice; *ö* [ö] Germ. hören; *au* [öy] French *feuille*; *ei, ey* [ei] ale. Length [:]; half-length [·].

326

sbdy, sth; *einhvern daginn* one of
these days (S. II, 7); *eitthvað
hundrað manns* about a (some)
hundred people; *eitthvað af fólki*
a few people (S. IV, **6**, 9).

einhvernveginn [eiŋ·hwɤdn(v)ei:jɪn,
eiŋ·hwɛrdnvei:jɪn; eiŋ·kʰvɤdn-, eiŋ·-
kvɤdn-; ·kʰvɛrdn-] adv. (=*einhvern
veginn*) somehow (literally: 'some
way').

eining, -ar, -ar [ei:niŋ̊, -aɹ] f.1 unit,
unity.

einka- [eiŋ·kʰa-, eiŋ·ka-] pref. private;
special, only.

einkasala, -sölu, -ur [eiŋ·kʰa-sa:la,
-sö:lɤ; eiŋ·ka-] wf.1 monopoly.

einkasonur, -ar, -synir [eiŋ·kʰa-sɔ:nɤɹ,
-aɹ, -sɪ:nɪɹ; eiŋ·ka-] m.3 only son.

einkenna, -kenndi, -kenndur (-kennt)
[eiŋ·kˌʰɛn·a, -kˌʰɛndɪ, -ɤɹ, -kˌʰɛntʰ;
-kˌʰɛnt] wv.2 characterize; *einkennandi (fyrir)* characteristic (of).

einkenni, -s, - [eiŋ·kˌʰɛn·ɪ(s)] n. mark,
sign, distinctive feature; insignia.

einkennilega [eiŋ·kˌʰɛn·ɪ-lɛ:qa] adv.
peculiarly.

einkennilegur [eiŋ·kˌʰɛn·ɪ-lɛ:qɤɹ] adj.
(see -*legur*) characteristic, peculiar,
queer; *einkennilegir menn* peculiar
characters.

einkum [eiŋ·kʰɤm, eiŋ·kɤm] adv.
especially.

einl. = *einleikur, einlægur.*

einleikur, -s, -ir [ein·lei·kʰɤɹ, -lei·kʰs,
-lei·kˌʰɪɹ; -lei·g̊ɤɹ, -lei·g̊ˌɪɹ] m.2 (instrumental) solo.

einlægur, -læg, -lægt [ein·lai·qɤɹ,
-lai·q, -laixt] adj. sincere; *þinn
(yðar) einlægur* yours sincerely;
yðar einlægur yours sincerely, yours
truly.

einmánuður, -aðar, -uðir [ein·mau·nyð-
ɤɹ, -aðaɹ, -yðɪɹ] m.3 from the middle
of March to the middle of April;
the last Icelandic month of winter.

einmitt [ein·mɪʰt·] adv. just; *einmitt
það!* just so, quite so, is that so!

1. einn, ein, eitt [eid·n̩, ei:n, eiʰt:]
num.card. (In. V, **2**, 2(a); 3, 3) one,
alone; *einn maður* one man; *þeir*

skildu hann eftir einan they left
him alone; *sá eini, sem vissi það*
the only one who knew it; *eini skólinn, sem* the only school that; *í einu
lagi* in one piece, in one phrase;
hún ein she alone. Plural *einir* in
distributive sense: *einir sokkar* a
pair of socks (stockings, hose).

2. einn, ein, eitt (pronounced and inflected as *einn* above) indef. pron.
(S. IV, **6**, 10) one, a certain (one);
maður einn a certain man (=*maður
nokkur*) (S. II, 1n1); *í einu orði
sagt* in a word; *einn sjómaður*
(num.) one sailor, *einn sjómaðurinn*
one of the sailors (=*einn af sjómönnunum, einn sjómannanna*) (S. II,
7); *ein sú versta hríð* one of the
worst blizzards; *einna* 'perhaps,'
einna beztur perhaps the best (S.
III, **5**, 3n); *það gildir einu* it is all
the same, it is just as well; *einu
sinni* adv. once, once upon a time
(*einu sinni var . . .*); *ekki einu
sinni það* not even that (S. VII,
4, 4); *þú einn* you alone.

einnig [eid·nɪq] adv. also.

eins [ein·s] adv. (gen. of *eitt*, see *einn*)
as, so; *hann er alveg eins* he is just
the same; *undir eins* adv. at once;
að eins (=*aðeins*) only; *eins og*
conj. as, as if; *eins . . . og* as . . . as,
as . . . as if, in the same way . . .
as; *eins gamall og ég* as old as I
(=*jafngamall mér*) (S. VI, **9**, *4*,
7; VIII, 3(g)).

einsamall, -sömul, -samalt [ein·-
sa·madl, -sö·mɤl, -sa·malt] adj. alone
(In. III, 2(a)7).

einsetja, -setti, -sett [ein·sɛ·tʰja,
-sɛʰt·ɪ, -sɛʰt·; -sɛ·dja] wv.1 *einsetja
sér* determine.

einseyringur, -s, -ar [ein·sei·riŋ̊ɤɹ,
-iŋs, -iŋ̊aɹ] m.1 a one-*eyrir* piece.

einsog conj. = *eins og.*

einstaka [ein·sta·kʰa; -sta·g̊a] adj.
indecl. single, solitary (In. III, 3,
3).

einstakur, -stök, -stakt [ein·sta·kʰɤɹ,

Consonants: [ð] breat*h*e; [g] *g*ood; [gⱼ] *g*yarden (garden); [hw] *wh*at; [j] *y*es; [kⱼ] *c*yan
(can); [ŋ] thi*ng*; [q] N. Germ. sa*g*en; [r] Scottish *r*; [x] approx. Germ. ac*h*; [þ] *th*in.
Voiceless: ○; [b̥, d̥, g̊] approx. *p, t, k*. Half-voiced: *italics*. Aspiration and preaspiration:
[ʰ]; [pʰ, tʰ, kʰ] *p-, t-, k-*. Others as in English.

327

-stö·kʰ, -staxt; -sta·ǧɣɽ, -stö·ǧ] adj. single.

einsömul, see *einsamall.*

einsöngur, -s, -söngvar [ein·söyŋǧɣɽ, -söyŋs, -söyŋǧvaɽ] m.1 solo.

eintala, -tölu, -ur [ein·tʰa·la, -tʰö·lɣ(ɽ)] wf.1 singular.

eintómur, -tóm, -tómt [ein·tʰou·mɣɽ, -tʰou·*m*, -tʰoumtʰ; -tʰoumt] adj. alone, exclusive(ly); *úr eintómri möl* from gravel exclusively.

einusinni [ei:nɣ·sɪn:ɪ] adv. (= *einu sinni,* see 2. *einn* and *sinn* n.) once.

einvera, -u [ein·vɛ·ra, -ɣ] wf.1 solitude.

einyrki, -yrkja, -jar [ei:nɪɽk₁ɪ, -ɪɽk₁a(ɽ)] wm.1 a farmer without help.

Eiríkur, -s [ei:ri·kʰɣɽ; -ri·ǧɣɽ; -rixs] m.1 Eric; *Eiríkur rauði* Eric the Red; settled in Greenland c. 985.

eista, -, -u, (-na) [eis·ta, -ɣ, eistna] wn. testicle.

eitt, see *einn.*

eitthvað, -hvert, see *einhver.*

eitur, (-ri), -urs [ei:tʰɣɽ, ei:tʰrɪ, ei:tʰɣɽs; ei:d·] n. poison.

ek, ekið, -inn, see *aka.*

ekkert, see *enginn.*

ekki [ɛʰk₁:ɪ] adv. not; *ekki það?* no? *ekki sízt* not least so; *ekki (eigi) aðeins . . . heldur einnig* conj. not only . . . but also (S. VIII, 2); *ekki* indef. pron. (old n. of *enginn*) *lítið sem ekki* hardly at all; *allt kom fyrir ekki* everything was in vain, everything came to nothing (In. VI, **6**, 2(g)).

ekkja, -ju, -jur, (ekkna) [ɛʰk₁:a, ɛʰk₁:ɣ(ɽ), ɛʰk·na] wf.1 widow.

ekla, -u [ɛʰk·la, -ɣ] wf.1 lack, dearth.

ekra, -u, -ur [ɛ:kʰra, -ɣ(ɽ); ɛ:ǧra] wf.1 field; acre (the American measure).

el, see *ala.*

él, -s, - [je:*l*, jɛl·s] n. squall.

elda, -aði, -að(ur) [ɛl·da, -aðɪ, -að, -aðɣɽ] wv.4 cook.

eldast, eltist, elzt [ɛl·dast, ɛl·tɪst, ɛlst] wv.2 (middle voice only) grow old (S. VI, **7**, 5).

eldavél, -ar, -ar [ɛl·da·vjɛ:*l*, -vjɛ:laɽ] f.1 kitchen stove.

eldfjall, -s, -fjöll [ɛl·dfjaḍl, -fjals, -fjödl] n. volcano.

eldgjá, -gjár, -gjár [ɛl·dg₁au·, -g₁au·*r*] f.1 crater, volcanic rift; ' Fire Gorge,' (a place name).

eldhús, -s, - [ɛl·ḍ(h)u·s, -(h)us·] n. kitchen.

eldhússbekkur, -bekkjar, -bekkir [ɛl·ḍ(h)us-bɛʰk:ɣɽ,-bɛʰk₁:aɽ,-bɛʰk₁:-ɪɽ] m.2 kitchen bench, kitchen table.

eldhússskápur, -s, -ar [ɛl·ḍ(h)us-skau:pʰɣɽ, -skau:pʰs, -skau:pʰaɽ; -skau:bɣɽ, -aɽ] m.1 kitchen cupboard, cabinet.

eldhætta, -u [ɛl·dhaiʰt·a, -ɣ] wf.1 firehazard.

eldri, see *gamall.*

eldspýta, -u, -ur [ɛl·dspi·tʰa, -ɣ(ɽ); -spi·da] wf.1 match.

eldstó, -stó(a)r, -stór [ɛl·dstou·, -stou··(a)ɽ] f.1 = *eldavél.*

eldstæði, -s, - [ɛl·dstai·ðɪ(s)] n. fireplace.

eldur, -s, -ar [ɛl·dɣɽ, ɛl·ds, ɛl·daɽ] m.1 fire.

Elín, -ar [ɛ:li·*n*, -naɽ] f.1 Eileen, Ellen.

Elísabet, -ar [ɛ:lisa·bɛ:tʰ, -aɽ, -bɛ:ḍ] f.1 Elizabeth.

Ella, -u, -ur [ɛl:a, -ɣ(ɽ)] wf.1 pet name for *Elín* (Pr. **3**, 2, 9n).

ellefti [ɛḍ·lɛftɪ] num.ord. eleventh.

ellefu [ɛḍ·lɛ·vɣ] num.card. eleven.

ellegar [ɛḍ·lɛ·qaɽ] conj. or (else) (S. VIII, 2).

ellistyrkur, -s, -ir, (-ja) [ɛḍ·lɪ-stɪɽ·kɣɽ, -stɪɽks, -stɪɽ·k₁ɪɽ, -k₁a] m.2 old age pension.

elska, -aði, -að(ur) [ɛl·ska, -aðɪ, -að, -aðɣɽ] wv.4 love (S. VI, **4**, *3*).

elta, elti, elt(ur) [ɛl·ta, ɛl·tɪ, ɛl·t(ɣɽ)] wv.2 pursue.

eltzur, see *gamall.*

embætti, -s, - [ɛm·baiʰt·ɪ(s)] n. office of civil service.

1. **en,** see 1. *enn.*

2. **en** [ɛn:] conj. but; *en þó* (but)

Vowels: *a* [a] approx. father; *á* [au] cow; *e* [ɛ] set; *é* [jɛ] yes; *i, y* [ɪ] sit; *í, ý* [i] feel; *o* [ɔ] law; *ó* [ou] note; *u* [ɣ] approx. Germ. Mütter; *ú* [u] school; *y* = *i*; *ý* = *í*; *œ* [ai] ice; *ö* [ö] Germ. hören; *au* [öy] French feuille; *ei, ey* [ei] ale. Length [:]; half-length [·].

328

still, yet; but even if; *en það er
nú svo, að* . . . ·but the fact· is that
. . . (S. VIII, 2); *en* after comparatives: than: *heldur en* rather
than; *áður en* before (= *fyrr en*);
eldri en ég older than I (= *mér
eldri*) (S. III, 4, 3; VIII, 3(g)).
1. **enda, -aði, -að(ur)** [ɛn·da, -aðɪ, -að,
-aðɏr̥] wv.4 end, terminate; *enda á
e-u* end (terminate) in sth; *enda
með því að* end in such a way
that, end with, end by; *endast* last,
suffice (*til* for); *svo langt, sem tími
endist til* as far as time will permit.
2. **enda** [ɛn·da] conj. and . . . also,
and . . . indeed, and, sure enough,
and that is why; *strákurinn var
óþægur, enda var hann flengdur* the
boy was naughty, and that is why
he was spanked (and he was also
(indeed) spanked); *það er langt
til Íslands, enda fara þangað fáir*
it is a long way to Iceland, hence
few will go there (S. VII, 3, 6;
VIII, 2).
endi, -a, -ar [ɛn·dɪ, -a(r̥)] wm.1 end;
á endanum in the end, at last.
endilega [ɛn·dɪ-lɛ:qa] adv. by all
means, necessarily.
endir, -is, -ar [ɛn·dɪr̥, -ɪs, -ar̥] m.1
end; *endir á e-u* the end of sth.
1. **endur**, see 2. *önd*.
2. **endur** [ɛn·dɏr̥] adv. of old, again;
endur fyrir löngu in times of yore.
endurnýja, -aði, -að(ur) [ɛn·dɏr-ni:ja,
-aðɪ, -að, -aðɏr̥] wv.4 renew.
endurreisa, -reisti, -reist(ur) [ɛn·dɏr-
rei:sa, -reis·tɪ, -ɏr̥, -reis·t] wv.2
re-establish.
1. **engi, -s, -** [eiɲ·g̊·ɪ(s)] n. meadow,
grassland.
2. **engi** = *enginn*.
enginn, engin, ekkert (engi, engi, ekki)
[eiɲ·g̊·ɪn, -ɪn, ɛʰkʲ·ɛr̥t; eiɲ·g̊·ɪ, ɛʰkʲ·ɪ],
acc. *engan, öngvan; enga, öngva;
ekkert* [eiɲ·g̊an, öyɲ·g̊van; eiɲ·g̊a,
öyɲ·g̊va], dat. *engum, öngvum;
engri, öngri; engu, öngvu* [eiɲ·g̊ɏm,
öyɲ·g̊vɏm; eiɲg̊rɪ; öyɲg̊rɪ; eiɲ·g̊ɏ,
öyɲ·g̊vɏ], gen. *einskis; engrar,*

öngrar; einskis [einsk‚ɪs; eiɲg̊rar̥,
öyɲg̊rar̥]; pl.nom. *engir, öngvir;
engar, öngvar; engin* [eiɲ·g̊‚ɪr̥,
öyɲ·g̊vɪr̥; eiɲ·g̊ar̥,öyɲ·g̊var̥; eiɲ·g̊‚ɪn],
acc. *enga, öngva; engar, öngvar;
engin* [eiɲ·g̊a, öyɲ·g̊va], dat. *engum,
öngvum* [eiɲ·g̊ɏm, öyɲ·g̊vɏm], gen.
engra, öngra [eiɲ·g̊ra, öyɲ·g̊ra] in-
def.pron. (only strong; In. VI, 6,
2(g)) no, none, nobody, no one;
enginn maður no man; *enginn veit*
no one knows; *ekkert* nothing; as
an adv.: not at all; *fyrir engan mun*
on no account; *segja ekkert* say
nothing; *engu (að) síður* none the
less; *svara engu* answer nothing;
eiga sér einskis ills von be wholly
without thought of danger (literally:
evil); *einskis virði* worth nothing,
of no value (S. I, 4, 2, 2). See also
S. IV, 6, 8.
engjar [eiɲ·g̊‚ar̥] f.l.pl. meadows,
grasslands, out-fields. Cf. 1. *engi* n.
England, -s [eiɲ·land(s), -lan·s] n.
England.
Englendingur, -s, -ar [eiɲ·lɛndiɲg̊ɏr̥,
- iɲs, -iɲg̊ar̥] m.1 an Englishman, pl.
Englishmen, the English (S. III, 3,
3n2).
1. **enn, en, eð** = *hinn, hin, hið* def. art.
2. **enn** [ɛn:] adv. (= *ennþá*) still;
ekki enn (þá) not yet; *enn betri*
still better; *enn aðrir* yet others;
enn fremur moreover, also, furthermore.
ennfremur [ɛn·frɛ·mɏr̥] adv. = *enn
fremur*.
enni, -s, - [ɛn:ɪ(s)] n. forehead.
ennþá [ɛn·þau·] adv. (= *enn þá*) still,
yet; *ennþá betri* still better, better
by far.
enska, -u [ɛnska, -ɏ] wf.1 English.
enskur, ensk, enskt [ɛnskɏr̥, ɛnsk,
ɛnst] adj. English.
eplagrautur, -ar, -ar [ɛʰp·la-gröy:tʰɏr̥,
-ar̥; -gröy:d-] m.1 apple pudding.
epli, -s, - [ɛʰp·lɪ(s)] n. apple.
1. **er, ert**, see *vera*.
2. **er** [ɛ:r] rel.pron. that, who, which
(In. VI, 4).

Consonants: [ð] brea*th*e; [g] *g*ood; [g‚] *gy*arden (garden); [hw̥] *wh*at; [j] *y*es; [kʲ] *cy*an
(can); [ŋ] thi*ng*; [q] N. Germ. sa*g*en; [r] Scottish *r*; [x] approx. Germ. a*ch*; [þ] *th*in.
Voiceless: ○; [b̥, d̥, g̊] approx. *p, t, k*. Half-voiced: *italics*. Aspiration and preaspiration:
[ʰ]; [pʰ, tʰ, kʰ] *p-, t-, k-*. Others as in English.

3. **er** [ɛ:r] conj. when (S. VIII, 3(h)).

erfa, erfði, erfður (erft) [ɛr·va, ɛr·(v)ðɪ, ɛr·(v)ðʏr̥, ɛr̥·(f)t] wv.2 inherit.

erfiður, -ið, -itt [ɛr·vɪ·ðʏr̥, -ɪ·ð, -ɪʰt·] adj. difficult.

erindi, -s, - [ɛ:rɪndɪ(s)] n. business, errand; *eiga erindi við e-n* have a business with someone; address, lecture, talk, speech, *flytja erindi* deliver a lecture, give a talk.

erja, -aði, -að [ɛr·ja, -aðɪ, -að] wv.4 *crjast við e-n* quarrel, bicker with somebody.

erlendur, -lend, -lent [ɛr·lɛndʏr̥, -lɛnd, -lɛntʰ; -lɛnt] adj. foreign; also a personal name: *Erlendur, -s (-ar).*

ermi, -ar, -ar [ɛr·mɪ, ɛr·mar̥] f.1 sleeve.

ernir, see *örn.*

ert, see *vera.*

erta, erti, ert(ur) [ɛr̥·ta, -ɪ, -ʏr̥, ɛr̥·t] wv.2 tease.

ertur [ɛr̥·tʏr̥] wf.1.pl. beans.

Esja, -u [ɛ:sja, -ʏ] wf.1 a mountain near Reykjavík; name of a boat.

eski, -s, - [ɛs·kjɪ(s)] n. ash (the wood) ; a box.

Eskifjörður, -fjarðar [ɛs·kjɪ-fjör·ðʏr̥, -fjar·ðar̥] m.3 'Ash Wood Fjord.'

Eskimói, -a, -ar [ɛs·kjɪ-mou:ɪ, -a(r̥)] wm.1 Eskimo.

éta (eta), ét (et), át, átum, étinn (etinn) (-ið) [jɛ:tʰa, ɛ:tʰa; jɛ:tʰ, ɛ:tʰ; au:tʰ,au:tʰʏm; jɛ:tʰɪn, ɛ:tʰɪn, -ɪð; jɛ:d·, ɛ:d·, au:d·] v.5 eat; *éta smjör við brauði* eat butter on bread; *hér vantar það, sem við á að éta* (proverbial) here the main thing (or an essential thing) is lacking (In. VII, **2**, *6*).

etja, atti, att [ɛ:tʰja, aʰt:(ɪ); ɛ:dja] wv.1 egg on.

Evrópa, -u [ɛv·rou·pʰa, -ʏ; -rou·ba] wf.1 Europe.

eyða, eyddi, eyddur (eytt) [ei:ða, eid:ɪ, -ʏr̥, eiʰt:] wv.2 spend, destroy; *eyða e-u* spend something; *eyðast* be emptied (of people), be destroyed.

eyði, -s, - [ei:ðɪ(s)] n. state of desolation, wilderness.

eyðiey, -eyjar, -eyjar [ei:ðɪ-ei:(jar̥)] f.1 desert island.

eyðublað, -s, -blöð [ei:ðʏ-bla:ð, -blað·s, -blö:ð] n. blank.

eygja, eygði, eygður (eygt) [ei:ja, eiɡ·ðɪ, -ʏr̥, eix·t; eiɡ̊·ðɪ, -ʏr̥] wv.2 see (far off), spot (with the eyes); pp. *eygður* literally: provided with eyes; *vel eygður* with beautiful eyes.

eyja, -u, -ur [ei:ja, -ʏ(r̥)] wf.1 island.

Eyjafjallajökull, -uls [ei:jafjadla-jö:kʰʏdl, -ʏls; -jö:ɡ̊ʏdl] m.1 'Ey Fell Glacier.'

Eyjafjörður, -fjarðar [ei:ja-fjör·ðʏr̥, -fjar·ðar̥] m.3 'Islands' Fjord.'

eyk, see *auka.*

eykt, -ar, -ir [eix·t, -ar̥, -ɪr̥] f.2 a period of three hours, the old Latin *hora.*

Eymundur, -ar (-s) [ei:mʏndʏr̥, -ar̥, -mʏn(d)s] m.1 personal name.

eyra, -u, (-na) [ei:ra, -ʏ, eir·dna] wn. ear (In. I, 7); *eyrun á mér* my ears (S. I, 4, *1*, 4).

eyri, -ar, -ar [ei:rɪ, -ar̥] f.1 sandbank, gravel bank, sand spit; also in place names: *-eyri, Eyrar-.*

-eyringur, -s, -ar [ei:riŋɡʏr̥, -iŋs, -iŋɡar̥] m.1 (in compounds only) a coin of one or more *aurar: eins-eyringur, fimmeyringur* etc., one-*eyrir* piece, five-*eyrir* piece, etc.

eyrir, -is, aurar [ei:rɪr̥, ei:rɪs, öy:rar̥] m.1 (In. I, **2**, *1*(b)8n) the smallest Icelandic coin, 0.01 *króna.*

eys, see 2. *ausa.*

eystra [eistra] adv. in the east.

eystri, austastur [eistrɪ, öys·tastʏr̥] adj. compar. & superl. (from *austur*) more eastern, more easterly, most easterly.

Eyvindur, -ar (-s) [ei:vɪn·dʏr̥, -ar̥] m.1 personal name (In. I, **2**, *1*(b) 11).

F.

1. **fá**, see *fár.*

2. **fá, fæ, fékk, fengum, fenginn (-ið)** [fau:, fai:, fjɛʰk:, feiŋ·ɡʏm, feiŋ·ɡʲ-

Vowels: *a* [a] approx. father; *á* [au] cow; *e* [ɛ] set; *é* [jɛ] yes; *i, y* [ɪ] sit; *í, ý* [i] feel; *o* [ɔ] law; *ó* [ou] note; *u* [ʏ] approx. Germ. Mütter; *ú* [u] school; *y = i; ý = í; æ* [ai] ice; *ö* [ö] Germ. hören; *au* [öy] French *feuille; ei, ey* [ei] ale. Length [:]; half-length [·].

330

ın, -ıð] v.7 be allowed, be able to; get, take; give. (1) Be allowed: *fá að tala* be allowed to speak; *gœti ég fengið að tala við* 'might I be allowed to speak to,' i. e. could I speak to; *má ég fá þetta?* may I have this? *má ég fá að gera þetta?* may I (be allowed to) do this? be able to: *enginn fœr gert við því* nobody can help that (S. VI, **12**, *2*, *3*); (2) get: *fáið yður sœti* take a seat; *fá sér bita* take a bite; *fá nóg af* get enough of; *fá veiki* get a sickness, get sick; *fá kvef* catch cold; *fá konunnar* marry the woman; *fá skift* get exchanged; *fá e-ð keypt* 'get sth bought,' i. e. get, buy; *fá sig klipptan* get one's hair cut, get a haircut; *fá e-ð út* get sth as a result of calculations; *fá e-n til e-s* (*til að gera e-ð*) get sbdy to do sth; impers.: (*það*) *má fá* (*þetta*) this may be had; middle voice: *fást* be obtainable, be to be had (S. VI, **7**, *3*); (3) give: *fá e-m e-ð* give sbdy sth, hand sth to sbdy, deliver sth to sbdy.

faðir, föður, feður [fa:ðɪr̥, fö:ðʏr̥, fɛ:ðʏr̥] m.4 father; *faðir minn* my father (S. I, **4**, *1*, 1).

faðirvor, -s [fa:ðɪr-vɔ:r, -vɔr̥·s] n. the Lord's Prayer.

faðmur, -s, -ar [fað·mʏr̥, faðms, fað·mar̥] m.1 fathom; *fjögra faðma dýpi* a depth of four fathoms.

fáeinir, -einar, -ein [fau:ei·nɪr̥, -ei·nar̥, -ei·n] adj.pl. a few.

fága, -aði, -að(ur) [fau:(q)a, -aðɪ, -að, -aðʏr̥] wv.4 polish, cleanse.

fagna, -aði, -að [faǧ·na, -aðɪ, -að] wv.4 rejoice; *f. e-u* rejoice in sth; *f. e-m* welcome sbdy.

fagnaðar, see *fögnuður*.

fagnaðarfundur, -ar, -ir [faǧ-naðar̥-fʏn·dʏr̥, -ar̥, -ɪr̥] m.3 'meeting of joy,' i. e. happy reunion, happy meeting.

fagur, fögur, fagurt; feg(ur)ri, fegurstur, fagrari, -astur [fa:qʏr̥, fö:qʏr̥, fa:qʏr̥t; fɛ:qʏr·ı, fɛq·rı,

fɛ:qʏr̥stʏr̥; faq·rarı, -astʏr̥] adj. beautiful, fair; *fögur þykir mér hönd þín* I think your hand is beautiful.

fágætur, -gæt, -gætt [fau:g₁ai·tʰʏr̥, -g₁ai·tʰ, -g₁aiʰt·; -g₁ai·d·] adj. rare.

fal, fal-ði, -inn, fálum, see *fela*.

fálki, -a, -ar [faul·k₁ʰı, faul·kʰa(r̥); faul·k₁ı, faul·ka(r̥)] wm.1 falcon (= *valur*); *Fálkinn* 'The Falcon,' a monthly.

falla, fell, féll, féllum, fallinn (-ið) [fað·la, fɛð·l, fjɛð·l, fjɛð·lʏm, fað·lın, -ið] v.7 fall, drop, tumble; be killed, be defeated; pp. *fallinn* fallen, killed, dead (S. VI, **3**, *3*).

fallbyssa, -u, -ur [fað·lbıs·a, -ʏ(r̥)] wf.1 cannon; pl. cannon(s); artillery.

fallbyssukúla, -u, -ur [fað·lbıs·ʏ-kʰu:la, -ʏ(r̥)] wf.1 cannon ball.

fallbyssustæði, -s, - [fað·lbıs·ʏ-stai:ðı(s)] n. artillery emplacement.

fallegur [fað·lɛ·qʏr̥] adj. (see *-legur*) handsome, beautiful.

fallhlíf, -ar, -ar [fað·(l)hlı·v, -hlı·var̥] f.1 parachute.

falskur, fölsk, falskt [falskʏr̥, fölsk, falst] adj. false.

fang, -s, föng [fauŋ·ǧ(s), fauŋ·s, föyŋ·ǧ] n. armful; hold, grasp; *eftir föngum* by all possible means, as far as one can.

fann, see *finna*.

fáorður, -orð, -ort [fau:ɔrðʏr̥, -ɔrð, -ɔrt] adj. of few words, silent, taciturn.

far, -s, för [fa:r, far·s, fö:r] n. fare, passage, journey; boat.

fár, fá, fátt; færri, fæstur [fau:r, fau:, fauʰt:; fair:ı, fais·tʏr̥] adj. (In. III, 3, *1*, 4; **4**, *3*) few; *fáir menn* few men; *fáir vildu* few (= nobody) wanted to; *ekki fáir* not few (= many); *fár veit, hverju fagna skal* few know what to welcome (proverbial); *fátt few things;* *fátt er verra* few things are worse; *fátt manna* few people (S. III, **1**, 4n; 3,

Consonants: [ð] brea*th*e; [g] *g*ood; [g₁] *gy*arden (garden); [hw̥] *wh*at; [j] *y*es; [k₁] *cy*an (can); [ŋ] thi*ng*; [q] N. Germ. sa*g*en; [r] Scottish *r*; [x] approx. Germ. a*ch*; [þ] *th*in. Voiceless: ○; [b̥, d̥, ǧ] approx. *p, t, k*. Half-voiced: *italics*. Aspiration and preaspiration: [ʰ]; [pʰ, tʰ, kʰ] *p-, t-, k-*. Others as in English.

1-2); *færri* fewer, very few; *fæstir* fewest, very few.

fara, fer, fór, fórum, farinn (-ið) [fa:ra, fɛ:r, fou:r, fou:rʏm, fa:rɪn, fa:rɪð] v.6 go; travel; fare; suit, fit; begin. (1) Go: *f. heim* go home, *f. út* go out; *hann er farinn* he has gone (S. VI, **3**, *3*); *fara veginn, heiðar, fjöll* (adv. acc.) go, travel the road, over the heaths, the mountains (S. I, **2**, *2*, 3); *fara sinn veg* go away; *fara ferða sinna* go about one's business (in one's own way); *fara svo eða svo* turn out so or so; *það fer vel* that will go well; *það mun fara bezt* that will be the best course to take; *svo fór, að . . .* it went so that . . . , it so turned out that . . . (S. VI, **14**, *4*); *fara illa* go badly; *nú fór verr en skyldi* this went worse than it should have; *þá væri verr farið en heima setið* ' in that case going out (the journey) would be worse than staying at home,' i. e. this would have been better undone; *sögur fara af e-u* stories are told of sth, cf. the story goes that . . . ; (2) *fara (e-m) vel (illa)* of clothes: fit (sbdy) well or badly, be becoming or not; (3) middle voice: *farast á mis* (recipr.) pass each other without meeting; pass without noticing each other; *farast* (intr.) perish, be lost; (4) auxiliary: begin: *fara að hátta* go to bed; *fara að sofa* go to sleep; *fara að skrifa* begin to write (S. VI, **5**); *hann fór að gifta sig* he went and married (worse luck!) (S. VI, **5**, **1n2**); (5) with preps and advs: *fara á fætur* get up, rise; *fara á hendur e-m* attack sbdy; *fara á bíó* go to the movies; *fara á skauta* go skating; *fara á hjóli* ride a bicycle; *fara á eftir* follow; *fara á (í) skóna* put on the shoes (literally: go into the shoes) (S. I, **4**, *1*, 3); *fara af skónum* take off the shoes; *fara eftir e-u* go according to sth, follow sth,

depend upon sth; *fara fram* proceed, go on; take place; *e-m fer fram* sbdy progresses or improves (bodily and mentally); *fara í föt (in)* dress; *fara í rúmið* go to bed; *fara í banka* go to a bank; *fara í búðir* go shopping; *fara í berjamó* go picking berries; *fara í fjallgöngu* go climbing mountains; *fara í bæinn* go into the (farm)house; go to town; go down town; *fara í laugar* go (in)to the swimming pool; *fara í kirkju* go to church; *fara í skóla* go to school; *í þær fara 3000 lítrar af nýmjólk* they take (consume, use up) 3000 liters of fresh milk; *fara inn* go in, enter; *fara með* take care of; *fara vel með sig* take good care of oneself; *fara með e-n* take sbdy, lead sbdy (to some place); *fara með e-m* go with sbdy, accompany sbdy (to some place); *fara með e-ð* go away with sth, take sth away; say, recite sth; *fara með e-ð til e-s* take sth to sbdy; *fara upp* go upstairs; *fara úr kápunni* take off one's coat (S. I, **4**, *1*, 3); *fara yfir* cross.

farangur, (-ri), -urs [fa:rauŋgʏr, -rɪ, -ʏrs] m.1 baggage, luggage.

farar, see 1. *för.*

farfugl, -s, -ar [far·fʏgl̥(s), -fʏg̊lar] m.1 bird of passage, migratory bird.

fargan, -ans [far·g̊an, -ans] n. racket.

farlama [far·la·ma] adj. indecl. disabled.

farmiði, -a, -ar [far·mɪ·ðɪ, -a(r)] wm.1 ticket.

farsæll, -sæl, -sælt; -sælli, sælastur [far·saidl̥, -sai·l̥, -sailt; -saidlɪ, -sai·lastʏr] adj. happy, lucky, prosperous.

farsællega [far·sail·ɛ·qa] adv. safely, happily.

farvegur, -vegar, -vegs; -vegir [far·-vɛ·qʏr, -vɛ·qar, -vɛxs, -vei·jɪr] m.2 and 3 (river) bed.

farþegi, -a, -ar [far·þei·jɪ, -þɛ·qa(r), -þei·ja(r)] wm.1 passenger.

Fáskrúðsfjörður, -fjarðar [fau(:)-

Vowels: *a* [a] approx. father; *á* [au] cow; *e* [ɛ] set; *é* [jɛ] yes; *i, y* [ɪ] sit; *í, ý* [i] feel; *o* [ɔ] law; *ó* [ou] note; *u* [ʏ] approx. Germ. Mütter; *ú* [u] school; *y = i; ý = i; æ* [ai] ice; *ö* [ö] Germ. hören; *au* [öy] French *feuille*; *ei, ey* [ei] ale. Length [:]; half-length [·].

332

skruðs-fjör·ðyr̥, -fjar·ðar̥] m.3
' Fáskrúð's Fjord.'

fasta, föstu, -ur [fas·ta, fös·tʏ(r̥)] wf.l
fast, Lent; *ekki mátti borða kjöt um
föstuna* meat must not be eaten during Lent (S. VI, 14, 8).

fasteign, -ar, -ir [fas·teiɡ̊n̥, -eiɡ̊nar̥,
-ir̥] f.2 real estate.

fastur, föst, fast [fas·tʏr̥, fös·t, fas·t]
adj. fast, fixed, firm, solid, permanent; *fast högg* smart blow;
fastur liður á dagskrá fixed item in
the program; *fastur gestur (á
matsöluhúsi)* habitual customer (at
a restaurant).

fat, -s, föt [fa:tʰ(s), fö:tʰ; fa:d̥, fö:d̥]
n. piece of cloᵗhing, garment; pl.
föt clothes, a suit of clothes; platter.

fatabúð, -ar, -ir [fa:tʰa-bu:ð, -ar̥, -ir̥;
fa:da-] f.2 clothing store.

fataefni, -s, - [fa:tʰ(a)-ɛb·nɪ(s);
fa:d̥(a)-] n. material (for clothes),
stuff, cloth.

fatakof(f)ort, -s, - [fa:tʰa-kʰɔ:fɔr̥t,
-kʰɔf:ɔr̥t; fa:da-] n. wardrobe trunk.

fatnaður, -aðar, -aðir [faʰt·naðʏr̥,
-aðar̥, -aðɪr] m.3 clothes, clothing;
tvennur fatnaður two suits of
clothes.

fátt, see *fár*.

fátækur, -tæk, -tækt [fau:tʰai·kʰʏr̥,
-tʰai·kʰ, -tʰaixt; tʰai·ɡ̊-] adj. poor.

fauk, see *fjúka*.

fax, -, föx [fax·s, föx·s] n. mane.

fé, fjár, pl. fé, fjám, fjá(a) [fjɛ:,
fjau:r, fjau:m, fjau:(a)] n. property, moneys; sheep, cattle, livestock (In. I, 4(b)3).

febr. =

febrúar [fɛ:bru·ar̥] m.indecl. February.

feðgar [fɛð·ɡ̊ar̥] wm.l.pl. father and son.

feðgin [fɛð·ɡ̊ɪn] n.pl. father and
daughter.

feður, see *faðir*.

feginn, -in, -ið; fegnari, -astur [fei:-
jɪn, -ɪn, -ɪð, feiɡ̊·narɪ, -astʏr̥] adj.
fain, glad; *verða e-u feginn* be glad
at (of) sth; be relieved at sth.

fegurð, -ar, -ir [fɛ:qʏrð, -ʏrðar̥, -ir̥]
f.2 beauty.

fegurri, fegurstur, see *fagur*.

feiti [fei:tʰɪ; fei:d̥ɪ] wf.2 fat, grease;
brilliantine, oil (for the hair).

feitur, feit, feitt [fei:tʰʏr̥, fei:tʰ,
feiʰt:; fei:d̥-] adj. fat.

fékk, see 2. *fá*.

fela, fel; fal, fálum; fól, fólum; falinn, fólginn (-ið) or fela, faldi,
falinn (-ið) [fɛ:la, fɛ:l, fa:l,
fau:lʏm, fou:l, fou:lʏm, fa:lɪn,
foul·ɡ̊ɪn, -ɪð; fal·d̥ɪ] v.4 and 6, or
wv.l conceal, hide; *vera í e-u falinn (fólginn)* consist of.

félag, -s, -lög [fjɛ:la·q, -laxs, -lö·q] n.
society.

félagi, -a, -ar [fjɛ:lai·jɪ, -la·qa(r̥);
-la·jɪ] wm.l companion, comrade,
fellow-member of a society.

1. fell, -s, - [fɛd̥·l̥, fɛl·s] n. isolated
hill, mountain; also in place names:
-*fell*, *Fells-*.

2. fell, féll, -um, see *falla*.

fella, felldi, felldur (fellt) [fɛd̥·la,
fɛl·d̥ɪ, -ʏr̥, fɛl·t] wv.2 fell (down),
throw down; slay, defeat; *fella við
e-ð* fit into sth; *fella sig við e-ð*
adapt oneself to sth, get used to
sth, like sth; *vera ekki við eina
fjölina felldur* not to be moulded
according to one pattern; be variegated; (of men) be philanderers.

fengið, -inn, -um, see 2. *fá*.

fenna, fennti, fennt(ur) [fɛn:a, fɛn·tʰɪ,
-ʏr̥, fɛn·tʰ; fɛn·t-] wv.2 fill with
snow, form snowdrifts; *fenna í kaf*
be covered with snow (S. VI, 14, 3).

ferð, -ar, -ir [fɛr·ð, -ðar̥, -ðɪr] f.2
journey, voyage; speed; *vera á ferðinni* be on the go, be up and about;
taka sér (takast) ferð á hendur undertake a journey, *fara ferð* make a
trip, *á ferð* on a journey.

ferðafélag, -s, -lög [fɛr·ða-fjɛ:laq, -laxs,
-löq] n. travellers' society, tourist
society; *Ferðafélagið = Ferðafélag
Íslands* ' The Tourist Society of
Iceland.'

ferðaföt [fɛr·ða-fö:tʰ; -fö:d̥] n.pl.
travelling outfit.

ferðalag, -s, -lög [fɛr·ða-la:q, -lax·s,

Consonants: [ð] brea*th*e; [g] *g*ood; [ɡ̊] *gy*arden (garden); [hw] *wh*at; [j] *y*es; [kɟ] *cy*an
(can); [ŋ] thi*ng*; [q] N. Germ. sa*g*en; [r] Scottish *r*; [x] approx. Germ. a*ch*; [þ] *th*in.
Voiceless: ○; [b̥, d̥, ɡ̊] approx. *p, t, k*. Half-voiced: *italics*. Aspiration and preaspiration:
[ʰ]; [pʰ, tʰ, kʰ] *p-, t-, k-*. Others as in English.

-lö:q] n. travelling, trip, journey, voyage.

ferðamaður, -manns, -menn [fer·ða-ma:ðYɹ̥, -man·s, -mɛn:] m.4 traveller, tourist.

ferðamannaskip, -s, - [fer·ðaman·a-skⱼI:pʰ, -skⱼIf·s; -skⱼI:b̥] n. tourist boat.

ferðast, -aðist, -azt [fer·ðast, -aðɪst, -ast] wv.2 (middle voice only) travel (S. VI, 7, 5); ferðast um landið travel through the country.

ferfaldur, -föld, -falt [feɹ̥·faldYɹ̥, -föld, -falt] adj. fourfold.

1. ferja, -u, -ur [fer·ja, -Y(ɹ̥)] wf.1 ferry, ferryboat.

2. ferja, -aði, -að(ur)[fer·ja, -aðɪ, -að, -aðYɹ̥] wv.4 ferry.

ferma, fermdi, fermdur (fermt)[fer·ma, fermdɪ, -Yɹ̥, fermtʰ; ferm̥t] wv.2 confirm (a child); load (a boat).

ferming, -ar, -ar [fer·miŋg̊, -aɹ̥] f.1 confirmation; loading of a boat.

fern, fern, fernt [ferdn̥, fed·n̥, fɛ(r)ntʰ; fen·tʰ; fɛ(r̥)nt; fen̥·t; fɛʰt:] distributive num. four of each, four of (in) a group; fernt a group of four (In. V, 3, 2).

ferskja, -u, -ur [ferskⱼa, -kⱼY(ɹ̥)] wf.1 peach.

fertugasti [fer·tɣqastɪ] num. ord. fortieth.

fertugur, -tug, -tugt [feɹ̥·tɣqYɹ̥, -tɣq, -tɣxt] adj. forty years old; forty fathoms deep (high, etc.) (In. V, 3, 1).

festa, festi, fest(ur) [fɛs·ta, -ɪ, -Yɹ̥, fɛs·t] wv.2 fasten, make fast, fix; snjó festir ekki the snow does not stick, the snow does not remain on the ground (S. VI, 14, 3).

festi, - (-ar), -ar[fɛs·tɪ, -aɹ̥]wf.2 (f.1) chain, pl. chains; betrothal (In. I, 6, 2).

fet, -s, - [fɛ:tʰ(s); fɛ:d̥] n. pace, step; foot (a measure); sex feta langur six foot long.

f. h. = fyrir hádegi.

fiðla, -u, -ur [fɪð·la, -Y(ɹ̥)] wf.1 violin, fiddle.

fiðluleikari, -a, -ar [fɪð·lY-lei:kʰarɪ, -a(ɹ̥); -lei:g̊-] wm.1 violinist, fiddler.

fiður, (-ri), -urs [fɪ:ðYɹ̥(s), fɪð·rɪ] n. feathers; fiðurundirsæng feather under bed, see undirsæng.

fífl, -s, - [fib̥·l̥(s)] n. fool; hvert fíflið any fool.

fíkja, -u, -ur [fi:kⱼʰa, -kⱼʰY(ɹ̥); fi:g̊ⱼa] wf.1 fig.

fimleikar [fɪm·lei·kʰaɹ̥; fɪ:m-; -lei·g̊aɹ̥] m.1 (or 2) pl. gymnastics.

1. fimm [fɪm:] num.card. five.

2. fimm, -s, - [fɪm:, fɪm·s] n. five (in cards).

fimma, -u, -ur [fɪm:a, -Y(ɹ̥)] wf.1 five (in cards).

fimmeyringur, -s, -ar [fɪm:ei·riŋg̊Yɹ̥, -iŋs, -iŋg̊aɹ̥] m.1 a five-aurar piece.

fimmfaldur, -föld, -falt [fɪm·faldYɹ̥, -föld, -falt] adj. fivefold.

fimmtán [fɪm·tʰau·n; fɪm̥·tau-n] num. card. fifteen.

fimmtándi [fɪm·tʰaundɪ; fɪm̥·taundɪ] num.ord. fifteenth.

fimmti [fɪm·tʰɪ; fɪm̥·tɪ] num.ord. fifth.

fimmtíu [fɪm·tʰi·jY; fɪm̥·ti·jY] num. card. fifty.

fimmtudagur, -s, -ar [fɪm·tʰY-da:qYɹ̥, -dax·s, -da:qaɹ̥; fɪm̥·tY-] m.1 Thursday.

fimmtugasti [fɪm·tʰYqastɪ; fɪm̥·t-] num.ord. fiftieth.

fimmtugur, -tug, -tugt [fɪm·tʰYqYɹ̥, -tʰYq, -tʰYxt; fɪm̥·t-] adj. fifty years old; fifty fathoms deep (high, etc.) (In. V, 3, 1).

fimmtungur, -s, -ar [fɪm·tʰuŋg̊Yɹ̥, -uŋs, -uŋg̊aɹ̥; fɪm̥·t-] m.1 one fifth, a fifth (of sth).

fingravettlingur, -s, -ar [fiŋ·g̊ra-vɛʰt·liŋg̊Yɹ̥, -iŋs, -iŋ·g̊aɹ̥] m.1 (woolen) glove.

fingur, (-ri), -urs, -ur [fiŋ·g̊Yɹ̥(s), fiŋ·g̊rɪ] m.4 finger; skera sig í fingur cut one's finger; telja á fingrum sér count on one's fingers (S. I, 4, 1, 5).

finn, fín, fínt [fid·n̥, fi:n, fin·tʰ; fid·nɪ, fi:nastYɹ̥; fin̥·t] adj. fine, dressy, elegant.

finna, finn, fann, fundum, fundinn

Vowels: a [a] approx. father; á [au] cow; e [ɛ] set; é [jɛ] yes; i, y [ɪ] sit; í, ý [i] feel; o [ɔ] law; ó [ou] note; u [Y] approx. Germ. Mütter; ú [u] school; y = i; ý = í; æ [ai] ice; ö [ö] Germ. hören; au [öy] French feuille; ei, ey [ei] ale. Length [:]; half-length [·].

(-ið) [fɪn:a, fɪn:, fan:, fɣn·d̥ɣm, -ɪn, -ɪð] v.3 (1) find, discover; meet, see (for a moment); feel; *finna sér eitthvað til* find some excuse or pretext; *finna e-n* see sbdy, visit sbdy; visit sbdy with hostile intent, get one: *finna e-n duglega* get one (visit one) with a vengeance; feel: *ég finn* I feel (for certain); *það var að finna (það fannst) á henni að* . . . one felt from what she said (uttered) that . . . (S. VI, **14**, 7); *finna til* feel sth, be hurt; *finna til e-s* feel sth; *finna til fótanna* feel one's feet; *finna til kulda* feel the cold; (2) middle voice: *finnast* (passive) be found; (recipr.) find each other (S. VI, **7**, *2-3*); *mér finnst* it seems to me, I think, I feel, I have a feeling; *mér finnst þeir of sterkir* I find them too strong; *finnast sem* feel as if (S. VI, **9**, *4*, 7).

Finni, -a, -ar [fɪn:ɪ, -a(r̥)] wm.1 a Finn, pl. Finns; the Finnish.

Finnur, -s, -ar [fɪn:ɣr̥, fɪn·s, fɪn:ar̥] m.1 pers. name.

firðir, see *fjörður.*

firma, -, -u [fɪr·ma, -ɣ] wn. firm, business, concern.

firnindi [fɪd̥·nɪndɪ; fɪrd̥n-] n.pl. usually in the phrase: *fjöll og firnindi* mountains and wildernesses.

firra, firrti, firrt(ur) [fɪr:a, fɪr̥·tɪ, -ɣr̥, fɪr̥·t] wv.2 *firra e-n e-u* deprive sbdy of sth.

fiskabollur (fiski-) [fɪs·ka-bɔl:ɣr̥, fɪs·kˌɪ-] wf.1.pl. fish balls.

fiskbúðingur, -s, -ar [fɪs·kbu·ðiŋ̊ɣr̥, -iŋs, -iŋ̊ar̥] m.1 fish pudding.

fiskistöng, -stangar, -stengur [fɪs·kˌɪ-stöyn·g̊, -staun·g̊ar̥, -steiŋ·g̊ɣr̥] f.3 fishing-tackle, fishing-rod.

fiskisúpa, -u, -ur [fɪs·kˌɪ·su:pʰa, -ɣ(r̥); -su:ba] wf.1 fish soup, fish broth.

fiskiveiðar [fis·kˌɪ-vei:ðar̥] f.1.pl. fishing.

fiskkippa, -u, -ur [fɪs·kkˌʰɪʰp·a, -ɣ(r̥)] wf.1 a bunch (mess) of fish.

fisktegund, -ar, -ir [fɪs·ktʰe·qɣnd̥, -ar̥, -ir̥] f.2 kind, species of fish.

fiskur, -s, -ar [fɪs·kɣr̥, fɪsks, fɪs·kar̥] m.1 fish, especially cod or haddock; *fiskur og síld* cod (haddock) and herring.

fiskverzlun, -unar, -anir [fɪs·kver̥slɣn, -ɣnar̥, -anɪr̥] f.2 fish store, fish market.

fjá(a), fjám, see *fé.*

fjaðrar, -ir, see *fjöður.*

fjalar, -ir, see 1. *fjöl.*

fjall, -s, fjöll [fjad̥·l̥, fjal·s, fjöd̥·l̥] n. mountain; *á fjöllum uppi* up in the mountains; *Fjöll* 'Mountains,' a district in the North East Uplands.

Fjallabaksvegur, -ar [fjad̥·labaxs-vɛ:qɣr̥, -vɛ:qar̥] m.3 'Way Behind the Mountains.'

Fjalla-Eyvindur, -ar [fjad̥·l̥(a)-ei:vɪndɣr̥, -ar̥] m.1 'Eyvindur of the Mountains,' an 18th century outlaw; subject of a famous play of that name by Jóhann Sigurjónsson.

fjallavættur, -ar, -ir [fjad̥·la-vaiʰt:ɣr̥, -ar̥, -ɪr̥] f.2 or m.3 mountain spirit.

fjalldrapi, -a [fjal·dra-pʰɪ, -a; fjad̥l·; -dra·bɪ] wm.1 dwarf birch.

fjallganga, -göngu, -ur [fjad̥·lgauŋ̊ga, -göyŋ̊ɣ(r̥)] wf.1 mountain climbing, trip to the mountains; pl. also the autumnal rounding up of sheep in the mountains (= *göngur*).

fjalllendi, -s, - [fjad̥·lendɪ(s)] n. mountains, mountainous parts.

fjallsrót, -ar, -rætur [fjal·srou·tʰ, -ar̥, -rai·tʰʏr̥; -rou·d̥, -rai·d̥ɣr̥] f.3 foot of a mountain.

fjandi, -a, fjendur (fjandur, fjandar) [fjan·dɪ, -a, fjɛn·dɣr̥, fjan·dɣr̥, fjan·dar̥] wm.2 enemy, fiend, devil; pl. *fjendur* enemies, *fjandar* devils (In. I, **5**, *2*).

fjár, see *fé.*

fjara, fjöru, -ur [fja:ra, fjö:rɣ(r̥)] wf.1 ebb, low tide; foreshore, beach; *milli fjalls og fjöru* between the mountains and the sea.

fjarðar, see *fjörður.*

fjarðarendi, -a, -ar [fjar·ðar-ɛn·dɪ, -a(r̥)] wm.1 end of a firth or fjord.

fjárframlag, -s, -lög [fjaur̥·framla:q,

Consonants: [ð] breat*h*e; [g] *g*ood; [gⱼ] *g*yarden (garden); [hw] *wh*at; [j] *y*es; [kⱼ] *c*yan (can); [ŋ] thi*ng*; [q] N. Germ. sa*g*en; [r] Scottish *r*; [x] approx. Germ. a*ch*; [þ] *th*in. Voiceless: ○; [b̥, d̥, g̊] approx. *p, t, k.* Half-voiced: *italics.* Aspiration and preaspiration: [ʰ]; [pʰ, tʰ, kʰ] *p-, t-, k-.* Others as in English.

335

-lax·s, -lö:*q*] n. sum of money, down payment.

fjárhagslega [fjau:r̥haxs-lɛ:qa] adv. financially, economically.

fjárhagur, -s, -ir [fjau:r̥ha·qɤr̥, -haxs, -hai·jır; -ha·jır̥] m.2 financial status.

fjárheimta, -u, -ur [fjau:r̥heimtʰa, -ɤ(r̥); -heim̥ta] wf.1 recovery of sheep (from the mountains in fall).

fjárhús, -s, - [fjau:r̥hu·s, -hus·] n. sheep shed, sheep barn.

fjarki, -a, -ar [fjar̥·k̡ı, fjar̥·ka(r̥)] wm.1 four (in cards).

fjarlægur, -læg, -lægt [fjar·lai·qɤr̥, -lai·*q*, -laixt] adj. distant; *fjarlægur e-m* far away from sbdy.

fjármálamaður, -manns, -menn [fjaur·· mau·la·ma:ðɤr̥, -man·s, -mɛn:] m.4 financier.

fjarri, fjær, fjærst [fjar:ı, fjai:*r*, fjair̥st] adv. far away; *fjarri mér* far away from me; *fjandinn fjarri mér*! keep away, devil!

fjárpest, -ar, -ir [fjaur̥·pʰɛst, -ar̥, -ır̥] f.2 sheep plague.

fjarskalega [fjas·ka-lɛ:qa, fjar̥ska-] adv. extremely, terribly, awfully.

fjarski, -a [fjar̥sk̡ı, fjar̥ska] wm.1 distance; *í fjarska* in the distance, far away.

fjendur, see *fjandi.*

fjórði [fjour·ðı] num.ord. fourth.

fjórðungur, -ungs, -ungar [fjour·ðuŋ· ĝɤr̥, -uŋs, -uŋ̊ar̥] m.1 one fourth, a weight of ten Icelandic pounds.

fjórir, fjórar, fjögur [fjou:rır̥,fjou:rar̥, fjö:qɤr̥], acc. *fjóra, fjórar, fjögur* [fjou:ra], dat. *fjórum* [fjou:rɤm], gen. *fjög(ur)ra* [fjöq·ra, fjö:qɤr·a] num.card. four (In. V, **2**, 2(d)).

fjórtán [fjour̥·tau·*n*] num.card. fourteen.

fjórtándi [fjour·taundı] num.ord. fourteenth.

fjós, -s, - [fjou:s, fjous:] n. cattle stable, cow shed, cow stable; also in place names: *Fjósa-.*

fjúka, fýk, fauk, fukum, fokinn (-ið) [fju:kʰa, fi:kʰ, föy:kʰ, fɤ:kʰɤm, fɔ:k̡ʰın, -ıð; fju:ĝa, fi:ĝ, föy:ĝ,

fɤ:ĝɤm, fɔ:ĝ̡ın] v.2 blow away, be carried away by the wind (S. VI, **14,** *3*).

fjær, comparative of *fjarri* and *fjærri.*

fjærri, fjær, fjærst [fjair:ı, fjai:*r*, fjair̥st] adv. far (away); *fjær* farther away; *fjærst* farthest away.

fjöður, fjaðrar, fjaðrir [fjö:ðɤr̥, fjað·· rar̥, fjað·rır̥] f.2 feather; (main) spring (of a watch).

fjögur, see *fjórir.*

fjög(ur)ra, see *fjórir.*

1. **fjöl, fjalar, -ir** [fjö:*l*, fja:lar̥, fja:· lır̥] f.2 flat piece of wood, thin board, deal; *vera ekki við eina fjölina felldur* be not moulded according to one pattern, be variegated; of a man: be a philanderer.
2. **fjöl-** [fjö:*l*-] pref. multi-, poly-.

fjölbreyttur, -breytt, -breytt [fjöl·· breiʰt·ɤr̥, -breiʰt·] adj. many-sided, diversified.

fjöldi, -a [fjöl·dı, -a] wm.1 multitude, a great many; *mikill fjöldi* a great number; *fjöldi af e-u* lots of sth.

fjölfræðingur, -s, -ar [fjöl·frai·ðiŋ̊ɤr̥, -iŋs, -iŋar̥] m.1 polymath.

fjölhæfur, -hæf, -hæft [fjö:lhai·vɤr̥, -hai·v, -haift] adj. versatile.

fjöll, see *fjall.*

fjölmenna, -mennti, -mennt(ur) [fjöl·· mɛn·a, -mɛntʰı, -ɤr̥, -mɛntʰ; -mɛn̠t-] wv.2 crowd, flock; come accompanied by a crowd, a flock; *það verður fjölmennt þar* many people will be there.

fjölskylda, -u, -ur [fjöl·sk̡ıldа, -ɤ(r̥)] wf.1 family.

fjör, (fjörvi), fjörs [fjö:*r*, fjör·vı, fjör·s] n. zest, spirit, pep, life.

fjörður, fjarðar, firðir [fjör·ðɤr̥, fjar·· ðar̥, fır·ðır̥] m.3 fjord, firth; in place names: *-fjörður, Fjarðar-; vestur á (í) Fjörðum* west in the Firths, usually: west in the Vestfirðir.

fjörgamall, -gömul, -gamalt [fjör·ga:· madl̥, -gö:mɤl, -ga:malt] adj. very old.

fjöru, -ur, see *fjara.*

Vowels: *a* [a] approx. *father*; *á* [au] *cow*; *e* [ɛ] *set*; *é* [jɛ] *yes*; *i, y* [ı] *sit*; *í, ý* [i] *feel*; *o* [ɔ] *law*; *ó* [ou] *note*; *u* [ɤ] approx. Germ. *Mütter*; *ú* [u] *school*; *y = i*; *ý = í*; *æ* [ai] *ice*; *ö* [ɵ̈] Germ. *hören*; *au* [öy] French *feuille*; *ei, ey* [ei] *ale*. Length [:]; half-length [·].

fjörutíu [fjö:rɤ-tʰi:jɤ] num. card.
forty.

1. flá, flæ, fló, flógum, fleginn (-ið)
[flau:, flai:, flou:, flou:(q)ɤm, flei:-
jɪn, -Ið] v.6 skin, flay; also:

2. flá, fláði, fláð(ur) [flau:, flau:ðɪ,
flau:ð, flau:ðɤr̥] wv.1.

flagð, -s, flögð [flaq·ð, flaqðs, flöq·ð;
flag̊·þ(s), flög̊·þ] n. monster, giantess.

flagg, -s, flögg [flag̊:(s), flög̊:] n. flag.

flaka, -aði, -að(ur) [fla:kʰa, -aðɪ, -að,
-aðɤr̥; fla:g̊a] wv.4 flap; flake.

flaksa, -aði, -að [flax·sa, -aðɪ, -að]
wv.4 flap.

flaska, flösku, -ur [flas·ka, flös·kɤ(r̥)]
wf.1 flask, bottle; þriggja pela flaska
a bottle of one and a half pints.

flatbrauð, -s [fla:tʰbröy·ð, -bröyðs;
fla:d̥-] n. 'flat bread,' i. e. flat unleavened rye-bread, baked in hot
embers.

flatkaka, -köku, -ur [fla:tʰkʰa·kʰa,
-kʰö·kʰɤ(r̥); fla:d̥kʰa·g̊a, -kʰö·g̊ɤ]
wf.1 'flat cake,' a loaf of flatbrauð.

flatti, flatt(ur), see fletja.

flaug, see fljúga.

flaut, see fljóta.

flegið, -inn, see 1. flá.

fleira, fleiri, see margur.

flesk, -s [fles·k(s)] n. pork, bacon.

flestir, see margur.

fletja, flatti, flatt(ur) [fle:tʰja, flaʰt:ɪ,
-ɤr̥, flaʰt:; fle:d̥ja] wv.1 flatten;
flake (a fish).

fleygja, fleygði, fleygður (fleygt) [flei:-
ja, fleiq·ðɪ, -ɤr̥, fleix·t; fleig̊·ðɪ] wv.2
fleygja e-u throw sth.

fleyta, fleytti, fleytt(ur) [flei:tʰa,
fleiʰt:ɪ, -ɤr̥, fleiʰt:; flei:da] wv.2
skim, float; fleyta sér literally:
'float oneself,' i. e. get by.

flibbi, -a, -ar [flɪb:ɪ, -a(r̥)] wm.1
collar; linur flibbi soft collar, harður
flibbi starched collar.

fljót, -s, - [fljou:tʰ(s), fljous:; fljou:d̥]
n. (= stórá) great river; 'fleet';
also in place names: -fljót, Fljóts-.

fljóta, flýt, flaut, flutum, flotinn (-ið)
[fljou:tʰa, fli:tʰ, flöy:tʰ, flɤ:tʰɤm,
flɔ:tʰɪn, -ið; fljou:da, fli:d̥, flöy:d̥,

flɤ:d̥ɤm, flɔ:d̥ɪn, -Ið] v.2 float, run,
stream.

Fljótsdalshérað, -s [fljous·dals·hje:-
rað, -aðs] n. 'Fleet Dale District.'

Fljótshlíð, -ar [fljous·hli·ð, -hl̥i·ðar̥]
f.1 'Fleet Slope,' a district of the
South.

fljótur, fljót, fljótt [fljou:tʰɤr̥, fljou:tʰ,
fljouʰt:; fljou:d̥-] adj. fast, quick,
swift; fljótur á sér quick, rash;
fljótt adv. quickly.

fljúga, flýg, flaug, flugum, floginn (-ið)
[flju:(q)a, fli:q, flöy:q, flɤ:qɤm,
flɔi:jɪn, -ið; flɔ:jɪn, -Ið] v.2 fly
(1. and 3. pers. subj. pres. fljúgi
[flju:ɪ] cf. Pr. 3, 4, 2n); fljúgandi
virki flying fortress; fuglinn fljúgandi a bird in flight.

fló, flógum, see 1. flá.

flóð, -s, - [flou:ð, flouð·s] n. flood,
flood tide, high tide.

flogið, -inn, see fljúga.

flói, -a, -ar [flou:ɪ, -a(r̥)] wm.1 bay
(of the sea); marshy country,
marshland, swamp; in place names:
-flói, Flóa-.

flokka, -aði, -að(ur) [flɔʰk:a, -aðɪ, -að,
-aðɤr̥] wv.4 classify.

flokkaglíma, -u, -ur [flɔʰk:a·gli:ma,
-ɤ(r̥)] wf.1 class wrestling.

flokkapólitík, -ur [flɔʰk:a·pʰou:lɪtʰi·kʰ,
-tʰi·kʰɤr̥; -tʰi·g̊-] f.3 party politics.

flokksblað, -s, -blöð [flɔx·sbla·ð, -blaðs,
-blö·ð; flɔʰk·s-] n. party paper,
party organ.

flokksfyrirliði, -a, -ar [flɔx·sfɪ·rɪ(r)lɪ:-
ðɪ, -a(r̥)] wm.1 lieutenant.

flokksleiðtogi, -a, -ar [flɔx·sleiðtʰɔi:jɪ,
-tʰɔ:qa(r̥); -tʰɔ:jɪ] wm.1 party
leader.

flokksræði, -s [flɔx·srai·ðɪ] n. party
rule.

flokkssjónarmið, -s, - [flɔx·(s)sjou·-
narmɪ·ð, -mɪð·s] n. point of view
of party politics.

flokkur, -s, -ar [flɔʰk:ɤr̥, flɔx·s;
flɔʰk·s, flɔʰk·ar̥] m.1 flock, company;
faction, (political) party.

flot, -s [flɔ:tʰ, flɔ:tʰs; flɔ:d̥] n. float-

Consonants: [ð] breathe; [g] good; [gɹ] gɹarden (garden); [hw̥] what; [j] yes; [kɹ] cɹan
(can); [ŋ] thing; [q] N. Germ. sagen; [r] Scottish r; [x] approx. Germ. ach; [þ] thin.
Voiceless: o; [b̥, d̥, g̊] approx. p, t, k. Half-voiced: italics. Aspiration and preaspiration:
[ʰ]; [pʰ, tʰ, kʰ] p-, t-, k-. Others as in English.

337

ing, *á flot* afloat; *á floti* floating; top-fat (in soups, etc.).

flotadeild, -ar, -ir [flɔ:tʰa-deil·d̩, -aṛ, -ɪṛ; flɔ:da-] f.2 fleet squadron; fleet division.

flotamálaráðherra, -a, -ar [flɔ:tʰamau-·la-rau:ðher·a(ṛ); flɔ:da-] wm.1 secretary of the navy (U.S.A.).

flotamálaráðuneyti, -s, - [flɔ:tʰamau-·la-rau:ðɤnei·tʰɪ(s); flɔ:da-, -nei·d̩ɪ] n. ministry of naval affairs, department of the navy.

flotastöð, -stöðvar, -var [flɔ:tʰa-stö:ð, -stöð·vaṛ; flɔ:da-] f.1 naval base.

floti, -a, -ar [flɔ:tʰɪ, -a(ṛ); flɔ:d̩ɪ] wm.1 fleet, navy.

flotið, -inn, see *fljóta.*

flótti, -a [flouʰt:ɪ, -a] wm.1 flight, *á flótta* in flight.

flú(a), flúði, flúð(ur), flúinn (-ið), see *flýja.*

fluga, -u, -ur, (-na) [flɤ:qa, -ɤ(ṛ), flɤg̊·na] wf.1 fly.

flugher, -s, -ir (-jar) [flɤ:qhe·r, -heṛ·s, -he·rɪṛ, -hɛɪ·jaṛ] m.1 & 3 air force, air fleet, Luftwaffe.

flugmaður,-manns,-menn [flɤq·ma·ðɤṛ, -mans, -mɛn·] m.4 aviator.

flugsandur, -s, -ar [flɤx·sandɤṛ, -san(d)s, -sandaṛ] m.1 = *foksandur.*

flugstöð, -stöðvar, -var [flɤx·stö·ð, -stöð·vaṛ] f.1 airport.

flugsveit, -ar, -ir [flɤx·svei·tʰ, -aṛ, -ɪṛ; -svei·d̩-] f.2 air squadron.

flugum, see *fljúga.*

flugvél, -ar, -ar [flɤq·vje·l, -vje·laṛ] f.1 airplane.

flugvélamóðurskip, -s, - [flɤq·vje·la-mou:ðɤrsk‚ɪ·pʰ, -sk‚ɪfs; -sk‚ɪ·b] n. =

flugvélaskip, -s, - [flɤq·vje·la-sk‚ɪ:pʰ, -sk‚ɪf·s; -sk‚ɪ:b̩] n. aircraft carrier, airplane carrier.

flugvöllur, -vallar, -vellir [flɤq·vödlɤṛ, -vadlaṛ, -vedlɪṛ] m.3 airfield, airdrome.

flutningasveit, -ar, -ir [flɤʰt·niŋga-svei:tʰ, -aṛ, -ɪṛ; -svei:d] f.2 transport service (in the army).

flutningsbíll, -bíls, -bílar [flɤʰt·niŋs-bid·l̩, -bil·s, -bi:laṛ] m.1 lorry; truck.

flutti, -ur, see *flytja.*

flutum, see *fljóta.*

flyðra, -u, -ur [flɪð·ra, -ɤ(ṛ)] wf.1 halibut, flounder.

flýg, see *fljúga.*

flygsa, -u, -ur [flɪx·sa, -ɤ(ṛ)] wf.1 wisp, tatter.

flýja (flú(a)); flý; flúði; flúinn (-ið), flúð(ur) [fli:ja, flu:(a), fli:, flu:ðɪ, flu:ɪn, -ɪð, flu:ð, flu:ðɤṛ] wv.1 & 3 flee, evade, run away from (In. VII, 3, *2*; 3, *2*, 3; 4, *10*).

flýt, see *fljóta.*

flýta, flýtti, flýtt [fli:tʰa, fliʰt:ɪ, fliʰt:; fli:da] wv.2 speed up, hasten; *flýta sér* hasten, hurry.

flytja, flutti, flutt(ur) [flɪ:tʰja, flɤ‚ʰt:ɪ, flɤ‚ʰt:(ɤṛ); flɪ:dja] wv.1 move transport; *flytja sig búferlum* move (from one home to another, see *búferli*); *flytja fyrirlestur* deliver a lecture.

flæ, see 1. *flá.*

flæða, flæddi, flæddur (flætt) [flai:ða, flaid̩:ɪ, -ɤṛ, flaiʰt:] wv.2 flood; impers.: *það flæðir* the flood is coming in; the tide is coming in; *flæða yfir* inundate, overflow.

flögð, see *flagð.*

flögg, see *flagg.*

flökun, -unar [flö:kʰɤn, -ɤnaṛ; flö:g̊ɤn] f.2 flaking.

flösku(r), see *flaska.*

Fnjóskadalur, -s [fnjous·ka-da:lɤṛ, -dal·s; hnjous·ka-] m.2 'Tinder Dale.'

fóðra, -aði, -að(ur) [fouð·ra, -aðɪ, -að, -aðɤṛ] wv.4 feed; *fóðra á e-u* feed with sth; line (garments).

fóður, (-ri), -urs, -ur [fou:ðɤṛ(s), fouð·rɪ] n. fodder; lining (in clothes).

fokinn, see *fjúka.*

foksandur, -s, -ar [fɔ:kʰsandɤṛ, -san(d)s, -sandaṛ; fɔ:g̊-] m.1 drifting, shifting sand(s).

fól, -um, see *fela.*

folald, -s, -öld [fɔ:lald̩(s), fɔ:löld̩] n. foal.

fólgið, -inn, see *fela.*

Vowels: *a* [a] approx. *father*; *á* [au] *cow*; *e* [ɛ] *set*; *é* [jɛ] *yes*; *i, y* [ɪ] *sit*; *í, ý* [i] *feel*; *o* [ɔ] *law*; *ó* [ou] *note*; *u* [ɤ] approx. Germ. *Mütter*; *ú* [u] *school*; *y = i*; *ý = í*; *æ* [ai] *ice*; *ö* [ö] Germ. *hören*; *au* [öy] French *feuille*; *ei, ey* [eiĬ] *ale*. Length [:]; half-length [·].

fólk, -s [foul·kʰ(s), foul·s, foulxs; foul·k] n. (the) people, household, folks (S. VI, **14, 2**).

fólksbíll, -bíls, -bílar [foul·sbiḍl̩, -bils, -bi·lar; foulxs·] m.1 bus, automobile for transporting people, passenger car.

fólksfjöldi, -a [foul·sfjölḍɪ, -a; foulxs·] wm.1 (number of) population; a great crowd of people.

1. for, -ar, -ir [fɔ:r, -rar, -rɪr] f.2 mud, muddy bog, swamp, marsh, fen.

2. for- [fɔ:r-] pref. fore-, pro-.

fór, -um, see *fara.*

forarflói, -a, -ar [fɔ:rar·flou:ɪ, -a(r̩)] wm.1 muddy bog, swamp, fen.

forboði, -a, -ar [fɔr·bɔ.ðɪ, -a(r̩)] wm.1 foreboding; precursor.

forboðinn, -in, -ið [fɔr·bɔ.ðɪn, -ɪn, -ɪð] adj. prohibited.

forða, -aði, -að [fɔr·ða, -aðɪ, -að] wv.4 save, *forða e·m* save sbdy; *forða e·u* prevent sth; *forðast e·ð* avoid sth.

foreldrar [fɔ:reldrar] wm.1.pl. parents.

forliði, -a, -ar [fɔr·lɪ·ðɪ, -a(r̩)] wm.1 pioneer (in the army).

form, -s, - [fɔr·m, fɔrms] n. form, pattern.

formsnillingur, -s, -ar [fɔr·msnɪdlɪŋg̊ʏr, -ɪŋs, -ɪŋgar] m.1 master of form.

forn, forn, fornt [fɔd·n̩, fɔ(r)ntʰ; fɔrdn̩, fɔ(r)nt] adj. old, ancient, antique; *að fornu og nýju* in old and modern times, of old and today.

fórn, -ar, -ir [fourdn̩, -nar, -nir] f.2 sacrifice; *færa fórnir* sacrifice; *færa þungar fórnir* suffer heavy losses.

fornbókabúð, -ar, -ir [fɔdnbou·kʰa·bu:ð, -ðar, -ðɪr; -bou:g̊a-] f.2 =

fornbóksala, -sölu, -ur [fɔd·nboukʰsa:·la, -sö:lʏ(r̩); fɔrdn̩·; -boug̊-] wf.1 antiquarian bookstore.

forníslenzka, -u [fɔd·ni·slenska, -ʏ; fɔrdn̩·] wf.1 Old Icelandic (Old Norse), = *norrœna.*

fornleifafélag, -s, -lög [fɔd·nlei·va·fje:laq, -laxs, -löq] n. archaeological society; *Hið íslenzka forn-*

leifafélag The Icelandic Archaeological Society.

Fornritafélag íslands [fɔd·nrɪ·tʰa·fje:·laq i:slan(d̩)s; -rɪda·; fɔrdn̩-] n. 'The Old Icelandic Text Society.'

fornsaga, -sögu, -ur [fɔd·nsa·qa, -sö··qʏ(r̩); fɔrdn̩-] wf.1 an Old Icelandic (family) saga.

fornsala, -sölu, -ur [fɔd·nsa·la, -sö··lʏ(r̩); fɔrdn̩-] wf.1 second hand bookstore, antique shop.

fornöld, -aldar, -ir [fɔd·nölḍ, -aldar, -ɪr; fɔrdn̩-] f.2 ancient times; in the history of Iceland: 874-1400.

forspjallsvísindi [fɔr·spja(d̩)ls-vi:sɪndɪ] n.pl. preparatory (propedeutic) sciences, i. e. logic and psychology.

forseti, -a, -ar [fɔr·se·tʰɪ, -a(r̩); -se·dɪ] wm.1 president.

forstofa, -u, -ur [fɔr·stɔ·va, -ʏ(r̩)] wf.1 hall, entrance hall.

forstöðukona, -u, -ur [fɔr·stö·ðʏ·kʰɔ:·na, -ʏ(r̩)] wf.1 headmistress (of a school), principal, director.

forsöngvari, -a, -ar [fɔr·söyŋg̊varɪ, -a(r̩)] wm.1 leader of the choir, precentor.

fortó, -s, - [fɔr·tʰou·(s)] n. sidewalk, = *gangstétt.*

forugur [fɔ:rʏqʏr̩] adj. (see *-ugur*) muddy.

forusta, -u [fɔ:rʏsta, -ʏ] wf.1 leadership.

forustuær, (-á), -ær, -ær [fɔ:rʏstʏ-ai:r, -au:] f.3 a ewe that leads the other sheep (cf. bellwether).

forviða [fɔr·vɪ·ða] adj.indecl. surprised, astonished.

forvitni [fɔr·vɪʰtnɪ] wf.2 curiosity.

forysta, -u [fɔ:rɪsta, -ʏ] wf.1 = *forusta.*

foss, -, -ar [fɔs:(ar̩)] m.1 waterfall, falls, Sc. force; also in place names: *-foss, Foss-.*

Fossá, -ár [fɔs:au·(r)] f.1 'Falls River.'

Fossnúpur, -s [fɔs·nu·pʰʏr, -nu·pʰs; -nu·bʏr] m.1 'Falls Knob.'

fótbrotna, -aði, -að [fou:tʰbrɔʰtna, -aðɪ, -að; fou:d̩-] wv.4 break a leg.

Consonants: [ð] brea*th*e; [g] *g*ood; [gj] *gy*arden (garden); [hw] *wh*at; [j] *y*es; [kj] *cy*an (can); [ŋ] thi*ng*; [q] N. Germ. sa*g*en; [r] Scottish *r*; [x] approx. Germ. a*ch*; [þ] *th*in. Voiceless: ○; [b̥, d̥, g̊] approx. *p, t, k.* Half-voiced: *italics.* Aspiration and preaspiration: [ʰ]; [pʰ, tʰ, kʰ] *p-, t-, k-.* Others as in English.

339

fótgöngulið, -s [fou:tʰgöyŋ̊g̊ɣlɪ:ð, -lɪð·s; fou:d̦-] n. infantry.

fótgönguliðs- [fou:tʰgöyŋ̊g̊ɣlɪð·s-; fou:d̦-] pref. infantry (adj.).

fótgönguliðsskriðdreki [fou:tʰgöyŋ̊g̊ɣ-lɪð(s)-skrɪð·drɛ·k̦ˌʰɪ, -drɛ·kʰa(r̦); fou:d̦-; -drɛ·g̊ˌɪ, -drɛ·g̊a(r̦)] wm.l infantry tank.

fótur, -ar, fætur [fou:tʰɣr̦, -ar̦, fai:-tʰɣr̦; fou:d̦-, fai:d̦-] m.4 foot, leg; á fjórum fótum on all fours; standa á öðrum fæti stand on one foot; komast á fætur get up; vera á fótum be up and about, be on one's feet; vera kalt á fótum have cold feet; ganga þurrum fótum 'walk with dry feet,' i.e. without wetting the feet (S. I, 3, 1, 2(e)); koma á fót establish, build.

fótviss, -viss, -visst [fou:tʰvɪs·, -vɪst; fou:d̦-] adj. surefooted.

foxtrott, -s [fɔx·stʰrɔʰt·(s)] n. foxtrot.

1. frá, see frár.

2. frá [frau:] prep. with dat. from: (1) of place: skammt frá staðnum a little way from the place, near by; frá dómkirkjunni starting from the cathedral; (2) of time: lög frá 1932 the law (act) of 1932; frá því að conj. from the time that (S. VIII, 3(h)); (3) other uses: segja frá e-u tell about sth, tell of sth, relate sth; tveir frá fjórum two subtracted from four; adverbially: skammt frá a short way off; þar upp frá up there; héðan í frá henceforth; til og frá to and fro.

frádráttur, -ar [frau:drauʰt·ɣr̦, -ar̦] m.3 subtraction.

fráfall, -falls, -föll [frau:fad̦l, -fals, -föd̦l] n. death, demise.

frágangur, -s [frau:gauŋg̊ɣr̦, -gauŋs] m.l make-up, getup, workmanship.

frakki, -a, -ar [fraʰkˌ:ɪ, fraʰk:a(r̦)] wm.l coat; Frakki Frenchman.

Frakkland, -s [fraʰk:land̦(s)] n. France.

fram [fram:] adv. forward, forth, out; (1) of direction: from the inner recesses of a house or a farm-stead to the door: koma fram come out, emerge; fara fram (a) go out (in the kitchen, to the door), (b) progress, (c) take place; (2) with preps and advs: fram á vellina down upon the fields, out on the plain; fram á hamarinn to the brink of the cliff; fram á nítjándu öld down into the nineteenth century; fram hjá e-m (e-u) by, past sbdy (sth); spýta fram úr sér disgorge; spit out; fram til up to (of time); fram undan e-u in front of sth; fram undir páska up to Easter; fram yfir over, past (a certain time); (3) prep. with acc.: fram dalinn up the valley (in the North of Iceland), down the valley (in the South of Iceland) (S. I, 2, 3, 3).

framan [fra:man] adv. (1) from the front; í framan in front, in the face; framan í e-n in(to) someone's face; framan af in the beginning, to begin with; hér að framan in the foregoing (pages); fyrir framan e-n (e-ð) in front of sbdy (sth); fram fyrir e-n (e-ð) to the front of sbdy (sth); before sbdy; (2) prep. with acc. framan dalinn down the valley (in the North of Iceland), up the valley (in the South of Iceland) (S. I, 2, 3, 3).

framar [fra:mar̦] adv. compar. farther on, more to the front; further; (any) more (of time); aldrei framar nevermore.

framdi, framið, -inn, see fremja.

framfaramál, -s, - [fram·fara·mau:l, -maul·s] n. matter of progress, matter of reform; progressive issue.

framför, -farar, -ir [fram·fö·r, -fa·rar̦, -ɪr̦] f.2 progress; usually in pl. framfarir; taka framförum make progress.

framgluggi, -a, -ar [fram.glɣg̊ˌ·ɪ, -glɣg̊·a(r̦)] wm.l windshield (of an automobile).

framhaldsmynd, -ar, -ir [fram·hal(d̦)s·mɪn·d̦, -ar̦, -ɪr̦] f.2 a motion picture shown by installments; a serial.

Vowels: a [a] approx. father; á [au] cow; e [ɛ] set; é [jɛ] yes; i, y [ɪ] sit; í, ý [i] feel; o [ɔ] law; ó [ou] note; u [ɣ] approx. Germ. Mütter; ú [u] school; y = i; ý = í; æ [ai] ice; ö [ö] Germ. hören; au [öy] French feuille; ei, ey [ei] ale. Length [:]; half-length [·].

340

framkoma, -u [fram·kʰɔ·ma, -ʏ] wf.1 manner, demeanor.

framkvæma, -kvæmdi, -kvæmdur (-kvæmt) [fram·kʰvai·ma, -kʰvaimdɪ, -ʏr̥, -kʰvaimtʰ; -kʰvaiṃt] wv.2 carry out.

framkvæmdir [fram·kʰvaimdɪr̥] f.2.pl. enterprises, works carried out to their completion.

framleiða, -leiddi, -leiddur (-leitt) [fram·lei·ða, -leid·ɪ, -ʏr̥, -leiʰt·] wv.2 produce.

framleiðsla, -u, [fram·leiðsla, -ʏ] wf.1 production, produce.

framleiðslutæki [fram·leiðslʏ-tʰai:-kⱼʰɪ, -tʰai:g̊ⱼɪ] n.pl. means of production.

framliði, -a, -ar [fram·lɪ·ðɪ, -a(r̥)] wm.1 soldier of an advanced post, pl. advanced posts.

frammi [fram:ɪ] adv. out; away from the center of the house, the *bœjarhús*; *frammi í stofu* (*eldhúsi*) out in the parlor (the kitchen); *frammi í dal* far up the valley; *frammi á sjó* far out at sea.

Framnesvegur, -ar [fram·nesve:qʏr̥, -ar̥] m.3 'Outer Ness Road,' in Reykjavík.

framorðið [fram:ɔrðɪð] pp.n. only in: *hvað er framorðið?* what time is it? how late is it; *það er orðið nokkuð framorðið* it has become pretty late.

framsókn, -ar, -ir [fram·souʰkn̥, -souʰknar̥, -ɪr̥] f.2 progress; *Framsókn = Framsóknarflokkurinn.*

framsóknarflokkur, -s, -ar [fram·souʰknar̥-flɔʰk:ʏr̥, -flɔʰk·s, -flɔx·s] m.1 a progressive party, *Framsóknarflokkurinn* 'The Progressive party.'

framsóknarmaður, -manns, -menn [fram·souʰknar-ma:ðʏr̥, -man·s, -men:] m.4 progressive; a man belonging to the *Framsókn* party.

framur, fröm, framt; framari, -astur [fra:mʏr̥, frö:m, fram·tʰ; fram·t; fra:marɪ, -astʏr̥] adj. forward, arrogant.

framvörður, -varðar, -verðir [fram·-

vörðʏr̥, -varðar̥, -verðɪr̥] m.3 front patrol.

franska, frönsku [franska, frönskʏ] wf.1 French (language).

franskbrauð, -s (franz-) [franskbröy·ð, -bröyðs, fran·s-] n. literally: ' French bread,' white bread.

franskur, frönsk, franskt [franskʏr̥, frönsk, franst] adj. French.

frár, frá, frátt; frárri, frá(a)stur [frau:r, frau:, frauʰt:; fraur:ɪ, frau:astʏr̥, fraus·tʏr̥] adj. swift; *frár á fœti* swift of foot.

fraus, see *frjósa.*

fregn, -ar, -ir [freg̊·n̥, -nar̥, -nɪr̥] f.2 a piece of news (= *frétt*), news; *hafa fregnir af e-m* have (get) news about sbdy, of sbdy.

freistni [freis(t)nɪ] wf.2 temptation.

frelsa, -aði, -að(ur) [frel·sa, -aðɪ, -að, -aðʏr̥] wv.4 save, liberate; *frelsa oss frá illu* deliver us from evil.

frelsishreyfing, -ar, -ar [frel·sɪs-hrei:-viŋ̊, -ar̥] f.1 movement for liberty, liberating movement.

fremja, framdi, framinn (-ið) [frem·-ja, fram·dɪ, fra:mɪn, -ɪð] wv.1 perform; *fremja prestsverk* perform the duties of a clergyman.

fremri, fremstur [frem·rɪ, fremstʏr̥] adj. compar. and superl. the foremost of two, of many; *fremstur* outstanding; cf. *framur* (In. III, 4, 4).

fremst [fremst] adv. most to the front, in front (in the theater: orchestra seats); farthest up (a valley), farthest out (on a brink).

fremur [fre:mʏr̥] adv. compar. (cf. *fram*) rather; *f. en* rather than.

frétt, -ar, -ir [frjeʰt:(ar̥), -ɪr̥] f.2 a piece of news, news; *hvað er í fréttum?* what news? *er nokkuð í fréttum?* any news?

frétta, frétti, frétt [frjeʰt:a, -ɪ, frjeʰt:] wv.2 hear, get news of; *fréttast* be heard, be rumored (S. VI, 7, 3).

fréttablað, -s, -blöð [frjeʰt:a-bla:ð, -blað·s, -blö:ð] n. newspaper.

Consonants: [ð] brea*th*e; [g] *g*ood; [gⱼ] *gy*arden (garden); [hw̥] *wh*at; [j] *y*es; [kⱼ] *cy*an (can); [ŋ] thi*ng*; [q] N. Germ. sa*g*en; [r] Scottish *r*; [x] approx. Germ. a*ch*; [þ] *th*in. Voiceless: ○; [b̥, d̥, g̊] approx. *p, t, k.* Half-voiced: *italics.* Aspiration and preaspiration: [ʰ]; [pʰ, tʰ, kʰ] *p-, t-, k-.* Others as in English.

frí, -s, - [fri:(s)] n. leave; free time, vacation, holiday, recess.

friða, -aði, -aður [frɪ:ða, -aðɪ, -að, -aðʏr̥] wv.4 pacify; protect by law *friða fyrir e-u* protect from sth.

Friðgeir, -s [frɪð·g₁ei·r, -g₁eir̥s] m.1 pers. name.

Friðjón, -s [frɪð·jou·n, -jouns] m.1 pers. name.

Friðrik, -s [frɪð·rɪ·kʰ, -rɪxs, -rɪ·kʰs; -rɪ·g̊] m.1 pers. name. Frederic.

fríkirkja, -u, -ur [fri:k₁ʰɪrk₁a, -k₁ʰɪr̥·k₁ʏ(r̥)] wf.1 free church, opposite of state church.

frímerki, -s, - [fri:mer̥k₁ɪ(s)] n. postage stamp, stamp.

frímínútur [fri:minu·tʰʏr̥; ·minu·dʏr̥] wf.1.pl. recess of ten minutes at the end of each hour in schools.

frískur, frísk, frískt [fris·k(ʏr̥), fris·t] adj. well, quite well, sound.

frjáls, frjáls, frjálst [frjaul·s, frjaulst] adj. free.

frjósa, frýs, fraus, frusum, frosinn (-ið) [frjou:sa, fri:s, fröy:s, frʏ:-sʏm, frɔ:sɪn, -ɪð] v.2 freeze; *hann frýs* it is freezing.

fróður, fróð, (frótt) [frou:ðʏr̥, frou:ð, (frouʰt:)] adj. learned.

frosið, -inn, see *frjósa.*

frú, -ar, frúr [fru:(ar̥), fru:r] f.1 Mrs., *frú A.B.* Mrs. A.B. (In. I, 3, *1* (b)4).

frum- [frʏ:m-] pref. proto-, primeval.

frumkvæði, -s, - [frʏm·kʰvai·ðɪ(s)] n. initiative, *eiga frumkvæði að e-u* have taken the initiative in some matter.

frumskógur, -ar, -ar [frʏm·skou·-(q)ʏr̥, -skou·(q)ar̥] m.1 primeval forest.

frusum, see *frjósa.*

frýja, frýði, frýð [fri:ja, fri:ðɪ, fri:ð] wv.1 taunt; *frýja e-m hugar* egg sbdy on.

frýs, see *frjósa.*

frystur, fryst, fryst [frɪs·tʏr̥, frɪs·t] adj. frosted, frozen.

fræði, -s, - [frai:ðɪ] wf.2 or n., usually pl., learning; in compounds (only f.) : -logy.

frægur, fræg, frægt; frægari (frægri), frægastur (frægstur) [frai:qʏr̥, frai:q, fraix·t; frai:qarɪ, fraiq·rɪ; frai:qastʏr̥, fraix·stʏr̥] adj. famous.

frændfólk, -s [frain·dfoulkʰ, -foul(x)s; -foulk] n. relatives, kinsfolk.

frændi, -a, -ur [frain.dɪ, -a, -ʏr̥] wm.2 relative, cousin.

frændkona, -u, -ur [frain·dkʰɔ·na, -ʏ(r̥)] wf.1 cousin, female relative.

frænka, -u, -ur [fraiŋ·kʰa, -ʏ(r̥); fraiŋ̊·ka] wf.1 cousin, female relative.

fröken, -ar, -ar [frö:kʰɛn, -nar̥; frö:-g̊ɛn] f.1 Miss; waitress.

fröm, see *framur.*

frönsk, see *franskur.*

fugl, -s, -ar [fʏg̊·l̥, fʏqls, fʏg̊·lar̥] m.1 bird, fowl; coll. masses of birds; *fuglinn fljúgandi* flying bird, a bird on the wing.

fuglalíf, -s [fʏg̊·la·li:v, -lif·s] n. bird life.

fukum, see *fjúka.*

fullorðinn, -in, -ið; -orðnari, -astur [fʏd·lɔrðɪn, -ɪn, -ɪð, fʏd·lɔrdnarɪ, -astʏr̥] adj. grown-up.

fullsmíðaður, -uð, -að [fʏd·lsmi·ðaðʏr̥, -smi·ðʏð, -smi·ðað] adj. (pp.) fully built.

fulltrúi, -a, -ar [fʏd·l̥tʰru·ɪ, -a(r̥)] wm.1 representative.

fullur, full, fullt; fyllri, fyllstur [fʏd·-lʏr̥, fʏd·l̥, fʏl̥·t; fɪdlrɪ, fɪlstʏr̥] adj. full, complete, entire; surfeited, drunk; *fullur af e-u* (also *fullur e-s, fullur með e-ð* full of sth, replete with sth; *fullur af víni* full (drunk) with wine; *fyrir fullt og allt* for good, completely.

fundið, -inn, -um, see *finna.*

fundur, -ar, -ir [fʏn·dʏr̥, -ar̥, -ɪr̥] m.3 finding, discovery; meeting, convention.

furða, -u, -ur [fʏr·ða, -ʏ(r̥)] wf.1 wonder, marvel, astonishment; pl. (supernatural) wonders, apparitions.

Vowels: *a* [a] approx. father; *á* [au] cow; *e* [ɛ] set; *é* [jɛ] yes; *i, y* [ɪ] sit; *í, ý* [i] feel; *o* [ɔ] law; *ó* [ou] note; *u* [ʏ] approx. Germ. Mütter; *ú* [u] school; *y = i; ý = í;* *æ* [ai] ice; *ö* [ö] Germ. hören; *au* [öy] French *feuille; ei, ey* [ei] ale. Length [:]; half-length [·].

342

fús, fús, fúst [fuːs, fusˑt] adj. willing,
eager.

fýk, see *fjúka*.

fylgd, -ar, -ir [fɪlqd̥, fɪlˑd̥, -ar̥, -ɪr̥]
f.2 guidance, companionship, following.

fylgdarlaus, -laus, -laust [fɪlˑdar-löyːs,
-löysˑt] adj. without guidance; *fylgdarlaust* adv. without guidance.

fylgdarmaður, -manns, -menn [fɪlˑ-
dar-maːð̥r̥, -manˑs, -mɛn:] m.4
guide.

fylgi, -s [fɪlˑg̊ˌɪ(s)] n. following,
support, help.

1. fylgja, -u, -ur [fɪlˑg̊ˌa, -g̊ˌʏ(r̥)] wf.1
fetch, wraith; a ghost that accom-
panies a certain person.

2. fylgja, fylgdi, fylgt [fɪlˑg̊ˌa, fɪl(q)-
dɪ, fɪlˑdɪ, fɪl(x)t, fɪlˑt] wv.2 follow,
fylgja e-m follow, guide, accompany
sbdy; *fylgja e-m heim* follow sbdy
home; take sbdy home; *fylgja e-m
til rúms* show sbdy his bed; *fylgja
e-m* follow, haunt (of ghosts called
fylgjur, see above); *fylgja lögum*
observe, obey the law; *e-ð fylgir
e-u* sth belongs to sth, is included
in sth, goes with sth; *fylgja ráðum*
follow advice.

fylgsni, -s, - [fɪl(x)snɪ(s)] n. hiding-
place, hideout.

fylking, -ar, -ar [fɪlˑkˌʰiŋg̊, -ar̥; fɪlˑ-
kˌiŋg̊]ˑf.1 battle array, troops in
battle array.

fylkingararmur, -s, -ar [fɪlˑkˌʰiŋg̊ar-
arˑmʏr̥, -s, -ar̥; fɪlˑkˌ-] m.1 flank.

fylkja, fylkti, fylkt(ur) [fɪlˑkˌʰa,
fɪlˑtɪ, fɪlˑt(ʏr̥); fɪlˑkˌa; fɪlxt-] wv.2
array; *fylkja sér* array oneself in
battle array, line up.

fylli [fɪd̥ˑlɪ] wf.2 fullness, satisfaction, surfeit.

fyllri, fyllstur, see *fullur*.

fyrir [fɪːrɪr̥] prep. with acc. and dat.
in front of, around, as, before, ago,
to; for, for the sake of, because of,
on account of. **A.** prep. with acc.
(1) of place (in phrases of movement): in front of: *fara fyrir
altarið* go in front of the altar;

fyrir ósinn blocking the front of the
estuary; *fyrir hornið* around the
corner; (2) of time: before: *fyrir
hádegi(ð)* a.m.; *fyrir helgina* before
the weekend, before Sunday; (3)
for: *gerðu það fyrir mig* do it for
me (for my sake) (S. I, **2**, *3*, 2);
fyrir e-ð, fyrir sakir e-s for the sake
of sth (sbdy), on account of; *fyrir
peninga, fyrir gjald* for money, for
payment; (4) for, as: *nota herbergi fyrir skrifstofu* use a room as
a study; *fyrir víst* for certain,
surely; *fyrir fullt og allt* for good.
B. prep. with dat. (1) of place (in
phrases denoting rest): in front
of, before: *vera fyrir altarinu* be
(stand) in front of the altar, at
the altar (S. I, **3**, *3*, 2); to, for:
*fyrir honum eru þúsund ár sem
einn dagur* to him (for him) a
thousand years are like one day;
þú ert fyrir mér you are in my
way, you hamper me; (2) of time:
ago: *fyrir þremur dögum* three days
ago; *fyrir mörgum árum* many
years ago; (3) because of, on account of: *ekkert heyrist fyrir fossinum* nothing is (can be) heard
because of the waterfall; *ég gat
ekki sofið fyrir hávaða* I could not
sleep because of the noise; *fyrir því
að* conj. because (S. VIII, 3(b));
(4) by: *ganga fyrir raforku* go by
electricity. **C.** With advs or preps
as an adv. or prep. with acc. (1)
*fyrir austan, vestan, norðan, sunn-
an*, in the east, west, etc.; *fyrir
innan, utan, ofan, neðan, austan*
(etc.) *eitthvað* inside of, outside of,
above, below, east of (etc.) something; *austur fyrir ána* crossing the
river to the east, *út fyrir ána* crossing over to the river's lower (outer)
bank (In. IV, **1**, 3n4); (2) adv. in
front as a team: *í sleða með hreindýrum fyrir* in a sleigh drawn by
reindeer; *verða naumt fyrir* be
rather too late, *verða seinn fyrir*
be late; *leggjast fyrir* lie down.

Consonants: [ð] brea*th*e; [g] *g*ood; [gˌ] *gy*arden (garden); [hw̥] *wh*at; [j] *y*es; [kˌ] *cy*an
(can); [ŋ] thi*ng*; [q] N. Germ. sa*g*en; [r] Scottish *r*; [x] approx. Germ. a*ch*; [þ] *th*in.
Voiceless: ○; [b̥, d̥, g̊] approx. *p, t, k*. Half-voiced: *italics*. Aspiration and preaspiration:
[ʰ]; [pʰ, tʰ, kʰ] *p-, t-, k-*. Others as in English.

fyrirfram [fɪːrɪ(r)fram:] adv. in advance, beforehand (also *fyrir fram*).

fyrirframgreiðsla, -u, -ur [fɪːrɪ(r̥)- fram-·greið·sla, -ɣ(r̥)] wf.1 payment in advance, down payment.

fyrirgefa, -gef, -gaf, -gáfum, -gefinn (-ið) [fɪːrɪ(r)gjɛ:va, -gjɛ:v, ga·v, -gau·vɣm, -gjɛ:vɪn, -ɪð] v.5 forgive; *fyrirgefið þér* excuse me, pardon me; don't mention it, you are welcome (a polite phrase used when sbdy thanks for sth).

fyrirlestur, -lestrar, -lestrar [fɪːrɪ(r)- les·tɣr̥, -lestrar̥] m.1 lecture.

fyrirmynd, -ar, -ir [fɪːrɪ(r)mɪn·d̥, -ar̥. -ɪr̥] f.2 pattern, model; ideal.

fyrirtak, -s [fɪːrɪ(r̥)tʰa:kʰ(s), -tʰax·s; -tʰa:g̊] n. an excellent thing; often in compounds: *fyrirtaks-* excellent; *f-kaffi* excellent coffee.

fyrirtæki, -s, - [fɪːrɪ(r̥)tʰai:kjʰɪ(s); -tʰai:g̊jɪ] n. enterprise, business; concern.

fyrr [fɪr:] adv. compar. (see *snemma*) before, earlier, sooner; *ekki fyrr en eftir þrjár vikur* not earlier than in three weeks' time; *fyrr en* conj. before, until, sooner than; *ekki fyrr . . . en* no sooner . . . than (S. VIII, 3(h)).

fyrra [fɪr:a] wn. only in *í fyrra* last year (from older (*h*)*ið fyrra* the former).

fyrradagur [fɪr:ada:qɣr̥] m.1 day before yesterday; only in: *í fyrra-dag* the day before yesterday (also: *í fyrra dag*).

fyrramál [fɪr:amau:l] n. only in: *í fyrramálið* (or *í fyrra málið*) early tomorrow morning; *snemma í fyrramálið* first thing in the morning.

fyrri, fyrstur [fɪr:ɪ, fɪrstɣr̥] adj. compar. and superl. former, first; *fyrri*: former, first of two; *í fyrra dag, sumar, vetur* the day before yesterday, last summer, last winter (also in compound words: *fyrradag,*

-sumar, -vetur, etc.); *eins og fyrri daginn* as usual.

fyrrmeir [fɪr·mei·r] adv. of old, in the good old days (In. IV, 2(d)).

fyrrnefndur, -nefnd, -nefnt [fɪr·nem-dɣr̥, -nɛmd, -nɛmtʰ; -nɛm̥t] adj. first named, aforenamed, mentioned before.

fyrrv. = fyrrverandi [fɪr·vɛ·randɪ] adj. former, ex-; *fyrrverandi ráðherra* ex-minister.

fyrst [fɪs·t, fɪr̥st] (see *snemma*) (1) adv. first, *sem fyrst* as soon as possible; (2) conj. since (S. VIII, 3(b)).

fyrstur, fyrst, fyrst [fɪs·tɣr̥, fɪs·t; fɪr̥st(ɣr̥)] num.ord. first; *fyrsti* the first; also superl. of *fyrri* (which see); *fyrst og fremst* first and foremost, in the first place, above all, primarily.

fæ, see 2. *fá*.

fæða, fæddi, fæddur [fai:ða, faid:ɪ, faid:ɣr̥, faiʰt:] wv.2 bear (a child); feed, bring up; *fæðast* be born (S. VI, 7, 3).

fæði, -s [fai:ðɪ(s)] n. food, board; *taka (mann) í fæði* board a person, take sbdy as a boarder; *fæði og húsnæði* board and lodgings (room).

fæðutegund, -ar, -ir [fai:ðɣtʰɛ:qɣnd, -ar̥, -ɪr̥] f.2 kind of food.

fær, fær, fært [fai:r, fair̥t] adj. able, capable; fit for use; *fær um (að gera) e-ð* able to do sth; *fært veður* passable weather, *fær vegur* passable road.

færa, færði, færður (fært) [fai:ra, fair·ðɪ, -ɣr̥, fair̥t] wv.2 bring, move, remove; *færa (e-m e-ð) að gjöf* bring (sbdy sth) as a gift; *færa e-m e-ð* bring sbdy sth, serve (food); middle voice: *færast í aukana* grow in power; *færast úr stað* move (from one place), move; *ylur færist í fæturna* heat moves into the feet, warmth penetrates the feet.

færð, -ar, -ir [fair·ð, -ðar̥, -ðɪr̥] f.2 going, condition of the roads or trails.

Vowels: *a* [a] approx. *father*; *á* [au] *cow*; *e* [ɛ] *set*; *é* [jɛ] *yes*; *i, y* [ɪ] *sit*; *í, ý* [i] *feel*; *o* [ɔ] *law*; *ó* [ou] *note*; *u* [ɣ] approx. Germ. *Mütter*; *ú* [u] *school*; *y = i*; *ý = í*; *æ* [ai] *ice*; *ö* [ö] Germ. *hören*; *au* [öy] French *feuille*; *ei, ey* [ei] *ale*. Length [:]; half-length [·].

færi, -s, - [fai:rɪ(s)] n. fishing line.
færri, see *fár.* **fæstur,** see *fár.*
fætur, see *fótur.*
föður, see *faðir.*
föður- [fö:ðʏr̥-] in compounds: paternal: *föður-afi, -amma, -bróðir, systir* paternal grandfather, grandmother, uncle, aunt.
föðurnafn, -s, -nöfn [fö:ðʏr-nab̥n̥, -nabns, -naf·s, -nöb̥·n̥] n. patronymic; like *Jónsson* = son of *Jón.*
fögnuður, fagnaðar [fög̊·nʏðʏr̥, fag̊·naðar̥] m.3 joy.
fögur, see *fagur.*
föl, -s [fö:l, föl·s] n. a thin film of snow covering the ground.
fölsk, see *falskur.*
fölur, föl, fölt [fö:lʏr̥, fö:l, föl·t] adj. pale.
fölva, -aði, -að [föl·va, -aðɪ, -að] wv.4 cover with a film of snow.
föng, see *fang.*
1. **för, farar, farir** [fö:r, fa:rar̥, fa:rɪr̥] f.2 journey, voyage; *segja sínar farir ekki sléttar* tell of one's having had a rough going; *vera á förum* be going away.
2. **för,** see *far.*
föst, see *fastur.*
föstu, -ur, see *fasta.*
föstudagur, -s, -ar [fös·tʏ-da:qʏr̥, -dax·s, -da:qar̥] m.1 Friday; *föstudagurinn langi* Good Friday.
föt, see *fat.*
föx, see *fax.*

G.

1. **gá, gáði, gáð** [gau:, gau:ðɪ, gau:ð] wv.3 look, heed; *gá til veðurs* look at the weather; *gá að e-u* look after sth; look for sth (= *gá e-s*).
2. **gá,** see *ganga.*
gaddavír, -vírs, (-vírar) [gad:avi:r, -vɪr̥·s, (-vi:rar̥)] m.1 barbed wire.
gaddur, -s, -ar [gad:ʏr̥, gad·s, gad:ar̥] m.1 spike, barb, thorn; hardfrozen snow and ice.
gaf, gáfum, see *gefa.*
gáfa, -u, -ur, (-na) [gau:va, -ʏ(r̥),

gaub̥·na] wf.1 gift; pl. *gáfur* gifts of the mind, ability.
gáfaður, -uð, -að; -aðri, -aðastur [gau:vaðʏr̥, -ʏð, -að, -aðrɪ, -aðas tʏr̥] adj. gifted, brilliant, able.
gaffalbiti, -a, -ar [gaf:al-bɪ:tʰɪ, -a(r̥); -bɪ:dɪ] wm.1 tidbit (of herring).
gaffall, -als, -lar [gaf:adl̥, -als, gaf·-lar̥] m.1 fork.
gafl, -s, -ar [gab̥·l̥, gabls, gab̥·lar̥] m.1 gable, end of a house.
gaflherbergi, -s, - [gab̥·l̥-herberg̊ɪ(s)] n. garret.
1. **gagn, -s, gögn** [gag̊·n̥, gag̊·ns, gax·s, gög̊·n̥] n. gain, advantage; help, use, profit; *hafa gagn af e-u* profit from sth; *vera til gagns* be advantageous; *það er gagn að e-u* there is (real) help in sth, sth helps, is of avail; *það er gagn* it is fortunate, fortunately; *landsins gagn og nauðsynjar* the public weal; *gögn* material, evidence; tools, utensils (thus in the compound *hús-gögn* furniture).
2. **gagn-** [gag̊·n̥-] pref. through; against.
gagna, -aði, -að [gag̊·na, -aðɪ, -að] wv.4 *gagna e-m* help sbdy; *það gagnar ekki* it does not avail, it is of no avail.
gagnárás, -ar, -ir [gag̊·nau·raus, -ar̥, -ɪr̥] f.2 counter attack.
gagnauga, -, -u, (-na) [gag̊·nöy·qa, -ʏ, -öyg̊·na] wn. temple.
gagnfræðaskóli, -a, -ar [gag̊·nfrai·ða-skou:lɪ, -a(r̥)] wm.1 middle school, secondary school; somewhat similar to high school.
gagnkvæmur, -kvæm, -kvæmt [gag̊·n-kʰvai·mʏr̥, -kʰvai·m, -kʰvaimtʰ; -kʰvaimt] adj. reciprocal.
gagnsær, -sæ, -sætt; -særri, -sæjastur [gag̊·nsai·r, -sai·, -saiʰt·, -sair·ɪ, -sai·jastʏr̥] adj. transparent.
gagnvart [gag̊·nvar̥t] prep. with dat. opposite.
gala, gel, gól, gólum, galinn (-ið) [ga:la, g̊ɛ:l, gou:l, gou:lʏm, ga:-lɪn, -ɪð] v.6 or (more commonly):
gala, -aði, -að [ga:la, -aðɪ, -að] wv.4

Consonants: [ð] brea*th*e; [g] *g*ood; [gɟ] *gy*arden (garden); [hw] *wh*at; [j] *y*es; [kɟ] *cy*an (can); [ŋ] thi*ng*; [q] N. Germ. sa*g*en; [r] Scottish *r*; [x] approx. Germ. a*ch*; [þ] *th*in. Voiceless: ○; [b̥, d̥, g̊] approx. *p, t, k.* Half-voiced: *italics.* Aspiration and preaspiration: [ʰ]; [pʰ, tʰ, kʰ] *p-, t-, k-.* Others as in English.

345

crow, sing; *fagurt galaði fuglinn sá* beautifully sang that bird; *haninn galar* the cock (rooster) crows.

Galdra-Loftur, -s [galdra-lɔf·ty̥r̥,-lɔfts] m.1 the greatest figure in Icelandic magic, an Icelandic Faust; a play by Jóhann Sigurjónsson.

galdramaður, -manns, -menn [gal·drama:ðy̥r̥, -man·s, -mɛn:] m.4 magician, sorcerer.

galdraöld, -aldar [gal·dra-öl·d̦, -al·dar̥] f.2 the age of magic (in Iceland the 17th century).

galdur, (-ri), -urs, -rar [gal·dy̥r̥(s), gal·drar] m.1 sorcery, magic; *brenndur fyrir galdra* burned for (the sake of) sorcery.

galinn, -in, -ið; galnari, galnastur; galdari, galdastur [ga:lɪn, -ɪn, -ið; gal·narɪ, -asty̥r̥; gal·darɪ, -asty̥r̥] adj. crazy; wild, insane.

1. gall, -s [gad·l̦, gal·s] n. gall.

2. gall, see 2. *gjalla.*

galli, -a, -ar [gad·lɪr, -a(r̥)] wm.1 drawback.

galt, see *gjalda.*

Galtalækur, -s [gal·ta-lai:kʰy̥r̥, -lai:kʰs; -lai·g̊-] m.1 'Hog Creek.'

galtar, see *göltur.*

gamall, gömul, gamalt; eldri, elztur [ga:madl, gö:mY̥l, ga:malt; ɛldrɪ, ɛlsty̥r̥] adj. old; *sá gamli* the old one; *í gamla daga* of old, in the (good) old days (In. III, 2(a)7; 3, 1; 4, 5); *gamla árið* 'the old year,' the past year.

gaman, (-ni), -ans [ga:man; gam·nɪ, gan:ɪ, ga:mans] n. fun; *hafa gaman af e-u* be amused by sth, be interested in sth, be fond of sth; *maður er manns gaman* (proverbial) man is pleased by man, man is consoled by man; *það væri gaman* that would be fun; *í gamni* in fun, facetiously.

gamlárskvöld, -s, - [gam·lau̥rs-kʰvöl·d̦, -s] n. New Year's Eve.

1. ganga, göngu, -ur [gauŋ·g̊a, göyŋ··g̊Y̥(r̥)] wf.1 walk; walking; pl.

göngur (= *fjallgöngur*) the round-up of sheep in the mountains, taking place in June and September every year.

2. ganga (gá) geng, gekk, gengum, genginn (-ið) [gauŋ·g̊a, gau:, g̊ɪeiŋ·g̊, g̊ɪɛk:, g̊ɪeiŋ·g̊Y̥m, g̊ɪeiŋ·g̊ɪɪn, -ið] v.7 go, walk, take a walk, climb; pass; go, run (of watches, engines); go so and so; extend; (1) go, walk; *gakk, gáttu* (imperative; In. VII, 4, 6, 1n3) go, walk; *koma gangandi* come walking; *ganga þurrum fótum* walk dry-shod; *hann er genginn burt* he has gone away (S. VI, 3, 3); *hvað ætli það sé lengi gengið?* how long a walk might it be? (2) go (of watches, engines, etc.): *ganga rétt* go true, keep time; *klukkan er farin að ganga tvö* the clock is past one, it is past one; *klukkan er langt gengin tvö* it is near two o'clock; (3) go so and so: *e-m gengur vel* (impers.) it goes well for sbdy; sbdy has good luck; *þetta gengur* this is the common (recurrent) thing; (4) of natural features: extend: *nes gekk út í vatnið* a ness (peninsula) extended into the lake; (5) with preps and advs: *ganga á fjall* climb a mountain; *ganga á hönd e-m* give oneself up to sbdy, surrender to sbdy; *ganga á* be going on, *hvað gengur á?* what is going on? *ganga á upphlut* wear upphlutur (a bodice) habitually; *ganga að e-u* walk up to sth; accept sth, agree to sth; be the matter with sth (*e-m* sbdy); *ganga aftur* walk (again) (of ghosts); haunt; *ganga frá e-m* go away from sbdy, leave sbdy; *ganga* (*vel, illa*) *frá e-u* do sth (well or badly); finish off; *ganga fyrir raforku* (*vatnsafli*) be driven by electricity (water power); *hann er að ganga í byl* a blizzard is coming up; *ganga í skóla* go to school; *ganga með ánni* (= *meðfram ánni*)

Vowels: *a* [a] approx. father; *á* [au] cow; *e* [ɛ] set; *é* [jɛ] yes; *i, y* [ɪ] sit; *í, ý* [i] feel; *o* [ɔ] law; *ó* [ou] note; *u* [Y̥] approx. Germ. Mütter; *ú* [u] school; *y* = *i*; *ý* = *í*; *æ* [ai] ice; *ö* [ö] Germ. hören; *au* [öy] French *feuille*; *ei, ey* [ei] ale. Length [:]; half-length [·].

346

walk along the river; *ganga með
e-ð* have sth; *ganga undir nafni*
go by a name, be called; *ganga
undir próf* take an examination;
ganga upp í ána (of the tide) flow
into; *ganga upp (í e-u)* of division:
come out even; *ganga við œrnar*
go inspecting the ewes.

gangstétt, -ar, -ir [gauŋ‧g̊stjeʰt‧(ar̥),
-ɪr] f.2 sidewalk.

gangur, -s, -ar [gauŋ‧g̊ʏr̥, gauŋ‧s,
gauŋ‧g̊ar̥] m.1 walk; passage, corridor; goings on (= *ógangur, lœti*),
racket, noise.

gardína, -u, -ur [gar‧di‧na, -ʏ(r̥)] wf.1
curtain.

garður, -s, -ar [gar‧ðʏr̥, garðs, gar‧-
ðar̥] m.1 vegetable garden, garden,
park; wall; *í garðinum* in the
garden; also = *heygarður* stackyard.

gárungi, -a, -ar [gau:ruŋg̊ɪ, -uŋg̊a(r̥)]
wm.1 wag.

gas, gass [ga:s, gas:] n. heating gas;
gas, poison gas (= *eiturgas*).

gassprengja, -u, -ur [ga:spreiŋg̊ɪa,
-g̊ɪʏ(r̥)] wf.1 gas shell.

1. gat, -s, göt [ga:tʰ, ga:tʰs, gö:tʰ;
ga:d, gö:d] n. hole; *bora gat á e-ð*
bore (drill) a hole in (through) sth.

2. gat, gátum, see *geta*.

gata, götu, -ur [ga:tʰa, gö:tʰʏ(r̥)]
wf.1 street; in street-names: *-gata*.

gáta, -u, -ur [gau:tʰa, -ʏ(r̥); gau:da]
wf.1 riddle.

gaumur, -s [göy:mʏr̥, göym‧s] m.1
attention, heed, consideration; *gefa
e-u fyllsta gaum* give the most careful attention to sth.

gaus, see *gjósa*.

gaut, see *gjóta*.

gefa, gef, gaf, gáfum, gefinn (-ið)
[g̊ɪɛ:va, g̊ɪɛ:v, ga:v, gau:vʏm,
g̊ɪɛ:vɪn, -ɪð] v.5 give, grant; serve
(food); deal (cards); *gefa e-m e-ð*
give sbdy sth; (1) give, grant:
gefa leyfi give leave, grant permission; *mér var gefið leyfi* I was
given leave (S. VI, 8, *3*); *gefa nafn*
give a name, call; *gefa gaum* pay
attention to, heed; *gefa sér tíma*

til e-s take the time for sth (to do
sth); (2) with preps and advs:
gefa af sér produce; *gefa e-ð í skyn*
hint sth, indicate sth; *gefa saman
hjón* marry a couple (the ceremony); *gefa út* publish.

gefandi, -a, -endur [g̊ɪɛ:vandɪ, -a,
-ɛndʏr̥] wm.2 giver.

Gefjun, -ar [g̊ɪɛv‧jʏn, -ʏnar̥] f.2 an
old Icelandic goddess; name of a
textile factory.

1. gegn [g̊ɪɛg̊‧n̥] prep. with dat.
against; *í gegn* adv. through; *í gegn
um e-ð* through sth; *gegn honum*
against him; *gegn ljósinu* against
the light.

2. gegn- [g̊ɪɛg̊‧n̥-] pref. through, trans-.

gegna, gegndi, gegnt [g̊ɪɛg̊‧na, g̊ɪeiŋ‧dɪ,
g̊ɪeiŋ‧tʰ; g̊ɪeiŋ̊‧t] wv.2 *gegna e-m* obey
sbdy *gegndu mér!* obey me! *gegna
e-u* obey, pay attention to sth, *ég
gegni því ekki* I pay no attention
to that.

gegnt [g̊ɪɛŋ‧tʰ; g̊ɪɛŋ̊‧t] prep. with dat.
opposite, against, facing; *hún sat
gegnt honum* she sat opposite him.

gegnum [g̊ɪɛg̊‧nʏm] prep. with acc.
(= *gegn um*) through.

geiri, -a, -ar [g̊ɪei:rɪ, -a(r̥)] wm.1
wedge-shaped strip, gore.

geisa, -aði, -að [g̊ɪei:sa, -aðɪ, -að]
wv.4 ravage.

geisli, -a, -ar [g̊ɪeis‧lɪ, -a(r̥)] wm.1
ray, beam.

geit, -ar, -ur [g̊ɪei:tʰ, -ar̥, -ʏr̥; g̊ɪei:d-]
f.3 goat.

gekk, see *ganga*.

gel, see *gala*.

geld, see *gjalda*.

gell, see 1. *gjalla*.

gelta, gelti, gelt [g̊ɪɛl‧ta, g̊ɪɛl‧tɪ,
g̊ɪɛl‧t] wv.2 bark; *gelta að e-m*
bark at sbdy.

geltir, see *göltur*.

geng, gengið, -inn, -um, see *ganga*.

gengi, -s [g̊ɪeiŋ‧g̊ɪ(s)] n. exchange,
rate of exchange; *gengið núna* the
current rate of exchange.

gera, gerði, gerður (gert) [g̊ɪɛ:ra,
g̊ɪer‧ðɪ, g̊ɪer‧ðʏr̥, g̊ɪer̥‧t] or:

Consonants: [ð] brea*th*e; [g] *g*ood; [g̊ɪ] *gy*arden (garden); [hw] *wh*at; [j] *y*es; [kɪ] *cy*an
(can); [ŋ] thi*ng*; [q] N. Germ. sa*g*en; [r] Scottish *r*; [x] approx. Germ. a*ch*; [þ] *th*in.
Voiceless: ○; [b̥, d̥, g̊] approx. *p, t, k*. Half-voiced: *italics*. Aspiration and preaspiration:
[ʰ]; [pʰ, tʰ, kʰ] *p-, t-, k-*. Others as in English.

gjöra, gjörði, gjörður (gjört) [g‚ö:ra, g‚ör·ðɪ, g‚ör·ðʏɽ, g‚ör̥·t] wv.2 do, make; (1) do, make: *hafa mikið að gera* have much to do, be busy; *hér er ekkert að gera* here (there) is nothing to be done (S. VI, 11, 6); *gerðu svo vel að* (*og*) . . . *gerið þér svo vel að* (*og*) literally: 'do so well as to,' be so kind as to, please; *gera at* stir up a riot; *gera innkaup* buy provisions, make purchases; *gera e-ð fyrir e-n* do sth for sbdy; *gera e-m gott* give sbdy a treat, treat sbdy with charity; *gera e-m e-ð* do sth to sbdy; *gera sig lítinn* make oneself small; (2) impers.: *gerði gott veður* (acc.) literally: 'it made good weather,' i. e. the weather became fine; (3) middle voice: *gerast* become; (4) auxiliary: *gerir syngja = syngur* does sing (only in poetry) (S. VI, 13, 11); (5) with preps and advs: *gera á hluta e-s* do injustice to sbdy, wrong one; *gera að e-u* do sth about sth, *hann gat eigi að gert* he could do nothing about it, *ég get ekki að því gert* I cannot help it, *ég get ekki að mér gert að hlœja* I cannot help laughing; *gera e-ð að e-u* make (turn) sth into sth; *gera sig að e-u* turn oneself into sth; take the shape of sth; *gera sér e-ð að góðu* put up with sth, accept sth with good grace; *gera lítið* (*mikið*) *að e-u* practise sth much (little), be given (averse) to doing sth; *hafa ekki mikið að gera í hendurnar á e-m* be no match for sbdy; *hafa að gera með e-n* (*e-ð*) have to do with sbdy (sth); *gera til* matter, *hvað gerir það til?* what does that matter, *það gerir ekkert til* that does not matter, it is all right; *gera e-ð úr e-u* make sth (out) of sth; *gera við úrið, bílinn* repair the watch, the car, *gera við* mend, repair, overhaul, rebuild.

gerð, -ar, -ir [g‚er·ð, -ðaɽ, -ðɪɽ] f.2 kind, make; *af nýjustu gerð* of the most recent make, the latest model.

gerði, -s, - [g‚er·ðɪ, -s] n. hedge, fence; also in place names: *-gerði.*

gerill, -ils, gerlar [g‚e:rɪḍl, -ɪls, g‚erd·lar] m.1 bacteria.

gerilsneyða, -sneyddi, -sneyddur (-sneytt) [g‚e:rɪl-snei·ða, -sneid·ɪ, -ʏr, -sneiʰt:] wv.2 pasteurize.

gerla (gjörla) [g‚erḍla, g‚örḍla] adv. clearly, thoroughly.

gerlafræði [g‚erḍla-frai:ðɪ] wf.2 bacteriology.

gersemi, -, -ar [g‚er·se·mɪ, -aɽ] wf.2 precious thing, gem.

gervi, -s, - [g‚er·vɪ(s)] n. guise, garb.

gestrisinn, -in, -ið; -risnari, -astur [g‚es·trɪ·sɪn, -ɪn, -ɪð; -rɪsnarɪ, -astʏr] adj. hospitable.

gestrisni [g‚es·trɪsnɪ] wf.2 hospitality.

gestur, -s, -ir [g‚es·tʏɽ, g‚ests, -g‚es·tɪɽ] m.2 guest; customer.

geta, get, gat, gátum, getinn (-ið) [g‚e:tʰa, g‚e:tʰ, ga:tʰ, gau:tʰʏm, g‚e:tʰɪn, -ɪð; g‚e:da, g‚e:d, ga:d, gau:dʏm, g‚e:dɪn, -ɪð] v.5 (1) beget: *geta son* beget a son; (2) mention, guess: *geta e-s* mention sth, guess sth; *geta um e-ð* mention sth; *þú getur því nærri að* you can imagine (guess) that . . . , impers.: *þess getur ekki = þess er ekki getið* it is not mentioned (S. VI, 14, 7); (3) auxiliary: be able to, may, can. In this sense the pp. is *getað*, and the verb is construed with a past participle; whereas the English *can* takes the infinitive (S. VI, 13, 3): *ég get komið* I can come; *geta gert e-ð* be able to do sth (S. VI, 12, 2, 3); *get ég . . . ?* may I . . . ? *get ég fengið e-ð* (or *að gera e-ð*)? can I get sth (or: may I do sth)? *gætirðu* (= *gaztu*) *fundið mig?* could you see me (for a moment)? (S. VI, 9, 2, 2); *við gætum reynt* we could try; *það getur verið* it may be; *það getur orðið* it may become (be); *út af þeirri reglu getur brugðið* that rule may be deviated from, broken.

Vowels: *a* [a] approx. father; *á* [au] cow; *e* [ɛ] set; *é* [jɛ] yes; *i, y* [ɪ] sit; *í, ý* [i] feel; *o* [ɔ] law; *ó* [ou] note; *u* [ʏ] approx. Germ. Mütter; *ú* [u] school; *y = i; ý = í;* æ [ai] ice; *ö* [ö] Germ. hören; *au* [öy] French feuille; *ei, ey* [ei] ale. Length [:]; half-length [·].

geyja, gey, gó, góum, - [g₁ei:ja, g₁ei:, gou:, gou:ɤm] v.6 bark (the usual word is *gelta*).

geyma, geymdi, geymdur (geymt) [g₁ei:ma, g₁eim·d̥ɪ, g₁eim·d̥ɤr, g₁eim·tʰ; geim̥·t] wv.2 put away, store, preserve, keep; *geyma e-ð* (also *geyma e-s*) preserve, keep sth.

geymsla, -u, -ur [g₁eimsla, -ɤ(r̥)] wf.1 keeping, preserving; storeroom, storage.

geysi- [g₁ei:sɪ-] pref. extremely, exceedingly.

geysimargur, -mörg, -margt; [g₁ei:sɪmar·g̊ɤr̥, -mör·g̊, -mar̥·t] adj. extremely many.

Geysir, -is [g₁ei:sɪr̥, -ɪs] m.1 'The Gusher,' the most famous hot spring in Iceland, from which the English word 'geyser' is derived.

geysistór, -stór, -stórt [g₁ei:sɪ-stou:r, -stour̥·t] adj. huge, gigantic.

gifta, gifti, gift(ur) [g₁ɪf·ta, g₁ɪf·tɪ, g₁ɪf·t(ɤr̥)] wv.2 marry, give in marriage; *gifta sig = giftast* marry, take a husband or wife; *hann gifti dóttur sína ríkum kaupmanni* he married his daughter to a rich merchant; *presturinn gifti þau* the parson married them.

gifting, -ar, -ar [g₁ɪf·tiŋg̊(ar̥)] f.1 marriage.

gigt, -ar [g₁ɪx·t, -ar̥] f.2 rheumatism, arthritis.

gil, -s, - [g₁ɪ:l, g₁ɪl·s] n. gorge, chasm, glen, gill, ravine; also in place names: *-gil*, *Gils-*, e. g. *Gils-á*.

gilda, gilti, gilt(ur) [g₁ɪl·da, g₁ɪl·tɪ, g₁ɪl·t(ɤr̥)] wv.2 be valid; *það gildir einu* it is all the same; *það gildir einu, þó að . . .* it is just as well, if . . .

gildi, -s, - [g₁ɪl·d̥ɪ(s)] n. worth, value (of money); *vera í gildi* (= *gilda*) retain one's value, be valid, current.

gildra, -u, -ur [g₁ɪl·dra, -ɤ(r̥)] wf.1 trap.

gildvaxinn, -in, -ið; -vaxnari, -astur [g₁ɪl·dvaxsɪn, -ɪn, -ɪð, -vaxsnarɪ, -astɤr̥] adj. square-built, thickset.

Gísli, -a, -ar [g₁is·lɪ, -a(r̥)] wm.1 pers. name; hero of *Gísla saga*.

gista, gisti, gist [g₁ɪs·ta, g₁ɪs·tɪ, g₁ɪs·t] wv.2 stay over night.

gistihús, -s, - [g₁ɪs·tɪhu:s, -hus:] n. hotel, inn.

gizka, -aði, -að [g₁ɪs·ka, -aðɪ, -að| wv.4 guess; *gizka á e-ð* guess (at) sth.

gjá, gjár, gjár [g₁au:(r)] f.1 rift, chasm, gorge, cleft.

gjafir, -ar, see *gjöf*.

gjald, -s, gjöld [g₁al·d̥(s), g₁öl·d̥] n. payment; *fyrir visst gjald* for a certain payment.

gjalda, geld, galt, guldum, goldinn (-ið) [g₁al·da, g₁el·d̥, gal·t, gɤl·d̥ɤm, gɔl·dɪn, -ið] v.3 pay: *gjalda skatt* pay tax(es); *gjalda e-s* pay for sth (figuratively speaking); have to take the consequences for sth.

gjaldeyrir, -is [g₁al·d̥ei·rɪr̥, -ɪs] m.1 currency.

1. gjalla, -aði, -að [g₁ad̥·la, -aðɪ, -að] wv.4 or:

2. gjalla, gell, gall, gullum, gollið [g₁ad̥·la, g₁ed̥·l, gad·l, gɤd·lɤm, gɔd·lɪð] v.3 speak loudly, yell.

gjamma, -aði, -að [g₁am:a, -aðɪ, -að] wv.4 bark, yelp.

gjár, see *gjá*.

gjárbakki, -a, -ar [g₁aur·baʰk₁·ɪ, -baʰk·ar̥] wm.1 bank, brink of a gorge.

gjarðar, see 2. *gjörð*.

gjarn, gjörn, gjarnt [g₁ad̥·n̥, g₁öd̥·n̥, g₁an·tʰ; g₁ard̥n̥, g₁örd̥n̥; g₁an̥·t] adj. eager.

gjarna(n); heldur, helzt [g₁ad̥·na(n); g₁ard̥na; hel·d̥ɤr̥, helst] adv. willingly, eagerly; more, most willingly, eagerly.

gjósa, gýs, gaus, gusum, gosinn (-ið) [g₁ou:sa, g₁i:s, göy:s, gɤ:sɤm, gɔ:sɪn, -ið] v.2 gush, spout, erupt.

gjóta, gýt, gaut, gutum, gotinn (-ið) [g₁ou:tʰa, g₁i:tʰ, göy:tʰ, gɤ:tʰɤm, gɔ:tʰɪn, -ɪð; g₁ou:da, g₁i:d̥, göy:d̥, gɤ:d̥ɤm, gɔ:dɪn, -ɪð] v.2 dart; *gjóta augum* dart the eyes, turn the eyes;

Consonants: [ð] brea*th*e; [g] *g*ood; [g₁] *gy*arden (garden); [hw] *wh*at; [j] *y*es; [k₁] *cy*an (can); [ŋ] thi*ng*; [q] N. Germ. sa*g*en; [r] Scottish *r*; [x] approx. Germ. a*ch*; [þ] *th*in. Voiceless: ○; [b̥, d̥, g̊] approx. *p, t, k*. Half-voiced: *italics*. Aspiration and preaspiration: [ʰ]; [pʰ, tʰ, kʰ] *p-, t-, k-*. Others as in English.

of dogs, foxes, cats, etc.: bear:
tíkin er gotin the bitch (tyke) has
had her whelps, has littered.

gjöf, gjafar, gjafir [g͵ö:*v*, g͵a:va͡ɾ,
-ɪ͡ɾ] f.2 gift, present; *að gjöf* as a
gift.

gjöld, see *gjald.*

gjöra, gjörði, gjört, see *gera.*

1. gjörð, see *gerð.*

2. gjörð, gjarðar, -ir [g͵ör·ð, g͵ar·ða͡ɾ,
-ɪ͡ɾ] f.2 girdle; girth, saddlegirth.

gjörla, see *gerla.*

gjörn, see *gjarn.*

gjörvuleikur, -s [g͵ör·vɤ·lei:kʰɤ͡ɾ,
-lei:kʰs; -lei:g̊-] m.2 accomplish-
ment, talent.

gladdi, -ur, see *gleðja.*

glaðlyndi, -s [glað·lɪndɪ(s)] n. cheerfulness, sunny disposition.

glaður, glöð, glatt [gla:ðɤ͡ɾ, glö:ð,
glaʰt:] adj. glad, pleased.

glampa, -aði, -að [glam·pʰa, -aðɪ, -að;
glam·pa] wv.4 gleam; *það glampar
á e-ð* sth gleams.

Glámur, -s [glau:mɤ͡ɾ, glaum·s] m.1
famous ghost in *Grettis saga.*

glápa, glápti, glápt [glau:pʰa, glauf·-
tɪ, glauf·t; glau:ba] wv.3 stare.

glas, -s, glös [gla:s, glas:, glö:s] n.
small bottle; a glass; *glas af mjólk*
(= *mjólkurglas*) a glass of milk,
glas af vatni (= *vatnsglas*) glass
of water.

glatt, see *glaður* and *gleðja.*

gleði, -, -ir [glɛ:ðɪ(͡ɾ)] wf.2 gladness,
good humor; comedy, pl. comedies.

gleðilegur [glɛ:ðɪ·lɛ:qɤ͡ɾ] adj. (see
-legur) joyous, joyful; *gleðileg jól*
happy Christmas; *gleðilegt nýjár*
happy New Year.

gleðja, gladdi, gladdur (glatt) [glɛð·ja,
glad:ɪ, -ɤ͡ɾ, glaʰt:] wv.1 please,
gladden; *gleðjast* rejoice (S. VI,
7, 4).

gleggri, gleggstur, see *glöggur.*

gleraugnalaus, -laus, -laust [glɛ:r-
öyg̊na-löy:s, -löys·t] adj. without
glasses; *gleraugnalaust* adv. without glasses.

gleraugu, -augna [glɛ:röy·qɤ, -öyg̊na]

n.pl. glasses, spectacles; *tvenn
gleraugu* two pairs of glasses.

glerhurð, -ar, -ir [glɛ:rhɤrð, -ða͡ɾ,
-ðɪ͡ɾ] f.2 glass door.

glervörur [glɛr·vö·rɤ͡ɾ] wf.1.pl. glass,
china and earthenware.

glervöruverzlun, -unar, -anir [glɛr·-
vörɤ-verslɤn, -yna͡ɾ, -anɪ͡ɾ] f.2 china
and earthenware store.

gletta, -u, -ur [glɛʰt:a, -ɤ(͡ɾ)] wf.1
prank; *gera e-m glettur* tease, play
pranks upon.

gleyma, gleymdi, gleymdur (gleymt)
[glei:ma, gleim·dɪ, gleim·dɤ͡ɾ,
gleim·tʰ; gleim·t] wv.2 forget;
gleyma e-u forget sth.

1. glíma, -u, -ur [gli:ma, -ɤ(͡ɾ)] wf.1
wrestling.

2. glíma, glímdi, glímdur (glímt)
[gli:ma, glim·dɪ, -ɤ͡ɾ, glim·tʰ;
glim·t] wv.2 wrestle; *glíma við e-n*
wrestle with sbdy; *glíma af snilld*
wrestle artistically.

glímufélag, -s, -lög [gli:mɤ-fjɛ:laq,
-laxs, -löq] n. wrestling club.

glímugarpur, -s, -ar [gli:mɤ-gar·pɤ͡ɾ,
-s, -a͡ɾ] m.1 =

glímukappi, -a, -ar [gli:mɤ-kʰaʰp:ɪ,
-a(͡ɾ)] wm.1 good wrestler, wrestling champion.

glímukóngur, -s, -ar [gli:mɤ-kʰouŋ·-
g̊ɤ͡ɾ, -kʰouŋ·s, -kʰouŋ·g̊a͡ɾ] m.1 wrestling champion.

glímumaður, -manns, -menn [gli:mɤ-
ma:ðɤ͡ɾ, -man·s, -mɛn:] m.4 wrestler.

glímusnillingur, -s, -ar [gli:mɤ-snɪd·-
liŋɤ͡ɾ, -iŋs, -iŋg̊a͡ɾ] m.1 wrestling
artist.

glitra, -aði, -að [glɪt:ʰra, -aðɪ, -að;
glɪ:dra] wv.4 glitter, gleam.

gljá, gljáði, gljáð [gljau:, gljau:ðɪ,
gljau:ð] wv.3 shine, glitter, gleam;
gljá(i)r sól á hlíð ' the sun glitters
on the hillside; ' the hillside gleams
in the sunshine.

gljúfur, (-ri), -urs, -ur [glju:vɤ͡ɾ(s),
gljuv·rɪ] n. gorge, glen, chasm,
ravine.

glóa, gló(a)ði, gló(a)ð [glou:a, -(a)ðɪ,
-(a)ð] wv.3 & 4 glow, shine.

Vowels: *a* [a] approx. father; *á* [au] cow; *e* [ɛ] set; *é* [jɛ] yes; *i, y* [ɪ] sit; *í, ý* [i] feel;
o [ɔ] law; *ó* [ou] note; *u* [ɤ] approx. Germ. Mütter; *ú* [u] school; *y* = *i*; *ý* = *í*; *æ* [ai] ice;
ö [ö] Germ. hören; *au* [öy] French *feuille*; *ei, ey* [ei] ale. Length [:]; half-length [·].

350

glóaldin, -s, - [glou:aldɪn, -ɪns] n.
= appelsína.

glóð, -ar, -ir; glæður [glou:ð, glou:-
ðar̥, -ɪr̥; glai:ðʏr̥] f.2 & 3 embers,
hot, glowing embers; ardor, fire.

glóðarbaka, -aði, -að(ur) [glou:ðar-
ba:kʰa, -aðɪ, -að, -aðʏr̥; -ba:g̊a]
wv.4 bake on hot embers.

glóðarsteikja, -steikti, -steikt(ur)
[glou:ðar̥-stei:k¸ʰa, -steix-tɪ, steix-t,
-ʏr̥, -stei:g̊¸a] wv.2 toast on hot
embers, roast on embers.

glotta, glotti, glott [glɔʰt:a, -ɪ, glɔʰt:]
wv.3 grin.

gluggatjald, -s, -tjöld [glʏg̊:a-tʰjal·d̥,
-s, -tʰjöl·d̥] n. = gardína, curtain.

gluggi, -a, -ar [glʏg̊¸:ɪ, glʏg̊:a(r̥)]
wm.1 window.

glæða, glæddi, glæddur (glætt) [glai:-
ða, glaid̥:ɪ, glaid̥:ʏr̥, glaiʰt:] wv.2
kindle; glæðast grow, increase.

glæður, see glóð.

glænýr, -ný, -nýtt [glai:ni·r̥, -ni·,
-niʰt·] adj. quite fresh.

glæpamaður, -manns, -menn [glai:pʰa-
ma:ðʏr̥, -man·s, -men:; glai:b̥a-]
m.4 criminal.

glöð, see glaður.

glöggur, glögg, glöggt; gleggri, gleggstur; glögg(v)ari, glögg(v)astur
[glög̊:ʏr̥, glög̊:, glöx·t; gleg̊·rɪ,
glɛxstʏr̥; glög̊:(v)arɪ, -astʏr̥] adj.
observant, keen; clear.

glöggva, -aði, -að [glög̊:va, -aðɪ, -að]
wv.4 make clear; glöggva sig á e-u
get a clearer picture (view) of sth.

glös, see glas.

gnýja, gnúði, gnúð(ur) [gni:ja, gnu:-
ðɪ, gnu:ð, -ðʏr̥] wv.1 storm, rage.

gnæfa, gnæfði, gnæft [gnai:va, gnaiv-
ðɪ, gnaif·t] wv.2 tower, loom, soar.

gó, góum, see geyja.

góa, -u, -ur [gou:a, -ʏ(r̥)] wf.1 from
the middle of February to the
middle of March; next to last
month before summer.

góð- [gou:ð-] pref. good.

góðgerð (-gjörð), -ar, -ir [gouð·g̊¸ɛrð,
-g̊¸erðar̥, -ɪr̥; -g̊¸örð] f.2 kind deed,

charitable deed; treat; cf. gera
e-m gott treat sbdy to sth.

góðgæti, -s [gouð·g̊¸ai·tʰɪ(s); -g̊¸ai·d̥ɪ]
n. things good to eat; goodies.

góðmenni, -s, - [gouð·mɛn·ɪ(s)] n.
kindhearted man, kind man.

góður, góð, gott; betri, beztur [gou:-
ðʏr̥, gou:ð, g̊ɔʰt:; bɛ:tʰrɪ, bɛs·tʏr̥;
bɛ:drɪ] adj. good, fine, smart; kind,
dear; góði vinur dear friend; góði
minn, góða mín my dear; góður við
e-n (góður e-m) good, kind to sbdy;
restored to health: hvernig ertu
(af gigtinni) núna? how are you
now (how is your arthritis now)?
Og ég er orðinn góður Oh, I have
gotten all right; hafa það gott be
fine; verði þér (yður) að góðu
'may you benefit by this,' you are
welcome (a polite phrase used in
answering an expression of thanks) ;
allt gott everything fine; með góðu
eða illu by fair means or foul;
launa illt með góðu requite evil
with good (S. III, 3, 2); gott er
að (inf.) it is good to; þér væri
betra að hætta you had better stop;
það er bezt ég hætti I'd better stop
(In. III, 2 (b)5a; 4, 5); betri
borgarar better citizens.

góðvild, -ar [gouð·vɪld̥(ar̥)] f.2 kindness, good will.

gól, gólum, see gala.

gola, -u, -ur [gɔ:la, -ʏ(r̥)] wf.1 breeze.

goldið, -inn, see gjalda.

gólf, -s, - [goul·v, goul·(v)s] n. floor.

gólfábreiða, -u, -ur [goul·vau-brei:ða,
-ʏ(r̥)] wf.1 =

gólfteppi, -s, - [goul·(v)tʰɛʰp·ɪ(s)] n.
rug.

gollið, see 2. gjalla.

gómur, -s, -ar [gou:mʏr̥, goum·s,
gou:mar̥] m.1 fingertip; palate;
þeim bar margt á góma 'many
things crossed their palates,' i. e.
they gossiped (spoke) of many
things.

góna, góndi, gónt [gou:na, goun·d̥ɪ,
goun·tʰ; goun·t] wv.3 stare.

gosi, -a, -ar [gɔ:sɪ, -a(r̥)] knave
(jack) (in cards).

Consonants: [ð] breathe; [g] good; [g¸] gyarden (garden); [hw] what; [j] yes; [k¸] cyan
(can); [ŋ] thing; [q] N. Germ. sagen; [r] Scottish r; [x] approx. Germ. ach; [þ] thin.
Voiceless: ○ ; [b̥, d̥, g̊] approx. p, t, k. Half-voiced: italics. Aspiration and preaspiration:
[ʰ]; [pʰ, tʰ, kʰ] p-, t-, k-. Others as in English.

gosið, -inn, see *gjósa*.

gotið, -inn, see *gjóta*.

gott, see *góður*.

gr. = *gramm*.

grá, see *grár*.

grafa, gref, gróf, grófum, grafinn (-ið) [gra:va, grɛ:v, grou:v, grou:vɣm, gra:vɪn, -ɪð] v.6 dig, bury; engrave; *grafa ósinn út* dig out the mouth of the river, open up the (blocked) estuary.

gráfíkja, -u, -ur [grau:fi·k‚a, -k‚ɣ(r̥); -fi·g̊‚a] wf.l fig. (= *fíkja*).

grafningur, -ings, -ingar [grab·niŋg̊ɣr̥, -iŋs, -iŋg̊ar̥] m.l ditch, trench.

gramm, -s, grömm [gram:, gram·s gröm:] n. gram.

grammófónn, -s, -ar [gram:ou·foud̥·n̥, -foun·s, -fou:nar̥] m.l grammophone.

grammófónplata, -plötu, -ur [gram:-oufoun-pʰla:tʰa,-pʰlö:tʰɣ(r̥); -pʰla:-da, -pʰlö:d̥ɣ(r̥)] wf.l grammophone record.

gramur, gröm, gramt [gra:mɣr̥, grö:m, gram·tʰ; gram̥·t] adj. angry, peeved, a little bit irritated; *gramur e·m* = *gramur við e·n* peeved with (at) sbdy.

granaldin, -s, - [gra:naldɪn, -ɪns] n. pineapple (= *ananas*).

grannur, grönn, grannt; grennri, grennstur [gran:ɣr̥, grön:, gran·tʰ; gran̥·t; grɛn:rɪ, grɛnstɣr̥] adj. slender; *grannt sérhljóð* 'lax' vowel (Pr. 2, 2, 3).

grannvaxinn, -in, -ið; -vaxnari, -astur [gran:vaxsɪn, -ɪn, -ɪð; -vaxsnarɪ, -astɣr̥] adj. slender.

grár, grá, grátt; grárri, gráastur [grau:r, grau:, grauʰt:; graur:ɪ, grau:astɣr̥] adj. grey; *grái hesturinn* the grey horse (S. II, 2); *sá grái = Gráni* the grey horse (S. III, 3, 3).

gras, -s, grös [gra:s, gras:, grö:s] n. grass.

grasgefinn, -in, -ið; -gefnari, -astur [gra:sg‚ɛ·vɪn, -ɪn, -ɪð; -g‚ɛb̥narɪ, -astɣr̥] adj. grassy; fertile.

grasigróinn, -in, -ið [gra:sɪ-grou:ɪn,

-ɪn, -ɪð] adj. grass-grown, covered with grass.

grastó, -tóar, -tór [gra:stʰou·(r), -tʰou·ar̥] f.l splotch of greensward in cliffs.

gráta, græt, grét, grétum, grátinn (-ið) [grau:tʰa, grai:tʰ, grjɛ:tʰ, grjɛ:tʰɣm, grau:tʰɪn, -ɪð; grau:d̥-, grai:d̥, grjɛ:d̥-] v.7 weep, *ekki að gráta* don't weep (S. VI, 10, 3).

grátt, see *grár*.

grautur, -ar, -ar [gröy:tʰɣr̥, -ar̥; gröy:d̥ɣr̥] m.l cooked cereal, porridge, pudding (In. I, 2, 1(b)11).

gref, see *grafa*.

greiða, greiddi, greiddur (greitt) [grei:ða, greid̥:ɪ, greid̥:ɣr̥, greiʰt:] wv.2 pay; unravel, comb; *greiða sér* comb one's hair.

greiði, -a, -ar [grei:ðɪ, -a(r̥)] wm.l favor, service, good turn; *gera e·m greiða* do sbdy a favor.

greiðsla, -u, -ur [greið·sla, -ɣ(r̥)] wf.l payment; combing of the hair, hairdressing, hair-do.

greiðvikinn, -in, -ið; -viknari, -astur [greið·vɪ·k‚ɪn, -ɪn, -ɪð; -vɪʰknarɪ, -astɣr̥] adj. obliging, ready to do a good turn or favor; *greiðvikinn við e·n* helpful to sbdy.

grein, -ar, -ar (-ir) [grei:n, -nar̥, -nɪr̥] f.l & 2 branch, bough; distinction, discernment; paragraph; essay; subject; *það kemur ekki til greina* that is out of the question, that is not to be considered or thought of.

greindur, greind, greint [grein·d̥ɣr̥, grein·d̥, grein·tʰ; grein̥·t] adj. intelligent, discerning; *greindur maður* an intelligent man.

1. greip, -ar, -ar [grei:pʰ, -ar̥; grei:b̥] f.l the space between the fingers, especially between thumb and fingers; *sækja ekki gull í greipar e·s* literally: ' not to (be able to) fetch gold from another's grip,' i. e. suffer ignominious defeat at the hands of sbdy

2. greip, see *grípa*.

greitt, see *greiða*.

grennd, -ar, -ir [grɛn·d̥, -ar̥, -ɪr̥] f.2

Vowels: *a* [a] approx. father; *á* [au] *cow*; *e* [ɛ] set; *é* [jɛ] *ye‥*; *i, y* [ɪ] sit; *í, ý* [i] *feel*; *o* [ɔ] law; *ó* [ou] note; *u* [ɣ] approx. Germ. Mütter; *ú* [u] school; *y = i*; *ý = í*; *æ* [ai] *ice*; *ö* [ö] Germ. hören; *au* [öy] French *feuille*; *ei, ey* [ei] *ale*. Length [:]; half-length [·].

neighborhood; *hér í grenndinni* in the neighborhood.

grennri, grennstur, see *grannur.*

greri, gréri, see *gróa.*

grét, -um, see *gráta.*

Gréta, -u [grjɛːtʰa, -ʏ; grjɛːd̥-] wf.1 pet name of *Margrét.*

Grettir, -is [grɛʰtːɪr̥, -ɪs] m.1 pers. name; hero of *Grettis saga.*

grimmilega [grɪmːɪ-lɛːqa] adv. fiercely.

grimmur, grimm, grimmt [grɪmːʏr̥, grɪmː, grɪmːtʰ; grɪm̥t] adj. fierce.

Grímsá, -ár [grim-sau-(r)] f.1 'Grímur's river.'

grípa, gríp, greip, gripum, gripinn (-ið) [griːpʰa, griːpʰ, greiːpʰ, grɪːpʰʏm, grɪːpʰɪn, -ɪð; griːb̥-, greiːb̥, grɪːb̥-] v.1 grab, grasp, seize.

gripahús, -s, - [grɪːpʰa-huːs, -husː; grɪːba-] n. usually in pl. houses, sheds, barns, stables for the domestic animals (*gripir*).

gripur, -s, -ir [grɪːpʰʏr̥, grɪːpʰs, grɪːpʰɪr̥; grɪːb̥-] m.2 domestic animal pl. livestock; thing of value; jewel(ry).

grís, -s, -ir (-ar) [griːs, grisː, griːsɪr̥, -ar] m.2 or 1 pig.

grjót, -s, - [grjouːtʰ(s); grjouːd̥] n. stones, rocks; pl. rocky ground.

grjótgarður, -s, -ar [grjouːtʰgarðʏr̥, -garðs, -garðar̥] m.1 stone wall.

gróa, græ; greri, gréri, gröri; gróinn (-ið) [grouːa, graiː, grɛːrɪ, grjɛːrɪ, gröːrɪ, grouːɪn, -ɪð] v.irreg. (In. VII, 5, 2), grow.

gróður, (-ri), -rar [grouːðʏr̥, grouð-rɪ, -rar̥] m.3 vegetation.

gróðurhús, -s, - [grouːðʏr̥-huːs, -husː] n. hothouse.

gróðurreitur, -s (-ar), -ir [grouːðʏ(r)-reiːtʰʏr̥, -s, -ar̥, -ɪr̥; -reiːd̥-] m.2 hotbed.

gróf, -um, see *grafa.*

Grótta, -u [grouʰtːa, -ʏ] wf.1 in Old Icelandic: the name of a famous mill; a low headland near Reykjavík.

gruna, -aði, -að(ur) [grʏːna, -aðɪ, -að, -aðʏr̥] wv.4 suspect; *mig grun-*

ar (e-ð) I suspect (sth) (S. I, 2, 1, 3; VI, 14, 5).

grund, -ar, -ir [grʏnd̥, -ar̥, -ɪr̥] f.2 dry level field of grass.

Grundarstígur, -s [grʏn-dar-stiːqʏr̥, -stixs] m.1 'Field Path,' in Reykjavík.

grunndiskur, -s, -ar [grʏnːdɪskʏr̥, -s, -ar̥] m.1 (shallow) plate.

grunnhygginn, -in, -ið; -hyggnari, -astur [grʏnːhɪɡ̊ɪn, -ɪn, -ɪð; -hɪɡ̊narɪ, -astʏr̥] adj. gullible, not too bright.

1. grunnur, -s, -ar [grʏnːʏr̥, grʏnːs, grʏnːar̥] m.1 foundation, base, background, backdrop; *á svörtum grunni* on a black background.

2. grunnur, grunn, grunnt; grynnri, grynnstur. [grʏnːʏr̥, grʏnː, grʏnːtʰ; grʏnːt; grɪnːrɪ, grɪnːstʏr̥] adj. shallow, flat; *grunnur diskur* a shallow plate (= *grunndiskur*).

Grýla, -u, -ur [griːla, -ʏ(r̥)] wf.1 an ogress in Icelandic folklore, used to scare children, a bugbear; name of a geyser.

grynnri, grynnstur, see *grunnur.*

græ, see *gróa.*

græðgi [graiðɡ̊ɪ] wf.2 greed.

grængolandi [graiŋgɔlandɪ] adj. deep and dark-green.

grænkál, -s [graiŋkʰauːl, -kʰauls] n. kale.

grænklæddur, -klædd, -klætt [graiŋ-kʰlaidʏr̥, -kʰlaid̥-, -kʰlaiʰt-] adj. clad in green.

Grænland, -s [grain-land̥, -lan(d̥)s] n. Greenland.

grænmeti, -s [grain-mɛtʰɪ(s), -mɛd̥ɪ] n. vegetables.

grænn, græn, grænt; grænni, grænastur [graid̥-n̥, graiːn, grain-tʰ; grain-t; graid̥-nɪ, grai-nastʏr̥] adj. green.

græskulaus, -laus, -laust [grais-kʏ-löyːs, -löys-t] adj. without malice, innocent; *græskulaust gaman* innocent fun.

græt, see *gráta.*

gröm, see *gramur.*

grömm, see *gramm.*

Consonants: [ð] breathe; [g] good; [ɡ̊] gyarden (garden); [hw] what; [j] yes; [kɟ] cyan (can); [ŋ] thing; [q] N. Germ. sagen; [r] Scottish r; [x] approx. Germ. ach; [þ] thin. Voiceless: ◌̥; [b̥, d̥, ɡ̊] approx. p, t, k. Half-voiced: italics. Aspiration and preaspiration: [ʰ]; [pʰ, tʰ, kʰ] p , t-, k-. Others as in English.

353

grönn, see *grannur*.

gröri, see *gróa*.

grös, see *gras*.

grösugur [grö:sʏqʏr̥] adj. (see -*ugur*) grassy.

guð, -s, -ir [gvʏ:ð, gvʏð·s, gvʏ:ðɪr̥] m.2 God (Pr. 3, 2, 5(a); In. I, 2, 2(b)2).

Guðbjörg, -bjargar [gvʏð·björǥ, -bjar- ǥar̥] f.2 pers. name.

Guðbrandur, -s (-ar) [gvʏð·brandʏr̥, -bran(d)s, -brandar̥] m.1 pers. name.

guðfræði [gvʏð·frai·ðɪ] wf.2 theology.

guðfræðideild, -ar, -ir [gvʏð·frai·ðɪ- deil·d̥, -ar̥, -ɪr̥] f.2 faculty (depart- ment) of theology.

guðfræðingur, -ings, -ingar [gvʏð·- frai·ðiŋǥʏr̥, -iŋs, -iŋǥar̥] m.1 theo- logian, student of theology.

guðfræðisdeild = guðfræðideild.

Guðjón, -s [gvʏð·jou·n, -jouns] m.1 pers. name.

Guðlaug, -ar [gvʏð·löy·q, -qar̥] f.1 pers. name.

Guðmundur, -ar (-s) [gvʏð·mʏndʏr̥, -mʏndar̥, -mʏn(d)s] m.1 pers. name; in patr.: *Guðmundsson, -dóttir*.

Guðni, -a [gvʏð·nɪ, -a] wm.1 pers. name.

Guðný, -nýjar [gvʏð·ni·(jar̥); gvʏ:- ni·(jar̥)] f.1 pers. name.

Guðríður, -ar [gvʏð·ri·ðʏr̥, -ar̥; gvʏ:- ri·ðʏr̥] f.1 pers. name.

Guðrún, -ar, -ar (-ir) [gvʏð·ru·n, -ru·nar̥, -ɪr̥] f.1 & 2 pers. name.

guðspjall, -s, spjöll [gvʏð·spjaɖl̥, -spjals, -spjöɖl] n. gospel.

guðspjallamaður,-manns,-menn [gvʏð·- spjaɖla·ma:ðʏr̥, -man·s, -mɛn:] m.4 evangelist.

guðsþjónusta, -u, -ur [gvʏð·sþjou·- nʏsta, -ʏ(r̥)] wf.1 divine service.

gufa, -u, -ur [gʏ:va, -ʏ(r̥)] wf.1 steam.

gufuhreinsun, -unar, -anir [gʏ:vʏ- hr̥ein·sʏn, -ʏnar̥, -anɪr̥] f.2 steam cleaning.

gufuhver, -s, -ar (-ir) [gʏ:vʏ·hwɛ:r, -hwɛr·s, -hwɛ:rar̥, -ɪr̥; -kʰvɛ:r, etc.] m.1 & 2 steam geyser; one spouting steam instead of water.

guldum, see *gjalda*.

gull, -s, - [gʏd·l̥, gʏl·s] n. gold; *úr gulli* of gold; pl. *gull* playthings, toys (S. II, 3).

gullbrúðkaup, -s, - [gʏd·lbruðkʰöy:pʰ, -kʰöyf·s; -kʰöy:b] n. golden anni- versary of a wedding.

gullbúinn, -in, -ið [gʏd·lbu·ɪn, -ɪn, -ɪð] adj. adorned with gold.

Gullfoss, - [gʏd·lfɔs·] m.1 'Gold Falls,' famous waterfall in the South of Iceland; name of a boat.

gullum, see 2. *gjalla*.

gulmórauður, -rauð, -rautt [gʏl·- mɔröy:ðʏr̥, -röy:ð, -röyʰt:; gʏl·- mou·-] adj. yellow-brown.

gulrót, -ar, -rætur [gʏl·rou·tʰ, -ar̥, -rai·tʰʏr̥; -rou·d̥, -rai·dʏr̥] f.3 carrot.

gulur, gul, gult [gʏ:lʏr̥, gʏ:l, gʏl·t] adj. yellow.

gúmmí, -s [gum:i·(s)] n. rubber.

gúmmískór, -s, -r [gum:i·skou:r, -skou:s] m.1 rubber shoe.

gúmmístígvél, -s, - [gum:i·stiq·vjɛl, -vjɛls] n. rubber boot.

Gunna, -u, -ur [gʏn:a, -ʏ(r̥)] wf.1 pet name for *Guðrún*.

Gunnar, -ars [gʏn:ar̥(s)] m.1 pers. name; a famous hero of *Njála*.

gúrka, -u, -ur [gur̥·ka, -ʏ(r̥)] wf.1 cucumber.

gusum, see *gjósa*.

gutl, -s [gʏʰtl̥(s)] n. dabbling.

gutum, see *gjóta*.

gyðingakökur, [g‚ɪ:ðiŋǥa-kʰö:kʰʏr̥, -kʰö:ǥʏr̥] wf.1.pl. sugar cookies.

Gyðingur, -ings, -ingar [g‚ɪ:ðiŋǥʏr̥, -iŋs, -iŋǥar̥] m.1 Jew; *gyðinga-* Jewish.

Gyllir, -is [gɪd·lɪr̥, -ɪs] m.1 in Old Icelandic myths: one of the horses of the gods; modern: the name of a trawler.

gýs, see *gjósa*.

gýt, see *gjóta*.

gæði [g‚ai:ðɪ] n.pl. kindness; (good) quality.

gæfa, -u [g‚ai:va, -ʏ] wf.1 good luck; *það er sitt hvað gæfa eða gjörvu- leikur* (proverbial) good luck and

---

Vowels: *a* [a] approx. *father*; *á* [au] *cow*; *e* [ɛ] *set*; *é* [jɛ] *yes*; *i, y* [ɪ] *sit*; *í, ý* [i] *feel*; *o* [ɔ] *law*; *ó* [ou] *note*; *u* [ʏ] approx. Germ. *Mütter*; *ú* [u] *school*; *y* = *i*; *ý* = *í*; *æ* [ai] *ice*; *ö* [ö] Germ. *hören*; *au* [öy] French *feuille*; *ei, ey* [ei] *ale*. Length [:]; half-length [·].

good looks (or talent) are different things.

gælunafn, -s, -nöfn [gˌai:lɣ-nab·n̩(s), -naf·s, -nöb·n̩] n. pet name, hypocoristic name.

gær [gˌai:r] adv. yesterday; only in the phrase: *í gær* yesterday.

gærdagur, -dags [gˌair·da·qɣr̩, -daxs] m.1 *í gærdag* yesterday.

gærkvöld, -s [gˌair·kʰvöld(s)] n. yesterday evening; *í gærkvöldi* last night.

gæta, gætti, gætt [gˌai:tʰa, gˌaiʰt:ɪ, gaiʰt:] wv.2 take care of, watch, heed, notice; consider; *gæta e-s, gæta að e-u* take care of sth, look after sth; *þegar þess er gætt* when you consider; impers.: *e-s gætir (ekki)* sth is (not) noticeable.

gögn, see *gagn*.

göltur, galtar, geltir [göl·tɣr̩, gal·tar̩, gˌɛl·tɪr̩] m.3 hog, boar.

gömul, see *gamall*.

göng, ganga [göyŋ·g̊, gauŋ·g̊a] n.pl. corridor, passage.

göngu(r), see *ganga*.

gönguskór [göyŋ·g̊ɣ-skou:r] m.1.pl. walking shoes.

göt, see *gat*.

götu, -ur, see *gata*.

götuhorn, -s, - [gö:tʰɣ-hɔd·n̩(s); -gö:dɣ-] n. street corner.

götunafn, -s, -nöfn [gö:tʰɣ-nab·n̩(s), -naf·s, -nöb·n̩; gö:dɣ-] n. streetname.

göturenna, -u, -ur [gö:tʰɣ-rɛn:a, -ɣ(r̩); gö:dɣ-] wf.1 gutter.

göturæsi, -s, - [gö:tʰɣ-rai:sɪ(s); gö:dɣ-] n. gutter.

H.

ha [ha:] interr. interj. what? beg your pardon! excuse me!

1. há, see 2. *hár*.

2. há, háði, háð(ur) [hau:, hau:ðɪ, hau:ðɣr̩] wv.3 hold a meeting (*há þing*); *há e-m* handicap sbdy.

3. há- [hau:-] pref. high.

háaustur, (-ri), -urs [hau:-öys·tɣr̩(s), -öystrɪ] n. due east.

hádagur, -s [hau:da·qɣr̩, -daxs] m.1 noontide; *um hádaginn* in the middle of the day.

hádegi, -s [hau:dei·jɪ(s)] n. noon, midday.

hádegisbil, -s [hau:dei·jɪs-bɪ:l, -bɪl·s] n. noontime, noontide; *um hádegisbilið* at noon, about noon.

hádegisleyti, -s [hau:dei·jɪs-lei:tʰɪ(s); -lei:dɪ] n. about noon.

hádegisstaður, -ar, -ir [hau:dei·jɪsta:-ðɣr̩, -ar̩, -ɪr̩] m.3 the place where the sun is at noon, south.

hádegisútvarp, -s, -vörp [hau:dei·jɪs-u:tʰvarp(s), -u:tʰvör̩p; -u:d-] n. noon broadcast.

hádegisverður, -ar, -ir [hau:dei·jɪs-vɛr·ðɣr̩, -ar̩, -ɪr̩] m.3 = *miðdegisverður* (*-matur*) lunch.

háði, -ur, see 2. *há*, and 2. *heyja*.

háður, háð, háð [hau:ðɣr̩, hau:ð] adj. dependent, unfree; *háður e-m* dependent on sbdy.

haf, -s, höf [ha:v, haf·s, hö:v] n. sea, ocean; *til hafsins* towards the sea; further out to sea, in the offing.

hafa; hef, hefi; hafði, hafður (haft) [ha·va, hɛ:v, hɛ:vɪ, hav·ðɪ, hav·ðɣr̩, haf·t] wv.3 & 1 have, keep, hold; get, take; have to (do); (1) have: *hafa e-ð* have sth; *hafa sýningu* have (hold, give) an exhibition; *hafa á sér helgi* have holiness, be sacred; *hafa mikið (lítið) að gera* have much (little) to do, be busy, not busy; *hafa lítið að gera í hendurnar á e-m* be no match for sbdy; *hafa að gera með e-n* have to do with sbdy; have to deal with sbdy; *hafa á að skipa* have available, have at one's disposal; *hafa betur* win; *láta hafa sig til e-s* let oneself be used for sth; (2) get: *hafa fregnir af* get news from, hear of; get, take: *hafðu þetta* take this; *látið þér mig hafa það* let me have it; *hafa Oddann* get the Oddi; (3) middle voice: *hafast (e-ð) að* do

---

Consonants: [ð] brea*th*e; [g] *g*ood; [gˌ] *gy*arden (garden); [hw] *wh*at; [j] *y*es; [kˌ] *cy*an (can); [ŋ] thi*ng*; [q] N. Germ. sa*g*en; [r] Scottish *r*; [x] approx. Germ. a*ch*; [þ] *th*in. Voiceless: ○; [b̥, d̥, g̥] approx. *p, t, k*. Half-voiced: *italics*. Aspiration and preaspiration: [ʰ]; [pʰ, tʰ, kʰ] *p-, t-, k-*. Others as in English.

sth, be occupied in doing sth; *hafast
við* dwell; (4) auxiliary: to have:
hafa verið have been; *ég hef (hafði)
verið* I have (had) been (S. VI,
1, *2*) ; *hafa farið* have gone (S. VI,
12, 2, 2) ; *hafðu sæll gert* good for
you to have done this, well done!
(S. VI, 9, *2*, 1n2) ; (5) with preps
and advs: *hafa e-ð eftir e-m* repeat
(quote) sth after sbdy; *hafa e-ð
fyrir e-ð* use sth as sth; *hafa mikið
(lítið) fyrir e-m* go to much (little)
trouble on sbdy's account; *hafa
með sér* take with one; *hafa til
(tilbúinn)* have ready, hold in
readiness; *hafa e-ð til* to have sth
in one's possession, in stock; be
liable to, be prone to (do sth);
hafa það til að be liable to; *hafa
e-n útundan* discriminate against
sbdy.

hafgola, -u, -ur [hav·gɔ·la, -ʏ(r̥)]
wf.1 sea breeze.

hafið, -inn, see *hefja.*

háflóð, -s, - [hau:flou·ð, -flouðs] n.
high tide.

hafnar, -ir, see *höfn.*

hafnarbakki, -a, -ar [hab̦·nar-baʰk̦:ɪ,
-baʰk:a(r̥)] wm.1 quay.

Hafnarfjörður, -fjarðar [hab̦·nar-fjör-
ðʏr̥, -fjar·ðar̥] m.3 'Haven Fjord.'

hafnargarður, -s, -ar [hab̦·nar-gar-
ðʏr̥, -garðs, -gar·ðar̥] m.1 'harbor
wall,' a mole.

hafnbann, -s, -bönn [hab̦·ṇban·, -bans,
-bön·] n. blockade.

hafnlaus, -laus, -laust [hab̦·nlöy·s,
-löyst] adj. without harbors.

hafragrautur, -ar, -ar [hav·ra-gröy:-
tʰʏr̥, -ar̥; -gröy:d̦·] m.1 oatmeal
(porridge).

haframjöl, -s [hav·ra-mjö:l, -mjöl·s]
n. oatmeal.

Hafstein, -s [haf·stei·n, -steins] m.1
family name; *Hannes Hafstein*
(1861-1922) poet and first prime
minister of Iceland.

1. haft, -s, höft [haf·t(s), höf·t] n.
hobble, fetter.

2. haft, see *hafa.*

Hafursey, -eyjar [ha:vʏr̥sei:, -ei:jar̥]

f.1 'Buck Island,' an isolated mountain in South Iceland.

hafvillur [hav:ɪdlʏr̥] wf.1.pl. being
off course at sea; loss of one's
course at sea.

Hagalín, -s [ha:qali:n, -lin·s] m.1
family name.

hagi, -a, -ar [hai:jɪ, ha:qa(r̥) ; ha:jɪ]
wm.1 pasture, land for grazing.

hagsmunir [hax·smʏ·nɪr̥] m.3.pl. interest, profit, *til hagsmuna fyrir
e-n* to profit sbdy, for sbdy's benefit.

hagur, -s, -ir [ha:qʏr̥, hax·s, hai:jɪr̥;
ha:jɪr̥] m.2 state, economic status;
condition.

halda, held, hélt, héldum, haldinn (-ið)
[hal·da, hɛl·d̦, hjɛl·t, hjɛl·dʏm, hal·-
dɪn, -ið] v.7 hold, keep; think, consider, hold; give, deliver; celebrate;
go, proceed; (1) with dat.: *halda
e-m (e-u)* keep, retain, detain sbdy
(sth), preserve sth; *halda vatni*
hold water, be watertight; (2) with
acc.: hold, think (with *að*-clause):
haldið þér (að þér) vilduð? do you
think you would . . .? *ég held (að)
ég taki* I think I shall (I'll) take
. . . , *hann hélt (að) skipið kæmi*
he thought the ship was coming;
with acc. and inf.: *halda e-n vera
e-ð* consider sbdy to be sth; (3)
with acc.: *halda fyrirlestur (um
e-ð)* give a lecture (on sth); *halda
hljómleika* give a concert; *halda
námskeið* give special courses for a
short period; *halda fund* hold a
meeting; *halda hátíð* celebrate a
festival; *halda heilagt* celebrate;
halda hjú keep servants; (4) middle voice: *haldast ekki við* not be
able to stick it out; *góða veðrið
hélzt* the good weather remained,
kept on; (5) with preps and advs:
halda á e-u hold sth (in the hand);
halda á e-u keep sth; *halda á (af)
stað* start, go, proceed (on a
journey); *halda áfram* keep going,
proceed, continue; *halda e-u áfram*
carry on with sth, continue sth;
halda heim(leiðis) go home, pro-

Vowels: *a* [a] approx. father; *á* [au] cow; *e* [ɛ] set; *é* [jɛ] yes; *i, y* [ɪ] sit; *í, ý* [i] feel;
o [ɔ] law; *ó* [ou] note; *u* [ʏ] approx. Germ. Mütter; *ú* [u] school; *y = i; ý = í; æ* [ai] ice;
ö [ö] Germ. hören; *au* [öy] French *feuille; ei, ey* [ei] ale. Length [:]; half-length [·].

356

ceed to go home; *halda í land* go
(row) ashore; *halda e-ð um e-ð*
hold, consider, think sth about sth;
halda upp á e-n (*e-ð*) celebrate,
like, be fond of sbdy (sth); *halda
sér við e-ð* keep to sth, stick to sth.

hálendi, -s, - [hau:lendɪ(s)] n. mountain plateau.

hálf- [haul·v-] pref. half; quite, somewhat.

hálfáttræður, -ræð, -rætt [haul·v-
auʰt:rai·ðʏr̥, -rai·ð, -raiʰt·] adj.
seventy-five years old.

Hálfdan, -ar (Hálfdán) [haul·(v)-
da(u)·n, -da(u)·nar̥] m.1 pers.
name Haldane.

hálffertugur, -tug, -tugt [haul·-fer̥·-
tʏqʏr̥, -tʏq, -tʏxt] adj. thirty-five
years old.

hálffimmtugur, -tug, -tugt [haul·-fɪm·-
tʰʏqʏr̥, -tʰʏq, -tʰʏxt; -fɪm̥·t-] adj.
forty-five years old.

hálffjögur [haul·fjö:qʏr̥] num. card.
n. of time: three thirty, half past
three.

hálfmánar [haul·(v)mau·nar̥] wm.1.
pl. turnovers (cookies).

hálfna, -aði, -að(ur) [haul·(v)na,
-aðɪ, -að, -aðʏr̥] wv.4 finish half of
sth; *hálfnaður* half done.

hálfsmánaðar- [haul·s·mau·naðar̥-]
pref. of a fortnight, of two weeks.

hálfsóla, -aði, -að(ur) [haul·(v)sou·-
la, -aðɪ, -að, -aðʏr̥] wv.4 half-sole
(a shoe).

hálftímagangur, -s [haul·tʰi·ma·gauŋ·-
ǧʏr̥, -gauŋ·s] m.1 half hour's walk.

hálftími, -a, -ar [haul·tʰi·mɪ -a(r̥)]
wm.1 half an hour.

hálftvö [haul·tʰvö:] num. card. n. of
time: one thirty, half past one.

hálfur, hálf, hálft [haul·vʏr̥, haul·v,
haul·t] adj. (mostly strong) half;
hálfur annar one and a half; *hálfur
þriðji* two and a half, etc.

hálfvilltur, -villt, -villt [haul·(v)-vɪl·-
tʏr̥, -vɪl̥·t] adj. half wild; quite
wild.

hálfþrítugur, -tug, -tugt [haul·þri:-

tʰʏqʏr̥, -tʰʏq, -tʰʏxt; -þri:d̥-] adj.
twenty-five years old.

hálfþrjú [haul·þrju:] num. card. n. of
time: two thirty, half past two.

hali, -a, -ar [ha:lɪ, -a(r̥)] wm.1 tail
(of a cow).

hálka, -u [haul·kʰa, -ʏ; haul̥·ka] wf.1
slipperiness.

háll, hál, hált [haud̥·l, hau:l, haul̥·t]
adj. slippery, smooth.

halla, -aði, -að [had·la, -aðɪ, -að] wv.4
slope, incline; *lítt hallandi* gently
sloping.

hallar, -ir, see *höll*.

Halldór, -s [hal·dou·r, -dour̥s] m.1
pers. name.

Halldóra, -u [hal·dou·ra, -ʏ] wf.1.pers.
name.

Hallgrímur, -s [had̥·lgri·mʏr̥, -grims]
m.1 pers. name.

halló [hal:ou:] interj. hello (used in
telephoning).

Hallormsstaður, -ar [had̥·lɔrm(s)-
sta:ðʏr̥, -ar̥] m.1 place name.

háls, -, -ar [haul·s(ar̥)] m.1 neck,
throat (= *kok*); ridge of land, hill;
góðir hálsar! gentlemen! (S. III,
2, 5n).

hálsbindi, -s, - [haul·sbɪndɪ(s)] n.
necktie.

hálsbólga, -u, -ur [haul·sboulǧa, -ʏ(r̥)]
wf.1 inflammation of the throat,
tonsilitis.

hálsbrotna, -aði, -að(ur) [haul·sbrɔʰt-
na, -aðɪ, -að, -aðʏr̥] wv.4 break
one's neck.

hálskirtill, -ils, -lar [haul·skjʰɪrtɪd̥l,
-ɪls, -lar̥] m.1 tonsil.

haltra, -aði, -að [hal·tra, -aðɪ, -að]
wv.4 limp; be lame, hobble.

haltur, hölt, halt [hal·tʏr̥, höl̥·t, hal̥·t]
adj. lame.

1. hamar, -ars, -rar [ha:mar(s), ham·-
rar̥] m.1 hammer; cliff, rock.

2. hamar, -ir, see *höm*.

hamast, -aðist, -azt [ha:mast, -aðɪst,
-ast] wv.4 (middle voice only)
hamast við e-ð work like a fury
at sth.

hamingja, -u, -ur [ha:miŋǧ̊ja, -ǧ̊jʏ(r̥)]

Consonants: [ð] brea*the*; [g] *g*ood; [gj] *gy*arden (garden); [hw] *wh*at; [j] *y*es; [kj] *cy*an
(can); [ŋ] thi*ng*; [q] N. Germ. sa*g*en; [r] Scottish *r*; [x] approx. Germ. a*ch*; [þ] *th*in.
Voiceless: ○; [b̥, d̥, g̊] approx. *p, t, k*. Half-voiced: *italics*. Aspiration and preaspiration:
[ʰ]; [pʰ, tʰ, kʰ] *p-, t-, k-*. Others as in English.

357

wf.1 luck, happiness; *til allrar hamingju* fortunately, luckily; *óska til hamingju* wish luck, extend felicitations to.

hamingjuósk, -ar, -ir [ha:mɪnǧᵣous·k, -aᵣ, -kⱼɪᵣ] f.2 felicitation.

hampur, -s [ham·pʰɣᵣ, -s, hampɣᵣ] m.1 hemp.

hana, see *hani* and *hún*.

handa [han·da] prep. with dat. for; *handa henni* for her.

handaband, -s, -bönd [han·da-ban·d(s), -bön·d] n. handshake; *heilsast með handabandi* shake hands with.

handan [han·dan] prep. with gen. on the other side of; *handan storms og strauma* beyond storms and stresses (currents).

handar, see *hönd*.

handklæði, -s, - [han·dkʰlai·ðɪ(s)] n. towel (= *þurrka*).

handleggur, -s, -ir, (-ja) [han·dlɛǧ·ɣᵣ, -lɛǧs, -lɛxs, -lɛgⱼɪᵣ, -lɛgⱼa] m.2 arm (= *armur*).

handleggsbrotna, -aði, -að [han·dlɛxsbrɔʰt·na, -aðɪ, -að] wv.4 break an arm.

handrið, -s, - [han·drɪ·ð, -rɪðs] n. railing.

handrit, -s, - [han·drɪ·tʰ(s); -rɪ·d] n. manuscript.

handsápa, -u, -ur [han·dsau·pʰa, -ɣ(ᵣ), -sau·ba] wf.1 face soap (literally: hand soap).

handsnyrting, -ar [han·dsnɪᵣtɪnǧ(aᵣ)] f.1 manicure.

handsprengja, -ju, -jur [han·dspreɪnǧⱼa, -ǧⱼɣ(ᵣ)] wf.1 hand grenade.

handtaska, -tösku, -ur [han·(d)tʰaska, -tʰöskɣ(ᵣ)] wf.1 handbag, suitcase, travelling bag.

1. hanga, hangi, hékk, héngum, hanginn (-ið) [hauŋ·ga, hauŋ·ǧⱼɪ, hⱼɛʰk:, hⱼeɪŋ·ǧɣm, hauŋ·ǧⱼɪn, -ɪð] v.7 or (more rarely):

2. hanga, hangdi, hangt [hauŋ·ga, hauŋ·dɪ, hauŋ·tʰ; hauŋ·t] wv.3 hang (intr.).

hangiket (-kjöt), -s [hauŋ·ǧⱼɪ-kⱼʰɛ:tʰ, kⱼʰö:tʰ, -s] n. smoked meat (usually mutton).

hanginn, -in, -ið [hauŋ·ǧⱼɪn, -ɪn, -ɪð] adj. hung, smoked (of meat).

hani, -a, -ar [ha:nɪ, -a(ᵣ)] wm.1 cock (rooster).

hankar, -ir, see *hönk*.

hann, hún, það [han:, hu:n, þa(:ð)], acc. *hann, hana, það* [ha:na], dat. *honum, henni, því* [hɔ:nɣm, hɛn:ɪ, þ(v)i:], gen. *hans, hennar, þess* [han·s, hɛn:aᵣ, þɛs:]; pl. *þeir, þær, þau* [þeiːr, þai:r, þöy:], acc. *þá, þær, þau* [þau:], dat. *þeim* [þei:m], gen. *þeirra* [þeir:a] third pers. pron. he, she, it, etc.; they, etc. (Pr. 4, 3; In. VI, 1, 3); impers.: (of the weather) *hann snjóar* it snows (S. IV, 1, 4(b); VI, 14, 3); *þeir Gunnar* they, those just mentioned and Gunnar; they, G. and his companions; *þau Gunnar* they, G. and a woman; *þau hjónin* they, the married couple (S. IV, 1, 3); *húsið hans Jóns* (= *hús Jóns*) John's house (S. II, 4); *hann Jón* John, our John; *hann boli* the (well known) bull; *það dimmir* it is getting dark; *það er bezt að hætta* it is best to cease (we had better cease); *það var einu sinni karl* there was once upon a time an old man (S. IV, 1, 5 a-c); *það er sagt* it is said; *þeir segja* they say, people say (S. VI, 14, 2).

Hannes, -ar (-s) [han:ɛ·s, -aᵣ] m.1 pers. name; patronymic: *Hannesson*.

hánorður, (-ri), -urs [hau:nɔr·ðɣᵣ(s), -nɔrðrɪ] n. due north.

hans, see *hann*.

hanzki, -a, -ar [hansk·ɪ, -ka(ᵣ)] wm.1 glove.

1. hár, -s, - [hau:r, hauᵣ·s] n. hair.

2. hár, há, hátt; hærri, hæstur [hau:r, hau:, hauʰt:; hair:ɪ, hais·tɣᵣ] adj. high, tall; loud; *tala hátt* speak loudly.

Haraldur, -s (-ar) [ha:raldɣᵣ, ha:·ral(d)s, -daᵣ] m.1 pers. name Harald,

Vowels: *a* [a] approx. father; *á* [au] cow; *e* [ɛ] set; *é* [jɛ] yes; *i, y* [ɪ] sit; *í, ý* [i] feel; *o* [ɔ] law; *ó* [ou] note; *u* [ɣ] approx. Germ. Mütter; *ú* [u] school; *y = i; ý = í;* *æ* [ai] ice; *ö* [ö] Germ. hören; *au* [öy] French *feuille; ei, ey* [ei] ale. Length [:]; half-length [·].

358

Harold; patronymic: *Haraldsson,
-dóttir.*

háralitur, -litar [hau:ra-lɪ:tʰʏr̩, -ar̩;
-lɪ:d̥-] m.3 color of the hair.

Haralz [ha:rals] m. indecl. family
name.

harðfiskur, -s, -ar [har-ð̥fɪskʏr̩, -fɪsks,
-fiskar̩] m.1 hard fish, dried fish
(cod, haddock), stockfish.

harðla [hardla] adv. very.

harðna, -aði, -að(ur) [hardn̥a, -aðɪ,
-að̥, -aðʏr̩] wv.4 harden, get hard,
get tough, toughen.

harðsoðinn, -in, -ið; -soðnari, -astur
[har-ð̥sɔ-ð̥ɪn, -ɪn, -ɪð̥, -sɔð̥narɪ,
-astʏr̩] adj. (pp.) hard-boiled.

harðsperra, -u, -ur [har-ð̥spɛr-a, -ʏ(r̩);
har̩-spɛr-a] wf.1 aching or stiffness
in limbs and muscles.

harður, hörð, hart [har-ð̥ʏr̩, hör-ð̥,
har̩-t] adj. hard, harsh, fast; *hart*
adv. hard, violently; *keyra hart*
drive fast.

harðvelli, -s [har-ð̥vɛdlɪ(s)] n. hard
(dry) field, dry ground.

harðvellisbali, -a, -ar [har-ð̥vɛdlɪs-
ba:lɪ, -a(r̩)] wm.1 hard level field.

harðýðgi [har-ð̥iðg̊ˌɪ] wf.2 hardness
of heart, harshness.

hárgreiða, -u, -ur [haur-grei-ð̥a, -ʏ(r̩)]
wf.1 comb.

hárgreiðslustofa, -u,-ur [haur-greiðslʏ-
-stɔ:va, -ʏ(r̩)] wf.1 hairdresser's
shop.

hárgreiðslustúlka, -u, -ur [haur-greið̥-
slʏ-stul-kʰa, -ʏ(r̩); -stul-ka] wf.1
hairdresser.

harmur, -s, -ar [har-mʏr̩, harms, har-
mar̩] m.1 sorrow, grief; *af harmi*
from (because of) grief.

harpa, hörpu, -ur [har̩-pa, hör̩-pʏ(r̩)]
wf.1 harp; first month of summer.

hárskeri, -a, -ar [haur̩-sk̩ˌɛ-rɪ, -a(r̩)]
wm.1 barber.

hárspíritus, -s [haur̩-spi-rɪtʰʏs; -d̥ʏs]
m.1 hair spirit, bay rum.

hárvatn, -s, -vötn [haur-vaʰtn̥, -vas·,
-vöʰtn̥] n. hair tonic, hair lotion.

hárþvottur, -ar [haur̩-þvɔʰt-ʏr̩, -ar̩]

m.1 (3) shampoo, washing of the
hair.

háseti, -a, -ar [hau:sɛ-tʰɪ, -a(r̩);
-sɛ-d̥ɪ] wm.1 sailor.

háskólabókasafn, -s, -söfn [hau:skou-
la-bou:kʰasabn̥(s), -söbn̥; -bou:g̊a-]
n. university library.

háskólafyrirlestur, -urs, -rar; -rar
[hau:skou-la-fɪ:rɪ(r)lɛstʏr̩(s), -les-
trar̩] m.1 lecture given at the university.

háskóli, -a, -ar [hau:skou-lɪ, -a(r̩)]
wm.1 university; *Háskólinn =Há-
skóli Íslands* The University of
Iceland.

háslétta, -u, -ur [hau:sljɛʰt-a, -ʏ(r̩)]
wf.1 plateau, tableland.

hasta, -aði, -að [has-ta, -aðɪ, -að̥]
wv.4 *hasta á e-n* rebuke one (reduce
to silence), call one down.

hastur, höst, hast [has-tʏr̩, hös-t,
has-t] adj. rough, hard-trotting (of
horses); harsh.

hásuður, (-ri), -urs [hau:sʏ:ð̥ʏr̩(s),
-sʏð̥-rɪ] n. due south.

hásumar, (-ri), -ars, -ur [hau:sʏ-
mar̩(s), -ʏr̩, -sʏmrɪ] n. high
summer.

hásæti, -s, - [hau:sai-tʰɪ(s); -sai-d̥ɪ]
n. high seat, dais.

hata, -aði, -að(ur) [ha:tʰa, -aðɪ, -að̥,
-aðʏr̩; ha:da] wv.4 hate.

hátíð, -ar, -ir [hau:tʰi-ð̥, -ðar̩, -ðɪr]
f.2 church holiday, holiday, feast
day, festival.

hátíðabúningur, -ings, -ingar [hau:-
tʰiða-bu:niŋg̊ʏr̩, -ɪŋs, -iŋg̊ar̩] m.1
formal dress.

hátíðahald, -s, -höld [hau:tʰi-ð̥a-
hal-d̥(s), -höl-d̥] n. celebration.

hátíðamatur, -ar [hau:tʰi-ð̥a-ma:tʰʏr̩,
-ar̩; -ma:d̥-] m.3 'food for holidays,' i. e. food for gourmets, great
delicacies.

hátíðisdagur, -s, -ar [hau:tʰiðɪs-da:-
qʏr̩, -dax-s, -da:qar̩] m.1 holiday,
feast day.

hátíðlegur [hau:tʰiðlɛ-qʏr̩] adj. (see
-legur) adj. solemn.

hátt, see 2. *hár.*

Consonants: [ð] brea*th*e; [g] *g*ood; [gⱼ] *gy*arden (garden); [hw̥] *wh*at; [j] *y*es; [kⱼ] *cy*an
(can); [ŋ] thi*ng*; [q] N. Germ. sa*gen*; [r] Scottish *r*; [x] approx. Germ. a*ch*; [þ] *th*in.
Voiceless: ○; [b̥, d̥, g̊] approx. *p, t, k.* Half-voiced: *italics.* Aspiration and preaspiration:
[ʰ]; [pʰ, tʰ, kʰ] *p-, t-, k-.* Others as in English.

1. **hátta, -aði, -að** [hauʰt:a, -aðɪ, -að]
wv.4 arrange, dispose; *hvernig e-u
er háttað* how sth is arranged.
2. **hátta, -aði, -að(ur)** [hauʰt:a, -aðɪ,
-að, -aðʏr̥] wv.4 intr.: go to bed;
trans.: *hátta e-n* put sbdy to bed.
hattur, -s, -ar [haʰt:ʏr̥, haʰt·s, haʰt:-
ar̥] m.1 hat; *hann tók ofan hattinn*
he took off his hat (S. I, 4, *1*, 3).
háttur, háttar, hættir [hauʰt:ʏr̥, -ar̥,
haiʰt:ɪr̥] m.3 mode, manner, way;
í háttum in manners, in appearance;
meter, rhythm; *á sama hátt* in the
same way; *mikils háttar maður* a
man of note; *lítils háttar* a little;
of small account, trifling (S. I,
4, *2*, 3).
hatur, (-ri), -urs [ha:tʰʏr̥(s); ha:d̥ʏr̥]
n. hate.
haugur, -s, -ar [höy:qʏr̥, höyx·s, höy:-
qar̥] m.1 mound, heap.
Haukadalur, -s [höy:kʰa-da:lʏr̥, -dal·s;
höy:g̊a-] m.2 'Hawk Valley.'
haus, -s, -ar [höy:s, höys:, höy:sar̥]
m.1 head (less polite than *höfuð*).
haust, -s, - [höys·t(s)] n. autumn,
fall; *á haustin* in the fall.
hausta, -aði, -að [höys·ta, -aðɪ, -að]
wv.4 *það haustar* fall is coming (S.
VI, 14, 3).
hávaðasamur, -söm, -samt [hau:va·ða-
sa:mʏr̥, -sö:*m*, -sam·tʰ; -sam̥·t] adj.
noisy.
hávaði, -a, -ar [hau:vaðɪ, -a(r̥)] wm.1
noise.
hávestur, (-ri), -urs [hau:vɛs·tʏr̥(s),
-vɛstrɪ] n. due west.
hef, see *hafa* and *hefja*.
hefð, -ar, -ir [hɛv·ð, -ðar̥, -ðɪr̥; hɛb̥·þ]
f.2 title, old custom.
hefi(r), see *hafa*.
hefja, hef, hóf, hófum, hafinn (-ið)
[hɛv·ja, hɛ:v, hou:v, hou:vʏm, ha:-
vɪn, -ɪð] v.6 lift, heave, raise, elevate; (auxiliary:) begin, start:
hóf að lesa began to read (literary;
fór að lesa is common) (S. VI, 5,
1); middle voice: *hefjast* (intr.)
begin (S. VI, 7, *4*).
hefna, hefndi, hefnt [hɛb̥·na, hɛm̥·dɪ,

hɛm̥·tʰ; hɛm̥·t] wv.2 avenge; *hefna
e-s* avenge sth (or sbdy); *hefna
fyrir e-ð* take vengeance for sth,
avenge sth.
hefnigjarn, -gjörn, -gjarnt [hɛb̥·nɪ-
g̊ˌad·n, -g̊ˌöd·n, -g̊ˌan·tʰ; -g̊ˌan·t;
-g̊ˌard̥n, -g̊ˌörd̥n] adj. revengeful.
hefta, hefti, heft(ur) [hɛf·ta, -ɪ, -ʏr̥,
hɛf·t] wv.2 hobble (a horse); fetter.
hefti, -s, - [hɛf·tɪ(s)] n. part (of a
book), number (of a periodical).
hegg, see *höggva*.
hégilja, -u, -ur [hˀjɛ:g̊ˌɪlja, -ʏ(r̥)] wf.1
trifle, superstition.
heiði, -ar, -ar [hei:ðɪ, -hei:ðar̥] f.1
heath, moor; mountain, mountain
pass.
heiðinn, -in, -ið; heiðnari, -astur [hei:-
ðɪn, -ɪn, -ɪð, heið·narɪ, -astʏr̥] adj.
heathen.
heiðra, -aði, -að(ur) [heið·ra, -aðɪ,
-að, -aðʏr̥] wv.4 honor, esteem,
heiðraður esteemed; *heiðraði herra*
'honored Sir,' Dear Sir.
1. **heiður, (-ri), -urs** [hei:ðʏr̥(s),
heið·rɪ] m.1 honor.
2. **heiður, heið, heitt** [hei:ðʏr̥, hei:ð,
heiʰt:] adj. clear, cloudless; *upp í
heiðan himininn* up into the clear
sky.
heiðursmaður, -manns, -menn [hei:-
ðʏrs·ma:ðʏr̥, -man·s, -mɛn:] m.4
man of honor, gentleman.
heilagfiski, -s [hei:laq·fɪs·kˌɪ(s)] n.
halibut.
heilagur, -lög, -lagt; -lagri, -lagastur
(also: **helgur, helg; helgari, -astur**)
[hei:laqʏr̥, -löq, -laxt; -laqrɪ, -la-
qastʏr̥; hɛl·g̊ʏr̥, hɛl·g̊, hɛl·g̊arɪ,
-astʏr̥] adj. holy, sacred (In. III,
2(b)9); *halda heilagt* celebrate.
heildós, -ar, -ir [heil·dou·s, -ar̥, -ɪr̥]
f.2 whole can (twice the amount
of *hálfdós* half a can).
heildsala, -sölu, -ur [heil·d̥sa·la, -sö:-
lʏ(r̥)] wf.1 wholesale house; wholesale.
heildsöluverzlun, -unar, -anir [heil·d̥-
sö·lʏ-vɛrslʏ*n*, -ʏnar̥, -anɪr̥] f.2
wholesale business.

Vowels: *a* [a] approx. father; *á* [au] cow; *e* [ɛ] set; *é* [jɛ] yes; *i, y* [ɪ] sit; *í, ý* [i] feel;
o [ɔ] law; *ó* [ou] note; *u* [ʏ] approx. Germ. Mütter; *ú* [u] school; *y* = *i*; *ý* = *í*; *æ* [ai] ice;
ö [ö] Germ. hören; *au* [öy] French feuille; *ei, ey* [ei] ale. Length [:]; half-length [·].

1. **heill, -ar, -ir** [heiḍ·l, -laṛ, -lɪṛ] f.2
luck, good (bad) o̤men; *heillin* my
dear, dearie.
2. **heill, heil, heilt; heilli, heilastur**
[heiḍ·l, hei:*l*, heil·t; heiḍ·lɪ, hei:-
lastʏṛ] adj. whole, entire; all; hale,
sound, healed.
heilmikill, -il, -ið [heil·mɪ·kₗʰɪd̥l, -i*l*,
-ið̥; -mɪ·g̊ₗ-] adj. quite great, quite
much; *heilmikið af e·u* quite an
amount of sth.
heilræði, -s, - [heil·rai·ðɪ(s)] n.
wholesome advice, wise counsel,
often in pl.
1. **heilsa, -u** [heil·sa, -ʏ] wf.1 health.
2. **heilsa, -ði, -ð** [heil·sa, -aðɪ, -að]
wv.4 greet, say how do you do;
heilsast greet each other; *ég bið að
heilsa honum* give him my regards,
= *heilsaðu honum frá mér.*
heilsufræði [heil·sʏ-frai:ðɪ] wf.2 hy-
giene, sanitation.
heilög, see *heilagur.*
heim [hei:*m*] (1) adv. home, *fara
heim* go home; (2) prep. with acc.
heim túnið home across the homefield (S. I, 2, *3*, 3).
heima [hei:ma] adv. at home; *eiga
heima* live (at a certain place).
heimafólk, -s [hei:ma-foul·kʰ,
-foul·(x)s; -foul·k] n. people of
the household.
heimahús [hei:ma-hu:s] n.pl (= *bœjarhús*) literally: ' home houses,'
the central building of a farm, opposed to *útihús* outhouses.
Heimaklettur, -s [hei:ma-kʰlɛʰt:ʏṛ,
-kʰlɛʰt·s] m.1 ' Home Cliff,' in
Vestmannaeyjar.
heimamaður, -manns, -menn [hei:ma-
ma:ðʏṛ, -man·s, -mɛn:] m.4 one of
the household; pl. people of the
place.
heiman [hei:ma*n*] adv. from home;
fara að heiman leave home.
heimastjórn, -ar [hei:ma-stjourd̥n,
-naṛ] f.2 home rule.
heimili, -s, - [hei:mɪlɪ(s)] n. home.
heimilisfang, -s, -föng [hei:mɪlɪs-

fauŋ·g̊(s), -fauŋ·s, -föyŋ·g̊] n. address.
heimill, -il, -ilt; -illi, -ilastur [hei:-
mɪd̥l, -i*l*, -ɪl̥t; -ɪd̥lɪ, -ɪlastʏṛ] (also:
heimull [hei:mʏd̥l], etc.) adj. at
free disposal.
heimkynni, -s, - [heim·kₗʰɪn·ɪ(s)] n.
home.
heimleiðis [heim·lei·ðɪs] adv. home,
homeward.
heimska, -u [heimska, -ʏ] wf.1 foolishness.
heimskaut, -s, - [heim·sköy·tʰ(s);
-sköy·d̥] n. pole; *norðurheimskaut*
north pole.
heimskautaland, -s, -lönd [heim·sköy-
tʰa·lan·d̥, -lan·s, -lön·d̥; -sköy·da-]
n. arctic (antarctic) country, polar
region.
heimskautsbaugur, -s, -ar [heim-
sköy·tʰs-böy:qʏṛ, -böyx·s, -böy:qaṛ;
-sköy·d̥s-] m.1 arctic (antarctic)
circle.
heimskur, heimsk, heimskt [heimskʏṛ,
heimsk, heimst] adj. stupid, foolish;
heimskt er heima alið barn (proverbial) a child brought up at home
remains foolish (i. e. inexperienced).
heimsmál, -s, - [heim·smau·*l*, -mauls]
n. world language.
heimsókn, -ar, -ir [heim·souʰkn̥, -naṛ,
-nɪṛ] f.2 visit; *fara í h-n* go visiting,
visit.
heimsóknartími, -a, -ar [heim·souʰk-
naṛ-tʰi:mɪ, -a(ṛ)] wm.1 visiting
hour.
heimsótt, -i, -ur, see *heimsœkja.*
heimspeki(s)deild, -ar, -ir [heim·spɛ-
kₗʰɪ(s)deil·d̥, -aṛ, -ɪṛ; -spɛ·g̊ₗɪs-] f.2
faculty (department) of philosophy.
heimsstríð, -s, - [heim·strí·ð, -stríðs]
n. =
heimsstyrjöld, -aldar, -aldir [heim·-
stɪrjöld̥, -aldaṛ, -aldɪṛ] f.2 World
War.
heimsækja, -sótti, -sótt(ur) [heim·-
sai·kₗʰa, -souʰt·ɪ, -ʏṛ; -souʰt·; -sai·-
g̊ₗa] wv.2 visit, call on; *heimsœkja
e·n* call on sbdy.
heimur, -s, -ar [hei:mʏṛ, heim·s, hei:-

Consonants: [ð] brea*th*e; [g] *g*ood; [gₗ] *gy*arden (garden); [hw̥] *wh*at; [j] *y*es; [kₗ] *cy*an
(can); [ŋ] thi*ng*; [q] N. Germ. sa*g*en; [r] Scottish *r*; [x] approx. Germ. a*ch*; [þ] *th*in.
Voiceless: ○; [b̥, d̥, g̊] approx. *p, t, k.* Half-voiced: *italics.* Aspiration and preaspiration:
[ʰ]; [pʰ, tʰ, kʰ] *p-, t-, k-.* Others as in English.

361

mar] m.1 world; *þessa heims og annars* in this and the other world (S. I, 4, *5*).

heita, heiti, hét, hétum, heitinn (-ið) [hei:tʰa, hei:tʰɪ, hjɛ:tʰ, hjɛ:tʰɤm, hei:tʰɪn, -ɪð; hei:d̥-, hjɛ:d̥-] v.7 be called, named, considered; promise; *heita e-m illu* promise sbdy evil things, threaten sbdy; *hvað heitið þér?* what is your name? *heita e-u nafni* be called by a certain name, be named; pp. *heitinn* late, *Jón heitinn* the late Mr. John; *hann lét það gott heita* (acc. with inf.) he said that it was all right (S. VI, 11, *4*).

heiti, -s, - [hei:tʰɪ(s); hei:d̥ɪ] n. name, term; *allt sem heiti hefur* 'everything that has (got) a name,' i. e. all you can think of; *spyrja e-n að heiti* ask sbdy's name.

heitt, see 2. *heiður* and *heitur*.

heitur, heit, heitt [hei:tʰɤr̥, hei:tʰ, heiʰt:; hei:d̥(ɤr̥)] adj. hot, warm, ardent; *heitt og kalt vatn* hot and cold (running) water; *Heitt og Kalt* (a restaurant) Hot and Cold (foods); *heitt* adv. hotly.

hékk, see 1. *hanga*.

hekl, -s [hɛʰk·l̥(s)] n. crotcheting.

1. Hekla, -u [hɛʰk·la, -ɤ] wf.1 'Cope,' a famous volcano in Iceland.

2. hekla, -aði, -að(ur) [hɛʰk·la, -aðɪ, -að, -aðɤr̥] wv.4 crotchet.

hektari, -a, -ar [hɛx·tarɪ, -a(r̥)] wm.1 hectare.

hektómetri, -a, -ar [hɛx·tou-mɛ:tʰrɪ, -a(r̥); -mɛ:d̥rɪ] wm.1 hectometer.

held, héldum, see *halda*.

heldri, helztur [hɛl·d̥rɪ, hɛlstɤr̥] adj. compar. and superl. notable, most notable; *heldri menn* 'better people,' gentry (S. III, 4, 6).

heldur [hɛl·d̥ɤr̥] (1) adv. compar. (see *gjarna*) rather, *heldur stór* rather big; a little (before comparatives): *heldur betur* a little better, *heldur minni* a little smaller; *heldur margir* rather many, (litotes) quite a few, too many (S. III, 4, 6n); *heldur ekki, ekki . . . heldur*

not . . . either; *heldur en ekki* (litotes) rather than not, more than a little, very great(ly); *vilja heldur* prefer (would rather); (2) conj. but (S. VIII, 2); *heldur annaðhvort . . . eða* but either . . . or; *heldur en* than, any more than (S. VIII, 3(g)); *hann leit ekki á hana, heldur en hún væri ekki til* he did not look at her any more than if she did not exist (S. VI, 9, *4*, 7).

1. Helga, -u, -ur [hɛl·g̊a, -ɤ(r̥)] wf.1 pers. name: Helga.

2. helga, -aði, -að(ur) [hɛl·g̊a, -aðɪ, -að, -aðɤr̥] wv.4 hallow, sanctify.

Helgafell, -s [hɛl·g̊a-fɛd·l̥, -fɛl·s] n. 'Holy Fell'; name of a mountain and a periodical.

1. Helgi, -a, -ar [hɛl·g̊jɪ, hɛl·g̊a(r̥)] wm.1 pers. name: Helgi.

2. helgi [hɛl·g̊jɪ] wf.2 holiness, sacredness.

3. helgi, -ar, -ar [hɛl·g̊jɪ, hɛl·g̊ar] f.1 holiday; *um helgina* on Sunday, over the weekend.

helgidagslæknir, -is, -ar [hɛl·g̊jɪdaxslaiʰk·nɪr̥, -ɪs, -ar] m.1 a doctor (physician) who is on duty on holidays.

helgisiður, -ar, -ir [hɛl·g̊jɪ-sɪ:ðɤr̥, -ar, -ɪr̥] m.3 rite.

helg, -ur, see *heilagur*.

hella, -u, -ur [hɛd·la, -ɤ(r̥)] wf.1 flat rock, flat stone.

hellir, -is, -ar [hɛd·lɪr̥, -ɪs, -ar] m.1 cave.

Hellisheiði, -ar [hɛd·lɪs-hei:ðɪ, -ar] f.1 'Cave Heath,' a mountain east of Reykjavík.

helluhraun, -s, - [hɛd·lɤ-hröy:n, -hröyn·s] n. flat rock lava.

helmingur, -s, -ar [hɛl·miŋg̊ɤr̥, -ɪns, -iŋg̊ar] m.1 half; *um allan helming* by leaps and bounds.

hélt, see *halda*.

helzt [hɛlst] adv. superl. (see *heldur* and *gjarna*) preferably, mostly, chiefly.

helztur, helzt, helzt [hɛlst(ɤr̥)] adj.

Vowels: *a* [a] approx. father; *á* [au] cow; *e* [ɛ] set; *é* [jɛ] yes; *i, y* [ɪ] sit; *í, ý* [i] feel; *o* [ɔ] law; *ó* [ou] note; *u* [ɤ] approx. Germ. Mütter; *ú* [u] school; *y* = *i*; *ý* = *í*; *æ* [ai] ice; *ö* [ö] Germ. hören; *au* [öy] French *feuille*; *ei, ey* [ei] ale. Length [:]; half-length [·].

superl. (see *heldri*) chief, principal, foremost, best.

hempa, -u, -ur [hɛm·pʰa, -ɤ(r̥); hɛm̥·pa] wf.1 cassock.

hendur, see *hönd*.

hengja, hengdi, hengdur (hengt) [heiŋ·g̊ɪa, heiŋ·dɪ, -ɤr̥, heiŋ·tʰ; heiŋ·t] wv.2 hang (trans.).

héngum, see 1. *hanga*.

hennar, henni, see *hann* (*hún*).

hentugur [hɛn·tʰɤqɤr̥; hɛn·t-] adj. (see *-ugur*) practical, handy.

heppilega [hɛʰp·ɪ·lɛːqa] adv. fortunately.

heppinn, -in, -ið; heppnari, -astur [hɛʰp:ɪn, -ɪn, -ɪð, hɛʰp·narɪ, -astɤr̥] adj. lucky; *Leifur heppni* Leif the Lucky.

her, -s, -ir, (-ja) [hɛːr, hɛr̥·s, hɛːrɪr̥, hɛr̥·ja] m.2 army, troops.

hér [hjɛːr] adv. here, in this case, in this matter; *hér í bæ* in this town; *hér á landi* in this country; *hér við land* at the coasts of this country, in the harbors of this country (In. IV, 1, 3); *hér um bil* about, circa.

hérað, -aðs, -öð (-uð) [hjɛ:rað, -aðs, -öð, -ɤð] n. region; (rural) district: *Hérað* = Fljótsdalshérað.

Héraðsflói, -a [hjɛ:raðs·flouːɪ, -a] wm.1 'District Bay.'

héraðsskóli, -a, -ar [hjɛ:rað(s)·skouːlɪ, -a(r)] wm.1 district school, folk high school in a rural district (= *lýðskóli*).

herbergi, -s, - [hɛr̥·bɛrg̊ɪ(s)] n. room; *herbergis-dyr* door of a room.

herða, herti, hert(ur) [hɛr̥·ða, hɛr̥·tɪ, hɛr̥·t(ɤr̥)] wv.2 harden; *herða fisk* dry fish.

herðar [hɛr̥·ðar̥] f.1.pl. shoulders.

herdeild, -ar, -ir [hɛr̥·deild, -ar̥, -ɪr̥] f.2 division of an army, also *stór herdeild*.

herflokkur, -s, -ar [hɛr̥·flɔʰk·ɤr̥, -flɔʰks, -flɔʰk·ar̥] m.1 troops; army corps.

herforingi, -ja, -jar [hɛr̥·fɔ·riŋg̊ɪɪ, -g̊ɪa(r)] wm.1 officer.

herforingjaráð [hɛr̥·fɔ·riŋg̊ɪa·rauːð, -rauð·s] n. general staff.

herfylki, -s, - [hɛr̥·fɪlkɪʰɪ(s); -fɪlk̥ɪɪ] n. battalion of the army.

hergögn, -gagna [hɛr̥·gögn̥, -gag̊na] n.pl. arms, ammunition.

herlæknir, -is, -ar [hɛr̥·laiʰknɪr̥, -ɪs, -ar̥] m.1 army doctor.

herlækningasveit, -ar, -ir [hɛr̥·laiʰk·niŋg̊a-sveiːtʰ, -ar̥, -ɪr̥; -svei:d] f.2 medical corps (of the army).

hermaður, -manns, -menn [hɛr̥·ma·ðɤr̥, -mans, -mɛn·] m.4 soldier.

hermálaráðherra, -, -ar [hɛr̥·mau·la·rauːðhɛr̥·a(r)] wm.1 minister of war; secretary of war (U. S. A.); secretary for war (England).

hérmeð [hjɛr̥·mɛ·ð] adv. (= *hér með*) herewith.

hérna [hjɛd·na; hjɛrdna] adv. here (pointing to sth); here (on this farm, etc.); *hérna í bœnum* in this town, in the town.

hernuminn, -in, -ið [hɛr̥·nɤ·mɪn, -ɪn, -ɪð] adj. occupied by armed forces.

herra, -, -ar [hɛr̥:a(r)] wm.1 (In. I, 5, 1) Mr., Sir; gentleman; *herra Jón Jónsson* Mr. J. J.; *kœri herra* Dear Sir; *herrar mínir!* gentlemen!

herramannsmatur, -ar [hɛr̥·amans·ma:tʰɤr̥, -ar̥; -ma:d·] m.3 food for gourmets.

hershöfðingi, -ja, -jar [hɛr̥·shövðiŋg̊ɪɪ, -iŋg̊ɪa(r); -höbð-] wm.1 general.

herskip, -s, - [hɛr̥·skɪʰpʰ, -skɪɪfs; -skɪɪ·b̥] n. man-of-war.

herstöð, -var, -var [hɛr̥·stö·ð, -stöðvar̥] f.1 army base.

herstöðvasjúkrahús, -s, -[hɛr̥·stöðva·sjuːkʰrahu·s, -hus·; -sju:g̊ra-] n. base hospital.

hersveit, -ar, -ir [hɛr̥·svei·tʰ, -ar̥, -ɪr̥; -svei·d] f.2 troops; regiment.

hersýning, -ar, -ar [hɛr̥·si·niŋg̊, -ar̥] f.1 review of troops.

1. hertaka, -töku, -ur [hɛr̥·tʰa·kʰa, -tʰö·kʰɤ(r); -tʰa·g̊a, -tʰö·g̊r] wf.1 occupation by an army.

2. hertaka, -tek, -tók, -tókum, -tekinn (-ið) [hɛr̥·tʰa·kʰa, -tʰɛ·kʰ, -tʰou·kʰ, -tʰou·kʰɤm, -tʰɛ·kɪʰɪn, -ɪð; -tʰa·g̊a,

Consonants: [ð] brea*the*; [g] *g*ood; [g̊ɪ] *gy*arden (garden); [hʍ] *wh*at; [j] *y*es; [kɪ] *cy*an (can); [ŋ] thi*ng*; [q] N. Germ. sa*g*en; [r] Scottish *r*; [x] approx. Germ. a*ch*; [þ] *th*in. Voiceless: ○; [b̥, d̥, g̊] approx. *p, t, k*. Half-voiced: *italics*. Aspiration and preaspiration: [ʰ]; [pʰ, tʰ, kʰ] *p-, t-, k-*. Others as in English.

363

-tʰɛ·g̊, -tʰou·g̊(ʏm), -tʰɛ·g̊ˌɪn] v.6 occupy by armed forces.

hertur, hert, hert [hɛr̥·t(ʏr̥)] adj. dried hard (of fish), dehydrated; hardened, tempered (of steel).

hérumbil [hj̊ɛ:rʏm-bɪ:l] adv. (= hér um bil) about, circa.

hespa, -u, -ur [hɛs·pa, -ʏ(r̥)] wf.1 hasp.

hestbak, -s [hɛs·(t)ba·kʰ(s); -ba·g̊] n. horseback; koma á hestbak have a ride, á hestbaki on horseback.

hesthús, -s, - [hɛs·t(h)u·s, -(h)us·] n. stable for horses.

hestur, -s, -ar [hɛs·tʏr̥; hɛsts, hɛs:; hɛs·tar̥] m.1 horse, pony.

hét, -um, see heita.

hetta, -u, -ur [hɛʰt:a, -ʏ(r̥)] wf.1 cap.

hettusótt, -ar, -ir [hɛʰt:ʏ-souʰt: -ar̥, -ɪr̥] f.2 mumps.

hey, -s, -, (-ja) [hei:(s), hei:ja] n. hay, straw; pl. stores of hay.

heyhirðing, -ar, -ar [hei:hɪrðiŋg̊, -ar̥] f.1 hauling hay (into the barn), ingathering of hay.

1. **heyja, -aði, -að(ur)** [hei:ja, -aði, -að, -aðʏr̥] wv.4 make hay; vel heyjaður well provided with hay.

2. **heyja, háði, háð(ur)** [hei:ja, hau:-ði, hau:ðʏr̥, hau:ð] wv.3 hold a meeting (heyja þing); heyja glímu perform, hold a wrestling match.

heyra, heyrði, heyrður (heyrt) [hei:-ra, heir·ði, -ʏr̥, heir̥·t] wv.2 hear, listen; (1) heyrðu mig (mér), heyrið þér! listen, I say! ég heyrði, að hann las (= heyrði hann lesa) I heard that he read (I heard him read) (S. VI, 9, 4, 1n2); heyrði hann kveðið í hólnum he heard sbdy singing in the hillock; að heyra til þín! (indignant) listen to you! (S. VI, 11, 2); það var að heyra á honum, að . . . one got the impression by listening to him that . . . (S. VI, 14, 7); (2) middle voice: heyrast be heard; láta e-ð heyrast á sér give a hint of sth (S. VI, 7, 3); það heyrist til hans he can be (is) heard (e. g. over the radio); mér heyrist e-ð I think I hear sth (S. VI, 14, 5); mér heyrist þér tala nógu vel I think you are speaking well enough; mér heyrðist hann koma (= að hann kæmi) I thought I heard him come (= that he came) (S. VI, 9, 4, 1n2).

h.f. = hlutafélag.

hið, see hinn def.art.

hífaður, -uð, -að [hi:vaðʏr̥, -ʏð, -að] adj. tipsy, tight.

hika, -aði, -að [hɪ:kʰa, -aði, -að; hɪ:g̊a] wv.4 hesitate.

Hildur, -ar [hɪl·dʏr̥, -ar̥] f.1 pers. name: Hild.

himinn, -ins, -nar [hɪ:mɪn, -ɪns, hɪm·-nar̥] m.1 heaven; á himnum in heaven.

hin, hina, -ar, -ir, see hinn 1. & 2.

hindber, -s, -, (-ja) [hɪn·dbɛ·r, -bɛr̥s, -bɛrja] n. raspberry.

hindberjasaft, -ar, [hɪn·dbɛrja-saf·t, -ar̥] f.2 raspberry juice.

hingað [hiŋ·g̊a(ð)] adv. hither, here; hingað til bæjarins to this town (Pr. 4, 2).

1. **hinn, hin, hið** [hɪn:, hɪ:n, hɪ:(ð)], acc. hinn, hina, hið [hɪ:na], dat. hinum, hinni, hinu [hɪ:nʏm, hɪn:ɪ, hɪ:nʏ], gen. hins, hinnar, hins [hɪn·s, hɪn:ar̥]; pl. hinir, hinar, hin [hɪ:nɪr̥, hɪ:nar̥, hɪ:n], acc. hina, hinar, hin [hɪ:na], dat. hinum [hɪ:nʏm], gen. hinna [hɪn:a] def. art. (In. II; S. II) the; hið fagra the beautiful; hið illa evil; hesturinn minn my horse; minn hestur, ekki yðar my horse, not yours (S. II, 2); hús-ið hans Jóns (= Jóns hús) John's house; hús-ið mitt (= mitt hús) my house; annað hús-ið one of the two houses; hitt hús-ið the other house (S. II, 4); það hús-ið, sem . . . the house which . . . (S. II, 7); einn sjómaðurinn one of the sailors (= einn af sjómönnu-num, einn sjómanna-nna). Note: The def. art. may drop the h in all forms: inn, in, ið.

2. **hinn, hin, hitt** [hɪn:, hɪ:n, hɪʰt:]

Vowels: a [a] approx. father; á [au] cow; e [ɛ] set; é [jɛ] yes; i, y [ɪ] sit; í, ý [i] feel; o [ɔ] law; ó [ou] note; u [ʏ] approx. Germ. Mütter; ú [u] school; y = i; ý = í; æ [ai] ice; ö [ö] Germ. hören; au [öy] French feuille; ei, ey [ei] ale. Length [:]; half-length [·].

364

dem. pron. (Except for *hitt* this pronoun is identical in form with the above, but *h* is never dropped in it), the other (one), that one; *ekki þessi, heldur hinn* not this, but the other one; *hinn daginn* the day after tomorrow (In. VI, **3**; S. IV, **3**, 4); *hitt* the remainder; *hinu megin, hinum megin* on the other side; *hins vegar* on the other hand.

hinna, -ar ,-i, see *hinn* 1. & 2.

hinztur, hinzt, hinzt [hɪnst(ʏr̥)] adj. superl. only: last; *ó hinzta degi* on the day of doom.

hins, see *hinn* 1. & 2.

hinsvegar [hɪn·sve·qar̥] adv. (= *hins vegar*) on the other hand, but.

hinu, see *hinn* 1. & 2.

hinum, see *hinn* 1. & 2.

hinumegin [hɪ:nʏ-mei:jɪn] (1) adv. (= *hinum* (*hinu*) *megin*) on the other side; (2) prep. with gen. *hinumegin árinnar* on the other side of the river.

hirða, hirti, hirtur (hirt) [hɪr̥·ða, hɪr̥·tɪ, -ʏr̥, hɪr̥·t] wv.2 tend, keep, take care of (animals); *hirða hey* gather in the hay, haul the hay; *hirða um* care for (about).

hirtir, see *hjörtur*.

hissa [hɪs:a] adj. indecl. surprised, astonished (S. III, 1, 2n).

hita, -aði, -að(ur) [hɪ:tʰa, -aðɪ, -að, -aðʏr̥; hɪ:da] wv.4 heat, prepare by boiling; *hita kaffi* 'heat coffee,' make coffee.

hiti, -a, -ar [hɪ:tʰɪ, -a(r̥); hɪ:dɪ] wm.1 heat, warmth, heating; fever; pl. *hitar* hot spells.

hitt, see 2. *hinn*.

hitta, hitti, hitt(ur) [hɪʰt:a, -ɪ, -ʏr̥; hɪʰt:] wv.2 hit; meet, come across, find; *hitta e-n* meet, catch sbdy; *hittast* meet each other (= *finnast*).

hittinn, -in, -ið [hɪʰt:ɪn, -ɪn, -ɪð] adj. clever at hitting.

hittni [hɪʰt·nɪ] wf.2 ability to hit.

hjá [hjạu:] prep. with dat. with, near, at sbdy's home; (1) with, near, at: *hjá barninu* with the

child; *hjá Hrísnesi* at H.-nes; (2) at: *hjá Jóni* at John's (S. I, 4, *1*, 2); (3) as a possessive: *hestarnir hjá honum* his horses, the horses of his (S. I, 4, *1*, 4); *nærfötin hjá ykkur* the underwear in your store (or: your underwear); *ponturnar hjá þeim sumum* the snuffboxes of some of them; (4) in case of, on, to: *hjá 'Gylli'* in case of *'Gyllir.'*

hjakka, -aði, -að(ur) [hjạʰk:a, -aðɪ, -að, -aðʏr̥] wv.4 hack again and again.

hjálpa, -aði, -að [hjạul·pʰa, -aðɪ, -að; hjạul·pa] wv.4 help; *hjálpa e-m með e-ð* help sbdy with sth, in doing sth.

hjálparbeitiskip, -s, - [hjạul·pʰarbei:tʰɪsk̬ɪ·pʰ, -sk̬ɪfs; hjạul·parbei:dɪsk̬ɪ·b̥] n. armed merchant cruiser.

hjálpsemi [hjạul·pʰse·mɪ; hjạul·p-] wf.2 helpfulness, readiness to help.

hjara, hjarði, hjarað [hjạ:ra, hjar·ðɪ, hjạ:rað] wv.3 barely live, vegetate.

hjarta, -, hjörtu, (hjartna) [hjạr̥·ta, hjör·tʏ, hjạrtna] wn. heart; *hjartað í mér* 'the heart in me,' my heart.

hjartar, see *hjörtur*.

hjó, see *höggva*.

hjól, -s, - [hjọu:l, hjọul·s] n. wheel; bicycle.

hjóla, -aði, -að [hjọu:la, -aðɪ, -að] wv.4 ride a bicycle.

hjólhestur, -s, -ar [hjọu:l·hestʏr̥; -hests, -hes·; -hestar] m.1 bicycle.

hjón [hjọu:n] n.pl. married couple; *hjónin* the master and the mistress of the house.

hjónaefni [hjọu:n(a)eb̥nɪ] n.pl. a betrothed couple.

hjú [hjụu:] n.pl. servants; *hjú* worthy couple (ironic and derogatory = *skötuhjú*).

hjuggum, see *höggva*.

hjúkra, -aði; -að [hjụu:kʰra, -aðɪ, -að; hjụu:g̥ra] wv.4 nurse.

hjúkrun, -unar [hjụu:kʰrʏn, -ʏnar̥; hjụu:g̥rʏn] f.2 nursing.

Consonants: [ð] brea*th*e; [g] *g*ood; [gʝ] *gy*arden (garden); [hw] *wh*at; [j] *y*es; [kʝ] *cy*an (can); [ŋ] thi*ng*; [q] N. Germ. sa*g*en; [r] Scottish *r*; [x] approx. Germ. a*ch*; [þ] *th*in. Voiceless: ○; [b̥, d̥, g̊] approx. *p, t, k*. Half-voiced: *italics*. Aspiration and preaspiration: [ʰ]; [pʰ, tʰ, kʰ] *p-, t-, k-*. Others as in English.

hjúkrunarkona, -u, -ur [hʲuːkʰrʏnar̥-kʰɔːna, -ʏ(r̥)]; hʲuːg̊rʏnar̥-] wf.1 nurse.

hjúkrunarstöð,-var,-var [hʲuːkʰrʏnar̥-stöːð, -stöð-var̥; hʲuːg̊rʏnar̥-] f.1 dressing station; casualty clearing station.

hjörtu, see *hjarta.*

hjörtur, hjartar, hirtir [hʲörˑtʏr̥, hʲar̥ˑtar̥, hɪrˑtɪr̥] m.3 hart, also pers. name.

hlað, -s, hlöð [hlaːð, hlaðˑs, hlöːð] n. a place, partly or fully paved, in front of a farmhouse; *ríða í hlað* ride up to the farmhouse(s).

1. hlaða, hlöðu, -ur [hlaːða, hlöː-ðʏ(r̥)] wf.1 barn; also in place names: *-hlaða, Hlöðu-.*

2. hlaða, hleð, hlóð, hlóðum, hlaðinn (-ið) [hlaːða, hlɛːð, hlouːð, hlouː-ðʏm, hlaːðɪn, -ɪð] v.6 build (a wall); pile up; load (a boat, a truck, a gun); *hlaða úr (heyi)* stack the hay; *hlaðast* be piled up.

hlaðborð, -s, -borð [hlaðˑbɔrð, -bɔrðs, -bɔrð] n. buffet.

hlakka, -aði, -að [hlaʰkːa, -aðɪ, -að] wv.4 cry (of birds of prey); exult; *hlakka til að gera e-ð* look forward to doing sth; *hlakka til e-s* look forward to sth.

hlána, -aði, -að [hlauːna, -aðɪ, -að] wv.4 thaw (S. VI, 14, 3).

hlaup, -s, - [hlöyːpʰ(s); hlöyːb] n. slide, landslide, landslip; alluvial cone or fan; barrel (of a gun).

hlaupa, hleyp, hljóp, hlupum, hlaupinn (-ið) [hlöyːpʰa, hleiːpʰ, hljouːpʰ, hlʏːpʰʏm, hlöyːpʰɪn, -ɪð; hlöyːb-, hleiːb, hljouːb, hlʏːbʏm] v.7 run; jump, leap; *hlaupa undir bagga með e-m* literally; run under the load with sbdy, i. e. come to the rescue of sbdy; *vöxtur hleypur í ána* the river is rising; *Skeiðará er hlaupin* Skeiðará has burst its bounds (S. VI, 3, 3).

hlaut, see *hljóta.*

hlé, -s [hljeː(s)] n. shelter, lee.

hleð, see 2. *hlaða.*

hlegið, -inn, see *hlæja.*

hleri, -a, -ar [hlɛːrɪ, -a, -ar̥] wm.1 trap door.

hlessa [hlɛsːa] adj. indecl. surprised, astonished, taken aback.

hleyp, see *hlaupa.*

1. hlið, -ar, -ar [hlɪːð, -ðar̥] f.1 side, flank.

2. hlið, -s, - [hlɪːð, hlɪðˑs] n. gate, port; entrance, hole.

hlíð, -ar, -ar [hliːð, -ðar̥] f.1 slope, mountain side; also in place names: *-hlíð, Hlíðar-.*

Hlíðarendi, -a [hliːðar-ɛnˑdɪ, -a] wm.1 'Slope's End,' a farmstead made famous by *Njála.*

Hlíðarendakot, -s [hliːðarenda-kʰɔːtʰ, -s, -kʰɔːd(s)] n. 'Slope's End Cot.'

hlíðarslakki, -a, -ar [hliːðar̥-slaʰkʲːɪ, -a(r̥)] wm.1 depression in the hillside.

hlífa, hlífði, hlíft [hliːva, hlivˑðɪ, hlifˑt; hlibˑðɪ] wv.2 spare, *hlífa e-m* spare sbdy.

hljóðbær, -bær, -bært [hljouðˑbaiˑr, -baiˑr, -bair̥ˑt] adj. carrying sound; *það er hljóðbært* sound is easily carried.

hljóðfall, -s [hljouðˑfadl̥, -fals] n. tempo, rhythm.

hljóðfæraverzlun, -unar, -anir [hljouð-faiˑra-verslʏn, -ʏnar̥, -anɪr̥] f.2 music store.

hljóðfæri, -s, - [hljouðˑfaiˑrɪ(s)] n. musical instrument.

hljómleikur, -s, -ar [hljoumˑleiˑkʰʏr̥, -leiˑkʰs, -leiˑkʰar̥; -leiˑg̊-] m.1 concert, music.

hljómlist, -ar [hljoumˑlɪst, -ar̥] f.2 music.

hljómlistarmaður, -manns, -menn [hljoumˑlɪstar-maːðʏr̥, -manˑs, -mɛnː] m.4 musician.

hljómlistarskóli, -a, -ar [hljoumˑlɪstar-skouːlɪ, -a(r̥)] wm.1 conservatory of music.

hljómplata,-plötu,-ur [hljoumˑpʰlaˑtʰa, -pʰlöˑtʰʏ(r̥); -pʰlaˑda, -pʰlöˑdʏ] wf.1 (grammophone) record.

Hljómskálagarður, -s [hljoumˑskauˑla-

Vowels: *a* [a] approx. father; *á* [au] cow; *e* [ɛ] set; *é* [jɛ] yes; *i, y* [ɪ] sit; *í, ý* [i] feel; *o* [ɔ] law; *ó* [ou] note; *u* [ʏ] approx. Germ. Mütter; *ú* [u] school; *y* = *i*; *ý* = *í*; *æ* [ai] ice; *ö* [ö] Germ. hören; *au* [öy] French feuille; *ei, ey* [ei] ale. Length [:]; half-length [ˑ].

366

gar·ðʏ̧r, -s] m.1 'Music Hall Park'
(hljómskáli music hall).

hljómsveit, -ar, -ir [hl̩joum·svei·tʰ, -ar̩,
-ɪr̩; -svei·d̩] f.2 band, orchestra.

hljóp, see hlaupa.

hljóta, hlýt, hlaut, hlutum, hlotinn
(-ið) [hl̩jou:tʰa, hl̩i:tʰ, hl̩öy:tʰ,
hlʏ:tʰʏm, hl̩ɔ:tʰɪn, -ɪð; hl̩jou:da,
hl̩i:d̩, hl̩öy:d̩, hl̩ʏ:dʏm, hl̩ɔ:dɪn]
v.2 get by lot, be allotted sth
(hljóta e·ð); must, have to, þetta
hlýtur að vera rétt this must be
right.

hló, see hlœja.

1. hlóð, -ar, -ir [hl̩ou:ð, -ðar̩, -ðɪr̩]
f.2 open fireplace (often in pl.
hlóðir).

2. hlóð, -um, see 2. hlaða.

hlógum, see hlœja.

hlotið, -inn, see hljóta.

hlúa, hlúði, hlúð [hl̩u:a, hlu:ðɪ, hlu:ð]
wv.3 cover up, hoe; hlúa að e·m
cover sbdy up.

hlúð, hlúði, see hlúa and hlýja.

hlupum, see hlaupa.

hlust, -ar, -ir [hl̩ʏs·t, -ar̩, -ɪr̩] f.2 ear-
hole, aperture of the ear, auditory
canal.

hlusta, -aði, -að [hl̩ʏs·ta, -aðɪ, -að]
wv.4 listen; h. á listen to.

hlustarverkur, -jar, -ir [hl̩ʏs·tar·ver̩·-
kʏr̩, -ver̩·k̩ar̩, -ver̩·k̩ɪr̩] m.2 earache.

hlutafélag, -s, -lög [hl̩ʏ:tʰa·fje:laq,
-laxs, -löq; hl̩ʏ:da-] n. joint-stock
company.

hluti, -a, -ar [hl̩ʏ:tʰɪ, -a(r̩); hl̩ʏ:dɪ]
wm.1 part, portion, share, lot; hluti
e·s part of sth; sbdy's share; gera
á hluta e·s do injustice to, wrong
someone.

hlutum, see hljóta.

hlutur, -ar, -ir [hl̩ʏ:tʰʏr̩, -ar̩, -ɪr̩;
hl̩ʏ:dʏr̩] m.3 thing, lot.

hlutverk, -s, - [hl̩ʏ:tʰverk(s); hl̩ʏ:d̩-]
n. role.

hlý, see hlýr.

hlýða, hlýddi, hlýtt [hl̩i:ða; hl̩id:ɪ,
hl̩iʰt:] wv.2 obey; hlýða e·m obey
sbdy; be proper, það hlýðir ekki,
að . . . it is not proper that . . . ,

it won't do to . . . ; listen: hlýða
á e·ð listen to sth, hlýða e·m yfir
e·ð hear sbdy repeat his lesson,
examine sbdy in sth.

hlýðinn, -in, -ið [hl̩i:ðɪn, -ɪn, -ɪð]
adj. obedient; hlýðinn e·m obedient
to sbdy.

hlýindi [hl̩i:jɪnd̩ɪ] n.pl. warmth, coziness.

hlýja, hlúði, hlúð [hl̩i:ja, hl̩u:ðɪ,
hl̩u:ð] wv.1 (cf. hlúa wv.3) warm,
cover up.

hlýna, -aði, -að [hl̩i:na, -aðɪ, -að]
wv.4 warm up; það hlýnar it is
warming up (S. VI, 14, 3).

hlynna, hlynnti, hlynnt(ur) [hl̩ɪn:a,
hl̩ɪn·tʰɪ, hl̩ɪn·tʰ(ʏr̩); hl̩ɪn·t-] wv.2
hlynna að e·u (c·m) support sth
(sbdy), help out; hlynntur e·m
favoring sbdy.

hlýr, hlý, hlýtt; hlýrri, hlýjastur
[hl̩i:r, hl̩i:, hl̩iʰt:; hl̩ir:ɪ, hl̩i:jast·
ʏr̩] adj. warm, cozy.

hlýt, see hljóta.

hlýtt, see hlýr and hlýða.

hlæja, hlæ, hló, hlógum, hleginn (-ið)
[hl̩ai:ja, hl̩ai:, hl̩ou:, hl̩ou:(q)ʏm,
hl̩ei:jɪn, -ɪð] v.6 laugh; hlæja að
e·u laugh at sth.

hlöð, see hlað.

hlöðu, see 1. hlaða.

hnakki, -a, -ar [hnaʰk̩:ɪ, hnaʰk:a(r̩)]
wm.1 back of the head.

hnakktaska, -tösku, -ur [hnaʰk:tʰaska,
-tʰöskʏ(r̩)] wf.1 saddlebag.

hnakkur, -s, -ar [hnaʰk:ʏr̩, hnaʰk·s,
hnaʰk:ar̩] m.1 man's saddle.

hnaut, see hnjóta.

1. hné, -s, - [hnje:(s)] n. knee.

2. hné, see hníga.

hneig, see hníga.

hnífapar, -s, -pör [hni:va·pʰa:r, ·pʰar̩·s,
-pʰö:r] n. knife and fork.

hnífur, -s, -ar [hni:vʏr̩, hnif·s, hni:v·
ar̩] m.1 knife; razor.

hníga, hníg, hneig (hné), hnigum,
hniginn (-ið) [hni:qa, hni:q, hnei:q,
hnje:, hnɪ:qʏm, hni:jɪn, -ɪð;
hnɪ(i):jɪn] v.1 fall, succumb.

hnippa, hnippti, hnippt [hnɪʰp:a,

Consonants: [ð] breathe; [g] good; [g̩] g̩arden (garden); [hw̩] what; [j] yes; [k̩] cyan
(can); [ŋ] thing; [q] N. Germ. sagen; [r] Scottish r; [x] approx. Germ. ach; [þ] thin.
Voiceless: ○; [b̩, d̩, g̩] approx. p, t, k. Half-voiced: italics. Aspiration and preaspiration:
[ʰ]; [pʰ, tʰ, kʰ] p-, t-, k-. Others as in English.

hníf·tɪ, hnɪf·t] wv.2 *hnippa í e·n* give sbdy a poke (in the ribs).

Hnitbjörg, -bjarga [hnɪ:tʰbjörg̊, -bjarga; hnɪ:d-] n. 'Locked Rocks,' The Einar Jónsson Art Museum.

hnjóta, hnýt, hnaut, hnutum, hnotinn (-ið) [hnjou:tʰa, hnɪ:tʰ, hnöy:tʰ, hnɣ:tʰʏm, hnɔ:tʰɪn, -ɪð; hnjou:d̥a, hni:d̥, hnöy:d̥, hnɣ:d̥ʏm, hnɔ:d̥ɪn] v.2 stumble.

1. hnoða, -, -u, (hnoðna) [hnɔ:ða, -ʏ, hnoð·na] wn. ball of yarn.

2. hnoða, -aði, -að(ur) [hnɔ:ða, -aðɪ, -að, -aðʏr] wv.4 knead.

hnokki, -a, -ar [hnɔʰkj:ɪ, hnɔʰk:a(r)] wm.1 small boy; *slíkur hnokki* such a little shaver.

hnotið, -inn, see *hnjóta.*

hnutum, see *hnjóta.*

hnýt, see *hnjóta.*

1. hóf, -s, - [hou:v, houf·s] n. moderation.

2. hóf, -um, see *hefja.*

hófsemi [houf·sɛ·mɪ] wf.2 moderation.

Hofsjökull, -uls [hɔf·s·jö·kʰʏd̥l, -ʏls; -jö·g̊-] m.1 'Temple Glacier.'

hófur, -s, -ar [hou:vʏr, houf·s, hou:var] m.1 hoof.

hol, -s, - [hɔ:l, hɔ:ls, hɔl·s] n. cavity, hollow; *á hol* into the cavity of the chest; *fara á hol* sink in.

hól, -s [hou:l, houl·s] n. praise.

hola, -u, -ur [hɔ:la, -ʏ(r)] wf.1 hole.

holdgun, -unar, -anir [hɔl·(d)g̊ʏn, -ʏnar, -anɪr] f.2 incarnation.

hólf, -s, - [houl·v, houl·(v)s] n. compartment; *í hólf og gólf* walls and floor alike.

hólfa, -aði, -aður [houl·va, -aðɪ, -að, -aðʏr] wv.4 divide into compartments.

hóll, -s, -ar [houd̥·l, houl·s, hou:lar] m.1 hill, hillock, knoll; also in place names: -*hóll, Hól(s)-.*

Hólmfríður, -ar [houl·(m)fri·ðʏr, -ar] f.1 pers. name.

hólmi, -a, -ar [houl·mɪ, -a(r)] wm.1 islet, small island.

Hólmsá, -ár [houl·msau·(r)] f.1 'Islet River,' *Hólmsárbrú* 'Islet River Bridge.'

hólmur, -s, -ar [houl·mʏr, houlms, houl·mar] m.1 small island, islet.

holt, -s, - [hɔl·t(s)] n. stony hill (bigger than *hóll*); foothill; also in place names: -*holt, Holts-.*

honum, see *hann.*

hóp, -s, - [hou:pʰ(s); hou:b̥(s)] n. a round lagoon, hope.

hópur, -s, -ar [hou:pʰʏr, hou:pʰs, -ar; hou:b̥-] m.1 flock, crowd.

horf, -s, - [hɔr·v, hɔrvs] n. direction; *halda í horfinu* keep (a thing, enterprise) going.

horfa, horfði, horft [hɔr·va, hɔr·(v)ðɪ, hɔr·(f)t] wv.3 look; *horfa á eftir e·m* watch sbdy going.

horfið, -inn, see *hverfa.*

horn, -s, - [hɔd̥·n(s); hɔrd̥n(s)] n. horn; corner (= *götuhorn*); *fyrir hornið* around the corner; *hafa allt illt á hornum sér* be as sour as a pickle (literally: have only evil things on one's horns) (S. I, 4, *1,* 5); *Horn* place name.

Hornafjörður, -fjarðar [hɔd̥·na·fjör·ðʏr, -fjar·ðar] m.3 'Horn Fjord.'

hótel, -s, - [hou:tʰɛl, hou:tʰɛls] n. hotel, *hótelþjónn* waiter, piccolo.

hrá, see *hrár.*

hraður, hröð, hratt [hra:ðʏr, hrö:ð, hraʰt:] adj. quick, swift, fast; *hratt* adv. quickly, fast; *of hratt* too fast.

hrafn, -s, -ar [hrab̥·n, hraf·s, hrab̥·nar] m.1 raven.

hrafnagervi, -s [hrab̥·na·g̊ʲɛr·vɪ(s)] n. the garb of ravens.

Hrafnagil, -s [hrab̥·na·g̊ʲɪ:l, -g̊ʲɪl·s] n. 'Raven Gill,' a parsonage, *Hrafnagils-hjónin* the master and mistress of H.

hrakið, -inn, hrakti, see *hrekja.*

hrár, hrá, hrátt; hrárri, hráastur [hrau:r, hrau:, hrauʰt:, hraur:ɪ, hrau:astʏr] adj. raw.

hratt, see *hraður* and *hrinda.*

hraun, -s, - [hröy:n, hröyn·s] n. lava, rocks.

hraundrangur, -s, -ar [hröyn·draung̊ʏr,

Vowels: *a* [a] approx. father; *á* [au] cow; *e* [ɛ] set; *é* [jɛ] yes; *i, y* [ɪ] sit; *í, ý* [i] feel; *o* [ɔ] law; *ó* [ou] note; *u* [ʏ] approx. Germ. Mütter; *ú* [u] school; *y = i; ý = í*; *æ* [ai] ice; *ö* [ö] Germ. hören; *au* [öy] French feuille; *ei, ey* [ei] ale. Length [:]; half-length [·].

368

-drauŋs, -drauŋg̊aṛ] m.1 lava pillar, lava rock.

hraungjót, -ar, -ir [hröyŋ·g̊ou·tʰ, -aṛ, -ıṛ; -g̊ou·d̥] f.2 lava cleft, lava chasm.

hraustlegur [hṛöys·tlε·qyṛ] adj. (see -legur) valiant, brave; brave-looking, strong-looking.

hraustur, hraust, hraust [hṛöys·t(yṛ)] adj. brave, courageous, valiant.

hreðka, -u, -ur [hṛeð·kʰa, -y(ṛ); hṛεþ·ka] wf.1 radish (= radísa).

hreiður, (-ri), -urs, -ur [hṛei:ðyṛ, hṛeið·rı, hṛei:ðyṛs] n. nest.

hreif, see 2. hrífa.

hrein, see hrína.

hreindýr, -s, - [hṛein·di·r, -dirs] n. reindeer.

hreinlæti, -s [hṛein·lai·tʰı(s), -lai·d̥ı] n. cleanliness.

hreinlætisvörur [hṛein·lai·tʰıs-vö:ryṛ; -lai·d̥ıs-] wf.1.pl. toilet articles; h-vöru-búðir toilet articles stores.

hreinn, hrein, hreint; hreinni, hreinastur [hṛeid·n, hṛei:n, hṛein·tʰ; hṛein·t; hṛeid·nı, hṛei:nastyṛ] adj. clean, clear, pure; sincere; hreinn og beinn straightforward; það er hreinasti óþarfi 'it is the purest extravagance,' it is quite unnecessary; hreint adv. purely.

hreinsa, -aði, -að(ur) [hṛein·sa, -aðı, -að, -aðyṛ] wv.4 clean, cleanse.

hreinskilni [hṛein·sk̥ıIlnı] wf.2 sincerity, candor.

hreinsun, -unar, -anir [hṛein·syn, -ynaṛ, -anıṛ] f.2 cleaning.

hreistur, (-ri), -urs, -ur [hṛeis·tyṛ(s), hṛeistrı] n. scales of fish.

hrekja, hrakti, hrakinn (-ið) [hṛε·k̥ıʰa, hṛax·tı, hṛa:k̥ʰın, -ıð; hṛε:g̊ıa, hṛa:g̊ıIn] wv.1 treat roughly, expose to bad weather, reject.

hrekk, see hrökkva.

hrekkja, hrekkti, hrekkt(ur) [hṛεʰk̥ı:a, hṛεx·tı, hṛεx·t(yṛ)] wv.2 play pranks upon sbdy, tease sbdy.

hrekkur, -s, -ir [hṛεʰk̥:yṛ, hṛεʰk̥·s, hṛεʰk̥ı:ıṛ] m.3 prank, practical joke.

hreppsnefnd, -ar, -ir [hṛεf·snεmd, -aṛ, -ıṛ; hṛεʰp·s-] f.2 the board of a hreppur, local board, 'township board.'

hreppstjóri, -a, -ar [hṛεʰp:stjou·rı, -a(ṛ)] wm.1 sheriff.

hreppur, -s, -ar [hṛεʰp:yṛ, hṛεʰp·s, hṛεf·s, hṛεʰp:aṛ] m.1 the smallest administrative unit in Iceland, 'township,' 'rape.'

hress, hress, hresst [hṛεs:, hṛεs·t] adj. in good spirits (health).

hressa, hressti, hresst(ur) [hṛεs:a, hṛεs·tı, hṛεs·t(yṛ)] wv.2 refresh, cheer up; hressast cheer up (intr.).

hressing, -ar, -ar [hṛεs:ıng̊, -aṛ] f.1 refreshment; fá sér hressingu get a refreshment, regale oneself.

hreyfa, hreyfði, hreyfður (hreyft) [hṛei:va, hṛeiv·ðı, -yṛ, hṛeif·t; hṛeib·ðı] wv.2 move.

hreyfing, -ar, -ar [hṛei:vıng̊, -aṛ] f.1 motion, movement.

hríð, -ar, -ir [hṛi:ð, -ðaṛ, -ðıṛ] f.2 rain or snowstorm, blizzard; throes (of pain); time, while; um langa hríð for a long while.

hríða, -aði, -að [hṛi:ða, -aðı, -að] wv.4 snow and sleet; það hríðar it is snowing (sleeting) (S. VI, 4, 3; 14, 3).

hríðskotabyssa, -u, -ur [hṛið·sk̥ɔ·tʰa-bıs:a, -y(ṛ); -sk̥ɔ·d̥a-] wf.1 automatic rifle.

1. hrífa, -u, -ur [hṛi:va, -y(ṛ)] wf.1 rake.

2. hrífa, hríf, hreif, hrifum, hrifinn (-ið) [hṛi:va, hṛi:v, hṛei:v, hṛı:-vym, hṛı:vın, -ıð] v.1 have effect; catch, move, touch, fascinate; vera hrifinn af e-u be fascinated by sth, admire sth.

hrífuendi, -a, -ar [hṛi:vy-εn·dı, -a(ṛ)] wm.1 the end of the rake (the handle of the rake).

hrífuskaft, -s, -sköft [hṛi:vy-skaf·t(s), -sköf·t] n. rake handle.

hrífuskaftsendi, -a, -ar [hṛi:vyskaf·ts-εn·dı, -a(ṛ)] wm.1 the end of the rake handle.

hrikalegur [hṛı:kʰa-lε·qyṛ; hṛı:g̊a-]

Consonants: [ð] breathe; [g] good; [gı] gyaıden (garden); [hw] what; [j] yes; [kı] cyan (can); [ŋ] thing; [q] N. Germ. sagen; [r] Scottish r; [x] approx. Germ. ach; [þ] thin. Voiceless: o; [b̥, d̥, g̊] approx. p, t, k. Half-voiced: italics. Aspiration and preaspiration: [ʰ]; [pʰ, tʰ, kʰ] p-, t-, k-. Others as in English.

adj. (see *-legur*) gigantic, grand, awe-inspiring.

hrína, hrín, hrein, hrinum, hrininn (-ið) [hr̥i:na, hr̥i:n, hr̥ei:n, hr̥i:- nʏm, hr̥i:nɪn, -ɪð] v.1 cry, bawl, (of children).

hrinda, hrind, hratt, hrundum, hrundinn (-ið) [hr̥ɪn·da, hr̥ɪn·d, hr̥aʰt:, hr̥ʏn·dʏm, hr̥ʏn·dɪn, -ɪð] v.3 push, reject; *hrinda e-m* push sbdy; imperative: *hritt þú, hrittu*, or *hrintu* push! *hrinda* repulse (an attack).

Hringbraut, -ar [hr̥ɪŋ·g̊bröy·tʰ, -ar̥; -bröy·d̥] f.2 'Roundabout Road.'

hringja, hringdi, hringt [hr̥ɪŋ·g̊ɹa, hr̥ɪŋ·dɪ, hr̥ɪŋ·tʰ; hr̥ɪŋ·t] wv.2 ring (bells); *hringja inn* sound the bell to enter church (or a class-room), opposite *hringja út*; *hringja* ring, phone, *hringja upp í síma* ring up (call up) on (over) the telephone.

hringla, -aði, -að [hr̥ɪŋ·la, -aðɪ, -að] wv.4 jingle, rattle.

hringleiksýning, -ar, -ar [hr̥ɪŋ·g̊·lei·kʰ- si·niŋ̊, -ar̥; -lei·g̊-] f.1 circus show.

hringur, -s, -ar, -ir, (-ja) [hr̥ɪŋ·g̊ʏr̥, hr̥ɪŋ·s, hr̥ɪŋ·g̊ar̥, hr̥ɪŋ·g̊ɪr̥, -g̊ɹa] m.1 & 2 ring; *liggja hringinn í kring um e-ð* encompass sth.

hrís, -s, - [hr̥i:s, hr̥is:] n. copse, underbrush; rice; pl. stretches covered with copse.

hrísgrjón [hr̥i:sgrjou·n] n.pl. rice.

hrísgrjónagrautur, -ar [hr̥i:sgrjou·na- gröy:tʰʏr̥, -ar̥; -gröy:d̥ʏr̥] m.1 rice cooked in milk.

hrísgrjónavellingur, -s [hr̥i:sgrjou·na- ved̥·liŋ̊ʏr̥, -iŋs] m.1 rice pudding.

hrísmjölsgrautur, -ar [hr̥i:smjöls- gröy:tʰʏr̥, -ar̥; -gröy:d̥ʏr̥] m.1 rice meal cooked in milk.

Hrísnes, -s [hr̥i:snɛ·s, -nɛs·] n. 'Copse Ness.'

hrjá, hrjáði, hrjáð(ur) [hr̥jau:, hr̥jau:- ðɪ, hr̥jau:ð, hr̥jau:ðʏr̥] wv.3 vex, harass.

hrognkelsi, -s, - [hr̥ɔg̊·ŋk̟ˌʰɛlsɪ(s)] n. lumpfish.

hrokkið, -inn, see *hrökkva*.

hross, -, - [hr̥ɔs:] n. horse.

hrossagaukur, -s, -ar [hr̥ɔs:a·göy:kʰʏr̥, -göyx·s, -göy:kʰar̥; -göy:g̊-] m.1 snipe.

hrossaket (-kjöt), -s [hr̥ɔs:a·k̟ˌʰɛ:tʰ, -k̟ˌʰö:tʰ(s); -k̟ˌʰɛ:d̥, -k̟ˌʰö:d̥] n. horse meat.

hrukkum, see *hrökkva*.

hrundið, -inn, -um, see *hrinda*.

Hruni, -a [hr̥ʏnɪ, -a] wm.1 place name; a parsonage.

hrútaber, -s, -, (-ja) [hr̥u:tʰa·bɛ:r̥, -bɛr·s, -bɛr·ja; hr̥u:da-] n. stone brambleberry.

hrútakofi, -a, -ar [hr̥u:tʰa·kʰɔ:vɪ, -a(r̥); hr̥u:da-] wm.1 ram shed.

hrútur, -s, -ar [hr̥u:tʰʏr̥, hr̥us:, hr̥u:tʰar̥; hr̥u:d̥-] m.1 wether, ram.

hryggur, -jar, -s; -ir, (-ja) [hr̥ɪg̊:ʏr̥, hr̥ɪg̊ˌ:ar̥, hr̥ɪg̊·s, hr̥ɪg̊ˌ:ɪr̥, -g̊ˌ:a] m.2 back, spine, spinal column; ridge (of a mountain, etc.).

hryssa, -u, -ur [hr̥ɪs:a, -ʏ(r̥)] wf.1 mare.

hræðast, hræddist, hræðzt [hr̥ai:ðast, hr̥aid:ɪst, hr̥aið·st] wv.2 (only middle voice) fear, *hrœðast dauðann* fear death, dread death (S. I, 2, 1, 1); *hrœðast* (intr.) be afraid (S. VI, 7, 4).

hræddur, hrædd, hrætt [hr̥aid:ʏr̥, hr̥aid:, hr̥aiʰt:] adj. afraid; *vera hræddur um að . . .* be afraid that, fear that . . .

hræsni [hr̥ais·nɪ] wf.2 hypocrisy.

hröð, see *hraður*.

hrökkbrauð, -s [hr̥öʰk:bröy·ð, -bröyð̥s] n. crisp bread, rye crackers, Swedish *knäckebröd*.

hrökkva, hrekk, hrökk, hrukkum, hrokkinn (-ið) [hr̥öʰk:va, hr̥eʰk:, hr̥öʰk:, hr̥ʏʰk:ʏm, hr̥ɔʰkˌ:ɪn, -ɪð] v.3 jerk, crack; *hrökkva við* jump, be startled.

húfa, -u, -ur [hu:(v)a, -ʏ(r̥)] wf.1 (Pr. 3, 4, 2) cap.

hugað, hugði, see 2. *hyggja*.

hugi, -a [hʏɣ·jɪ, hʏ:qa; hʏ:jɪ] wm.1 mind.

hugmynd, -ar, -ir [hʏq·mɪnd̥, -ar̥, -ɪr̥] f.2 idea; *hafa hugmynd um e-ð* have

---

Vowels: *a* [a] approx. father; *á* [au] cow; *e* [ɛ] set; *é* [jɛ] yes; *ı, y* [ɪ] sit; *í, ý* [i] feel; *o* [ɔ] law; *ó* [ou] note; *u* [ʏ] approx. Germ. Mütter; *ú* [u] school; *y = i*; *ý = í*; *œ* [ai] ice; *ö* [ö] Germ. hören; *au* [öy] French *feuille*; *ei, ey* [ei] ale. Length [:]: half-length [·].

an idea of sth; *hugmynd mín er sú, að* . . . I have an idea that . . . , my plan is to . . .

hugsa, -aði, -að(ur) [hʏx·sa, -aðɪ, -að, -aðʏr̥] wv.4 think; *hugsa sér* imagine; *hugsa um* think of; take care of, provide for; *hugsa um að gera e-ð* think of doing sth.

hugsi [hʏx·sɪ] adj. indecl. in thought; *hann var hugsi* he was lost in thought (S. III, 1, 2n).

hugsjón, -ar, -ir [hʏx·sjou·*n*, -nar̥, -nɪr̥] f.2 ideal.

hugur, -ar, -ir [hʏ:qʏr̥, -ar̥; hʏʏ:jɪr̥] m.3 mind, heart, courage; imagination; *hugur fylgir máli* something is spoken from the heart, sth is meant.

húka, húkti, húkt [hu:kʰa, hux·tɪ, hux·t; hu:g̊a] wv.3 squat.

huldi, hulið, -inn, see *hylja.*

huldudalur, -s, -ir [hʏl·dʏ·da:lʏr̥, -dal·s, -da:lɪr̥] m.2 concealed, hidden valley.

huldufólk, -s [hʏl·dʏ·foul·kʰ, -foul·s; -foul·k] n. elves, fairies, fairy folk, 'hidden folk.'

huldumaður, -manns, -menn [hʏl·dʏ·ma:ðʏr̥, -man·s, -mɛn:] m.4 fairy man, elf.

hún, see *hann.*

Húnaflói, -a [hu:na·flou:ɪ, -a] wm.1 'Bear Cub Bay.'

hunang, -s [hʏ:nauŋg̊, -auŋs] n. honey.

hundheiðinn, -in, -ið; -heiðnari, -astur [hʏn·dhei·ðɪn, -ɪ*n*, -ɪð; -heiðnarɪ, -astʏr̥] adj. heathen as a dog, utterly heathen.

hundrað, -aðs, -uð [hʏn·dra.ð, -aðs, -ʏð] n. num. card. hundred.

hundraðasti [hʏn·draðastɪ] num. ord. one hundredth.

hundraðfaldur, -föld, -falt [hʏn·dra.ð·fal.dʏr̥, -föl·d, -fal·t] adj. hundred-fold.

hundsa, -aði, -að(ur) [hʏn·sa, -aðɪ, -að, -aðʏr̥] wv.4 ignore (as one would ignore a dog).

hundsgarmur, -s, -ar [hʏn·s·garmʏr̥, -garms, -garmar̥] m.1 poor dog, wretch of a dog.

hundur, -s, -ar [hʏn·dʏr̥, hʏn·s, hʏn·d̥·ar̥] m.1 dog (especially the male; the female: *tík*).

hurð, -ar, -ir [hʏr·ð, -ðar̥, -ðɪr̥] f.2 door; *hurð á hjörum* door on hinges.

hurfum, see *hverfa.*

hús, -s, - [hu:s, hus:] n. house; pl. often = *bæjarhús*; in place names: *-hús, Húsa-.*

húsaskipun, -unar [hu:sa·sk₁ɪ:pʰʏn, -ʏnar̥; -sk₁ɪ:b̥ʏn] f.2 arrangement of buildings.

húsasmíðameistari, -a, -ar [hu:sa·smi·ða·meis·tarɪ, -a(r̥)] wm.1 builder.

húsbóndi, -a, -bændur [hus·boundɪ, -a, -baindʏr̥] wm.2 master of the house, head of the family.

húsdýr, -s, - [hu:sdi·r̥, -dɪr̥s] n. domestic animal.

húsfreyja, -u, -ur [hu:sfrei·ja, -ʏ(r̥), hus·-] wf.1 mistress of the house.

húsgagnaverzlun, -unar, -anir [hu:s·gag̊na·vɛrslʏn, -ʏnar̥, -anɪr̥; hus·-] f.2 furniture store.

húsgögn, -gagna [hu:sgög̊n, -gag̊na; hus·-] n.pl. furniture.

húshorn, -s, - [hu:shɔðn(s), -hɔrðn̥] n. corner of the (a) house.

húskveðja, -u, -ur [hu:skʰvɛðja, -ʏ(r̥)] wf.1 'funeral farewell,' a brief oration delivered at the home of the deceased.

húsmæðraskóli, -a, -ar [hu:smaiðra·skou:lɪ, -a(r̥)] wm.1 school for housewives, school of home economics.

hússtjórnarskóli, -a, -ar [hus:-(s)tjourdnar̥·skou:lɪ, -a(r̥)] wm.1 school of home economics.

hvá, hváði, hváð [hwau:, hwau:ðɪ, hwau:ð; kʰvau:(ðɪ), etc.] wv.3 say *hvað?* (= what?), say 'beg your pardon.'

1. hvað [hwa:(ð), kʰva:(ð)] interr. pron. n. (see 2. *hver*) (Pr. 4, 2; In. VI, 5) what; *hvað var það?* what was it (for you), what do you want? *hvað annað?* what else? as

Consonants: [ð] brea*th*e; [g] *g*ood; [g₁] *gy*arden (garden); [hw̥] *wh*at; [j] *y*es; [k₁] *cy*an (can); [ŋ] thi*ng*; [q] N. Germ. sa*g*en; [r] Scottish *r*; [x] approx. Germ. a*ch*; [þ] *th*in. Voiceless: ○; [b̥, d̥, g̊] approx. *p, t, k*. Half-voiced: *italics*. Aspiration and preaspiration: [ʰ]; [pʰ, tʰ, kʰ] *p-, t-, k-*. Others as in English.

371

an adv.: *hvað lengi* (= *hve lengi*)?
how long? *hvað stór?* how big?
2. **hvað** [hwa:(ð); kʰva:(ð)] indef.
pron. (see 3. *hver*) *hvað . . . nú*
whatever; *hvað e-ð snertir* concerning sth; *allt hvað hann getur*
(= *það sem*) all that he can; *hvað
annað . . . sem* whatever else.
1. **hvaða** [hwa:ða; kʰva:ða] interr.
pron. indecl. (In. VI, **5**) what; what
kind of; *hvaða maður er þetta?*
'what man is this?' who is this
man? or: what kind of a man is
this? (S. IV, 5, 2).
2. **hvaða** [hwa:ða; kʰva:ða] indef.
pron. indecl. (in correlative phrases)
whatever, any; *á hvaða tíma* (*dags*)
sem er at whatever time (of day)
it is, at any time (hour); *hvaða
. . . sem er* any . . . whatever.
hvaðan [hwa:ðan; kʰva:ðan] adv.
whence, where from (In. IV, 1, 2-3);
hvaðan . . . sem rel. conj. whence-
so-ever, wherever . . . from (S. VIII,
3(j)).
Hvalfjörður, -fjarðar [hwal·fjörðʏr,
-fjarðar; kʰval·-] m.3 'Whale Fjord.'
hvar [hwa:r; kʰva:r] adv. where;
hvar er hann? where is he? *sér hann,
hvar kemur . . .* he sees where
(= that) there comes . . . ; *víðast
hvar* in most places (In. IV, 1, 2-3);
hvar . . . sem rel. conj. wherever
(S. VIII, 3(j)).
1. **hvarf, -s, hvörf** [hwar·v, hwarvs,
hwör·v; kʰvar·v, kʰvör·v] n. dis-
appearance; hill concealing things
from view.
2. **hvarf,** see *hverfa.*
hvarfla, -aði, -að [hwardla, -aðɪ, -að;
kʰvardla] wv.4 waver, loiter, wander, stroll.
hvass, hvöss, hvasst [hwas:, hwös:,
hwas·t; kʰvas:, etc.] adj. keen-
edged, strong (of wind), sharp,
piercing.
hvatti, -ur, see *hvetja.*
hve [hwe:; kʰve:] adv. how; *hve
mikið?* how much? (In. IV, 1, 2).
hvein, see *hvína.*

hveiti, -s [hwei:tʰɪ(s); hwei:dɪ;
kʰvei:-] n. wheat.
hveitibrauð, -s, - [hwei:tʰɪ-bröy:ð,
-bröyð·s; hwei:dɪ-; kʰvei:-] n. literally: 'wheat bread,' white bread.
hvenær [hwʏ.nair, hwʏ:nar; hwe:-
nair; kʰvʏ:-, kʰve:-] adv. (Pr. 2, *1,*
3n2; In. IV, 1, 2) when; rel. conj.
whenever (S. VIII, 3(j)).
1. **hver, -s; -ar, -ir** [hwe:r, hwer·s,
hwe:rar, -ɪr: kʰve:r, etc.] m.1 & 2
geyser, hot spring.
2. **hver, hver, hvert; hvað** [hwʏ:r,
hwʏr·t, hwa:ð; kʰvʏ:r, kʰvʏr·t;
hwe:r, hwer·t; kʰve:r, kʰver·t;
kʰva:ð], acc. *hvern, hverja, hvert;
hvað* [hwʏd·n, hwʏr·ja; kʰvʏd·n,
kʰvʏr·ja; hwerdn, hwer·ja; kʰverdn,
kʰver·ja], dat. *hverjum, hverri,
hverju* [hwʏr·jʏm, hwʏr:ɪ, hwʏr·jʏ;
kʰvʏr·jʏ(m), kʰvʏr:ɪ; hwer·jʏ(m),
hwer:ɪ; kʰver·jʏ(m), kʰver:ɪ], gen.
hvers, hverrar, hvers [hwʏr·s, hwʏr:-
ar; kʰvʏr·s, kʰvʏr:ar; hwer·s, hwer:-
ar; kʰver·s, kʰver:ar]; plural: *hverjir, hverjar, hver* [hwʏr·jɪr, hwʏr·jar,
hwʏ:r; kʰvʏr·jɪr, kʰvʏr·jar, kʰvʏ:r;
hwer·jɪr, hwer·jar, hwe:r; kʰver·jɪr,
kʰver·jar, kʰve:r], acc. *hverja, hverjar, hver* [hwʏr·ja; kʰvʏr·ja; hwer·ja;
kʰver·ja], dat. *hverjum* [hwʏr·jʏm;
kʰvʏr·jʏm; hwer·jʏm; kʰver·jʏm],
gen. *hverra* [hwʏr:a; kʰvʏr:a;
hwer:a, kʰver:a] (Pr. **2,** *1,* 3n2)
interr. pron. (only strong; In. VI,
5) who, which, what; *hver var það?*
who was it? *hver þeirra?* which of
them? *hann vissi, við hverja hann
átti* he knew what kind of men he
was dealing with; *hvert ykkar?*
which of you (children or a mixed
group)? *hvert?* whither? *hvað?*
what? excuse me! what did you
say? *hvað mörg ár varstu þar?* how
many years were you there? *sjáðu,
hvað* (= *hve*) *vel þetta er gert* look
how well done this is; *en hvað það
var skrítið!* how funny (it was)!
hvers vegna? why? See S. III, 1, 4;
IV, 5, 1; VI, 9, *4,* 2; VII, 2, 2 & 3.

Vowels: *a* [a] approx. *father*; *á* [au] *cow*; *e* [ɛ] *set*; *é* [jɛ] *yes*; *i, y* [ɪ] *sit*; *í, ý* [i] *feel*;
o [ɔ] *law*; *ó* [ou] *note*; *u* [ʏ] approx. Germ. Mütter; *ú* [u] *school*; *y = i*; *ý = í*; *æ* [ai] *ice*;
ö [ö] Germ. *hören*; *au* [öy] French *feuille*; *ei, ey* [ei] *ale*. Length [:]; half-length [·].

3. **hver, hver, hvert; hvað** indef. pron. (forms and pronunciation identical with 2. *hver* above) (In. VI, 6, 2(c)) each, every; *hver sem* whoever, whichever; *hver sem er* whoever there is, anyone; *hvað sem á gengur* whatever is going on; *hvert sem er* whichever place you want to go, to any place; *gef hverjum sitt* give each his due; *hverjum þykir sinn fugl fagur* (proverbial) 'each considers his bird the fair(est) one,' *hvert ofan á annað* each on top of the other; *þriðja hvert ár* every third year; *hvað af hverju* any time now; *hvað um það* even so, in spite of everything; *hvað beztur* (= *einna beztur*) perhaps the best (S. III, 5, 3n1). See S. IV, 6, 11.

hverabrauð, -s, - [hwe̥:ra-brö̥y:ð, -brö̥yð.s; kʰve̥:ra-] n. black bread baked in the steam or hot water of geysers (*scytt brauð*).

Hveragerði, -s [hwe̥:ra-g̥ᵢer·ði(s); kʰve̥:ra-] n. 'Geysers' Hedge,' a town east of Reykjavík.

hverasvæði, -s, - [hwe̥:ra-svai:ði(s); kʰve̥:ra-] n. region with geysers, or hot springs.

Hveravellir, -valla [hwe̥:ra-ved·lɪr, -vad·la; kʰve̥:ra-] m.3.pl. 'Geysers' Field,' deep in the interior of Iceland.

hverfa, hverf, hvarf, hurfum, horfinn (-ið) [hwe̥r·va, hwe̥r·v, hwar·v, hʏr·vʏm, hɔr·vɪn, -ɪð; kʰve̥r·va, kʰver·v, kʰvar·v] v.3 disappear; *hverfa sjónum* vanish from sight; *hverfa* go away.

hverfi, -s, - [hwe̥r·vɪ(s); kʰver·vɪ] n. quarter (in a town or city), neighborhood.

Hverfisgata, -götu [hwe̥r·vɪs-ga:tʰa, -gö:tʰʏ; kʰver·vɪs-; -ga:da, -gö:dʏ] wf.1 'Quarter Street.'

hvergi [hwʏr·g̥ᵢɪ; kʰvʏr·g̥ᵢɪ; hwe̥r·g̥ᵢɪ, kʰver·g̥ᵢɪ] adv. nowhere (Pr. 2, *1*, 3n2).

hverndags- [hwʏn·daxs-; kʰvʏn·daxs-] pref. everyday.

hvernig [hwʏd·nɪɡ, kʰvʏd·nɪɡ, also: hwʏd·nɪn, kʰvʏd·nɪn; hwerdnɪɡ, kʰverdnɪɡ] adv. (Pr. **2**, *1*, 3n2) how; *hvernig er með þetta?* how about this? *hvernig sem* rel. conj. however; *hvernig sem þetta fer* however this may go (S. VIII, 3(j)).

hverskonar [hwe̥r·skʰɔ·nar; kʰve̥r·s-; hwʏr·s-, kʰvʏr·s-] adv. (also *hvers konar*) what kind of.

hversslags [hwʏr·slaxs; kʰvʏr·-] (Pr. **2**, *1*, 3n2) adj. indecl. what kind of *hversslags er þetta!* what *is* this!

hversu [hwe̥r·sʏ, kʰve̥r·sʏ; hwʏr·sʏ, kʰvʏr·sʏ] adv. how (In. IV, *1*, 2).

hversvegna [hwʏr·sve̥g̥na, hwe̥r·s-; kʰvʏr·s-, kʰve̥r·s-] adv. why (also *hvers vegna*).

hvert [hwʏr·t, kʰvʏr·t; hwe̥r·t, kʰver·t] (1) neuter of *hver* 2 & 3; (2) adv. whither, where (Pr. **2**, *1*, 3n2; In. IV, 1, 2-3); (3) *hvert sem* rel. conj. wherever, to any place whatever (S. VIII, 3(j)).

hvessa, hvessti, hvesst(ur) [hwe̥s:a, hwe̥s·tɪ, -ʏr; hwe̥s·t; kʰves:a, etc.] wv.2 sharpen; rise (of storms), increase in velocity; *hann er að hvessa* the storm is rising.

hvetja, hvatti, hvatt(ur) [hwe̥:tʰja, hwaʰt:ɪ, -ʏr, hwaʰt:; kʰve̥:tʰja, kʰvaʰt:, -ɪ, -ʏr; hwe̥:dja; kʰve̥:dja] wv.1 exhort, encourage, whet.

hví [hwi:; kʰvi:] adv. why (In. IV, 1, 2); *hví slœr þú mig?* why do you strike me?

hvíla, hvíldi, hvíldur (hvílt) [hwi:la, hwil·dɪ, -ʏr, hwil·t; kʰvi:la, kʰvil·dɪ, kʰvil·t] wv.2 rest (trans.); *hvíla hestana* rest the horses; *hvíla sig* rest (oneself); *hvílast* rest (intr.).

hvíld, -ar, -ir [hwil·d; -ar, -ɪr; kʰvil·d] f.2 rest; *með hvíldum* by taking a rest every now and then, intermittently.

hvílíkur, -lík, -líkt [hwi:li·kʰʏr, -li·kʰ, -lixt; -li:g̥-; kʰvi:-] interr. pron. what kind of, what (In. VI, **5**; S. IV, 5, 4).

Consonants: [ð] brea*the*; [g] *g*ood; [g̥ᵢ] *gy*arden (garden); [hw] *wh*at; [j] *y*es; [k̥ᵢ] *cy*an (*can*); [ŋ] thi*ng*; [q] N. Germ. sa*g*en; [r] Scottish *r*; [x] approx. Germ. a*ch*; [þ] *th*in. Voiceless: ∘; [b̥, d̥, g̥] approx. *p, t, k*. Half-voiced: *italics*. Aspiration and preaspiration: [ʰ]; [pʰ, tʰ, kʰ] *p-, t-, k-*. Others as in English.

hvína, hvín, hvein, hvinum, hviniŏ [hwɪ:na, hwi:n, hwei:n, hwɪ:nʏm, hwɪ:nɪð; kʰvi:n-, kʰvei:n, kʰvɪ:n-] v.1 whiz, whistle.

Hvítá, -ár [hwi:tʰau.; kʰvi:tʰau.; hwi:dau.; kʰvi:dau.] f.1 'White River.'

hvítabjörn, -bjarnar, -birnir [hwi:tʰa-bjöd.n, -bjad.nar, -bɪd.nɪr; kʰvi:tʰa-; hwi:da-; kʰvi:da-; -björdn, -bjard-nar, -bɪrdnɪr] m.3 polar bear.

hvítasunna, -u, -ur [hwi:tʰa-sʏn:a, -ʏ(r); kʰvi:tʰa-; hwi:da-, kʰvi:da-] wf.1 Whitsun(day); annar í hvíta-sunnu Whitmonday.

hvítkál, -s [hwi:tʰkʰau.l, -kʰauls; kʰvi:tʰ-; hwi:d-, kʰvi:d-] n. white cabbage.

hvítur, hvít, hvítt [hwi:tʰʏr, hwi:tʰ, hwiʰt:; kʰvi:tʰ(ʏr),kʰviʰt:; hwi:d-(ʏr), kʰvi:d(ʏr)] adj. white.

hvolfa, hvolfdi, hvolft [hwɔl.va, hwɔl.-dɪ, hwɔl.t; kʰvɔl.va, kʰvɔl.dɪ, kʰvɔl.t] wv.3 capsize; bátnum hvolfdi (impers.) the boat capsized.

1. hvor, hvor hvort [hwɔ:r, hwɔr.t; kʰvɔ:r, kʰvɔr.t], acc. hvorn, hvora, hvort [hwɔd.n, hwɔ:ra; kʰvɔd.n, kʰvɔ:ra, hwɔrdn, kʰvɔrdn], dat. hvorum, hvorri, hvoru [hwɔ:rʏ(m), hwɔr.ɪ; kʰvɔ:rʏ(m), kʰvɔr:ɪ], gen. hvors, hvorrar, hvors [hwɔr.s, hwɔr:ar; kʰvɔr.s,kʰvɔr:ar]; plural: hvorir, hvorar, hvor [hwɔ:rɪr, -ar, hwɔ:r; kʰvɔ:rɪr, -ar, kʰvɔ:r], acc. hvora, hvorar, hvor [hwɔ:ra; kʰvɔ:ra], dat. hvorum [hwɔ:rʏm; kʰvɔ:rʏm], gen. hvorra [hwɔr:a; kʰvɔr:a] (Instead of [ɔ] this pronoun may be pronounced with an [ʏ] throughout, cf. Pr. 2, 1, 7n3, and is then identical in form with 2. hver) interr. pron. which of two; hvor þeirra var það? which of them was it? (In. VI, 5; S. IV, 5, 3).

2. hvor, hvor, hvort indef. pron. (forms identical with 1. hvor above) indef. pron. each of two = hvor um sig, either; sitt hvoru(m) megin (hvorumegin) við ána on each side

of the river; hvor . . . annan each other; hvor frá annari from each other; hvort sem er (var) in any case (S. IV, 6, 12); þrjár sneiðar af hvoru three slices of each.

hvorki [hwɔr.k,ɪ; kʰvɔr.k,ɪ; hwʏr.k,ɪ, kʰvʏr.k,ɪ] conj· hvorki . . . né neither . . . nor (Pr. 2, 1, 7n3; S. VIII, 2).

hvort [hwɔr.t, kʰvɔr.t; hwʏr.t, kʰvʏr.t] conj. (= neuter of 1. hvor) whether, if; hvort . . . eða whether . . . or; hvort heldur . . . eða whether . . . or; hvort sem er . . . eða whether (it is) . . . or (S. VIII, 2 & 3(i)).

hvortveggja, hvortveggja, hvorttveggja [hwɔr.tʰveg̊,.a; kʰvɔr.-; hwʏr.-, kʰvʏr.-] indef.pron. each of two, both; það er hvorttveggja . . . enda not only . . . but also (In. VI, 6, 2(e); S. IV, 6, 14).

hvorugur, hvorug, hvorugt [hwɔ:rʏqʏr, hwɔ:rʏq,hwɔ:rʏxt; kʰvɔ:r-; hwʏ:r-, kʰvʏ:r-] indef.pron. (Pr. 2, 1, 7n3; In. VI, 6, 2(b)) neither (of two); hvorugt augað neither eye, neither of the eyes (S. II, 7; III, 1, 4; IV, 6, 13).

hvumsa [hwʏm.sa, kʰvʏm.sa] adj. indecl. surprised, astonished, startled.

hvuti, -a, -ar [hwʏ:tʰɪ, -a(r); kʰvʏ:-tʰɪ; hwʏ:dɪ, kʰvʏ:dɪ] wm.1 dog, doggy.

hvörf, see 1. hvarf.

hvöss, see hvass.

1. hyggja, -u, -ur [hɪg̊,:a, -g̊,:ʏ(r)] wf.1 thought, mind; hafa í hyggju intend, plan, have in mind.

2. hyggja, hugði, hugað [hɪg̊,:a, hʏq.-ðɪ, hʏ:qað] wv.1 & 3 think.

hylja, huldi, hulinn (-ið) [hɪl.ja, hʏl.-dɪ, hʏ:lɪn, -ɪð] wv.1 cover, conceal, hide.

hylli [hɪd.lɪ] wf.2 favor, loyalty.

hýrga, -aði, -að(ur) [hir.g̊a, -aðɪ, -að, -aðʏr] wv.4 gladden, pep up.

hýsa, hýsti, hýst(ur) [hi:sa, his.tɪ, his.t(ʏr)] wv.2 house, harbor.

hæð, -ar, -ir [hai:ð, -ðar, -ðɪr] f.2 height, hill; floor, story.

Vowels: a [a] approx. father; á [au] cow; e [ɛ] set; é [jɛ] yes; i, y [ɪ] sit; í, ý [i] feel; o [ɔ] law; ó [ou] note; u [ʏ] approx. Germ. Mütter; ú [u] school; y = i; ý = í; æ [ai] ice; ö [ö] Germ. hören; au [öy] French feuille; ei, ey [ei] ale. Length [:]; half-length [·].

hæfa, hæfði, hæfður (hæft) [hai:va,
haiv·ðɪ, haiv·ðʏr̥, haif·t; haib·ðɪ,
-ʏr̥] wv.2 hit, score a hit.

hæg, see *hægur.*

hægð, -ar, -ir [haiq·ð, -ðar̥, -ðɪr̥;
haig̊·þ] f.2 ease; *í hægðum sínum*
at a leisurely pace, slowly.

hægfara [haiq·fa·ra] adj. indecl. slow,
tardy; (politically) conservative.

hægindastóll, -s, -ar [hai:jɪnda-
stoud·l̥, -stoul·s, -stou:lar̥] m.1 easy
chair.

hægri [haiq·rɪ] adj. compar. (of
hægur) right; *hægri hönd* right
hand; *hægra megin* on the right
side.

hægur, hæg, hægt; hægri, hægastur
[hai:qʏr̥, hai:q, haix·t; haiq·rɪ,
hai:qastʏr̥] adj. slow, gentle, easy,
possible; *hægur vindur, hæg átt*
gentle wind; *það kynni að vera
hægt* it might be possible; (*það*)
er hægt að . . . it is possible to
. . . ; adv. *hægt* slowly; *farðu
hægt!* go slow! *hægara* more
slow(ly), easier; *það er hægara
sagt en gert* it is easier said than
done; *hægri hönd* right hand, cf.
above.

hækka, -aði, -að(ur) [haiʰk:a, -aðɪ,
-að, -aðʏr̥] wv.4 grow taller;
heighten, elevate.

hæll, -s, -ar [haid·l̥, hail·s, hai:lar̥]
m.1 heel; *setja hæla á skó* put
heels on shoes.

hæna, -u, -ur [hai:na, -ʏ(r̥)] wf.1
hen.

hænsnaket (-kjöt), -s [hainsna-k,ʰɛ:tʰ,
-k,ʰö:tʰ(s); -k,ʰɛ:d̥, -k,ʰö:d̥] n.
chicken meat, chicken; fowl.

hænsni, -s, - [hainsnɪ(s)] n. chicken.

hærri, hæstur, see 2. *hár.*

1. hætta, -u, -ur [haiʰt:a, -ʏ(r̥)]
wf.1 danger.

2. hætta, hætti, hætt [haiʰt:a, -ɪ,
haiʰt:] wv.2 put in danger, en-
danger, stake, risk; *hætta lífi sínu*
risk one's life; *e-m hættir við e-u*
sbdy is liable to (have) sth (e.g.
some sickness).

3. hætta, hætti, hætt(ur) [haiʰt:a, -ɪ,
-ʏr̥, haiʰt:] wv.2 leave off, cease;
hætta e-u, hætta að gera e-ð cease
sth, cease doing sth.

hættir, see *háttur* and *hætta* 2. & 3.

hættulegur [haiʰt:ʏ-lɛ:qʏr̥] adj. (see
-legur) dangerous.

höf, see *haf.*

höfðingi, -ja, -jar [höv·ðiŋg̊,ɪ, -iŋ·
g̊,a(r̥); höb·ð-] wm.1 chieftain,
chief.

höfn, hafnar, hafnir [höb·n̥, hab·nar̥,
-ɪr̥] f.2 harbor; *á h·ina* into the
harbor.

höft, see 1. *haft* and *hafa.*

höfuð, -uðs, -uð [hö:vʏð, -ʏðs] n.
head; *með hatt á höfði* with hat(s)
on his (their) head(s); *láta e-ð
ekki undir höfuð leggjast* not to
neglect sth, not leave sth undone.

höfuðbað, -baðs, -böð [hö:vʏð-ba:ð,
-bað·s, -bö:ð] n. shampoo.

höfuðdeild, -ar, -ir [hö:vʏð-deil·d̥, -ar̥,
-ɪr̥] f.2 army corps.

höfuðverkur, -jar, -ir, (-ja) [hö:vʏð-
vɛr̥·kʏr̥, -vɛr̥·k,ar̥, -k,ɪr̥] m.2 headache.

höfuðþáttur, -ar, -þættir [hö:vʏð-
þauʰt:ʏr̥, -ar̥, -þaiʰt:ɪr̥] m.3 chief
strand, element.

höfundur, -ar, -ar [hö:vʏndʏr̥, -ar̥]
m.1 author.

högg, (-vi), -s, - [hög̊:(vɪ), hög̊·s] n.
blow, knock.

höggva, hegg, hjó, hjuggum, höggvinn
(-ið) [hög̊:va, hɛg̊:, hjou:, hjʏg̊:-
ʏm, hög̊:vɪn, -ɪð] v.7 hew, strike.

hökull, -uls, -lar [hö:kʰʏdl̥, -ʏls, höʰk·l·
ar̥; hö:g̊-] m.1 chasuble.

höll, hallar, hallir [höd·l̥, had·lar̥,
had·lɪr̥] f.2 palace.

hölt, see *haltur.*

höm, hamar, hamir [hö:m, ha:mar̥,
-ɪr̥] f.2 haunch, buttock.

hönd, handar, hendur [hön·d̥, han·dar̥,
hɛn·dʏr̥] f.3 hand; *í hendinni* in
the hand; *á vinstri hönd* to the
left; *til beggja handa* on both
sides; *njóttu heill handa!* bravo
for you to have done this! (S.

Consonants: [ð] brea*th*e; [g] *g*ood; [g,ɪ] *gy*arden (garden); [hʍ] *wh*at; [j] *y*es; [k,ɪ] *cy*an
(can); [ŋ] thi*ng*; [q] N. Germ. sa*g*en; [r] Scottish *r*; [x] approx. Germ. ach; [þ] *th*in.
Voiceless: o; [b̥, d̥, g̊] approx. *p, t, k.* Half-voiced: *italics.* Aspiration and preaspiration:
[ʰ]; [pʰ, tʰ, kʰ] *p-, t-, k-.* Others as in English.

VI, **10**, 5); *þeir ráku óvinina af
höndum sér* they drove their
enemies off (their hands) (S. I,
4, *1*, 3 & 5); *taka e-n höndum*
arrest sbdy (S. I, **3**, *1*, 2(e)); *hafa
lítið að gera í hendurnar á e-m* be
no match for sbdy; *fyrir hönd e-s*
on behalf of sbdy; *ganga á hönd
e-m* surrender to sbdy; become
vassal to sbdy; *láta af hendi* give
up, deliver (up); *af náttúrunnar
hendi* by nature, of natural causes,
natural; *vera fyrir hendi* be at
hand, exist; *takast á hendur* undertake; *allra handa* of all kinds, all
kinds of.

hönk, hankar, hankir [höyŋ·kʰ, hauŋ·-
kʰaṛ, hauŋ·kˌʰɪṛ; höyⁿ̥·k, hauⁿ̥·kaṛ,
hauⁿ̥·kˌɪṛ] f.2 hank, coil.

hörð, see *harður*.

Höskuldur, -s, (-ar) [hös·kɤldɤṛ, -aṛ;
hös·kɤl(d̥)s] m.1 pers. name; patronymics: *Höskuldsson, -dóttir,
Höskuldar-dóttir*.

höst, see **hastur**.

I.

í [i:] **A.** prep. with acc. (mostly in
phrases of motion) in, into, for,
as, to (S. I. **2**, *3*, 2): (1) of place:
in, into: *inn í skólann* into the
schoolhouse; *fara í kaupstaðinn* go
to town; *líta í bók* look into (at)
a book; *leggja í ferð* start a
journey; *í burtu* away; *í suður*
south; *í bak og brjóst* behind and
in front; (2) with preps and advs:
í gegnum (í gegn um) prep. with
acc. through; *í kringum (í kring
um)* prep. with acc. around, round
ıbout; (3) in, for, as: *taka e-n í
'æði* board sbdy, give sbdy board;
í kostnað for expenses; *í jólagjöf*
as a Christmas gift; *tvo í tólf hefur
maður sex sinnum* two is contained
six times in twelve; (4) denoting
rest, of place: *í efra, í neðra, í
ytra, í innra* in the upper, lower,
outer, inner regions (from *hið efra*,

etc.); (5) of time: in, during, for:
*í dag, í kvöld, í nótt, í morgun,
í sumar (vor, vetur, haust)* today,
tonight (= in the evening), tonight
(= during the night), this morning,
this summer (spring, winter, fall);
at a certain time: *í fyrradag* the
day before yesterday; *í gær* yesterday; *í gamla daga* in the (good)
old days, of yore; *í langan tíma* for
a long time (= *um langan tíma*);
í hvert sinn each time.
B. prep. with dat. (in phrases
denoting rest; S. I, **3**, *3*, 2):
(1) of space: in, on, at: *í húsinu*
in the house; *í kirkjunni* in the
church; *í fjörunni* on the shore
(beach); *í Frakklandi* in France;
í suðri in the south, due south;
góður í e-u good at sth; *lesa í bók*
read (in) a book; *í góðum fötum*
wearing good clothes; *augun í mér*
my eyes (literally: 'the eyes in
me') (S. I, **4**, *1*, 4); (2) of time:
in: *í því* in that moment (= *í því
bili*); *í þessum mánuði* this month.

íbúð, -ar, -ir [i:bu·ð̥, -ð̥aṛ, -ð̥ɪṛ] f.2
apartment (or a house), habitation;
til íbúðar for habitation.

iðja, -u, -ur [ɪð̥·ja, -ɤ(ṛ)] wf.1 occupation, industry.

iðjusemi [ɪð̥·jɤ·sɛ:mɪ] wf.2 industry.

iðn, -ar, -ir [ɪð̥·n̥, -naṛ, -nɪṛ] f.2 trade,
handicraft.

iðnaðarmaður, -manns, -menn [ɪð̥·nað̥-
ar·ma:ð̥ɤṛ, -man·s, -mɛn:] m.4
handicraftsman, artisan.

iðnaður, -aðar [ɪð̥·nað̥ɤṛ, -að̥aṛ] m.3
industry.

iðnmál [ɪð̥·nmau·l̥] n.pl. issues, affairs,
matters concerning or pertaining to
the handicrafts.

iðnskóli, -a, -ar [ɪð̥·nskou·lɪ, -a(ṛ)]
wm.1 technical school, vocational
school, handicrafts school.

iðnþing, -s, - [ɪð̥·nþiŋ̊, -þiŋs] n. convention of handicraftsmen.

iðra, -aði, -að [ɪð̥·ra, -að̥ɪ, -að̥] wv.4
repent; *mig iðrar e-s* I repent of
sth; but usually in the middle

Vowels: *a* [a] approx. father; *á* [au] cow; *e* [ɛ] set; *é* [jɛ] yes; *i, y* [ɪ] sit; *í, ý* [i] feel;
o [ɔ] law; *ó* [ou] note; *u* [ɤ] approx. Germ. Mütter; *ú* [u] school; *y = i; ý = í;* *œ* [ai] ice;
ö [ö] Germ. hören; *au* [öy] French *feuille; ei, ey* [ei] ale. Length [:]; half-length [·].

voice: *iðrast e-s* repent of sth; *ég iðrast þess* I repent of it; *iðrast eftir e-u* (*e-ð*) repent of sth.

Iðunn, -unnar [ɪ:ðʏn, -ʏn·aṛ] f.2 the goddess of youth in Old Icelandic mythology; name of a drugstore in Reykjavík.

ígerð, -ar, -ir [i:gˌerð, -ðaṛ, -ðɪṛ] f.2 boil.

íhald, -s [i:halḍ(s)] n. conservatism, coll. the Conservatives.

íhaldsflokkur, -s, -ar [i:hal(ḍ)s-flɔʰk:-ʏṛ, -flɔʰk·s, -flɔʰk:aṛ] m.1 Conservative party; *Íhaldsflokkurinn* 'the Conservative party.'

íhaldsmaður,-manns,-menn [i:hal(ḍ)s-ma:ðʏṛ, -man·s, -men:] m.4 conservative.

il, iljar, iljar [ɪ:l, ɪl·jaṛ] f.1 sole of the foot.

ill, see *illur*.

illa; verr, verst [idˌla, ɪdˌla, ver:, verst] adv. badly, worse, worst (In. IV, 2(d)); *nú fór illa* this went badly.

illfýsi [idˌlfi·sɪ] wf.2 malice.

illfær, -fær, -fært [idˌlfai·r, -faiṛt] adj. hardly passable, hardly possible to execute.

illska, -u [il·ska, -ʏ] wf.1 evil, hatred; *fullur illsku* (gen.) full of evil (hatred).

illur, ill, illt; verri, verstur [idˌlʏṛ, idˌl, idˌl·t; ɪdˌlʏṛ, ɪdˌl, ɪl·t; ver:ɪ, verstʏṛ] adj. (Pr. 2, 1, 5n2; In. III, 4, 5) bad, ill, evil; worse, worst; *mér er* (*verður*) *illt* I am (getting) sick, ill; *illt* evil; *launa illt með góðu* requite evil with good (S. III, 3, 2); *hið illa* evil; *þeim var ég verst, er ég unni mest* I was worst to him I loved the most (S. III, 5, 1); *illur yfirferðar* hard to pass; *nú er illt í efni* worse luck!

ilmsmyrsl(i), -s, - [ɪl·msmɪṛsl, -s, -lɪ, -s] n. toilet cream, face cream.

ilmur, -s [ɪl·mʏṛ, ɪlms] m.1 odor, fragrance, scent.

ilmvatn, -s, -vötn [ɪl·mvaʰtn, -vas·, -vöʰtn] n. toilet water, perfume.

Ingibjörg, -bjargar, -bjargir [iŋ·ĝˌɪ-björ·ĝ, -bjar·ĝaṛ, -bjar·ĝˌɪṛ] f.2 pers. name.

Ingileif, -ar, -ar [iŋ·ĝˌɪ-lei·v, -vaṛ] f.1 pers. name.

Ingólfur, -s [iŋ·ĝoulvʏṛ, -oul(v)s] m.1 pers. name; *Ingólfur Arnarson* (fl. 874) first settler of Iceland.

Ingveldur, -ar, -ar [iŋ·ĝveldʏṛ, -aṛ] f.1 pers. name.

1. inn [ɪn:] (1) adv. (In. IV, 1, 3) in, into; *ganga inn* go in, enter; *fara inn í húsið* go into the house; *inn af e-u* inwards from some point, extending upwards from some point; *inn fyrir* (motion) inside, in beyond (a point or limit); *inn fyrir þröskuldinn* crossing the threshold going in; *inn fyrir bæ* crossing the city limits going inland; (2) prep. with acc.; *inn dalinn* up the valley (S. I, 2, 3, 3).

2. inn, in, ið, see 1. *hinn, hin, hið.*

innan [ɪn:an] (1) adv. (In. IV, 1, 3; S. I, 2, 3, 3) from within (= out); *innan að* from within, from the inside, from the interior (of the country); *fyrir innan* adv. inside (rest); prep. with acc.: *fyrir innan hurðina* inside the door; *fyrir innan bæinn* up above the farmstead (the town), or: on that side of the farmstead (town) which faces inland; (2) prep. with acc. *innan dalinn* down the valley; (3) prep. with gen. of time: *innan skamms* shortly, within a short time; also of space, but mostly in compounds: *innanlands* within the country.

innangengt [ɪn:an-gˌeiŋ·tʰ; -gˌeiŋ·t] ppn. passable from within; *það er innangengt í fjósið* there is a passage leading from the *bær* (= the main group of houses) to the cow shed.

innanlands [ɪn:an-lan·s] adv. within the country.

innanlandsmál [ɪn:anlans-mau:l] n. pl. domestic affairs.

innar, innst [ɪn:aṛ, ɪn·st] adv. (com

Consonants: [ð] brea*the*; [g] *g*ood; [gⱼ] *g*yarden (garden); [hw] *wh*at; [j] *y*es; [kⱼ] *c*yan (can); [ŋ] thi*ng*; [q] N. Germ. sa*g*en; [r] Scottish *r*; [x] approx. Germ. a*ch*; [þ] *th*in. Voiceless: ○; [b̥, d̥, g̊] approx. *p, t, k*. Half-voiced: *italics*. Aspiration and preaspiration: [ʰ]; [pʰ, tʰ, kʰ] *p-, t-, k-*. Others as in English.

377

par. and superl. of *inni* within)
farther within, farthest within.

innflúenza, -u, -ur [ɪn·flu·ɛn·sa, -ʏ(r̥)]
wf.1 influenza (also: *flenza* = flu).

innflutningur, -s, -ar [ɪn·flʏʰtniŋ·g̊ʏr̥,
-iŋ·s, -iŋ·g̊ar̥] m.1 import.

innfluttur, -flutt, -flutt [ɪn·flʏʰt·(ʏr̥)]
adj. (pp. of *flytja inn*) imported.

inngangsorð, -s, - [ɪŋ·gauŋs·ɔr·ð, -ɔrðs]
n. password.

inngangur, -s, -ar [ɪŋ·gauŋg̊ʏr̥, -gauŋs,
-gauŋg̊ar̥] m.1 entrance.

1. innheimta, -u, -ur [ɪn:heimtʰa,
-ʏ(r̥); -heimta] wf.1 collecting (of
debts, etc.).

2. innheimta, -heimti, -heimt(ur) [ɪn:-
heimtʰa, -heimtʰɪ, -ʏr̥, -heimtʰ;
-heimt-] wv.2 collect (debts, taxes,
etc.).

innheimtukostnaður, -aðar [ɪn:heim-
tʰʏ·kɔstnaðʏr̥, -ar̥; -heimtʏ-] m.3
cost of collecting; *í innheimtukostnað* for the cost of collecting.

inni [ɪn:ɪ] adv. inside, indoors, in,
within; *inni í húsinu* inside the
house (In. IV, 1, 3).

innifalinn, -in, -ið [ɪn:ɪ·fa:lɪn, -ɪn,
-ɪð] adj. (pp.) *i. í* included in.

innilegur [ɪn:ɪ·lɛ·qʏr̥] adj. (see
-legur) cordial, heartfelt.

inniskór [ɪn:ɪ·skou:r̥] m.1.pl. slippers.

innkaup, -s, - [ɪŋ·kʰöy·pʰ, -kʰöyfs;
-kʰöy·b] n. wholesale buying (from
a foreign country); pl. *innkaup*
purchases; *gera innkaup* make purchases.

innleiða, -leiddi, -leiddur (-leitt)
[ɪn·lei·ða, -leid·ɪ, -ʏr̥, -leiʰt·] wv.2
introduce (the metric system).

innlendur, -lend, -lent [ɪn·lɛnd(ʏr̥),
-lɛntʰ; -lɛnt] adj. domestic, native;
innlendur markaður home market.

innrás, -ar, -ir [ɪn·rau·s, -ar̥, -ɪr̥] f.2
invasion, attack.

innri, innstur [ɪn·rɪ, ɪnstʏr̥] adj.
compar. and superl. inner, interior,
innermost; *innri maður* the inner
being, one's true self.

inntaka, -töku, -ur [ɪn·tʰa·kʰa, -tʰö·-
kʰʏ(r̥); -tʰa·g̊-, -tʰö·g̊-] wf.1 admis-

sion (to a school); dose (of a
medicine).

Írland, -s [ir·land(s)] n. Ireland, Eire.

írskur, írsk, írskt [irskʏr̥, irsk, irst]
adj. Irish.

ís, -s, -ar [i:s, is:, i:sar̥] m.1 ice.

Ísafjarðardjúp, -s [i:safjarðar·dju:pʰ,
-s; -dju:b] n. 'Ice Fjord Deep.'

Ísafjörður, °-fjarðar [i:sa·fjör·ðʏr̥,
-fjar·ðar̥] m.3 'Ice Fjord.'

ísbjörn, -bjarnar, -birnir [i:sbjödn,
-bjadnar̥, -bɪdnɪr̥; -björdn, -bjardnar̥,
-bɪrdnɪr̥] m.3 polar bear.

Ísland, -s [i:sland, -lan(d)s] n. Iceland.

Íslandsglíman, -unnar [i:slan(d)s-
gli:man, -gli:mʏn·ar̥] wf.1 with the
def. art. 'The Iceland Wrestling
Match.'

Íslendingasögur, -sagna [i:slɛndiŋga·
sö:qʏr̥, -sag̊·na] wf.1.pl. the Icelandic family sagas, the sagas of
the Icelanders.

Íslendingur, -s, -ar [i:slɛndiŋg̊ʏr̥, -iŋs,
-iŋg̊ar̥] m.1 Icelander.

íslenzka, -u [i:slɛnska, -ʏ] wf.1 Icelandic.

íslenzkur, -lenzk, -lenzkt [i:slɛnskʏr̥,
-lɛnsk, -lɛnst] adj. Icelandic; *Íslenzk fornrit* Old Icelandic Texts,
comprising the Sagas, the Eddas,
Chronicles of the Norwegian Kings,
the Mythical-heroic sagas (*fornald-
arsögur*), etc.

issi, sissi [ɪs:ɪ, sɪs:ɪ] interj. tish, tush.

ístað, -s, -stöð [i:sta·ð, -staðs, -stö·ð]
n. stirrup.

ívið [i:vɪ·ð] adv. a little bit; *ívið
betri* a little bit better, slightly
better.

Íþaka, -þöku [i:þa·kʰa, -þö·kʰʏ; -þa·g̊a,
-þö·g̊ʏ] wf.1 Ithaca; the library of
Menntaskólinn, Reykjavík.

íþrótt, -ar, -ir [i:þrouʰt·, -ar̥, -ɪr̥] f.2
sport.

íþróttamaður, -manns, -menn [i:-
þrouʰt·a·ma·ðʏr̥, -man·s, -mɛn:] m.4
sportsman, athlete.

íþróttaskóli, -a, -ar [i:þrouʰt·a·skou:-

Vowels: *a* [a] approx. father; *á* [au] cow; *e* [ɛ] set; *é* [jɛ] yes; *i, y* [ɪ] sit; *í, ý* [i] feel;
o [ɔ] law; *ó* [ou] note; *u* [ʏ] approx. Germ. Mütter; *ú* [u] school; *y* = *i*; *ý* = *í*; *æ* [ai] ice;
ö [ö] Germ. hören; *au* [öy] French *feuille*; *ei, ey* [ei] ale. Length [:]; half-length [·].

lí, -a(r̯)] wm.1 sports school, athletic school.

íþróttaviðburður, -ar, -ir [i:þrou^hta·
við·bɤrðɤr̯, -ar̯, -ir̯] m.3 sport event.

íþróttavöllur, -vallar, -vellir [i:-
þrou^ht·a·vöd̯·lɤr̯, -vad̯·lar̯, -ved̯·lir̯]
m.3 arena, stadium, sports field;
íþróttavöllurinn ' The Sports Field,'
(of Reykjavík).

J.

ja [ja(:)] interj. well.

já [jau:] adv. yes (in answer to
affirmative questions); *er hann
heima?* *já* is he at home? yes; but:
er hann ekki heima? *jú* is he not at
home? yes, he is.

1. jafn, jöfn, jafnt [jab̯·n̯, jöb̯·n̯,
jam·t^h; jam̯·t; jaf·t] adj. even,
equal.

2. jafn- [jab̯·n̯-] pref. even, equal,
equally.

jafna, -aði, -að(ur) [jab̯·na, -aði, -að,
-aðɤr̯] wv.4 make even, set right;
compare; *jafna til e-s* cite, quote
sth in comparison.

jafnaðar, see *jöfnuður*.

jafnaðargeð, -s [jab̯·naðar-g̯ɛ:ð,
-g̯ɛð·s] n. even temper.

jafnaðarmaður, -manns, -menn [jab̯·-
naðar-ma:ðɤr̯, -man·s, -mɛn:] m.4
socialist.

jafnaðarstefna, -u [jab̯·naðar̯-stɛb̯·na,
-ɤ] wf.1 socialism.

jafnan [jab̯·nan] adv. always, commonly.

jafnfætis [jab̯·nfai·t^hɪs; -fai·d̯ɪs] adv.
standa jafnfætis e-m be on equal
standing with sbdy, be one's equal.

jafngamall, -gömul, -gamalt [jab̯·nga·-
mad̯l, -gö·mɤl, -ga·malt; jam·-] adj.
jafngamall mér of the same age as I
(S. I, 3, *2*, 1).

jafnlyndi, -s [jab̯·nlɪndɪ(s)] n. even
temper, equanimity.

jafnnær [jab̯·nai:r] adj. indecl. or
adv. equally near (to a goal) *þau
komu jafnnær aftur* they returned
as wise as they went.

jafnóðum [jab̯·nou·ðɤm] adv. as soon,
just as quickly.

jafnskjótt [jab̯·nsk̯ɪou^ht·] adv. (just)
as soon; *jafnskjótt sem* conj. as
soon as = *jafnskjótt og* (S. VIII,
3(h) & 4).

jafnvel [jab̯·nvɛ·l] adv. even.

jakkaföt, -fata [ja^hk:a-fö:t^h, -fa:t^ha;
-fö:d̯, -fa:d̯a] n.pl. men's clothes.

jakki, -a, -ar [ja^hk̯ɪ:ɪ, -k:a(r̯)] wm.1
jacket (man's or woman's).

Jakob, -s [ja:k^hɔ·b̯(s), ja:g̯ɔ·b̯(s)]
m.1 Jacob, James.

jan. =

janúar [ja:nu·ar] m. indecl. January.

jarða, -aði, -að(ur) [jar·ða, -aðɪ, -að,
-aðɤr̯] wv.4 bury, inter.

jarðar, -ir, see *jörð*.

jarðarber, -s, -, (-ja) [jar·ðar-bɛ:r,
-bɛr·s, -bɛr·ja] n. strawberry.

jarðarför, -farar, -farir [jar·ðar̯-fö:r,
-fa:rar̯, -ɪr] f.2 funeral.

jarðfræði [jar·ðfrai·ðɪ] wf.2 geology.

jarðvegur, -vegs, -vegir [jar·ðvɛ·qɤr̯,
-vɛxs, -vei·jɪr̯] m.2 soil.

járn, -s, - [jaud̯·n̯, jaud̯·n̯s; jaurd̯n̯(s)]
n. iron.

járnvörudeild, -ar, -ir [jaud̯·nvö·rɤ-
deil·d̯, -ar̯, -ɪr̯] f.2 hardware department.

járnvöruverzlun, -unar, -anir [jaud̯·n-
vö·rɤ-verslɤn, -ɤnar̯, -anɪr̯] f.2 hardware store.

jarpur, jörp, jarpt [jar·pɤr̯, jör·p,
jar·(p)t] adj. bay (of horses only);
sá jarpi = *Jarpur* the bay horse;
sú jarpa = *Irpa* the bay mare (S.
III, 3, 3); brown.

Jarþrúður, -ar [jar·þru·ðɤr̯, -ar̯] f.1
pers. name.

játa, -aði, -að [jau:t^ha, -aðɪ, -að;
jau:d̯a] wv.4 *játa e-u* say yes to
sth, agree to sth; own, admit sth;
assent, consent to sth.

Jesús, -ú (-úsar) [jɛ:su·s, -u·; -u·sar̯]
m.1 Jesus.

Jóhann, -s [jou:han·(s)] m.1 Johan,
John.

Jóhanna, -hönnu [jou:han·a, -hön·ɤ]
wf.1 Joan.

Consonants: [ð] brea*th*e; [g] *g*ood; [g̯ɪ] *gy*arden (garden); [hw̯] *wh*at; [j] *y*es; [k̯ɪ] *cy*an
(can); [ŋ] thi*ng*; [q] N. Germ. sa*g*en; [r] Scottish *r*; [x] approx. Germ. a*ch*; [þ] *th*in.
Voiceless: ○; [b̯, d̯, g̯] approx. *p*, *t*, *k*. Half-voiced: *italics*. Aspiration and preaspiration:
[^h]; [p^h, t^h, k^h] *p*-, *t*-, *k*-. Others as in English.

Jóhannes, -ar (-s) [jou:han·es, -aɽ]
m.1 John patronymic: Jóhannesson.
jók, see auka.
jól [jou:l] n.pl. Christmas; á jólunum
at Christmas; annar í jólum the
second day of Christmas.
jóladagur, -s, -ar [jou:la-da:qɣɽ,
-dax·s, -da:qaɽ] m.1 Christmas Day.
jólakaka, -köku, -ur [jou:la-kʰa:kʰa,
-kʰö:kʰɣ(r̥); -kʰa:g̊a,-kʰö:g̊ɣɽ] wf.1
raisin bread; raisin cake.
jólakort, -s, - [jou:la-kʰɔr̥·t(s)] n.
Christmas card.
jólamatur, -ar [jou:la-ma:tʰɣɽ, -aɽ;
-ma:dɣɽ]m.3 Christmas fare (food).
jólanótt, -nætur, -nætur [jou:la-
nouʰt:; -nai:tʰɣr; -nai:dɣɽ] f.3
Christmas eve.
jólasveinn, -s, -ar [jou:la-sveid·n̥,
-svein·s, -svei:naɽ] m.1 Yule goblin.
Jón, -s, -ar [jou:n, joun·s, jou:naɽ]
m.1 John; Jón Sigurðsson (1811-79)
famous statesman.
Jónas, -ar (-s) [jou:na·s, -ar] m.1
Jonas; patronymic: Jónasson.
Jónína, -u [jou:ni·na, -ɣ] wf.1 pers.
name.
jórtur, (-ri), -urs [jour̥·tɣr(s), jour̥trɪ]
n. the cud; chewing the cud.
jós, see 2. ausa.
jú [ju:] adv. yes (answering a negative question); er hann ekki heima?
jú is he not at home? yes, he is.
jukum, see auka.
júlí [ju:li·] m. indecl. July.
júní [ju:ni·] m. indecl. June.
jusum, see 2. ausa.
jæja [jai:ja] interj. well, all right.
jöfn, see 1. jafn.
jöfnuður, jafnaðar [jöb·nɣðɣɽ, jab··
naðaɽ] m.3 equal proportion, equity,
fairness; til jafnaðar on the average.
jökulá, -ár, -ár [jö:kʰɣl-au:(r); jö:g̊·]
f.1 glacier river.
Jökulgil, -s, - [jö:kʰɣl-g̊ˌɪ:l, -g̊ˌɪl·s;
jö:g̊ɣl-] n. 'Glacier Gorge.'
jökull, -uls, -lar [jö:kʰɣdl, -ɣls, jöʰk·l-
aɽ; jö:g̊·] m.1 glacier.
jökulvatn, -s, -vötn [jö:kʰɣl-vaʰt·n̥,

-vas:, -vöt·n̥; -jö:g̊·] n. glacier
river.
jörð, jarðar, -ir [jör·ð, jar·ðaɽ, jar·ðɪɽ]
f.2 earth, ground; farm, estate;
pl. farmsteads, estates.
jörp, see jarpur.
Jörundur, -ar (-s) [jö:rɣndɣɽ, -ɣndaɽ,
-ɣnd̥s] m.1 pers. name.

K.

kaf, -s, köf [kʰa:v, kʰaf·s, kʰö:v] n.
plunge into water; deep water;
dense smoke or steam; fara á kaf
go under water.
kafa, -aði, -að [kʰa:va, -aðɪ, -að] wv.4
dive, plunge in, submerge oneself,
in water, etc.
kafbátur, -s, -ar [kʰav-bau·tʰɣɽ;
-bau·tʰs, -baus·; -bau·tʰaɽ; -bau·d̥-]
m.1 submarine, u-boat.
kafði, kafið, -inn, see kefja.
kaffi, -s [kʰaf:ɪ(s)] n. coffee.
kaffibrauð, -s [kʰaf:ɪ-bröy:ð, -bröyð·s]
n. cakes or cookies served with
coffee.
kaffihús, -s, - [kʰaf:ɪ-hu:s, -hus:] n.
café.
kaffikanna, -könnu, -ur [kʰaf:ɪ-kʰan:a,
-kʰön:ɣ(r̥)] wf.1 coffeepot.
kaffisopi, -a, -ar [kʰaf:ɪ-sɔ:pʰɪ, -a(r̥);
-sɔ:bɪ] wm.1 'a sip of coffee,' i. e.
a cup of coffee, coffee.
kaffistell, -s, - [kʰaf:ɪ-stɛl:, -stɛl·s]
n. coffee set (Pr. 3, 2, 9n).
kaka, köku, -ur [kʰa:kʰa, kʰö:kʰɣ(r̥);
kʰa:g̊a, kʰö:g̊ɣɽ] wf.1 cake, cookie,
pastry.
kál, -s [kʰau:l, kʰaul·s] n. turnip or
rutabaga greens; kale; cabbage;
ekki er sopið kálið, þó í ausuna sé
komið 'the cabbage soup is not yet
sipped even if it is already in the
ladle,' i. e. there is many a slip
betwixt cup and lip.
kala, kelur (or kell), kól, kólum,
kalinn (-ið) [kʰa:la; kˌʰe:lɣɽ,
kˌʰed·l; kʰou:l, kʰou:lɣm, kʰa:lɪn,
-ɪð] v.6 impers.: mig kelur (kell)
I freeze, I become frostbitten; það

Vowels: a [a] approx. father; á [au] cow; e [ɛ] set; é [jɛ] yes; i, y [ɪ] sit; í, ý [i] feel;
o [ɔ] law; ó [ou] note; u [ɣ] approx. Germ. Mütter; ú [u] school; y = i; ý = í; æ [ai] ice;
ö [ö] Germ. hören; au [öy] French feuille; ei, ey [ei] ale. Length [:]; half-length [·].

kól af honum fótinn he lost his foot through frostbite.

kaldavermsl, -s [kʰal·da-vermsl̥(s)] n. spring, cold in summer but not subject to freezing in winter.

kaldi, -a [kʰal·dɪ, -a] wm.l light breeze; cold, not too strong wind.

kaldur, köld, kalt [kʰal·dʏr̥, kʰöl·d̥, kʰal·t] adj. cold; *mér verður kalt* I shall be cold.

kálfi, -a, -ar [kʰaul·vɪ, -a(r̥)] wm.l calf of the leg.

kálfur, -s, -ar [kʰaul·vʏr̥, kʰaul·(v)s, kʰaul·var̥] m.l calf; also pers. name.

kalla, -aði, -að(ur) [kʰad̥·la, -aðɪ, -að, -aðʏr̥] wv.4 call, name; say, consider; *kalla e-n e-ð* call sbdy sth, consider sbdy to be sth; *kalla sig* call oneself; *ég kalla það gott* I consider that fine (S. VI, 11, 4); *kalla á e-n* call, summon sbdy; *kalla upp* call out, cry out; middle voice: *kallast* be called.

Kalli, -a, -ar [kʰal·ɪ, -a(r̥)] wm.l pet name of *Karl* (Pr. 3, 2, 9n).

kamar, -ars, -rar [kʰa:mar̥(s), kʰam·-rar̥] m.l toilet, W.C.

kambgarn, -s [kʰam·(b)gad̥n(s); kʰam·bgardn] n. worsted.

kambur, -s, -ar [kʰam·bʏr̥, kʰam·(b)s, kʰam·bar̥] m.l comb; card; ledge of rock.

kandídat, -s, -ar [kʰan·di·da:tʰ(s), -ar̥; -da:d̥] m.l graduate of the University.

kanel, -s [kʰa:nɛ·l, -ɛls] m.l cinnamon.

kann, see *kunna.*

kanna, könnu, -ur [kʰan:a, kʰön:ʏ(r̥)] wf.l pot, coffeepot, teapot; *vera með kaffi á könnunni* have coffee (boiling) in the pot.

kannske [kʰan·sk₁ɛ·] adv. perhaps; *kannske þér vilduð* perhaps you would. . . .

kápa, -u, -ur [kʰau:pʰa, -ʏ(r̥); kʰau:-b̥a] wf.l coat, cope.

kapp, -s, köpp [kʰaʰp:, kʰaʰp·s, kʰöʰp:] n. contention, zeal; *af kappi* eagerly; *leggja kapp á e-ð* strive for sth.

kapphlaup, -s, - [kʰaʰp:hl̥öy·pʰ(s); -hl̥öy·b̥] n. race.

karfa, körfu, -ur [kʰar·va, kʰör·vʏ(r̥)] wf.l basket.

kargaþýfi, -s [kʰar·ga-þi:vɪ(s)] n. very hillocky (humpy) field.

kári, -a, -ar [kʰau:rɪ, -a(r̥)] wm.l wind; also pers. name.

karl, -s, -ar [kʰad̥·l, kʰal·s, kʰad̥·lar̥; kʰardl̥, kʰarls, kʰardlar̥] m.l man; old man, old fellow; also *Karl* pers. name; rock, shaped like a man.

karlakór, -s, -ar [kʰad̥·la-kʰou:r, -kʰour·s, -kʰou:rar̥; kʰardla-] m.l men's choir.

karlmaður, -manns, -menn [kʰad̥·lma·-ðʏr̥, -mans, -mɛn·] m.4 man, opposed woman (= *kvennmaður*).

karlmannsföt, -fata [kʰad̥·lmans-fö:tʰ -fa:tʰa; kʰardl̥-; -fö:d̥, -fa:d̥a] n.pl. men's clothes.

karlmannsnafn, -s, -nöfn [kʰad̥·lmans-nab·n; -nabn̥s, -naf·s; -nöb·n̥; kʰardl̥-] n. man's name.

karlsdóttir, -dóttur, -dætur [kʰal·s-douʰt·ɪr, -ʏr̥, -dai·tʰʏr̥; kʰarls-; -dai·dʏr̥] f.3 daughter of the old man, the churl.

karlsson(ur), -sonar, -synir [kʰal·sɔ·n, -sɔ·nʏr̥, -sɔ·nar̥, -sɪ·nɪr̥; kʰarl·] m.3 son of the old man, the churl.

karltötur, (-ri), -urs, -ur [kʰad̥·ltʰö·-tʰʏr̥(s), -tʰö·tʰrɪ; -tʰö·d̥·; kʰardl̥-] n. rag of an old man; poor old man.

kartafla, -öflu, -ur [kʰar·tabla, -töb·-lʏ(r̥)] wf.l potato.

kartöflujafningur, -s, -ar [kʰar·töblʏ-jab·ningʏr̥, -ins, -ingar̥] m.l creamed potatoes.

kasta, -aði, -að(ur) [kʰas·ta, -aðɪ, -að, -aðʏr̥] wv.4 throw, cast, fling, *kasta steini* throw a stone; *steini var kastað* a stone was thrown (S. VI, 8, 4); *kasta sprengjum á* throw bombs on, bomb; *kasta kveðju á e-n* greet (in words only, opposite to *heilsa með handabandi*); *kasta* (of mares and dogs) foal, have a litter; *kasta upp* throw up, vomit.

Katla, Kötlu [kʰaʰt·la, kʰöʰt·lʏ] wf.l

Consonants: [ð] brea*th*e; [g] *g*ood; [gȷ] *g*yarden (garden); [hʍ] *wh*at; [j] *y*es; [kȷ] *cy*an (can); [ŋ] thi*ng*; [q] N. Germ. sa*g*en; [r] Scottish *r*; [x] approx. Germ. a*ch*; [þ] *th*in. Voiceless: ○; [b̥, d̥, g̊] approx. *p, t, k*. Half-voiced: *italics*. Aspiration and preaspiration: [ʰ]; [pʰ, tʰ, kʰ] *p-, t-, k-*. Others as in English.

pers. name; name of a well known volcano.

katlar, -i, see *ketill*.

Katrín, -ar [kʰa:tʰri·n, -naṛ; kʰa:-dri·n] f.1 pers. name Catherine.

kattur, see *köttur*.

kauði, -a, -ar [kʰöy:ðɪ, -a(ṛ)] wm.1 rogue, wag.

kaup, -s, - [kʰöy:pʰ(s), kʰöyf·s; kʰöy:b̥] n. buy, bargain; *verða af kaupinu* lose the bargain.

kaupa, keypti, keypt(ur) [kʰöy:pʰa, kⱼʰeif·tɪ, -yṛ, kⱼʰeif·t; kʰöy:ba] wv.2 buy, *kaupa e-ð* buy sth; *kaupa sér* buy (for oneself); *kaupa e-u* make a certain bargain, make a deal, strike a bargain (In. VII, *3, 3*, 5).

kaupfélag, -s, -lög [kʰöy:pʰfjɛ·laq, -laxs, -löq; kʰöy:fjɛ·-, kʰöyf:jɛ·-] n. co-operative society, co-operative store; *K. Reykjavíkur og nágrennis* ' The Co-operative Society of R. and Neighborhood.'

kaupgreiðsludeild, -ar, -ir [kʰöy:pʰ-greiðslɤ-deil·d̥, -aṛ, -ɪṛ; kʰöy:b̥-] f.2 pay service (in the army).

kaupm. =

kaupmaður, -manns, -menn [kʰöypʰ:-ma·ðɤṛ, -mans, -mɛn·; kʰöy:pʰ-, kʰöy:b̥-] m.4 merchant, businessman.

kaupstaðarferð, -ar, -ir [kʰöyf·staðaṛ-fɛr·ð, -ðaṛ, -ðɪṛ; kʰöy:pʰ-, kʰöy:b̥-] f.2 journey, trip to the trading place, trip to town.

kaupstaður, -ar, -ir [kʰöyf·sta·ðɤṛ, -aṛ, -ɪṛ; kʰöy:pʰ-, kʰöy:b̥-] m.3 trading place, market town, village, town.

kaus, see *kjósa*.

kaþólskur, -þólsk, -þólskt [kʰa:þoulsk-yṛ; -þoulsk; -þoulst] adj. catholic.

kefja, kafði, kafinn (-ið) [kⱼʰɛv·ja, kʰav·ðɪ, kʰa:vɪn, -ɪð] wv.1 dip, submerge, suppress, suffocate; *vera önnum kafinn* be busy as a bee.

keila, -u, -ur [kⱼʰei:la, -ɤ(ṛ)] wf.1 cone; (a fish: torsk).

Keilir, -is [kⱼʰei:lɪṛ, -ɪs] m.1 ' the Cone,' a mountain south of Reykjavík.

keilumyndaður, -uð, -að [kⱼʰei:lɤ-mɪn·daðɤṛ, -ɤð, -að] adj. cone-shaped.

kelda, -u, -ur [kⱼʰɛl·da, -ɤ(ṛ)] wf.1 muddy watercourse in a bog, quagmire, slough.

Keli, -a, -ar [kⱼʰɛ:lɪ, -a(ṛ)] wm.1 pet name for *Þorkell*.

kell, kelur, see *kala*.

kem, see 2. *koma*.

kemba, kembdi, kembdur (kembt) [kⱼʰɛm·ba, kⱼʰɛm·dɪ, -yṛ, kⱼʰɛm·tʰ; kⱼʰɛm·t] wv.2 comb, card.

kenna, kenndi, kenndur (kennt) [kⱼʰɛn:a, kⱼʰɛn·dɪ, -yṛ, kⱼʰɛn·tʰ; kⱼʰɛn·t] wv.2 teach; *kenna e-m e-ð* teach sbdy sth; attribute, ascribe sth to sbdy; *kenna e-m um e-ð* blame sbdy for sth; *vera e-u að kenna* be attributable to sth, be caused by sth, be blamable on sth; *kenna e-m að stafa* teach sbdy to spell, read; *þeim var kennt* they were taught.

kennaraskóli, -a, -ar [kⱼʰɛn:ara-skou:-lɪ, -a(ṛ)] wm.1 school for teachers; normal school.

kennarasæti, -s, - [kⱼʰɛn:ara-sai:-tʰɪ(s); -sai:dɪ] n. teacher's chair.

kennari, -a, -ar [kⱼʰɛn:arɪ, -a(ṛ)] wm.1 teacher.

kenndur, kennd, kennt [kⱼʰɛn·dɤṛ, kⱼʰɛn·d̥, kⱼʰɛn·tʰ; kⱼʰɛn·t] adj. (pp.) (slightly) tipsy.

kennsla, -u [kⱼʰɛnsla, -ɤ] wf.1 teaching.

kennslubók, -ar, -bækur [kⱼʰɛnslɤ-bou:kʰ(aṛ), -bai:kʰyṛ; -bou:g̊, -bai:g̊yṛ] f.3 textbook.

kennslukona, -u, -ur [kⱼʰɛnslɤ-kʰɔ:na, -ɤ(ṛ)] wf.1 teacher (female).

kennslustofa, -u, -ur [kⱼʰɛnslɤ-stɔ:va, -ɤ(ṛ)] wf.1 classroom, auditorium.

kennslustund, -ar, -ir [kⱼʰɛnslɤ-stɤn·d̥, -aṛ, -ɪṛ] f.2 class, hour (of teaching).

keppa, keppti, keppt [kⱼʰɛʰp:a, kⱼʰɛf·-tɪ, kⱼʰɛf·t] wv.2 contend; *keppa um e-ð* compete for sth; *keppast við að gera e-ð* exert oneself in doing sth.

Vowels: *a* [a] approx. father; *á* [au] cow; *e* [ɛ] set; *é* [jɛ] yes; *i, y* [ɪ] sit; *í, ý* [i] feel; *o* [ɔ] law; *ó* [ou] note; *u* [ɤ] approx. Germ. Mütter; *ú* [u] school; *y* = *i*; *ý* = *í*; *æ* [ai] ice; *ö* [ö] Germ. hören; *au* [öy] French *feuille*; *ei, ey* [ei] ale. Length [:]; half-length [·].

keppandi, -a, -endur [kˌʰɛʰp:anḍɪ, -a, -ɛndɣɾ] wm.2 contestant.

kerling, -ar, -ar [kˌʰɛd·liŋg̊, -aɾ; kˌʰɛrdl-] f.1 old woman, carline; rock, shaped like a woman.

ket (kjöt), -s [kˌʰɛːtʰ, kˌʰöːtʰ, -s; kˌʰɛːḍ, kˌʰöːd] n. meat, flesh.

ketbúð, -ar, -ir (kjöt-) [kˌʰɛːtʰbu·ð, -ðaɾ, -ðɪɾ, kˌʰöːtʰ-; kˌʰɛːḍ-, kˌʰöːḍ-] f.2 meat store, meat market.

ketill, -ils, -katlar [kˌʰɛːtʰɪdl, -ɪls, kʰaʰt·laɾ; kˌʰɛːḍ-] m.1 kettle, cauldron; also place name: Katlar, and pers. name: Ketill.

ketsúpa, -u, -ur (kjöt-) [kˌʰɛːtʰsu·pʰa, -ɣ(ɾ); kˌʰöːtʰ-; kˌʰɛːḍ-, kˌʰöːḍ-, -suːba] wf.1 meat soup, broth.

ketti(r̊), see köttur.

kex [kˌʰɛx·s] n. (coll.) crackers.

keypti, -ur, see kaupa.

keyra, keyrði, keyrður (keyrt) [kˌʰeiːra, kˌʰeir·ðɪ, -ɣɾ, kˌʰeiɾ·t] wv.2 to drive (a car), whip, spur (a horse).

kg. = kíló (gramm).

kgl. = konunglegur.

Kiddi, -a [kˌʰɪḍːɪ, -a] wm.1 pet name for Kristján; Kiddabúðir chain stores in Reykjavík.

kíghósti, (kík-), -a [kˌʰiːqhoustɪ, -a; kˌʰiːkʰ-, kˌʰiːg̊-] wm.1 whooping cough.

kíkir, -is, -(ir)ar [kˌʰiːkˌʰɪɾ, -ɪs, -ɪraɾ; kˌʰiːkˌʰaɾ; kˌʰiːg̊ˌ-] m.1 field glass (= sjónauki).

Kiljan, -s [kˌʰɪl·jan, -ans] m.1 pers. name.

kíll, kils, kílar [kˌʰiḍ·l, kˌʰil·s, kˌʰiːlaɾ] m.1 inlet, creek, canal.

kíló, -s, - [kˌʰiːlou·(s)] n. =

kílógramm, -s [kˌʰiːlou·gram·(s)] n. kilogram (ca. two pounds).

kílómetri, -a, -ar [kˌʰiːlou·mɛːtʰrɪ, -a(ɾ); -mɛːdrɪ] wm.1 kilometer.

kind, -ar, -ur [kˌʰɪn·ḍ, -aɾ, -ɣɾ] f.3 sheep.

kindaket (-kjöt), -s [kˌʰɪn·da·kˌʰɛːtʰ, -s, -kˌʰöːtʰ(s); -kˌʰɛːd, -kˌʰöːḍ] n. mutton.

kinn, -ar, -ar [kˌʰɪn:(aɾ)] f.1 cheek.

kirkja, -u, -ur, (-na) [kʰɪɾ·kˌa, -kˌɣ(ɾ), kˌʰɪɾkna] wf.1 church, kirk.

Kirkjubæjarklaustur, (-ri), -urs [kˌʰɪɾ·- kˌɣbai·jaɾ-kʰlöys·tɣɾ(s), -kʰlöystrɪ] n. 'Kirk By Cloister,' (klaustur = monastery).

Kirkjubær, -bæjar [kʰɪɾ kˌɣ-bai:r, -bai:jaɾ] m.2 'Church Place,' 'Parsonage.'

kirkjuhljómleikar [kˌʰɪɾ·kˌɣ-hljoum·- lei·kʰaɾ; -lei·g̊aɾ] m.1 pl. church organ recital.

kirkjuklukka,-u,-ur [kˌʰɪɾ·kˌɣ-kʰlɣʰk:- a, -ɣ(ɾ)] wf.1 church bell.

kirkjusmiður, -s,-ir [kˌʰɪɾ·kˌɣ-smɪ:ðɣɾ, -smɪð·s, -smɪːðɪɾ] m.2 church builder.

kirkjustaður, -ar, -ir [kˌʰɪɾ·kˌɣ-sta:- ðɣɾ, -aɾ, -ɪɾ] m.3 a parsonage.

kirkjusöngur, -s [kˌʰɪɾ·kˌɣ-söyŋ·g̊ɣɾ, -söyŋ·s] m.1 church music.

kirsiber, -s, -, (-ja) [kˌʰɪɾ·sɪ-bɛ:r, -bɛr·s, -bɛr·ja] n. cherry.

kirsiberjasaft, -ar [kˌʰɪɾ·sɪbɛrja-saf·t, -aɾ] f.2 cherry juice.

kirtill, -ils, -lar [kˌʰɪɾ·tɪdl, -ɪls, kˌʰɪɾtlaɾ] m.1 gland.

kista, -u, -ur, (-na) [kˌʰɪs·ta, -ɣ(ɾ), kˌʰɪstna] wf.1 chest.

kistuhandraði, -a, -ar [kˌʰɪs·tɣ-han·d- raðɪ, -a(ɾ)] wm.1 locker (in a chest).

kjaftshögg, -s, - [kˌʰaf·(t)shög̊:, -hög̊·s] n. blow on the mouth, a buffet, slap.

kjaftur, -s, -ar [kˌʰaf·tɣɾ, kˌʰaf·(t)s, kˌʰaf·taɾ] m.1 mouth (disrespectful), muzzle, snout, chops; haltu kjafti hold your tongue.

kjallari, -a, -ar [kˌʰad·larɪ, -a, -aɾ] wm.1 cellar, basement.

kjáni, -a, -ar [kˌʰauːnɪ, -a(ɾ)] wm.1 (little) fool.

Kjartan, -s [kˌʰaɾ·tan, -ans] m.1 pers. name; the hero of Laxdœla saga.

Kjarval, -s [kˌʰar·val, -vals] m.1 family name; a famous Icelandic painter: Jóhannes Kjarval.

kjói, -a, -ar [kˌʰouː:ɪ, -a(ɾ)] wm.1 arctic skua.

Consonants: [ð] breathe; [g] good; [gˌ] gˌarden (garden); [hw] what; [j] yes; [kˌ] cˌyan (can); [ŋ] thing; [q] N. Germ. sagen; [r] Scottish r; [x] approx. Germ. ach; [þ] thin. Voiceless: ○; [b̥, d̥, g̊] approx. p, t, k. Half-voiced: italics. Aspiration and preaspiration: [ʰ]; [pʰ, tʰ, kʰ] p-, t-, k-. Others as in English.

383

kjólföt, -fata [kˌʰoul·fö·tʰ, -fa·tʰa; -fö·d̥, -fa·da] n. pl. (= kjóll) dress coat, full dress, tails.

kjólkragi, -a, -ar [kˌʰoul·kʰrai·jɪ, -a(r̥); -kʰra·jɪ] wm.1 dress collar.

kjóll, -s, -ar [kˌʰoud·l, kˌʰoul·s, kˌʰou:lar̥] m.1 dress (for women); dress coat, full dress (for men).

kjóllaf, -s, -löf [kˌʰoul:a·v, -lafs, -lö·v] n. coat tail.

Kjós, -ar [kˌʰou:s, -ar̥] f.2 a place name.

kjósa, kýs, kaus, kusum, kosinn (or kjörinn) (-ið) [kˌʰou:sa, kˌʰi:s, kʰöy:s, kʰʏ:sʏm, kʰɔ:sɪn (kˌʰö:rɪn), -ɪð] v.2 choose, select; elect, return; kjósa þingmann return an M. P.; elect a member of the parliament; kjósa um e-ð choose between things; kjósa e-n borgarstjóra elect sbdy mayor (S. I, 2, 1, 2); kjósa e-ð heldur prefer sth; kjörinn elected.

kjör, -s, - [kˌʰö:r, kˌʰör·s] n. election, choice; pl. condition, circumstances; góð kjör fine circumstances; lifa við betri kjör live in better circumstances; fá e-ð með góðum kjörum get sth cheap.

kjörgengi, -s [kˌʰör·g̥ˌeiŋ̊ɪ(s)] n. eligibility; réttur til kjörgengis the right to be elected.

kjörinn, see kjósa.

kjöt, -s [kˌʰö:tʰ(s), kˌʰö:d̥] n. = ket; also in compounds.

kl. = klukkan.

klak, -s [kʰla:kʰ(s); kʰla:g̊] n. hatching of fish.

klaki, -a, -ar [kʰla:kˌʰɪ, -kʰa(r̥); kla:-g̊ˌɪ, -g̊a] wm.1 ice, chunk of ice.

klakkur, -s, -ar [kʰlaʰk:ʏr̥, kʰlaʰk·s, kʰlax·s, kʰlaʰk:ar̥] m.1 peg of a packsaddle.

Klapparstígur, -s [kʰlaʰp:ar·sti:qʏr̥, -stix·s] m.1 'Flat Rock Path,' in Reykjavík.

Klara, Klöru [kʰla:ra, kʰlö:rʏ] wf.1 Clare.

1. klauf, -ar, -ir [kʰlöy:v, -var̥, -vɪr̥] f.2 cloven hoof; slit (of trousers).

2. klauf, see kljúfa.

klaufi, -a, -ar [kʰlöy:vɪ, -a(r̥)] wm.1 a clumsy fellow, fool.

klaustur, (-ri), -urs, -ur [kʰlöys·tʏr(s), kʰlöystrɪ] n. monastery; mostly in place names: -klaustur.

1. kleif, -ar, -ir [kʰlei:v, -var̥, -vɪr̥] f.2 ridge of cliffs, rock ascent.

2. kleif, see klífa.

kleina, -u, -ur [kʰlei:na, -ʏ(r̥)] wf.1 twisted doughnut.

klerkur, -s, -ar [kʰler̥·kʏr̥, kʰler̥ks, kʰler̥·kar̥] m.1 a clergyman, pl. the clergy.

klettur, -s, -ar [kʰleʰt:ʏr̥, kʰleʰt·s, kʰleʰt:ar̥] m.1 rock, cliff.

klífa, klíf, kleif, klifum, klifinn (-ið) [kʰli:va, kʰli:v, kʰlei:v, kʰlɪ:vʏm, kʰlɪ:vɪn, -ɪð] v.1 climb; klífa þrítugan hamarinn (proverbial) 'climb a cliff thirty fathoms high,' attempt and accomplish the impossible.

klifra, -aði, -að [kʰlɪv·ra, -aðɪ, -að] wv.4 = klifrast, climb (ofan down).

klippa, klippti, klippt(ur) [kʰlɪʰp:a, kʰlɪf·tɪ, -ʏr̥, kʰlif·t] wv.2 clip, cut, shear; cut the hair.

klipping, -ar, -ar [kʰlɪʰp:iŋ̊, -ar̥] f.1 haircut.

kljúfa, klýf, klauf, klufum, klofinn (-ið) [kʰlju:va, kʰli:v, kʰlöy:v, kʰlʏ:vʏm, kʰlɔ:vɪn, -ɪð] v.2 split, cleave.

kló, -ar, klær [kʰlou:(ar̥), kʰlai:r] f.3 claw, clutch.

klof, -s, - [kʰlɔ:v, kʰlɔf·s] n. crutch or crotch.

klofið, -inn, see kljúfa.

klofna, -aði, -að [kʰlɔb·na, -aðɪ, -að] wv.4 split, be divided.

klofvega [kʰlɔv:ɛ·qa] adv. astride.

klufum, see kljúfa.

klukka, -u, -ur, (-na) [kʰlʏʰk:a, -ʏ(r̥), kʰlʏʰk·na] wf.1 clock, bell; watch; klukkan þrjú (at) three o'clock; klukkuna vantar kortér í þrjú it is quarter of (to) three.

klukkustund, -ar, -ir [kʰlʏʰk:ʏ·stʏn·d̥, -ar̥, -ɪr̥] f.2 =

klukkutími, -a, -ar [kʰlʏʰk:ʏ·tʰi:mɪ, -a(r̥)] wm.1 hour (= stund).

Vowels: a [a] approx. father; á [au] cow; e [ɛ] set; é [jɛ] yes; i, y [ɪ] sit; í, ý [i] feel; o [ɔ] law; ó [ou] note; u [ʏ] approx. Germ. Mütter; ú [u] school; y = i; ý = í; æ [ai] ice; ö [ö] Germ. hören; au [öy] French feuille; ei, ey [ei] ale. Length [:]; half-length [·].

klýf, see *kljúfa*.

klyf, -jar, -jar [kʰlɪ:*v*, kʰlɪv·jaɾ] f.1 a bundle of ca. 100 pds, carried on one side by a packhorse (*klyfja-hestur, hestur undir klyfjum*).

klyfberi, -a, -ar [kʰlɪv·be·rɪ, -a(ɾ); kʰlɪb:ɛ·rɪ] wm.1 packsaddle.

klæða, klæddi, klæddur (klætt) [kʰlai:-ða, kʰlaid:ɪ, -Yɾ, kʰlaiʰt:] wv.2 cloth, dress; *klæða sig* dress (oneself) *k·sig í* put on; with dat. clothe, cover: *klæða grasi* cover with grass.

klæðaverksmiðja, -u, -ur [kʰlai:ða-veɾ·ksmɪðja, -Y(ɾ)] wf.1 textile factory, woolen cloth manufactory, cloth mill.

klæði, -s, - [kʰlai:ðɪ(s)] n. cloth, stuff; broadcloth; pl. clothes.

klæðskeri, -a, -ar [kʰlaið·skɟe:rɪ, -a, -aɾ] wm.1 tailor, dressmaker.

klæja, -aði, -að [kʰlai:ja, -aðɪ, -að] wv.4 itch; *mig klæjar* I itch; *mig klæjar lófann* (acc.) the palm of my hand itches.

Klængur, -s [kʰlaiŋ· g̊Yɾ, kʰlaiŋ·s] m.1 pers. name.

klær, see *kló*.

klöpp, klappar, -ir [kʰlöʰp:, kʰlaʰp:aɾ, -ɪɾ] f.2 flat rock.

km. = *kílómetri*.

knár, kná, knátt; knárri, knástur [kʰnau:*r*, kʰnau:, kʰnauʰt:, kʰnaur:ɪ, kʰnaus·tYɾ] adj. strong, doughty; *margur er knár, þó hann sé smár* many a man is strong, though he is small.

Knútur, -s, -ar [kʰnu:tʰYɾ, kʰnu:tʰs, kʰnu:tʰaɾ; kʰnu:d̥-] m.1 literally: knot; pers. name: Canute.

knýja, knúði, knúinn (-ið) [kʰni:ja, kʰnu:ðɪ, kʰnu:ɪn, -ɪð] wv.1 compel, force.

kobbi, -a, -ar [kʰɔb̥:ɪ, -a(ɾ)] wm.1 young seal (pet name for *kópur* young seal; also pet name for *Jakob*, pers. name).

koddi, -a, -ar [kʰɔd̥:ɪ, -a(ɾ)] wm.1 pillow (to sleep on).

koffort, -s, - (kofort) [kʰɔf:ɔɾt(s); kʰɔ:fɔɾt(s)] n. trunk.

kofi, -a, -ar [kʰɔ:vɪ, -a(ɾ)] wm.1 hut, shed, shack.

kok, -s [kʰɔ:kʰ(s), kʰɔ:g̊(s)] n. throat, pharynx.

kol [kʰɔ:*l*] n.pl. coal.

kól, see *kala*.

kolageymsla, -u, -ur [kʰɔ:la·g̊ɟeimsla, -Y(ɾ)] wf.1 coal storage.

koli, -a, -ar [kʰɔ:lɪ, -a(ɾ)] wm.1 plaice, dab.

kollgáta, -u, -ur [kʰɔd̥·l̥·gau:tʰa, -Y(ɾ); -gau:da] wf.1 the true answer to the riddle; *eiga kollgátuna* guess right.

kollóttur, -ótt, -ótt [kʰɔd̥·louʰt·Yɾ, -ouʰt·] adj. rounded in shape (of sheep and cows without horns); with a round top (of mountains).

kollur, -s, -ar [kʰɔd̥·lYɾ, kʰɔl·s, kʰɔd̥·laɾ] m.1 head, top.

kolmórauður, -rauð, -rautt [kʰɔl·-mɔ:röy·ðYɾ, -röy·ð, röyʰt·; -mou:-] adj. dark and muddy (of water), dark brown.

kolugur [kʰɔ:lYqYɾ] adj. (see -*ugur*) dirty, blackened with coal (or: as if by coal), sooty. Note: the troll objected to the 'sooty snout' of the girl, because she had just received the Eucharist.

kólum, see *kala*.

1. koma, -u, -ur [kʰɔ:ma, -Y(ɾ)] wf.1 coming, arrival.

2. koma, kem, kom, komum, kominn (ið) [kʰɔ:ma, kɟʰe:*m*, kʰɔ:*m*, kʰɔ:-mYm, kʰɔ:mɪn, -ɪð] v.4 A. Intransitive: to come, arrive; come to pass; pass, advance; (1) come: *koma gangandi, ríðandi* come walking, riding (S. VI, **12**, *1*, 1); *komdu sæll, komið þér sælir* how do you do (S. IV, 1, 2); *á sunnudaginn kemur* this coming Sunday; *koma í veg fyrir e-ð* prevent sth; *koma í stað e-s* take the place of sth; (2) impersonal: *vera kominn* have come, have arrived, be there; *er komið á gluggann* sbdy comes to the win-

---

Consonants: [ð] brea*th*e; [g] *g*ood; [g̊] *g*yarden (garden); [hw] *wh*at; [j] *y*es; [kɟ] *cy*an (can); [ŋ] thi*ng*; [q] N. Germ. sa*g*en; [r] Scottish *r*; [x] approx. Germ. a*ch*; [þ] *th*in. Voiceless: ○; [b̥, d̥, g̊] approx. *p, t, k*. Half-voiced: *italics*. Aspiration and preaspiration: [ʰ]; [pʰ, tʰ, kʰ] *p-, t-, k-*. Others as in English.

dow; *það er komið fram undir hádegi* it is almost noon; *nú er svo komið, að* . . . things have come to such a pass that . . . (S. VI, **14, 4**); *e-ð kemur e-m fyrir sjónir* sth appears (so or so) to sbdy; *það kæmi mér ekki á óvart* I would not be surprised (by it). **B.** Transitive with dative: *koma e-u (e-m) e-ð* get sth (sbdy) to some place (S. I, **3, 1,** 2(d)); *koma e-u í póst* get sth into the mails; *koma e-m á land* get sbdy ashore; *koma e-u á fót* establish sth; *koma sér e-ð* arrange (for oneself) to stay at a place; *koma sér fyrir* arrange for board and lodgings, get lodgings for oneself; *koma sér vel (illa)* (a) come in handy (be inconvenient), (b) get along well (badly) with others, be liked (disliked). **C.** Middle voice: *komast* (intr.) get (somewhere) (S. VI, **7, 4**); *komast að e-u* (a) get to sth, (b) get wind of sth, hear of sth; *komast heim* get home; *komast þangað* get there; *komast yfir e-ð* (a) get across sth (a river, a mountain), (b) get into one's possession; *komast ofan í glasið* get (down) into the bottle; *komast upp á e-ð* (a) get on top of sth, (b) get the knack of sth; *komast til e-s* find time to do sth, get around to doing sth. **D.** With preps and advs: *koma að* get, come to a place; *þegar að var komið* when people got there; *koma af* come from; *koma aftur* come back, be back; *koma fyrir* happen; *koma í vatn* be in water; *koma inn* enter, come in; visit; *koma með e-m* accompany sbdy; *koma með e-ð (e-n)* bring sth (sbdy); *koma ofan* come downstairs; *koma til* come to; *til komi þitt ríki* thy kingdom come; *koma e-u upp* erect, build sth, finish (a building); *vera undir e-u kominn* depend upon sth; *koma út* be published; be the outcome; *koma við* visit, *koma við hjá e-m* visit some-

one; *koma við e-n* touch sbdy, affect sbdy; *koma e-u (e-m) við* concern sth, concern, be the business of sbdy; *það kemur þér ekkert við* it (that) is no business of yours, *það kemur þessu ekkert við* that has nothing to do with it.

komma, -u, -ur [kʰɔm:a -ʏ(r̥)] wf.1 comma.

kommi, -a, -ar [kʰɔm:ɪ, -a(r̥)] wm.1 nickname for *kommúnisti*.

kommóða, -u, -ur [kʰɔm:ou·ða, -ʏ(r̥)] wf.1 (= *dragkista*) chest of drawers.

kommúnistaflokkur, -s, -ar [kʰɔm:u·nɪsta-flɔʰk:ʏr̥; -flɔx·s,-flɔʰk·s; -flɔʰk:·ar̥] m.1 Communist party.

kommúnisti, -a, -ar [kʰɔm:u·nɪstɪ, -a(r̥)] wm.1 Communist.

komumaður, -manns, -menn [kʰɔ:mʏ·ma:ðʏr̥, -man·s, -mɛn:] m.4 newcomer.

kona, -u, -ur, (kvenna) [kʰɔ:na, -ʏ(r̥), kʰvɛn:a] wf.1 woman (In. I, **6, 1**); the wife, the mistress of the house.

konar [kʰɔ:nar̥] adv. of kind, of type; *eins konar* a certain type of; of a certain type; *þrenns konar* of three types; *margs konar* of many types, kinds, many kinds of; also in compounds: *einskonar*, etc.

kóngsbarn, -s, -börn [kʰouŋ·sbaðn̥, -bas·, -bödn̥] n. king's child.

kóngsdóttir, -dóttur, -dætur [kʰouŋ·s-douʰt·ɪr̥, -ʏr̥, -dai·tʰʏr̥; -dai·dʏr̥] f.3 king's daughter, princess.

kóngsgersemi, -, -ar [kʰouŋ·s·g‚ɛrsɛ·mɪ, -ar̥] wf.2 treasured possession of a king, a gift fit for princes.

kóngssonur, -sonar, -synir [kʰouŋ·sɔ·-nʏr̥, -ar̥, -sɪ·nɪr̥] m.3 king's son, prince.

kóngur, -s, -ar [kʰouŋ· g̊ʏr̥, kʰouŋ·s, kʰouŋ·g̊ar̥] m.1 king (less formal than *konungur*); *kóngur í spilum* king (playing cards).

konunglegur [kʰɔ:nuŋ̊·lɛ·qʏr̥] adj. (see -*legur*) royal.

konungsstjórn, -ar, -ir [kʰɔ:nuŋ(s)-stjourðn̥, -nar̥, -nɪr̥] f.2 government by a king, monarchy.

Vowels: *a* [a] approx. father; *á* [au] cow; *e* [ɛ] set; *é* [jɛ] yes; *i, y* [ɪ] sit; *í, ý* [i] feel; *o* [ɔ] law; *ó* [ou] note; *u* [ʏ] approx. Germ. Mütter; *ú* [u] school; *y* = *i*; *ý* = *í*; *æ* [ai] ice; *ö* [ö] Germ. hören; *au* [öy] French *feuille*; *ei, ey* [ei] ale. Length [:]; half-length [·].

konungur, -s, -ar [kʰɔ:nuŋg̊ʏr̥, -uŋs,
-ungar̥] m.1 king.
kopar, -ars [kʰɔ:pʰar̥(s); kʰɔ:bar̥]
m.1 copper.
kór, -s, -ar [kʰou:r, kʰour̥·s, kʰou:rar̥]
m.1 chancel (in a church); choir,
quire.
kórdyr [kʰour·dɪ·r] f.3.pl. door of the
chancel in Icelandic churches.
korkur, -s, -ar [kʰɔr̥·kʏr̥, kʰɔr̥ks, kʰɔr̥·-
kar̥] m.1 cork.
korn, -s, - [kʰɔd·n̥(s), kʰɔrdn̥(s)] n.
corn, grain, especially rye; pl. korn
grains of sth.
kornvara, -vöru, -ur [kʰɔd·nva·ra,
-vö·rʏ(r̥); kʰɔrdn̥-] wf.1 grain.
korriró [kʰɔr:ɪrou:] imitative baby
talk for kúr(ðu) í ró sleep in peace.
kort, -s, - [kʰɔr̥·t(s)] n. map, card.
kortér, -s, - [kʰɔr̥·tje·r, -jers̥] n. quarter
of an hour.
korvetta, -u, -ur [kɔr·veʰt·a, -ʏ(r̥)]
wf.1 corvette.
kosið, -inn, see kjósa.
kosning, -ar, -ar [kʰɔs·niŋg̊(ar̥)] f.1
election.
kosningaréttur, -ar [kʰɔs·niŋga-rjeʰt:-
ʏr̥, -ar] m.3 franchise, right to vote.
koss, -, -ar [kʰɔs:(ar̥)] m.1 kiss.
kossaleit, -ar [kʰɔs:a-lei:tʰ(ar̥);
-lei:d] f.2 seeking (looking for)
kisses (the title of a poem).
kosta, -aði, -að(ur) [kʰɔs·ta, -aðɪ, -að,
-aðʏr̥] wv.4 cost; hvað kostar
þetta? what does this cost? það
kostar krónu it costs a crown;
kosta e-n (trans.) pay the expenses
of sbdy.
kostamikill, -il, -ið; -meiri, mestur
[kʰɔs·ta-mɪ:kₗʰɪdl, -ɪl, -ɪð; -mɪ:-
g̊ₗɪdl; -mei:rɪ, -mɛs·tʏr̥] adj. rich,
full of good qualities.
kostnaður, -aðar [kʰɔstnaðʏr̥, -aðar̥]
m.3 cost.
kostur, -ar, -ir [kʰɔs·tʏr̥, -ar̥, -ɪr̥] m.3
choice, terms; conditions; chance,
opportunity; en að öðrum kosti but
otherwise, or else; að minnsta kosti
at least, at any rate.
kot, -s, - [kʰɔ:tʰ(s), kʰɔ:d] n. shack,

hut, croft, cottage; also in place
names: -kot, Kot-.
kr. = króna.
krafa, kröfu, -ur [kʰra:va, kʰrö:-
vʏ(r̥)] wf.1 demand.
krafði, -ur, krafið, -inn, see krefja.
kraftaskáld, -s, - [kʰraf·ta-skaul·d(s)]
n. poet magician.
krakkaskinn, -s, - [kʰraʰk:a-skₗɪn:,
-skₗɪn·s] n. poor child, poor kid.
krakki, -a, -ar [kʰraʰkⱼ:ɪ, kʰraʰk:a(r̥)]
wm.1 child, kid, brat.
krambúð, -ar, -ir [kʰram·bu·ð, -ðar̥,
-ðɪr̥] f.2 general store.
krankur, krönk, krankt [kʰrauŋ·kʰʏr̥,
kʰröyŋ·kʰ, kʰrauŋ·tʰ; kʰrauŋ·kʏr̥,
kʰröyŋ̊·k, kʰrauŋ̊·t] adj. sick, not
well.
krappur, kröpp, krappt [kʰraʰp:ʏr̥,
kʰröʰp:, kʰraf·t] adj. narrow, strait.
krati, -a, -ar [kʰra:tʰɪ, -a(r̥)] wm.1
a nickname for sósialdemókrati.
krefja, krafði, krafður, krafinn (-ið)
[kʰrɛv·ja, kʰrav·ðɪ, -ʏr̥, kʰra:vɪn,
-ɪð] wv.1 demand; krefjast e-s
demand sth.
kreppa, -u, -ur [kʰrɛʰp:a, -ʏ(r̥)] wf.1
straits, fix; depression.
krepputímar [kʰrɛʰp:ʏ-tʰi:mar̥] wm.1.
pl. times of depression.
kría, -u, -ur [kʰri:ja, -jʏ(r̥)] wf.1
arctic tern.
kring [kʰriŋ·g̊] adv. round; í kring
um e-ð (acc.) around sth (= í
kringum).
kringla, -u, -ur [kʰriŋ·la, -ʏ(r̥)] wf.1
pretzel.
kringlóttur, -ótt, -ótt [kʰriŋ·louʰt·-
(ʏr̥)] adj. round; nokkrar kringl-
óttar some round ones (i. e. krónur
crowns, money).
kringum [kʰriŋ·g̊ʏm] prep. with acc.
í kringum bæinn around the farmhouses.
Kristín, -ar, -ar [kʰrɪs·ti·n, -nar̥] f.1
pers. name Christina.
kristinn, -in, -ið; kristnari, -astur
[kʰrɪs·tɪn, -ɪn, -ɪð, kʰrɪs(t)narɪ,
-astʏr̥] adj. Christian; kristin fræði
Christian doctrine, religion (to be

Consonants: [ð] breathe; [g] good; [gⱼ] gyarden (garden); [hw̥] what; [j] yes; [kⱼ] cyan
(can); [ŋ] thing; [q] N. Germ. sagen; [r] Scottish r; [x] approx. Germ. ach; [þ] thin.
Voiceless: ◦; [b̥, d̥, g̊] approx. p, t, k. Half-voiced: italics. Aspiration and preaspiration:
[ʰ]; [pʰ, tʰ, kʰ] p-, t-, k-. Others as in English.

387

studied before confirmation); *kristinn dómur* (or *kristindómur*)
Christianity, religion; *Kristinn, -ins*
m.1 pers. name.

Kristján, -s [kʰrɪs·tjau·n, -auns] m.1
Christian.

Kristjana, -jönu [kʰrɪs·tja·na, -jö·nʏ]
wf.1 Christiana.

Kristmann, -s [kʰrɪs·tman·, ·mans]
m.1 pers. name.

kristni [kʰrɪs(t)nɪ] wf.2 Christianity,
religion.

Kristskirkja, -u [kʰrɪs·-kⱼʰɪrkⱼa, -kⱼʏ]
wf.1 'Christ's Church,' the Catholic
cathedral in Reykjavík.

króna, -u, -ur [kʰrou·na, -ʏ(r̥)] wf.1
króna, crown, the Icelandic mint
unit (at present: 1.-dollar = 6.51
krónur).

krónupeningur, -s, -ar [kʰrou·nʏ-
pʰɛ·niŋ g̊ʏr̥, -iŋs, -iŋg̊ar̥] m.1 a coin
of one *króna*.

krónuseðill, -ils, -seðlar [kʰrou·nʏ-
-sɛ·ðɪd̥l, -ɪls, -seð·lar̥] m.1 a bill
(banknote) of one *króna*.

kroppa, -aði, -að(ur) [kʰrɔʰp·a, -aðɪ,
-að, -aðʏr̥] wv.4 to graze, crop;
pick; *kroppa gras* graze, nibble
grass.

kross, -, -ar [kʰrɔs·(ar̥)] m.1 cross.

krossa, -aði, -að(ur) [kʰrɔs·a, -aðɪ,
-að, -aðʏr̥] wv.4 sign with a cross.

krummi, -a, -ar [kʰrʏm·ɪ, -a(r̥)] wm.1
pet name for *hrafn* raven.

krúna, -u, -ur [kʰru·na, -ʏ(r̥)] wf.1
crown.

krydd, -s [kʰrɪd̥·(s)] n. spices.

kryddsíld, -ar [kʰrɪd̥·sild̥(ar̥)] f.2
spiced herring.

krýna, krýndi, krýndur (krýnt) [kʰri·-
na, kʰrin·dɪ, -ʏr̥, kʰrin·tʰ; kʰrin·t]
wv.2 crown; pp. *krýndur* crowned.

krystall, -als, -allar [kʰrɪs·tad̥l, -als,
-ad̥lar̥] m.1 crystal.

krækiber, -s, -, (-ja) [kʰrai·kⱼʰɪ·bɛ·r,
-bɛr·s, -ber·ja; kʰrai·g̊ⱼɪ-] n. crowberry.

krækja, krækti, krækt(ur) [kʰrai·kⱼʰa,
kʰraix·tɪ, -ʏr̥, kʰraix·t; kʰrai·g̊ⱼa]

wv.2 hook, clasp; *krækja aftur
hurðina* lock or latch the door.

kröftugur [kʰröf·tʏqʏr̥] adj. (see
-ugur) mighty, powerful.

kröfu, see *krafa.*

krönk, see *krankur.*

kröpp, see *krappur.*

ku, see *kveða* (= *kvað*).

kú, kúa, see *kýr.*

kúga, -aði, -að(ur) [kʰu·(q)a, -aðɪ,
-að, -aðʏr̥] wv.4 force, compel, cow.

kúgildi, -s, - [kʰu·g̊ⱼɪld̥ɪ(s)] n. the
value of a cow.

kúla, -u, -ur, (-na) [kʰu·la, -ʏ(r̥),
kʰul·na] wf.1 ball, projectile, bullet.

kunna, kann, kunnum, kunni, kunnað
[kʰʏn·a, kʰan·, kʰʏn·ʏm, kʰʏn·ɪ,
kʰʏn·að] pret. pres. v. (In. VII, **5**,
1) (1) know how to; *kunna að
skrifa* know how to write; *eitthvað
kannt þú* you know sth (sc. in
magic); *kunna upp á sínar tíu
fingur* have sth at one's fingers'
ends; (2) like so and so: *kunna
betur við e-ð* like sth better, prefer;
kunna við sig be at ease, like it
(= *kunna vel við sig*) (3) auxiliary: may: *það kann að batna*
it may improve; *ef ég kann að
koma þar* if I happen to come there
(S. VI, **13**, 4).

kunnáttumaður,-manns,-menn [kʰʏn·-
auʰt·ʏ·ma·ðʏr̥, -man·s, -mɛn·] m.4
expert; a man who knows more
than the average person; a magician, sorcerer.

kunningi, -ja, -jar [kʰʏn·iŋg̊ⱼɪ,
-iŋg̊ⱼa(r̥)] wm.1 acquaintance.

kunningjabréf, -s, - [kʰʏn·iŋg̊ⱼa-
brjɛ·v, -brjɛf·s] n. letter to an
acquaintance, informal letter.

kunningjahópur, -s, -ar [kʰʏn·iŋg̊ⱼa-
hou·pʰʏr̥, -hou·pʰs, -ar̥; -hou·b̥-]
m.1 crowd of acquaintances.

kunnugur [kʰʏn·ʏqʏr̥] adj. (see *-ugur*)
kunnugur e-u familiar with sth.

kunnur, kunn (kunnt) [kʰʏn·ʏr̥, kʰʏn·,
kʏn·tʰ; kʏn·t] adj. known; *lítt
kunnur* little known; *kunnur e-m*

Vowels: *a* [a] approx. father; *á* [au] cow; *e* [ɛ] set; *é* [jɛ] yes; *i, y* [ɪ] sit; *í, ý* [i] feel;
o [ɔ] law; *ó* [ou] note; *u* [ʏ] approx. Germ. Mütter; *ú* [u] school; *y* = *i*; *ý* = *í*; *æ* [ai] ice;
ö [ö] Germ. hören; *au* [öy] French *feuille*; *ei, ey* [ei] ale. Length [:]; half-length [·].

388

known to sbdy; *kunnur að e-u* known for sth.

kúra, kúrði, kúrt [kʰu:ra, kʰur·ðɪ, kʰur·t] wv.3 lie, rest; mope.

kúrenå, -u, -ur [kʰu:rɛ·na, -ɣ(r̥)] wf.1 currant.

kurteis, -eis, -eist [kʰɣr̥·tei·s, -eist] adj. polite, courteous.

kurteislega [kʰɣr̥·teis-lɛ:qa] adv. politely.

kusum, see *kjósa.*

kussa, -u, -ur [kʰɣs:a, -ɣ(r̥)] wf.1 pet name for *kýr* cow.

kvað, kváðum, see *kveða.*

kvaddi, -ur, kvatt, see 2. *kveðja.*

kvaldi, kvalið, -inn, see *kvelja.*

Kvaran, -s [kʰva:ran, -ans] m.1 family name; Einar H. Kvaran (1859-1938) novelist.

kveða, kveð, kvað (ku), kváðum, kveðinn (-ið) [kʰvɛ:ða, kʰvɛ:ð, kʰva:ð, kʰɣ:, kʰvau:ðɣm, kʰvɛ:ðɪn, -ið] v.5 (1) say; acc. with inf.: *hann kvað það satt vera* he said that it was true (he declared it to be true); impers.: *hann kvað (ku) vera ríkur* he is said to be rich; *hann kvað ætla að* . . . he is said to be going to . . . ; *í orði kveðnu* in name, on paper, in theory; middle voice: *kveðast* say, say that, *hann kvaðst vera latur* he said that he (himself) was lazy (S. VI, 9, 5, 2); (2) recite, sing, chant, croon: *kveða við barn* lull a baby to sleep with song; *kveða vísu* compose a song; (3) impers.: *það kveður að e-u (e-m)* sth (sbdy) is of importance, sth (sbdy) is significant, sbdy is a great personality.

kveðandi [kʰvɛ:ðanḍɪ] wf.2 metrum; singing.

1. kveðja, -u, -ur [kʰvɛð·ja, -ɣ(r̥)] wf.1 greeting, regards; *með beztu kveðjum* with best regards (phrase in ending a letter). Cf. *kasta.*

2. kveðja, kvaddi, kvaddur (kvatt) [kʰvɛð·ja, kʰvad:ɪ, kʰvad:ɣr̥, kʰvaʰt:] wv.1 greet, say goodbye; *kveðjast* say goodbye to each other.

kvef, -s [kʰvɛ:v, kʰvɛf·s] n. cold; *fá kvef* catch cold.

kveið, see *kvíða.*

kveikja, kveikti, kveikt(ur) [kʰvei:-kₗʰa, kʰveix·tɪ, -ɣr̥, kʰveix·t; kʰvei:-g̊ₗa] wv.2 light, kindle; *kveikja ljós* light a light; *kveikja á lampa (raljósi)* light a lamp; turn on the (electric) light; *kveikja í e-u* set fire to, set on fire.

kveisa, -u, -ur [kʰvei:sa, -ɣ(r̥)] wf.1 bellyache, colic, gripes.

kveld, see *kvöld.*

kvelja, kvaldi, kvalinn (-ið) [kʰvɛl·ja, kʰval·dɪ, kʰva:lɪn, -ið] wv. 1 torture; *kveljast* suffer (pain) (S. VI, 7, 4).

kvenna, see *kona.*

kvennaskóli, -a, -ar [kʰvɛn:a-skou:lɪ, -a(r̥)] wm.1 school for girls; (senior) high school, (junior) college for girls.

kvennfólk, -s (kven-) [kʰvɛn-foulkʰ, -foul(x)s; -foulk] n. women (folks).

kvennmaður, -manns, -menn (kven-) [kʰvɛn·ma·ðɣr̥, -mans, -mɛn·] m.4 woman.

kvennmannsföt, -fata (kven-) [kʰvɛn·-mans-fö:tʰ, -fa:tʰa; -fö:ḍ, -fa:ḍa] n.pl. women's clothes.

kvennmannsnafn, -s, -nöfn (kven-) [kʰvɛn·mans-nab·ṇ(s),-naf·s,-nöb·ṇ] n. woman's name.

kver, -s, - [kʰvɛ:r, kʰvɛr̥·s] n. booklet; catechism.

kvíða, kvíði, kveið, kviðum, kviðið [kʰvi:ða, kʰvi:ðɪ, kʰvei:ð, kʰvɪ:ðɣm, kvɪ:ðɪð] v.1 *kvíða e-u* fear for sth, fear that sth will or will not happen. Note: Present *kvíði* is as if from wv.2.

1. kviður, -ar, -ir [kʰvɪ:ðɣr̥, -ar̥, -ɪr̥] m.3 belly, abdomen.

2. kviður, -ar, -ir [kʰvɪ:ðɣr̥, -ar̥, -ɪr̥] m.3 jury.

kvika, -aði, -að [kʰvɪ:kʰa, -aðɪ, -að; kʰvɪ:g̊a] wv.4 move.

kvikfé, -fjár [kʰvɪ:kʰfjɛ·, -fjau·r; kʰvɪ:g̊-] n. livestock.

Consonants: [ð] brea*th*e; [g] *g*ood; [gⱼ] *gy*arden (garden); [hʍ] *wh*at; [j] *y*es; [kⱼ] *cy*an (can); [ŋ] thi*ng*; [q] N. Germ. sa*g*en; [r] Scottish *r*; [x] approx. Germ. a*ch*; [þ] *th*in. Voiceless: o; [b̥, ḍ, g̊] approx. *p, t, k.* Half-voiced: *italics.* Aspiration and preaspiration. [ʰ]; [pʰ, tʰ, kʰ] *p-, t-, k-.* Others as in English.

kvikfénaður, -ar [kʰvɪ:kʰfjɛ·naðʏr̥, -ar; kʰvɪ:g̊-] m.3 livestock.

kvikfjárrækt, -ar [kʰvɪ:kʰfjaur-raix·t, -ar̥; kʰvɪ:g̊-] f.2 animal husbandry, livestock raising.

kvikmynd, -ar, -ir [kʰvɪ:kʰmɪnd, -ar̥, -ɪr̥; kʰvɪ:g̊-] f.2 film, motion picture, movie.

kvikmyndahús, -s, - [kʰvɪ:kʰmɪnda-hu:s, -hus:; kʰvɪ:g̊-] n. motion picture house, movie-house, movie (= bíó).

kvikmyndaleikari, -a, -ar [kʰvɪ:kʰmɪnda-lei:kʰarɪ, -a, -ar̥; kʰvɪ:g̊-, -lei:g̊arɪ] wm.1 motion picture actor, movie actor, film actor.

kviksyndi, -s [kʰvɪ:kʰsɪndɪ(s); kʰvɪ:g̊-] n. quagmire, quicksand.

kvikur, kvik, kvikt [kʰvɪ:kʰʏr̥, kʰvɪ:kʰ, kʰvɪx·t; kʰvɪ:g̊(ʏr̥)] adj. alive, moving, vivacious.

kvilli, -a, -ar [kʰvɪd·lɪ, -a, -ar̥] wm.1 ailment, ailing.

kvintett, -s, -ar [kʰvɪn·tʰɛʰt·(s), -ar̥; kʰvɪn·tɛʰt·] m.1 quintet.

kvæði, -s, - [kʰvai:ðɪ(s)] n. poem.

kvöld, -s, - (kveld) [kʰvöl·d(s), kʰvɛl·d(s)] n. evening; að kvöldi dags in the evening; annað kvöld tomorrow night; í kvöld tonight; gott kvöld good evening; þessi kvöldin these evenings (cf. these days).

kvöldmatur, -ar [kʰvöl·dma·tʰʏr̥, -ar̥; -ma·dʏr̥] m.3 supper, evening meal.

kvöldverður, -ar, -ir [kʰvöl·dverðʏr̥, -ar̥, -ɪr̥] m.3 supper.

Kýlingar [kˌʰi:liŋg̊ar̥] m.1.pl. a place name.

kyn, -s, -, (-ja) [kˌʰɪ:n, kˌʰɪn·s, kˌʰɪn·ja] n. kin; gender.

kynna, kynnti, kynnt(ur) [kˌʰɪn:a, kˌʰɪn·tʰɪ, -ʏr̥, kˌʰɪn·tʰ; kˌʰɪn·t, -ɪ, -ʏr̥] wv.2 make known; introduce; kynna e-n e-m introduce sbdy to sbdy; kynna sér e-ð acquaint oneself with sth; kynnast get acquainted with.

kynning, -ar, -ar [kˌʰɪn:iŋg̊, -ar̥] f.1 introduction, acquaintance with.

kýr, (kú), kýr, kýr, (kúa) [kˌʰi:r, kʰu:, kʰu:a] f.3 cow.

kyrr, kyrr, kyrrt [kˌʰɪr:, kˌʰɪr̥·t; kˌʰɪ:r; kˌʰʏr:, kˌʰʏ:r, kˌʰʏr̥·t] adj. quiet, calm, still; not moving, running; hér er kyrrt og gott here is good and quiet; vertu kyrr! be quiet, halt! (Pr. 2, 1, 11n).

kýs, see kjósa.

kyssa, kyssti, kysst(ur) [kˌʰɪs:a, kˌʰɪs·t, -ɪ, -ʏr̥; kˌʰʏs:a, kˌʰʏs·t] wv.2 kiss.

kæla, kældi, kældur (kælt) [kˌʰai:la, kˌʰail·dɪ, -ʏr̥, kˌʰail·t] wv.2 cool.

kær, kær, kært; kærari, -astur; kærri, kærstur [kˌʰai:r, kˌʰair·t, kˌʰai:rarɪ, -astʏr̥, kˌʰair:ɪ, kˌʰairstʏr̥] adj. dear, beloved; kæri vinur dear friend (common informal beginning of letters; S. III, 2, 5); kær mér dear to me; kærar kveðjur cordial greetings.

1. kæra, -u, -ur [kˌʰai:ra, -ʏ(r̥)] wf.1 complaint.

2. kæra, kærði, kærður (kært) [kˌʰai:ra, kˌʰair·ðɪ, -ʏr̥, kˌʰair·t] wv.2 accuse.

kærandi, -a, -endur [kˌʰai:randɪ, -a, -endʏr̥] wm.2 accuser, the plaintiff.

kærður, kærð, kært [kˌʰair·ðʏr̥, kˌʰair·ð, kˌʰair·t] adj. accused; hinn kærði the accused, the defendant.

köf, see kaf.

köku, -ur, see kaka.

kökudiskur, -s, -ar [kʰö:kʰʏ-dɪs·kʏr̥, -dɪsks, -dɪs·kar̥; kʰö:g̊ʏ-] m.1 cake plate.

köld, see kaldur.

kölski, -a [kʰölsk·ɪ, -ka] wm.1 the devil.

könnu, -ur, see kanna.

könnunarflokkur, -s, -ar [kʰön:ʏnar-flɔʰk·ʏr̥, -flɔʰk·s, -flɔʰk:ar̥] m.1 patrol.

köpp, see kapp.

körfu, -ur, see karfa.

körfustóll, -s, -ar [kʰör·vʏ-stoud·l, -stoul·s, -stou:lar̥] m.1 wicker chair.

Kötlu, see Katla.

Vowels: a [a] approx. father; á [au] cow; e [ɛ] set; é [jɛ] yes; i, y [ɪ] sit; í, ý [i] feel; o [ɔ] law; ó [ou] note; u [ʏ] approx. Germ. Mütter; ú [u] school; y = i; ý = í; æ [ai] ice; ö [ö] Germ. hören; au [öy] French feuille; ei, ey [ei] ale. Length [:]; half-length [·].

390

köttur, kattar, kettir [kʰöʰt:ʏr̥, kʰaʰt:-
ar̥, kɪʰcʰt:ɪr̥] m.3 cat.

L.

1. lá, láði, láð [lau:, lau:ðɪ, lau:ð]
wv.3 *lá e-m e-ð* blame sbdy for sth;
only with negation: *ég lái þér það
ekki* I do not blame you for it.
2. lá, see *liggja*.

labba, -aði, -að [lab:a, -aðɪ, -að] wv.4
walk leisurely, take a walk, stroll,
saunter; *ég labbaði (mig) upp í
skóla* I strolled up to the school
(S. I, **2**, *1*, 4).

lafa, lafði, lafað [la:va, lav·ðɪ, la:vað;
lab·ðɪ] wv.3 hang limply.

lag, -s, lög [la:q, lax·s, lö:q] n. layer;
shape, condition; stab; lull between
two breakers, opportunity; *sæta
lagi* take the opportunity; song,
tune, melody; pl. *lög* law; *gera e-ð
með lagi* do sth in an efficient way,
hafa lag á e-u have the knack of
sth (of doing sth); *setja í lag*
adjust, fix, put in good order *fara
í samt lag* resume the original
(same) shape; *í góðu lagi* in good
condition; (opposite: *í ólagi*); *er
nokkurt lag á þessu?* is there any
rime or reason in this? *allt í lagi!*
everything in order, O.K.; *í einu
lagi* in one piece, in one phrase;
í tvennu lagi in two parts, in two;
í fyrsta (öðru) lagi in the first
(second) place; *í síðasta lagi* latest.

lág, -ar, -ir [lau:(q), lau:(q)ar̥,
lau:jɪr̥] f.2 hollow, depression.

laga, -aði, -að(ur) [la:qa, -aðɪ, -að,
-aðʏr̥] wv.4 fix, repair, adjust, *laga
e-ð* fix sth; *laga sig til* fix oneself.

laga- og hagfræði-deild, -ar, -ir [la:qa-
ɔ(q)-hax·frai·ðɪ·deil·d, -ar̥, -ɪr̥] f.2
faculty (department) of law (juris-
prudence) and political economy.

lagar, see *lögur*.

Lagarfoss, - [la:qar·fɔs:] m.1 'Loch
Falls,' waterfall and a boat's name.

lagði, -ur, see *leggja*.

lagðsíður, -síð, -sítt [laq·ðsi·ðʏr̥, -si·ð,

-siʰt·; lag·þ-] adj. longhaired (of
sheep).

lagður, lögð, lagt [laq·ðʏr̥, löq·ð,
lax·t; lag·ðʏr̥, lög·þ] adj. laid over
with ice, frozen.

laginn, -in, -ið; lagnari, -astur [lai:-
jɪn, -ɪn, -ɪð, la(i)g·narɪ, -astʏr̥;
la:jɪn] adj. adept, skilful.

lagkaka, -köku, -ur [lax·kʰa·kʰa, -kʰö·-
kʰʏ(r); -kʰa·ga, -kʰö·gʏ] wf.1 layer
cake.

laglegur [laq·lɛ·qʏr̥] adj. (see -*legur*)
pretty, handsome, good-looking.

láglendi, -s, - [lau:(q)lendɪ(s)] n.
lowland.

láglendisræma, -u, -ur [lau:(q)lendɪs-
rai:ma, -ʏ(r̥)] wf.1 rim of lowland.

lagning, -ar, -ar [lag·ning, -ar̥] f.1
laying (of nets, roads, etc.); water
wave (in hairdressing).

lagskiftur, -skift, -skift [lax·sk,ɪftʏr̥,
-sk,ɪft] adj. formed by layers, divided by layers.

lagskona, -u, -ur [lax·skʰɔ·na, -ʏ(r̥)]
wf.1 comrade (female).

lagsmaður, -manns, -menn [lax·sma·-
ðʏr̥, -mans, -men·] m.4 comrade
(male).

lágum, see *liggja*.

lágur, lág, lágt; lægri, lægstur [lau:-
(qʏ)r̥, .lau:(q), laux·t; lauʰt:;
laiq·rɪ, laixstʏr̥] adj. low, low-
lying; short of stature; *lægri
skólar* lower schools (i.e. *barna-
skólar òg gagnfræðaskólar* primary
and secondary (middle) schools).

1. lak, -s, lök [la:kʰ(s), lö:kʰ; la:g,
lö:g] n. bedsheet.
2. lak, lákum, see *leka*.

lamb, -s, lömb [lam·b, lam·(b)s.
löm·b] n. lamb.

lambaket, -s (-kjöt) [lam·ba·k,ʰc:tʰ(s).
-k,ʰö:tʰ; -k,ʰc:d, -k,ʰö:d] n. lamb
(meat); = *ket af lambi* meat of
lamb.

lambasteik, -ar, -ur [lam·ba·stei:kʰ,
-ar̥, -ʏr̥; -stei:g] f.3 roast lamb.

lambhús, -s, - [lam·b(h)u·s, -hus·] n.
lamb shed.

lán, -s, - [lau:n, laun·s] n. loan; *taka*

Consonants: [ð] brea*the*; [g] *g*ood; [gɪ] *gy*arden (garden); [hw] *wh*at; [j] *y*es; [kɪ] *cy*an
(can); [ŋ] thi*ng*; [q] N. Germ. sa*gen*; [r] Scottish *r*; [x] approx. Germ. a*ch*; [þ] *th*in.
Voiceless: ο; [b̥, d̥, g̥] approx. *p, t, k*. Half-voiced: *italics*. Aspiration and preaspiration:
[ʰ]; [pʰ, tʰ, kʰ] *p-, t-, k-*. Others as in English.

lán take a loan; *fá e-ð að láni* borrow sth.

lána, -aði, -að(ur) [lau:na, -aðɪ, -að, -aðʏṛ] wv.4 lend; *lána e-m e-ð* lend sbdy sth; *fá e-ð lánað hjá e-m* borrow sth from sbdy.

land, -s, lönd [lan·d, lan·(d̥)s, lön·d̥] n. land, country; *hér á landi* in this country; *um allt land* throughout the country; *kominn undir land á Íslandi* come near the coast of Iceland; *komast á land* reach the shore, get ashore; *til lands og sjávar* on land and sea; *út á land* into the country; land; estate, farm; so in place names: *-land; Land* a district in the South of Iceland.

landafræði [lan·d̥a-frai:ðɪ] wf.2 geography.

landafræði(s)bók, -ar, -bækur [lan·d̥(a)frai·ðɪ(s)·bou:kʰ, -aṛ, -bai:kʰʏṛ; -bou:g̊, -bai:g̊ʏṛ] f.3 geography book.

landafurðir [lan·d̥a·vʏrðɪṛ] f.2.pl. produce of the land, farm products.

landbúnaður, -ar [lan·d̥bu·naðʏṛ, -aṛ] m.3 animal husbandry, agriculture, livestock raising.

landfarssótt, -ar, -ir [lan·d̥faṛ(s)·souʰt:, -aṛ, -ɪṛ] f.2 epidemic.

landferð, -ar, -ir [lan·d̥ferð, -ðaṛ, -ðɪṛ] f.2 travel by land, journey.

landfugl, -s, -ar [lan·d̥fʏg̊l(s), -fʏg̊laṛ] m.1 land bird.

landganga, -göngu, -ur [lan·d̥gauŋg̊a, -göyŋg̊ʏ(ṛ)] wf.1 landing, walking ashore, invading a coast.

landgöngumenn, -manna [lan·d̥göyŋg̊ʏ-mɛn:, -man:a] m.4.pl. marines.

landgöngusveit, -ar, -ir [lan·d̥göyŋg̊ʏ-svei:tʰ, -aṛ, -ɪṛ; -svei:d̥] f.2 troops for landing, marines.

landi, -a, -ar [lan·d̥ɪ, -a, -aṛ] wm.1 compatriot, fellow-countryman.

landleyfi, -s, - [lan·d̥lei·vɪ(s)] n. permission to go ashore, shore leave.

Landmannaleið, -ar [lan·d̥man·a·lei:ð, -ðaṛ] f.2 'the Road of *Landmenn*.'

Landmannahellir, -is [lan·d̥man·a-

heð·lɪr, -ɪs] m.1 'the Cave of *Landmenn*.'

Landmenn, -manna [lan·d̥mɛn·, -man·a] m.4.pl. the inhabitants of the district Land.

landnám, -s, - [lan·d̥nau·m, -naums] n. taking of land, settling on land; the first settlement of Iceland.

Landnáma, -u [lan·d̥nau·ma, -ʏ] wf.1 'The Book of the Settlements,' describing the earliest settlements and the pioneers in Iceland (874-930).

landnámsmaður, -manns, -menn [lan·d̥naums·ma:ðʏṛ, -man·s, -mɛn:] m.4 settler, pioneer.

landnámstíð, -ar [lan·d̥naums-ti:ð, -ðaṛ] f.2 the time of the settlement of Iceland (874-930).

landnorður, (-ri), -urs [lan·d̥norðʏṛ(s), -norðrɪ] n. northeast.

landplága, -u, -ur [lan·d̥pʰlau·(q)a, -pʰlau·(q)ʏ(ṛ)] wf.1 plague.

Landsbanki Íslands [lan·(d̥)sbauŋk,ʰɪ i:slan(d̥)s; -bauŋ̊k,ɪ] wm.1 'The National Bank of Iceland.'

Landsbókasafnið, -sins [lan·(d̥)sbou·kʰa·sab·nɪð, -sabnsɪns; -bou·g̊a-] n. with the def. art. 'The National Library.'

landshorn, -s, - [lan·(d̥)shɔdn(s); -hordn(s)] n. 'corner of the land,' lands end.

landslag, -s [lan·(d̥)sla·q, -laxs] n. nature, physical condition of a country, features of the country, scenery.

landsmaður, -manns, -menn [lan·(d̥)s-ma·ðʏṛ, -mans, -mɛn·] m.4 inhabitant, native; pl. people of the land.

landsmál [lan·(d̥)smau·l] n.pl. public affairs.

landsmálasamtök [lan·(d̥)smau·la-sam·tʰök, -tʰög̊] n.pl. league to further public affairs; *Landsmálasamtök Þjóðveldismanna* 'The League of Nationalists.' Cf. *Þjóðveldismenn*.

landssamband, -s [lan·(d̥s)samband(s)] n. country-wide union, federation; *Landssamband iðnaðar-*

Vowels: *a* [a] approx. *father;* *á* [au] *cow;* *e* [ɛ] *set;* *é* [jɛ] *yes;* *i, y* [ɪ] *sit;* *í, ý* [i] *feel;* *o* [ɔ] *law;* *ó* [ou] *note;* *u* [ʏ] approx. Germ. M*ü*tter; *ú* [u] *school;* *y* = *i;* *ý* = *í;* *æ* [ai] *ice;* *ö* [ö] Germ. h*ö*ren; *au* [öy] French f*eui*lle; *ei, ey* [ei] *ale.* Length [:]; half-length [·].

392

manna 'The Federation of Icelandic Handicraftsmen.'

Landssímastööin, -stöövarinnar [lan·(d̥)si·ma·stö:ðɪn, -stöð·varɪn·ar] f.1 with def. art. 'The State Telegraph and Telephone Office.'

Landssíminn, -ans [lan·(d̥s)si·mɪn, -si·mans] wm.1 with the def. art. 'The State Telegraph (and Telephone),' long distance (in telephoning).

Landsspítalinn, -ans [lan·(d̥s)spi·tʰalɪn, -ans; -spi·d̥-] wm.1 with the def. art. 'The State Hospital.'

landsuður, (-ri), -urs [lan·d̥sʏ·ðʏr̥(s), -sʏðrɪ] n. southeast.

landsýn, -ar [lan·d̥si·n, -si·nar̥] f.2 landfall; *í landsýn* in sight of land.

lang- [lauŋ·g̊-] pref. completely, by far (S. III, 5, 3).

langa, -aði, -að [lauŋ·g̊a, -aðɪ, -að] wv.4 want, desire; *mig langar að* (or: *til að*) *gera e-ð* I want to do sth; *mig hefði langað* (*til*) *að* I should have liked to; *mig langar í e-ð* I want sth, I long for sth, I have a craving for sth (S. I, 2, *1*, 3; VI, 14, *5*).

Langaðráttur, -ar [lauŋ·g̊a·drauʰt:ʏr̥, -ar̥] m.3 'Long Draught,' a place in a river where long nets can be laid and hauled. Also *Langidráttur, Langadráttar.*

langafi, -a, -ar [lauŋ·g̊a·vɪ, -a(r̥)] wm.1 great-grandfather.

langa-langafi, -a, -ar [lauŋ·g̊a-lauŋ·g̊a·vɪ, -a(r̥)] wm.1 great-great-grandfather.

langa-langamma, -ömmu, -ur [lauŋ·g̊a-lauŋ·g̊am·a, -öm·ʏ(r̥)] wf.1 great-great-grandmother.

langamma, -ömmu, -ur [lauŋ·g̊am·a, -öm·ʏ(r̥)] wf.1 grandmother.

Langanes, -s [lauŋ·g̊a·nɛ:s, -nɛs:] n. 'Long Ness.'

langflestir, -flestar, -flest [lauŋ·g̊-flɛs·tɪr̥, -flɛs·tar̥, -flɛs·t] adj. pl. superl. by far the most numerous; by far the most.

Langjökull, -uls [lauŋ·g̊jö·kʰʏdl, -ʏls; -jö·g̊ʏdl] m.1 'Long Glacier.'

langlína, -u, -ur [lauŋ·g̊li·na, -ʏ(r̥)] wf.1 long distance (in telephoning).

langtum [lauŋ·tʰʏm, lauŋ·tʏm] adv. by far; *langtum betri* by far the better one.

langur, löng, langt; lengri, lengstur [lauŋ·g̊ʏr̥, löyŋ·g̊, lauŋ·tʰ; lauŋ·t; leiŋg̊rɪ, leiŋstʏr̥] adj. long; *langt* far, long way; long time; *fyrir löngu* long ago (S. III, 3, 2); *svo langt sem* as far as; *áður en langt um líður* before long; *vita lengra en nef manns nær* 'know further than one's nose reaches,' be a magician; *lengst* (*af*) for the longest time, almost all the time.

lapið, -inn, lapti, see *lepja*.

Lappi, -a, -ar [laʰp:ɪ, -a(r̥)] wm.1 a Lap; a common dog's name.

lár, -s, -ar [lau:r, laur̥·s, lau:rar̥] m.1 wool box.

Lárus, -ar (-s) [lau:rʏs, -ar̥] m.1 Lawrence; patr. *Lárusson.*

las, lásum, see *lesa*.

lasinn, -in, -ið; lasnari, -astur [la:sɪn, -ɪn, -ɪð; las·narɪ, -astʏr̥] adj. sick, ill, indisposed, not well.

laska, -aði, -að(ur) [las·ka, -aðɪ, -að, -aðʏr̥] wv.4 damage.

lát, -s, - [lau:tʰ(s); lau:d̥] n. giving way, loss, death.

láta, læt, lét, létum, látinn (-ið) [lau:tʰa, lai:tʰ, lje:tʰ, lje:tʰʏm, lau:tʰɪn, -ɪð; lau:da, lai:d̥, lje:d̥, lje:dʏm, lau:dɪn, -ɪð] v.7 let; have (done); let, leave, yield, die; put; behave, act; say, allege, pretend (*látast*); (1) let: *látum oss* let us (in the liturgy chiefly, otherwise: *við skulum*); *láta heillast* let oneself be bewitched (spellbound); *láta e-n hafa* (*fá*) *e-ð* let one have sth; *láta e-ð af hendi* (*við e-n*) deliver sth (up to sbdy); (2) after *láta* an infinitive of a transitive verb must usually be translated by a passive infinitive (or with 'have' and a past participle) in English:

Consonants: [ð] brea*th*e; [g] *g*ood; [gj] *gy*arden (garden); [hʍ] *wh*at; [j] *y*es; [kj] *cy*an (can); [ŋ] thi*ng*; [q] N. Germ. sa*g*en; [r] Scottish *r*; [x] approx. Germ. a*ch*; [þ] *th*in. Voiceless: ○; [b̥, d̥, g̊] approx. *p, t, k.* Half-voiced: *italics.* Aspiration and preaspiration: [ʰ]; [pʰ, tʰ, kʰ] *p-, t-, k-.* Others as in English.

láta sauma let be sewn, have sewn (S. VI, **14**, *9*) ; *láta gera e-ð* have sth done; *láta raka sig* have oneself shaven; *láta bursta skóna* have the shoes brushed; *láta þurrka þau* have them dried; *láta vekja e-n* have sbdy awakened; *láta færa sér kaffi* have coffee brought (served) ; *láta fara vel um sig* make oneself comfortable; *láta undir höfuð leggjast* neglect ('leave sth lying under one's head').; *láta vitja* have (sbdy, sth) fetched; (3) let, leave alone: *láta vera* let be, leave alone; *láta (e-n) eiga sig* (literally: 'let one own oneself') let (sbdy) be, leave alone (S. VI, **11**, *6*) ; *ég læt það vera* (literally: 'I let it be') that is all right; *láta undan* yield, give in; *láta undan fæti* give way under the foot; *látast* die, *látinn* dead; (4) put: *láta út fyrir* put outside; (5) behave: *láta vel, illa, grimmilega* behave well, badly, act fiercely (of dogs); *því læturðu svona?* why do you carry on (cut up) like that? *láta vel(illa) yfir e-u* be contented (discontented) with sth, praise (blame) sth; *vel látinn* well esteemed, much liked; (6) middle voice: *látast* pretend, let on; *hann lézt ekki heyra* he pretended not to hear (S. VI, **9**, *5*, *2*).

latína, -u [la:tʰi·na, -ʏ; la:ᵭi·na] wf.1 Latin.

latur, löt, latt [la:tʰʏr, lö:tʰ, laʰt:; la:dʏr, lö:d] adj. lazy.

Laufásvegur, -ar [löy:vau·s-ve:qʏr, -ve:qar] m.3 'Leaf Ridge Way.'

1. laug, -ar, -ar [löy:q, -qar] f.1 bath, hot spring; *Laugarnar* 'The Hot Springs' near Reykjavík, an open air swimming pool.

2. laug, see *ljúga.*

laugahiti, -a [löy:qa-hɪ:tʰɪ, -a; -hɪ:dɪ] wm.1 heat from hot springs.

laugahitun, -ar [löy:qa-hɪ:tʰʏn, -ʏnar; -hɪ:dʏn] f.2 heating by water from hot springs.

Laugahraun, -s [löy:qa-hᵣöy:n, -hᵣöyn·s] n. 'Hot Springs Lava.'

Laugar [löy:qar] f.1.pl. 'Hot Springs,' a common place name; the open air swimming pool of Reykjavík.

laugardagur, -s, -ar [löy:qar-da:qʏr, -dax·s, -da:qar] m.1 Saturday.

Laugarvatn, -s [löy:qar-vaʰt·n̥, -vas:] n. 'Hot Spring Lake,' a well known rural district school (folk high school) in the South.

laugavatn, -s [löy:qa-vaʰt·n̥, -vas:] n. water from hot springs.

Laugavegur, -ar [löy:qa-vɛ:qʏr, -vɛ:qar] m.3 'Hot Springs Way,' one of the chief streets of Reykjavík.

lauk, see *ljúka.*

laus, laus, laust [löy:s, löys·t] adj. loose, free, vacant; *síminn er laus* the line (phone) is free; *brauðið er laust* the benefice (pastorate) is vacant; *laus allra mála* free of all concern (obligation) to; *laus við e-ð* free from sth.

lauslega [löy:slɛ·qa] adv. loosely, approximately, in a rough manner.

laust, see *laus* and *ljósta.*

1. laut, -ar, -ir [löy:tʰ, -ar, -ɪr; löy:d] f.2 hollow, depression in the ground.

2. laut, see *lúta.*

lautinant, -s, -ar [löy:tʰɪnan·tʰ, -s, -ar; löy:dɪnan·t] m.1 lieutenant.

lax, -, -ar [lax·s(ar)] m.1 salmon.

laxá, -ár, -ár [lax·sau·(r)] f.1 salmon river; also a place name.

laxaklak, -s [lax·sa-kʰla:kʰ(s); -kʰla:g̊] n. salmon hatching.

Laxnes, -s [lax·snɛ·s, -nɛs] n. place name, 'Salmon Ness'; gen. used as family name: *Laxness.*

laxveiðaá, -ár, -ár [lax·svei·ða-au:(r)] f.1 salmon (fishing) river.

laxveiðasvæði, -s, - [lax·svei·ða-svai:ðɪ(s)] n. salmon fishing region.

laxveiði, -ar, -ar [lax·svei·ðɪ, -vei·ðar] f.1 salmon fishing.

laxveiðilög, -laga [lax·svei·ðɪ-lö:q, -la·qa] n.pl. (The) Salmon Fishing Act.

Vowels: *a* [a] approx. father; *á* [au] cow; *e* [ɛ] set; *é* [jɛ] *yes*; *i, y* [ɪ] sit; *í, ý* [i] feel; *ö* [ö] Germ. hören; *au* [öy] French *feuille*; *ei, ey* [ei] ale. Length [:]; half-length [·]. Consonants: [ð] brea*the*; [g] *g*ood; [gɹ] *gy*arden (garden); [hw̥] *wh*at; [j] *y*es; [kɹ] *cy*an

394

léð, -i, -ur, see *ljá*.

leður, (-ri), -urs [lε:ðʏṛ(s), lεð·rɪ] n. leather.

leggja, legg, lagði, lagður (lagt) [lεg̊ʲ:a, lεg̊:, laq·ðɪ, -ʏṛ, lax·t; lag̊·ðɪ, -ʏṛ] wv.1 (1) transitive with acc.: lay, place, put; lay down, put in shape; lay out, build; apply; put: *leggja e-ð innan í bréf* inclose sth in a letter; lay: *leggja veg* lay out a road, build a road; *leggja hárið* wave the hair (with water); *leggja kapp á e-ð* strive for sth; *leggja stund á e-ð* practice, apply oneself to sth; (2) transitive with acc. and dat.: cover: *leggja e-ð e-u* cover (overlay) sth with sth; *þakið er lagt grænum þakhellum* the roof is covered with green tiles; (ísi) *lagður* covered with ice; with dat. (instrumental) only: *leggja báti að bryggju* lay a boat up at a pier, bring the boat up to the pier; (3) impersonal: be moved or carried: *reykinn* (acc.) *leggur upp* the smoke is carried up; *þokuna* (acc.) *leggur inn fjörðinn* the fog is spreading up the fjord; (4) middle voice: *leggjast* 'lay oneself,' lie down; go to bed (with some sickness); *leggjast á e-ð* fall upon sth; *leggjast fyrir* lie down; *leggjast í rúmið* take to one's bed, be laid up; *leggjast út* become an outlaw; *láta undir höfuð leggjast* (literally: 'let sth be laid under one's head') neglect; *hann er lagztur* he has lain down (S. VI, 3, 3, 2); (5) with preps and advs: *leggja á e-n* put a spell upon sbdy; *legg ég á og mæli ég um* I solemnly pronounce this spell; *leggja á (af) stað* start on a journey; *leggja á skarðið, leiruna, fjörðinn* start going over the pass, the mud flat, the fjord; *leggja í ferð* start a journey; *leggja inn* put into, deliver to; *leggja niður* lay down, discontinue; *leggja saman* add; *leggja til* propose; *sverja og sárt við leggja* swear, invoking

heavy penalties on oneself (if the oath be false).

legið, -inn, see *liggja*.

legir, see *lögur*.

legubekkur, -bekkjar, -bekkir [lε:qʏbεʰk:ʏṛ, -bεʰkʲ:aṛ, -bεʰkʲ:ɪṛ] m.2 sofa, couch.

-legur, -leg, -legt; -legri, -legastur [-lε:qʏṛ, -lε:q, -lεx·t; -lεq·rɪ, -lε:qastʏṛ] adj. suffix -ly.

1. leið, -ar, -ir [lei:ð, -ðaṛ, -ðɪṛ] f.2 way, road, route; *alla leið* all the way; *á leiðinni* on the way; *um leið* at the same time; *þeir fóru þessa leið* they took this route (S. I, 2, 2, 3).

2. leið, see *leiður* and *líða*.

leiða, leiddi, leiddur (leitt) [lei:ða, leid:ɪ, -ʏṛ; leiʰt:] wv.2 lead; *leiða e-n* lead sbdy; *leiðast* lead each other, walk hand in hand.

leiðast, leiddist, leiðzt [lei:ðast, leid:ɪst, leið·st] wv.2 (middle voice only) be bored; *mér leiðist* I am bored, I am sorry (S. VI, 4, 3; 6, 2; 7, 5).

leiðinlegur, [lei:ðɪn·lε:qʏṛ] adj. (see *-legur*) tedious, tiresome, irksome; *það er leiðinlegt, að* it is too bad that . . . , it is a pity that. . . .

leiður, leið, leitt [lei:ðʏṛ, lei:ð, leiʰt:] adj. loathsome; peeved, disgruntled; *leiður við e-n* hateful to sbdy (= *leiður e-m*); *mér er leitt* I am tired of, I hate to; *það var leitt, að* . . . it was too bad that . . . , I am sorry that . . . , unfortunately.

leifar [lei:vaṛ] f.1.pl. remnants, leftovers.

leiftur, (-ri), -urs, -ur [leif·tʏṛ(s), leiftrɪ] n. lightning.

leiftursókn, -ar, -ir [leif·tʏṛ·souʰk·n̥, -naṛ, -nɪṛ] f.2 Blitz offensive.

Leifur, -s [lei:vʏṛ, leif·s] m.1 pers. name; *Leifur heppni* Leif the Lucky; found *Vínland hið góða* (i. e. America) ca. 1000.

leiga, -u, -ur, (-na) [lei:qa, -ʏ(ṛ), leig̊·na] wf.1 rent.

Consonants: [ð] brea*the*; [g] *g*ood; [gʲ] *gy*arden (garden); [hw] *wh*at; [j] *y*es; [kʲ] *cy*an (can); [ŋ] thi*ng*; [q] N. Germ. sa*g*en; [r] Scottish *r*; [x] approx. Germ. a*ch*; [þ] *th*in. Voiceless: ○; [b̥, d̥, g̊] approx. *p, t, k.* Half-voiced: *italics.* Aspiration and preaspiration: [ʰ]; [pʰ, tʰ, kʰ] *p-, t-, k-.* Others as in English.

leigja, leigði, leigður (leigt) [lei:ja,
leiq·ðɪ, -ʏr̥, leix·t; leig̊·ðɪ, -ʏr̥] wv.2
rent, charter; *leigja sér* rent (for
oneself), hire; *leigja sér bíl* hire a
car, take a taxi; *leigja út* let (out).

leigubíll, -bíls, -bílar [lei:qʏ-bið·l̥,
-bil·s, bi:lar̥] m.1 taxi, hired car.

leika, leik, lék, lékum, leikinn (-ið)
[lei:kʰa, lei:kʰ, lje:kʰ, lje:kʰʏm,
lei:k̯ʰɪn, -ɪð; lei:g̊a, lei:g̊, lje:g̊,
lje:g̊ʏm, lei:g̊ɪn, -ɪð] v.7 play, act;
leika sér play; *leika á e-n* trick
sbdy, play a prank upon sbdy; *leika
á hljóðfœri* play an instrument;
leika í kvikmynd act in a film, in
a motion picture; *leika Hamlet*
play, act Hamlet.

leikari, -a, -ar [lei:kʰarɪ, -a(r̥);
lei:g̊arɪ] wm.1 actor.

leikfélag, -s, -lög [lei:kʰfje·laq, -laxs,
-löq; lei:g̊-] n. theater guild, actors'
guild, *Leikfélag Reykjavíkur* 'The
Theater Society of Reykjavík.'

leikfimi [lei:kʰfɪ·mɪ; lei:g̊-] wf.2
gymnastics.

leikhús, -húss, -hús [lei:kʰhu·s, -hus·;
lei:g̊-] n. theater.

leikrit, -s, - [lei:kʰrɪ·tʰ(s); lei:g̊-]
n. play.

leiksveinn, -s, -ar [lei:kʰsveiðn̥, -sveins,
-svei·nar̥; lei:g̊-] m.1 playmate.

leiksystir, -ur, -ur [lei:kʰsɪstɪr̥, -ʏr̥;
lei:g̊-] f.3 playmate (girl).

leiksystkin [lei:kʰsɪsk̯ɪn; lei:g̊-] n.pl.
playmates (boy and girl).

leikur, -s, -ir (-ar), (-ja, -a) [lei:kʰʏr̥,
lei:kʰs, lei:k̯ʰɪr̥, lei:kʰar; lei:k̯ʰa,
lei:kʰa; lei:g̊ʏr̥, lei:g̊ɪr̥, etc.] m.2
& 1 play.

leir, -s [lei:r, leir̥·s] m.1 clay, mud;
bad poetry.

leira, -u, -ur [lei:ra, -ʏ(r̥)] wf.1 mud
flat at the end of a fjord, or along
a river.

leirkelda, -u, -ur [leir̥·k̯ɪɛlda, -ʏ(r̥)]
wf.1 clay slough, mud slough.

leirpyttur, -s, -ir [leir̥·pɪʰt·ʏr̥, -pɪʰts,
-pɪʰt·ɪr̥] m.2 a pit of loam, clay,
mud.

leirskáld, -s, - [leir̥·skauld̥(s)] n. bad
poet, poetaster.

leirtau, -s [leir̥·tʰöy·(s)] n. crockery,
porcelain.

1. leit, -ar, -ir [lei:tʰ, -ar̥, -ɪr̥; lei:d̥]
f.2 search.

2. leit, see *líta*.

leita, -aði, -að [lei:tʰa, -aðɪ, -að;
lei:da] wv.4 look for, search, *leita
að e-u = leita eftir e-u (leita e-s)*
seek, search, look for sth.

lék, -um, see *leika*.

leka, lek, lak, lákum, lekinn (-ið)
[lɛ:kʰa, lɛ:kʰ, la:kʰ, lau:kʰʏm,
lɛ:k̯ʰɪn, -ɪð; lɛ:g̊a, lɛ:g̊, la:g̊,
lau:g̊ʏm, lɛ:g̊ɪn, -ɪð] v.5 leak.

leki, -a [lɛ:k̯ʰɪ, lɛ:kʰa; lɛ:g̊ɪ, lɛ:g̊a]
wm.1 leak.

lengd, -ar, -ir [leiŋ·d̥, -ar̥, -ɪr̥] f.2
length.

lengdarmál, -s [leiŋ·dar-mau:l,
-maul·s] n. measure of length.

lengi, lengur, lengst [leiŋ·g̊ɪ, leiŋ·g̊ʏr̥,
leiŋst] adv. long, for a long time;
lengi sumars for a good part of the
summer (S. I, **4**, *2*, 5).

lengja, lengdi, lengdur (lengt) [leiŋ·-
g̊ja, leiŋ·dɪ, -ʏr̥, leiŋ·tʰ; leiŋ̊·t] wv.2
prolong, lengthen; *daginn lengir* the
days are growing longer (S. VI,
14, *3*); *lengja eftir e-m* long for
sbdy's arrival; grow impatient
waiting for sbdy.

lengri, lengstur, see *langur*.

lepja, lapti, lapinn (-ið) [lɛ:pʰja,
laf·tɪ, la:pʰɪn, -ɪð; lɛ:bja, la:bɪn]
wv.1 lap up (of dogs, cats).

léreft, -s, - [lje:rɛft(s)] n. linen;
fimm metrar af lérefti five meters
of linen.

lesa, les, las, lásum, lesinn (-ið)
[lɛ:sa, lɛ:s, la:s, lau:sʏm, lɛ:sɪn,
-ɪð] v.5 read; study; *þú lest* you
are reading; *lesa bœn* read (say)
a prayer; *vel lesinn* (active sense)
well read; *mikið lesin bók* (passive)
much read book (S. VI, **12**, *2*, 1);
lesa undir morgundaginn prepare
one's lesson for the morning; *lesa*

Vowels: *a* [a] approx. *father*; *á* [au] *cow*; *e* [ɛ] *set*; *é* [jɛ] *yes*; *i, y* [ɪ] *sit*; *í, ý* [i] *feel*;
o [ɔ] *law*; *ó* [ou] *note*; *u* [ʏ] approx. Germ. Mütter; *ú* [u] *school*; *y = i*; *ý = í*; *œ* [ai] *ice*;
ö [ö] Germ. *hören*; *au* [öy] French *feuille*; *ei, ey* [ei] *ale*. Length [:]; half-length [·].

upp review (a subject); recite, give a recital.

lest, -ar, -ir [lɛs·t, -a*r*, -ɪ*r*] f.2 caravan, caravan of packhorses.

lét, -um, see *láta*.

létta, létti, létt [ljɛʰt:a, -ɪ, ljɛʰt:] wv.2 lighten (a burden, a task), brighten up; be relieved; *þokunni léttir* the fog clears; *hann léttir til* it (the weather) clears up; *mér létti* I was relieved.

léttur, létt, létt [ljɛʰt:ʏ*r*, ljɛʰt:] adj. light; *léttur skriðdreki* light tank.

lexía, -u, -ur [lɛx·si·ja, -ʏ(*r*)] wf.1 lesson.

leyfa, leyfði, leyfður (leyft) [lei:va, leiv·ðɪ, -ʏ*r*, leif·t; leib·ðɪ] wv.2 allow, permit; *leyfa e-m að gera e-ð* allow sbdy to do sth; *leyfa e-m e-ð* allow sbdy sth.

leyfi, -s, -[lei:vɪ(s)] n. leave, permission; *með leyfi* by (your) leave, with (your) permission; licence (= *veiðileyfi* licence to fish).

leysa, leysti, leyst(ur) [lei:sa leis·tɪ, -ʏ*r*: leis·t] wv.2 loose, loosen, release; ransom; undo, untie, make free; *leysa hnút* untie a knot; *leysa úr álögum* disenchant, release (free) from a spell; *leysa barn frá móður* deliver a mother of her child; impers.: *snjóa* (acc.) *leysir* snow melts, the snow is melting (S. VI, 14, 3).

leyti, -s [lei:tʰɪ(s); lei:dɪ] n. part, time; *um það leyti* about that time; *um miðaftansleytið* about four-five o'clock; *að nokkru leyti* partly, to some extent; *að mestu leyti* mostly; *að sínu leyti* proportionally; *að mörgu leyti* in many ways.

lið, -s [lɪ:ð, lɪð·s] n. (coll.) force, troops, army.

liða, -aði, -að(ur) [lɪ:ða, -aðɪ, -að, aðʏ*r*] wv.4 wave (the hair); *liðast fall in waves.

líða, líð, leið, liðum, liðinn (-ið) [lɪ:ða, li:ð, lei:ð, lɪ:ðʏm, lɪ:ðɪn, -ɪð] v.l glide, pass, proceed; feel, suffer; (1) pass (of time): *vikuna*

sem leið last week; *áður en langt um líður* before long; *þegar líður á daginn* when it gets late in the day, towards evening; *að þeim tíma liðnum* after that time; (of pain, etc.) *líða frá* pass away; (2) be, be coming along: *hvað líður kaffinu?* how is the coffee coming along? *hvað líður tímanum?* what about the time? what time is it? (3) feel: *líða vel* feel well, feel fine; *hvernig líður þér?* how are you feeling? (4) suffer: *hann hefur liðið mikið* he has suffered much; *ég get ekki liðið tóbaksreyk* I cannot stand tobacco smoke.

liðsforingi, -ja, -jar [lɪð·sfɔ·riŋɡ̊ˌɪ, -iŋɡ̊ˌa(*r*)] wm.1 officer.

liðun, -unar [lɪ:ðʏn, -ʏna*r*] f.2 waving (of hair).

liður, -ar, -ir [lɪ:ðʏ*r*, -a*r*, -ɪ*r*] m.3 limb, joint, link, part (of a compound word), generation; *allt í níunda lið* up to the ninth generation; item: *fastur liður á dagskrá* fixed item on the (daily) program.

liðþjálfi, -a, -ar [lɪð·þjaulvɪ, -a(*r*)] wm.1 sergeant (= *undirforingi*).

líf, -s, - [li:v, lif·s] n. life; *morgunn lífsins* the morning of life (S. I, 4, 1, 1); *á lífi* alive.

lifa, lifði, lifað [lɪ:va, lɪv·ðɪ, lɪ:vað; lɪb·ðɪ] wv.3 live; *lifa á e·u* live on (by) sth; *lifa við betri kjör* live in better circumstances, have a higher standard of living; *ekki nokkur lifandi maður* not a living soul; *lifandi skelfing* how awfully (S. VI, 4, 3; 12, 1, 2).

lífdagar [liv·da·qa*r*] m.1.pl. life; *saddur lífdaga* of ripe old age; ready to die, eager to die.

lífga, -aði, -að(ur) [liv·g̊a, -aðɪ, -að, -aðʏ*r*] wv.4 call to life, revive, resuscitate.

lifrarpylsa, -u, -ur [lɪv·ra*r*·pʰɪl·sa, -ʏ(*r*)] wf.1 liver sausage, made of crushed liver, rye flour, suet, and water; eaten fresh or pickled.

lífseigur, -seig, -seigt [lif·sei·qʏ*r*,

Consonants: [ð] brea*th*e; [g] *g*ood; [gⱼ] *gy*arden (garden); [hw] *wh*at; [j] *y*es; [kⱼ] *cy*an (can); [ŋ] thi*ng*; [q] N. Germ. sa*g*en; [r] Scottish *r*; [x] approx. Germ. a*ch*; [þ] *th*in. Voiceless: ○; [b̥, d̥, g̊] approx. *p, t, k*. Half-voiced: *italics*. Aspiration and preaspiration: [ʰ]; [pʰ, tʰ, kʰ] *p-, t-, k-*. Others as in English.

-sei·*q*, -seixt] adj. tough, tenacious, clinging to life.

lifur, lifrar, lifrar [lɪ:vʏr̥, lɪv·rar̥] f.1 liver; *lifrarpylsa.*

liggja, ligg, lá, lágum, leginn (-ið) [lɪg̊ˌ:a, lɪg̊:, lau:, lau:(q)ʏm, lei:jɪn, -ɪð] v.5 lie, be (sick) in bed; be situated; extend; lead (of doorways, roads, streets) ; *liggja úti* camp out, stay out over night; be an outlaw; *ekkert liggur á* this is not urgent, there is no hurry; *liggja við* be at stake; *líf liggur við* a life is at stake; *það liggur við, að* . . . it almost happens that . . . , someone barely escapes doing sth (S. VI, **4**, *3*; **6**, *2*).

1. **lík, -s, -** [li:kʰ(s) ; li:g̊] n. dead body, corpse.

2. **lík**, see *líkur.*

1. **líka, -aði, -að** [li:kʰa, -aðɪ, -að; li:g̊a] wv.4 please, like; *mér líkar það ekki* I do not like it, I am not satisfied with it; *e-m líkar vel (illa) við e-n* sbdy likes (dislikes) someone (S. I, **3**, *1*, 2; VI, **4**, *3*).

2. **líka** [li:kʰa; li:g̊a] adv. also, too; *þessi líka litlu læti* (litotes) quite a little disturbance (or rather the opposite) ; *þá er hann líka sloppinn* then he is really through.

líkami, -a, -ar [li:kʰa·mɪ, -a(r̥) ; li:g̊-] wm.1 body.

líkan, -ans, -ön [li:kʰan, -ans, -ön; li:g̊an] n. monument, statue.

líki, -s [li:kjˡʰɪ(s) ; lɪ:g̊ˌɪ] n. shape.

líkja, líkti, líkt [li:kjˡʰa, lix·tɪ, lix·t; li:g̊ˌa] wv.2 *líkja eftir e-u* imitate sth; *líkjast e-u (e-m)* resemble sth (sbdy), be similar to sth (sbdy).

líklega [li:kʰlɛ·qa; li:g̊-; lihk·-] adv. probably, likely.

líkneski, -s, - [lihk·neskˌɪ(s)] n. monument, statue.

líkur, lík, líkt [li:kʏr̥, li:kʰ, lix·t; li:g̊ʏr̥, li:g̊] adj. similar, like; *líkur e-m* similar to sbdy; *líkt og e-ð* like sth.

lilja, -u, -ur [lil·ja, -ʏ(r̥)] wf.1 lily;

name of a famous poem·; pers. name: *Lilja.*

lím, -s [li:*m*, lim·s] n. glue, paste.

líma, límdi, límdur (límt) [li:ma, lim·dɪ, -ʏr̥, lim·tʰ; lim̥·t] wv.2 glue, paste.

lin, see *linur.*

lín, -s, - [li:*n*, lin·s] n. linen.

lína, -u, -ur [li:na, -ʏ(r̥)] wf.1 line; letter.

línlak, -s, -lök [lin·la·kʰ(s), -lö·kʰ; -la·g̊, -lö·g̊] n. linen bedsheets.

linsoðinn, -in, -ið [lɪn·sɔ·ðɪn, -ɪn, -ɪð] adj. (pp.) softboiled.

linur, lin, lint [lɪ:nʏr̥, lɪ:*n*, lɪn·tʰ; lin̥·t] adj. soft.

lipur, lipur, lipurt; liprari, -astur [lɪ:pʰʏr̥, lɪ:pʰʏrt; lɪ:pʰrari, -astʏr̥; lɪ:br̥ʏr̥(t), lɪ:br̥arɪ] adj. nimble, supple; obliging, friendly.

list, -ar, -ir [lɪs·t, -ar̥, -ɪr̥] f.2 art, artistry; *stutt er líf, en listin löng* short is life, but art is long, ars longa, vita brevis; *glíma af list* wrestle artistically.

listamaður, -manns, -menn [lɪs·ta·ma:ðʏr̥, -man·s, -men:] m.4 artist.

listasafn, -s, -söfn [lɪs·ta·sab·n̥, -sabn̥s, -söb·n̥] n. museum, collection of art objects.

listastefna, -u, -ur [lɪs·ta·stɛb·na, -ʏ(r̥)] wf.1 tendency in arts.

listaverk, -s, - [lɪs·ta·vɛr̥·k(s)] n. work of art.

listmálari, -a, -ar [lɪs·tmau·larɪ, -a(r̥)] wm.1 painter.

lita, -aði, -að(ur) [lɪ:tʰa, -aðɪ, ·að, -aðʏr̥; lɪ:da] wv.4 color, tint, paint.

líta, lít, leit, litum, litið [li:tʰa, li:tʰ, lei:tʰ, lɪ:tʰʏm, lɪ:tʰɪð; li:da, li:d̥, lei:d̥, lɪ:dʏm, lɪ:dɪð] v.1 look, see, behold; (1) *líta á e-ð* look at sth; *líta eftir e-u* look after sth, take care of sth; *líta út* look, *hvernig lítur hann út?* how does he look? *það lítur ekki út fyrir, að* . . . it does not look as if . . . (S. VI, **14**, *7*) ; *líta við* look up, look around; (2) middle voice: *e-m líst á e-ð* sbdy likes sth; *e-m líst ekki á e-n*

Vowels: *a* [a] approx. father; *á* [au] *cow;* *e* [ɛ] set; *é* [jɛ] *yes;* *i, y* [ɪ] sit; *í, ý* [i] feel; *o* [ɔ] *law;* *ó* [ou] note; *u* [ʏ] approx. Germ. Mütter; *ú* [u] school; *y = i;* *ý = í;* *æ* [ai] ice; *ö* [ö] Germ. hören; *au* [öy] French *feuille;* *ei, ey* [ei] ale. Length [:]; half-length [·].

398

sbdy does not like (the looks of) someone; *mér lízt vel* (*illa*) *á e-ð* I like (dislike) sth; *mér lízt svo á manninn, að* . . . it is my impression of the man that . . . (S. VI, 14, 5); *honum lízt vel á stúlkuna* he likes (is falling in love with) the girl.

litast, -aðist, -azt [lɪ:tʰast, -aðɪst, -ast; lɪ:dast] wv.4 (only middle voice) *litast um* look about, look around.

lítill, lítil, lítið; minni, minnstur [li:tʰɪdl, -ɪl, -ɪð, mɪn:ɪ, mɪnstʏr̥; li:dɪdl] adj. (In. III, 2(a)8; (b)8 & 9; 3, 1; 4, 5) little, small; *hinn litli* the small one; *lítill fyrir sér* of small account; *lítils háttar* of little account; a little; *það er nú lítið* that is really not much; *lítið um e-ð* little of sth; *það er lítið um það* not much, not at all; *litlu* by a little, a little bit, *litlu sunnar* a little more to the south; *það minnsta, sem þú getur gert, er að* . . . the least you can do is to . . . *bókin er minnst 100 ára gömul* the book is at least 100 years old.

lítri, -a, -ar [li:tʰrɪ, -a(r̥); li:drɪ] wm.1 liter.

lítt; miður, minnst [liʰt:, mɪ:ðʏr̥, mɪnst] adv. little, less, least; *lítt vanur e-u* little used to sth (In. IV, 2(d)).

ljá, ljæ, léði, léð(ur) [ljau:, ljai:, ljɛ:ðɪ, -ʏr̥, ljɛ:ð] wv.1 lend; *ljá e-m e-ð* lend sbdy sth, give sbdy sth; *ljáðu mér bókina* give me the book.

ljár, -s, -ir [ljau:r, ljau:s, ljau:ɪr̥] m.2 scythe.

ljóð, -s, - [ljou:ð, ljouð·s] n. poem, song.

ljóma, -aði, -að [ljou:ma, -aðɪ, -að] wv.4 gleam, shine with splendor; *ljómandi* gleaming, resplendent; *ljómandi fallegur* very beautiful.

1. ljós, -s, - [ljou:s, ljous:] n. light.

2. ljós, ljós, ljóst [ljou:s, ljous·t] adj. bright, light.

ljósgulur, -gul, -gult [ljou:sgʏ·lʏr̥, -gʏ·l, -gʏlt] adj. bright yellow.

ljósleitur, -leit, -leitt [ljou:slei·tʰʏr̥, -lei·tʰ, -leiʰt·; -lei·d(ʏr̥)] adj. light-colored.

ljósmyndavél, -ar, -ar [ljou:smɪnda-vje:l, -vje:lar̥] f.1 camera, kodak.

ljósta, lýst, laust, lustum, lostinn (-ið) [ljous·ta, lis·t, löys·t, lʏs·tʏm, lɔs·tɪn, -ɪð] v.2 strike, smite.

ljótur, ljót, ljótt [ljou:tʰ(ʏr̥), ljouʰt:; ljou:d(ʏr̥)] adj. ugly; *ljótur er hann núna* what ugly (threatening) weather (S. IV, 1, 4(b)).

ljúfur, ljúf, ljúft [lju:vʏr̥, lju:v, ljuf·t] adj. dear, gentle, mild; *ljúfur við e-n* gentle towards sbdy; *mér er ljúft, að* . . . I am pleased to . . .

ljúga, lýg, laug, lugum, loginn (-ið) [lju:(q)a, li:q, löy:q, lʏ:qʏm, lɔi:jɪn, -ɪð; lɔ:jɪn] v.2 lie, tell a lie; (1 and 3 pers. pres. subj. *ljúgi* [lju:ɪ] cf. Pr. 3, 4, 2n).

ljúka, (lúka), lýk, lauk, lukum, lokinn (-ið) [lju:kʰa, lu:kʰa, li:kʰ, löy:kʰ, lʏ:kʰʏm, lɔ:k̩ʰɪn, -ɪð; lju:g̊a, lu:g̊a, li:g̊, löy:g̊, lʏ:g̊ʏm, lɔ:g̊ɪn] v.2 end, bring to an end, finish; pay up; *ljúka við e-ð* finish sth (= *ljúka e-u*); *ljúka námi* finish study; *að e-u loknu* sth having been finished, after sth; *því var lokið* it was over; impers.: *hér lýkur sögunni* here the story ends (S. VI, 14, 4).

ljæ, see *ljá*.

lóa, -u, -ur [lou:a, -ʏ(r̥)] wf.1 golden plover.

loða, loddi, loðað [lɔ:ða, lɔd̩:ɪ, lɔ:ðað] wv.3 *loða við* stick to.

loðdýr, -s, - [lɔð·di·r, -dir̥s] n. fur-bearing animal.

loðdýrabúskapur, -ar [lɔð·di·ra·bu:-ska·pʰʏr̥, -ar̥; -ska·bʏr̥] m.3 fur-bearing animal farming; fox and mink farming.

loðkápa, -u, -ur [lɔð·kʰau·pʰa, -ʏ(r̥); -kʰau·ba] wf.1 fur coat.

loðkragi, -a, -ar [lɔð·kʰrai·jɪ, -kʰra·qa; -kʰra·jɪ] wm.1 fur collar.

Consonants: [ð] brea*th*e; [g] *g*ood; [gj] *g*yarden (garden); [hw] *wh*at; [j] *y*es; [kj] *c*yan (can); [ŋ] thi*ng*; [q] N. Germ. sa*g*en; [r] Scottish *r*; [x] approx. Germ. ach; [þ] *th*in. Voiceless: ○; [b̥, d̥, g̊] approx. *p, t, k*. Half-voiced: *italics*. Aspiration and preaspiration: [ʰ]; [pʰ, tʰ, kʰ] *p-, t-, k-*. Others as in English.

Loðmundur, -ar [lɔð·mʏndʏr̥, -ar̥] m.1
a personal name; a place name
(mountain); *Loðmundarfjörður*
'Loðmundur's Fjord.'

lof, -s [lɔ:*v*, lɔf·s] n. praise.

lofa, -aði, -að(ur) [lɔ:va, -aðɪ, -að,
-aðʏr̥] wv.4 allow, permit; promise;
praise; *lofa e·m e·ð* (*að gera e·ð*)
allow sbdy sth (to do sth); *lofa
(e·m) e·u* promise (sbdy) sth (S.
I, 3, *1*, 2n); *lofa guð* praise the
Lord.

lófi, -a, -ar [lou:(v)ɪ, -a(r̥)] wm.1
(Pr. 3, *4*, 2) palm of the hand.

loft, -s, - [lɔf·t(s)] n. sky, air, airs;
ceiling; loft, second floor, upper
story; *bera við loft* loom against
the sky; *vera mikill á lofti* be stuck
up, be conceited, give oneself airs;
loftið í skemmunni (= *skemmuloft-
ið*) the loft of the storage house.

loftárás, -ar, -ir [lɔf·tau·rau·s, -ar̥,
-ɪr̥] f.2 air attack, air raid.

loftbelgur, -s, -ir [lɔf·tbel̥g̊ʏr̥, -bel̥g̊s,
-bel̥g̊ˌɪr̥] m.2 balloon.

loftfar, -s, -för [lɔf·tfa·r, -far̥s, -fö·r]
n. dirigible, airship.

loftskeytatæki [lɔf·tskˌei·tʰa·tʰai:-
kˌʰɪ; -skˌei·da·tʰai:g̊ˌɪ] n.pl. radio
(receiver and transmitter), radio
apparatus.

loftskeyti, -s, - [lɔf·tskˌei·tʰɪ(s);
-skˌei·dɪ] n. radiogram.

Loftur, -s [lɔf·tʏr̥, lɔfts] m.1 pers.
name.

loftvarnarbyssa, -u, -ur [lɔf·tvardnar-
bɪs:a, -ʏ(r̥)] wf.1 anti-aircraft gun.

loftvarnarmerki, -s, - [lɔf·tvardnar-
·mer̥·kˌɪ(s)] n. air raid signal.

loftvarnir [lɔf·tvardnɪr̥] f.2.pl. anti-
aircraft defense.

loftvog, -ar, -ir [lɔf·tvɔ·q, -vɔ·qar̥,
-vɔi·jɪr̥; -vɔ·jɪr̥] f.2 barometer.

logi, -a, -ar [lɔi:jɪ, lɔ:qa(r̥); lɔ:jɪ]
wm.1 fire, flame.

logið, -inn, see *ljúga*.

1. loka, -u, -ur [lɔ:kʰa, -ʏ(r̥); lɔ:g̊a]
wf.1 lock; flap.

2. loka, -aði, -að(ur) [lɔ:kʰa, -aðɪ,

-að, -aðʏr̥; lɔ:g̊a] wv.4 close, shut;
loka dyrunum close the door.

lokið, -inn, see *ljúka*.

loks, loksins [lɔx·s, lɔx·sɪns] adv. at
last, finally (S. I, 4, *5*).

Lóló [lou:lou:] f. indecl. pet name.

lón, -s, - [lou:*n*, loun·s] n. lagoon;
also a place name: *Lón*.

lostið, -inn, see *ljósta*.

lotið, -inn, see *lúta*.

lúða, -u, -ur [lu:ða, -ʏ(r̥)] wf.1
halibut, flounder.

lúði, lúið, -inn, see *lýja*.

lúðrakonsert, -ar, -ir [luð·ra·kʰɔn·sert̥,
-ar̥, -ɪr̥] f.2 band concert; trumpet
concert; horn concert.

lúðrasveit, -ar, -ir [luð·ra·svei:tʰ, -ar̥,
-ɪr̥; -svei:d] f.2 brass band.

lúður, -urs, -rar [lu:ðʏr̥(s), luð·rar̥]
m.1 trumpet, horn.

Lúðvík, -s (-víg) [luð·vi·kʰ; -vi·g̊;
-vi·q; -vixs] m.1 Ludwig.

lugum, see *ljúga*.

lúka, see *ljúka*.

lukka, -u, -ur [lʏʰk:a, -ʏ(r̥)] wf.1
luck, happiness; *til allrar lukku*
fortunately.

lukti, -ur, see *lykja*.

lukum, see *ljúka* (*lúka*).

lumma, -u, -ur [lʏm:a, -ʏ(r̥)] wf.1
pancake; (small) palm of the hand,
small hand.

lunga, -, -u, (-na) [luŋ·g̊a, -ʏ, luŋ·na,
lu:na] wn. lung.

lungnabólga, -u, -ur [luŋ·na·boul·g̊a,
-ʏ(r̥); lu:na-] wf.1 pneumonia.

lúra, -u, -ur [lu:ra, -ʏ(r̥)] wf.1 plaice,
dab.

lustum, see *ljósta*.

lúta, lýt, laut, lutum, lotinn (-ið)
[lu:tʰa, li:tʰ, löy:tʰ, lʏ:tʰʏm, lɔ:-
tʰɪn, -ɪð; lu:da, li:d, löy:d, lʏ:-
dʏm, lɔ:dɪn] v.2 bend over, bow.

lúterstrú, -ar [lu:tʰers·tʰru:(ar̥);
lu:ders-] f.1 Lutheran denomina-
tion, Lutheranism.

lutum, see *lúta*.

lýðræði, -s [lið·rai·ðɪ(s)] n. democracy.

lýðskóli, -a, -ar [lið·skou:lɪ, -a(r̥)]

Vowels: *a* [a] approx. father; *á* [au] *cow*; *e* [ɛ] *set*; *é* [jɛ] *yes*; *i, y* [ɪ] *sit*; *í, ý* [i] *feel*;
o [ɔ] *law*; *ó* [ou] *note*; *u* [ʏ] approx. Germ. Mütter; *ú* [u] *school*; *y = i*; *ý = í*; *æ* [ai] *ice*;
ö [ö] Germ. hören; *au* [öy] French *feuille*; *ei, ey* [ei] *ale*. Length [:]; half-length [·].

wm.1 school for the people, folk high school.

lýður, -s, -ir [li:ðy̜r̩, lið·s, li:ðɪr̩] m.2 people, crowd, mass.

lýðveldi, -s, - [lið·vɛl̜dɪ(s)] n. republic, democracy.

lyf, -s, - [lɪ:v, lɪf·s] n. drug, medicine.

lyfjabúð, -ar, -ir [lɪv·ja·bu:ð, -ðar̩, -ðɪr̩] f.2 (= apótek) drugstore.

lyfjafræði [lɪv·ja·frai:ðɪ] wf.2 pharmacology.

lýg, see ljúga.

lygi, -, -ar [lɪi:jɪ, lɪ:qar̩; li:jɪ, lɪ:jɪ] wf.2 lie.

lygn, lygn, lygnt; lygn(a)ri, -astur [lɪg̊·n̩, lɪŋ·tʰ; lɪn̥·t; lɪg̊nrɪ, lɪg̊·narɪ, lɪg̊·nasty̜r̩] adj. calm (wind or sea).

lýja, lúði, lúinn (-ið) [li:ja, lu:ðɪ, lu:ɪn, -ɪð] wv.1 (& 3) tire out; ég er lúinn I am tired.

lýk, see ljúka (lúka).

lykill, -ils, -lar [lɪ:k̟ʲʰɪdl, -ɪls, lɪʰk·lar̩; lɪ:g̊ʲɪdl, -ɪls; lɪʰk̟ʲ:ɪdl̥] m.1 key.

lykja, lukti, lukt(ur) [lɪ:k̟ʲʰa, lʏx·tɪ, lʏx·t(y̜r̩); lɪ:g̊ʲa] wv.1 lock up, enclose, encompass.

lykta, -aði, -að [lɪx·ta, -aðɪ, -að] wv.4 smell; fiskurinn lyktar illa the fish smells bad; hundurinn lyktaði af fötunum the dog smelled (sniffed) the clothes.

lyng, -s [lɪŋ·g̊(s), lin·s] n. heather; leaves and stems of several berry-bearing plants that live together: heather, blueberries, crowberries, bilberries, etc.

lýsa, lýsti, lýst [li:sa, lis·tɪ, lis·t] wv.2 describe; lýsa e-u (e-m) describe sth (sbdy); light up, illuminate lýsa kirkjuna illuminate the church; lýsa e-u yfir declare sth (solemnly).

lýsi, -s [li:sɪ(s)] n. fish liver oil.

lyst, -ar, -ir [lɪs·t, -ar̩, -ɪr̩] f.2 appetite (= matarlyst).

lýst, see ljósta, and lýsa.

lýt, see lúta.

lægð, -ar, -ir [laiq·ð, -ðar̩, -ðɪr̩; laig̊·þ] f.2 low lying area, hollow, depression; low (in meteorology).

lægðarmiðja, -u, -ur [laiq·ðar-mɪð·ja, -ɣ(r̩); laig̊·ðar-] wf.1 center of a low (in meteorology).

lægri, lægstur, see lágur.

Lækjargata, -götu [lai:k̟ʲʰar·ga:tʰa, -gö:tʰɣ; lai:g̊ʲar·ga:da, -gö:dɣ] wf.1 'Brook Street.'

lækna, -aði, -að(ur) [laiʰk·na, -aðɪ, -að, -aðy̜r̩] wv.4 cure, heal.

læknadeild, -ar, -ir [laiʰk·na-deil·d̥, -ar̩, -ɪr̩] f.2 faculty (department) of medicine.

læknir, -is, -(ir)ar [laiʰk·nɪr̩, -ɪs, -ar̩, -(ɪr)ar̩] m.1 medical doctor, physician.

læknishérað, -aðs, -öð [laiʰk·nɪs-hjɛ:ra ð, -aðs, -öð] n. district of a (country) doctor.

lækur, læks, lækir, (-ja) [lai:kʰy̜r̩, lai:kʰs, lai:k̟ʲʰɪr̩, lai:k̟ʲʰa; lai:g̊ʲy̜r̩, lai:g̊s, lai:g̊ʲɪr̩, lai:g̊ʲa] m.2 brook, run, creek.

læna, -u, -ur [lai:na, -ɣ(r̩)] wf.1 rill, streamlet, Sc. lane.

lær (læri), -s, - [lai:r, lai:rɪ(s); lair·s] n. thigh; í mitt lær up to the middle of the thigh.

læra, lærði, lærður (lært) [lai:ra, lair·ðɪ, lair·ðy̜r̩, lair·t] wv.2 learn; transitive: teach, vera lærður be learned, have been taught.

lærdómsdeild, -ar, -ir [lair·doums-deil·d̥, -ar̩, -ɪr̩] f.2 the three higher classes of menntaskóli (Gymnasium), corresponding roughly to the first two college years in America.

lærdómsmaður, -manns, -menn[lair·-doums-ma:ðy̜r̩, -man·s, -mɛn:] m.4 scholar.

læt, see láta.

læti, láta [lai:tʰɪ, lau:tʰa; lai:dɪ, lau:da] n.pl. noise, racket, disturbance; þessi líka litlu læti (litotes) quite a little disturbance!

lög, laga [lö:q, la:qa] n.pl. (see lag) the law; með lögum by law; á móti lögum against the law; lög frá 1932 the Act of 1932.

Consonants: [ð] breathe; [g] good; [gj] gyarden (garden); [hw] what; [j] yes; [kj] cyan (can); [ŋ] thing; [q] N. Germ. sagen; [r] Scottish r; [x] approx. Germ. ach; [þ] thin. Voiceless: ○; [b̥, d̥, g̊] approx. p, t, k. Half-voiced: italics. Aspiration and preaspiration: [ʰ]; [pʰ, tʰ, kʰ] p-, t-, k-. Others as in English.

401

Lögberg, -s [löq·ber͜g, -s] n. 'Law Rock.'

lögð, see *lagður.*

lögfræðingur, -s, -ar [löx·frai·ðin͜gyr̥, -ins, -in͜gar̥] m.1 lawyer.

lögregla, -u [löq·re͜gla, -y] wf.1 police.

lögreglueftirlit, -s [löq·re͜gly·cf·tir·lɪt·tʰ(s); -lɪ·d̥] n. police control; *hafa lögreglueftirlit með e-u* exercise police control, see to it that . . .

lögreglustöð, -stöðvar [löq·re͜gly·stö:ð, -stöð·var̥] f.1 police station.

lögsögumaður, -manns, -menn [löx·sö·· qy·ma:ðyr̥, -man·s, -mɛn:] m.4 law-speaker, an officer (president) of the Old Icelandic *Alþingi,* whose duty it was to recite all existing law in three consecutive summers (*segja upp lög*).

lögur, lagar, legir [lö:qyr̥, la:qar̥, lei:jɪr̥; lɛ:jɪr̥] m.3 liquid; a long narrow lake (= *Lagarfljót*).

lök, see *lak.*

lömb, see *lamb.*

lönd, see *land.*

löng, see *langur.*

löt, see *latur.*

M.

m. = *metri.*

m. a. = *meðal annars* among other things.

1. má, máði, máð(ur) [mau:, mau:ðɪ, -yr̥, mau:ð] wv.3 erase, make fade.

2. má, see *mega.*

maður, manns, menn, manna [ma:- ðyr̥, man·s, mɛn:, man:a] m.4 man; husband; person; gentleman; indef. pron. sg.: one, pl. people, they; *maður er manns gaman* (proverbial) man is pleased (consoled) by man; *verða ekki að manni* not attain to a man's estate, not grow to be a man, remain undeveloped; *innri maður* one's true self; *fimm manns* five persons, *hundrað manns* one hundred people, *hundruð manna* hundreds of men (persons) (S. I, **4, 2, 5**); *maður minn!* my dear

fellow! *maðurinn minn* my husband (S. II, 2); *manna sterkastur* strongest of men, very strong (S. III, **5, 2**); indef. pron.: *maður heyrir þetta* one hears this; *menn segja* people say (S. VI, **14, 2**).

máfur, -s, -ar [mau:vyr̥, mauf·s, mau:var̥] m.1 seagull.

magáll, -áls, -álar [ma:qaudl, -auls, -au·lar̥] m.1 flank (of mutton or beef).

magaveikur, -veik, -veikt [ma:qa- vei:kʰyr̥, -vei:kʰ, -veix·t; -vei:g͜yr̥, -vei:g͜] adj. having a weak (sick) stomach.

magaverkur, -jar, -ir [ma:qa-ver·kyr̥, -verk₁ar̥, -ɪr̥] m.2 stomach ache.

magi, -a, -ar [mai:jɪ, ma:qa(r̥); ma:jɪ] wm.1 stomach.

mágkona, -u, -ur [mau:(q)kʰɔ·na, -y(r̥)] wf.1 sister-in-law.

magna, -aði, -að(ur) [ma͜g·na, -aðɪ, -að, -aðyr̥] wv.4 strengthen; *magnast* increase, be strengthened, be intensified.

Magnús, -ar (-s) [ma͜g·nu·s, ma͜g·nu·· sar̥, ma͜g·nus·] m.1 pers. name: Magnus; patronymics: *Magnússon, -dóttir.*

magur, mögur, magurt; magrari, -astur; meg(ur)ri, megurstur [ma:- qyr̥, mö:qyr̥, ma:qyr̥t; maq·rarɪ, -astyr̥; mɛ:qyr·ɪ, mɛq·rɪ; mɛ:qyr̥st-yr̥] adj. lean; thin.

mágur, -s, -ar [mau:(q)yr̥, maux·s, mau:(q)ar̥] m.1 brother-in-law.

maí [mai:] m. indecl. May.

maís [mai:s] m. indecl. corn.

major, -s, -ar [ma:jou·r, -jour̥s, -jou·· rar̥] m.1 major.

makki, -a, -ar [maʰk₁:ɪ, maʰk:a(r̥)] wm.1 neck of a horse.

maklegur [ma:kʰlɛ·qyr̥; ma:g͜-] adj. (see *-legur*) deserved, just.

1. mál, -s, - [mau:l, maul·s] n. speech, power of speech; language, tongue; *Mál og menning* 'Language and Culture,' a literary society; matter, affair, cause; suit, action, case; *mjög alvarlegt mál* a very serious

Vowels: *a* [a] approx. father; *á* [au] cow; *e* [ɛ] set; *é* [jɛ] yes; *i, y* [ɪ] sit; *í, ý* [i] feel; *o* [ɔ] law; *ó* [ou] note; *u* [y] approx. Germ. Mütter; *ú* [u] school; *y = i; ý = í; æ* [ai] ice; *ö* [ö] Germ. hören; *au* [öy] French *feuille; ei, ey* [ei] ale. Length [:]; half-length [·].

matter, a matter for great concern.
2. mál, -s, - [mau:l, maul·s] n. measure; measurement; *taka mál af e-m* take one's measure.
1. mala, -aði, -að(ur) [ma:la, -aði, -að, -aðʏr] wv.4 or (rarely):
2. mala, mel, mól, mólum, malinn (-ið) [ma:la, me:l, mou:l, mou:lʏm, ma:lɪn, -ɪð] v.6 grind.
mála, -aði, -að(ur) [mau:la, -aði, -að, -aðʏr] wv.4 paint.
máladeild, -ar, -ir [mau:la-deil·d, -aᵣ, -ɪᵣ] f.2 the language division in the *menntaskóli* (Gymnasium), a curriculum specializing in (modern) languages.
málagjöld [mau:la-gˌöl·d] n.pl. (literally: payment of wages) retribution; *makleg málagjöld* just retribution.
malar, -ir, see *möl.*
málari, -a, -ar [mau:larɪ, -a(ᵣ)] wm.1 painter.
malarslétta, -u, -ur [ma:laᵣ-sljeʰt:a, -ʏ(ᵣ)] wf.1 gravel plain.
malbikaður, -uð, -að [mal·bɪ·kʰaðʏr, -ʏð, -að; -bɪ:g̊-] adj. (pp.) macadamized; covered with gravel and pitch or oil.
málfræði [maul·frai·ði] wf.2 grammar, linguistics, philology.
málfræðislega [maul·frai·ðɪs·le:qa] adv. grammatically.
málgagn, -s, -gögn [maul·gag̊n; -gag̊ns, -gaxs; -gög̊n] n. organ, mouthpiece (of a political party).
máltíð, -ar, -ir [maul·tʰi·ð, -ðaᵣ, -ðɪᵣ] f.2 meal.
málverk, -s, - [maul·veᵣk(s)] n. painting.
málverkasafn, -s, -söfn [maul·veᵣka-sab·n(s), -söb·n] n. collection of paintings; *Málverkasafn ríkisins* 'The National Gallery.'
málverkasýning, -ar, -ar [maul·veᵣka-si:nig̊, -aᵣ] f.1 exhibition of paintings.
mamma, mömmu, -ur [mam:a, möm:-ʏ(ᵣ)] wf.1 mother, mummy.
man, see *muna.*
mann, -a, see *maður.*

mannahendur, -handa [man:a-hen·dʏᵣ, -han·da] f.3 only in pl. human hands; *gerður af mannahöndum* man made; *komast undir mannahendur* get caught by the law.
mannaket (-kjöt),-s[man:a-kₛʰe:tʰ(s), -kˌʰö:tʰ(s); -kˌʰe:d, -kˌʰö:d] n. human flesh.
mannanöfn, -nafna [man:a-nöb·n, -nab·na] n.pl. personal names (sg. *mannsnafn*).
mannfall, -s [man·fadl, -fals] n. casualties.
mannheimar [man:hei·maᵣ] m.l.pl. abodes of men, the world of humans, the upper world.
mannkyn, -s [man·kˌʰɪ·n, -kˌʰɪns] n. mankind.
manns, see *maður.*
mannsaldur, -urs, -rar [man·saldʏᵣ(s), -aldraᵣ] m.1 generation.
mannséttskyrta, -u, -ur [man·sjeʰt·-skˌɪᵣ·ta, -ʏ(ᵣ)] wf.1 shirt with stiff cuffs.
mannskratti, -a, -ar [man·skraʰt·ɪ, -a(ᵣ)] wm.1 deuce of a fellow.
mannsnafn, -s [man·snab̥n(s)] n. personal name; pl. *mannanöfn.*
manntjón, -s, - [man·tʰjou·n, -tʰjouns] n. loss of men, casualties.
mannvirki, -s, - [man·vɪᵣkˌɪ(s)] n. work of man; monument(s) of man's ingenuity.
mánudagur, -dags, -dagar [mau:nʏ-da:qʏᵣ, -dax·s,-da:qaᵣ]m.1 Monday; *mánudags-kvöld* Monday evening.
mánuður, -aðar, -uðir (-aðir) [mau:-nʏðʏᵣ, -aðaᵣ, -ʏðɪᵣ, -aðɪᵣ] m.3 month.
marði, marið, -inn, see *merja.*
margfalda, -aði, -að(ur) [mar·g̊falda, -aðɪ, -að, -aðʏᵣ] wv.4 multiply.
margföldun, -unar, -faldanir [mar·g̊-földʏn, -ʏnaᵣ, -faldanɪᵣ] f.2 multiplication.
margföldunartafla, -töflu, -ur [mar·g̊-földʏnar-tʰab·la, -tʰöblʏ(ᵣ)] wf.1 multiplication table.
Margrét, -ar [mar·grje·tʰ(aᵣ), -grje·d·(aᵣ)] f.1 pers. name: Margaret.

Consonants: [ð] brea*th*e; [g] *g*ood; [gˌ] *gy*arden (garden); [hw] *wh*at; [j] *y*es; [kˌ] *cy*an (can); [ŋ] thi*ng*; [q] N. Germ. sa*g*en; [r] Scottish *r*; [x] approx. Germ. a*ch*; [þ] *th*in. Voiceless: ○ ; [b̥, d̥, g̊] approx. *p, t, k.* Half-voiced: *italics.* Aspiration and preaspiration: [ʰ]; [pʰ, tʰ, kʰ] *p-, t-, k-.* Others as in English.

403

margur, mörg, margt; fleiri, flestur [mar·g̊ʏr̥, mör·g̊, mar̥·t; flei:rɪ, fles·tʏr̥] adj. (never weak in sg. Ĭn. IIÍ, **3**, *1*, 4; **4**, *5*) many; *margur maðurinn* many a man (S. II, 7); *margir menn* many men (persons, people); *á marga vegu* in many ways; *margir segja* many people say; *margt* many things; *margt er skritið* many things are funny; *margt manna* many (of) people (S. III, 1, 4n; **3**, 1-2); *margt af e-u* a great number of sth; *nokkuð fleira?* anything else? anything more? *flestir* most people; *flestir þeirra* most of them.

marhnútur, -s, -ar [mar̥·hnu·tʰʏr̥, -hnu·tʰs, -hnu·tʰar̥; -hnu·d̥·] m.1 sea-scorpion, bullhead, father-lasher.

María, -u [ma:ri·ja, -ʏ] wf.1 Mary.

máríuerla, -u, -ur [mau:ri(jʏ)·er·d̥la, -ʏ(r̥); mau:rija·ʰt·la, -öʰt·lʏ(r̥); mau:rijauʰt·la, -ʏ(r̥)] wf.1 white wagtail.

markaður, -aðs, -aðar; -aðir [mar̥·kaðʏr̥, -aðs, -aðar̥, -aðɪr̥] m.2 & 3 market.

markar, see *mörk*.

marmelaði, -s [mar·mela·ðɪ(s)] n. marmelade.

marz [mar̥·s] m. indecl. March.

mása, -aðĭ, -að [mau:sa, -aðɪ, -að] wv.4 wheeze, be short of breath.

máske [maus·k₁ɛ·, mau:sk₁ɛ:] adv. = *kannske*, perhaps.

mastur, (-ri), -urs, möstur [mas·tʏr̥(s), mastrɪ, mös·tʏr̥] n. mast.

mat, mátum, see *meta*.

mata, -aði, -að(ur) [ma:tʰa, -aðɪ, -að, -aðʏr̥; ma:d̥a] wv.4 *mata e-n* give sbdy food, feed sbdy; *matast* eat (S. VI, **7**, *4*).

matarlyst, -ar [ma:tʰar·lɪs·t, -ar̥; ma:dar·] f.2 appetite.

matarþurfi [ma:tʰar̥·þʏr·vɪ; ma:dar̥·] adj. indecl. in need of food.

máti, -a, -ar [mau:tʰɪ, -a(r̥); mau:dɪ] wm.1 manner, mode; *í sama máta* in the same way, likewise, also.

matmál, -s, - [ma:tʰmau·l, -mauls; ma:d-] n. time to eat, mealtime.

matmálsfrí, -s, - [ma:tʰmauls·fri:(s); ma:d̥-] n. recess for eating (lunch).

matmálstími, -a, -ar [ma:tʰmauls·tʰi:mɪ, -a(r̥); ma:d̥·] wm.1 mealtime.

matreiða, -reiddi, -reiddur (-reitt) [ma:tʰrei·ða, -reid̥:ɪ, -ʏr̥, -reiʰt·; ma:d̥-] wv.2 prepare food, cook.

matreiðslubók, -ar, -bækur [ma:tʰreið-slʏ·bou:kʰ, -ar̥, -bai:kʰʏr̥; ma:d̥-, -bou:g̊, -bai:g̊ʏr̥] f.3 cook book.

matsala, -sölu, -ur [ma:tʰsa·la, -sö·lʏ(r̥); ma:d̥-] wf.1 selling of food, place where food is served, restaurant.

matseðill, -ils, -lar [ma:tʰsɛ·ðɪd̥l, -ɪls, -sɛðlar; ma:d̥-] m.1 menu.

matskeið, -ar, -ir [ma:tʰsk₁ei·ð, -ðar̥, -ðɪr; ma:d̥·] f.2 tablespoon.

matsöluhús, -s, - [ma:tʰsö·lʏ·hu:s, -hus·; ma:d̥-] n. restaurant, boarding-house, pension.

mátt, -i, see *mega*.

Matteus, -ar [maʰt:ɛ·ʏs(ar̥)] m.1 Matthew =

Mattías, -ar, (-s) [maʰt:ija·s, -a·sar̥] m.1 patronymic: *Mattíasson*.

máttugur [mauʰt:ʏqʏr̥] adj. (see *-ugur*) powerful, mighty.

máttur, -ar, mættir [mauʰt:ʏr̥, -ar̥, maiʰt:ɪr̥] m.3 might, power, strength.

mátulegur [mau:tʰʏ·le:qʏr̥; mau:dʏ-] adj. (see *-legur*) just right.

matur, -ar [ma:tʰʏr̥, -ar̥; ma:dʏr̥] m.3 food.

matvara, -vöru, -ur [ma:tʰva·ra, -vö·rʏ(r̥); ma:d̥-] wf.1, usually in pl. food, foodstuff.

matvöruverzlun, -unar, -anir [ma:tʰvö·rʏ·verslʏn, -ʏnar̥, -anɪr̥; ma:d̥-] f.2 food store.

Mbl. = *Morgunblaðið* 'The Morning News.'

með [mɛ:ð, mɛ(:)] **A.** prep. with dat. (S. I, **3**, *3*, 2) with, through, by; along; at, in (of time); between, among; (1) with, by: *með þessu* with this, through this; *með sölu* through selling; *með lögum* by

Vowels: *a* [a] approx. father; *á* [au] cow; *e* [ɛ] set; *é* [jɛ] yes; *i, y* [ɪ] sit; *í, ý* [i] feel; *o* [ɔ] law; *ó* [ou] note; *u* [ʏ] approx. Germ. Mütter; *ú* [u] school; *y* = *i*; *ý* = *í*; *æ* [ai] ice; *ö* [ö] Germ. hören; *au* [öy] French feuille; *ei, ey* [ei] ale. Length [:]; half-length [·].

404

law; *lömb með mömmum sínum*
lambs with their mothers; *fara
með e-m* go with sbdy, accompany
sbdy; *með skipi* by boat, on a boat;
(2) of place: along: *ganga með
klettum* walk along rocks; *með
ströndum fram* along the shores,
in coastal traffic; (3) of time:
in, at: *með morgninum* (first
thing) in the morning; *með hádeginu* at noon; (4) among: *með
þeim* between them (of two), among
them (of many); (5) *með því
að* conj. since (S. VIII, 3(b));
B. prep. with acc. (S. I, 2, *3*, 2)
with; concerning: *fara með e-n* take
sbdy (somewhere); *koma með e-ð*
bring sth; *ánægður með e-ð* pleased
with sth, satisfied with sth; *verzla
með e-ð* deal in sth; *hvernig er með
þetta?* how is it concerning this,
how about this? C. adv. *með* too:
nóttina með the night too, the
night also.

1. **meðal, -als, -öl** [mɛːðal, -als, -öl]
n. medicine, drug.

2. **meðal** [mɛːðal] prep. with gen.
between (two), among (many);
meðal þeirra among them; *meðal
annars* among other things; *meðal
annara orða* by the way.

meðan [mɛːðan] (1) adv. *meðan, á
meðan* meanwhile, in the meantime;
(2) conj. while: *meðan það var*
while it lasted; *meðan hann væri
þar* while he was there.

meðfram [mɛð·fram·] prep. with dat.
(also *með . . . fram*) along: *meðfram ströndum = með ströndum
fram* along the coasts, coastwise.

meðhjálpari, -a, -ar [mɛð·hjaulpʰarɪ,
-a(r̥); -hjaulp-] wm.1 parish-clerk.

meðmælabréf, -s, - [mɛð·mai·la-brjɛːv,
-brjɛf·s] n. letter of recommendation.

meðmæli, -s, - [mɛð·mai·lɪ(s)] n.
usually in pl. recommendation.

mega, má, megum, mátti, mátt
[mɛiːqa, mauː, mɛiːqʏm, mauʰtːɪ,
mauʰt:] pret. pres. v. (In. VII, **5**, *1*)
may, must (not), have to; shall,

will; be permitted, be allowed; be
able to; (1) *má ég (mætti ég)
spyrja?* may I (might I) ask? *þú
mátt ekki fara* you must not go;
*menn mega vara sig á því (. . . á
að gera e-ð)* people should (had
better) beware of that (. . . of
doing sth); *þú mátt fara* you may
(are allowed to) go; *og mátti
kauði kúra þar* and the rogue had
to (litotes) stay there; *ég held ég
megi taka það* I think I will take
it; *mega vera að e-u* have time
(leisure) to do sth (= *hafa tíma
til e-s*); *ég má til (með) að gera
það* I must (I have to) do it;
(2) impersonal: *(það) má* one can,
one may, it is possible; *má vera,
að . . .* may be that . . . , it is
possible that . . . ; impers. *má* with
active inf. is usually to be translated 'may' with a passive inf.; *má
flokka* may be classified; *hvað má
bjóða yður?* 'what may be offered
to you?' what may I offer you?
mátti heyra one could hear, it was
possible to hear, it could be heard;
sjá má (= það má sjá) it may be
seen; *ekki má* one must not; *mikið
má, ef vel vill* much can be done
with good will (or: if things turn
out right). See VI, 2, 5n; **4**, *3*;
9, *2*, 2; **11**, *6*; **13**, 5; **14**, 8.

megin [mɛiːjɪn] adv. or prep. with
gen. mostly in the combinations:
öðru(m) megin on one side,
hinu(m) megin on the other side,
báðu(m) megin on both sides of;
báðum megin árinnar on both sides
of the river; *austan megin árinnar*
on the east side of the river. (Also
öðrumegin, hinumegin, báðumegin).

megn, megn, megnt; megnri, -astur
[mɛg̊·n̥, mɛn̥·tʰ; mɛn̥·t; mɛg̊nrɪ,
mɛg̊·nastʏr̥] adj. strong, pungent.

megurri, megurstur, see *magur*.

meiða, meiddi, meiddur (meitt) [mei:-
ða, meid:ɪ, -ʏr̥, meiʰt:] wv.2 hurt;
meiða sig hurt oneself, get hurt;
meiða e-n hurt sbdy; *skórnir meiða*

Consonants: [ð] brea*th*e; [g] *g*ood; [gɪ] *g*yarden (garden); [hw̥] *wh*at; [j] *y*es; [kɪ] *c*yan
(can); [ŋ] thi*ng*; [q] N. Germ. sa*g*en; [r] Scottish *r*; [x] approx. Germ. a*ch*; [þ] *th*in.
Voiceless: ○; [b̥, d̥, g̊] approx. *p, t, k*. Half-voiced: *italics*. Aspiration and preaspiration:
[ʰ]; [pʰ, tʰ, kʰ] *p-, t-, k-*. Others as in English.

405

mig á fótunum the shoes hurt my feet.

meiddur, meidd, meitt [meid:ɪr, meid:, meiʰt:] adj. (pp.) hurt, *meiddur hestur* injured horse.

meig, see *míga.*

mein, -s, - [mei:n, mein·s] n. harm, hurt, damage; *vertu engum að meini* do not harm anyone.

1. **meina, -aði, -að** [mei:na, -aði, -að] wv.4 *meina e-m e-ð* hinder sbdy in doing sth, prevent sbdy from doing sth.

2. **meina, meinti, meint(ur)** [mei:na, mein·tʰɪ, -ɪr; mein·tʰ; mein·t·] wv.2 mean; *hvað meinar hann með þessu?* what does he mean by this?

meinlaus, -laus, -laust [mein·löy·s, -löyst] adj. harmless; *(e-m) að meinlausu* so that no harm is done (to anybody).

meinsemd, -ar, -ir [mein·semd, -ar, -ɪr] f.2 disease, tumor.

meir, see *mjög.*

meiri, see *mikill.*

meistari, -a, -ar [meis·tarɪ, -a(r)] wm.1 master; master of arts.

meitt, see *meiða,* and *meiddur.*

mel, see 2. *mala.*

melóna, -u, -ur [mɛ:lou·na, -ɪ(r)] wf.1 melon.

Melrakkaslétta, -u [mɛl·raʰk·a·slje ʰt:a, -ɪ] wf.1 'Fox Plain.'

melur, -s, -ar [mɛ:lɪr, mɛl·s, mɛ:lar] m.1 gravel or sandy hill, sand flat; also in street-names: -*melur, Melar,* 'Gravel Flats,' and place names.

menn, see *maður.*

menning, -ar, -ar [mɛn·iŋg, -ar] f.1 culture, civilization.

Menningarsjóður, -s [mɛn:iŋgar·sjou:·ðɪr, -sjouð·s] m.2 'Culture Fund,' to aid in study of Icelandic culture and in publication of popular books.

mennskur, mennsk, mennskt [mɛnsk·ɪr, mɛnsk, mɛnst] adj. human (in opposition to supernatural).

mennta, -aði, -að(ur) [mɛn·tʰa, -aðɪ, -að, -aðɪr; mɛn·ta] wv.4 educate,

mennta sig educate oneself, improve one's mind.

menntaður, -uð, -að [mɛn·tʰaðɪr, -ɪð, -að; mɛn·taðɪr] adj. (pp.) cultured, civilized; educated; *hinn menntaði heimur* the civilized world.

Menntaskólahlið, -s [mɛn·tʰaskou·la·hlɪ:ð, -hlɪð·s; mɛn·ta-] n. the gate of *Menntaskólinn.*

menntaskólapiltur, -s, -ar [mɛn·tʰa·skou·la·pʰɪl·tɪr, -pɪlts, -pɪl·tar; mɛn·ta-] m.1 student of *Menntaskólinn.*

menntaskóli, -a, -ar [mɛn·tʰa·skou:lɪ, -a, -ar; mɛn·ta-] wm.1 a gymnasium of six years, combining a *gagnfræðadeild* (three years) and a *lærdómsdeild* (three years), the latter corresponding to the last year of high school and the first two years of college in America. *Menntaskólinn* 'The Gymnasium' in Reykjavík.

mér, dat. of *ég.*

meri, -ar, -ar [mɛ:rɪ, -a(r)] wf.1 mare.

merja, marði, marinn (-ið) [mɛr·ja, mar·ðɪ, ma:rɪn, -ɪð] wv.1 crush; squeeze; *merja sig* crush some part of one's anatomy; *merja sig á fingri, á fæti* crush a finger, a foot.

merki, -s, - [mɛr·kjɪ(s)] n. signal; *gefa merki* signal.

merkilegur [mɛr·kjɪ·lɛ:qʏr] adj. (see -*legur*) notable, significant, important.

merking, -ar, -ar [mɛr·kjɪŋg, -ar] f.1 significance, meaning.

merkja, merkti, merkt(ur) [mɛr·kjₐa, mɛr·(x)tɪ, -ʏr, mɛr·(x)t] wv.2 mark, sign; signify.

1. **merkur,** see *mörk.*

2. **merkur, merk, merkt** [mɛr·kʏr, mɛr·k, mɛr·(x)t] adj. notable, significant, important.

1. **messa, -u, -ur** [mɛs:a, -ʏ(r)] wf.1 mass.

2. **messa, -aði, -að** [mɛs:a, -aðɪ, -að] wv.4 hold divine service in a church; say mass, conduct mass.

mest, mestur, see *mjög* and *mikill.*

mestallur, -öll, -allt [mɛs·taðlʏr, -öðl,

Vowels: *a* [a] approx. *father; á* [au] *cow; e* [ɛ] *set; é* [jɛ] *yes; i, y* [ɪ] *sit; í, ý* [i] *feel; o* [ɔ] *law; ó* [ou] *note; u* [ʏ] approx. Germ. *Mütter; ú* [u] *school; y = i; ý = í; æ* [ai] *ice; ö* [ö] Germ. *hören; au* [öy] French *feuille; ei, ey* [ei] *ale.* Length [:]; half-length [·].

GLOSSARY

-alt] adj. almost all, *mestallt* almost everything·

mestmegnis [mɛs·tmɛg̊nɪs] adv. mostly.

met, -s, - [mɛ:tʰ(s); mɛ:d(s)] n. record; *setja met í e-u* establish a record in sth.

meta, met, mat, mátum, metinn (-ið) [mɛ:tʰa, mɛ:tʰ, ma:tʰ, mau:tʰʏm, mɛ:tʰɪn, -ið; mɛ:da, mɛ:d̥, ma:d̥, mau:d̥ʏm, mɛ:dɪn] v.5 value, esteem; *meta mikils* value highly.

metrakerfi, -s [mɛ:tʰra·kʲ,ʰɛr·vɪ(s); mɛ:dra-] n. metric system.

metri, -a, -ar [mɛ:tʰrɪ, -a(r̥); mɛ:d̥rɪ] wm.1 meter.

mettur, mett, mett [mɛʰt:ʏr̥, mɛʰt:] adj. satisfied by food, sated.

1. mið, -s, - [mɪ:ð, mɪð·s] n. (fishing) bank, landmark; taking of bearings.
2. mið, see 1. *miður*.
3. mið- [mɪ:ð-] pref. mid-.

miða, -aði, -að [mɪ:ða, -aðɪ, -að] wv.4 aim, point to; *miða á* aim at, draw a bead on; *miða við* compare to; *miða* take bearings.

miðaftan, -s [mɪ:ðaftan, -ans] n. four to six in the afternoon.

miðaftanskaffi, -s [mɪ:ðaftans·kʰaf:·ɪ(s)] n. afternoon coffee; also called *eftirmiðdagskaffi*.

miðaftansleyti, -s [mɪ:ðaftans·lei:·tʰɪ(s); -lei:dɪ] n. around four to six in the afternoon.

miðaftanste, -s [mɪ:ðaftans·tʰɛ:(s)] n. afternoon tea.

Miðbær, -bæjar [mɪð·bai·r̥, -bai·jar̥] m.2 'Mid-town,' the middle of the town.

miðdagsmatur, -ar [mɪd̥·axs·ma·tʰʏr̥, -ar̥; -ma:d̥ʏr̥] m.3 = *miðdegisverður* lunch, dinner (at 12-1 o'clock).

miðdagur, -s, -ar [mɪð·da·qʏr̥, -daxs, -da·qar̥; mɪd̥:a·qʏr̥] m.1 dinner (at 6-7 o'clock).

miðdegis- [mɪð·dei·jɪs-; mɪd̥·ei·jɪs-] pref. noon-; *m·tónleikar* noon concert.

miðdegisverður, -ar, -ir [mɪð·dei·jɪs·ver·ðʏr̥, -ar̥, -ɪr̥; mɪd̥:-] m.3 dinner.

miði, -a, -ar [mɪ:ðɪ, -a(r̥)] wm.1 piece of paper; sticker; ticket.

miðnætti, -s, - [mɪð·nai ʰt·ɪ(s)] n. twelve at night, midnight.

miðskóli, -a, -ar [mɪð·skou·lɪ, -a(r̥)] wm.1 middle school, secondary school.

miðstöð, -stöðvar, -var [mɪð·stö·ð, -stöð·var̥] f.1 center; *miðstöð andlegrar menningar* center of (spiritual) culture; central or head office; central telephone office; central heating plant.

miðstöðvarhitun, -ar [mɪð·stöðvar·hɪ:tʰʏn, -hɪ:tʰʏnar̥; -hɪ:d̥-] f.2 central heating.

miðstöðvarstúlka, -u, -ur [mɪð·stöð·var·stul·kʰa, -ʏ(r̥); -stul·ka] wf.1 operator (in the central telephone office).

1. miður, mið, mitt (acc. miðjan, miðja, mitt) [mɪ:ðʏr̥, mɪ:ð, mɪʰt:; mɪð·jan, mɪð·ja] adj. (In. III, 2(a)4 & (b)10; 3, 1, 4) mid-, in the middle (of), middle; *í mitt lær* up to the middle of the thigh; *áin var á miðjar síður* the river reached up to the middle of the sides of the horses.
2. miður [mɪ:ðʏr̥] adv. (compar. of *lítt*) less, worse; *því miður* unfortunately.

miðvikudagur, -s, -ar [mɪð·vɪkʰʏ·da:qʏr̥, -dax·s, -da:qar̥; -vɪg̊·] m.1 Wednesday.

mig, acc. of *ég*.

míga, míg, meig, migum, miginn (-ið) [mi:qa, mi:q, mei:q, mɪ:qʏm, mɪi:jɪn, -ið, mi:jɪn, -ið] v.1 piss; *míga e-u* piss sth; *mígandi rigning* pouring rain (polite for *míga*: *kasta af sér vatni*).

mikill, -il, -ið; meiri, mestur [mɪ:·kʲ,ʰɪdl, -ɪl, -ið, mei:rɪ, mɛs·tʏr̥; mɪ:g̊,ɪdl] adj. (In. III, 2(a)8 & (b)8-9; 4, 5) great, large, big; *mikill maður* a great man (but: *stór maður* a big man); *áin var mikil* the river was swollen; *mikið* much; *mikið af e-u* great amount

Consonants: [ð] brea*the*; [g] *g*ood; [gʲ] *gy*arden (garden); [hw] *wh*at; [j] *y*es; [kʲ] *cy*an (can); [ŋ] thi*ng*; [q] N. Germ. sa*g*en; [r] Scottish *r*; [x] approx. Germ. a*ch*; [þ] *th*in. Voiceless: ○; [b̥, d̥, g̊] approx. *p, t, k*. Half-voiced: *italics*. Aspiration and preaspiration: [ʰ]; [pʰ, tʰ, kʰ] *p-, t-, k-*. Others as in English.

407

of sth, much of sth; *mikið er af
e-u* there is plenty of sth, sth is
very plentiful; *mikill vexti* great
in stature, tall (S. I, **3**, *2*, 3);
mikill á lofti conceited, stuck up;
miklu much; *miklu betur* much
better; *miklu stærri* much larger,
bigger (S. I, **3**, *2*, 5); *mikils virði*
worth much; *meira eða minna* more
or less; *að meira eða minna leyti*
more or less, to greater or less
extent; *meira að segja* even, believe
it or not; *öllum meiri* greater than
all (= *meiri en allir aðrir*) (S. I,
3, *2*, 4); *þeirra mestur* greatest of
them; *mesti nytjafugl* a bird of
great use; *mest* mostly.

míla, -u, -ur, (-na) [miːla, -ʏ(r̥),
mil·na] wf.1 mile, usually = *dönsk
míla* Danish mile = 7.5 km; *ensk
míla* English mile (U. S. A.) =
1.6 km.

mildur, mild, milt [mɪl·dʏr̥, mɪl·d̥,
mɪl·t] adj. mild.

milla, -u, -ur [mɪl·a, -ʏ(r̥)] wf.1 an
ornamented metal (silver) loop
(used on the embroidered bodice
called *upphlutur*) (Pr. 3, *2*, 9n).

milli [mɪd̥·lɪ] prep. with gen. between
(two), among (many); *milli ánna*
between the rivers; *milli árinnar og
fjallsins* between the river and the
mountain; also *á milli*; *sín á milli*
among themselves; *milli landa* between (foreign) countries (and
Iceland).

millímetri, -a, -ar [mɪl·iːmɛ·tʰrɪ,
-a(r̥); -mɛːdrɪ] wm.1 millimeter
(Pr. 3, *2*, 9n).

millipils, -, - [mɪd̥·lɪ·pʰɪl·s] n. slip.

milljón, -ar, -ir [mɪl·joun, -nar̥, -nɪr̥]
f.2 million.

millum [mɪd̥·lʏm] prep. with gen. =
milli.

milta, -, -u [mɪl·tʰa, -ʏ] n. milt,
spleen.

mín, see *ég* and *minn.*

minjar [mɪn·jar̥] f.1.pl. memorials,
traces of former times, monuments.

minn, mín, mitt [mɪn:, miːn, mɪʰt:]

poss. pron. (In. III, 2(b)5e & 8;
VI, **2**) my, mine; *ég og mínir* I and
mine, I and my family (household); *húsið mitt* (= *mitt hús*) my
house (S. II, 4); *minn hestur,*
usually *hesturinn minn* my horse
(S. III, **2**, 4); *Finnur minn* my
good F. See also S. IV, **2**, 7.

minna, minnti, minnt(ur) [mɪn:a,
mɪn·tʰ, -ɪ, -ʏr̥; mɪn·t] wv.2 remind
of; *minna e-n á e-ð* remind sbdy of
sth; impersonal: *mig minnir, að*
. . . I think I remember that . . . ,
I seem to remember that . . . (S.
I, **2**, *1*, 3; VI, **14**, 5); middle voice:
minnast e-s remember sth; mention
sth; *minnast á e-ð (e-n)* mention
sth (sbdy) (S. VI, **7**, *4*); *þessa
verður minnzt* this will be remembered (S. VI, **14**, 6).

1. **minni, -s** [mɪn:ɪ(s)] n. memory,
hafa gott minni have a good
memory; *í manna minnum* within
the memory of living men.

2. **minni, minnstur,** see *lítill.*

minning, -ar, -ar [mɪn:iŋg, -ar̥] f.1
memory, remembrance, recollection;
commemoration.

minningarorð [mɪn:iŋgar·ɔr·ð] n.pl.
obituary (notice); *minningarorð
um e-n* obituary of sbdy; com-
memorative speech or article.

minnst, minnstur, see *lítt* and *lítill.*

mínúta, -u, -ur [miːnu·tʰa, -ʏ(r̥);
-u·d̥a] wf.1 minute.

mis- [mɪːs-] pref. mis-; adv. see *fara.*

misdægurt [mɪːsdai·qʏrt] n. adj. only
in the phrase: *verða aldrei misdægurt* 'never have a day different
from another,' never get sick.

misendismaður, -manns, -menn [mɪːs-
ɛndɪs·maːðʏr̥, -man·s, -mɛn:; mɪːs-
ɪndɪs-] m.4 illreputed person, rascal; a dangerous man.

misjafn, -jöfn, -jafnt [mɪːsjabn̥,
-jöbn̥, -jamtʰ; -jamt, -jaft] adj.
different, uneven; evil; *misjafn að
gæðum* uneven in quality.

miskunn, -ar [mɪs·kʏn, -ʏn, -nar̥] f.2
mercy.

Vowels: *a* [a] approx. father; *á* [au] cow; *e* [ɛ] set; *é* [jɛ] yes; *i, y* [ɪ] sit; *í, ý* [i] feel;
o [ɔ] law; *ó* [ou] note; *u* [ʏ] approx. Germ. Mütter; *ú* [u] school; *y* = *i*; *ý* = *í*; *æ* [ai] ice;
ö [ö] Germ. hören; *au* [öy] French *feuille*; *ei, ey* [ei] ale. Length [:]; half-length [·].

miskunnarlaus, -laus, -laust [mɪs.-kynar-löy:s, -löys·t] adj. merciless, cruel.

mislíka, -aði, -að [mɪ:sli·kʰa, -aðɪ, -að; -li·ga] wv.4 *mér mislíkar það* it displeases me; I do not like it (S. I, 3, *1*, 2(b); VI, 4, *3*).

mislingar [mɪs·liṇgar] m.l.pl. measles.

mislitur, -lit, -litt [mɪ:slɪ·tʰyr, -lɪ·tʰ, -lɪʰt; -lɪ·d·] adj. colored, varicolored, motley.

missa, missti, misst(ur) [mɪs:a, mɪs·t, -ɪ, -yr] wv.2 lose, drop; *missa e-ð niður* drop sth; *þeir verða að missa, sem eiga* (proverbial) those who own must take losses; *missa af e-u* miss sth, lose sth; *hann missti af strætisvagninum* he missed the bus.

misseri, -s, - [mɪs:erɪ(s)] n. half year, semester; six months.

misskilja, -skildi, -skilinn (-ið) [mɪ:-sk₁ɪlja, -sk₁ɪldɪ, -sk₁ɪ·lɪn, -ɪð] wv.1 misunderstand (*e-ð* sth; *e-n* sbdy).

missýnast, -sýndist, -sýnzt [mɪ:si·nast, -sindɪst, -sinst] wv.2 (middle voice only) see wrongly; *mér missýnist* my eyes deceive me (S. VI, **7**, *5*).

mitt, see l. *miður* and *minn*.

mitti, -s, - [mɪʰt:ɪ(s)] n. waist; *í mitti* up to the waist; *snjórinn var í mitti* the snow was up to the waist.

mjaltir [mjal·tɪr] f.2.pl. milking time.

mjó, see *mjór*.

mjólk, -ur [mjoul·kʰ, -yr; mjoul·k] f.3 milk; *með mjólk út á* with milk [on it].

mjólkurbúð, -ar, -ir [mjoul·kʰyr-bu:ð, -ðar, -ðɪr; mjoul·kyr-] f.2 milk shop, milk store, dairy products store.

mjólkurgrautur, -ar, -ar [mjoul·kʰyr-gröy:tʰyr, -ar; mjoul·kyr-gröy:dyr] m.l cereal cooked in milk.

mjólkurmatur, -ar [mjoul·kʰyr-ma:-tʰyr, -ar; mjoul·kyr-ma:dyr] m.3 milk food.

mjólkurostur, -s, -ar [mjoul·kʰyr-ɔs·tyr, -ɔsts, -ɔs·tar; mjoul·kyr-] m.l (milk) cheese (to differentiate from *mysuostur* whey cheese, q. v.), = *ostur*.

mjór, mjó, mjótt; mjórri, mjóstur [mjou:r, mjou:, mjouʰt:; mjour:ɪ, mjous·tyr] adj. thin, slender, narrow.

mjúkur, mjúk, mjúkt; mýkri, mýkstur [mju:kʰyr, mju:kʰ; mjux·t; mi:-kʰrɪ, mix·styr; mju:g, -yr, mi:grɪ] adj. soft, smooth.

mjög; meir, mest [mjö:q, mei:r, mɛs·t] adv. very, much; more, most; *mjög gamall* very old; *mér þykir mjög vænt um hann* I love him very much, I am very fond of him (In. IV, 2(d); S. VII, 4, 2).

móar, see *mór*.

móberg, -s [mou:berg(s)] n. tuff.

móbergsfjall, -s, -fjöll [mou:bergs-fjad·l, -fjal·s, -fjöd·l] n. a mountain of tuff.

1. móða, -u, -ur [mou:ða, -y(r)] wf.l mist.

2. móða, -u, -ur [mou:ða, -y(r)] wf.l big river.

móðir, -ur, mæður [mou:ðɪr, -yr, mai:ðyr] f.3 mother, *móðir mín* my mother.

móður- [mou:ðyr] in compounds: *móður-afi, -amma, -bróðir, -systir* maternal grandfather, grandmother, uncle, aunt.

móðurmynd, -ar, -ir [mou:ðyr-mɪn·d, -ar, -ɪr] f.2 'what is supposed to be a mother' (a mock derogatory term that a mother might use of herself).

mói, -a, -ar [mou:ɪ, -a(r)] wm.l ground covered with heather and other creeping brushes, crowberries, blueberries, etc. cf. *mór*.

mól, -um, see 2. *mala*.

mold, -ar, -ir [mɔl·d, -ar, -ɪr] f.2 mould, earth, dirt; pl. ashes.

moldarflag, -s, -flög [mɔl·dar-fla:q, -flax·s, -flö:q] n. patch of ground destitute of greensward.

moll, -s [mɔl:(s)] m.l minor (in music) (Pr. 3, *2*, 9n).

mór, mós, móar [mou:r, mou:s, mou:ar] m.l ground covered with heather, crowberries, blueberries and other creeping brushes, moor, heath; it is usually dry, often humpy.

Consonants: [ð] brea*the*; [g] *g*ood; [gj] *g*yarden (garden); [hw] *wh*at; [j] *y*es; [kj] *c*yan (can); [ŋ] thi*ng*; [q] N. Germ. sa*g*en; [r] Scottish *r*; [x] approx. Germ. a*ch*; [þ] *th*in. Voiceless: ○; [b̥, d̥, g̥] approx. *p, t, k*. Half-voiced: *italics*. Aspiration and preaspiration: [ʰ]; [pʰ, tʰ, kʰ] *p-, t-, k-*. Others as in English.

mórauður, -rauð, -rautt [mɔːröy·ðʏr̥, -röy·ð, -röyʰt·; mou:-] adj. yellowish brown, tan (of animals only sheep can be so colored).

morgunblað, -s, -blöð [mɔr·g̊ʏn-bla:ð, -blað·s, -blö:ð] n. morning news-paper, *Morgunblaðið* 'The Morning News.'

morgundagur, -s [mɔr·g̊ʏn-da:qʏr̥, -dax·s] m.l (the day) tomorrow.

morgungyðja, -u, -ur [mɔr·g̊ʏn-g‚ɪð·ja, -ʏ(r̥)] wf.l goddess of dawn (Aurora).

morgunkaffi, -s [mɔr·g̊ʏn-kʰaf:ɪ(s)] n. breakfast (coffee).

morgunmatur, -ar [mɔr·g̊ʏn-ma:tʰʏr̥, -ar̥; -ma:dʏr̥] m.3 breakfast.

morgunn, -uns, -nar [mɔr·g̊ʏn, -ʏns, mɔ(r)dnar̥] m.l morning; *á morgun* tomorrow morning; *í morgun* this morning; *með morgninum* next morning, first thing in the morning; *að morgni* next morning; *um morgun-inn eftir* next morning.

morguntónleikar [mɔr·g̊ʏn-tʰoun·lei·kʰar̥; -lei·g̊ar̥] m.l.pl. morning con-cert.

morgunverður, -ar, -ir [mɔr·g̊ʏn-ver·ðʏr̥, -ar̥, -ɪr̥] m.3 breakfast.

móri, -a, -ar [mou:rɪ, -a(r̥)] wm.l brown- or tan-colored animal or ghost (male).

mós, see *mór.*

mosavaxinn, -in, -ið [mɔ:sa-vax·sɪn, -ɪn, -ɪð] adj. grown over with moss, moss-covered.

Mosfellsheiði, ·-ar [mɔ:sfɛls-hei:ðɪ, -ar̥] f.l 'Moss Fell Heath,' a moun-tain NE of Reykjavík.

mosi, -a, -ar [mɔ:sɪ, -a(r̥)] wm.l moss.

mót, -s, - [mou:tʰ(s); mou:d] n. meeting, rendezvous; mode, way, manner; *mæla sér mót* appoint a meeting place, rendezvous; *með tvennu móti* in two ways; *með öllu móti* in every way.

mótgangur,-s [mou:tʰgauŋg̊ʏr̥,-gauŋs; mou:d·] m.l adversity.

móti [mou:tʰɪ; mou:dɪ] prep. with dat. (dat. of *mót* above) against, to meet; *maður kom á móti honum* a man came against him; *hann talaði (á) móti honum* he spoke against him; *á móti suðri* facing south.

mótmæla, -mælti, -mælt(ur) [mou:tʰ-mai.la, -mailt, -ɪ, -ʏr̥; mou:d-] wv.2 speak against, oppose, deny.

mótmælandi, -a, -endur [mou:tʰmai·-landɪ, -a, -ɛndʏr̥; mou:d-] wm.2 Protestant; opponent.

mótor, -s, -ar [mou:tʰɔr̥, -ɔr̥s, -ɔrar̥; mou:d-] m.l motor (= *vél*).

mótorbátur, -s, -ar [mou:tʰɔr-bau:-tʰʏr̥, -baus:, -bau:tʰar̥; mou:dɔr-bau:dʏr̥] m.l motorboat; *mótorbáta-útgerð* motorboat fisheries.

Múlakot, -s [mu:la-kʰɔ:tʰ(s), -kʰɔ:d] n. place name, 'Spur Cot.'

Múlasýsla, -u, -ur [mu:la-sis·la, -ʏ(r̥)] wf.l 'Spur District.'

muldi, mulið, -inn, see *mylja.*

múli, -a, -ar [mu:lɪ, -a(r̥)] wm.l end of a mountain, spur, head, headland.

mun, see *munu.*

muna, man, munum, mundi, munað [mʏ:na, ma:n, mʏ:nʏm, mʏn·dɪ, mʏ:nað] pret. pres. v. (In. VII, 5, 1) remember, call to mind, recol-lect; *ég man ekki* I forget; *muna e-m e-ð* remember sth for or against sbdy (S. VI, 4, 3).

Mundi, -a [mʏn·dɪ, -a] wm.l pet name for *Guðmundur.*

munkur, -s, -ar [muŋ·kʰʏr̥, muŋ·kʰs, muŋ·kʰar̥; muŋ·k-] m.l monk.

munnstykki, -s, - [mʏn·stɪʰkj·ɪ(s)] n. mouthpiece.

munntóbak, -s [mʏn·tʰou·bakʰ, -baxs; -bag̊] n. chewing tobacco.

munu, mun, munum, mundi, pret. inf. mundu [mʏ:nʏ, mʏ:n, mʏ:nʏm, mʏn·dɪ, -ʏ] pret. pres. v. (auxiliary only) shall, will, may; *ég mun fara* I shall go, I shall probably go; *ég mun hafa farið* I shall have gone, I may have gone, I probably went; (S. VI, 2, 5-7); *ég mun hafa séð*

Vowels: a [a] approx. father; á [au] cow; e [ɛ] set; é [jɛ] yes; i, y [ɪ] sit; í, ý [i] feel; o [ɔ] law; ó [ou] note; u [ʏ] approx. Germ. Mütter; ú [u] school; y = i; ý = í; æ [ai] ice; ö [ö] Germ. hören; au [öy] French feuille; ei, ey [ei] ale. Length [:]; half-length [·].

410

hann áður I may have seen him before, I probably have seen him before (S. VI, **2**, *3*n) ; *það mun þó ekki hafa verið ýsa?* it was not haddock by any chance, was it? *ég mundi (myndi) hafa = ég hefði* I would have; *ég mundi (myndi) vilja = ég vildi* I would like to (S. VI, **9**, *2*, 2n1-2); pret. inf. *mundu* (or *mundi*): *hann sagðist mundu (mundi) koma* he said he would come (S. VI, **11**, *1*); *mun = mun vera; hann mun (vera) dauður* he is probably dead (S. VI, 11, *6*n1); *hann kvað þá mundu dauða (vera)* he said they were probably dead.

munur, -ar, -ir [mɣ:nʏr̥, -ar̥, -ɪr̥] m.3 thing, difference; *fyrir engan mun* by no means, on no account, *fyrir alla muni* by all means, above all; *til muna* to a great extent; *þeim mun meira . . . því meira* the more . . . the more (S. I, **3**, *2*, 5).

murta, -u, -ur [mʏr̥·ta, -ɣ(r̥)] wf.1 a small thing; a species of small trout found in Þingvallavatn.

mús, -ar, **mýs** [mu:s, -ar̥, mi:s] f.3 mouse.

músík, -ur [mu:si·kʰ, -ʏr̥; mu:si·g̊] f.3 music.

mý, -s [mi:(s)] n. (coll.; the individual is *mýfluga*) buffalo gnats and mosquitoes; swarm of these flies; *fullt af mýi* full of buffalo gnats.

mýbit, -s [mi:bɪ·tʰ(s)] n. the bite of buffalo gnats; buffalo gnats (= *mý*).

mýfluga, -u, -ur [mi:flɣ·qa, -ɣ(r̥)] wf.1 buffalo gnat, mosquito.

mýkri, **mýkstur**, see *mjúkur*.

mylja, **muldi**, **mulinn** (-ið) [mɪl·ja, mʏl·dɪ, mʏ:lɪn, -ɪð] wv.1 crush.

mylla, -u, -ur [mɪl:a, -ɣ(r̥)] wf.1 (Pr. 3, *2*, 9n) mill.

mynd, -ar, -ir [mɪn·d, -ar̥, -ɪr̥] f.2 picture, image; motion picture (= *kvikmynd*), movie; form, *í breyttri mynd* in a different form.

mynda, -aði, -að(ur) [mɪn·da, -aðɪ,

-að, -aðʏr̥] wv.4 *mynda e-ð* form sth; *myndast* form, take shape.

myndastytta, -u, -ur [mɪn·da-stɪʰt:a, -ɣ(r̥)] wf.1 monument.

myndhöggvari, -a, -ar [mɪn·d̥hög̊·varɪ, -a(r̥)] wm.1 sculptor.

mynt, -ar, -ir [mɪn·tʰ, -ar̥, -ɪr̥; mɪn̥·t] f.2 coin; mint.

Mýrdalsjökull, -uls [mir·dals-jö:kʰʏdl, -ʏls; -jö:g̊ʏdl] m.1 'Marsh Dale Glacier.'

Mýrdalur, -s [mir·da·lʏr̥, -dals] m.2 'Moor Dale,' or 'Marsh Dale'; *Mýrdals-sandur* 'Moor Dale Sand.'

mýri, -ar, -ar [mi:rɪ, -ar̥] f.1 swamp, marsh, morass, bog.

myrkfælinn, -in, -ið [mɪr̥·kfai·lɪn, -ɪn, -ɪð] adj. afraid of the darkness.

myrkur, (-ri), -urs, -ur [mɪr̥·kʏr̥(s), mɪr̥krɪ] n. darkness.

myrkvi, -a, -ar [mɪr̥·kvɪ, -a(r̥)] wm.1 darkness, shadow, cloud; eclipse of sun or moon (*sól-, tungl-*).

mýs, see *mús*.

mysa, -u [mɪ:sa, -ɣ] wf.1 whey.

mysuostur, -s, -ar [mɪ:sɔstʏr̥, -ɔsts, -ɔstar̥] m.1 'whey cheese,' of the same type as the Norwegian 'Getost.'

mývargur, -s [mi:varg̊ʏr̥, -varg̊s] m.1 = *mý*, plague of buffalo gnats or mosquitoes.

Mývatn, -s [mi:vaʰtn, -vas] n. 'Buffalo gnat Lake,' or 'Mosquito Lake.'

mæðgin [maið·g̊ɪn] n.pl. mother and son.

mæðgur, **mæðgna** [maið·g̊ʏr̥, maið·g̊na] wf.1.pl. mother and daughter.

mæður, see *móðir*.

mægð, -ar, -ir [maiq·ð, -ðar̥, -ðɪr̥; maig̊·þ] f.2, usually in pl.: relationship by marriage.

mægjast, **mægðist**, **mægzt** [mai:jast, maiq·ðɪst, maix·st; maig̊·ðɪst] wv.2 (only in middle voice) become related by marriage.

1. **mæla**, **mælti**, **mælt(ur)** [mai:la, mail·t, -ɪ, -ʏr̥] wv.2 speak; appoint; *mæla móti* deny; *mæla sér mót* appoint a rendezvous; *mæla um*

411

speak a (magic) formula; *mæli ég um og legg það á* I solemnly pronounce this spell.

2. **mæla, mældi, mældur** (mælt) [mai:la, mail·dɪ, -ʏɾ, mail·t] wv.2 measure.

mælikvarði, -a, -ar [mai:lɪ·kʰvar·ðɪ, -a(ɾ)] wm.1 scale; standard; *á útlendan mælikvarða* by foreign standards.

mænir, -is, -(ir)ar [mai:nɪɾ, -ɪs, -(ɪr)aɾ] m.1 ridge of the roof.

mæta, mætti, mætt(ur) [mai:tʰa, maiʰt:, -ɪ, -ʏɾ; mai:da] wv.2 meet; *mæta e-m* meet sbdy; *mætast* meet each other.

mættir, see *máttur, mega.*

mögur, see *magur.*

möl, malar, -ir [mö:l, ma:laɾ, -ɪɾ] f.2 gravel; pl. gravel flats.

mölva, -aði, -að(ur) [möl·va, -aðɪ, -að, -aðʏɾ] wv.4 smash, break.

mömmu, -ur, see *mamma.*

möndull, -uls, -lar [mön·dʏdl, -ʏls, möndlaɾ] m.1 cylinder, axis.

mönduiveldi, -s, - [mön·dʏl·vel·dɪ(s)] n. axis power.

mör, -s, mörvar [mö:r, mör·s, mör·vaɾ] m.1 suet, caul (= *netja*).

mörg, see *margur.*

mörk; markar, merkur; merkur [mör·k, mar·kaɾ, mer·kʏɾ] f.3 pint, half a pound; woods, forest.

möttull, -uls, -lar [möʰt:ʏdl, -ʏls, möʰt·laɾ] m.1 mantle, cope.

N.

1. **ná, næ** (or **nái**), **náði, náð** [nau:, nai:, nau:ɪ, nau:ðɪ, nau:ð] wv.1 or 3 get, catch, reach; attain, overtake, come up with; extend; (1) get, catch: *ná heyi saman* rake (get) the hay together; *ná e-m* catch up with sbdy, overtake sbdy; *ná í e-n* get sbdy, get hold of sbdy; (2) reach, extend: *ná upp í loftið* reach up to the ceiling, extend up to the ceiling; *ná hingað* reach to here, get here, be here; *ná frá . . . til* reach

from . . . to . . . ; (3) auxiliary: *náir syngja = syngur* (poetic) does sing (S. VI, **13,** 11).

2. **ná-** [nau:-] pref. closely.
NA-átt = *norðaustanátt* wind from northeast.

náð, -ar, -ir [nau:ð, -ðaɾ, -ðɪɾ] f.2 grace; *drottins náð* grace of God; pl. *náðir* peace; *vertu í eilífri náðinni* 'be in eternal grace,' by all means!

nafn, -s, nöfn [nab·n, naf·s, nöb·n] n. name, term; *nafn á e-u* name of sth, term for sth; *fullu nafni* with a name written out in full; *að nafni* by name; *bera nafn* have a name, be named, bear the name.

nafnlaus, -laus, -laust [nab·nlöy·s, -löyst] adj. without a name.

naggra, -aði, -að [naɡ̊:ra, -aðɪ, -að] wv.4 reach (scrape) bottom = *naggra niðri* (of boats and horses).

naglar, see *nagli* and *nögl.*

nagli, -a, -ar [naɡ̊·lɪ, -a(ɾ)] wm.1 nail.

nágrenni, -s, - [nau:ɡren·ɪ(s)] n. vicinity, neighborhood.

náinn, -in, -ið; nánari, -astur [nau:ɪn, -ɪn, -ɪð, nau:narɪ, -astʏɾ] adj. near; closely related; close; *nánari* more precise, more specific.

nákvæmlega [nau:kʰvaim·lɛ:qa] adv. exactly.

nál, -ar, -ar [nau:l, -laɾ] f.1 needle.

nálarauga, -, -u [nau:lar·öy:qa, -ʏ] wn. the eye of a needle.

nálgast, -aðist, -azt [naul·ɡ̊ast, -aðɪst, -ast] wv.4 (middle voice only) approach; *nálgast e-n* (*e-ð*) approach sbdy (sth) (S. VI, **7,** 5).

nálægur, -læg, -lægt; -lægari, -astur [nau:lai·qʏɾ, -lai·q, -laixt, -lai·qarɪ, -astʏɾ] adj. near; *nálægt e-m* (*e-u*) near to sbdy (sth); *nálægt því* near, nearly, almost; *þar nálægt* near there (S. I, **3,** 2, 1); *hér nálægt* near here, in the neighborhood.

nam, námum, see 1. *nema.*

Vowels: *a* [a] approx. father; *á* [au] cow; *e* [ɛ] set; *é* [jɛ] yes; *i, y* [ɪ] sit; *í, ý* [i] feel; *o* [ɔ] law; *ó* [ou] note; *u* [ʏ] approx. Germ. Mütter; *ú* [u] school; *y = i; ý = í; æ* [ai] ice; *ö* [ö] Germ. hören; *au* [öy] French feuille; *ei, ey* [ei] ale. Length [:]; half-length [·].

nám, -s, - [nau:*m*, naum·s] n. study; *halda áfram námi* continue studying.

námsgrein, -ar; -ar, -ir [naum·sgrei·*n*, -nar, -nɪr] f.l & 2 subject, study.

námskeið, -s, - [naum·sk₁ei·ð, -sk₁eiðs] n. course of study, usually special or extra-curricular courses.

nasar, -ir, see *nös*.

nátengdur, -tengd, -tengt [nau:tʰeiŋ·dɥr, -tʰeiŋd, -tʰeiŋtʰ; -tʰeiŋt] adj. closely related, closely connected with.

nátt, -ar, nætur, (nátta) [nauʰt:, -ar, nai:tʰɥr, nauʰt:a; nai:dɥr] f.3 = *nótt*.
N-átt = *norðanátt* wind from the north.

náttborð, -s, - [nauʰt:borð, -borðs] n. night table, bedroom table.

náttmál [nauʰt:mau·l] n.pl. nine in the evening.

nátttröll, -s, - [nauʰtʰ:rödl, -tʰröls] n. night troll.

náttúra, -u, -ur [nauʰt:ura, -ɣ(r)] wf.l nature; (supernatural) virtue, power; pl. characteristics; *mannleg náttúra* human nature.

náttúrufegurð, -ar [nauʰt:urɣ·fɛ:-qɥrð, -ðar] f.2 beauty of nature.

náttúrufræði [nauʰt:urɣ·frai:ðɪ] wf.2 natural science.

náttúrugripasafn, -s, -söfn [nauʰt:-urɣgrɪ·pʰa·sab·n, -s, -söb·n; -grɪ·ba-] n. museum of natural history; *Náttúrugripasafnið* 'The Museum of Natural History.'

náttúrugripur, -s, -ir [nauʰt:urɣ-grɪ:pʰɥr, -grɪ:pʰs, -ɪr; grɪ:b̥-] m.2 object of nature.

nauðsyn, -synjar, -synjar [nöyð·sɪ·*n*, -sɪnjar] f.l necessity, pl. necessities.

nauðsynlega [nöyð·sɪn·lɛ:qa] adv. needs, necessarily; *ég þarf nauðsyn-lega að gera e·ð* I must necessarily do sth, I have to do sth.

naumur, naum, naumt [nöy:mɥr, nöy:*m*, nöym·tʰ; nöym·t] adj. short, close, stingy; *verða naumt fyrir með e·ð* get pushed for time in doing sth, run short of time.

náungi, -a, -ar [nau:uŋg̊₁ɪ, -g̊a(r̥)] wm.l neighbor, fellow man; the other fellow, a fellow.

naust, -s, - [nöys·t(s)] n. boathouse; in place names; *-naust*.

1. naut, -s, - [nöy:tʰ(s), nöys:; nöy:d] n. bull, bullock; pl. cattle; in place names: *Nauta-, Nautabú*, etc.

2. naut, see *njóta*.

nautaket (-kjöt), -s [nöy:tʰa·k₁ʰɛ:tʰ, -s, -k₁ʰö:tʰ(s); nöy:da·k₁ʰɛ:d, -k₁ʰö:d] n. beef.

nautgripur, -s, -ir [nöy:tʰgrɪ·pʰɥr, -grɪ·pʰs, -ɪr; nöy:dgrɪ·b̥ɥr] m.2 cow or bull; pl. cattle (cows).

neðan [nɛ:ðan] (1) adv. from below; *að neðan* from below; *fyrir neðan hólinn* (acc.) below the hill; (In. IV, 1, 3); (2) prep. with acc. *neðan brekkuna* up the slope; (3) prep. with gen. *neðan brekk-unnar* below the slope.

neðanundir [nɛ:ðan·ɥn·dɪr] adv. and prep. with dat. below; *neðanundir brekkunni* below the slope (also *neðan undir*).

neðar, neðst [nɛ:ðar, nɛðst] adv. compar. and superl. farther down, farthest down.

nef, -s, -, (-ja) [nɛ:*v*, nɛf·s, nɛv·ja] n. nose, bill, beak; *nefið á mér* my nose; *skattur á nef hvert* head tax (S. I, 4, *1*, 4).

nefna, nefndi, nefndur (nefnt) [nɛb·na, nɛm·dɪ, -ɥr, nɛm·tʰ; nɛm·t] wv.2 call, name, mention, speak of; *má nefna* may be mentioned; *svo nefnd-ur* so-called.

nefnari, -a, -ar [nɛb·narɪ, -a(r̥)] wm.l denominator.

neftóbak, -s [nɛf·tʰou·bakʰ, -baxs] n. snuff (= 'nose tobacco').

neglur, see *nögl*.

nei [nei:] adv. no; *nei þakk, nei takk* no thank you.

neinn, nein, neitt [neid·n, nei:*n*, neiʰt:] indef. pron. (only strong) used only after negation: (*ekki*) *neinn* (not) any one, no one; *ekki*

Consonants: [ð] brea*the*; [g] *g*ood; [g₁] *gy*arden (garden); [hw̥] *wh*at; [j] *y*es; [k₁] *cy*an (can); [ŋ] thi*ng*; [q] N. Germ. sa*g*en; [r] Scottish *r*; [x] approx. Germ. a*ch*; [þ] *th*in. Voiceless: ○; [b̥, d̥, g̊] approx. *p, t, k*. Half-voiced: *italics*. Aspiration and preaspiration: [ʰ]; [pʰ, tʰ, kʰ] *p-, t-, k-*. Others as in English.

413

af neinu for no (special) reason; *ekki til neins* of no use; (In. VI, 6, 2(a); S. IV, 6, 15).

neita, -aði, -að [nei:tʰa, -aðɪ, -að; nei:da] wv.4 deny, say no, refuse; *neita e-u* deny sth; *neita e-m um e-ð* deny sbdy sth, refuse sth to sbdy.

1. nema, nem, nam, námum, numinn (-ið) [nɛ:ma, nɛ:m, na:m, nau:-mʏm, nʏ:mɪn, -ɪð] v.4 take; *nema land* take land, settle a place, a country; *nema (burt)* take away, kidnap; *nema lög* learn, study law; *nema staðar* stop; *þetta nam 100 krónum* this amounted to 100 crowns.

2. nema [nɛ:ma] conj. except, save, but, unless; *enginn, nema hann* nobody but he; *hann fór hvergi, nema honum væri skipað* he went nowhere, unless he was ordered to do so; *nema helzt* except perhaps; *ekki nema* not more than, only; not except, not unless; *ekki nema því meira liggi við* not unless sth very serious be at stake (S. I, 3, 2, 5); *nema hvað* except that; (S. VI, 9, 3, 3; VIII, 3(c)).

nemandi, -a, -endur [nɛ:mandɪ, -a, -endʏr] wm.2 pupil, student.

nenna, nennti, nennt [nɛn:a, nɛn·tʰ, -ɪ; nɛn·t] wv.2 only in a question or with a negation: *hann nennir ekki að lesa* he does not want to read, he is too lazy to read; *nennir þú að lesa þetta?* do you want to take time to read this, can you get yourself to read this?

neri, néri, see *núa.*

nes, ness, nes [nɛ:s, nɛs:] n. ness, point, headland, peninsula; in place names *-nes.*

nesta, -aði, -að(ur) [nɛs·ta, -aðɪ, -að, -aðʏr] wv.4 provide with food (for a trip, a picnic, etc.).

nesti, -s [nɛs·tɪ(s)] n. provisions, food (on a journey, picnic, etc.).

net, -s, -, (-ja) [nɛ:tʰ(s), nɛ:tʰja; nɛ:d] n. net, seine.

netjalagning, -ar, -ar [nɛ:tʰja-lag·nin�....g, -ar; nɛ:dja-] f.1 casting of nets.

neyða, neyddi, neyddur (neytt) [nei:-ða, neid:ɪ, -ʏr, neiʰt:] wv.2 compel; *neyðast* be compelled (by circumstances).

nía, -u, -ur [ni:ja, -ʏ(r)] wf.1 nine (in cards).

niðri [nɪð·rɪ] adv. down, below, downstairs; (in the theatre) orchestra seats; under; *niðri í vatninu* under the surface of the water; *ná sér niðri á e-m* get even with sbdy (In. IV, 1, 3).

niður [nɪ:ðʏr] (1) adv. down, downwards; *detta niður* fall down; *leggjast niður* lie down; *skifta niður* classify; *niður í* down into; *niður úr* down from (In. IV, 1, 3); (2) prep. with acc. (= *ofan*) *niður brekkuna* down the slope (S. I, 2, 3, 3).

niðursoðinn, -in, -ið [nɪ:ðʏr-sɔ:ðɪn, -ɪn, -ɪð] adj. (pp.) preserved, canned; *niðursoðinn matur* canned food (goods), tinned food.

niðursuða, -u [nɪ:ðʏr-sʏ:ða, -ʏ] wf.1 canning, preserving; *n. á síld* canning of herring.

niðursuðuverksmiðja, -u, -ur [nɪ:-ðʏrsʏ·ðʏ-vɛr·ksmɪðja, -ʏ(r)] wf.1 canning factory.

niðursuðuvörur [nɪ:ðʏrsʏ·ðʏ-vö:rʏr] wf.1.pl. canned goods.

nífaldur, -föld, -falt [ni:faldʏr, -föld, -falt] adj. ninefold.

nikkel, -s [nɪʰk:el, -els] n. nickel.

níræður, -ræð, -rætt [ni:rai·ðʏr, -rai·ð, -raiʰt·] adj. ninety years old.

nítján [ni:tʰjau·n, ni:djau·n̩] num. card. nineteen.

nítjándi [ni:tʰjaundɪ, ni:d-] num.ord. nineteenth.

nítugasti [ni:tʰʏ·qastɪ, ni:d-] num. ord. ninetieth.

níu [ni:jʏ] num. card. nine.

níundi [ni:jʏndɪ] num. ord. ninth.

níutíu [ni:jʏ-tʰi:jʏ] num.card. ninety.

Njála, -u [njau:la, -ʏ] wf.1 the saga

Vowels: *a* [a] approx. *father;* *á* [au] *cow;* *e* [ɛ] *set;* *é* [jɛ] *yes;* *i, y* [ɪ] *sit;* *í, ý* [i] *feel;* *o* [ɔ] *law;* *ó* [ou] *note;* *u* [ʏ] approx. Germ. *Mütter;* *ú* [u] *school;* *y = i;* *ý = í;* *æ* [ai] *ice;* *ö* [ö] Germ. *hören;* *au* [öy] French *feuille;* *ei, ey* [ei] *ale.* Length [:]; half-length [·].

414

of *Njáll Þorgeirsson,* most famous
of the Icelandic (family) sagas.
njósn, -ar, -ir [njous·*n,* -nar̥, -nɪr̥] f.2
spying; news gotten by spying.
njósna, -aði, -að [njous·na, -aðɪ, -að]
wv.4 spy, reconnoitre.
njósnari, -a, -ar [njous·narɪ, -a(r̥)]
wm.1 spy.
njósnarflokkur, -s, -ar [njous·nar̥-
flɔʰk:ʏr̥, -flɔx·s, -flɔʰk:ar̥] m.1
patrol,°a flock of spies.
njóta, nýt, naut, nutum, notið [njou:-
tʰa, ni:tʰ, nöy:tʰ, nʏ:tʰʏm, nɔ:tʰɪð;
njou:da, ni:d̥, nöy:d̥, nʏ:d̥ʏm,
hɔ:dɪð̥] v.2 enjoy; *njóta e·s* enjoy
sth,°benefit from sth, get advantage
from sth; *njóta sín* enjoy oneself,
enjoy one's faculties; *ég naut mín
ekki* I was not myself.
n. k. = *næstkomandi* next.
N-kaldi = *norðankaldi* light breeze
from the north.
nóg [nou:(*q*)] n. enough; *meira en
nóg* more than enough; *nóg af e-u*
enough, plenty of sth.
nógsamlega [nou:(q)sam-lɛ:qa] adv.
enough.
nógu [nou:(q)ʏ] adv. enough; *nógu
vel* well enough.
nógur, nóg, nógt [nou:(q)ʏr̥, nou:(*q*),
noux·t] adj. (never weak) enough,
sufficient, plentiful; *nógur matur*
enough food.
nokkuð [nɔʰk:ʏð] adv. somewhat
(see *nokkur*) (S. VII, **4**, 2).
nokkur, nokkur, nokkurt, nokkuð
[nɔʰk:ʏr̥, nɔʰk:ʏr̥t, nɔʰk:ʏð] indef.
pron. (only strong; In. VI, **6**, 2 (b))
some, somebody, someone; *nokkrir
menn* some men (people, persons);
nokkrir segja some say; *maður
nokkur* a certain man (person);
any, anybody, anyone; *er nokkur
hér?* is there anybody here? *ekki
nokkur sál* not a soul; *nokkrar
klukkustundir* a few hours; *nokkur
skipin* some of the ships (S. II, 7);
ef hún er nokkur if she (i. e. it)
exists at all; *nokkuð* anything:
(*er*) *nokkuð að frétta?* (is there)

any news? *þó nokkuð* quite a bit;
fyrir nokkru a short while ago; *að
nokkru* to some extent; *a. n. l. = að
nokkru leyti* partly, to some extent;
nokkuð seint somewhat late. (S.
III, 1, 4; IV, **6**, 16).
nokkurntíma [nɔʰk:ʏn-tʰi:ma, nɔʰk:-
ʏdn-] adv. (also *nokkurn tíma*)
ever, any time.
nokkurskonar [nɔʰk:ʏr̥s-kʰɔ:nar̥] adv.
(also *nokkurs konar*) a kind of,
some sort of.
nokkursstaðar [nɔʰk:ʏr̥(s)-sta:ðar̥]
adv. (also *nokkurs staðar*) anywhere.
nón [nou:*n,* noun·s] n. three in the
afternoon. This was the original
time for noon, even in England.
Nonni, -a, -ar [nɔn:ɪ, -a(r̥)] wm.1
pet name for *Jón.*
Nora-magasín, -s [nou:ra-ma:g̊asi·*n,*
-sins] n. a store in Reykjavík.
Nordal, -s [nɔr·da·*l,* -dals] m.1 family
name; *Sigurður N.* an authority on
Icelandic literature.
norðan [nɔr·ðan] (1) adv. from the
north (= *að norðan*); *vindurinn er
á norðan* the wind blows from the
north; *fyrir norðan* north of, in
the North; *norður fyrir* passing
north of, rounding (the country)
to the north; (2) prep. with acc.
norðan heiðina from the north
across the heath; (3) prep. with
gen. north of: *norðan fjarðar* (also
in one word: *norðanfjarðar*) north
of the fjord. (In. IV, 1, 3).
norðanátt, -ar [nɔr·ðan-auʰt:, -ar̥]
f.2 (prevailing) wind from the north.
norðangarður, -s [nɔr·ðan-gar·ðʏr̥,
-garðs] m.1 spell of storms from
the north.
norðangarri, -a [nɔr·ðan-gar:ɪ, -a]
wm.1 = *norðangarður.*
norðankaldi, -a [nɔr·ðan-kʰal·d̥ɪ, -a]
wm.1 light breeze from the north.
norðar, norðast, nyrzt [nɔr·ðar̥, -ast,
nɪr̥st] adv. compar. and superl.
more to the north, most to the
north.

Consonants: [ð] brea*the;* [g] *g*ood; [gj] *gy*arden (garden); [hw̥] *wh*at; [j] *y*es; [kj] *cy*an
(can); [ŋ] thi*ng;* [q] N. Germ. sa*g*en; [r] Scottish *r;* [x] approx. Germ. a*ch;* [þ] *th*in.
Voiceless: ○; [b̥, d̥, g̊] approx. *p, t, k.* Half-voiced: *italics.* Aspiration and preaspiration:
[ʰ]; [pʰ, tʰ, kʰ] *p-, t-, k-.* Others as in English.

norðarlega [nɔr·ðaðlɛ·qa, nɔr·ðar-]
adv. northerly; *norðarlega í Atlantshafi* in the northern Atlantic.

norðaustanátt, -ar [nɔr·ðöystan-auʰt:,
-aṛ] f.2 (prevailing) wind from the
northeast.

Norðfjörður, -fjarðar [nɔṛ·fjörðYṛ,
-fjarðar; nɔr·ð-] m.3 'North Fjord.'

Norðlendíngur, -s, -ar [nɔṛdlendiŋ̊Yṛ,
-iŋs, -iŋgaṛ, nɔr·ð-] m.1 man, person
from the North of Iceland.

Norðmaður, -manns, -menn [nɔr·ðma·
ðYṛ, -mans, -mɛn·] m.4 Norwegian,
Norseman.

1. norður, (-ri), -urs [nɔr·ðYṛ(s),
nɔrðrɪ] n. north; *í n-i* in the north.
2. norður [nɔr·ðYṛ] adv. north, northwards; *norður í land* to the North
of Iceland; *norður í landi* in the
North of Iceland (In. IV, 1, 3).

norðurheimskaut, -s [nɔr·ðYṛ-heim·
sköy·tʰ(s); -sköy·d] n. north pole.

norðurheimskautsland, -s, -lönd [nɔr·
ðYṛheimsköytʰs-lan·d, -s; -sköyds-]
n. north polar (arctic) region.

Norðurland, -s [nɔr·ðYṛ-lan·d, -lan·s]
n. the North of Iceland.

Norðurlandaþjóð, -ar, -ir [nɔr·ðYṛ-
landa-þjou:ð, -ðaṛ, -ðɪṛ] f.2 Scandinavian nation.

norðurljós, -s, - [nɔr·ðYṛ-ljou:s,
-ljous:] n. aurora borealis, northern
lights.

Norðurlönd, -landa [nɔr·ðYṛ-lön·d,
-lan·da] n.pl. The North, Scandinavia.

norðurströnd, -strandar, -strendur
[nɔr·ðYṛ-strön·d, -stran·daṛ, -stren·
dYṛ] f.3 northern shore, coast.

norðvestan [nɔr·ðvɛstan] adv. from
the northwest.

norðvestanlands [nɔr·ðvɛstan-
lan·(d)s] adv. in the North West
of Iceland.

Noregur, -s [nɔ:rɛ·qYṛ, -ɛxs] m.1
Norway; *Noregskonungur* King of
Norway.

normalbrauð, -s, - [nɔr·mal·bröy:ð,
-bröyð·s] n. ryebread (from sifted
rye flour).

norn, -ar, -ir [nɔrdn, -naṛ, -nɪṛ] f.2
Norn (one of the fatal sisters) pl.
Fates, Destinies (of Icelandic mythology); witch.

nornalög, -laga [nɔrdna-lö:q, -la:qa]
n.pl. norn melodies.

norræna, -u [nɔr:ai·na, -Y] wf.1 Old
Norse-Icelandic.

norrænn, -ræn, -rænt; -rænni, -rænastur [nɔr:aiðn, -rai·n, -raintʰ; -raint;
-raidnɪ, -rai·nastYṛ] adj. Norse,
Nordic, Scandinavian, Northern.

norrænufræðingur, -ings, -ingar [nɔr:
ainY-frai:ðiŋ̊Yṛ, -iŋs, -iŋgaṛ] m.1
expert or scholar in the Old Norse-
Icelandic language and literature.

norskur, norsk, norskt [nɔrskYṛ, nɔrsk,
nɔrst] adj. Norwegian.

nota, -aði, -að(ur) [nɔ:tʰa, -aðɪ, -að,
-aðYṛ; nɔ:da] wv.4 use, make use
of; *nota e-ð fyrir e-ð* use sth as
sth; *notast við e-ð* make shift to
use sth.

notalegur [nɔ:tʰa-lɛ:qYṛ; nɔ:da-] adj.
(see *-legur*) comfortable, cozy.

notið, see *njóta.*

nótt, nætur, nætur, nótta [nouʰt:,
nai:tʰYṛ; nai:dYṛ; nouʰt:a] f.3
night; *góða nótt* good night; *í nótt*
tonight; *í nótt sem var* last night;
á nóttunni at night; *að nóttu til*
at night; *tvær nætur* (acc.) for two
nights (S. I, 2, 2, 2).

nóv. =

nóvember [nou:vɛmbɛ·r] m. indecl.
November.

nú [nu:] adv. now; *nú á dögum*
nowadays, in our time; *nú í vikunni*
this week; *hvað . . . nú* whatever;
nú is that so, yes, why, really (often
hard to translate into English).
Talið þér íslenzku? Það er nú lítið.
Do you speak Icelandic? Why, very
little, indeed. *Nú, mér heyrist þér
tala nógu vel* Why, I think you
speak well enough; *þú getur nú
ekki gert það* why, you cannot do
that; *ég held nú það* I should say so.

núa, ný; neri, néri, nöri; núinn (-ið)
[nu:a, ni:, nɛ:rɪ, njɛ:rɪ, nö:rɪ,

Vowels: *a* [a] approx. father; *á* [au] cow; *e* [ɛ] set; *é* [jɛ] yes; *i, y* [ɪ] sit; *í, ý* [i] feel;
o [ɔ] law; *ó* [ou] note; *u* [Y] approx. Germ. M*ü*tter; *ú* [u] school; *y* = *i*; *ý* = *í*; *æ* [ai] ice;
ö [ö] Germ. hören; *au* [öy] French *feuille*; *ei, ey* [ei] ale. Length [:]; half-length [·].

416

nu:ɪn, -ɪð] wv.1 and irreg. (In. VII, 5, 2) rub.

núlifandi [nu:lɪ·vandɪ] adj. now living; contemporary.

núll, -s, - [nul:, nul·s] n. zero; 0.33 (núll komma þrjátíu og þrír) zero point three three (Pr. 3, 2, 9n).

númer, -s, - [nu:mɛ·r, nu:mers] n. number; (= símanúmer) phone number.

numið, see 1. nema.

núna [nu:na] adv. now; ekki núna not now.

núpur, -s, -ar [nu:pʰʏr, nu:pʰs, nu:-pʰar; nu:b·] m.1 knoll, knob; also in place names: -núpur, Núps-.

nútímamaður, -manns, -menn [nu:-tʰi·ma-ma:ðʏr, -man·s, -mɛn:] m.4 a modern man, a modern.

nútími, -a [nu:tʰi·mɪ, -a] wm.1 the present time, the present times, modern times (nútíminn).

nutum, see njóta.

NV = norðvestan from the northwest.

1. ný, see núa and nýr.

2. ný- [ni:-] pref. newly, just recently.

nýborinn, -in, -ið [ni:bɔ:rɪn, -ɪn, -ɪð] adj. (pp.) recently, just born; having just given birth to; ærin er nýborin the ewe has just lambed; but: lambið er nýborið the lamb has just been born (S. VI, 12, 2, 1).

nýfarinn, -in, -ið [ni:fa:rɪn, -ɪn, -ɪð] adj. (pp.) just gone, just departed.

nýgiftur, -gift, -gift [ni:gɪf·tʏr, -g₁ɪf·t] adj. (pp.) newly wed.

nýjár, -s, - [ni:jau.r, -aurs] n. New Year, New Year's Day.

nýjársdagur, -dags, -dagar [ni:jaurs-da:qʏr, -dax·s, -da:qar] m.1 New Years Day.

nýjársnótt, -nætur, -nætur [ni:jaurs-nouʰt:, -nai:tʰʏr; -nai:dʏr] f.3 New Years Eve (= gamlárskvöld).

nýlega [ni:lɛ·qa] adv. recently, newly.

nýlenda, -u, -ur [ni:lɛnda, -ʏ(r)] wf.1 colony.

nýlenduvöruverzlun, -unar, -anir [ni:-lɛndʏvörʏ-verslʏn, -ʏnar, -anɪr] f.2 grocery store.

nýmeti, -s [ni:mɛ·tʰɪ(s), -mɛ·dɪ] n. fresh food (fish or meat).

nýmjólk, -ur [ni:mjoulkʰ, -ʏr; -mjoulk] f.3 fresh milk, whole milk.

nýr, ný, nýtt; nýjastur [ni:r, ni:, niʰt:, nir:ɪ, ni:jastʏr] adj. new, fresh, recent; að (af) nýju afresh; nýtt kjöt fresh meat.

nýra, -, -u [ni:ra, -ʏ] wn. kidney.

nyrðri, nyrztur [nɪrðrɪ, nɪrstʏr] adj. compar. and superl. more, most northerly; (í) nyrðra adv. in the north.

nyrzt, see norðar.

nýt, see njóta and nýtur.

nýtízku- [ni:tʰis·kʏ-] pref. modern (is-tic).

nýtízkuhús, -s, - [ni:tʰiskʏ-hu:s, -hus:] n. house according to the newest fashion, modern house, modernistic house.

nytjafugl, -s, -ar [nɪ:tʰja-fʏg̊·l, -fʏqls, -fʏg̊·lar; nɪ:dja-] m.1 a bird of some use.

nytsamur, -söm, -samt [nɪ:tʰsa·mʏr, -sö·m; -samtʰ; -samt; nɪ:d·] adj. useful; nytsamur fyrir e-n (e-m) useful to sbdy.

nýtur, nýt, nýtt [ni:tʰʏr, ni:tʰ, niʰt:; ni:dʏr, ni:d] adj. useful; einskis nýtur of no use.

næ, see 1. ná.

nægur, næg, nægt [nai:qʏr, nai:q, naix·t] adj. plentiful, sufficient, enough.

næla, -u, -ur [nai:la, -ʏ(r)] wf.1 pin, brooch.

næpa, -u, -ur [nai:pʰa, -ʏ(r); nai:ba] wf.1 turnip.

nær [nai:r] (comparative of nærri) adv. nearer; færast nær (e-u) approach (sth) þér væri nær að hætta you had better stop; almost, nearly nær dauður almost dead; = hvenær, when.

nærbuxur, -buxna [nair·bʏxsʏr, -bʏx-sna] wf.1.pl. drawers, pants; kvenn-manns nærbuxur woman's pants.

nærföt, -fata [nair·fö·tʰ, -fa·tʰa; -fö·d, -fa·da] n.pl. underwear.

Consonants: [ð] breathe; [g] good; [g₁] gyarden (garden); [hʍ] what; [j] yes; [k₁] cyan (can); [ŋ] thing; [q] N. Germ. sagen; [r] Scottish r; [x] approx. Germ. ach; [þ] thin. Voiceless: o; [b̥, d̥, g̊] approx. p, t, k. Half-voiced: italics. Aspiration and preaspiration: [ʰ]; [pʰ, tʰ, kʰ] p-, t-, k-. Others as in English.

nærri [nair:ɪ] adv. near, almost;
nærri e-m near to sbdy; *nærri
dauður* almost dead; *þú getur því
nærri, að* . . . you can imagine
that. . . .

nærskyrta, -u, -ur [nair·sk₁ɪrta, -ɣ(r̥)]
wf.1 undershirt; (for women) vest,
chemise.

nærsveitir [nair·svei·tʰɪr̥, -svei·dɪr] f.2
surrounding country, districts of
the vicinity.

næst [nais·t] adv. (n. of *næstur*)
nearest, next; *þar næst* next to
that, thereupon, = *því næst*.

næsta, -u [nais·ta, -ɣ] wf.1 *á næstunni*
in the nearest future, in the immediate future.

næstelztur, -elzt, -elzt [nais·tɛlstɣr̥,
-ɛlst] adj. next in age below.

næstkomandi [nais·tkʰɔ·mandɪ] adj.
next.

næstum [nais·tɣm] adv. almost,
= *næstum því*.

næstur, næst, næst [nais·t, -ɣr̥] adj.
superl. (of *nærri*) nearest, next;
til næsta bæjar to the next farmstead; *hver er sjálfum sér næstur*
'each is his own neighbor,' everyone
for himself.

nætur, see *nátt, nótt*.

næturklúbbur, -s, -ar [nai:tʰɣr·
kʰlub:ɣr̥, -kʰlub·s, -kʰlub:ar; nai:-
dɣr̥·] m.1 night club.

næturlæknir, -is, -ar [nai:tʰɣr-laiʰk·-
nɪr̥, -ɪs, -ar̥; nai:dɣr̥·] m.1 'night
doctor,' a physician who is on duty
all night.

nætursakir [nai:tʰɣr·sa:k₁ʰɪr̥, nai:-
dɣr̥·sa:g̊₁ɪr̥] adv. over night, for a
night; *vera (um) nætursakir einhvers staðar* stay over night somewhere.

næturvörður, -varðar, -verðir [nai:-
tʰɣr·vör·ðɣr̥, -var·ðar̥, -vɛr·ðɪr̥;
nai:dɣr·] m.3 night watchman.

nöfn, see *nafn*.

nögl, naglar, neglur [nög̊·l, nag̊·lar̥,
nɛg̊·lɣr̥] f.3 nail (finger- toe-).

nöri, see *núa*.

nös, nasar, nasir [nö:s, na:sar̥, -ɪr̥]
f.2 nostril.

O.

o, ó [ɔ:, ou:] interj. oh; *o jæja* well;
oh, why.

ó- [ou:-] negative pref. un-, in-.

óalandi [ou:a·landɪ] adj. (pr. p.) not
tó be fed.

óbrúaður, -uð, -að [ou:bru·aðɣr̥, -ɣð,
-að] adj. (pp.) unbridged.

óbyggð, -ar, -ir [ou:bɪqð, -ðar̥, -ðɪr̥;
-bɪg̊þ] f.2 often in pl. uninhabited
parts, wilderness, the interior (of
the country).

óbyggður, -byggð, -byggt [ou:bɪqðɣr̥,
-bɪqð, -bɪxt; -bɪg̊ð-, bɪg̊þ] adj. uninhabited, unsettled.

óð, -um, see *vaða*.

óðar, óðara [ou:ðar̥, -ara] adv. (compar. of *óður*) at once; *óðar(a) en*
conj. sooner than, as soon as (S.
VIII, 3(h)).

oddi, -a, -ar [ɔd:ɪ, -a(r̥)] wm.1 a
tongue-shaped spit of land between
rivers (or jutting out into a river,
or a lake, or the sea); *Oddi* a
famous parsonage in the South of
Iceland, seat of a fine school in the
twelfth century; home of *Sæmundur
fróði*.

Óðinn, -ins [ou:ðɪn, -ɪns] m.1 Odin,
chief of the gods in Old Icelandic
mythology.

óðinshani, -a, -ar [ou:ðɪns-ha:nɪ,
-a(r̥)] wm.1 'Odin's cock,' phalarope.

ódýr, -dýrt, -dýrt [ou:di·r, -dɪrt] adj.
cheap, inexpensive.

1. of [ɔ:v, ɔv·, ɔf·] adv. too, too much;
of snemma too early; *það er ýmist
of eða van* it is either too much or
too little.

2. of- [ɔ:v-, ɔv·-] pref. too.

óf, -um, ofið, -inn, see *vefa*.

ofan [ɔ:van, ɔ:n-] (Pr. 4, *3*; In. IV,
1, 3) (1) adv. from above, down,
downstairs; *fara ofan* go downstairs; *taka ofan* take off the hat;
(2) with preps: *ofan á (oná)* on

Vowels: *a* [a] approx. father; *á* [au] cow; *e* [ɛ] set; *é* [jɛ] yes; *i, y* [ɪ] sit; *í, ý* [i] feel;
o [ɔ] law; *ó* [ou] note; *u* [ɣ] approx. Germ. Mütter; *ú* [u] school; *y* = *i*; *ý* = *í*; *æ* [ai] ice;
ö [ö] Germ. hören; *au* [öy] French *feuille*; *ei, ey* [ei] ale. Length [:]; half-length [·].

418

top; *ofan á e-u* on top of sth; *ofan á e-ð* down on (to) sth; *ofan að (onað) e-u* down to sth; *ofan af (onaf) e-u* from the top of sth; *ofan fyrir e-ð* down below sth (motion); *fyrir ofan e-ð* above sth (rest); *ofan hjá e-u* down by sth; *ofan í (oní) e-ð* down into sth; *ofan með e-u* down along sth; *ofan um (onum) e-ð* down through sth; *ofan yfir (onyfir) heiði* down across the heath (mountain); (3) prep. with acc. *ofan fjallið, dalinn* down the mountain, the valley (S. I, **2**, **3**, 3); (4) prep. with gen. *ofan sjávar* (also a compound: *ofan-sjávar*) on or above the surface of the sea, afloat.

ofát, -s [ɔ:vau·tʰ(s), -au·d̥] n. over-eating.

ofdrykkja, -u [ɔv·drɪʰkⱼ·a, -ᵇkⱼ·ʏ] wf.1 intemperance.

óferjandi [ou:fɛr·jand̥ɪ] adj. (pr.p.) not to be ferried.

oféta, -ét, -át, -átum, -étinn (-ið) [ɔv·je·tʰa, -je·tʰ, -au·tʰ, -au·tʰʏm, -je·tʰɪn, -ɪð; -je·d̥·, -au·d̥·] v.5 eat too much; *oféta sig* overeat (oneself); *o. sig á* over indulge in.

offra, -aði, -að [ɔf:ra, -aðɪ, -að] wv.4 sacrifice.

o. fl. = *og fleira.*

ófreskja, -u, -ur [ou:frɛskⱼa, -kⱼʏ(r̥)] wf.1 monster.

ófriðaður, -uð, -að [ou:frɪ:ðaðʏr̥, -ʏð, -að] adj. (pp.) unprotected.

ófriður, -ar [ou:frɪ·ðʏr̥, -ar̥] m.3 war; disturbance(s).

ófríður, -fríð, -frítt [ou:fri:ðʏr̥, -fri:ð, -friʰt:] adj. ugly (opposite to *fríður* beautiful).

ofsaga, -sögu, -ur [ɔf·sa·qa, -sö·qʏ(r̥)] wf.1 only in: *ekki er ofsögum af því sagt* the stories (descriptions, etc.) of that are not exaggerated.

ofsi, -a [ɔf·sɪ, -a] wm.1 violence, impetuosity.

oft [ɔf·t] adv. often, frequently; *oftast* most often, usually.

ófúinn, -in, -ið; -fúnari, -astur [ou:- fu:ɪn, -ɪn, -ɪð, -fu:narɪ, -astʏr̥] adj. not rotted, not spoiled by rot; whole, sound.

ófullgerður, -gerð, -gert (-gjörður) [ou:fʏd̥l·g̊ⱼɛr·ðʏr̥, -g̊ⱼɛr·ð, -g̊ⱼɛr̥·t; -g̊ⱼör·ðʏr̥] adj. (pp.) incomplete, unfinished.

ófær, -fær, -fært [ou:fai·r, -fair̥t] adj. impassable; *áin er ófær hestum* the river is impassable (unfordable) for horses.

ófæra, -u, -ur [ou:fai·ra, -ʏ(r̥)] wf.1 an impassable place; often in place names: *Ófæra* 'Impasse,' *Ófærufoss* 'Impasse Falls,' *Ófærugil* 'Impassable Gorge.'

1. og [ɔ:g̊, ɔ:, ɔ] (Pr. **4**, **2**; S. VI, 9, *4*, 7; VIII, 2) (1) conj. and, as; *bæði . . . og* both . . . and; *sami . . . og* same . . . as; plus: *tveir og tveir eru fjórir* 2 + 2 = 4; (2) adv. also, too (= *einnig*).

2. og [ɔ:, ɔ] interj. = *o*, oh; *og sussu nei!* oh, no, no! *og vertu ekki að þessu!* oh, leave off, if you please!

óg, -um, see *vega.*

ógangur, -s [ou:g̊auŋg̊ʏr̥, -g̊auŋs] m.1 noise, racket.

ógleðjast, -gladdist, -glaðzt [ou:g̊lɛð·jast, -g̊lad̥·ɪst, -g̊laðst] wv.1 (only middle voice) get sad, get downcast; lose heart, flag in spirit.

ógn, -ar, -ir [ou̯g̊·n̥, -nar̥, -nɪr̥] f.2 terror, fear; a terrible thing.

ógna(r)stór, -stór, -stórt [ou̯g̊·na(r̥)- stou:r, -stour̥·t] adj. awfully big.

ógrynni, -s [ou:g̊rɪn·ɪ(s)] n. plenty; *ógrynni fjár* immeasurable wealth (S. I, 4, 2, 5).

óhamingja, -u [ou:ha·miŋg̊ⱼa, -g̊ⱼʏ] wf.1 bad luck; *til allrar óhamingju* unfortunately.

óhapp, -s, -höpp [ou:haʰp·(s), -höʰp·] n. bad luck, misfortune, accident.

óhentugur [ou:hɛntʰʏqʏr̥; -hɛntʏqʏr̥] adj. (see *-ugur*) unsuited, unsuitable; awkward, impractical.

óheppinn, -in, -ið; óheppnari, -astur [ou:heʰp·ɪn, -ɪn, -ɪð, -heʰp·narɪ,

---

Consonants: [ð] brea*th*e; [g] *g*ood; [gⱼ] *gy*arden (garden); [hw̥] *wh*at; [j] *y*es; [kⱼ] *cy*an (can); [ŋ] thi*ng*; [q] N. Germ. sa*g*en; [r] Scottish *r*; [x] approx. Germ. a*ch*; [þ] *th*in. Voiceless: ○; [b̥, d̥, g̊] approx. *p, t, k.* Half-voiced: *italics.* Aspiration and preaspiration: [ʰ]; [pʰ, tʰ, kʰ] *p-, t-, k-.* Others as in English.

-astʏr̥] adj. unlucky, having bad
luck.
óhlýðinn, -in, -ið; óhlýðnari, -astur
[ou:hli·ðɪn, -ɪn, -ɪð, -hliðnarɪ,
-astʏr̥] adj. disobedient; óhlýðinn
e-m, óhlýðinn við e-n disobedient to
sbdy.
óhreinindi [ou:hr̥ei·nɪndɪ] n.pl. dirt.
óhreinn, -hrein, -hreint; óhreinni,
-hreinastur [ou:hr̥eidn, -hr̥ei·n,
-hr̥eintʰ; -hr̥eint; ou:hr̥eidnɪ, -hr̥ei·-
nastʏr̥] adj. dirty, unclean.
óhultur, -hult, -hult [ou:hʏltʏr̥,
-hʏlt] adj. safe (ó. fyrir safe from).
óhættur, -hætt, -hætt [ou:haiʰt·ʏr̥,
-haiʰt·] adj. safe; e-m er óhætt sbdy
is safe, it is safe for sbdy.
óhöpp, see óhapp.
ók, -um, see aka.
ókenndur, -kennd,-kennt [ou:kʲʰendʏr̥,
-kʲʰend, -kʲʰentʰ; -kʲʰent] adj. (pp.)
unknown.
ókennilegur [ou:kʲʰen·ɪ-le:qʏr̥] adj.
(see -legur) unrecognizable, unknown; strange.
ókeypis [ou:kʲʰei·pʰɪs, -kʲʰei·bɪs] adv.
free, gratuitous.
okkar, gen. pl. of ég; of us; einn
okkar one of us.
okkur, dat. pl. of ég; us.
okt. =
október [ɔx·toube·r] m.indecl. October.
ókunnugur [ou:kʰʏn·ʏqʏr̥] adj. (see
-ugur) unfamiliar, strange; ég er
ókunnugur hér I am a stranger
here; bréf til ókunnugs manns
letter to a stranger, a formal letter;
ókunnugir strangers.
okur, (-ri), -urs [ɔ:kʰʏr̥(s), ɔ:kʰrɪ;
ɔ:g̊ʏr̥, ɔ:g̊rɪ] n. usury.
ókurteis, -eis, -eist [ou:kʰʏr̥tei·s,
-eist] adj. impolite, rude.
ókurteisi [ou:kʰʏr̥tei·sɪ] wf.2 im-
politeness, rudeness.
ól, -um, see ala.
Ólafur, -s, -ar [ou:la·vʏr̥, -lafs, -la·var̥]
m.1 pers.name: Olaf, Olav; patronymic: Ólafsson, -dóttir.
óláta, see ólæti.

óli, -a [ou:lɪ, -a] wm.1 pet name for
Ólafur; also pers. name.
olía, -u, -ur [ɔ:li·ja, -ʏ(r̥)] wf.1 oil,
petroleum (= steinolía), kerosene;
motor oil (= mótor olía).
ólíkur, -lík, -líkt [ou:li·kʰʏr̥, -li·kʰ,
-lixt; -li·g̊(ʏr̥)] adj. unlike, dissimilar; það var ekki ólíkt honum
it was not unlike him (litotes: it
was just like him, it was just what
you could expect from him).
olíuföt, -fata [ɔ:li·jʏ-fö:tʰ; -fa:tʰa;
-fö:d, -fa:da] n.pl. oilskin.
olla, olli, ollað (pret. subj. ylli) [ɔd·la,
ɔd·lɪ, ɔd·lað, ɪd·lɪ] wv.3 (irreg.)
cause (= valda) (In. VII, 3, 4,
5 (d)).
olli, see valda.
ollið, -inn, see vella.
ólmur, ólm, ólmt [oul·mʏr̥, oul·m,
oulmtʰ; oulmt] adj. mad, eager,
raging.
olnbogi, -a, -ar [ɔl·bɔi·jɪ, ·bɔ:qa(r̥);
ɔl·n-] wm.1 elbow.
óloft, -s [ou:lɔft(s)] n. bad, polluted
air.
oltið, -inn, see l. velta.
ólyginn, -in, -ið; -lygnari, -astur
[ou:lɪi·jɪn, -ɪn, -ɪð; -li·jɪn; -lɪ·jɪn;
-lig̊·narɪ, -astʏr̥] adj. unlying,
truthful.
ólæti, -láta [ou:lai·tʰɪ, -lau·tʰa; -lai·dɪ,
-lau·da] n.pl. noise, racket, trouble.
Ólöf, -lafar [ou:lö·v, -la·var̥] f.1 pers.
name.
ómengaður, -uð, -að [ou:meiŋ·gaðʏr̥,
-ʏð, -að] adj. unmixed.
o. m. fl. = og margt fleira and many
other things.
ómissandi [ou:mɪs·andɪ] adj. (pr.p.)
indispensable.
ómótt [ou:mouʰt·] adj. n. only in:
vera ómótt (with dat.) be indisposed, feel weary, exhausted.
ómögulega [ou:mö·qʏ-le:qa] adv. im-
possibly, by no means.
ómögulegur [ou:mö·qʏ-le:qʏr̥] adj.
(see -legur) impossible, not possible.
oná [ɔ:nau·] (Pr. 4, 3) = ofan á, see
ofan.

Vowels: a [a] approx. father; á [au] cow; e [ɛ] set; é [jɛ] yes; i, y [ɪ] sit; í, ý [i] feel;
o [ɔ] law; ó [ou] note; u [ʏ] approx. Germ. Mütter; ú [u] school; y = i; ý = í; æ [ai] ice;
ö [ö] Germ. hören; au [öy] French feuille; ei, ey [ei] ale. Length [:]; half-length [·].

ónáð, -ar [ou:nau·ð̥, -ðar̥] f.2 disgrace, lack of favor.

ónáða, -aði, -að(ur) [ou:nau·ða, -aðɪ, -að̥, -aðɣr̥] wv.4 ónáða e-n disturb sbdy.

oní [ɔ:ni·] (Pr. 4, 3) = ofan í, see ofan.

onum [ɔ:nɣm] (Pr. 4, 3) = ofan um, see ofan.

onyfir [ɔ:nɪ·vɪr̥] (Pr. 4, 3) = ofan yfir, see ofan.

ónýti, -s [ou:ni·tʰɪ(s); -ni·dɪ(s)] n. a useless thing; only in: til ónýtis in vain, to no purpose; fara til ónýtis be spoiled.

ónæði, -s, - [ou:nai·ðɪ(s)] n. trouble, inconvenience, disturbance.

ónæðissamur, -söm, -samt [ou:nai·-ðɪ(s)-sa:mɣr̥,-sö:m,-sam·tʰ;-sam̥·t] adj. full of disturbances, not quiet; noisy.

opinber, -ber, -bert [ɔ:pʰɪn-bɛ:r, -bɛr̥·t; ɔ:bɪn-] adj. public.

opinbera, -aði, -að(ur) [ɔ:pʰɪn-bɛ:ra, -aðɪ, -að̥, -aðɣr̥; ɔ:bɪn-] wv.4 make public, announce, reveal; opinbera trúlofun sína announce one's betrothal.

opinn, -in, -ið [ɔ:pʰɪn, -ɪn, -ɪð̥; ɔ:bɪn] adj.open; standa opinn be,stay open.

opna, -aði, -að(ur) [ɔʰp·na, -aðɪ, -að̥, aðɣr̥] wv.4 open; opna hurðina open the door; opna sýningu open an exhibition, open a show; opnast be opened.

óráðandi [ou:rau·ðandɪ] adj. (pr. p.) óráðandi nokkrum bjargráðum not to be helped in any way (by helpful advice).

óragur, -rög, -ragt [ou:ra·qɣr̥, -rö·q, -raxt] adj. brave, not cowardly, courageous.

orð, -s, - [ɔr·ð̥, ɔrð̥s] n. word; hafa orð á e-u mention sth, make a remark about sth; í orði kveðnu in name, on paper, in theory; með öðrum orðum (m. ö. o.) in other words.

orðabók, -ar, -bækur [ɔr·ða-bou:kʰ, -ar̥, -bai:kʰɣr̥; -bou:g̊, -bai:g̊ɣr̥] f.3 dictionary.

orðið, -inn, see verða.

1. óreiður, -reið, -reitt [ou:rei·ðɣr̥, -rei·ð̥, -reiʰt·] adj. not angry.

2. óreiður, -reið, -reitt [ou:rei·ðɣr̥, -rei·ð̥, -reiʰt·] adj. impassable on horseback; unfordable; áin er óreið og svo mikil, að hún flæðir yfir alla bakka the river is unfordable and so swollen that it floods all its banks.

organ, -s, -ön [ɔr·g̊an, -ans, -ön] n. organ.

organleikari, -a, -ar [ɔr·g̊an-lei:kʰarɪ, -a(r̥); -lei:g̊arɪ] wm.1 organist, organ player.

orgel, -s, - [ɔr·g̊ɛl, -ɛls] n. organ; small organ for the home.

1. orka, -u [ɔr·ka, -ɣ] wf.1 power, force, strength.

2. orka, -aði, -að [ɔr·ka, -aðɪ, -að̥] wv.4 orka e-u be able (have strength) to do a thing.

orpið, -inn, see 1. verpa.

orsök, -sakar, -ir [ɔr·sö·kʰ, -sa·kʰar, -sa·kˌɪr̥] f.2 cause, reason; orsök til e-s reason why (sth happens).

ort, -i, -ur, see yrkja.

orusta, -u, -ur [ɔ:rɣsta, -ɣ(r̥)] wf.1 battle, fight.

orustuskip, -s, - [ɔ:rɣstɣ-skˌɪ:pʰ, -skˌɪf·s; -skˌɪ:b] n. battleship.

orustuflugvél, -ar, -ar [ɔ:rɣstɣ-flɣq·-vje·l, -lar̥] f.1 fighter (airplane).

óræktaður, -uð, -að [ou:raixtaðɣr̥, -ɣð̥, -að̥] adj. (pp.) uncultivated (soil).

órög, see óragur.

ós, óss, ósar [ou:s, ous:, ou:sar̥] m.1 estuary, mouth of a river or a lake; verpti fyrir ós Grímsár the estuary of G. got dammed up.

óseyddur, -seydd, -seytt [ou:seid·ɣr̥, -seid·, -seiʰt·] adj. (pp.) not baked (or cooked) long.

o. s. frv. = og svo framvegis and so forth, etc.

ósigrandi [ou:sɪqrandɪ] adj. (pr. p.) invincible.

ósk, -ar, -ir [ous·k, -ar̥, ous·kˌɪr̥] f.2 wish.

421

óska, -aði, -að [ous·ka, -aðɪ, -að] wv.4
wish; *óska eftir e-u* wish for sth,
want sth (= *óska e-s*); *óska e-m e-s*
wish sbdy sth; *óskast* be wanted,
be desired; *óskandi væri* it is to
be hoped (S. VI, 12, 1, 3).

Óskar, -s [ous·kar̥(s)] m.l pers. name.

óskyldur, -skyld, -skylt [ou:sk₁ɪldɪr̥,
-sk₁ɪld, -sk₁ɪlt] adj. un-related, not
related to (*óskyldur e-m*).

ósköp [ou:skö·pʰ, ous·kɪpʰ, ous·kʏ;
ou:skö·b̥, etc.] n.pl. literally: evil
fate; used as an adv.: very; awfully, frightfully, terribly.

ósnortinn, -in, -ið [ou:snɔrtɪn, -ɪn, -ɪð]
adj. (pp.) untouched.

oss, honorific acc. and dat. of *ég*; us.

ostur, -s, -ar [ɔs·tɪr̥, ɔsts, ɔs·tar̥] m.l
cheese.

ósvinna, -u [ou:svɪn·a, -ʏ] wf.1 ill-
breeding, rudeness.

ósýrður, -sýrð, -sýrt [ou:sirðʏr̥, -sirð,
-sirt] adj. (pp.) unleavened.

ótal [ou:tʰa·l] n. used as adj., but
indecl. innumerable (multitude);
ótal æfintýri innumerable folk tales
(*märchen*).

ótíður, -tíð, -títt [ou:tʰi·ðʏr̥, -tʰi·ð,
-tʰiʰt·] adj. infrequent; *ekki ótíður*
(litotes) not infrequent = quite
frequent.

ótraustur, -traust, -traust [ou:tʰröys-
t(ʏr̥)] adj. unsafe, weak.

ótrúlega [ou:tʰru·le·qa] adv. un-
believably, incredibly.

ótrúlegur [ou:tʰru·le·qʏr̥] adj. (see
-*legur*] unbelievable, incredible.

ótryggur, -trygg, -tryggt [ou:tʰrɪg̊·ʏr̥,
-tʰrɪg̊·, -tʰrɪx·t] adj. treacherous,
unsafe.

ótta, -u, -ur [ouʰt:a, -ʏ(r̥)] wf.1 three
o'clock in the morning.

óttast, -aðist, -azt [ouʰt:ast, -aðɪst,
-ast] wv.4 (middle voice only) fear;
óttast e-n (*e-ð*) fear sbdy (sth);
óttast um e-n fear for sbdy (S. VI,
4, 3; 7, 5).

ótti, -a [ouʰt:ɪ, -a] wm.1 fear; *ótti
drottins* fear of God (S. I, 4, 2, 6).

óvanalegur [ou:va·na·le·qʏr̥] adj. (see

-*legur*) unusual; adv. -*lega* unusually.

óvani, -a [ou:va·nɪ, -a] wm.l bad
habit.

óvanur, -vön, -vant [ou:va·nʏr̥, -vö·n,
-vantʰ; -vant] adj. unused to;
óvanur e-u, *óvanur við e-ð* not used
to sth.

óvarkár, -kár, -kárt [ou:var̥·kʰau·r,
-kʰaur̥t] adj. careless, incautious,
unwary.

óvarkárni [ou:var̥kʰaurḍnɪ] wf.2 care-
lessness, imprudence.

óveður, (-ri), -urs, -ur [ou:ve·ðʏr̥(s),
-veðrɪ] n. bad weather, storm,
blizzard.

óvenjulegur [ou:venjʏ·le·qʏr̥] adj.
(see -*legur*) unusual; adv. -*lega*
unusually.

óvinur, -ar, -ir [ou:vɪ·nʏr̥, -ar̥, -ɪr̥]
m.3 enemy.

óx, see *vaxa*.

óþarfi, -a [ou:þarvɪ, -a] wm.1 something not necessary, not needed;
something superfluous; article(s)
of luxury; extravagance.

óþarfur, -þörf, -þarft [ou:þarvʏr̥,
-þörv, -þar̥(f)t] adj. needless, useless, superfluous; *sá er ekki óþarfur*
(litotes) he is not quite useless (or
rather the opposite); *vera óþarfur
e-m* be not useful to sbdy (litotes:
be very inconvenient, harmful,
damaging to sbdy).

óþekktur, -þekkt, -þekkt [ou:þextʏr̥,
-þext] adj. unknown.

óþveginn, -in, -ið [ou:þvei·jɪn, -ɪn,
-ɪð] adj. (pp.) unwashed; unflat-
tering, uncomplimentary.

óþægur, -þæg, -þægt [ou:þai·qʏr̥,
-þai·q, -þaixt] adj. naughty, unruly.

P.

pabbi, -a, -ar [pʰab̥:ɪ, -a, -ar̥] wm.1
daddy, father.

pakki, -a, -ar [pʰaʰk̥ɪ:ɪ, -ʰk̥:a(r̥)] wm.1
packet, package.

Páll, -s, -ar [pʰaud̥·l, pʰaul·s, pʰau:-
lar̥] m.l Paul.

Vowels: *a* [a] approx. father; *á* [au] cow; *e* [ɛ] set; *é* [jɛ] yes; *i, y* [ɪ] sit; *í, ý* [i] feel;
o [ɔ] law; *ó* [ou] note; *u* [ʏ] approx. Germ. Mütter; *ú* [u] school; *y = i*; *ý = í*; *æ* [ai] ice;
ö [ö] Germ. hören; *au* [ɵy] French feuille; *ei, ey* [ei] ale. Length [:]; half-length [·].

pallur, -s, -ar [pʰadˑlɣr̥, pʰalˑs, pʰadˑ- lar̥] m.1 loft; *sat́ á palli* was sitting in the loft.

pálmasunnudagur, -s, -ar [pʰaulˑma- sɣn:ɣdaˑqɣr̥, -daxs, -daˑqar̥] m.1 Palm Sunday.

pálmi, -a, -ar [pʰaulˑmɪ, -a(r̥)] wm.1 palm; also pers. name.

panna, pönnu, -ur [pʰan:a, pʰön:ɣ(r̥)] wf.1 pan, skillet, frying pan.

panta, -aði, -að(ur) [pʰanˑtʰa, -aðɪ, -að, -aðɣr̥; pʰanˑta] wv.4 order.

partur, -s, -ar [pʰar̥ˑtɣr̥, -ar̥, pʰar̥ts] m.1 part.

páskar [pʰausˑkar̥] m.1.pl. Easter; *páskavika* Easter week.

passa, -aði, -að(ur) [pʰas:a, -aðɪ, -að, -aðɣr̥] wv.4 take care; *passa e-n* take care of sbdy; fit: *fötin passa mér* the suit of clothes fits me.

Passíusálmar [pʰas:iˑjɣ-saulˑmar̥] m. 1.pl. Passion Psalms; *Passíusálmarn- ir* the famous Passion Psalms of Hallgrímur Pétursson (1614-74), the greatest of Icelandic hymn writers.

Patreksfjörður, -fjarðar [pʰa:tʰrexs- fjörˑðɣr̥, -fjarˑðar̥; pʰa:drexs-] m.3 'Patric's Fjord.'

pd. = *pund, punda* pound.

peli, -a, -ar [pʰɛ:lɪ, -a(r̥)] wm.1 half a pint; a baby's bottle.

peningur, -s, -ar [pʰɛ:niŋg̊ɣr̥, -iŋs, -iŋg̊ar̥] m.1 coin; pl. money.

penni, -a, -ar [pʰɛn:ɪ, -a(r̥)] wm.1 pen.

pera, -u, -ur [pʰɛ:ra, -ɣ(r̥)] wf.1 pear.

pest, -ar, -ir [pʰɛsˑt, -ar̥, -ɪr̥] f.2 plague.

Pétur, (-ri), -urs [pʰjɛ:tʰɣr̥(s), pʰjɛ:- tʰrɪ; pʰjɛ:dɣr̥, pʰjɛ:drɪ] m.1 Peter.

peysa, -u, -ur [pʰei:sa, -ɣ(r̥)] wf.1 sweater; the bodice of *peysuföt.*

peysuföt, -fata [pʰei:sɣ-fö:tʰ, -fa:tʰa; -fö:d̥, -fa:da] n.pl. a national cos- tume of Icelandic women.

píanó, -s, - [pʰi:janouˑ, -ouˑs] n. piano.

píanóleikari, -a, -ar [pʰi:janouˑlei:- kʰarɪ, -a(r̥); -lei:g̊-] wm.1 pianist.

píanóundirspil, -s [pʰi:janouˑɣn- dɪr̥spɪˑl, -spɪls] n. piano accom- paniment.

pils, -, - [pʰɪlˑs] n. skirt.

piltur, -s, -ar [pʰɪlˑtɣr̥, -ar̥, pʰɪlts] m.1 boy, lad; schoolboy; farm-hand; *piltar* the boys.

pípa, -u, -ur, (-na) [pʰi:pʰa, -ɣ(r̥); pʰi:ba; pʰiʰpˑna] wf.1 pipe.

pipar, -ars [pʰɪ:pʰar̥(s); pʰɪ:bar̥] m.1 pepper.

piparkökur [pʰɪ:pʰar̥-kʰö:kʰɣr̥; pʰɪ:- bar̥-kʰö:g̊ɣr̥] wf.1.pl. pepper (gin- ger) snaps.

pípuhattur, -s, -ar [pʰi:pʰɣ-haʰt:ɣr̥, -ar̥, -haʰtˑs; pʰi:bɣ-] m.1 high hat, top hat.

pípukragi, -a, -ar [pʰi:pʰɣ-kʰrai:jɪ, -kʰʰa:qa(r̥); pʰi:bɣ-, -kʰra:jɪ] wm.1 (= *prestakragi*) clergyman's ruff.

pískur, -s, -ar [pʰis-kɣr̥, pʰisks, pʰisˑ- kar̥] m.1 = *svipa.*

pistill, -ils, -lar [pʰɪsˑtɪd̥l, -ɪls, pʰɪstˑ lar̥] m.1 epistle.

1. planta, plöntu, -ur [pʰlanˑtʰa, pʰlönˑ- tʰɣ(r̥); pʰlanˑta, pʰlönˑtɣ(r̥)] wf.1 plant, herb.

2. planta, -aði, -að(ur) [pʰlanˑtʰa, -aðɪ, -að, -aðɣr̥; pʰlanˑta] wv.4 plant.

plata, plötu, -ur [pʰla:tʰa, pʰlö:tʰɣ(r̥); pʰla:da, pʰlö:dɣr̥] wf.1 plate; (grammophone) record.

plöntu, -ur, see 1. *planta.*

plötu, -ur, see *plata.*

poki, -a, -ar [pʰɔ:kʰɪ, -kʰa(r̥); pʰɔ:- g̊ˌɪ, -g̊a(r̥)] wm.1 bag.

pólitík, -ur [pouˑlɪ-tʰi:kʰ(ɣr̥), -tʰi:- g̊(ɣr̥)] f.3 politics.

pólitískur, -tísk, -tískt [pouˑlɪ-tʰisˑ- kɣr̥, -tʰisˑk, -tʰisˑt] adj. political.

pollur, -s, -ar [pʰɔdˑlɣr̥, pʰɔdls, pʰɔdˑ- lar̥] m.1 pool, puddle, pit.

ponta, -u, -ur [pʰɔnˑtʰa, -ɣ(r̥); pʰɔnˑta] wf.1 snuff box (horn); pulpit.

port, -s, - [pʰɔr̥ˑt(s)] n. gate, narrow lane between houses, or through a house.

póstafgreiðsla, -u, -ur [pʰousˑtavgreið-

Consonants: [ð] brea*th*e; [g] *g*ood; [gɪ] *gy*arden (garden); [hw] *wh*at; [j] *y*es; [kɪ] *cy*an (can); [ŋ] thi*ng*; [q] N. Germ. sa*g*en; [r] Scottish *r*; [x] approx. Germ. a*ch*; [þ] *th*in. Voiceless: ○; [b̥, d̥, g̊] approx. *p, t, k.* Half-voiced: *italics.* Aspiration and preaspiration: [ʰ]; [pʰ, tʰ, kʰ] *p-, t-, k-.* Others as in English.

423

sla, -ʏ(r̥)] wf.1 first class post office.

póstávísun, -unar, -anir [pʰous·tau·- vi:sʏn, -ʏnar̥, -anir̥] f.2 money order; postal money order.

pósthólf, -s, - [pʰous·thoulv, -houlvs] n. post box.

pósthús, -s, - [pʰous·t(h)u·s, -hus·] n. post office.

pósthússdyr [pʰous·t(h)us·-dɪ:r] f.3. pl. door of the post office.

Pósthússstræti, -s [pʰous·t(h)us·- strai:tʰɪ(s); -strai:dɪ] n. ' Post Office Street.'

póstkassi, -a, -ar [pʰous·tkʰas·ɪ, -a (r̥)] wm.1 mailbox.

póstkrafa, -kröfu, -ur [pʰous·tkʰra·va, -kʰrö·vʏ(r̥)] wf.1 C. O. D. package.

postuli, -a, -ar [pʰɔs·tʏlɪ, -a(r̥)] wm.1 apostle.

postulín, -s [pʰɔs·tʏ-li:n, -lin·s] n. porcelain, china.

póstur, -s, -ar [pʰous·tʏr̥, -ar̥, pousts, pous:] m.1 mail; mailman; pósturinn er kominn, hann hafði mikinn póst the mailman has arrived; he had a great deal of mail.

póstþjónn, -s, -ar [pʰous·tþjoudn, -þjouns, -þjou·nar̥] m.1 post office employee.

póstþjónusta, -u [pʰous·tþjou·nʏsta, -ʏ] wf.1 postal service.

pottbrauð, -s [pʰɔʰt·bröy·ð, -bröyðs] n. homemade ryebread, baked under a pot.

pottur, -s, -ar [pʰɔʰt:ʏr̥, -ar̥, pʰɔʰt·s] m.1 pot, pan; quart (a measure); sjóða mat í potti cook food in a pot; pottur á hlóðum pot on an open fireplace; það er víða pottur brotinn (proverbial) in most places there is sth amiss (' a pot is broken '), ' it happens in the best families.'

prédika, -aði, -að [pʰrje:dɪ·kʰa, -aðɪ, -að; -dɪ·g̊a] wv.4 preach, deliver a sermon.

prédikun, -unar, -anir [pʰrje:dɪ·kʰʏn, -ʏnar̥, -anir̥; -dɪ·g̊·] f.2 sermon; flytja prédikun deliver a sermon, preach.

prédikunarstóll, -s, -ar [pʰrje:dɪ- kʰʏnar·stoud·l, -stoul·s, -stou:lar̥; -dɪ·g̊·] m.1 pulpit.

pressa, -aði, -að(ur) [pʰres:a, -aðɪ, -að, -aðʏr̥] wv.4 press; pressa föt press a suit of clothes.

prestakragi, -a, -ar [pʰres·ta·kʰrai:jɪ, -kʰra:qa(r̥); -kʰra:jɪ] wm.1 clergyman's ruff.

prestssetur, (-ri), -urs, -ur [pʰres:e·- tʰʏr̥, pʰres·tse·tʰʏr̥; -ʏr̥s, -se·tʰrɪ; -se·d·] n. parsonage.

prestsverk, -s, - [pʰres:ver̥k(s); pʰrestsver̥k] n. clerical duties, clerical rites.

prestur, -s, -ar [pʰres·tʏr̥, pʰres:, pʰres·tar̥] m.1 minister, clergyman, parson, priest.

próf, -s, - [pʰrou:v, pʰrouf·s] n. examination, test; meira próf (of chauffeurs) advanced test for driving; taka próf upp úr skóla take the final examination at a school.

prófa, -aði, -að(ur) [pʰrou:va, -aðɪ, -að, -aðʏr̥] wv.4 examine, test, try; give an examination.

prófessor, -s, -ar [pʰrou:fes:ɔr̥, -ɔr̥s, -ɔrar] m.1 professor.

prósent [pʰrou:sentʰ; -sent] adv. = af hundraði = % per cent.

prúðmenni, -s, - [pʰruð·men·ɪ(s)] n. a well mannered man, person; a gentleman.

prúðmennska, -u [pʰruð·menska, -ʏ] wf.1 good manners.

prúður, prúð, prútt [pʰru:ðʏr̥, pʰru:ð, pʰruʰt:] adj. well mannered, gentle; stately.

prýði [pʰri:ðɪ] wf.2 ornament; distinguished manner.

prýðilegur [pʰri:ðɪ·le:qʏr̥] adj. (see -legur) splendid, excellent, distinguished.

púðra, -aði, -að(ur) [pʰuð·ra, -aðɪ, -að, -aðʏr̥] wv.4 powder.

púður, (-ri), -urs [pʰu:ðʏr̥(s), pʰuð·- rɪ] n. powder; gunpowder.

pund, -s, - [pʰʏn·d, pʰʏn(d)s] n. pound (= 1.10 pd.).

Vowels: a [a] approx. father; á [au] cow; e [ɛ] set; é [jɛ] yes; i, y [ɪ] sit; í, ý [i] feel; o [ɔ] law; ó [ou] note; u [ʏ] approx. Germ. Mütter; ú [u] school; y = i; ý = í; æ [ai] ice; ö [ö] Germ. hören; au [öy] French feuille; ei, ey [ei] ale. Length [:]; half-length [·].

pönnu, -ur, see *panna*.

pönnukaka,-köku,-ur [pʰön:ʏ-kʰa:kʰa, -kʰö:kʰʏ(r̥); -kʰa:g̊a, -kʰö:g̊ʏ] wf.1 Icelandic pancake.

pöntun, -unar, pantanir [pʰön·tʰʏn, -ʏnar̥, pʰan·tʰanɪr̥; pʰön·tʏn, pʰan̥·tanɪr̥] f.2 order.

pyttur, -s, -ir [pʰɪʰt:ʏr̥, -ɪr̥, pʰɪʰt·s] m.2 pit, pool.

R.

rabarbaragrautur, -ar, -ar [ra:barba·-ra-gröy:tʰʏr̥, -ar̥; -gröy:d̥ʏr̥] m.1 rhubarb sago or potato starch pudding.

rabarbarasúpa, -u, -ur [ra:barba·ra-su:pʰa, -ʏ(r̥); -su:b̥a] wf.1 rhubarb soup.

rabarbari, -a [ra:barba:rɪ, -a] wm.1 rhubarb.

rabba, -aði, -að [rab̥:a, -aðɪ, -að] wv.4 talk, chat, prate; *rabba saman* talk (to each other), discuss things.

ráð, -s, - [rau:ð, rauð·s] n. counsel, advice; means, expedient; plan, design; condition, way of life; *gera ráð fyrir e-u* plan sth; *gera ráð fyrir að byrja* plan to begin, expect to begin; *leita ráða hjá e-m (e-s)* seek one's advice; *hvað á nú til ráðs (or bragðs) að taka?* what is now to be done? *fylgja ráðum e-s* follow one's advice.

ráða, ræð, réð (réði), réðum, ráðinn (-ið) [rau:ða, rai:ð, rje:ð, rje:ðɪ, rje:ðʏm, rau:ðm, -ɪð] v.7 (pret. *réði* according to wv.1) advise, counsel; resolve, decide; rule, wield, have power over; have one's way; (1) *ráða e-m e-ð* advise sbdy (to do) sth; *þeir réðu það með sér* they decided (that) among themselves (S. IV, 2, 2); *ráða e-u* have one's way about sth; *þú ræður því* (you can) do as you please; *ráða sér ekki fyrir fögnuði* be beside oneself with joy; *ráða sér ekki fyrir stormi* hardly to be able to stand on one's feet for the storm;

(2) with preps and advs: *ráða (e-ð) af e-u* guess, conclude (sth) from sth; *ráða e-ð af* decide sth; *ráða fyrir landi* govern, rule a realm; *ráða við e-n (or e-ð)* be able to manage sbdy (or sth); (3) auxiliary: *ræður syngja = syngur* does sing (poetical) (S. VI, 13, 11).

ráðagerð, -ar, -ir [rau:ða-g̊ˌer·ð, -ðar̥, -ðɪr̥] f.2 plan, planning.

raðar, -ir, see *röð*.

raddar, -ir, see *rödd*.

ráðgera, -gerði, -gerður (-gert); (-gjöra, etc.) [rauð·g̊ˌe·ra, -gjerðɪ, -ʏr̥, -g̊ˌer̥t; -g̊ˌö·ra, etc.] wv.2 project, plan; *ráðgera e-ð* plan sth = *gera ráð fyrir e-u.*

ráðgjafi, -a, -ar [rauð·g̊ˌa·vɪ, -a(r̥)] wm.1 counselor, minister.

ráðherra, -, -ar [rau:ðher·a, -ar̥] wm.1 cabinet or government minister; *forsætis-ráðherra* premier, prime minister; *dómsmála-ráðherra* attorney general; *kirkjumála-ráðherra* minister of public worship; *kennslu-mála-ráðherra* minister of education; *atvinnumála-ráðherra* minister of industry; *fjármála-ráðherra* minister of finance; *utanríkismála-ráðherra* minister of foreign affairs.

radísa, -u, -ur [ra:di·sa, -ʏ(r̥)] wf.1 radish.

ráðleggja, -lagði, -lagt [rauð·leg̊ˌ·a, -laqðɪ, -laxt] wv.1 advise; *ráðleggja e-m e-ð* advise sbdy (to do) sth.

ráðunautur, -s, -ar [rau:ðʏ-nöy:tʰʏr̥, -s, -nöy:tʰar̥; -nöy:d̥·] m.1 adviser; expert.

ráðuneyti, -s, - [rau:ðʏ-nei:tʰɪ(s); -nei:dɪ] n. ministry, department; *fjármálaráðuneyti* ministry of finance, treasury department.

ráðvandur, -vönd, -vant [rauð·vandʏr̥, -vönd̥, -vantʰ; -vant̥] adj. honest.

raf, rafs [ra:v, raf·s] n. amber; Latin *electrum.*

ráfa, -aði, -að [rau:va, -aðɪ, -að] wv.1 wander (aimlessly), stroll, loiter.

Consonants: [ð] brea*th*e; [g] *g*ood; [gˌ] *gy*arden (garden); [hʍ] *wh*at; [j] *y*es; [kˌ] *cy*an (can); [ŋ] thi*ng*; [q] N. Germ. sa*g*en; [r] Scottish *r*; [x] approx. Germ. a*ch*; [þ] *th*in. Voiceless: ○; [b̥, d̥, g̊] approx. *p, t, k.* Half-voiced: *italics.* Aspiration and preaspiration: [ʰ]; [pʰ, tʰ, kʰ] *p-, t-, k-.* Others as in English.

rafeldavél, -ar, -ar [ra:v-ɛl·davje·l, -laṟ] f.1 electric stove.

rafeldstó, -stó(a)r, -stór [ra:veldstou·, -stou·aṟ, -stou·r] f.1 electric stove.

rafljós, -s, - [rav·ljou·s, -ljous·] n. electric light.

rafljósakróna, -u, -ur [rav·ljou·sa- kʰrou:na, -ɣ(ṟ)] wf.1 electric chandelier.

rafmagn, -s [ram:aǥn, ram:ax·s; rav·maǥn(s)] n. electricity.

rafmagnseldavél, -ar, -ar [ram:axs- el·davje:l, -laṟ] f.1 electric stove.

raforka, -u [ra:vɔrka, -ɣ] wf.1 elec- tric power, electricity; ganga fyrir raforku go by electric power.

rafstó, -stó(a)r, -stór [raf·stou·(aṟ), -stou·r] f.1 electric stove.

Ragnheiður, -ar [raǥ·ŋhei·ðɣṟ, -aṟ] f.1 pers. name.

Ragnhildur, -ar [rag·nhɪldɣṟ, -aṟ] f.1 pers. name; Ragnild.

ragur, rög, ragt [ra:qɣṟ, rö:q, rax·t] adj. cowardly.

rak, rákum, see reka.

1. raka, -aði, -að(ur) [ra:kʰa, -aðɪ, -að, -aðɣṟ; ra:ǥa] wv.4 rake; shave; scrape together; raka dreifar re- rake, rake up the remnants of the hay; raka sig shave (oneself); raka af sér skeggið shave off one's beard.

2. raka, see rök.

rakáhöld, -halda [ra:kʰau·höl·d, -hal· da; ra:ǥ-] n.pl. shaving kit (outfit).

rakari, -a, -ar [ra:kʰarɪ, -a, -aṟ; ra:ǥ-] wm.1 barber.

rakarastofa, -u, -ur [ra:kʰara-stɔ:va, -ɣ(ṟ); ra:ǥara-] wf.1 barber shop.

rakbursti, -a, -ar [ra:kʰbɣ(ṟ)stɪ, -a(ṟ); ra:ǥ-] wm.1 shaving brush.

rakhnífur, -s, -ar [ra:khnı·vɣṟ, -hnıfs, -hni·vaṟ; ra:ǥ-] m.1 razor.

raksápa, -u, -ur [ra:kʰsau·pʰa, -ɣ(ṟ); ra:ǥsau·ba] wf.1 shaving cream.

rakstur, -urs (-rar) [raxstɣṟ(s), raxs- traṟ] m.1 raking of hay; shave.

rakvél, -ar, -ar [ra:kʰvje·l, -laṟ; ra:ǥ-] f.1 safety razor.

rammgöldróttur, -ótt, -ótt[ram:göl·-

drouʰt·ɣṟ, -ouʰt·] adj. full of wizardry, full of witchcraft.

rammur, römm, rammt [ram:ɣṟ, röm:, ram·tʰ; ram̦·t] adj. strong; pungent.

rán, -s, - [rau:n, raun·s] n. robbery.

Rán, -ar [rau:n, -naṟ] f.2 goddess of the sea in Old Icel. myths.

Ránargata, -götu [rau:nar-ga:tʰa, -gö:tʰɣ; -ga:da, -gö:dɣ] wf.1 street in Reykjavík.

ránfugl, -s, -ar [raun·fɣǥl(s), -fɣqls, -fɣǥlaṟ] m.1 bird of prey.

Rangá, -ár, -ár [rauŋ·ǥau·(r)] f.1 'Rib River' (?).

Rangárvellir, -valla [rauŋ·ǥaur-ved·lɪṟ, -vad·la] m.3.pl. 'Plains of Rangá.'

rangur, röng, rangt [rauŋ·ǥɣṟ, röyŋ·ǥ, rauŋ·tʰ; rauŋ·t] adj. wrong; mis- taken; með réttu eða röngu with right or wrong (S. III, 3, 2).

rann, see 2. renna.

Rannveig, -ar [ran:vei·q, -qaṟ] f.1 pers. name.

rányrkja, -u [rau:nɪrk̦a, -k̦ɣ] wf.1 exploitation.

rata, -aði, -að [ra:tʰa, -aðɪ, -að; ra:- da] wv.4 find one's way; rata í ógæfu meet with misfortune.

rauðgrautur, -ar [röyð·gröy·tʰɣṟ, -aṟ; -gröy·dɣṟ] m.1 red sago or potato starch pudding, Danish dessert.

Rauðhamrar [röy:ðhamraṟ] m.1.pl. 'Red Cliffs' or 'Red Rocks.'

rauðkál, -s [röyð·kʰau·l, -kʰauls) n. red cabbage.

rauðrófa, -u, -ur [röyð·rou·(v)a, -ɣ(ṟ)] wf.1 (red) beet.

rauðspretta, -u, -ur [röyð·spreʰt·a, -ɣ(ṟ)] wf.1 (= koli, skarkoli) plaice.

rauður, rauð, rautt [röy:ðɣṟ, röy:ð, röyʰt:] adj. red; Eiríkur rauði Eric the Red.

rauf, see rjúfa.

rauk, see rjúka.

raun, -ar, -ir [röy:n, -naṟ, -nɪṟ] f.2 trial, test, experience; grief; pl. troubles, sufferings, woes.

Vowels: a [a] approx. father; á [au] cow; e [ɛ] set; é [jɛ] yes; i, y [ɪ] sit; í, ý [i] feel; o [ɔ] law; ó [ou] note; u [ɣ] approx. Germ. Mütter; ú [u] school; y = i; ý = í; æ [ai] ice; ö [ö] Germ. hören; au [öy] French feuille; ei, ey [ei] ale. Length [:]; half-length [·].

raunar [röy:naṟ] adv. (gen. of *raun*) really, indeed, in reality.

raunsær, -sæ, -sætt; -særri, -sæjastur [röyn·sai·r, -sai·, -saiʰt·, -sair·ɪ, -sai·jastʏṟ] adj. realistic.

rausn, -ar [röys·n̩, -naṟ] f.2 munificence.

rautt, see *rauður*.

réð, réði, réðum, see *ráða*.

refabú, -s, - [rɛ:va·bu:(s)] n. fox farm.

refsing, -ar, -ar [rɛf·sing̊, -aṟ] f.1 punishment.

refur, refs, refar (-ir) [rɛ:vʏṟ, rɛf·s, rɛ:vaṟ, -ɪṟ] m.1 (2) fox; fox collar.

regla, -u, -ur [rɛg̊·la, -ʏ(ṟ)] wf.1 rule, norm, code; *gera sér e-ð að reglu* make it a rule (S. IV, 1, 5(b)).

reglulegur [rɛg̊·lʏ-lɛ:qʏṟ] adj. (see *-legur*) regular.

reglusamur, -söm, -samt [rɛg̊·lʏ-sa:mʏṟ, -sö:m, -sam·tʰ; -sam̩·t] adj. orderly.

reglusemi [rɛg̊·lʏ-sɛ:mɪ] wf.2 orderliness, regularity.

regn, -s, - [rɛg̊·n̩(s)] n. rain.

regnfrakki, -a, -ar [rɛg̊·nfraʰkɟ·ɪ, -fraʰk·a(ṟ)] wm.1 combined windbreaker and raincoat.

regnkápa, -u, -ur [rɛg̊·nkʰau·pʰa, -ʏ(ṟ); -kʰau·ba] wf.1 raincoat.

regnskúr, -ar,-iṟ or -s,-ar [rɛg̊·nsku·r, -raṟ, -rɪṟ; -skuṟs] f.2 or m.1 shower of rain.

1. reið, -ar, -ir [rei:ð, -ðaṟ, -ðɪṟ] f.2 riding; *hafa tvo* (sc. *hesta*) *til reiðar* have two riding horses; *tveggja tíma reið* a ride of two hours (S. I, 4, 2, 1).

2. reið, see *ríða*.

reiðfæri, -s, - [reið·fai·rɪ(s)] n. packsaddle (Icelandic).

reiðföt, -fata [reið·fö·tʰ, -fa·tʰa; -fö·d̩, -fa·da] n.pl. riding apparel, riding outfit.

reiðhestur, -s, -ar [rei:ðhestʏṟ, -hests, -hestaṟ] m.1 riding horse.

reiðhjól, -s, - [reið·hjou·l, -hjouls] n. = *hjól*, bicycle.

1. reiði, -a, -ar [rei:ðɪ, -a(ṟ)] m.1 rigging, tackle; crupper (of a saddle).

2. reiði [rei:ðɪ] wf.2 wrath.

reiðigjarn, -gjörn, -gjarnt [rei:ðɪ-g̊ɟad·n̩, -g̊ɟöd·n̩, -g̊ɟan·tʰ; -g̊ɟan̩·t; -g̊ɟardn̩, -g̊ɟördṇ] adj. hot-tempered, irascible.

reiðingur, -s, -ar [rei:ðing̊ʏṟ, -ins, -ingaṟ] m.1 an Icelandic packsaddle.

reiðstígvél [reið·stiq·vjɛ·l] n.pl. riding boots.

1. reiður, reið, reitt [rei:ðʏṟ, rei:ð, reiʰt:] adj. angry; *reiður e-m*, *reiður við e-n* angry at sbdy.

2. reiður, reið, reitt [rei:ðʏṟ, rei:ð, reiʰt:] adj. passable on horseback; fordable (of rivers).

reif, see *rífa*.

reik, -s [rei:kʰ(s); rei:g̊] n. fluctuation, wandering; *vera á reiki* fluctuate.

reika, -aði, -að [rei:kʰa, -aðɪ, -að; rei:g̊a] wv.4 wander around, stroll, rove.

reikna, -aði, -að(ur) [reiʰk·na, -aðɪ, -að; -aðʏṟ] wv.4 reckon, calculate, do arithmetic.

reikningur, -ings, -ingar [reiʰk·ning̊ʏṟ, -ins, -ingaṟ] m.1 arithmetic; bill: *borga reikninginn* pay the bill; *reikningur fyrir e-u* a bill for sth.

reimt [reim·tʰ; reim̩·t] adj.n. haunted; *þar varð reimt* the place became haunted.

reipi, -s, - [rei:pʰɪ(s), rei:bɪ] n. rope; especially one braided from horse hair, used for binding hay.

reis, see *rísa*.

reisa, reisti, reist(ur) [rei:sa, reis·tɪ, -ʏṟ, reis·t] wv.2 build, erect.

reist, see *rísta*.

reitt, see *reiður* 1. & 2.

reka, rek, rak, rákum, rekinn (-ið) [rɛ:kʰa, rɛ:kʰ, ra:kʰ, rau:kʰʏm, rɛ:kɟʰɪn, -ɪð; rɛ:g̊a, rɛ:g̊, ra:g̊, rau:g̊ʏm, rɛ:g̊ɟɪn, -ɪð] v.5 (1) drive; *reka hesta* drive horses; pursue, follow; run, thrust: *reka (e-ð) undir (e-ð)* run (sth) under (sth); carry on: *reka verzlun* carry on

Consonants: [ð] brea*th*e; [g] *g*ood; [gɟ] *gy*arden (garden); [hw̥] *wh*at; [j] *y*es; [kɟ] *cy*an (can); [ŋ] thi*ng*; [q] N. Germ. sa*g*en; [r] Scottish *r*; [x] approx. Germ. a*ch*; [þ] *th*in. Voiceless: o; [b̥, d̥, g̊] approx. *p, t, k*. Half-voiced: *italics*. Aspiration and preaspiration: [ʰ]; [pʰ, tʰ, kʰ] *p-, t-, k-*. Others as in English.

427

trade; (2) impersonal: *e-n* (*e-ð* (acc.)) *rekur* (*upp*) sbdy (sth) is driven ashore, sbdy (sth) drifts ashore; *skipið* (acc.) *rak á land* the ship drifted ashore (S. VI, 14, *3*(c)); *nöglina* (acc.) *rekur fram* the (finger) nail is driven forth, it falls off.

rekkja,-u,-ur,(-na)[rɛʰkʲ:a,-ʰkʲ:ʏ(r̥), rɛʰk·na] wf.1 bed.

rekstur, -urs, -rar [rɛxstʏr̥(s), rɛxs-trar̥] m.1 business, activity, production; a flock of sheep that is being driven from one place to another.

1. renna, -u, -ur [rɛn:a, -ʏ(r̥)] wf.1 gutter, course, run.

2. renna, renn, rann, runnum, runninn (-ið) [rɛn:a, rɛn:, ran:, rʏn:ʏm, rʏn:ɪn, -ıð] v.3 run; *áin rennur* the river flows; flee; melt, dissolve; *dagur rennur* day breaks; *sól rennur til viðar* the sun goes under; *renna úr* run from, drain, flow out of; *laxinn rennur* (*í ána*) the salmon run (up the river).

3. renna, renndi, renndur (rennt) [rɛn:a, rɛn·dɪ, -ʏr̥, rɛn·tʰ; rɛn·t] wv.2 let run, make run; *renna færi* run out a fishing line; *renna e-u undir e-ð* run sth under sth.

reri, réri, see *róa*.

rétt, see 2. *réttur*.

rétta, rétti, rétt(ur) [rjɛʰt:a, rjɛʰt:ɪ, -ʏr̥, rjɛʰt:] wv.2 make straight, straighten, stretch out; *rétta úr sér* stretch oneself (= *rétta sig*); *rétta upp* stretch up; *rétta e-m e-ð* hand sbdy sth, pass sbdy sth.

réttindi [rjɛʰt:ɪndɪ] n.pl. rights.

réttlátur, -lát, -látt [rjɛʰt:lau·tʰʏr̥, -lau·tʰ,-lauʰt·; -lau·d̥·] adj. righteous.

réttlæti, -s [rjɛʰt:lai·tʰɪ(s); -lai·d̥ɪ] n. justice.

réttnefni, -s, - [rjɛʰt:nɛb·nɪ(s)] n. true name, fitting term.

1. réttur, -ar, -ir [rjɛʰt:ʏr̥, -ar̥, -ɪr̥] m.3 right, law, title; court; course, dish; *ég hef rétt til að* I am en-titled to; *eiga rétt á e-u* have a right to sth.

2. réttur, rétt, rétt [rjɛʰt:ʏr̥, rjɛʰt:] adj. straight; right, correct, just, due; *á réttri leið* on the right road; *það er réttast að hætta* it is best to cease; *það mun* (*vera*) *réttast* that will be best; *rétt* adv. just, exactly; *rétt aðeins* just barely: *rétt að segja* almost.

revýa, -u, -ur [rɛ·vi·ja, -ʏ(r̥)] wf.1 revue, variety show.

Reyðarfjörður, -fjarðar [rei:ðar̥-fjör·-ðʏr̥, -fjar·ðar̥] m.3 'Whale Fjord.'

reyður, -ar, -ar [rei:ðʏr̥, -ar̥] f.1 salmon trout.

reykhús, -s, - [rei:khu·s, -hus·; rei:g̊-] n. smoke house.

reyking, -ar, -ar [rei:kʲʰiŋg̊(ar̥); rei:g̊ɪ-] f.1 smoking; *reykingar eru bannaðar hér* smoking is forbidden here.

reykingaborð, -s, - [rei:kʲʰiŋg̊a-bɔr·ð, -bɔrð̥s; rei:g̊ɪ-] n. smoking stand (table), tobacco table.

Reykir, see *reykur.*

reykja, reykti, reykt(ur) [rei:kʲʰa, reix·tɪ, -ʏr̥, reix·t; rei:g̊ɪa] wv.2 smoke; *reykja pípu* smoke a pipe; *reykja kjöt* cure meat by smoking.

Reykjanes, -s [rei:kʲʰa-nɛ:s, -nɛs:; rei:g̊ɪa-] n. 'Smoke Ness.'

Reykjavík, -ur [rei:kʲʰa-vi:kʰ(ʏr̥); rei:g̊ɪa-vi:g̊] f.3 'Smoke Bay,' the capital of Iceland; *Reykjavíkurbær* the city of R.

reyksprengja, -u, -ur [rei:kʰspreiŋg̊ɪa, -g̊ɪʏ(r̥); rei:g̊-] wf.1 smoke shell.

reyktóbak, -s [rei:kʰtʰou·bakʰ, -baxs; rei:g̊tʰou·bag̊] n. tobacco (for smoking).

reyktur, reykt, reykt [reix·tʏr̥, reix·t] adj. (pp. of *reykja*) smoked; *reyktur lax* smoked salmon.

reykur, -jar, -ir [rei:kʰʏr̥, rei:kʲʰar̥, rei:kʲʰɪr̥; rei:g̊ʏr̥, rei:g̊ɪ-] m.2 smoke; *Reykir* 'Smokes,' a place name; also in *Reykja-.*

reykvískur, -vísk, -vískt [rei:kʰviskʏr̥, -visk, -vist; rei:g̊-] adj. of Reykjavík.

Vowels: *a* [a] approx. father; *á* [au] cow; *e* [ɛ] set; *é* [jɛ] yes; *i, y* [ɪ] sit; *í, ý* [i] feel; *o* [ɔ] law; *ó* [ou] note; *u* [ʏ] approx. Germ. Mütter; *ú* [u] school; *y = i; ý = í; æ* [ai] ice; *ö* [ö] Germ. hören; *au* [öy] French feuille; *ei, ey* [ei] ale. Length [:]; half-length [·].

428

reyna, reyndi, reyndur (reynt) [rei:-
na, rein·dɪ, -Yr̥, rein·tʰ; rein̥·t] wv.2
try, endeavor; *reyna e-ð, reyna til
e-s, reyna að gera e-ð* try (to do)
sth; *reynast* prove (to be), be
proven (S. VI, **7**, *3*).

reynd, -ar [rein·d̥(ar̥)] f.2 experience,
fact; *í reynd(inni)* in (actual) fact
(opposite *í orði kveðnu*); *af eigin
sjón og reynd* by (one's) own ob-
servation; *reyndar* adv. in fact.

reyndar [rein·dar̥] adv. in fact.

reyndur, reynd, reynt [rein·dʏr̥, rein·d̥,
rein·tʰ; rein̥·t] adj. experienced.

Reynir, -is [rei:nɪr̥, -ɪs] m.1 place
name; dat. *Reyn(i)*.

ríða, ríð, reið, riðum, riðinn (-ið)
[ri:ða, ri:ð, rei:ð, rɪ:ðʏm, rɪ:ðɪn,
-ið] v.1 ride; *ríða hesti* ride a
horse; *ríða hart* ride fast; *ríða
veginn* (acc.) ride along the road;
ríða húsum ride astride the ridge
of the roof; ride the house(s) (of
spooks); *það ríður á e-u* sth is important; *mér ríður á því* it is
(very) important for me.

riddaralið, -s [rɪd̥:ara-lɪ:ð, -lɪð·s] n.
cavalry.

rífa, ríf, reif, rifum, rifinn (-ið) [ri:va,
ri:v, rei:v, rɪ:vʏm, rɪ:vɪn, -ið] v.1
tear, tear up; rend; demolish; *hann
er að rífa sig upp í norðangarra*
a stubborn blizzard (or storm) from
the north is brewing (S. VI, **14**, *3*).

riffilkúla, -u, -ur [rɪf:ɪl-kʰu:la, -ʏ(r̥)]
wf.1 rifle bullet.

riffill, -ils, -lar [rɪf:ɪd̥l̥, -ɪls, rif·lar̥]
m.1 rifle.

riffilsprengikúla, -u, -ur [rɪf:ɪl-spreiŋ·-
g̊ɪkʰu·la, -ʏ(r̥)] wf.1 rifle grenade.

rifjasteik, -ar, -ur [rɪv·ja-stei:kʰ,
-stei:g̊, -ar̥, -ʏr̥] f.3 chops, lamb
chops.

rífka, -aði, -að(ur) [rif·ka, -aðɪ, -að,
-aðʏr̥] wv.4 enlarge, extend; liber-
alize.

rifrildi, -s, - [rɪv·rɪld̥ɪ(s)] n. quarrel;
banter.

rigna, rigndi, rigndur (rignt) [rɪg̊·na,
rɪŋ·dɪ, rɪŋ·dʏr̥, rɪŋ·tʰ; rɪŋ̥·t] wv.2

rain; *hann rignir* it rains, it is
raining (S. VI, **4**, *3*).

rigning, -ar, -ar [rɪg̊·niŋ̊, -ar̥] f.1
rain; pl. rainy spells.

rigningarlegur [rɪg̊·niŋ̊ar-lɛ:qʏr̥] adj.
(see *-legur*) (looking) like (it is
going to) rain; adv. *-lega; r-lega
leit út* it looked like rain.

rigningasveit, -ar, -ir [rɪg̊·niŋ̊a-svei:tʰ,
-ar̥, -ɪr̥; -svei:d̥] f.2 rainy district.

rigningatíð, -ar, -ir [rɪg̊·niŋ̊a-tʰi:ð,
-ðar̥, -ðɪr̥] f.2 rainy spell.

ríki, -s, -, (-ja) [ri:kjʰɪ(s), ri:kjʰa;
ri:g̊ɪ(s), ri:g̊ja] n. state; kingdom, realm.

ríkur, rík, ríkt [ri:kʰʏr̥, ri:kʰ, rix·t;
ri:g̊(ʏr̥)] adj. rich.

ríma, -u, -ur, (-na) [ri:ma, -ʏ(r̥),
rim·na] wf.1 rime, ballad; canto;
rímur a rimed romance in many
cantos, of different meters.

rísa, rís, reis, risum, risinn (-ið) [ri:sa,
ri:s, rei:s, rɪ:sʏm, rɪ:sɪn, -ið] v.1
rise, arise; *rísa upp* arise; *risa upp
frá dauðum* arise from the dead.

rismál [ri:smau·l] n.pl. six in the
morning; time to rise.

1. **rista, risti, rist(ur)** [rɪs·ta, -ɪ, -ʏr̥,
rɪs·t] wv.2 or rarely (old):

rísta, ríst, reist, ristum, ristinn (-ið)
[ris·ta, ris·t, reis·t, rɪs·tʏm, rɪs·tɪn,
-ið] v.1 cut, slash, slit; carve.

2. **rista, risti, rist(ur)** [rɪs·ta, rɪs·tɪ,
rɪs·t(ʏr̥)] wv.2 toast; *rista brauð*
toast bread; *rist brauð* toasted
bread.

rit, -s, - [rɪ:tʰ(s); rɪ:d̥(s)] n. written
work, work, book.

rithöfundur, -ar, -ar [rɪ:tʰhö·vʏndʏr̥,
-ar̥; rɪ:d̥-] m.1 writer, author.

ritsímastöð, -stöðvar, -var [rɪ:tʰsi·ma-
stö:ð, -stöð·var̥; rɪ:d̥-] f.1 Telegraph office (Building).

ritsími, -a, -ar [rɪ:tʰsi·mɪ, -a(r̥);
rɪ:d̥-] wm.1 telegraph.

ritstjóri, -a, -ar [rɪ:tʰstjou·rɪ, -a(r̥);
rɪ:d̥-] wm.1 editor.

ritstjórn, -ar, -ir [rɪ:tʰstjourdn̥, -nar̥,
-nɪr̥; rɪ:d̥-] f.2 editorial board.

rjómagrautur, -ar [rjou·ma-gröy:tʰʏr̥,

Consonants: [ð] brea*the*; [g] *g*ood; [gʲ] *gy*arden (garden); [hw] *wh*at; [j] *y*es; [kʲ] *cy*an
(can); [ŋ] thi*ng*; [q] N. Germ. sa*g*en; [r] Scottish *r*; [x] approx. Germ. a*ch*; [þ] *th*in.
Voiceless: ○; [b̥, d̥, g̊] approx. *p, t, k*. Half-voiced: *italics*. Aspiration and preaspiration:
[ʰ]; [pʰ, tʰ, kʰ] *p-, t-, k-*. Others as in English.

429

-aŗ; -gröy:dɣŗ] m.1 thick rice cooked in milk.

rjómakaka, -köku, -ur [rjou:ma·kʰa:-kʰa, -kʰö:kʰɣ(ŗ); -kʰa:ga̭, -kʰö:g̭ɣ] wf.1 pastry, Danish pastry.

rjómakanna, -könnu, -ur [rjou:ma-kʰan:a, -kʰön:ɣ(ŗ)] wf.1 cream pitcher.

rjómaterta, -u, -ur [rjou:ma·tʰeŗ·ta, -ɣ(ŗ)] wf.1 cream cake.

rjómi, -a [rjou:mɪ, -a] wm.1 cream.

rjúfa, rýf, rauf, rufum, rofinn (-ið) [rju:va, ri:v, röy:v, rɣ:vɣm, rɔ:vɪn, -ɪð] v.2 break, tear up, demolish.

rjúka, rýk, rauk, rukum, rokinn (-ið) [rju:kʰa, ri:kʰ, röy:kʰ, rɣ:kʰɣm, rɔ:kˌʰɪn, -ɪð; rju:ga̭, ri:g̭, röy:g̭, rɣ:g̭ɣm, rɔ:g̭ˌɪn, -ɪð] v.2 smoke, emit smoke or steam.

rjúpa, -u, -ur [rju:pʰa, -ɣ(ŗ); rju:ba̭] wf.1 ptarmigan.

róa, ræ; reri, réri, röri; róinn (-ið) [rou:a, rai:, rɛ:rɪ, rje:rɪ, rö:rɪ, rou:ɪn, -ɪð] v.irreg. (In. VII, 5, 2) row, row out to sea fishing; róa (á) báti row a boat.

róður, róðrar, róðrar [rou:ðɣŗ, rouð·-raŗ] m.1 rowing, trip on a rowboat; fishing trip.

rófa, -u, -ur, (-na) [rou:(v)a, -ɣ, roub̭·na] wf.1 tail (of a dog); rutabaga.

rofið, -inn, see rjúfa.

rokið, -inn, see rjúka.

rokkur, -s, -ar [rɔʰk:ɣŗ, rɔʰk:s, rɔʰk:-aŗ] m.1 spinning wheel.

rómantík, -ur [rou:mantʰi·kʰ, -ɣŗ; -tʰi·g̭] f.3 romanticism.

rómantískur, -tísk, -tískt [rou:man-tʰis·kɣŗ, -tʰis·k, -tʰis·t] adj. romantic.

rósfingraður, -uð, -að [rou:s·fiŋ·graðɣŗ, -ɣð, -að] adj. rose-fingered.

roskinn, -in, -ið; rosknari, -astur [rɔs·kˌɪn, -ɪn, -ɪð; rɔsknarɪ, -astɣŗ] adj. middle-aged, elderly.

rósóttur, -ótt, -ótt [rou:souʰt·ɣŗ, -ouʰt·] adj. with floral design, with a design of roses.

rostungur, -ungs, -ungar [rɔs·tuŋg̭ɣŗ, -uŋs, -uŋg̭aŗ] m.1 walrus.

rót, -ar, rætur [rou:tʰ, -aŗ, rai:tʰɣŗ; rou:ḓ, rai:dɣŗ] f.3 root.

rótarsvörður, -svarðar [rou:tʰar·svör·-ðɣŗ, -svar·ða̭ŗ; rou:daŗ] m.3 'root sward,' fen sward, the intertwined roots of vegetation in bogs.

rótlaus, -laus, -laust [rou:tʰlöy·s, -löys·t; rou:ḓ·] adj. rootless, without (the intertwined) roots (of plants).

róttækur, -tæk, -tækt [rou:(t)tʰai·-kʰɣŗ, -tʰai·kʰ, -tʰaixt; -tʰai·g̭·] adj. radical.

rúða, -u, -ur [ru:ða, -ɣ(ŗ)] wf.1 (window) pane.

ruddi, -ur, see ryðja.

rúði, rúið, -inn, see rýja.

rufum, see rjúfa.

rúgbrauð, -s, - [ru:(q)bröy·ð, -bröyðs] n. rye bread, pumpernickel.

rugl, -s [rɣg̭·l, rɣg̭ls] n. nonsense, twaddle.

rúgmjöl, -s [ru:(q)mjö·l, -mjöls] n. rye flour.

rúgur, -s [ru:(q)ɣŗ, rux·s] m.1 rye.

rukum, see rjúka.

rúllupylsa, -u, -ur [rul:ɣ·pʰɪl·sa, -ɣ(ŗ)] wf.1 (a roll of) spiced flank of lamb.

rúm, -s, - [ru:m, rum·s] n. place, space; bed.

rúmur, rúm, rúmt [ru:mɣŗ, ru:m, rum·tʰ; rum·t] adj. spacious, ample, roomy, a little over; rúmar tvær álnir a little over two ells.

rumba, -u, -ur [rɣm·ba̭, -ɣ(ŗ)] wf.1 a spell of bad weather; rhumba.

rúml. = rúmlest or rúmlega.

rúmlega [rum·lɛ·qa] adv. amply, a little more than.

rúmlest, -ar, -ir [rum·lɛst, -aŗ, -ɪŗ] f.2 = tonn, ton.

Rúna, -u [ru:na, -ɣ] wf.1 pet name for Guðrún or Sigrún.

runnið, -inn, -um, see 2. renna.

rupl, -s [rɣʰp·l, rɣʰpls] n. plundering.

rúsína, -u, -ur [ru:si·na, -ɣ(ŗ)] wf.1 raisin.

Vowels: a [a] approx. father; á [au] cow; e [ɛ] set; é [jɛ] yes; i, y [ɪ] sit; í, ý [i] feel; o [ɔ] law; ó [ou] note; u [ɣ] approx. Germ. Mütter; ú [u] school; y = i; ý = í; æ [ai] ice; ö [ö] Germ. hören; au [öy] French feuille; ei, ey [ei] ale. Length [:]; half-length [·].

rusl, -s [rʏs·l̠, rʏsls] n. rubbish.

Rússi, -a, -ar [rus:ɪ, -a(r̠)] wm.l Russian.

Rússland, -s [rus:land̠, -lan(d̠)s] n. Russia.

rússneska, -u [rus:ncska, -ʏ] wf.l Russian (language).

rússneskur, -nesk, -neskt [rus:ncskʏr̠, -ncsk, -ncst] adj. Russian.

rutt, see ryðja.

Rvík = Reykjavík.

ryðja, ruddi, ruddur (rutt) [rɪð·ja, rʏd̠:ɪ, -ʏr̠, rʏʰt:] wv.l clear (out of °the way), clear (a road), excavate (a river bed).

rýf, see rjúfa.

rýja (rúa), rý(i), rúði, rúinn (-ið), rúð(ur) [ri:ja, ru:a, ri:(jɪ), ru:ðɪ, ru:ɪn, -ɪð; ru:ð, ru:ðʏr̠] wv.l & 3 shear (sheep), fleece.

ryk, -s [rɪ:kʰ(s); rɪ:g̊(s)] n. dust.

rýk, see rjúka.

rykkilín, -s, - [rɪ¹ʰk₁:ɪ-li:n, -lin·s] n. surplice.

rýmri, rýmstur, see rúmur.

rýr, rýr, rýrt [ri:r, rir̠·t] adj. lean, shrunken; meager.

rýrna, -aði, -að(ur) [rird̠na, -aðɪ, -að, -ðʏr̠] wv.4 shrink.

rýrnun, -ar [rird̠nʏn, -ʏnar̠] f.2 shrinkage.

ræ, see róa.

ræð, see ráða.

1. ræða, -u, -ur [rai:ða, -ʏ(r̠)] wf.l speech, oration.

2. ræða, ræddi, ræddur (rætt) [rai:ða, raid̠:ɪ, -ʏr̠, raiʰt:] wv.2 converse, speak; ræða um speak about; ₁nema um e-ð sé að ræða unless the'question is about sth; ræða e-ð discuss sth.

rækja, rækti, rækt(ur) [rai:k₁ʰa, raix·tɪ, raix·t(ʏr̠); rai:g̊₁a] wv.2 observe, heed, respect; rækja helgar tíðir attend mass (regularly), perform mass.

rækt, -ar [raix·t, -ar̠] f.2 love, affection; cultivation.

rækta, -aði, -að(ur) [raix·ta, -aðɪ, -að, -aðʏr̠] wv.4 cultivate (land).

ræna, rændi (rænti), rændur (ræntur) (rænt) [rai:na, rain·dɪ (rain·tʰɪ; rain·tɪ), rain·dʏr̠ (rain·tʰʏr̠; rain·-tʏr̠), rain·tʰ; rain·t] wv.2 rob; ræna e·n e-u rob sbdy of sth (S. I, 3, 1, 2(f)).

ræningi, -ja, -jar [rai:niŋg̊₁ɪ, -g̊₁a(r̠)] wm.l robber.

Rænka, -u, -ur [raiŋ·kʰa, -ʏ(r̠); raiŋ̊·ka] wf.l pet name for Ragnheiður or Ragnhildur.

ræsi, -s, - [rai:sɪ(s)] n. (in bogs) drain, rill, watercourse; (in cities) gutter, sewer.

rætt, see 2. ræða.

rætur, see rót.

röð, raðar, -ir [rö:ð, ra:ðar̠, -ɪr̠] f.2 order, row; þriðji í röðinni third in (the) order, third in the row.

rödd, raddar, -ir [röd̠:, rad̠:ar̠, -ɪr̠] f.2 voice.

rög, see ragur.

rök, raka [rö:kʰ, ra:kʰa; rö:g̊, ra:g̊a] n.pl. reasons, reasoning, arguments.

rökfræði [rö:kʰfrai:ðɪ; rö:g-] wf.2 logic.

rökkur, (-ri), -urs, -ur [röʰk:ʏr̠(s), röʰk:rɪ] n. twilight.

rökkva, -aði, -að [röʰk:va, -aðɪ, -að] wv.4 grow dark; það er farið að rökkva it is beginning to grow dark.

römm, see rammur.

rönd, randar, rendur [rön·d̠, ran·dar̠, ren·dʏr̠] f.3 stripe, streak; edge, border, rim.

röndóttur, -ótt, -ótt [rön·douʰt·ʏr̠, -ouʰt·] adj. striped.

röng, see rangur.

röntgengeislar [rön·tʰgcn-g₁eis·lar̠; rön·t-] wm.l.pl. X-rays.

röri, see róa.

röskur, rösk, röskt [rös·kʏr̠, rös·k, rös·(k)t] adj. vigorous, brave, active; ample; röskur hálftímagangur a good half hour's walk.

S.

SA = suðaustan from the southeast.

1. sá, sái, sáði (old: seri, söri),

Consonants: [ð] breathe; [g] good; [g₁] gyarden (garden); [hw̥] what; [j] yes; [k₁] cyan (can); [ŋ] thing; [q] N. Germ. sagen; [r] Scottish r; [x] approx. Germ. ach; [þ] thin. Voiceless: ○; [b̥, d̥, g̊] approx. p, t, k. Half-voiced: italics. Aspiration and preaspiration: [ʰ]; [pʰ, tʰ, kʰ] p-, t-, k-. Others as in English.

431

sáð (old: **sáinn, -ið**) [sau:, sau:ı, sau:ðı, (sɛ:rı, sjɛ:rı, sö:rı), sau:ð (sau:ın, -ıð)] wv.3 & irreg. (cf. In. VII, **5**, *2*) sow.

2. **sá, sáum,** see *sjá.*

3. **sá, sú, það** [sau:, su:, þa:ð, þa(:)], acc. *þann, þá, það* [þan:, þau:], dat. *þeim, þeirri, því* [þei:*m*, þeir:ı, þvi:, þi:], gen. *þess, þeirrar, þess* [þɛs:, þeir:a*r*]; plural *þeir, þær, þau* [þei:*r*, þai:*r*, þöy:], acc. *þá, þær, þau* [þau:], dat. *þeim* [þei:*m*], gen. *þeirra* [þeir:a] dem. pron. (Pr. **4,** *2*; In. VI, **3**) that, that one, he (who), she, it (who); it; *sá þeirra, sem* the one of them who; *þeir verða að missa, sem eiga* (proverbial) those who own (sth) must take losses; *á þeim degi* on that day (previously mentioned, or to be mentioned); *sá eldri* the older one; *sá gamli* the old one, the old man (S. III, **3,** *3*); *sá rauði = Rauður* the red (horse) (S. III, **2,** *3*); *sá er góður!* he is a good one! (sarcastically); *sá klaufi!* such a fool! *en sá hiti!* what heat! *sá einn* (*sem*) he alone (who); *það er . . .* it is . . . , there is . . . ; *það rignir* it rains (= *hann rignir*) (S. VI, **14,** *3*); *það sama* the same; *það eitt . . . , sem* that alone which, those things alone . . . which; *og það* and that; *það er nú það* that is that; *hann var það vitrari, að . . .* he was so (that) much wiser that . . . ; *það* to such an extent: *áin var það mikil, að hún var óreið* the river was so high that it was unfordable; *því fremur* all the more so; *því næst* next to that, then; *því miður* unfortunately; *því . . . því* the (more) . . . the (more); *nema veðrið verði því verra* unless the weather should get very bad indeed (S. I, **3,** *2,* 5; III, **4,** 4 & 5); *því* adv. therefore; *því?* why; *af því að* because; *þess vegna* therefore; *þess . . . þess* the

. . . the (S. VIII, 3(g)). See S. IV, **3,** 1-2.

saddi, saddur, see *seðja.*

saddur, södd, satt [sad:ʏ*r*, söd:, sa^ht:] adj. satisfied, full; *saddur af mat* appetite satisfied; *saddur lífdaga* ready to die, of ripe old age.

safn, -s, söfn [sab·n, sabns, söb·n̥] n. collection, library.

safna, -aði, -að(ur) [sab·na, -aðı, -að, -aðʏr] wv.4 gather; *safna bókum* collect books; *safnast saman* gather (intr.).

safnaðar, -ir, see *söfnuður.*

Safnahús, -s [sab·n(a)-hu:s, -hus:] n. 'The Museum' (National Library, etc.).

saft, -ar, -ir [saf·t, -a*r*, -ı*r*] f.2 fruit juice.

sag, -s [sa:q, sax·s] n. sawdust.

saga, sögu, -ur, (sagna) [sa:qa, sö:-qʏ(*r*), saǥ·na] wf.1 story, tale; *saga,* history; *sagan af e-m* the story of sbdy; *segja upp alla sögu* tell the whole story; *vera úr sögunni* 'be out of the story,' be extinct, be forgotten; *saga um e-ð* story about sth.

sagar, -ir, see *sög.*

sagði, -ur, sagt, see *segja.*

sagnar, -ir, see *sögn.*

sagógrjón [sa:ǥou·-grjou:*n*] n.pl. sago.

sakar, -ir, see *sök.*

sakir [sa:k¡ʰır; sa:ǥ¡ır] prep. with gen. (see *sök*) on account of; *sakir þess* because of that; *sakir þess að* conj. because (S. VIII, 3(b)).

sakna, -aði, -að [sa^hk·na, -aðı, -að] wv.4 *sakna e-s* miss sbdy; *ég sakna þín* I miss you.

saknaðar, see *söknuður.*

sál, -ar, -ir [sau:*l*, -la*r*, -lı*r*] f.2 soul; bag.

sala, sölu, -ur [sa:la, sö:lʏ(*r*)] wf.1 sale; *til sölu* for sale.

sála, -u, -ur, (-na) [sau:la, -ʏ(*r*), saul·na] wf.1 soul; *engin sála* not a soul.

sálarfræði [sau:la*r*-frai:ðı] wf.2 psychology.

Vowels: *a* [a] approx. father; *á* [au] cow; *e* [ɛ] set; *é* [jɛ] yes; *i, y* [ı] sit; *í, ý* [i] feel; *o* [ɔ] law; *ó* [ou] note; *u* [ʏ] approx. Germ. Mütter; *ú* [u] school; *y = i; ý = í; æ* [ai] ice; *ö* [ö] Germ. hören; *au* [öy] French *feuille; ei, ey* [ei] ale. Length [:]; half-length [·].

432

sálast, -aðist, -azt (sálaður) [sau:-
last, -aðɪst, -ast; sau:laðʏr̥] wv.4
(middle voice only) die, pass away;
give up the ghost.

salat, -ats, -öt [sa:latʰ(s), -ötʰ; -aḍ,
-öḍ] n. lettuce.

salerni, -s, - [sa:lerdnɪ(s)] n. toilet,
W. C.

sálmaskáld, -s, - [saul·ma·skaul·d̥(s)]
n. hymn writer, psalmist.

sálmur, -s, -ar [saul·mʏr̥, saulms,
saul·mar] m.1 hymn, psalm.

salt, -s, sölt [sal̥·t, salts, söl̥·t] n.
salt; vega salt see-saw.

salta, -aði, -að(ur) [sal̥·ta, -aðɪ, -að,
-aðʏr̥] wv.4 salt, season; saltaður
salted, corned (beef, mutton).

Saltari, -a, -ar [sal̥·tarɪ, -a(r̥)] wm.1
the Psalter.

saltfiskur, -s [sal̥·tfɪskʏr̥, -s] m.1
salted fish; clipfish.

saltket, -s (kjöt) [sal̥·tkⱼʰɛ·tʰ(s);
-kⱼʰɛ·d̥; -kⱼʰö·t; -kⱼʰö·d̥] n. salted,
corned meat.

saltur, sölt, salt [sal̥·tʏr̥, söl̥·t, sal̥·t]
adj. salted, corned; salty.

salur, -s, -ir [sa:lʏr̥, -ɪr̥, sal·s] m.2
hall, auditorium.

saman [sa:man] adv. together, between them; allir saman all together; smám saman gradually;
koma saman gather, come together.

samband, -s, -bönd [sam·band(s),
-bönd] n. connection (e. g. in telephoning); federation, union; Samband hinna íslenzku kaupfélaga,
Samband íslenzkra samvinnufélaga
Union of the Icelandic Co-operative
Societies; samband Íslands og Danmerkur the Union of Iceland and
Denmark (ended in 1944).

sambandslög, -laga [sam·ban(d)s-lö:q,
-la:qa] n.pl. Act of Union (between
Iceland and Denmark, running out
and not renewed in 1944).

samdi, samið, -inn, see semja.

sameina, -aði, -að(ur) [sa:mei·na,
-aðɪ, -að, -að(ʏr̥)] wv.4 unite
(trans.), combine; sameinast unite
(intr.).

samgöngur, -gangna [sam·göyŋg̊ʏr̥,
-gauŋ(g̊)na] wf.1.pl. intercourse,
communications.

samhygð, -ar [sa:mhɪqð, -ðar̥; -hɪg̊þ]
f.2 = samúð, sympathy; name of a
wrestling club.

samkomulag, -s [sam·kʰɔmʏ·la:q,
-lax·s] n. agreement.

samkvæmur, -kvæm, -kvæmt [sam·-
kʰvai.mʏr̥, -kʰvai·m, -kʰvaimtʰ,
-kʰvaimt] adj. in agreement with;
samkvæmur e-u in agreement with
sth; samkvæmt því in agreement
with that, according to that.

samlagning, -ar [sam·laḡniŋg̊, -ar̥] f.1
addition.

samningur, -s, -ar [sam·niŋg̊ʏr̥, -iŋs,
-iŋg̊ar̥] m.1 agreement, treaty, con-
tract.

samræmi, -s [sam·rai·mɪ(s)] n. ac-
cord, harmony; í samræmi við e-ð
in accordance with sth.

samsafn, -s, -söfn [sam·sabn̥, -sab̥n̥s,
-söb̥n̥] n. collection, group.

samstæða, -u, -ur [sam·stai·ða, -ʏ(r̥)]
wf.1 set (of sth).

1. samt [sam·tʰ; sam̥·t] adv. (n. of
samur) still, yet, however, nevertheless, all the same; þakk fyrir
samt thank you all the same.

2. samt. = samtals.

samtal, -s, -töl [sam·tʰa·l, -tʰals; -tʰö·l]
n. talk, conversation.

samtals [sam·tʰals] adv. all told,
altogether.

samtími, -a [sam·tʰi·mɪ, -a] wm.1 the
present age = samtíminn.

samtímis [sam·tʰi·mɪs] adv. coeval
with, contemporaneous with; samtímis e-m contemporary with sbdy.

samúð, -ar [sa:mu·ð, -u·ðar̥] f.2 sympathy; condolence; votta e-m samúð
offer sbdy condolences.

samur, söm, samt [sa:mʏr̥, sö:m,
sam·tʰ, sam̥·t] adj. (dem. pron. In.
VI, 3n2) (the) same; sá sami the
same; sami ... og same ... as;
á sama stað og in the same place
as; í sama bili the same moment;
mér er sama it is all one to me,

Consonants: [ð] breathe; [g] good; [gⱼ] gyarden (garden); [hw] what; [j] yes; [kⱼ] cyan
(can); [ŋ] thing; [q] N. Germ. sagen; [r] Scottish r; [x] approx. Germ. ach; [þ] thin.
Voiceless: ○; [b̥, d̥, g̊] approx. p, t, k.   Half-voiced: italics.   Aspiration and preaspiration:
[ʰ]; [pʰ, tʰ, kʰ] p-, t-, k-.   Others as in English.

433

it is all the same to me, it makes no difference to me; *hann varð aldrei samur eftir skurðinn* he was never the same after the operation; *það (hið) sama* the same (S. IV, 3, 5); *sama* the same; *sama er að segja um það* the same may be said of it (is to be said of it); *fara í samt lag, komast í samt lag* resume the original shape, recuperate; *samt* adv. nevertheless, anyway, = *samt sem áður*.

samvinna, -u, -ur [sam·vɪn·a, -ʏ(r̥)] wf.1 co-operation; *vera í samvinnu við e-n* co-operate with sbdy, work together with sbdy.

samvinnufélag, -s, -lög [sam·vɪn·ʏ-fjɛ:laq, -laxs, -löq] n. co-operative society, association, company.

samvinnuskóli, -a [sam·vɪn·ʏ-skou:lɪ, -a] wm.1 a school where the theory of co-operation in business and elsewhere is taught.

samvizka, -u, -ur [sam·vɪska, -ʏ(r̥)] wf.1 conscience; *hafa vonda samvizku = vera með mórauða samvizku* have bad conscience.

samþykki, -s, - [sam·þɪʰkj·ɪ(s)] n. consent, assent, approval.

samþykkja, -þykkti, -þykkt(ur) [sam·-þɪʰkj·a, -þɪxtɪ, -ʏr̥, -þɪxt] wv.2 consent, agree to; *samþykkja lög* pass a law, enact a law; carry a proposition.

sandfok, -s, - [san·dfɔ·kʰ(s); -fɔ·g̊] n. dust, dust storm, sand storm.

sandkorn, -s, - [san·dkʰɔdn̥(s); -kʰɔrdn̥] n. a grain of sand.

Sandskeið, -s [san·dskj₁ei·ð, -skj₁eiðs] n. 'Sand Run,' 'Sand Race.'

sandur, -s, -ar [san·dʏr̥, san·(d̥)s, san·dar̥] m.1 sand, sandy desert, gravel plain; also place name: *Sandur*.

sanna, -aði, -að(ur) [san:a, -aðɪ, -að, -aðʏr̥] wv.4 prove; *sanna e-ð* prove sth; *sanna e-m e-ð* prove sth to sbdy, demonstrate sth to sbdy.

sannarlega [san:ar·lɛ:qa] adv. truly, certainly.

sanngjarn, -gjörn, -gjarnt [saŋ·gj₁adn̥, -gj₁ödn̥, -gj₁antʰ; -gj₁ant; -gj₁ardn̥, -gj₁ördn̥] adj. fair (price), equitable.

sannur, sönn, satt [san:ʏr̥, sön:, saʰt:] adj. true; *betur satt væri* (short for: *það væri betur, að satt væri*) would it were true! I wish it were true; *segja satt* tell the truth (S. III, 3, 2); *segja e-ð satt* tell the truth about sth; *ég segi það satt!* I declare!

sápa, -u, -ur [sau:pʰa, -ʏ(r̥); sau:ba] wf.1 soap.

Sápubúð, -ar [sau:pʰʏ-bu:ð, -ðar̥] f.2

Sápuhús, -s [sau:pʰʏ-hu:s, -hus:; sau:bʏ-] n. 'Soap Store.'

1. **sár, -s, -** [sau:r, saur̥·s] n. wound.

2. **sár, sár, sárt** [sau:r, saur̥·t] adj. sore, wounded; aching, painful; sore, angry; *e-ð er sárt* sth hurts; *sverja og sárt við leggja* swear, invoking heavy (sore) penalties upon oneself, in case the oath be false.

sardína, -u, -ur [sar·di·na, -ʏ(r̥)] wf.1 sardine.

sárna, -aði, -að [saurdna, -aðɪ, -að] wv.4 get sore, get tender; impersonal: *mér sárnar* it grieves me.

sat, sátum, see *sitja*.

sáta, -u, -ur [sau:tʰa, -ʏ(r̥); sau:da] wf.1 truss of hay; haycock.

Satan, -s [sa:tʰan; sa:dan, -ans] m.1 Satan.

satt, see *saddur, sannur,* and *seðja*.

sauð, see *sjóða*.

sauðaket (-kjöt), -s [söy:ða-kj₁ʰɛ:tʰ(s), -kj₁ʰö:tʰ; -kj₁ʰɛ:d̥, -kj₁ʰö:d̥] n. lamb, mutton.

sauðarlæri, -s, - [söy:ðar-lai:rɪ(s)] n. leg of mutton (lamb).

sauðburður, -ar [söyð·bʏrðʏr̥, -ar̥] m.3 lambing season.

sauðfé, -fjár [söyð·fjɛ·, -fjau·r] n. (coll.) sheep.

sauðhús, -s, - [söy:ðhu·s, -hus·] n. sheep shed.

sauðskinn, -s, - [söyð·skj₁ɪn·, -skj₁ɪns] n. sheepskin, sheep hide (= *gæra*).

sauðskinnsskór [söyð·skj₁ɪn(s)-skou:r]

Vowels: *a* [a] approx. father; *á* [au] cow; *e* [ɛ] set; *é* [jɛ] yes; *i, y* [ɪ] sit; *í, ý* [i] feel; *o* [ɔ] law; *ó* [ou] note; *u* [ʏ] approx. Germ. Mütter; *ú* [u] school; *y = i; ý = i;* æ [ai] ice; *ö* [ö] Germ. hören; *au* [öy] French feuille; *ei, ey* [ei] ale. Length [:]; half-length [·].

m.1.pl. Icelandic shoes (moccasins) made of sheepskin.

sauður, -ar, -ir [söy:ðyr̥, -ar̥, -ɪr̥] m.3 sheep; especially a castrated ram.

saug, see *sjúga.*

sauma, -aði, -að(ur) [söy:ma, -aðɪ, -að, -aðyr̥] wv.4 sew, make; *sauma á sig* sew for oneself; *láta sauma á sig* have sewn (for oneself).

saup, see 2. *súpa.*

saur, -s [söy:r, söyr̥·s] m.1 dirt.

sautján (seytján) [söy:tʰjau·n, sei:-tʰjau·n; söy:d̦-, sei:d̦-] num. card. seventeen.

sautjándi (seytjándi) [söy:tʰjaundɪ, sei:tʰjaundɪ; söy:d̦-, sei:d̦-] num. ord. seventeenth.

sé, see *sjá* and *vera.*

seðill, -ils, -lar [sɛ:ðɪdl, -ɪls, sɛð·lar̥] m.1 bill, banknote; piece of paper.

seðja, saddi, saddur (satt) [sɛð·ja, sad:ɪ, -yr̥, saʰt:] wv.1 satisfy (appetite), fill.

séð(ur), see *sjá.*

1. **sef, -s** [sɛ:v, sɛf·s] n. rush, sedge.
2. **sef,** see *sofa.*

séffot, sifjott, -s [sjɛ:vijɔ·tʰ(s), sɪv·-jɔʰt(s)] n. cheviot.

segja, sagði, sagður (sagt) [sei:ja, saq·ðɪ, saq·ðyr̥, sax·t; sag̊·ðɪ, -yr̥] wv.3 say; (1) say, tell; *segja e-m e-ð* tell sbdy sth; *segja hvor öðrum* tell to each other; *rétt að segja* so to speak, almost; *strákur sagði það vera* (acc. with inf.) the boy (urchin) said that it was so (i. e. that he could); (2) impersonal: *nú segir ekki af honum . . .* now nothing is said (heard) of him . . . (S. VI, 14, 7); *sagt er* it is said, sbdy says; (3) middle voice: *segjast* (followed by an indirect speech infinitive, cf. *kveðast*) say that . . . ; *segjast hafa* say that one has (S. VI, 9, 5, 1 & 2); *segjast vera* say that one is, claim to be; (4) with preps and advs: *segja frá* tell (about sth); *segja til* say, indicate; *segja e-m til e-s* inform sbdy of sth; *segja til vegar* tell the right way, give

directions; *segja e-ð um e-n* say sth about sbdy, *segja e-ð um e-ð* use some expression about sth; *segja upp alla sögu* tell the whole story; *segja upp lög* recite, proclaim the law (this was the duty of the old Icelandic lawspeaker *lögsögumaður*); *segja (e-ð) við e-n* say (sth) to sbdy. See also S. VI, **14, 2.**

seig, see *síga.*

seigur, seig, seigt [sei:qyr̥, sei:q, seix·t] adj. tough, stubborn.

seinn, sein, seint; seinni, seinastur [seid·n, sei:n, sein·tʰ; sein·t; seid·-nɪ, sei:nastyr̥] adj. slow, late, tardy; *seinn á sér* slow (in motion); *á seinni öldum* in later times (literally: ages, centuries); *seint* adv. slowly, not easily; late (litotes: never); *betra er seint en aldrei* better late than never.

sekk, see 1. *sökkva.*

sekúnda, -u, -ur [sɛ:kʰunda, -ʏ(r̥); sɛ:g̊-] wf.1 second.

sekúnduvísir, -is, -(ir)ar [sɛ:kʰundʏ-vi:sɪr̥, -ɪs, -(ɪr)ar̥; sɛ:g̊-] m.1 second-hand (of a watch or clock).

sel, -s, -, (-ja) [sɛ:l, sɛl·s, sɛl·ja] n. shieling; a place in which sheep and cows were kept in summer time in order to get the fullest benefit of their milk; in place names: *-sel, Sels-, Selja-.*

selja, seldi, seldur (selt) [sɛl·ja, sɛl·dɪ, -yr̥, sɛl·t] wv.1 sell, deliver; *selja e-ð af hendi* deliver sth, give up sth; *selja e-m e-ð* sell sth to sbdy.

sellýsi, -s [sɛl:i·sɪ(s)] n. seal oil.

selskinn, -s, - [sɛl·sk‚ɪn·, -sk‚ɪns] n. sealskin.

selskinnsföt, -fata [sɛl·sk‚ɪns-fö:tʰ, -fa:tʰa; -fö:d̦, -fa:da] n.pl. sealskin clothes.

selslíki, -s [sɛl·sli·k‚ʰɪ(s); -li·g̊‚ɪ] n. the shape of a seal.

Seltjarnarnes, -s [sɛl·tʰjaðnar-nɛ:s, -nɛs:] n. 'Seal Pond (Tarn) Ness.'

selur, sels, selir [sɛ:lyr̥, sɛl·s, sɛ:lɪr̥] m.2 seal; *honum fór ekki að verða* *um sel* he began to get uneasy, he was getting the creeps.

1. **sem** [sɛ:m] rel. pron. that; who, which (In. VI, **4**; S. IV, **4**; VII, **2**, 3).

2. **sem** [sɛ:m] conj. as, like; (1) comparison: *hratt sem fugl flýgi* swift as a bird in flight; *hvítur sem snjór* white as snow; *koma sem þjófur á nóttu* come like a thief in the night (S. VI, **9**, *4*, 7; VIII, 3(g)); *sem fyrst* as soon as possible; *sem mest* at maximum; *sem verst* as bad as possible, at its worst (thus with superlatives) (S. III, **5**, 3n2); *sem móðir kvæði við barn* as if a mother sang to a baby; (2) temporal: as, when: *en sem hann sá þetta* but as he saw this (S. VIII, 3(h)).

semja, samdi, saminn (-ið) [sɛm·ja, sam·dɪ, sa:mɪn, -ɪð] wv.1 agree, settle, come to terms; *semja um e-ð* come to terms about sth; write, compose; *semja bók* write a book; *semja lag* compose a melody.

senda, sendi, sendur (sent) [sɛn·da, -ɪ, -ʏr̥, sɛn·tʰ; sɛn̥·t] wv.2 send, forward, despatch; throw, cast; *senda bréf* send a letter; *senda steini* throw a stone; *senda eftir e-m* send for sbdy; *senda á fé* send to attack the sheep; middle voice: *sendast* be sent, *sendist* should be sent.

sendiherra, -, -ar [sɛn·dɪ·her̥:a, -ar̥] wm.1 ambassador, minister.

sending, -ar, -ar [sɛn·dɪŋ̊, -ar̥] f.1 sth sent; parcel, package; a ghost or spirit raised and sent to harm sbdy.

sendinn, -in, -ið; sendnari, -astur [sɛn·dɪn, -ɪn, -ɪð; sɛndnarɪ, -astʏr̥; sɛn(d̥)n-] adj. sandy; *sendinn jarðvegur* sandy soil.

senn [sɛn:] adv. soon, presently.

sent, -s, - [sɛn·tʰ(s); sɛn̥·t] n. cent; *fimmtíu senta glas* a fifty cents' bottle; *5 og 10 senta búð* 5 and 10 cent store.

sentímetri, -a, -ar [sɛn·tʰi·me:tʰrɪ, -a(r̥); sɛn̥·ti·me:d̥rɪ] wm.1 centimeter.

september [sɛf·tɛmbɛ·r] m. indecl. September.

sér, see *sig*.

séra, síra [sjɛ:ra, si:ra] m. indecl. Reverend; *séra Jón Jónsson* (the) Rev(erend) J. J.

sérhver, -hver, -hvert; -hvað [sjɛr̥·hwʏ·r, -hwʏr̥t, -hwa·ð; -kʰvʏ·r, -kʰvʏr̥t, -kʰva·ð; -ʰwɛ·r, -hwɛr̥t; -kʰvɛ·r, -kʰvɛr̥t] indef. pron. (only strong) each, every, every one; (In. VI, **6**, 2(c); S. III, **1**, 4; IV, **6**, 17).

sérhæfður, -hæfð, -hæft [sjɛ:rhaivð̥ʏr̥, -haivð̥, -haift; -haibð̥ʏr̥, -haibþ] adj. specialized.

seri, séri, see 1. *sá*.

sérkennilegur [sjɛr̥·k̥ˌʰɛn·ɪ·lɛ:qʏr̥] adj. (see *-legur*) peculiar, characteristic.

sérstakur, -stök, -stakt [sjɛr̥·sta·kʰʏr̥, -stö·kʰ, -staxt; -sta·ɣ̊ʏr̥, -stö·g̊] adj. separate, apart, certain, specific; special, particular, extraordinary.

sess, -, -ar [sɛs:(ar̥)] m.1 seat.

sessa, -u, -ur [sɛs:a, -ʏ(r̥)] wf.1 pillow (to sit on).

sessi, -a, -ar [sɛs:ɪ, -a(r̥)] wm.1 (seat) companion.

set, -s, - [sɛ:tʰ, sɛ:tʰs; sɛ:d̥] n. sitting place, seat; *færa sig um set* change one's place (position).

seta, -u, -ur [sɛ:tʰa, -ʏ(r̥); sɛ:d̥a] wf.1 seat; *setan í stólnum* the seat of the chair; *setan í buxunum* the seat of the pants.

setið, -inn, see *sitja*.

setja, setti, settur (sett) [sɛ:tʰja, sɛʰt:ɪ, -ʏr̥, sɛʰt:; sɛ:d̥ja] wv.1 (1) set, place, put; establish; *setja bréf í póst* mail a letter; *setja inn í hús* put (take) into a house; *setja í lag* adjust, fix; *setja á fót* (= *stofna*) establish, found; *setja e-m e-ð fyrir* assign (a lesson) to sbdy; *setja upp sátur* set up haycocks, cock the hay; *setja ofan í súrt* pickle (in sour whey); *setja sig til burðar* (of ewes) run away

Vowels: *a* [a] approx. *father*; *á* [au] *cow*; *e* [ɛ] *set*; *é* [jɛ] *yes*; *i, y* [ɪ] *sit*; *í, ý* [i] *feel*; *o* [ɔ] *law*; *ó* [ou] *note*; *u* [ʏ] approx. Germ. M*ü*tter; *ú* [u] *school*; *y = i*; *ý = í*; *æ* [ai] *ice*; *ö* [ö] Germ. h*ö*ren; *au* [öy] French *feuille*; *ei, ey* [ei] *ale*. Length [:]; half-length [·].

436

to lamb; reflexive: *setja sig niður* sit down; more commonly: (2) middle voice: *setjast (niður)* sit down, take a seat; *hann er setztur* he has sat down (S. VI, 3, *3*, 2); impersonal: *setzt er* sbdy sits down (S. VI, **7**, *6*).

setulið, -s [sɛ:tʰʏ·lɪ:ð̤, -lɪð̤·s; sɛ:d̤ʏ-] n. garrison.

setur, (-ri), -urs, -ur [sɛ:tʰʏr̥(s), sɛ:-tʰrɪ; sɛ:d̤ʏr̥, sɛ:d̤rɪ] n. dwelling place, residence.

setustofa, -u, -ur [sɛ:tʰʏ·stɔ:va, -ʏ(r̥); sɛ:d̤ʏ-] wf.1 sitting room.

sex [sɛx·s] num. card. six.

sex, -, - [sɛx·s] n. six (in cards).

sexa, -u, -ur [sɛx·sa, -ʏ(r̥)] wf.1 six (in cards).

sexfaldur, -föld, -falt [sɛx·s·faldʏr̥, -föld, -falt] adj. sixfold.

sextán [sɛx·stau·n] num. card. sixteen.

sextándi [sɛx·staund̤ɪ] num. ord. sixteenth.

sextíu [sɛx·stʰi·jʏ] num. card. sixty.

sextugasti [sɛx·stʏqastɪ] num. ord. sixtieth.

sextugur, -tug, -tugt [sɛx·stʏqʏr̥, -ʏq, -ʏxt] adj. sixty years of age; sixty fathom deep (high).

Seyðisfjörður, -fjarðar [sei:ð̤ɪs·fjör·-ð̤ʏr̥, -fjar·ð̤ar̥] m.3 'Cooking Pit Fjord.'

seyddur, seydd, seytt [seid̤:ʏr̥, seid̤:, seiʰt:] adj. baked or cooked long with moderate heat.

sí- [si:-] pref. always, continually.

1. **síð, síðla** [si:ð̤, sið̤·la] adv. late; *síð* is positive to *síðar* and *síður*, which see.

2. **síð**, see 1. *síður*.

síða, -u, -ur [si:ð̤a, -ʏ(r̥)] wf.1 side; flank.

siða, -aði, -að(ur) [sɪ:ð̤a, -að̤ɪ, -að̤, -að̤ʏr̥] wv.4 civilize, polish; *siðaður maður* civilized person, well-mannered person.

síðan [si:ð̤an] (1) adv. then, thereupon, after that, since; *síðan á landnámstíð* since the pioneering days; *síðan um aldamót* since the turn of the century; *síðan fóru þeir* thereupon they went; *hann hefur ekki sézt síðan* he has not been seen since; (2) conj. since; *en síðan þeir fóru, hefur ekki spurzt til þeirra* but since they left, they have not been heard of (S. VIII, 3(h)).

síðar, síðast [si:ð̤ar̥, si:ð̤ast] adv. compar. and superl. (of *síð*) later; latest, last; *litlu síðar* a little later.

síðari, síðastur [si:ð̤arɪ, si:ð̤astʏr̥] adj. compar. and superl. later, latest; latter, last; *þakka fyrir síðast* thank for the last time one spent together (a common polite phrase in Icelandic).

síðarnefndur, -nefnd, -nefnt [si:ð̤ar̥-nɛm·d̤ʏr̥, -nɛm·d̤, -nɛm·tʰ; -nɛm·t] adj. (pp.) the last named; the latter.

síðaskifti [si:ð̤a·skɪf·tɪ] n.pl. 'change of custom,' 'change of belief,' the Reformation.

síðdegis [sið̤·dei·jɪs] adv. p.m., in the afternoon.

síðkast [sið̤·kʰast] n. only in: *upp á síðkastið* of late.

siður, -ar, -ir [sɪ:ð̤ʏr̥, -ar, -ɪr] m.3 custom, habit, usage; religion, faith; *hafa e-n sið* have some habit, be used to; *heiðinn siður* paganism, heathendom; *kristinn siður* Christianity; *hinn nýi siður* the new faith; (*það*) *var siður* it was customary.

1. **síður, síð, sítt** [si:ð̤ʏr̥, si:ð̤, siʰt:] adj. low, long (down); *sitt skegg* long beard; *síður kjóll* long dress.

2. **síður** [si:ð̤ʏr̥] adv. compar. (see *varla, valla*) less; rather not; *engu síður, eigi að síður* no less, nevertheless; *miklu síður* much less; *vilja síður* want rather not, prefer not to; *síður en svo* far from it.

sifjott, -s = *séfíot*.

sig, sér, sín [sɪ:q, sjɛ:r, si:n] refl. pron. him- (her-, it-) self (In. VI, 1, 3); refl.: *meiða sig* hurt oneself; (S. IV, *2*, 1); recipr.: *tala sín á milli* speak to each other, speak

---

Consonants: [ð̤] brea*th*e; [g] *g*ood; [ɡ̊] *gy*arden (garden); [hw̥] *wh*at; [j] *y*es; [kɟ] *cy*an (can); [ŋ] thi*ng*; [q] N. Germ. sa*g*en; [r] Scottish *r*; [x] approx. Germ. a*ch*; [þ] *th*in. Voiceless: ○; [b̥, d̤, g̊] approx. *p, t, k*. Half-voiced: *italics*. Aspiration and preaspiration: [ʰ]; [pʰ, tʰ, kʰ] *p*-, *t*-, *k*-. Others as in English.

among themselves (S. IV, **2**, 2);
vera sér be alone, separated from
others, be by oneself.

síga, síg, seig, sigum, siginn (-ið)
[si:qa, si:*q*, sei:*q*, sɪ:qʏm, sɪi:jɪn,
-ɪð; si:jɪn, sɪ:jɪn] v.1 fall, sink,
drain.

sígaretta, -u, -ur [si:ga-rɛʰt:a, -ʏ(r̥)]
wf.1 cigaret, = *vindlingur*.

Sigbjörn, -bjarnar, (-björns) [sɪq·-
bjödn, -bjaḍnar̥, -bjös·] m.3 pers.
name; patronymic: *Sigbjörnsson.*

Sigfús, -ar (-s) [sɪx·fu·s(ar̥), -fus.]
m.1 pers. name; patronymic:
Sigfússon.

Sigga, -u, -ur [sɪg̊:a, -ʏ(r̥)] wf.1 pet
name for *Sigríður.*

Siggi, -a, -ar [sɪg̊ʲ:ɪ, -g̊:a(r̥)] wm.1
pet name for *Sigurður.*

1. **sigla, -u, -ur** [sɪg̊·la, -ʏ(r̥)] wf.1
= *mastur*, mast.

2. **sigla, sigldi, sigldur (siglt)** [sɪg̊·la,
sɪqldɪ, -ʏr̥, sɪqltʰ, sɪxlt] wv.2 sail;
ply the seas.

sigling, -ar, -ar [sɪg̊·liŋg, -ar̥] f.1 sailing, voyage.

Siglufjörður, -fjarðar [sɪg̊·lʏ-fjör·ðʏr̥,
-fjar·ðar̥] m.3 'Mast Fjord.'

Signý, -nýjar [sɪg̊·ni·(jar̥)] f.1 pers.
name.

Sigríður, -ar [sɪq·ri·ðʏr̥, -ar̥] f.1 pers.
name: Sigrid.

Sigrún, -ar [sɪq·ru·*n*, -ru·nar̥] f.1 pers.
name.

sigtibrauð, -s, - [sɪx·tɪ-bröy:ð,-bröyð·s]
n. rye bread made of strained rye
and wheat.

Sigurbjörg, -bjargar [sɪ:qʏr-björ·g̊,
-bjar·g̊ar̥] f.2 pers. name.

Sigurbjörn, -bjarnar (-björns) [sɪ:qʏr-
bjöd·n, -bjad·nar̥, -bjös:] m.3 pers.
name; patronymic: *Sigurbjörnsson.*

Sigurður, -ar (-s) [sɪ:qʏrðʏr̥, -ar̥,
-ʏr(ð)s] m.1 Sigurd; patronymic:
Sigurðsson, Sigurðardóttir.

Sigurgísli, -a [sɪ:qʏr-g̊ʲis·lɪ, -a] wm.1
pers. name.

Sigurjón, -s [sɪ:qʏr-jou:*n*, -joun·s]
m.1 pers. name.

Sigurliði, -a [sɪ:qʏr-lɪ:ðɪ, -a] wm.1
pers. name.

síki, -s, - [si:kʲ,ʰɪ(s); si:g̊ʲ,ɪ] n. Sc.
sike; a streamlet, rill flowing
through marshy ground.

síld, -ar, -ir [sil·d, -ar̥, -ir] f.2 herring.

síldarflak, -s, -flök [sil·dar-fla:kʰ(s);
-flö:kʰ; -fla:g̊, -flö:g̊] n. herring
flake; *reykt síldarflök* kippers.

síldarverksmiðja, -u, -ur [sil·dar-vɛr·k-
smɪðja, -ʏ(r̥)] wf.1 herring oil
and meal factory.

silfur, (-ri), -urs [sɪl·vʏr̥(s), sɪlvrɪ]
n. silver.

silfurbakki, -a, -ar [sɪl·vʏr-baʰkʲ,:ɪ,
-ʰk:a(r̥)] wm.1 silver tray.

silki, -s [sɪl·kʲ,ʰɪ(s); sɪl·kʲ,ɪ] n. silk.

silkisokkur, -s, -ar [sɪl·kʲ,ʰɪ-sɔʰk:ʏr̥,
-sɔʰk·s, -sɔʰk:ar̥; sɪl·kʲ,ɪ-] m.1 silk
stocking, hose.

silkisvunta, -u, -ur [sɪl·kʲ,ʰɪ-svʏn·tʰa,
-ʏ(r̥); sɪl·kʲ,ɪ-svʏn·ta] wf.1 silk
apron.

Silli, -a [sɪl:ɪ, -a] wm.1 pet name for
Sigurliði; Silli og Valdi chain
stores in Reykjavík.

silungsveiði, -ar, -ar [sɪ:luŋs-vei:ðɪ,
-ar̥] f.1 trout fishing.

silungur, -s, -ar [sɪ:luŋg̊ʏr̥, -uŋs, -uŋ-
g̊ar̥] m.1 trout.

síma, -aði, -að [si:ma, -aðɪ, -að] wv.4
telephone, phone; *síma á stöðina*
phone to the station, call up the
station.

símanúmer, -s, - [si:ma-nu:mɛr(s)]
n. telephone number (= *númer*).

símaskrá, -skrár, -skrár [si:ma-
skrau:(r)] f.1 telephone directory.

síma-staur, -s, -ar [si:ma-stöy:r,
-stöʏr·s, -stöy:rar̥] m.1 telephone
(telegraph) pole.

símastöð, -stöðvar, -var [si:ma-stö:ð,
-stöð·var̥] f.1 telephone (telegraph)
station.

símatæki, -s, - [si:ma-tʰai:kʲ,ʰɪ(s);
-tʰai:g̊ʲ,ɪ] n. the phone apparatus,
the dial phone.

sími, -a, -ar [si:mɪ, -a, -ar̥] wm.1 telephone, phone (= *talsími*); telegraph
(= *ritsími*).

Vowels: *a* [a] approx. *father*; *á* [au] *cow*; *e* [ɛ] *set*; *é* [jɛ] *yes*; *i, y* [ɪ] *sit*; *í, ý* [i] *feel*;
o [ɔ] *law*; *ó* [ou] *note*; *u* [ʏ] approx. Germ. Mütter; *ú* [u] *school*; *y* = *i*; *ý* = *í*; *æ* [ai] *ice*;
ö [ö] Germ. hören; *au* [öy] French *feuille*; *ei, ey* [eiʲ] *ale*. Length [:]; half-length [·].

símskeytaform, -s, - [sim·sk₁ei·tʰa-
for·m, -forms; -sk₁ei·d̥a-] n. telegram blank.
símskeyti, -s, - [sim·sk₁ei·tʰɪ(s),
-sk₁ei·d̥ɪ(s)] n. telegram.
sín, see *sig* and 2. *sinn.*
sindur, (-ri), -urs, -ur [sɪn·d̥ʏr̥(s),
sɪnd̥rɪ] n. glowing iron scales, dross,
slag.
sindursprengja, -u, -ur [sɪn·d̥ʏr̥-
sprein·g̊₁a, -g̊₁ʏ(r̥)] wf.1 star shell.
1. sinn, -s, - [sɪn:, sɪn·s] n. time occasion; *í fyrra sinnið* the first time,
the former time; *í fyrsta sinn* for
the first time; *í síðasta sinn* last
time; *í hvert sinn* each time; *fimm
sinnum sex* five times six; *mörgum
sinnum* many times; *að þessu sinni*
this time, for the time being; *einu
sinni* once; *einu sinni var . . .* once
upon a time there was . . . ; *ekki
einu sinni* not once; not even.
2. sinn, sín, sitt [sɪn:, si:n, sɪʰt:]
poss. pron. (In. III, 2(b)5e & 8;
VI, 2) his, her (hers), its, one's;
their (theirs); *hann tók hestinn
sinn* (more rarely: *sinn hest*) he
took his horse (S. III, 2, 4); *hann
tók hattinn sinn* he took his own
hat, but: *hann tók hattinn hans* he
took his (the other fellow's) hat;
þau fluttu í nýja húsið sitt they
moved into their new house (S. I,
4, 1, 1); *sín eigin börn* their own
children; *gjalda hverjum sitt* pay
each his due; *þeir tóku sinn hestinn
hvor* they took a horse each (but:
hvor sinn hest each his own horse);
sitt hvað each one's own thing, this
and that; *það er sitt hvað* it is
different; *sitt hvoru(m) megin við*
on each side of, on both sides of.
See also S. IV, 2, 3 & 5 & 7.
sinna, sinnti, sinnt [sɪn:a, sɪn·tʰɪ;
sɪn·tʰ; sɪn·t(ɪ)] wv.2 pay attention
to, take care of (*sinna e-m*).
sinni, -a, -ar [sɪn:ɪ, -a, -ar̥] wm.1 fol-
lower, partisan of.
síra = *séra.*
sirz, - [sɪr̥·s] n. (coll.) chintzes.

sitja, sit, sat, sátum, setinn, -ið
[sɪ:tʰja, sɪ:tʰ, sa:tʰ, sau:tʰʏm,
sɛ:tʰɪn, -ɪð; sɪ:dja, sɪ:d̥, sa:d̥,
sau:d̥ʏm, sɛ:d̥ɪn, -ɪð] v.5 sit, be
seated; stay, remain; *sitja hjá e-m*
sit by sbdy; *sitja heima* stay at
home; *þá væri verr farið en heima
setið* (proverbial) this would have
been better not done; *sitja yfir kaffi*
sit over coffee cups, sit at the coffee
table; *sitja yfir* act as a midwife
(*yfirsetukona*), assist in calving,
lambing, childbirth; *sitja undir e-m*
have sbdy on one's lap. See also
S. VI, 4, 3; 6, 2.
sítróna, -u, -ur [si:tʰrou·na, -ʏ(r̥);
si:drou·na] wf.1 lemon.
sitt, see 2. *sinn.*
sítt, from 1. *síður.*
síungur, -ung, -ungt [si:-uŋ·g̊ʏr̥, -uŋ·g̊,
-uŋ·tʰ; -uŋ̊·t] adj. always, ever
young.
sívinnandi [si:vɪn:andɪ] adj. (pr. p.)
continually working.
sízt [sis·t] adv. superl. of 2. *síður* (cf.
varla) least (of all); *síðast en ekki
sízt* last but not least; *ekki sízt* not
least so.
sjá, sé, sá, sáum, séð(ur) [sjau:, sjɛ:,
sau:, sau:ʏm, sjɛ:ðʏr̥, sjɛ:ð] v.5
(In. VII, 2, 6) (1) see, look at;
understand; visit; *ég sé þig á
morgun* I shall see you tomorrow;
ég sé í blöðunum I see (have seen)
in the newspapers; *ég sá, að hann
skrifaði* (= *sá hann skrifa*) I saw
that he wrote (= saw him write)
(S. VI, 9, 4, 1n2 & 2); *ég sá hann
koma* (acc. with inf.) I saw him
come (coming) (S. VI, 11, 3);
*hann er ekki allur, þar sem hann
er séður* (proverbial) he is not all
he seems to be, i. e. he is quite
shrewd; (2) impersonal: *sjá má*
(it) may be seen; *er svo að sjá,
sem . . . it* looks as if . . . ; *það
sér ekki á* (*e-u* or *e-m*) it cannot
be seen (on sbdy or sth); *það sér
ekki út úr augunum* 'one cannot
see out of one's eyes' (S. VI, 14,

Consonants: [ð] brea*th*e; [g] *g*ood; [g₁] *gy*arden (garden); [hw̥] *wh*at; [j] *y*es; [k₁] *cy*an
(can); [ŋ] thi*ng*; [q] N. Germ. sa*g*en; [r] Scottish *r*; [x] approx. Germ. ac*h*; [þ] *th*in.
Voiceless: ○; [b̥, d̥, g̊] approx. *p, t, k.* Half-voiced: *italics.* Aspiration and preaspiration:
[ʰ]; [pʰ, tʰ, kʰ] *p-, t-, k-*. Others as in English.

7); (3) middle voice: *sjást* be seen (pass.), see each other (recipr.) (S. VI, **7**, *3*); with preps and advs: *sjá til* see, wait and see; *sjá til e-s* see, discover (sbdy coming), watch; *sjá til e-s* see to sth, take care of sth (sbdy); *sjá um e-ð* take care of sth, direct some work, look after sth.

sjaldan, sjaldnar, sjaldnast [sjal·da̠n, sjaldnar̠, sjaldnast] adv. seldom, more seldom, most rarely.

sjaldgæfur, -gæf, -gæft [sjal·dg̦ai·vr̠, -g̦ai·v, -g̦aift] adj. rare.

sjaldséður, -séð, -séð [sjal·dsjɛ·ðr̠, -sjɛ·ð] adj. rarely seen.

sjálfsagður, -sögð, -sagt [sjaul·(v)-saqðr̠, -söqð, -saxt; -sag̊ðr̠, -sög̊þ] adj. self-evident; *að sjálfsögðu* of course; as a matter of course, undoubtedly, = *sjálfsagt*.

sjálfskeiðingur, -s, -ar [sjaul·(v)sk̦ei·-ðiŋr̠, -iŋs, -iŋar̠] m.1 pocket knife.

sjálfstjórn, -ar, -ir [sjaul·(v)stjourd̦n, -nar̠, -nir̠] f.2 self-rule, self-government.

sjálfstæði, -s [sjaul·(v)stai·ðɪ(s)] n. independence.

sjálfstæðisbarátta, -u, -ur [sjaul·(v)-stai·ðɪs-ba:rauʰta, -ɣ(r̠)] wf.1 fight for independence.

sjálfstæðisflokkur, -s, -ar [sjaul·(v)-stai·ðɪs-flɔʰk:ɣr̠, -flɔx·s, -flɔʰk·s, -flɔʰk:ar̠] m.1 independence party, *Sjálfstæðisflokkurinn* 'The Independence party.'

sjálfstæðismaður, -manns, -menn [sjaul·(v)stai·ðɪs-ma:ðr̠, -man·s, -mɛn:] m.4 an independent, a member of the Independence party.

sjálfsæfisaga, -sögu, -ur [sjaul·(v)s-ai·vɪsa·qa, -sö·qɣ(r̠)] wf.1 autobiography.

sjálfur, sjálf, sjálft [sjaul·vr̠, sjaul·v, sjaul·t; sjaulft] dem. pron. (always strong; In. III, **3**, *1*, 4; VI, 1n) self (myself, yourself, himself, herself, itself, ourselves, yourselves, themselves); *hver er sjálfum sér*

næstur everybody for himself (S. IV, 1, 6); *lá við sjálft, að Rússar ynnu* the Russians were on the point of winning,—they almost won; *sjálf messan* the mass itself.

sjálfvirkur, -virk, -virkt [sjaul·(v)-vɪr̠kɣr̠, -vɪr̠k, -vɪr̠(x)t] adj. automatic; *sjálfvirkur sími* dial phone.

sjálfþakkað [sjaul·(v)þaʰk·að] pp. n. *það er sjálfþakkað* (or simply: *sjálfþakkað!*) 'that is automatically thanked for,' 'you should thank yourself for it'; (a polite phrase often used to answer thanks), you are welcome.

sjár, see *sjór.*

sjatna, -aði, -að(ur) [sjaʰt·na, -aðɪ, -að, -aðɣr̠] wv.4 settle down.

sjávar, see *sjór.*

sjávarútvegur, -ar (-s) [sjau·var-u:tʰvɛ·qɣr̠, -vɛ·qar̠, -vɛxs; -u:d-] m̦.3 or 2 fisheries.

sjóða, sýð, sauð, suðum, soðinn (-ið) [sjou:ða, si:ð, söy:ð, sɣ:ðɣm, sɔ:-ðɪn, -ɪð] v.2 boil, seethe, cook; *sjóða við gufu* boil by steam.

sjódraugur, -s, -ar [sjou:dröy·qɣr̠, -dröyxs, -dröy·qar̠] m.1 sea ghost, the ghost of a drowned man.

sjóferð, -ar, -ir [sjou:fɛrð, -ðar̠, -ðɪr̠] f.2 voyage; fishing trip.

sjófugl, -s, -ar [sjou:fɣ̊l̦(s), -lar̠] m.1 sea bird.

sjólið, -s [sjou:lɪ·ð, -lɪðs] n. sailors of the navy, the navy.

sjóliði, -a, -ar [sjou:lɪ·ðɪ, -a(r̠)] wm.1 sailor of the navy.

sjómaður, -manns, -menn [sjou:ma·-ðr̠, -mans, -mɛn.] m.4 sailor, fisherman.

sjómannasögur [sjou:man·a·sö:qɣr̠] wf.1.pl. sailors' stories, sailors' yarns.

sjón, -ar, -ir [sjou:n, -nar̠, -nɪr̠] f.2 sight, vision; *koma e-m fyrir sjónir* appear to sbdy; *eigin sjón og reynd* own seeing and experiencing.

sjónauki, -a, -ar [sjou:nöy·k̦ʰɪ, -öy·-kʰa(r̠); -öy·g̦̊ɪ, -öy·g̊a(r̠)] wm.1 field glass.

Vowels: *a* [a] approx. father; *á* [au] cow; *e* [ɛ] set; *é* [jɛ] yes; *i, y* [ɪ] sit; *í, ý* [i] feel; *o* [ɔ] law; *ó* [ou] note; *u* [ɣ] approx. Germ. Mütter; *ú* [u] school; *y* = *i*; *ý* = *í*; *æ* [ai] ice; *ö* [ö] Germ. hören; *au* [öy] French feuille; *ei, ey* [ei] ale. Length [:]; half-length [·].

440

sjóndeildarhringur, -s [sjoun·deildar̨·
hr̨iŋ·ɡ̊ɣr̨, -hr̨iŋ·s] m.l horizon.

sjór, sjár, sær; sjóar, sjávar, sævar,
sjós; sjóar,sjóir, sjáir, sævar [sjou:r,
sjau:r, sai:r; sjou:ar̨, sjau:var̨,
sai:var̨, sjou:s; sjou:ar̨, sjou:ir̨,
sjau:ir̨, sai:var̨] m.l (In. I, 2,
1(b)9) sea, seawater; pl. waves;
úti á sjó out at sea; róa á sjó row
out to sea fishing, go out fishing;
til lands og sjávar on land and sea;
á sjó eða landi on sea or land.

sjúga, sýg, saug, sugum, soginn (-ið)
[sju:(q)a, si:q, söy:q, sɤ:qɤm,
sɔi:jIn, -Ið; sɔ:jIn] v.2 suck.

sjúkdómur, -s, -ar [sju:kʰdou·mɤr̨,
-doums, -dou·mar̨; sju:g̊-] m.l sickness, malady; af sjúkdómum from
sicknesses.

sjúklingur, -s, -ar [sjuʰk·liŋɡ̊ɣr̨, -iŋs,
-iŋg̊ar̨] m.l patient.

sjúkrabörur [sju:kʰra·bö:rɣr̨; sju:-
g̊ra-] wf.l.pl. stretcher.

sjúkrahús, -húss, -hús [sju:kʰra·hu:s,
-hus:, sju:g̊ra-] n. hospital (=
spítali).

sjúkrasamlag, -s, -lög [sju:kʰra·sam-
laq, -laxs, -löq; sju:g̊ra-] n. sickness
benefit society, sick club.

sjúkravagn, -s, -ar [sju:kʰra·vag̊·n(s),
-nar̨; sju:g̊ra-] m.l ambulance.

sjúkur, sjúk, sjúkt [sju:kʰɣr̨, sju:kʰ,
sjux·t; sju:g̊ɣr̨, sju:g̊] adj. sick,
ill (= veikur).

1. sjö [sjö:] num. card. seven.

2. sjö, -s, - [sjö:, sjö:s] n. seven (in
cards).

sjöa, -u, -ur [sjö:a, -ɣ(r̨)] wf.l seven
(in cards).

sjöfaldur, -föld, -falt [sjö:faldɣr̨,
-föld, -falt] adj. sevenfold.

sjötíu [sjö:tʰi·jɣ] num. card. seventy.

sjötti [sjöʰt:I] num.ord. sixth, á sjötta
ári going on six.

sjöttungur, -s, -ar [sjöʰt:uŋɡ̊ɣr̨, -uŋs,
-uŋg̊ar̨] m.l one seventh.

sjötugasti [sjö:tʰɤqastI; sjö:d̨-] num.
ord. seventieth.

sjötugur, -tug, -tugt [sjö:tʰɤqɣr̨, -ɤq,
-ɤxt; sjö:d̨-] adj. seventy years of
age.

sjöundi [sjö:ɤnd̨I] num. ord. seventh.

sjövetlingur, -s, -ar [sjö:veʰt·liŋɡ̊ɣr̨,
-iŋs, -iŋg̊ar̨] m.l seven years old
child.

skaða, -aði, -að(ur) [ska:ða, -aðI,
-að, -aðɤr̨] wv.4 harm, hurt.

skaðbrenna, -brenn, -brann, -brunnum,
-brunninn (-ið) [skað·bren·a, -bren·,
-bran·, -brɤn·ɤm, -brɤn·In, -Ið] v.3
burn dangerously (intr.).

skaði, -a, -ar [ska:ðI, -a, -ar̨] wm.l
detriment, harm, loss; verða fyrir
sköðum take losses, suffer damages.

skaðlegur [skað·lɛ·qɣr̨] adj. (see
-legur) harmful, injurious.

skafa, skef, skóf, skófum, skafinn (-ið)
[ska:va, sk¸ɛ:v, skou:v, skou:vɤm,
ska:vIn, -Ið] v.6 scrape.

skaft, -s, sköft [skaf·t, skafts, köf·t]
n. shaft, handle.

Skaftá, -ár [skaf·tau·, -au·r] f.l
'Shaft River'; Skaftártunga 'Shaft
River Tongue,' a tongueshaped piece
of land between Skaftá and Hólmsá.

Skaftafells-sýsla,-u,-ur [skaf·tafɛl(s)-
sis·la, -ɣ(r̨)] wf.l 'The District of
Skaftafell.'

Skagafjörður, -fjarðar [ska:qa-fjör··
ðɣr̨, -fjar·ðar̨] m.3 'Headland
Fjord,' 'Skaw Fjord.'

skaka, skek, skók, skókum, skekinn
(-ið) [ska:kʰa, sk¸ɛ:kʰ, skou:kʰ,
skou:kʰɤm, sk¸ɛ:k¸In, -Ið; ska:g̊a,
sk¸ɛ:g̊, skou:g̊, skou:g̊ɤm, sk¸ɛ:g̊¸In,
-Ið] v.6 shake; churn (butter).

skal, see skulu.

skál, -ar; -ar, -ir [skau:l, -lar̨, -lIr̨]
f.l or 2 bowl; skál! skoal! to your
health!

skáld, -s, - [skaul·d̨, skauld̨s] n. poet,
writer of poetry or novels.

skáldgáfa, -u [skaul·d̨gau·va, -ɤ] wf.l
gift of (composing) poetry.

skáldsaga, -sögu, -ur [skaul·d̨sa·qa,
-sö·qɤ(r̨)] wf.l novel.

skáldsagnahöfundur, -ar, -ar [skaul·d̨-
sag̊na-hö:vɤnd̨ɣr̨, -ar̨] m.l novel
writer, writer of fiction.

Consonants: [ð] breathe; [g] good; [ɡ̊ɹ] gyarden (garden); [hw] what; [j] yes; [kɹ] cyan
(can); [ŋ] thing; [q] N. Germ. sagen; [r] Scottish r; [x] approx. Germ. ach; [þ] thin.
Voiceless: o; [b̥, d̥, g̊] approx. p, t, k. Half-voiced: italics. Aspiration and preaspiration:
[ʰ]; [pʰ, tʰ, kʰ] p-, t-, k-. Others as in English.

441

skáldskapur, -ar [skaul·dska·pʰʏr̥, -ar̥; -ska·bʏr̥] m.3 poetry.

skalf, see skjálfa.

skall, see 1. skella.

skálm, -ar; -ar, -ir [skaul·m, -mar̥, -mɪr̥] f.1 & 2 trouser leg; big knife.

skamma, -aði, -að(ur) [skam:a, -aðɪ, -að, -aðʏr̥] wv.4 scold, abuse, revile; skammast sín be ashamed of oneself; skammastu þín! be ashamed of yourself! shame on you!

skammbyssa, -u, -ur [skam·bɪs·a, -ʏ(r̥)] wf.1 pistol, revolver.

skammstafaður, -stöfuð, -stafað [skam·sta·vaðʏr̥, -stö·vʏð, -sta·vað] adj. (pp.) abbreviated.

skammur, skömm, skammt; skemmri, skemmstur [skam:ʏr̥, sköm:, skam·tʰ; skam̩·t; sk̩ɛm:rɪ, sk̩ɛmst-ʏr̥] adj. short, brief; skammt short way, short time; skammt frá near by, a short way off; skammt til Reykjavíkur a short way to R.; fyrir skömmu a short while ago; skömmu seinna a little later (S. III, 3, 2); skemmsta leið the shortest road; til skamms tíma until recently.

skána, -aði, -að [skau:na, -aðɪ, -að] wv.4 get better; mér er að skána I am getting better.

skap, -s [ska:pʰ(s), skaf·s; ska:b(s)] n. temper, mood; í þungu skapi in a downcast mood.

1. skapa, -aði, -að(ur) [ska:pʰa, -aðɪ, -að, -aðʏr̥; ska:ba] wv.4 or (rarely, old):

2. skapa, skep, skóp, skópum, skapinn (-ið); skaptur [ska:pʰa, sk̩ɛ:pʰ, skou:pʰ, skou:pʰʏm, ska:pʰɪn, -ɪð, skaf·tʏr̥; ska:ba, sk̩ɛ:b, skou:b, skou:bʏm, ska:bɪn, -ɪð] v.6 (wv.3) shape, create, make; skapast be created, arise.

skápur, -s, -ar [skau:pʰʏr̥, skau:pʰs, skau:pʰar̥; skau:b-] m.1 cupboard, wardrobe, locker, (book)case.

skar, skárum, see skera.

skár, skást [skau:r, skaus·t] adv. compar. and superl. better, best under the circumstances.

skara, -aði, -að [ska:ra, -aðɪ, -að] wv.4 poke, rake; skara í eldinn poke the fire; skara e-u frá shove sth aside.

skarð, -s, skörð [skar·ð, skarðs, skar̥·s, skör·ð] n. mountain pass; 'Pass.'

skarðsbrekkur, -brekkna [skarðsbrɛʰk·-ʏr̥, -brɛʰkna, skar̥·s-] wf.1.pl. the slopes of a mountain leading to a pass; place name: 'Mountain Pass Slopes.'

skarfur, -s, -ar [skar·vʏr̥, skarvs, skar·var̥] m.1 cormorant; éta eins og skarfur eat like a glutton, eat like a pig.

skarlatssótt, -ar [skar·latʰ(s)-souʰt:, -ar̥; skal:atʰs-] f.2 scarlet fever.

skárri, skástur [skaur:ɪ, skaus·tʏr̥] adj. compar. and superl. better, best under the (bad) circumstances; comparatively better, best.

skarsúð, -ar, -ir [skar̥·su·ð, -ðar̥, -ðɪr̥] f.2 clincher roof.

skást, see skár.

skástur, see skárri.

skata, skötu, -ur [ska:tʰa, skö:tʰʏ, -ʏr̥; ska:da, skö:dʏ] wf.1 skate.

skattur, -s, -ar [skaʰt:ʏr̥, -ar̥, skaʰt·s] m.1 tax.

1. skaut, -s, - [sköy:tʰ(s); sköy:d] n. a pointed headdress worn with skautbúningur; corner, sheet (of a sail); pole.

2. skaut, see skjóta.

skautbúningur, -s, -ar [sköy:tʰbu·niŋ̊ʏr̥, -ɪns, -iŋ̊ar̥; sköy:d·] m.1 national dress of Icelandic women, worn on most festive occasions.

skauti, -a, -ar [sköy:tʰɪ, -a(r̥); sköy:-dɪ] wm.1 skate; fara á skautum skate.

skauttreyja, -u, -ur [sköy:(t)tʰrei·ja, -ʏ(r̥); sköy:d·] wf.1 bodice belonging to skautbúningur.

ske, skeði, skeð [sk̩ɛ:, sk̩ɛ:ðɪ, sk̩ɛ:ð] wv.3 irreg. (present: sker or skeður) (In. VII, 4, 7) happen; hvað skeður? what happens?

skef, see skafa.

1. skeið, -ar; -ar, -ir [sk̩ei:ð, -ðar̥,

Vowels: a [a] approx. father; á [au] cow; e [ɛ] set; é [jɛ] yes; i, y [ɪ] sit; í, ý [i] feel; o [ɔ] law; ó [ou] note; u [ʏ] approx. Germ. Mütter; ú [u] school; y = i; ý = í; æ [ai] ice; ö [ö] Germ. hören; au [öy] French feuille; ei, ey [ei] ale. Length [:]; half-length [·].

442

-ðir] f.1 & 2 spoon; sheath (pl.);
(natural) bridge.

2. skeið, -s, - [sk̦ei:ð, sk̦eið·s] n.
space, race, run; ambling (of
horses); time; *um skeið* for a while.

Skeiðará, -ár [sk̦ei:ðar·au:(r)] f.1
one of the most dangerous glacial
rivers in Iceland; *Skeiðarár-sandur*
' The Sand of Skeiðará.' Cf. 1. *skeið*.

skeifa, -u, -ur, (-na) [sk̦ei:va, -ɤ(r̦);
sk̦eib·na] wf.1 horseshoe.

skein, see *skína*.

skek, skekinn, see *skaka* and *skekja*.

skekja, skek, skók, skókum, skekinn
(-ið) [sk̦ɛ:k̦ʰa, sk̦ɛ:kʰ, skou:kʰ,
skou:kʰɤm, sk̦ɛ:k̦ʰɪn, -ɪð; sk̦ɛ:g̦̦a,
sk̦ɛ:g̦, skou:g̦, skou:g̦ɤm, sk̦ɛ:g̦̦ɪn,
-ɪð] v.6 shake (rare for *skaka*).

skel, -jar, -jar [sk̦ɛ:l, sk̦ɛl·jar̦] f.1
shell, mussel.

skelf, see *skjálfa*.

skelfing, -ar, -ar [sk̦ɛl·viŋg̦, -ar̦] f.1
terror; *mikil skelfing* how dreadful;
mikil lifandi skelfing how perfectly
awful (ly).

1. skella, skell, skall, skullum, skoll-
inn (-ið) [sk̦ɛd·la, sk̦ɛd·l, skad·l,
skɤd·lɤm, skɔd·lɪn, -ɪð] v.3 (intr.)
crash, fall with a clash, come (suddenly) on; *skella á* break out.

2. skella, skellti, skellt(ur) [sk̦ɛd·la,
sk̦ɛl·tɪ, -ɤr̦, sk̦ɛl·t] wv.2 (trans.)
slam; *skella hurð* slam a door;
clash, slap; *skella saman lófunum*
clap the hands together; throw,
skella e-m niður throw sbdy down.

1. skemma, -u, -ur [sk̦ɛm:a, -ɤ(r̦)]
wf.1 storeroom, storehouse, storage;
bower.

2. skemma, skemmdi, skemmdur
(skemmt) [sk̦ɛm:a, sk̦ɛm·dɪ, -ɤr̦,
sk̦ɛm·tʰ; sk̦ɛm·t] wv.2 spoil,
damage.

skemmd, -ar, -ir [sk̦ɛm·d, -ar̦, -ɪr̦] f.2
injury, damage, sabotage.

skemmdarverk, -s, - [sk̦ɛm·dar·ver̦·k,
-s] n. damage, injury, sabotage.

skemmri, skemmstur, see *skammur*.

skemmta, skemmti, skemmt [sk̦ɛm·-
tʰa, -ɪ, sk̦ɛm·tʰ; sk̦ɛm·t, -a, -ɪ]

wv.2 amuse, divert, entertain;
skemmta e-m entertain sbdy;
skemmta sér amuse or enjoy oneself, have a good time.

skemmtiför, -farar, -farir [sk̦ɛm·tʰɪ·
fö:r, -fa:rar̦, -ɪr̦; sk̦ɛm·tɪ·] f.2
pleasure trip.

skemmtilega [sk̦ɛm·tʰɪ·lɛ:qa; sk̦ɛm·-
tɪ-] adv. pleasantly, interestingly,
in an entertaining manner.

skemmtilegur[sk̦ɛm·tʰɪ·lɛ:qɤr̦;sk̦ɛm·-
tɪ-] adj. (see -*legur*) pleasant, nice,
interesting, amusing, entertaining.

skemmtiskrá, -skrár, -skrár [sk̦ɛm·-
tʰɪ-skrau:(r); sk̦ɛm·tɪ-] f.1 program.

skemmtun, -unar, -anir [sk̦ɛm·tʰɤn,
-ɤnar̦, -anɪr̦; sk̦ɛm·tɤn] f.2 enjoyment, fun, good time, amusement,
pleasure, diversion, entertainment.

skemmuloft, -s, - [sk̦ɛm:ɤ·lɔf·t(s)]
n. store room loft.

skenkja, skenkti, skenkt(ur) [sk̦eiŋ·-
k̦ʰa,sk̦eiŋ·tʰɪ,-ɤr̦; sk̦eiŋ·tʰ; sk̦eiŋ·-
k̦a, sk̦eiŋ·t, -ɪ, -ɤr̦] wv.2 pour (tea,
coffee, wine).

skep, see 2. *skapa* (*skóp*).

skepna, -u, -ur [sk̦ɛʰp·na, -ɤ(r̦)] wf.1
beast; domestic animal, creature;
skepnurnar the livestock; the domestic animals; *það voru allar
skepnurnar* that was all there was
of domestic animals.

sker, -s, -, (-ja) [sk̦ɛ:r, sk̦ɛr̦·s,
sk̦ɛr·ja] n. skerry, crag.

skera, sker, skar, skárum, skorinn
(-ið) [sk̦ɛ:ra, sk̦ɛ:r, ska:r, skau:-
rɤm, skɔ:rɪn, -ɪð] v.4 cut, slaughter;
carve; *skera sig* cut oneself; *skera
e-n*, (*e-ð*) cut sbdy (sth); *skera
e-n upp* operate on sbdy; *skera úr*
cut away; decide; *skera sundur* cut
asunder, cut up.

skessa, -u, -ur [sk̦ɛs:a, -ɤ(r̦)] wf.1
troll woman, giantess.

skeyti, -s, - [sk̦ei:tʰɪ(s); sk̦ei:dɪ(s)]
n. missile; telegram.

skíðabrekka, -u, -ur [sk̦i:ða-brɛʰk:a,
-ɤ(r̦)] wf.1 ski run, ski slope.

Consonants: [ð] brea*th*e; [g] *g*ood; [gⱼ] *gy*arden (garden); [hw] *wh*at; [j] *y*es; [kⱼ] *cy*an
(can); [ŋ] thi*ng*; [q] N. Germ. sa*g*en; [r] Scottish *r*; [x] approx. Germ. a*ch*; [þ] *th*in.
Voiceless: ○; [b̦, d̦, g̦] approx. *p, t, k*. Half-voiced: *italics*. Aspiration and preaspiration:
[ʰ]; [pʰ, tʰ, kʰ] *p-, t-, k-*. Others as in English.

443

skíði, -s, - [sk̦i:ðɪ(s)] n. ski; *farä á skíðum* to ski.

skífa, -u, -ur [sk̦i:va, -ɣ(r̦)] wf.1 dial, face; *skífa á úri* a watch dial; *skífa á klukku* the face of a clock.

skifta, skifti, skift(ur) [sk̦ɪf·ta, -ɪ, -ɣr̦, sk̦ɪf·t] wv.2 (1) divide, exchange, share; *skifta í tvennt* divide in two parts; *skifta verkum* divide (or exchange) one's work; *skifta hárinu* part the hair; *svo dögum skiftir* many days at a stretch; *svo árum skiftir* for years; (2) with preps and advs: *skifta sér af e-u* meddle with sth; *skifta í smátt* exchange for small change, give change for; *skiftast í* be divided into; *skifta niður* divide, classify; *skifta um olíu* change oil; *skifta við e-n* deal (trade) with sbdy.

skifti, -s, - [sk̦ɪf·tɪ(s)] n. division, sharing; time; (*í*) *bœði skiftin* both times.

skiftimynt, -ar, -ir [sk̦ɪf·tɪ·mɪn·tʰ, -ar̦, -ɪr̦; -mɪn·t] f.2 change, small change.

skila, -aði, -að [sk̦ɪ:la, -aðɪ, -að] wv.4 deliver, give back, return; *skila e-u* deliver a message (or sth) (*til e-s* to sbdy).

skildir, see *skjöldur.*

skilja, skildi, skilinn (-ið) [sk̦ɪl·ja, sk̦ɪl·dɪ, sk̦ɪ:lɪn, -ɪð] wv.1 (1) separate, divide; discern, understand; *skilja e-ð frá e-u* separate sth from sth (e. g. cream from skimmed milk); *þeir skildu vinir* they parted as friends; *þau skildu* they were divorced; *ég skildi, að þetta var rétt* I understood that this was right (S. VI, 9, 4, 1n2 & 2); (2) middle voice: *skiljast* be understood; *hann skildist ekki* he was not (could not be) understood (S. VI, 7, 3); *skiljast* part, depart (S. VI, 7, 4); *mér skildist þú segja* (= *að þú segðir*) 'I thought I understood that you said' I thought you said, I understood you to say (S. VI, 9, 4, 1n2); (3) with preps and advs: *skilja á um e-ð* differ about sth, fall out about sth; *skilja e-ð eftir* leave sth (behind).

skilnaður, -ar, -ir [sk̦ɪl·naðʏr̦, -ar̦, -ɪr̦] m.3 separation (e. g. of Iceland and Denmark); divorce (= *hjóna-skilnaður*).

skilningur, -s [sk̦ɪl·nɪŋ̊ɣr̦, -ɪŋs] m.1 understanding.

skilrúm, -s, - [sk̦ɪl·ru·m, -rum·s] n. partition.

skilti, -s, - [sk̦ɪl·tɪ(s)] n. sign, signboard.

skilyrði, -s, - [sk̦ɪ:lɪrðɪ(s)] n. condition; *hin beztu skilyrði* ideal conditions; *skilyrði fyrir e-ð* condition(s) for sth.

skína, skín, skein, skinum, skininn (-ið) [sk̦i:na, sk̦i:n, sk̦ei:n, sk̦ɪ:-nʏm, sk̦ɪ:nɪn, -ɪð] v.1 shine, gleam; *sólin skín* the sun shines (is shining); *það skín í e-ð* sth is exposed to view.

skip, -s, - [sk̦ɪ:pʰ, sk̦ɪf·s; sk̦ɪ:b] n. ship, boat.

skipa, -aði, -að(ur) [sk̦ɪ:pʰa, -aðɪ, -að, -aðɣr̦; sk̦ɪ:ba] wv.4 order, bid, tell, command; *skipa e-m e-ð* command sbdy (to do) sth; with an active inf. to be translated with a passive inf.: *þeir skipa að slökkva ljósin* they order (command) the lights to be put out (S. VI, 14, 9); command; arrange; *hafa á að skipa* have available; *skipa e-n til e-s* appoint sbdy to (do) sth.

skipaeign, -ar, -ir [sk̦ɪ:pʰa-eig̊·n, -nar̦, -nɪr̦; sk̦ɪ:ba-] f.2 ship possession, ships possessed.

skipalest, -ar, -ir [sk̦ɪ:pʰa-les·t, -ar̦, -ɪr̦; sk̦ɪ:ba-] f.2 convoy.

skipasmíð, -ar, -ar [sk̦ɪ:pʰa-smi:ð, -ðar̦; sk̦ɪ:ba-] f.1 shipbuilding.

skipasmíðastöð, -stöðvar, -var [sk̦ɪ:-pʰasmi·ða-stö:ð, -stöð·var̦; sk̦ɪ:ba-] f.1 shipbuilding station, shipyard.

skipastóll, -s, -ar [sk̦ɪ:pʰa-stoud·l, -stoul·s, -stou:lar̦; sk̦ɪ:ba-] m.1 supply of ships, fleet.

skiprúm, -s, - [sk̦ɪ:pʰru·m, -rums;

Vowels: *a* [a] approx. father; *á* [au] cow; *e* [ɛ] set; *é* [jɛ] yes; *i, y* [ɪ] sit; *í, ý* [i] feel; *o* [ɔ] law; *ó* [ou] note; *u* [ʏ] approx. Germ. Mütter; *ú* [u] school; *y* = *i*; *ý* = *í*; *æ* [ai] ice; *ö* [ö] Germ. hören; *au* [öy] French feuille; *ei, ey* [ei] ale. Length [:]; half-length [·].

444

sk‚ɪꟸb‚-] n. berth, job on board a ship.

skipstjóri, -a, -ar [sk‚ɪːpʰstjouˑrɪ, -a(r̥); sk‚ɪf‑-] wm.1 captain.

skipun, -unar, -anir [sk‚ɪːpʰʏn, -ʏnar̥, -anɪr̥; sk‚ɪːb‚-] f.2 order, command, appointment.

skíra, skírði, skírður (skírt) [sk‚iːra, sk‚irˑðɪ, -ʏr̥, sk‚irˑt] wv.2 baptize.

skírdagur, -s, -ar [sk‚irˑda·qʏr̥, -daxs, -da·qar̥] m.1 Maundy-Thursday.

skírnarnafn, -s, -nöfn [skirðnar-nab·n̥; -nabn̥s, -naf·s; -nöb·n̥] n. Christian name, first name, given name.

Skírnir, -is [sk‚irðnɪr̥, -ɪs] m.1 in Old Icelandic myths, the messenger of Freyr; name of the oldest Icelandic (and Scandinavian) periodical (1827-).

skjaldar, see skjöldur.

Skjaldbreiður, -s [sk‚al·dbrei·ðʏr̥, -breiðs] m. 'Broad Shield,' a dome-shaped mountain northeast of Þingvellir.

skjálfa, skelf, skalf, skulfum, skolfinn (-ið) [sk‚aul·va, sk‚el·v, skal·v, skʏl·vʏm, skɔl·vɪn, -ɪð] v.3 shiver (with cold, etc.).

Skjálfandi, -a [sk‚aul·vandɪ, -a] wm.2 'The Shiverer,' a fjord in the North.

skjátlast, -aðist, -azt [sk‚auʰt·last, -aðɪst, -ast] wv.4 (middle voice only) be mistaken; mér skjátlast I am mistaken (S. VI, 7, 5).

skjóta, skýt, skaut, skutum, skotinn (-ið) [sk‚ouːtʰa, sk‚iːtʰ, sköyːtʰ, skʏːtʰʏm, skɔːtʰɪn, -ɪð; sk‚ouːda, sk‚iːd̥, sköyːd̥, skʏːdʏm, skɔːdɪn] v.2 shoot, shove; skjóta kúlu (dat.) shoot a projectile, a bullet; skjóta fugl (acc.) shoot a bird; skjótið! fire! skjóta á shoot at, bombard; skjóta niður shoot down; skjóta báti fram shove a boat forth, launch a boat; skjótast dart, run.

skjóttur, skjótt, skjótt [sk‚ouʰt:ʏr̥, sk‚ouʰt:] adj. piebald (of horses only); sá skjótti = Skjóni the piebald horse (S. III, 3, 3).

skjökta, skjökti, skjökt [sk‚öx·ta, -ɪ, sk‚öx·t] wv.2 limp.

skjöldur, skjaldar, skildir [sk‚öl·dʏr̥, sk‚al·dar̥, sk‚ɪl·dɪr̥] m.3 shield.

skóáburður, -ar [skouːau·bʏr·ðʏr̥, -ar̥] m.3 shoe polish.

skoða, -aði, -að [skɔːða, -aðɪ, -að, -aðʏr̥] wv.4 inspect, look at; look upon, consider; skoða e-ð look at sth; ég skoða það rétt I look upon it as right (consider it right) (S. VI, 4, 3); skoða sig um look around, see the sights.

skoðun, -unar, -anir [skɔːðʏn, -ʏnar̥, -anɪr̥] f.2 view, opinion.

skóf, -um, see skafa.

skógarleifar [skouː(q)ar-lei:var̥] f.1. pl. remnants of woods.

skógarmaður, -manns, -menn [skouː-(q)ar-ma:ðʏr̥, -man·s, -mɛn:] m.4 'man of the woods,' an outlaw (in Old Icelandic).

skógur, -ar, -ar [skouː(q)ʏr̥, -ar̥] m.1 woods, forest, birch copse; birchwood.

skóhlíf, -ar, -ar [skouːhl̥i·v, -var̥] f.1 rubber, galosh.

skók, -um, see skaka, skekja.

skólapiltur, -s, -ar [skouːla-pʰɪl·tʏr̥, -ar̥, -pʰɪlts] m.1 schoolboy.

skólaskyldur, -skyld, -skylt [skouːla-sk‚ɪl·dʏr̥, -sk‚ɪl·d̥, -sk‚ɪl·t] adj. compelled by law to go to school.

skólastofa, -u, -ur [skouːla-stɔːva, -ʏ(r̥)] wf.1 schoolroom.

Skólavörðuholt, -s [skouːlavör·ðʏ-hol·t, -hɔlts] n. 'School Cairn Hill,' in Reykjavík.

Skólavörðustígur, -s [skouːlavörðʏ-sti:qʏr̥, -stix·s] m.1 'School Cairn Path,' in Reykjavík.

skolfið, -inn, see skjálfa.

skóli, -a, -ar [skouːlɪ, -a(r̥)] wm.1 school.

skolla, skolli, skollað [skɔd·la, skɔd·lɪ, skɔd·lað] wv.3 (irreg. In. VII, 3, 4, 5(d)) hang loosely.

skolleitur, -leit, -leitt [skɔl·ei·tʰʏr̥, -l:ei·tʰ, -l:eiʰt·; -l:ei·d̥] adj. ashblond.

Consonants: [ð] breathe; [g] good; [gɹ] gyarden (garden); [hw] what; [j] yes; [kɹ] cyan (can); [ŋ] thing; [q] N. Germ. sagen; [r] Scottish r; [x] approx. Germ. ach; [þ] thin. Voiceless: o; [b̥, d̥, g̊] approx. p, t, k. Half-voiced: italics. Aspiration and preaspiration: [ʰ]; [pʰ, tʰ, kʰ] p-, t-, k-. Others as in English.

445

skollið, -inn, see 1. *skella*.

skólprenna, -u, -ur [skoul·pʰrɛn·a, -ʏ(r̥); skoul̥·p·] wf.1 waste pipe, gutter.

skóp, -um, see 2. *skapa*.

skopleikur, -s, -ar (-ir) [skɔ:pʰlei·kʰʏr̥, -lei·kʰs, -leixs, -lei·kʰar̥, -lei:k‚ʰɪr̥; skɔ:blei·ǥʏr̥, -ar̥, -lei·ǥs, -lei:ǥ‚ɪr̥] m.1 (or 2) comedy.

skopra, -aði, -að [skɔ:pʰra, -aðɪ, -að, -aðʏr̥; skɔ:bra] wv.4 roll.

skór, skós, skór [skou:r, skou:s] m.1 shoe.

skora, -u, -ur [skɔ:ra, -ʏ(r̥)] wf.1 cut, score, rift, chasm.

skorða, -u, -ur [skɔr·ða, -ʏ(r̥)] wf.1 prop, shore.

skorið, -inn, see *skera*.

skorta, skorti, skort [skɔr̥·ta, -ɪ, skɔr̥·t] wv.3 lack; *mig skortir ekkert* (acc.) I lack nothing (S. I, 2, *1*, 3).

skortur, -s [skɔr̥·tʏr̥, skɔr̥ts] m.1 lack, want; *skortur á e-u* lack of sth.

skósíður, -síð, -sítt [skou:si·ðʏr̥, -si·ð, -siʰt·] adj. reaching down to the shoes (of a low hanging garment).

skósmiður, -s, -ir [skou:smɪ·ðʏr̥, -smɪðs, -smɪ·ðɪr̥] m.2 shoemaker.

skósverta, -u, -ur [skou:svɛr̥ta, -ʏ(r̥)] wf.1 shoeblack.

skot, -s, - [skɔ:tʰ, skɔ:tʰs; skɔ:d̥(s)] n. shot; nook, cranny.

skotbyrgi, -s, - [skɔ:tʰbɪrǥ‚ɪ(s); skɔ:d̥-] n. dug-out.

skotfæradeild, -ar, -ir (-sveit, -ar, -ir) [skɔ:tʰfai·ra-deil·d̥, -ar̥, -ɪr̥; skɔ:d̥-; -svei:tʰ, -ar̥; -ɪr̥; -svei:d̥] f.2 ammunition service.

skotfæri [skɔ:tʰfai·rɪ; skɔ:d̥-] n.pl. ammunition.

skotgrafabyssa, -u, -ur [skɔ:tʰgra·va-bɪs:a, -ʏ(r̥); skɔ:d̥-] wf.1 trench mortar.

skotgröf, -grafar, -ir [skɔ:tʰgrö·v, -gra·var̥, -ɪr̥; skɔ:d̥-] f.2 trench, pl. trenches, entrenchments.

skotheldur, -held, -helt [skɔ:tʰɛldʏr̥, -hɛld̥; -hɛl̥t; skɔ:d̥-] adj. shotproof, bombproof.

skothríð, -ar, -ir [skɔ:tʰr̥i·ð, ·ðar̥, ·ðɪr̥;

skɔ:d̥-] f.2 shower, rain of bullets, bombardment.

skotið, -inn, see *skjóta*.

skotvígi, -s, - [skɔ:tʰvi·jɪ(s); skɔ:d̥-] n. battery.

skotæfing, -ar, -ar [skɔ:tʰai·viŋ, -ar̥; skɔ:d̥-] f.1 gunnery practice, target practice, rifle practice.

skott, -s, - [skɔ‚ʰt:, skɔ‚ʰt·s] n. tail; *skottið á hundinum* the tail of the dog (S. I, 4, *1*, 4); *skott á húfu* tassel of a cap.

skotta, -u, -ur [skɔ‚ʰt:a, -ʏ(r̥)] wf.1 a female ghost.

skotthúfa, -u, -ur [skɔ‚ʰt:hu·(v)a, -hu·(v)ʏ(r̥)] wf.1 a tasseled cap used with *peysuföt*.

skóverkstæði, -s, - [skou:vɛr̥·kstai·-ðɪ(s)] n. shoe repair shop.

skóverzlun, -unar, -anir [skou:vɛrslʏn, -ʏnar̥, -anɪr̥] f.2 shoe store.

1. skrá, skrár, skrár [skrau:(r)] f.1 list, register, catalogue; *skrá yfir e-ð* list of sth.; lock.

2. skrá, skráði, skráð(ur) [skrau:, skrau:ðɪ, -ʏr̥, skrau:ð] wv.3 write, register, list.

skrafa, -aði, -að [skra:va, -aðɪ, -að] wv.4 talk, chat, prate.

skrapp, see *skreppa*.

skrásetja, -setti, -sett(ur) [skrau:sɛ·tʰja, -scʰt·ɪ, -ʏr̥, -scʰt·; -sɛ·d̥ja] wv.1 register; *skrásetja vörumerki* register a trade-mark; *skrásetja bréf* register a letter; *skrásetja drauga-sögur* write up ghost stories.

skreið, see *skríða*.

skreiðast, skreiddist, skreiðzt [skrei:-ðast, skreid̥:ɪst, skreiðst] wv.4 (middle voice only) creep (with difficulty).

skreppa, skrepp, skrapp, skruppum, skroppinn (-ið) [skrɛʰp:a, skrɛʰp:, skraʰp:, skrʏʰp:ʏm, skrɔʰp:ɪn, -ɪð] v.3 go for a moment, run, slip, dash for; *skreppa inn* drop in (at a drug-store); *skreppa heim* run home; *skreppa til næsta bæjar* make a short visit (trip) to the next farm-

Vowels: *a* [a] approx. father; *á* [au] cow; *e* [ɛ] set; *é* [jɛ] yes; *i, y* [ɪ] sit; *í, ý* [i] feel; *o* [ɔ] law; *ó* [ou] note; *u* [ʏ] approx. Germ. Mütter; *ú* [u] school; *y* = *i*; *ý* = *í*; *œ* [ai] ice; *ö* [ö] Germ. hören; *au* [öy] French feuille; *ei, ey* [ei] ale. Length [:]; half-length [·].

446

stead; *skreppa út í bœ* run out
(into the town) for a moment.

skríða, -u, -ur [skrɪ:ða, -ʏ(r̥)] wf.1
slide, land-slide, rock-slide.

skríða, skríð, skreið, skriðum, skriðinn
(-ið) [skri:ða, skri:ðᵊ, skrei:ð,
skrɪ:ðʏm, skrɪ:ðɪn, -ɪð] v.1 creep,
crawl; glide.

skriðdrekabyssa, -u, -ur [skrɪð·drɛ·kʰa-
bɪs:a, -ʏ(r̥); -drɛ·g̊a-] wf.1 antitank gun, antitank rifle.

skriðdreki, -a, -ar [skrɪð·drɛ·kjʰɪ,
-drɛ·kʰa(r̥); -drɛ·g̊ⱼɪ, -drɛ·g̊a] wm.1
' crawling dragon,' tank.

skriðjökull, -uls, -lar [skrɪð·jö·kʰʏdl̥,
-ʏls, -jöʰklar̥] m.1 (crawling, moving) glacier, gletcher; *skriðjökuls-
tunga* tongue of glacier.

skriðsund, -s [skrɪð·sʏnd̥(s)] n. crawl
(swimming).

skrifa, -aði, -að(ur) [skrɪ:va, -aðɪ,
-að, -aðʏr̥] wv.4 write; *skrifast á*
write to each other; *skrifa bréf*
write a letter; *skrifa e-m* write to
sbdy.

skrifstofa, -u, -ur [skrɪf·stɔ·va, -ʏ(r̥)]
wf.1 office, study.

skrifstofumaður, -manns, -menn [skrɪf·-
stɔ·vʏ·ma:ðʏr̥, -man·s, -mɛn:] m.4
office worker, white collar worker.

skrifstofustörf, -starfa [skrɪf·stɔ·vʏ-
stör·v, -star·va] n.pl. office work.

skrítinn, -in, -ið; skrítnari, -astur
[skri:tʰɪn, -ɪn, -ɪð; skri:d̥·; skriʰt·-
narɪ, -astʏr̥] adj. funny, peculiar, odd.

skrolla, skrolli, skrollað [skrɔd·la, -ɪ,
-að] wv.3 (irreg. In. VII, 3, 4, 5 (d))
hang loosely.

skroppið, -inn, see *skreppa*.

skrúði, -a, -ar [skru:ðɪ, -a(r̥)] wm.1
vestments.

skrúfa, -u, -ur, (-na) [skru:va, -ʏ(r);
skrub·na] wf.1 screw.

skruppum, see *skreppa*.

skræfa, -u, -ur [skrai:va, -ʏ(r̥)] wf.1
coward.

skrælingi, -ja, -jar [skrai:liŋg̊ⱼɪ,
-g̊ⱼa(r̥)] wm.1 barbarian; Eskimo.

skrökva, -aði, -að [skrö:kʰva, -aðɪ,

-að; skrö:g̊va] wv.4 not tell the
truth (weaker than *ljúga* lie).

skúffa, -u, -ur [skuf:a, -ʏ(r̥)] wf.1
drawer.

skuggamynd, -ar, -ir [skʏg̊:a·mɪn·d̥,
-ar̥, -ɪr̥] f.2 picture projected or
thrown on a screen; *sýna skuggamyndir* show pictures, illustrate
with slides.

skuggi, -a, -ar [skʏg̊ⱼ:ɪ, skʏg̊:a(r̥)]
wm.1 shadow.

skuld, -ar, -ir [skʏl·d̥, -ar̥, -ɪr̥] f.2
debt.

skulda, -aði, -að [skʏl·da, -aðɪ, -að]
wv.4 owe; *skulda e-m e-ð* owe sbdy
sth.

skuldunautur, -ar, -ar [skʏl·dʏ·nöy:-
tʰʏr̥, -ar̥; -nöy:dʏr̥] m.1 debtor.

skulfum, see *skjálfa*.

Skúli, -a [sku:lɪ, -a] wm.1 pers. name.

skulu, skal, skulum, skyldi, pret. inf.
skyldu [skʏ:lʏ, ska:l, skʏ:lʏm,
sk,ɪl·dɪ, sk,ɪl·dʏ] pret. pres. v. (In.
VII, 5, 1) shall, will; (1) *ég skal*
I will, *þú skalt* you shall, *við
skulum* (a) we will, (b) let us;
(2) *hvað skal segja?* what is to be
done (decided, said) ? (S. VI, 11, 6;
14, 8); *hér skal aðeins minnzt á
það* here only this shall be mentioned; *skyldi bóndi segja honum
nafn hans* the farmer was to tell
him his (the other person's) name;
(3) *skal* (*skyldi*) *hann fara?* I
wonder whether he will go; *skyldi
það?* I wonder (whether it is so)
(S. VI, 9, 2, 2); *það skyldi þó
aldrei hafa verið?* it couldn't have
been . . . could it? it wouldn't,
I suppose, have been? I wonder
whether that was not . . . (so);
nú fór verr en skyldi this went
worse than it should have; (4) *skulu*
(or *skuli*) inf. pres.: *hún segist
skuli reyna það* she says that she
will try it; *skyldu* (or *skyldi*) inf.
pret.: *hann sagðist skyldu koma* he
said that he would come (S. VI,
11, 1). See also S. VI, 2, 5n; 4, 3;
13, 6.

Consonants: [ð] brea*the*; [g] *g*ood; [gⱼ] *gy*arden (garden); [hw] *wh*at; [j] *y*es; [kⱼ] *cy*an
(can); [ŋ] thi*ng*; [q] N. Germ. sa*g*en; [r] Scottish *r*; [x] approx. Germ. a*ch*; [þ] *th*in.
Voiceless: ○ ; [b̥, d̥, g̊] approx. *p, t, k*. Half-voiced: *italics*. Aspiration and preaspiration:
[ʰ]; [pʰ, tʰ, kʰ] *p-, t-, k-*. Others as in English.

skullum, see 1. *skella*.

skurður, -ar, -ir [skɪr·ðʏr̥, -ar̥, -ɪr̥] m.3 cut, operation; trench, canal, ditch.

1. skúta, -u, -ur [sku:tʰa, -ʏ(r); sku:da] wf.1 small craft, vessel, smack.

2. skúta, skútti, skútt [sku:tʰa, skuʰt:ɪ, skuʰt:; sku:d·] wv.3 overhang.

skúti, -a, -ar [sku:tʰɪ, -a(r̥); sku:dɪ] wm.1 cave; *það er lakur skúti, sem ekki er betri en úti* ' it is a miserable cave that is not better than being outside.'

skutum, see *skjóta*.

ský, -s, - [skji:(s)] n. cloud.

skyggn, skyggn, skyggnt [skjɪg̊·n̥, skjɪŋ·tʰ; skjɪŋ̊·t] adj. clairvoyant.

skylda, -u, -ur [skjɪl·da, -ʏ(r̥)] wf.1 duty.

skyldfólk, -s [skjɪl·d̥foulkʰ; -foulkʰs, -fouls; -foulk] n. (coll.) relatives.

skyldi, -u, see *skulu*.

skyldur, skyld, skylt [skjɪl·d̥ʏr̥, skjɪl·d̥, skjɪl·t] adj. related; in duty bound; *hann er skyldur mér* he is related to me (S. I, 3, 2, 1).

skyn, -s [skjɪ:n, skjɪn·s] n. sense, understanding; *gefa e-ð í skyn* hint sth; *bera skyn á e-ð* understand about sth, be an expert on sth.

skyndi- [skjɪn·dɪ·] pref. rush-, quick, blitz-.

skyndiárás [skjɪn·dɪ·au:rau·s, -ar̥, -ɪr̥] f.2 rush-attack, blitz-attack.

skynja, -aði, -að [skjɪn·ja, -aðɪ, -að, -aðʏr̥] wv.4 sense, perceive, understand, make out.

skyr, -s [skjɪ:r, skjɪr̥·s] n. Icelandic curds (or cream cheese).

skýra, skýrði, skýrður (skýrt) [skji:ra, skjir·ðɪ, -ʏr̥, skjir̥·t] wv.2 explain, interpret; *skýra frá e-u* tell of sth.

skyrblanda, -blöndu [skjɪr·blanda, -blöndʏr̥] wf.1 sour Icelandic curds mixed with water.

skýring, -ar, -ar [skji:riŋ̊, -ar̥] f.1

explanation; *til skýringar* in explanation, to illustrate.

skýrsla, -u, -ur [skjɪr̥sla, -ʏ(r̥)] wf.1 report.

skyrta, -u, -ur [skjɪr̥·ta, -ʏ(r̥)] wf.1 shirt (= *manséttskyrta*).

skyrtuhnappur, -s, -ar [skjɪr̥·tʏ·hnaʰp:-ʏr̥, -ar̥, -hnaʰp·s] m.1 stud.

skýt, see *skjóta*.

skytta, -u, -ur [skjɪʰt:a, -ʏ(r̥)] wf.1 sharpshooter, shot.

skæður, skæð, skætt [skjai:ðʏr̥, skjai:ð, skjaiʰt:] adj. dangerous; *skæður e-m* dangerous for sbdy.

skæla, skældi, skældur (skælt) [skjai:-la, skjail·dɪ, skjail·dʏr̥, skjail·t] wv.2 cry (of children); *skæla sig* make faces; *skældur* distorted.

sköft, see *skaft*.

skömm, skammar, -ir [sköm:, skam:-ar̥, -ɪr̥] f.2 shame; *hafðu skömm fyrir* shame on you for this.

skömm, see *skammur*.

skörð, see *skarð*.

skötu, see *skata*.

s.l. = *síðastliðinn* last, past.

slá, slæ, sló, slógum, sleginn (-ið) [slau:, slai:, slou:, slou:(g)ʏm, slei:jɪn, -ɪð] v.6 beat, strike, smite, knock, kick, slap; mow, cut grass; kill, slay, etc. (1) beat, strike: *slá e-n högg* give sbdy a blow; *slá ösku úr pípu* knock the ashes from a pipe; *slá botn í* (originally:) ' hammer a bottom into a barrel,' end (a letter); *slá tvær flugur í einu höggi* swat two flies at one blow, i. e. do two things at the same time; *slá túnið* mow the homefield; (2) impersonal: *öllu slær í dúnalogn* everything becomes dead calm; (3) with preps: strike: *slá e-u í e-n* strike sbdy with sth; *slá (svipunni) í hestinn* strike the horse with the whip, spur the horse; *slá upp dansi* strike up a dance, dance.

S-land = *Suðurland* The South of Iceland.

slapp, see 1. *sleppa*.

Vowels: *a* [a] approx. father; *á* [au] cow; *e* [ɛ] set; *é* [jɛ] yes; *i, y* [ɪ] sit; *í, ý* [i] feel; *o* [ɔ] law; *ó* [ou] note; *u* [ʏ] approx. Germ. Mütter; *ú* [u] school; *y = i*; *ý = í*; *æ* [ai] ice; *ö* [ö] Germ. hören; *au* [öy] French feuille; *ei, ey* [ei] ale. Length [:]; half-length [·].

slátra, -aði, -að [slau:tʰra, -aðɪ, -að; slau:dra] wv.4 slaughter; *slátra nauti* slaughter a bull.

slátur, (-ri), -urs, -ur [slau:tʰʏr̥(s), slau:tʰrɪ; slau:dʏr̥, slau:drɪ] n. Icelandic blood and liver sausages.

sláturfélag, -s, -lög [slau:tʰʏr̥-fje:laq, -laxs, -lög; slau:dʏr̥-] n. co-operative butchery; *Sláturfélag Suður-lands* ' The Co-operative Butcheries of the South.'

sláturtíð, -ar, -ir [slau:tʰʏr̥-tʰi:ð, -ðar̥, -ðɪr̥; slau:dʏr̥-] f.2 the season of slaughtering (the lambs in the fall).

sláttulok [slauʰt:ʏ-lɔ:kʰ; -lɔ:g̊] n.pl. the end of the haymaking season (also: *sláttarlok*).

sláttur, -ar, slættir [slauʰt:ʏr̥, -ar̥, slaiʰt:ɪr̥] m.3 mowing season, hay-making season; *fyrir, eftir slátt* before, after the haymaking season; *á slætti* during the haymaking season.

slaufa, -u, -ur [slöy:fa, -ʏ(r̥)] wf.1 tie, a bow (used with full dress).

sleði, -a, -ar [slɛ:ðɪ, -a(r̥)] wm.1 sleigh, sledge, sled.

slegið, -inn, see *slá.*

sleit, see *slíta.*

slekk, see 1. *slökkva.*

1. sleppa, slepp, slapp, sluppum, slopp--inn (-ið) [slɛʰp:a, slɛʰp:, slaʰp:, slʏʰp:ʏm, slɔʰp:ɪn, -ɪð] v.3 (intr.) escape, get off.

2. sleppa, sleppti, sleppt [slɛʰp:a, slɛf--tɪ, slɛf·t] wv.2 (trans.) let go; *sleppa e-m* let sbdy go, leave hold of; release, set free.

1. slétta, -u, -ur [sljɛʰt:a, -ʏ(r̥)] wf.1 plain.

2. slétta, slétti, slétt(ur) or -aði, -að(ur) [sljɛʰt:a, -ɪ, -ʏr̥, sljɛʰt:; -aðɪ, -að, -aðʏr̥] wv.2 & 4 make level.

sléttur, slétt, slétt [sljɛʰt:ʏr̥, sljɛʰt:] adj. smooth, level, plain.

slíður, (-ri), -urs, -ur [sli:ðʏr̥(s), slið·rɪ] n. scabbard, sheath.

slifsi, -s, - [slɪf·sɪ(s)] n. (1) a broad

tie (scarf) used with *peysuföt*; (2) men's tie, = *bindi.*

slíkur, slík, slíkt [sli:kʰʏr̥, sli:kʰ, slix·t; sli:g̊ʏr̥, sli:g̊] adj. (dem. pron. In. VI, 3n2) such; *slíkur maður* such a man; *sem slíkur* as such; *slíkt og þvílíkt!* the idea of it! (S. IV, 3, 5).

slíta, slít, sleit, slitum, slitinn (-ið) [sli:tʰa, sli:tʰ, slei:tʰ, slɪ:tʰʏm, slɪ:tʰɪn, -ɪð; sli:da, sli:d, slei:d, slɪ:dʏm, slɪ:dɪn] v.1 break, tear apart, break off, dissolve (trans.); *slíta sambandi* dissolve, abrogate a union.

sljór, sljó, sljótt; sljórri, sljóastur [sljou:r, sljou:, sljouʰt:, sljour:ɪ, sljou:astʏr̥] adj. dull, unsensitive.

sló, see *slá.*

slóð, -ar, -ir [slou:ð, -ðar̥, -ðɪr̥] f.2 track; tract; *hér um slóðir* in these parts.

slógum, see *slá.*

sloppið, -inn, see 1. *sleppa.*

slóra, slórði (slóraði), slórt, slórað [slou:ra,slour·ðɪ(slou:raðɪ),slour̥·t, slou:rað] wv.3 & 4 loaf, tarry.

sluppum, see 1. *sleppa.*

slúta, slútti, slútt [slu:tʰa, sluʰt:(ɪ); slu:da] wv.3 project, hang down.

slyngur, slyng, slyngt [sliŋ·g̊ʏr̥, sliŋ·g̊, sliŋ·tʰ; sliŋ·t] adj. capable, shrewd; skilled, expert.

slys, -s, - [slɪ:s, slɪs:] n. accident.

slysa, -aði, -að(ur) [slɪ:sa, -aðɪ, -að, -aðʏr̥] wv.4 make one have an accident (*slys*); *slysast* have an accident.

slæ, see *slá.*

slæða, -u, -ur [slai:ða, -ʏ(r̥)] wf.1 veil.

slæmur, slæm, slæmt; verri, verstur [slai:mʏr̥, slai:m, slaim·tʰ; slaiɱ·t; ver:ɪ, verstʏr̥] adj. bad, unwell; *það er slæmt* it is a pity; *slæmt samband (í síma)* bad connection (on the phone).

1. slökkva, slekk, slökk, - [slöʰk:va, slɛʰk:, slöʰk:] v.3 or more commonly:

2. slökkva, slökkti, slökkt(ur) [slöʰk :-
va, slöx·tɪ, -ʏr̥, slöx·t] wv.2 extinguish, put out (light, fire).
slöngva, -aði, -að(ur) [slöyŋ·g̊va, -aðɪ,
-að, -aðʏr̥] wv.4 sling, hurl; slöngva
steini hurl a stone.
1. smá, see smár.
2. smá- [smau:-] pref. small, little,
etc.
smáflotadeild, -ar, -ir [smau:-flɔ:tʰa-
deil·d̥, -ar̥, -ɪr̥; flɔ:d̥a-] f.2 fleet division (four vessels), small part of
a fleet.
smáfugl, -s, -ar [smau:fʏg̊l̥(s), -fʏg̊l-
ar̥] m.l small bird.
smákökur [smau:kʰö·kʰʏr̥, -kʰö·g̊ʏr̥]
wf.1.pl. cookies.
smala, -aði, -að(ur) [sma:la, -aðɪ,
-að, -aðʏr̥] wv.4 smala fénu gather
the sheep (from the mountain pas-
tures); smala atkvæðum canvass
for votes.
smalamaður, -manns, -menn [sma:la-
ma:ðʏr̥, -man·s, -mɛn:] m.4 (=
smali) shepherd.
smalastúlka, -u, -ur [sma:la-stul·kʰa,
-ʏ(r̥); -stul·ka] wf.1 shepherdess.
smali, -a, -ar [sma:lɪ, -a(r̥)] wm.l
shepherd; (= búsmali, fé) sheep.
small, see smella.
smáminnka, -aði, -að [smau:miŋ·kʰa,
-aðɪ, -að, -miŋ·ka] wv.4 dwindle;
get smaller and smaller.
smámunur, -ar, -ir [smau:mʏ·nʏr̥, -ar̥,
-ɪr̥] m.3 a little thing, trifle.
smápeningur, -s, -ar [smau:pʰɛ·niŋg̊ʏr̥,
-iŋs, -iŋg̊ar̥] m.l a small coin, pl.
(small) change.
smár, smá, smátt; smærri, smæstur
[smau:r, smau:, smauʰt:, smair:ɪ,
smais·tʏr̥] adj. small, little, fine;
smám (dat.pl.) saman = smátt og
smátt by degrees; smátt small
things, change.
Smáragata, -götu [smau:ra-ga:tʰa,
-gö:tʰʏ; -ga:d̥a, -gö:d̥ʏ] wf.1 'Clover
Street.'
smári, -a, -ar [smau:rɪ, -a(r̥)] wm.l
clover; also a family name.

smásaga, -sögu, -ur [smau:sa·qa, -sö·-
qʏ(r̥)] wf.l short story.
smásala, -sölu, -ur [smau:sa·la, -sö·-
lʏ(r̥)] wf.l retail (business).
smáskip, -s, - [smau:skⱼɪ·pʰ, -skⱼɪfs]
n. little ship, small ship.
smáskæra, -u, -ur [smau:skⱼai·ra,
-ʏ(r̥)] wf.l guerilla fighting.
smáskæruflokkur, -s, -ar [smau:skⱼai·-
rʏ-flɔʰk:ʏr̥, -flɔʰk·s, -flɔx·s, -flɔʰk:ar̥]
m.l guerilla band.
smásöluverzlun, -unar, -anir [smau:-
sö·lʏ-verslʏn, -ʏnar̥, -anɪr̥] f.2 retail
business.
smátt, see smár.
smaug, see smjúga.
smáútræði, -s [smau:-u·tʰrai·ðɪ, -s;
-u·d̥-] n. small scale fishing.
smávaxa, -vex, -óx, -uxum, -vaxinn
(-ið) [smau:-vax·sa, -vex·s, -oux·s,
-ʏx·sʏm, -vax·sɪn, -ɪð] v.7 grow by
degrees; pp. smávaxinn small of
stature, little of stature.
smekkur, -s [smɛʰk:ʏr̥, smɛʰk·s] m.2
taste.
smekkvísi [smɛʰk:vi·sɪ] wf.2 taste,
good taste.
smella, smell, small, smullum, smoll-
inn (-ið) [smɛd·la, smɛd·l̥, smad·l̥,
smʏd·lʏm, smʊd̥·lɪn, -ɪð] v.3 clash,
crack.
smíð, -ar, -ar [smi:ð, -ðar̥, -ðar̥] f.l
building; a thing built, forged or
made by a smiður (= smíði).
smíða, -aði, -að(ur) [smi:ða, -aðɪ, -að,
-aðʏr̥] wv.4 work in wood or metals;
forge, make, build; smíða kirkju
build a church; smíða undir hest
make shoes for a horse.
smíði, -ar, -ar [smi:ðɪ, -ar̥] f.l building; í smíðum a-building.
smiðja, -u, -ur [smɪð·ja, -ʏ(r̥)] wf.l
smithy, forge.
smiður, -s, -ir [smɪ:ðʏr̥, smɪð·s, smɪ:-
ðɪr̥] m.2 smith, blacksmith, car-
penter, builder, (gold-, silver-) smith.
smjúga, smýg, smaug, smugum, smog-
inn (-ið) [smju:qa, smi:q, smöy:q,
smʏ:qʏm, smɔi:jɪn, -ɪð; smɔ:jɪn]
v.2 creep.

smjör, -s [smjö:*r*, smjö*r̥*·s] n. butter;
brætt smjör melted butter.

smjörgrautur, -ar [smjör·gröy:t*ʰ*Y*r̥*,
-a*r̥*; -gröy·dY*r̥*] m.1 wheat flour
cooked in milk and butter.

smogið, -inn, see *smjúga*.

smóking, -s, -ar [smou:k₁*ʰ*iŋg̊, -iŋs,
-iŋg̊a*r̥*; smou:g̊₁·] m.1 dinner jacket,
tuxedo.

smollið, -inn, see *smella*.

smugum, see *smjúga*.

smullum, see *smella*.

smurði, smurður, see *smyrja*.

smýg, see *smjúga*.

smyrja, smurði, smurður (smurt)
[smIr·ja, smYr·ðI, smYr·ðY*r̥*, smYr·t;
smYr·ja] wv.1 (Pr. *2, 1*, 1ĺn)
butter, smear, grease; anoint;
smurt brauð bread and butter.

smærri, smæstur, see *smár*.

snáfa, -aði, -að [snau:va, -aðI, -að]
wv.4 retreat shamefully; *snáfaðu
burtu* go away, pack off, away with
you, scram!

snagi, -a, -ar [snai:jI, sna:qa(*r̥*);
sna:jI] wm.1 clothes-peg.

snar, snör, snart [sna:*r*, snö:*r*, sna*r̥*·t]
adj. quick, gallant; hard-spun.

snarar, -ir, see *snör*.

snarpur, snörp, snarpt [snar̥·pY*r̥*,
snör̥·p, sna*r̥*·(f)t] adj. rough to the
touch; sharp; dashing, brisk, active.

snart, see *snar* and 2. *snerta*.

1. sneið, -ar; -ar, -ir [snei:ð, -ðar,
-ðI*r̥*] f.1 & 2 slice; *sneið af brauði*
slice of bread.

2. sneið, see *sníða*.

snemma, fyrr, fyrst [snɛm:a, fIr:,
fI*r̥*st] adv. (In. IV, **2**(d)) early,
earlier, earliest; *snemma dags* early
in the day; *snemma um daginn*
early (in) that day (S. I, **4**, *2, 5*).

sneri, snéri, see *snúa*.

1. snerta, snerti, snert(ur) [snɛr̥·ta,
-I, -Y*r̥*, snɛr̥·t] wv.2 or (more
rarely):

2. snerta, (snerti), snart, snurtum,
snortinn (-ið) [snɛr̥·ta, snɛr̥·tI,
snar̥·t, snYr̥·tYm, snɔr̥·tIn, -Ið] v.3

touch; *hvað . . . snertir* concerning;
pp. *snortinn* touched.

sníða, sníð, sneið, sniðum, sniðinn
(-ið) [sni:ða, sni:ð, snei:ð, snI:-
ðYm, snI:ðIn, -Ið] v.1 cut.

snjá, snjáði, snjáð(ur) [snjau:, snjau:-
ðI, snjau:ð, snjau:ðY*r̥*] wv.3 wear
threadbare, make threadbare; *snjást*
become threadbare.

snjall, snjöll, snjallt [snjad·l, snjöd·l,
snjal·t] adj. masterful, ingenious,
excellent.

snjár, snjávar, see *snjór*.

snjóa, -aði, -að(ur) [snjou:a, -aðI,
-að, -aðY*r̥*] wv.4 snow; *hann (það)
snjóar* it is snowing (S. VI, **4**, *3*).

snjór, snjár, snær; snjóar, snjávar, snævar; snjóar [snjou:*r*, snjau:*r*,
snai:*r*, snjou:a*r̥*, snjau:va*r̥*, snai:-
va*r̥*; snjou:a*r̥*] m.1 (In. I, **2**, *1*(b)**9**)
snow; pl. spells of snowfalls, snow-
storms.

snjótittlingur, -ings, -ingar [snjou:-
t*ʰ*ɪ*ʰ*t·liŋg̊Y*r̥*, -iŋs, -iŋg̊a*r̥*] m.1 snow
bunting (in winter feathers); cf.
sólskríkja.

snjöll, see *snjallur*.

Snorri, -a [snɔr:I, -a] m.1 pers.
name; *Snorri Sturluson* (1179-1241)
famous author; cf. *Edda* and *Sturlunga*.

snortið, -inn, see 2. *snerta*.

snotur, snotur, snoturt; snotrari,
-astur [snɔ:t*ʰ*Y*r̥*, snɔ:t*ʰ*Y*r̥*t, snɔ:-
t*ʰ*rarI, -astY*r̥*; snɔ:dY*r̥*(t), snɔ:-
drarI] adj. pretty, handsome, good-
looking, nice-looking.

snúa (snú) sný; sneri, snéri, snöri;
snúinn (-ið) [snu:a, snu:, sni:,
snɛ:rI, snjɛ:rI, snö:rI, snu:In, -Ið]
v. irreg. (In. VII, **5**, *2*) turn (in a
certain direction); *snúa e-u* turn
sth; *snúa sér* turn oneself, turn;
snúa til vinstri turn to the left;
snúast við e-u react to sth, take a
certain course in a case.

snúður, -ar (-s), -ar [snu:ðY*r̥*, -a*r̥*,
snuð·s] m.1 bun.

snurtum, see 2. *snerta*.

sný, see *snúa*.

Consonants: [ð] brea*th*e; [g] *g*ood; [g₁] *gy*arden (garden); [hw̥] *wh*at; [j] *y*es; [k₁] *cy*an
(can); [ŋ] thi*ng*; [q] N. Germ. sa*g*en; [r] Scottish *r*; [x] approx. Germ. a*ch*; [þ] *th*in.
Voiceless: ○; [b̥, d̥, g̊] approx. *p, t, k*. Half-voiced: *italics*. Aspiration and preaspiration:
[*ʰ*]; [p*ʰ*, t*ʰ*, k*ʰ*] *p*-, *t*-, *k*-. Others as in English.

451

snyrta, snyrti, snyrt(ur) [snɪr̥·ta, -ɪ, -ʏr̥, snɪr̥·t] wv.2 dress, fix up; manicure.

snyrtiborð, -s, - [snɪr̥·tɪ·bɔr·ð, -bɔrðs] n. dressing table.

snyrtivörur [snɪr̥·tɪ·vö:rʏr̥] wf.1.pl. cosmetics, toilet articles.

snæða, snæddi, snæddur (snætt) [snai:ða, snaid̥:ɪ, -ʏr̥, snaiʰt:] wv.2 eat.

Snæfell, -s [snai:fed̥l, -fɛls] n. 'Snow Fell.'

Snæfellsnes, -s [snai:fɛls·nɛ:s, -nɛs:] n. 'Snow Fell Ness.'

snær, snævar, see snjór.

snætt, see snæða.

snöggklippa, -klippti, -klippt(ur) [snö̊g̊ɪ·kʰlɪʰp·a, -kʰlɪf·tɪ, -ʏr̥, -kʰlɪf·t] wv.2 cut (the hair) close.

snögglega [snö̊g̊:lɛ·qa] adv. suddenly.

snöggur, snögg, snöggt; snögg(v)ari, -(v)astur [snög̊:ʏr̥, snög̊:, snöx·t; snög̊:(v)arɪ, -(v)astʏr̥] adj. sudden; short (of hair, grass); quick; snöggvast adv. just for a moment.

1. snör, snarar, -ir [snö:r, sna:rar̥, -ɪr̥] f.2 Old Icelandic: daughter-in-law; now: poetic word for woman.

2. snör, see snar.

snöri, see snúa.

snörp, see snarpur.

soð, -s [sɔ:ð, sɔð·s] n. broth.

sóðakaka, -köku, -ur [sou:da·kʰa:kʰa, -kʰö:kʰʏ(r̥); -kʰa:g̊a, -kʰö:g̊ʏ(r̥)] wf.1 plain cake.

soðið, -inn, see sjóða.

sogið, -inn, see sjúga.

sofa, sef, svaf, sváfum, sofinn (-ið) [sɔ:va, sɛ:v, sva:v, svau:vʏm, sɔ:-vɪn, -ɪð] v.5 sleep; sofa við teppi sleep with blankets; sofa yfir sig oversleep; (S. VI, 4, 3; 6, 2).

sófi, (sóffi), -a, -ar [sou:fɪ, souf:ɪ, -a, -ar̥] wm.1 sofa.

sofna, -aði, -að(ur) [sɔb·na, -aðɪ, -að, -aðʏr̥] wv.4 fall asleep (S. VI, 6, 2); ég var að sofna I was falling asleep; hann er sofnaður he has fallen asleep.

Sog, -s [sɔ:q, sɔx·s] n. 'The Sucker,' a big river draining the Þingvalla-vatn.

sokkaband, -s, -bönd [sɔʰk:a·ban·d̥(s), -bön·d̥] n. garter.

sokkabandsbelti, -s, - [sɔʰk:aban(d̥)s·bɛl·tɪ(s)] n. girdle.

sokkið, -inn, see 1. sökkva.

sokkur, -s, -ar [sɔʰk:ʏr̥, -ar̥, sɔʰk·s] m.1 stocking, sock, hose; einir sokk-ar one pair of socks; vera í tvenn-um sokkum wear (have on) two pair of socks.

sókn, -ar, -ir [souʰk·n̥, -nar̥, -nɪr̥] f.2 the act of seeking, visiting, at-tacking; = kirkjusókn, prestakall parish; attack, offensive.

sóknarnefnd, -ar, -ir [souʰk·nar·nɛm·d̥, -ar̥, -ɪr̥] f.2 parish board.

sóknarprestur, -s, -ar [souʰk·nar·pʰres-·tʏr̥, -pʰrɛs:, -pʰrɛs·tar̥] m.1 parish priest, parson.

sól, -ar, -ir, (-na) [sou:l, -lar̥, -lɪr̥; soul·na] f.2 (wf.1) sun.

sóla, -aði, -að(ur) [sou:la, -aðɪ, -að, -aðʏr̥] wv.4 sole (a shoe).

sólarhringur, -s, -ar [sou:la(r̥)·hrɪŋ-·g̊ʏr̥, -hrɪŋ·s, -hrɪŋ·g̊ar̥] m.1 twenty-four hours; day and night.

solgið, -inn, see 1. svelgja.

sóli, -a, -ar [sou:lɪ, -a(r̥)] wm.1 sole.

sólskin, -s, - [soul·skɪ·n, -skₗɪns] n. sunshine.

sólskríkja, -u, -ur [soul·skri·kₗʰa, -kₗʰʏ(r̥); -skri·g̊ₗ·] wf.1 snow bunt-ing (in summer feathers); cf. snjótittlingur.

soltið, -inn, see 1. svelta.

Sólvallagata, -götu [soul·vadla·ga:tʰa, -gö:tʰʏ, -ga:da, -gö:d̥ʏ] wf.1 'Sunny Field Road.'

Solveig, -ar [sɔl·vɛi·q, -qar̥] f.1 pers. name.

sónata, -ötu, -ötur [sou:na·tʰa, -ö·tʰ-ʏ(r̥), -a·da, -ö·d̥ʏ(r̥)] wf.1 sonata.

son(ur), -ar, synir [sɔ:nʏr̥, sɔ:n, sɔ:nar̥, sɪ:nɪr̥] m.3 son; as a part of patronymics always: -son.

sópa, -aði, -að(ur) [sou:pʰa, -aðɪ, -að, -aðʏr̥; sou:ba] wv.4 sweep, brush.

sopið, -inn, see súpa.

Vowels: a [a] approx. father; á [au] cow; e [ɛ] set; é [jɛ] yes; i, y [ɪ] sit; í, ý [i] feel; o [ɔ] law; ó [ou] note; u [ʏ] approx. Germ. Mütter; ú [u] school; y = i; ý = í; æ [ai] ice; ö [ö] Germ. hören; au [öy] French feuille; ei, ey [ei] ale. Length [:]; half-length [·].

sór, -um, see *sverja*.

sorfið, -inn, see *sverfa*.

sortna, -aði, -að(ur) [sɔrtna, -aðɪ, -að, -aðʏr̥] wv.4 darken, blacken.

sósíaldemókrati, -a, -ar [sou:sijalde:moukʰra·tʰɪ, -a, -ar̥; -kʰra·dɪ] wm.1 (= *krati*) social democrat.

sósíalisti, -a, -ar [sou:sijalɪs·tɪ, -a(r̥)] wm.1 socialist.

sosum [sɔ:sʏm] adv. = *svo sem*.

sót, -s [sou:tʰ(s), sou:d̥] n. soot.

Sóti, -a, -ar [sou:tʰɪ, -a(r̥); sou:dɪ] wm.1 'Sooty,' a rustbrown (= *sótrauður*) horse.

sótt, -ar, -ir [souʰt:, -ar̥, -ɪr̥] f.2 sickness.

sótti, -ur, see *sœkja*.

1. spá, spár, spár [spau:(r)] f.1 prophecy.

2. spá, spáði, spáð [spau:, spau:ðɪ, spau:ð] wv.3 prophesy; *því var spáð, að* . . . it was prophesied that. . . .

spakur, spök, spakt [spa:kʰʏr̥, spö:kʰ, spax·t; spa:g̊ʏr̥, spö:g̊] adj. quiet, gentle; wise.

spann, see *spinna*.

spar, spör, spart [spa:r, spö:r, spar̥·t] adj. sparing, thrifty.

spara, -aði, -að(ur) [spa:ra, -aðɪ, -að, -aðʏr̥] wv.4 save, economize; spare.

sparneytinn, -in, -ið; -neytnari, -astur [spar·nei·tʰɪn, -ɪn, -ɪð; -neiʰt·narɪ, -astʏr̥; -nei·dɪn] adj. frugal.

sparneytni [spar·neiʰt·nɪ] wf.2 frugality.

sparsamur, -söm, -samt [spar̥·sa·mʏr̥, -sö·m, -samtʰ; -samt] adj. thrifty, sparing.

sparsemi [spar̥·sɛ·mɪ] wf.2 thrift, economy.

spegill, -ils, -lar [spei:jɪd̥l, -ɪls, speig̊·lar̥] m.1 mirror; *Spegillinn* 'The Mirror,' or 'The Speculum,' a periodical.

spegilskyggður, -skyggð, -skyggt [spei:jɪl-skɪg̊·ðʏr̥, -skɪg̊·ð, -skɪx·t; -skɪg̊·ðʏr̥, -skɪg̊·þ] adj. polished like a mirror.

spil [spɪ:l] n.pl. cards; *spila á spil*

play at cards; *tvenn spil* two decks of cards.

spínat, -s [spi:na·tʰ(s), -a·d̥(s)] n. spinach.

spinna, spinn, spann, spunnum, spunninn, -ið [spɪn:a, spɪn:, span:, spʏn:ʏm, spʏn:ɪn, -ɪð] v.3 spin; *spinna á rokk* spin on a spinning wheel.

spítali, -a, -ar [spi:tʰalɪ, -a(r̥); spi:dalɪ] wm.1 = *sjúkrahús*, hospital.

spjald, -s, spjöld [spjal·d̥, spjald̥s, spjöl·d̥] n. board; book cover; *lesa spjaldanna á milli* read from cover to cover.

spói, -a, -ar [spou:ɪ, -a(r̥)] wm.1 curlew.

spóka, -aði, -að [spou:kʰa, -aðɪ, -að; spou:g̊a] wv.4 *spóka sig* stalk, strut, sport.

spónn, spóns, spænir [spoud̥·n̥, spoun·s, spai·nɪr̥] m.3 spoon (made of horn); shavings of wood.

sportvöruverzlun, -unar, -anir [spɔr̥·t-vö·rʏ-vɛrslʏn, -ʏnar̥, -anɪr̥] f.2 = *íþróttavöruverzlun*, sports outfitters' store.

spraka, spröku, -ur, [spra:kʰa, sprö:-kʰʏ(r̥); spra:g̊a, sprö:g̊ʏ] wf.1 halibut.

sprakk, see *springa*.

spratt, see *spretta*.

sprengigröf, -grafar, -ir [spreiŋ·g̊ɪ-grö:v, -gra:var̥, -ɪr̥] f.2 land mine.

sprengikúla, -u, -ur [spreiŋ·g̊ɪ-kʰu:la, -ʏ(r̥)] wf.1 shell, cannon ball.

sprenging, -ar, -ar [spreiŋ·g̊ɪŋ, -ɪŋar̥] f.1 explosion.

1. sprengja, -u, -ur [spreiŋ·g̊ɪa, -g̊ɪʏ(r̥)] wf.1 bomb; *varpa, kasta sprengjum* throw bombs, bomb, raid.

2. sprengja, sprengdi, sprengdur (sprengt) [spreiŋ·g̊ɪa, spreiŋ·dɪ, -ʏr̥, spreiŋ·tʰ; spreiŋ·t] wv.2 explode (trans.), blast, tear, break.

sprengjuflugvél, -ar, -ar [spreiŋ·g̊ɪʏ-flʏx·vjɛ·l, -lar̥] f.1 bomber.

sprengjuheldur, -held, -helt [spreiŋ·g̊ɪʏ-hɛl·dʏr̥, -hɛl·d̥, -hɛl·t] adj. bombproof.

spretta, sprett, spratt, spruttum,

Consonants: [ð] brea*the*; [g] *g*ood; [gj] *gy*arden (garden); [hw̥] *wh*at; [j] *y*es; [kj] *cy*an (can); [ŋ] thi*ng*; [q] N. Germ. sa*g*en; [r] Scottish *r*; [x] approx. Germ. a*ch*; [þ] *th*in. Voiceless: ∘; [b̥, d̥, g̊] approx. *p, t, k*. Half-voiced: *italics*. Aspiration and preaspiration: [ʰ]; [pʰ, tʰ, kʰ] *p-, t-, k-*. Others as in English.

453

sprottinn (-ið) [spreʰt:a, spreʰt:, spraʰt:, sprɣʰt:ʏm, sprɔʰt:ɪn, -ið] v.3 sprout, grow; *spretta upp* jump up.

springa, spring, sprakk, sprungum, sprunginn (-ið) [sprɪŋ·g̊a, sprɪŋ·g̊, spraʰk:, sprʊŋ·g̊ʏm, sprʊŋ·g̊ˌɪn, -ið] v.3 burst (intr.), explode.

sprottið, -inn, see *spretta*.

sprunga, -u, -ur [sprʊŋ·g̊a, -ʏ(r̥)] wf.1 rift, cleft, chasm.

sprungið, -inn, -um, see *springa*.

spruttum, see *spretta*.

spröku, -ur, see *spraka*.

spúa, spúi, spúði, spúður, see *spýja*.

spunnið, -inn, -um, see *spinna*.

spurði, -ur, see *spyrja*.

spýja (spúa), spý(spúi), spúði, spúð- (ur) [spi:ja (spu:a), spi: (spu:ɪ), spu:ðɪ, spu:ðʏr̥, spu:ð] wv.1 & 3 spew, vomit; emit.

spyrja, spurði, spurður (spurt) [spɪr·ja, spʏr·ðɪ, -ʏr̥, spʏr̥·t; spʏr·ja] wv.1 (Pr. 2, *1*, 11n) ask, question, inquire, hear (as a result of questioning); (1) *ég spyr, hver það sé* I ask who that is; *ég spurði, hver það væri* I asked who that was (S. VI, 9, *4*, 2); *hin spyr, hvaða fiskur það hafi verið* the other asks what fish that was; *ef spurt er* if it is asked; (2) middle voice: *spyrjast* be heard (pass.); *það spurðist, að . . .* it was heard that . . . the news spread that . . . (S. VI, 7, *3*); (3) with preps and advs: *spyrja að e-m* ask about sbdy; *spyrja eftir e-m* (*e-u*) ask for sbdy (sth); *spyrja e-n um e-ð* (= *spyrja e-n e-s*) ask sbdy about sth; *spyrjast til vegar* ask one's way.

1. spýta, -u, -ur [spi:tʰa, -ʏ(r̥); spi:- da] wf.1 a piece of wood.

2. spýta, spýtti, spýtt(ur) [spi:tʰa, spiʰt:ɪ, -ʏr̥, spiʰt:; spi:da] wv.2 *spýta e-u* spit, disgorge sth; *spýta bjór* nail up and stretch a skin.

spænir, see *spónn*.

spök, see *spakur*.

spör, see *spar*.

staðfugl, -s, -ar [stað·fʏg̊l(s), -fʏg̊lar̥] m.1 non-migratory bird.

staddur, stödd, statt [stad:ʏr̥, stöd:, staʰt:] adj. placed; *vera staddur* be placed, happen to be (in a place), happen to be present, *vera staddur á* be standing on.

staðhættir, -hátta [sta:ðhaiʰt·ɪr̥, -hauʰt·a] m.3.pl. qualities of a place; local conditions.

staðið, -inn, see *standa*.

staðnaður, stöðnuð, staðnað [stað·- naðʏr̥, stöð·nʏð, stað·nað] adj. (pp.) stagnant (water).

staður, -ar, -ir [sta:ðʏr̥, sta:ðar̥, sta:ðɪr̥] m.3 place, spot; town; parsonage (= *kirkjustaður*); farmstead, thus in place names, whose first part is a person's name: 'the place of sbdy,': but mostly in plural: *Þorvalds-staðir* 'the farm (place) of *Þorvaldur*;' *á staðnum* on (of) the place; *í staðinn fyrir* instead of; *í stað e-s, í staðinn* instead of sth (sbdy); *fara, leggja á* (*af*) *stað* start a journey (trip); *færast úr stað* move.

stafa, -aði, -að(ur) [sta:va, -aðɪ, -að. -aðʏr̥] wv.4 spell; *láta e-n stafa* have sbdy spell; *sólin stafar geislum á vatnið* the sun projects its rays on the water.

stafn, -s, -ar [stab·n, stabns, stab·nar̥] m.1 = *gafl* gable; stem, prow, stern (of a ship, boat).

stafngluggi, -a, -ar [stab·nglʏg̊ˌ·ɪ, -a(r̥)] wm.1 window on a gable (end of the house).

stafur, -s, -ir [sta:vʏr̥, staf·s, sta:vɪr̥] m.2 staff, stick; letter (= *bókstafur*), *stór stafur* capital (big letter).

stakk, see *stinga*.

stal, stálum, see *stela*.

stál, -s, - [stau:l, staul·s] n. steel; a perpendicular haystack in a barn.

stálheldur, -held, -helt [stau:l-hel·dʏr̥, -hel·d, -hel·t] adj. supporting one like steel (of ice).

stálheppinn, -in, -ið [stau:l-heʰp:ɪn, -ɪn, -ið] adj. very lucky; *stálhepp-*

Vowels: *a* [a] approx. father; *á* [au] cow; *e* [ɛ] set; *é* [jɛ] yes; *i, y* [ɪ] sit; *í, ý* [i] feel; *o* [ɔ] law; *ó* [ou] note; *u* [ʏ] approx. Germ. Mütter; *ú* [u] school; *y* = *i*; *ý* = *í*; *æ* [ai] ice; *ö* [ö] Germ. hören; *au* [öy] French *feuille*; *ei, ey* [ei] ale. Length [:]; half-length [·].

inn með e-ð very lucky with sth, in respect to sth.

stand, -s [stan·d̦(s)] n. condition; *í góðu standi* in good condition.

standa, stend, stóð, stóðum, staðinn (-ið) [stan·da, stɛn·d̦, stou:ð, stou:-ðʏm, sta:ðɪn, -ǐð] v.6 stand, be standing; stay, remain, be; stick; last; stand, endure; (1) *stattu* (= *statt þú* imperative) stand, stay, remain; *stattu kyrr* halt, be quiet! *ég er búinn að standa hér síðan í morgun* I have been standing here since this morning (S. VI, **6**, *2*); *þar sem hún stóð* 'where she (it) stood,' i. e. on the spot; *standa opinn* stay open; *standa fastur* stick, be stuck; *standa í blóma* flourish; *standa í blaðinu* be in the newspaper, be said in the newspaper; *standa í blautu* have wet garments, especially wet socks; *standa lengi* stand, last long; *svo búið má ekki standa* things cannot be left at such a pass; (2) impersonal: *það stendur á hádegi* it is exactly (at) noon; *meðan á því stendur* while it lasts; (3) reflexive: *standa sig vel (illa)* acquit oneself with honor (badly); (4) middle voice: *standast e-ð* stand sth, endure sth; *standast ekki e-ð* not be able to stand sth; (5) with preps and advs: *standa fyrir e-u* organize sth, arrange sth, sponsor sth; *standa upp* rise; *standa við* stop; *standa yfir* be going on.

stangar, see *stöng.*

stanza, -aði, -að(ur) [stan·sa, -aðɪ, -að, -aðʏr] wv.4 stop.

stara, starði, starað [sta:ra, star·ðɪ, sta:rað] wv.3 stare.

starf, -s, störf [star·v, starvs, stör·v] n. work, task, job.

starfsemi [star·vsɛ·mɪ] wf.2 activity, business.

stássstofa, -u, -ur [staus:(s)tɔ·va, -ʏ(r̦)] wf.1 drawing room.

statt, see *staddur.*

sté, see *stíga.*

Stefán, -s [stɛ:fau·n, stɛf:au·n] m.1 Steven, Stephen.

1. **stefna, -u, -ur** [stɛb̦·na, -ʏ(r̦)] wf.1 direction, course; movement (in art, literature); platform (of a party).
2. **stefna, stefndi, stefndur (stefnt)** [stɛb̦·na, stɛm·dɪ, -ʏr̦, stɛm·tʰ, stɛm·t] wv.2 take a course; *að hverju ber að stefna* which course should be taken; stand, steer; summon; *stefna e-m fyrir rétt* summon sbdy to appear before a court.

stefnuskrá, -skrár, -skrár [stɛb̦·nʏ-skrau:(r)] f.1 program; platform.

stefnuvargur, -s [stɛb̦·nʏ-var·ǧʏr̦] m.1 beasts of prey, vermin (foxes, rats, mice) summoned (*stefnt*) and sent by sorcerers to plague their victims.

steig, see *stíga.*

steik, -ar (-ur), -ur [stei:kʰ, -ar̦, -ʏr̦; stei:ǧ] f.3 roast; animal for roasting; *hér hleypur steik um stiga* 'look at the roast running over the paths.'

steikja, steikti, steikt(ur) [stei:kᵢʰa, steix·tɪ, -ʏr̦, steix·t; stei:ǧᵢa] wv.2 roast, cook in deep fat; broil, fry; *steikt brauð* bread cooked in fat; *steikt egg* fried eggs.

steindepill, -ils, -lar [stein·dɛ·pʰɪdl̦, -ɪls, -dɛʰplar̦] m.1 wheatear.

Steindór, -s [stein·dou·r, -dours] m.1 pers. name.

steingerður, -gerð, -gert (-gjörður, etc.) [steiŋ·g̦ᵢɛrðʏr̦, -g̦ᵢɛrð, -g̦ᵢɛrt; -g̦ᵢör-ðʏr̦] adj. petrified.

Steingrímur, -s [steiŋ·gri·mʏr̦, -gríms] m.1 pers. name.

steinhús, -s, - [stei:nhu·s, -hus·] n. stone house; house built of concrete.

steinn, -s, -ar [steid̦·n̦, stein·s, stei:-nar̦] m.1 stone; also pers. name: *Steinn.*

steinsteypa, -u [stein·stei·pʰa, -ʏ; stein·stei·b̦a] wf.1 concrete; pouring of concrete.

Steinunn; -unnar [stei:nʏn, -ʏnar̦] f.1 pers. name.

steinuppgefinn, -in, -ið [stei:n-ʏʰp:-

Consonants: [ð] brea*th*e; [g] *g*ood; [gⱼ] *gy*arden (garden); [hʍ] *wh*at; [j] *y*es; [kⱼ] *cy*an (can); [ŋ] thi*ng*; [q] N. Germ. sa*g*en; [r] Scottish *r*; [x] approx. Germ. a*ch*; [þ] *th*in. Voiceless: ○; [b̦, d̦, g̦] approx. *p, t, k.* Half-voiced: *italics.* Aspiration and preaspiration: [ʰ]; [pʰ, tʰ, kʰ] *p-, t-, k-.* Others as in English.

455

gје·vɪn, -ɪn, -ɪð] adj. dog-tired,
exhausted.

stekk, see 1. *stökkva.*

stekkur, -jar (-s), -ir, (-ja) [steʰk:ʏr̥,
steʰkⱼ:ar̥, steʰk·s, stex·s, steʰkⱼ:ɪr̥,
-ʰkⱼ:a] m.2 a sheepfold or pen where
the lambs were weaned from (*stíað
frá*) their mothers; also in place
names: *-stekkur, Stekkjar-.*

stela, stel, stal, stálum, stolinn (-ið)
[stɛ:la, stɛ:l, sta:l, stau:lʏm, stɔ:-
lɪn, -ɪð] v.4 steal; *stela e-u frá e-m*
steal sth from sbdy; *stelast til að
gera e-ð* do sth by stealth.

stelpa, -u, -ur, (-na) [stɛl·pʰa, -ʏ(r̥),
stɛlpʰna; stɛl·pa, stɛlpna] wf.1
hussy, wench.

stend, see *standa.*

stengur, see *stöng.*

sterkur, sterk, sterkt [stɛr̥·kʏr̥, stɛr̥·k,
stɛr̥·t] adj. strong; potent; *sterkur
maður* strong man; *sterkt kaffi*
strong coffee.

stétt, -ar, -ir [stjɛʰt:, -ar̥, -ɪr̥] f.2
class.

steypa, steypti, steypt(ur) [stei:pʰa,
steif·tɪ, -ʏr̥, steif·t; stei:ba] wv.2
throw, hurl; pour out; cast, found,
make of concrete (streets); *steypa
yfir sig kápu* throw a cape over
oneself.

steypiflugvél, -ar, -ar [stei:pʰɪ-flʏq·-
vjɛ·l, -lar̥; stei:bɪ-] wf.1 dive bomber.

steypiregn, -s, - [stei:pʰɪ-rɛg̊·n̥(s);
stei:bɪ-] n. downpour.

stífla, -aði, -að(ur) [stib̥·la, -aðɪ, -að,
-aðʏr̥] wv.4 dam up; *stíflast* be
dammed up.

**stíga, stíg, steig (sté), stigum, stig-
inn (-ið)** [sti:qa, sti:q, stei:q, stje:,
stɪ:qʏm, stɪi:jɪn, -ɪð, sti:jɪn, stɪ:-
jɪn] v.1 step, tread; stride; ascend;
stíga í fótinn step on (one's own)
foot; *stíga á fótinn* step on (sbdy
else's) foot; *stíga af baki* alight
from a horse; *stíga í stólinn* go up
into the pulpit, preach; *loftvogin
stígur* the barometer is rising.

stigi, -a, -ar [stɪi:jɪ, -a, -ar̥; sti:jɪ,
stɪ:jɪ] wm.1 flight of stairs, ladder.

stigur, stigs, stigar (-ir) [stɪ:qʏr̥,
stɪx·s, stɪi:qar̥, stɪi:jɪr̥] =

stígur, stígs, stígar (-ir) [sti:qʏr̥,
stix·s, sti:qar̥, sti:jɪr̥] m.1 & 2
path; *-stígur* in street-names.

stígvél, -s, - [stiq·vjɛ·l, -vjɛls] n. boot.

still, -s, -ar (stýll) [stid̥·l̥, stil·s, sti:-
lar̥] m.1 style; exercise, composi-
tion; scale; *í stórum stíl* on a large
scale.

stilla, stillti, stillt(ur) [stɪd̥·la, stɪl̥·tɪ,
-ʏr̥, stɪl̥·t] wv.2 still, calm, quiet,
appease; *stilla sig* calm oneself,
control oneself.

stilltur, stillt, stillt [stɪl̥·tʏr̥, stɪl̥·t]
adj. calm, quiet, steady, composed.

Stína, -u [sti:na, -ʏ] wf.1 pet name
of *Kristín.*

**stinga, sting, stakk, stungum, stung-
inn (-ið)** [stiŋ·g̊a, stiŋ·g̊, staʰk:,
stuŋ·g̊ʏm, stuŋ·g̊ⱼɪn, -ɪð] v.3 prick,
stab, sting, pierce; put, thrust,
stick; *stinga bréfum í póstkassa*
put letters into the mailbox; *stinga
e-u undir e-ð* run (thrust) sth
under sth.

stirður, stirð, stirt [stɪr̥·ðʏr̥, stɪr̥·ð,
stɪr̥·t] adj. stiff, clumsy, rigid.

stirndur, stirnd, stirnt [stɪ(r)nd̥ʏr̥,
stɪ(r)nd, stɪ(r)ntʰ; stɪ(r̥)nt] adj.
set with stars; *stirndur himinn*
heaven full of stars.

stjórn, -ar, -ir [stjourd̥n̥, -nar̥, -nɪr̥]
f.2 (1) government of a country;
(2) board of directors, directors,
officers, committee; direction; *undir
stjórn e-s* under the direction of
sbdy, directed by sbdy.

stjórna, -aði, -að [stjourdna, -aðɪ,
-að] wv.4 *stjórna e-u* govern sth.

stjórnandi, -a, -endur [stjourdnandɪ,
-a, -ɛndʏr̥] wm.2 director, dirigent
(of an orchestra).

stjórnarráð, -s [stjourdna(r)·rau:ð,
-rauð·s] n. government, cabinet;
Government House (= *Stjórnarráðshúsið*).

stjórnarskrá, -skrár, -skrár [stjourdn-
ar̥·skrau:(r)] f.1 constitution.

Vowels: *a* [a] approx. father; *á* [au] cow; *e* [ɛ] set; *é* [jɛ] yes; *i, y* [ɪ] sit; *í, ý* [i] feel;
o [ɔ] law; *ó* [ou] note; *u* [ʏ] approx. Germ. Mütter; *ú* [u] school; *y* = *i*; *ý* = *í*; *æ* [ai] ice;
ö [ö] Germ. hören; *au* [öy] French *feuille*; *ei, ey* [ei] ale. Length [:]; half-length [·].

stjórnmál [stjourd̦n·mau·*l*] n.pl. politics.

stjórnmálamaður, -manns, -menn [stjourd̦nmau·la·ma:ðʏr̦, -man·s, -mɛn:]̦ m.4 statesman, politician, political leader.

stjúp- [stju:pʰ-; stju:b̦-] pref. step-; *stjúp-faðir, -móðir, -dóttir -sonur* step-father, -mother, -daughter, -son.

stjúpi, -a, -ar [stju:pʰɪ, -a, -ar̦; stju:-bɪ] wm.1 stepfather.

stjúpmæðrasaga, -sögu, -ur [stju:pʰ-maiðra-sa:qa, -sö:qʏ(r̦); stju:b̦-] wf.1 story of a stepmother, a stepmother tale.

stjörnufræði [stjöd̦·nʏ-frai:ðɪ; stjör-dnʏ-] wf.2 astronomy.

stó̦, stóar, stór [stou:, stou:ar̦, stou:*r*] f.1 iron stove.

1. stóð, -s [stou:ð, stouð·s] n. a flock of breeding horses; flock of horses (stud).

2. stóð, -um, see *standa.*

stofa, -u, -ur [stɔ:va, -ʏ(r̦)] wf.1 guest room, drawing room.

stofnsetja, -setti, -sett(ur) [stɔb·nsɛ·-tʰja, -sɛʰt·ɪ, -ʏr̦, -sɛʰt·; -sɛ·d̦ˌa]̦ wv.1 establish.

stofnun, -unar, -anir [stɔb·nʏn, -ʏnar̦, -anɪr̦] f.2 establishment; *með stofnun Alþingis* with the establishment of the Alþingi.

stofuhurð, -ar, -ir [stɔ:vʏ-hʏr·ð, -ðar̦, -ðɪr̦] f.2 guest room door.

stokkabelti, -s, - [stɔʰk:a-bɛl·tɪ(s)] n. belt made of heavy silver or gold(en) links, belonging to *skautbúningur.*

stokkið, -inn, see 1. *stökkva.*

stolið, -inn, see *stela.*

stóll, -s, -ar [stoud·l̦, stoul·s, stou:lar̦] m.1 chair; pulpit (in church); *á stólnum* in the pulpit.

stoppa, -aði, -að(ur) [stɔʰp:a, -aðɪ, -að, -aðʏr̦] wv.4 stop; *stoppa e-ð með (úr) e-u* stuff sth with sth; *stoppa sokka* darn socks; *strætisvagninn stoppar hér* the bus stops here.

stoppstaður, -ar, -ir [stɔʰp:sta:ðʏr̦,

-ar̦, -ɪr]̦ m.3 bus stop (= *viðkomustaður*).

1. stór, stór, stórt; stærri, stærstur [stou:*r*, stour·t, stair:ɪ, stais·tʏr̦; stair̦stʏr̦] adj. big, great, large; *stór maður* a big man (*mikill maður* a great man); *stór flotadeild* (fleet) squadron.

2. stór- [stou:*r*-] pref. big, large, great.

3. stór, see *stó.*

stórá, -ár, -ár [stou:rau·(*r*)] f.1 great river.

stórfylki, -s, - [stour̦·fɪlk,ʰɪ, -s; -fɪl̦k,ɪ] n. brigade.

stórgrýttur, -grýtt, -grýtt [stour̦-griʰt·ʏr̦, -griʰt·] adj. of big rocks or boulders; rocky.

stórhátíð, -ar, -ir (-ar) [stou:rhau·-tʰi·ð, -ðar̦, -ðɪr̦] f.2 (f.1) major (church) feast-day; major holyday (of the church).

storkna, -aði, -að(ur) [stɔr̦kna, -aðɪ, -að, -aðʏr̦; stor̦tna] wv.4 coagulate, congeal.

stórkostlegur [stour̦·kʰɔst-lɛ:qʏr̦] adj. (see *-legur*) grand, colossal, magnificent.

stórskorinn, -in, -ið [stour̦·skɔ·rɪn, -ɪn, -ɪð] adj. big-faced, big-featured.

stórskotafylki, -s, - [stour̦·skɔ·tʰa-fɪl·k,ʰɪ(s); -skɔ·da-fɪl·k,ɪ] n. battery (smallest unit of field artillery).

stórskotalið, -s [stour̦·skɔ·tʰa-lɪ:ð, -lɪð·s; -skɔ·da-] n. artillery.

stórstígur, -stíg, -stígt [stour̦·sti·qʏr̦, -sti·q, -stixt] adj. taking long steps or strides.

stórum [stou:rʏm] adv. greatly.

stórvaxinn, -in, -ið [stour̦·vaxsɪn, -ɪn, -ɪð] adj. large of stature, huge.

1. strá, -s, - [strau:(s)] n. straw, blade of grass.

2. strá, stráði, stráð(ur) [strau:, strau:ðɪ, -ʏr, strau:ð] wv.3 strew, scatter; *strá e-ð e-u* strew sth (e.g. the floor) with sth.

strádýna, -u, -ur [strau:di·na, -ʏ(r̦)] wf.1 straw mattress, hay mattress.

strákgrey, -s, - [strau:kʰ-grei·(s), strau:(g̊)-] n. poor boy.

strákur, -s, -ar [strau:kʰYr̥, straux·s, strau:kʰar̥; strau:g̊Yr̥, -ar̥] m.l boy (less polite than *drengur*), brat, urchin.

strandar, see *strönd*.

strandferð, -ar, -ir [stran·dferð̊, -ðar̥, -ðIr̥] f.2 coastal voyage, a trip along the coasts of Iceland.

strandhögg, -s, - [stran·dhög̊·, -hög̊·s] n. commando raid, raid upon an enemy coast.

strandhöggssveit, -ar, -ir [stran·d-hög̊(s)-svei:tʰ, -ar̥, -Ir̥; -svei:d̥] f.2 commandos, commando raiders, coastal raiders.

strauk, see *strjúka*.

strax [strax·s] adv. right away, at once; *rétt strax* almost at once, almost right away; *strax og* conj. as soon as (S. VIII, 3(h) and 4).

strendur, see *strönd*.

stríð, -s, - [stri:ð̊, strið·s] n. war (= *styrjöld*) *meðan á stríðinu stendur* for the duration (of the war); *að stríðinu loknu* after the war.

stríða, stríddi, strítt [stri:ða, strið:I, striht:] wv.2 *stríða e-m* irritate, tease sbdy; *stríða* (rare) carry on warfare.

stríðshaukur, -s, -ar [strið·shöy·kʰYr̥, -höy·kʰs, -höyxs, -höy·kʰar̥; -höy·g̊-] m.l war hawk airplane.

stríðsmaður, -manns, -menn [strið·s-ma·ðYr̥, -mans, -men·] m.4 warrior.

strjúka, strýk, strauk, strukum, strok-
-inn (-ið) [strju:kʰa, stri:kʰ, ströy:kʰ, strY:kʰYm, strɔ:k̥ʰIn, -Ið̊; strju:g̊a, stri:g̊, ströy:g̊, strY:g̊Ym, strɔ:g̊ˌIn] v.2 escape, elope, run away, (of horses:) run home; stroke.

strok, -s [strɔ:kʰ(s); strɔ:g̊] n. running away; *það er strok í hestinum* the horse is liable to run away (back to its home).

strokið, -inn, see *strjúka*.

strompur, -s, -ar [strɔm·pʰYr̥, -s, -ar̥; strɔm·pYr̥] m.l chimney pot, skylight.

strukum, see *strjúka*.

strýk, see *strjúka*.

stræti, -s, - [strai:tʰI(s); strai:dI] n. street; in street-names: -stræti.

strætisvagn, -s, -ar [strai:tʰIs-vag̊·n(s), -vag̊·nar̥; strai:dIs-] m.l bus; *fara á strætisvagni* ride a bus.

strönd, strandar, strendur, strandir [strön·d, stran·dar̥, stren·dYr̥, stran·-dIr̥] f.3 shore, coast, strand; *með ströndum fram* coastwise; *Strandir = Hornstrandir*, a district of Vestfirðir.

studdi, -ur, stutt, see *styðja*.

stúdent, -s, -ar [stu:dentʰ(s), -ar̥; stu:dent̥] m.l student, graduate of a gymnasium (*menntaskóli*).

stúdentspróf, -s, - [stu:dentʰs-pʰrou:v, -pʰrouf·s; -dents-] n. examen artium, the comprehensive final examination at the end of a *menntaskóli* (gymnasium), entitling the graduate to matriculate in Icelandic, Scandinavian, and German universities.

stúka, -u, -ur [stu:kʰa, -Y(r̥); stu:g̊a] wf.l box (in the theater); lodge (Good-Templar).

stukkum, see 1. *stökkva*.

stúlka, -u, -ur, (-na) [stul·kʰa, -Y(r̥), stulkʰna, stultʰna; stul·ka, stulkna, stultna] wf.l girl.

stund, -ar, -ir [stYn·d, -ar̥, -Ir̥] f.2 hour; while, short time; *leggja stund á* apply oneself to.

stundarsakir [stYndar-sa:kˌʰIr̥, -sa:-g̊ˌIr̥] adv. (= *stundar sakir*) *um stundarsakir* for a while.

stundum [stYn·dYm] adv. sometimes.

stungið, -inn, -um, see *stinga*.

Sturla, -u [stYrdla, -Y; stYd·la] wf.l in form, but masc. pers. name; *Snorri Sturlu-son*, a famous historian (1179-1241).

Sturlunga, -u [stYrdluŋ̊a, -Y] wf.l 'Book of the Sturlungs,' a chronicle containing the history of twelfth and thirteenth century Iceland, the

---

Vowels: *a* [a] approx. *father*; *á* [au] *cow*; *e* [ɛ] *set*; *é* [jɛ] *yes*; *i, y* [ɪ] *sit*; *í, ý* [i] *feel*; *o* [ɔ] *law*; *ó* [ou] *note*; *u* [Y] approx. Germ. *Mütter*; *ú* [u] *school*; *y = i*; *ý = í*; *œ* [ai] *ice*; *ö* [ö] Germ. *hören*; *au* [öy] French *feuille*; *ei, ey* [ei] *ale*. Length [:]; half-length [·].

age of the classical Icelandic literature. The Sturlungs: *Sturlungar*
were the sons and descendants of
Sturla Þórðarson, father of *Þórður,
Sighvatur,* and *Snorri Sturlusynir.*
stuttpilsuð [styʰt:pʰɪlsyð] adj. f.
wearing short skirts.
stuttur, stutt, stutt; styttri, stytztur
[styʰt:yr̥, styʰt:, stɪʰt·rɪ, stɪs·tyr̥]
adj. short.
styðja, studdi, studdur (stutt) [stɪð·-
ja, styd:ɪ, -yr̥, styʰt:] wv.1 support.
stýfa, stýfði, stýfður (stýft) [sti:va,
stiv·ðɪ, stiv.ðyr̥, stif·t] wv.2 cut,
chop off; cut the hair; *stýfa krónuna*
cut the value of the crown, de-
valuate the *króna.*
stýfing, -ar, -ar [sti:viŋg, -ar̥] f.1
haircut; *stýfing krónunnar* the de-
valuation of the *króna.*
styggur, stygg, styggt [stɪg̊:yr̥, stɪg̊:,
stɪx·t] adj. nervous, jumpy, cross;
styggur í skapi short of temper;
(of animals) shying; *styggur hestur* a shying horse, skittish horse.
stýll, -s, -ar [stid·l̥, stil·s, sti:lar̥] m.1
= *still.*
stýra, stýrði, stýrður (stýrt) [sti:ra,
stir·ðɪ, -yr̥, stir·t] wv.2 *stýra báti,
skipi* steer a boat, a ship; *stýra
fundi* conduct a meeting; *stýra liði*
govern, command troops.
stýri, -s, - [sti:rɪ(s)] n. rudder.
stýrimaður, -manns, -menn [sti:rɪ-
ma:ðyr̥, -man·s, -men:] m.4 mate,
helmsman; *fyrsti, annar stýrimaður*
first, second mate.
stýrimannaskóli, -a, -ar [sti:rɪman·a-
skou:lɪ, -a(r̥)] wm.1 nautical
school, navigation school.
styrjöld, -aldar, -aldir [stɪr·jöld, -ald-
ar̥, -aldɪr̥] f.2 (= *stríð*) war;
heimsstyrjöld World War.
styrkja, styrkti, styrkt(ur) [stɪr·kja,
stɪr·(x)tɪ, -yr̥, stɪr·(x)t] wv.2 help,
aid; subsidize; strengthen.
styrkur, -s, -ir [stɪr·kyr̥, stɪrks, stɪr·-
k₁ɪr̥] m.2 stipend, grant; *styrkur
til náms* (= *námsstyrkur*) stipend,
scholarship.

1. stytta, -u, -ur [stɪʰt:a, -y(r̥)] wf.1
= *myndastytta* monument.
2. stytta, stytti, stytt(ur) [stɪʰt:a,
stɪʰt:ɪ, -yr̥, stɪʰt:] wv.2 shorten,
abridge; *stytta upp* stop raining
(snowing).
styttri, stytztur, see *stuttur.*
stæði, -s, - [stai:ðɪ(s)] n. standing
room (in a theater).
stærð, -ar, -ir [stair·ð, -ðar̥, -ðɪr̥] f.2
size; *á stærð við e-ð* similar in
size to sth.
stærðfræði [stair·ðfrai·ðɪ] wf.2 mathematics.
stærðfræði(s)deild, -ar -ir [stair·ð-
frai·ðɪ(s)·deil·d, -ar̥, -ɪr̥] f.2 division of mathematics, department
of mathematics (in the gymnasium).
stærri, stærstur, see 1. *stór.*
stöð, stöðvar, -var [stö:ð, stöð·var]
f.1 station; = *bílastöð;* = *símastöð;*
á stöðina to the station.
stödd, see *staddur.*
stöðnuð, see *staðnaður.*
stöðull, -uls, -lar [stö:ðyd̥l, -yls, stöð·-
lar̥] m.1 milking place (for ewes or
cows); also in place names -*stöðull.*
stöðuvatn, -s, -vötn [stö:ðy·vaʰt·n̥(s),
-vas:, -vöʰt·n̥] n. (= *vatn*) lake.
stöðva, -aði, -að(ur) [stöð·va, -aðɪ,
-að, -aðyr̥] wv.4 stop; *stöðva e-ð*
stop sth.
stökk, -s, - [stöʰk:, stöʰk·s] n. jump,
bound, spring, leap; gallop.
stökk, see 1. *stökkva.*
stökkpallur, -palls, -pallar [stöʰk:pʰad·
lyr̥, -pʰals, -pʰadlar̥] m.1 springboard.
stökkull, -uls, -lar [stöʰk:ydl, -yls,
-stöʰk·lar̥] m.1 springe (a whale).
stökkur, stökk, stökkt [stöʰk:yr̥,
stöʰk:, stöx·t] adj. brittle; *stökkur
í sér* brittle of (by) nature.
1. stökkva, stekk, stökk, stukkum,
stokkinn (-ið) [stöʰk:va, steʰk:,
stöʰk:, styʰk:ym, stɔʰk:j₁:ɪn, -ɪð] v.3
jump, spring, bound, leap, gallop;
stökkva upp spring up, arise.
2. stökkva, stökkti, stökkt [stöʰk:va,
stöx·t(ɪ)] wv.2 spray; *stökkva
vatni á e-ð* sprinkle water on sth.

Consonants: [ð] brea*th*e; [g] *g*ood; [gⱼ] *gy*arden (garden); [hw̥] *wh*at; [j] *y*es; [kⱼ] *cy*an
(can); [ŋ] thi*ng*; [q] N. Germ. sa*g*en; [r] Scottish *r*; [x] approx. Germ. a*ch*; [þ] *th*in.
Voiceless: ᵒ; [b̥, d̥, g̊] approx. *p, t, k.* Half-voiced: *italics.* Aspiration and preaspiration:
[ʰ]; [pʰ, tʰ, kʰ] *p-, t-, k-.* Others as in English.

459

stöng, stangar, stengur [stöyŋ·g̊, stauŋ·g̊ar̥, steiŋ·g̊yr̥] f.3 pole; fishing-rod; (beizlis-) branch (of a bridle).

störf, see 3. starf.

sú, see 3. sá.

suða, -u [sy:ða, -y] wf.1 boiling; chattering.

suðaustan [sy:ðöystan] adv. from the southeast; fyrir suðaustan e-ð southeast of sth.

sudda, -aði, -að [syd̥:a, -aðɪ, -að] wv.4 drizzle; hann suddar it drizzles (= það suddar) (S. VI, 4, 3).

suðrænn, -ræn, -rænt; -rænni, -rænast-ur [syð·raiðn̥, -rai·n, -raintʰ; -raint; -raidnɪ, -rai·nastyr̥] adj. southern, tropical.

suðum, see sjóða.

1. suður, (-ri), -urs [sy:ðyr̥(s), syð·-rɪ] n. the south; í suðri in the south; í suður south, southwards.

2. suður [sy:ðyr̥] adv. south, suður yfir ána south across the river (= suður fyrir ána); suður um land south across (over) the coun-try (In. IV, 1, 3).

suðurátt, -ar [sy:ðyr̥-auʰt:, -ar̥] f.2 south.

Suðurgata, -götu [sy:ðyr̥-ga:tʰa, -gö:-tʰy; -ga:d̥a, -gö:d̥y] wf.1 'South Street.'

Suðurland, -s [sy:ðyr̥-lan·d̥, -lan·(d̥)s] n. the South (of Iceland).

Suðurlandsundirlendi, -s [sy:ðyr̥lan·s-·yn·dɪrlen·d̥ɪ(s)] n. the Southern Lowlands of Iceland.

suðvestur [syð·vestyr̥] adv. southwest.

suðvesturströnd, -strandar [syð·ves-tyr̥·strön·d̥, -stran·d̥ar̥] f.3 south-west coast.

Súgandafjörður, -fjarðar [su:qanda-fjör·ðyr̥, -fjar·ðar̥] m.3 'Súgandi's Fjord.'

sugum, see sjúga.

súgur, -s [su:(q)yr̥, sux·s, dat. su:jɪ] m.1 draft; fara í súginn be spent, wasted.

súkkulaði, -s [suʰk:y·la:ðɪ(s)] n. chocolate.

sukkum, see 1. sökkva.

sulgum, see 1. svelgja.

sultum, see 1. svelta.

sultutau, -s [syl̥·tx·tʰöy:(s)] n. jam, jelly, preserves.

sumar, (-ri), -ars, -ur [sy:mar̥(s), sym·rɪ, sy:myr̥] n. summer; í sumar this summer; að sumri next sum-mer (= næsta sumar); í sumar leið last summer; að sumrinu (til) during the summer.

sumardagur, -s, -ar [sy:mar-da:qyr̥, -dax·s, -da:qar̥] m.1 summer day; sumardagurinn fyrsti the first day of summer.

sumardvöl, -dvalar, -dvalir [sy:mar-dvö:l, -dva:lar̥, -ɪr̥] f.2 summer sojourn.

sumarfrí, -s, - [sy:mar̥-fri:(s)] n. summer vacation.

sumarmál [sy:mar-mau:l] n.pl. a few days before the first day of summer.

sumarsól, -ar [sy:mar̥-sou:l, -lar̥] f.2 summer sun.

sumir, see sumur.

summa, -u, -ur [sym:a, -y(r̥)] wf.1 sum, total.

sumsstaðar [sym·sta·ðar̥] adv. (= sums staðar) at some place, in places, some place.

sumur, sum, sumt [sy:myr̥, sy:m, sym·tʰ; sym·t] indef. pron. (always strong, In. VI, 6, 2(b)) some; sumir af some of; sumir segja some say; sumt er gott some things are good; það er allt og sumt that is all; sums staðar = sumsstaðar; (S. IV, 6, 18; VI, 14, 2).

sund, -s, - [syn·d̥(s)] n. sound (arm of the sea); lane (between houses; thus in street-names: -sund); pas-sage, pass between hills; swimming; öll sund eru lokuð all avenues are barred.

Sundhöllin, -hallarinnar [syn·dhöd̥lɪn, -hadlarɪn·ar̥] f.2 'The Swimming Hall,' an indoor swimming pool in Reykjavík.

sundkennari, -a, -ar [syn·dk̥ʰen·arɪ, -a(r̥)] wm.1 teacher of swimming.

Vowels: a [a] approx. father; á [au] cow; e [ɛ] set; é [jɛ] yes; i, y [ɪ] sit; í, ý [i] feel; o [ɔ] law; ó [ou] note; u [y] approx. Germ. Mütter; ú [u] school; y = i; ý = í; æ [ai] ice; ö [ö] Germ. hören; au [öy] French feuille; ei, ey [ei] ale. Length [:]; half-length [·].

460

sundla, -aði, -að [sʏn·la, sʏndla, -aðɪ, -að] wv.4 get dizzy (in high places or rivers).

sundlaug, -ar, -ar [sʏn·dlöy·q, -löy·qar] f.1 swimming pool.

sundsýning, -ar, -ar [sʏn·dsi·ning, -ar] f.1 swimming show.

sundur [sʏn·dʏr] adv. asunder (= í sundur), to pieces.

sundurgrafinn, -in, -ið [sʏn·dʏr-gra:-vɪn, -ɪn, -ɪð] adj. cut up, cut asunder.

sundurtættur, -tætt, -tætt [sʏn·dʏr-tʰaiʰt:(ʏr)] adj. torn apart, torn to pieces, cut up.

sungið, -inn, -um, see syngja.

sunnan [sʏn:an] adv. (In. IV, 1, 3) from the south (= að sunnan); fyrir sunnan in the south, south of; fyrir sunnan land in the south of Iceland, south of Iceland; sunnan við south of; (2) prep. with acc. sunnan dalinn from the south along the valley; (3) prep. with gen. south of; sunnan túns south of the homefield.

sunnanlands [sʏn:an-lan·s, -lands] adv. of (in) the south of Iceland; (to the) south of Iceland; sigla sunnanlands sail south of Iceland.

sunnudagur, -s, -ar [sʏn:ʏ-da:qʏr, -dax·s, -da:qar] m.1 Sunday.

1. súpa, -u, -ur [su:pʰa, -ʏ(r); su:ba] wf.1 soup.

2. súpa, sýp, saup, supum, sopinn (-ið) [su:pʰa, si:pʰ, söy:pʰ, sʏ:pʰʏm, sɔ:pʰɪn, -ɪð; su:ba, si:b, söy:b, sʏ:bʏm, sɔ:bɪn] v.2 sip, drink; ekki er sopið kálið, þó í ausuna sé komið there is many a slip betwixt cup and lip.

súpuskál, -ar; -ar, -ir [su:pʰʏ-skau:l, -lar, -lɪr; su:bʏ-] f.1 & 2 tureen, soup bowl.

súr, súr, súrt [su:r, sur·t] adj. sour, acid; setja ofan í súrt pickle things in sour whey; upp úr súru from out of the sour whey, pickled; súrt slátur pickled blood and liver sausages.

súrbrauð, -s, - [sur·bröy·ð, -bröyðs] n. 'sour bread,' a kind of white bread.

surfum, see sverfa.

súrsætur, -sæt, -sætt [sur·sai·tʰʏr, -sai·tʰ, -saiʰt·; -sai·d-] adj. sweet and sour.

sussu, [sʏs:ʏ] interj. og sussu nei why, of course not!

svaf, sváfum, see sofa.

svalg, see 1. svelgja.

svalir [sva:lɪr] f.2.pl. balcony.

svalt, see 1. svelta and svalur.

svalur, svöl, svalt [sva:lʏr, svö:l, sval·t] adj. cool.

svangur, svöng, svangt; svengri, svengstur [svauŋ·g̊ʏr, svöyŋ·g̊, svauŋ·tʰ; svauŋ̊·t; sveiŋgrɪ, sveiŋst-ʏr] adj. hungry.

svanur, -s, -ir [sva:nʏr, svan·s, sva:-nɪr] m.2 (= álft) whooper swan.

svar, -s, svör [sva:r, svar·s, svö:r] n. answer, response; svar við e-u the answer to sth.

svara, -aði, -að [sva:ra, -aðɪ, -að] wv.4 answer, reply; svara e-m answer sbdy; svara e-u answer sth; svara til e-s correspond to sth.

svarf, see sverfa.

svarið, -inn, see sverja.

Svartagil, -s [svar·ta-g̊ɪ:l, -g̊ɪl·s] n. 'Black Ravine,' 'Black Gill.'

svartfugl, -s [svar·tfʏg̊l(s)] m. (coll.) auks and guillemots.

Svartiskóli, Svartiskóla [svar·tɪ-skou:lɪ, -askou:la] wm.1 'Black School,' name of a famed legendary school of eleventh century France (sometimes (wrongly) identified with the University of Paris) where the devil was schoolmaster.

svartur, svört, svart [svar·tʏr, svör·t, svar·t] adj. black; svartur á hár with black hair.

svefn, -s [sveb·n, svebns] m.1 sleep.

svefnherbergi, -s, - [sveb·nherber-g̊ɪ(s)] n. bedroom.

svei [svei:] adv. fie; svei þér! fie on you! shame on you!

sveið, see svíða.

sveif, see svífa.

sveik, see *svíkja*.

Sveinbjörn, -bjarnar [svein·bjöd̦n̦, ·bjad̦nar̦] m.3 pers. name.

sveinn, -s [sveid·n̦, svein·s] m.1 boy; male child; also: pers. name: *Sveinn* Swain.

sveipa, -aði, -að(ur) [svei:pʰa, -aðɪ, -að, -aðɣr̦; svei:ba] wv.4 cover, wrap in; *sveipa e·n e·u* wrap sbdy up in sth.

sveit, -ar, -ir [svei:tʰ, -ar̦, -ɪr̦; svei:d̦] f.2 rural district, rural settlement, usually = *hreppur*; country (opposite *bœir* towns); crowd, troops.

sveitabóndi, -a, -bændur [svei:tʰa-boun·dɪ, -a, -bain·dɣr̦; svei·da·] wm.2 farmer (in a rural district, opposite: *sjávarbóndi* a farmer who is partly or altogether a fisherman).

sveitalíf, -s [svei:tʰa-li:*v*, -lif·s; svei:-da·] n. rural life.

sveitarstjórn, -ar, -ir [svei:tʰar-stjourd̦n̦, -nar̦, -nɪr̦; svei:d̦ar̦·] f.2 = *hreppsstjórn*.

1. svelgja, svelg, svalg, sulgum, solginn (-ið) [svɛl·ǧ̦ja, svɛl·ǧ̦, sval·ǧ̦, sɣl·-ǧ̦ɣm, sɔl·ǧ̦ɪn, -ɪð] v.3 or (more commonly):

2. svelgja, svelgdi, svelgt [svɛl·ǧ̦ja, svɛl·(q)d̦ɪ, svɛl·(q)tʰ, svɛl·(x)t] wv.2 swallow; *mér svelgist á e·u* I am swallowing sth the wrong way (S. VI, 14, 5).

1. svelta, svelt, svalt, sultum, soltinn (-ið) [svɛl·ta, svɛl·t, sval·t, sɣl·tɣm, sɔl·tɪn, -ɪð] v.3 be hungry, starve (intr.).

2. svelta, svelti, svelt(ur) [svɛl·ta, svɛl·tɪ, -ɣr̦, svɛl·t] wv.2 starve (trans.).

sverfa, sverf, svarf, surfum, sorfinn (-ið) [svɛr·va, svɛr·*v*, svar·*v*, sɣr·-vɣm, sɔr·vɪn, -ɪð] v.3 file; erode.

sverja, sver, sór, sórum, svarinn (-ið) [svɛr·ja, svɛ:*r*, sou:*r*, sou:rɣm, sva:rɪn, -ɪð] v.6 swear; *sverja og sárt við leggja* swear invoking heavy (sore) penalties on oneself, if the oath be false; cf. cross my heart and hope to die.

sveskja, -u, -ur [svɛs·k̦ja, -k̦ɪɣ(r̦)] wf.1 prune.

sveskjugrautur, -ar [svɛs·k̦ɪɣ-gröy:-tʰɣr̦, -ar̦; -gröy:d̦ɣr̦] m.1 prune pudding.

sví- [svi:-] pref. derogatory prefix, dis-.

svið [svɪ:ð] n.pl. the singed head(s) (and feet) of sheep, eaten fresh or pickled.

svíða, svíð, sveið, sviðum, sviðinn (-ið) [svi:ða, svi:ð, svei:ð, svɪ:ðɣm, svɪ:ðɪn, -ɪð] v.1 singe, burn; *svíða svið* singe the hair off the heads of sheep; impersonal: *mig svíður* I have a burning sensation (*í fótinn, augað* (acc.) in my foot, my eye; my eye, my foot hurts me) (S. I, 4, 1, 3).

sviði, -a [svɪ:ðɪ, -a] wm.1 burning sensation, hurt.

svífa, svíf, sveif, svifum, svifinn (-ið) [svi:va, svi:*v*, svei:*v*, svɪ:vɣm, svɪ:vɪn, -ɪð] v.1 soar, hover.

svifblys, -s, - [svɪv·blɪ·s, -blɪs·] n. parachute torch.

Svíi, -a, -ar [svi:jɪ, -a(r̦)] wm.1 Swede.

svíkja, svík, sveik, svikum, svikinn (-ið) [svi:k̦ʰa, svi:kʰ, svei:kʰ, svɪ:-kʰɣm, svɪ:k̦ʰɪn, -ɪð; svi:ǧ̦ja, svi:ǧ̦, svei:ǧ̦, svɪ:ǧ̦ɣm, svɪ:ǧ̦ɪn] v.1 deceive, betray.

svili, -a, -ar [svɪ:lɪ, -a, -ar̦] wm.1 a man married to the sister of another man's wife.

svín, -s, - [svi:*n*, svin·s] n. swine, pig, hog.

svínaket (-kjöt), -s [svi:na-k̦ʰɛ:tʰ, k̦ʰö:tʰ(s); -k̦ʰɛ:d̦, -k̦ʰö:d̦] n. pork.

svínarækt, -ar [svi:na-raix·ț, -ar̦] f.2 swine raising, hog raising.

svínsflesk, -s [svin·sflɛsk(s)] n. pork, bacon.

svínslæri, -s, - [svin·slai·rɪ(s)] n. ham.

1. svipa, -u, -ur [svɪ:pʰa, -ɣ(r̦); svɪ:ba] wf.1 whip.

2. svipa, -aði, -að(ur) [svɪ:pʰa, -aðɪ, -að, -aðɣr̦; svɪ:b-] wv.4 be similar to, be like sbdy; *e·m svipar til e·s* sbdy is somewhat like sbdy; pp. *svipaður e·m* similar to sbdy; *á svipaðan hátt* in a similar way.

Vowels: *a* [a] approx. father; *á* [au] cow; *e* [ɛ] set; *é* [jɛ] yes; *i, y* [ɪ] sit; *í, ý* [i] feel; *o* [ɔ] law; *ó* [ou] note; *u* [ɣ] approx. Germ. Mütter; *ú* [u] school; *y* = *i*; *ý* = *í*; *æ* [ai] ice; *ö* [ö] Germ. hören; *au* [öy] French feuille; *ei, ey* [ei] ale. Length [:]; half-length [·].

svipta, svipti, svipt(ur) [svɪf·ta, -ɪ, -ʏr̥, svɪf·t] wv.2 deprive; *svifta e-n e-u* deprive sbdy of sth (S. I, *3*, *1*, 2(f)).

svipur, -s, -ir [svɪ:pʰʏr̥, -s, -ɪr̥; svɪ:b̥-] m.2 characteristic appearance, features, trait; ghost, spirit, wraith; *svipatrú* belief in spirits.

svívirða, -virti, -virt(ur) [svi:vɪrða, -vɪr̥tɪ, -ʏr̥, -vɪr̥t] wv.2 dishonor, disgrace, violate the honor of, ravish.

Svíþjóð, -ar [svi:þjou·ð, -ðar̥] f.3 Sweden.

1. **svo** [svɔ:, sɔ:, sɔ] adv. (Pr. *3*, *2*, 16n; *4*, *3*) (1) of manner: so, thus, that: *svo nefndur* so-called; *svo mælti hann* thus he spoke; *svo búið má ekki standa* things cannot be left at such a pass; *síður en svo* anything but that, quite the contrary; (2) of quantity: so, that: *svo mikið* so much; *svo gamall* that old; (3) of time: then: *svo kvöddu þeir* then (thereupon) they took leave; (*og*) *svo* (and) then (enumerating); (4) *svo sem* such as, as f. inst.; *svo sem, svosem, sosum* [s(v)ɔ:sɛ·m, sɔ:sʏm] just about: *svo sem tvö fet frá húsinu* (just) about two feet from the house; really: *það er svo sem* (*sosum*) *ekki til mikils* it is really not of much (litotes: = any) use; *það er svo sem sýnilegt* it (that) is really evident, it is quite obvious; *það er nú svo sem* (*sosum*) *óþarfi* that is really quite unnecessary (superfluous); *og svosem ekki neitt* oh, nothing, really.

2. **svo, svo að** [s(v)ɔ:, s(v)ɔ: a·ð] (1) conj. (effect or result) so that, also: *svo . . . að* so . . . that; *enginn gerir, svo að öllum líki* 'nobody works so that all will like it,' i. e. no one does (works) to the satisfaction of all; (S. VI, *9*, *4*, 4; VIII, 3(d)); (2) conj. (of purpose) so that, *svo að . . . ekki* lest, so as not to (S. VI, *9*, *4*, 5; VIII, 3(f)); (3) conj. (comparison) as;

svo . . . sem as . . . as, so . . . as; *svo sem vér og fyrirgefum vorum skuldunautum* as we, too, forgive our debtors; *er svo að sjá, sem it* looks as if; (S. VIII, 3(g)); *svo framarlega sem* conj. (conditional) provided (S. VIII, 3(c)).

svolítill, -il, -ið [s(v)ɔ:li·tʰɪd̥l, -ɪl, -ɪð; -li·dɪd̥l] adj. very little, tiny; *svolítið* a little bit.

svona [s(v)ɔ:na] (Pr. *4*, *3*) adv. thus; like this; about, perhaps; now, there, there.

svonefndur, -nefnd, -nefnt [s(v)ɔ:nɛmd̥ʏr̥, -nɛmd̥, -nɛmtʰ; -nɛmt] adj. so-called (also *svo nefndur*).

svunta, -u, -ur [svʏn·tʰa, -ʏ(r̥); svʏn̥·ta] wf.1 apron.

svæði, -s, - [svai:ðɪ(s)] n. region; space, tract of land.

svör, see *svar*.

svört, see *svartur*.

sýð, see *sjóða*.

syðra [sɪð·ra] adv. in the south (= *í* (old: *hið*) *syðra*).

syfja, -aði, -að(ur) [sɪv·ja, -aðɪ, -að, -aðʏr̥] wv.4 *mig syfjar* I get sleepy; *ég er syfjaður* I am sleepy (S. I, *2*, *1*, 3; VI, **14**, *5*).

sýg, see *sjúga*.

sykur, (-ri), -urs [sɪ:kʰʏr̥(s), sɪ:kʰrɪ; sɪ:g̊-] m.1 or n. sugar.

sykurker, -s, - [sɪ:kʰʏr̥-k̠ʰɛːr, -k̠ʰɛr·s; sɪ:g̊ʏr̥-] n. sugar bowl.

sykurkringla, -u, -ur [sɪ:kʰʏr̥-kʰriŋ·la, -ʏ(r̥); sɪ:g̊ʏr̥-] wf.1 coffee ring.

symfónía, -u, -ur [sɪm·fou·nija, -ʏ(r̥)] wf.1 symphony.

sýn, -ar, -ir [si:n, -nar̥, -nɪr̥] f.2 vision, sight; *blindir fá sýn* the blind receive the sight.

sýna, sýndi, sýndur (sýnt) [si:na, sin·dɪ, -ʏr̥, sin·tʰ; sin·t] wv.2 (1) show, exhibit, perform; *sýna e-m e-ð* show sbdy sth; (2) middle voice: *mér sýnist e-ð* I think I see sth (S. VI, **14**, *5*); *mér sýndist hann koma* (= *að hann kæmi*) I thought I saw him come (coming)

Consonants: [ð] brea*th*e; [g] *g*ood; [gj] *gy*arden (garden); [hw] *wh*at; [j] *y*es; [kj] *cy*an (can); [ŋ] thi*ng*; [q] N. Germ. sa*g*en; [r] Scottish *r*; [x] approx. Germ. a*ch*; [þ] *th*in. Voiceless: ○; [b̥, d̥, g̊] approx. *p, t, k*. Half-voiced: *italics*. Aspiration and preaspiration: [ʰ]; [pʰ, tʰ, kʰ] *p-, t-, k-*. Others as in English.

(= that he came) (S. VI, **9**, **4**, 1n2); *sýnast sem* seem as if (S. VI, **9**, **4**, 7); *sýnast sitt hvað* be of different (opposite) opinions.

synd, -ar, -ir [sɪn·d̥, -ar̥, -ɪr̥] f.2 sin.

synda, synti, synt [sɪn·d̥a, sɪn·tʰɪ, sɪn·tʰ; sɪn·t·] wv.2 swim; *synda með e-n* swim with sbdy (i. e. taking sbdy with him).

syndari, -a, -ar [sɪn·d̥arɪ, -a, -ar̥] wm.1 sinner.

syndga, -aði, -að [sɪŋ·g̊a, -aðɪ, -að; sɪn·d̥g̊a] wv.4 to sin.

syndur, synd, synt [sɪn·d̥ʏr̥, sɪn·d̥, sɪn·tʰ; sɪn·t] adj. able to swim.

syngja, syng, söng, sungum, sunginn (-ið) [sɪŋ·g̊ja, sɪŋ·g̊, söyŋ·g̊, suŋ·g̊ʏm, suŋ·g̊jɪn, -ɪð] v.3 sing.

sýni, -s [si:nɪ(s)] n. visibility; *gott sýni* fine visibility; *til sýnis* for show, for inspection.

sýning, -ar, -ar [si:niŋ̊, -ar̥] f.1 exhibition, show (= *leiksýning* at the theater, *kvikmyndasýning* at the movie).

synja, -aði, -að [sɪn·ja, -aðɪ, -að] wv.4 *synja e-m e-s, synja e-m um e-ð* deny sbdy sth.

sýnn, sýn, sýnt; sýnni, sýnstur [sid̥·n̥, si:n, sin·tʰ; sin·t; sid̥·nɪ, sinstʏr̥] adj. obvious, visible.

sýp, see 2. *súpa.*

sýr, (sú), sýr, sýr, (súa) [si:r, su:(a)] f.3 sow (obsolete).

syrgja, syrgði, syrgður (syrgt) [sɪr·g̊ja, sɪr·ðɪ, -ʏr̥, sɪr̥·t; sɪrqðɪ, -ʏr̥, sɪr̥xt] wv.2 mourn.

1. **sýsla, -u, -ur** [sis·la, -ʏ(r̥)] wf.1 occupation; work; (administrative) district of *sýslumaður,* ' county.'

2. **sýsla, -aði, -að** [sis·la, -aðɪ, -að] wv.4 be busy with sth, be working; *eitthvað (sitt hvað) að sýsla* doing this and that.

sýslumaður, -manns, -menn [sis·lʏma:ðʏr̥, -man·s, -mɛn:] m.4 district magistrate, prefect.

sýslunefnd, -ar, -ir [sis·lʏ-nɛm·d̥, -ar̥, -ɪr] f.2 district board, 'county board.'

systir, -ur, -ur [sɪs·tɪr̥, -ʏr̥] f.3 sister.

systkin [sɪs·kjɪ·n] n.pl. brother and sister.

systkina-börn, -synir, -dætur [sɪs·-kjɪna-böd̥·n̥, -sɪ:nɪr̥, -dai:tʰʏr̥; -dai:-d̥ʏr̥] n., m., f. pl. first cousins: children, sons, daughters of brother and sister.

systra-börn, -synir, -dætur [sɪs·tra-böd̥·n̥, -sɪ:nɪr̥, -dai:tʰʏr̥; -dai:d̥ʏr̥] n., m., f. pl. first cousins: children, sons, daughters of sisters.

sýta, sýtti, sýtt [si:tʰa, siʰt:ɪ, siʰt:; si:d̥a] wv.2 whimper, sorrow.

sæbrattur, -brött, -bratt [sai:braʰt·ʏr̥, -bröʰt·, -braʰt·] adj. rising steeply out of the sea.

sækja, sótti, sótt(ur) [sai:kjʰa,souʰt:ɪ, -ʏr̥, souʰt:; sai:g̊ja] wv.2 seek, fetch, take, go and get; *sækja heim* (= *heimsækja*) visit, call on; *sækja um styrk* ' seek to obtain a grant,' apply for a grant or stipend or scholarship; *sækja ekki gull í greipar e-m (e-s)* 'not to get gold at sbdy's hands,' i. e. suffer defeat at the hands of sbdy; *sækja að* attack, molest; *sækja (vel, illa) að e-m* attack one in the spirit, affect one; it was believed that a visitor's accompanying spirit (*fylgja*) preceded him and affected the man he wanted to visit in some way (good or bad, often by making him sleepy) before the guest arrived. Hence the common question: *hvernig sæki ég að þér?* how do I affect you? how are you?

sæll, sæl, sælt; sælli, sælastur [said̥·l, sai:l, sail·t, said̥·lɪ, sai:lastʏr̥] adj. happy, blessed; in greetings: *komdu sæll* how do you do, how are you? *vertu sæll* goodbye; (informal:) *sæli(r) nú* hello; *komið þér sælir (-ar)* (polite) how do you do (S. IV, 1, 2; V, 4, 5).

sæludalur, -s, -ir [sai:lʏ-da:lʏr̥, -dal·s, -da:lɪr̥] m.2 valley of bliss.

Vowels: *a* [a] approx. father; *á* [au] cow; *e* [ɛ] set; *é* [jɛ] yes; *i, y* [ɪ] sit; *í, ý* [i] feel; *o* [ɔ] law; *ó* [ou] note; *u* [ʏ] approx. Germ. Mütter; *ú* [u] school; *y* = i; *ý* = í; *æ* [ai] ice; *ö* [ö] Germ. hören; *au* [öy] French *feuille*; *ei, ey* [ei] ale. Length [:]; half-length [·].

464

Sæmundur, -ar (-s) [sai:mɤndᶘɤᶘ, -aᶘ; -mɤn(d)s] m.l pers. name; patronymic: *Sæmundsson, -dóttir*; *Sæmundur fróði* (1056-1133) priest at Oddi, famed for his learning, in later folklore for his magic.

sæng, -ur, -ur [saiŋ·ğ, -ɤᶘ] f.3 bed, bedcover, featherbed.

sænska, -u [sainska, -ɤ] wf.l Swedish.

sænskur, sænsk, sænskt [sainskɤᶘ, sainsk, sainst] adj. Swedish.

sær, sævar, see *sjór.*

særður, særð, sært [sair·ðɤᶘ, sair·ð, sair·t] adj. wounded.

1. sæta, sætti, sætt (-ið) [sai:tʰa, saiʰt:ɪ, saiʰt:; sai:da] wv.2 *sæta færi, lagi* take the opportunity; *hverju sætir það?* what is the reason?

2. sæta, sætti, sætt [sai:tʰa, saiʰt:- (ɪ); sai:da] wv.2 set up a small haystack or haycock (which later may be tied in a bundle).

sæti, -s, - [sai:tʰɪ(s); sai:dɪ] n. seat; *fá sér sæti* take a seat, have a seat; a group of *sátur* (= small haystacks or haycocks).

sætsúpa, -u, -ur [sai:tʰsu·pʰa, -ɤ(ᶘ); sai:dsu·ba] wf.l sweet soup made with fruit juices, fruit soup.

sætt, see *sæta* and *sætur.*

sætur, sæt, sætt [sai:tʰɤr, sai:tʰ, saiʰt:; sai:dɤᶘ, sai:d] adj. sweet.

södd, see *saddur.*

söðull, -uls, -lar [sö:ðɤdl, -ɤls, söð·- laᶘ] m.l woman's saddle.

söfn, see *safn.*

söfnuður, safnaðar, -ir [söb·nɤðɤᶘ, sab·naðaᶘ, -ıᶘ] m.3 congregation.

sög, sagar, sagir [sö:q, sa:qaᶘ, sai:jıᶘ; sa:jıᶘ] f.2 saw.

sögn, sagnar, -ir [söğ·n, sağ·naᶘ, -ıᶘ] f.2 story, (hear) say, legend, tale; (in grammar) verb.

sögu, -ur, see *saga.*

Sögueyja, -u [sö:qɤ-ei:ja, -ei:jɤ] wf.l Saga Island, i. e. Iceland.

sögufrægur, -fræg, -frægt [sö:qɤ- frai:qɤᶘ, -frai:q, -fraix·t] adj. of historic fame.

sögulegur [sö:qɤ-le:qɤᶘ] adj. (see *-legur*) historical; interesting.

sögustaður, -ar, -ir [sö:qɤ-sta:ðɤᶘ, -aᶘ, -ıᶘ] m.3 historic place; sagastead.

sök, sakar, sakir [sö:kʰ, sa:kʰaᶘ, sa:- kᶘʰɪᶘ; sö:ğ, sa:ğaᶘ, sa:ğᶘɪᶘ] f.2 matter, thing; guilt, charge, offence; suit, case, action; *vera viss í sinni sök* be certain of the matter; *fyrir þá sök* because of the fact; *fyrir sakir e-s* for the sake of sth (sbdy), because of sth (sbdy).

1. sökkva, sekk, sökk, sukkum, sokkinn (-ið) [söʰk:va, seᶜʰk:, söʰk:, sɤʰk:ɤm, soʰkᶨ:ın, -ıð] v.3 sink (intr.); *sökkva í* sink in.

2. sökkva, sökkti, sökkt [söʰk:va, söx·tɪ, söx·t] wv.2 sink (trans.) *sökkva skipi* sink a boat.

söknuður, saknaðar [söʰk·nɤðɤᶘ, saʰk·- naðaᶘ] m.3 sense of loss, sorrow.

sökum [sö:kʰɤm; sö:ğᶘm] prep. with gen. (dat.pl. of *sök*) on account of; *sökum þess* on account of that; *sökum þess að . . .* conj. because (S. VIII, 3(b)).

sölt, see *salt* and *saltur.*

sölu, -ur, see *sala.*

söluumboð, -s, - [sö:lɤ-ɤm·bɔ·ð, -bɔðs] n. commission to sell; *hafa söluumboð* have a commission, be commissioned; *söluumboð til e-s* authorization (permission) to sell to sbdy.

söm, see *samur.*

sömuleiðis [sö:mɤ-lei:ðɪs] adv. likewise, also, too.

söng, see *syngja.*

söngkraftar [söyŋ·ğkʰraftaᶘ] m.l song capacities, talents.

sönglag, -s, -lög [söyŋ·ğla·q, -laxs, -lö·q] n. melody, song.

sönglíf, -s [söyŋ·ğli·v, -lifs] n. musical life, musical activity.

söngur, söngs, söngvar [söyŋ·ğɤᶘ, söyŋ·s, söyŋ·ğvaᶘ] m.l song.

söngvari, -a, -ar [söyŋ·ğvarɪ, -a(ᶘ)] wm.l singer.

sönn, see *sannur.*

söri, see 1. *sá.*

Consonants: [ð] brea*th*e; [g] *g*ood; [ɡɹ] *gy*arden (garden); [hʍ] *wh*at; [j] *y*es; [kɹ] *cy*an (can); [ŋ] thi*ng*; [q] N. Germ. sa*g*en; [r] Scottish *r*; [x] approx. Germ. a*ch*; [þ] *th*in Voiceless: o; [ḅ, ḍ, g̊] approx. *p, t, k*. Half-voiced: *italics*. Aspiration and preaspiration [ʰ]; [pʰ, tʰ, kʰ] *p-, t-, k-*. Others as in English.

T.

tá, táar, tær [tʰau:, tʰau:aṛ, tʰai:r]
f.3 toe; *á tánum* on the toes.

taða, tööu [tʰa:ða, tʰö:ðɤ] wf.1 hay
from the manured homefield (from
tað n. manure).

táði, táið, -inn, see *tæja.*

tafði, tafið, -inn, see *tefja.*

tag [tʰa:q] dat. **tagi** [tʰai:jɪ; tʰa:jɪ]
n. only in: *af . . . tagi* of (this,
etc.) kind, sort. Cf. also *tæi.*

tagl, -s, tögl [tʰag̊·l̥(s), tʰög̊·l̥] n. tail
of a horse.

tak, -s, tök [tʰa:kʰ, tʰa:kʰs, tʰö:kʰ;
tʰa:g̊, tʰö:g̊] n. hold, grasp; piercing
pain, stabbing pain.

taka, tek, tók, tókum, tekinn (-ið)
[tʰa:kʰa, tʰɛ:kʰ, tʰou:kʰ, tʰou:kʰɤm,
tʰɛ:k₁ʰɪn, -ɪð; tʰa:g̊a, tʰɛ:g̊, tʰou:g̊,
tʰou:g̊ɤm, tʰɛ:g̊₁ɪn] v.6 take, seize,
catch, grasp, hold; buy; overtake,
surprise; take (time); receive,
accept; succeed; begin; (1) with
acc.: *taka (leigu)bíl á götunni* hail
a taxi in the street; *taka mynd* take
a picture, snap a picture; *taka e-n
í skóla* admit sbdy to a school; *taka
tíma* take lessons, take courses
(= *vera í tímum hjá e-m*); *taka
próf* take an examination; *taktu
þennan hatt* buy this hat; *taka ost*
make cheese; *ef dagur tæki þau* if
day should surprise them; *höfnin
tekur 100 skip* the harbor holds 100
ships; *taka aftur gleði sína* recover
one's good humor; *taka sér far* take
passage, buy a ticket; (2) with a
double acc.: *það tók mig langan
tíma* it took me a long time;
(3) with dat.: *taka e-m* receive,
welcome sbdy; *taka e-m (vel, illa)*
receive sbdy (well, in an unfriendly
manner); *taka e-u* put up with,
accept sth; resign oneself to sth;
taka framförum make progress;
taka ástfóstri við center one's affections in, grow fond of; (4) middle voice: *takast vel (illa)* succeed,

be a success, go well (badly);
góðar ástir tókust með þeim true
love sprang up between them;
takast af cease, be abolished;
takast (= taka sér) e-ð á hendur
undertake sth; (5) impersonal:
mig tekur í fótinn my foot hurts
me (S. I, **4,** *1,* 3); (6) auxiliary:
begin: *veðrið tók að batna* the
weather began to improve (S. VI,
5, *1*); (7) with preps and advs:
taka á touch, take; *taka á móti*
receive, welcome; *taka að sér* take
in hand, take over; *taka e-ð af e-m*
take sth away from sbdy; *taka
eftir e-u* notice sth; *taka í nefið
(tóbak)* take snuff; *taka ofan* take
off one's hat; unload the pack
horses; *taka til e-s* begin sth; *taka
til fótanna* take to one's heels; *taka
til ára* take to the oars, grasp the
oars; *taka undir* (= *anza, svara*)
respond; *taka upp* adopt, begin;
pick up; draw from one's pocket;
lift; *taka upp hjá sér* dig out of
one's pockets; *taka e-n upp* call on
sbdy (in class); *taka upp í sig*
chew tobacco; *taka við* receive;
taka við e-u receive, accept, take
sth; *taka við af e-u* be next in
order, follow.

takk [tʰaʰk:] = *þakk,* thanks.

takmarka, -aði, -að(ur) [tʰa:kʰmarka,
-aðɪ, -að, -aðɤṛ; tʰa:g̊-] wv.4 limit,
curb.

tal, -s [tʰa:l, tʰal·s] n. talk, conversation, speech; *vera á tali* (in telephoning) be speaking; the line is
busy; *koma til tals* come up in the
course of conversation.

1. **tala, tölu, -ur** [tʰa:la, tʰö:lɤ(ṛ)]
   wf.1 figure, number; speech; button.
2. **tala, -aði, -að** [tʰa:la, -aðɪ, -að]
   wv.4 speak, talk; *tala um e-ð* speak
   about sth; *tala ensku* speak English;
   tala við e-n speak to sbdy.

taldi, talið, -inn, see *telja.*

Tálknafjörður, -fjarðar [tʰaulkʰna-
fjör·ðɤṛ, -fjar·ðaṛ; tʰaulkna-, tʰault-
na-] m.3 'Tálkni's Fjord.'

Vowels: *a* [a] approx. father; *á* [au] cow; *e* [ɛ] set; *é* [jɛ] yes; *i, y* [ɪ] sit; *í, ý* [i] feel;
o [ɔ] law; *ó* [ou] note; *u* [ɤ] approx. Germ. Mütter; *ú* [u] school; *y* = *i*; *ý* = *í*; *æ* [ai] ice;
ö [ö] Germ. hören; *au* [öy] French *feuille*; *ei, ey* [ei] ale. Length [:]; half-length [·].

talsverður, -verð, -vert [tʰal·sverðYr̥,
-verð, -ver̥t] adj. considerable.

tamdi, tamið, -inn, see *temja*.

tangó, -s [tʰaŋ·g̊ou·(s)] m.1 tango.

tannar, see *tönn*.

tannbursti, -a, -ar [tʰan·bY(r̥)stɪ,
-a(r̥)] wm.1 toothbrush.

tannduft, -s [tʰan·dYft, -s] n. tooth
powder.

tannpasta [tʰan·pʰasta] n.indecl. tooth
paste.

tannpína, -u [tʰan·pʰi·na, -Y; tʰam··]
wf.1 toothache.

tannverkur, -jar (-s), -ir, (-ja) [tʰan··
ver̥kYr̥, -ver̥k₁a(r̥), -k₁ɪr̥, -ver̥ks]
m.2 toothache.

tap, -s, töp [tʰa:pʰ(s), tʰö:pʰ; tʰa:b̥,
tʰö:b̥] n. loss.

tapa, -aði, -að(ur) [tʰa:pʰa, -aðɪ, -að,
-aðYr̥; tʰa:b̥a] wv.4 lose; *tapa e-u*
lose sth.

tarna [tʰad̥·na, tʰar̥d̥na] adv. chiefly
in: *að °tarna* [a· tʰad̥·na] = *það
þarna* this here; *hvað er að tarna?*
what *is* this!

taumur, -s, -ar [tʰöy:mYr̥, tʰöym·s,
tʰöy:mar̥] m.1 rein; *taka í taumana*
take the reins; *hafa hest í taumi*
lead a horse by the bridle.

t. d. = *til dæmis* for instance.

te, -s [tʰɛ:(s)] n. tea.

tefja, tafði, tafinn (-ið) [tʰɛv·ja, tʰav··
ðɪ, tʰa:vɪn, -ɪð] wv.1 delay, hinder
(trans.); tarry (intr.); *og megi
hann ekki tefja* and that he must
not tarry.

tegund, -ar, -ir [tʰɛ:qYnd̥, -ar̥, -ɪr̥] f.2
kind, species.

tek, tekið, -inn, see *taka*.

tekanna, -könnu, -ur [tʰɛ:kʰan·a,
-kʰön·Y(r)] wf.1 teapot.

tekjur, tekna [tʰɛ:k₁ʰYr̥, tʰɛʰk·na] wf.
1.pl. income.

telgja, telgdi, telgdur (telgt) [tʰɛl·g̊₁a,
tʰɛlqdɪ, -Yr̥, tʰɛlxt; tʰɛqld̥ɪ, -Yr̥,
tʰɛxl̥t] wv.2 whittle.

telja, taldi, talinn (-ið) [tʰɛl·ja, tʰal·dɪ,
tʰa:lɪn; -ɪð] wv.1 count, reckon,
consider; enumerate; *telja e-n
(vera) e-ð* consider sbdy (to be)

sth; *telja e-n góðan* consider sbdy
good (S. I, 2, *1*, 2); *telja e-ð víst*
consider sth certain; *telja (e-ð)
til e-s* count (sth) as sth; include
(sth) in sth; *telja upp* count, mention, enumerate; *talið er* it is considered, thought.

teljari, -a, -ar [tʰɛl·jarɪ, -a(r̥)] wm.1
numerator (in fractions).

telpa, -u, -ur [tʰɛl·pʰa, -Y(r̥); tʰɛl·pa]
wf.1 little girl (baby talk for
stelpa).

temja, tamdi, taminn (-ið) [tʰɛm·ja,
tʰam·dɪ, tʰa:mɪn, -ɪð] wv.1 tame,
break in; *temja hest* break in a
horse (colt); *temja sér e-ð* exercise
oneself in sth, train oneself in sth.

tengda-faðir, -móðir, -dóttir, -sonur
[tʰeiŋ·da-fa:ðɪr̥, -mou:ðɪr̥, -douʰt:-
ɪr̥, -sɔ:nYr̥] m.4, f.3, f.3, m.3 father-,
mother-, daughter-, son-in-law.

tengdafólk, -s [tʰeiŋ·da-foul·kʰ,
-foul·(x)s; -foul·k] n. people related by marriage, in-laws.

tengdir [tʰeiŋ·dɪr̥] f.2.pl. relationship
by marriage.

tengdur, tengd, tengt [tʰeiŋ·dYr̥,tʰeiŋ·d̥,
tʰeiŋ·tʰ; tʰeiŋ·t] adj. *tengdur e-m*
connected with sbdy; related to sbdy
by marriage.

tengja, tengdi, tengdur (tengt) [tʰeiŋ··
g̊₁a, tʰeiŋ·dɪ, -Yr̥, tʰeiŋ·tʰ; tʰeiŋ·t]
wv.2 join, connect, unite; *tengjast*
become related by marriage.

tennur, see *tönn*.

teppi, -s, - [tʰɛʰp:ɪ(s)] n. blanket,
cover; tapestry (= *veggteppi*); rug
(= *gólfteppi*).

terta, -u, -ur [tʰɛr̥·ta, -Y(r̥)] wf.1
tart; cream cake.

teskeið, -ar, -ir [tʰɛ:sk₁ei·ð, -ðar̥, -ðɪr̥]
f.2 teaspoon.

Theódór, -s [tʰɛ:ou·dou:r, -dour̥s]
m.1 Theodor.

Theódóra, -u [tʰɛ:ou·dou:ra, -Y] wf.1
Theodora.

Thorarensen [tʰou:rarɛnsɛ·n] m.1
family name.

Thoroddsen [tʰou:rɔd̥·sɛ·n] m.1 family
name.

Consonants: [ð] brea*the*; [g] *g*ood; [g₁] *gy*arden (garden); [hw] *wh*at; [j] *y*es; [k₁] *cy*an
(can); [ŋ] thi*ng*; [q] N. Germ. sa*g*en; [r] Scottish *r*; [x] approx. Germ. a*ch*; [þ] *th*in.
Voiceless: ○; [b̥, d̥, g̊] approx. *p, t, k*. Half-voiced: *italics*. Aspiration and preaspiration:
[ʰ]; [pʰ, tʰ, kʰ] *p-, t-, k-*. Others as in English.

467

Thorvaldsen [tʰɔr·val(d)sɛ·n] m.1 family name; *Albert Thorvaldsen* (1779-1844) famous Danish-Icelandic sculptor.

tía, -u, -ur [tʰi:ja, -ɣ(r̥)] wf.1 ten (in cards).

tíð, -ar, -ir [tʰi:ð, -ðar̥, -ðIr̥] f.2 time; season, weather; *góð tíð* a spell of good weather; tense (in grammar); pl. *tíðir* divine services; *fara til tíða* go to church.

tíðarfar, -s [tʰi:ðar̥·fa:r, -far̥·s] n. weather conditions, climate.

tíðindi [tʰi:ðIndI] n.pl. news, tidings.

tíðka, -aði, -að(ur) [tʰi·ð·kʰa, -aðI, -að, -aðɣr̥; tʰip·ka] wv.4 be accustomed to; *tíðkast* be usual, be customary.

tíeyringur, -s, -ar [tʰi:jei·riŋɣr̥, -Iŋs, -iŋar̥] m.1 a ten-*aurar* piece.

tífaldur, -föld, -falt [tʰi:faldɣr̥, -föld, -falt] adj. tenfold.

tigur, see *tugur.*

tík, -ar, -ur [tʰi:kʰ, -ar̥, -ɣr̥; tʰi:g̊] f.3 she-dog, tyke, bitch.

til [tʰi:l, tʰIl·] **A.** prep. with gen. to, towards; to, for; for, in order to, to; in, on, under, to—extent; up to, until, for (a while); (1) to, towards: *til Íslands* to Iceland; *fara, koma til e-s* go, come to sbdy, go visiting; (2) in, on: *til sveita* in the rural districts; *til lands og sjávar* on land and sea; (3) to, for: *til hvers?* what for (= *af hverju*)? why? *til þess* for that purpose, to (do so); *skip til umráða* ships at (his) disposal; *til fararinnar* for the journey; *ætla til íbúðar* intend for habitation; *til vinnu* (a) for work, (b) to work; *til sölu* for sale; *t. d. = til dæmis* for instance; *til þess að* or *til að* (with inf.) in order to, for; *til (þess) að fara til þeirra* for going to them; (with *að*-clause) *til þess að hann færi* in order that he should go (S. VI, 9, 4, 5; 11, 3; VIII, 3(f)); *til þess er* conj. until (S. VIII, 3(h)); (4) other senses: *til minningar um* in memory of; *til jafnaðar* on the average; *til muna* to a considerable (or great) extent; *koma til greina* be taken under consideration, be possible; (5) of time: up to, until: *til áramóta* to the end of the (present) year (and the beginning of the next); *til skamms tíma* up to recently; *til skemmri tíma* for a shorter time.

B. adv. in addition: *tvær sneiðar til* two more slices; *að sumrinu til* during the summer; with verbs: *bera til* happen; *bjóðast til* offer; *vera til* exist; be ready, available; *verða til e-s* take sth upon oneself.

C. conj. to: *tveir til þrír* two to three.

tilboð, -s, - [tʰIl·bɔ·ð, -bɔðs] n. offer.

tilbúinn, -in, -ið [tʰIl·bu·In, -In, -Ið] adj. (pp.) ready; *ertu tilbúinn?* are you ready? ready made (clothes).

tilfinnanlegur [tʰIl·fIn·an·le:qɣr̥] adj. (see *-legur*) perceptible.

tilfinning, -ar, -ar [tʰIl·fIn·iŋg, -ar̥] f.1 feeling.

tilhögun, -unar [tʰI:lhö·qɣn, -ɣnar̥] f.2 arrangement.

tilkomumikill, -il, -ið; -meiri, -mestur [tʰIl·kʰɔ·mɣ·mI:kj ʰIdl, -Il, -Ið; -mI:-g̊ Idl; -mei:rI, -mes·tɣr̥] adj. grand, impressive.

tilkynna, -kynnti, -kynnt(ur) [tʰIl··kj ʰIn·a, -kj ʰIntʰI, -ɣr̥, -kj ʰIntʰ; -kj ʰInt·] wv.2 notify, inform, inform of, let know sth (*tilkynna e-ð*).

tilkynning, -ar, -ar [tʰIl·kj ʰIn·iŋg, -ar̥] f.1 announcement, notification; proclamation; report.

tillaga, -lögu, -ur [tʰIl·a:qa, tʰIl·ö·qɣ(r̥)] wf.1 proposal.

tiltala, -tölu, -ur [tʰIl·tʰa·la, -tʰö·lɣ(r̥)] wf.1 proportion; *að tiltölu við e-ð* in proportion to sth.

tiltölulega [tʰIl·tʰö·lɣ·le:qa] adv. comparatively.

tíma, tímdi, tímt [tʰi:ma, tʰim·dI, tʰim·tʰ; tʰim·t] wv.2 have the heart to, be willing to (only with negation): *tíma ekki að gera e-ð* be reluctant, unwilling to do sth.

Vowels: *a* [a] approx. father; *á* [au] cow; *e* [ɛ] set; *é* [jɛ] yes; *i, y* [I] sit; *í, ý* [i] feel; *o* [ɔ] law; *ó* [ou] note; *u* [ɣ] approx. Germ. Mütter; *ú* [u] school; *y = i*; *ý = í*; *æ* [ai] ice; *ö* [ö] Germ. hören; *au* [öy] French feuille; *ei, ey* [ei] ale. Length [:]; half-length [·].

468

tímarit, -s, - [tʰi:ma-rɪ:tʰ, -s; -rɪ:d̥]
n. periodical.

tímatal, -tals, -töl [tʰi:ma-tʰa:l, -tʰal·s,
-tʰö:l] n. chronology.

timbur, (-ri), -urs [tʰɪm·b̥ʏr̥(s),
tʰɪmb̥rɪ] n. timber, wood.

timburáðdrættir [tʰɪm·b̥ʏr-að-draiʰt·-
ɪr̥] m.3 transportation of timber.

timburhús, -húss, - [tʰɪm·b̥ʏr̥-hu:s,
-hus:] n. wooden frame house.

timburskortur, -s [tʰɪm·b̥ʏr̥-sk̥ɔr̥·tʏr̥,
-sk̥ɔr̥ts] m.1 lack of timber.

timburverzlun, -unar, -anir [tʰɪm·b̥ʏr-
ver̥slʏn, -ʏnar̥, -anɪr̥] f.2 lumber-
yard.

tími, -a, -ar [tʰi:mɪ, -a(r̥)] wm.1
time; while, hour (= klukkutími,
klukkustund); um tíma for a while;
að þeim tíma liðnum after that time
(literally: that time passed);
tvennir tímar two different times;
pl. tímar lessons, courses; Tíminn
'The Times,' a newspaper.

tindóttur, -ótt, -ótt [tʰɪn·douʰt·(ʏr̥)]
adj. full of peaks, summits, crags.

tindur, -s, -ar [tʰɪn·d̥ʏr̥, -ar̥, tʰɪnd̥s]
m.1 peak, summit.

tíræður, -ræð, -rætt [tʰi:rai·ðʏr̥,
-rai·ð, -raiʰt·] adj. hundred years of
age, hundred fathoms deep, high.

titra, -aði, -að [tʰɪ:tʰra, -aðɪ, -að;
tʰɪ:dra] wv.4 shiver, vibrate.

tittlingur, -s, -ar [tʰɪʰt·liŋg̊ʏr̥, -iŋs,
-iŋg̊ar̥] m.1 sparrow.

tittur, -s, -ir [tʰɪʰt·ʏr̥, -ɪr̥, tʰɪʰt·s] m.2
peg, tack, pin.

tíu [tʰi:jʏ] num. card. ten.

tíund,-ar,-ir [tʰi:jʏnd̥,-ar̥,-ɪr̥] f.2 tithe.

tíundi [tʰi:jʏndɪ] num. ord. tenth.

tjá, tjáði, tjáð(ur) [tʰjau:, tʰjau:ðɪ,
-ʏr̥, tjau:ð] wv.3 tell, say, explain,
mention; tjá sig apologize.

tjald, -s, tjöld [tʰjal·d̥, tʰjalds, tʰjöl·d̥]
n. tent.

tjarnar, -ir, see tjörn.

Tjarnargata, -götu [tʰjad̥·nar-ga:tʰa,
-gö:tʰʏ; -ga:d̥-, -gö:d̥-; tʰjard̥nar-]
wf.1 'Pond Street' in Reykjavík.

tjóður, (-ri), -urs, -ur [tʰjou:ðʏr̥(s),
tʰjouð·rɪ] n. tether.

tjón, -s, - [tʰjou:n, tʰjoun·s] n. loss,
damage, detriment.

tjöld, see tjald.

tjörn, tjarnar, -ir [tʰjöd̥·n, tʰjad̥·nar̥,
-ɪr̥; tʰjörd̥n, tʰjard̥nar̥] f.2 pond,
tarn; small (shallow) lake; Tjörnin
'The Pond,' in Reykjavík.

tó, tóar, tór [tʰou:(ar̥), tʰou:r̥] f.1
grassy spot in rocks; also in place
names, Tó, Tóar·.

tóbak, -s [tʰou:ba·kʰ(s), -baxs; -ba·g̊]
n. tobacco.

tóbaksbaukur, -s, -ar [tʰou:baxs-böy:-
kʰʏr̥, -böy:kʰs, -böy:kʰar̥; -böy:g̊·]
m.1 snuff box, snuff horn (= ponta).

tóbaksbúð, -ar, -ir [tʰou:baxs-bu:ð,
-ðar̥, -ðɪr̥] f.2 tobacco shop; tobacco
store.

tóbakseinkasala, -sölu, -ur [tʰou:baxs-
eiŋ·kʰasa·la, -sö:lʏ(r̥); -eiŋ·ka-] wf.1
trade monopoly on tobacco; Tóbakseinkasalan, Tóbakseinkasala ríkisins 'The State Tobacco Monopoly.'

tóbakslaus, -laus, -laust [tʰou:baxs-
löy:s, -löys·t] adj. having no tobacco, run out of tobacco.

tóbaksreykur, -jar [tʰou:baxs-rei:kʰʏr̥,
-k̩ʰar̥; -rei:g̊ʏr̥, -g̊ͅar̥] m.2 tobacco
smoke.

tóbaksverzlun, -unar, -anir [tʰou:baxs-
ver̥slʏn, -ʏnar̥, -anɪr̥] f.2 tobacco
shop; tobacco trade.

tófa, -u, -ur (tóa) [tʰou:(v)a, -ʏ(r̥)]
wf.1 (female) fox, vixen.

tófugervi, -s [tʰou:(v)ʏ-g̩er·vɪ, -s] n.
the garb of a fox.

tóft, -ar, -ir (tótt) [tʰouʰt:, touf·t,
-ar̥, -ɪr̥] f.2 the four (earthen) walls
surrounding a house without a roof;
a ruin; also in place names: -tóft
(-tótt).

togari, -a, -ar [tʰɔ:qarɪ, -a(r̥)] wm.1
trawler; beam-trawler; togaraútgerð trawler-fisheries.

tók, -um, see taka.

tólf [tʰoul·v] num. card. twelve.

tólfræður, -ræð, -rætt [tʰoul·(v)rai·-
ðʏr̥, -rai·ð, -raiʰt·] adj. tólfrætt
dýpi a depth of 120 fathoms.

tólfti [tʰoul·tɪ, tʰoul̥ftɪ] num. ord.
twelfth.

tólftungur, -ungs, -ungar [tʰoul··
tuŋg̊ʏr̥, ·uŋs, -uŋg̊ar̥; tʰoul̥ft-] m.1
one twelfth.

tolla, tolldi, tollað [tʰɔd·la, tʰɔl·dɪ,
tʰɔd·lað] wv.3 stick, cleave to.

tollur, -s, -ar [tʰɔd·lʏr̥, tʰɔdls, tʰɔd··
lar̥] m.1 tariff.

Tómas, -s (-ar) [tʰou:ma·s, -ar̥] m.1
Thomas.

tómati, -a, -ar [tʰou:ma·tʰɪ, -a(r̥)]
wm.1 tomato.

tóna, -aði, -að [tʰou:na, -aðɪ, -að,
-aðʏr̥] wv.4 chant, intone.

tónleikur, -s, -ar [tʰoun·lei·kʰʏr̥;
-lei·kʰs, -leixs; -lei·kʰar̥; -lei:g̊-]
m.1 (or 2) concert; program of
music.

tónlist, -ar [tʰoun·lɪst, -ar̥] f.2 music.

Tónlistarfélagið, -sins [tʰoun·lɪstar-
fje:laijɪð, -laxsɪns] n. with the def.
art. 'The Music Society.'

tónn, -s, -ar [tʰoud·n̥, tʰoun·s, tʰou:-
nar̥] m.1 tone.

tor- [tʰɔ:r-] pref. difficult, with difficulty.

torf, -s [tɔr·v, tɔrfs] n. green turf,
sod.

torfþak, -s, -þök [tɔr·fþa·kʰ, -þa·kʰs,
-þö·kʰ] n. roof thatched with sod.

torsóttur, -sótt, -sótt [tʰɔr·souʰt·ʏr̥,
-souʰt·] adj. difficult to get.

tótt, see tóft.

tóvinna, -u [tʰou:vɪn·a, -ʏ] wf.1 wool
home industry.

traðar, -ir, see tröð.

trappa, tröppu, -ur [tʰraʰp:a, tʰröp:-
ʏ(r̥)] wf.1 step; pl. tröppur steps,
short flight of steps.

traust, -s [tʰröys·t, tʰröysts] n. confidence; trust, reliance; bera traust
til e-s have confidence in sbdy.

traustur, traust, traust [tʰröys·tʏr̥,
tʰröys·t] adj. safe, faithful, reliable.

tré, -s, - [tʰrjɛ:(s)] n. tree; wood.

treð, see troða.

tregi, -a [tʰrei:jɪ, tʰrɛ:qa; tʰrɛ:jɪ]
wm.1 grief.

treyja, -u, -ur [tʰrei:ja, -ʏ(r̥)] wf.1
(woman's) jacket.

trjóna, -u, -ur [tʰrjou:na, -ʏ(r̥)] wf.1
snout, ram.

troða, treð, tróð, tróðum, troðinn (-ið)
[tʰrɔ:ða, tʰrɛ:ð, tʰrou:ð, tʰrou:ðʏm,
tʰrɔ:ðɪn, -ɪð] v.6 tread (on), tram-
ple (on) (troða (á)); with dat.
stuff, cram; troða sér inn í cram
oneself into.

1. trú, -ar [tʰru:, tʰru:ar̥] f.1 religion; belief; trú á e-ð belief in
sth.

2. trú, see trúr.

trúa, trúði, trúað [tʰru:a, tʰru:ðɪ,
tʰru:að] wv.3 believe; trúa á guð
believe in God; trúa á mátt sinn
og megin believe in one's own
strength and power; trúa e-u believe sth; trúa e-m believe, trust
sbdy; pp. trúaður believing, re-
ligious; því er ekki trúandi that is
not to be trusted.

trúlofa, -aði, -aður [tʰru:lɔ·va, -aðɪ,
-að, -aðʏr̥] wv.4 engage, betroth;
trúlofa sig or more commonly:
trúlofast become engaged.

trúlofun, -unar, -anir [tʰru:lɔ·vʏn,
-ʏnar, -anɪr̥] f.2 betrothal.

trúr, trú, trútt; trúrri, trúastur
[tʰru:r, tʰru:, tʰruʰt:; tʰrur:ɪ,
tʰru:astʏr̥] adj. faithful; trúr e-m
faithful to sbdy.

trygging, -ar, -ar [tʰrɪg̊;:iŋg̊, -ar̥] f.1
guarantee.

tryggur, trygg, tryggt [tʰrɪg̊:ʏr̥, tʰrɪg̊:,
tʰrɪx·t] adj. faithful; tryggur e-m,
tryggur við e-n faithful to sbdy.

tryppi, -s, - [tʰrɪʰp:ɪ(s)] n. colt,
young horse.

tröð, traðar, -ir [tʰrö:ð, tʰra:ðar̥,
tʰra:ðɪr̥] f.2 pavement; pl. traðir
a way with walls on each side
leading up to the farmhouse through
the tún; also in place names: -tröð,
Traðar-.

tröll, -s, - [tʰröd·l̥, tʰröl·s] n. troll.

tröllatrú, -ar [tʰröd·la-tʰru:(ar̥)] f.1
belief in trolls (trúin á tröllin).

tröllatryggð, -ar, -ir [tʰröd·la-tʰrɪq·ð,

470

-ðar̯, -ðır̯; -tʰrɪg̊·þ] f.2 'troll faith,' extreme faithfulness.

tröllskessa, -u, -ur [tʰröd·lsk₁ɛs·a, -ɣ(r̯)] wf.1 troll woman, giantess.

tröppu, -ur see trappa.

tugabrot, -s, - [tʰɣ:qa-brɔ:tʰ(s), -brɔ:d] n. decimal fraction(s).

tugga, -u, -ur [tʰɣg̊:a, -ɣ(r̯)] wf.1 a mouthful, cud; a wisp of hay.

tuggði, tuggið, -inn, see tyggja.

tugur, -ar, -ir [tʰɣ:qɣr̯, -ar̯, tʰɣy:jır̯; tʰɣ:jır] m.3 ten, decade.

tún, -s, - [tʰu:n, tʰun·s] n. homefield, a manured field nearest to the farm-houses (usually surrounding them); also in place and street-names: -tún.

túnasláttur, -ar, -slættir [tʰu:na-slauʰt:ɣr̯, -ar̯, -slaiʰt:ır] m.3 home-field mowing, haymaking in the homefield.

tundur, (-ri), -urs [tʰɣn·dɣr̯(s), tɣn-drı] n. tinder, inflammable material; explosives.

tundurdufl, -s, - [tʰɣn·dɣr-dɣb·l(s)] n. mine.

tundurskeyti, -s, - [tʰɣn·dɣr-sk₁ei:-tʰı(s); -sk₁ei:dı(s)] n. torpedo.

tundurspillir, -is, -(ir)ar [tʰɣn·dɣr-spıd·lır̯, -ıs, (-ir)ar̯] m.1 torpedo boat.

tunga, -u, -ur, (-na) [tʰuŋ·g̊a, -ɣ(r̯), tʰuŋ·na, tʰu:na] wf.1 tongue; tongue-shaped land between two rivers, tongue-shaped glacier between two mountains; in place names: -tunga, Tungu-, Tungna-; tungan í mér ('the tongue in me') my tongue (S. I, 4, 1, 4); language.

tungl, -s, - [tʰuŋ·l, tʰuŋls; tʰuŋ·s] n. moon; heavenly body.

tunglsljós, -s [tʰuŋ·lsljou:s, -ljous·; tʰuŋ·sljou:s] n. moonlight.

tunna, -u, -ur [tʰɣn:a, -ɣ(r̯)] wf.1 barrel.

tuttugasti [tʰɣʰt:ɣqastı] num. ord. twentieth.

tuttugu [tʰɣʰt:ɣqɣ] num. card. twenty.

tuttugu-og-fimm-eyringur [tʰɣʰt:ɣq·

ɔ··fım:-ei·riŋg̊ɣr̯, -ıŋs, -ıŋg̊ar̯] m.1 a twenty-five-aurar piece.

tveggja, see tveir.

tveggjaeyringur, -s, -ar [tʰvɛg̊₁:ei·-riŋg̊ɣr̯, -ıŋs, -ıŋg̊ar̯] m.1 a two-aurar piece.

tveir, tvær, tvö [tʰvei:r,tʰvai:r,tʰvö:], acc. tvo, tvær, tvö [tʰvɔ:], dat. tveim(ur) [tʰvei:m(ɣr̯)], gen. tveggja [tʰvɛg̊₁:a] num. card. two (In. V, 2, 2(b)).

tvennur, tvenn, tvennt [tʰvɛn:ɣr, tʰvɛn:, tʰvɛn·tʰ; tʰvɛn·t] distribu-tive num. tvennir sokkar two pair of socks; tvennt a group of two; vera í tvennu (= í tvennum sokkum) wear two pair of stockings (In. V, 3, 3).

tvíbökur [tʰvi:bö·kʰɣr̯; -bö·g̊ɣr̯] wf.1 pl. zwieback (sg. tvíbaka).

Tvídægra, -u [tʰvi:daiqra, -ɣ] wf.1 'Two Days Heath.'

tvífylki, -s, - [tʰvi:fılk₁ʰı(s); -fılk₁ı] n. regiment.

tvíheilagur, -ög, -agt [tʰvi:hei·laqɣr̯, -öq, -axt] adj. having two holidays.

tvíhnepptur, -hneppt, -hneppt [tʰvi:-hnɛf·tɣr̯, -hnɛf·t] adj. double-breasted.

tvílyftur, -lyft, -lyft [tʰvi:lıf·t(ɣr̯)] adj. two-story (house).

tvímælalaust [tʰvi:mai·la-löys·t] adv. without doubt.

tvisttau, -s, - [tʰvıs·tʰöy·(s)] n. tweeds.

tvistur, -s, -ir [tʰvıs·tɣr̯, -ır, tʰvısts] m.3 tweeds; (in cards) deuce.

tvisvar [tʰvı:sva·r] adv. twice (= tvisvar sinnum).

tvítugsaldur, (-ri), -urs [tʰvi:tʰɣxs-al·dɣr̯(s), -aldrı; tʰvi:dɣxs-] m.1 age of twenty, teens; vera á tvítugs-aldri be in the (late) teens, be about twenty.

tvítugur [tʰvi:tʰɣqɣr̯; tʰvi:dɣqɣr̯] adj. (see -ugur) twenty years of age; vera milli tvítugs og þrítugs be in the twenties; tvítugt (= tví-tugsaldur) age of twenty (In. V, 3, 1; S. III, 3, 2).

Consonants: [ð] breathe; [g] good; [g₁] gyarden (garden); [hw̥] what; [j] yes; [k₁] cyan (can); [ŋ] thing; [q] N. Germ. sagen; [r] Scottish r; [x] approx. Germ. ach; [þ] thin. Voiceless: ○; [b̥, d̥, g̊] approx. v, t, k. Half-voiced: italics. Aspiration and preaspiration: [ʰ]; [pʰ, tʰ, kʰ] p-, t-, k-. Others as in English.

471

tvo, see *tveir.*

tvær, see *tveir.*

tvö, see *tveir.*

tvöfaldur, -föld, -falt [tʰvö:faldɣɾ, -föld, -falt] adj. double; false; *tvöfalt bréf* a letter requiring double postage, weighing 20-125 gr.

tyggja, tuggði, tugginn (-ið) [tʰɪg̊ˌ:a, tʰɣq·ðɪ, tʰɣg̊ˌ:ɪn, -ɪð; tʰɣg̊·ðɪ] wv.1 chew; *tyggja tóbak* chew tobacco.

tylft, -ar, -ir [tʰɪlft; tʰɪl·t, -aɾ, -ɪɾ] f.2 dozen.

týna, týndi, týndur (týnt) [tʰi:na, tʰin·dɪ, -ɣɾ, tʰin·tʰ; tʰin·t] wv.2 lose; *týna e-u* lose sth; *týnast* get lost.

tyrkneskur, -nesk, -neskt [tʰɪr·knes·kɣɾ, -nesk, -nest] adj. Turkish.

tæi (also written tagi, dat. sg. of tag) [tʰai:jɪ] only in *af því tæi (tagi)* of that kind; *af ýmsu tæi* of different kinds.

tæja, táði, táinn (-ið) [tʰai:ja, tʰau:-ðɪ, tʰau:ɪn, -ɪð] wv.1 tease, pick wool.

tækifæri, -s, - [tʰai:kˌʰɪ·fai:rɪ(s); tʰai:g̊ˌɪ-] n. occasion, opportunity; *hafa tækifæri til e-s (til að gera e-ð)* have an opportunity to sth (to do sth); *fá tækifæri til að* get an opportunity to; *við hátíðleg tækifæri* on solemn occasions.

tæpitunga, -u, -ur [tʰai:pʰɪ·tʰuŋ·g̊a, -ɣ(ɾ); tʰai:bɪ-] wf.1 baby talk.

tæpitungunöfn, -nafna [tʰai:pʰɪ·tʰuŋ·g̊ɣ-nöb·n, -nab·na; tʰai:bɪ-] n.pl. baby talk names.

tær, see *tá.*

töðu, see *taða.*

tögl, see *tagl.*

tök, see *tak.*

tölu, see 1. *tala.*

tölustafur, -s, -ir [tʰö:lɣ·sta:vɣɾ, -staf·s, -sta:vɪɾ] m.2 numerical character, figure.

tönn, tannar, tennur (tönnur) [tʰön:, tʰan:aɾ, tʰen:ɣɾ, tʰön:ɣɾ] f.3 tooth.

töp, see *tap.*

tötur, (-ri), -urs, -rar or -ur [tʰö:tʰɣɾ(s), tʰö:tʰrɪ, tʰö:tʰraɾ; tʰö:d·]

m.1 or n. tatter, rag, poor fellow; pl. *tötrar* tatters, rags, *tötur* poor fellows.

U.

úfinn, -in, -ið; úfnari, -astur [u:vɪn, -ɪn, -ɪð; ub·narɪ, -astɣɾ] adj. rough, tussled (hair).

ufsi, -a, -ar [ɣf·sɪ, -a(ɾ)] wm.1 pollock, coalfish.

ugga, uggði, uggað [ɣg̊:a, ɣq·ðɪ, ɣg̊:að; ɣg̊·ðɪ] wv.3 fear, apprehend; *ugga að sér, að . . .* fear that . . . not.

-ugur, -ug, -ugt; -ugri, -ugastur [-ɣ(·)qɣɾ, -ɣ(·)q, -ɣxt; -ɣqrɪ, -ɣ(·)-qastɣɾ] adj. suffix. (In. III, 2(b)9; 4, 4).

úldinn, -in, -ið; úldnari, -astur [ul·dɪn, -ɪn, -ɪð; ul(d)narɪ, -astɣɾ] adj. putrid.

úldna, -aði, -að(ur) [ul·(d)na, -aðɪ, -að, -aðɣɾ] wv.4 get putrid.

úlfar, -ars [ul·var(s)] m.1 pers. name.

úlfur, -s, -ar [ul·vɣɾ, ulfs, ul·vaɾ] m.1 wolf.

ull, -ar [ɣd·l, ɣd·laɾ] f.1 wool; *úr ull* of wool; woolen; *ganga úr ull(u)* shed the fleece (of sheep).

ullardúkur, -s, -ar [ɣd·lar·du:kʰɣɾ, -du:kʰs, -dux·s; -du:kʰaɾ; -du:g̊-] m.1 woolen (cloth).

ullarsokkur, -s, -ar [ɣd·lar·sɔʰk:ɣɾ, -sɔʰk·s, -sɔʰk:aɾ] m.1 woolen stockings, socks, hose.

ullartau, -s, - [ɣd·lar·tʰöy:(s)] n. woolen (stuff).

ullarvettlingur, -s, -ar [ɣd·lar·veʰt·-liŋɣɾ, -iŋs, -iŋaɾ] m.1 woolen mitten.

ullum, see *valda* and *vella.*

ultum, see 1. *velta.*

um [ɣm:] prep. with acc. around, round; over, across, through, throughout, by way of; about, circa; at, during, for (of time); per (of time); about, on, concerning, regarding, of; to the amount of; (1) around: *ganga kring um bæinn* walk around the farmstead; *um herðarnar* on the shoulders, across

---

Vowels: *a* [a] approx. *father*; *á* [au] *cow*; *e* [ɛ] *set*; *é* [jɛ] *yes*; *i, y* [ɪ] *sit*; *í, ý* [i] *feel*; *o* [ɔ] *law*; *ó* [ou] *note*; *u* [ɣ] approx. Germ. *Mütter*; *ú* [u] *school*; *y* = *i*; *ý* = *í*; *æ* [ai] *ice*; *ö* [ö] Germ. *hören*; *au* [öy] French *feuille*; *ei, ey* [ei] *ale*. Length [:]; half-length [·].

the shoulders, round the shoulders; (2) of space: over, across: *suður um Þingvallavatn* south across Þingvellir lake; *um borð* on board; *út um gluggann* through the window; *um göturnar* in the streets; *um hlið* through a gate; *um ósa* through estuaries, through the mouths (of lagoons, rivers); *um Foss* by way of Foss; *við gengum um allt skipið* we went all over the ship; *víða um land* in many places throughout the country; *um sveitirnar* through the (rural) districts; *um Norðurlönd* throughout Scandinavia; (3) about, circa: *það er um hádegisbilið* it is about noon (= *það er um það að vera hádegi*); (4) at (of time): *um morguninn eftir* next morning; *um áramót* at the turn of the year; *um leið* at the same time; *um leið og* conj. as soon as, at the same time as (S. VIII, 3(h)); *um vor* one spring, during one spring; *um nóttina* during the night, over night; *um tíma* for a time, for a while; *um nokkur ár* for several years; *um stundarsakir* for a while; *um mánuðinn* per month; (5) with verbs etc.: *tala um e-ð* speak about sth; talk about sth; *fyrirlestur um e-ð* a lecture on sth; *um innlendar fréttir* concerning domestic news; *þegja um e-ð* be silent about (concerning) sth; *sameinast um e-ð* unite in defense of sth; *skiftast í flokka um e-ð* be divided in parties on the issue of sth; *keppa um hylli lýðsins* contend for the favor of the (people) masses; *hvað er um að vera?* what is going on? (6) to the amount of: *þyngjast um pund* gain a pound in weight; *hækka um þumlung* grow one inch.

ꞏimbót, -ar, -bætur [ʏm·bouꞏtʰ, -aɾ̥, -baiꞏtʰʏɾ; -bouꞏd̥, -baiꞏd̥ʏɾ] f.3 improvement.

U. M. F. = ungmennafélag Youth League, Youth Association.

umferð, -ar, -ir [ʏm·fɛrð, -ðaɾ̥, -ðɪɾ̥] f.2 traffic; round.

umfram [ʏm·fram·] prep. with acc. over and above; *umfram allt* above all (also *um fram*) (S. I, 2, 3, 1).

umhverfis [ʏm·hwɛrvɪs; -kʰvɛrvɪs] prep. with acc. around; *umhverfis bæinn* around the houses (the farmstead) (S. I, 2, 3, 1).

ummæli [ʏm:aiꞏlɪ] n.pl. words, formula.

umráð [ʏm·rauꞏð] n.pl. disposal; *til umráða* at one's disposal.

umsát, -ar, -ir [ʏm·sauꞏtʰ, -aɾ̥, -ɪɾ̥; -sauꞏd̥] f.2 siege.

umskiftingur, -s, -ar [ʏm·sk̜ꞏɪftiŋɡ̊ʏɾ̥, -iŋs, -iŋɡaɾ̥] m.1 changeling.

umtal, -s [ʏm·tʰaꞏl, -tʰals] n. reference, discussion.

una, undi, unað [ʏ:na, ʏn·d̥ɪ, ʏ:na ð] wv.3 be content, satisfied; *una e-u = una við e-ð* be happy with sth, acquiesce in sth.

undan [ʏn·d̥an] prep. with dat. from under, before, in front of; (racing) away from; born of; *hundurinn kom undan stólnum* the dog came (emerged) from under the chair; *undan rigningunni* from the rain; (á) *undan e-u* before sth (time); *á undan e-m* before sbdy (in space or time); *gekk á undan honum* walked in front of him; *Grána er undan Rauðku gömlu* the Gray mare is out of (born of) the old Red mare.

undanrenna, -u [ʏn·d̥an·rɛn:a, -ʏ] wf.1 skim(med) milk.

undarlega [ʏn·d̥ar·lɛ:qa] adv. curiously, peculiarly, marvelously.

undið, -inn, -um, see 1. *vinda.*

undir [ʏn·d̥ɪɾ̥] prep. with acc. or dat., or adv. under, below, underneath; near, at, close to; during. A. prep. with acc. in phrases of motion (S. I, 2, 3, 2): under, below, near, close to; for: *skríða undir borðið* creep under the table; *undir hádegi* close to noon; *koma undir land* come near land (the coast); *borga undir bréf* pay for a letter. B. prep. with

---

Consonants: [ð] brea*the*; [g] *g*ood; [gɹ] *g*yarden (garden); [hw̥] *wh*at; [j] *y*es; [k̜ɹ] *cy*an (can); [ŋ] thi*ng*; [q] N. Germ. sa*g*en; [r] Scottish *r*; [x] approx. Germ. a*ch*; [þ] *th*in. Voiceless: ○; [b̥, d̥, g̊] approx. *p, t, k*. Half-voiced: *italics*. Aspiration and preaspiration: [ʰ]; [pʰ, tʰ, kʰ] *p-, t-, k-*. Others as in English.

473

dat. in phrases denoting rest (S.
I, **3**, *3*, 2) : (1) *undir borðinu*
under the table; *undir fótum sér*
below one's (his, her, etc.) feet;
undir berum himni out in the open,
outside; *undir fossi* under or behind
a waterfall; *sitja undir e-m* have
sbdy sitting on one's lap; (2) at,
near: *undir fjallsrótum* at the foot
of the mountain; *norður undir
fjalli* up north near the mountain;
(3) miscellaneous: *undir áhrifum*
under the influence; *vera undir e-u
kominn* depend upon sth; *undir
messu* during mass. **C**. adv. *undir
eins* at once, directly (= *undireins*);
undir eins og conj. as soon as (S.
VIII, 3 (h)); *neðan undir* below.
undirbúningur, -s [ʏn·dɪr·bu:niŋ̊ɣr̥,
·iŋs] m.1 preparation(s).
undirdeild, -ar, -ir [ʏn·dɪr-deil·d̥, -ar̥,
-ɪr] f.2 subdivision, sub-department.
undireins [ʏn·dɪr-ein·s] adv. (= *undir
eins*) at once.
undirforingi, -ja, -jar [ʏn·dɪr̥·fɔ:riŋ̊ɪ,
·g̊ˌa(r̥)] wm.1 subordinate officer,
petty officer, noncommissioned officer (sergeant, corporal).
undirkjóll, -s, -ar [ʏn·dɪr-kˌʰoud̥·l,
-kˌʰoul·s, -kˌʰou:lar] m.1 slip.
undirskál, -ar; -ar, -ir [ʏn·dɪr-skau:l,
-lar̥, -lɪr̥] f.1 & 2 saucer.
undirspil, -s [ʏn·dɪr-spɪ:l, -spɪl·s] n.
accompaniment.
undirsæng, -ur, -ur [ʏn·dɪr-saiŋ·g̊,
-ʏ(r̥)] f.3 a soft feather mattress,
under feather bed.
undur, (-ri), -urs, -ur [ʏn·dʏr̥(s),
ʏndrɪ] n. wonder; *það eru engin
undur, þó að* . . . it is no wonder,
if. . . .
ungdæmi, -s [uŋ·g̊dai·mɪ(s)] n. youth,
younger days; *í mínu ungdæmi* in
my younger days.
ungfrú, -ar, -frúr [uŋ·g̊fru·, -fru·ar̥,
-fru·r] f.1 Miss.
unglingur, -s, -ar [uŋ·liŋ̊ɣr̥, -liŋs,
-liŋ̊ar̥; uŋ·g̊-] m.1 youth, young
person.
ungmennafélag, -s, -lög [un·g̊men·a-

fjɛ:laɡ, -laxs, -löɡ] n. Youth league,
association of young men and women.
ungmenni, -s, - [uŋ·g̊men·ɪ(s)] n.
youth, young man or woman.
ungur, ung, ungt; yngri, yngstur
[uŋ·g̊ʏr̥, uŋ·g̊, uŋ·tʰ; uŋ̊·t; iŋ̊grɪ,
iŋstʏr̥] adj. young.
unna, ann, unnum, unni, unnað [ʏn:a,
an:, ʏn:ʏm, ʏn:ɪ, ʏn:að] pret. pres.
v. (In. VII, 5, *1*) *unna e-m* love
sbdy; *unnast* love each other; *unna
e-m e-s* not grudge sbdy sth (S. VI,
4, *3*).
unnið, -inn, -um, see 2. *vinna*.
unun, -unar [ʏ:nʏn, -ʏnar̥] f.2 delight,
pleasure; *unun er* it is a pleasure.
unz [ʏn·s] conj. until (S. VIII, 3 (h)).
upp [ʏʰp:] (1) adv. (In. IV, 1, 3)
up, upon, upstairs; ashore; over
again; from . . . onwards, etc.; *fara
upp* (*á loft*) go upstairs; *þar upp
frá* up there; *upp í sveit* out into
the country (from town); up into
the country; *upp til sveita* up in
the country (rural districts); *upp
aftur og aftur* over and over again;
upp frá því from then onwards; *þvo
upp* (*úr vatni*) wash up (in water);
upp úr súru from out of the sour
whey, pickled; *komast upp úr bekk*
be promoted at the end of a school
year, make the grade; (2) prep.
with acc. *upp fjallið* up the mountain (S. I, **2**, *3*, 3).
uppáhalds- [ʏʰp:au·hal·(d̥)s-] pref.
favorite.
uppáhaldsmatur, -ar [ʏʰp:au·hal(d̥)s-
ma:tʰʏr̥; -ar̥; -ma·dʏr̥] m.3 favorite dish.
uppboð, -s [ʏʰp:bɔ·ð, -bɔðs] n. auction.
uppbót, -ar, -bætur [ʏʰp:bou·tʰ, -ar̥,
-bai:tʰʏr̥; -bou·d̥, -bai·dʏr̥] f.3 com-
pensation.
uppbrot, -s, - [ʏʰp:brɔ·tʰ, -s; -brɔ·d̥]
n. cuff (on trousers).
uppganga, -göngu, -ur [ʏʰp:gauŋ̊a,
-göyŋ̊ɣʏ(r̥)] wf.1 stairway; ascent;
going ashore, landing place.
uppgróinn, -in, -ið [ʏʰp:grou·ɪn, -ɪn,

Vowels: *a* [a] approx. *father*; *á* [au] *cow*; *e* [ɛ] *set*; *é* [jɛ] *yes*; *i, y* [ɪ] *sit*; *í, ý* [i] *feel*;
o [ɔ] *law*; *ó* [ou] *note*; *u* [ʏ] approx. Germ. *Mütter*; *ú* [u] *school*; *y = i*; *ý = í*; *æ* [ai] *ice*;
ö [ö] Germ. *hören*; *au* [öy] French *feuille*; *ei, ey* [ei] *ale*. Length [:]; half-length [·].

-ið] adj. covered (again) with vegetation.

uppgötva, -aði, -að(ur) [ʏʰp:gö·tʰva, -aðɪ, -að, -aðʏ̣; -gö·d̯va] wv.4 discover.

upphaf, -s, -höf [ʏʰp:ha·v, -hafs, -hö·v] n. beginning; origin; upphaf á e-u beginning of sth.

upphaflega [ʏʰp:hav-lɛ:qa] adv. originally.

upphlutur, -ar, -ir [ʏʰp:hl̥ʏ·tʰʏ̣, -ar̥, -ɪr̥; -hl̥ʏ·d̯-] m.3 bodice.

upphæð, -ar, -ir [ʏʰp:hai·ð, -ðar̥, -ðɪr̥] f.2 amount; in pl. also: highest heavens.

uppi [ʏʰp:ɪ] adv. (In. IV, 1, 3) up above, upstairs; uppi í sveit in the country (opposite í kaupstað or í bænum in the town, the city); á landi uppi up in the land, ashore; uppi á fjöllum (= á fjöllum uppi) up in the mountains; vera uppi be upstairs; flourish, live.

uppiskroppa [ʏʰp:ɪ-skrɔʰp:a] adj. indecl. having nothing left; uppiskroppa með e-ð (run) out of sth.

uppköst, -kasta [ʏʰp:kʰöst, -kʰasta] n.pl. vomiting.

uppl. = upplýsing(ar).

upplestur, -urs (-rar), -rar [ʏʰp:lɛs-tʏ̣(s), -lɛstrar̥] m.1 recital, reading aloud.

upplýsing, -ar, -ar [ʏʰp:li·siŋg̊, -ar̥] f.1 information (commonly in pl.).

uppnæmur, -næm, -næmt [ʏʰp:nai·-mʏ̣, -nai·m, -naimtʰ; -naimt̯] adj. taken aback, helpless; vera ekki uppnæmur fyrir e-u not to be helpless in face of sth.

uppskurður, -ar, -ir [ʏʰp:skʏrðʏ̣, -ar̥, -ɪr̥] m.3 (surgical) operation.

uppspretta, -u, -ur [ʏʰp:sprɛʰt·a, -ʏ(r̥)] wf.1 spring, well.

uppstigningardagur, -s, -ar [ʏʰp:stɪg̊-niŋg̊ar-da:qʏ̣, -dax·s, -da:qar̥] m.1 Ascension Day.

upptekinn, -in, -ið [ʏʰp:tʰɛ·k̥ʰ ɪn, -ɪn, -ɪð; -tʰɛ·g̊ˌɪn] adj. occupied.

uppvakningur, -s, -ar [ʏʰp:vaʰkniŋg̊ʏ̣,

-ɪŋs, -iŋg̊ar̥] m.1 a ghost that has been raised.

1. úr, -s, - [u:r, ur̥·s] n. watch.

2. úr [u:r] prep. with dat. out of, from; from the cause of; (out) of (a material), etc.; (1) úr dyrunum from the doorway; neðan úr out from below, up; kroppa augu úr lambi pick the eyes out of the lamb; (2) from: sálast úr forvitni die (be dying) from curiosity; (3) of: úr hverju? of what material? vera úr e-u be made of sth; úr ull of wool, woolen; úr timbri of wood, of timber; byggðir úr torfi og grjóti built of turf (sod) and stones; (4) úr því að conj. since (S. VIII, 3(b)).

urðum, see verða.

úrkoma, -u, -ur [ur̥·kʰɔ·ma, -ʏ(r̥)] wf.1 precipitation, rain or snowfall; pl. rainy spells, rains; úrkomu-laus without rainfall.

urpum, see 1. verpa.

urriði, -a, -ar [ʏr̥:ɪ·ðɪ, -a, -ar̥] wm.1 trout, sea trout, lake trout.

úrsmiður, -s, -ir [ur̥·smɪ·ðʏ̣, -smɪðs, -smɪ·ðɪr̥] m.2 watchmaker.

úrval, -s [ur̥·va·l̥, -vals] n. selection.

úrvalsbók, -ar, -bækur [ur·vals·bou:kʰ, -ar̥, -bai:kʰʏ̣; -bou:g̊, -bai:g̊ʏ̣] f.3 select book.

úrvalshersveit, -ar, -ir [ur·vals·hɛr̥·-svei·tʰ, -ar̥, -ɪr̥; -svei·d̯] f.2 select troops, task troops.

út [u:tʰ, u:d̯] adv. (In.IV,1,3) out; (1) fara út go out; (2) with preps and advs: mjólk út á with milk (on it); út af e-u on account of sth; út af fyrir sig by oneself, apart; út fyrir out crossing the limits of sth, out beyond; út í out into; út í vatnið in(to) the water; út um land out into the country; út um tún out in the homefield; út úr e-u out of sth; (3) prep. with acc.: út dalinn down the valley (S. I, 2, 3, 3); út nóttina throughout the night.

utan [ʏ:tʰan, ʏ:d̯an] (1) adv. (In.

Consonants: [ð] breathe; [g] good; [g̊ɪ] gyarden (garden); [hw̥] what; [j] yes; [k̥ɪ] cyan (can); [ŋ] thing; [q] N. Germ. sagen; [r] Scottish r; [x] approx. Germ. ach; [þ] thin. Voiceless: ○; [b̥, d̥, g̊] approx. p, t, k. Half-voiced: italics. Aspiration and preaspiration: [ʰ]; [pʰ, tʰ, kʰ] p-, t-, k-. Others as in English.

475

IV, **1**, 3; S. I, **2**, *3*, 3) from the
outside (= *að utan*) ; abroad ; *fara
utan* go abroad, *vera utan* be
abroad ; *utan á* on the outside
of ; *utan af landi* from the
country ; *utan í hól* on the slope of
a hill(ock) ; *utan við* outside of ;
utan við sig absentminded, distracted ; (2) prep. with acc.: *utan
dalinn* up the valley ; *fyrir utan
e-ð* outside of sth ; (3) prep. with
gen.: outside of : *utan túns* outside
the homefield ; (4) conj. *utan einu
sinni* except once.

utanáskrift, -ar, -ir [ʏ:tʰan·au·skrif·t,
-aṛ, -ɪṛ; ʏ:dan-] f.2 address (on a
letter).

utanlands [ʏ:tʰan-lan·(d̥)s; ʏ:dan-]
adv. abroad.

utanlandssigling, -ar, -ar [ʏ:tʰan-
lan(d̥s)-sɪg̊·liŋg̊, -aṛ; ʏ:dan-] f.1
journey abroad.

utanríkismál [ʏ:tʰanri·kʲʰɪs-mau:l;
ʏ:danri·g̊ʲɪs-] n.pl. foreign affairs.

utanríkisráðherra, -a, -ar [ʏ:tʰanri·
kʲʰɪs-rau:ðher·a(ṛ); ʏ:danri·g̊ʲɪs-]
wm.1 foreign minister.

utanríkisráðuneyti,-s,- [ʏ:tʰanri·kʰʲɪs-
rau:ðʏnei·tʰɪ(s) ; ʏ:danri·g̊ʲɪs-rau:-
ðʏnei·dɪ] n. foreign office; ministry
of foreign affairs, department of
state (U. S. A.).

**útbúa, -bý, -bjó, -bjuggum, -búinn
(-ið)** [u:tʰbu·a, -bi·, -bjou·, -bjʏg̊·ʏm,
-bu·ɪn, -ɪð; u:d̥-] v.7 prepare, fit out.

útbúnaður, -aðar [u:tʰbu·naðʏṛ, -aðaṛ;
u:d̥-] m.3 outfit.

útengi, -s [u:tʰeiŋg̊ʲɪ(s); u:d̥-] n.
(coll.) outlying meadows.

útengjasláttur, -ar [u:tʰeiŋg̊ʲa-slauʰt:-
ʏṛ, -aṛ; u:d̥-] m.3 haymaking in
the (outlying) meadows.

útgáfa, -u, -ur [u:tʰgau·va, -ʏ(ṛ);
u:d̥-] wf.1 publishing; edition.

útganga, -göngu, -ur [u:tʰgauŋg̊a,
-göyŋg̊ʏ(ṛ); u:d̥-] wf.1 going out,
exit.

útgerð, -ar, -ir [u:tʰgʲɛrð, -ðaṛ, -ðɪṛ;
u:d̥-] f.2 outfitting of fishing boats,
motorboat business; trawler business.

útgerðarmaður, -manns, -menn [u:tʰ-
gʲɛrðar-ma:ðʏṛ, -man·s, -mɛn:;
u:d̥-] m.4 shipowner, motorboat
owner, trawler owner.

útgjöld, -gjalda [u:tʰg̊ʲöld, -g̊ʲalda;
u:d̥-] n.pl. expenditure, expenses.

útgöngusálmur, -s, -ar [u:tʰgöyŋg̊ʏ-
saul·mʏṛ, -saulms, -saul·maṛ; u:d̥-]
m.1 recessional hymn.

úthagi, -a, -ar [u:thai·jɪ, -ha·qa(ṛ);
u:d̥-, -ha·jɪ] wm.1 outlying pasture.

úti [u:tʰɪ; u:d̥ɪ] adv. (In. IV, 1, 3)
out, outside, in an outhouse, out
of doors; over, up, finished; *úti og
inni* outdoors and indoors; *úti í
garðinum* in the garden; *úti um
land* in the country (opposite: in
town: *í bænum*); *vera úti við* be
out (not in the house); *öll von var
úti* all hope was over.

útibú, -s, - [u:tʰɪ-bu:(s); u:d̥ɪ-] n.
branch farm; branch office, branch
store or chain store.

útibúsverzlun, -unar, -anir [u:tʰɪbu·s-
vɛrslʏn, -ʏnaṛ, -anɪṛ; u:d̥ɪ-] f.2
chain store.

útidyr [u:tʰɪ-dɪ:r; u:d̥ɪ-] f.3.pl. front
door.

útiföt, -fata [u:tʰɪ-fö:tʰ, -fa:tʰa;
u:d̥ɪ-fö:d̥, -fa:d̥a] n.pl. (tailored)
suit; street clothes.

útihús, -s, - [u:tʰɪ-hu:s, -hus:; u:d̥ɪ-]
n. outhouse, a house (shed, barn)
far from the central group on the
farm.

útilaug, -ar, -ar [u:tʰɪ-löy:q, -qaṛ;
u:d̥ɪ-] f.1 outdoor swimming pool.

útilegumaður, -manns, -menn [u:tʰɪlɛ-
qʏ-ma:ðʏṛ; -man·s, -mɛn:; u:d̥ɪ-]
m.4 outlaw, usually thought to inhabit the desert interior of the
country.

útilegumannatrú, -ar [u:tʰɪlɛ·qʏman·a-
tʰru:, -aṛ; u:d̥ɪ-] f.1 belief in outlaws.

útiloka, -aði, -að(ur) [u:tʰɪ-lɔ:kʰa,
-aðɪ, -að, -aðʏṛ; u:d̥ɪ-lɔ:g̊a] wv.4
exclude.

Vowels: *a* [a] approx. *father*; *á* [au] *cow*; *e* [ɛ] *set*; *é* [jɛ] *yes*; *i, y* [ɪ] *sit*; *í, ý* [i] *feel*;
o [ɔ] *law*; *ó* [ou] *note*; *u* [ʏ] approx. Germ. *Mütter*; *ú* [u] *school*; *y* = *i*; *ý* = *í*; *æ* [ai] *ice*;
ö [ö] Germ. *hören*; *au* [öy] French *feuille*; *ei, ey* [ei] *ale*. Length [:]; half-length [·].

útjaðar, -ars, -rar [u:tʰja·ðar̥(s),
-jaðrar̥; u:d̥-] m.1 border, suburb.

útkoma, -u, -ur [u:tʰkʰɔ·ma, -ɣ(r̥);
u:d̥-] wf.1 outcome; answer, total
(in calculations), result, quotient.

útlagi, -a, -ar [u:tʰlai·jɪ, -la·qa(r̥);
u:d̥-; -la·jɪ] wm.1 outlaw.

útlendingur, -s, -ar [u:tʰlendiŋɣr̥,
-ins, -iŋgar̥] m.1 foreigner.

útlendur, -lend, -lent [u:tʰlendɣr̥,
-lend, -lentʰ; u:d̥-; -lent̥] adj.
foreign.

útlit, -s [u:tʰlɪ·tʰ(s); u:dlɪ·d̥] n. appearance, look, prospect; *i útliti* in
appearance; *það er útlit fyrir e-ð
(fyrir að e-ð gerist)* it looks as if
(sth is going to happen).

útlönd, -landa [u:tʰlönd, -landa; u:d̥-]
n.pl. foreign countries; *vera í
útlöndum* be abroad; *fara til útlanda*
go abroad.

1. útnorður, (-ri), -urs [u:tʰnɔrðɣr̥(s),
-nɔrðrɪ; u:d̥-] n. northwest.

2. útnorður [u:tʰnɔrðɣr̥; u:d̥-] adv.
northwest.

útrýma, -rýmdi, -rýmt [u:tʰri·ma,
-rimdɪ, -rimtʰ; -rimt̥; u:d̥-] wv.2
útrýma e-u extinguish sth.

útsauma, -aði, -að(ur) [u:tʰsöy·ma,
-aðɪ, -að, -aðɣr̥; u:d̥-] wv.4 em-
broider; *útsaumaður* embroidered.

útskrifa, -aði, -að(ur) [u:tʰskrɪ·va,
-aðɪ, -að, -aðɣr̥; u:d̥-] wv.4 give
degrees; *útskrifaður* graduated.

útsýni, -s, - [u:tʰsi·nɪ(s); u:d̥-] n.
view, visibility.

útundan [u:tʰɣndan; u:d̥-] adv. *hafa
e-n útundan* discriminate against
sbdy; treat sbdy worse than others.

útvarp, -s [u:tʰvarp(s); u:d̥-] n.
broadcasting, broadcast, radio;
syngja (tala) í útvarpið sing
(speak) over the radio; *Útvarpið
= Ríkisútvarpið* 'The Iceland
Broadcasting Service.'

útvarpa, -aði, -að [u:tʰvarpa, -aðɪ,
-að; u:d̥-] wv.4 broadcast; *útvarpa
e-u* broadcast sth.

útvarpstæki, -tækja [u:tʰvarps-tʰai:-

k̥ɪhɪ, -tʰai:k̥ɪha; u:d̥-; -tʰai:g̥ɪ,I, -a]
n.pl. radio, radio receiving set.

útvega, -aði, -að [u:tʰvɛ·qa, -aðɪ, -að;
u:d̥-] wv.4 *útvega e-m e-ð* get, procure sth for sbdy; *útvega sér* get
(for oneself), procure.

tvegsbanki Íslands [u:tʰvɛxs-bauŋ·k̥ɪhɪ,
i:slan(d)s; u:dvɛxs-bauŋ·k̥ɪI] wm.1
'The Fishing Trade Bank of Iceland.'

útvegur, -ar, -vegs [u:tʰvɛ·qɣr̥, -ar̥,
-vɛxs; u:d̥-] m.2 = *sjávarútvegur*,
fisheries, fishing.

uxum, see *vaxa*.

V.

vað, -s, vöð [va:ð, vað·s, vö:ð] n.
ford (on a river).

vaða, veð, óð, óðum, vaðinn (-ið)
[va:ða, vɛ:ð, ou:ð, ou:ðɣm, va:ðɪn,
-ið] v.6 wade; *vaða ána* wade the
river; *vaða í fætur* wet one's feet.

vaðmál, -s, - [vað·mau·l, -mauls] n.
homespun, wadmal.

vafði, vafið, -inn, see *vefja*.

vafi, -a [va:vɪ, -a] wm.1 doubt; *það
er enginn vafi á því* there is no
doubt about it.

vagga, vöggu, -ur [vag̥:a, vög̥:ɣ(r̥)]
wf.1 cradle.

Vaglar [vag̥·lar̥] f.1.pl. place name.

vagn, -s, -ar [vag̥·n̥, vag̥n̥s, vag̥·nar̥]
m.1 wagon.

vaka, vakti, vakað [va:kʰa, vax·tɪ,
va:kʰað; va:g̥a(ð)] wv.3 be awake;
watch; *láta í veðri vaka* intimate,
hint, make believe (S. VI, **4**, *3*).

vakar, -ir, see *vök*.

vakið, -inn, vakti, see *vekja*.

vakna, -aði, -að(ur) [vahk·na, -aðɪ,
-að, -aðɣr̥] wv.4 awake (S. VI,
5, *2*; **6**, *2*).

valar, see *völur*.

vald, -s, völd [val·d̥, valds, völ·d̥] n.
power.

valda, veld, olli, ullum, valdið [val·da,
vɛl·d̥, ɔd·lɪ, ɣd·lɪm, val·dɪð] v.7
valda e-u cause sth (In. VII, **2**, *8n4*).

1. **Valdi, -a, -ar** [val·dɪ, -a(r̥)] wm.1
pet name for Þorvaldur, Valdimar.
2. **valdi, valið, -inn,** see velja.
Valdimar, -s [val·dɪ-ma·r, -mar̥·s] m.1
pers. name.
Valgerður, -ar [val·g₍e̥rðʏr̥, -ar̥] f.1
pers. name.
vall, see vella.
valla, = varla.
vallar, see völlur.
vals, -, -ar [val·s, val·sar̥] m.1 waltz.
valt, see 1. velta.
Valtýr, -týs [val·tʰi·r, -tʰi·s] m.1 pers.
name.
valur, -s, -ir [va:lʏr̥, val·s, va:lɪr̥]
m.2 = fálki, falcon.
van- [va:n-, van·-] pref. negative:
in-, incomplete.
vanalegur [va:na-lɛ:qʏr̥] adj. (see
-legur) usual, common, ordinary.
vandaður, vönduð, vandað [van·daðʏr̥,
vön·dʏð, van·dað] adj. well done,
substantial, elaborate; hið vandaðasta most elaborate.
vandamaður, -manns, -menn [van·da-
ma:ðʏr̥, -man·s, -mɛn:] m.4 relative, guardian (even if not related).
1. **vandi, -a** [van·dɪ, -a] wm.1 custom,
habit; difficulty; eiga vanda fyrir
e-u get something (a sickness)
habitually, be prone to sth.
2. **vandi, vaninn,** see 2. venja.
vandlega [van·dlɛ·qa] adv. carefully.
vandrataður, -rötuð, -ratað [van·dra·-
tʰaðʏr̥, -rö·tʰʏð, -ra·tʰað; -ra·d·,
-rö·d·] adj. difficult to find or follow
(of roads).
vangá, -gár [vaŋ·gau·(r)] f.1 inadvertence.
vanheilsa, -u [va:nheilsa, -ʏ] wf.1
bad health, poor health.
vani, -a [va:nɪ, -a] wm.1 habit.
vann, see 2. vinna.
vanta, -aði, -að [van·tʰa, -aðɪ, -að;
van·ta] wv.4 impersonal with double
acc.: mig vantar skó I lack (need)
shoes (S. I, 2, 1, 3; VII, 3, 1).
vanur, vön, vant [va:nʏr̥, vö:n, van·tʰ;
van·t] adj. used to, experienced;
vanur e-u = vanur við e-ð used to

sth, familiar with sth; vera vanur
að use to, be used to.
1. **var, vör, vart** [va:r, vö:r, var̥·t]
adj. aware; cautious; verða e-s var
become aware of sth = verða var
við e-ð; gera vart við sig make
one's coming known to the inhabitants of the house (farm).
2. **var,** see vera.
1. **vara, vöru, -ur** [va:ra, vö:rʏ(r̥)]
wf.1 ware, goods, merchandise.
2. **vara, -aði, -að(ur)** [va:ra, -aðɪ,
-að, -aðʏr̥] wv.4 warn; vara e-n við
e-u warn sbdy of sth; vara e-n við
að gera e-ð warn sbdy not to do
sth; vara sig beware; varaðu þig!
beware! vara sig á e-u (á að gera
e-ð) beware of sth (of doing sth);
varast e-ð avoid sth.
3. **vara, varði, varað** [va:ra, var·ðɪ,
va:rað] wv.3 suspect; verður það
oft, þá varir minnst (proverbial)
it often happens when you least
suspect it.
varalitur, -ar, -ir [va:ra-lɪ:tʰʏr̥, -ar̥,
-ɪr̥; -lɪ:dʏr̥] m.3 lipstick.
varar, see 1. vör.
varð, see verða.
varða, vörðu, -ur [var·ða, vör·ðʏ(r̥)]
wf.1 cairn.
varðar, see vörður.
varði, varið, -inn, see 2. verja.
varðveita, -veitti, -veittur [var·ðvei·-
tʰa, -veiʰt·ɪ, -ʏr̥, -veiʰt·] wv.2 preserve, keep, conserve.
vargefinn, -in, -ið [var·g₍e·vɪn, -ɪn,
-ɪð] adj. (pp.) ill matched (in
marriage).
varla (valla); síður, sízt [vad·la,
vardla, si:ðʏr̥, sis·t] adv. hardly,
less, least.
varmur, vörm, varmt [var·mʏr̥, vör·m,
varmtʰ; varm̥t] adj. warm; little
used except in the idiom; að vörmu
spori 'the step still being warm,'
i. e. at once.
varna, -aði, -að [vardna, -aðɪ, -að]
wv.4 varna e-m e-s deny, refuse sbdy
sth; keep sbdy from doing (getting)
sth.

Vowels: a [a] approx. father; á [au] cow; e [ɛ] set; é [jɛ] yes; i, y [ɪ] sit; í, ý [i] feel;
o [ɔ] law; ó [ou] note; u [ʏ] approx. Germ. Mütter; ú [u] school; y = i; ý = í; æ [ai] ice;
ö [ö] Germ. hören; au [öy] French feuille; ei, ey [ei] ale. Length [:]; half-length [·].

varnar, -ir, see *vörn.*
varnarlína, -u, -ur [varḍnar-li:na, -ʏ(r̥)] wf.1 line of defense.
varp, see 1. *verpa.*
varpa, -aði, -að [var̥·pa, -aðɪ, -að] wv.4 throw; *varpa e-u* throw sth; *varpa sprengjum* throw bombs.
vart, see 1. *var.*
varúð, -ar [va:ru·ð, -ðar̥] f.2 caution.
vasaklútur, -s, -ar [va:sa-kʰlu:tʰʏr̥, -kʰlu:tʰs, -kʰlu:tʰar̥; -kʰlu:ḍ-] m.1 handkerchief.
vasaúr, -s, - [va:sa-u:r, -ur̥·s] n. pocket watch.
vasi, -a, -ar [va:sɪ, -a(r̥)] wm.1 pocket; vase.
1. vaskur, -s, -ar [vas·kʏr̥, vasks, vas·kar̥] m.1 sink.
2. vaskur, vösk, vaskt [vas·kʏr̥, vös·k, vas·(k)t] adj. brave, valiant.
vatn, -s, vötn [vaʰt·n̥, vas:, vöʰt·n̥] n. water; lake; river, pl. especially large rivers; *glas af vatni* glass of water (S. II, 3).
vatnahestur, -s, -ar [vaʰt·na-hes·tʏr̥, -hes:, -hes·tar̥] m.1 'river horse,' a horse adept at wading over the big and treacherous glacier rivers.
Vatnajökull, -uls [vaʰt·na-jö:kʰʏdl, -ʏls; -jö:ǵʏdl] m.1 'River Glacier.'
vatnsglas, -s, -glös [vas:-gla·s, -glas·, -glö·s] n. tumbler, glass; glass of water.
vatnskanna, -könnu, -ur [vas:-kʰan·a, -kʰön·ʏ(r̥)] wf.1 water pitcher, jug.
vatnsleiðsla, -u, -ur [vas:-leiðsla, -ʏ(r̥)] wf.1 water pipes; running water in the house.
vatnsrás, -ar, -ir [vas:-rau·s, -ar̥, -ɪr̥] f.2 watercourse; water conduit.
vatnssalerni, -s, - [vas:(s)a·lerḍnɪ(s)] n. W. C.
vatt, see 1. *vinda.*
vaxa, vex, óx, uxum, vaxinn (-ið) [vax·sa, vex·s, oux·s, ʏx·sʏm, vax·-sɪn, -ɪð] v.7 grow, increase; *vaxa í þá átt* grow in that direction; pp. *vaxinn* grown; *lyngi vaxinn* covered with leather; *grasi vaxinn* grown covered) with grass (S. I, 3, *1*, 2(e)).

vaxtar, see *vöxtur.*
1. veð, -s, - [vɛ:ð, veð·s] n. mortgage.
2. veð, see *vaða.*
veðréttur, -ar, -ir [veð·rjeʰt·ʏr̥, -ar̥, -ɪr̥] m.3 mortgage; *fyrsti veðréttur* first mortgage.
veður, (-ri), -urs, -ur [ve:ðʏr̥(s), veð·rɪ] n. weather, the weather; wind; *láta í veðri vaka* intimate, hint, make believe.
veðurbarinn, -in, -ið [ve:ðʏr-ba:rɪn, -ɪn, -ɪð] adj. weatherbeaten, weathered.
veðurdagur [ve:ðʏr-da:qʏr̥] m.1 only in: *einn góðan veðurdag* one fine day.
veðurfregn, -ar, -ir [ve:ðʏr-frɛǵ·n, -nar̥, -nɪr̥] f.2 weather forecast, weather news.
veðurútlit, -s [ve:ðʏr-u:tʰlɪ·tʰ(s); -u:dlɪ·ḍ] n. weather forecast, prospect.
vefa, vef, óf, ófum, ofinn (-ið) [ve:va, vɛ:v, ou:v, ou:vʏm, ɔ:vɪn, -ɪð] v.6 weave.
vefja, vafði, vafinn (-ið) [vɛv·ja, vav·ðɪ, va:vɪn, -ɪð; vab·ðɪ] wv.1 wrap up; *vefja e-ð (innan) í e-u* wrap sth up in sth.
vefnaðarvörudeild, -ar, -ir [vɛb·-naðar-vö·rʏ-deil·ḍ, -ar̥, -ɪr̥] f.2 dry goods (textile) department.
vefnaðarvöruverzlun,-unar,-anir [vɛb·-naðarvö·rʏ-verslʏn, -ʏnar̥, -anɪr̥] f.2 dry goods store, dry goods business.
vega, veg, vó ((v)óg), vógum (ógum), veginn (-ið) [ve:qa, vɛ:q, vou:(q), vou:(q)ʏm, ou:(q)ʏm, vei:jɪn, -ɪð] v.6 weigh; kill.
vegalengd, -ar, -ir [vɛ:qa-leiŋ·ḍ, -ar̥, -ɪr̥] f.2 distance.
vegfarandi, -a, -endur [vɛx·fa·randɪ, -a, -ɛndʏr̥] wm.2 wayfarer, traveler.
veggfóður, (-ri), -urs [vɛǵ:fou·ðʏr̥(s), -fouðrɪ] n. wallpaper.
veggur, veggjar (veggs), veggir, (-ja) [vɛǵ:ʏr̥, vɛǵ̠ː ar̥, vɛǵ·s, vɛǵ̠ː ɪr̥, vɛǵ̠ː a] m.2 wall.
vegleysa, -u, -ur [vɛq·lei·sa, -ʏ(r̥)]

Consonants: [ð] brea*th*e; [g] *g*ood; [gɪ] *gy*arden (garden); [hw] *wh*at; [j] *y*es; [kɪ] *cy*an (can); [ŋ] thi*ng*; [q] N. Germ. sa*g*en; [r] Scottish *r*; [x] approx. Germ. a*ch*; [þ] *th*in. Voiceless: ○; [b̥, ḍ, g̥] approx. *p, t, k.* Half-voiced: *italics.* Aspiration and preaspiration: [ʰ]; [pʰ, tʰ, kʰ] *p-, t-, k-.* Others as in English.

479

wf.1 bad way, bad road; no road
at all.

vegna [veg̊·na] prep. with gen. (gen.
pl. of *vegur*) because of, on account
of; *þeirra vegna* on account of them
(also: *vegna þeirra*) *hvers vegna*
(= *hversvegna*)? wherefore, why?
þess vegna (= *þessvegna*) therefore;
vegna þess að conj. because (S.
VIII, 3(b)).

vegur, -ar (-s), -ir [ve:qɣr̥, -ar̥
(vex·s), vei:jir̥] m.3 (or 2) way,
road; way, mode, manner; in street-
names -*vegur*; *vera kominn nokkuð
á veg* have covered part of the way
(work); *fara sinn veg* go one's
way; *koma í veg fyrir e-ð* prevent
sth; *annars vegar . . . hins vegar*
on the one hand . . . on the other
hand; *beggja vegna* on both sides
(S. I, 4, 5); *einhvern veginn* some
way, somehow; *á marga vegu* in
many ways.

veiða, veiddi, veiddur (veitt) [vei:ða,
veid:ɪ, -ɣr̥, veiʰt:] wv.2 hunt, fish.

veiðarfæri [vei:ðar̥·fai:rɪ] n.pl. fishing tackle, hunting outfit.

veiði, -ar, -ar [vei:ðɪ, vei:ðar̥] f.1
hunting, fishing.

veiðiá, -ár, -ár [vei:ðɪ-au:(r)] f.1
fishing river.

veiðifugl, -s, -ar [vei:ðɪ-fɣg̊·l, -fɣqls,
-fɣg̊·lar̥] m.1 bird subject to
hunting.

veiðileyfi, -s, - [vei:ðɪ-lei:vɪ(s)] n.
hunting, fishing license.

veiðiskip, -s, - [vei:ðɪ-skjɪ:pʰ, -skjɪf·s;
-skjɪ:b] n. fishing vessel.

veiðiskipafloti, -a, -ar [vei:ðɪskjɪ·pʰa-
flɔ:tʰɪ, -a(r̥); -skjɪ·ba-flɔ:dɪ] wm.1
fishing fleet.

veiðivatn, -s, -vötn [vei:ðɪ·vaʰt·n̥,
-vas:, -vöʰt·n̥] n. lake good for
fishing.

veik, see *víkja* and *veikur*.

veiki [vei:kjʰɪ, vei:g̊jɪ] wf.2 sickness.

veikindi [vei:kjʰɪndɪ; vei:g̊jɪndɪ] n.pl.
sickness.

veikja, veikti, veikt(ur) [vei:kjʰa,
veix·tɪ, -ɣr̥, veix·t; vei:g̊jа] wv.2

weaken, enfeeble; *veikjast(af)* get
sick, be taken ill (with).

veikur, veik, veikt [vei:kʰɣr̥, vei:kʰ,
veix·t; vei:g̊(ɣr̥)] adj. weak; sick,
ill.

veit, see *vita*.

1. veita, veitti, veitt(ur) [vei:tʰa,
veiʰt:ɪ, -ɣr̥, veiʰt:; vei:da] wv.2
grant, give, afford, bestow; *veita
e-m e-ð* grant sbdy sth; *ekki veitir
af því* one has use for it, it cannot
be left unused, there is nothing to
spare; *mér veitir ekki af því* I cannot do with less than that.

2. veita, veitti, veitt [vei:tʰa, veiʰt:ɪ,
veiʰt:; vei:da] wv.2 irrigate; *veita
vatni á, veita á* irrigate (with
water), *veita vatni* convey water.

veizla, -u, -ur [veis·la, -ɣ(r̥)] wf.1
feast, celebration, banquet.

vekja, vakti, vakinn (-ið) [ve:kjʰa,
vax·tɪ, va:kjʰɪn, -ið; ve:g̊ja, va:-
g̊jɪn] wv.1 awaken, rouse, arouse;
vekja e-n awake sbdy; *vekja upp
draug* raise a ghost, conjure up a
ghost.

vekjaraklukka, -u, -ur [ve:kjʰara-
kʰlɣʰk:a, -ɣ(r̥); ve:g̊jara-] wf.1
alarm clock.

vel, betur, bezt [ve:l, be:tʰɣr̥, bes·t;
be:dɣr̥] adv. (In. IV, 2(d)) well,
quite; *það fór vel* that went as it
should; *ekki vel ánægður* not quite
satisfied; *ef vel á að vera* if things
go as they should; *hafa betur* get
the upper hand, win.

vél, -ar, -ar [vje:l, -lar̥] f.1 engine,
machine, motor; pl. machinery;
artifice, deceit.

vélahersveit, -ar, -ir [vje:la-her̥·svei·tʰ,
-ar̥, -ɪr̥; -svei·d] f.2 mechanized
troops.

vélbúinn, -in, -ið [vjel·bu·ɪn, -ɪn, -ɪð]
adj. armored; *vélbúið lið* armored
troops, mechanized troops.

vélbyssa, -u, -ur [vjel·bɪs·a, -ɣ(r̥)]
wf.1 machine gun.

vélbyssuhreiður, (-ri), -urs, -ur [vjel·-
bɪs·ɣ-hrei:ðɣr̥(s), -hreið·rɪ] n. machine gun nest.

Vowels: *a* [a] approx. *father*; *á* [au] *cow*; *e* [ɛ] *set*; *é* [jɛ] *yes*; *i, y* [ɪ] *sit*; *í, ý* [i] *feel*;
o [ɔ] *law*; *ó* [ou] *note*; *u* [ɣ] approx. Germ. M*ü*tter; *ú* [u] *school*; *y* = *i*; *ý* = *í*; *œ* [ai] *ice*;
ö [ö] Germ. h*ö*ren; *au* [öy] French *feuille*; *ei, ey* [ei] *ale*. Length [:]; half-length [·].

vélbyssulið, -s [vjɛl·bɪs·ʏ·lɪː·ð, -lɪð·s]
n. machine gun troops.

veld, see *valda.*

velferð, -ar [vɛl·fɛrð, -ðar̥] f.2 welfare.

1. **velgja, -u** [vɛl·g̊ja, -g̊jʏ] wf.1
nausea; *fá velgju* get nauseated;
hafa velgju be, feel nauseated.

2. **velgja, velgdi, velgður (velgt)** [vɛl-
g̊ja, vɛl·(q)di, -ʏr̥, vɛl(x)t] wv.2
mig velgir við e-u I am nauseated
at sth; *velgja vatn* warm water.

velir, see *völur.*

velja, valdi, valinn (-ið) [vɛl·ja, val·dɪ,
va:lɪn, -ɪð] wv.1 select, choose, pick
out; select the number on the phone
dial, dial; elect, *velja þingmann*
elect a member of parliament.

velkja, velkti, velkt(ur) [vɛl·kjʰa,
vɛl·(x)t, -ɪ, -ʏr̥; vɛl·kja] wv.2 soil,
maltreat.

velkominn, -in, -ið [vɛl·kʰɔ·mɪn, -ɪn,
-ɪð] adj. welcome; *það er velkomið*
'it is welcome,' you are welcome to
it, with pleasure!

vella, vell, vall, ullum, ollið [vɛd̥·la,
vɛd̥·l, vad̥·l, ʏd·lʏm, ɔd·lɪð] v.3 cook,
boil, well up; *spóinn vellur* the
curlew sings.

vellir, see *völlur.*

vellingur, -s, -ar [vɛd̥·liŋ̊ʏr̥, -iŋs,
-iŋgar̥] m.1 porridge, cooked cereal.

vélstjóraskóli, -a, -ar [vjɛl·stjou·ra-
skou:lɪ, -a(r̥)] wm.1 school for
marine engineers.

vélstjóri, -a, -ar [vjɛl·stjou·rɪ, -a(r̥)]
wm.1 machinist; marine engineer.

1. **velta, velt, valt, ultum, oltinn (-ið)**
[vɛl·ta, vɛl·t, val·t, ʏl·tʏm, ɔl·tɪn,
-ɪð] v.3 roll (intr.), tumble, fall.

2. **velta, velti, velt** [vɛl·ta, vɛl·t, -ɪ]
wv.2 roll (trans.) *velta e-u* roll
sth; *velta tunnu* roll a barrel.

1. **venja, -u, -ur** [vɛn·ja, -ʏ(r̥)] wf.1
habit, custom; *eins og venja er til*
as (it) is customary; *það er venja,
venjan er* the custom is, it is usual.

2. **venja, vandi, vaninn (-ið)** [vɛn·ja,
van·dɪ, va:nɪn, -ɪð] wv.1 train, accustom to; *venja e-n á e-ð* train

sbdy to do sth, accustom sbdy (to
do) sth.

venjulega [vɛn·jʏ·lɛ:qa] adv. usually,
customarily.

venjulegur [vɛn·jʏ·lɛ:qʏr̥] adj. (see
-legur) usual, customary, common.

venzlaður, -uð, -að [vɛnslaðʏr̥, -ʏð,
-að] adj. related by marriage; *venzlaður e-m* related to sbdy by
marriage.

vér honorific pl. of *ég.*

**vera; er, ert; var; vorum, vórum;
verið** [vɛ:ra, ɛ:r, ɛr̥·t, va:r, vɔ:rʏm,
vou:rʏm, vɛ:rɪð] v.irreg. (In. VII,
2, 6; 5, 3) to be, exist, constitute,
consist of; equal; stay, remain;
(auxiliary) be, have; (1) *vera
góður* be good; *vertu sæll* goodbye;
vera e-r trúar be of some denomina-
tion, belong to some religion; *vera
til altaris* receive communion; *vera
í félagi* be member of a society;
vera þáttur í constitute a part of;
sem aldrei skyldi verið hafa which
never should have been allowed to
happen; *skeytið er fimmtán orð* the
telegram is (= consists of) fifteen
words; *tveir og tveir eru fjórir
2 + 2 = 4; hvað var það fyrir
yður?* what did (do) you want?
what can I do for you? *var það
nokkuð fleira?* anything more? *það
væri gaman* that would be fun (S.
VI, 9, 2, 2); *á sunnudaginn var*
last Sunday; (2) stay: *ég var þar
ár(ið)* I stayed there a year, I remained there a year; *biðja um að
lofa sér að vera* ask for night's
lodgings (ask to be allowed to stay
overnight); *veri þeir, sem vera
vilja* let those, who want to, stay;
(3) impersonal uses: *þér er bezt
að* (with inf.) it is best for you
to . . . , you had better . . . ; *það
er bezt fyrir e-n* it is best for sbdy,
one had better; *það eru engin undur*
it is no wonder (S. V, 4, 3); *þér
væri nær að hætta* you had better
stop; *mér er heitt, kalt, illt* I am
warm, cold, ill (S. VI, *14, 5*); *vera*

Consonants: [ð] brea*th*e; [g] *g*ood; [gj] *gy*arden (garden); [hw] *wh*at; [j] *y*es; [kj] *cy*an
(can); [ŋ] thi*ng*; [q] N. Germ. sa*g*en; [r] Scottish *r*; [x] approx. Germ. a*ch*; [þ] *th*in.
Voiceless: ○; [b̥, d̥, g̊] approx. *p, t, k.* Half-voiced: *italics.* Aspiration and preaspiration:
[ʰ]; [pʰ, tʰ, kʰ] *p-, t-, k-.* Others as in English.

481

vel be fine, be all right; *ef vel á að vera* if things go as they should; *er svo að sjá, sem* . . . it looks as if . . . ; *sama er að segja um* the same is to be (may be) said about; *þá er að byrja* then we shall begin, let's begin; *hvað er að frétta?* what news? (S. VI, **14**, *8*); compound tenses: passive: *það var byggt af kappi* building went on eagerly; intrans. v. of motion: *nú var riðið í hlað* sbdy rode up to the front of the house(s); middle voice: *þar var barizt tvo daga* there they fought two days (S. VI, **14**, *6*); (4) auxiliary uses: with intrans. verbs of motion: *vera farinn* have gone; *vera lagztur* have lain down (S. VI, **1**, *2*; **3**; **12**, *2, 2*); durative action: *vera að lesa* be reading (S. VI, **4**; **4**, *3*); *vertu ekki að gráta* don't weep (S. VI, **10**, 4); *vera að verða* be on the point of becoming (getting); completed action: *vera búinn að lesa* have finished reading (S. VI, **6**; *6, 2*); *vera búinn að vera* be through; passive voice: *vera tekinn* be taken (S. VI, **8**); *vera* is often omitted in acc. with inf. phrases: *þeir töldu hann (vera) efnaðan* they considered him (to be) wealthy; *þeir sögðu hann (vera) dauðan* they said that he was dead, etc.; also in: *hann mun (vera) farinn* he has probably gone, *hann mundi (vera) farinn* he would (probably) have gone, etc. (S. VI, **11**, *6*n1); (5) with preps and advs: *e-ð er að e-u* sth is wrong with sth, sth is the matter with sth; *er eitthvað að?* is anything wrong? *hvað er að?* what is wrong? *mega vera að e-u* have time to do sth; *vera án e-s* be without sth, do without sth; *vera eftir* be left; *það sem eftir er dagsins* in what is left of the day; *vera heima* stay at home, be home; *vera í* be in, make; *í potti eru fjórir pelar* there are four half-pints to a quart; *vera í e-u* wear sth

(clothes) *vera með e-ð* have (hold) sth; be occupied with sth; *vera með e-m (e-u)* be for sbdy (sth); *drottinn sé með yður* God be with you; *vera saman* be together; *vera til* exist, be available, be found; *vera um e-ð* deal with, treat (of); *bókin er um Ísland* the book is about Iceland; *hvað er um að vera?* what is the matter? what is it all about? *ég sá, hvað um var að vera* I saw what was going on; *vera uppi* be upstairs; live, flourish; *vera úti* be outside; (= *vera liðinn, vera búinn*) expire, be over; *vera við e-ð* be present at sth, participate in sth.

verð, -s [ver·ð, verðs] n. price, value, worth; *verð á e-u* price of sth.

verða, verð, varð, urðum, orðinn (-ið) [ver·ða, ver·ð, var·ð, ɣr·ðɣm, ɔr·ðɪn, -ɪð] (imperative vertu [ver·tɣ]) v.3 become, be; grow, get, turn; happen; remain, stay; must, have to; (auxiliary) shall have, should have; (1) become: *verða feginn* be(come) glad; *verða tilbúinn* be(come) ready; *verða á vegi e-s* happen to be in one's way, happen to meet with sbdy; *þetta verða fimmtán krónur* this will be (come to) fifteen krónur; *verða lengi að gera e-ð* be long in doing sth; *það er nú lítið orðið* it is not much now; *nú orðið* now; *ég er (var) orðinn* I have (had) become (S. VI, **3**, *3*); *hann varð kyrr* he remained, he decided to remain (S. VI, **4**, *3*); (2) impersonal uses: *verði yður að góðu* 'may you enjoy it,' a polite phrase with which the host answers his guest when the latter thanks him for a meal; also used as a greeting in entering a room where people are having meals; *e-m verður gott af e-u* sth agrees with sbdy; *mér varð illt (bilt) við* I was startled, I got scared at (sth); *mér varð það á* . . . I had the (slight) misfortune . . . (S. VI, **14**, *5 & 8*); (3) to have to, have

Vowels: *a* [a] approx. father; *á* [au] cow; *e* [ɛ] set; *é* [jɛ] yes; *i, y* [ɪ] sit; *í, ý* [i] feel; *o* [ɔ] law; *ó* [ou] note; *u* [ɣ] approx. Germ. Mütter; *ú* [u] school; *y* = *i*; *ý* = *í*; *æ* [ai] ice; *ö* [ö] Germ. hören; *au* [öy] French *feuille*; *ei, ey* [ei] ale. Length [:]; half-length [·].

482

got to, must: *ég verð að fara* I must go (S. VI, **2**, *5*n; **13**, 7); (4) auxiliary: *ég verð kominn* I shall have come, *ég yrði kominn* I should have come; *það verða* (= *munu verða*) *vandræði* (*með það*) that will cause difficulties (S. V, **4**, 3); *hann varð ekki tekinn* he could not be taken; *honum varð ekki bjargað* he could not be saved (S. VI, **8**, *5*); *hann verður farinn* (= *mun verða farinn*) he will have gone (S. VI, **12**, *2*, 2); (5) with preps and advs: *verða að* be(come) the matter with, happen to (of accidents); *verða að e-u* become sth, turn into sth; *verða að manni* grow up to be a man; *vertu að steini* turn into a stone; *verða af e-u* lose sth; become of sth; *verða eftir* be left, remain; *verða fyrir e-u* be hit by, be affected by sth; *verða fyrir vonbrigðum* be disappointed, disillusioned; *verða til e-s*, *verða til að gera e-ð* come forth to do sth, take sth upon oneself, undertake sth; *verða um e-ð* become of sth; *verða úr e-u* (= *verða af e-u*) happen, be realized; *úr því gat ekki orðið* that could not be done, realized; *verða úti* die from exposure.

verðir, see *vörður*.

verður, verð, vert [vɛr·ðʏr̥, vɛr·ð, vɛr̥·t] adj. worth, worthy; *einskis verður* worth nothing, of no value; *þess vert, að* . . . worthy of. . . .

1. verja, -u, -ur [vɛr·ja, -ʏ(r̥)] wf.1 outer garment; defense, defense measures; defensive weapon, armor (against *gegn*).

2. verja, varði, varinn (-ið) [vɛr·ja, var·ðɪ, va:rɪn, -ɪð] wv.1 defend, guard against; *verja e-n e-u* guard sbdy against sth; *verjast* defend oneself; *eiga í vök að verjast* 'have to defend oneself in a hole in the ice,' i. e. be hard pressed, be in a bad fix; *verja fyrir e-u* defend against sth.

verk, -s, - [vɛr̥·k(s)] n. work, task, labor; opus; *vinsælt verk* a popular task; *óvinsælt verk* a thankless job; *taka til verka* take to working, begin work.

verkamaður, -manns, -menn [vɛr·kama:ðʏr̥, -man·s, -mɛn:] m.4 laborer, workman, worker.

verkfræði [vɛr̥·kfrai·ðɪ] wf.2 engineering.

verkfræðideild, -ar, -ir [vɛr·kfrai·ðɪdeil·d, -ar̥, -ɪr̥] f.2 faculty (department) of engineering.

verkfræðingasveit, -ar, -ir [vɛr·kfrai·-ðiŋga-svei:tʰ, -ar̥, -ɪr̥; -svei:d] f.2 engineers (corps of).

verkfræðingur, -s, -ar [vɛr·kfrai·ðiŋg-ʏr̥, -ɪŋs, -iŋgar̥] m.1 engineer.

verkja, -aði, -að [vɛr̥·kja, -aðɪ, -að] wv.4 pain, hurt; *mig verkjar í fótinn* I have a (constant) pain in my foot (S. I, **4**, *1*, 3).

verksmiðja, -u, -ur [vɛr̥·ksmɪðja, -ʏ(r̥)] wf.1 factory, mill.

verksmiðjustjóri, -a, -ar [vɛr̥·ksmɪðjʏrstjou:rɪ, -a(r̥)] wm.1 director of a factory.

verkur, verkjar (verks), verkir, (-ja) [vɛr̥·kʏr̥, vɛr̥·kjar̥, vɛr̥ks, vɛr̥·kjɪr̥, -kja] m.2 pain, ache; *ég finn til verkjar í fætinum* I feel a pain in my foot.

verma, vermdi, vermdur (vermt) [vɛr·ma, vɛrmdɪ, -ʏr̥, vɛrmtʰ; vɛrmt] wv.2 warm, heat.

vermireitur, -s, -ir [vɛr·mɪ-rei:tʰʏr̥, -rei:tʰs, -ɪr̥; -rei:d-] m.2 hotbed.

vernd, -ar, -ir [vɛrnd, vɛn·d, -ar̥, -ɪr̥] f.2 protection, defense.

vernda, -aði, -að(ur) [vɛrnda, -aðɪ, -að, -aðʏr̥; vɛn·da] wv.2 protect, defend, guard.

1. verpa, verp, varp, urpum, orpinn (-ið) [vɛr̥·pa, vɛr̥·p, var̥·p, ʏr̥·pʏm, ɔr̥·pɪn, -ɪð] v.3 throw; *verpa e-u* throw sth; *verpa eggjum* lay eggs; *verpa sandi* cover with sand.

2. verpa, verpti, verpt(ur) [vɛr̥·pa, vɛr̥·(p)tɪ, -ʏr̥, vɛr̥·(p)t] wv.2 lay eggs; *hænan verpir vel* the hen lays

---

Consonants: [ð] brea*th*e; [g] *g*ood; [gʲ] *gy*arden (garden); [hw] *wh*at; [j] *y*es; [kʲ] *cy*an (can); [ŋ] thi*ng*; [q] N. Germ. sa*g*en; [r] Scottish *r*; [x] approx. Germ. a*ch*; [þ] *th*in. Voiceless: ○; [b̥, d̥, g̊] approx. *p, t, k.* Half-voiced: *italics.* Aspiration and preaspiration: [ʰ]; [pʰ, tʰ, kʰ] *p-, t-, k-.* Others as in English.

well (copiously); throw up a sand-bank, form a dam, dam up: *það verpir fyrir ósinn* the estuary is (being) dammed up.

verr, verri, see *illa, illur, slæmur, vondur.*

vers, -, - [ver̥·s; ves:] n. verse, stanza, strophe, especially of a hymn.

versna, -aði, -að [ves·na, -aðɪ, -að; ver̥sna] wv.4 get worse, grow worse, deteriorate; *honum versnar* he is getting worse.

verst(ur), see *illa, illur, slæmur, vondur.*

verzla, -aði, -að [ver̥sla, -aðɪ, -að] wv.4 carry on business; *verzla með e-ð* deal in sth; *verzla við e-n* deal with sbdy.

verzlun, -unar, -anir [ver̥slʏn, -ʏnar̥, -anɪr̥] f.2 trade, business, concern; store, shop.

verzlunarbréf, -s, - [ver̥slʏnar·brje:v, -brjef·s] n. commercial letter.

verzlunarmenntun, -unar [ver̥slʏnar-men·tʰʏn, -ʏnar̥; -men·tʏn] f.2 commercial training.

verzlunarskóli, -a, -ar [ver̥slʏnar-skou:lɪ, -a(r̥)] wm.1 commercial school.

veröld, -aldar, -aldir [ve:röld, -aldar̥, -aldɪr̥] f.2 world.

vesall, vesöl, vesalt; (veslari, -astur) [ve:sadl̥, ve:söl, ve:salt, ves·larɪ, -astʏr̥] adj. sick(ly), ailing, poor, wretched, miserable.

vestan [ves·tan] (1) adv. from the west (= *að vestan*); *fyrir vestan ána* west of the river; *rétt vestan við ána* just west of the river (In. IV, 1, 3); (2) prep. with acc. *vestan túnið* from the west across the homefield; (3) prep. with gen. west of: *vestan hafs* 'west of the ocean,' i. e. in America.

Vestfirðir, -fjarða [ves·tfɪrðɪr̥, -fjarða] m.3 'The West Fjords,' a fjord-indented peninsula in the northwest corner of Iceland.

vesti, -s, - [ves·tɪ(s)] n. vest, waistcoat.

Vestmannaeyjar [ves·tman·(a)-ei:jar̥] f.1.pl. 'The Westmen Islands,' a group south of Iceland.

vestra [vestra] adv. in the west.

vestri (vestari), vestastur [vestrɪ, ves·tarɪ, -astʏr̥] adj. compar. and superl. more westerly, most westerly.

1. **vestur, (-ri), -urs** [ves·tʏr̥(s), vestrɪ] n. (the) west.

2. **vestur** [ves·tʏr̥] (1) adv. (In. IV, 1, 3) west, towards the west, in the west; *fara vestur fyrir* (or *yfir*) *ána* cross the river going west; *vestur í Dalasýslu* in Dalasýsla in the west (or: west towards Dalasýsla); (2) prep. with acc. *vestur túnið* west across the home-field.

Vesturbærinn, -bæjarins [ves·tʏr-bai:-rɪn, -bai:jarɪns] m.2 with the def. art. 'The West Town,' in Reykjavík.

Vesturgata, -götu [ves·tʏr-ga:tʰa, -gö:tʰʏ; -ga:da, -gö:dʏ] wf.1 'West Street,' in Reykjavík.

Vesturheimur, -s [ves·tʏr-hei:mʏr̥, -heim·s] m.1 America.

Vestur-Íslendingur, -s, -ar [ves·tʏr-i:slɛndiŋɡʏr̥, -iŋs, -iŋɡar̥] m.1 American-Icelander.

Vesturland, -s [ves·tʏr-lan·d, -lan·(d)s] n. 'The West' of Iceland.

vesæll, -sæl, -sælt; -sælli, -sælastur [ve:saidl̥, -sai·l, -sailt, -saidlɪ, -sai·lastʏr̥] adj. sick(ly), poor, wretched, miserable, cf. *vesall.*

vettlingur, -s, -ar [vɛʰt·liŋɡʏr̥, -iŋs, -iŋɡar̥] m.1 mitten, glove.

vetra, -aði, -að [ve:tʰra, -aðɪ, -að; ve:dra] wv.4 *það vetrar snemma* winter is coming early (S. VI, 14, 3).

vetur, -rar, -ur [ve:tʰʏr̥, ve:tʰrar̥; ve:dʏr̥, -rar̥] m.4 winter; *tveggja vetra tryppi* a two years old colt (S. I, 4, 2, 3) (= *tvæveturt tryppi*), *sjö vetra gamall* seven years old; *á vetrum, á veturna* in winter.

veturnætur, -nátta [ve:tʰʏr-nai:tʰʏr̥, -nauʰt:a; ve:dʏr-nai:dʏr̥] f.3.pl. a

---

Vowels: *a* [a] approx. father; *á* [au] cow; *e* [ɛ] set; *é* [jɛ] yes; *i, y* [ɪ] sit; *í, ý* [i] feel; *o* [ɔ] law; *ó* [ou] note; *u* [ʏ] approx. Germ. Mütter; *ú* [u] school; *y = i*; *ý = í*; *æ* [ai] ice; *ö* [ö] Germ. hören; *au* [öy] French feuille; *ei, ey* [ei] ale. Length [:]; half-length [·].

few days before the first day of winter.

vex, see *vaxa*.

vextir, see *vöxtur*.

1. **við** pl. of *ég*.

2. **við** [vɪ:ð, vɪ:, vɪ] (Pr. **4**, *2*) A. prep. with acc. against, with; at, near, on, facing, against; of; at (of time); at, occupied with; to, for; as adv. often not translated; (1) *berjast við e-n* fight against sbdy; *leika við e-n* play with sbdy; *tala við e-n* speak to sbdy; (2) of space: *við gluggann* at the window; *við Menntaskólann* near the Menntaskóli (Gymnasium); *við Bókhlöðustíg* facing Bókhlöðu-stígur; *við ströndina* near the shore; *við sjó* at the sea (shore), on the sea (shore); *vera við kirkju* be at church, attend church; *við loft* against the sky; (3) of direction: *austan við* east of; *á hœgri hönd við hann* ' on the right side of him,' on his right side; (4) of time: *við þessi orð* at these words; (5) miscellaneous: *vera við nám* be (occupied with) studying; *við betri kjör* in better circumstances; *vinna við e-ð* work in (at) sth; *lög við ljóð* tunes for poems (texts); *sönglag við kvœði* song for a text; *kveða við barn* lull a baby to sleep with song; sing to a baby; *að tiltölu við e-ð* in proportion to sth; (6) adverbially: *vera úti við* be out, be outdoors; *vera við* be present, be at hand. **B**. prep. with dat. against, for: *við góðu verði* for a good price (S. I, 3, *3*, 2).

1. **við** [vi:ð] f. (1 ?) only in the phrase: *á víð og dreif* scattered.

2. **við**, see *viður*.

víða [vi:ða] adv. widely, in many places; through many places; *víða um lönd* in many lands (countries); *víða og lengi* far and wide and for a long time; *og víðar* and in more places; and elsewhere.

víðátta, -u, -ur [vi:ðauʰt·a, -ʏ(r̥)] wf.1 expanse.

víðáttumikill, -il, -ið [vi:ðauʰt·ʏ-mɪ:k₁ʰɪd̥l̥, -ɪl, -ɪð; -mɪ:g̊₁ɪd̥l̥] adj. extensive.

viðbein, -s, - [vɪð·bei·n, -beins) n. collarbone.

viðbeinsbrotna, -aði, -að [vɪð·beins-brɔʰt·na, -aðɪ, -að] wv.4 break the collarbone.

viðbót, -ar, -bætur [vɪð·bou·tʰ, -ar̥, -bai·tʰʏr̥; -bou·d̥, -bai·dʏr̥] f.3 addition; *í viðbót* in addition; *einn í viðbót* one more.

viðburður, -ar, -ir [vɪð·bʏrðʏr̥, -ar̥, -ɪr̥] m.3 event.

viðdvöl, -dvalar, -ir [vɪð·dvö·l, -dva·-lar̥, -ɪr̥] f.2 stay; *hafa stutta viðdvöl* stay for a short time.

viðfelldinn, -in, -ið; -felldnari, -astur [vɪð·feld̥ɪn, -ɪn, -ɪð, -feld̥narɪ, -astʏr̥] adj. agreeable, affable.

viðgerð, -ar, -ir (viðgjörð) [vɪð·g₁erð, -ðar̥, -ðɪr̥; vɪð·g₁jörð] f.2 repair, mending, rebuilding; *viðgerð á skóm* repair of shoes.

viðhöfn, -hafnar [vɪːðhöbn̥, -habnar̥] f.2 show, pomp, ceremony.

víðikjarr, -s, -kjörr [vi:ðɪ-k₁ʰar:, -k₁ʰar:s, -k₁ʰör:] n. willow copse.

víðir, -is [vi:ðɪr̥, -ɪs] m.1 willow.

viðkoma, -u, -ur [vɪð·kʰɔ·ma, -ʏ(r̥)] wf.1 touch; stop; fertility (in animals).

viðkomustaður, -ar, -ir [vɪð·kʰɔ·mʏ-sta:ðʏr̥, -ar̥, -ɪr̥] m.3 (bus) stop, stopping place; port of call.

viðlátinn, -in, -ið [vɪð·lau·tʰɪn, -ɪn, -ɪð; -lau·d̥·] adj. at hand, at leisure, not engaged; *ekki viðlátinn* occupied.

viðnám, -s [vɪð·nau·m, -naums] n. resistance.

viðskiptavinur, -ar, -ir [vɪð·sk₁ɪfta-vɪ:nʏr̥, -ar̥, -ɪr̥] m.3 customer.

viðskifti [vɪð·sk₁ɪftɪ] n.pl. dealings, intercourse, commerce.

viðstaða, -stöðu, -ur [vɪð·sta·ða, -stö·-ðʏ(r̥)] wf.1 stop, stoppage, stay.

Consonants: [ð] brea*th*e; [g] *g*ood; [g₁] *gy*arden (garden); [hw] *wh*at; [j] *y*es; [k₁] *cy*an (can); [ŋ] thi*ng*; [q] N. Germ. sa*g*en; [r] Scottish *r*; [x] approx. Germ. a*ch*; [þ] *th*in. Voiceless: ○; [b̥, d̥, g̊] approx. *p, t, k*. Half-voiced: *italics*. Aspiration and preaspiration: [ʰ]; [pʰ, tʰ, kʰ] *p-, t-, k-*. Others as in English.

viðstaddur, -stödd, -statt [vɪð·stað·ʏr̥, -stöð·, -staʰt·] adj. present.

víðsvegar [við·sve·qar̥] adv. (= *víðs vegar*) in many places, scattered about.

viðtal, -s, -töl [vɪð·tʰa·l, -tʰals, -tʰö·l] n. talk, interview; *eiga viðtal við e-n* have a talk (interview) with sbdy.

viðtæki, -s, - [vɪð·tʰai·k₁ʰɪ(s); -tʰai·g̊₁ɪ] n. radio receiving set (= *útvarpstæki*).

viðtækjaverzlun, -unar, -anir [vɪð·tʰai·k₁ʰa·veᵣslʏn, -ʏnar̥, -anɪr̥; -tʰai·g̊₁a-] f.2 radio receiving sets business; *V. ríkisins* 'The State Monopoly of Radios.'

viðundur, (-ri), -urs, -ur [vɪ·ðʏn·dʏr̥(s), -ʏndrɪ] n. fool; *verða að viðundri* act like a fool.

viður, -ar, -ir [vɪ·ðʏr̥, -ar̥, -ɪr̥] m.3 wood; pl. logs, timber.

víður, víð, vítt [vi·ðʏr̥, vi·ð, viʰt:] adj. wide, large, extensive; loose; *víðs vegar* scattered about, in many places.

viðurkenna, -kenndi,-kenndur (-kennt) [vɪ·ðʏr̥-k₁ʰen:a, -k₁ʰen·dɪ, -ʏr̥, -k₁ʰen·tʰ; -k₁ʰen·t] wv.2 acknowledge.

viðurnefni, -s, - [vɪ·ðʏr·neb·nɪ(s)] n. nickname.

viðvíkjandi [vɪð·vi·k₁ʰandɪ; -vi·g̊₁andɪ] pr.p. with dat. *viðvíkjandi e-u* concerning sth.

víg, -s, - [vi·q, vix·s] n. killing.

Vigfús, -ar, (-s) [vɪx·fu·s, -fu·sar̥, -fus·] m.1 pers. name; patronymic: *Vigfússon*.

víggirða, -girti, -girt(ur) [viq·g̊₁ɪrða, -g̊₁ɪrtɪ, -ʏr̥, -g̊₁ɪr̥t] wv.2 fortify.

víggirðing, -ar, -ar [viq·g̊₁ɪrðiŋ̊, -ar̥] f.1 fortification.

vígi, -s, - [vi·jɪ(s)] n. fortress.

vígja, vígði, vígður (vígt) [vi·ja, viq·ðɪ, -ʏr̥, vix·t; vig̊·ð-] wv.2 consecrate, hallow; *vígður prestur* ordained parson.

Vignir, -is [vɪg̊·nɪr̥, -ɪs] m.1 pers. name.

vígstöðvar [vix·stöðvar̥] f.1.pl. front, battle line(s).

vigt, -ar, -ir [vɪx·t, -ar̥, -ɪr̥] f.2 weight.

vik, -s, - [vɪ:kʰ(s); vɪ:g̊] n. bend, turn; *það er hægt um vik* 'it is an easy turn,' it is easy.

vík, -ur, -ur [vi:kʰ, -ʏr̥; vi:g̊] f.3 a small bay or inlet; frequent in place names: *-vík, Víkur-*.

vika, -u, -ur, (-na) [vɪ:kʰa, -ʏ(r̥); vɪ:g̊a; vɪʰk·na] wf.1 week; *viku fyrir jól* a week before Christmas; *í næstu viku* next week; *viku af sumri* one week (passed) of the summer; *viku eftir jól* a week after Christmas; *það rigndi vikuna, sem leið* it rained last week (S. I, 2, 2, 1); *Vikan* 'The Week,' a periodical.

víkja, vík, veik, vikum, vikinn (-ið) [vi:k₁ʰa, vi:kʰ, vei:kʰ, vɪ:kʰʏm, vɪ:k₁ʰɪn, -ɪð; vi:g̊₁a, vi:g̊, vei:g̊, vɪ:g̊ʏm, vɪ:g̊₁ɪn] v.1 turn, deviate, go, yield; *aldrei að víkja!* never to yield! *víkjum nú aftur að því* let us now turn again to that; *því víkur svo við, að . . .* it so happens that; *sögunni víkur til* the tale turns to (S. VI, 14, 4).

vikudagur, -dags, -dagar [vɪ:kʰʏ·da:·qʏr̥, -dax·s, -da:qar̥; vɪ:g̊ʏ-] m.1 weekday.

vikutími, -a [vɪ:kʰʏ-tʰi:mɪ, -a; vɪ:g̊ʏ-] wm.1 week's time.

Vilborg, -ar, -ir [vɪl·borg̊, -ar̥, -g̊₁ɪr̥] f.2 pers. name.

Vilhjálmur, -s|[vɪl·hʲaulmʏr̥, -hʲaulms] m.1 William.

vilja, vil, viljum, vildi, viljað [vɪl·ja, vɪ:l, vɪl·jʏm, vɪl·dɪ, vɪl·jað] pret. pres. v. (In. VII, 5, 1) (1) want to, wish to, be willing; *vilja heldur (helzt)* prefer; *vilja síður* prefer not to; *hvað villtu?* what do you want? *ég vil ekki segja* I would not say; *vilduð þér sjá bréfið?* would you like to see the letter (S. VI, 9, 2, 2) ; *það vildi ég, að hann kæmi* I wish (that) he'd come; *ég vildi gjarnan* I'd like to; *vilja e-m e-ð*

Vowels: *a* [a] approx. father; *á* [au] cow; *e* [ɛ] set; *é* [jɛ] yes; *i, y* [ɪ] sit; *í, ý* [i] feel; *o* [ɔ] law; *ó* [ou] note; *u* [ʏ] approx. Germ. Mütter; *ú* [u] school; *y = i; ý = í;* æ [ai] ice; *ö* [ö] Germ. hören; *au* [öy] French feuille; *ei, ey* [ei] ale. Length [:]; half-length [·].

486

want to speak to sbdy about sth,
have business with sbdy; (2) auxiliary: *eins og oft vill verða* as (it)
often will happen (S. VI, **2**, 5n;
13, 8); (3) *vilja til* happen; *það
vill svo til* it so happens; *ef til vill*
perhaps.

vilji, -a, -ar [vɪl·jɪ, -a(r̥)] wm.1 will.

1. **villa, -u, -ur** [vɪd·la, -ʏ(r̥)] wf.1
going astray; error,mistake; heresy.

2. **villa, villti, villt(ur)** [vɪd·la, vɪl̥·tɪ,
-ʏr̥, vɪl̥·t] wv.2 lead astray, mis-
lead; bewilder; *villa fyrir e-m* lead
sbdy astray; *villast* get lost, go
astray; *ekki verður um villzt* there
can be no mistake about it (S. VI,
7, *6*).

villtur, villt, villt [vɪl̥·tʏr̥, vɪl̥·t] adj.
wild, savage; lost, bewildered, wan-
dered astray.

vín, -s, - [vi:n, vin·s] n. wine.

vínarbrauð, -s, - [vi:nar-bröy:ð,
-bröyð·s] n. Danish pastry.

vinátta, -u [vɪ:nauʰt·a, -ʏ] wf.1
friendship.

vínber, -s, -, (-ja) [vin·be·r, -ber̥s,
-berja] n. grape.

1. **vinda, vind, vatt, undum, undinn
(-ið)** [vɪn·da, vɪn·d, vaʰt:, ʏn·dʏm,
ʏn·dɪn, -ɪð] v.3 wind, wring; twist,
turn; *vindast* get twisted; *vindast
um ökklann* turn one's ankle; *vinda
bráðan bug að e-u* hurry up sth, do
sth without delay, lose no time in
doing sth; *vinda upp segl* hoist
sail; imperative: *vitt þú, vittu*
wind, wring (In. VII, **4**, *6*, 1n3).

2. **vinda, -aði, -að** [vɪn·da, -aðɪ, -að]
wv.4 begin to blow; *það vindar,
hann vindar* it is beginning to blow.

vindátt, -ar, -ir [vɪn·dauʰt·, -ar̥, -ɪr̥]
f.2 direction from which the wind
blows.

vindauga, -u [vɪn·döy·qa, -ʏ] wn. barn
'window,' a door high up on the
gable of the barn where the bundles
of hay are rolled in.

vindill, -ils, -lar [vɪn·dɪdl, -ɪls, vɪn·dlar̥]
m.1 cigar.

vindlahylki, -s, - [vɪn·dla-hɪl·kɪʰɪ(s);
-hɪl·kɪ] n. cigar case, cigaret case.

vindlingur, -s, -ar [vɪn·dliŋ̊ʏr̥, -ɪŋs,
-iŋgar̥] m.1 cigaret.

vindur, -s, -ar [vɪn·dʏr̥, vɪnds, vɪn·dar̥]
m.1 wind.

vingast, -aðist, -azt [vɪŋ·gast, -aðɪst,
-ast] wv.4 (middle voice only) *vingast við e-n* get friendly with, become friends with sbdy.

vingjarnlega [vɪŋ·g̊ɪadn-lɛ:qa] adv. in
a friendly way.

1. **vinna, -u** [vɪn:a, -ʏ] wf.1 work,
labor, employment; *við vinnu* at
work.

2. **vinna, vinn, vann, unnum, unninn
(-ið)** [vɪn:a, vɪn:, van:, ʏn:ʏm,
ʏn:ɪn, -ɪð] v.3 work (at sth), labor;
do, perform, achieve; win, gain,
conquer; *vinna við e-ð* work in sth,
at sth; *vinnast* be won; *vinnast
fljótt og vel* get done quickly and
well.

vinnufólk, -s [vɪn·ʏ-foul·kʰ, -foul·(x)s,
-foul·k] n. servants; farmhands.

vinnumaður, -manns, -menn [vɪn·ʏ-
ma:ðʏr̥, ·man·s, -mɛn:] m.4 farm-
hand, man-servant on a farm.

vinnustofa, -u, -ur [vɪn·ʏ-stɔ:va,
-ʏ(r̥)] wf.1 studio (of an artist).

vinsamlega [vɪn·sam-lɛ·qa] adv. friendly,kindly; *vinsamlegast* with kindest
regards; kindly.

vinsemd, -ar [vɪn·sɛmd, -ar̥] f.2
friendliness; *með vinsemd* in all
friendliness, with kind regards, sincerely yours (ending letters).

vinstri [vɪnstrɪ] adj. compar. left;
vinstra megin á e-u on the left side
of sth; *vinstri höndin* the left hand;
á vinstri hönd to the left.

vinsæll, -sæl, -sælt; -sælli, -sælastur
[vɪn·saidl, -sai·l, -sailt, -saidlɪ,
-sai·lastʏr̥] adj. popular.

vinur, -ar, -ir [vɪ:nʏr̥, -ar̥, -ɪr̥] m.3
friend; *kæri vinur, góði vinur* dear
friend (beginning letters).

vinveittur, -veitt, -veitt [vɪn·veiʰt·ʏr̥,
-veiʰt·] adj. friendly; *vinveittur
e-m* friendly to sbdy.

Consonants: [ð] brea*th*e; [g] *g*ood; [gɪ] *gy*arden (garden); [hʏ] *wh*at; [j] *y*es; [kɪ] *cy*an
(can); [ŋ] thi*ng*, [q] N. Germ. sa*g*en; [r] Scottish *r*; [x] approx. Germ. a*ch*; [þ] *th*in.
Voiceless: ∘; [b̥, d̥, g̊] approx. *p, t, k*. Half-voiced: *italics*. Aspiration and preaspiration:
[ʰ]; [pʰ, tʰ, kʰ] *p-, t-, k-*. Others as in English.

vinza, -aði, -að(ur) [vɪn·sa, -aðɪ, -að, -aðʏr̥] wv.4 winnow, sift; *vinza úr e-u* winnow from sth, glean from sth.

virða, virti, virt(ur) [vɪr̥·ða, vɪr̥·tɪ, -ʏr̥, vɪr̥·t] wv.2 value; esteem, honor; think (much, little) of; appraise, estimate; *virða mikils* value highly; *virða e-ð fyrir sér* look (reflectively) at sth; *virðast* seem; *e-m virðist e-ð* sbdy thinks sth, sth seems to sbdy (S. VI, 7, *3*); *virðast sem* seem (feel) as if (S. VI, 9, *4*, 7).

virði, -s [vɪr̥·ðɪ(s)] n. value; *eignin er 3000 kr. virði* the property is worth 3000 *krónur* (S. I, 4, *2*, 2).

virðing, -ar, -ar [vɪr̥·ðɪ̊ŋg̊, -ar̥] f.1 honor, esteem; *með vinsemd og virðingu* 'friendly and respectfully,' i. e. yours truly (ending letters).

virðingarfyllst [vɪr̥·ðɪ̊ŋg̊ar̥·fɪlst] adv. superl. very respectfully, yours (very) truly (ending letters).

virki, -s, - [vɪr̥·kjɪ(s)] n. fortress, stronghold.

virkisfallbyssur [vɪr̥·kjɪs-fad̥·l̥bɪs·ʏr̥] wf.1.pl. fortress artillery.

virkislið, -s [vɪr̥·kjɪs-lɪ:ð̊, -lɪð·s] n. fortress troops.

virkisveggur, -veggjar, -veggir [vɪr̥··kjɪs-veg̊:ʏr̥, -veg̊j:ar̥, -veg̊j:ɪr̥] m.2 fortress wall.

vís, vís, víst [vi:s, vis·t] adj. wise; certain; *að vísu* 'according to what is certain,' i. e. to be sure (S. III, 3, 2); *verða e-s vís (vísari)* ascertain sth, become aware of sth.

1. vísa, -u, -ur [vi:sa, -ʏ(r̥)] wf.1 verse, stanza, lyric; *gera (yrkja) vísu* make (compose) a short lyric.

2. vísa, -aði, -að [vi:sa, -aðɪ, -að] wv.4 *vísa e-m á e-ð* show, guide sbdy to sth; *vísa á rétta leið* show the right road; *vísa til rúms* show (one) one's bed.

vísir, -is, -(ir)ar [vi:sɪr̥, -ɪs, -(ɪr)ar̥] m.1 germ, sprout, embryo; *vísir til e-s* embryonic beginning of sth; *Vísir* a daily, so called because it

was the first 'germ' of a daily in Iceland; *vísir* hand on a clock.

visna, -aði, -að(ur) [vɪs·na, -aðɪ, -að, -aðʏr̥] wv.4 wither.

viss, viss, visst [vɪs:, vɪs·t] adj. certain, sure; fixed; *vera viss í sinni sök* be certain (positive) about a matter; *visst gjald* a fixed payment.

vissi, see *vita*.

vissulega [vɪs:ʏ-lɛ:qa] adv. certainly, verily.

víst [vis·t] adv. (n. of *vís* certain) surely, probably.

vist, -ar, -ir [vɪs·t, -ar̥, -ɪr̥] f.2 stay, sojourn; term of service; pl. provisions (food), supplies.

vistadeild, -ar, -ir (-sveit, -ar, -ir) [vɪs·ta-deil·d̥, -ar̥, -ɪr̥ (-svei:tʰ, -ar̥, -ɪr̥; -svei:d̥)] f.1 service of supply (in the army), quartermaster corps.

vit, -s, - [vɪ:tʰ(s); vɪ:d(s)] n. intelligence, understanding, sense, reason; pl. the senses; *hafa vit á e-u* be a judge of sth, understand about sth; *koma vitinu fyrir e-n* bring sbdy to reason.

vita, veit, vitum, vissi, vitað [vɪ:tʰa, vei:tʰ, vɪ:tʰʏm, vɪs:ɪ, vɪ:tʰað; vɪ:da, vei:d̥, vɪ:dʏm, vɪ:dað] pret. pres. v. (In. VII, 5, *1*) know, be aware of; turn, face; *ég veit ekki* I do not know; *vita ekki til sín* have lost consciousness; *vita hvorki upp né niður í e-u* understand less than nothing of sth; *vita upp á sína tíu fingur* know for certain; *vita lengra en nef manns nær* 'know further than one's nose reaches,' i. e. know (much) more than the average person, be shrewd, be versed in magic lore; *ég vissi, að hann fór* I knew that he went (S. VI, 9, *4*, 1n2); *ég skal vita, hvort (hvernig)* . . . I will see whether (how) . . . ; *glugginn veit út að götunni* the window faces the street.

vitja, -aði, -að [vɪ:tʰja, -aðɪ, -að; vɪ:dja] wv.4 call on, visit; fetch; look after; *vitja um e-n* visit sbdy,

Vowels: *a* [a] approx. father; *á* [au] cow; *e* [ɛ] set; *é* [jɛ] yes; *i, y* [ɪ] sit; *í, ý* [i] feel; *o* [ɔ] law; *ó* [ou] note; *u* [ʏ] approx. Germ. M*ü*tter; *ú* [u] school; *y = i*; *ý = í*; *æ* [ai] ice; *ö* [ö] Germ. h*ö*ren; *au* [öy] French *feuille*; *ei, ey* [ei] ale. Length [:]; half-length [·].

look after sbdy; *vitja læknis* fetch
a doctor.
vitlaus, -laus, -laust [vɪʰt·löy·s, -löyst;
vɪ:tʰ-, vɪ:d̦-] adj. mad, crazy, (witless), *vitlaus í e-ð* crazy for sth,
vitlaus í að gera e-ð madly eager
to do sth; *ertu vitlaus!* are you
crazy?
vitlegur [vɪ:tʰlɛ·qʏr̦, vɪ:d̦-] adj. (see
-legur) wise (usually in a sarcastic
sense): *það hefði verið vitlegt eða
hitt þó heldur* that would have been
wise or rather the opposite (litotes).
vitleysa, -u, -ur [vɪʰt·lei·sa, -ʏ(r̦)]
wf.1 foolishness.
vitni, -s, - [vɪʰt·nɪ(s)] n. witness.
vítt, see *víður.*
vitur, vitur, viturt; vitrari, -astur
[vɪ:tʰʏr̦, vɪ:tʰʏr̦t; vɪ:tʰrarɪ, -astʏr̦;
vɪ:d̦ʏr̦(t), vɪ:d̦rarɪ] adj. intelligent, wise.
vizka, -u [vɪs·ka, -ʏ] wf.1 wisdom.
vó, see *vega.*
1. **vofa, -u, -ur** [vɔ:va, -ʏ(r̦)] wf.1
spirit, wraith, specter.
2. **vofa, vofði, vofað** [vɔ:va, vɔv·ðɪ,
vɔ:vað; vɔb·ðɪ] wv.3 *vofa yfir*
threaten, be imminent.
vog, -ar, -ir [vɔ:q, -qar̦, vɔi:jɪr̦;
vɔ:jɪr̦] f.2 weight.
vó(g), vógum, see *vega.*
volgna, -aði, -að [vɔl·na, -aðɪ, -að]
wv.4 get lukewarm, warm up.
(intr.).
volgur, volg, volgt [vɔl·ɡʏr̦, vɔl·ɡ,
vɔl̦·t; vɔl(x)t] adj. tepid, lukewarm.
von, -ar, -ir [vɔ:n, -nar̦, -nɪr̦] f.2 hope,
expectation; *það er ekki von* that
is not to be expected, no wonder;
það er von á e-u (e-m) one may
expect sth (sbdy); *eiga von á e-u
(e-m)* expect sth (sbdy); *eiga sér
einskis ills von* be completely unsuspecting of evil.
vona, -aði, -að [vɔ:na, -aðɪ, -að] wv.4
hope, expect; *ég vona það* I hope so,
vonandi I hope; *vonast til* hope,
expect, *vonast eftir* hope for.
vonbrigði [vɔn·brɪqðɪ; vɔm·-] n.pl.
disappointment.

vondur, vond, vont; verri, verstur
[vɔn·dʏr̦, vɔn·d, vɔn·tʰ; vɔn·t; ver:ɪ,
vɛs·tʏr̦, vɛrstʏr̦] adj. bad, evil,
wicked; *vont veður* bad weather;
*vera e-m vondur = vera vondur við
e-n* be unkind to sbdy, treat sbdy
badly (In. III, 2(b)5b; 4, 5).
vopn, -s, - [vɔʰp·n, vɔʰpns] n. weapon.
Vopnafjörður, -fjarðar [vɔʰp·na·fjör-·
ðʏr̦, -fjar·ðar̦] m.3 'Vopni's Fjord.'
vopnahlé, -s, - [vɔʰp·na·hljɛ:(s)] n.
armistice.
1. **vor, -s, -** [vɔ:r, vɔr̦·s] n. spring;
í vor this spring, last spring; *að
vori* next spring; *á vorin* in spring;
vor og haust in spring and in fall.
2. **vor, vor, vort** [vɔ:r, vɔr̦·t] poss.
pron. (In. VI, 2) our (referring to
the honorific pl. *vér*); *faðir vor* our
Father; *vor guð* our God (S. III,
2, 4).
3. **vor,** honorific gen. pl. of *ég.*
vora, -aði, -að [vɔ:ra, -aðɪ, -að] wv.4
það vorar spring is coming (S. VI,
14, 3).
vorkunn, -ar [vɔr̦·kʏn, -ʏn(·)ar̦] f.2
excuse, pity; *honum er vorkunn* he
is excusable, or: he is to be pitied.
vorum, vórum, see *vera.*
votur, vot, vott [vɔ:tʰʏr̦, vɔ:tʰ, vɔʰt:;
vɔ:d(ʏr̦)] adj. wet, drenched.
voveiflega [vɔ:veiv·lɛ:qa] adv. in a
violent manner, by accident.
vænn, væn, vænt; vænni, vænstur
[vaid·n, vai:n, vain·tʰ; vain·t; vaid·-
nɪ, vainstʏr̦] adj. promising, hope-
ful; handsome, beautiful; big; *e-m
þykir vænt um e-n* sbdy likes (loves)
sbdy.
vænta, vænti, vænt [vain·tʰa, vain·tʰɪ,
vain·tʰ; vain·t-] wv.2 hope for,
expect; *vænta e-s* expect sth; *ekki
vænti ég, að það hafi nú verið
stökkull* I don't expect that it was
a springe? I suppose it was not a
springe?
væntanlega [vain·tʰan·lɛ:qa; vain·-
tan-] adv. in all probability,
probably.
væntanlegur [vain·tʰan·lɛ:qʏr̦; vain·-

Consonants: [ð] brea*th*e; [g] *g*ood; [ɡ̑] *gy*arden (garden); [hw̦] *wh*at; [j] *y*es; [k̑] *cy*an
(can); [ŋ] thi*ng*; [q] N. Germ. sa*g*en; [r] Scottish *r*; [x] approx. Germ. a*ch*; [þ] *th*in.
Voiceless: ○; [b̦, d̦, ɡ̦] approx. *p, t, k.* Half-voiced: *italics.* Aspiration and preaspiration:
[ʰ]; [pʰ, tʰ, kʰ] *p-, t-, k-.* Others as in English.

tan-] adj. (see -legur) to be expected; pósturinn er væntanlegur í kvöld the mailman may be expected tonight.

1. **væta, -u, -ur** [vai:tʰa, -ɤ(r̥); vai:ḏa] wf.1 wetness, moisture, rain; það er blessuð vætan! that's a good rain! (sincerely or sarcastically).

2. **væta, vætti, vætt(ur)** [vai:tʰa, vaiʰt:I, -ɤr̥; vai:ḏa] wv.2 wet, moisten.

vætt, -ar, -ir [vaiʰt:, -ar̥, -Ir̥] f.2 hundredweight (= 10 fjórðungar), cwt.

vættur, -ar, -ir [vaiʰt:ɤr̥, -ar̥, -Ir̥] f.2 (or m.3) wight, spirit, demon, troll.

vöð, see vað.

vöggu, -ur, see vagga.

vök, vakar, vakir [vö:kʰ, va:kʰar̥, va:k₁ʰIr̥; vö:g̊, va:g̊ar̥, va:g̊₁Ir̥] f.2 hole in the ice; cf. 2. verja.

vökna, -aði, -að(ur) [vöʰk·na, -aðI, -að, -aðɤr̥] wv.4 get wet, get moist; enginn er verri, þó hann vökni (proverbial) no one is the worse for getting (a little) wet; mér vöknaði um augu my eyes grew moist (S. I, **4**, 1, 5).

vökva, -aði, -að(ur) [vö:kʰva, -aðI, -að, -aðɤr̥; vö:g̊va] wv.4 water, wet; vökva blóm water flowers.

völ [vö:l] f.2 (only in this form) choice; völ er á e-u sth is available.

völd, see vald.

völur, valar, velir [vö:lɤr̥, va:lar̥, vɛ:lIr̥] m.3 rod.

völlur, vallar, vellir [vöd·lɤr̥, vad·lar̥, vɛd·lIr̥] m.3 plain, field; leggja að velli slay; halda velli hold one's ground.

vön, see vanur.

vönduð, see vandaður.

1. **vör, varar, varir** [vö:r, va:rar̥, -Ir̥] f.2 lip; landing place.

2. **vör,** see 1. var.

vörðu, -ur, see varða.

vörður, varðar, verðir [vör·ðɤr̥, var·ðar̥, vɛr·ðIr̥] m.3 guard; vera á verði be on guard (also figuratively).

vörm, see varmur.

vörn, varnar, -ir [vördn̥, vardnar̥, -Ir̥] f.2 defense.

vöru, -ur, see 1. vara.

vörubíll, -s, -ar [vö:rɤ-biḏ·l̥, -bil·s, -bi:lar̥] m.1 lorry, truck.

vörudeildahús, -s, - [vö:rɤdeil·da-hu:s, -hus:] n. department store.

vöruhús, -s, - [vö:rɤ-hu:s, -hus:] n. warehouse; Vöruhúsið a dry goods store in Reykjavík.

vörumerki, -s, - [vö:rɤ-mer·k₁I(s)] n. trade-mark.

vörutegund, -ar, -ir [vö:rɤ-tʰɛ:qɤnd, -ar̥, -Ir̥] f.2 kind of goods, ware.

vösk, see 2. vaskur.

vötn, see vatn.

vöxtur, vaxtar, vextir [vöxstɤr̥, vaxstar̥, vɛxstIr̥] m.3 growth, increase, rising (of rivers); pl. vextir interest; setja fé á vöxtu put out money at interest.

Y.

yðar, yður, see þú.

yfir [I:vIr̥] prep. with acc. or dat. or adv. (1) prep. with acc. in phrases of motion (S. I, 2, 3, 2); over, across, beyond: settu ljósið yfir dyrnar put the light over the door; fara yfir ána go over the river, cross the river; of time: yfir hádegi over (past) noon; yfir mánuðinn for the month, per month; (2) prep. with dat. in phrases denoting rest (S. I, 3, 3, 2): over, above: ljósið er yfir dyrunum the light is above the door; (3) adv. over: yfir á, yfir í over yonder, yfir um over, yfir frá over yonder (sometimes yfrá, yfrí, yfrum); more than: yfir 40 þúsundir over forty thousand.

yfirferð, -ar, -ir [I:vIr̥-fɛr·ð, -ðar̥, -ðIr̥] f.2 crossing, traversing; (the act of) passing; illur (góður) yfirferðar difficult (easy) to pass.

yfirflotaforingi [I:vIr̥-flɔ:tʰafɔ·ring₁I, -g̊₁a(r̥); -flɔ:ḏa-] wm.1 chief admiral.

Vowels: a [a] approx. father; á [au] cow; e [ɛ] set; é [jɛ] yes; i, y [I] sit; í, ý [i] feel; o [ɔ] law; ó [ou] note; u [ɤ] approx. Germ. Mütter; ú [u] school; y = i; ý = í; æ [ai] ice; ö [ö] Germ. hören; au [öy] French feuille; ei, ey [ei] ale. Length [:]; half-length [·].

490

yfirfrakki, -a, -ar [ɪ:vɪr̥·fraʰk₁:ɪ, -ʰk:a(r̥)] wm.1 overcoat.

yfirgnæfandi [ɪ:vɪr-gnai:vand̥ɪ] pr. p. dominating.

yfirhöfn, -hafnar, -ir [ɪ:vɪr̥·höb·n̥, -hab·nar̥, -hab·nɪr̥] f.2 overcoat.

yfirleður, (-ri), -urs [ɪ:vɪr-lɛ:ðɣr̥(s), -lɛð·rɪ] n. top leather.

yfirleitt [ɪ:vɪr-leiʰt:] adv. generally speaking.

yfirmaður, -manns, -menn [ɪ:vɪr-ma:-ðɣr̥, -man·s, -mɛn:] m.4 chief, chief of staff, commander in chief; yfirmaður Bandaríkjahers commander in chief of the U.S.A. army.

yfirráð [ɪ:vɪ(r)-rau:ð] n.pl. rule, sway.

yfirsæng, -ur, -ur [ɪ:vɪr̥-saiŋ·g̊, -ɣr̥] f.3 bedcover, comfort.

yfirvararskegg, -s [ɪ:vɪrva·rar̥-sk₁ɛg̊:, -sk₁ɛg̊·s] n. moustache.

yfrá [ɪv·rau·, ɣv·rau·] (Pr. 4, 3), see yfir (á).

yfri [ɪv·ri·, ɣv·ri·] (Pr. 4, 3), see yfir (i).

yfrum [ɪv·rɣm, ɣv·rɣm] (Pr. 4, 3), see yfir (um).

ýkjur [i:k₁ʰɣr̥; i:g̊₁ɣr̥] wf.1.pl. exaggeration(s).

ykkar, ykkur, see þú.

ylur, -s (-jar) [ɪ:lɣr̥, ɪl·s, ɪl·jar̥] m.2 warmth.

ým(i)s, ým(i)s, ýmist [im·s, i:mɪ·s, i:mɪst] adj. now this now that, various, diverse, different; af ýmsu tagi of various kinds; pl. ýmsir, ýmsar, several, sundry; á ýmsum tímum at different times; ýmist . . . eða conj. either . . . or, sometimes . . . sometimes (S. VIII, 2).

ýmislegur [i:mɪs-lɛ:qɣr̥] adj. (see -legur) different, various; ýmislegt various things.

yngri, yngstur, see ungur.

ýra, ýrði, ýrður (ýrt) [i:ra, ir·ði, -ɣr̥, ir̥·t] wv.2 drizzle; það ýrir úr honum it is drizzling (S. VI, 4, 3).

yrkja, orti, ort(ur) [ɪr·k₁a, ɔr̥·tɪ, ɔr̥·t(ɣr̥)] wv.2 (In. VII, 3, 3, 5) compose a poem; be a poet; yrkja

um e·ð (e·n) sing about sth (sbdy).

ýsa, -u, -ur [i:sa, -ɣ(r̥)] wf.1 haddock.

ytri, yztur [ɪ:tʰrɪ, ɪs·tɣr̥; ɪ:d̥rɪ] adj. compar. and superl. outer, outermost.

Þ.

þ. = þann.

1. þá [þau:] adv. (In. IV, 1, 2) (1) then, at that time, thereupon; þá og síðar then and later; þá . . . þá then . . . then (in enumerating things); og . . . þá in that case; þá og þegar, þá og þá at any moment; (2) redundant (not to be translated) at the beginning of a main sentence that follows its subordinate clause: ef . . . , þá . . . , fyrst . . . , þá . . . , etc.: ef þú villt koma á morgun, þá skal ég vera heima if you will (want to) come tomorrow, (then) I shall be at home; fyrst þú sveikst mig, þá vil eg ekkert hafa með þig since you betrayed me, I will have nothing to do with you; (3) þá er (= þegar) conj. when (S. VIII, 3(h)); þá er (= þegar) þetta heyrðist when this was heard (rumored). . . .

2. þá, see hann and 3. sá.

3. þá, see 1. þiggja.

það, see hann and 3. sá.

þáð, þáði, see 2. þiggja.

þaðan [þa:ðan] adv. thence, from there; þaðan í frá thenceforth (In. IV, 1, 2-3); þaðan sem (þaðan er) rel. conj. whence (S. VIII, 3(j)).

þagði, þagað, see þegja.

þagga, -aði, -að [þag̊:a, -aðɪ, -að] wv.4 silence, dampen; þagga niður í e·m hush up, quiet sbdy.

þagmælska, -u [þaq·mailska, -ɣ] wf.1 reticence, discreetness.

þágum, see 1. þiggja.

þak, -s, þök [þa:kʰ(s), þö:kʰ; þa:g̊, þö:g̊] n. roof.

þakhella, -u, -ur [þa:khed̥la, -ɣ(r̥)] wf.1 slate, tile.

þakið, -inn, þakti, -ur, see þekja.

þakk, takk [þaʰk:, tʰaʰk:] interj.

(short for (*ég*) *þakka*) thank you, thanks; *þakk fyrir* thank you, thanks; *já, þakk, jú, þakk* yes, thank you; *þakk fyrir síðast* 'thank you for the last time we spent together' (a polite phrase), usually answered by: *þakka þér sjálfum* or *sjálfþakkað* 'thank yourself'; or rather: *sömuleiðis* 'likewise,' and: (*þakka þér*) *miklu fremur* '(thank you) even more.'

þakka, -aði, -að [þa^hk:a, -aðɪ, -að] wv.4 thank; *þakka fyrir* thank for; *þakka fyrir sig* thank on one's own behalf; *þakka fyrir matinn* thank for the food (in Iceland grace is not said, but you thank your host for the food after the meal); *ekkert að þakka* 'nothing to thank for,' don't mention it, you are welcome (to it); *þakka e-m fyrir e-ð* thank sbdy for sth; *þakka e-m e-ð* thank sbdy for sth (thanks to him), attribute sth to sbdy; *þakka fyrir gamla árið* 'thank for the old year' (an Icelandic polite custom), cf. *þakk fyrir síðast* above.

þakkar, -ir, see **þökk.**

þakklæti, -s [þa^hk:lai·t^hɪ(s); -lai·dɪ] n. thanks, gratitude (*fyrir e-ð* for sth).

þangað [þauŋ·ga(ð)] adv. (Pr. 4, 2; In. IV, 1, 2-3) thither, to that place, there; *hingað og þangað* hither and thither; *þangað til* adv. until then; *þangað til* (*að*) conj. until; *þangað til* (= *þar til*) (*að*) *hann kemur* until he comes (S. VIII, 3(h)); *þangað sem* rel. conj. where, whither (S. VIII, 3(j)).

þann, see **3. sá.**

þannig [þan:ɪq] adv. (In. IV, 1, 2) thus.

þar [þa:r] (1) adv. (In. IV, 1, 2-3) there, at that place; *hann er þar* he is there; with preps and advs: *þar á meðal* among these; *þar í landi* in that country; *þar að auki* in addition; *þar af leiðir, að* . . . (thence) it follows, that . . . ; *þar*

með er ekki sagt, að . . . 'therewith is not said that . . . ,' it does not follow that . . . ; *þar til* adv. until then; *þar til um hádegi* until about noon; *þar upp frá* up there; *þar næst* next to that, then, thereupon; (2) *þar eð* conj. since, whereas (S. VII, **2,** 3; VIII, 3(b)); (3) *þar sem* rel. conj. where, whereas; since (S. VIII, 3(b) & (j)); *húsið* . . . *þar sem við vorum í gær* the house . . . where we were yesterday; *þar sem oss hefur borizt til eyrna* . . . since the rumor has reached our ears . . . ; (3) *þar til* (*að*) conj. until; *þar til hann kemur* until he comes; *þar til er* conj. until (S. VIII, 3(h)).

þarf, see **þurfa.**

þarfar, -ir, see **þörf.**

þarfnast, -aðist, -azt [þardnast, -aðɪst, -ast] wv.4 (middle voice only) *þarfnast e-s* need sth.

þarfur, þörf, þarft [þar·vʏr, þör·v, þar·(f)t] adj. useful; *þarfur e-m* useful to sbdy (S. I, 3, 2, 1).

þarna [þad·na, þardna] adv. there (pointing); *þarna á borðinu* there on that table, on this table.

þátttaka, -töku [þau^ht:t^ha·k^ha; -t^hö·k^hʏ; -t^ha·ga, -t^hö·gʏ] wf.1 participation.

þáttur, -ar, þættir [þau^ht:ʏr, -ar, þai^ht:ɪr] m.3 strand, piece, element, part of, share; act (in a play); *taka þátt í e-u* take part in sth, share sth; *vera þáttur í* be a constituent of, an element of.

þau, pl. of **það,** see **3. sá.**

þaut, see **þjóta.**

þ. e. = *það er* = **i. e.,** that is.

þegar [þɛ:qar] (1) adv. already, at once; *þegar um vorið* already in the spring; *hann hætti þegar* (= *þegar í stað* = *undir eins*) he stopped at once; (2) conj. when (S. VIII, 3(h) & 4); *þegar sólin kom upp* when the sun rose; *þegar hann heyrði þetta, þá sagði hann* when he heard this, (then) he said (S.

Vowels: *a* [a] approx. *father*; *á* [au] *cow*; *e* [ɛ] *set*; *é* [jɛ] *yes*; *i, y* [ɪ] *sit*; *í, ý* [i] *feel*; *o* [ɔ] *law*; *ó* [ou] *note*; *u* [ʏ] approx. Germ. *Mütter*; *ú* [u] *school*; *y* = *i*; *ý* = *í*; *æ* [ai] *ice*; *ö* [ö] Germ. *hören*; *au* [öy] French *feuille*; *ei, ey* [ei] *ale*. Length [:]; half-length [·].

VII, 3, 6); (3) *þegar er* conj. as
soon as; *þegar er sólin kom upp*
as soon as the sun rose.

þegið, -inn, see 1. *þiggja.*

þegja, þagði, þagað [þei:ja, þaq·ðɪ,
þa:qað; þaǥ·ðɪ] wv.3 be silent;
remain silent, be quiet; *þegiðu*
(= *þegi þú*)! hold your tongue!
shut up! *þegja yfir e-u* keep silent
(mum) about sth.

þeim, see *hann* and 3. *sá.*

þeir, see *hann* and 3. *sá.*

þeirra, see *hann* and 3. *sá.*

þeirrar, see 3. *sá* (*sú*).

þeirri, see 3. *sá* (*sú*).

þekja, þakti, þakinn (-ið), þakt(ur)
[þɛ:kₗʰa, þax·tɪ, -ʏr̥, þax·t, þa:kₗʰɪn,
-ɪð; þɛ:ǥₗa, þa:ǥₗɪn] wv.1 cover,
thatch.

þekking, -ar [þɛʰkₗ:iŋǥ, -ar̥] f.1
knowledge.

þekkja, þekkti, þekkt(ur) [þɛʰkₗ:a,
þɛx·tɪ, -ʏr̥, þɛx·t] wv.2 know, recognize; *þekkja e-n aftur* recognize
sbdy; *ég þekkti hann vel* I knew
him (I used to know him) well;
þekktur known, well-known; *þekktur
fyrir e-ð* known for (on account of)
sth; *þú getur ekki verið þekktur
fyrir það* 'you cannot let yourself
be known for that,' i. e. you should
be ashamed of doing that; *þekkjast*
know each other.

þenna(n), see *þessi.*

þér, see *þú.*

þéra, -aði, -að(ur) [þjɛ:ra, -aðɪ, -að,
-aðʏr̥] wv.4 say *þér* 'you.' to sbdy;
þérast say *þér* to each other (S.
IV, 1, 2).

þerna, -u, -ur [þɛrdna, -ʏ(r̥)] wf.1
waitress.

þess, see *hann* and 3. *sá* (*það*).

þessi, þessi, þetta [þɛs:ɪ, þɛʰt:a], acc.
þenna(n), þessa, þetta [þɛn:a(n),
þɛs:a], dat. *þessum, þessari, þessu*
[þɛs:ʏm, þɛs:arɪ, þɛs:ʏ], gen. *þessa,
þessarar, þessa* [þɛs:arar̥]; pl.
þessir, þessar, þessi [þɛs:ɪr̥, þɛs:ar̥],
acc. *þessa, þessar, þessi,* dat. *þessum,*
gen. *þessara* [þɛs:ara] dem. pron.

this that; *þessi* this one; *þessi
maður* this man; *þetta er laglegur
hestur* this is a handsome pony;
ekki þetta heldur hitt augað not
this but the other eye (S. II, 7);
þessi kvöldin 'these evenings';
þessa mánaðar (= *þ. m.*) of this
month; *með þessu* with, through
this; *þetta* adv. with difficulty, just
barely; *hann baxar þetta í áttina*
oh, he is striving (with difficulty)
to move in the right direction (In.
VI, 3; S. IV, 3, 3).

þessvegna [þɛs:vɛǥna] adv. (= *þess
vegna*) therefore, on account of that
(In. IV, 1, 2).

þetta, see *þessi.*

þið, see *þú.*

1. þíða, -u, -ur [þi:ða, -ʏ(r̥)] wf.1
thaw, pl. spells of thawing.

2. þíða, þíddi, þíddur (þítt) [þi:ða,
þid:ɪ, -ʏr̥, þiʰt:] wv.2 thaw out;
þíða fötin sín thaw out one's
clothes.

þig, see *þú.*

1. þiggja, þigg, þá, þágum, þeginn
(-ið) [þɪǥₗ:a, þɪǥ:, þau:, þau:-
(q)ʏm, þei:jɪn, -ɪð] v.6 or (more
commonly):

2. þiggja, þáði, (þáð) [þɪǥₗ:a, þau:ðɪ,
(þau:ð)] wv.1 accept, *þiggja e-ð*
accept sth; *þiggja boð* accept an
invitation.

þil, -s, -, (-ja) [þɪ:l, þɪl·s, þɪl·ja] n.
wooden panel, partition.

þilja, -aði, -að(ur) [þɪl·ja, -aðɪ, -að,
-aðʏr̥] wv.4 line (with wooden
boards).

þín, see *þinn* and *þú.*

þing, -s, - [þiŋ·ǥ, þiŋ·s] n. meeting,
convention, assembly, parliament,
thing; = *Alþingi* the Icelandic
Parliament.

þingbundinn, -in, -ið [þiŋ·ǥbʏndɪn,
-ɪn, -ɪð] adj. constitutional, limited
by the power of parliament.

þingheimur, -s [þiŋ·ǥhei·mʏr̥, -heims]
m.1 (assembly of) people participating in a *þing.*

Consonants: [ð] brea*th*e; [g] *g*ood; [gɪ] *gy*arden (garden); [hw̥] *wh*at; [j] *y*es; [kɪ] *cy*an
(can); [ŋ] thi*ng*; [q] N. Germ. sa*g*en; [r] Scottish *r*; [x] approx. Germ. a*ch*; [þ] *th*in.
Voiceless: ○; [b̥, d̥, ǥ] approx. *p, t, k.* Half-voiced: *italics.* Aspiration and preaspiration:
[ʰ]; [pʰ, tʰ, kʰ] *p*-, *t*-, *k*-. Others as in English.

þingræði, -s [þiŋ·g̊rai·ði(s)] n. parlamentarism.

þingsályktun, -unar, -anir [þiŋ·sau·lɪx·tʏn, -ʏnar̥, -anɪr̥] f.2 resolution of parliament.

þingsályktunartillaga, -lögu, -ur [þiŋ·sau·lɪx·tʏnar̥·tʰɪl:aqa, -tʰɪl:öqʏ(r̥)] wf.1 proposition resolved by parliament, resolution of parliament.

Þingvallavatn, -s [þiŋ·g̊vadla·vaʰt·n̥, -vas:] n. 'Lake of Þingvellir.'

Þingvellir, -valla [þiŋ·g̊vedlɪr̥, -vadla] m.3.pl. 'Plains of the Thing,' where the Old Icelandic Alþingi met.

þinn, þín, þitt [þɪn:, þi:n, þɪʰt:] poss. pron. of the second pers. (In. III, 2(b)5e; (b)8; VI, 2) thy, thine; your, yours (S. IV, 2, 7) þinn hestur, usually: hesturinn þinn your horse (S. III, 2, 4); kjáninn þinn you (little) fool (S. IV, 2, 6).

Þistilfjörður, -fjarðar [þɪs·tɪl·fjör·ðʏr̥, -fjar·ðar̥] m.3 'Thistle Fjord.'

þitt, see þinn.

þjá, þjáði, þjáð(ur) [þjau:, þjau·ði, þjau:ðʏr̥, þjau:ð] wv.3 afflict, torment; pp. þjáður suffering.

þjálfaður, -uð, -að [þjaul·vaðʏr̥, -ʏð, -að] adj. drilled, trained.

þjóð, -ar, -ir [þjou:ð, -ðar̥, -ðɪr̥] f.2 nation, people.

þjóðerni, -s [þjou:ðɛrdnɪ(s)] n. nationality.

þjóðernissinni, -a, -ar [þjou:ðɛrdnɪ(s)·sɪn:ɪ, -a(r̥)] wm.1 nationalist, National socialist.

þjóðkirkja, -u, -ur [þjouð·k̥ʲ ʰɪr̥k̥ʲa, -ʏ(r̥)] wf.1 state church.

þjóðleikhús, -s [þjouð·lei·khu·s, -hus·] n. national theater.

þjóðminjasafnið, -sins [þjouð·mɪnjasab·nɪð, -sabnsɪns] n. with def. art. 'The National Museum.'

Þjóðólfur, -s [þjou:ðoulvʏr̥, -oul(v)s] m.1 'Theodolph,' a newspaper.

þjóðréttur, -ar, -ir [þjouð·rjɛʰt·ʏr̥, -ar̥, -ɪr̥] m.3 national (favorite) food or dish.

þjóðsaga, -sögu, -ur [þjouð·sa·qa, -sö·qʏ(r̥)] wf.1 folk tale.

Þjóðskjalasafnið, -sins [þjouð·sk̥ʲ a·lasab·nɪð, -sabnsɪns] n. with def. art. 'The National Archives.'

þjóðstjórn, -ar, -ir [þjouð·stjourdn̥, -nar̥, -nɪr̥] f.2 national government.

þjóðtrú, -ar [þjouð·tʰru·, -tʰru·ar̥] f.1 popular beliefs, folk beliefs.

þjóðvegur, -ar, -ir [þjouð·vɛ·qʏr̥, -ar̥, -vei·jɪr̥] m.3 highway; við þjóðveginn on the highway.

þjóðveldi, -s [þjouð·vɛldɪ(s)] n. commonwealth, republic; a centralized form of government.

þjóðveldismenn, -manna [þjouð·vɛldɪsmɛn:, -man:a] m.4.pl. (members of) a party that favors a strong central government and tries to curb party rule.

Þjóðverji, -a, -ar [þjouð·verjɪ, -ja(r̥)] wm.1 a German, pl. Germans.

Þjóðviljinn, -ans [þjouð·vɪljɪn, -jans] wm.1 with def. art. 'The Will of the People,' a newspaper.

Þjóðvinafélagið, -sins [þjouð·vɪ·na·fjɛ:lai·jɪð, -laxsɪns] n. with def. art. = Hið íslenzka þjóðvinafélag 'The Friends of the Icelandic Nation Society,' a literary society.

þjóðþrif [þjouð·þrɪ·v] n.pl. national prosperity; til þjóðþrifa for the benefit of the nation.

þjónn, -s, -ar [þjoud·n̥, þjoun·s, þjou:nar̥] m.1 servant, waiter, piccolo.

þjórfé, -fjár [þjour̥·fjɛ:, -fjau·r̥] n. tips (= drykkjupeningar) í þjórfé in tips, as tips.

þjóta, þýt, þaut, þutum, þotinn (-ið) [þjou:tʰa, þi:tʰ, þöy:tʰ, þʏ:tʰʏm, þɔ:tʰɪn, -ɪð; þjou:da, þi:d, þöy:d, þʏ:d̥ʏm, þɔ:dɪn] v.2 rush, speed.

þ. m. = þessa mánaðar of this month, inst.

1. þó, see 1. þvo.

2. þó [þou:] (1) adv. yet, however (= samt), still, nevertheless; þó svo, að . . . yet so that . . . , yet in such a manner that . . . ; (2) þó (að), þótt conj. (with subj.) although, though, even if, if; þó svo væri even if it were so, even so;

Vowels: a [a] approx. father; á [au] cow; e [ɛ] set; é [jɛ] yes; i, y [ɪ] sit; í, ý [i] feel; o [ɔ] law; ó [ou] note; u [ʏ] approx. Germ. Mütter; ú [u] school; y = i; ý = í; æ [ai] ice; ö [ö] Germ. hören; au [öy] French feuille; ei, ey [ei] ale. Length [:]; half-length [·].

þó aldrei nema það sé satt even if
it be true, granted that it be true;
enda þótt even if; jafnvel þótt even
if (S. VI, 9, 4, 6; VIII, 3(e) & 4).

þófta, -u, -ur (þótta) [þouf·ta, -ʏ(ɾ̥);
þouʰt:a] wf.1 thwart.

þógum, see 1. þvo.

þoka, -u, -ur [þɔ:kʰa, -ʏ(ɾ̥); þɔ:g̊a]
wf.1 fog; pl. foggy weather.

þóknast, -aðist, -azt [þouʰk·nast,
-aðɪst, -ast] wv.4 (middle voice
only) please; þóknast e-m please
sbdy, find favor with sbdy; e-m
þóknast e-ð sth pleases sbdy; hvað
þóknast yður? what would you
like?

þola, þoldi, þolað [þɔ:la, þɔl·dɪ, þɔ:-
lað] wv.3 suffer, endure, stand
(= líða).

Þór, -s [þou:r, þouɾ̥·s] m.1 Thor, Old
Icelandic god; pers. name.

þora, þorði, þorað [þɔ:ra, þɔr·ðɪ,
þɔ:rað] wv.3 dare; ég þori það ekki
I dare not.

Þóra, -u [þou:ra, -ʏ] wf.1 pers. name.

Þórarinn, (-arni), -arins [þou:rarɪn,
-ardnɪ, -arɪns] m.1 pers. name.

Þórbergur, -s [þour·berg̊ʏɾ̥, -berg̊s;
þɔr·-] m.1 pers. name.

Þorbjörg, -bjargar [þɔr·björg̊,·bjarg̊aɾ̥]
f.2 pers. name.

Þórdís, -ar [þour·di·s(aɾ̥)] f.2 pers.
name.

Þórður, -ar [þour·ðʏɾ̥, -aɾ̥] m.1 pers.
name.

Þórey, -eyjar [þou:rei·, -ei·jaɾ̥] f.1
pers. name.

Þorgerður, -ar [þɔr·g̊ɪerðʏɾ̥, -aɾ̥] f.1
pers. name.

Þórhildur, -ar [þou:rhɪldʏɾ̥, -aɾ̥] f.1
pers. name.

Þorkell, -s [þɔr·kɪʰedl̥, -kɪʰels] m.1
pers. name.

Þorleifur, -s [þɔd·lei·vʏɾ̥, -leifs] m.1
pers. name.

þorp, -s, - [þɔr̥·p(s)] n. village.

þorri, -a, -ar [þɔr:ɪ, -a(ɾ̥)] wm.1 from
the middle of January to the middle
of February; the first month after
midwinter.

þorrið, -inn, see 1. þverra.

þorskur, -s, -ar [þɔs·kʏɾ̥, þɔsks, þɔs·-
kaɾ̥; þɔrsk-] m.1 cod; as a term of
vilification: fool, stupid fellow.

Þorsteinn, -s [þɔs·teid̥n̥, -steins; þɔɾ̥·-
steid̥n] m.1 pers. name Thorsten.

Þórunn, -ar [þou:rʏn, -ʏn(·)aɾ̥] f.1
pers. name.

Þorvaldsstaðir [þɔr·val(d̥s)sta:ðɪɾ̥]
m.3.pl. place name.

Þorvaldur, -s [þɔr·valdʏɾ̥, -val(d̥)s]
m.1 pers. name.

Þorvarður, -ar (-s) [þɔr·varðʏɾ̥, -aɾ̥,
-varðs] m.1 pers. name, patronymic:
Þorvarðarson.

þotið, -inn, see þjóta.

þótt, see 2. þó (að) and þykja.

þótta, see þófta.

þótti, see þykja.

þrá, þráði, þráð [þrau:, þrau·ðɪ,
þrau:ð] wv.3 long for; þrá e-ð long
for sth.

þrár, þrá, þrátt; þrárri, þráastur
[þrau:r, þrau:, þrauʰt:; þraur:ɪ,
þrau·astʏr] adj. stubborn; rancid;
þrátt adv. frequently; þrátt fyrir
e-ð in spite of sth; þrátt fyrir allt
in spite of all; þrátt fyrir það,
að . . . in spite of the fact that . . .
(S. VIII, 3(e)).

þraut, see þrjóta.

þrefaldur, -föld, -falt [þre:faldʏɾ̥,
-föld, -falt] adj. triple, threefold.

þreif, see þrífa.

þreifa, -aði, -að [þrei:va, -aðɪ, -að]
wv.4 touch, feel with the hands;
þreifa á e-u touch with the hands;
þreifandi myrkur 'groping darkness' (S. VI, 12, 1, 3).

þrem(ur), see þrír.

þrengri, þrengstur, see þröngur.

þrenning, -ar, -ar [þrɛn:ing̊, -aɾ̥] f.1
trinity.

þrennskonar [þrɛn·skʰɔ·naɾ̥] adv. (=
þrenns konar) of three types, of
three kinds.

þrennur, þrenn, þrennt [þrɛn:ʏɾ̥,
þrɛn:, þrɛn·tʰ; þrɛn·t] distributive
num. triple, threefold; þrennt three

Consonants: [ð] breathe; [g] good; [gɪ] gɪarden (garden); [hw] what; [j] yes; [kɪ] cɪan
(can); [ŋ] thing; [q] N. Germ. sagen; [r] Scottish r; [x] approx. Germ. ach; [þ] thin.
Voiceless: ∘; [b̥, d̥, g̊] approx. p, t, k. Half-voiced: italics. Aspiration and preaspiration:
[ʰ]; [pʰ, tʰ, kʰ] p-, t-, k-. Others as in English.

things, a group of three; *þrenn föt* three suits of clothes; *þrenns konar* of three kinds; *allt er þegar þrennt er* (proverbial) three times makes the thing complete; *skifta í þrennt* divide in three parts (In. V, **3**, 3).

þrettán [þrɛʰt:aun] num. card. thirteen.

1. **þrettándi** [þrɛʰt:aundɪ] num. ord. thirteenth.

2. **þrettándi, -a, -ar** [þrɛʰt:aundɪ, -a(r̥)] wm.1 Epiphany, Twelfth-day.

þreyja, þreyði, þreyð(ur) [þrei:ja, þrei:ðɪ, þrei:ðɣr̥, þrei:ð] wv.2 wait patiently; long for; *þreyja e-n* long for sbdy; *hægt er að þreyja þorrann og góuna* (proverbial) one can always stand the two midwinter months.

þreyta, þreytti, þreytt(ur) [þrei:tʰa, þreiʰt:ɪ, -ɣr̥, þreiʰt:; þrei:da] wv.2 tire out; *þreyta e-n* tire sbdy out.

þreytast, þreyttist, þreytzt [þrei:tʰast, þreiʰt:ɪst, þreis·t; þrei:dast] wv.2 (middle voice) get tired; *þreytast á e-u* get tired of sth.

þreyttur, þreytt, þreytt [þreiʰt:(ɣr̥)] adj. tired, fatigued (*á* of).

þriðji [þrɪð·jɪ] num. ord. third.

þriðjudagur, -s, -ar [þrɪð·jɣ-da:qɣr̥, -dax·s, -da:qar] m.1 Tuesday; *þriðju-dags-kvöld, -morgunn* Tuesday evening, morning.

þriðjungur, -s, -ar [þrɪð·juŋg̊ɣr̥, -uŋs, -uŋg̊ar̥] m.1 one third; *fullur þriðjungur* fully one third.

þrífa, þríf, þreif, þrifum, þrifinn (-ið) [þri:va, þri:v, þrei:v, þrɪ:vɣm, þrɪ:vɪn, -ɪð] v.1 catch, grab; *þrífast* thrive (S. VI, **7**, *4*).

þriggja, see *þrír.*

Þríhamrar [þri:hamrar̥] m.1.pl. ' Three Rocks.'

þríheilagur, -lög, -lagt [þri:hei·laqɣr̥, -löq, -laxt] adj. having three consecutive holidays.

þrír, þrjár, þrjú [þri:r, þrjau:r, þrju:], acc. *þrjá, þrjár, þrjú* [þrjau:], dat. *þrem(ur)* [þrɛ:m, þrɛ:mɣr̥], gen. *þriggja* [þrɪg̊ʲ:a] num. card. three

(In. V, **2**, 2(c)); *þau þrjú* they three, the three of them.

þristur, -s, -ir [þrɪs·tɣr̥, þrɪsts, þrɪs·-tɪr̥] m.2 trey.

þrisvar [þrɪ:sva·r] adv. thrice, three times (= *þrem sinnum*).

þrítugasti [þri:tʰɣqastɪ; þri:dɣqastɪ] num. ord. thirtieth.

þrítugfaldur, -föld, -falt [þri:tʰɣx-fal·dɣr̥, -föl·d, -fal·t; þri:dɣx-] adj. thirtyfold.

þrítugnættur, -nætt, -nætt [þri:tʰɣq-naiʰt:(ɣr̥); þri:dɣq-] adj. having thirty nights; *þrítugnættur mánuð-ur* a month of thirty nights (days).

þrítugsaldur, (-ri), -urs [þri:tʰɣxs-al·dɣr̥(s), -al·drɪ; þri:dɣxs-] m.1 age of thirty; the twenties; *vera á þrítugsaldri* be in the (late) twenties (= *vera milli tvítugs og þrítugs*).

þrítugur, -tug, -tugt [þri:tʰɣqɣr̥, -ɣq, -ɣxt; þri:dɣqɣr̥] adj. thirty (years of age); *þrítugt* (= *þrítugsaldur*) age of thirty (In. V, **3**, 1); *hálf-þrítugur* twenty-five years of age.

þrjá, þrjár, see *þrír.*

þrjátíu [þrjau:tʰi·jɣ] num. card. thirty.

þrjóta, þrýt, þraut, þrutum, þrotinn (-ið) [þrjou:tʰa, þri:tʰ, þröy:tʰ, þrɣ:tʰɣm, þrɔ:tʰɪn, -ɪð; þrjou:da, þri:d, þröy:d, þrɣ:dɣm, þrɔ:dɪn] v.2 give out; cease, come to an end.

þrjótur, -s, -ar [þrjou:tʰɣr̥, þrjou:tʰs, þrjou:tʰar̥; þrjou:d·] m.1 rascal, villain.

þrjú, see *þrír.*

þrotið, -inn, see *þrjóta.*

þrutum, see *þrjóta.*

þrýt, see *þrjóta.*

þröng, þröngvar, -var [þröyŋ·g̊, þröyŋ·-g̊var̥] f.1 crowd, throng; a narrow pass.

þröngur, þröng, þröngt; þrengri, þrengstur [þröyŋ·g̊ɣr̥, þröyŋ·g̊, þröyŋ·tʰ; þröyŋ·t; þreiŋ̊grɪ, þreiŋst-ɣr̥] adj. narrow, tight.

þröngva, -aði, -að [þröyŋ·g̊va, -aðɪ, -að] wv.4 compel; force; *þröngva*

Vowels: *a* [a] approx. father; *á* [au] cow; *e* [ɛ] set; *é* [jɛ] yes; *i, y* [ɪ] sit; *í, ý* [i] feel; *o* [ɔ] law; *ó* [ou] note; *u* [ɣ] approx. Germ. Mütter; *ú* [u] school; *y = i; ý = í;* *œ* [ai] ice; *ö* [ö] Germ. hören; *au* [öy] French *feuille*; *ei, ey* [ei] ale. Length [:]; half-length [·].

e-m til e-s (*til að gera e-ð*) force, press sbdy to (do) sth.

þú, þig, þér, þín [þu:, þɪ:q, þɪq, þje:r, þjɛr, þi:n] second pers. pron. thou, you; thee, you; thee, you; of thee, of you (Pr. **4**, *4*; In. VI, 1, 2); *ertu* (= *ert þú*)? are you? *bréf til þín* a letter to you; *gættu þín* take care of yourself; *hann bíður þín* he waits for you; plural (originally dual): þið, ykkur, ykkur; ykkar [þɪ:ð, þɪ(:), ɪʰk:ʏr̥, ɪʰk:ar̥; ʏʰk:-ʏr̥, ʏʰk:ar̥] you; of you, your, yours (Pr. **2**, *1*, 11n; **4**, *2*; In. VI, 1, 2); *þið meiðið ykkur* you hurt yourselves; *hann þekkti ykkur* he knew you; *hvað sýnist ykkur?* what do you think? *gætið ykkar* be careful; *hestarnir ykkar* your horses; *þið Gunnar* you and Gunnar (S. IV, 1, 3); honorific plural: þér, yður, yður; yðar [þje:r, ɪ:ðʏr̥, ɪ:ðar̥] you; you; of you, your, yours (In. VI, 1, 2; S. IV, 1, 2); *gerið þér svo vel, fáið þér yður sæti* please, take a seat (for yourself); *ég þekkti yður strax* I knew you at once; *hatturinn yðar* your hat; *var þetta yðar hattur?* was this your hat? (S. III, 2, 4); *þér verkamenn!* you workers! *yðar hátign* your majesty.

þúa, -aði, -að(ur) [þu:a, -aðɪ, -að, -aðʏr̥] wv.4 say *þú* 'thou' to sbdy (*þúa e-n*); *þúast* say *þú* to each other (S. IV, 1, 2).

þúfa, -u, -ur, (-na) [þu:va, -ʏ(r̥); þub·na] wf.1 hump, hummock.

þúfnakargi, -a, -ar [þub·na-kʰar·g̊ɪ, -g̊a(r̥)] wm.1 a field covered with humps (hummocks).

þumalfingur, (-ri), -urs, -ur [þʏ:mal-fiŋ·g̊ʏr̥(s), -fiŋg̊rɪ] m.4 =

þumall, -als, -lar [þʏ:madl̥, -als, þʏm·-lar̥] m.1 thumb; also: the thumb of a glove.

þumlungur, -s, -ar [þʏm·luŋg̊ʏr̥, -uŋs, -uŋg̊ar̥] m.1 thumb of a glove; inch.

þungavara, -vöru, -ur [þuŋ·g̊a-va:ra, -vö:rʏ(r̥)] wf.1 heavy goods.

þungi, -a [þuŋ·g̊ˌɪ, -g̊a] wm.1 weight; load, burden; drowsyness.

þungur, þung, þungt; þyngri, þyngstur [þuŋ·g̊ʏr̥, þuŋ·g̊, þuŋ·tʰ; þuŋ̊·t; þiŋg̊rɪ, þiŋstʏr̥] adj. heavy, ponderous; downcast; difficult, hard; *þungur skriðdreki* heavy tank; *þungir kostir* onerous conditions.

þunnur, þunn, þunnt; þynnri, þynnstur [þʏn:ʏr̥, þʏn:, þʏn·tʰ; þʏn̊·t; þɪn:rɪ, þɪnstʏr̥] adj. thin; *þunn plata* thin plate (but: *mjór vír* thin wire, *magur maður* thin (lean) man).

þurfa, þarf, þurfum, þurfti, þurft [þʏr·va, þar·v, þʏr·vʏm, þʏr̥·(f)tɪ, þʏr̥·(f)t] pret. pres. v. (In. VII, **5**, *1*) need, have to, be necessary; (1) *þurfa e-ð, þurfa e-s* (*með*) need sth; *hún þarf þess með* . . . she (certainly) needs it . . . (2) auxiliary: need, have to: *ég þarf að fara* I have to go, I must go (S. VI, 2, 5n; 4, 3; 13, 9); *ég þyrfti að fá mér skó* I should need to get me a pair of shoes (S. VI, 9, 2, 2); *þurfa að láta gera e-ð* have to have sth done; (3) impersonal: *það* (*þess*) *þarf ekki* that is not necessary; *þá þarf ekkert að vera að hugsa um* . . . then it is not at all necessary to think of (be thinking of) . . . (S. VI, 14, 8).

þurfi [þʏr·vɪ] adj. indecl. with gen. *einskis þurfi* needing nothing, in need of nothing.

Þuríður, -ar [þʏ:ri·ðʏr̥, -ar̥] f.1 pers. name.

þurr, þurr, þurrt [þʏr:, þʏr̥·t; þʏ:r] adj. dry; arid.

1. þurrka, -u, -ur [þʏr̥·ka, -ʏ(r̥)] wf.1 towel.

2. þurrka, -aði, -að(ur) [þʏr̥·ka, -aðɪ, -að, -aðʏr̥] wv.4 dry, wipe dry, wipe; *þurrka sér* wipe one's face (= *þurrka sér í framan*); *þurrka sér um hendur*(nar), *augun, nefið* wipe one's hands, eyes, nose; *þurrka af diskum* wipe the dishes; *þurrka*

Consonants: [ð] brea*th*e; [g] *g*ood; [gj] *gj*arden (garden); [hw] *wh*at; [j] *y*es; [kj] *cy*an (can); [ŋ] thi*ng*; [q] N. Germ. sa*g*en; [r] Scottish *r*; [x] approx. Germ. a*ch*; [þ] *th*in. Voiceless: ○; [b̥, d̥, g̊] approx. *p, t, k*. Half-voiced: *italics*. Aspiration and preaspiration: [ʰ]; [pʰ, tʰ, kʰ] *p-, t-, k-*. Others as in English.

hey dry the hay; *þurrka fisk* dry (cure) the fish.

þurrkatíð, -ar, -ir [þʏɾ·ka-tʰi:ð̥, -ð̥aɾ̥, -ð̥ɪɾ̥] f.2 dry spell.

þurrkur, -s, -ar [þʏɾ·kʏɾ̥, þʏɾks, þʏɾ·kaɾ] m.1 dry weather; pl. dry spells.

þurrkví, -kvíar, -ar [þʏr:kʰvi·, -kʰvi·-jaɾ] f.1 dry dock.

þurrlendi, -s [þʏr:lend̥ɪ(s)] n. the dry land (opposite of bogs, marshes).

þurrlendur, -lend, -lent [þʏr:lend̥ʏɾ̥, -lend̥, -lentʰ; -lent] adj. dry (of land); *hér er þurrlent* here the land (ground) is dry.

þurrum, see 1. *þverra.*

þursi, -a, -ar (þussi) [þʏɾ·sɪ, -a, -aɾ̥; þʏs:ɪ] wm.1 giant, troll.

þúsund, -ar, -ir [þu:sʏnd̥, -aɾ̥, -ɪɾ̥] f.2 thousand.

þúsundárahátíð, -ar, -ir [þu:sʏnd̥au·-ra-hau:tʰi·ð̥, -ð̥aɾ̥, -ð̥ɪɾ̥] f.2 millenary, millenary celebration.

þúsundfaldur, -föld, -falt [þu:sʏnd̥-fal·d̥ʏɾ̥, -föl·d̥, -fal̥·t] adj. thousand-fold.

þutum, see *þjóta.*

þvaður, (-ri), -urs [þva:ðʏɾ̥(s), þvað̥-rɪ] n. gossip.

þvarr, see 1. *þverra.*

þvegið, -inn, see *þvo* 1 & 2.

þver, þver, þvert [þvɛ:r, þvɛɾ̥·t] adj. lying athwart, transverse; obstinate, unyielding; contrary, adverse; *þvert á móti* on the contrary; *þvert á móti e-u* quite contrary to sth, exactly opposite to sth; *þvert í gegnum* straight through.

þverá, -ár, -ár [þvɛ:rau·(r)] f.1 tributary river; also a place name.

þvergata, -götu, -ur [þvɛr·ga·tʰa, -gö·-tʰʏ(r̥); -ga·d̥a, -gö·d̥ʏ] wf.1 crossroad.

þverhníptur, -hnípt, -hnípt [þvɛɾ·hnif-tʏɾ̥, -hnift] adj. perpendicular, steep.

1. þverra, þverr, þvarr, þurrum, þorrinn (-ið) [þvɛr:a, þvɛr:, þvar:, þʏr:ʏm, þɔr:ɪn, -ɪð̥] v.3 or:

2. þverra, -aði, -að [þvɛr:a, -aðɪ, -að̥] wv.4 dwindle, diminish.

þvert, see *þver.*

því [þvi:, þɪ:] (Pr. 3, *2*, 16n; *4, 3*; In. IV, 1, 2) (1) adv. (dat. of *það,* see 3. *sá, hann*) therefore; *enska er heimsmál, því læra menn hana* English is a world language, therefore people learn it; (2) *því (að)* conj. for, because (S. VIII, 3(b)); *Íslendingar læra ensku, því hún er heimsmál* Icelanders learn English, for it is a world language (explanation); *af því (að)* because; *Íslendingar læra ensku, af því hún er heimsmál* Icelanders learn English, because it is a world language (cause); (3) *því . . . því* conj. the . . . the; *því . . . þeim mun* conj. the . . . the (S. VIII, 3(g)).

þvílíkur, -lík, -líkt [þvi:li·kʰʏɾ̥, -li·kʰ, -lixt; -li·g̊(ʏɾ̥)] dem. pron. (In. VI, 3n2) such; what; *þvílíkur fjöldi* such multitude (S. IV, 5, 4n).

1. þvo, þvæ, (þó, þógum), þveginn (-ið) [þvɔ:, þvai:, þou:, þou:(q)-ʏm, þvei:jɪn, -ɪð̥] v.6 or:

2. þvo, þvæ, þvoði, þveginn (-ið), (þvoð(ur)) [þvɔ:, þvai:, þvɔ:ðɪ, þvei:jɪn, -ɪð̥, þvɔ:ðʏɾ̥, þvɔ:ð̥] wv.1 wash; launder; *þvo þvott* launder the wash; *þvo sér* wash, wash oneself; *þvo sér í framan og um hendur* wash one's face and hands; *þvo upp úr vatni* wash in water.

þvottahús, -húss, -hús [þvɔʰt:a-hu:s, -hus:] n. laundry; washroom.

þvottakona, -u, -ur [þvɔʰt:a-kʰɔ:na, -ʏ(r̥)] wf.1 laundress.

þvottalaug, -ar, -ar [þvɔʰt:a-löy:q, -qaɾ̥] f.1 hot spring for washing.

þvottasápa, -u, -ur [þvɔʰt:a-sau:pʰa, -ʏ(r̥); -sau:b̥a] wf.1 laundry or kitchen soap.

þvottaþró, -ar, -r [þvɔʰt:a-þrou:; -þrou:(a)ɾ̥, -þrou:r] f.1 sink (= *vaskur*).

þvottur, -ar, -ar [þvɔʰt:ʏɾ̥, -aɾ̥] m.1

Vowels: *a* [a] approx. *father;* *á* [au] *cow;* *e* [ɛ] *set;* *é* [jɛ] *yes;* *i, y* [ɪ] *sit;* *í, ý* [i] *feel;* *o* [ɔ] *law;* *ó* [ou] *note;* *u* [ʏ] approx. Germ. *Mütter;* *ú* [u] *school;* *y = i;* *ý = í;* *æ* [ai] *ice;* *ö* [ö] Germ. *hören;* *au* [öy] French *feuille;* *ei, ey* [eiˈ] *ale.* Length [:]; half-length [·].

washing; wash; laundry; *til þvotta* for washing.

þvæ, see *þvo* 1 & 2.

þýða, þýddi, þýddur (þýtt) [þi:ða, þid:ɪ, -ʏɽ, þiʰt:] wv.2 mean, translate; *þetta þýðir* this means; *þýða bók* translate a book; *þetta þýðir ekki neitt* this is of no use.

þýðing, -ar, -ar [þi:ðiŋg̊, -aɽ] f.1 meaning, significance, importance; translation.

þýðingarmikill, -il, -ið; -meiri, -mestur [þi:ðiŋg̊ar-mɪ:k̲ˌʰɪdl̥, -ɪl, -ɪð; -mei:rɪ, -mɛs·tʏɽ] adj. important, significant; *ein þýðingar-mestu framleiðslutæki* among (one of) the most important means of production.

þýður, þýð, þýtt [þi:ðʏɽ, þi:ð, þiʰt:] adj. gentle, affable; smooth-paced (of horses).

þýfður, þýfð, þýft [þiv·ðʏɽ, þiv·ð, þif·t; þib·ðʏɽ, þib·þ] adj. with humps, humpy (of land); *hér er þúft* here the ground is full of humps.

þykja, þótti, þótt [þɪ:k̲ʰa, þouʰt:ɪ, þouʰt:; þɪ:g̊ˌa] wv.2 seem, think, feel; be considered, etc. (1) impersonal: *mér þykir* it seems to me, I think, I feel; *mér þótti þið fljótir* I thought you were quick (S. V, 4, 4); *mér þykir það dýrt* I think (feel) that is expensive; *e-m þykir e-ð gott (illt)* sbdy likes (dislikes) sth; *mér þótti sem . . . it seemed to me as if . . .* (S. VI, 9, 4, 7); *mér þykir vænt um e-n (e-ð)* I like (I love) sbdy (sth); *mér þykir illt, að . . . I am sorry that . . .* (S. VI, 14, 5); *mér þætti vænt um, ef . . . (að . . .)* I'd like it, if . . . (S. VI, 9, 2, 2); (2) middle voice: *þykjast sjá* think that one sees, pretend to see; *ég þóttist góður* I was satisfied with myself, I deemed myself lucky; *menn þóttust fara að verða varir við draugagang* people thought that they began to notice spooks; *þykjast* (= *látast*) let on,

say, pretend (with indirect speech inf.) *hann þóttist ekki hafa komizt til að skrifa* he pretended that he had not found time to write (S. VI, 9, 5, 2); (3) personal: be considered: *hann þykir góður* he is considered good (but: *hann þykist góður* he considers himself good) (S. VI, 11, 5); *þóttu þetta ill tíðindi* this was considered bad news.

þykkna, -aði, -að [þɪʰk·na, -aðɪ, -að] wv.4 become thick; *þykkna upp* become overcast (of the weather).

þykkur, þykk, þykkt; þykkri, þykkstur; þykk(v)ari, -(v)astur [þɪʰk·ʏɽ, þɪʰk:, þɪx·t; þɪʰk·rɪ, þɪx·stʏɽ; þɪʰk:(v)arɪ, -(v)astʏɽ] adj. thick; overcast (sky); *hann er þykkur til hafsins* the sky is overcast in the offing.

þyngd, -ar, -ir [þiŋ·d̥, -aɽ, -ɪɽ] f.2 weight.

þyngja, þyngdi, þyngdur (þyngt) [þiŋ·g̊ˌa, þiŋ·dɪ, -ʏɽ, þiŋ·tʰ; þiŋ·t] wv.2 make heavy; *þyngjast* gain in weight, get heavy.

þyngri, þyngstur, see *þungur*.

þynnri, þynnstur, see *þunnur*.

þyrsta, þyrsti, þyrst [þɪs·ta, -ɪ, þɪs·t; þɪrsta, -ɪ, þɪrst] wv.2 impersonal: *mig þyrstir* I am getting thirsty, I get thirsty (S. I, 2, 1, 3).

þyrstur, þyrst, þyrst [þɪs·t(ʏɽ); þɪrst(ʏɽ)] adj. thirsty; *ég er þyrstur* I am thirsty.

þýt, see *þjóta*.

þýtt, see *þýða* and *þýður*.

þýzka, -u [þis·ka, -ʏ] wf.1 German (language).

Þýzkaland, -s [þis·ka-lan·d̥, -lan·(d̥)s] n. Germany.

þýzkur, þýzk, þýzkt [þis·kʏɽ, þis·k, þis·t] adj. German.

þægilegur [þai:jɪ-lɛ:qʏɽ] adj. (see *-legur*) comfortable; easy; polite.

þægur, þæg, þægt [þai:qʏɽ, þai:q, þaix·t] adj. easy, obedient; *þægur e-m = þægur við e-n* obedient to sbdy; *vera e-m ekki þægur ljár í*

Consonants: [ð] brea*the*; [g] *g*ood; [gˌ] *gy*arden (garden); [hw] *wh*at; [j] *y*es; [kˌ] *cy*an (can); [ŋ] thi*ng*; [q] N. Germ. sa*gen*; [r] Scottish *r*; [x] approx. Germ. a*ch*; [þ] *th*in. Voiceless: ○; [b̥, d̥, g̊] approx. *p, t, k*. Half-voiced: *italics*. Aspiration and preaspiration: [ʰ]; [pʰ, tʰ, kʰ] *p-, t-, k-*. Others as in English.

þúfu (proverbial) 'be not an easy scythe to handle in humpy ground for sbdy,' be difficult to handle for sbdy.

þær, see *hann*, 3. *sá.*

þættir, see *þáttur.*

þögull, -ul, -ult; -ulli, -ulastur [þö:-qɤdl, -ɤl, -ɤlt; þö:qɤdlɪ, -ɤlastyɾ̥] adj. taciturn.

þök, see *þak.*

þökk, þakkar, -ir [þöʰk:, þaʰk:aɾ̥, þaʰkⱼ:ɪɾ̥] f.2 thanks.

1. þörf, þarfar, -ir [þör·v, þar·vaɾ̥, -ɪɾ̥] f.2 need, requirement; necessity *eftir þörfum* according to need, as occasion requires; *nú er þörf að duga* now there is urgent need to show one's mettle.

2. þörf, see *þarfur.*

Æ.

1. æ [ai:] adv. ever; *æ síðan* for ever afterwards.

2. æ [ai:] interj. oh, ouch.

æðarfugl, -s, -ar [ai:ðar·fɤg̊·l, -fɤg̊ls, -fɤqls, -fɤg̊·laɾ̥] m.1 eider duck(s).

æðarkolla, -u, -ur [ai:ðar·kʰɔd·la, -ɤ(ɾ̥)] wf.1 eider duck (the female).

æði, -s [ai:ðɪ(s)] n. (raving) madness, furor.

æðisgenginn, -in, -ið [ai:ðɪs-g̊ⱼeiŋ·g̊ⱼɪn, -ɪn, -ɪð] adj. mad, raving mad.

æður, -ar, -ar [ai:ðyɾ̥, -aɾ̥] f.1 eider duck.

æfi, -, -ir [ai:vɪ, ai:vɪɾ̥] wf.2 life; pl. lives (= biographies).

æfing, -ar, -ar [ai:viŋg̊, -aɾ̥] f.1 drill, practice, exercise.

æfintýri, -s, - [ai:vɪn-tʰi:rɪ(s)] n. folk tale, *märchen*; adventure.

æja, áði, -áð [ai:ja, au:ðɪ, -au:ð] wv.3 rest, graze (horses); cf. 3. *á.*

ær, (á), ær, ær, (áa) [ai:r, au:, au:a] f.3 ewe.

æra, ærði, ærður (ært) [ai:ra, air·ðɪ, -ɤɾ̥, air·t] wv.2 drive mad, deafen with noise.

ærhús, -s, - [ai:rhu·s, -hus·] n. shed for ewes.

æskja, æskti, æskt [ais·kⱼa, ais·tɪ, ais·t; ais(k)t(ɪ)] wv.2 *æskja e-s* wish for sth.

ætla, -aði, -að(ur) [aiʰt·la, -aðɪ, -að, -aðyɾ̥; aʰt·la] wv.4 (Pr. 2, *1*, 12n) (1) auxiliary: (S. VI, 2, 5n; 4, *3*; 13, 10); intend to, be going to; *ætla að fara* intend to go; verbs of motion are often dropped after *ætla*: *ég ætla út* I am going out; *hvert ætlar þú?* where are you going? where do you intend to go; *ætla lengra* intend to proceed on one's journey, be going further; *allt fór sem ætlað var* everything went (came off) as planned (according to schedule); *ætla til e-s* intend for sth; (2) think, believe: *menn ætluðu, að það væru útilegumenn* people thought that they were outlaws.

ætli [aiʰt·lɪ; aʰt·lɪ] interrog. adv. with. subj. I wonder if . . . ; *hvað ætli klukkan sé?* I wonder what time it is? *ætli það?* I wonder; *hvað ætli það sé lengi gengið* how long a walk would that be?

ætlun, -unar, -anir [aiʰt·lɤn, -ɤnaɾ̥, -anɪɾ̥] f.2 intention, plan.

ætt, -ar, -ir [aiʰt:, -aɾ̥, -ɪɾ̥] f.2 family, lineage, extraction; *af góðum ættum* of good family, of good stock.

ættarnafn, -s, -nöfn [aiʰt:ar·nab·n, -nabns, -nöb·n̥] n. family name.

ættjarðarást, -ar [aiʰt:jarðar-aus·t, -aɾ̥] f.2 love of country.

ættjörð, -jarðar, -ir [aiʰt:jörð, -jarðaɾ̥, -ɪɾ̥] f.2 native land, mother country.

Ö.

öðru(m), see *annar.*

öfl, see *afl.*

öflun, -unar [öb·lɤn, -ɤnaɾ̥] f.2 procuring.

öfugur. -ug, -ugt [ö:vɤqɤɾ̥, -ɤq, -ɤxt] adj. backward, awkward.

öfund, -ar [ö:vɤnd, -aɾ̥] f.2 envy.

ökkli, -a, -ar [öʰk·lɪ, -a(ɾ̥)] wm.1 ankle.

ökklaliður, -ar (-s), -ir [öʰk·la-lɪ:ðyɾ̥,

Vowels: *a* [a] approx. *father*; *á* [au] *cow*; *e* [ɛ] *set*; *é* [jɛ] *yes*; *ι, y* [ɪ] *sit*; *í, ý* [i] *feel*; *o* [ɔ] *law*; *ó* [ou] *note*; *u* [ɤ] approx. Germ. *Mütter*; *ú* [u] *school*; *y = i*; *ý = í*; *æ* [ai] *ice*; *ö* [ö] Germ. *hören*; *au* [öy] French *feuille*; *ei, ey* [ei] *ale*. Length [:]; half-length [·].

-aṛ, -iṛ, -lɪð·s] m.3 (2) the joint of the ankle, ankle.

öl, -s [ö:l, öl·s] n. beer, ale.

öld, aldar, -ir [öl·d, al·dar, -iṛ] f.2 age, century; *um aldir alda* for ever and ever, in secula seculorum; *átjánda og nítjánda öldin* the eighteenth and nineteenth centuries; *á 19. öldinni* in the nineteenth century.

öldu, see *alda*.

Ólfus, -s [öl·vɣ·s, -ɣs·] n. a district of the South.

öll, -u, -um, see *allur*.

öllsömul, -sömun, see *allursaman*.

ölturu, see *altari*.

ölvaður, -uð, -að [öl·vaðɣṛ, -ɣð, -að] adj. (pp.) intoxicated.

ölvast, -aðist, -azt [öl·vast, -aðɪst, -ast] wv.4 become intoxicated.

ömmu, -ur, see *amma*.

1. önd, andar [ön·d, an·daṛ] f.2 breath, life; *gefa upp öndina* give up the ghost, die.

2. önd, andar, endur [ön·d, an·daṛ, ɛn·dɣṛ] f.3 duck.

Önnu, see *Anna*.

önnur, see *annar*.

önnurhver, see *annarhver*.

önnurhvor, see *annarhvor*.

önnurtveggja, see *annartveggja*.

Önundarfjörður, -fjarðar [ö:nɣndar·fjör·ðɣṛ, -fjar·ðaṛ] m.3 'Önundur's Fjord.'

1. ör, -s, - [ö:r, -öṛ·s] n. skar.

2. ör, örvar, -var [ö:r, ör·vaṛ] f.1 arrow.

3. ör, ör, ört; ör(v)ari, ör(v)astur [ö:r, öṛ·t; ör·varɪ, -astɣṛ, ö:rarɪ, -astɣṛ] adj. ready, prompt; vehement; liberal; sensitive; *ört* quickly.

4. ör- [ö:ṛ-] pref. very, extremely; also negative pref.

öreigi, -a, -ar [ö:rei·jɪ, -ei·qa(ṛ)] wm.1 indigent person; proletarian.

örfár, -fá, -fátt [öṛ·fau:r, -fau:, -fauʰt:] adj. *örfáir* very few; *örfátt* very few things.

örmagna [ör·maǧna] adj. indecl. exhausted.

örmjór, -mjó, -mjótt [ör·mjou:r, -mjou:, -mjouʰt:] adj. very slender, extremely thin.

örn, arnar, ernir [ördn, ardnaṛ, ɛrdnɪṛ] f.2 or m.3 eagle; also pers. name.

örorkubót, -ar, -bætur [ö:rɔrkɣ·bou:tʰ, -aṛ, -bai:tʰɣṛ; -bou:d, -bai:-dɣṛ] f.3 disability pension.

örskammur, -skömm, -skammt [öṛ·skam:ɣṛ, -sköm:, -skam·tʰ; -skam·t] adj. very short; *örskammt* very short way, very short time.

örva, -aði, -að(ur) [ör·va, -aðɪ, -að, -aðɣṛ] wv.4 encourage.

örvænta, -vænti, -vænt [ör·vaintʰa, -ɪ, -vaintʰ; -vaint, -a, -ɪ] wv.2 despair; *örvænta um e-ð* despair of sth.

öræfi [ö:rai·vɪ] n.pl. (mountain) wilderness; a wild harborless shore; *Öræfi* 'The Wilderness,' 'The Wild Shores' (?), a district of the South.

ösku, see *aska*.

öskubakki, -a, -ar [ös·kɣ·baʰkj:ɪ, -ʰk:a(ṛ)] wm.1 ashtray.

öskur, (-ri), -urs, -ur [ös·kɣṛ(s), öskrɪ] n. cry, roar.

öt, see *at*.

öx, öxi, axar, axir [öx·s, öx·sɪ, ax·saṛ, -ɪṛ] f.2 axe.

Öxará, -ár [öx·sar·au:(r)] f.1 'Axe River.'

öxl, axlar, -ir [öxsl, axslaṛ, -ɪṛ] f.2 shoulder.

Consonants: [ð] brea*th*e; [g] *g*ood; [gj] *gy*arden (garden); [hw] *wh*at; [j] *y*es; [kj] *cy*an (can); [ŋ] thi*ng*; [q] N. Germ. sa*g*en; [r] Scottish *r*; [x] approx. Germ. a*ch*; [þ] *th*in. Voiceless: ○; [b̥, d̥, g̥] approx. *p, t, k*. Half-voiced: *italics*. Aspiration and preaspiration: [ʰ]; [pʰ, tʰ, kʰ] *p-, t-, k-*. Others as in English.

ADDITIONS.

aðkomumaður, -manns, -menn [að·kʰɔ-
mʏma:ðʏɾ, -man·s, -mɛn:] m.4 newcomer.

ánægja, -u [au:nai·ja, -ʏ] wf.1
pleasure.

blýantur, -s, -ar [bli:jantʰʏɾ; -an̪t·;
-s, -aɾ] m.1 lead pencil.

brennivín, -s [bren:ɪvi:n, -vin·s] n.
gin.

dimmur, dimm, dimmt [dɪm:(ʏɾ),
dɪm·tʰ, dɪm̪·t] adj. dark, dim.

dufl, -s, - [dʏb̪·l(s)] n. buoy.

2. en but; sometimes to be translated
'and.' Þjálfi hét sonur hans en
Röskva dóttir his son's name was Þ.
and R. his daughter's.

fylla, fyllti, fyllt(ur) [fɪd̪·la, fɪl̪·tɪ,
-ʏɾ] wv.2 fill.

haka, höku, -ur [ha:kʰa, hö:kʰʏ(ɾ);
ha:ǧ·, hö:ǧ·] wf.1 chin.

heilla, -aði, -að(ur) [heid̪·la, -aðɪ,
-aðʏɾ, -að] wv.4 fascinate, bewitch;
heillast be bewitched.

heyrn, -ar, -ir [heir·d̪n̪, -naɾ, -nɪɾ] f.2
hearing.

hleypa, hleypti, hleypt(ur) [hl̪ei:pʰa,
hl̪eif·tɪ, -ʏɾ; hl̪ei:ba] wv.2 let run,
prick.

hylla, -u, -ur [hɪd̪·la, -ʏ(ɾ)] wf.1
shelf.

klæðaskápur, -s, -ar [kʰlai:ða -skau:-
pʰʏɾ, -skau:pʰs; -skau:b̪·] m.1 wardrobe.

kærlega [k̪ʰair·lɛ·qa] adv. kindly,
very much.

lampi, -a, -ar [lam·pʰɪ, -a(ɾ); lam̪·pɪ]
wm.1 lamp.

leistur, -s, -ar [leis·tʏɾ, -s, -aɾ] m.1
sock.

líknarbelgur, -s, -ir [liʰk·nar -bɛl·ǧʏɾ,
-ǧs, -bɛl·ǧ̪ɪɾ] m.2 amnion.

mál, -s, - [mau:l] n. time, mál að
gera e-ð time to do sth.

munnur, -s, -ar [mʏn:ʏɾ, -aɾ, mʏn·s]
m.1 mouth.

náttúrlega [nauʰt:ur·lɛ·(q)a] adv.
naturally.

Norðurálfa, -u [nɔr·ðʏr -aul·va, -ʏ]
wf.1 Europe.

ofn, -s, -ar [ɔb̪·n̪(s), -naɾ] m.1 stowe,
oven.

ólán, -s [ou:lau·n, -laun·s] n. misfortune.

pappír, -s [pʰaʰp:ir, -irs] m.1 paper.

regnhlíf, -ar, -ar [rɛǧ·nhl̪i·v, -hl̪i·vaɾ]
f.1 umbrella.

skammta, -aði, -að(ur) [skam·tʰa,
-aðɪ, -aðʏɾ, -að; skam̪·ta] wv.4 dole
out, give each one a portion; ration.

skegg, -s, - [sk̪ɛǧ:, sk̪ɛǧ·s] n. beard.

spor, -s, - [spɔ:r, spɔɾ·s] n. footstep,
footprint, track.

spurning, -ar, -ar [spʏr(d̪)niŋǧ, -ǧaɾ]
f.1 question.

staup, -s, - [stöy:pʰ, -s; stöy:b̪] n.
goblet, beaker, glass.

tau, -s, - [tʰöy:(s)] n. stuff, material,
cloth.

502